THE LAW OF PUBLIC COMMUNICATION

The twelfth edition of this classic textbook provides an overview of communication and media law including the most current legal developments. It explains laws affecting the daily work of writers, broadcasters, public relations practitioners, photographers, bloggers and other public communicators.

By providing statutes and cases in an accessible manner, even to students studying law for the first time, the authors ensure that students acquire a firm grasp of the legal issues affecting the media. The book examines legal topics such as libel, privacy, intellectual property, obscenity and access to information, considering the development and current standing of relevant laws and important cases. It examines how these laws affect public, political and commercial communication. The twelfth edition discusses hot topics such as proposals to modify Section 230 of the Communications Decency Act, net neutrality legislation, participant monitoring, the "actual malice" standard for litigation against journalists and the Julian Assange Espionage Act prosecution. It also explores social media issues, such as whether social media use by public officials constitutes a public forum, liability for defamation and the operation of Facebook's Oversight Board.

The Law of Public Communication is an ideal core textbook for undergraduate and graduate courses in communication law and mass media law.

Online resources include a test bank and PowerPoint slides.

William E. Lee is Professor Emeritus of Journalism at the Grady College of Journalism and Mass Communication, University of Georgia.

Daxton R. Stewart is an attorney and Professor of Journalism in the Bob Schieffer College of Communication at Texas Christian University.

Jonathan Peters is an attorney and a media law professor at the University of Georgia, with faculty appointments in the Grady College of Journalism and Mass Communication and the School of Law.

THE LAW OF PUBLIC COMMUNICATION

12TH EDITION

William E. Lee

Daxton R. Stewart

Jonathan Peters

Routledge
Taylor & Francis Group

NEW YORK AND LONDON

Cover image: © andipantz/Getty Images

Twelfth edition published 2023
by Routledge
605 Third Avenue, New York, NY 10158

and by Routledge
4 Park Square, Milton Park, Abingdon, Oxon, OX14 4RN

Routledge is an imprint of the Taylor & Francis Group, an informa business

First edition published by Longman Publishing Group 1988
Eleventh edition published by Routledge 2021

Library of Congress Cataloging-in-Publication Data
A catalog record for this book has been requested

ISBN: 978-1-032-20695-0 (hbk)
ISBN: 978-1-032-19312-0 (pbk)
ISBN: 978-1-003-26473-6 (ebk)

DOI: 10.4324/9781003264736

Typeset in Garamond Std
by Apex CoVantage, LLC

Access the Support Material: www.routledge.com/9781032193120

For Theresa, for Kara and for Kristen

CONTENTS

PREFACE

The Law of Public Communication provides practical, professional training in a book grounded in the liberal arts. Professors who assign this book wish to teach legal principles, demonstrate methods of analyzing cases and provide practical knowledge for future communicators. The text explains the law as it applies to the daily work of writers, broadcasters, advertisers, cable operators, Internet service providers, public relations practitioners, photographers, bloggers and other public communicators. The many statutes and cases are presented in a cohesive narrative that is understandable even to students studying law for the first time. While presenting much of the rich complexity of communication law, we strive for readability. To help ensure understanding, we tell the legal story through actual cases, reinforcing the narrative with frequent summaries of major points. Always, we hope to convey the fascination we maintain with the dynamic field of communication law.

In addition to acquiring practical knowledge, students learn legal principles and methods of analysis necessary to evaluate and keep abreast of a rapidly changing subject. We discuss cases in sufficient detail—often with quotations—for students to understand legal issues, identify court holdings and appreciate the courts' rationale. We explain constitutional doctrine, theories of media regulation and judicial tests in Chapter 2. Chapter 3 addresses prior restraints, postpublication penalties and content-neutral regulations. We apply the theories and tools presented in Chapters 2 and 3 repeatedly throughout the text. As was true in earlier editions, the twelfth edition contains extensive but unobtrusive footnotes to document the scholarship on which assertions are based and to suggest further reading for the student and professor.

The authors recognize that publishers, broadcasters and other media owners are not the only speakers with First Amendment rights. Thus, we cover the law of public relations and advertising as it affects political campaign coordinators, corporate spokespersons and commercial advertisers. We offer separate chapters on commercial and political speech, while integrating issues of commercial communication into traditional chapters of libel, privacy, copyright and access to courts. The book also speaks to the growing number of independent media entrepreneurs, including community journalists, bloggers and freelancers.

All areas of communication law—including libel, privacy, copyright, corporate speech and public records laws—are constantly evolving, often in response to new technologies. Each chapter of *The Law of Public Communication* includes cases and regulations resulting from new technologies; the twelfth edition also offers new sections on drones, hate speech in social media, revenge porn sites, "dark money" in election campaigns and the European right to be forgotten.

The Law of Public Communication focuses on the law regulating the content of public communication, not on laws regulating the structure of corporate media, newsroom safety or labor-management contracts. Thus, for example, taxes on the media are discussed in cases where they restrict what might be said or published. Important business and economic issues that do not directly affect the content of the media are left to courses in business law and communication management.

William E. Lee

Daxton R. Stewart

Jonathan Peters

NEW TO THE TWELFTH EDITION

Updates the extradition proceedings of WikiLeaks founder Julian Assange and the Biden administration's decision to continue prosecuting Assange for violating the Espionage Act.

Notes the confiscation by the United States of $5.2 million from Edward Snowden because he did not comply with his secrecy agreement prior to publishing his book.

Explains the Fourth Circuit's decision to dismiss the suit by former national security officials challenging the government's review of proposed books and other forms of expression discussing classified information.

Discusses the extraordinary attempt by the Trump administration to block publication of a book by former National Security Advisor John Bolton and the Biden administration's unexpected settlement with Bolton allowing him to keep his book profits.

Notes new voting patterns at the U.S. Supreme Court, including the emergence of four justices as the swing vote.

Explains why Senate Democrats expedited the confirmation of Justice Breyer's replacement, Ketanji Brown Jackson, and why Jackson is unlikely to alter the Court's current 6–3 conservative/liberal split.

Presents the use of "dark money" in the 2020 federal elections and notes the inability of Senate Democrats to alter Senate rules to enable enactment of legislation requiring disclosure of dark money donors.

Describes the U.S. Supreme Court ruling in *Mahanoy Area School District v. B.L.*, which offers First Amendment protection to students engaging in profane off-campus social media postings.

Analyzes the U.S. Supreme Court ruling in *Americans for Prosperity Foundation v. Bonta* and presents the implications of that ruling for donor disclosure requirements.

Updates developments in lobbying regulation, including the Biden administration's new ethics rules.

Notes the issues in *Cruz v. FEC*, a case before the U.S. Supreme Court involving a challenge to a statute restricting the use of donor funds to pay back candidate loans.

Explores the issues regarding voir dire in high-publicity trials presented by *United States v. Tsarnaev*, a case decided by the U.S. Supreme Court in 2022.

Describes the impact of the COVID-19 pandemic on electronic coverage of federal court proceedings, including livestreaming of Supreme Court oral arguments.

Critiques the unusual prior restraint preventing the *New York Times* from publishing Project Veritas' attorney-client memos.

Discusses the Trump administration's subpoenas of the email and phone records of eight journalists and the Biden administration's efforts to remake Department of Justice policies to better protect journalists.

Notes changes to the Patriot Act "business records" provisions.

Explains the Third Circuit's ruling in *Free Speech Coalition v. Attorney General*, creating an exemption from age-verification requirements for those producers of sexual imagery not featuring young-looking performers.

Contrasts the political advertising policies of social media platforms, such as Twitter, with the legal obligations of broadcasters and shows the increasing use of social media platforms by candidates.

Discusses state legislation designed to police perceived bias in the content practices and policies of social media companies.

Updates the analysis of net neutrality under the Trump and Biden administrations, and notes efforts at the federal and state levels to pass net neutrality legislation.

Notes the spread of viral misinformation during the COVID-19 pandemic, and updates the discussion of Facebook's approach to identifying and reviewing viral misinformation.

Explains the purpose of the newly established Facebook Oversight Board and how it operates to uphold or reverse Facebook content decisions in light of the company's stated values and policies.

Presents a new Eighth Circuit case holding that a government official's social media campaign account may not be a designated public forum.

Notes the Supreme Court of California's case upholding the constitutionality of prohibitions on participant monitoring.

Updates the FAA rules regarding drone use, discussing one that allows for drones to be flown over people, at night and over moving vehicles, without the need to seek waivers.

Analyzes the commercialization rights of college athletes, in light of the Supreme Court's 2021 case *NCAA v. Alston* and the NCAA's new interim policy suspending its name, image and likeness rules.

Notes the dismissal of Roy Moore's privacy claims against Sacha Baron Cohen for his satirical Showtime program.

Presents the 2020 Supreme Court decision holding that a state may not copyright its entire official code that includes both the laws and annotations interpreting them.

Observes the rise of the NFT art market and the copyright issues raised by people stealing digital art and passing it off as their own to sell.

Explains the purpose of the newly established Copyright Claims Board and how it operates to provide an efficient way to resolve certain disputes that involve claims of less than $30,000.

Discusses high-profile ongoing defamation litigation by voting machine companies and poll workers against broadcasters such as Fox News, One America News and Newsmax, who they accuse of harming their reputations by broadcasting lies about the 2020 election.

Updates criminal libel law, which a federal judge upheld against a First Amendment challenge in 2021.

Notes huge damage award against a celebrity blogger in a case brought by rapper Cardi B, topping $4 million after a jury trial.

Analyzes liability for reposting images found on social media with defamatory information added, as when MSNBC's Joy Reid was found responsible as a "solo author" for images initially shared by another person on Twitter when she reposted them on Instagram.

Reviews bills under consideration by Congress to reform or repeal Section 230 of the Communications Decency Act, and the First Amendment challenges they will face if passed, along with review of the Florida and Texas state law efforts to subvert Section 230, both of which were halted by federal district courts in 2021. Also updates First Amendment challenges to the Fight Online Sex Trafficking Act (FOSTA), a revision to Section 230 made by Congress in 2018.

Describes current challenges to the "actual malice" standard of *New York Times v. Sullivan*, the bedrock of American defamation law, including the possibility of the Supreme Court reconsidering the case, and lower courts finding ways around it to continue litigation against journalists.

Comments on recent litigation by politicians like Donald Trump and Sarah Palin against media for publishing opinion pieces, looking to get to trial on what they believe are false statements embedded in those columns.

Presents recent Ninth Circuit case on the "reasonable consumer" standard, finding that Trader Joe's "100% Manuka Honey" that contained well less than that percentage was not deceptive.

Offers more detail on puffery, including *Leonard v. PepsiCo* (soon to be a docuseries on Apple TV+), in which a court ruled that a television ad in which a teenager used Pepsi Points to buy a fighter jet was not an actual offer that could be redeemed.

Explains FTC enforcement efforts against deceptive advertising and marketing in cryptocurrency schemes.

Updates First Amendment cases on access to social media accounts of public officials who block users and journalists, including *Knight First Amendment Institute v. Trump*.

Notes recent FOIA litigation to get access to source materials and unredacted versions of the Mueller Report.

ACKNOWLEDGMENTS

We thank the many people who have helped and encouraged us, particularly the scores of professors and students who have told us our book is comprehensive, accurate and interesting. We appreciate our critics and reviewers who have pointed out errors and offered many suggestions we have incorporated into the text. Once again, we thank Kent Middleton for his excellent work on this book for more than 30 years. Even though he is no longer contributing to the book, his insistence on clear and engaging writing continues to guide us.

William E. Lee
University of Georgia
weyrelee@uga.edu

Daxton R. (Chip) Stewart
Texas Christian University
d.stewart@tcu.edu

Jonathan Peters
University of Georgia
jonathan.peters@uga.edu

Public Communication and the Law

Parents, upset by teenagers posting vulgar messages on social media, have turned to school officials demanding that "spill the tea" accounts be shut down. School officials, in turn, respond that they have no authority over social media platforms.[1] And when school officials consider punishing students for inappropriate social media postings, their authority is confined by a landmark 2021 U.S. Supreme Court ruling protecting off-campus student speech.

For more than 50 years courts have protected peaceful political expression on campus if the expression does not disrupt the school. As the Supreme Court in 1969 stated in *Tinker v. Des Moines Independent Community School District*, public school students do not "shed their constitutional rights to freedom of speech or expression at the schoolhouse gate."[2] But in cases after *Tinker*, the Court ruled that due to the unique circumstances of the high school environment, vulgar speech

---

[1] Julie Jargon, "The New Cyberbullying Tactic," *Wall St. J.*, Dec. 20, 2021, at A13.
[2] 393 U.S. 503, 506 (1969).

DOI: 10.4324/9781003264736-1

at school assemblies could be punished.[3] Moreover, speech in a school-sponsored newspaper could be regulated by the principal.[4]

Tinker and the Court's subsequent student speech cases did not anticipate the problems created by off-campus student speech, such as social media postings threatening or bullying teachers and other students. In recent years, courts have struggled to define the appropriate level of administrators' control over off-campus speech, but in 2021, in *Mahanoy Area School District v. B.L.*, the Supreme Court ruled that schools may only punish off-campus speech in narrow circumstances.[5] The Court cautioned that school administrators also have a duty to inculcate values respecting freedom of speech.

Mahanoy stemmed from a Snapchat post by Brandi Levy, who was unsuccessful in her effort to make her high school's varsity cheerleading squad. On the weekend after learning that her tryout was unsuccessful, Levy posted a photo on Snapchat showing Levy and a friend with middle fingers raised; the caption said, "Fuck school fuck softball fuck cheer fuck everything." Another student took a screenshot of Levy's post and instead of disappearing, the image soon spread throughout the school community, resulting in school officials disciplining Levy because her "negativity" could impact students. Levy and her parents sued the school district, claiming a violation of Brandi's First Amendment rights.

A federal district court found Levy's post had not caused substantial disruption at the school, a conclusion sustained by the Court of Appeals for the Third Circuit. The appellate court, however, also issued a categorical rule preventing schools from punishing off-campus speech.[6] In a concurring opinion, Judge Thomas Ambro said Levy's speech should be protected because it was not disruptive, but the majority was wrong to protect all off-campus speech.

By an 8–1 vote, the Supreme Court agreed with Ambro's approach. Even off-campus speech could be punished if it involved bullying, harassment, or threats aimed at teachers or other students. Levy's speech, though, did not target anyone, nor did her vulgarity meet the legal definition of obscenity. The school's interest in punishing vulgar language was weakened because Levy's post occurred on the weekend off campus and did not disrupt school activities.

The Court was wary of giving administrators too much latitude to punish off-campus speech, explaining that parents are better suited than administrators to supervise what students say off campus. Moreover, the prospect of school officials monitoring off-campus speech continuously was at odds with free speech values. Most importantly, schools have a role to play in teaching that unpopular speech is worthy of protection. Justice Stephen Breyer, writing for the Court, said "America's public schools are the nurseries of democracy. Our representative democracy only works if we protect the 'marketplace of ideas.'" Justice Breyer concluded by noting it might be tempting to dismiss Levy's Snapchat post as "unworthy" of robust First Amendment protection, "But sometimes it is necessary to protect the superfluous in order to preserve the necessary."

Mahanoy illustrates that in in contemporary First Amendment doctrine, context often defines the level of First Amendment protection. As will be discussed in Chapter 2, the rights of high school students are generally different than those of

---

[3] Bethel Sch. Dist. No. 403 v. Fraser, 478 U.S. 675 (1986).
[4] Hazelwood Sch. Dist. v. Kuhlmeier, 484 U.S. 260 (1988).
[5] 141 S. Ct. 2038 (2021).
[6] 964 F.3d 170 (3rd Cir. 2020).

college students. Similarly, speech by government employees at work can be limited in ways that would be impermissible if applied to the public. Where speech occurs often defines its protection. If Levy had spoken her message of displeasure in class, or at an assembly, school officials would have been able to punish her.

Mahanoy is also significant because it illustrates the current Court's philosophical preference for free speech. Moreover, due to the split between the liberal and conservative blocs at the Court, discussed later in this chapter, *Mahanoy* shows that to obtain a majority, opinions must often be exceedingly narrow and therefore offer little guidance to lower courts. Indeed, apart from *Mahanoy*'s philosophical preference for free speech, Justice Clarence Thomas claimed in a dissenting opinion that lower courts "will almost certainly be at a loss as to what exactly the Court's opinion today means."

This book explains the legal protections available to public communicators and emphasizes the First Amendment to the U.S. Constitution, adopted in 1791. As interpreted by the U.S. Supreme Court, the First Amendment largely insulates public communicators from liability for publication on issues of public importance. The First Amendment makes it almost impossible for the government to stop publication before news reports and opinion, some of it hyperbolic, false, and even classified, can "see the light of day."

The framers of the Constitution recognized that the guarantee of freedom of expression rests not just on limiting the power of government but also on the attitudes of the public. As Alexander Hamilton wrote in *The Federalist No. 84*, the security of liberty of the press "must altogether depend upon public opinion, and on the general spirit of the people."

Americans in 2022 are sharply divided in their trust and support of news media; there are strong social forces seeking to punish the press for its excesses and mistakes. Much of this book discusses the ways by which society holds public communicators accountable, but also explains why the First Amendment generally protects the freedom to publish. Important concepts, such as the line between private information and newsworthy information—concepts that in are flux due to changing social customs—are also explored.

This book also shows that the First Amendment's protection is not limited to journalists working for mainstream media outlets. As the Supreme Court has noted in a variety of cases, street-corner speakers have the same First Amendment protection as journalists. Or, stated in contemporary terms, bloggers have the same constitutional status as the journalists writing for the *Wall Street Journal*.

This chapter examines legal concepts and procedures that are important to an understanding of the law of public communication. It explains the purpose and organization of law and describes court procedures. Finally, this chapter discusses how communicators work with lawyers.

THE SOURCES OF LAW

Law can be defined in many ways, but for our purposes, law is the system of rules that govern society. The system of rules serves many functions in our society, including regulating the behavior of citizens and corporations. Law prohibits murder and restricts what advertisers can say about their products. It provides a vehicle to settle disputes, such as when a reporter refuses to testify in court. Furthermore, law limits the government's power to interfere with individual rights, such as the right to speak and publish.

The law in the United States comes primarily from six sources: constitutions, statutes, administrative rules and regulations, executive actions, the **common law**[7] and the law of equity.

Constitutional Law

Constitutions are the supreme source of law in the United States and are the most direct reflection of the kind of government desired by the people. Constitutions of both the federal and state governments supersede all other declarations of public policy. The Constitution of the federal government and the constitutions of the 50 states establish the framework for governing. They outline the structure of government and define governmental authority and responsibilities.

Frequently, a constitution limits the powers of government, as in the case of the Bill of Rights, the first ten amendments to the U.S. Constitution. The Bill of Rights protects the rights and liberties of U.S. citizens against infringement by government. The First Amendment, particularly its prohibition against laws abridging freedom of speech and the press, provides the foundation for communication law.

The federal constitution is the country's ultimate legal authority. Any federal law, state law or state constitution that contradicts the U.S. Constitution cannot be implemented; the U.S. Constitution prevails. Similarly, a state constitution prevails in conflicts with either the **statutory law** or the common law in the same state. However, federal and state laws that do not conflict with the federal constitution can provide more protection for communicators than is available under the First Amendment alone. For example, most states shield journalists from revealing confidential news sources in more circumstances than the First Amendment as interpreted by the U.S. Supreme Court.

The Supreme Court, the nation's supreme judicial body, has the last word on the meaning of the federal constitution. Each state's supreme court is the interpreter of that state's constitution. Only the U.S. Supreme Court can resolve conflicts between the federal and state constitutions. The courts make constitutional law when they decide a case or controversy by interpreting a constitution. Constitutional law can be understood only by reading the opinions of the courts.

The U.S. Constitution is hard to amend and therefore is changed infrequently. Amendments to the U.S. Constitution can be proposed only by two-thirds of the members of both houses of Congress or by a convention called by two-thirds of the state legislatures. Amendments must be ratified by three-fourths of the state legislatures or by state constitutional conventions in three-fourths of the states.

Statutory Law

A major source of law in the United States is the collection of statutes and ordinances written by legislative bodies—the U.S. Congress, the 50 state legislatures, county commissions, city councils and countless other lawmaking bodies. Statutes set forth enforceable rules to govern social behavior. Areas of communication law controlled by statutes include advertising, copyright, electronic media, obscenity and access to government-held information.

Almost all this country's criminal law, including a prohibition against the distribution of obscenity, is statutory. Statutes not only prohibit antisocial acts but also frequently provide for the oversight of acceptable behavior. For example, the

---

[7] Definitions for terms printed in boldface can be found in the glossary at the end of the book.

federal Communications Act of 1934 was adopted so that the broadcast spectrum would be used for the public good.

The process of adopting statutes allows lawmakers to carefully study a complicated issue—such as how to regulate the use of the electromagnetic spectrum—and write an appropriate law. The process permits anyone or any group to make suggestions through letters, personal contacts and hearings. In practice, well-organized special interests such as broadcasters and telecommunications companies substantially influence the legislative process. As shown in Chapter 7, highly regulated industries have the largest lobbying expenditures.

The adoption of a statute does not conclude the lawmaking process. Executive branch officials often must interpret statutes through administrative rules. Judges add meaning when either the statutes themselves or their application are challenged in court. Judges explain how statutes apply in specific cases, as when the U.S. Supreme Court ruled in 2005 that providers of peer-to-peer file-sharing services may be "contributory infringers" of material protected under the Copyright Act.[8] In 2011, the U.S. Supreme Court held that corporations have no "personal privacy" under a section of the Freedom of Information Act.[9] Consequently, information obtained from AT&T during the course of a federal investigation could be disclosed.

The courts can invalidate state and local laws that conflict with federal laws or the U.S. Constitution, including the First Amendment. For example, in 2011, the U.S. Supreme Court declared unconstitutional a California statute restricting children's access to violent video games.[10]

Sometimes federal laws **preempt** state regulation, thereby monopolizing governmental control over a specific subject. Article VI, Paragraph 2 of the U.S. Constitution, known as the Supremacy Clause, provides that state law cannot supersede federal law. Thus, the U.S. Supreme Court nullified an Oklahoma statute banning the advertising of wine on cable television because it conflicted with federal law prohibiting the editing of national and regional television programming carried by cable systems.[11]

Administrative Law

Federal agencies such as the Federal Communications Commission (FCC) and the Federal Trade Commission (FTC) develop rules and decisions known as **administrative law**. These agencies dominate several areas of communication law. The FCC regulates the broadcast, cable, satellite and telephone industries. The FTC regulates advertising and telemarketing. Other agencies overseeing communication include the Securities and Exchange Commission (SEC), which controls communication related to the securities industry; the Federal Election Commission (FEC), which regulates political campaign contributions and expenditures; and the Food and Drug Administration (FDA), which regulates prescription drug and medical product advertising, and tobacco product advertising. Table 1.1 lists these agencies, their areas of regulation and key regulations.

Administrative agencies are often founded on the premise that they will be independent bodies of experts who set policy solely by analyzing facts. However,

---

[8] Metro-Goldwyn-Mayer Studios, Inc. v. Grokster, Ltd., 545 U.S. 913 (2005).
[9] FCC v. AT&T, Inc., 562 U.S. 397 (2011).
[10] Brown v. Entm't Merchant Ass'n, 564 U.S. 786 (2011).
[11] Capital Cities Cable, Inc. v. Crisp, 467 U.S. 691 (1984).

Table 1.1 Federal Regulatory Agencies

Agency	Areas of Regulation	Key Regulations
Federal Communications Commission (FCC)	Radio, television, cable, satellite, telephone	Political broadcasting rules, indecency regulations, children's television regulations
Federal Election Commission (FEC)	Federal elections	Contribution limits and prohibitions, disclosure of campaign finances, campaign expenditures
Federal Trade Commission (FTC)	Advertising (except prescription drugs and medical devices), telemarketing	Deceptive advertising, product labeling, unfair consumer practices, children's online privacy, tobacco health warnings
Food and Drug Administration (FDA)	Food, drugs, medical devices, cosmetics, tobacco	Prescription drug advertising, medical device advertising, food, drug, cosmetic labels, tobacco advertising
Securities and Exchange Commission (SEC)	Securities brokers, investment advisors, stock exchanges	Insider trading, false/misleading information

regulation by administrative agencies is an intensely political process involving complex interactions among the regulatory agency, the regulated industry, Congress, the president and public interest groups. The president influences an agency by naming commissioners, subject to approval by the Senate, and designating an agency's chair. Through the Office of Management and Budget, the executive branch reviews proposed regulations to determine consistency with the president's policies. Congress shapes regulation by telling agencies which industries or practices they can regulate. Moreover, Congress controls the budgets of agencies, and congressional committees closely monitor the actions of agencies. Regulated industries, such as telecommunications, are among the largest contributors to political campaigns. These industries use their ties to elected officials to influence regulatory agencies.

Congress creates administrative agencies to supervise activities or industries that require more attention than legislators can provide. Administrative agencies serve a variety of functions, unique in the American system of government. First, agencies engage in **rulemaking**, a process that is like the legislative function. For example, the FCC developed a rule prohibiting a company from owning a television station and a newspaper in the same city. Second, agencies **adjudicate** disputes, resolving complaints initiated by business competitors, the public or the agency itself. Administrative law judges conduct hearings resembling judicial proceedings at which evidence is submitted and witnesses are examined and cross-examined. After a hearing, an FTC administrative law judge found that advertisements for Extra Strength Doan's Pills were deceptive because they contained an unsubstantiated claim that Doan's Pills relieved pain more effectively than competing brands such as Tylenol. Third, agencies perform executive branch functions when they enforce rules against a firm or individual. In recent years, the FCC has fined broadcasters for violating indecency regulations by broadcasting sexual language. Before making its ruling, the agency reviewed the complaints of listeners and responses of broadcast licensees.

Regulatory agencies are bound by the requirements of the Administrative Procedure Act (APA).[12] This statute specifies the procedures that must be employed when an agency enacts rules or enforces regulations. For example, the APA requires that parties can comment on proposed rules. Parties may also petition an agency to issue, amend, or repeal a rule. Under the APA, a party may seek judicial review of an agency action on several grounds, such as the agency has exceeded its statutory authority. Federal judges reviewing agency actions ensure that administrative agencies act within the boundaries set by the Constitution and statutory law.

An administrative action may be challenged on the ground that the agency has exceeded its statutory authority. For example, in 2000, the Supreme Court agreed with tobacco manufacturers that the FDA exceeded its authority when the agency banned outdoor tobacco advertisements near schools and playgrounds. Although the Supreme Court agreed that tobacco poses a serious health threat, the Court found Congress excluded tobacco products from the FDA's jurisdiction at that time. The Court stated, "an administrative agency's power to regulate in the public interest must always be grounded in a valid grant of authority from Congress."[13] (Congress conferred power on the FDA to regulate tobacco product advertising in 2009, a development discussed in Chapter 8.) Similarly, in 2019, a federal district found that a Trump administration rule requiring drug makers to put prices in television advertisements exceeded the statutory authority of the Department of Health and Human Services.[14]

An agency's action may be challenged on the ground that it is arbitrary and capricious. A federal appeals court ruled in 2009 that the FCC acted arbitrarily when it capped at 30 percent the national market share of any cable company. Given the presence of competitors, such as direct broadcast satellite (DBS) systems, the court found there was no proof that a cable operator serving more than 30 percent of subscribers would pose a threat to competition.[15] In contrast, the Supreme Court ruled in 2021 the FCC did not act capriciously when it eliminated a ban on newspaper-broadcast combinations in the same market.[16] The FCC found the ban was obsolete due to the impact of new media outlets such as cable and Internet-based news and entertainment platforms, a conclusion supported by evidence regarding competition.

An agency's action may also be challenged as unconstitutional. The Supreme Court ruled that the FEC acted unconstitutionally when it sought to punish the Colorado Republican Party for purchasing radio advertising in a political campaign.[17] The Supreme Court ruled that a political party's advertising expenditures, like those of other individuals or groups, are constitutionally protected speech that cannot be limited if the expenditures are not coordinated with any candidate.

Executive Actions

The president and other governmental executive officers can also make law. The president exercises power by appointing regulators, issuing executive orders and proclamations, and forging executive agreements with foreign countries. Much of the president's authority derives from Article 2 of the U.S. Constitution, requiring

---

[12] 5 U.S.C. § 551 et seq.
[13] FDA v. Brown & Williamson Tobacco Co., 529 U.S. 120, 161 (2000).
[14] Merck & Co. v. Dep't of Health and Human Serv., 385 F. Supp. 3d 81 (D.D.C. 2019).
[15] Comcast v. FCC, 579 F.3d 1 (D.C. Cir. 2009).
[16] FCC v. Prometheus Radio Project, 141 S. Ct. 1150 (2021).
[17] Colorado Republican Campaign Committee v. FEC, 518 U.S. 604 (1996).

the president to "take Care that the Laws be faithfully executed." The Supreme Court has allowed the chief executive broad regulatory powers under the clause. In addition, Congress often grants the president the authority to administer statutes.

Perhaps the president's greatest influence on communication law comes from the power to nominate judges to the federal courts, including the U.S. Supreme Court. The political and judicial philosophies of the judges, and particularly their interpretation of the First Amendment, determine the boundaries of freedom for communicators. The president also nominates the members of several administrative agencies, including the FCC, the FTC and the SEC. The president seldom issues executive orders that directly affect the law of public communication. An exception is the order that determines the documents that should be "classified" and thereby withheld from public disclosure to protect national security.

Common Law

The common law, often called judge-made law, was the most important source of law during the early development of this country. Unlike the general rules adopted as statutes by legislatures, the common law is the accumulation of rulings made by the courts in individual disputes. Judges, not legislatures, largely created the law of privacy, which allows individuals to collect damage awards for media disclosure of highly offensive personal information.

Common law in the United States grew out of the English common law. For centuries, judges in England, under the authority of the king, decided controversies based on tradition and custom. These rulings established **precedents** that, together, became the law of the land. When the English colonized America, they brought the common law, including the precedents, with them.

The common law recognizes the importance of stability and predictability in the law. The common law is based on the judicial policy of **stare decisis**, which roughly means "let past decisions stand." In the common law, a judge decides a case by applying the law established by other judges in earlier, similar cases. The reliance on precedent not only provides continuity but also restricts judicial abuse of discretion. Thus, editors can use previous case law to help them determine whether a picture they want to publish is likely to be considered a violation of someone's privacy.

Although the common law promotes stability, it also allows for flexibility. The common law can adjust to fit changing circumstances because each judge can interpret and modify the law. Judges have five options when considering a case. They can (1) apply a precedent directly, (2) modify a precedent to fit new facts, (3) establish a new precedent by distinguishing the new case from previous cases, (4) overrule a previous precedent as no longer appropriate or (5) ignore precedent. In most cases, precedent is either followed or adjusted to meet the facts at hand. Judges only rarely overrule previous precedents directly. Ignoring precedents greatly increases the risks of an opinion being overturned by a higher court.

Constitutional law and statutory law have a higher legal status than the common law, and, therefore, the common law is relied on only when a statute or constitutional provision is not applicable. Concepts developed in common law can become part of statutes when legislatures incorporate those concepts into a statute, a process called codification. For example, in 1976, Congress rewrote the federal copyright statute to codify a judicially created exception to a copyright owner's absolute control of a book, film or musical score.

Sometimes, people confuse the common law with constitutional law. Both are created in part by judicial opinions based on precedent. However, constitutional law is based on judicial interpretation of a constitution, whereas common law is based on custom and practice.

The common law is not written down in one book. It can be understood only by reading recorded court decisions in hundreds of different volumes. Although the 1976 copyright statute is in one volume of the United States Code, the common law of privacy can be discovered only by synthesizing numerous state and federal judicial opinions.

Common law is primarily state law. Each state has its own judicial traditions. However, as shown in Chapter 11, the Federal Rules of Evidence now allow federal judges to create common-law testimonial privileges. In 1996, the U.S. Supreme Court ruled that a federal common-law privilege covered confidential communications between therapists and patients.[18] Recently, journalists have argued that a federal common-law privilege should also protect journalist-source relations. These claims have been rejected.

Law of Equity

The sixth source of law, equity, is historically related to the common law. Although **equity** is a legal term, it means what it sounds like. The law of equity allows courts to take action that is fair or just.

The law of equity developed because English common law allowed individuals to collect only monetary compensation after an injury had occurred. Under the law of equity, a **litigant** could petition the king to "do right for the love of God and by way of charity."[19] The law of equity allowed for preventive action and for remedial action other than monetary compensation. Although judges sitting in equity must consider precedent, they have substantial discretion to order a remedy they believe fair and appropriate.

Unlike England, the United States and most of the 50 states have never had separate courts of equity. Equity developed in the same courts that decided common-law cases. However, juries are never used in equity suits.

Equity is significant in communication law primarily because of its preventive possibilities. Judges, for example, might use equity to halt the publication of a story considered a danger to national security. Punishment after publication would not protect national security.

■ SUMMARY ■

Law in the United States comes from constitutions, statutes, administrative agencies, executive orders, common law and equity. Constitutions outline the structure of government and define governmental authority and responsibilities. In the United States, the First Amendment to the federal Constitution protects the right to free speech and to a free press. Statutes are enforceable rules written by legislative bodies to govern social behavior. Administrative agencies make law as they adopt rules and adjudicate disputes, as authorized by statute. Executive orders are issued by the top officer in the executive branch of government. The common law is a collection of judicial decisions based on custom and tradition. Equity provides alternatives to the legal remedies available through the common law.

---

[18] Jaffee v. Redmond, 518 U.S. 1 (1996).
[19] Henry Abraham, *The Judicial Process* 14 (1986).

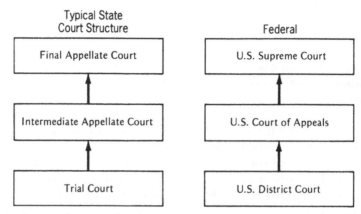

FIGURE 1.1 Comparative examples of state and federal court structures.

THE COURTS

Although agencies in all three branches of government in the United States make law, the judiciary is particularly important to a student of the law of public communication. There are 52 court systems in the country: the federal system, a system for each state and another in the District of Columbia. The structures of the 52 systems are similar, but the state systems operate independently of the federal system under the authority of the state constitutions and laws.

Most court systems consist of three layers (see Figure 1.1). At the lowest level are the trial courts, where the facts of each case are evaluated in light of the applicable law. The middle layer for both the federal system and many states is an intermediate **appellate court**. Finally, all court systems include a court of ultimate appeal, usually called a supreme court. The federal court system is the most important for the law of public communication.

The Federal System

The U.S. Constitution mandates only one federal court, the U.S. Supreme Court, but provides for "such inferior courts as the Congress may from time to time ordain and establish."[20] The Constitution also spells out the **jurisdiction**, or areas of responsibility, of the federal courts. The federal courts exercise ultimate authority over the meaning of the Constitution, including the constitutionality of statutes that impinge on the First Amendment. The federal courts also resolve conflicts in the interpretation of federal statutory law. The federal courts hear controversies involving the United States, such as when the Department of Justice seeks a court order to obtain the name of a confidential news source. The federal courts can hear controversies between citizens or corporations of different states. Frequently, for example, the two parties in a libel suit—the person suing, and the publisher or broadcaster being sued—live in different states. Matters not specifically assigned to the federal courts by the Constitution are tried in state courts.

Congress created the federal judicial system in 1789 with the adoption of the Federal Judiciary Act. The federal system includes 94 trial courts, the U.S. district

---

[20] U.S. Const. art. III, § 1.

courts; 13 intermediate appellate courts, the judicial circuits of the U.S. Courts of Appeals; and the highest appellate court, the U.S. Supreme Court. Courts with special jurisdiction, such as the U.S. Tax Court, are not generally important to the law of public communication.

TRIAL COURTS Almost all court cases begin in the trial courts, the U.S. district courts. These are also called courts of **original jurisdiction**. Trial courts examine the facts, or evidence, in a case and then apply the appropriate law. Only trial courts employ juries.

There are 94 U.S. district courts. There is at least one federal district court in every state. Some states, such as Alaska, have only one district court. Other states, such as New York, have multiple districts. District courts also exist in the District of Columbia and in territories such as Guam. Many districts have more than one judge. By 2020, Congress had authorized 677 district court judgeships.

INTERMEDIATE APPELLATE COURTS Every person who loses in a trial court has the right to at least one **appeal**. In the federal system, that appeal is made to an intermediate appellate court. Appellate courts do not hold new trials and generally do not reevaluate the facts of cases. Rather, their responsibility is to ensure that trial courts use the proper procedures and apply the law correctly.

Appellate court judges decide cases primarily based on lower court records and lawyers' written arguments, called *briefs*. The judges also hear a short oral argument by attorneys for both sides. If an appellate court discovers that a trial court has erred, the higher court may reverse, or overturn, the lower court and **remand** the case or send it back to a lower court for a new trial.

An appeal of a federal district court decision will ordinarily be considered in one of the 13 circuits of the U.S. Courts of Appeals (see Figure 1.2). The jurisdictions of 12 of these courts are defined geographically. The thirteenth, the U.S. Court of Appeals for the Federal Circuit, handles only specialized appeals.

By 2020, Congress had authorized 179 appellate court judgeships. The Ninth Circuit, with 29 judges, has the largest number of judges; the First Circuit, with six

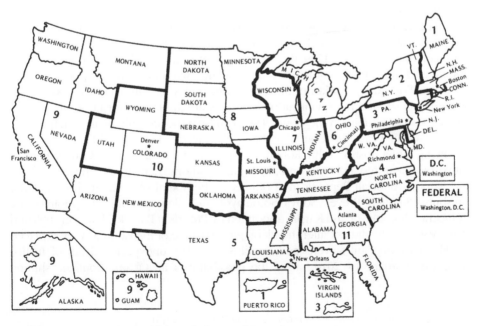

FIGURE 1.2 The 13 circuits of the U.S. Courts of Appeals.

judges, has the smallest number. Most cases are heard by a panel of three judges. Particularly important cases will be heard **en banc**, that is, by all the judges of the court. For example, in 2007, the U.S. Court of Appeals for the D.C. Circuit ruled en banc that Congressman Jim McDermott violated House ethics rules when he passed to journalists a tape recording he knew had been illegally created by a Florida couple.[21]

The decisions of the U.S. Courts of Appeals must be followed by the federal district courts under their jurisdiction. Opinions of the Courts of Appeals may be persuasive authority but are not binding on state courts in the same jurisdiction deciding similar issues. Although federal appeals court decisions are not binding outside their jurisdiction, they are frequently influential.

Three circuits of the U.S. Courts of Appeals are particularly important to communication law. The Second Circuit, which hears appeals from federal courts in New York, decides many media cases because New York City is the headquarters for many magazines, book publishers, advertising and public relations agencies. The Court of Appeals for the D.C. Circuit hears most of the appeals of decisions by the FCC and the FTC and many of the cases involving the federal Freedom of Information Act. The Ninth Circuit, with jurisdiction over Hollywood and Silicon Valley, frequently decides film, television, and copyright cases.

THE U.S. SUPREME COURT Although the U.S. Supreme Court can exercise both original and appellate jurisdiction, it is primarily an appellate court. The Constitution specifically limits the occasions when the Supreme Court can be the first court to consider a legal controversy, and the Court has decided cases in that capacity fewer than 250 times in the history of the country. Original jurisdiction cases are increasingly rare on the Court's docket; in recent years the Court has generally disposed of only one original jurisdiction case each term, and in 2012 and 2013, it disposed of no original jurisdiction cases.[22] However, because the Court has the last word in the interpretation of federal law, the Court's appellate duties make it one of the most powerful institutions in the world. Appellate cases reach the Court from all other federal courts, federal regulatory agencies and state supreme courts.

The nine Supreme Court justices, like all federal judges, are appointed by the president and confirmed by the Senate, a process that recently has become extremely partisan. Since 1789, the Senate has refused to confirm 12 Supreme Court nominees. Eleven nominations have been withdrawn when strong opposition was apparent. For example, Harriet Miers's nomination was withdrawn in 2005 when Senators questioned her qualifications. Justices are appointed for life or as long as they choose to remain on the Court. They can be removed only by impeachment.[23]

In recent years the Court has been sharply divided along ideological lines. Following Chief Justice John Roberts's appointment in 2005, the Court's conservative bloc featured Roberts, Antonin Scalia, Anthony Kennedy, Clarence Thomas and Samuel Alito, all Republican appointees. The liberal bloc featured Ruth Bader Ginsburg, Stephen Breyer, Sonya Sotomayor and Elena Kagan, all appointed by Democrats. Sotomayor and Kagan, appointed by President Barack Obama in 2009 and 2010, respectively, did not alter the ideological balance of the Court as they replaced the liberals John Paul Stevens and David Souter. The unexpected death of Justice Scalia on February 13, 2016, raised the possibility of an Obama nominee shifting

---

[21] 484 F.3d 573 (D.C. Cir. 2007).

[22] Lee Epstein et al., *The Supreme Court Compendium* 78 (6th ed. 2015).

[23] U.S. Const. art. III, § 1; *see also* Samuel Mermin, *Law and the Legal System* 327 (2nd ed. 1982).

PHOTO 1.1 Justices of the U.S. Supreme Court, October Term 2021. Front row, left to right: Associate Justice Samuel A. Alito Jr., Associate Justice Clarence Thomas, Chief Justice John G. Roberts Jr., Associate Justice Stephen G. Breyer, and Associate Justice Sonia Sotomayor. Back row, left to right: Associate Justice Brett M. Kavanaugh, Associate Justice Elena Kagan, Associate Justice Neil M. Gorsuch, and Associate Justice Amy Coney Barrett. In January 2022, Justice Breyer announced he would retire at the end of the Court's current Term.

Source: Fred Schilling, Collection of the Supreme Court of the United States.

the Court's ideological lineup, perhaps for a generation. Senate Republican majority leader Mitch McConnell announced that any Obama nominee would be blocked, stating, "This nomination will be determined by whoever wins the presidency."

President Obama countered that it was his constitutional duty to nominate; on March 16, 2016, he nominated Merrick Garland, chief judge of the Court of Appeals for the D.C. Circuit. Minutes after the announcement, Senator McConnell reiterated that the Senate acts as a check on the president; Senate Republicans refused to vote on Garland, and his nomination expired in early January 2017.

The gamble by the Senate Republican leadership paid off with the election of Donald Trump. During the 2016 campaign, Trump repeatedly stated if elected, he would appoint a justice in the mold of Scalia. On January 31, 2017, Trump nominated Neil M. Gorsuch, a federal appeals court judge in Denver who shares the conservative legal philosophy of Scalia. Democrats, embittered by the Republican refusal to consider Garland, filibustered Gorsuch's nomination, causing Republicans to change Senate rules meant to ensure bipartisan cooperation in considering Supreme Court nominees. Republicans lowered the threshold on Supreme Court nominations from 60 votes to a simple majority vote, eliminating the ability of the minority party to block a nominee.[24] Gorsuch was confirmed on April 7 and participated in a handful of cases argued during April 2017.

---

[24] Matt Flegenheimer, "Republicans Gut Filibuster Rule to Lift Gorsuch," *N.Y. Times*, Apr. 7, 2017, at A1.

When the Court is sharply divided, one justice poised between the two blocs emerges as the critical swing vote. During the period from 1994 to 2005, Sandra Day O'Connor was often the swing vote. From 2005 until his 2018 retirement, Justice Kennedy was the swing vote.[25] Although Kennedy voted more often with the conservative bloc than the liberal bloc, he abandoned the conservatives in several important 5–4 cases.[26] Most significantly, Kennedy joined the liberal bloc in the landmark 2015 *Obergefell v. Hodges* decision striking down state laws prohibiting same-sex marriage.[27] Kennedy's replacement, Brett Kavanaugh, was confirmed in 2018 after a bruising confirmation fight over sexual assault allegations. His appointment retained the Court's 5–4 conservative/liberal split.

The death of liberal icon Ruth Bader Ginsberg in September 2020 gave President Trump the opportunity to shift the Court's ideological balance. Democrats, still furious over the treatment of Garland in 2016, argued that it was "illegitimate" for Republicans to confirm a Republican nominee so close to the 2020 presidential election. Republicans responded that the accusations of hypocrisy were an "unwarranted tantrum from the left," and confirmed Amy Coney Barrett by a 52–48 vote, with every Democrat in opposition. Justice Barrett is the first justice since 1870 to be confirmed without single vote from the Senate minority party.

The late January 2022 retirement announcement by Justice Breyer gave President Joe Biden the opportunity to fulfil a campaign promise to nominate a black woman to the Supreme Court. The announcement was met with relief by Democrats who feared that a Senate takeover by Republicans after the 2022 elections could block Biden from fulfilling any vacancies. Biden's nominee, Judge Ketanji Brown Jackson, was approved by the Senate on April 7, 2022, and will join the Court when Breyer retires in summer 2022. Jackson clerked for Breyer and shares a similar judicial philosophy. Her appointment is unlikely to alter the dominance of the Court's conservative majority.

With a 6–3 conservative/liberal split, the days of a single swing justice may be over. Instead, based on the 2020 Term, the center of the Court includes four justices, Chief Justice Roberts, and Justices Gorsuch, Kavanaugh, and Barrett, who occasionally joined the three-member liberal wing to form majorities in divided cases. For example, Justices Breyer, Sotomayor and Kagan, along with Gorsuch and Kavanaugh, joined an opinion authored by Justice Barrett that held a policeman did not illegally obtain information from a law enforcement database.[28]

While there were six cases in the 2020 Term where the Court divided 6–3 along conservative/liberal lines,[29] the Court was unanimous in 46 percent of its cases, a significantly greater percentage than the average for the previous 80 years.[30]

Nonetheless, Democrats, fearful of the Court advancing a conservative agenda on issues such as abortion and the right to bear arms, pressed President Biden to support a plan to "pack" the Court by adding justices. Biden, though, chose to appoint a commission to study potential changes to the Court. The Commission's report, published in December 2021, made no specific recommendations for change, but gave an analysis of the pros and cons of reform proposals,

[25] Adam Liptak, "Roberts Court Shifts Right, Tipped by Kennedy," *N.Y. Times*, July 1, 2009, at A1; Jess Bravin, "Lawyers Swing for Kennedy Vote," *Wall St. J.*, Oct. 3, 2006, at A2.
[26] *See, e.g.*, Caperton v. Massey Coal Co., Inc., 556 U.S. 868 (2009); Kennedy v. Louisiana, 554 U.S. 407 (2008); Boumediene v. Bush, 553 U.S. 723 (2008).
[27] 135 S. Ct. 2584 (2015).
[28] Van Buren v. United States, 141 S. Ct. 1648 (2021).
[29] *See, e.g.*, Americans for Prosperity Found. v. Bonta, 141 S. Ct. 2373 (2021).
[30] Adam Liptak, "An Unpredictable Term Ends With a Turn to the Right," *N.Y. Times*, July 3, 2021, at A1.

Table 1.2 U.S. Supreme Court Caseload, 1964–2020 Terms						
	1964 Term (Warren, C.J.)	**1974 Term (Burger, C.J.)**	**1984 Term (Burger, C.J.)**	**1994 Term (Rehnquist, C.J.)**	**2004 Term (Rehnquist, C.J.)**	**2020 Term (Roberts, C.J.)**
Cases filed	2,288	3,661	4,046	6,996	7,496	5,307
Cases disposed of by full opinions	103	144	159	90	87	69
Disposed of by per curiam opinions	17	20	11	3	2	3

Sources: Administrative Office of the United States Courts, *Judicial Business of the United States Courts: 2005 Annual Report of the Director*; United States Supreme Court, *Chief Justice's Year-End Report on the Federal Judiciary*, 2021; Lee Epstein et al., *The Supreme Court Compendium* (2003).

such as term limits.[31] Advocates of reform described the Commission as producing a "milquetoast report." Imposing term limits requires a constitutional amendment, a highly unlikely event in the current polarized political environment.

The justices who are considered "conservative" and those who are considered "liberal" do not always vote as blocs, nor do conservatives or liberals always have predictable votes in free expression cases. Many of the conservative justices have joined their more liberal colleagues to support freedom of expression. For example, all the conservatives, except Justice Thomas, joined with the liberals to protect the speech of Brandi Levy in the *Mahanoy* case discussed earlier in this chapter. Justice Kennedy and Chief Justice Roberts joined with liberal Justices Ginsburg, Breyer, Sotomayor and Kagan to strike down a federal law punishing false claims about receiving a military decoration or medal.[32] Similarly, Chief Justice Roberts and Justices Scalia, Kennedy and Thomas joined with Ginsburg, Breyer, Sotomayor and Kagan to rule that Westboro Baptist Church was shielded from liability for its funeral picketing.[33]

As shown in Table 1.2, the number of cases filed with the Supreme Court has dramatically increased since 1954. While the number of cases accepted for oral argument and disposed of with a full opinion increased during the tenure of Chief Justices Earl Warren (1953–1969) and Warren E. Burger (1969–1986), Chief Justice Rehnquist (1986–2005) sought to reduce the number during his tenure. In the later part of Rehnquist's tenure, the Court usually received nearly 8,000 petitions annually and agreed to hear arguments in fewer than 100 cases a term.

Although Chief Justice Roberts stated during his confirmation hearings he thought the Court could "contribute more to the clarity and uniformity of the law by taking more cases," the Court has yet to increase its caseload under Roberts. The number of cases filed with the Court has recently declined, dropping from 8,857 in the 2006 Term to 5,307 in the 2020 Term. Also, the number of cases accepted for oral argument has been declining slightly under Roberts. In the 2005 Term, the Court's first with Roberts as chief justice, the Court heard oral arguments in 87 cases; in the 2020 Term, the Court heard arguments in 72 cases. This is down markedly from the 1980s when the Court typically heard 150 or more cases each term. The decline is partly due to congressional action increasing the Court's control

---

[31] Presidential Comm'n on the Supreme Court of the United States, *Draft Final Report* (Dec. 2021).
[32] United States v. Alvarez, 132 S. Ct. 2537 (2012).
[33] Snyder v. Phelps, 562 U.S. 443 (2011).

over its docket. In 1988, Congress passed legislation giving the Supreme Court nearly total discretion in selecting the cases it will hear.[34] Until then, the Court was required to hear several kinds of appeals accounting for 20 percent of its caseload. Now, even more than before, most cases reach the Court by a writ of **certiorari**, a Latin term indicating the Court is willing to review a case. As the Office of the Clerk of the Supreme Court explains,

> review by this Court by means of a writ of certiorari is not a matter of right, but of judicial discretion. The primary concern of the Supreme Court is not to correct errors in lower court decisions, but to decide cases presenting issues of national importance beyond the particular facts and parties involved.[35]

The process of submitting a case to the Supreme Court for review begins when an attorney files a written argument, called a petition for certiorari, asking the Court to review a decision by a federal court or state supreme court. Four Supreme Court justices must vote yes if the Court is to grant a writ of certiorari and put the case onto its calendar. The Court rejects about 99 percent of the petitions for certiorari, usually with no explanation. When a petition for certiorari is denied, the lower court decision stands. The Supreme Court's refusal to accept a case does not affirm a lower court's opinion. Denial of certiorari "signifies only that the Court has chosen not to accept the case for review and does not express the Court's view of the merits of the case."[36] The Court denies certiorari for many reasons, perhaps because a case lacks legal significance or because there is no significant conflict in the lower courts to resolve.

If the Supreme Court accepts a case, the review process is much the same as for other appellate courts. The attorneys file briefs arguing their position. The briefs generally present the facts of the case, the issues involved, a review of the actions of the lower courts and legal arguments. The Supreme Court justices review the written arguments and then listen to what is usually a half hour of oral argument from each attorney. The justices often interrupt attorneys to ask questions or challenge the arguments being presented. The time limit is precise. An attorney arguing before the Court is expected to stop in the middle of a sentence if the light in front of the lectern signals that time has expired.

Following oral arguments, the justices meet in the Justices' Conference Room to discuss the case. No one except the justices is permitted in the room. Once the justices have voted, a justice voting with the majority will be designated to write the Court's opinion. If the chief justice is part of the majority, he or she decides who will write the opinion of the Court. If the chief justice votes in the minority, the most senior justice in the majority decides who will write the Court's opinion. The choice of author for an opinion is significant because the author of the Court's opinion can weave in his or her political philosophy, view of the role of the Court and interpretation of law.

After a justice drafts an opinion for the Court, the draft is circulated to the other justices for editing and comment. Drafts of dissenting opinions may be shared

---

[34] Supreme Court Case Selections, Pub. L. No. 100–352, 102 Stat. 662 (1988) (amending 28 U.S.C. §§ 1254, 1257, 1258).

[35] Office of Clerk, United States Supreme Court, *Guide for Prospective Indigent Petitioners for Writs of Certiorari* at 1, Oct. 2005.

[36] *Id.*

as well. The justices may bargain over the language in the drafts. Votes may shift. Ordinarily, at least a few justices will join the opinion of the Court without adding their own comments. However, justices often write their own **concurring** or **dissenting opinions** to explain their votes. They can also join, or sign on to, opinions written by other justices.

Sometimes none of the draft opinions presented to the Court attracts the five votes necessary for a majority. In such a situation, the draft with the most support becomes the **plurality** opinion of the Court, as occurred in *Richmond Newspapers v. Virginia*. Although the justices in *Richmond Newspapers* voted 7–1 that the First Amendment requires trials to be open to the public, no more than three justices agreed to any one opinion explaining why courtrooms should remain open during trials.[37] If many of the justices write their own opinions rather than joining an opinion of the Court, the high court offers little guidance to lower courts facing similar circumstances. A majority of the justices deciding a case, usually five, must agree to any point of law for the Court's opinion to become binding precedent.

In what is known as the Pentagon Papers case, discussed in Chapter 3, each of the nine justices wrote his own opinion. Although the Court voted 6–3 that the *New York Times* and the *Washington Post* could report a secret Defense Department study, the only opinion issued on behalf of the six-justice majority was an unsigned, three-paragraph **per curiam** opinion. A per curiam opinion is "by the court" rather than an opinion attributed to any one justice. The Court's opinion in the Pentagon Papers case said only that the government had not sufficiently justified barring news stories based on the Defense Department study.[38] The justices could not agree on the reasons a **prior restraint** was unjustified.

Technically, the Supreme Court's decisions apply only to the case being decided. The Supreme Court's opinions do not establish statute-like law. However, lower courts assume the Supreme Court will decide similar cases in similar ways, so they adjudicate conflicts before them accordingly. Otherwise, lower court judges risk having their decisions overturned.

The Supreme Court, in its role as interpreter of the U.S. Constitution, can review the constitutionality of all legislation. This means that the Supreme Court can invalidate an act of Congress that violates the Constitution. The Court has declared all or part of a federal statute unconstitutional about 180 times in the history of the country. The Court has also declared provisions of about 1,325 state laws and constitutions to be unconstitutional.[39] The Supreme Court has frequently expanded freedom of expression by invalidating state and federal statutes found to conflict with the First Amendment.

Neither the Supreme Court nor any other court can enforce its own decisions. The courts have no troops or police to force compliance. The executive branch enforces court decisions. Law enforcement officers ensure that fines are paid and sentences are served. When the Supreme Court rules against the executive branch, it relies on tradition and its own prestige to achieve compliance. In 1974, public respect for the Court forced President Richard Nixon to obey an order to release secret White House tapes to a special prosecutor who was investigating the Watergate scandal.[40]

---

[37] 448 U.S. 555 (1980).
[38] N.Y. Times Co. v. United States, 403 U.S. 713 (1971).
[39] Congressional Research Service, *The Constitution of the United States of America: Analysis and Interpretation of the Constitution, Centennial Edition*, S. Doc. No. 112–9 (2016).
[40] United States v. Nixon, 418 U.S. 683 (1974).

The State Systems

Most state court systems are organized much like the federal courts. Each state has trial courts, similar to the federal district courts, which handle nearly every kind of civil or criminal case. These courts, often called county courts, are ordinarily the first state courts to consider libel or privacy cases. These trial courts also handle appeals for a number of subordinate trial courts responsible for minor civil matters, traffic violations and criminal misdemeanors. Most state court judges are elected, usually in nonpartisan elections.

State court systems provide either one or two levels of appellate courts. In some states, appeals go directly from the county courts to what is usually called the state supreme court. However, many states have intermediate appellate courts to moderate the workload of the supreme court. State courts of appeals, like the federal circuit courts, often use small panels of judges. State appellate court decisions interpreting state law are binding on both lower state courts and federal courts in the same jurisdiction.

The decisions of state supreme courts, usually made up of seven to nine justices, constitute the law of the state and are binding on all of the state's courts. Each state supreme court is the final arbiter of its own state constitution, provided there is no conflict with the federal Constitution. A losing **party** in a state supreme court case may have recourse before the U.S. Supreme Court only if a substantial federal question is involved.

■ SUMMARY ■

There are 52 court systems: one for the federal government, one for the District of Columbia and one for each state. Most court cases originate in the trial courts, where the law is applied to the facts of each case. Appeals courts ensure that the trial courts use the proper procedures and apply the law correctly. The federal court system consists of federal district courts, the 13 circuits of the U.S. Courts of Appeals and the U.S. Supreme Court.

THE LITIGATION PROCESS: CIVIL AND CRIMINAL

In criminal law, the government punishes individuals who commit illegal acts such as murder. Civil law ordinarily resolves disputes between two private parties, such as over a news story. Most communication cases are brought in civil court rather than criminal court.

A crime is an antisocial act defined by law, usually a statute adopted by a state legislature. State criminal statutes forbid behavior such as murder and specify punishment, usually a jail sentence, a fine, or both. Criminal law is enforced by government law enforcement officers. Once suspects are arrested, they are prosecuted by government attorneys. The state must prove its case beyond a reasonable doubt, a heavy **burden of proof** demanding that jurors be all but certain that the government's version of events is correct. One example of criminal law discussed in this book is obscenity, explored in Chapter 9.

In contrast to criminal cases intended to punish illegal behavior, civil cases often involve claims by individuals or organizations seeking legal redress for a violation of their interests. A person or organization filing a civil suit usually seeks compensation for harm suffered because of the actions of another. A woman may sue a newspaper for defamation if the paper inaccurately reports that she deals illegal drugs. A legal wrong committed by one person against another is often called a **tort**. Civil law provides the opportunity for a "peaceful" resolution when one person accuses another of committing a tort. A person whose reputation is harmed by false statements is supposed to sue for defamation, not challenge the detractor to a duel.

Litigants in civil cases can win by proving their cases by a preponderance of the evidence. Unlike criminal prosecutors, lawyers representing civil plaintiffs do not have to prove wrong beyond a reasonable doubt. Preponderance of the evidence means that litigants must convince jurors that their version of events is more probable—if by a narrow margin—than that of the opposing party. If the person suing wins a civil case, he or she often recovers monetary **damages**. If the person being sued wins, frequently no money changes hands except to pay the lawyers' fees. In civil law, there are no jail terms and usually no fines.

Civil law, including libel and privacy, is a significant part of the law of public communication. Civil suits are more likely to be based on common law than on statutory law. In media law the government is not ordinarily involved except to provide neutral facilities—the judge, the jury and the courthouse—to help settle the dispute. However, a civil suit can be based on a statute, and a person or group can sue, or be sued by, the government. Some states' open meetings and open records laws allow private citizens to sue officials to secure public access.

A Civil Suit

A civil case begins when the person suing, called the **plaintiff**, files a legal complaint against the person being sued, the **defendant**. In April 1976, Dr. Ronald Hutchinson, then the research director at a Michigan state mental hospital, filed a civil complaint against Senator William Proxmire of Wisconsin in the District Court for the Western District of Wisconsin. Proxmire announced during a 1975 speech that he was awarding a "Golden Fleece" award to the federal agencies that had sponsored Hutchinson's research on why monkeys clench their jaws when exposed to stressful stimuli. Proxmire's speech included the following:

> The funding of this nonsense makes me almost angry enough to scream and kick or even clench my jaw. It seems to me it is outrageous. Dr. Hutchinson's studies should make the taxpayers as well as his monkeys grind their teeth. . . . It is time for the Federal Government to get out of this "monkey business."

Hutchinson complained that Proxmire had defamed him by describing his research as worthless and in a civil complaint sought $8 million in damages. Hutchinson's complaint said Proxmire's speech had humiliated him, held him up to public scorn, damaged his professional and academic standing, and damaged his ability to attract research grants.[41]

Once a complaint has been filed at the courthouse, a defendant (in this case Senator Proxmire) is served with a summons, a notice to appear in court. If defendants fail to appear, courts may hold them in contempt and require them to forfeit their cases. Defendants often respond to complaints by denying the accusations. Senator Proxmire "answered" the complaint, in part, by filing a motion for

---

[41] Hutchinson v. Proxmire, 443 U.S. 111 (1979).

summary judgment, a common defense tactic in communication cases. A judge can grant a summary judgment to either a defendant or a plaintiff if the judge believes that the two sides in a case agree on the facts of the dispute and that one side should win as a matter of law. A summary judgment terminates a suit in its early stages, saving attorney fees and avoiding the often-unpredictable outcome of a jury trial. Summary judgments in defamation cases are discussed more thoroughly in Chapter 4.

Hutchinson's complaint, Proxmire's answer, and a reply by Hutchinson are called the *pleadings*, documents stating the nature of a case. Sometimes the two sides in a dispute file a series of documents to narrow the issues and thereby limit the length and expense of a trial. Frequently, the two sides will ask a judge for a pretrial conference in another attempt to narrow the issues or even to settle the case.

Meanwhile, the parties, sometimes called litigants, begin what is called **discovery**. Discovery is the information-gathering process. During discovery—which in major cases can take several years—each side finds out as much as possible about the evidence possessed by the other party. The lawyers often prepare interrogatories, written questions that must be answered under oath by people who might have relevant information. Then lawyers frequently take depositions, that is, ask questions in person that also must be answered under oath.

During discovery, lawyers may request that the judge issue a **subpoena** requiring a journalist or someone else to testify or bring documents or other evidence to court. A subpoena must be served to the person named in it. Failure to comply with a subpoena can result in a contempt of court ruling. Journalists frequently fight subpoenas on the grounds that revealing sources or evidence will limit their ability to gather news, a subject discussed in Chapter 11.

In the *Hutchinson* case, the judge granted time for discovery after receiving Senator Proxmire's motion for summary judgment. The two parties exchanged interrogatories and subsequently the answers. Hutchinson requested a jury trial. He also asked to amend his complaint, a motion that was granted over the objection of Senator Proxmire. In the amended complaint, Hutchinson said the Golden Fleece announcement not only defamed him but also infringed on his rights of privacy and peace and tranquility. Both Hutchinson, the plaintiff, and Proxmire, the defendant, filed the results of depositions. Shortly thereafter, Hutchinson filed a brief, along with five volumes of exhibits, arguing against Proxmire's motion for summary judgment. Senator Proxmire filed a reply brief with exhibits.

About a year after Hutchinson filed his complaint, the district court judge granted Senator Proxmire's motion for summary judgment.[42] If the summary judgment had not been granted, the case would have gone to trial.

A jury trial is required if the two parties disagree on the facts of a case and one of the parties insists on a jury. After both sides present their cases, the judge explains the relevant law to the jurors. The jury is asked to apply the law to the facts, and it may set monetary damages as part of the verdict. If a judge believes the jury verdict is contrary to law or that the damage award is excessive, he or she can overturn the jury's decision. This occurred when a judge decided that a jury verdict in favor of Mobil Oil president William Tavoulareas and against the *Washington Post* was contrary to libel law.[43]

---

[42] 431 F. Supp. 1311 (W.D. Wis. 1977).

[43] Tavoulareas v. Washington Post Co., 567 F. Supp. 651 (D.D.C. 1983), *aff'd*, 817 F.2d 762 (D.C. Cir. 1987) (en banc).

Once a judgment has been recorded in a case, either party can appeal. The person who appeals is known as the **petitioner**; the person fighting the appeal is called the **respondent**. In Hutchinson's suit, Hutchinson became a petitioner when he appealed the grant of summary judgment to the U.S. Court of Appeals for the Seventh Circuit, where it was upheld.[44] Hutchinson's petition for certiorari to the U.S. Supreme Court was granted. Proxmire was the respondent before both the Seventh Circuit and the Supreme Court. The Supreme Court reversed the decision of the Seventh Circuit and remanded the case to the lower courts. Hutchinson and Proxmire eventually settled out of court. Hutchinson received $10,000 in damages and an apology from Senator Proxmire. The Supreme Court opinion, *Hutchinson v. Proxmire*, is discussed in Chapter 4.

A Criminal Case

The key steps in a criminal prosecution are substantially the same in most states. The procedures may be labeled differently or occur in a different sequence.

A criminal action begins with a law enforcement investigation. The case of Dr. Sam Sheppard, a Cleveland, Ohio, osteopath, began with the bludgeoning death of his wife, Marilyn, on July 4, 1954. This sensational case has often been described as the "crime of the century" and served as the inspiration for the top-rated 1960s television series *The Fugitive* and a 1990s Oscar-winning movie of the same name. As the Ohio Supreme Court described the case: "Murder and mystery, society, sex and suspense were combined in this case in such a manner as to intrigue and captivate the public fancy to a degree perhaps unparalleled in recent annals."[45]

Sensational publicity began immediately with the news of Marilyn Sheppard's death and continued through Sam Sheppard's conviction for second-degree murder. Sheppard told investigators that he awoke to his wife's screams and then struggled with an unidentified "form" he found standing next to his wife's bed. As he struggled with the "form," Sheppard was knocked unconscious. Upon regaining consciousness, Sheppard followed the "form" outside of the house where he again grappled with it until losing consciousness a second time. Sheppard reenacted his version of these events at his home for the coroner, police investigators and journalists. Press coverage of the police investigation and coroner's inquest emphasized evidence incriminating Dr. Sheppard and included headlines such as "Why Isn't Sam Sheppard in Jail?" The extensive, sensational publicity is discussed more fully in Chapter 10.

After a nearly one-month investigation, Sam Sheppard was arrested on a charge of murder on July 30. The investigation established that Mrs. Sheppard had been killed with a blunt instrument, that Dr. Sheppard was in the house at the time, that no money was missing from the home and that no readable fingerprints could be found.[46]

After an arrest, the person accused of a crime appears before a magistrate for a preliminary hearing. At the hearing, the person is advised of the nature of the crime and reminded of his or her right to counsel and the right to remain silent. The primary purpose of a preliminary hearing is to determine if there is sufficient evidence, or **probable cause**, to justify further detention or a trial. Sheppard

[44] 579 F.2d 1027 (7th Cir. 1978).
[45] State v. Sheppard, 135 N.E.2d 340, 342 (Ohio 1956).
[46] State v. Sheppard, 128 N.E.2d 471 (Ohio Ct. App. 1955).

appeared before a magistrate, was informed of the murder charge, and was bound over to the grand jury.

If the magistrate decides that there is probable cause, he or she will set the bail, that is, announce the amount of money that must be posted before the accused can be released from jail. The bail is intended to ensure that the accused appears in court. Sheppard was denied bail.

The next step, depending on the state, could be the filing by the prosecutor of a criminal information, a document formally accusing the person of a crime. Or the prosecutor may take the evidence to a grand jury to seek an **indictment**, a formal accusation by a grand jury. Not all states have grand juries, and their role in the criminal justice system varies. On August 17, 1954, a grand jury in Ohio indicted Sheppard for first-degree murder.[47]

An arraignment usually follows the formal accusation. The arraignment is the official, formal reading of the indictment or information to the accused. The accused is asked to plead guilty or not guilty.

If the defendant pleads not guilty, the focus turns to pretrial preparation and negotiation. Both the prosecution and defense engage in discovery, the pretrial fact-finding. Both sides may submit a variety of motions to the judge. The defense may move for an adjustment or dismissal of the charges. Or, as in Sam Sheppard's case, a defense attorney may ask that a trial be relocated or delayed because of extensive pretrial publicity. The judge in the Sheppard trial denied both motions.

During the pretrial maneuvers, the prosecution and defense may agree to resolve the case through a plea bargain. In plea bargaining, a trial is avoided because the defendant is willing to plead guilty, often to reduced charges. Roughly 90 percent of criminal defendants plead guilty, thereby avoiding a trial.[48] Plea bargains not only save time and money but also avoid the uncertainty inherent in a trial.

A trial can take place before a judge or a jury. Criminal defendants can waive their right to a jury trial. After the jury announces the verdict of guilty or not guilty, a judge pronounces the sentence. A jury in the Common Pleas Court of Cuyahoga County, Ohio, decided that Sheppard "purposely and maliciously" killed his wife, the requirement for second-degree murder in Ohio. The judge sentenced Sheppard to life in prison, the mandatory penalty in Ohio for the crime of second-degree murder.

Sheppard appealed to the Court of Appeals of Ohio for Cuyahoga County, an intermediate appellate court. He argued that there were nearly 40 errors in the conduct of the trial, including the denial of motions to move the trial and to postpone the trial. He also argued that the jury had been improperly selected and prejudicial evidence had been improperly allowed during the trial. The three-judge panel decided that Sheppard "has been afforded a fair trial by an impartial jury and . . . substantial justice has been done."[49] Sheppard also lost a 1956 appeal in the Ohio Supreme Court.[50] The U.S. Supreme Court denied certiorari the same year.[51] Nine years later, the U.S. Supreme Court agreed to consider Sheppard's contention that he was denied a fair trial because of sensational media coverage. That story is told in Chapter 10.

---

[47] *Id*; Sheppard v. Maxwell, 384 U.S. 333 (1966).

[48] American Bar Association, *Law and the Courts: A Handbook of Courtroom Procedures* 44 (1995).

[49] State v. Sheppard, 128 N.E.2d 471, 504 (Ohio Ct. App. 1955), *aff'd*, 135 N.E.2d 340 (Ohio 1956), *cert. denied*, 352 U.S. 910 (1956).

[50] State v. Sheppard, 135 N.E.2d 340 (Ohio 1956).

[51] Sheppard v. Ohio, 352 U.S. 910 (1956).

▓ SUMMARY ▓

Criminal law prohibits antisocial behavior as defined by statute. Violations are punishable by jail sentences and fines. Criminal law is enforced by the government. A criminal action begins with an investigation and an arrest. A preliminary hearing is held to determine if there is sufficient evidence to justify a trial. Then either a prosecutor or a grand jury formally accuses a person of a crime. After the accused responds to the charge during an arraignment, the prosecution and the defense engage in pretrial fact-finding, known as discovery. Civil law ordinarily involves disputes between two private parties. A plaintiff sues a defendant for damages. After the plaintiff files a civil complaint and the defendant responds, the two parties engage in discovery. Civil and criminal cases can be dismissed or otherwise resolved before trial.

WORKING WITH THE LAW

Working With Lawyers

Because public communication often raises questions of law, professional communicators frequently need lawyers. Communicators should not fear or avoid lawyers; rather, communicators should use lawyers intelligently.

Most communicators will not have direct access to a lawyer in their first job. Television stations, for example, generally prefer journalists to take legal questions to the news director, who ordinarily can answer routine legal questions and decide when a lawyer should be consulted. Some large media outlets hire staff lawyers, known as in-house attorneys. Other media companies engage a law firm they can call as needed. Even the smallest communications organization should have experienced legal counsel to call when questions arise.

A lawyer should be consulted in the following cases:

- When a communicator is served with a subpoena, a summons or an arrest warrant. Communicators need the advice of a lawyer before responding to a legal document.
- When there is a concern that a story being considered for publication could lead to a libel or privacy suit. Attorneys can assess the risks of stories and suggest modifications.
- When a news medium is asked to print retractions or corrections. Some well-intentioned corrections can increase, rather than decrease, the risk of a suit if a lawyer is not consulted.
- When a communicator is approached by a lawyer hired by someone else. A layperson should not respond to the legal moves of a legal adversary.
- When a communicator is considering an action that may be illegal. Reporters pursuing a story sometimes consider trespassing, tape recording or obtaining stolen documents. Sometimes it is obvious when an act is illegal; often it is not. Reporters need to understand the legal consequences of their actions.

Lawyers can do more than help limit the legal jeopardy of communication professionals. They can also help communicators do their jobs. For example, lawyers can help journalists obtain access to closed records or meetings by explaining to officials the rights of the public and press.

Lawyers can help resolve a legal conflict, but they cannot eliminate the sloppy writing or editing that may have caused a suit. Attorneys can explain the probable risks and consequences of a story or an ad. They can discuss the factors that ought to be considered in deciding how to avoid **liability**. An attorney should know the questions an opposing attorney will ask about a story and what arguments are likely to be made in a libel trial. The job of a lawyer, according to James Goodale, a prominent media attorney, should be "to figure out how to get the story published," not trimmed or killed.[52] The lawyer should explain legal risks; the communicator should make the editorial decisions after weighing those risks.

Public communicators may sometimes need a personal attorney. An employer might refuse to represent an employee in court, especially if the employee acts contrary to instructions. In the early 1970s, the *New York Times* refused to defend one of its reporters, Earl Caldwell, when he declined to testify before a grand jury. Lawyers from the *Times* initially represented Caldwell and obtained a protective order limiting the questions that could be asked of him. However, Caldwell refused even to enter the grand jury room, which is closed to the public and the press, claiming that to do so would imperil his sensitive relations with the Black Panthers. Caldwell was cited for contempt of court and the *Times* did not support his appeals; the company's general counsel James Goodale regarded Caldwell's refusal even to appear as "far out" and feared an adverse appellate court ruling.[53] Caldwell's case was considered by the Supreme Court in *Branzburg v. Hayes*, a case discussed in Chapter 11.

SUMMARY

Legal advice can be an expensive but necessary part of modern communication. Lawyers should be called when a communicator must respond to an official document or someone else's attorney. Lawyers should be consulted when a communicator is considering an act that may be illegal. Lawyers should review stories that could lead to libel or privacy suits. Lawyers can explain the risks of publishing a story, but they should not be allowed to act as editors.

LIMITATIONS OF THE LAW

This book focuses on the law. Professional communicators need to know the law to do their jobs effectively and without unnecessary risk. However, the law does not resolve all questions that may arise in public communication.

The law may allow behavior that exceeds professional ethics. Ethics is the consideration of moral rights and wrongs; it also involves respect for the emotional well-being, dignity, and physical safety of others. The law, however, does not always parallel professional codes of conduct. The First Amendment frequently permits expression, such as the publication of the names of sexual assault complainants, which many journalists consider unethical. Communicators base decisions to publish on whether behavior is morally "right" or "wrong" as well as on its legality. However, a discussion of ethics is left for another book. The purpose of this book is to help professional communicators understand the law that affects their performance.

---

[52] Ann Rambo, "Litigious Age Gives Rise to Media Law," *Presstime*, Nov. 1981, at 7.
[53] James C. Goodale, *Fighting for the Press* 25 (2013).

2

The First Amendment

A mericans enjoy greater freedom of expression than any other people. Other democracies protect freedom of expression but not to the degree that the U.S. Constitution does. Unlike the citizens of many foreign lands, Americans are free to burn their country's flag, call the president a crook, carry swastikas in public demonstrations and watch endless violence on television.

The legal foundation of the American freedom to speak and publish is the First Amendment. "Congress shall make no law," the First Amendment says, "respecting an establishment of religion, or prohibiting the free exercise thereof; or abridging the freedom of speech, or of the press; or the right of the people peaceably to assemble, and to petition the government for a redress of grievances." The categorical language of the First Amendment, prohibiting government interference with

DOI: 10.4324/9781003264736-2

freedom of expression, gives Americans a broad right to speak, publish, broadcast, blog and demonstrate on matters of conscience and consequence—and on trivial matters, too—without fear of government reprisal. Freedom of expression is in large measure a negative freedom: freedom from government interference.

Despite the categorical prohibition against government interference, the First Amendment does not establish absolute freedom for citizens to speak and publish. Sometimes expression may be halted or punished if it endangers national security, incites a riot, contains "fighting words" or infringes a copyright. Expression may also be punished after dissemination if it damages the reputation of others or invades their privacy. Communication law, the subject of this book, is the system by which society determines which expression is protected and which may be punished, when, and why. Exceptions to freedom of expression depend on what is said, who is speaking, and the harm that speech or writing causes. Whether speech may be prohibited or punished also depends on the standards of judgment employed by the courts and on the theory or purposes underpinning freedom of expression.

THEORY OF FREEDOM OF EXPRESSION

A theory is a set of assumptions, principles and procedures that categorize knowledge and explain behavior. Einstein's theory of relativity helps scientists to understand the relationship of time, space and matter. Able scholars have attempted to formulate theories to explain when expression should be free and when it should be restricted. The researchers seek a set of assumptions, principles and procedures that can consistently explain why freedom of expression should—or should not—protect such diverse expression as reporting a city council meeting, publishing stolen government documents, burning draft cards, stating the alcohol content of a beer on the label and broadcasting four-letter words.

Forming a coherent theory of free expression might seem quite easy, considering the elegant economy of the First Amendment itself: "Congress shall make no law . . . abridging the freedom of speech or of the press." Yet few agree on the range of speakers, expression and circumstances that such a theory should encompass.

Many thoughtful scholars have illuminated various values and purposes served by freedom of expression. Professor Vincent Blasi has emphasized the importance of protecting the powerful media that "check" government's power.[1] Professor Lee Bollinger stresses the importance of freedom of expression as a way to develop—and reflect—a tolerant society.[2] Yet, despite these and many other contributions to First Amendment theory, no all-encompassing theory of freedom of expression has emerged. This is because freedom of expression involves so many different media, social conflicts and competing philosophies.

In the absence of a single theory of freedom of expression, perhaps one should adopt Professor Frederick Schauer's suggestion that there are several First Amendments, each with different theoretical justifications for different circumstances. One First Amendment, according to Schauer, serves the goals of democratic governance by forbidding government to suppress the political speech of its critics. Another First Amendment is justified by the search for truth in the "marketplace of ideas." This First Amendment protects open inquiry into the sciences

---

[1] Vincent Blasi, "The Checking Value in First Amendment Theory," *Am. B. Found. Res. J.* 521 (1977).
[2] Lee Bollinger, *The Tolerant Society* (1986).

at academic institutions. A third First Amendment, Schauer suggests, protects individual fulfillment by safeguarding expression in the arts.[3]

Like Schauer, the late law professor Harry Kalven saw so many conflicting values and complex facts in freedom of expression controversies that he thought it fruitless to try to construct an overarching theory. It is better, Kalven said, to "think small,"[4] deciding each court case as it arises without attempting to reconcile every decision with every other in a consistent structure. Thinking small offers the benefit of flexibility; if we treat each case separately, we do not necessarily have to protect the soap salesman's free speech to the same degree or for the same reasons we protect the speech of the soapbox orator. However, Kalven's particularized approach presents the drawback of complexity; if every free speech case is different, the First Amendment doctrine may become as complex as the Internal Revenue Code. Lawyers charging $500 per hour might welcome complexity, but publishers, broadcasters, bloggers and podcasters prefer simpler guides to freedom of expression.

If decisions determining freedom of expression cannot be predicted or rationalized within an all-encompassing theory, neither must decisions about freedom of expression be abandoned to the whims of judges and government administrators. Communication law is guided by a number of procedures, traditions and values that create unifying themes if not a consistent theory. Americans agree on the broad purposes and values of freedom of expression, even as they may disagree about when the government may curb that freedom. Important values served by freedom of expression include the social goals of attaining the truth, making decisions in a democracy, checking government power and managing change. Freedom of expression also serves the related personal value of individual fulfillment.

Attainment of Truth

The argument that freedom of expression aids the search for truth assumes that rational decisions emerge from consideration of all facts and arguments. An individual who seeks knowledge and truth, said the late Professor Thomas Emerson, carries on a continuous Socratic dialogue. He said that a citizen who seeks truth

> must hear all sides of the question, especially as presented by those who feel strongly and argue militantly for a different view. He must consider all alternatives, test his judgment by exposing it to opposition, make full use of different minds to sift the true from the false. Conversely, suppression of information, discussion, or the clash of opinion prevents one from reaching the most rational judgment, blocks the generation of new ideas, and tends to perpetuate error.[5]

The belief that freedom of expression speeds the search for truth is frequently summarized in the metaphor of the marketplace of ideas. The best test of truth, according to the late Supreme Court Justice Oliver Wendell Holmes, is the power of a thought "to get itself accepted in the competition of the market."[6] Just as shoppers in the commercial marketplace are said to seek the best products, participants in

---

[3] Frederick Schauer, "Must Speech Be Special," 78 *Nw. U. L. Rev.* 1284 (1983).
[4] *See* Kenneth L. Karst, "The First Amendment and Harry Kalven: An Appreciative Comment on the Advantages of Thinking Small," 13 *UCLA L. Rev.* 1 (1965).
[5] Thomas Emerson, *Toward a General Theory of the First Amendment* 7 (1966).
[6] Abrams v. United States, 250 U.S. 616 (1919).

the marketplace of ideas are said to seek the most original, truthful or useful information. Like commercial shoppers, consumers of ideas must be wary that they do not accept inferior goods. In theory, good ideas—political, scientific and social—will prevail in a free market.

The marketplace-of-ideas metaphor can be traced to the bad marriage of John Milton, the English poet and essayist. In 1644, Milton published an essay titled *Areopagitica*, which was Milton's response to criticism he had received for publishing without a government license. Milton had published a tract urging that English divorce laws be liberalized so that he could dissolve an unpleasant union. In *Areopagitica*, Milton argued that Parliament should allow unlicensed printing.

Milton said that licensing is a bad idea because it deprives citizens of knowledge and ideas that could improve their lives. Furthermore, he argued, censorship is impractical because the censor's pencil does not prevent the circulation of influential ideas. In addition, Milton said that most people are not fit to be censors. Those with the intelligence to be discerning censors would not want such a boring and unrewarding task. Besides, he concluded, citizens benefit from having to distinguish good ideas from bad. In his most famous passage, Milton said that the free competition of ideas furthered the search for truth:

> And though all the winds of doctrine were let loose to play upon the earth, so Truth be in the field, we do injuriously, by licensing and prohibiting, to mis-doubt her strength. Let her and Falsehood grapple; who ever knew Truth put to the worse, in a free and open encounter?[7]

Despite his laissez-faire argument, Milton did not believe that all expression should be permitted. As a Puritan, he was not ready to allow free discussion of Catholicism or atheism.

Nineteenth-century philosopher John Stuart Mill thought it "idle sentimentality" to argue, as Milton did, that truth would not be "put to the worse" in combat with falsehood. "History teems," Mill wrote, "with instances of truth put down by persecution." Yet Mill valued free speech fully as much as Milton, not because truth would always prevail but because truth has no chance to prevail without freedom of expression. Silencing the opinion of even one person robs the human race, Mill said. If a correct statement is suppressed, he said, people are "deprived of the opportunity of exchanging error for truth." If a false statement is suppressed, people "lose, what is almost as great a benefit, the clearer perception and livelier impression of truth, produced by its collision with error."[8]

Not all students of freedom of expression embrace the metaphor of the marketplace of ideas. One commentator questions whether citizens are sufficiently rational to choose truth over falsehood.[9] A Stanford University study found that students often lack the ability to evaluate the accuracy and credibility of information they find on social media sites.[10] Many citizens thought the proliferation of misinformation and disinformation during the 2016 and 2020 presidential elections challenged the proposition that truth will prevail in a free marketplace of speech.

---

[7] John Milton, *Areopagitica*, in 32 *Great Books of the Western World* 409 (1952).
[8] John Stuart Mill, *On Liberty* 24 (Gateway 1955).
[9] C. Edwin Baker, "Scope of the First Amendment Freedom of Speech," 25 *UCLA L. Rev.* 964 (1978).
[10] Sue Shellenbarger, "Most Students Don't Know When News Is Fake, Stanford Study Finds," *Wall St. J.*, Nov. 21, 2016.

Feminist scholar Catharine MacKinnon argues that the marketplace of ideas is an abstraction of little value to women because women are often too poor to buy speech. Indeed, MacKinnon argues that women are victimized in the marketplace by an avalanche of pornography depicting them as sexual objects. To MacKinnon, well-financed and often violent pornography constitutes the "free speech of men" that "silences the free speech of women."[11]

Critics of the marketplace metaphor have questioned for decades whether consolidation of the media unduly restricts the circulation of ideas and search for truth. The marketplace of ideas would mean little to minorities, dissidents and fringe groups if they could not gain access to monopoly media. Professor Jerome Barron was concerned in the 1970s that insufficiently diverse ideas were allowed access to metropolitan daily newspapers then monopolizing most American cities.[12] Barron echoed the Commission on Freedom of the Press, a panel of scholars and intellectuals who warned in 1947 that concentration of media ownership threatened to create a private censorship as restrictive as government censorship.[13] More recently, the U.S. government and some foreign governments professed concerns that American telephone–Internet media companies, such as Comcast and AT&T, may dominate access to the Internet, while other technology companies, such as Google and Amazon, may dominate search, content and storage of information.[14] In 2015, the FCC imposed "**net neutrality**" rules on Internet service providers (ISPs) requiring them—like telephone companies—to allow equal access for all Internet content.[15] Those rules were challenged, as discussed later in this chapter.

Although several large companies control vast holdings of publications, broadcast stations, cable companies, entertainment production facilities, Internet media and data, there are still many voices in the marketplace of ideas. Once-dominant metropolitan newspapers have been displaced by competitive niche publications, cable and the Internet. Cable television, offering scores of specialized channels, lures viewers from the once-preeminent broadcast networks, while telephone companies compete for local cable and mobile audiences. Satellite radio companies merge to compete with terrestrial radio. Social media allow billions of users worldwide to share news, ideas and personal information. Internet service providers and content creators combine and compete to serve and profit from the public's limitless appetite for interactive video, audio and print.

Governance

Besides aiding the search for truth, freedom of expression contributes to democratic governance. "The root purpose of the First Amendment," Professor Thomas Emerson said, "is to assure an effective system of freedom of expression in a democratic society."[16] Alexander Meiklejohn, an influential philosopher and academic leader, was the best-known proponent of the theory that freedom of expression is to be valued primarily for its contribution to governance. For Meiklejohn, freedom of expression was more valued for its role in democratic governance than as a route toward truth. "No one can deny," Meiklejohn wrote, "that the winning of

---

[11] Catharine MacKinnon, *Feminism Unmodified: Discourses on Life and Law* (1987).

[12] Jerome Barron, *Freedom of the Press for Whom?* 6 (1973). *See also* Jerome Barron, "Access to the Press—A New First Amendment Right," 80 *Harv. L. Rev.* 1641 (1967).

[13] Commission on Freedom of the Press, *A Free and Responsible Press* (1947).

[14] *See* Mark Scott, "What U.S. Tech Giants Face in Europe in 2017," *N.Y. Times*, Jan. 1, 2017.

[15] FCC, "Protecting and Promoting the Open Internet, Final Rule," 80 *Fed. Reg.* 19738, Apr. 13, 2015.

[16] Thomas Emerson, *System of Freedom of Expression* 17 (1970).

the truth is important for the purposes of self-government." However, Meiklejohn said, truth is not our "deepest need." Meiklejohn said the First Amendment is an important device "for winning of new truth," but the First Amendment is even more important as a "device for the sharing of whatever truth has been won." To Meiklejohn, the informed voter was crucial. The purpose of free speech, he said, "is to give to every voting member of the body politic the fullest possible participation in the understanding of those problems with which the citizens of a self-governing society must deal."[17] Therefore, he said, "no idea, no opinion, no doubt, no belief, no counter belief, no relevant information" may be kept from the people.

Meiklejohn is often referred to as an "absolutist" because he said speech that contributes to "the business of government" should be absolutely protected from government intervention. Meiklejohn hoped that freedom of expression would protect discussion, beliefs and associations necessary for responsible voting because, to him, voting was the key act of self-governance. Voting, he said, is "the official expression of a self-governing man's judgment on issues of public policy."

In response to criticism that his focus on political expression was too narrow, Meiklejohn expanded his definition of political speech. He said that governance in a democracy requires absolute First Amendment protection, not only for speech about elections and politics but also for communications about education, philosophy, science, literature, the arts and public issues. From discussion of philosophy, science and the arts, the voter derives the knowledge and sensitivity to human values necessary for "sane and objective judgment" in the voting booth, Meiklejohn said.[18] His expansive definition of political speech meriting "absolute" protection made it difficult to determine which expressions would not deserve protection.

Check on Government Power

Professor Vincent Blasi offers a variation on the argument that freedom of expression serves primarily to further democratic governance. He argues that freedom of expression is to be valued as a check on abuses of governmental authority. He therefore sees the media as an institutional counterweight to government. To Blasi, freedom of expression, particularly as exercised by the larger media, is a countervailing power to federal, state and local governments, in which corruption seems to increase with their budgets. Abuse of government, he says, "is an especially serious evil—more serious than the abuse of private power, even by institutions such as large corporations which can affect the lives of millions of people."[19]

The First Amendment, Blasi argues, is most valuable during such "pathological" periods as Watergate, when the pressure on democratic institutions is so intense that government may be tempted to suppress free expression.[20] He does not deny that freedom of expression serves other values besides checking government power, values such as promoting self-governance and enhancing individual dignity. But Blasi is more interested in power relationships. To him, the press can

---

[17] Alexander Meiklejohn, *Free Speech and Its Relation to Self-Government* 88–9 (1948). *See also* Robert Bork, "Neutral Principles and Some First Amendment Problems," 47 *Indiana L.J.* 1 (1971).
[18] Alexander Meiklejohn, "The First Amendment Is an Absolute," *Sup. Ct. Rev.* 245, 256–7 (1961). For criticism, *see* Zechariah Chafee, "Book Review," 62 *Harv. L. Rev.* 891 (1949).
[19] Vincent Blasi, "The Checking Value in First Amendment Theory," 1977 *Am. B. Found. Res. J.* 521, 538.
[20] Vincent Blasi, "The Pathological Perspective and the First Amendment," 85 *Colum. L. Rev.* 449 (1985). *See also* Floyd Abrams, "The Press is Different: Reflections on Justice Stewart and the Autonomous Press," 7 *Hofstra L. Rev.* 563 (1979).

expose political corruption if it scrutinizes government operations in a system that recognizes the First Amendment checking function of the press.

Change With Stability

Another value related to governance is the contribution of free speech to orderly change. Free expression can act as a safety valve, allowing critics to participate in peaceful change rather than seek influence through antidemocratic acts. Those who believe this argue that racist militia groups must be allowed to express themselves at meetings and over the Internet. Suppression drives the opposition underground, Professor Emerson warned, "leaving those suppressed either apathetic or desperate. It thus saps the vitality of the society or makes resort to force more likely."[21]

If freedom of expression promotes change with stability, dissidents may work their ideas into the social fabric without resorting to a violent underground cell. Worthless ideas can be rejected with little threat to the equilibrium of society. Where freedom prevails, consensus may support orderly change. Free expression therefore promotes both stability and flexibility, tradition and change. As Emerson said, where there is freedom of expression, society is better able to maintain "the precarious balance between healthy cleavage and necessary consensus."

Fulfillment

Freedom of expression is valued not only because of the social values it promotes but also because speaking and publishing enrich one's life. Freedom of expression, Professor Emerson said, is justified as a right of the individual "purely in his capacity as an individual. It derives from the widely accepted premise of Western thought that the proper end of man is the realization of his character and potentialities as a human being." Freedom of expression is a fundamental good, says Professor Laurence Tribe, "an end in itself, an expression of the sort of society we wish to become and the sort of persons we wish to be."[22]

The notion that freedom of expression is necessary to protect the integrity of the individual reflects the influence of natural law in American jurisprudence. Natural law, popular in the seventeenth and eighteenth centuries, posited that people are born, as English philosopher John Locke said, with fundamental rights of life, liberty and property, rights that the government is bound by contract with its citizens to protect.[23] The influence of natural law can be seen in the American Declaration of Independence and in the guarantees of liberty and equality in the Bill of Rights. The Bill of Rights protects the integrity of the individual not only from government suppression of free speech but also from unreasonable searches and forced confessions.

Self-fulfillment is not an isolated value. When people fulfill themselves by speaking and writing, they also serve the social and political values of free speech. One might say that the individual's rights of liberty and equality find their highest fulfillment when a citizen participates in what Lincoln called "Government of the People."[24] Professor Steven Shiffrin captures a relationship between individual fulfillment and political speech when he suggests that the organizing symbol of the First Amendment should be neither fulfillment nor the marketplace, but the

---

[21] Thomas Emerson, *Toward a General Theory of the First Amendment* 12 (1966).
[22] Laurence Tribe, *American Constitutional Law* 785 (2nd ed. 1988).
[23] John Locke, *Of Civil Government* (1955). *See also* Jean-Jacques Rousseau, *The Social Contract* (1960).
[24] *See* Wolfgang Friedman, *Legal Theory* 419–20 (5th ed. 1967).

dissenter. Citing Ralph Waldo Emerson, Shiffrin argues that a major purpose of the First Amendment is "to protect romantics—those who would break out of classical forms: the dissenters, the unorthodox, the outcasts." The First Amendment, Shiffrin says, sponsors individualism, rebelliousness and antiauthoritarianism.[25]

Some writers find the concept of natural rights too vague and sentimental for making principled decisions in free speech cases.[26] Does one's natural right to self-expression include the right to shout obscenities? Burn a draft card? Shoot an adversary? It is hard to answer these questions when freedom of expression is justified on the grounds of an unprovable natural right to fulfillment. Nevertheless, the American legal system, particularly the Bill of Rights, has been molded by the principles of natural law.[27] To most Americans, freedom of expression is an end in itself as well as a means to other ends.

■ SUMMARY ■

Despite many attempts, scholars have failed to articulate a comprehensive theory of freedom of expression. Nevertheless, it is generally agreed that freedom of expression serves several important values, among them the search for truth, promotion of democratic governance, a check on government abuses and orderly change. Freedom of expression is also valued because it contributes to human fulfillment.

REGULATING EXPRESSION

The First Amendment's language may appear to be categorical, but its protections are not absolute. The language telling Congress it can pass "no law" abridging free expression has never meant absolutely no law. Justice Hugo Black argued that the federal government was "without any power whatever under the Constitution to put any type of burden on speech and expression of ideas of any kind."[28] But Justice Black's **absolutism** never enjoyed the support of even a significant minority of the Supreme Court.

Other justices, with the exception of William Douglas, found Black's absolutism unrealistic. The Court's majority has concluded that there are times when freedom of expression must give way to other personal and social interests such as national security or public tranquility. Even Justice Black conceded it was reasonable to limit when and where a constitutionally protected demonstration might be held.[29] Absolutists presumably would also concede that the government may abridge perjury and fraudulent speech.

Although absolutism has not prevailed as First Amendment doctrine, the First Amendment does protect two kinds of speech absolutely. One is speech critical of the government. Newspapers, broadcasters and bloggers can say whatever they want about a city, state or other government,[30] although the media may be sued if they defame individuals within the government. Another absolute protection is afforded to broadcasters fulfilling equal time requirements mandated by federal communications law. Because broadcast stations are required to provide

---

[25] Steven Shiffrin, *The First Amendment, Democracy, and Romance* 5 (1990).

[26] *See, e.g.*, Frederick Schauer, "The Role of the People in First Amendment Theory," 74 *Calif. L. Rev.* 761 (1986).

[27] Wolfgang Friedmann, *Legal Theory* 136–7 (5th ed. 1967).

[28] Ginzburg v. United States, 383 U.S. 463, 476 (1966) (dissenting opinion).

[29] Adderley v. Florida, 385 U.S. 39 (1966).

[30] *E.g.*, Philadelphia v. Washington Post, 482 F. Supp. 897 (E.D. Pa. 1979).

opportunities of equal access for political candidates, the broadcasters are abso-lutely protected from libel suits resulting from those broadcasts.[31]

With absolutism failing to muster sufficient support, courts have developed tests to determine the point at which freedom of expression must give way to con-flicting social interests, such as national security, individual reputation, orderly streets and honest commercial markets. Whether regulations are constitutional depends on many factors, including the type of expression, who is speaking and the medium of expression. These factors, in turn, determine the rigor with which the courts rule on the legality of regulations on expression. Generally speaking, the courts are less tolerant of regulations on political speech than on commercial speech or sexual expression. Generally, the courts are less tolerant of regulations on the print media than on broadcasting. Similarly, regulations on speech by adults are less likely to be constitutional than regulations on expression by students.

Judges determining the legality of media regulations employ a number of analytical and procedural tools designed to maximize freedom of expression. The assumptions and procedures that judges bring to their First Amendment decisions help ensure that their rulings will not be arbitrary, but will be consistent and unbi-ased. Among the most important judicial practices guaranteeing maximum freedom of expression are (1) judicial review, (2) First Amendment due process and (3) a bias against regulating expressive content.

Judicial Review and the Fourteenth Amendment

Under the Constitution, judges have a duty to uphold the individual rights pro-tected by the Bill of Rights. Because each federal court has the power of constitu-tional review, any federal judge has the authority to determine whether a law or regulation in the judge's jurisdiction unconstitutionally restricts freedom of speech or the press. Federal judges are the final arbiters of freedom of expression, deciding whether state and federal legislators, administrators or lower courts have abridged freedom of expression in violation of the First Amendment.

It is proper that federal judges rather than legislators or executive branch administrators be the final guardians of free expression. Federal judges, appointed for life, can be objective, free of political pressures. The late Professor Alexander Bickel pointed out that judges have "the leisure, the training, and the insulation to follow the ways of the scholar in pursuing the ends of government."[32] Only a judi-cial determination in First Amendment cases, the Supreme Court has said, "ensures the necessary sensitivity to freedom of expression."[33] Recognizing the importance of an independent judiciary as a guarantor of individual rights, emerging democra-cies often establish constitutional courts with the power to nullify legislation that infringes on freedom of speech, freedom of religion and other civil rights.

The authority of American federal courts to review the constitutionality of state laws restricting speech derives from the **Fourteenth Amendment**. Without the Fourteenth Amendment, the First Amendment would only protect American citizens from abridgments of free expression by the federal government. The Fourteenth Amendment protects citizens and the media from "**state action**" abridg-ing free speech. The Fourteenth Amendment prohibits any state from enforcing a law that would (1) abridge the privileges or immunities of citizens of the United

---

[31] Farmers Educ. and Coop. Union of Am. v. WDAY, Inc., 360 U.S. 525 (1959).
[32] Alexander Bickel, *The Least Dangerous Branch* 25–6 (1962).
[33] Freedman v. Maryland, 380 U.S. 51 (1965).

States, (2) deprive any person of life, liberty or property, without due process of law or (3) deny any person equal protection of the laws. The First Amendment and Bill of Rights do not protect citizens from commercial corporations or media companies that might deny citizens access for their views.

The Fourteenth Amendment, adopted in 1868, was meant by its author, Representative John Bingham of Ohio, to end the "dual citizenship" under which Americans had lived from the time the Constitution was ratified through the Civil War.[34] Before the Civil War, Americans had two distinct citizenships: one state, one federal. A state legislature could limit speech, schooling, voting, or other rights in ways that the federal government could not.[35] This was because the Bill of Rights originally barred only Congress from passing legislation violating the First Amendment, the Fourth Amendment and other amendments guaranteeing a citizen's rights. States could adopt poll taxes, create separate schools for blacks or close a newspaper without violating the Constitution.

The Fourteenth Amendment was supposed to give blacks full citizenship after the Civil War, guaranteeing to citizens of every state the same rights they enjoyed as citizens of the United States. However, it was not until the late nineteenth century that the Supreme Court, employing the Fourteenth Amendment, began to challenge state laws—state action—that violated a citizen's constitutional rights. By the twentieth century, the Supreme Court had begun to employ the Fourteenth Amendment to strike down state laws that denied citizens freedom of expression, freedom of religion, the right to a fair trial and other rights guaranteed by the Bill of Rights. In several cases, the Supreme Court ruled that restrictive state laws violate a citizen's constitutional rights by denying the privileges and immunities, due process or equal protection guaranteed by the Bill of Rights and the Fourteenth Amendment.

In the 1925 case of *Gitlow v. New York*, the Court said it "assumed" that First Amendment rights protected from abridgment by Congress are "among the fundamental personal rights and 'liberties' protected by the due process clause of the Fourteenth Amendment from impairment by the states."[36] But the Court did not strike down a New York statute under which Benjamin Gitlow was convicted for publishing a little-noticed manifesto urging the overthrow of the government. The Supreme Court first struck down a state statute violating freedom of the press six years later in *Near v. Minnesota*.[37] The Minnesota statute declared unconstitutional in *Near* permitted prepublication restraints on "malicious, scandalous, and defamatory" publications. In declaring the restraints on publication unconstitutional, Chief Justice Charles Evans Hughes wrote:

> It is no longer open to doubt that the liberty of the press, and of speech, is within the liberty safeguarded by the due process clause of the Fourteenth Amendment from invasion by state action. It was found impossible to conclude that this essential personal liberty of the citizen was left unprotected by the general guaranty of fundamental rights of person and property.

Since *Near v. Minnesota*, almost all of the clauses of the Bill of Rights have been applied to the states in a process frequently called **incorporation**. Case by case,

---

[34] Irving Brant, *The Bill of Rights* 325 (1965).
[35] *See* Barron v. Baltimore, 32 U.S. (7 Pet.) 243 (1833).
[36] 268 U.S. 652, 666 (1925).
[37] 283 U.S. 697 (1931).

the Supreme Court incorporated the various clauses of the Bill of Rights into the Fourteenth Amendment, ruling that the state laws violate the Constitution by denying citizens either their privileges and immunities, equal protection of the law or due process. Because the Fourteenth Amendment requires state and local governments to honor the federal Bill of Rights, an ordinance permitting a county sheriff to arbitrarily refuse a parade permit denies citizens their First Amendment rights as surely as if the U.S. attorney general denied the permit. Similarly, an unreasonable search by a county sheriff violates the Fourth Amendment just as if the illegal search were conducted by the FBI.

Because individuals and private organizations—including the media—are not government entities, they control their messages and can deny access to their speech platforms without engaging in "censorship." Broadcasters and newspapers do not violate the First Amendment if they refuse to carry a controversial issue advertisement.[38] Twitter and YouTube do not violate the First Amendment if they remove videos of beheadings in the Mideast or faked photos of a celebrity suicide.[39] A private college does not violate the First Amendment when it shuts down the campus newspaper. In each case, there is no unconstitutional state action, because private broadcasters, colleges and Twitter publishers are not state agents.

In its most recent state action case, *Manhattan Community Access Corp. v. Halleck*, decided in 2019, the Supreme Court concluded: "The Free Speech Clause prohibits only governmental abridgment of speech. [It] does not prohibit private abridgment."[40] The opinion later observed: "By enforcing that . . . boundary between the governmental and the private, the state-action doctrine protects a robust sphere of individual liberty." Notably, *Halleck* involved a private nonprofit corporation that operated a public access channel for a city, and the Court noted that "merely hosting speech by others . . . does not alone transform private entities into state actors subject to First Amendment constraints."

Against that background, several states, most notably Florida and Texas, have enacted legislation to police perceived ideological bias in the practices and policies of social media companies. The Florida law, signed in May 2021, prohibited social media companies from "willfully deplatforming" state political candidates by suspending or barring them. A federal judge blocked state officials from enforcing the law, and the U.S. Court of Appeals for the Eleventh Circuit held that most parts of the law were likely unconstitutional.[41] The Texas law, signed in September 2021, prohibited social media companies from moderating content based on "the viewpoint of the user." A federal judge blocked the law, and the U.S. Court of Appeals for the Fifth Circuit later reinstated it. The U.S. Supreme Court is expected to review both laws.[42]

When media companies receive a government benefit, the public interest may require that they open their channels of communication in circumscribed ways. The government requires broadcasters to provide "reasonable access" for political candidates, a public interest regulation required of broadcasters because they are licensed to operate on the limited public broadcast spectrum.[43] Similarly, the government can require private cable companies to open channels for public,

---

[38] CBS, Inc. v. Democratic Nat'l Comm., 412 U.S. 94 (1973); Miami Herald Publishing Co. v. Tornillo, 418 U.S. 241 (1974).

[39] Nancy Scola, "Foley Video, Photos Being Scrubbed from Twitter," *Wash. Post*, Aug. 19, 2014.

[40] 139 S. Ct. 1921 (2019).

[41] NetChoice, LLC v. Moody, www.rcfp.org/briefs-comments/netchoice-llc-v-moody/.

[42] NetChoice v. Paxton, www.rcfp.org/briefs-comments/netchoice-v-paxton/.

[43] CBS, Inc. v. FCC, 453 U.S. 367 (1981).

educational and government programming—known as PEG channels—because the cable companies have been granted franchises to lay cable over public rights of way.[44] "Common carrier" telephone companies are required to carry the messages of all customers.

In 2017, the Federal Communications Commission, with a new Republican majority, began the process of overturning "net neutrality" regulations imposed on Internet service providers by the Obama-era FCC. The agency voted to start rolling back the rules requiring ISPs to transmit all Internet traffic equally,[45] then voted again to repeal the rules, and in June 2018 the repeal took effect. In short, the Obama-era FCC, in a move upheld by the federal courts, had classified ISPs as "telecommunications services"—the same as telephone companies that are not allowed to speed up, halt, or slow content of favored or disfavored content providers or business partners. Net neutrality rules were meant to foster innovation, competition and consumer choice,[46] but Ajit Pai, chairman of the Trump-era FCC, said that requiring net neutrality would curtail investment and innovation.[47] Since then, the U.S. Congress has tried unsuccessfully to pass net neutrality legislation, and individual states have tried to do the same, with California succeeding. Under the Biden administration, Jessica Rosenworcel, the FCC's acting chairwoman, has voiced support for restoring net neutrality regulations.

First Amendment Due Process

If the government wishes to ban an obscene movie, deny a parade permit, close a courtroom or otherwise restrict expression, the First Amendment requires that careful procedures be followed. Procedures that are sometimes called **First Amendment due process** require that judges determine what restrictions are allowed after the government meets its burden of proving that a regulation is necessary.[48]

First Amendment due process requires the government to prove that speech is unprotected by the First Amendment rather than requiring the media to prove the expression is protected. The government bears the burden of proof so that the media will not become defensive and censor themselves. Citizens who know they must prove their conduct is lawful, the Supreme Court has said, will "steer far wider of the unlawful zone than if the State must bear these burdens."[49] Thus, the government must prove a film is obscene and therefore should not be shown; it is unconstitutional for the courts to assume that a film is obscene and then require a theater owner to prove that it is not.[50] Similarly, the government bears the burden of proving why a publication might be so dangerous to the national security that publication should be halted,[51] or why a courtroom must be closed to the public to ensure a fair trial.[52]

When the government proposes halting freedom of expression, due process usually requires that the government post notice of a hearing at which media

---

[44] Denver Area Educ. Telecommunications Consortium, Inc. v. FCC, 518 U.S. 727 (1996).

[45] Brian Fong, "FCC Votes to Start Rolling Back Landmark Net Neutrality Rules," *Wash. Post*, May 18, 2017.

[46] FCC, "Protecting and Promoting the Open Internet, Final Rule," 80 *Fed. Reg.* 19738 (Apr. 13, 2015).

[47] Associated Press, "'Net Neutrality' Foe Ajit Pai Is New FCC Head," *N.Y. Times*, Jan. 23, 2017.

[48] *See* Henry Monaghan, "First Amendment 'Due Process'," 83 *Harv. L. Rev.* 518 (1970).

[49] Speiser v. Randall, 357 U.S. 513 (1958).

[50] Freedman v. Maryland, 380 U.S. 51 (1965).

[51] New York Times v. United States, 403 U.S. 713 (1971).

[52] Richmond Newspapers, Inc. v. Virginia, 448 U.S. 555 (1980).

attorneys can challenge the proposed restriction.[53] At the hearing, attorneys for the media argue that the government cannot demonstrate a sufficient need for the restriction it proposes. In obscenity cases, due process requires that a censorship board hold a hearing at which attorneys for theater owners can argue against government charges that a work is obscene.[54]

Due process also requires that administrators regulating expression not act arbitrarily, but follow objective standards and explain how they arrived at their decision. Thus, it is unconstitutional for a government official to arbitrarily determine whether a fee will be charged for a parade permit and what that fee will be.[55] All demonstrators seeking a parade permit must pay the same reasonable fee, if any.

If an administrative board bans speech, due process also requires that the would-be speaker or theater owner be allowed a rapid appeal to a federal court. Only a judge can make the final determination whether expression can be banned. Statutes sometimes require a rapid—or expedited—judicial review.

Content Regulations

Central to First Amendment doctrine is the assumption that the government should not regulate the content of expression. Unless the government has a compelling interest to regulate, the Supreme Court has said, the constitutional guarantee of freedom of expression means that "government has no power to restrict expression because of its message, its ideas, its subject matter, or its content."[56] Where regulations restrict the content of political, social and artistic expression, skeptical judges subject the regulations to an analysis called **strict scrutiny**—or exacting scrutiny—to ensure that the regulations (1) are justified by a compelling government interest and (2) are narrowly drawn so as to impose the minimum abridgment of free expression. If the government lacks a compelling interest in regulating content, or if the regulation is too broad, the regulation is unconstitutional.

The Constitution is more tolerant toward content-neutral regulations than it is toward content regulations. The government does not have to demonstrate a compelling interest to justify content-neutral regulations, such as restrictions on the times and routes of parades, regulations that ensure minimum disruption but do not curtail the message of the parade participants. The government may more easily justify content-neutral regulations because they are not aimed at regulating content and only minimally impinge on freedom of expression, if at all. Content-neutral regulations are discussed in Chapter 3.

The application of strict scrutiny to content regulations reflects the skepticism with which judges view regulations that restrict a fundamental right such as freedom of expression. When courts review restrictions on a fundamental right, they abandon their usual deference to the legislature, a coequal branch of government. Instead, the courts adopt a skeptical attitude of "prove to me this regulation is not unconstitutional." Deference to a legislative finding "cannot limit judicial inquiry when First Amendment rights are at stake," the Supreme Court has said.[57]

Content regulations may regulate a whole subject or category of speech, such as anonymous political flyers or violent video games. Content regulations might also regulate the viewpoint of a speaker, requiring a speaker to express or

---

[53] *See* Laurence Tribe, *American Constitutional Law* 1059–60 (2nd ed. 1988).
[54] Freedman v. Maryland, 380 U.S. 51 (1965).
[55] Forsyth County v. Nationalist Movement, 505 U.S. 123 (1992).
[56] Police Dep't v. Mosley, 408 U.S. 92 (1972).
[57] Landmark Communications, Inc. v. Virginia, 435 U.S. 829 (1978).

not express a certain viewpoint, such as favoring a government official or opposing a government policy. The First Amendment particularly frowns on government attempts to control the viewpoint of a speaker or publisher.

If a court applying strict scrutiny decides the government lacks a compelling interest to justify the content regulation, the regulation is unconstitutional. If the government has a compelling interest in the regulation, the regulation is still unconstitutional if it is not narrowly drawn so it regulates only speech the government has a compelling need to regulate, such as speech that might lead to the sexual exploitation of children. Seldom does the government successfully argue that it has a compelling need to regulate speech or that a content regulation is sufficiently narrow to meet constitutional standards.

SUBJECT MATTER REGULATIONS The Supreme Court subjects content regulations to strict scrutiny, whether the regulations control subject matter or viewpoint. In a 1995 case involving subject matter, the Supreme Court employed strict scrutiny to strike down an Ohio law prohibiting anonymous campaign literature "designed to influence voters." In *McIntyre v. Ohio Elections Commission*, the Court invalidated this subject matter regulation, in part, because it unconstitutionally banned a category of political speech—anonymous flyers and other publications designed to influence voters in an election or referendum. Under the state statute, someone could lawfully distribute anonymous brochures about American literature but could not distribute anonymous brochures about political issues—such as school taxes—that citizens might vote on.[58]

Margaret McIntyre, her son and a friend distributed anonymous flyers opposing a school tax in Westerville, Ohio. McIntyre was fined $100 for violating the state law requiring the sponsor's name and address on all flyers, handbills, posters, direct mailings and other publications supporting or opposing candidates, referenda issues, tax proposals or other publications designed to influence voters.

The Court recognized the statute as a regulation on the content of speech. The state law regulated a category of speech—anonymous publications designed to influence voters—requiring them to prominently display the name and residence or business address of the person or organization responsible for the publication. The Court noted the subject matter regulation was evenhanded with regard to viewpoint, requiring the sponsors' names on all political flyers designed to influence voters, whether the authors favored or opposed a candidate, ballot issue, tax or other public issues. Ms. McIntyre would have violated the law even if she had not expressed her view opposing a proposed tax.

The Supreme Court ruled the Ohio statute unconstitutionally interfered with a category of political speech at the heart of American democracy. Distributing controversial, perhaps influential, leaflets is the "essence of First Amendment expression," the Court said. Imposing "exacting scrutiny," the Supreme Court found less than compelling Ohio's argument that the prohibition on anonymous leaflets was necessary to provide relevant information to voters and to prevent fraud and libel. Writers, the Court said, have a First Amendment right to determine the content of their publications, including whether they wish to sign their names. Authors' names are no more relevant to voters than other content in a political publication, the Court said.

The Court recognized the state has an interest in preventing fraud in an election, but other statutes address that issue directly, the Court said. The statute that

---

[58] 514 U.S. 334 (1994).

Ms. McIntyre violated unconstitutionally banned all unsigned flyers designed to influence voters, whether or not the publications contained fraud or libel. The statute banned anonymous flyers in elections, where there is a strong state interest in preventing fraud, but also in ballot issues and in other public issues where fraud might be a less serious or non-existent threat. Thus, the Ohio statute was much broader than necessary to prevent what would be relatively few instances of fraud and libel in political publications. The Court noted anonymous political publications enjoy a long, proud history, including the *Federalist Papers* in which Alexander Hamilton, John Jay and James Madison signed fictitious names to their arguments favoring ratification of the Constitution.

In another case involving content regulations, the Supreme Court in 2011 struck down a California statute that prohibited the sale of very violent interactive video games to minors. Applying strict scrutiny in *Brown v. Entertainment Merchants Association*, the Court ruled 7–2 that the State of California lacked a compelling need to justify prohibiting the sale of a category of constitutionally protected speech—violent video games.[59] While the Court was sympathetic to the state's interest in curbing antisocial behavior, the Court said the state presented minimal evidence—certainly not compelling evidence—that violent video games cause minors to act aggressively. Similarly, the Court noted that Grimms' fairy tales, Homer's *Odyssey*, Saturday morning cartoons and violent comic books and films have not been proven to cause children to become aggressively antisocial. Therefore, the Court refused to place the content category of violent video games outside First Amendment protection. *Entertainment Merchants* is discussed in detail in Chapter 9.

VIEWPOINT DISCRIMINATION A particularly egregious form of content regulation is **viewpoint discrimination**. When the government engages in viewpoint discrimination, it does not regulate a whole category of subject matter, such as political speech or violent video games, but favors or disfavors a point of view within a category. In 1989, the Supreme Court struck down a law punishing desecration of the American flag because the law unconstitutionally punished flag burners for their political viewpoints. In *Texas v. Johnson*, the Court overturned the conviction of Gregory Lee Johnson, who doused a flag with kerosene and set it on fire outside the 1984 Republican National Convention in Dallas to protest the policies of the Reagan administration. Johnson was convicted under a Texas law prohibiting intentional desecration of the flag where it caused "serious offense."[60] The Court ruled 5–4 that the statute unconstitutionally punished political expression. Indeed, many bystanders were offended by Johnson's incendiary act, but "offense" does not justify punishment for constitutionally protected speech that does not result in imminent lawless action. "If there is a bedrock principle underlying the First Amendment," Justice William Brennan wrote for the Court majority, "it is that the Government may not prohibit the expression of an idea simply because society finds the idea itself offensive or disagreeable."

The Court found no compelling interest in the desire of Texas to preserve the peace or to preserve the flag as a symbol of national unity. Johnson's incendiary act posed no danger of a riot in Dallas, the Court noted. Brennan said the symbolic value of the flag would be better preserved not by punishing flag burners but by trying to persuade protesters they are wrong. A government, Brennan said, "cannot

---

[59] 564 U.S. 786 (2011).
[60] 491 U.S. 397 (1989).

carve out a symbol of unity and prescribe a set of approved messages to be associated with that symbol." Quoting an earlier case, Brennan wrote:

> If there is any fixed star in our constitutional constellation, it is that no official, high or petty, can prescribe what shall be orthodox in politics, nationalism, religion, or other matters of opinion or force citizens to confess by word or act their faith therein.

In dissent, Chief Justice Rehnquist, joined by two other justices, said burning the flag—a symbol of American unity—is not expression that should be protected by the First Amendment. Public burning of the American flag, Rehnquist wrote, "was no essential part of any exposition of ideas, and at the same time it had a tendency to incite a breach of the peace."

In another viewpoint case, *Rosenberger v. University of Virginia*, the Supreme Court struck down a state university regulation that prohibited funding a religious publication, "Wide Awake: A Christian Perspective at the University of Virginia." At the same time the university funded 15 other student publications, including "The Yellow Journal," a humor magazine that satirized Christianity, and "Al-Salam," a publication that promoted a better understanding of Islam at the university.[61] Given the wide array of religious and antireligious subject matter, the university could not discriminate against one religious viewpoint in "Wide Awake," a viewpoint based on faith in a deity, the Court said.

In 2011, the Supreme Court ruled members of a church could not be punished by jurors who might disagree with the hateful, anti-gay viewpoints expressed on signs carried by church members near the funeral service of an American soldier. In *Snyder v. Phelps*,[62] the Court held the First Amendment was violated by a $5 million jury award for emotional distress allegedly caused by members of the Westboro Baptist Church carrying signs near the funeral proclaiming "God Hates the USA/Thank God for 9/11," "America Is Doomed," "God Hates Fags" and "Pope in Hell." While the signs were crude and offensive, the Court said they were protected viewpoints because they highlighted issues of public importance—"the political and moral conduct of the United States and its citizens, the fate of our Nation, homosexuality in the military, and scandals involving the Catholic clergy."

Vagueness and Overbreadth

When scrutinizing a law or regulation for constitutionality, the Supreme Court is often making sure that the restriction is easily understandable and does not overreach into areas of protected expression. In legal terms, the courts examine content and content-neutral regulations for **vagueness** and **overbreadth**. Normally, citizens cannot challenge the constitutionality of a law unless the law has been invoked against them. However, a citizen can challenge a vague or overbroad law that restricts expression even if the plaintiff is not a victim of the law. That is to say, an overbroad or vague law that restricts freedom of expression can be challenged "on its face" because the very existence of the law may curtail freedom of expression.[63]

---

[61] 515 U.S. 819 (1995).
[62] 562 U.S. 443 (2011).
[63] New York v. Ferber, 458 U.S. 747 (1982); Brockett v. Spokane Arcades, Inc., 472 U.S. 491 (1985).

An unconstitutionally vague law is one that is written so unclearly that persons "of common intelligence must necessarily guess at its meaning and differ as to its application."[64] A vague law is unconstitutional because it inhibits speech by making speakers unnecessarily cautious.[65] A federal judge struck down a vague University of Michigan policy banning speech or action that "stigmatizes or victimizes."[66] The policy was designed to halt racial jokes, slurs and other hate speech against women, minorities and gays on campus. In contemporary campus debate, critics might call the policy an attempt to impose political correctness on the campus.

Striking the code down for being unconstitutionally vague, the court said that both "stigmatize" and "victimize" are general terms that elude precise definition. A university lawyer admitted to the judge that he could not distinguish between speech that is merely offensive, and therefore protected, and speech that stigmatizes or victimizes, and therefore would not be protected. A policy that does not define the line between protected and unprotected speech will inhibit speech and is therefore unconstitutionally vague.

An overbroad law, unlike a vague one, may be quite clear about what it prohibits, but it prohibits too much. The Supreme Court ruled that the Communications Decency Act was overbroad because it not only banned Internet sales to minors of indecent pictures and texts—a ban that would be constitutional—but also prohibited parents from searching the web for indecency with their children. The government cannot ban indecent expression for adults, whether or not the adults wish to show it to their children. The Court suggested the Communications Decency Act might have been constitutional if it could effectively limit indecency on the Internet only to minors, but the statute was unconstitutionally overbroad because it prohibited all Internet indecency. Similarly, the University of Michigan policy designed to halt racist and sexist speech was also overbroad. The federal court said the policy was too broad because it not only prohibited disruptive or obscene speech—speech that could be constitutionally prohibited—but also prohibited distasteful speech protected by the First Amendment.[67]

■ SUMMARY ■

Federal courts, which have jurisdiction to determine what expression is protected by the Constitution, have the power under the Fourteenth Amendment to invalidate laws under which state actors violate the First Amendment. In reviewing the constitutionality of restrictions on free speech, the courts operate with a bias against regulations that limit the content of expression—whether subject matter or viewpoint—a bias manifest through the application of strict scrutiny, the requirement that the government establish a compelling need if a narrowly drawn regulation is to be constitutional. Because of the important values at stake in freedom-of-expression cases, appellate courts do not assume the constitutionality of legislation or lower court decisions restricting speech. Furthermore, courts scrutinize restrictive rules for overbreadth and vagueness to ensure minimum curbs on freedom of expression. When considering banning or limiting expression, the courts also ensure First Amendment due process by placing the burden of justifying restrictions

---

[64] Connally v. General Constr. Co., 269 U.S. 385, 391 (1926).
[65] *See* Anthony Amsterdam, "The Void for Vagueness Doctrine," 109 *U. Pa. L. Rev.* 67 (1960).
[66] Doe v. University of Michigan, 721 F. Supp. 852 (E.D. Mich. 1989).
[67] *Id.*

on the government and providing for adversary hearings at which the media may challenge restrictions.

TESTS

A frequently employed test at the turn of the century was the now-discredited bad-tendency test, by which judges could easily punish expression that presented even a slight tendency to cause harm. More recently, courts have tested the constitutionality of some restrictions by whether the speech presents a clear and present danger to society. Another test, frequently employed, is a balancing test, by which the Court weighs interests in free speech against conflicting social interests.

Bad-Tendency Test

The discredited **bad-tendency test**, accepted by a majority of the Supreme Court in the early twentieth century, provides virtually no First Amendment protection for speech. Under the bad-tendency test, expression may be halted or punished if it presents the slightest "tendency" to cause a substantial evil. The bad-tendency test is unconstitutionally vague because it fails to warn a speaker when speech may be punished.[68] The most innocuous threat might have a tendency—though extremely remote—to cause a disturbance.

The Supreme Court cited the bad-tendency test in *Gitlow v. New York* when it said the state could punish those who abuse freedom of expression by words that, among other things, are "inimical to the public welfare" or "tend . . . to corrupt public morals."[69] Under the bad-tendency test, virtually any social or public interest justifies suppression of expression. The bad-tendency test therefore cuts off expression long before it poses a danger to society. Under the bad-tendency test, speech might be punished merely because the speaker intended harm, even if the speech was unlikely to cause harm.

Clear-and-Present-Danger Test

The repressive bad-tendency test was gradually replaced by the **clear-and-present-danger test**, which today protects much more speech than the bad-tendency test. The clear-and-present-danger test was first stated by Justice Oliver Wendell Holmes in *Schenck v. United States*.[70] Expression should be punished, Holmes said in the 1919 case, only when words "are used in such circumstances and are of such a nature as to create a clear and present danger that they will bring about the substantive evils that Congress has a right to prevent."

Despite the requirement that speech present a "clear" and "present" danger, Charles Schenck and another socialist, Elizabeth Baer, were punished for distributing a circular that presented no immediate danger to anyone. Schenck's antidraft circular contained "impassioned language" urging that citizens were duty bound to oppose the draft because "conscription was despotism in its worst form and a monstrous wrong against humanity in the interest of Wall Street's chosen few." Evidence at Schenck's trial established that at least a few conscripts received a flyer, but it apparently persuaded no one to avoid the draft. Schenck was convicted of

---

[68] Thomas Emerson, *Toward a General Theory of the First Amendment* 50–1 (1963); Zechariah Chafee, *Free Speech in the United States* 42–51 (1969).
[69] 268 U.S. 652, 667 (1925).
[70] 249 U.S. 47 (1919).

conspiring to violate the Espionage Act of 1917, which, as strengthened in 1918, made it a crime to willfully cause or attempt to cause insubordination or disloyalty in military forces or to obstruct recruiting.[71] Convictions could result in fines of up to $10,000 and prison terms of up to 20 years.

Holmes could easily conclude that Schenck's ineffectual, one-page circulars presented a clear and present danger worthy of conviction because Holmes did not view the flyer as political speech. To Holmes, Schenck's flyers, which the justice noted were being distributed during wartime, were not speech on political matters so much as they were interjections, like falsely yelling "Fire!" in a theater, the punishment of which raised no First Amendment conflicts.[72]

Furthermore, freedom of expression enjoyed no special status in Holmes's mind at the time, despite his articulation of the clear-and-present-danger test. In fact, Holmes insisted at the time that free speech "stand[s] no differently than freedom from vaccination," a "freedom" that a legislative majority could constitutionally curtail.[73] To Holmes and the Supreme Court in 1919, speech that presented a clear and present danger, like speech that presented a bad tendency, could be punished if it might cause harm at some time in the distant future.

That same year, Holmes began to see that freedom of expression enjoys little protection if speakers can be jailed because their speech has a tendency to cause some undefined harm at some undefined time. Giving voice to his new understanding, Holmes dissented when the Supreme Court upheld the conviction of five Russian aliens for distributing political flyers. In his famous dissent in *Abrams v. United States*,[74] Holmes said that even opinions we "loathe and believe to be fraught with death" should not be suppressed "unless they so imminently threaten immediate interference with the lawful and pressing purposes of the law that an immediate check is required to save the country." Holmes thought Abrams's flyers opposing the dispatch of American troops to Russia were opinions that presented no such imminent danger.

Several times after *Schenck* and *Abrams*, the Supreme Court purported to apply a clear-and-present-danger test but upheld convictions for expression that presented no imminent threat. During the McCarthy era in the 1950s, a Supreme Court plurality upheld the conviction of nearly a dozen members of the Communist Party for "conspiring" to advocate the forcible overthrow of the government.[75] The defendants' crime in the case, *Dennis v. United States*, was belonging to the Communist Party.

While applying a version of the clear-and-present-danger test in *Dennis*, the plurality admitted that the defendant and his comrades posed no immediate danger of violence. Nevertheless, the Court upheld the conviction, saying the government need not wait to stop speech "until the catalyst is added" if "the ingredients of the reaction are present." It was enough, the Court said, that Dennis and his friends established a "highly organized conspiracy, with rigidly disciplined members subject to call when the leaders . . . felt the time had come for action."

The Court's version of the clear-and-present-danger test in *Dennis* amounted to little more than a one-time balancing of free speech interests against general

---

[71] Espionage Act of June 15, 1917, 40 Stat. 217.
[72] *See* Jeremy Cohen, *Congress Shall Make No Law: Oliver Wendell Holmes, the First Amendment, and Judicial Decision Making* (1989).
[73] Letter of Oliver Wendell Holmes Jr. to Judge Learned Hand, June 24, 1918, in Gerald Gunther, *Learned Hand: The Man and the Judge* 163 (1994).
[74] 50 U.S. 616 (1919) (dissenting opinion).
[75] 341 U.S. 494 (1951).

security considerations during a politically charged era. Whether or not one agrees with the Court's results, the justices in the plurality did not rigorously scrutinize the speech of Dennis and his cohorts to determine whether it presented a clear and present danger.

By 1957, the Court had begun to examine the facts of cases more carefully to determine if speech in fact presented an imminent danger. In *Yates v. United States*, the Court applied the clear-and-present-danger test more literally than before, ruling that a conspiracy to advocate the overthrow of the government was too far removed from immediate danger to be punished. The Court said that a clear and present danger could be found only if there were advocacy of direct illegal action.[76]

In 1969, in a decision that is still active precedent, the Court employed a variation of the clear-and-present-danger test requiring that speech be punished only if it incites lawless action. In the 1969 case *Brandenburg v. Ohio*,[77] the Court overturned the conviction of Ku Klux Klan members for racist provocations. The Court struck down an Ohio criminal syndicalism statute under which a Ku Klux Klan leader had been convicted for advocating unlawful methods of industrial or political reform. Brandenburg was fined $1,000 and sentenced from one to ten years in prison for telling Klansmen at a televised meeting:

> We're not a revengent organization, but if our President, our Congress, our Supreme Court, continues to suppress the white, Caucasian race, it's possible that there might have to be some revengence taken.

Brandenburg then told of plans to march on Congress "four hundred thousand strong" on the Fourth of July. The Supreme Court overturned Brandenburg's conviction because the statute permitted convictions for "mere advocacy" of illegal action at some distant time. To be constitutional, the Court said, an advocacy statute can punish only speech that "is directed to inciting or producing imminent lawless action and is likely to incite or produce such actions."

Four years later, the Court again employed its incitement variation of the clear-and-present-danger test to overturn the conviction of a street protester. In *Hess v. Indiana*, the Court reversed the conviction of a demonstrator who was arrested during an antiwar demonstration on a college campus for shouting, "We'll take the fucking street later."[78] The Court concluded that Hess's statement, at worst, "amounted to nothing more than advocacy of illegal action at some indefinite future time." To sustain a conviction, the Court said, it was necessary to show that the words "were intended to produce, and likely to produce, imminent disorder."

Balancing Test

The clear-and-present-danger test sets a standard for halting or punishing speech that presents an immediate danger of unlawful action. In many cases, however, such as those involving defamation or invasion of privacy, speech may be sufficiently harmful to justify compensation for an injured party, although the expression may not present immediate danger of unlawful action justifying a prior restraint or a

---

[76] 354 U.S. 298 (1957).

[77] 395 U.S. 444 (1969) (per curiam). *See* Hans Linde, "'Clear and Present Danger' Re-examined: Dissonance in the Brandenburg Concerto," 22 *Stan. L. Rev.* 1163, 1166 (1970).

[78] 414 U.S. 105 (1973). *See also* Healy v. James, 408 U.S. 169 (1972).

criminal punishment. In such cases, which are much more common than cases in which speech incites unlawful action, the clear-and-present-danger test might not be appropriate. Instead, courts often employ a balancing test in such cases.

In effect, all judicial standards, including the clear-and-present-danger test, involve balancing of conflicting interests,[79] but judges employing the balancing test consciously weigh conflicting interests against each other. Chief Justice Vinson explained balancing when he said that it is the duty of the courts to determine which of two conflicting interests demands the greater protection in particular circumstances.[80]

Courts engage in what is called **ad hoc balancing** when judges treat each case separately, placing speech considerations on one side of the scales and conflicting values—such as individual reputation—on the other side. In ad hoc balancing, there are no definitions or single standards for guidance. Ad hoc balancing provides great flexibility because a judge can assign different weights to different facts of a case. One time, a judge could rule that freedom of expression was more important; another time, the judge could decide that a person's reputation outweighed freedom of expression.

But what is gained in flexibility is lost in predictability. In fact, ad hoc balancing risks making First Amendment protection indefinable; judges balancing speech interests against other personal and social interests may rule for either side in any case.[81] Ad hoc balancing creates opportunities for biased judgments because judges may impose their own values where there are no objective standards.

To put more uniformity and predictability into balancing, courts engage in what is sometimes called **definitional balancing**. In definitional balancing, courts define the outer limit of free speech before the balancing test is applied in individual cases. Thus, definitional balancing reduces the vagueness of ad hoc balancing by providing defined standards that can be applied in similar cases.

For example, in libel cases involving the media and a public official, the media's freedom of expression is balanced against the official's right to a good reputation. However, the media bring a defined advantage to the scales in each case. This is because the Supreme Court has ruled that the media's freedom of expression includes protection to publish false, defamatory statements about public officials, provided that the false statements are not published knowingly or recklessly, either of which constitutes what is called **actual malice**.

Because the Supreme Court has ruled that public officials must prove the media published defamatory statements with actual malice, officials know before they file a libel suit that the courts will not engage in ad hoc balancing of the officials' interest in reputation against the media's First Amendment rights. The media's constitutional freedom to make false but non-malicious statements is defined beforehand.[82] Thus, the media have a preferred position—one mandated by the First Amendment because of the importance that political speech be robust and uninhibited—when an official's reputation is balanced against the media's freedom of expression. Public officials who sue the media for libel know at the outset they will have difficulty proving the defamatory statements were published with malice.

---

[79] Paul Freund, *The Supreme Court of the United States* 42–4 (1961).
[80] American Communications Ass'n v. Douds, 339 U.S. 382 (1950).
[81] Rodney Smolla, *Smolla and Nimmer on Freedom of Speech* secs. 2:58–2:60 at 2–56 to 2–62 (1999).
[82] N.Y. Times v. Sullivan, 376 U.S. 254 (1964).

■ **SUMMARY** ■

The First Amendment does not create absolute protection for freedom of expression, the courts say. Courts therefore apply tests in individual cases to determine whether freedom of expression or conflicting social and personal values will prevail. The discredited bad-tendency test permitted suppression of almost any expression that presented a vague danger to social or personal interests. A clear-and-present-danger test, if applied literally, provides more protection for freedom of expression by prohibiting speech only when there is clear evidence of an incitement to lawless action. Most often, the courts employ a balancing test. Ad hoc balancing gives judges great flexibility but makes First Amendment protections unpredictable. Definitional balancing brings more uniform standards to First Amendment adjudication.

THE HIERARCHY OF PROTECTED EXPRESSION

The First Amendment says that Congress shall make no law abridging freedom of expression, and the Supreme Court has ruled that the constitutionality of content regulations on political speech will be subjected to strict scrutiny. Despite the staunch protections for content, however, not every type of content is protected by the First Amendment, and not every type of content that is protected is protected equally. Indeed, some content is so low in the hierarchy of freedom of expression that it is excluded from First Amendment protection and therefore can be banned.

In the constitutional hierarchy of content, the most favored speech is political and social content, the regulation of which must be subjected to strict scrutiny. Less protected are advertising and nonobscene sexual expression, the regulation of which is subjected to more relaxed scrutiny or intermediate scrutiny. Excluded from constitutional protection are false advertising, fraud, child pornography, fighting words and true threats. The Supreme Court, which is reluctant to add new categories of unprotected speech, has refused to exclude depictions of animal cruelty[83] or false claims of military valor[84] from First Amendment protection.

Political and Social Expression

The most valued and most protected speech—the expression that arguably contributes most to individual fulfillment as well as to democratic governance—is expression dealing with political, social, religious and cultural issues. Protected subject matter includes debate about elections, referenda, labor, race, health, agriculture, religion, education and other political and social issues.

Protected political and social expression may take many forms. Protected content may be printed in newspapers, magazines, editorial advertisements, posters and poetry. Protected content may be expressed orally through speeches, lectures, films and broadcasts. It may be delivered symbolically through black armbands,[85] political campaign contributions,[86] marches, slogans and political symbols.[87] One court ruled that a rugby match between the United States and South Africa was protected by the First Amendment and could not be canceled by the governor of New

---

[83] United States v. Stevens, 559 U.S. 460 (2010).
[84] United States v. Alvarez, 132 S. Ct. 2537 (2012).
[85] Tinker v. Des Moines Indep. Community Sch. Dist., 393 U.S. 503 (1969).
[86] Buckley v. Valeo, 424 U.S. 1 (1976).
[87] Spence v. Washington, 418 U.S. 405 (1974).

York because of the "singularly dramatic racial issue involved."[88] The Constitution, the Supreme Court has said, "looks beyond written or spoken words as mediums of expression."[89] Instead of protecting only "particularized" messages, the First Amendment also protects the "painting of Jackson Pollock, music of Arnold Schoenberg, or Jabberwocky verse of Lewis Carroll."

Commercial and Sexual Expression

Despite the bias in First Amendment jurisprudence against content regulation, the Constitution tolerates more regulation on advertising and pornography because they are supposedly less valuable than political speech. Commercial advertising was once among the categories of speech excluded by definition from constitutional protection, but truthful commercial speech now enjoys some constitutional protection from government regulation, although false advertising does not.

Commercial advertising, the Supreme Court says, may be more heavily regulated than political and cultural expression because advertising, being motivated by economic gain, is hardier and can therefore withstand more regulation. Advertising is also more easily verified, the Court says.[90] Because of the hardiness and verifiability of commercial speech, the Supreme Court says there is less reason for society to tolerate inaccurate or misleading commercial speech than to tolerate false political speech. Political speech is said to be more vulnerable and less verifiable. Advertising will be discussed in Chapter 8.

Regulations on nonobscene sexual expression are also subject to less exacting scrutiny than regulations on political content. Nude dancing, the Supreme Court has said, enjoys less First Amendment protection than political speech because it is expressive conduct within the outer perimeters of the First Amendment.[91] Nonobscene sexual films, plays and magazines may be examined for obscenity before distribution, whereas political and other more highly valued expression may not.[92] Furthermore, the display of nonobscene sexual plays, movies and printed materials can be restricted to certain zones within a city without violating the First Amendment.[93]

Some expression is less protected if it is broadcast rather than printed. Indecency, which may be thought of as four-letter words, is fully protected content in magazines, books and other printed media, but is less protected in broadcasting. The Supreme Court justifies less rigorous First Amendment protection for broadcast indecency because broadcasts supposedly intrude into the home, assailing vulnerable children.[94] Obscenity, "patently offensive" depictions of sexual and excretory acts, is excluded from constitutional protection. Obscenity, indecency and violence are discussed in Chapter 9. The section in Chapter 3 on content-neutral regulations explores the relaxed constitutional standards the Supreme Court applies to regulations on marches, demonstrations and other speech in public forums. Two categories of expression excluded from constitutional protection are discussed here: fighting words and true threats, both often falling into the non-legal category of hate speech.

---

[88] Selfridge v. Carey, 522 F. Supp. 693 (N.D.N.Y. 1981).
[89] Hurley v. Irish-American Gay, Lesbian, and Bisexual Group of Boston, 515 U.S. 557 (1995).
[90] Virginia State Bd. of Pharmacy v. Virginia Citizens Consumer Council, Inc., 425 U.S. 748 (1976).
[91] City of Erie v. Pap's A.M., 529 U.S. 277 (2000).
[92] Freedman v. Maryland, 380 U.S. 51 (1965).
[93] City of Renton v. Playtime Theatres, Inc., 475 U.S. 41 (1986).
[94] See Glen Robinson, "The Electronic First Amendment," 47 Duke L.J. 899 (1998).

Hate Speech

Hate speech, a problem worldwide, consists of written or spoken words that insult and degrade groups identified by race, gender, ethnic group, religion or sexual orientation. Hate speech includes the swastikas neo-Nazi marchers carry in a Jewish neighborhood, the ethnic "joke" on a campus radio station, the derogatory slur directed at a Muslim, and the burning cross in a black family's front yard.

Professor Richard Delgado argues that racist speech "injures the dignity and self-regard of the person to whom it is addressed, communicating the message that distinctions of race are distinctions of merit, dignity, status and personhood."[95] Similarly, Professor Mari Matsuda argues that a government's failure to punish racial and ethnic invective amounts to state support for hate speech—speech that denies personhood.[96] Although many would agree that hateful expressions "rape the soul" and undermine community tolerance,[97] support for legal sanctions against hate speech is not universal. Prohibitions on hate speech, it is argued, will have little beneficial effect because law cannot eradicate the prejudice and bias that motivate hate speech. Instead of benefiting society, it is argued, punishing hate speech may harm society by driving hate groups into dangerous underground cells. Furthermore, hate speech laws may be used to stifle the minorities the laws are supposed to protect.[98]

Most countries outside the United States punish hate speech. Under a United Nations resolution, member nations are supposed to declare illegal "all dissemination of ideas based on racial superiority or hatred, [and] incitement to racial discrimination."[99] In Canada, it is a crime to willfully promote hatred in public against an identifiable group, such as a religious or racial minority.[100] France criminalizes incitement to discrimination, hatred or violence based on ethnicity, race or religion;[101] French law and German law prohibit trade in Nazi memorabilia and denying the Holocaust.[102] Facebook, Twitter and other American media companies increasingly run afoul of foreign hate speech laws. Under pressure from foreign governments and public opinion, Facebook and other social media are adopting policies to combat hate speech as well as false speech and fake news.

The United States is unique in that the First Amendment protects expression of much hate speech. However, two categories of speech, fighting words and true threats, are not protected by the First Amendment.

FIGHTING WORDS The Supreme Court defines **fighting words** as those that "by their very utterance inflict injury or tend to incite an immediate breach of the peace."[103] Expression constitutes fighting words only if it is so offensive as to

---

[95] Richard Delgado, "Words That Wound: A Tort Action for Racial Insults, Epithets, and Name-Calling," 17 *Harv. Civ. Rts.-Civ. Lib. L. Rev.* 133–6 (1982).

[96] Mari J. Matsuda, "Public Response to Racist Speech: Considering the Victim's Story," 87 *Mich. L. Rev.* 2320 (1989).

[97] Rodney Smolla, *Free Speech in an Open Society* 153 (1992).

[98] *See, e.g.*, Sandra Coliver, "Hate Speech Laws: Do They Work?" in *Striking a Balance: Hate Speech, Freedom of Expression and Non-discrimination* 367 (Sandra Coliver ed., 1992).

[99] *International Convention on the Elimination of All Forms of Racial Discrimination* art. 4(a), General Assembly Resolution 2106A of Dec. 21, 1965, entered into force Jan. 4, 1969.

[100] *See* John Manwaring, "Legal Regulation of Hate Propaganda in Canada," in *Striking a Balance* 107–8 (Sandra Coliver ed., 1992).

[101] *See* Roger Errera, "In Defense of Civility: Racial Incitement and Group Libel in French Law," in *Striking a Balance* 147 (Sandra Coliver ed., 1992).

[102] *See* Yahoo! Inc. v. La Ligue Contre Le Racism et L'Antisemitisme, 433 F.3d 1199, *cert. denied*, 126 S. Ct. 2332 (2006); German Criminal Code, § 130 (Bohlander translation).

[103] Chaplinsky v. New Hampshire, 315 U.S. 568 (1942).

have "a direct tendency to cause acts of violence by the person to whom, individually, the remark is addressed."[104] Fighting words may be prohibited because they provoke a breach of the peace, not merely because their content offends. It is difficult for an aggrieved plaintiff to win a fighting words suit because the words at issue seldom provoke a face-to-face confrontation.

The fighting words doctrine originated in the case of *Chaplinsky v. New Hampshire* in 1941.[105] Chaplinsky was convicted for calling a marshal in Rochester, New Hampshire, a "goddamned racketeer and a damned Fascist." Although the marshal did not strike Chaplinsky, the court said that "goddamned racketeer" and "damned Fascist" were epithets likely to provoke the average person to physical retaliation. Chaplinsky therefore had no First Amendment protection because he had uttered fighting words. Fighting words are outside of constitutional protection, the Court said, because they are "no essential part of any exposition of ideas, and are of such slight social value as a step to truth that any benefit that may be derived from them is clearly outweighed by the social interest in order and morality."

In 1971, the Court overturned the conviction of a war protester because the slogan on the back of his jacket—"Fuck the Draft"—did not constitute fighting words. In *Cohen v. California*, the Court said the slogan on Cohen's jacket, which he wore in a California courthouse, was a constitutionally protected comment on the unpopular war the country was then waging in Vietnam. Cohen's message did not constitute fighting words because it presented no immediate danger of a violent physical reaction in a face-to-face confrontation. No one, the Court said, could regard the words on Cohen's jacket as "a direct personal insult."[106]

University codes designed to curb hate speech on campus have also been declared unconstitutional, in part because they are not narrowly drawn to prohibit only fighting words. As discussed earlier, a federal court struck down a University of Michigan regulation that prohibited verbal or physical behavior that "stigmatizes or victimizes" because the policy punished speech that was vaguely offensive. The court said the university might prohibit obscenity, fighting words, criminal incitement and sexual harassment in the workplace, but not speech that is merely offensive.[107] The court said that the university enforced the policy "broadly and indiscriminately" in classrooms and other places.

The Supreme Court overturned the conviction of a St. Paul, Minnesota, racist because of a faulty fighting words ordinance. The Supreme Court reversed the conviction of 17-year-old Robert A. Victoria, who was charged for burning a cross inside the fenced yard of the home of Russ and Laura Jones, a black couple, in violation of a city disorderly conduct ordinance. The ordinance made it a misdemeanor for anyone to place a symbol, object or graffiti, including a swastika or burning cross, on public or private property if it was likely to arouse "anger, alarm, or resentment in others on the basis of race, color, creed, religion or gender."

Writing for the Court majority in *R.A.V. v. City of St. Paul*,[108] Justice Antonin Scalia said the St. Paul ordinance was unconstitutional because it prohibited only fighting words based on "race, color, creed, religion, or gender," while presumably permitting hate speech motivated by political party, union membership, homosexuality or other protected interests. Finding an unconstitutional content regulation,

---

[104] Gooding v. Wilson, 405 U.S. 518 (1972).
[105] 315 U.S. 568 (1941).
[106] 403 U.S. 15, 20 (1971).
[107] Doe v. University of Michigan, 721 F. Supp. 852 (E.D. Mich. 1989).
[108] 505 U.S. 377 (1992).

Justice Scalia said, "The First Amendment does not permit St. Paul to impose special prohibitions on those speakers who express views on disfavored subjects."

Scalia said the cross burning might have been punished under laws that do not curb speech but prohibit illegal actions such as arson, terroristic threats or criminal damage to property. After the *R.A.V.* decision, Arthur Morris Miller, the only adult convicted under the St. Paul ordinance for the cross burning at the Jones home, pled guilty to the federal misdemeanor of interfering with the Jones's right of access to housing by conspiring to burn crosses in the couple's yard.

Although speech cannot be punished simply because it is motivated by racial, ethnic, religious or gender bias, the Supreme Court has ruled that crimes that do not involve speech may be more severely punished if they are motivated by racial and ethnic bias. In *Wisconsin v. Mitchell*, the Supreme Court upheld a statute providing for higher penalties if a criminal selects victims because of their race, religion or sexual orientation.[109] The Supreme Court upheld the punishment of a black Kenosha man whose sentence for aggravated battery had been increased because he selected his victim because he was white.

TRUE THREATS This is a category of speech, like fighting words, that is excluded from First Amendment protection. The Supreme Court defines a **true threat** as speech or symbolic expression "intended to create a pervasive fear in victims that they are a target of violence."[110] A true threat is intended to intimidate the target of the threat. It is not enough that the target of the threat fears for his or her physical safety; the person making a true threat must intend to intimidate the person threatened. The Supreme Court has not been clear about how the intent to intimidate should be proven. There is no intent to intimidate if the threat is lighthearted or can't be taken seriously. There is no intent to intimidate if the threat is vague.

The Supreme Court ruled that burning a cross may constitute a true threat if the purpose of the burning is to intimidate. Writing for the Court in *Virginia v. Black*, Justice Sandra Day O'Connor said cross burning is constitutionally protected if not intended to intimidate—such as burning a cross in a film—but is beyond constitutional protection if intended to intimidate—such as burning a cross in a black family's yard.[111] Context is important. Noting that cross burning is intertwined with the reign of terror imposed by the Ku Klux Klan following the Civil War, O'Connor said punishing cross burning with intent to intimidate punishes "a particularly virulent form of intimidation." O'Connor said the Virginia statute, unlike the ordinance prohibiting cross burning invalidated in *R.A.V. v. City of St. Paul*, did not punish expression on a disfavored topic. The Virginia statute punished all cross burning engaged in with the intent to intimidate, whereas the St. Paul ordinance punished cross burning that intended to intimidate only if the hateful symbolic speech were motivated by racial, gender or religious animosity but not by other hateful animosities. The Virginia statute, the Court said, was constitutional insofar as it did not single out for opprobrium only that speech directed toward one of the specified disfavored topics.

While the majority of the Court in *Virginia v. Black* held that cross burning that is intended to intimidate constitutes an unprotected true threat, the majority also ruled that the Virginia statute at issue in *Virginia v. Black* was unconstitutional because it allowed a jury to infer that anyone who burned a cross intended to

[109] 508 U.S. 476 (1993).
[110] Virginia v. Black, 538 U.S. 343 (2003).
[111] *Id.*

intimidate. The First Amendment requires a more detailed inquiry into intent in each case of cross burning, O'Connor said.

In 2015, the Supreme Court ruled that prosecutors in Internet threat cases must prove that the defendant intended to threaten the victim, but the Court left unclear how intent was to be established. In *Elonis v. United States*, the Court reversed a lower court ruling allowing convictions for Internet threats if a reasonable person would perceive a threat; the lower court had not required proof the defendant intended to threaten the victim.

The Court remanded the case to determine if Anthony Elonis intended to threaten his estranged wife when he posted several Facebook messages—some in rap format—including:

> If I only knew then what I know now, I would have smothered your ass
> with a pillow, dumped your body in the back seat, dropped you off in
> Toad Creek, and made it look like a rape and murder.

A lower court had sentenced Elonis to prison for 44 months, concluding a reasonable person would view the communications as intending to threaten.[112] Elonis claimed he had a First Amendment right to post his messages and that he did not intend to threaten his wife.

In its 8–1 decision, the Supreme Court did not specify what mental state must be proven—such as recklessness or a purpose to threaten—to convict for threatening posts on the Internet. The Court did not rule on First Amendment issues.

In an earlier non-Internet case, *Watts v. United States*,[113] the Supreme Court ruled that Watts, an 18-year-old opponent of the Vietnam War, had not threatened the life of the president when he told a discussion group at a Washington, D.C., rally that he might shoot Lyndon B. Johnson. Watts said he wanted to get L.B.J. "in my sights" if he were inducted into the Army and made to carry a rifle. Watts and his audience then laughed. The Supreme Court considered Watts's warning, which drew laughter and was contingent on his induction into the Army, to be "pure" political speech posing no threat to the president.

Social Media

Hostile speech has escalated in the United States, particularly on social media. Much of it is protected, hyperbolic political speech directed at government officials or institutions like the police, or extremist speech denigrating immigrants and racial or ethnic minorities. Hate speech flourishes on social media in part because some platforms allow anonymous posts, and a few do not restrict hate speech in any way.

Hundreds of social media users have been charged under federal and state laws with criminal threats, sometimes terroristic threats, usually because they either threatened police or supported the Islamic State. A man was charged in Buffalo, New York, with threatening to injure police officers for an alleged Facebook post saying, "Let's Start Killin Police Lets See How Dey Like It." In a two-week period following the killing of police in Dallas and Baton Rouge, Louisiana, federal and state authorities arrested at least eight people for posting threats against police.[114]

---

[112] 135 S. Ct. 2001 (2015).
[113] 394 U.S. 705 (1969) (per curiam).
[114] Nicole Hong, "Police Ramp Up Scrutiny of Online Threats," *Wall St. J.*, July 20, 2016.

Between 2014 and 2016, the government gained guilty pleas—without proof at trial of the seriousness of the threat or the intent of the speaker—in almost all of 100 cases where defendants were charged with support of the Islamic State.[115] In one widely reported case, Safya Roe Yassin, 39, a Muslim woman born in the United States, pleaded guilty to charges she intended to threaten by retweeting messages supporting the Islamic State. Yassin allegedly retweeted a message containing "Wanted to kill" and the names, addresses and phone numbers of U.S. law enforcement employees and military members.[116] The retweet did not specify a time or place for carrying out the threat. Before the retweet, U.S. Air Force members who were identified in Islamic State tweets received anonymous death threats. Twitter's terms of service, like terms of service of other social media companies, prohibit violent threats or promoting terrorism.[117] Ultimately, Yassin was sentenced to nine years in federal prison without parole.

The U.S. government cannot compel social media to limit or prohibit hateful speech, but some foreign governments can, at least on sites aimed at users in those countries. American social media companies voluntarily combat hateful and threatening speech on the Internet. In a six-month period, Twitter suspended more than 235,000 accounts that allegedly promoted terrorism.[118] And, in 2018, a California state appeals court dismissed a claim against Twitter by a self-proclaimed "racialist" and "white advocate" who alleged that the platform violated his First Amendment rights when it permanently deleted his accounts.[119]

Twitter has increased training of teams to recognize and delete hateful and threatening expression and has made it easier for users to report abusive behavior. Twitter makes it harder for users whose accounts have been shut down to reopen a new account. For personal peace, Twitter allows users to block or mute words, phrases and conversations they do not want to hear.[120]

American social media also combat hate speech and threats abroad, sometimes under threat of prosecution under foreign hate speech laws and raising questions whether global American media companies must remove an expression that violates foreign laws but would be protected in the United States. In 2016, Facebook reluctantly removed the name and address of a Berlin restaurant owned by Yorai Feinberg, a 35-year-old Israeli. Feinberg's address was posted on a Facebook map without Feinberg's knowledge by a far-right group under the banner "Jews Among Us." Also posted were names and addresses of Jewish institutions and Israeli-owned businesses. Feinberg soon received anonymous phone calls telling him, "I hate Jews." At first, Facebook refused to delete the page, claiming the posting met the company's community standards. But Facebook deleted the page after many complaints on social media, in newspapers and from German authorities, who threatened to invoke laws prohibiting inciting hatred against minorities and denying the Holocaust.[121] Much of the hate speech in Germany is directed at immigrants from Syria, Afghanistan and other war-torn countries.

---

[115] *Id.*

[116] Criminal Complaint, United States v. Yassin, No. 16-mj-2009DPR (W.D. Mo., Feb. 17, 2016).

[117] Twitter, "The Twitter Rules," https://help.twitter.com/en/rules-and-policies/twitter-rules; Facebook, Community Standards, "Direct Threats," www.facebook.com/communitystandards/; Nicole Hong, "ISIS Retweet Arrest Raises Free Speech Issues," *Wall St. J.*, Aug. 12, 2016.

[118] Katie Benner, "Twitter Suspends 235,000 More Accounts Over Extremism," *Wall St. J.*, Aug. 18, 2016.

[119] Robert Burnson, "Twitter Beats Censorship Lawsuit by Banned White Nationalist," *Bloomberg*, Aug. 23, 2018.

[120] Katie Benner, "Twitter Adds New Ways to Curb Abuse and Hate Speech," *N.Y. Times*, Nov. 15, 2016.

[121] Mark Scott and Melissa Eddy, "Facebook Runs Up Against German Hate Speech Laws," *N.Y. Times*, Nov. 28, 2016.

Facebook has updated its global community standards for its billions of users to curb hate speech in the United States and abroad, attempting to strike a balance between freedom of expression and the protection of vulnerable minorities. Facebook's action comes after much pressure from foreign countries, particularly Germany, which has more stringent laws against hate speech and a citizenry that remembers the mass murder of Jews during World War II followed by decades of Communist rule in the Eastern bloc.

False, Fake or Cruel

False or fake news is easy to find on social media, from claims that Bill Gates is controlling minds through COVID-19 vaccines to those that President Obama was a Muslim, from reports that Pope Francis endorsed Donald Trump for president to those of U.S. voter fraud illustrated with footage from Russian polling stations.[122] There is a vast ecosystem of misinformation that includes Google, Twitter and Facebook; message boards like 4chan and Reddit; and certain cable channels and print media. Moreover, algorithms have made it possible to synthesize fictitious video, images, voice and text. For example, photos of imaginary faces can be fabricated by computers, and faces can be swapped from one body to another, creating "deepfakes" and threats to both reputation and privacy. Journalists should develop strategies to assess whether content was produced by a media-synthesis algorithm.[123]

By and large, false speech is protected by the First Amendment in the United States. While fraud, perjury and false advertising are beyond constitutional protection, false statements in the political, religious and social realm—that is, the most consequential realms of speech—are constitutionally protected. American law does not require that politicians, the news media or social media be truthful. Indeed, the First Amendment explicitly protects much falsehood, including false statements that defame public officials—unless the statements are published with "actual malice." Erroneous statement is inevitable in free debate, the Supreme Court has said, and must be protected if the freedom of expression is to have the "breathing space" it needs to survive.[124]

In 2012, a 6–3 majority of the Supreme Court refused to declare that falsity is beyond constitutional protection. In *U.S. v. Alvarez*, the Court struck down the federal Stolen Valor Act, a law that criminalized falsely claiming to have won a military medal. Xavier Alvarez falsely told fellow members of a California water board he had been awarded the Congressional Medal of Honor. Permitting the government to criminalize false claims of military valor, Justice Kennedy said, "would endorse government authority to compile a list of subjects about which false statements are punishable. That governmental power has no clear limiting principle." Citing Orwell's *Nineteen Eighty-Four*, Kennedy said, "Our constitutional tradition stands against the idea that we need Oceania's Ministry of Truth."[125]

If falsehood is protected by the First Amendment, truth will be determined, if at all, through ethical journalism and principled civic dialogue in the marketplace of ideas. To promote truth and reduce falsity in the public sphere, social media

---

[122] Deepa Seetharaman, "Social Media Companies Forced to Confront Misinformation and Harassment," *Wall. St. J.*, Jan. 12, 2017.
[123] Nicholas Diakopoulos, "Reporting in a Machine Reality: Deepfakes, Misinformation, and What Journalists Can Do About Them," *Colum. Journalism Rev.*, May 15, 2018.
[124] New York Times v. Sullivan, 376 U.S. 254 (1964).
[125] United States v. Alvarez, 132 S. Ct. 2537 (2012); United States v. Swisher, 811 F.3d 299 (9th Cir. 2016).

companies are adopting policies and practices, sometimes reluctantly, to reduce the spread of falsehoods and to increase the spread of truthful information on their platforms. Let's use Facebook as an example.

Mark Zuckerberg, founder and chief executive officer of Facebook, generally has viewed Facebook as a neutral platform whose primary function was allowing friends and family to share pictures and posts where it would be inappropriate for Facebook management to become the "arbiter of truth." He once said that "news and media are not primary things people do on Facebook."[126] In 2019, Zuckerberg delivered a speech in which he defended Facebook as a champion of free expression.[127] He said again that the platform should not be an arbiter of speech, and he defended the site's decision earlier that year not to fact-check political ads, saying, "I don't think it's right for a private company to censor politicians or the news in a democracy." And while acknowledging Facebook's power, he said the more important reality is that his company has "decentralized power by putting it directly into people's hands," which he said "at scale is a new kind of force in the world—a Fifth Estate." Public reaction to the speech was generally negative. A related *New Yorker* column ran under the headline "Mark Zuckerberg Still Doesn't Get It"[128] and argued that Zuckerberg's "thesis was that free speech is good," while the largely unanswered question was "whether free speech is the only good worth pursuing."

Facebook is an influential media company where billions of people post, read and view news, including fake news. Forty-four percent of Americans get at least some of their news from Facebook, often in their news feed, typically a user's first daily stop.[129] Studies show that Facebook content has "directly influenced political self-expression, information seeking and real-world voting behavior of millions of people."[130] In response to those realities and the growing chorus of critics who have said for years that the company has not done enough to moderate user content, Facebook has undertaken initiatives to reduce misinformation and to support the spread of high-quality journalism.

For example, Facebook has partnered with independent third-party fact-checkers—involving more than 80 organizations working in more than 60 languages—to identify and review viral misinformation, defined as "provably false claims, particularly those that have the potential to mislead or harm."[131] The site has also made it harder for false news to gain advertising support on Facebook, and the site has tweaked its algorithms so accurate journalism has a better chance than false, sensational information of appearing at the top of a user's feed. There is still, however, much more work to be done, as the COVID-19 pandemic has made clear, as viral misinformation has spread with relative ease throughout the public health crisis.

Another relevant layer of governance at Facebook is its recently established Oversight Board. Its members, from around the world, select content cases for review—with the power to uphold or reverse Facebook's content decisions in light

---

[126] Deepa Seetharaman, "Zuckerberg Continues to Defend Facebook Against Election Criticism," *Wall St. J.*, Nov. 14, 2016.

[127] Mark Zuckerberg, "Standing for Voice and Free Expression," *Facebook*, Oct. 17, 2019, www.facebook.com/notes/mark-zuckerberg/standing-for-voice-and-freeexpression/10157267502546634/.

[128] Andrew Marantz, "Mark Zuckerberg Still Doesn't Get It," *New Yorker*, Oct. 19, 2019.

[129] Deepa Seetharaman, "Facebook to Push for Better Journalism," *Wall St. J.*, Jan. 12, 2017.

[130] *See, e.g.*, Deepa Seetharaman, "Zuckerberg Continues to Defend Facebook Against Election Criticism," *Wall St. J.*, Nov. 14, 2016.

[131] "How Facebook's Third-Party Fact-Checking Program Works" (June 1, 2021), www.facebook.com/journalismproject/programs/third-party-fact-checking/how-it-works.

of the company's stated values and policies. The board's actions are binding, meaning Facebook must implement them, unless doing so would violate the law. The board is also empowered to make recommendations regarding Facebook content policy. As the Facebook "community grew to more than 2 billion people, it became increasingly clear to the . . . company that it shouldn't be making so many decisions about speech and online safety on its own."[132] But as one commentator put it, the board is "like Damocles, working just beneath the double-edged sword of free expression on one side, and other human rights prerogatives on the other. It's not an easy or enviable task."[133]

ANIMAL CRUELTY In 2010, the Supreme Court refused to add depictions of animal cruelty to the short list of categories of expression excluded from constitutional consideration. In *United States v. Stevens*, the Court declared unconstitutionally broad a federal statute adopted to punish "crush videos," sexual fetish films in which women step on insects or small animals with their bare feet or high heels.[134] In fact, the statute had only been used to prosecute images of animals fighting, including the dog-fight videos sold by Robert J. Stevens.

In an 8–1 ruling written by Chief Justice Roberts, the Supreme Court reiterated its reluctance to create new categories of speech beyond constitutional protection. Roberts said the statute was overbroad because it not only punished crush videos but also provided for up to five years in prison for anyone who violated a state law forbidding picturing a living animal being intentionally maimed, mutilated, tortured, wounded or killed. Roberts said it would be illegal under the overbroad law to sell in Washington, D.C., a magazine or video depicting hunting because hunting is unlawful in the District of Columbia. After the *Stevens* decision, Congress adopted and President Obama signed a narrower law punishing illegal animal cruelty—wanton torturing, killing, burning, drowning, suffocating and impaling of animals—not depictions of hunting or dogs fighting. A federal appeals court ruled the second statute constitutional where the cruelty to animals in the crush videos was also obscene because of the appeal of cruelty to those with atypical sexual appetites.[135] See discussion of atypical tastes in Chapter 9.

■ SUMMARY ■

Despite the categorical language of the First Amendment prohibiting abridgments of free expression, the Supreme Court has structured a hierarchy of protected expression. Political and social commentary sit at the top of the hierarchy, enjoying the most protection under the First Amendment. Lower down and protected under a more relaxed constitutional scrutiny are commercial speech and nonobscene sexual expression. Excluded or enjoying almost no protection under the First Amendment are obscenity, false advertising, fighting words and true threats. Mushrooming false and fake speech is generally protected by the First Amendment in the United States, but American social media companies, which are becoming increasingly important sources of news, are pressured by foreign governments to remove false, fake and hateful speech. Facebook and other social media companies are combatting such speech by engaging fact-checkers, putting questionable

---

[132] Oversight Board, Facebook, https://oversightboard.com/.
[133] Ross Ufberg, "The Oversight Board at 6 Months: Will Facebook Rue the Day?" MLRC (June 2021), https://medialaw.org/the-oversight-board-at-6-months-will-facebook-rue-the-day/.
[134] United States v. Stevens, 559 U.S. 460 (2010).
[135] United States v. Richards, 755 F.3d 269 (5th Cir. 2014).

stories lower in the news feed, and educating consumers about how to tell fact from falsehood.

WHO IS PROTECTED?

The First Amendment prohibits government from interfering with "the freedom of speech" but does not state whether all people and corporations enjoy the same degree of free expression. Do children have the same rights as adults? Do prison inmates have the same rights as the *New York Times*? Not surprisingly, perhaps, the courts have ruled that different speakers enjoy different levels of First Amendment protection, just as different categories of speech are protected differently. The average adult has greater First Amendment rights than students and government employees. Publishers enjoy fuller freedoms of expression than broadcasters and nonmedia corporations. But for most individuals, including publishers, the First Amendment guarantees a wide range of entitlements, including the right to speak, publish, receive information and refuse to speak.

Adults

SPEAKING AND PUBLISHING The right to speak and publish is basic to freedom of expression. The First Amendment prohibits the government from interfering with citizens' rights of speech and of the press. Every person enjoys the right to converse on a public sidewalk or expound on a political or religious theme at a public meeting or on a blog. Any citizen with sufficient resources may publish and distribute a newspaper, pamphlet or book. Some argue that the government has an affirmative obligation to encourage speech in "public forums" such as public parks and sidewalks.

Freedom of expression includes the individual's right to participate in symbolic forms of expression such as marching, demonstrating, contributing money to a political campaign and even burning the American flag. Symbolic expression, which is speech melded with conduct, is not permitted in all places and at all times but is nevertheless protected by the First Amendment along with more "pure" speech and publishing. As was noted earlier, anonymous speech is also protected, lessening the chances that outcasts will be persecuted for their unpopular viewpoints.

RECEIVING INFORMATION The First Amendment does not protect just the right to talk, write and associate; it protects the interchange of ideas. Speaking and publishing mean little if one cannot also hear or acquire information. The right to speak and publish therefore implies an audience to hear, to read and to respond.

The Supreme Court has recognized a limited constitutional right to receive information.[136] Workers, for example, have a right to hear what a labor organizer has to say.[137] Consumers have a right to receive some forms of commercial advertising[138] and corporate communication.[139] Regulations on broadcasting, too, are supposed to promote the rights of listeners and viewers to receive information.[140]

---

[136] Martin v. Struthers, 319 U.S. 141 (1943).
[137] Thomas v. Collins, 323 U.S. 516 (1945).
[138] Virginia State Bd. of Pharmacy v. Virginia Citizens Consumer Council, Inc., 425 U.S. 748 (1976).
[139] First Nat'l Bank of Boston v. Bellotti, 435 U.S. 765 (1978).
[140] Red Lion Broadcasting Co. v. FCC, 395 U.S. 367 (1969). *See generally* William Lee, "The Supreme Court and the Right to Receive Expression," *Sup. Ct. Rev.* 303 (1987).

The constitutional right of a citizen to receive information is not as strong as the right to speak and publish. The right to receive derives from, and is subsidiary to, the right to speak and publish.[141] The right to receive, therefore, is difficult to assert. Indeed, in most circumstances, the government is not required to provide information, and citizens usually have no constitutional right of access to information. The Supreme Court has recognized a limited constitutional right of access to courtrooms,[142] but no constitutional right of access for the press and public to prisons,[143] to foreign countries that have been declared off-limits by the State Department[144] or to the words of foreigners denied visas to speak in the United States.[145] Likewise, public access to government records and meetings depends on state and federal statutes,[146] not on a First Amendment right of access serving a public right to receive information.

COMPELLING SPEECH The freedom of expression belonging to individuals and associations includes freedom from compelled speech. "The right to speak and the right to refrain from speaking are complementary components of the broader concept of 'individual freedom of mind,'" the Supreme Court has said.[147] Therefore, the government cannot compel schoolchildren to salute the flag if their families' religious beliefs forbid it.[148] Nor can the government, consistent with the First Amendment, compel citizens to affirm a belief in God,[149] associate with a political party in order to get a job,[150] adhere to an ideology[151] or place their names on political campaign literature.[152]

In 1995, a unanimous Supreme Court ruled that private citizens who organize a parade may not be forced to include marchers conveying a message that the organizers do not wish to convey. In *Hurley v. Irish-American Gay, Lesbian, and Bisexual Group of Boston*, the Court said that a veterans group that organized a St. Patrick's Day parade in Boston could exclude marchers expressing gay pride, a message the veterans said was inconsistent with their theme of traditional religious and social values.[153]

Writing for the Court, Justice David H. Souter said that the veterans' exclusion of gays did not constitute discrimination based on sexual orientation. Gays were permitted to march in the parade if they did not march under a gay banner. A private speaker—such as the Veterans Council—may permit "multifarious voices" in a parade without forfeiting the right to exclude others, including those who would openly celebrate being gay, Souter said.

The government is not supposed to withhold privileges or benefits from an association or compel disclosure of a group's membership.[154] Because of the right of association, minor political parties may be exempted from laws requiring disclosure of political contributions and expenditures if disclosure might subject the

---

[141] Ronald Dworkin, *Taking Rights Seriously* 93 (1977).
[142] Richmond Newspapers, Inc. v. Virginia, 448 U.S. 555 (1980).
[143] Houchins v. KQED, 438 U.S. 1 (1978).
[144] Zemel v. Rusk, 381 U.S. 1 (1965).
[145] Kleindienst v. Mandel, 408 U.S. 753 (1972).
[146] *See, e.g.*, Freedom of Information Act, 5 U.S.C. § 552a.
[147] Wooley v. Maynard, 430 U.S. 705 (1977).
[148] West Virginia State Bd. of Educ. v. Barnette, 319 U.S. 624 (1943).
[149] Torcaso v. Watkins, 367 U.S. 488 (1961).
[150] Elrod v. Burns, 427 U.S. 347 (1976).
[151] Wooley v. Maynard, 430 U.S. 705 (1977).
[152] McIntyre v. Ohio Elections Comm'n, 514 U.S. 334 (1995).
[153] 515 U.S. 557 (1995).
[154] Laurence Tribe, *American Constitutional Law* 1010–22 (2nd ed. 1988).

parties to threats, harassment or reprisals.[155] An unpopular church might have difficulty collecting contributions, the Supreme Court has said, if the church were required to disclose the names of its members.[156]

A private newspaper may not be compelled to publish news stories, advertisements, letters or replies. In *Miami Herald Publishing Co. v. Tornillo*,[157] the Supreme Court struck down a section of the Florida Election Code requiring a publisher to print a free reply by candidates attacked by a paper. The case arose when the *Miami Herald* refused to publish a reply to the paper's criticism of Pat Tornillo, a candidate for the state legislature. The paper charged that Tornillo, the executive director of the Classroom Teachers Association of Miami, had led an illegal teachers' strike a few years earlier.

Tornillo argued that the First Amendment rights of the public would be served if dominant newspapers like the *Herald* were required to print replies from political candidates. However, the Supreme Court ruled that compelling newspaper editors to publish replies violates the First Amendment. The Court said that requiring publication would unconstitutionally dampen the vigor and limit the variety of public debate because the replies would increase the cost of printing, require additional composing time and take up space that could be devoted to other subjects. The Court also feared that editors forced to run political replies would avoid controversial election coverage, thus limiting public debate. Furthermore, the unanimous Court said that compelling publication would interfere with the function of editors:

> The choice of material to go into a newspaper, and the decisions made as to limitations on the size of the paper, and content, and treatment of public issues and public officials—whether fair or unfair—constitute the exercise of editorial control and judgment. It has yet to be demonstrated how government regulation of this crucial process can be exercised consistent with First Amendment guarantees of a free press.

Several years after *Tornillo*, the Supreme Court ruled that a public utility is protected from having to carry messages from a consumer group in the company's billing envelopes. The government cannot compel a utility, as it cannot compel a newspaper or an individual, to associate with political or social commentary it opposes.[158] Nevertheless, the First Amendment does permit the government to require a number of disclosures by individuals and groups. Later chapters discuss constitutionally acceptable compulsory disclosure by advertisers, corporations, lobbyists, contributors to political campaigns and journalists ordered to testify before grand juries and courts.

The First Amendment also allows public access to electronic media. While citizens may not demand space in a newspaper or magazine, the Supreme Court has ruled that political candidates must be accorded "reasonable access" to broadcast channels. Cable operators, too, may be required to provide "access" channels for programs produced by local citizens. Access to the telecommunications media is discussed in Chapter 7.

---

[155] Buckley v. Valeo, 424 U.S. 1 (1976) (per curiam).
[156] Seattle Times v. Rhinehart, 467 U.S. 20 (1984).
[157] 418 U.S. 241 (1974).
[158] Pacific Gas & Elec. Co. v. Public Utilities Comm'n., 475 U.S. 1 (1986).

Public Forums

The government owns and manages numerous properties where communication occurs. People speak and distribute flyers on sidewalks built and maintained by government for public use; companies post mouthwash advertisements on government-owned buses; citizen groups discuss macrame and Islam in classrooms operated by local boards of education. Although the government owns and operates property, the government does not necessarily control the expression that takes place there. The degree of government control depends on the degree to which the property is a **public forum**.

The Supreme Court identifies three kinds of forums: traditional, dedicated and nonpublic. Traditional public forums have historically been open for public discourse. They include streets, parks and other public places that the Supreme Court says have "immemorially been held in trust for the use of the public" for assembly, communicating and discussing public questions.[159] Speakers generally have as much right to discuss ideas and distribute information in traditional public forums as they would in their own front yards. The government can impose reasonable regulations on the loudness and hours of speech in a traditional forum, but the government can exclude speakers only by demonstrating a compelling interest—such as stopping a riot—and the exclusion is narrowly tailored. The government cannot favor one viewpoint over another in any forum.

A dedicated public forum is property that the government intentionally designates for public discourse. A state university dedicates a public forum in campus facilities when it allows registered student groups to meet there.[160] A state legislature creates public forums when it declares citizens must be allowed to speak at school board meetings.[161] A municipal auditorium dedicated to expressive activities is a public forum.[162] Even a public official's social media page may be a designated public forum if used for official purposes and interacting with citizens.[163] That means the official may not, on the basis of viewpoint, block users from the account or otherwise limit their speech on it. For example, the U.S. Court of Appeals for the Second Circuit held in 2019 that President Donald Trump's practice of blocking critics from his Twitter feed was a form of unconstitutional viewpoint discrimination. However, the same rule may not apply to a public official's campaign account. In 2021, the U.S. Court of Appeals for the Eighth Circuit held that a state legislator did not violate the First Amendment when she blocked a constituent from her Twitter account because the legislator operated it "in a private capacity, namely, as a campaigner for public office" and therefore not "under color of state law."[164] Chapter 12 features a more detailed discussion of government officials' social media accounts and the public forum doctrine.

As with a traditional public forum, a speaker may be excluded from a dedicated forum only if the government has a compelling interest that is narrowly tailored. The government also cannot favor one viewpoint over another. But contrary

---

[159] Hague v. Committee for Indus. Org., 307 U.S. 496 (1939).

[160] Widmar v. Vincent, 454 U.S. 263 (1981).

[161] Madison Joint School Dist. v. Wisconsin Employment Relations Comm'n., 429 U.S. 167 (1976).

[162] Southeastern Promotions, Ltd. v. Conrad, 420 U.S. 546 (1975).

[163] Davison v. Randall, 912 F.3d 666 (4th Cir. 2019); Knight First Amendment Inst. Columbia v. Trump, 928 F.3d 226 (2d. Cir. 2019); Knight First Amendment Institute v. Trump, 302 F. Supp. 3d 541 (S.D.N.Y. 2018).

[164] Eugene Volokh, "Legislator Free to Block Users from Her Campaign-Focused Twitter Account," *Reason*, Jan. 28, 2021, https://reason.com/volokh/2021/01/28/legislator-free-to-block-users-from-her-campaign-focused-twitter-account/.

to practice in a traditional forum, the government can limit the dedicated forum to certain speakers and topics in order to preserve the purpose for which the forum was created. Indeed, a dedicated public forum is often called a limited forum. Thus, a university that opens rooms after classes might limit access to student organizations discussing political and social issues, but the university cannot discriminate against viewpoints expressed by students on those issues. In a decision discussed earlier, the Supreme Court ruled in *Rosenberger v. University of Virginia* that barring funding for "Wide Awake" was unconstitutional viewpoint discrimination.[165] The university was under no obligation to fund any student publications, but once it chose to do so, it could not discriminate on the basis of viewpoint, the viewpoint supporting faith in a deity.

The Supreme Court's third type of forum, the nonpublic forum, is property that is neither traditionally open for public debate nor dedicated by policy to public discourse. A military base is a nonpublic forum, dedicated to the training and discipline of soldiers, not to the exploration of ideas. The government "has power to preserve the property under its control for the use to which it is lawfully dedicated," the Supreme Court has said.[166] In nonpublic forums, the government may permit speech, but the government need demonstrate no compelling reasons to justify barring speech. In nonpublic forums, the government needs only reasonable regulations that preserve the property for the purpose to which it is lawfully dedicated. As in all forums, the government may not favor one viewpoint over another.

Government and Business Employees

The right to speak and publish does not belong only to private citizens. The government and its employees also share the right, but with limits. Government officials have a right, sometimes a legislated duty, to communicate with the public through press conferences, press releases, state of the union addresses, public reports and paid public notices. Furthermore, government employees, like other citizens, may speak as private persons on public issues and vote for political candidates. The Supreme Court has ruled that midlevel government employees may accept payment for talks and articles they produce off the job.[167]

In *Pickering v. Board of Education*, the Supreme Court ruled that a public school teacher has a First Amendment right, like any citizen, to write a letter to the editor criticizing the school board without fear of retaliation. Relying on *Pickering*, the Court ruled in 2014 that Edward R. Lane, a former employee of a community college, had a First Amendment right to testify as a citizen in court on a matter of public concern—not related to his employment—without fear of retaliation from the college. Lane testified in the corruption trial of a former state representative.[168]

In 2013, a federal appeals court ruled that jailors employed by a sheriff had a First Amendment right to "like" a candidate on Facebook. The court said Sheriff B.J. Roberts of Hampton, Virginia, violated the First Amendment rights of jailors by failing to reappoint them after they "liked" a candidate opposing Roberts for sheriff. Political loyalty is not a requirement for the job of jailor, the court said. Employees have a right to select the "like" icon just as they have a right to erect a political sign.[169]

---

[165] 515 U.S. 819 (1995).
[166] Greer v. Spock, 424 U.S. 828 (1976).
[167] United States v. National Treasury Employees Union, 513 U.S. 454 (1995).
[168] Pickering v. Bd. of Educ., 391 U.S. 563 (1968); Lane v. Franks, 134 S. Ct. 2369 (2014).
[169] Bland v. Roberts, 730 F.3d 368 (4th Cir. 2013).

The law also recognizes special obligations on public employees that are not imposed on private citizens. Public employees must not distort the political process, disrupt the efficient operation of an agency, compromise the safety of fellow employees or reveal confidential information, such as tax and health data, entrusted to an agency. The law therefore permits the government to restrict the speech of government employees and some private employees in ways that would not be permitted on speech by the general public.

Since the founding of the country, the government has attempted to preserve the neutrality of government officials by limiting their political participation. Thomas Jefferson ordered officers of his administration not "to influence the votes of others nor take any part in the business of electioneering, that being deemed inconsistent with the spirit of the Constitution and his duties to it." The Hatch Act prohibits most federal executive branch employees from engaging in political activities on the job, running for political office, campaigning for or against a candidate and collecting contributions for partisan candidates.[170]

To ensure government efficiency, the Supreme Court has acknowledged wide authority for government supervisors to punish work-related speech that might be disruptive. In a very restrictive decision, the Court in 2006 ruled that government employees have no First Amendment protection if employers retaliate against them for statements made "pursuant to their official duties"—as opposed to protected statements that contribute to "civic discourse." In *Garcetti v. Ceballos*, the Court ruled that Los Angeles County did not violate the First Amendment rights of Deputy District Attorney Richard Ceballos when the county demoted him after Ceballos wrote a memorandum to a supervisor questioning the truthfulness of a deputy sheriff's application for a search warrant.[171] "We hold," Justice Kennedy wrote for the 5–4 majority, "that when public employees make statements pursuant to their official duties, the employees are not speaking as citizens for First Amendment purposes, and the Constitution does not insulate their communications from employer discipline."

WHISTLEBLOWERS Government employees, as well as corporate employees, need freedom to reveal internal wrongs and cover-ups that might waste money and compromise the public interest. Government employees are supposed to be protected if they "blow the whistle" on mismanagement and illegalities within their agencies. The Whistleblower Protection Act of 1989 is supposed to protect federal employees from retaliation if they reveal violations of law or regulations, gross mismanagement, waste of funds, abuse of authority or substantial danger to public health or safety.[172] Federal law also protects whistleblowing employees from retaliation in certain high-risk areas of private commerce, such as the nuclear and aviation industries, and employees in important policy areas, such as occupational safety, the environment and civil rights. Following the scandals at Enron and Tyco Industries, Congress passed legislation to protect employees against retaliation if they reveal securities law violations or fraud. Many states also have laws to protect whistleblowers.

Although employees may be protected if they reveal mismanagement and illegalities in the workplace, government and private employees are not protected if they leak confidential information about security, foreign policy or competitive

---

[170] James Richardson, *A Compilation of the Messages and Papers of the Presidents* 10, 1789–1897, at 98–9 (1898); Hatch Act, 5 U.S.C. §§ 7321–6.

[171] 547 U.S. 410 (2006).

[172] 5 U.S.C. § 2301(b)(9).

practices. Often the leaker of information will be punished, but not the journalist who publishes the leaked information. President Obama was the most aggressive prosecutor of leaks since the Nixon administration. As of late 2013, the Obama administration had convicted six government officials or contractors for leaks of government documents. The Obama administration had prosecuted eight leaks, five more than had been prosecuted in all previous administrations.[173]

Indeed, the Obama administration was faced with many more substantial leaks than previous administrations, some of them targeted to reveal government corruption and wrongdoing, some of them massive and apparently indiscriminate. Massive disclosures of classified information were carried out by Edward Snowden and Pfc. Bradley (now Chelsea) Manning. Snowden, who was employed by a government contractor, passed some 1.7 million documents to journalists about classified government surveillance programs before he took refuge in Russia. Manning, while on duty in Iraq, delivered 750,000 computer documents to Julian Assange's WikiLeaks, including 250,000 diplomatic cables and a video of American troops in a helicopter shooting civilians in Iraq. In 2013, a military court sentenced Manning to 35 years in prison, the longest sentence ever handed down in the case of a leak of U.S. government information.[174] President Obama commuted Manning's sentence in 2017. Chapter 3 discusses the constructive trust imposed on Snowden and the extradition of Assange to face Espionage Act charges.

Several other government officials have faced sanctions for disclosing classified information. In 2015, former CIA officer Jeffrey Sterling was convicted of espionage for disclosing to *New York Times* reporter and book author James Risen a covert CIA program that disrupted Iran's development of nuclear weapons. Only after the Sterling trial began did the Department of Justice (DOJ) drop its demand that Risen either disclose Sterling as his source or testify at Sterling's trial. In another case, highly decorated General David H. Petraeus pleaded guilty to a misdemeanor for passing highly classified journals to his mistress when he was the director of the CIA.[175]

In 2014, Stephen J. Kim, a former State Department contractor, pleaded guilty to leaking information in 2009 to Fox News reporter James Rosen from a highly classified report about North Korea. Rather than face prosecution under the Espionage Act, Kim agreed to a 13-month sentence. Rosen, who received the information, was not prosecuted. The media vehemently protested when they learned the DOJ had acquired Rosen's emails. The DOJ has since revised its guidelines for subpoenaing information from the press, as discussed in Chapter 11.[176]

Students

First Amendment rights are not the exclusive property of adults. Young people also have rights to speak and publish. As the Supreme Court said in 1969, students' First Amendment rights "do not stop at the schoolhouse gate."[177] However, the First Amendment rights of students at public high schools are weak. The Supreme

[173] TheGuardian.com, "Obama's Efforts to Control Leaks 'Most Aggressive Since Nixon', Report Finds," Oct. 10, 2013.

[174] Charlie Savage and Emmarie Huetteman, "Manning Sentenced to 35 Years for a Pivotal Leak of U.S. Files," *N.Y. Times*, Aug. 21, 2013.

[175] Matt Apuzzo, "C.I.A. Officer Is Found Guilty in Leak Tied to Times Reporter," *N.Y. Times*, Jan. 26, 2015; Michael S. Schmidt and Matt Apuzzo, "Petraeus Reaches Plea Deal Over Giving Classified Data to His Lover," *N.Y. Times*, Mar. 3, 2015.

[176] Charlie Savage, "Ex-Contractor at State Dept. Pleads Guilty in Leak Case," *N.Y. Times*, Feb. 7, 2014.

[177] Tinker v. Des Moines Indep. Community Sch. Dist., 393 U.S. 503 (1969).

Court has ruled that high school officials can regulate student speech that is disruptive, lewd or otherwise "inappropriate" in campus newspapers, school assemblies and other "school sponsored" settings. Whereas high school officials generally lack authority to regulate students' off-campus speech, appellate courts do permit high school authorities to punish students for off-campus speech, including postings on websites and in social media, if the speech disrupts teaching, poses an immediate likelihood of disruption, bullies students or causes a true threat. The Supreme Court refused to review several high school cases, thus passing up opportunities to clarify the high school authorities' control of students' off-campus postings.

Students at state colleges and universities have sounder First Amendment freedoms than high school students, generally being free to say or publish whatever they wish as long as the speech does not disrupt the educational program. However, some courts are ruling that state college and university students can be regulated under the looser First Amendment standards that courts allow high school officials to employ.

HIGH SCHOOLS For many years, courts ruling on student expression in high schools followed the Supreme Court's 1969 ruling in *Tinker v. Des Moines Independent Community School District,* a case in which the Court said that the First Amendment protects expression by high school students as long as it does not disrupt school functions, is not obscene and does not violate the rights of other students. In *Tinker,* the Court upheld the right of high school students to wear black armbands as a silent political protest to the war in Vietnam. High school students, the Court said, can express their opinions on campus, "even on controversial subjects like the conflict in Vietnam, if the student does so without 'materially and

PHOTO 2.1 Mary Beth Tinker and her brother, John, display two black armbands, the objects of the Supreme Court's case addressing how far public schools may go in limiting the wearing of political symbols. They were suspended from classes, along with three other students, for wearing the bands to mourn the Vietnam War dead.

Source: Getty Images. Used by permission.

substantially interfer[ing] with the requirements of appropriate discipline in the operation of the school' and without colliding with the rights of others." Nothing about the students' symbolic expression, the Court concluded, would have allowed Des Moines school officials "to forecast substantial disruption of or material interference with school activities."[178]

Distinguishing *Tinker*, federal courts have ruled that high school officials do have wide authority to ban clothing and symbols, such as the Confederate flag, that are disruptive or potentially disruptive. The Ninth Circuit Court of Appeals ruled a principal could ban whites from wearing T-shirts displaying the American flag, a provocative act on Cinco de Mayo, a day when the school was celebrating Hispanic culture. Earlier there had been confrontations and fights between white and Mexican students at the school. The court said high school officials are not required to wait until there is violence, but have wide discretion to forestall violence and protect student safety.[179]

SCHOOL-SPONSORED SPEECH While *Tinker* held that students might import nondisruptive speech onto campus, the Court ruled in 1986 that high school administrators could punish vulgar student expression at school-sponsored events, even if no substantial disruption is threatened. In *Bethel School District No. 403 v. Fraser*, the Court ruled a school could constitutionally suspend a student for delivering a sexually suggestive nominating speech for a candidate for student office at a school assembly that "was part of a school-sponsored educational program."[180] Matthew Fraser was suspended for three days and removed from the list of student graduation speakers after he delivered a provocative speech resulting in hooting and yelling at an assembly students were required to attend. Fraser told fellow students his nominee was "a man who will go to the very end—even the climax—for each and every one of you." The Court said a student has no First Amendment right to deliver speech containing pervasive, offensive sexual innuendo within the school context.

Two years later, the Supreme Court extended *Fraser*, ruling a principal could censor a nondisruptive school-sponsored newspaper containing no offensive innuendo if the censorship reasonably served the educational mission of the school. In *Hazelwood School District v. Kuhlmeier*, the Court upheld deletions of two stories from *Spectrum*, the student newspaper at Hazelwood East High School near St. Louis.[181] Principal Robert Reynolds deleted an article about teen pregnancies and one about divorce.

Central to the decision was the Court's ruling that *Spectrum* was not a public forum where school officials would be constrained from regulating expression. The Court said *Spectrum* was not a public forum because it had never been dedicated "by policy or by practice" to use by the public. Rather, the paper was produced in a journalism class under supervision of a teacher for academic credit. The Court said a school could impose virtually any reasonable regulation on school-sponsored expression, speech that includes student publications, plays, speeches at assemblies and any other expression that the public might associate with a school. It was constitutional for the principal to remove the *Spectrum* articles, the Court said, to protect younger students from "inappropriate" material, to allow the school to "disassociate itself" from expression it disliked, and to protect the privacy of students

---

[178] Tinker v. Des Moines Independent Community School District, 393 U.S. 503 (1969).
[179] Dariano v. Morgan Hill Unified School Dist., 745 F.3d 354 (9th Cir. 2014).
[180] 478 U.S. 675 (1986).
[181] 484 U.S. 260 (1988).

and parents. Thus, after *Kuhlmeier*, high school administrators can impose almost any "reasonable" regulation on school-sponsored student expression.

In 2007, a divided Supreme Court extended school control over school-sponsored student speech to school-approved off-campus events. In *Morse v. Frederick*, the Court upheld the suspension of 18-year-old Joseph Frederick for hoisting a "Bong Hits 4 Jesus" banner on a sidewalk across from his high school as Frederick watched an Olympic torch parade with fellow students.[182] Writing for five members of the Court, Chief Justice Roberts said a high school principal may constitutionally restrict student speech at approved school events when the speech is "reasonably viewed as promoting illegal drug use" in violation of high school rules.

As in earlier cases, the Court noted Frederick's limited speech rights because of the "special characteristics of the school environment." Frederick was subject to rules of his high school in Juneau, Alaska, the Court said, because he was attending a school-sanctioned event with fellow students during school hours. Teachers were also released from school to observe the parade and monitor students. Deterring drug use by school children is an important, perhaps compelling interest, Chief Justice Roberts wrote. Justice Stevens argued in a dissenting opinion, joined by Justices Souter and Ginsburg, that Frederick's banner ("Bong Hits 4 Jesus") was "nonsense" that should be protected by the First Amendment because it neither violated any rule nor expressly advocated illegal or harmful conduct.

Relying on *Fraser* and *Hazelwood*, the Second Circuit Court of Appeals in 2011 upheld censorship of a school-sponsored newspaper and an independent newspaper at Ithaca High School in New York, each of which contained the same lewd cartoon in which stick figures engage in sexual acts.[183] The court said the principal had authority under the *Fraser* ruling to remove lewd material from a school-sponsored newspaper and prohibit campus distribution of an independent off-campus paper.

However, relying on *Tinker* and distinguishing *Fraser*, the U.S. Court of Appeals for the Third Circuit ruled in 2013 two female students at a Pennsylvania middle school had a First Amendment right to wear "I Love Boobies" bracelets, which the girls purchased with their mothers to support the fight against breast cancer.[184]

Like the black armband in *Tinker*, the bracelets did not disrupt school activities beyond a few giggles by immature boys. Unlike the crude *Fraser* speech, the bracelets clearly were not lewd or vulgar, the court said. Equally clear, the court said, the bracelets did not invade anyone's rights.

Importantly, although the Supreme Court's decisions permit school officials to censor nondisruptive school-sponsored expression, the Court's rulings do not require administrators to censor. The decisions say only that censorship of expression bearing the imprimatur of the school does not violate the First Amendment if reasonable regulations serve the school's educational purposes. In fact, several states, including California, Massachusetts and Iowa, limit school officials' powers of censorship far more than *Hazelwood* allows. Iowa adopted a law guaranteeing public school students freedom of expression similar to that guaranteed by the Supreme Court's 1969 ruling in *Tinker*. The Iowa statute protects student expression except when speech is disruptive, obscene, defamatory or would incite students to

---

[182] 551 U.S. 393 (2007).
[183] R.O. v. Ithaca City School Dist., 645 F.3d 533 (2d Cir. 2011), *cert. denied* 132 S. Ct. 422 (2011).
[184] B.H. v. Easton Area School District, 725 F.3d 293 (3d Cir. 2013) (en banc).

break the law.[185] To protect schools from liability for student speech, the Iowa law, like one in Massachusetts,[186] says student expression is not to be deemed an expression of school policy, nor is the school system liable if it fails to censor.

OFF-CAMPUS SPEECH As discussed in Chapter 1, the Supreme Court decided in 2021 the landmark case *Mahanoy Area School District v. B.L.*, which held that schools may punish off-campus student speech only in narrow circumstances.[187] Recall that the case arose from a Snapchat post by Brandi Levy, who, as a freshman, was unsuccessful in her effort to make her school's varsity cheerleading squad. On the weekend after learning that she did not make the team, Levy posted a photo on Snapchat showing Levy and a friend with middle fingers raised, and the caption said, "Fuck school fuck softball fuck cheer fuck everything." Another student took a screenshot of it, and the photo soon spread throughout the school community, where officials disciplined Levy because her "negativity" could impact students. Levy and her parents sued the school district, claiming a First Amendment violation.

A federal trial court found that Levy's post had not caused substantial disruption at the school, a conclusion sustained by the Third Circuit. The appellate court set out a categorical rule preventing schools from punishing off-campus speech.[188] In a concurring opinion, Judge Thomas Ambro said that Levy's speech should be protected because it was not disruptive but that the majority was wrong to protect all off-campus speech.

At the Supreme Court, by an 8–1 vote, the justices agreed generally with Ambro's approach, finding that the "special characteristics that give schools additional license to regulate student speech do not always disappear when that speech takes place off campus." The majority went on to observe that the "circumstances that may implicate a school's regulatory interests," on campus or off campus, include serious or severe bullying or harassment targeting individuals, as well as threats aimed at teachers or students. Levy's speech did not target anyone, nor did her vulgarity meet the legal definition of obscenity. Moreover, the school's regulatory interests were diminished because Levy's posts appeared outside of school hours from a location outside the school, and she transmitted them through a personal cell phone to an audience of her private circle of friends.

Mahanoy was significant in part because it resolved numerous questions raised or left open by the lower courts, which had been called on for years to address the authority of schools to punish off-campus student speech. For example, the Third Circuit had ruled twice that a school cannot punish high school students for tasteless, offensive off-campus web posts that are not disruptive.[189] In one case, the Third Circuit ruled that Hermitage School District in Pennsylvania could not suspend Justin Layshock, 17, for an offensive "parody profile" of school principal Eric W. Trosch, created after school on Layshock's MySpace page at his grandmother's house. Layshock's posting, accompanied by a photograph of Trosch, said Trosch was a "big fag," a "big steroid freak" and a "big whore."[190] The appeals court decided there was no disruption: no cancelled classes, no widespread disorder, no

---

[185] Iowa Code § 280.22.
[186] Mass. Ann. Laws ch. 71 § 82.
[187] 141 S. Ct. 2038 (2021).
[188] 964 F.3d 170 (3rd Cir. 2020).
[189] Layshock v. Hermitage Sch. Dist., 650 F.3d 205 (3d Cir. 2011); J.S. v. Blue Mt. Sch. Dist., 650 F.3d 915 (3d Cir. 2011).
[190] Layshock v. Hermitage Sch. Dist., 650 F.3d 205 (3d Cir. 2011).

violence or actions requiring discipline. Nor would the court allow the school to "stretch its authority" to Justin's grandmother's house to punish him for the offensive posting.

The Eighth Circuit ruled that a student could be suspended for presenting a true threat in instant messages. The student had talked about acquiring a gun and shooting other students.[191] After police were notified of the threats, the student was suspended, expelled and placed in juvenile detention. The Fourth Circuit ruled that it is constitutional to punish students who engage in disruptive bullying of other students through social media.[192] The Second Circuit ruled that high school administrators could punish a student for an off-campus blog post that posed a serious risk of disrupting the school, where a student government representative called administrators "douchebags."[193]

STATE COLLEGES AND UNIVERSITIES The *Hazelwood* decision, which allows officials to regulate high school expression, said nothing about the greater First Amendment freedoms usually enjoyed by students at state colleges and universities.[194] In 1972, the Supreme Court said that First Amendment protections apply with the same force on college campuses as in the larger community.[195] A year later, the Court ruled that state university officials lack the authority to ban offensive student expression "in the name alone of the 'conventions of decency.'"[196]

In 2001, a federal appeals court reaffirmed that students at state universities and colleges enjoy more First Amendment freedoms than high school students do.[197] The U.S. Court of Appeals for the Sixth Circuit ruled that Kentucky State University violated the First Amendment when administrators confiscated 2,000 yearbooks because administrators objected to the "poor quality" and the theme, "destination unknown." Finding the yearbook to be a limited public forum, the appeals court rejected the university's claim that the Supreme Court's *Hazelwood* ruling allows university administrators to impose "reasonable" regulations as high school officials can. The Sixth Circuit ruled that Kentucky State had failed to demonstrate the compelling interest needed to justify a prior restraint on content in a public forum at a state university.

However, in 2005, the U.S. Court of Appeals for the Seventh Circuit ruled that state university and college students enjoy no more freedom from administrative censorship than high school students. In a decision the Supreme Court did not review, an 11-member appellate court in Chicago ruled that Governors State University might censor the campus paper, the *Innovator*, like a high school paper if it was not designated a public forum. In 2007, the Illinois legislature nullified the ruling in the state by passing a statute declaring media at public colleges to be public forums and prohibiting prior review. Prior review at public colleges would still be permissible in Indiana and Wisconsin, the other states in the Seventh Circuit.[198]

---

[191] D.J.M. v. Hannibal Public School District #60, 647 F.3d 754 (8th Cir. 2011).

[192] Kowalski v. Berkeley Co. Schools, 652 F.3d 565 (4th Cir. 2011).

[193] Doninger v. Niehoff, 642 F.3d 334 (2d Cir. 2011).

[194] *See* Student Gov't Ass'n v. Board of Trustees, 868 F.2d 473 (1st Cir. 1989).

[195] Healy v. James, 408 U.S. 169 (1972).

[196] Papish v. Board of Curators, 410 U.S. 667 (1973).

[197] Kincaid v. Gibson, 236 F.3d 342 (6th Cir. 2001).

[198] Hosty v. Carter, 412 F.3d 731 (7th Cir. 2005), *cert. denied*, 546 U.S. 1169 (2006); College Campus Press Act, 110 ILCS 13/1.

Nonmedia and Media Corporations

While First Amendment rights for adults, students and government employees may differ, so, too, do rights of expression enjoyed by different media and nonmedia profit-making corporations.

Profit-making nonmedia corporations, such as Coca-Cola or Microsoft, have First Amendment rights to spend from the corporate treasury for all manner of product advertising and issue advertising to bolster the corporate image and comment on public affairs. Corporate rights include the ability to buy advertising supporting or opposing ballot issues, such as whether a state should require a deposit on beverage containers to encourage conservation. In a decision discussed in Chapter 7, the Supreme Court ruled that profit-making nonmedia corporations can buy advertising on behalf of candidates in federal elections, a right previously denied to corporations and unions. Commercial media corporations, such as newspapers and broadcasters, have a First Amendment right to criticize and comment on candidates.

The Supreme Court has ruled each medium of communication presents "peculiar problems." Consequently, different media enjoy different levels of protection under the First Amendment. For example, the government regulates newspaper publishers to a lesser degree than broadcasters. The degree of freedom a medium enjoys depends on several factors, including the availability of channels, the pervasiveness and intrusiveness of the medium, and the historic relationship between the government and the medium. As print, voice and video merge into digital multimedia, the law struggles to find appropriate analogies in older media to categorize and regulate the new.

The print medium—the press mentioned in the Constitution—has historically enjoyed the most protection under the First Amendment. The First Amendment stoutly protects the right of newspaper, book and pamphlet publishers to publish all manner of political and social commentary, whether tasteless or profound.

Broadcasters, who acquire a government license to operate over government-allocated frequencies, are—unlike newspapers—required to operate "in the **public interest**." Unlike newspaper publishers, broadcasters must allow equal opportunities for political candidates to access their channels during the election cycle. The government also regulates the "decency" of broadcast programs during day and early evening hours because broadcasting is said to be an intrusive medium that might harm children if indecency were permitted.

Cable operators are licensed by local governments. However, the content of cable program channels is generally subject to minimal government control. For example, the courts see less need for control of indecency on cable than in broadcasting because cable is considered a less intrusive medium than broadcasting. Cable is a medium, like newspapers, that customers choose by purchasing it. The Internet, like newspapers, is generally unregulated.

■ SUMMARY ■

First Amendment freedoms are enjoyed to a greater or lesser degree by average citizens, government employees, students and corporations. The First Amendment freedoms of adults and ideological associations include the freedom to speak, publish, join with others, receive information, solicit funds and refuse to speak. High school students may distribute nondisruptive personal communication on campus, but high school administrators may impose "reasonable"—highly restrictive—regulations on school-sponsored expression to advance the school's educational mission. Schools may punish off-campus student speech only in narrow circumstances. Government employees may speak and vote as private citizens, but high-level employees are barred from participating in political campaigns. Profit-making nonmedia corporations enjoy First Amendment freedoms to buy commercial and issue advertising, including advertising supporting the election of political candidates. Among the media, print enjoys the most First Amendment protection; the Internet enjoys nearly the same. Broadcasters are subject to more control because of the limited public spectrum on which they operate and because of the intrusive nature of broadcasting. Cable operators enjoy less freedom than publishers, but more than broadcasters.

3

Methods of Control

Because the First Amendment does not protect all expression, the question arises how best to curb unprotected expression that defames, invades privacy, incites riots, damages national security or causes other harms. Should harmful expression be stopped by government censors before it is disseminated or punished after dissemination?

A consistent thread in the law of public communication favors the second choice, punishing the dissemination of harmful expression, not censoring speech before it is disseminated. In legal terms, First Amendment doctrine presumes that prior restraints on publication are unconstitutional. Nevertheless, a few prior restraints on communication are permitted. The government can block false advertising, copyright violations and dispatches from military combat sites.

This chapter explains the various forms of prior restraint. The chapter also explains why the Supreme Court generally disfavors licensing but allows licensing in special contexts such as broadcasting. Finally, this chapter discusses the Court's tests for determining the constitutionality of content-neutral regulations.

PRIOR RESTRAINTS

The legal bias against prior restraints precedes adoption of the First Amendment. William Blackstone, the English jurist, wrote long before the First Amendment was ratified that liberty of the press

DOI: 10.4324/9781003264736-3

consists in laying no *previous* restraints upon publications, and not in freedom from censure for criminal matter when published. Every freeman has an undoubted right to lay what sentiments he pleases before the public: to forbid this is to destroy the freedom of the press: but if he publishes what is improper, mischievous, or illegal, he must take the consequences of his own temerity.[1]

While prior restraints were imposed infrequently in the American colonies, the founders, who were familiar with Blackstone, adopted the First Amendment in part to end prior restraints.[2] The importance of having no restraints before publication has also been noted by the modern Supreme Court. "Prior restraints on speech and publication," the Supreme Court has said, "are the most serious and the least tolerable infringement on First Amendment rights."[3] Because of the presumption that prior restraints are unconstitutional, the courts will strictly scrutinize any proposal to restrict dissemination of news or information.

Prior restraints are thought to be more inhibiting to free expression than subsequent punishment.[4] For the publisher, prior restraints are a direct curb on publication, whereas the possibility of prosecution after publication is a more remote and perhaps less inhibiting threat.

Prior restraints may also bring a wider range of expression under government scrutiny than postpublication prosecution. Under a system of prior restraints, the government may require that all public expression be censored by a central authority. This creates a bottleneck that intimidates speakers and greatly diminishes the valuable facts and ideas the public receives. Where prior restraints are permitted, the public has no opportunity to judge the worth of suppressed ideas or to offer criticism that might strengthen weak proposals.

Though financial penalties or jail sentences imposed after publication may intimidate speakers, postpublication punishments offer the advantage of allowing ideas to circulate because expression is not throttled by a bureaucratic bottleneck. Furthermore, where a government engages in postpublication punishments instead of prior restraints, the government may lack the resources to prosecute every publisher it would have censored if given the opportunity.[5]

The Supreme Court established the presumption that prior restraints are unconstitutional in the 1931 case of *Near v. Minnesota*.[6] In *Near*, the Court struck down a state nuisance statute that permitted an **injunction** to halt "malicious, scandalous, or defamatory" publications. Under the statute, publishers could avoid an injunction if they could prove that a publication was true and made with good motives for justifiable ends. Publishers who printed in defiance of an injunction could be held in contempt of court.

The constitutionality of the statute was tested by Jay Near, an anti-Semitic publisher from Duluth whose *Saturday Press* accused Minneapolis police chief Frank Brunskill of failure to pursue a "Jewish gangster" who allegedly controlled gambling, bootlegging and racketeering in the city. Near's publication asserted that

---

[1] *Commentaries on the Laws of England* 4, 151–2 (Gifford 1820) (emphasis in the original).
[2] Leonard Levy, *Emergence of a Free Press* (1985).
[3] Nebraska Press Ass'n v. Stuart, 427 U.S. 539 (1976).
[4] *But see* Martin Redish, *Freedom of Expression: A Critical Analysis* 127–71 (1984).
[5] Thomas Emerson, *The System of Freedom of Expression* 506 (1970).
[6] 283 U.S. 697 (1931).

"[p]ractically every vendor of vile hooch, every owner of a moonshine still, every snake-faced gangster and embryonic yegg in the Twin Cities is a JEW." The trial court declared the paper a nuisance and issued an injunction to bar Near from publishing more defamatory and scandalous matter. The Minnesota Supreme Court upheld the trial court, but in a 5–4 decision the U.S. Supreme Court reversed.

Chief Justice Charles Evans Hughes, citing Blackstone and Madison, wrote that the main purpose of the guarantee of freedom of expression is to prevent previous restraints on publication. Hughes said the prohibition on prior restraints was even more important in the twentieth century than it was in the eighteenth because press exposures of official corruption—expression the government would most like to censor—multiply as the government becomes more complex.

Hughes said the Minnesota statute imposed unconstitutional prior restraints because it permitted courts to enjoin publication of expression critical of public officials. It is the essence of censorship, Hughes said, to suppress a newspaper, under threat of being held in contempt, for publishing charges of official dereliction. Defamed officials may sue a newspaper after publication for libel, the Court said, but it is unconstitutional to bar all publication because statements might be libelous.

The Court also rejected imposing prior restraints because a publication might be "scandalous." Charges of government misconduct may indeed cause public scandal, the Court said, but "a more serious public evil would be caused by authority to prevent publication."

The Court found unacceptable the statutory requirement that publishers trying to avoid injunctions prove their good motives, justifiable ends and the truth of their publications. Under such vague standards, a legislature or court would have complete discretion to determine what "justifiable ends" are and to "restrain publication accordingly," Hughes said.

Chief Justice Hughes did not say that the constitutional prohibition on prior restraints is absolute. The Court suggested that prior restraints might be permissible in wartime to bar expression obstructing military recruiting or announcing the number and location of troops or the sailing dates of troop transports. Hughes also suggested prior restraints might be acceptable on obscene expression and on incitement to violence or to the forceful overthrow of the government. "The constitutional guaranty of free speech," Hughes said, does not "protect a man from an injunction against uttering words that may have all the effect of force."

Prior restraints may take many forms. They may appear as an injunction—the "classic" prior restraint—like that issued in the *Near* case, or they may appear as licensing, in contracts or other agreements, and in discriminatory taxes.

Injunctions

Injunctions are quite easily permitted in some contexts. Courts willingly issue injunctions to halt obscenity, false advertising and fraud, speech that is outside constitutional protection. As Professor Laurence Tribe suggests, prior restraints are justified in obscenity and commercial cases because the courts may determine as easily before publication as after whether a statement is obscene, false or fraudulent.[7] Furthermore, delaying dissemination of such expression is less damaging to freedom of expression than delaying political speech, it is argued, because of the lesser value accorded to commercial and sexual expression.

---

[7] Laurence Tribe, *American Constitutional Law* 1048 (2nd ed. 1988).

The courts are less likely to issue a prior restraint on political speech and other expression in which the harm may be difficult to determine ahead of time and in which the harm caused by a restraint may be severe. *New York Times v. United States* is a dramatic case demonstrating the Supreme Court's unwillingness to grant prior restraints on political speech when the government cannot make a clear showing that publication will cause a severe harm.[8]

In *New York Times v. United States*, frequently referred to as the Pentagon Papers case, the Supreme Court refused to bar publication of a series of stories in the *New York Times* and other newspapers based on a secret Pentagon study of the Vietnam War. The Pentagon Papers, a 47-volume classified history of American involvement in Vietnam, were commissioned by Defense Secretary Robert McNamara before he left office in 1968. The papers documented how Republican and Democratic administrations had misled the American people about the nation's objectives in Southeast Asia. One of the minor authors of the Pentagon Papers, Daniel Ellsberg, acting without authorization, provided the classified documents to the *Times* and later to the *Washington Post*.

After publication began in the *Times* on Sunday, June 13, 1971, President Nixon asked the Justice Department to seek an injunction on the grounds that continued publication would cause irreparable danger to the national interest. The government argued that publication would prolong the war in Vietnam and disrupt the administration's diplomacy. The country learned later that the Nixon administration also feared that publication of the Pentagon Papers might frighten the Chinese from then-secret negotiations to open diplomatic relations with the United States. The administration feared the Chinese would be wary of conducting confidential discussions with the United States if the details of the confidential Pentagon Papers were being exposed on the front page of the *New York Times*.

In New York, the U.S. Court of Appeals for the Second Circuit enjoined publication of the papers in the *Times*, but the Court of Appeals for the D.C. Circuit refused to stop publication in the *Post*. The Supreme Court temporarily stopped publication in the *Post* and, on June 25, granted expedited review of both cases. After oral arguments, the Court delivered its opinion in less than a week.

The Supreme Court ruled, 6–3, that the First Amendment did not permit an injunction. A brief, unsigned opinion for the court—a per curiam opinion—freed the papers to publish because the government, the Court said, had not met its "heavy burden" of proof to overcome the presumption that prior restraints are unconstitutional. While the newspapers were pleased to resume publication, the Court's opinion provided little guidance about when injunctions violate the First Amendment. The terse majority opinion did not define the government's heavy burden or explain why the government had not met the burden in the Pentagon Papers case.

The Court's "real" opinion is found in nine separate opinions written by the six concurring and three dissenting justices. On the majority side, Justices Black and Douglas asserted their absolutism, arguing they could not imagine a situation in which the government could meet its "heavy burden" to justify a prior restraint. Justice Brennan, citing *Near v. Minnesota*, said prior restraints might be justified in wartime if the government presented clear evidence that publication presented an imminent danger. However, Congress had not declared war in Vietnam, and Brennan saw no evidence that publication of the Pentagon Papers presented an immediate danger to national security.

---

[8] 403 U.S. 713 (1971). *See generally* David Rudenstine, *The Day the Presses Stopped* (1996).

PHOTO 3.1   Daniel Ellsberg speaks at a July 1, 1971, press conference concerning the U.S. Supreme Court's Pentagon Papers ruling. Ellsberg admitted he gave the classified documents to the press, stating "I could no longer cooperate in concealing this information from the American public. I did this clearly at my own jeopardy and I am prepared to answer to all the consequences of this decision." Ellsberg was prosecuted under the Espionage Act, but charges were dismissed in 1973 when it was revealed that the White House plumbers—a group designed to stop leaks—had broken into the office of Ellsberg's psychiatrist and the FBI had illegally wiretapped Ellsberg's phones. The judge ruled the government's misconduct "incurably infected the prosecution of this case."

Source: Getty Images. Used by permission.

Three other justices in the majority, Potter Stewart, Byron White and Thurgood Marshall, said a prior restraint might be justified if congressional legislation had authorized one in such a case. Justice Stewart, in an opinion joined by Justice White, suggested the Court might uphold an injunction against the *New York Times* even without congressional authorization if the government proved publication would "surely result in direct, immediate, and irreparable damage" to the nation. In any case, the government had not met that burden, Stewart said, although he was convinced that publication of the Pentagon Papers would cause some harm.

The three dissenters, Chief Justice Burger and Justices Harlan and Blackmun, thought the Pentagon Papers case should not be decided so swiftly. The chief justice was also disappointed that the newspaper did not return the "stolen" papers as, in his view, any responsible citizen would return lost property to its owner.

Although the press considered the Pentagon Papers decision a great victory, the decision revealed for the first time that a majority of the Supreme Court might be willing to enjoin publication of political speech if a publication presented an immediate, irreparable danger to national security. The press was also put on notice that the government might prosecute the press under criminal statutes for publishing classified information. As shown later in this chapter, Attorney General Alberto Gonzales warned the press in 2006 that the government has the authority to punish those who publish classified information.

The government's power to halt national security publications was tested again in 1979, when a federal court in Wisconsin stopped publication of an article about the hydrogen bomb. The article, which described in general terms how easy it might be to build a bomb, was to appear in the small-circulation *Progressive* magazine. Using Justice Stewart's suggested test from the Pentagon Papers case, District Judge Robert Warren ruled that the article, "The H-Bomb Secret: How We Got It; Why We're Telling It," presented an "immediate, direct, irreparable harm to the interests of the United States."[9]

Even though the article was based in large measure on public information, the court found an imminent danger in publication of "concepts that are not found in the public realm, concepts are vital to the operation of the bomb." The court said the article could allow a medium-sized nation to move faster in developing a hydrogen weapon than it otherwise might and thus irreparably harm the security of the United States. Publication also violated provisions of the Atomic Energy Act prohibiting disclosure of "restricted data," including information about the design and manufacture of atomic weapons. The media did not learn whether an appeals court would uphold the prior restraint on *Progressive* because the government dropped its suit after information like that in the *Progressive* article was published elsewhere.

In a 2021 action that departs from prior restraint doctrine, a New York judge temporarily prevented the *New York Times* from publishing information contained in attorney-client memoranda written by a lawyer for Project Veritas, a group known for using unusual information gathering techniques such as fake identities and hidden cameras to ensnare gullible targets. Project Veritas is suing the *Times* for defamation stemming from a 2020 story about a video the group produced alleging voter fraud. (Separately, the group is being investigated by the FBI regarding the theft of Ashley Biden's diary; a search warrant used in that investigation is discussed in Chapter 11.)

On November 11, 2021, the *Times* first published an article quoting extensively from memos prepared in 2017 and 2018 by the group's lawyer, Benjamin Barr, who answered questions about the legality of unusual reporting techniques, such as whether Project Veritas "operatives" could use the dating app Tinder to meet government employees. "Project Veritas has long occupied a gray area between investigative journalism and political spying," the *Times* stated, and the internal documents "reveal the extent to which the group has worked with its lawyers to gauge how far its deceptive reporting practices can go before running afoul of federal laws."[10]

Project Veritas accused the *Times* of improperly obtaining privileged material to embarrass a litigation opponent, and on November 18, New York trial court Justice Charles Wood ordered the *Times* to temporarily refrain from further publication of the confidential materials in its possession or from seeking out such documents.[11]

Under *Seattle Times Co. v. Rhinehart*,[12] a Supreme Court opinion discussed in Chapter 10, courts supervising the discovery process can prevent publication of

---

[9] United States v. Progressive, Inc., 467 F. Supp. 990 (W.D. Wis. 1979), *dismissed*, 610 F.2d 819 (7th Cir. 1979).

[10] Adam Goldman and Mark Mazzetti, "Is It Journalism or Political Spycraft?" *N.Y. Times*, Nov. 12, 2020, at B1.

[11] Order to Show Cause, Project Veritas v. The N.Y. Times Co., Index No. 63921/2020 (Sup. Ct. of N.Y., Nov. 18, 2021). The temporary restraint was continued by a December 23, 2021 order. Decision and Order, Project Veritas v. The N.Y. Times Co., Index No. 63921/2020 (Sup. Ct. of N.Y., Dec. 23, 2021).

[12] 467 U.S. 20 (1984).

information a litigant obtains through compulsory legal disclosure, but the identical information could be published if acquired through means other than discovery. Although the discovery process in the Project Veritas defamation suit against the *Times* had not yet begun, Justice Wood read *Seattle Times* narrowly, stating the case allowed the press to publish information obtained from "traditional" public sources such as interviews or public records.[13]

There was no evidence showing the *Times* illegally obtained the memos, but Justice Wood criticized the *Times*' lawyers for "vaguely" stating that the memos were gathered through "newsgathering efforts." He concluded that Project Veritas' assertion that the memos were obtained by "irregular means" was sufficient.[14] Judge Wood also assessed whether the memos were a matter of public concern, determining that advice a client receives from a lawyer is "not the public's business . . . it is quintessentially personal, not public in nature."[15] This conclusion ignores the public benefits from other unauthorized disclosures of attorney-client communications, such as the reporting that Brown & Williamson Tobacco Corporation refused to disclose the health risks associated with cigarettes.[16]

Justice Wood discounted the importance freedom of the press, concluding that "the erosion of the attorney-client privilege is a far more imminent concern." Moreover, the *Times* gained a strategic advantage in the defamation lawsuit because the memos provided its lawyers with insight into the workings of Project Veritas.

A New York state appeals court in February 2022 temporarily stayed Wood's order until a formal appeal could be heard, allowing the *Times* to continue publishing information from the documents.[17]

Prepublication Agreements

Besides injunctions, prior restraints may take the form of a government contract or restrictive prepublication agreement. Although government employees have a right to speak as private citizens, their speech may be restricted in several ways. Just as private corporations may prohibit employees from revealing confidential business information, the government may prohibit its employees from divulging information that would jeopardize national security, reveal business secrets or invade privacy.

Federal employees throughout the executive branch sign so-called standard nondisclosure forms prohibiting disclosure of "classified" and, on some forms, "classifiable" information. Employees who divulge information in violation of the agreements may lose their security clearances or their jobs.

CIA employees must sign an employment contract that subjects them to a lifetime obligation not to publish information about the agency or intelligence activities without first submitting manuscripts to the CIA. Former CIA intelligence officer Frank Snepp paid a heavy price for violating his agreement with the CIA; Snepp published a book critical of the rapid American evacuation of Vietnam without submitting the manuscript to the CIA, as his secrecy agreement required. Although

---

[13] Decision and Order at 10, Project Veritas v. The N.Y. Times Co., Index No. 63921/2020 (Sup. Ct. of N.Y., Dec. 23, 2021).

[14] *Id.* at 7.

[15] Decision and Order at 24, Project Veritas v. The N.Y. Times Co., Index No. 63921/2020 (Sup. Ct. of N.Y., Dec. 23, 2021).

[16] Philip Hilts, "Tobacco Company Was Silent on Hazards," *N.Y. Times*, May 7, 1994, at A1.

[17] Decision and Order on Motion, Project Veritas v. The N.Y. Times Co., No. 2021–09551 (N.Y. Appellate Div., Feb. 9, 2022).

the CIA conceded Snepp's book, *Decent Interval*, contained no classified material, the agency brought a suit for breach of contract. Upholding the CIA's contractual claims, the Supreme Court rejected Snepp's argument that the CIA imposed an unconstitutional prior restraint by subjecting all his expression to prepublication review.[18]

Even Snepp's publication of unclassified material relating to intelligence activities might damage national interests, the Court said. Snepp's publication, it said, might inadvertently reveal classified information and perhaps inhibit sources from confiding in the CIA if they thought the agency could not keep a secret.

In a footnote, the Court suggested that the CIA's censorship powers did not depend exclusively on the prepublication contract. Even in the absence of an agreement, the Court said, "the CIA could have acted to protect substantial government interests by imposing reasonable restrictions on employee activity that in other contexts might be protected by the First Amendment." To punish Snepp, the Supreme Court approved the imposition of a "constructive trust" on all his earnings from the book, as well as earnings on movies and talks resulting from his work as an intelligence officer in Vietnam. Earnings in the trust reverted to the government.[19]

Since the *Snepp* case, the CIA or other intelligence agencies have rarely sued their former officers for breach of contract. However, the government has successfully confiscated profits in cases where a secrecy agreement was violated. In 2016, Matt Bissonnette, a former member of Navy Seal Team 6 whose best-selling book *No Easy Day* described the raid that killed Osama bin Laden, agreed to forfeit $6.8 million in book royalties and speaking fees because he did not clear his disclosures with the Pentagon.[20] In 2020, the government established a constructive trust preventing $5.2 million in royalties and any future royalties from being disbursed to Edward Snowden, who gained worldwide fame in 2013 when he disclosed top-secret documents about National Security Agency (NSA) surveillance programs and fled to Russia to avoid criminal prosecution for violating the Espionage Act. In his memoir, *Permanent Record*, published in September 2019, Snowden described how he leaked classified documents to journalists. Deputy Attorney General Jeffrey Rosen said, "Edward Snowden violated his legal obligations to the United States, and therefore, his unlawful financial gains must be relinquished to the government."[21]

CIA officers subject to secrecy agreements may negotiate with the agency's Publication Review Board (PRB), but courts are reluctant to overturn the PRB's determination of harmful material. For example, in 2009, the agency won a case brought by former CIA employee Valerie Plame.[22] When Plame joined the CIA, she accepted lifelong restrictions on her ability to disclose classified information. Plame was publicly identified as a CIA operative in 2003, a revelation that led to a leak investigation and prosecution of White House official "Scooter" Libby. (Aspects of the Plame leak case are discussed in Chapter 11.) After retiring from the CIA, Plame prepared a memoir and submitted her manuscript to the PRB; it blocked

---

[18] Snepp v. United States, 444 U.S. 507 (1980). *See generally* Frank Snepp, *Irreparable Harm: A Firsthand Account of How One Agent Took on the CIA in an Epic Battle Over Secrecy and Free Speech* (1999).

[19] In 1990, a federal appeals court denied Snepp's attempt to modify his prior censorship agreement with the government. United States v. Snepp, 897 F.2d 138 (4th Cir. 1990).

[20] Christopher Drew, "Ex-SEAL Member Who Wrote Book on Bin Laden Raid Forfeits $6.8 Million," *N.Y. Times*, Aug. 19, 2016, at A9.

[21] Office of Public Affairs, Dep't of Justice, *United States Obtains Final Judgment and Permanent Injunction Against Edward Snowden*, Oct. 1, 2020.

[22] Wilson v. CIA, 586 F.3d 171 (2d Cir. 2009).

publication of passages relating to her possible pre-2002 CIA service, which the agency regarded as classified information. The Second Circuit Court of Appeals ruled that facts relating to Plame's possible pre-2002 service were properly classified and the CIA could, consistent with the First Amendment, prohibit her from publishing such information under the terms of her secrecy agreement. Plame's memoir, *Fair Game: My Life as a Spy, My Betrayal by the White House*, was published with the CIA-ordered redactions rendered in the text as blacked-out lines.

At the time of the 1980 *Snepp* ruling, only the CIA and NSA required prepublication review. In 2022, every U.S. intelligence agency imposed a lifetime prepublication review requirement on at least a subset of former employees. The review process varies wildly across agencies, and manuscripts are sometimes reviewed by multiple agencies, each of which has varying standards of what may be disclosed. Moreover, the amount of material submitted for review has markedly increased since the 1970s, resulting in lengthy delays in the review process. In 1977, the CIA received 43 submissions for review. In 2015, the agency received more than 8,400 submissions. Recognizing the problems in the system of review, the House and Senate Intelligence Committees in 2017 instructed the Director of National Intelligence (DNI) to prepare a prepublication review policy applicable to all intelligence agencies "that yielded timely, reasoned, and impartial decisions." The DNI announced in 2018 that an intelligence community-wide process was being formulated, but to date it has not been issued.

In 2019 a group of former intelligence officials filed suit, contending the prepublication review process violates the First Amendment. The suit asserted that the ambiguous and vague standards place too much discretionary power in reviewing officials who can discriminate against low-ranking critics, while quickly clearing favorable memoirs of senior officials.[23] The case was dismissed by a district court which concluded the prepublication review processes were "reasonable" measures to protect sensitive information and did not violate the plaintiffs' First Amendment rights. The Fourth Circuit affirmed in 2021, drawing upon *Snepp* for the conclusion that the plaintiffs voluntarily signed the agreements and therefore knowingly waived their First Amendment rights.[24] According to the appellate court, *Snepp* required no more than a reasonableness test balancing the government's compelling interest in the secrecy of national security information against the interests of an employee to comment on matters of public concern.

Claims of political manipulation of the publication review process permeated the Trump administration's 2020 efforts to prevent publication of former national security advisor John Bolton's best-selling memoir *The Room Where It Happened*, which portrayed Trump as corrupt and erratic. Bolton submitted his manuscript for review in December 2019 and for several months worked to delete classified information with Ellen Knight, a career National Security Council employee with extensive publication review experience. Knight informed Bolton on April 27, 2020, that she no longer considered the manuscript to contain classified material; the Trump administration then began delaying tactics, assigning Michael Ellis, a political appointee with no experience, to conduct another review of Bolton's manuscript. White House officials also pressured Knight to change her views about the manuscript.

---

[23] Complaint for Declaratory and Injunctive Relief, Timothy Edgar v. Daniel Coats, No. 8:19-cv-00985-GJH (E.D. Md. Apr. 2, 2019). *See generally* Kevin Casey, Note, "Till Death Do Us Part: Prepublication Review in the Intelligence Community," 115 *Colum. L. Rev.* 417 (2015).

[24] Edgar v. Haines, 2 F.4th 298 (4th Cir. 2021).

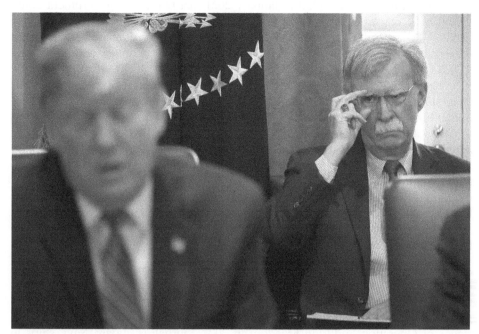

PHOTO 3.2 National Security Advisor John Bolton listens to President Trump during a February 12, 2019, cabinet meeting. Bolton served from April 2018 to September 2019. After leaving the White House, Bolton wrote a memoir containing criticism of Trump; fearful of the book's impact on the 2020 election, Trump administration officials unsuccessfully sought to prevent publication of the book and to confiscate Bolton's royalties, claiming Bolton had not complied with the prepublication review process imposed on members of the intelligence community. The Biden administration's 2021 settlement with Bolton allowed him to keep all profits.

Source: Getty Images. Used by permission.

Bolton decided to submit the manuscript to his publisher, Simon and Schuster, without receiving written clearance from the government. The publisher scheduled release of the book for June 23 and prior to that date printed and shipped 200,000 copies to bookstores around the world and gave review copies to media outlets. On June 16, the Department of Justice took the extraordinary step of seeking an injunction preventing publication; it also initiated a civil suit to confiscate Bolton's royalties and opened a criminal investigation assessing whether Bolton had disclosed classified information.

Federal judge Royce Lambert on June 20, 2020, refused to halt publication.[25] Noting that excerpts from the book were widely available online and that copies of the book had been shipped to booksellers around the world, Lambert said "the horse is not just out of the barn—it is out of the country." Lambert did, however, strongly criticize Bolton's decision to proceed without written authorization. Based on declarations from government officials and his own review, Lambert concluded Bolton likely jeopardized national security by disclosing classified information in violation of his nondisclosure obligations. Lambert ruled the government could continue its efforts to establish a "constructive trust."[26]

---

[25] Memorandum Order, United States v. Bolton, 1:20-cv-1580 (D.D.C. June 20, 2020).
[26] Memorandum Opinion, United States v. Bolton, 1:20-cv-1580 (D.D.C. Oct. 1, 2020).

Judge Lambert later ruled in January 2021 that before the government could establish a "constructive trust" over Bolton's book profits, it must have "clean hands."[27] Thus, Bolton was authorized to conduct discovery into whether Trump officials acted with bad faith by delaying the prepublication review and attempting to influence classification decisions.

Faced with the prospect of damaging publicity about government officials attempting to manipulate the prepublication review process, the Biden administration in June 2021 dropped the criminal investigation of Bolton and ceased the effort to confiscate Bolton's profits. In a settlement agreement, the Department of Justice agreed to never again sue Bolton over *The Room Where It Happened*, and Bolton agreed that any future writing based on his government service would be submitted for prepublication review.[28] Charles Cooper, Bolton's lawyer, said that by ending the actions against Bolton, the Biden administration "tacitly acknowledged that President Trump and his White House officials acted illegitimately."

Military Security Review

Another and broader prior restraint is imposed by the military on press coverage of combat operations. American military officials carefully control press access to military bases and military operations. As a condition of access, the military imposes ground rules restricting what the press publishes. For example, during the opening stages of Operation Enduring Freedom in 2001, journalists aboard Navy ships in the Arabian Sea were not allowed to publish the full names of military personnel. Journalists accompanying Air Force flights over Afghanistan were not allowed to disclose sensitive information such as altitude and route. (The ground rules for coverage of Operation Iraqi Freedom are discussed in Chapter 12.) Journalists who violate the ground rules may be expelled from the combat zone.

Under Department of Defense policy, military commanders in the field have the option of subjecting news stories to review by military officials. Known as **security review**, this process is intended to ensure that journalists comply with the ground rules. Some commanders, fearful that the press will inadvertently disseminate information useful to the enemy, insist on security review of all news coverage. Other commanders carefully explain to journalists what can and cannot be reported and then trust journalists to follow the rules. In Operation Iraqi Freedom, security review was authorized when briefing of journalists did not sufficiently protect sensitive information.

Although Pentagon guidelines provide that security review be used only to excise information harmful to operational security, the system has also been used to control the military's image. During the 1991 Gulf War, military officers who supervised journalists understood that they "risked being called to task" by their commanders for negative stories.[29] This institutional imperative to burnish the organization's image is not unique to military officers; it is inherent in any system in which government officials engage in prepublication review. As Professor Thomas Emerson wrote:

> The function of the censor is to censor. He has a professional interest in finding things to suppress. . ... The long history of prior restraint

---

[27] Memorandum Opinion, United States v. Bolton, 1:20-cv-1580 (D.D.C. Jan. 14, 2021).

[28] Settlement Agreement in the Matter of United States v. Bolton, 1:20-cv-01580 (D.D.C. June 16, 2021).

[29] Jason DeParle, "After the War: Long Series of Military Decisions Led to Gulf War News Censorship," *N.Y. Times*, May 5, 1991, at A1.

reveals over and over that the personal and institutional forces inherent in the system nearly always end in a stupid, unnecessary, and extreme suppression.[30]

Although members of the press have filed legal challenges to restrictions on access to battlefield settings, the system of security review has never been challenged. The press prefers that security review not occur but will accept it as a condition of gaining access to military operations or facilities.[31]

With the proliferation of modern communication technologies available to military personnel, the American military has developed rules relating to blogging by its personnel. Bloggers must inform their commanding officer when establishing a blog and are taught by operations security officers not to discuss "planned or ongoing military operations or tactics, techniques, and procedures" that have not been officially released, nor to divulge classified information. While commanders have the authority to require submissions for prepublication review, some prefer bloggers be taught to use proper judgment.[32] In a highly publicized action in 2008, the Army ordered Lt. Matthew Gallagher to cease blogging from Iraq because he posted material without having it vetted by a supervisor. Gallagher's blog provided "raw and insightful snapshots" of the Iraq War; the blog was drawing tens of thousands of visitors at the time it was ordered taken down.[33]

Licensing ✕

Prior restraint by licensing was well known to the framers of the Constitution. In 1643, the English Parliament passed a law forbidding publication of any book, pamphlet or paper without registration with the Stationers' Company, a group of 97 London stationers who were given a monopoly by the Crown on all printing. Milton wrote *Areopagitica*, his famous pamphlet championing a free press, in opposition to this act.

Under the Printing Act of 1662, London stationers controlled the printing, importing and selling of all publications. Nothing could be printed, imported or sold that was "heretical, seditious, schismatical, or offensive" to the Church of England. It was also forbidden to print anything offensive to any officer of government, to a corporation or to any private person.[34] By the 1690s, economically powerful commercial printers forced an end to English licensing, but licensing continued in the colonies until the mid-1720s.

Contemporary First Amendment doctrine is hostile to licensing schemes in which government officials have unbridled discretion to control what may be communicated in public forums, motion pictures and other media. In special contexts such as broadcasting, though, the Court allows licensing that would be unconstitutional in other media.

Anyone may start a newspaper without seeking a license from the government; newspaper publishers do not interfere with the voices of other publishers.

---

[30] Thomas Emerson, "The Doctrine of Prior Restraint," 20 *Law & Contemp. Probs.* 648, 659 (1955).

[31] *See generally* William Lee, "'Security Review' and the First Amendment," 25 *Harv. J. L. & Pub. Pol'y* 743 (2002).

[32] *See, e.g.,* Noah Schatman, "Army Squeezes Soldier Blogs, Maybe to Death," *Wired,* May 2, 2007; Army Regulation AR 530–1, Operations Security (Sept. 2014).

[33] Ernesto Londono, "Silent Posting: With His Blog Kaboom, a Young Soldier Told of His War. Last Month, the Army Made Him Shut It Down," *Wash. Post,* July 24, 2008, at C1.

[34] Fredrick Siebert, *Freedom of the Press in England 1476–1776,* at 239–41 (1952).

The Court, however, believes that licensing of broadcasting is necessary to prevent interference among broadcasters and other users of the electromagnetic spectrum. Similarly, to minimize disruption of public streets and rights-of-way, cable-system operators are required to obtain franchises from local governments. As with print media, communicators using the Internet do not need licenses; the Court believes the Internet lacks physical limitations like those of broadcasting.

PUBLIC FORUMS The modern Supreme Court has recognized that certain forms of public expression, such as the use of a street for a parade, require a license to protect public safety. However, the Supreme Court has consistently decried subjective licensing standards that allow government officials to discriminate among potential speakers based on their messages. Licensing schemes for First Amendment activity on public property must contain "narrow, objective, and definite" standards to guide the licensing authority.

The Supreme Court believes that public facilities, such as streets, must be available to all, regardless of whether government officials agree with the views expressed. Subjective licensing laws are presumed unconstitutional, and plaintiffs challenging these laws need not prove that content discrimination has occurred. The Supreme Court believes that

> the danger of censorship and of abridgment of our precious First Amendment freedoms is too great where officials have unbridled discretion over a forum's use. Our distaste for censorship—reflecting the natural distaste of a free people—is deep-written in our law.[35]

The line between permissible and impermissible licensing of public assemblies is illustrated in *Shuttlesworth v. City of Birmingham*, in which the Supreme Court found unconstitutional a Birmingham, Alabama, parade ordinance.[36] The law gave members of the city commission the authority to deny permits to parades that were harmful to the "public welfare," "morals" or "good order" of the community. The Court condemned the local officials' "virtually unbridled and absolute power" to prohibit parades. Writing for a unanimous Court, Justice Stewart said,

> a municipality may not empower its licensing officials to roam essentially at will, dispensing or withholding permission to speak, assemble, picket, or parade, according to their own opinions regarding the potential effect of the activity in question on the "welfare," "decency," or "morals of the community."

Justice Stewart contrasted the Birmingham ordinance with a New Hampshire statute that had been found to be constitutional in *Cox v. New Hampshire*.[37] The New Hampshire law did not allow government officials to withhold a license if they disliked the message of a parade. Under the New Hampshire statute, marchers had a right to a license, subject only to content-neutral "time, place and manner" regulations designed to accommodate competing demands for public use of the streets. Unlike content-based licensing, the Court believes content-neutral licensing for public assemblies or marches does not raise the specter of censorship.[38]

---

[35] Southeastern Promotions, Ltd. v. Conrad, 420 U.S. 546, 553 (1975).
[36] 394 U.S. 147 (1969).
[37] 312 U.S. 569 (1941).
[38] Thomas v. Chicago Park District, 534 U.S. 316 (2002).

Some forms of public expression are exempt from licensing. In *Watchtower Bible & Tract Society v. Village of Stratton*, the Supreme Court invalidated a municipal licensing requirement for advocates of religious and political causes who sought to engage in door-to-door advocacy.[39] Justice Stevens wrote for the Court:

> It is offensive—not only to the values protected by the First Amendment, but to the very notion of a free society—that in the context of everyday public discourse a citizen must first inform the government of her desire to speak to her neighbors and then obtain a permit to do so.

MOTION PICTURES The Supreme Court believes that each medium of communication presents "peculiar problems." The Court has ruled that local governments may license motion pictures as a means of dealing with the "peculiar problems" posed by the film medium. The Court has also ruled, however, that film licensing must follow stringent procedural protections. In addition, a film licensing standard must not be unconstitutionally vague. Faced with these strict requirements, local governments no longer license films, even though they have the legal authority to do so.

After the inception of motion pictures in the 1890s, government officials, fearful of the power of this new medium, began licensing films in various jurisdictions. Motion pictures were not initially believed to be part of the press but were regarded as being like circuses and other "shows and spectacles" subject to government control without First Amendment limitations. In 1915, the U.S. Supreme Court unanimously upheld an Ohio statute requiring film licensing; only those films of a "moral, educational or amusing and harmless character" could be exhibited.[40] The Court reasoned that motion pictures were not "organs of public opinion" but were "mere representations of events, of ideas and sentiments known." In addition, films were "capable of evil," especially because of "their attractiveness and manner of exhibition."

In the 1952 decision *Joseph Burstyn, Inc. v. Wilson*, the Court reversed itself and concluded that motion pictures are important organs of public opinion, even though they are "designed to entertain as well as inform."[41] Furthermore, the "capacity for evil, particularly among the youth of a community" did not disqualify all motion pictures from First Amendment protection. The Court held that a New York licensing statute, which prohibited the exhibition of "sacrilegious" films, gave unbridled censorship powers to government officials. "It is not the business of government in our nation to suppress real or imagined attacks upon a particular religious doctrine, whether they appear in publications, speeches, or motion pictures," the Court wrote.

Although licensing is permitted to bar distribution of obscene films, the Supreme Court imposes strict procedural requirements to minimize unnecessary curbs on protected expression. In *Freedman v. Maryland* the Court unanimously ruled unconstitutional a Maryland film-licensing statute because it lacked the procedural protections necessary to protect free expression.[42] The Court ruled that a system of film licensing must contain strict procedural safeguards. These safeguards, discussed more fully in Chapter 9, place the burden of proving that a film

---

[39] 536 U.S. 150 (2002).
[40] Mutual Film Corp. v. Industrial Comm'n of Ohio, 236 U.S. 230 (1915).
[41] 343 U.S. 495 (1952).
[42] 380 U.S. 51 (1965).

is unprotected upon the government. Further, because the "censor's business is to censor," the Court required that the decisions of film licensors be subjected to prompt review by judges who are believed to be more responsive to free expression than licensors.

A film-licensing scheme with careful procedures may nonetheless be unconstitutional if the licensing standard is vague. In *Interstate Circuit, Inc. v. Dallas*, the Court found unconstitutionally vague a municipal licensing scheme that classified films as "suitable for young persons" and "not suitable for young persons."[43] Unsuitable films included the portrayal of "brutality, criminal violence or depravity" and "sexual promiscuity" in a manner that encouraged crime or sexual promiscuity by young people. The ordinance did not define terms such as "sexual promiscuity," leading the Court to conclude that the licensing board was "adrift upon a boundless sea."

During the social upheaval of the 1960s, American society became more tolerant of graphic film portrayals. Also, in 1968, the Motion Picture Association of America (MPAA) introduced its film rating system to offer parents advance information about films. This system of industry rating, discussed in detail in Chapter 9, reduced governmental interest in licensing films. These developments, along with the strict requirements of *Freedman* and *Interstate Circuit*, led to the dissolution of most film licensing boards in the late 1960s and early 1970s. The last state licensing body, the Maryland State Board of Censors, was disbanded in 1981. The nation's last municipal film licensing entity, the Dallas Motion Picture Classification Board, was disbanded by city officials in 1993.

BROADCASTING The medium of mass communication receiving the least amount of First Amendment protection is broadcasting. The Court has approved licensing and content regulation for broadcasting that would be unconstitutional for the print media. The Court does not regard licensing of a broadcaster as a prior restraint, nor is FCC review of broadcast programming considered to be censorship. Nevertheless, the power to revoke or not renew a license for programming-related reasons has rarely been used. The threat of loss of license is sufficient deterrent to ensure that most broadcasters comply with programming regulations.

The Supreme Court has ruled that the physical limitations of the electromagnetic **spectrum** justify government licensing of broadcasters. Broadcast licensees, in return for receiving one of a limited number of spectrum assignments available, may be required to serve the **public interest** in ways not required of the print media. For example, the government cannot compel newspapers to provide space to political candidates. However, broadcasters are required to provide airtime to federal candidates, a requirement the Supreme Court regards as permissible under the First Amendment.[44]

To operate a radio or television station legally in the United States, a company or individual must have a license granted by the FCC. In *Red Lion Broadcasting Co. v. FCC*, the Supreme Court's most important discussion of the First Amendment and broadcasting, the Court described the electromagnetic spectrum as a scarce resource that requires a system of government allocation.[45] Justice White said as long as demand for spectrum space exceeds the frequencies available, no one can claim a First Amendment right to broadcast "comparable to the right of every individual to speak, write, or publish." Therefore, White said, the right to free speech is

---

[43] 390 U.S. 676 (1968).
[44] CBS v. FCC, 453 U.S. 367 (1981).
[45] 395 U.S. 367 (1969).

not violated when the FCC acts to ensure that the spectrum is used to benefit the public.

Red Lion introduced a new element to First Amendment analysis: the collective right of the people to receive expression justifies government regulation. "It is the right of the viewers and listeners, not the right of the broadcasters, which is paramount," the Court said.

To promote the public's interest in diverse views, Congress and the FCC have established limits on the number and types of media one licensee may own. For example, for many years a broadcaster could not own a newspaper in the same market. When the FCC adopted this rule in 1975, it ordered the divestiture of 16 newspaper-broadcast combinations in small communities that had only one daily newspaper and one broadcast station. All other existing combinations were allowed to continue, but no new newspaper-broadcast combinations were permitted. The Supreme Court in 1978 unanimously affirmed the FCC's authority to impose these conditions on broadcast licensees.[46] Citing *Red Lion*, the Court held that newspaper publishers had no First Amendment right to a broadcast license. Further, the FCC could use licensing criteria to promote more diverse media ownership. In recent years the FCC has modified its ownership rules in response to a rapidly changing media landscape. In 2017, the FCC repealed the newspaper-broadcast cross-ownership ban, concluding it was no longer necessary due to the multiplicity of news sources and the diminished role of daily newspapers.[47] The Supreme Court unanimously upheld the FCC's decision in 2021, concluding that for the purposes of the Administrative Procedure Act, the FCC had not acted in an arbitrary and capricious manner. The FCC reasonably concluded that the ownership rules were no longer necessary to serve the public interest goals of competition, localism, and viewpoint diversity.[48]

Until the 1990s, programming was also a significant factor considered by the FCC in awarding and renewing licenses. Despite the obvious dangers, courts permitted the agency to make licensing decisions based on subjective evaluations of the value of broadcast programming. If the FCC did not review the content of a specific program prior to its broadcast, there was no impermissible prior restraint. The government's authority to revoke or not renew a broadcast license for programming-related reasons stands in marked contrast to the limits on government power to control newspaper publishing.

Trinity Methodist Church, South v. FRC illustrates the distinction between the broadcasting and print media.[49] "Fighting Bob" Shuler, a Methodist minister, used his Los Angeles radio station to attack local government corruption; his broadcasts were laced with references to "pimps" and "prostitutes" as well as attacks on the Catholic Church. Shuler's broadcasts were strikingly similar to the newspaper attacks of Jay Near. In *Near v. Minnesota*, discussed earlier in this chapter, the Supreme Court ruled the government could not enjoin Near from publishing libelous and scandalous material. In the case of Shuler, though, a federal appellate court ruled that the Federal Radio Commission (FRC), the predecessor of the FCC, did not violate the First Amendment by refusing to renew Shuler's license because of defamatory and racist broadcasts. The appellate court said the FRC's action was neither "censorship nor previous restraint." Shuler remained free to continue his attacks

---

[46] FCC v. National Citizens Comm. for Broadcasting, 436 U.S. 775 (1978).
[47] FCC, Quadrennial Review Order, 32 F.C.C.R. 9802 (2017).
[48] FCC v. Prometheus Radio Project, 141 S. Ct. 1150 (2021).
[49] 62 F.2d 850 (D.C. Cir. 1932).

on public officials in other forums, but he had no right to a broadcast license. To the appellate court, the power of the federal government to regulate interstate commerce meant that a broadcast licensee received a license "subject to the power of government, in the public interest, to withdraw it without compensation."

Despite the government's authority to revoke or not renew a broadcast license for programming-related reasons, such actions have been rare. As will be shown in Chapter 9, the FCC prefers to use sanctions such as fines to punish broadcasters for violations of programming rules. Also, Congress in 1996 substantially reduced the FCC's ability to evaluate programming in licensing decisions.

Before 1996, the FCC would hold a comparative hearing if more than one applicant wanted the same broadcast license. Among the criteria used were factors such as proposed program service and past broadcast record.[50] Congress significantly altered broadcast licensing in 1996, preventing the FCC from considering competing applications in license renewals.[51] Congress further altered broadcast licensing in 1997, giving the FCC the authority to award contested licenses for new nondigital commercial frequencies via an auction process; contested licenses for nondigital noncommercial licenses are awarded through a lottery process.[52] Comparative hearings were not held for new digital television licenses; these frequencies were reserved for existing television broadcasters.

Currently, broadcasters have a renewal expectancy unless they have committed serious violations of statutory and regulatory requirements.[53] Broadcasters have an incentive to retain their valuable licenses and rarely offer programming that would justify the loss of a license.

CABLE Cable signals are sent to homes through **coaxial cable** or **fiber-optic cable**. The cable is strung on utility poles or installed underground. Because local cable signals are not sent "over the air" through the broadcast spectrum, cable operators are not required to obtain broadcast licenses from the FCC. However, because cable installation involves disruption of city streets and the stringing of cable on utility poles, local or state governments grant licenses known as a **franchise** to cable operators. The franchise authorizes the construction and operation of a cable system.

During the 1970s and 1980s, the height of initial franchising, municipal governments generally followed a competitive bidding process to award a single cable franchise.[54] In *Los Angeles v. Preferred Communications, Inc.*, the Supreme Court unanimously held that the cable-franchising process would be subject to constitutional scrutiny.[55] The Court acknowledged for the first time that cable system operators are entitled to First Amendment protection; cities could no longer award exclusive franchises based on assertions about the need to minimize the demands on public property.

Preferred involved a challenge to the franchise process in Los Angeles. The city was divided into different areas, and after a competitive bidding process, a single franchise was awarded for each area. Preferred Communications, Inc. (PCI) did not participate in the bidding process. Nonetheless, PCI asked the city for an additional franchise to serve the South Central district. After this request was denied,

---

[50] Policy Statement on Comparative Broadcast Hearings, 1 F.C.C.2d 393 (1965).

[51] 47 U.S.C. § 309(k).

[52] 47 U.S.C. § 309(i), (j).

[53] 47 U.S.C. § 309(k).

[54] *See generally* William Lee, "Cable Franchising and the First Amendment," 36 *Vand. L. Rev.* 867 (1983).

[55] 476 U.S. 488 (1986).

PCI brought suit, claiming that its First Amendment right to construct and operate a cable system was violated by the city's exclusive franchising scheme.

The Supreme Court unanimously affirmed an appellate court ruling that Los Angeles violated the First Amendment when it prohibited competition among cable operators. Significantly, the Court held that cable television "partakes of some of the aspects of speech and the communication of ideas as do the traditional enterprises of newspaper and book publishers, public speakers, and pamphleteers." Specifically, cable operators exercise editorial discretion through original programming or by selecting which television stations or cable program services, such as CNN and MTV, to offer to the public. However, the Court indicated that PCI's First Amendment rights would have to be balanced against the impact on the city caused by an additional cable operator stringing cable on poles and digging up city streets.

The Court remanded the *Preferred* case to the lower courts to develop more information about the impact of multiple cable systems on public property. In doing so, the Court rejected the claim that courts should defer to the city's judgment as to the need for exclusive franchising. Because the franchising scheme restricted speech protected by the First Amendment, the Court held that lower courts could not assume that the exclusive scheme actually served the city's interests. Los Angeles would have to prove that the installation of a second cable system was so disruptive that exclusive franchising was justified.

On remand, the district court found that the disruption the city feared was not sufficient to warrant an exclusive franchise scheme. The Court of Appeals for the Ninth Circuit affirmed; the appellate court held that although the interests advanced by the city were substantial, "[c]ompetition in the marketplace of ideas—as in every other market—leads to a far greater diversity of viewpoints (and better service) than if a single vendor is granted a . . . monopoly."[56] Moreover, exclusive franchising created the risk that the cable operator would be a captive of city hall. The Supreme Court refused to hear the case for a second time.[57]

Congress has enacted several statutory provisions relating to cable franchising. Cable operators are required to have a franchise, but local governments may not grant an exclusive franchise.[58] Local governments may require cable operators to set aside channel capacity for public, educational and governmental access channels and to pay franchise fees up to 5 percent of gross revenue.[59] Although franchising authorities may establish requirements for "broad categories of video programming," such as sports, news and public affairs, and children's programming, Congress said that franchising authorities could not require a particular program service, such as CNN or ESPN.[60] If both the cable operator and the local franchising authority agree, a franchise may be renewed through negotiations. However, to protect cable operators from an arbitrary denial of a renewal, Congress has created procedures and standards that may be invoked for renewals.[61] For example, Congress said that local franchising authorities may consider the "quality of the operator's service," but this refers only to matters such as billing and response to consumer complaints, not to the quality or level of program services.

---

[56] 13 F.3d 1327, 1330 (9th Cir. 1994), *cert. denied*, 512 U.S. 1235 (1994).
[57] 512 U.S. 1235 (1994).
[58] 47 U.S.C. § 541.
[59] 47 U.S.C. §§ 531, 542.
[60] 47 U.S.C. § 544. *See also* Time Warner Cable v. City of New York, 943 F. Supp. 1357 (S.D.N.Y. 1996), *aff'd sub nom.* Time Warner Cable v. Bloomberg L.P., 118 F.3d 917 (2d Cir. 1997).
[61] 47 U.S.C. § 546.

Since the early 2000s, telephone companies such as Verizon and AT&T have built fiber networks capable of carrying voice, video and Internet communication. However, to offer video service on these networks, the telephone companies needed cable franchises. Telephone companies claimed the process of gaining permission from thousands of individual communities delays implementation of this service. Thus, the telephone companies lobbied state legislatures for laws authorizing state-issued video franchises and a streamlining of the franchising process. Twenty-five states have enacted laws allowing state-issued franchises since 2005.[62]

The phone companies also sought federal streamlining of franchising. In 2006, the FCC adopted rules designed to make it easier for phone companies to enter the cable television business.[63] The FCC found that local governments were acting unreasonably by delaying action on franchise applications and requiring franchise applicants to pay for the building of public swimming pools, recreation centers and landscaping for parks. The FCC adopted rules requiring local franchise authorities to act on applications within 90 days, and the costs of in-kind contributions are counted toward the 5 percent cap on franchise fees.

INTERNET American citizens may establish websites, write blogs and create their own pages on social media such as Facebook without government licensing. The Supreme Court first confronted the constitutional status of Internet communication in 1997, ruling that unlike licensed media such as broadcasting, the First Amendment fully protected the Internet. In *Reno v. ACLU*, the Court rejected claims that the Internet had attributes, like broadcasting, justifying diminished constitutional protection.[64] The Internet is not as "invasive" as radio or television because Internet communications do not "invade" an individual's home or appear on one's computer screen unbidden. "Users seldom encounter content 'by accident,'" the Court said. In addition, there were no physical attributes that justify licensing. "Unlike the conditions that prevailed when Congress first authorized regulation of the broadcast spectrum, the Internet can hardly be considered a 'scarce' expressive commodity. It provides relatively unlimited, low-cost capacity for communication of all kinds," the Court wrote.

Unlike some countries, where going online is considered a dissident act or where websites of political opposition groups have been banned or blocked, Americans have unfettered access to content described by the Court "as diverse as human thought." Promoting free access to the Internet is an aspect of American foreign policy; in January 2010, then–Secretary of State Hillary Clinton announced a program to help expand Internet access in the Middle East and North Africa and condemned efforts by foreign governments to restrict citizen use of the Internet.[65] The United States has spent more than $145 million since 2008 on Internet freedom. For example, the United States trains human rights workers to secure communication from surveillance, evade government firewalls and operate mobile networks when government shuts down connection to the Internet.[66] The Trump administra-

---

[62] *See, e.g.*, S.C. Code Ann. § 58–12–310; Tex. Util. Code § 66.

[63] Implementation of Section 621(a)(1) of the Cable Communications Policy Act, Report and Order and Further Notice of Proposed Rulemaking (FCC 06–180) (Dec. 20, 2006).

[64] 521 U.S. 844 (1997).

[65] Brian Knowlton, "Clinton Urges a Global Response to Internet Attacks," *N.Y. Times*, Jan. 22, 2010, at A6.

[66] James Glanz and John Markoff, "U.S. Underwrites Internet Detour Around Censors," *N.Y. Times*, June 12, 2011, at 1.

tion continued to support technology solutions that provide "uncensored access to the free and open internet."[67]

In addition to efforts by the U.S. State Department, the U.S. Agency for Global Media (USAGM), which operates global information services such as the Voice of America, also operates the Office of Internet Freedom, and financially supports the Open Technology Fund (OTF), a developer of technologies to circumvent censorship. For the last seven years, USAGM has invested more than $100 million in projects to promote Internet freedom in the world's most restricted environments. For example, when USAGM news sites were abruptly blocked in Pakistan, the OTF created mirror sites to ensure USAGM content remained available. OTF in 2019 developed the Bypass Censorship browser extension, which delivers censorship-resistant duplicate sites allowing users to circumvent government-imposed blocks.

Discriminatory Taxation

After licensing ended in England, the government controlled the press by taxing publications and advertisements. A discriminatory tax, or a "tax on knowledge" as it was called in colonial times, is not a prior restraint on a specific story. But a tax on the press may be considered a prior restraint because it curtails publishers' ability to disseminate information and, consequently, citizens' ability to receive it. Taxation by the English Crown made publications less profitable, thus making them vulnerable to control through government subsidies and bribery.[68] Taxes on the press did not end in England until 1855. The notorious Stamp Acts under which colonial publications were taxed helped precipitate the American Revolution.

The First Amendment does not exempt publishers and broadcasters from the laws regulating all businesses. The media must abide by tax, safety, antitrust, labor and other laws that regulate businesses. However, the First Amendment may be used to strike down business regulations that are based on content or that place a disproportionate burden on the media.

The Supreme Court has consistently ruled that discriminatory taxes on the media are unconstitutional. In 1936, the Court struck down a tax on large newspapers in Louisiana because it was not a general business tax. The law imposed a license tax of 2 percent on the gross receipts of the 13 newspapers in the state that had a circulation of more than 20,000 copies. Publishers subject to the tax were required to file sworn financial reports every three months under penalty of a fine of up to $500 and imprisonment of up to six months.

The tax was adopted to diminish criticism of Governor Huey Long by the large papers in the state. Notable among the more critical papers was the *New Orleans Times-Picayune*. Governor Long did not see the tax as a tax on knowledge but rather as a tax on lying because, in his view, the big papers in the state lied about him. But to Justice George Sutherland, who delivered the opinion in *Grosjean v. American Press Co.*, the tax was an unconstitutional restraint on the press because it limited advertising revenue and restricted circulation.[69]

The Court said that owners of newspapers are not immune from any of "the ordinary forms of taxation for support of the government," but they cannot be subjected to taxes "single in kind" that place a restraint on the press. Such a tax

---

[67] Department of State, Bureau of Democracy, Human Rights, and Labor, *Advancing Freedom and Democracy Report 2017–2018* (Sept. 6, 2018).

[68] Fredrick Siebert, *Freedom of the Press in England 1476–1776*, at 305–22 (1952).

[69] 297 U.S. 233 (1936).

violates the First and Fourteenth Amendments, Justice Sutherland said, because it is "a deliberate and calculated device in the guise of a tax to limit the circulation of information to which the public is entitled."

Since *Grosjean*, the Court struck down a Minnesota tax on newspapers that used large amounts of ink and paper. The Court found that Minnesota had no compelling justification for taxing large newspapers differently than small newspapers.[70] Similarly, the Supreme Court ruled an Arkansas sales tax imposed on general-circulation magazines, but not on religious, professional, trade or sports journals, was unconstitutionally discriminatory.[71]

However, in 1991, the Supreme Court upheld for the first time the constitutionality of imposing a general business tax on one medium while exempting others. In *Leathers v. Medlock*, the Court ruled that Arkansas could apply a sales tax to cable television and satellite services while exempting the print media.[72] In a 7–2 opinion written by Justice Sandra Day O'Connor, the Court ruled that the state could constitutionally impose a 4 percent general business tax on programs delivered by cable and satellite because the tax was not based on content.

The Court said the Arkansas tax was unlike the unconstitutional taxes in the Louisiana and Minnesota cases, in which a small group of newspapers was singled out for a burdensome tax. In contrast, the Court noted that the Arkansas tax was applied to nearly 100 cable and satellite delivery systems.

Nor did the Court view the Arkansas tax on cable and satellite services like the unconstitutional Arkansas sales tax that applied to general-interest magazines but not to religious and sports magazines. The tax on cable and satellite programming, the Court said, was not discriminatory but was a general tax applying equally to several services besides cable, including natural gas, electricity, water and telephone.

The Supreme Court regards laws that impose a financial burden on speakers because of the content of their speech as being like discriminatory taxes. In *Simon & Schuster v. New York State Crime Victims Board*, the Court struck down a law requiring convicted criminals and those accused of crimes to deposit income from works describing their crimes in an account for the criminals' victims and creditors.[73] The "Son of Sam" law was enacted in 1977 to prevent serial killer David Berkowitz, known as Son of Sam, from profiting from the story of his crimes while families of Berkowitz's five dead victims and other injured people received nothing.

The Supreme Court found that the New York statute, like a discriminatory tax, would discourage creation of protected expression. Although the state had a compelling interest in ensuring that victims of crime are compensated by those who harm them, the law was not properly tailored to serve this interest. The law was too narrow because it singled out profits from crime stories but did not require profits from drug sales or other criminal activities to be paid to victims. The law was too broad because it applied to any work in which the author admitted to committing a crime, even if the crime was petty and the reference only incidental.

---

[70] Minneapolis Star & Tribune Co. v. Minnesota Comm'r of Revenue, 460 U.S. 575 (1983).
[71] Arkansas Writers' Project, Inc. v. Ragland, 481 U.S. 221 (1987). *See also* Texas Monthly, Inc. v. Bullock, 489 U.S. 1 (1989).
[72] 499 U.S. 439 (1991).
[73] 502 U.S. 105 (1991).

The federal government[74] and 45 states[75] have laws preventing criminals from profiting from the sale of their memoirs.

▓ SUMMARY ▓

Although prior restraints on content are presumed to be unconstitutional, they are permitted on a few types of expression. Injunctions may be imposed in national security cases, but only if the government meets an undefined "heavy" evidentiary burden. Injunctions may also be imposed on false advertising, publications that would violate a copyright and obscenity. The courts have upheld contracts in which government employees agree to have all writings reviewed before publication. Courts also approve of general business taxes on the media, but discriminatory taxes based on the content of what is published are unconstitutional. Licensing that leaves unbridled discretion to government officials is an unconstitutional prior restraint, but the Supreme Court has approved licensing for broadcasting that would be unconstitutional for print media. Municipalities can issue nonexclusive cable franchises.

PUNISHMENT AFTER PUBLICATION ✕

The Blackstonian view of press freedom, discussed earlier in this chapter, regarded prior restraints as impermissible but left unchecked the government's power to impose sanctions after publication. Even in the early 1900s, the Supreme Court described the First Amendment as preventing prior restraints, but allowing subsequent punishment of communications "deemed contrary to the public welfare."[76] Beginning in the 1930s, the Court expanded its view of press freedom, announcing that the "mere exemption from previous censorship" was "too narrow a view of the liberty of the press."[77] Modern Supreme Court doctrine acknowledges the "chilling effect" or self-censorship that occurs when postpublication sanctions are severe.[78]

The Court continues to regard prior restraints as the "most serious and least tolerable" form of regulating expression.[79] Thus, punishment after publication, rather than prior restraint, is the more common method of curbing harmful expression. Most of this book discusses the circumstances under which communicators may be liable for disseminating dangerous, false, defamatory, private or obscene material.

Of considerable legal and practical interest to communicators is whether they can be punished for publishing confidential information that they lawfully acquire from someone who deliberately leaks it or who inadvertently gives it to the media. In *Smith v. Daily Mail Publishing Co.*, the Court expressed the following principle: "If a newspaper lawfully obtains truthful information about a matter of public significance then state officials may not constitutionally punish publication of that information, absent a need to further a state interest of the highest order."[80] This principle indicates it is extraordinarily difficult for the state to punish the publication of lawfully acquired truthful information of public significance.

---

[74] 18 U.S.C. § 3681.
[75] *See, e.g.*, Ala. Code § 41–9–80; Cal. Civ. Proc. Code § 340.3.
[76] Patterson v. Colorado, 205 U.S. 454, 462 (1907).
[77] Grosjean v. American Press Co., 297 U.S. 233, 246 (1936).
[78] *See, e.g.*, New York Times Co. v. Sullivan, 376 U.S. 254, 278 (1964).
[79] Nebraska Press Ass'n v. Stuart, 427 U.S. 539, 559 (1976).
[80] 443 U.S. 97, 103 (1979).

While the contours of the phrase "lawful newsgathering" are imprecise, the Court's cases regard the mere receipt of information from a source to be legal, even when the source obtains the information illegally or is not supposed to disclose it. For example, in *Bartnicki v. Vopper*, the Court held that a radio talk show host acted lawfully when he received a copy of a recording of a telephone conversation that was illegally recorded by someone else.[81] Similarly, in *Florida Star v. B.J.F.*, police officials mistakenly gave the name of a rape victim to a reporter; the Court held that the receipt of this information by the press was lawful.[82]

In both *Bartnicki* and *Florida Star*, the Court ruled that privacy interests did not outweigh the right of the press to publish truthful information. Likewise, the Court ruled in *Daily Mail* that protecting the anonymity of juvenile offenders did not justify punishing the press for publishing a name that was lawfully acquired by monitoring the police band radio frequency and by questioning police and other officials. The Court has yet to find an interest of the "highest order" to warrant sanctions on the publication of truthful information.

An important theme appearing in cases applying the *Daily Mail* principle is the "chilling effect," which may occur if the press is punished for publishing truthful information. Especially when truthful information is lawfully obtained from government sources, the Court believes that a press subject to "self-censorship" is unable to "inform citizens about the public business."[83]

As explained in Chapter 5, unlawful information gathering, such as trespass, can be punished. And as shown in Chapter 12, the government may withhold information from the press. Nonetheless, as Justice Potter Stewart wrote, though the government "may deny access to information and punish its theft, government may not prohibit or punish the publication of that information once it falls into the hands of the press, unless the need for secrecy is manifestly overwhelming."[84]

Stewart's reference to the need for secrecy left open the possibility that in rare cases, such as national security, punishment of publication would be constitutional. However, it is unclear that the existing espionage laws apply to press publication of classified information.

The unsuccessful 1942 attempt by the Roosevelt administration to get a grand jury to indict the *Chicago Tribune* for its coverage of the Battle of Midway serves as a powerful reminder to government officials of the obstacles to punishing the press for disclosure of classified information, such as proving the press acted with bad faith.[85] However, in May 2006, then–Attorney General Gonzales "fired a shot across journalism's bow, raising the possibility that news outlets might be criminally prosecuted if they publish classified government secrets."[86]

During 2005 and 2006, the press reported a series of secret government actions aimed at terrorists, such as the CIA's operation of secret prisons in Eastern Europe. Each story was based on leaks of classified information. After the press revealed these secret programs, the Bush administration began a series of leak investigations.

---

[81] 532 U.S. 514 (2001).
[82] 491 U.S. 524 (1989).
[83] Cox Broadcasting Corp. v. Cohn, 420 U.S. 469, 496 (1975).
[84] Landmark Communications, Inc. v. Virginia, 435 U.S. 829, 849 (1978) (Stewart, J., concurring in the judgment).
[85] Michael S. Sweeney and Patrick S. Washburn, "'Ain't Justice Wonderful:' The *Chicago Tribune*'s Battle of Midway Story and the Government's Attempt at an Espionage Act Indictment in 1942," *Journalism & Communication Monographs* (Spring 2014).
[86] "Chill Wind Blows in D.C.," *Boston Herald*, May 24, 2006, at 32.

Amidst the crackdown on leaks, Attorney General Gonzales told a television news audience the government has the legal authority under the espionage laws to prosecute the press for publishing classified information.[87] Gonzales's claim, along with the leak investigations, prompted two congressional committees to hold hearings in 2006 on the issues raised by national security leaks.[88] Some prominent members of Congress disputed Gonzales's claim, arguing that Congress has not authorized punishment of the press for publishing classified information.

Following the massive disclosure of classified information by WikiLeaks in 2010, the Obama administration considered prosecuting Julian Assange, founder of WikiLeaks; this idea was abandoned after press advocates argued that prosecuting Assange would set a dangerous precedent because mainstream news outlets regularly publish leaked classified information. Government action targeting the source of the leak, Army Pvt. Bradley Manning (now known as Chelsea Manning), rested on a stronger ground. Manning was sentenced in 2013 to 35 years for unlawful disclosure of classified information, a sentence commuted by Obama in January 2017. Similarly, federal prosecutors in 2013 charged Edward Snowden with three felonies in connection with leaks about secret U.S. surveillance programs.[89] The Obama administration did not charge the journalists who published classified material leaked by Snowden.

As a presidential candidate in 2016, Donald Trump praised WikiLeaks for publishing Clinton campaign emails, but shortly after Trump became president, WikiLeaks published a collection of stolen classified documents revealing the CIA's hacking tools. Mike Pompeo, Trump's first CIA chief and later Secretary of State, called WikiLeaks a "nonstate hostile intelligence service."[90] When Assange was indicted for violating the Espionage Act in May 2019, John Demers, head of the National Security Division of the Department of Justice, said it was not DOJ policy to target journalists for reporting, adding "Julian Assange is no journalist."[91]

The indictment charges Assange with conspiring with Manning to gain unauthorized access to a computer network used by the Department of Defense for classified documents and for publishing classified documents relating to the wars in Afghanistan and Iraq, including the names of Afghan and Iraqi locals who helped the United States. The indictment alleges that Assange knew publication of this information endangered lives.[92] Press advocates feared the prosecution would chill journalism based on leaks of government documents.

Assange, who had been living in the Ecuadorian embassy in London since 2012, was arrested in 2019 by British police after Ecuador revoked his immunity. After serving a 50-week sentence in Britain for skipping bail relating to a now-closed Swedish investigation into rape allegations against him, Assange has been

---

[87] Adam Liptak, "Gonzales Says Prosecutions of Journalists Are Possible," *N.Y. Times*, May 22, 2006, at A14.

[88] *Examining DOJ's Investigation of Journalists Who Publish Classified Information: Hearing Before the S. Comm. on the Judiciary*, 109th Cong. (June 6, 2006); *Media's Role and Responsibilities in Leaks of Classified Information: Hearing Before the H. Permanent Select Comm. on Intelligence*, 109th Cong. (May 26, 2006).

[89] Peter Finn and Sari Horwitz, "U.S. Charges Snowden with Espionage," *Wash. Post*, June 22, 2013, at A1.

[90] Julian Barnes, Adam Goldman, and Charlie Savage, "Assange's Path from Protected to Prosecuted," *N.Y. Times*, Nov. 17, 2018, at A1. *See also* Warren Strobel, "From Internet Warrior to Jailed Suspect," *Wall St. J.*, Apr. 12, 2019, at A8.

[91] Michael Grynbaum and Marc Tracy, "'That's Called News Gathering': Charges Alarm Advocates of Press Freedom," *N.Y. Times*, May 24, 2019, at A8.

[92] Superseding Indictment, United States v. Julian Paul Assange, No. 1:18-cr-111 (CMH) (E.D. Va. May 23, 2019).

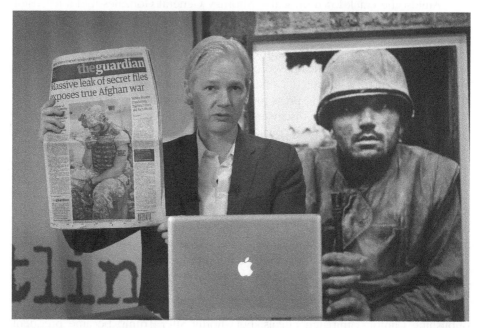

PHOTO 3.3 Julian Assange, founder of WikiLeaks, came to international attention in 2010 when WikiLeaks posted classified U.S. documents relating to the wars in Iraq and Afghanistan. The *Guardian* (Britain), *Der Spiegel* (Germany) and the *New York Times* published stories based on the leaked documents.

Source: Getty Images. Used by permission.

kept in custody, as the U.S. sought his extradition. In January 2021, a British judge ruled Assange could not be extradited, citing the risk of suicide and Assange's diminished mental health. In one of its last official acts, the Trump administration filed an appeal; soon after taking office, the Biden administration decided to continue the extradition effort. At a hearing at the British High Court in October 2021, U.S. representatives made binding assurances that before or after a trial, Assange would not be placed in solitary confinement or put in a "supermax" prison. The High Court was satisfied by these assurances and in December 2021 ruled that Assange could be extradited.[93] In January 2022, the High Court allowed Assange to appeal to the British Supreme Court on the narrow point that the U.S. assurances should have come earlier in the extradition process. If extradited, Assange's case will measure the First Amendment right to publish against the Espionage Act's prohibition on publication of information harmful to national security.

Because the press has never been prosecuted for violating the espionage laws, judicial analysis of the application of these laws to the press is sparse. The federal district court considering the government's request for an injunction against the *New York Times* in the Pentagon Papers case ruled these laws to be inapplicable to "publishing."[94] The government in the Pentagon Papers case was not seeking to punish the press for publishing classified information; the government sought to rely on the espionage laws as support for an injunction. An authoritative 1973 study by two legal scholars concluded, "Neither the Congresses that wrote the laws nor

---

[93] Government of the United States of America v. Assange, [2021] EWHC 3313 (Dec. 10.2021).
[94] United States v. N.Y. Times, 328 F. Supp. 324, 328–9 (S.D.N.Y. 1971).

the Executives who enforced them have behaved in a manner consistent with the belief that the general espionage statutes forbid acts of publication."[95]

■ SUMMARY ■

Postpublication punishments are permitted for some libelous, false, fraudulent and private communications. The Supreme Court has also said that the media may be liable for publication of confidential government information. However, the Court has never held the media liable for such a publication. The prosecution of WikiLeaks founder Julian Assange may clarify the applicability of the Espionage Act to publishing.

CONTENT-NEUTRAL REGULATIONS ✕

As was shown in Chapter 2, one of the most significant distinctions in the Supreme Court's contemporary First Amendment doctrine is between content-based and content-neutral regulations. Although content restrictions will generally be found unconstitutional under the strict scrutiny courts engage in, content-neutral regulations are subject to a less rigorous, ad hoc balancing process.

Not all content-neutral regulations are treated alike. Governments rarely ban an entire form of expression, preferring to enact more limited time, place and manner restrictions. Total bans, even when content-neutral, are generally unconstitutional. For example, in *Ladue v. Gilleo*, the Court found a city's complete ban on political signs on residential property to be unconstitutional.[96] Justice Stevens wrote that the city's interest in minimizing the visual clutter of signs was not sufficiently important to justify the ban on this "unique and important" form of expression. "A special respect for individual liberty in the home has long been part of our culture and law," Justice Stevens wrote, and this principle "has special resonance when the government seeks to constrain a person's ability to *speak* there."

In contrast, more limited restrictions are generally found to be constitutional under the **time, place and manner test**.[97] In this test, courts first must assess whether the regulation is content-neutral; that is, whether the government has adopted the regulation to control something other than the message conveyed by expressive activities. A content-neutral regulation must not be based on government hostility to particular messages.[98] Second, courts assess whether the regulation is narrowly tailored to serve a significant governmental interest, such as preserving park property or keeping streets clean. The time, place and manner test also asks whether the regulation leaves open "ample" alternative channels for communication.

Content Neutrality

One of the most important cases in the development of the Court's content-neutral methodology is *United States v. O'Brien*.[99] The Court upheld a military draft law prohibiting men from destroying or mutilating their draft cards, even when it was

---

[95] Harold Edgar and Benno Schmidt, Jr., "The Espionage Statutes and Publication of Defense Information," 73 *Colum. L. Rev.* 929, 1077 (1973).
[96] 512 U.S. 43 (1994).
[97] Clark v. Community for Creative Non-Violence, 468 U.S. 288, 293 (1984).
[98] Ward v. Rock Against Racism, 491 U.S. 781, 791 (1989).
[99] 391 U.S. 367 (1968).

applied to a Vietnam War protestor who publicly burned his draft card. Writing for the Court, Chief Justice Warren noted that the law did not single out public protestors but applied to all men who destroyed their draft cards, even those privately destroying their cards without any communicative intent. The draft card law was content neutral, the Court said, because it was adopted not to punish dissent but to allow the government to raise armies quickly and efficiently by requiring eligible men to carry classification certificates.

Another example of a content-neutral law restricting expressive behavior is a federal regulation prohibiting camping in Lafayette Park and other parks located near the White House. In *Clark v. Community for Creative Non-Violence*, the Court held that this law did not violate the First Amendment rights of protestors who sought to sleep in Lafayette Park to protest the Reagan administration's policies and to portray the plight of the homeless.[100] The Court held that the ban on camping, and on sleeping specifically, was not motivated by disagreement with the demonstrators' message. The government's substantial interest in preserving park property was served by uniformly applicable measures designed to limit wear and tear on parks.

Although viewpoint-based restrictions are "egregious,"[101] in 2015 the Court ruled unconstitutional restrictions based on subject matter. In striking down a municipal sign ordinance treating political signs differently than signs discussing other topics, the Court said "a speech regulation targeted at specific subject matter is content based even if it does not discriminate among viewpoints within the subject matter."[102] Content-neutral measures treating all signs alike were available.

Tailoring

After determining that a regulation is content-neutral, courts ask whether the regulation is narrowly drawn to advance a significant or substantial governmental interest. This prong of content-neutral analysis has three components: (1) assessing the substantiality of the government's interest, (2) determining whether the regulation advances that interest and (3) examining the narrowness of the restriction.

SUBSTANTIAL GOVERNMENT INTEREST The Court requires a *compelling* governmental interest in cases involving a serious restriction on First Amendment rights, such as a content-based exclusion from a public forum. Because the Court regards content-neutral restrictions as less harmful to free expression than content-based restrictions, it applies the less demanding standard of a significant or *substantial* governmental interest. Such mundane interests as preserving the free flow of traffic or ensuring uncluttered sidewalks usually constitute a substantial interest.

ADVANCING THE INTEREST Under the time, place and manner test, the Court defers to the judgment of legislators or other officials as to the efficacy of a regulation. For example, in *Clark v. Community for Creative Non-Violence*, the Court accepted the judgment of the Park Service as to the necessity of a ban on camping as a means of preserving park property. The demonstrators sought an exemption from the ban, claiming that their activities would not be harmful to the park. The Court deferred to the expertise of Park Service officials, stating that the judiciary lacked "the competence to judge how much protection of park lands is wise and how that level of conservation is to be attained."

---

[100] 468 U.S. 288 (1984).
[101] Rosenberger v. Rector and Visitors of Univ. of Va., 515 U.S. 819, 829 (1995).
[102] Reed v. Town of Gilbert, 135 S. Ct. 2218 (2015).

NARROWNESS In time, place and manner cases, the Court does not require that the government use the least restrictive methods to advance the interest. Rather, a time, place and manner regulation is narrowly tailored as long as the method of regulation does not capture behaviors unrelated to the interest the state seeks to protect.

Ward v. Rock Against Racism illustrates this aspect of time, place and manner analysis.[103] The Court upheld a New York ordinance requiring that performers utilizing a stage area in Central Park use sound amplification equipment and a sound technician provided by the city. The city enacted the requirement so that performances would not be so loud as to disturb nearby residences. Rock bands, however, claimed the law interfered with their artistic freedom. The Court held that this type of regulation "need not be the least restrictive or least intrusive means" of serving the government interest. Because the regulation did not include measures unrelated to the asserted interest of residential privacy, it was properly tailored. Had the law controlled amplified sound *and* banned pantomimes, it would not have been a narrowly tailored means of protecting nearby residences from loud noise.

Alternative Channels

In addition to narrowly advancing a content-neutral governmental interest, a constitutional time, place and manner regulation must also leave open adequate alternative channels of communication.

The ban on camping in parks in the District of Columbia was constitutional in part because demonstrators could convey the plight of the homeless without sleeping in the parks. Similarly, the control of amplified sound in Central Park had "no effect on the quantity or content of that expression beyond regulating the extent of amplification." And a ban on picketing taking place solely in front of a particular residence still allowed protestors to march through a neighborhood and hand out literature.[104]

In contrast, the ban on residential signs in Ladue, Missouri, restricted "a venerable means of communication that is both unique and important." The alternative means of communication were either too expensive or time-consuming to be constitutionally adequate, the Court said. "Even for the affluent," Justice Stevens wrote,

> the added costs in money or time of taking out a newspaper advertisement, handing out leaflets on the street, or standing in front of one's house with a hand-held sign may make the difference between participating and not participating in some public debate.

■ SUMMARY ■

Content-neutral time, place and manner regulations are constitutional if they serve a substantial government interest, are narrowly written and leave alternative channels of communication. The Court has ruled that officials may not ban citizens' use of public streets and parks but may limit expression to preserve public order, the integrity of parks, the privacy of residences and the smooth flow of pedestrians and traffic.

---

[103] 491 U.S. 781 (1989).
[104] Frisby v. Schultz, 487 U.S. 474 (1988).

CHAPTER

4

Libel

Shakespeare, in 1604, recognized the importance of reputation:

Who steals my purse steals trash; tis something, nothing;
Twas mine; tis his, and has been slave to thousands;
But he that filches from me my good name
Robs me of that which not enriches him,
And makes me poor indeed.[1]

Four centuries later, the U.S. Supreme Court still recognizes **reputation** as one of a person's most important possessions. Society's willingness to protect individual reputation from "unjustified invasion and wrongful hurt," the late Justice Potter

---

[1] *Othello*, act III, scene 3.

DOI: 10.4324/9781003264736-4

Stewart said, reflects the value that society attaches to the "dignity and worth of every human being."[2]

Stewart pointed to libel law, "as imperfect as it is," as the only legal means to vindicate or recover a falsely tarnished reputation. In the United States, people can sue for printed or spoken words that "diminish the esteem, respect, good will or confidence" others have in them or for language that incites "adverse, derogatory or unpleasant feelings or opinions" about them.[3] People who believe they have been libeled can sue to recover monetary compensation.

The law that allows individuals to sue for damaged reputations creates financial risks for newspaper reporters, broadcasters, bloggers and tweeters. Between 2010 and 2014, the average damage award against media defendants in the United States in libel and privacy cases was $2.6 million, the median $1 million.[4] The largest damage award against a newspaper was nearly $223 million, awarded by a Texas jury in 1997.[5]

Most cases are dropped, dismissed or settled before trial. According to the Media Law Resource Center, only about four to five libel cases go to trial per year in the United States, down from about 27 per year in 1980.[6]

Nevertheless, defamation can be costly. After their errant and misleading reporting, conservative broadcasters faced several lawsuits by voting machine companies and poll workers the networks credulously accused of rigging the 2020 presidential election. Dominion Voting Systems sued Fox for $1.6 billion, a claim a Delaware judge allowed to proceed, finding it "reasonably conceivable that Dominion has a claim for defamation."[7] Smartmatic, another voting machine company, said in its lawsuits that it lost $2 billion in value from the false and defamatory broadcasts of One America News and Newsmax.[8]

Litigating a case can cost hundreds of thousands or, in high-profile cases, millions of dollars in attorney fees and costs for publishers—even if they ultimately win the lawsuit. One of the highest-profile libel cases in the twentieth century, General William Westmoreland's lawsuit against CBS regarding a documentary about the Vietnam War, was estimated to cost the parties more than $8 million in legal fees over a three-year period.[9]

Such lawsuits can be existential threats for publishers. A man who claimed that he invented email sued Techdirt, a blog founded by Mike Masnick in 1997 covering technology, government policy and legal matters, after the blog challenged that claim. Facing a $15 million damage claim, Masnick said the litigation "could very well be the end of Techdirt, even if we are completely on the right side of the law." A judge dismissed the case nine months later, and Techdirt continues to publish.[10]

---

[2] Rosenblatt v. Baer, 383 U.S. 75 (1966) (concurring opinion).

[3] W. Page Keeton et al., *Prosser and Keeton on the Law of Torts* § 111, at 773 (5th ed. 1984).

[4] Media Law Resource Center, "MLRC 2014 Report on Trials and Damages," Jan. 2014.

[5] MMAR Group, Inc. v. Dow Jones & Co. 187 F.R.D. 282 (S.D. Tex. 1999) (new trial ordered), *case dismissed at request of plaintiff*, No. 95-CV-1262 (S.D. Tex. Jan. 5, 2000).

[6] First Amendment Watch, "Media Law Expert George Freeman Talks About the Internet, Political Polarization, and Defamation Law," Jan. 6, 2020.

[7] Katie Robertson & Jonah E. Bromwich, "Fox News's Request to Dismiss Suit is Rejected," *N.Y. Times*, Dec. 18, 2021, B3.

[8] Jan Wolfe & Helen Coster, "Newsmax, One America News Sued by Voting Technology Firm Smartmatic," *Reuters*, Nov. 3, 2021.

[9] Alexander Alben, "The Truth Defense—Lessons Learned from Westmoreland v. CBS," 10 *Loy. L.A. Ent. L. Rev.* 397, 399 (1989).

[10] Mike Masnick, "Techdirt's First Amendment Fight for Its Life," *Techdirt*, Jan. 11, 2017.

The fear of costly libel suits impeding robust public affairs journalism makes defamation one of the most important issues in the law of public communication. It also has become one of the most visible challenges facing journalists both in the United States and elsewhere in the world, as politicians and celebrities use the courts to intimidate and silence critics. During his ultimately successful campaign for the presidency, Donald Trump said he would like to "open up our libel laws" to make it easier to sue news media, a threat that drew intense pushback from the press and First Amendment advocates.[11] As part of his anti-media message in his reelection efforts, Trump himself unsuccessfully sued the *New York Times* for an opinion column alleging quid pro quo connections between his presidential campaign and Russia, a case dismissed in 2021 when a court recognized that an opinion of this kind is not proper grounds for a lawsuit, and that even if it were, he would be unable to meet the First Amendment requirement as a public official of proving "actual malice" to prevail.[12] One of Trump's fiercest allies in Congress, Rep. Devin Nunes, filed six lawsuits in 2019 against journalists, media companies, anonymous Twitter users—such as a parody account pretending to be his mother—and Twitter itself, and he threatened more lawsuits to come against his critics. Experts estimated the lawsuits were costing him hundreds of thousands of dollars in legal fees to file, even though the odds of him succeeding in any of them were very slim.[13]

Internationally, libel remains a challenge, especially in countries without robust free speech protections. In Turkey, between 2014 and 2016, more than 1,800 criminal cases were filed against citizens, journalists and even children who were accused of insulting President Recep Tayyip Erdogan, including one case in which a physician was fired from his government job and faced a two-year jail sentence for sharing a meme online comparing photos of Erdogan to Gollum from "Lord of the Rings."[14] And in South Korea, embattled President Park Geun-hye brought dozens of libel actions, both criminal and civil, against her critics, earning the scorn of the United Nations Human Rights Committee.[15]

Besides being a common threat to publishers, libel also is one of the most complicated. Libel law is complex in part because it originated in 50 versions as state law. In addition, the U.S. Supreme Court added a transforming constitutional dimension by applying the First Amendment to libel in 1964. A 1996 federal statute immunizes Internet service providers from suits when people post libelous comments on the providers' sites. Finally, many aspects of libel law are illogical. In the words of a prominent legal scholar, "It must be confessed at the beginning that there is a great deal of the law of defamation which makes no sense."[16]

This chapter explains the principles and application of libel law. The chapter begins with a discussion of libel terminology and the legal burden borne by the plaintiff suing for libel. The chapter then reviews libel damage awards. Finally, defenses to a libel suit are discussed along with media tactics to deter libel suits and libel reform proposals.

---

[11] Sydney Ember, "If Trump Sought to Change Libel Laws, It Would Be No Easy Task," *N.Y. Times*, Nov. 14, 2016, B6.
[12] Eriq Gardner, "Donald Trump Loses Libel Lawsuit Against N.Y. Times," *Hollywood Reporter*, March 10, 2021.
[13] Kate Irby, "Devin Nunes Lives on a Congressman's Salary. How Is He Funding So Many Lawsuits?" *Fresno Bee*, Dec. 4, 2019.
[14] Safak Timur, "Turkey Cracks Down on Insults to President," *N.Y. Times*, Mar. 3, 2016, A8.
[15] Choe Sang-Hun, "Defamation Laws Give South Korea an Anti-Dissent Tool," *N.Y. Times*, Mar. 6, 2016, A8.
[16] William Prosser, *Prosser on Torts* § 111, at 737 (4th ed. 1971).

LIBEL TERMINOLOGY

Defamation is expression that tends to damage a person's standing in the community through words that attack an individual's character or professional abilities. Defamation also can cause people to avoid contact with the person attacked. Defamation can take the form of either libel or slander. Almost all defamation cases are taken to civil rather than criminal court.

Libel and Slander

Traditionally, written or printed defamation is **libel**, whereas spoken defamation is **slander**. Historically, plaintiffs could win larger damage awards in libel suits than in slander suits, in part because written defamation was believed to cause more harm to a person's reputation. The printed word was more enduring than speech and could be circulated more widely. In addition, the author of libelous words was considered to have deliberately damaged someone's reputation, whereas slanderers were considered to have spoken spontaneously.[17] Because slander is considered less harmful, successful slander plaintiffs may have to show that the defamation caused them a financial loss. Only rarely do libel plaintiffs have to prove monetary loss.

However, broadcasting blurs the distinction between libel and slander because broadcasting carries the spoken defamation to a large audience. The ***Restatement (Second) of Torts***, an influential summary of tort law, argues that defamation by broadcast should be treated in the same way as print defamation because defamation in radio and television can damage a reputation as badly as defamation in print. In addition, the *Restatement* contends, broadcasting can damage a reputation as easily as print because, as a mass medium, it has the same credibility and prestige.[18] Courts also find defamation on the Internet and on social media platforms to be libel rather than slander.[19]

Criminal Libel and Civil Libel

Most early libel law was criminal law. Governments adopted criminal libel statutes to prevent breaches of the peace and punish criticism of government. The government prosecuted defamation of public officials, disrespect for the dead and aspersions on the chastity of women because such defamation—whether true or false—might cause disorder and violence. The defendant, if found guilty, could be fined or jailed. Government prosecution on behalf of the defamed, though not protective of free speech, was a civilizing improvement over earlier "self-help" remedies when the defamed sought to restore their honor by dueling or fighting.

Today, most libel cases in the United States are civil suits. The defamed sue for money damages. The government usually seeks no jail term or fine in criminal libel proceedings. The development of civil libel has given Americans an alternative to putting people in jail for something they say. The move away from criminal libel has come in spite of a 1952 Supreme Court opinion, *Beauharnais v. Illinois*, in which a divided Court upheld an Illinois statute that criminalized any publication that "portrays depravity, criminality, unchastity, or lack of virtue in any class of

---

[17] Rice v. Simmons, 2 Del. (2 Harr.) 417, 422 (1838). *See Restatement (Second) of Torts* § 568(3).
[18] *Restatement (Second) of Torts* § 568A and 568A comment a.
[19] *E.g.*, Blumenthal v. Drudge, 992 F. Supp. 44 (D.D.C. 1998); Gordon v. Love, No. B256367, Court of Appeals. Cal. (Feb. 1, 2016).

citizens of any race, color, creed or religion." The law had been used to prosecute a hatemonger who distributed racist literature. In a 5–4 decision, the U.S. Supreme Court ruled that a state law targeting libelous remarks directed at ethnic and racial groups was permissible under the First Amendment.[20]

Although *Beauharnais* never has been overturned, the decision has been eclipsed by more recent decisions abandoning breach of the peace as a justification for libel convictions. Under current libel law, ethnic and racial slurs directed at large groups are not considered defamatory because slurs on large groups do not identify a single individual. Today, a libel plaintiff typically must establish that he or she was identified individually.

In addition, the Supreme Court has ruled unconstitutional a state statute punishing speech that tends to breach the peace, thus knocking out an important rationale for criminal libel prosecutions. In *Ashton v. Kentucky*, the Court unanimously overturned the conviction of Steve Ashton under Kentucky criminal libel law allowing the state to punish conduct "calculated to create disturbances of the peace." Ashton had been fined $3,000 and sentenced to six months in prison for printing a pamphlet during a bitter labor dispute in Hazard, Kentucky. The pamphlet attacked the chief of police, the sheriff and the co-owner of the *Hazard Herald* for their failure to support striking miners. The pamphlet said Sheriff Charles Combs had bribed a jury after "intentionally blinding a boy with tear-gas" and beating him while his hands were cuffed. The U.S. Supreme Court said Kentucky's law was too vague and imprecise to withstand constitutional scrutiny.[21]

The Court also has ruled that criminal prosecutions for criticism of the public conduct of public officials are unconstitutional unless the publication is false and made knowingly or recklessly. The Court reversed the conviction of New Orleans prosecutor Jim Garrison, who had accused eight judges of being lazy, inefficient and sympathetic to "racketeer influences."[22] About a dozen states still permitted criminal libel prosecutions as of 2022, though these laws had been on the decline across the country.[23] However, a federal judge in 2021 upheld New Hampshire's criminal libel law against a challenge that it was unconstitutionally overbroad and vague, brought by a man who had twice been charged for criminal defamation for online posts he made about a fitness coach on Craigslist and a police officer he accused of corruption in the comments section of a newspaper article.[24]

THE PLAINTIFF

A person who files a libel complaint becomes the plaintiff in a libel suit. Any individual, business, nonprofit corporation or unincorporated association can legally sue for lost reputation. A government or government agency may not sue for libel, although government officials may bring defamation suits.

Living Individuals

Every individual has a personal right to sue to protect his or her reputation. However, because reputation is personal to each individual, no person can sue for damage to the reputation of another. Relatives, partners or subordinates of

---

[20] 343 U.S. 250 (1952).
[21] 384 U.S. 195 (1996).
[22] Garrison v. Louisiana, 379 U.S. 64 (1964).
[23] Eugene Volokh, "Anti-Libel Injunctions," 167 *U. Pa. L. Rev.* 73, 80 (2019).
[24] Frese v. MacDonald, 512 F. Supp. 273 (D.N.H. 2021).

someone named in a defamatory story cannot ordinarily win suits by claiming that they were libeled. Because damage to reputation is an individual matter, defamation of one person does not "rub off" on another, even to close relatives or business associates.[25] Friends, relatives or associates of a person libeled can successfully sue for libel only if they have been defamed themselves.

The right to sue for damage to reputation dies with each individual. No relative can sue on behalf of a dead person whose reputation may be defiled.[26] Although people can bequeath houses, cars, copyright in books and other property to heirs, they cannot bequeath personal rights such as reputation or privacy. However, a relative may be able to continue a libel suit filed by an individual who dies before the suit is concluded. The U.S. Supreme Court ruled that the widow of famed attorney Johnnie L. Cochran Jr. could substitute for her husband in a libel suit the famous lawyer filed against a former client who picketed Cochran's offices, shouting insults and obscenities and claiming Cochran owed him money.[27]

Some plaintiffs are "libel proof" because their reputations are "so hopelessly bad . . . that no words can affect [them] harmfully."[28] Libel-proof plaintiffs are relatively rare, but courts may find them in serial criminals such as John Cerasani—who pleaded guilty to charges of racketeering, conspiracy to rob a bank and possession of illegal drugs—making him unable to successfully sue the producers of a 1997 film that depicted him viciously beating a truck driver and participating in a gruesome murder.[29] In 2020, when notorious outfielder Lenny Dykstra sued his former Mets teammate Ron Darling for stories told in his book *108 Stitches: Loose Threads, Ripping Yarns, and the Darndest Characters from My Time in the Game*, a New York judge ruled that Dykstra was libel-proof, noting that the ballplayer was "infamous for being, among other things, racist, misogynist, and anti-gay, as well as a sexual predator, a drug-abuser, a thief, and an embezzler."[30]

However, some jurisdictions recognize the "incremental harm" doctrine, which allows plaintiffs to win libel suits even if they have terrible reputations, as long as there is new harm.[31] For example, in 2009, a federal judge refused summary judgment for a book author who argued that model Anna Nicole Smith's former attorney and companion was libel proof. The judge ruled that even though the attorney, Howard K. Stern, had a bad reputation, his reputation could be further damaged by a book accusing him of taped sex acts at a party, pimping Smith to other men when she was drugged, and contributing to her death 12 years after the death of her 90-year-old billionaire husband.[32]

Organizations

A business can sue for defamatory false stories about business practices, such as financial mismanagement or attempts to deceive the public through advertising.[33] Nonprofit corporations, such as churches and charitable organizations, can sue for

---

[25] *Restatement (Second) of Torts* § 564 and comment e.

[26] *Restatement (Second) of Torts* § 560. *See also* Gugliuzza v. KCMC Inc., 593 So. 2d 845 (La. 1992).

[27] Tory v. Cochran, 544 U.S. 734 (2005).

[28] *Restatement (Second) of Torts* § 559 comment d.

[29] Cerasani v. Sony Corp., 991 F. Supp. 343, 346 (S.D.N.Y. 1998).

[30] Dykstra v. St. Martin's Press LLC, 2020 N.Y. Misc. LEXIS 2659 (New York Cnty., N.Y., 2020).

[31] Kevin L. Kite, "Incremental Identities: Libel-Proof Plaintiffs, Substantial Truth, and the Future of the Incremental Harm Doctrine," 73 *N.Y.U. L. Rev.* 529 (1998).

[32] Stern v. Cosby, 645 F. Supp. 2d 258 (S.D.N.Y. 2009).

[33] *See* Dun & Bradstreet, Inc. v. Greenmoss Builders, 472 U.S. 749 (1985).

language that damages their ability to obtain donations.[34] Unincorporated associations, including labor unions, can sue for false stories that would damage their ability to attract members, conduct business or obtain financial support.[35]

Government

Units of government cannot sue for criticism of governmental conduct. Governments cannot sue on their own behalf, on behalf of employees or on behalf of the public they serve, no matter how false or unreasonable the criticism. Appellate courts consistently have held that governments cannot be defamed.[36] The U.S. Supreme Court has declared that libel suits by government institutions are unconstitutional.[37] The right to criticize government has been held to be too important to self-government for the law to permit governments to sue for libel.

The U.S. Supreme Court implicitly has endorsed the Illinois Supreme Court's rejection in 1923 of a libel suit by the City of Chicago. The Illinois court said, "no court of last resort in this country has ever held, or even suggested, that prosecutions for libel on government have any place in the American system of jurisprudence." The City of Chicago had sued the *Chicago Tribune* for printing that the city was "broke," its "credit was shot to pieces" and bankruptcy for the city was "just around the corner." The city claimed the articles damaged its credit in the bond market and accounted for a substantial financial loss. The Illinois Supreme Court said that even if the *Tribune*'s stories resulted in an increase in taxes, it was better that irresponsible individuals or newspapers go unpunished than for all citizens to be "in jeopardy of imprisonment or economic subjection" for criticizing "an inefficient or corrupt government."[38]

The fact that government cannot be libeled should not encourage careless statements about government. Besides, government employees can sue as individuals if they are defamed.

■ SUMMARY ■

Defamation is expression that damages a person's reputation. Printed defamation, online defamation and most broadcast defamation are considered to be libel. Slander is spoken defamation. Civil libel law—whereby one person or organization sues another for monetary damages—is most common, replacing criminal libel law, which is aimed at preventing breaches of the peace. Individuals and organizations, including businesses, may sue for libel, but governments may not.

THE PLAINTIFF'S BURDEN OF PROOF

To win damages in a libel suit, a plaintiff must establish certain claims to the satisfaction of a jury. This obligation is called the plaintiff's **burden of proof**. To sue successfully for libel, most plaintiffs must prove

1. defamation—that there was defamatory language.
2. identification—that the defamation was about the plaintiff.

---

[34] *Restatement (Second) of Torts* § 561, 562, and 562 comment a.

[35] *Id.* at § 562 and 562 comment a.

[36] *See* College Savings Bank v. Florida Prepaid Postsecondary Educ. Expense Bd., 919 F. Supp. 756, *claim dismissed, in part, complaint dismissed*, 948 F. Supp. 400 (D.N.J. 1996), *aff'd*, 131 F.3d 353 (3d Cir. 1997), *aff'd in part*, 527 U.S. 666 (1999), *rev'd in part*, 527 U.S. 627 (1999).

[37] *See* Rosenblatt v. Baer, 383 U.S. 75 (1966); N.Y. Times Co. v. Sullivan, 376 U.S. 254 (1964).

[38] City of Chicago v. Tribune Co., 139 N.E. 86, 91 (1923).

3. publication—that the defamation was disseminated.

4. fault—that the defamation was published as a result of negligence or recklessness.

5. falsity—that the statement was false, a burden only for persons suing for defamation related to matters of public concern.

6. personal harm—such as a loss to reputation, emotional distress or the loss of business revenues.

Most plaintiffs have to satisfy all six elements of a libel suit. To prove only one—defamation, for example—is not enough to win a libel suit. However, even if libel plaintiffs meet their burden of proof, they might not win their suits. Defendants will present defenses based on the First Amendment and the common law, defenses that a plaintiff must refute. The defendant's case will be discussed later in the chapter.

Defamation

The *Restatement (Second) of Torts* defines defamation as statements that tend to expose a person "to hatred, ridicule or contempt." Defamation may reflect unfavorably on someone's morality or integrity or discredit a person in his or her occupation. Defamation may restrict a person's social contacts by asserting that the individual has a mental illness or a particularly undesirable and contagious disease.[39] Defamation can occur in news stories, press releases, advertising, broadcasts, in-house memos, blogs, social media posts and speeches.

In court, a judge usually determines whether a message is capable of a defamatory meaning. A jury determines whether that message, in its everyday meaning, defamed the person who is suing.[40]

DEFAMATORY CONTENT The words and phrases most often involved in libel suits are those stating or suggesting criminal activity, serious moral failings, or incompetence in business or professional life. Words also defame if they imply that a person is unpatriotic, mentally incompetent, alcoholic or infected by a loathsome disease.

Crime Stories about crime make up a significant proportion of the news. Asserting that someone committed or has been accused of committing a crime is defamatory on its face. If a newspaper or broadcast station falsely reports that someone is suspected or convicted of rape, drug use or drunken driving, that person may be able to win a libel suit. A court ruled the *Washington Post* printed libel when it erroneously reported that Michael Donaldson had pleaded guilty to a charge of murder. In fact, Donaldson was acquitted of the charge.[41] Context of these statements matters as well. A court found that a magazine story calling a person an "eel" could be defamatory because everyone else called an eel in the story was "someone who has been convicted of or has plead guilty to violations of the Endangered Species Act."[42] The court said the story implied the plaintiff also had engaged in criminal activity.

Similarly, spewing insults online that imply criminal behavior can be costly. A Georgia jury awarded rapper Cardi B $4 million in actual damages, punitive damages and attorney fees in 2022 in her lawsuit against a celebrity blogger who had

---

[39] *Restatement (Second) of Torts* § 559.
[40] *Id.* at §§ 559 comment e, 563 comment c, and 614.
[41] Donaldson v. Washington Post Co., 3 Media L. Rep. 1436 (D.C. Super. Ct. 1977).
[42] Snider v. National Audubon Soc'y, Inc., 20 Media L. Rep. 1218 (E.D. Cal. 1992).

made false allegations that Cardi B was a cocaine user, had been a prostitute, and had herpes.[43]

Occupation Allegations of criminal activity, unethical practices and incompetence related to work accounted for more than three-quarters of the libel cases in the aforementioned study.[44] Charges of corruption may be defamatory. An Illinois jury awarded business executive Robert Crinkley $2.25 million for a *Wall Street Journal* article accusing him of making payoffs to foreign governments. The *Journal* falsely reported that Crinkley, president of a division of a pharmaceutical company, resigned after disclosures that he made payments to foreign governments in order to obtain business. The court said the false allegations impugned Crinkley's integrity even though such payments were not illegal.[45]

Of course, not every story that generates a complaint is libelous. A federal appeals court said that criticism of a law class at Stanford University did not impugn the reputation of the professor. The magazine that published the story said that Professor Stanley Kaplan's criminal law course was "recognized as the easiest five credits" at Stanford. The article reported that some students listened to the lectures over the radio while they sunned themselves by the pool, the professor required only a midterm and a final, the grades "exactly mirror the curve" for grades at Stanford, and two students took the final exam in top hats and three-piece suits while drinking champagne. The U.S. Court of Appeals for the Ninth Circuit said that the story said nothing directly about the teacher's ability or integrity and maybe nothing derogatory about the course. The court said that any implication that the class was worthless because it was easy was "strained."[46]

Business Businesses may sue for stories claiming they provide poor service or have committed a crime. Businesses also may sue for language asserting they cheat their customers, are financially insolvent, or intentionally are selling harmful or ineffective products. Businesses can sue only for damage to the corporate reputation and not for damage to any individual's reputation.

Charges that a business is deceptive could cause the loss of customers. A federal court said a broadcast report that a retail meat company deceptively advertised the price and quality of its beef could be defamatory. Donna Deaner, a reporter for WTAE-TV in Pittsburgh, broadcast that a Steaks Unlimited sales agent said the beef at a sale was "lovely, fully dressed and trimmed" and a "fantastic bargain." But Deaner said the beef came from "old tough animals" and was tenderized "with a variety of chemicals to make it palatable." She also said the meat was not much cheaper than what could be purchased in supermarkets. Although the U.S. Court of Appeals for the Third Circuit said the report could be defamatory, it ruled Steaks Unlimited could not meet the other elements of its burden of proof to win a suit.[47]

The reputation of a business also can be damaged by false allegations that it is financially unstable or insolvent, reports that could damage bank credit and result in the loss of customers. In a case that will be discussed more thoroughly later in the chapter, a construction company named Greenmoss Builders won $350,000 when a credit-reporting agency falsely said the company had filed for bankruptcy.

---

[43] Nancy Dillon, "Cardi B Defamation Award Now Tops $4 Million," *Rolling Stone*, Jan. 25, 2022.
[44] Marc Franklin, "Winners and Losers and Why: A Study of Defamation Litigation," *Am. B. Found. Res. J.* 455, 477–8, 482 (1980).
[45] "*Wall Street Journal* Loses $2.25 Million Libel Judgment," *Editor & Publisher*, June 1, 1991, at 19; Crinkley v. Dow Jones & Co., 456 N.E.2d 138 (Ill. App. Ct. 1983).
[46] Kaplan v. Newsweek Magazine, Inc., 776 F.2d 1053 (9th Cir. 1985).
[47] Steaks Unlimited, Inc. v. Deaner, 623 F.2d 264 (3d Cir. 1980).

A 17-year-old employee of the credit agency had inadvertently attributed the bank-ruptcy petition of a former Greenmoss employee to the company itself.[48]

A business also may be able to win a libel suit if a publication or broadcast contends that it manufactures or promotes products that could damage the public health or safety. The Brown & Williamson Tobacco Corporation won $3.5 million in damages after a Chicago television commentator accused the company of trying to sell Viceroy cigarettes to children. Walter Jacobson of WBBM-TV said Viceroy's strategy was to convince young people that smoking cigarettes was an "illicit plea-sure" like drinking alcoholic beverages, smoking pot and engaging in sexual activi-ties. Jacobson said Viceroy wanted to "present the cigarette as an initiation into the adult world" and a "declaration of independence." Jacobson's commentary said Viceroy lied when it contended it was not trying to sell cigarettes to children. However, Brown & Williamson proved the accusation false—the company had rejected the "illicit pleasure" strategy aimed at children and fired the ad agency that proposed it.[49]

At least a few states limit libel suits related to business and occupation through what is called the *single instance rule.* Courts in New York and Florida have held that "language charging a professional person with ignorance or error on a single occasion" is not defamatory without proof of specific monetary loss.[50] The courts have suggested that readers and viewers know that everyone makes mistakes at some time, and therefore a report of a single error will not damage a professional's reputation.

Product Disparagement or Trade Libel Libel of products—called **product disparagement** or **trade libel**—defames the quality or usefulness of a commercial product rather than the company that produced it. Stories suggesting that a brand of scissors cannot cut, a manufacturer's basketball does not bounce, or a prescrip-tion drug causes cancer are examples of product disparagement. The assertions criticize the products without contending that the companies are trying to cheat their customers. Product disparagement awards compensate for the loss of sales rather than for damage to reputation.

Plaintiffs have difficulty winning product disparagement suits. They not only must meet the burden of proof required of all libel plaintiffs but also must prove financial loss and malice. Bob Diefenderfer, a businessman in Sheridan, Wyoming, lost a libel suit because he was unable to prove financial loss after a radio station suggested merchandise he wanted to sell after a fire was not

> worth the paper cartons it was packed in. . . .. Radios had picked up moisture, dishes and glassware, subjected to terrific heat, were brit-tle. . . .. The Navajo rugs were scorched and the colors ran together. The record stock was wet and useless.[51]

A trial judge ruled the merchandise on sale at Bob's War Surplus Store was worth more than the paper cartons. However, the judge said Diefenderfer had not proven his store had lost money because of the broadcast. Diefenderfer's claims of trade damage were "uncertain, conjectural and speculative."

---

[48] Dun & Bradstreet, Inc. v. Greenmoss Builders, Inc., 472 U.S. 749 (1985).
[49] Brown & Williamson Tobacco Corp. v. Jacobson, 644 F. Supp. 1240 (N.D. Ill. 1986), *aff'd in part*, 827 F.2d 1119 (7th Cir. 1987), *cert. denied*, 485 U.S. 993 (1988).
[50] Porcari v. Gannett, 36 Media L. Rep. 2402 (N.Y. Ct. App. 2008).
[51] Diefenderfer v. Totman, 280 P.2d 284 (Wyo. 1955).

In addition to proving a loss of business, a plaintiff in a product disparage-ment case must establish that defamation was published with either **common-law malice**—intent to do harm—or **actual malice**—knowledge of falsity or reckless disregard for the truth.[52] The malice requirement prevented the Bose Corporation from winning damages for a false statement printed in *Consumer Reports* about the Bose 901 speaker system. The magazine said that sound from the speakers wan-dered "about the room." A violin appeared to be "10 feet wide and a piano stretched from wall to wall." A district court judge was persuaded that the publication caused an eight-month decline in the sales growth of the speaker system, a loss for which Bose should be compensated. However, a federal appeals court overturned the ruling, deciding that Bose had not adequately established that *Consumer Reports* knew the publication was false, a requirement imposed by the First Amendment. That ruling was upheld by the U.S. Supreme Court.[53]

In a highly publicized case, a federal appeals court ruled that the *Oprah Winfrey Show* did not defame Texas beef in violation of a state food disparagement statute.[54] Texas, like more than a dozen states, has a "veggie libel statute" that makes the media liable if they knowingly disseminate false information about the safety of a perishable food. The U.S. Court of Appeals for the Fifth Circuit ruled that guests on the show presented protected opinion when one warned that the deadly mad cow disease could migrate rapidly from Great Britain, and another guest compared mad cow disease to AIDS. Sales of Texas beef plummeted after the show.

The appeals court said the opinion about the spread of mad cow disease was protected because it was based on known facts about how cattle were fed at the time. The comparison of mad cow disease to AIDS was protected exaggeration. The court did not determine whether a lower court had correctly ruled that cattle pro-ducers could not sue under the Texas statute because cattle were not "perishable."

Although Oprah won the Texas case, the media were not able to challenge the constitutionality of the Texas statute successfully. The Texas law and so-called veggie libel statutes in other states are vulnerable to constitutional attack because they inhibit food critics, environmental writers and agricultural experts who criti-cize how American foods are grown and processed. The First Amendment protects wide-open debate on public issues—a debate in which experts often disagree—but the veggie libel statutes make critics responsible for large payments unless their statements are based on scientific fact. However, environmentalists, biologists, agronomists, geneticists and other scientists often disagree even about facts.

Character, Habits and Obligations Although a majority of libel suits have involved criticism of people for their work, a libel study demonstrated that many suits are filed for attacks on personal character traits or lifestyle. For example, per-sonal reputations can be damaged by stories that suggest people are dishonest, cruel or do not live up to their social obligations. A federal district court said that a broadcast news segment that could be interpreted to portray Amrit Lal as a slum landlord could be defamatory. The court said WCAU-TV in Philadelphia may have defamed Lal when it reported an allegation by students that he refused to make necessary repairs on his property. The tenants complained of leaky roofs, faulty wiring and "other eyesores." The court said the broadcast could be interpreted as

---

[52] *E.g., Restatement (Second) of Torts* §§ 623A comment d, 626, 633, 634; Rodney Smolla, *The Law of Defamation* § 11.02[2] [e], at 11–33 (1998).

[53] Bose Corp. v. Consumers Union of United States, Inc., 508 F. Supp. 1249, *enforced*, 529 F. Supp. 357 (D. Mass. 1981), *rev'd*, 692 F.2d 189 (1st Cir. 1982), *aff'd*, 466 U.S. 485 (1984).

[54] Engler v. Winfrey, 201 7.3d 680 (5th Cir. 2000).

accusing Lal of being an "unscrupulous" person who "preys upon the economically disadvantaged."[55] The court said the report could deter people from associating or dealing with Lal, an issue that needed to be determined at trial. Other courts have said that people were libeled when they were accused of being hypocrites, liars, cowards or cheats, or unwilling to pay their bills.[56]

Assertions that either a husband or wife has not fulfilled marital or familial obligations also may be libelous. A court said a woman defamed her ex-husband when she said, "he abandoned me, made no provisions for my support, treated me with complete indifference and did not display any affection or regard for me."[57]

Assertions that a person's sexual conduct deviates from generally accepted norms usually are defamatory. A jury awarded a Virginia woman $25,000 after the *Charlottesville Daily Progress* falsely said she was pregnant and unmarried.[58] False allegations of homosexuality are generally defamatory, though jurisdictions are split on whether such allegations are libelous "per se" (that is, on their face) or whether additional proof is necessary to show that the plaintiff was harmed by such an allegation. For example, a New York appeals court in 2020 determined that false accusations of homosexuality were no longer defamatory per se, recognizing the "profound and notable transformation of cultural attitudes and governmental protective laws" such as laws barring discrimination against people for sexual orientation and state and federal courts' recognition of same-sex marriages.[59] However, other courts have found differently. A Texas appeals court, for example, determined that a restaurant owner's derogatory implication of a patron's sexuality in a public setting was slanderous per se and supported a $5,000 jury verdict.[60]

Although alcoholism is legally an illness, false accusations that someone is an alcoholic, a drunkard, a drunk driver or a member of Alcoholics Anonymous may be libelous.[61] To say that someone had a drink is not defamatory under most circumstances, but a report of raucous activity because of drinking can be. Actress Carol Burnett settled out of court with the *National Enquirer* for an undisclosed amount of money after the publication inaccurately reported that she drank too much and became obnoxious at the Rive Gauche, a restaurant in Washington, D.C.[62]

A story can be libelous if it has a tendency to inhibit personal contact. Persons reported to have a particularly undesirable and contagious disease may be shunned.[63] Therefore, people can successfully sue for inaccurate reports that they have a sexually transmitted disease such as AIDS, genital herpes or syphilis. Cancer is not believed to be contagious and is not considered to be damaging to esteem or reputation.[64]

Politics, Religion and Race People can lose face if a story questions their patriotism or accuses them of being aligned with a political group that is considered a threat to the nation's well-being. It can be defamatory to assert falsely that

---

[55] Lal v. CBS, 551 F. Supp. 356 (E.D. Pa. 1982), *aff'd*, 726 F.2d 97 (1984).

[56] *Restatement (Second) of Torts* § 569(g); W. Page Keeton et al., *Prosser and Keeton on the Law of Torts* § 111, at 775 (5th ed. 1984).

[57] Brown v. Du Frey, 134 N.E.2d 469 (N.Y. 1956).

[58] *E.g.*, Gazette Inc., v. Harris, 325 S.E.2d 713 (Va. 1985).

[59] Laguerre v. Morris, 192 A.D.3d 44 (N.Y. App., 2nd Div., 2020)

[60] Van Meter v. Morris, 2011 Tex. App. LEXIS 9847 (Texas Ct. App. 2011).

[61] W. Page Keeton et al., *Prosser and Keeton on the Law of Torts* § 111, at 775 (5th ed. 1984).

[62] Burnett v. National Enquirer, Inc., 144 Cal. App. 3d 991 (Cal. Ct. App. 1983), *appeal dismissed*, 465 U.S. 1014 (1984); "Settlement in Burnett-Enquirer Suit," *United Press International*, Dec. 19, 1984, BC cycle.

[63] *Restatement (Second) of Torts* § 559(c).

[64] Chuy v. Philadelphia Eagles Football Club, 595 F.2d 1265 (3d Cir. 1979).

someone is a traitor or a spy, believes in anarchy or wants to overthrow the government by force. A former Arizona state attorney general was awarded $485,000 after an editorial in the *Arizona Republic* said he had Communist sympathies.[65] A story falsely reporting that an individual is a member of a discredited organization—such as the Nazi Party—is defamatory.[66] In 2016, actor James Woods tweeted a photo of a woman giving a "Heil Hitler" salute at a rally for then-candidate Donald Trump, and included the words, "So-called #Trump 'Nazi' is a #BernieSanders agitator/operative?" It turned out the woman he accused was not who he said she was, but rather another woman who was an actual Trump supporter. The woman Woods targeted sued, and the U.S. Court of Appeals for the Sixth Circuit found that being accused of giving a Nazi salute was indeed defamatory. However, because Woods posed the tweet as a question, the court said the statement could also be interpreted to have a non-defamatory meaning, and thus under the state of Ohio's "innocent construction" rule (see below) that privileges statements with possible non-defamatory meaning, it was not, in the end, actionable.[67]

Courts have also held that the use of derogatory nationalistic and racial terms might not damage reputation. An individual might be able to win a libel suit only if there is proof of harm to reputation. Ordinarily, the courts say that highly offensive terms do not reflect on the individual character or beliefs of the persons subjected to the verbal abuse.

Humor and Ridicule A publication that generates laughs at someone's expense or makes a person the butt of a joke is not necessarily libelous. But humor can become libelous if it subjects people to ridicule by suggesting they do not deserve respect. A major difficulty for writers is that even the courts disagree on where to draw the line between nondefamatory humor and defamatory ridicule.

"The reports of my death are greatly exaggerated," Mark Twain is reported to have said after his obituary appeared prematurely in a New York newspaper. Most courts have ruled that false obituaries, even those planted in newspapers, may be bad jokes but are not libelous.[68] A New York court ruled that it was not defamatory to assert that the corpse of someone who was very much alive was lying in state at the address of a saloon. Even if readers had known the address was that of a bar, the judge said, the obituary did not expose the plaintiff to public hatred, shame, odium, ridicule, aversion or disgrace. The judge said that, at worst, the publication "might cause some amusement to plaintiff's friends."[69]

FORMS OF LIBEL Libel suits most often result from words printed or broadcast in news stories, editorials, letters to editors and press releases. But defamation can also appear in headlines and advertisements. Sometimes words are defamatory only in combination or because of circumstances not known to a reasonably prudent writer or editor. Libel also can occur in the use of photographs, cartoons, caricatures and video in all media. Increasingly, posts on social media sites such as Twitter and Facebook are leading to defamation lawsuits, particularly outside of the United States.[70]

---

[65] Phoenix Newspapers, Inc. v. Church, 537 P.2d 1345 (Ariz. 1975), *appeal dismissed*, 425 U.S. 908 (1976), *reb'g denied*, 425 U.S. 985 (1976).
[66] Holy Spirit Ass'n v. Sequoia Elsevier Publishing Co., 4 Media L. Rep. 1744 (N.Y. Sup. Ct. 1978).
[67] Boulger v. Woods, 917 F.3d 471 (6th Cir. 2019).
[68] *E.g.*, Cohen v. New York Times Co., 138 N.Y.S. 206 (1912).
[69] Cardiff v. Brooklyn Eagle, Inc., 75 N.Y.S.2d 222 (Kings Co. 1947).
[70] Ian Burrell, "Libel Cases Prompted by Social Media Posts Rise 300% in a Year," *The Independent*, Oct. 19, 2014.

Words Some words are defamatory on their face; they are "libelous per se." Courts have held that these words can, by themselves, damage a person's repu- tation. Words that are libelous per se have clear, unambiguous and commonly agreed-upon meanings. Among the many "red flag" words that are defamatory on their face are "unethical," "adulterer," "thief," "drunkard" and "cheat" (see Box "Red Flag Words").

RED FLAG WORDS

Abused, abuser	Deviate, deviant	Mistreat
Addiction	Drinking, drunk, drunken,	Molested
Adultery	drunkard	Murdered
Affair	Drug problem	Perjury
AIDS	Embezzled	Prostitute, prostitution
Alcoholism, alcoholic	Fraud or fraudulent	Rioted
Arrested	Gay	Robbed, robbery
Assaulted	Harass, harassment	Scandal
Attacked	HIV	Sex, sexual
Bankrupt, bankruptcy	Homosexual	Sexually transmitted
Beat	Ill, illness	disease
Bisexual	Illegal	Slept with
Breached	Illicit	Smuggled
Burglary	Immoral	Spied
Came out of the closet	Infringed	Steal, stole, stolen
Charged	Killed	Theft, thief
Cheat, cheated	Lesbian	Trespassed
Convicted	Lied	Underage
Cover up	Mismanaged	Waste, wasted

Quotation marks indicate to readers that a speaker's words are being repro- duced verbatim. Therefore, fabricated quotes can defame speakers by attributing untrue assertions to them. Fabricated quotes may also tar people with unattractive personal traits they do not possess.[71]

Many words and phrases have more than one meaning. Some states have adopted what is called the **innocent construction rule**, which provides that language should be considered nondefamatory if it can be read that way. The Illinois Supreme Court said courts should find no libel if words, "considered in con- text and given their natural and obvious meaning," can reasonably be interpreted "innocently."[72] Applying the innocent construction rule, an Illinois appellate court said it was not defamatory for a school board member, Charles Garrison, to say that "legal ramifications" from a state investigation might result in school superintendent Gene Cartwright's losing certification and being fined or jailed. Cartwright said Garrison's statements libeled him by suggesting he was a criminal. But the Illinois court said Cartwright was not defamed because Garrison did not imply Cartwright was unfit to be a school administrator. Relying on the innocent construction rule, the court said Garrison's comment could reasonably be interpreted to mean he

---

[71] Masson v. New Yorker Magazine, 501 U.S. 496 (1991).
[72] Green v. Rogers, 917 N.E.2d 450, 500 (Ill. 2009). *See also* Kyu Ho Youm, "The Innocent Construction Rule: Ten Years After Modification," 14 *Comm. & L.* 49 (Dec. 1992).

was leaving to the state's attorney whether Cartwright had done anything "legally wrong" that might result in "legal ramifications."[73]

In a libel case, the meaning of words must usually be considered in the context of a complete article, book or broadcast.[74] A plaintiff cannot successfully contend that an isolated word or sentence is defamatory when the thrust of the article or book in which it appears creates a neutral or favorable impression of the person.

Words also have to be considered in their social context. In 1976, a federal judge ruled that falsely asserting that a citizen worked for the CIA could be defamatory, a ruling that would have been unlikely 20 years earlier. For many years following World War II, being wrongly associated with the CIA would not make most people an object of hatred, contempt or ridicule. But the judge said falsely calling someone an employee of the CIA during the 1960s and 1970s might be defamatory because many citizens during that period believed the CIA engaged in illegal activities.[75]

Implication, Innuendo and Circumstance Whereas some defamatory words are libelous on their face, others defame more subtly by implication or **innuendo**. The Tennessee Supreme Court, in remanding a case for trial, said omissions in a newspaper "so distorted the truth" that the story libeled Ruth Ann Nichols and her husband by falsely accusing her of adultery. The story in the *Memphis Press-Scimitar* truthfully reported that Mrs. Nichols was shot by a Mrs. Newton who "arrived at the Nichols home and found her husband there with Mrs. Nichols." Although the story, gathered from a police arrest report, was true, it omitted information from a second police report noting that Mr. Nichols and two neighbors were talking in the living room when Mrs. Newton arrived in the middle of the afternoon. The court said that readers could not have "conceivably" concluded that Mrs. Nichols was committing adultery if a complete account of the incident had been reported.[76] Nevertheless, a jury later ruled in favor of the newspaper at a trial in which Mrs. Nichols failed to meet her burden of proving defamation, falsity, fault and damages.[77]

Libel by implication or innuendo or otherwise only apparent from the context or circumstances is called *libel per quod*.[78] More frequently, *libel per quod* means libel that is apparent only to readers who know facts not included in the story. For example, birth notices mistakenly naming the parents of a baby are usually not libelous. However, a birth notice wrongly identifying a new father might be libelous if readers know that the named father is single or happily married to someone other than the correctly identified mother.[79]

The distinction between *libel per se* and *libel per quod* can be important when it comes to damages. In most jurisdictions, presumed damages are only available when the libel is per se, while libel per quod requires the plaintiff to prove actual harm or loss to receive damages.[80] The New Jersey Supreme Court, for example, noted that in a case of a private person accused online of sexually assaulting a

---

[73] Cartwright v. Garrison, 447 N.E.2d 446 (Ill. App. Ct. 1983).

[74] *Restatement (Second) of Torts* § 563 comment d.

[75] *See* Oliver v. Village Voice, Inc., 417 F. Supp. 235 (S.D.N.Y. 1976).

[76] Memphis Publishing Co. v. Nichols, 569 S.W.2d 412 (Tenn. 1978).

[77] Barbara Dill, *The Journalist's Handbook on Libel and Privacy* 64–7 (1986).

[78] *See, e.g.*, Bruck v. Cincotta, 371 N.E.2d 874 (Ill. App. Ct. 1978).

[79] *See* W. Page Keeton et al., *Prosser and Keeton on the Law of Torts* § 111, at 776 (5th ed. 1984); Karrigan v. Valentine, 339 P.2d 52 (Kan. 1959).

[80] See Michael K. Steenson, "Presumed Damages in Defamation Law," 40 *Wm. Mitchell L. Rev.* 1492 (2014).

minor, clearly libelous per se, that presumed damages in such cases protect the peace of mind of private citizens, who would otherwise be forced "to ferret out proof of loss of reputation from any of the world-wide potential viewers of defamatory Internet content about that otherwise private person."[81]

Headlines Courts are split over whether a headline alone can result in a successful libel suit. In many jurisdictions, a suit will not be successful if a defamatory headline is clarified in the accompanying story. In those states, the headline and article must be read as a whole.

However, some courts hold that a headline by itself may be considered libelous even if the article provides clarification. As the *Restatement (Second) of Torts* notes, readers often miss important parts of a story because they see only the headlines or read an article "hastily or imperfectly."[82] The *New Orleans Times-Picayune* paid $10,000 in damages for the headline "Bid Specs Reported 'Rigged.'" The article below the headline correctly reported that a consultant concluded that bid specifications for a school for the deaf appeared to favor specific manufacturers. A Louisiana appellate court said that favoring some manufacturers over others may or may not be illegal or improper but that the word *rigged* in the headline was defamatory because it denoted "fraudulent, illegal, and improper" activity.[83]

"Clickbait" headlines could also result in libel claims. Harvard Law School professor Lawrence Lessig sued the *New York Times* over a headline in 2019 about an opinion piece he had written about sex offender Jeffrey Epstein's controversial charitable donations. The headline in the *Times* read, "A Harvard Professor Doubles Down: If You Take Epstein's Money, Do It in Secret," even though the column Lessig wrote was mostly aimed at what he saw as unfair scapegoating of the M.I.T. Media Lab director who had accepted Epstein's donations, which the underlying article detailed accurately. Lessig dropped the lawsuit after the *Times* changed the headline to "What Are the Ethics of Taking Funds?"[84]

Photographs, Cartoons and Layout Photographs can also be the basis of a successful libel suit if the lens creates an illusion or the picture is altered.[85] More often, however, defamation occurs because of the combination of a picture and a nearby headline, story or cutline. The Supreme Judicial Court of Massachusetts said a Boston lawyer was entitled to a jury trial to determine whether he had been libeled when his name and picture appeared just below a headline reporting a kickback in a land scandal. Mitchell Mabardi's picture and name, without further explanation, appeared in the *Boston Herald-Traveler* immediately below the headline "Settlement Upped $2,000: $400 Kickback Told." The headline applied to a story about an official—pictured and named in the story—who had been convicted for taking a kickback in a government land purchase. Mabardi had nothing to do with the kickback story. Mabardi's picture was supposed to appear next to another story on the page about a different land deal.[86]

These situations are similar to the tort of "false light" by distortion, discussed more in Chapter 5. However, because not every state recognizes the false light tort, plaintiffs may bring suit under libel law instead in those jurisdictions. For example,

---

[81] W.J.A. v. D.A., 43 A.3d 1148, 1160 (N.J. 2012).

[82] *Restatement (Second) of Torts* § 563 comment d.

[83] Forrest v. Lynch, 347 So. 2d 1255 (La. Ct. App. 1977).

[84] Mike Masnick, "Lessig Withdraws 'Clickbait Defamation' Lawsuit Against NY Times After Changed Headline," *Techdirt*, April 14, 2020.

[85] *See* Robert Sack and Sandra Baron, *Libel, Slander, and Related Problems* 101–4 (1994); Rodney Smolla, *Law of Defamation* § 4.07[2] [a], at 4–28.6 to 4–28.8 (1998).

[86] Mabardi v. Boston Herald-Traveler Corp., 198 N.E.2d 304 (Mass. 1964).

in the aftermath of the Boston Marathon bombing in 2013, the *New York Post* ran a photograph with two young men on its cover, under the headline "BAG MEN," with a sub-headline reading "Feds seek this duo pictured at the Boston Marathon." The men were not involved in the bombing at all, nor were they considered suspects by the FBI. Because Massachusetts does not recognize the false light tort, the men sued for defamation, providing evidence that their reputations had been harmed by their treatment by the *Post*. A state court judge agreed, allowing their case to proceed because "a reasonable reader could construe the publication as expressly saying that law enforcement personnel were seeking not only to identify the plaintiffs, but also to find them, and as implying that the plaintiffs were the bombers."[87]

■ SUMMARY ■

Libel plaintiffs must establish that a publication or broadcast holds them up to hatred, ridicule or contempt. Most defamation involves assertions that individuals committed a crime or are incompetent or unethical in their occupation. Both businesses and products can be defamed. Also defamatory are suggestions of deviant sexual habits, irresponsible or unethical behavior, mental deficiencies, loathsome diseases and a lack of patriotism. Defamation can occur because of photographs, layouts and headlines as well as stories. Judges determine whether words are capable of defamatory meaning, and jurors determine whether the person suing was actually defamed. Isolated words taken out of context cannot be defamatory. However, a person can be libeled by the implication of words or by words that take on a defamatory meaning because of facts known to some readers but not to writers and editors.

Identification

Libel plaintiffs, in addition to establishing that an expression is defamatory, must also prove that the defamatory language is about them individually. Persons who are part of a large group that is libeled are usually unable to sue because they cannot show the defamation is about them individually.

IDENTIFYING INDIVIDUALS The identification requirement means that plaintiffs must prove the defamatory language is "of and concerning" them. They must show that at least one reader or viewer could identify them as the object of the defamatory remarks. A person can be identified by name, picture, description, nickname, signature, caricature or set of circumstances.[88] For example, a newspaper printed an article with the headline "Whitewater counsel kicks off first prosecution." Two photographs accompanied the article, one appearing over the name "Fitzhugh." The article discussed a defendant named "Eugene Fitzhugh" and then used the name "Fitzhugh," without a first name, seven times. The photograph was of a J. Michael Fitzhugh, who was not connected with the Whitewater case and who sued the newspaper for libel. Several people testified that at first they thought the article was about J. Michael Fitzhugh. The Arkansas Supreme Court said there was sufficient evidence allowing the impression J. Michael Fitzhugh had been charged with a crime.[89]

---

[87] Barhoum v. NYP Holdings, Inc., 42 Media L. Rep. 1401 (Mass. Super. 2014).
[88] *See Restatement (Second) of Torts* § 564; W. Page Keeton et al., *Prosser and Keeton on the Law of Torts* § 111, at 783 (5th ed. 1984).
[89] Little Rock Newspaper, Inc. v. Fitzhugh, 954 S.W.2d 914 (Ark. 1997), *cert. denied*, 523 U.S. 1095 (1998).

Many libel suits involve the inadvertent naming of the wrong person. A careless police reporter can erroneously copy the name "Adams" instead of "Adamson" from police records. Or a reporter might use the wrong middle initial or address. In a case of a wrong address, the *Springfield (Massachusetts) Union* lost a $60,000 suit for reporting that Anthony Liquori of Agawam had pleaded guilty to conspiring to break into two businesses. A reporter for the paper obtained Anthony Liquori's name from the court record. Because the court record did not include Liquori's address, the reporter wrote the address of the only Anthony Liquori listed in the Agawam telephone book. Unfortunately for the paper, the Anthony Liquori who had pleaded guilty was then living in Springfield, not Agawam, and the Anthony Liquori listed in the Agawam phone book successfully sued for libel.[90]

The Liquori case demonstrates that checking identification in one place is not always enough. The case also demonstrates the importance of a thorough identification. Media lawyers recommend identifying story subjects three ways: full name, including a middle initial; address; and occupation. Listing ages can also help to identify people with certainty. In 1980, the now-defunct *Washington Star* won a libel suit because it printed a complete identification, including name, age and address. The paper, relying on a police officer at the scene, said the person who shot Dr. Michael Halberstam was Jerry Summerlin, 22, of the 5500 block of Dana Place, N.W., Washington, D.C. Jerry Gene Summerlin of 8809 Plymouth Street in Silver Spring, Maryland, sued, claiming he had been wrongfully identified as the man who killed Halberstam. But a federal district court judge said the *Star*'s story had provided enough information to ensure that someone with the same name as the murder suspect would not be erroneously identified and unfairly stigmatized. Jerry Gene Summerlin was not 22 and did not live on Dana Place. Furthermore, Jerry Gene Summerlin had not been hospitalized with internal injuries, as the man arrested for Halberstam's murder had been. Halberstam had hit his assailant with his car as he was driving himself to the hospital.[91]

Courts have ruled that libel plaintiffs can establish a libelous story "of or concerning" them even if their name does not appear in the story. The Supreme Court of Massachusetts ruled that Haim Eyal, the owner of Haim's Delicatessen in Brookline, Massachusetts, might be able to prove that he was identified by a broadcast that said, "The owner of a Brookline delicatessen and seven other people are arrested in connection with an international cocaine ring."[92] Although the broadcast did not name Haim or his delicatessen, the court noted that a significant number of residents thought the report referred to Haim.

People who provide the basis for unflattering characters in fiction may sue for libel if the author fails to adequately disguise the fictionalized characters.[93] In a case in which a real person and a fictionalized character had the same name, a federal appeals court ruled Melanie Geisler should have the chance to prove in court that she was identified as the central character in a fictionalized book titled *Match Set* about a trans woman who helped fix tennis tournaments and participated in graphic sexual conduct. Geisler said she was defamed because she was an "upstanding individual" and the mother of two children.[94]

---

[90] Liquori v. Republican Co., 396 N.E.2d 726 (Mass. App. Ct. 1979).
[91] Summerlin v. Washington Star Co., 7 Media L. Rep. 2460 (D.D.C. 1981).
[92] Eyal v. Helen Broadcasting Corp., 583 N.E.2d 228 (Mass. 1991).
[93] *E.g.*, Rodney Smolla, *The Law of Defamation* § 4.09[7][a], at 4–40 (1998).
[94] Geisler v. Petrocelli, 616 F.2d 636 (2d Cir. 1980).

GROUP LIBEL Because defamation is a matter of personal reputation, large groups—such as union members, doctors, Republicans, or Mexican Americans—cannot usually sue successfully for libel over comments made about their group. Individual members of large groups cannot successfully sue for such allegations as "all doctors are quacks" or "most politicians are corrupt." The courts consistently rule that people belonging to groups of more than 100 members cannot claim that defamatory comments about the group as a whole are "of and concerning" them individually.[95]

The Kentucky Supreme Court ruled that a Kentucky Fried Chicken outlet in Bowling Green, Kentucky, belonged to too large a group to be identified when Colonel Harland Sanders, the chain's original owner, criticized the food produced and served by the chain. The Bowling Green outlet sued Sanders for telling the *Louisville Courier-Journal* that the gravy the chain served was a combination of "wallpaper paste" and "sludge" and the crispy recipe was "nothing in the world but a damn fried doughball stuck on some chicken." The court said that nothing in the article identified the Bowling Green restaurant from the more than 5,000 Kentucky Fried Chicken outlets around the world. A reference to all did not identify one.[96]

The smaller the group, the more likely it is that every individual in it might be able to sue. Courts have suggested that defamatory language aimed at groups of fewer than 15 people may be "of or concerning" each of the individuals in the group. A Michigan appellate court said that two officers of a union local could sue the *Detroit News* for accusing the local union leadership of being "thieves," "thugs" and "union hoods." The court allowed the president and secretary-treasurer of the local to sue for libel because the reference was to a group of seven leaders, "whose identities are readily ascertainable from the content of the article."[97]

However, members of even relatively small groups may fail to establish they were identified if defamation does not slur the whole group. For example, a federal court dismissed a libel lawsuit by three brothers of the Phi Kappa Psi fraternity at the University of Virginia, who had argued that rape allegations made in a *Rolling Stone* article and podcast were "of and concerning" them because they implied that rape was part of an "initiation ritual" at the fraternity. The court found that the reporter was merely speculating about the sexual assault claim, which ultimately turned out to be made up. Two members of the fraternity were able to establish that the report was "of and concerning" them because the article and connected podcast referred to them with more detail, one by the location of his bedroom in the fraternity house and the other by his status as rush chair. But the court said another fraternity member was not identified merely by being a member of the graduating class and occasionally riding a bicycle on campus, as referenced in the article.[98] The fraternity itself, as an organization, settled its lawsuit against *Rolling Stone* for $1.65 million in 2017.[99]

■ SUMMARY ■

Libel plaintiffs must demonstrate that defamatory language refers to them individually. Many suits result from inaccurate identification. People who can show they can

[95] *Restatement (Second) of Torts* § 564A; W. Page Keeton et al., *Prosser and Keeton on the Law of Torts* § 111, at 784 (5th ed. 1984).

[96] Kentucky Fried Chicken, Inc. v. Sanders, 563 S.W.2d 8 (1978).

[97] Lins v. Evening News Ass'n, 342 N.W.2d 573 (Mich. Ct. App. 1983).

[98] Elias v. Rolling Stone, 872 F.3d 97 (2d Cir. 2016).

[99] Sydney Ember, "Rolling Stone to Settle Suit Over Article Citing Rape," *N.Y. Times*, June 13, 2017, B4.

be recognized as characters in defamatory works of fiction may be able to successfully sue for libel. Communicators should be careful that libelous language about a group will not be considered to identify any single individual. Defamation of groups larger than 100 people is reasonably safe. However, individuals may be able to sue successfully for defamatory language pertaining to all members of groups of fewer than 100. For groups of fewer than 100, restrictive phrases such as "a few of" or "a couple of" can sometimes thwart individuals' claims that they were identified. Any member of a small group of 15 or fewer might claim identification in stories defaming members of the group.

Publication

Libel plaintiffs, in addition to proving that defamatory language identifies them, must prove that the libel is communicated to someone beyond the defamed. The *publication* of defamation, in the legal sense, requires at least three persons—the person uttering or publishing the defamation, the person being defamed and a person hearing or seeing the defamation. A third person must be exposed to the defamation before the person defamed can suffer damage to reputation.

Newspapers and magazines *publish* when they circulate one copy of one issue. Radio and television stations publish when they air a broadcast. Bloggers publish when they hit the send key. A libel plaintiff is not required to prove that subscribers or viewers heard or read a defamatory publication; courts assume publications and broadcast signals reach an audience.[100]

Libel can be *published* not only in newspapers and broadcasts but also in press releases, interoffice memos, conversations, interviews, business letters, blogs and websites. A defamation lawsuit against musician Courtney Love from a fashion designer she called a "nasty lying hosebag thief" and a "drug-pushing prostitute" in 2011 was the first celebrity case involving Twitter, and the platform has been the subject of several lawsuits since, with some commentators calling such cases "Twibel."[101]

Communicators are usually liable for repeating, or *republishing*, defamation if the defamation does not have an official government source. Plaintiffs are not restricted to suing the first person to utter or write a libelous comment; they can also sue anyone—including the media—who disseminates the libel. As several courts have noted in the context of defamation, "Tale-bearers are as bad as tale-makers."[102] A citizen who accuses a doctor of malpractice can be sued for libel, but so can the reporter who quotes the accusation in a news story, the editors who review the copy and the newspaper's publisher. Similarly, a reader who is libeled in a letter to the editor can sue the editor and publisher of the newspaper as well as the author of the letter.[103] Persons responsible for the republication of defamation are liable even if they properly attribute stories or indicate they are "only publishing a rumor."[104]

In the United States, Twitter users are liable for their defamatory tweets, but Twitter and other Internet service providers are not liable for defamatory posts on

---

[100] *See Restatement (Second) of Torts* § 559 comment e; Hornby v. Hunter, 385 S.W.2d 473 (Tex. Civ. App. 1964).

[101] Ellyn M. Angelotti, "Twibel Law: What Defamation and Its Remedies Look Like in the Age of Twitter," 13 *J. High Tech. L.* 433 (2013).

[102] *E.g.*, Harris v. Minvielle, 19 So. 925 (La. 1896).

[103] *See, e.g.*, W. Page Keeton et al., *Prosser and Keeton on the Law of Torts* § 113, at 799 (5th ed. 1984); Weaver v. Pryor Jeffersonian, 569 P.2d 967 (Okla. 1977).

[104] *Restatement (Second) of Torts* § 578 comments a, b; W. Page Keeton et al., *Prosser and Keeton on the Law of Torts* § 113, at 799 (5th ed. 1984).

their sites because of Section 230 of the Communications Decency Act of 1996, discussed later. In England, up to 10,000 Twitter users were potential defendants after tweeting and retweeting false allegations of child molestation contained in a BBC news report. The BBC report mistakenly accused former Conservative official Alistair McAlpine of child molestation. The BBC settled McAlpine's lawsuit for £185,000 (about $300,000). McAlpine dropped suits against tweeters with fewer than 500 followers in return for modest contributions to a BBC children's charity, but McAlpine continued a libel suit against a prominent politician's wife who allegedly tweeted false statements to 56,000 followers.[105] Liability for retweets as a kind of republication was possible in the United Kingdom, whereas in the United States, users of social media platforms who share posts via retweet are shielded from liability by Section 230.[106]

Publishing companies and broadcasters are responsible for libel because their employees select, write, edit and distribute information to the public. With the publishers' control of content comes liability for defamation. Thus, **common carriers**, such as telephone companies and some microwave system operators, are not responsible for libelous messages because they typically exercise no control over the information they transmit. Common carriers simply carry the messages of others, unedited, for a fee. Owners of bookstores, too, have been absolved of liability for defamatory and obscene materials that the store owners have no reason to know are contained in the books they sell.[107] Bookstore owners are not publishers who control the content of their offerings, and asking owners to review each book for libel would unconstitutionally hinder the flow of information.

ONLINE PUBLISHERS Under American law, operators of online platforms and discussion groups, like common carriers and bookstore operators, are not considered to be publishers responsible for libel posted to their electronic information services. Even if an electronic service provider attempts to screen libelous and obscene messages from the service, the system operator is not liable for defamatory and offensive postings on the system. In Section 230 of the Communications Decency Act of 1996, Congress established, "No provider or user of an interactive computer service shall be treated as the publisher or speaker of any information provided by another information content provider."[108] Because of the cushion Section 230 gave to online companies to avoid liability for the acts of users in the early days of the Web, "foster[ing] the innovation and freedom that has allowed an industry to grow and thrive for more than two decades," U.S. Naval Academy cybersecurity professor Jeff Kosseff calls Section 230 "The Twenty-Six Words That Created the Internet."[109]

Section 230 was intended to overturn a New York court ruling that made electronic service operators liable for defamation if they, like a publisher, attempted to control the content of their system.[110] Shortly after Section 230 was passed, a federal appeals panel used it to bar a libel suit against an Internet service provider over third-party postings, even if the service provider is notified that libelous material has been posted. In the case, Kenneth Zeran sued America Online (AOL) over anonymous Internet advertisements for T-shirts, advertisements linking Zeran to

---

[105] Josh Halliday, "Lord McAlpine Drops Some Twitter Defamation Cases," *The Guardian*, Feb. 21, 2013.
[106] Daxton R. Stewart, "When Retweets Attack: Are Twitter Users Liable for Republishing the Defamatory Tweets of Others?" 90 *Journalism & Mass Comm. Q.* 233 (2013).
[107] *E.g.*, Smith v. California, 361 U.S. 147 (1959).
[108] 47 U.S.C. § 230.
[109] Jeff Kosseff, *The Twenty-Six Words That Created the Internet* 7 (2019).
[110] Peter Lewis, "Judge Allows Libel Lawsuit Against Prodigy to Proceed," *N.Y. Times*, May 26, 1995, at D4.

offensive messages about the bombing of the Alfred P. Murrah Federal Building in Oklahoma City.[111] One advertisement said, "Visit Oklahoma . . . It's a BLAST!!!" Another proclaimed, "McVeigh for President 1996." Readers were invited to call "Ken" at Kenneth Zeran's phone number in Seattle. Zeran, a commercial publisher with no connection to the Oklahoma City bombings, tried to sue AOL for negligently allowing libelous material to appear on its bulletin board, even after Zeran asked that it be removed. Zeran received many abusive phone calls after AOL disseminated the bogus advertisements.

Ruling for AOL, the federal court said the Telecommunications Act of 1996 exempts Internet providers from liability when third parties post libelous electronic messages. Freedom of expression would be chilled, the court said, if online service providers were saddled with the "staggering" task of reviewing the millions of interactive messages disseminated daily on their electronic networks. An equally impossible burden would be placed on electronic service providers if they were held responsible for removing libelous messages after being "notified" of their presence, the court concluded. "In light of the vast amount of speech communicated through interactive computer services," the court said, "these notices could produce an impossible burden for service providers, who would be faced with ceaseless choices of suppressing controversial speech or sustaining prohibitive liability."

Courts have established Section 230 as a strong shield against liability for online services and social media platforms in libel cases, ruling consistently that such Internet service providers are not responsible for the acts of their users. Self-described celebrity "asshole" Tucker Max, who hosted a message board on his website, was found to be protected against a libel lawsuit by blueberry fortune heir Anthony DiMeo, who complained that the commenters on the message board had disparaged him and his disastrous New Year's Eve party, which was short on food and alcohol and devolved into what the judge described as the "party from hell."[112] A schoolteacher and Cincinnati Bengals cheerleader also found herself unable to receive damages after anonymous commenters known as "The Dirty Army" posted on the website TheDirty.com that she "slept with every other Bengal football player" and likely had chlamydia and gonorrhea. The site's operator, Nik Richie, had engaged in the comments section as well, and a jury awarded the woman $338,000 in damages for libel against Richie and his site. But a federal appeals court struck down the verdict, ruling that Section 230 shielded Richie and the site from the acts of the anonymous commenters, regardless of the fact that Richie encouraged the behavior, because it fell short of being what the court described as "material contribution" to the libelous comments.[113]

This does not mean that social media posts will be entirely immune from liability, even if they are based in the original post. If the post is made and adds new information, that may amount to a separate publication. For example, in 2018, a woman spoke at a city council meeting in California opposing sanctuary city laws aimed at protecting immigrants, and a photo of the woman "with an open mouth in front of a minority teenager" was posted on Twitter, with a caption saying she "yelled specific racist remarks at the young man in the photo." This turned out not to be true; both the woman and the teenager said they were having a civil discussion. Cable news host Joy Reid retweeted the photo, an act that was protected from defamation claims by Section 230. However, she later posted the photo on a

---

[111] Zeran v. America Online, Inc., 129 F.3d 327 (4th Cir. 1997), *cert. denied*, 524 U.S. 937 (1998).
[112] DiMeo v. Max, 433 F. Supp. 2d 523 (E.D. Pa. 2006).
[113] Jones v. Dirty World Entertainment Recordings, 755 F.3d 398 (6th Cir. 2014).

separate social media platform, Instagram, and repeated the claim that the woman was shouting racist comments at the teenager. A federal appeals court allowed the libel suit to proceed against Reid in 2020, saying that she was the "sole author" of the Instagram post, and not merely a non-material contributor sharing someone else's post.[114]

While Section 230's broad shield against liability has allowed anonymous gossip sites and apps such as The Dirty and YikYak to survive, at least temporarily,[115] it has also provided freedom for online developers and companies such as Google and Facebook to grow without the threat of constant litigation. For example, courts have found that Google is not responsible for reputational damage caused by search engine results,[116] nor is the customer review site Yelp liable for the critical posts of its users.[117]

As tech companies have grown in power and influence, Section 230 has faced increasing scrutiny from politicians and critics across the political spectrum, to the point that both the Democratic and Republican candidates for president called for the law to be repealed in their 2020 campaigns. Eighteen bills were filed in 2020 to repeal or massively reform Section 230, and another 18 were introduced in 2021, though none seemed close to passage due to deep divides on the goals of repeal or reform. If passed, any of the bills would face significant First Amendment challenges. Free speech and free press protections extend to online companies such as Facebook, Google and Amazon, who have discretion as private actors to determine what content they will (and will not) host on their platforms. Efforts by state legislatures to curb Section 230 protections have struggled to overcome the First Amendment, as federal courts halted laws passed in 2021 in both Texas and Florida that would have made online platforms liable for their content moderation decisions and aimed to prevent bans on politicians and speakers who violated their terms of service by spreading health misinformation or false information about the 2020 election that was associated with the January 6, 2021 mob assault on the U.S. Capitol.[118]

Through its first 25 years, Section 230 remained largely untouched as a strong shield for online content hosts—whether a newspaper allowing comments section under a story, a citizen inviting discussion on a blog, or a social media platform enabling users to post and comment. Entering 2022, the law had been consistently applied as a way to protect online hosts, treating them more as distributors (such as bookstores or newsstands) than publishers of the content their users created and shared on their platforms. However, legislators and even some jurists have signaled that reconsideration of what has been a bedrock of online law in the United States may be coming. Concurring in a decision dismissing an effort to prevent former president Trump from blocking followers on Twitter, Justice Thomas decried the First Amendment implications of the "concentrated control of so much speech in the hands of a few private parties" and suggested that tech platforms such as Twitter may be properly treated as common carriers or places of public accommodation, reasoning that such an interpretation might open the door for legislators to place more restrictions or burdens on those platforms.[119] Such efforts have already

---

[114] La Liberte v. Reid, 966 F.3d 79 (2nd Cir. 2020).

[115] Jonathan Mahler, "Who Spewed That Abuse? Yik Yak Isn't Telling," *N.Y. Times*, Mar. 9, 2015, A1.

[116] Manchanda v. Google, Inc., 2016 U.S. Dist. LEXIS 158458 (S.D.N.Y. 2016).

[117] Kimzey v. Yelp!, Inc., 836 F.3d 1263 (9th Cir. 2016).

[118] *See* NetChoice v. Moody, No. 21-12355 (11th Cir., May 23, 2022); NetChoice v. Paxton, 1:21-CV-840-RP (W.D. Texas, Dec. 2, 2021).

[119] Biden v. Knight First Amendment Institute, 141 S. Ct. 1220 (2021) (J. Thomas, concurring).

been made in other countries that allow lawsuits against tech companies for the content they host. Australia's High Court, for example, ruled in 2021 that online hosts could be liable for content posted by users, a decision that led CNN to block Australians from their Facebook pages and several public officials to disable comments on their Facebook pages as well.[120]

When U.S. courts have made exceptions to Section 230, they have typically involved federal regulations, product liability and commercial transactions, which are discussed in more detail in Chapter 8.

FOREIGN JURISDICTIONS Foreign courts—particularly British courts—sometimes hold American journalists and authors liable for publishing defamation even though the same publication would not be punishable in the United States. At one point, London was known as the "libel capital of the world" because celebrities and the wealthy frequently filed there because libel suits are difficult to defend in the United Kingdom. Khalid bin Mahfouz, a deceased Saudi billionaire, received large settlements and apologies from publishers in several of the more than 24 libel suits he filed in Britain, where the defendant has the burden to prove the truth when defamation is charged.[121]

To combat "libel tourism," President Obama in 2010 signed the SPEECH Act, a law that prohibits federal courts from enforcing foreign libel judgments that the First Amendment would not allow in U.S. courts, including judgments that do not require public officials or public figures to prove actual malice as an element of their libel claims.[122] This is important because most countries around the world have rejected the stricter fault requirements of U.S. defamation law, including Canada, England, France, Germany and Australia. Countries that have adopted actual malice requirements for public figures include the Philippines, Argentina, Taiwan and Hungary.[123]

Libel tourism laws include "Rachel's law," a New York statute adopted to protect Rachel Ehrenfeld from enforcement of a £110,000 British libel judgment for her book on Bin Mahfouz, even though the book was not sold or distributed in England. Decisions of this kind led to calls for reform and, ultimately, enactment of England's Defamation Act 2013, which makes plaintiffs establish that England is the most appropriate venue for the case and requires proof of serious financial loss or reputational damage.[124]

■ SUMMARY ■

Publication, one element of the burden of proof for libel plaintiffs, means that defamation is communicated to a third party. Anyone participating in the process of publishing defamation may be liable. A republication of a libel is a new libel. Although print companies and broadcasters, who control the content of their media, are publishers responsible for libel, common carriers and bookstore owners are not. Operators of interactive computer services, like common carriers, do

---

[120] Byron Kaye, "CNN Denies Australians Access to Its Facebook," *Reuters*, Sept. 29, 2021.
[121] Mark Sweney, "Surge in 'Libel Tourism' Brings 11% Rise in Cases," *Guardian.co.uk*, Nov. 20, 2009; Dennis Cummings, "Congress Looks to End 'Libel' Tourism," *Finding Dulcinea*, Oct. 9, 2008.
[122] Securing the Protection of Our Enduring and Established Constitutional Heritage Act, 28 U.S.C. §§ 4101–4105.
[123] Kyu Ho Youm, "The 'Actual Malice' of New York Times Co. v. Sullivan: A Free Speech Touchstone in a Global Century," 19 *Comm. Law & Policy* 185 (2014).
[124] Ari Shapiro, "On Libel and the Law, U.S. And U.K. Go Separate Ways," *NPR*, Mar. 21, 2015; Sarah Lyall, "Libel Cases Now Harder to Bring in England," *N.Y. Times*, Apr. 26, 2013, at A4.

not assume the responsibility of publishers for obscene, defamatory and otherwise objectionable postings by third parties on their electronic services.

Fault

A libel plaintiff proving defamation, identification and publication also must prove that a medium erred in the preparation of a story. The U.S. Supreme Court has said that the First Amendment bars plaintiffs from collecting damages for loss of reputation unless they can show that defendants published or broadcast with **fault**, usually **negligence** for private plaintiffs and recklessness for public officials and figures. The Court revolutionized libel law in the United States by providing consti- tutional protection for false, defamatory statements when the journalist's error does not rise—or sink—to the level of negligence or recklessness. The degree of the journalist's fault is the central issue in many libel suits.[125]

The degree of fault that a plaintiff must prove depends on who is suing. Public officials and public figures have the heavy burden of establishing that the media published defamation knowing that their story was false or that they reck- lessly disregarded the truth. The burden of proof for private persons suing for libel depends on state law. Most states require that private persons prove the publisher acted negligently, which is much easier to prove than proving knowing falsehood or reckless disregard for the truth.

In 1964, the U.S. Supreme Court declared unconstitutional the common law of strict liability—that is, responsibility regardless of the intent of the publisher— when the media defame a public official. In *New York Times v. Sullivan*, the Court "constitutionalized" libel law by ruling that the robust political debate necessary in a democracy is inadequately protected by a common law that failed to require public officials to prove that defamation was false and published with fault. Indeed, the Court said some false statements must be protected by the First Amendment in political debate if freedom of expression is to have the "breathing space" needed to flourish.[126] The large jury awards often accompanying libel judgments in the common-law regime of strict liability inhibited press freedom, the Court said, just as physical punishments inhibited freedom under the English and colonial criminal law of seditious libel.

SEDITIOUS LIBEL IN THE UNITED STATES During the formative years of the United States, the country relied substantially on English common law. In England during the seventeenth and eighteenth centuries, criticism of government officials—always proclaimed by the officials to be false, scandalous and malicious— was called **seditious libel**. A person convicted of seditious libel could be fined, imprisoned, pilloried and whipped. The government said seditious libel should be punished to prevent public unrest—a breach of the peace—that criticism of govern- ment would often provoke. Truth was no defense to seditious libel charges because true criticism, officials said, was more likely to provoke violence than false state- ments. The legal adage "the greater the truth, the greater the libel" was accurate at a time when the criminal law of seditious libel was designed to prevent breaches of the peace. Moreover, judges decided the legal question of whether expression was

---

[125] *See* John Soloski, "The Study and the Libel Plaintiff: Who Sues for Libel," 71 *Iowa L. Rev.* 217, 218 (1985); Randall Bezanson, "Libel Law and Realities of Litigation: Setting the Record Straight," 71 *Iowa L. Rev.* 226, 229–31 (1985).
[126] 376 U.S. 254 (1964).

"By no means," exclaimed Hamilton, in his clear, thrilling, silvery voice. "It is not the bare, printing and publishing of a paper that will make it a libel; the words themselves must be libelous, that is, false, scandalous, and seditious, else my client is not guilty." (Page 553)

FIGURE 4.1   A scene from the seditious libel trial of John Peter Zenger in 1735.

seditious. The members of the public sitting on the jury could determine only the fact of whether the accused printed or said the words as charged.[127]

In a famous case, a colonial jury in New York rebelled against the common law of seditious libel. In 1735, the jury found the now-legendary printer John Peter Zenger, publisher of the *New York Weekly Journal,* not guilty of seditious libel even though he had printed stories of New York Governor William Cosby's high-handed land deals and manipulation of the courts. Zenger's lawyer, Andrew Hamilton, conceded that Zenger had published the remarks critical of Cosby, thereby conceding the only fact the jury could legally determine. However, the jury, affirming a citizen's right to truthfully criticize public officials, returned a verdict of not guilty. The judge could have overturned the jury verdict but chose not to.

The Zenger verdict, as welcome as it was to advocates of unfettered political expression, did not change the law. Zenger was acquitted in spite of the law. When the Bill of Rights was adopted in 1791, decades after the Zenger trial, critics of government could still be jailed and fined for truthful statements ruled to constitute seditious libel. Even when the First Amendment was adopted, truth was not a defense in libel cases, and juries were still limited to determining whether the defamation had been published as charged.

In fact, seven years after the Bill of Rights was ratified, Congress passed a seditious libel statute. Despite the First Amendment, Federalists in Congress adopted the Alien and Sedition Acts in 1798 to punish their Republican critics, led by Thomas Jefferson. The Federalists were afraid that the Republicans would destroy the young American republic by fostering the radical ideas that had led to the French Revolution. The Alien Act allowed the president to deport anyone not

---

[127] Leonard Levy, *Emergence of a Free Press* 9 (1985).

born in the United States who was "dangerous to the peace" or suspected of "secret machinations against the government." The Sedition Act prohibited any conspiracy to oppose the government and "any false, scandalous and malicious writing" against the government or government officials. Violators could be punished by fines of up to $2,000 and jail terms for as long as two years.[128]

Ironically, the Sedition Act did bring reform. The Sedition Act permitted the defense of truth and accorded juries the power to determine, as a matter of law, whether publications were seditious. But these reforms meant little because juries were dominated by Federalists. In addition, literal Federalist judges required the accused to prove the truth "to the marrow"—documenting every word of every statement. Critical opinions that could not be proven true were judged false.

The Federalists prosecuted more than a dozen people under the Sedition Act, including newspaper editors and writers in Boston, Philadelphia and Richmond. Congressman Matthew Lyon was fined $1,000 and sentenced to four months in jail after he wrote for the *Vermont Journal* that President Adams was continually grasping for power and possessed "an unbounded thirst for ridiculous pomp, foolish adulation, and selfish avarice."[129] Individual Supreme Court justices sat on circuit courts that prosecuted government critics under the act.

The Federalists shrewdly wrote the Alien and Sedition Acts so that the laws could not be used against them. In today's terminology, the Alien and Sedition Acts were written with a sunset clause. The acts expired at the end of Federalist President John Adams's term. This was a precaution in case the Federalists lost the election of 1800—which they did, to Thomas Jefferson and the Republicans. Jefferson did not renew the acts when the Republicans took office in 1801.

The Republicans argued that the Alien and Sedition Acts violated the First Amendment because they punished criticism of government. However, historian Leonard Levy contended that the statutes reflected the conventional understanding of the term *freedom of the press* at the time. Levy argued that most politicians in the late eighteenth century believed in freedom of expression as it was defined by famed English legal commentator William Blackstone. Blackstone said liberty of the press meant only freedom from prior restraint on publication and not freedom from punishment for publishing words that were "improper, mischievous, or illegal."[130]

Levy contended that prosecutions under the Alien and Sedition Acts helped to sensitize Americans to the dangers of punishing criticism of government and government officials. Republican theorists argued fiercely that freedom of expression was hollow unless criticism of government—including false statements—was tolerated, and their message seems to have been heard.[131] In 1812, the Supreme Court terminated the federal common law of seditious libel.[132] In 1840, Congress repaid fines levied under the Sedition Act on the grounds that the law was unconstitutional.[133] Prosecutions for seditious libel under state statutes became less frequent, and the courts declared that the government itself could not be libeled; only individuals within a government might pursue a defamation suit. The constitutionality of the Sedition Act of 1798 was never tested before the Supreme Court, but in 1964 the Supreme Court stated in *New York Times v. Sullivan* that the Sedition Act of 1798 had been unconstitutional.

---

[128] James Morton Smith, *Freedom's Fetters* 321, 438–42 (1956).

[129] *Id.* at 226, 235, 421–2.

[130] William Blackstone, *Commentaries on the Laws of England*, London, 1765–9, book 4, 151–2. *See generally* Leonard Levy, *Emergence of a Free Press* (1985).

[131] Leonard Levy, "Liberty and the First Amendment: 1790–1800," 68 *Am. Hist. Rev.* 29 (1962).

[132] United States v. Hudson & Goodwin, 11 U.S. (7 Cranch) 32 (1812).

[133] *See* N.Y. Times Co. v. Sullivan, 376 U.S. 254, 276 (1964).

CONSTITUTIONAL PROTECTION FOR LIBEL ABOUT PUBLIC OFFICIALS In *New York Times v. Sullivan*, the Supreme Court said for the first time that the First Amendment protects criticism of government officials even if the remarks are false and defamatory. The Court said that public officials cannot successfully sue for libel unless they establish that defamation has been published with **actual malice**: knowing falsity or reckless disregard for the truth. This burden of proof for public officials has come to be known as *New York Times* actual malice. The new constitutional protection for criticism of public officials announced in *New York Times v. Sullivan* effectively ended the law of seditious libel in the 50 states.

Breathing Space for Falsity The case that provided the media with constitutional protection for the criticism of public officials was a product of the civil rights struggle in the South in the early 1960s. L.B. Sullivan, a police official in Montgomery, Alabama, sued the *New York Times* for publishing a March 29, 1960, advertisement purchased by a committee of civil rights activists, including the well-known labor leader A. Philip Randolph. The full-page ad, titled "Heed Their Rising Voices," said that "thousands of Southern Negro students are engaged in widespread nonviolent demonstrations" affirming "the right to live in human dignity." The efforts were being met, the ad said, "by an unprecedented wave of terror." The ad purported to document the "wave of terror" and sought support for the civil rights movement in the South and for its leader, Dr. Martin Luther King, Jr. (see ad, Figure 4.2).

The ad contained several false statements, some of them minor inaccuracies. Nine student leaders were not expelled for singing at the state capitol, as the ad stated. The students were expelled for demanding service at a Montgomery courthouse lunch counter. Contrary to statements in the ad, the dining hall at the Alabama State College campus had not been padlocked, and there was no attempt "to starve" students into "submission." The only students barred were those without tickets. The police, although deployed in large numbers, had not "ringed" the campus, as the advertisement claimed. Nor had King been arrested seven times, as the ad declared. King had been arrested four times. There was conflicting evidence about the ad's claim that King had been assaulted. The *New York Times* ad staff could have checked the accuracy of the ad against the *Times*' news stories of the same events, but the newspaper staff did not.

The Montgomery commissioner in charge of police, L.B. Sullivan, demanded that the *Times* publish a retraction. The paper refused, asking Sullivan why he believed the ad referred to him. Sullivan did not respond but sued the *Times* for $3 million along with three other Montgomery officials and the Alabama governor, John Patterson. At the trial, Sullivan argued the charges of police abuse in the advertisement defamed him—even though he was not named in the advertisement—because he supervised the police department. The Alabama judge trying the case instructed the jury that the ad was libelous on its face and that damage to reputation need not be proved.

The judge told the jury that it had to decide only that the statements were published in the *Times* and were "of and concerning" Sullivan. Under rules of strict liability in effect at that time, a newspaper was liable for defamation regardless of the intent of the publisher or the care the paper exercised publishing a libelous story. The jury awarded Sullivan $500,000, the largest libel judgment in Alabama to that time.[134] The judgment was upheld by the Supreme Court of Alabama. This

---

[134] Anthony Lewis, "Annals of Law: The Sullivan Case," *New Yorker*, Nov. 5, 1984, at 52, 55.

"*The growing movement of peaceful mass demonstrations by Negroes is something new in the South, something understandable.... Let Congress heed their rising voices, for they will be heard.*"

—*New York Times editorial*
Saturday, March 19, 1960

Heed Their Rising Voices

As the whole world knows by now, thousands of Southern Negro students are engaged in wide-spread non-violent demonstrations in positive affirmation of the right to live in human dignity as guaranteed by the U. S. Constitution and the Bill of Rights. In their efforts to uphold these guarantees, they are being met by an unprecedented wave of terror by those who would deny and negate that document which the whole world looks upon as setting the pattern for modern freedom....

In Orangeburg, South Carolina, when 400 students peacefully sought to buy doughnuts and coffee at lunch counters in the business district, they were forcibly ejected, tear-gassed, soaked to the skin in freezing weather with fire hoses, arrested en masse and herded into an open barbed-wire stockade to stand for hours in the bitter cold.

In Montgomery, Alabama, after students sang "My Country, 'Tis of Thee" on the State Capitol steps, their leaders were expelled from school, and truck-loads of police armed with shotguns and tear-gas ringed the Alabama State College Campus. When the entire student body protested to state authorities by refusing to re-register, their dining hall was pad-locked in an attempt to starve them into submission.

In Tallahassee, Atlanta, Nashville, Savannah, Greensboro, Memphis, Richmond, Charlotte, and a host of other cities in the South, young American teen-agers, in face of the entire weight of official state apparatus and police power, have boldly stepped forth as protagonists of democracy. Their courage and amazing restraint have inspired millions and given a new dignity to the cause of freedom.

Small wonder that the Southern violators of the Constitution fear this new, non-violent brand of freedom fighter ... even as they fear the upswelling right-to-vote movement. Small wonder that they are determined to destroy the one man who, more than any other, symbolizes the new spirit now sweeping the South—the Rev. Dr. Martin Luther King, Jr., world-famous leader of the Montgomery Bus Protest. For it is his doctrine of non-violence which has inspired and guided the students in their widening wave of sit-ins; and it this same Dr. King who founded and is president of the Southern Christian Leadership Conference—the organization which is spearheading the surging right-to-vote movement. Under Dr. King's direction the Leadership Conference conducts Student Workshops and Seminars in the philosophy and technique of non-violent resistance.

Again and again the Southern violators have answered Dr. King's peaceful protests with intimidation and violence. They have bombed his home almost killing his wife and child. They have assaulted his person. They have arrested him seven times—for "speeding," "loitering" and similar "offenses." And now they have charged him with "perjury"—a *felony* under which they could imprison him for *ten years*. Obviously, their real purpose is to remove him physically as the leader to whom the students and millions

of others—look for guidance and support, and thereby to intimidate *all* leaders who may rise in the South. Their strategy is to behead this affirmative movement, and thus to demoralize Negro Americans and weaken their will to struggle. The defense of Martin Luther King, spiritual leader of the student sit-in movement, clearly, therefore, is an integral part of the total struggle for freedom in the South.

Decent-minded Americans cannot help but applaud the creative daring of the students and the quiet heroism of Dr. King. But this is one of those moments in the stormy history of Freedom when men and women of good will must do more than applaud the rising-to-glory of others. The America whose good name hangs in the balance before a watchful world, the America whose heritage of Liberty these Southern Upholders of the Constitution are defending, is *our* America as well as theirs ...

We must heed their rising voices—yes—but we must add our own.

We must extend ourselves above and beyond moral support and render the material help so urgently needed by those who are taking the risks, facing jail, and even death in a glorious re-affirmation of our Constitution and its Bill of Rights.

We urge you to join hands with our fellow Americans in the South by supporting, with your dollars, this Combined Appeal for all three needs—the defense of Martin Luther King—the support of the embattled students—and the struggle for the right-to-vote.

Your Help Is Urgently Needed . . . NOW !!

Stella Adler	Dr. Alan Knight Chalmers	Anthony Franciosa	John Killens	L. Joseph Overton	Maureen Stapleton
Raymond Pace Alexander	Richard Coe	Lorraine Hansbury	Eartha Kitt	Clarence Pickett	Frank Silvera
Harry Van Arsdale	Nat King Cole	Rev. Donald Harrington	Rabbi Edward Klein	Shad Polier	Hope Stevens
Harry Belafonte	Cheryl Crawford	Nat Hentoff	Hope Lange	Sidney Poitier	George Tabori
Julie Belafonte	Dorothy Dandridge	James Hicks	John Lewis	A. Philip Randolph	Rev. Gardner C. Taylor
Dr. Algernon Black	Ossie Davis	Mary Hinkson	Viveca Lindfors	John Raitt	
Marc Blitzstein	Sammy Davis, Jr.	Van Heflin	Carl Murphy	Elmer Rice	Norman Thomas
William Branch	Ruby Dee	Langston Hughes	Don Murray	Jackie Robinson	Kenneth Tynan
Marlon Brando	Dr. Philip Elliott	Morris Iushewitz	John Murray	Mrs. Eleanor Roosevelt	Charles White
Mrs. Ralph Bunche	Dr. Harry Emerson	Mahalia Jackson	A. J. Muste	Bayard Rustin	Shelley Winters
Diahann Carroll	Fosdick	Mordecai Johnson	Frederick O'Neal	Robert Ryan	Max Youngstein

We in the south who are struggling daily for dignity and freedom warmly endorse this appeal

Rev. Ralph D. Abernathy (Montgomery, Ala.)	Rev. Matthew D. McCollom (Orangeburg, S. C.)	Rev. Walter L. Hamilton (Norfolk, Va.)	Rev. A. L. Davis (New Orleans, La.)
Rev. Fred L. Shuttlesworth (Birmingham, Ala.)	Rev. William Holmes Borders (Atlanta, Ga.)	I. S. Levy (Columbia, S. C.)	Mrs. Katie E. Whickham (New Orleans, La.)
Rev. Kelley Miller Smith (Nashville, Tenn.)		Rev. Martin Luther King, Sr. (Atlanta, Ga.)	Rev. W. H. Hall (Hattiesburg, Miss.)
Rev. W. A. Dennis (Chattanooga, Tenn.)	Rev. Douglas Moore (Durham, N. C.)	Rev. Henry C. Bunton (Memphis, Tenn.)	Rev. J. E. Lowery (Mobile, Ala.)
Rev. C. K. Steele (Tallahassee, Fla.)	Rev. Wyatt Tee Walker (Petersburg, Va.)	Rev. S. S. Seay, Sr. (Montgomery, Ala.)	Rev. T. J. Jemison (Baton Rouge, La.)
		Rev. Samuel W. Williams (Atlanta, Ga.)	

COMMITTEE TO DEFEND MARTIN LUTHER KING AND THE STRUGGLE FOR FREEDOM IN THE SOUTH

312 West 125th Street, New York 27, N. Y. UNiversity 6-1700

Chairmen: A. Philip Randolph, Dr. Gardner C. Taylor; *Chairmen of Cultural Division:* Harry Belafonte, Sidney Poitier; *Treasurer:* Nat King Cole; *Executive Director:* Bayard Rustin; *Chairmen of Church Division:* Father George B. Ford, Rev. Harry Emerson Fosdick, Rev. Thomas Kilgore, Jr., Rabbi Edward E. Klein; *Chairman of Labor Division:* Morris Iushewitz

Please mail this coupon TODAY!

Committee To Defend Martin Luther King
and
The Struggle For Freedom In The South

312 West 125th Street, New York 27, N. Y.
UNiversity 6-1700

I am enclosing my contribution of $_____
for the work of the Committee.

Name _____
(PLEASE PRINT)

Address _____

City _____ Zone ___ State ____

☐ I want to help   ☐ Please send further information

Please make checks payable to:
Committee To Defend Martin Luther King

FIGURE 4.2 Advertisement published March 29, 1960, that led to the U.S. Supreme Court decision in *New York Times v. Sullivan*.

was a typical outcome in cases against news media reporting on civil rights matters and other instances of violence and oppression by white government officials and law enforcement officers against black citizens. They were early efforts of what we now recognize as strategic lawsuits against public participation (SLAPPs), which will be discussed later in this chapter. Libel law was being used and abused by Southern officials in a way that amounted to a modern version of sedition law, with "an object to proscribe and quash press coverage of the civil rights struggle," as detailed by legal scholar Aimee Edmondson, who wrote about dozens of such cases before the *Sullivan* case reached the Supreme Court.[135]

In *New York Times v. Sullivan*, the U.S. Supreme Court recognized this trend of public officials bringing lawsuits to harass and silence critics in the civil rights era. The Court voted unanimously to reverse the Alabama court. Justice William Brennan Jr., writing for the Supreme Court, said that Alabama's libel law, which presumed defamation to be both false and harmful to reputation, did not adequately safeguard freedom of speech and press as required by the First and the Fourteenth Amendments. Brennan said that at issue was "a profound national commitment to the principle that debate on public issues should be uninhibited, robust and wide-open, and that it may well include vehement, caustic and sometimes unpleasantly sharp attacks on government and public officials."

Brennan said that a civil libel suit brought by a public official such as Sullivan created the same kind of dangers to First Amendment freedoms as a seditious libel prosecution initiated by the government. He said "the court of history" had found that the Sedition Act of 1798, which had authorized punishment for criticism of government and public officials, was inconsistent with the First Amendment. He argued that the media's fear of large damage awards under civil libel laws such as the one in Alabama created greater "hazards to protected freedoms" than the criminal penalties of seditious libel laws. Brennan said First Amendment freedoms could not survive if a "pall of fear and timidity" was imposed on those who otherwise offer public criticism.

Brennan said a privilege to criticize official conduct was "appropriately analogous" to protection accorded a public official sued for libel by a private citizen. Private citizens cannot sue public officials for libelous statements uttered in their official capacity in a legislative chamber, in an executive statement, or from the bench. Officials speaking in an official capacity are immune from libel suits so that they are not inhibited from engaging in "fearless, vigorous, and effective administration." The "citizen-critic" who libels an official should have a similar immunity, Brennan said. "It is as much his duty to criticize as it is the official's duty to administer."

Brennan rejected Sullivan's argument that constitutional guarantees did not protect the *Times* because the defamation had occurred in an advertisement. Sullivan had cited the Supreme Court's 1942 decision in *Valentine v. Chrestensen*, in which the Court denied constitutional protection to a handbill it had called "purely commercial advertising."[136] In *Sullivan*, however, Brennan argued that the civil rights ad in the *Times* was not purely commercial speech. Although the ad had been purchased, it was political speech that "communicated information, expressed opinion, recited grievances and sought financial support" on behalf of a cause "of

---

[135] Aimee Edmondson, *In Sullivan's Shadow: The Use and Abuse of Libel Law During the Long Civil Rights Struggle* 5 (2019).
[136] *See* 316 U.S. 52 (1942).

the highest public concern." Brennan said the fact that the *Times* was paid for the ad was as immaterial as the fact that books and newspapers are sold. He added:

> Any other conclusion would discourage newspapers from carrying "editorial advertisements" of this type, and so might shut off an important outlet for the promulgation of information and ideas by persons who do not themselves have access to publishing facilities.

Brennan also rejected the argument that falsehoods cannot be protected by the First Amendment. He said constitutional protection did not depend on the "truth, popularity, or social utility" of the ideas and beliefs expressed. The national commitment to the free expression of political beliefs presumed exaggeration and error. Indeed, truth for one person could be error for another, Brennan said. If critics of public officials could be penalized for false statements, Brennan said, they would tend to avoid controversy:

> A rule compelling the critic of official conduct to guarantee the truth of all of his factual assertions—and to do so on pain of libel judgments virtually unlimited in amount—leads to a comparable "self-censorship."

Brennan said potential critics of government could be "chilled" from even speaking the truth for fear of the expense and uncertainty of a libel trial.

Because a requirement that defendants prove the truth of their remarks "dampens the vigor and limits the variety of public debate," the Supreme Court established a new constitutional rule to provide better protection for the criticism of public officials. No longer would courts, such as those in Alabama, be able to presume the falsity of defamation and require the defendant to prove the truth, often a very difficult task. Instead, the Court said that plaintiffs—public officials—must shoulder the heavy responsibility of proving published statements about them are false and defamatory. Not only that, but public officials must also prove that libelous statements about their official conduct were published with "actual malice." To prove *New York Times* actual malice, an official has to establish that a defendant published the statement either (1) knowing it was false or (2) exercising reckless disregard for the truth.

The Court ruled the ad in the *Times* had not been published with actual malice. The Court said the fact that stories contradicting the ad existed in the *Times*' own files did not mean that employees responsible for the ad knew it was false. Brennan said a statement by a *Times* employee that he thought the advertisement was "substantially correct" was reasonable and suggested the employee did not know the ad was false. The *Times*' failure to check the ad against the news stories might be evidence of negligence, the Court said, but it did not demonstrate recklessness. The Court was also satisfied with the *Times*' reliance for the accuracy of the advertisement on the good reputation of those listed as sponsors of the ad, particularly Randolph, the chair of the "committee" submitting the ad. Furthermore, the Court said the *Times*' failure to retract the errors in the ad was not evidence of actual malice. The *Times* reasonably responded to Sullivan's request for a retraction by asking him why he believed the ad referred to him, the Court said. The *Times*' unacknowledged letter to Sullivan did not constitute a final refusal to retract.

Although the Supreme Court ruled the *New York Times* was not liable for the civil rights ad, the *Sullivan* opinion left many unanswered questions about the new constitutional protection for libel. For example, who would be considered a public official? What kind of conduct constituted *New York Times* actual malice? Would anyone besides public officials have to prove *New York Times* actual malice to win a libel suit?

Defining Public Officials The Sullivan Court said that public officials would have to prove actual malice to collect damages for defamation relating to their official conduct, but the Court did not define *public official* or *official conduct*. The Court said only that Sullivan was a public official because he was an elected commissioner, and the allegations in the ad related to his conduct as the commissioner in charge of the police department.

Since *Sullivan*, courts have ruled that public officials include persons elected to public office and nonelected government employees who play major roles in the development of public policy. Public officials include federal and state legislators, mayors, town council members, school board members and elected judges.[137] In addition, courts have said that nonelected government employees responsible for public policy are public officials. Shortly after *New York Times v. Sullivan*, the Supreme Court declared that a former supervisor of a county-owned ski resort might be a public official. In that case, *Rosenblatt v. Baer*, the Court said the decision in *New York Times v. Sullivan* was motivated by "a strong interest in debate" about public issues and the people in positions to significantly influence the resolution of those issues. Therefore, the Court said, public officials are government employees "who have, or appear to the public to have, substantial responsibility for or control over the conduct of governmental affairs."[138] It is not necessary that officials exercise great power or possess a lofty title. Rosenblatt was only the supervisor of a ski resort, but the Court said he might be a public official if his position "would invite public scrutiny and discussion of the person holding it."

Lower courts have ruled that persons supervising public funds and maintaining the public health and welfare are public officials. The likelihood of being designated a public official increases as an employee's contact with the public and authority to make governmental decisions increase. Among public employees designated public officials are a school superintendent, a town tax assessor, an administrator of a county motor pool, a county medical examiner, a director of financial aid at a state college, a director of an antipoverty agency and various military officers. Paid consultants, police informants and the director of a university print shop were ruled not to be public officials because they lacked influence over public policy.[139]

The courts' criteria indicate that the head of a city public works department would be considered a public official because of the position's inherent responsibility for public policy, public safety and public funds. An auditor might be a public official. An auditor is usually not responsible for public policy but does play a key role in the government's use of public funds. Receptionists and janitors are generally not public officials. They exercise little if any control over public policy and do not, in their government jobs, play an important role in the debate of public issues.

Law enforcement personnel, regardless of rank, are ordinarily considered public officials. The courts have said that a police chief, a deputy sheriff and a federal drug enforcement agent are public officials. Frequently, police officers without rank, "the cops on the beat," are also categorized as public officials. The courts are conscious of the frequent contact the police have with the public, their authority

---

[137] Bruce Sanford, *Libel and Privacy* § 7.2.3.1, at 264–7 (2nd ed. 1999).
[138] Rosenblatt v. Baer, 383 U.S. 85.
[139] *See* Bruce Sanford, *Libel and Privacy* § 7.2.2.2, at 260–4 (2nd ed. 1999).

and their ability to exercise force. That force "can result in significant deprivation of constitutional rights and personal freedoms, not to mention bodily injury and financial loss."[140]

Public officials are required to prove *New York Times* actual malice only for defamatory statements about their official conduct, not for statements about their private lives. However, the Supreme Court has interpreted official conduct broadly. In *Garrison v. Louisiana*, the Court said that an assertion that judges were lazy, "vacation-minded" and sympathetic to criminals was a comment about their official conduct. The Court unanimously reversed the Louisiana Supreme Court's determination in a criminal libel case that Jim Garrison, the district attorney for New Orleans Parish, had attacked the judges' private reputations rather than their official or public reputations. Writing for the Supreme Court, Justice Brennan conceded that accusing the judges of dishonesty, malfeasance and improper motivation affected their private as well as public reputations. But, Justice Brennan said, the *New York Times* rule protects the free flow of criticism about the public conduct of an official even if the criticism hurts an official's private as well as public reputation. Indeed, Brennan said, the *New York Times* rule is so broad that it protects any statements "which might touch on an official's fitness for office." Brennan said few personal attributes were more germane to an official's fitness for office "than dishonesty, malfeasance, or improper motivation."[141]

A few years later, the Court said that any accusation that a public official had committed a crime was related to the person's fitness for office. The Court ruled that Leonard Damron, the mayor of Crystal River, Florida, had to prove actual malice to win a suit he had filed against the Ocala Star-Banner Company over a false report in the *Star-Banner* that Damron had been charged with perjury.[142] The courts have routinely held that discussions of the official conduct of former public officials is protected under the *New York Times v. Sullivan* rule.

■ SUMMARY ■

In *New York Times v. Sullivan*, the U.S. Supreme Court ruled for the first time that the First Amendment protects the publication of false statements that may damage an official's reputation. The Court said that public officials suing the media for statements about their official conduct must prove that defamation was published with knowing falsehood or reckless disregard for the truth. The Court said that such a heavy burden of proof on public officials was necessary to protect a robust debate on public issues. *New York Times v. Sullivan* eliminated state common law holding that officials could win libel suits by showing only that the media had disseminated defamatory information about them. After *New York Times v. Sullivan*, courts have defined public officials to include anyone elected to public office as well as government employees responsible for policy making or for public funds, health or safety.

EXTENDING *NEW YORK TIMES* TO PUBLIC FIGURES As we have seen, the courts extended the *New York Times* actual malice requirement to a wide range of public officials, all the way down to fairly low-level former government employees. In 1967, three years after *Sullivan*, the Court in effect extended the *New York Times* malice requirement to **public figures**. In *Curtis Publishing Co. v. Butts* and *Associated Press v. Walker*, the Court required two well-known libel plaintiffs, a

---

[140] Gray v. Udevitz, 656 F.2d 588 (10th Cir. 1981).
[141] Garrison v. Louisiana, 379 U.S. 64 (1964).
[142] Ocala Star-Banner Co. v. Damron, 401 U.S. 295 (1971).

football coach and a segregationist former U.S. Army major general, to prove that defamatory statements about them were published with what amounted to *New York Times* actual malice.[143] Public figures, the Court said, include those who are "intimately involved in the resolution of important public questions or, by reason of their fame, shape events in areas of concern to society at large."

The Court, however, would not extend the actual malice requirement to private citizens acting in matters of public concern. In 1974, the Supreme Court ruled in *Gertz v. Welch* that private libel plaintiffs—those who are neither public officials nor public figures—are not required to prove *New York Times* actual malice. But, the Court said private libel plaintiffs, like public officials and public figures, would have to prove more than the fact that they were defamed. Private libel plaintiffs, too, would have to prove that a libelous publication was published with fault, but a lesser degree of fault than the malice that public figures and officials were required to prove. *Gertz* ended strict liability for the press in private-person libel suits just as *Sullivan* ended strict liability in cases of public officials.

Elmer Gertz was a prominent Chicago civil rights attorney who was libeled by *American Opinion*, a magazine representing the right-wing John Birch Society. The libelous article said Gertz engineered a frame-up of Richard Nuccio, a Chicago police officer convicted of second-degree murder for killing a boy. Gertz represented the parents of the boy in a civil suit filed against Officer Nuccio; Gertz had nothing to do with Nuccio's criminal trial.

Besides accusing Gertz of a frame-up, *American Opinion* pictured Gertz as part of a nationwide conspiracy to discredit local law enforcement agencies and replace them with a national police force that would support a Communist dictatorship. Gertz was inaccurately called a "Leninist," a "Communist-fronter" and an official of the Marxist League for Industrial Democracy. *American Opinion* also said that Gertz had been an officer of the National Lawyers Guild, which the magazine described as a Communist organization. The magazine falsely reported that the police had a file on Gertz that took "a big Irish cop to lift."[144]

The trial court and appeals court ruled that Gertz was involved in an issue of public interest and therefore had to prove that *American Opinion* published the defamatory article with *New York Times* actual malice. The trial court and an appellate court said Gertz was involved in an issue of public importance because Gertz represented the family in a well-publicized suit against Richard Nuccio over the death of their son. The lower courts said the public had a legitimate interest in trials of a police officer and the broader controversy of a nationwide conspiracy to discredit local police officers. The Supreme Court reversed the lower court decisions, 5–4, ruling that Gertz was a private person who did not have to prove actual malice to win his libel suit.

Writing for the Court, Justice Lewis Powell identified two kinds of public figures, since labeled (1) "all-purpose" and (2) "limited," or "vortex," public figures. All-purpose public figures "occupy positions of such pervasive power and influence that they are deemed public figures for all purposes." More commonly, Powell said, those classed as public figures have "thrust themselves to the forefront of particular public controversies in order to influence the resolution of the issues involved." Powell implied that individuals who voluntarily inject themselves into a public controversy would have to prove *New York Times* actual malice only for

---

[143] 388 U.S. 130 (1967).
[144] Gertz v. Robert Welch, Inc., 418 U.S. 323 (1974).

defamatory falsehoods related to that controversy, thus the labels of "limited" and "vortex" public figures. Private persons, like Elmer Gertz, who are involuntarily drawn into public issues would seldom have to prove actual malice, Powell said.

The Court said public figures, like public officials, should meet heavier burdens of proof when suing the media for libel than private plaintiffs meet. Powell said libel law should be more generous to private plaintiffs than to public figures because public figures expect to be commented on and have better means of self-defense. Public figures, unlike private citizens, invite attention and comment; they seek their status by playing an influential role in the affairs of society and thereby voluntarily expose themselves to an increased risk of public scrutiny and defamatory falsehoods. Private persons, on the other hand, have not embraced the risk of public exposure. The private person has relinquished "no part of his interest in the protection of his own good name, and consequently he has a more compelling call on the courts for redress of injury inflicted by defamatory falsehood."

Public figures, unlike private citizens, also have access to "channels of effective communication" so that they can counteract false statements about them, Powell said. Because of their access to media, public figures can minimize damage to their reputations; they can "contradict the lie or correct the error." In contrast, private persons, Powell said, are more "vulnerable to injury"; they lack effective opportunities for rebuttal.

Powell said that Gertz was neither an all-purpose public figure nor a vortex public figure. Although Gertz had published several books and articles on legal subjects and had served as an official in several civic and professional associations, he was not an all-purpose public figure. None of the jurors at the libel trial had heard of him. In any case, Powell said that a citizen who participates in community and professional affairs does not become a public personality "for all aspects of his life" unless there is "clear evidence of general fame or notoriety in the community, and pervasive involvement in the affairs of society."

If Gertz did not have widespread fame and notoriety, neither had he "thrust himself into the vortex" of the public issue involving the trials of the police officer Richard Nuccio. Gertz had not "engage[d] the public's attention in an attempt to influence" the outcome of an issue, the Court said. Gertz never discussed the criminal or civil litigation in the press. A lawyer did not become a public figure simply by representing a client in a controversial case.

After determining that Gertz was a private person who did not have to show actual malice, the Court sent the case back to the trial court. In 1983, more than 14 years after Gertz sued, he was awarded $482,000 in damages, interest and court fees.[145]

The *Gertz* case, like *New York Times v. Sullivan*, raised several questions. Justice Powell used several terms—*fame, notoriety, pervasive power, influence, voluntarily thrust* and *public controversies*—that he did not define. Shortly after *Gertz*, one federal judge said trying to define a public figure is "much like trying to nail a jellyfish to the wall."[146] Lower courts still struggle to distinguish between public figures and private persons.

All-Purpose Public Figures One of Powell's two categories of public figures in Gertz included people with special prominence in society—those who exercise general power or influence and those who occupy a position of continuing news

---

[145] Anthony Lewis, "Annals of Law: The Sullivan Case," *New Yorker*, Nov. 5, 1984, at 52, 79.
[146] Rosanova v. Playboy Enterprises, Inc., 411 F. Supp. 440 (S.D. Ga. 1976), *aff'd*, 580 F.2d 859 (5th Cir. 1978).

value. Such *all-purpose* public figures have achieved widespread fame or notoriety. The public figures must prove *New York Times* actual malice for libelous stories about their private lives as well as their public activities.

One federal appeals court said that the all-purpose public figure is a well-known "celebrity," his name a "household word." The public recognizes him and follows his words and deeds, either because it regards his ideas, conduct, or judgment as worthy of its attention or because he actively pursues that consideration.[147]

Courts have had limited opportunities to categorize nationally known persons as all-purpose public figures. A federal appeals court said the long-time host of a popular television program was an all-purpose public figure.[148] Other federal courts put a prominent political writer, William F. Buckley Jr.,[149] and a publicly owned insurance company with assets of a billion dollars into the all-purpose public figure category.[150] Actress Carol Burnett was presumed without explanation to be a public figure in her suit against the *National Enquirer*.[151]

In a series of cases, the U.S. Supreme Court ruled that plaintiffs who may be quite well known in their own professional or social circles nevertheless may remain private persons as libel plaintiffs. The Supreme Court ruled that a prominent member of Palm Beach society and former wife of Firestone tire heir Russell Firestone was not a public figure.[152]

Mary Alice Firestone sued *Time* magazine after a "Milestones" item incorrectly reported that Russell Firestone had won a divorce on the grounds "of extreme cruelty and adultery." Although cruelty and adultery were issues in the divorce trial, the trial court did not say they were the reasons the divorce was granted.

The Supreme Court categorized Firestone as a private person for the purpose of her suit even though she was "prominent among the '400' of Palm Beach Society" and an "active" member of the "sporting set." She subscribed to a clipping service to keep track of the times she was mentioned in the newspapers. Her marital difficulties were "well known," and her suit for divorce became a "veritable cause célèbre in social circles across the country." However, the Supreme Court said that Firestone remained a private person because she "did not assume any role of especial prominence in the affairs of society, other than perhaps Palm Beach society."

Limited, or Vortex, Public Figures Justice Powell's second category of public figures in *Gertz* included people who inject themselves into a public controversy to affect its outcome. Such people are *limited* public figures, who have to prove *New York Times* actual malice only for defamation directly connected to their voluntary acts. These limited public figures remain private persons for libelous statements about their private lives. The Supreme Court said Elmer Gertz was a private person because he had not actively thrust himself into any issue related to the trials of policeman Richard Nuccio. Gertz had not tried to influence public opinion.

In cases after *Gertz*, the Supreme Court has made it clear that persons will be classified as limited, or vortex, public figures only if (1) the alleged defamation involves a public controversy, (2) the person suing for libel has voluntarily participated in the discussion of that controversy and (3) the person suing for libel has tried to affect the outcome of the controversy.

---

[147] Waldbaum v. Fairchild Publications, Inc., 627 F.2d 1287 (D.C. Cir.), *cert. denied*, 449 U.S. 898 (1980).

[148] Carson v. Allied News Co., 529 F.2d 206 (7th Cir. 1976).

[149] Buckley v. Littell, 539 F.2d 882 (2d Cir. 1976), *cert. denied*, 429 U.S. 1062 (1977).

[150] Reliance Ins. Co. v. Barrons, 442 F. Supp. 1341 (S.D.N.Y. 1977).

[151] Burnett v. National Enquirer, Inc., 144 Cal. App. 3d 991 (Cal. Ct. App. 1983).

[152] Time, Inc. v. Firestone, 424 U.S. 448 (1976).

All three criteria must be met before a person will be considered a limited public figure, although court discussions of the last two criteria are frequently merged. In addition, lower courts sometimes consider other factors discussed by the Supreme Court in *Gertz*, including access to the media for the purpose of rebutting a defamatory remark.

The Court has not carefully defined the term *public controversy*, in which vortex figures become involved. However, the Court has indicated that public controversy should be understood narrowly. In *Time v. Firestone*, the Court said the term did not refer to all controversies that attracted the public's interest. When the Court declared that Firestone was not a public figure, it asserted that a divorce proceeding was not the sort of "public controversy" referred to in *Gertz*, even though the marital difficulties of extremely wealthy individuals may be of interest to some members of the public.

The U.S. Court of Appeals for the D.C. Circuit said that a public controversy has to be a "real dispute" over a specific issue affecting a segment of the general public. In *Waldbaum v. Fairchild Publications*, the D.C. Circuit said the outcome of a public controversy has "foreseeable and substantial ramifications" for those not directly participating in the debate. News coverage is an indication of a public controversy, the court said, but newsworthiness itself is not a sufficient criterion.[153]

The D.C. Circuit said Eric Waldbaum was a public figure in his suit against a trade publication called *Supermarket News* because he injected himself into controversy as the president of an innovative consumer cooperative, Greenbelt Consumer Services. Greenbelt, the second of its kind in the country, owned retail supermarkets, furniture and gift outlets, and service stations. Waldbaum sued *Supermarket News* over a five-sentence item that announced his ouster as Greenbelt president. The article said that the co-op had been "losing money" and "retrenching" with Waldbaum in charge.

The D.C. Circuit said Waldbaum was a limited public figure because he set policies and standards in the supermarket industry. The court said Waldbaum thrust himself into public controversies over unit pricing and open dating in supermarkets by fighting traditional industry practices. He also invited the public and press to meetings about topics ranging from "supermarket practices to energy legislation and fuel allocation." The court said that Waldbaum's activities generated considerable comment from trade journals and newspapers, including the *Washington Post*. His policies were debated within the supermarket industry and by retailers and consumers in the Washington, D.C., area.

Public controversies identified by the courts, in addition to supermarket business practices, include the value of protein supplements in the human diet[154] and alleged recruiting violations in a college basketball program.[155] A court said the infamous rape trial of black youths known nationally as the "Scottsboro Boys" focused on the controversy of fair justice for blacks in the court system.[156] The courts have also considered controversial a campaign to recall city council members,[157] the

[153] 627 F.2d at 1292.

[154] Hoffman v. Washington Post Co., 433 F. Supp. 600 (D.D.C. 1977).

[155] Barry v. Time, Inc., 584 F. Supp. 1110 (N.D. Cal. 1984).

[156] Street v. NBC, 645 F.2d 1227 (6th Cir.), *cert. granted*, 454 U.S. 815, *cert. dismissed*, 454 U.S. 1095 (1981).

[157] Weingarten v. Block, 102 Cal. App. 2d 129, *cert. denied*, 449 U.S. 899 (1980).

firing of an administrator of a large public hospital,[158] and the impact on a community when a company closes a manufacturing plant.[159]

Issues that the courts have not considered to be public controversies include a fight among company stockholders that would have no impact on the general public[160] and the demonstration of an air-powered automobile. A court said the car may be of some interest to the public but had not been part of a dispute.[161]

Once the courts determine that a story is about a public controversy, they must determine the nature and purpose of a person's participation in that controversy. Five years after *Gertz*, the Supreme Court said that limited public figures must thrust themselves into controversies with the intent of affecting the outcomes. Public figures must initiate their own participation in the debate over a public controversy. It is not enough for someone to become involuntarily involved in a controversy or to do something controversial, such as using government funds for questionable research or committing a crime. Public figures must also make an effort to affect the resolution of the controversy.

In *Hutchinson v. Proxmire*, the Supreme Court said that receiving substantial federal funds did not make a research scientist a public figure. Neither did the scientist's publication of research findings in professional journals. The scientist, Dr. Ronald Hutchinson, sued Senator William Proxmire for criticizing the half-million dollars spent by three government agencies on Hutchinson's study of monkeys. Senator Proxmire gave one of his Golden Fleece awards for wasteful government spending to the National Science Foundation, the Office of Naval Research, and the National Aeronautics and Space Administration for sponsoring Hutchinson's research. Hutchinson was trying to help federal agencies resolve problems faced by humans confined in close quarters in space and under the ocean. He was looking for visible ways to determine aggressive tendencies in animals, such as the clenching of jaws. Senator Proxmire ridiculed the research on the U.S. Senate floor, in a newsletter to constituents and in comments made on a nationally televised talk show. Proxmire said that Hutchinson "has made a fortune from his monkeys and in the process made a monkey out of the American taxpayer." Hutchinson contended that the comments had damaged both his reputation among his professional colleagues and his ability to obtain research grants.

The Supreme Court, in an opinion written by Chief Justice Warren Burger, said that simply being the recipient of public money does not make a person a public figure. If such were the case, Burger said, "everyone who received or benefited from the myriad public grants for research could be classified as a public figure." Burger said that Hutchinson had not thrust himself or his views into a public controversy for the purpose of influencing others. Hutchinson had become involved in a controversy created by Senator Proxmire, but Hutchinson had never assumed a role of prominence in the broad question of how public money should be spent, Burger said. "Neither his applications for federal grants nor his publications in professional journals can be said to have invited that degree of public attention and comment . . . essential to meet the public figure level."[162] In addition, Burger noted that Hutchinson had not enjoyed the regular access to the media necessary for a public figure. He was offered access only after Proxmire directed attention to him.

---

158 Gadd v. News-Press Publishing Co., 10 Media L. Rep. 2362 (Fla. Cir. Ct. 1984).
159 Thompson v. National Catholic Reporter Pub. Co., 4 F. Supp. 2d 833 (E.D. Wis. 1998).
160 Denny v. Mertz, 318 N.W.2d 141 (Wis. 1982).
161 Re v. Gannett Co., 480 A.2d 662 (Del. Super. Ct. 1984).
162 443 U.S. 111 (1979).

If Ronald Hutchinson is a private person, despite his prominence, it is unlikely that many private libel plaintiffs will have to prove malice if they are involuntarily drawn into issues of public importance. Indeed, the Court in *Gertz* said that only in "exceedingly rare" circumstances would private persons become public figures through no purposeful action on their part. Lower courts rarely determine that a plaintiff is an involuntary public figure.[163]

Instead, the courts almost always find that people who do not seek public attention or controversy are not public figures, even though they may be controversial themselves. A California court said that Virginia Franklin, a high school teacher who became the focus of a book-banning controversy, did not become a public figure because there was no evidence that she intentionally triggered a controversy when she told students to read a book of underground writings of the 1960s. A parent complained about the book to a chapter of the Elks Lodge, and protests of the lodge led to a public hearing before the school board and an administrative evaluation. The court said Franklin did not initiate media contact. She participated in the controversy only to the extent required by her job.[164]

Businesspeople do not ordinarily become public figures simply because their business practices or products are criticized, even if they respond to the charges.[165] Nor will they usually be considered to have injected themselves into controversial public issues solely because they advertised or practiced public relations.[166] However, businesses or businesspeople may become public figures if they initiate aggressive advertising or public relations campaigns related to controversial issues. A federal appeals court categorized Greenbelt co-op executive Eric Waldbaum as a public figure because he promoted precedent-breaking business policies vigorously. Waldbaum, who knew how to use the news media, held press conferences to discuss Greenbelt's policies and operations. He conducted an aggressive consumer education campaign in a monthly newspaper, *Co-op Consumer*. In the words of the trial judge, Waldbaum was "an activist, projecting his own image and that of the cooperative."[167]

Courts regularly conclude that political candidates are public figures if defamatory comments are made about their candidacies. The Supreme Court has said that criticism about political candidates must be accorded as much constitutional protection as criticism about officeholders. In *Monitor Patriot v. Roy*, a losing candidate for a New Hampshire seat in the U.S. Senate sued after a syndicated political columnist called him a former small-time bootlegger. The Court said that the candidate, Alphonse Roy, was a public figure who, like most political candidates, puts before the voters "every conceivable aspect of his public and private life that he thinks may lead the electorate to gain a good impression of him."[168] The Court said that a candidate's integrity or qualities as a father or husband may become matters of public concern.

Courts usually decide that people who voluntarily try to change the minds of others about public issues are limited public figures. Among persons the courts have determined to be public figures for trying to affect the outcome of public

---

[163] *E.g.*, Rodney Smolla, *Law of Defamation* § 2–14[1], at 2–43 (1998). *But see, e.g.*, Dameron v. Washington Magazine, Inc., 779 F.2d 736 (D.C. Cir. 1985).

[164] Franklin v. Lodge No. 1108, 97 Cal. App. 3d 915 (Cal. Ct. App. 1979).

[165] *E.g.*, General Prod. Co. v. Meredith Corp., 526 F. Supp. 546 (E.D. Va. 1981).

[166] *See, e.g.*, Vegod Corp. v. ABC, 603 P.2d 14 (Cal. 1980). *But see* Steaks Unlimited, Inc. v. Deaner, 468 F. Supp. 779 (W.D. Pa. 1979), *aff'd*, 623 F.2d 264 (3d Cir. 1980).

[167] Waldbaum v. Fairchild Publications, Inc., 627 F.2d 1300.

[168] *See* Monitor Patriot Co. v. Roy, 401 U.S. 265 (1971).

controversies were an outspoken foe of fluoridating water[169] and a person who circulated a petition and purchased advertising to oppose county land acquisition.[170] Also designated a limited public figure was Liberty Lobby, a self-avowed citizens' lobby. Liberty Lobby claims to promote "patriotism, nationalism, lawfulness, protection of the national interests of the United States and the economic interests of its citizens."[171] College professors and administrators have also been found to be limited purpose public figures, rather than public officials, such as an associate dean at the University of Virginia, who sued *Rolling Stone* magazine after its description of her response to reports of gang rape at a fraternity on campus turned out to be invented by an unreliable source.[172]

Other Limited Public Figures Besides recognizing the all-purpose public figure and the vortex figure, some courts confer limited public figure status on entertainers, athletes and others who attract attention because of visible careers. Public figures in this category do not have the widespread fame or notoriety of an all-purpose public figure, nor have they injected themselves into a controversial public issue with the intent of affecting the outcome. Nevertheless, many lower courts believe those who seek public attention during their careers ought to have to prove *New York Times* actual malice for the limited purpose of defamation about their public performances.[173]

Indeed, while the U.S. Supreme Court has not directly recognized this category of public figure in *Gertz* or since, one of the first public figures to be recognized by the Court would probably fit. In a case to be discussed later, University of Georgia athletic director Wally Butts was considered a public figure in his suit against the *Saturday Evening Post* after the *Post* said that Butts plotted to fix a football game. Although Butts was what the Supreme Court called a "well-known and respected figure in coaching ranks," his fame did not extend beyond the sports world, nor had Butts voluntarily injected himself into a controversy. Yet the Supreme Court recognized Butts as a public figure.[174]

Similarly, the U.S. Court of Appeals for the Fifth Circuit said entertainer Anita Brewer was a public figure for a story that focused on her romance with Elvis Presley, a relationship that advanced her career. The Fifth Circuit said Brewer had entered a profession that required public appearances and invited press attention.[175] Other plaintiffs treated similarly include a football player,[176] a prominent writer for *Sports Illustrated*,[177] a person promoting newly acquired radio stations,[178] and a seminude dancer.[179]

Time Lapse The Supreme Court has not said whether a public figure becomes a private person over time. In the absence of Supreme Court direction, several lower courts have said that public figures do not lose their public figure status with a lapse of time, at least when the libel concerns the same issues that led to the public attention in the first place.

---

[169] Yiamouyiannis v. Consumers Union of the United States, 619 F.2d 932 (2d Cir. 1980).

[170] Cloyd v. Press, Inc., 629 S.W.2d 24 (Tenn. App. 1981).

[171] Liberty Lobby, Inc. v. Anderson, 562 F. Supp. 201 (D.D.C. 1983), *aff'd*, 746 F.2d 1563 (D.C. Cir. 1984), *vacated on other grounds*, 477 U.S. 242 (1986).

[172] Eramo v. Rolling Stone, LLC, 209 F. Supp. 3d 862 (W.D. Va. 2016).

[173] *See, e.g.*, Bruce Sanford, *Libel and Privacy* § 7.4.2, at 317–22 (2nd ed. 1999).

[174] Curtis Publishing Co. v. Butts, 388 U.S. 130, 155 (1967).

[175] Brewer v. Memphis Publishing Co., 626 F.2d 1238 (1980).

[176] *E.g.*, Chuy v. Philadelphia Eagles Football Club, 595 F.2d 1265 (3d Cir. 1979) (en banc).

[177] Maule v. NYM Corp., 429 N.E.2d 416 (N.Y. 1981).

[178] Howard v. Buffalo Evening News, Inc., 453 N.Y.S.2d 516 (App. Div. 1982).

[179] Griffin v. Kentucky Post, 10 Media L. Rep. 1159 (Ky. Cir. Ct. 1983).

For example, a federal appeals court said that Victoria Price Street, who accused the nine black "Scottsboro Boys" of raping her in 1931, was a public figure 50 years later. Street sued NBC for a network docudrama that portrayed her as a woman trying to send innocent young men to the electric chair. The U.S. Court of Appeals for the Sixth Circuit said that Street had been a public figure in the 1930s because of her prominent role in the controversy over justice for blacks, her access to the media and her effort to aggressively promote her version of the case outside of the courtroom. She was still a public figure nearly 50 years later because "once a person becomes a public figure in connection with a particular controversy, that person remains a public figure for purposes of later commentary or treatment of *that controversy*" (emphasis in original).

Public figures of the past do not lose access to the media where they can discuss their role in a continuing controversy, the court said. In addition, the Sixth Circuit said, vigorous public debate must be protected even though fading memories and disappearing sources make it more difficult for the media to verify the accuracy of their reports. At the same time, the court said the passage of time "does not automatically diminish the significance of events or the public's need for information." The Sixth Circuit said the case of the Scottsboro Boys, "the most famous rape case of the twentieth century," focused the nation's attention on the courts' treatment of blacks. The court said the Scottsboro case would remain "a living controversy" as long as fair justice for blacks is an issue.[180]

▓ SUMMARY ▓

The Supreme Court said in *Gertz v. Welch* that public figures are either persons of widespread fame or notoriety or people who inject themselves into the debate about controversial public issues for the purpose of affecting the outcome. Public figures, unlike private libel plaintiffs, voluntarily subject themselves to public exposure and have ready access to the media, in which they can rebut defamatory remarks. The Supreme Court said that persons of widespread fame and notoriety are public figures for all purposes either because of their prominence or because of the influence they exercise in society. Limited public figures are persons who voluntarily thrust themselves into a public controversy with the intent of having an impact on the way that controversy is resolved. Limited public figures must prove *New York Times* actual malice only for media discussion of that issue.

***NEW YORK TIMES* ACTUAL MALICE** Once a court decides that a person is a public official, a public figure or a private person, the focus of the libel case turns to the question of *fault*, that is, whether communicators published the alleged libel carelessly or maliciously. To win a libel suit, each plaintiff must prove not only that the publication was false and defamatory but also that it was published with fault. Private persons must prove that a publisher acted negligently or carelessly. Public officials and public figures must prove *New York Times* actual malice: that the publisher knew the publication was false or published it with reckless disregard for the truth. Actual malice, which must be proven with "clear and convincing evidence,"[181] is a subjective decision, not susceptible to a precise definition. But a communicator who acts with actual malice demonstrates much more than ill will or carelessness. *New York Times* actual malice is also more flagrant than an "extreme

---

[180] Street v. NBC, 645 F.2d at 1235, *cert. granted*, 454 U.S. 815, *cert. dismissed*, 454 U.S. 1095 (1981).
[181] *See, e.g.*, Philadelphia Newspapers Inc. v. Hepps, 475 U.S. 767 (1986).

departure" from the professional journalistic practices that most communicators would follow.[182]

Reckless Disregard for the Truth Public officials and public figures most often try to prove *New York Times* actual malice by establishing that communicators demonstrated a reckless disregard for the truth. The Supreme Court has said that plaintiffs can establish reckless disregard only if they can prove that defamatory statements were made with a "high degree of awareness of their probable falsity."[183] In *St. Amant v. Thompson,* the Court said a candidate for sheriff in Baton Rouge did not exercise reckless disregard because he believed the truth of false statements he made in a televised speech. Phil St. Amant implied during his speech that his opponent, a deputy sheriff named Herman Thompson, had been bribed by a local union officer. St. Amant based his charges on an affidavit of a union member, but St. Amant did not consider that his accusations might be defamatory and made no effort to verify his information. The U.S. Supreme Court, finding no reckless disregard for the truth, overturned lower court rulings for Thompson.

Justice Byron White, writing for the Court's eight-person majority, said reckless conduct is not measured by whether a reasonably prudent person would have published or investigated before publishing. Rather, White said, "There must be sufficient evidence to permit the conclusion that the defendant in fact entertained serious doubts as to the truth of his publication."[184]

However, White emphasized that the Court's decision did not automatically protect journalists who argue they believe their stories are true. A journalist cannot successfully contend a story is written in good faith if there are "obvious reasons" to doubt the credibility of a source or the accuracy of the source's information, White said. Nor can remarks be "based wholly on an unverified anonymous telephone call." White said courts may find *New York Times* actual malice if defamatory remarks are fabricated or "so inherently improbable that only a reckless man would have put them into circulation."

The inquiry into whether a journalist entertained "serious doubts" about the truth or falsity of a story requires the courts to try to reconstruct the publishing process. The courts ask whether a journalist adequately investigated a story given the time available. The courts consider whether the reporter chose reliable sources, ignored warnings that the story was wrong, or disregarded inconsistencies. Other factors that could contribute to a finding of actual malice include a mistake in interpretation, the use of the wrong terms and a biased selection of facts. Proof of motives such as ill will or hatred could be one of the factors in actual malice. So could a publisher's intent to print sensational stories to attract readers and the failure to print a retraction. Ordinarily, one of these items alone is not sufficient evidence of reckless disregard for the truth; actual malice is usually a combination of reckless practices.

The Supreme Court found actual malice in an Ohio case in which journalists, according to the Court, purposely avoided the truth. The *Hamilton (Ohio) Journal News* deliberately evaded the truth, the Court said, when the paper relied on a highly questionable source and failed to investigate contradictions before publishing a front-page story charging a judicial candidate with planning blackmail and promising favors for help in smearing his opponent. The story said that the unsuccessful judicial challenger, Daniel Connaughton, promised Alice Thompson and her

---

[182] Harte-Hanks Communications, Inc. v. Connaughton, 491 U.S. 657 (1989).

[183] Garrison v. Louisiana, 379 U.S. at 74.

[184] 390 U.S. 727 (1968).

sister jobs, a trip to Florida and fancy dinners "in appreciation" for their help in the investigation of corruption in the incumbent judge's office. Connaughton suppos-edly made these unethical promises during a taped conversation with Thompson and her sister, a conversation at which several other people were present. The paper also reported that Thompson said Connaughton planned to quietly blackmail the incumbent judge with a tape of the sisters' damning information.

Connaughton denied threatening blackmail and offering the sisters favors, a denial supported by five others who witnessed the taped conversation between Connaughton and the sisters. The Supreme Court upheld the jury's award of $200,000, finding that the newspaper published with actual malice.[185]

The Court cited several reportorial practices that added up to actual malice:

- Relying on a questionable source—Thompson, who had a criminal record, had been treated for mental instability, and had told the paper that she opposed Connaughton's candidacy.
- Failing to interview Thompson's sister and several other people who later refuted Thompson.
- Failing to listen to the tape, which Connaughton made available to the news-paper, a tape that would have corroborated or disproved Thompson's claims of Connaughton's offers and threats.
- Ignoring Connaughton's denials.
- Ignoring the improbability that Connaughton would quietly blackmail the incumbent judge with the taped interview when the newspaper knew Connaughton had already given the tape to the police.
- Revealing the newspaper's prejudice by publishing an editorial accurately predicting the conclusions of the investigative story it later published about Connaughton.
- Claiming that staff members were assigned to conduct key interviews that staffers testified they had not been assigned.

In sum, the Supreme Court concluded that the *Journal News* had published with actual malice by its "deliberate decision not to acquire knowledge of facts that might confirm the probable falsity of Thompson's charges. Although failure to investigate will not alone support a finding of actual malice," the Court said, "the purposeful avoidance of the truth is in a different category."

The Court saw similarities between the Connaughton case and an earlier case in which the *Saturday Evening Post* lost a libel suit because of slipshod investiga-tory techniques that three justices thought constituted actual malice. In the earlier case, *Curtis Publishing Co. v. Butts*, reporters failed before publication to check the story of an unreliable source who said that Georgia football coach Wally Butts had fixed a football game with Alabama. Although the staff of the *Saturday Evening Post* was under no deadline pressure, it failed to interview witnesses or view game films. The *Post* instead relied on the unsupported testimony of a check forger who claimed he acquired information about the fix when he was mysteriously con-nected to a telephone conversation between Butts and Alabama coach Bear Bryant.

In a case decided at the same time as *Butts*, a unanimous Court determined that the Associated Press (AP) had acted responsibly when it reported that retired Army Major General Edwin Walker had encouraged violence and led a charge against federal marshals during the integration of the University of Mississippi in

---

[185] Harte-Hanks Communications, Inc. v. Connaughton, 491 U.S. 657 (1989).

1962. In *Associated Press v. Walker*, the Court reversed a $500,000 award for Walker, who denied that he encouraged violence.

The AP reporter, the Court said, gave "every indication of being trustworthy and competent." He checked his story with apparently reliable sources, leaving no reason for AP editors to doubt the reporter's story about a former general known for his vehement opposition to integration. Furthermore, the Court recognized that some errors might creep into a news story written under deadline pressure.[186]

Knowing Falsehood Although public officials and public figures who have to prove actual malice usually try to establish reckless disregard for the truth, a few cases provide evidence that journalists published with knowledge that a defamatory story was false. Potent evidence of knowing falsehood is fabrication—a journalist who makes up a story knowing it is false.

In *Cantrell v. Forest City Publishing Co.*, a case that will be discussed in Chapter 5, the U.S. Supreme Court said that a reporter acted with actual malice when he fabricated an interview with a West Virginia widow named Margaret Cantrell. Although Cantrell was not home when the *Cleveland Plain Dealer* reporter visited the Cantrell home, he nevertheless quoted her in his story. The story also exaggerated the family poverty following the death of Cantrell's husband in a bridge accident.[187]

In *Goldwater v. Ginzburg*, the U.S. Court of Appeals for the Second Circuit said that *Fact* magazine knowingly published defamatory falsehoods about 1964 presidential candidate Barry Goldwater. In *Goldwater*, the court said *Fact* editor Ralph Ginzburg and managing editor Warren Boroson decided shortly after the Republican nominating convention to attack Goldwater's character "on preconceived psychiatric or psychological grounds of their own fabrication."[188] Before Boroson had begun his research, the court said, he wrote that the Goldwater profile would say that the candidate had "deep-seated doubts about his masculinity." Ginzburg wrote in one of the magazine's articles that Goldwater had experienced two nervous breakdowns, although Ginzburg knew that Goldwater and his physician denied the charge. Ginzburg also asserted, without consulting experts in psychiatry, that Goldwater suffered from a serious mental disease. For a second article in *Fact*, Ginzburg edited psychiatrists' responses to a mail survey to distort the doctors' comments about Goldwater. The Second Circuit, noting that Ginzburg had created numerous false statements to support his predetermined views about Goldwater's mental condition, affirmed a jury verdict that the *Fact* articles were published with actual malice.

Performer Carol Burnett proved that the *National Enquirer* knowingly printed a false story when it said she made a fool of herself in an expensive Washington, D.C., restaurant. The four-sentence item in the *Enquirer* said that "a boisterous" Carol Burnett argued with former Secretary of State Henry Kissinger. Burnett supposedly "traipsed around the place offering everyone a bite of her dessert" and "really raised eyebrows when she accidentally knocked a glass of wine over one diner and started giggling instead of apologizing."

The trial court established that the story was based on tips from a freelancer who emphasized that Burnett was not drunk. One *Enquirer* writer expressed doubts that the tip about Burnett's behavior could be trusted. Another could verify only that Burnett shared her dessert and "carried on a good-natured conversation"

---

[186] Curtis Publishing Co. v. Butts, 388 U.S. 130, 155 (1967).
[187] 419 U.S. 245 (1974).
[188] 414 F.2d 324 (2d Cir. 1969).

with Kissinger. No one told *Enquirer* columnist Brian Walker, the author of the story, that Burnett and Kissinger had an argument. The reports of Burnett's "boisterous" behavior and the wine spilling were only unverified hearsay. The trial judge suggested that Walker added "embellishment . . . 'to spice up' the item." The judge said the *Enquirer* published with actual malice because Walker had serious doubts about the truth of the publication and there was "a high degree of probability" that he fabricated part of the story.[189]

Although fabrication by itself can constitute *New York Times* actual malice, the Supreme Court has ruled that a writer who deliberately modifies a speaker's words within quotation marks does not necessarily knowingly falsify the speaker's statement. Unless the change substantially increases damage to a person's reputation, altering the words in quotation marks is not "knowing falsehood," the Court said. In *Masson v. New Yorker Magazine, Inc.*, the Court rejected, 7–2, Freudian scholar Jeffrey Masson's argument that writers act with actual malice when they deliberately change a speaker's remarks inside quotation.

Masson sued *New Yorker* author Janet Malcolm for falsely quoting him as calling himself an "intellectual gigolo" and "the greatest analyst who ever lived." Masson claimed these phrases were exaggerations that made him appear unscholarly, irresponsible, vain and lacking honesty and moral integrity. Malcolm said her quotes were accurate.[190]

Without deciding whether the altered quotes libeled Masson, the Court noted that minor inaccuracies do not amount to falsity as long as "the substance, the gist, the sting, of the libelous charge be justified." Furthermore, a "deliberate alteration of the words uttered by a plaintiff does not equate with knowledge of falsity," the Court said, "unless the alteration results in a material change in the meaning conveyed by the statement." In a more recent case involving Air Wisconsin Airlines, the Court reiterated that actual malice requires that libelous falsehoods be "material," not merely minor inaccuracies.[191]

The Court said in *Masson* that writers must be left some leeway to recreate quotes that reflect the substance if not the exact words spoken in an interview. Writers, the Court said, often alter words inside of quotation marks to correct grammar and syntax, including making intelligible the remarks of "rambling" speakers. In addition, the Court said, writers working from notes often put into quotation marks statements that are incomplete or inexact. Only if the alterations add significantly to defamatory meaning would the alterations constitute knowing falsehood.[192]

Inquiry Into a Journalist's Mind The proof necessary for *New York Times* actual malice, evidence of knowing falsehood or reckless disregard of the truth, seemingly requires courts to know what journalists think as they prepare a story. The need to prove knowing falsehood or a "high degree of awareness" of the probable falsity encourages plaintiffs' lawyers to examine the thought processes, or "the state of mind," of journalists. Plaintiffs' lawyers ask writers whether they believed what their sources told them. Editors are asked whether they doubted the truth of the story and, if so, whether they told reporters to provide more documentation. Both writers and editors are asked how they decided what to publish.

---

[189] Burnett v. National Enquirer, Inc., 7 Media L. Rep. 1321 (Cal. Super. Ct. 1981), *aff'd on other grounds*, 144 Cal. App. 3d 991 (Cal. Ct. App. 1983).
[190] 501 U.S. 496 (1991).
[191] Air Wisconsin Airlines Corp. v. Hoeper, 134 S. Ct. 852 (2014).
[192] 501 U.S. at 515.

Many journalists argue that detailed examinations of news decisions violate the First Amendment by interfering with editorial processes. They contend that writers and editors are reluctant to express doubts about a story in the newsroom if those doubts might be used against them in court. Journalists claim that juries cannot understand why journalists under deadline pressure might decline to pursue tips that could make a story more complete. Nevertheless, in *Herbert v. Lando*, the Court said the First Amendment does not bar inquiry into the editorial process.

In *Lando*, the Court said a producer for *60 Minutes* could be asked how he evaluated information for a segment on Colonel Anthony Herbert, a controversial retired Army officer. A 1973 *60 Minutes* broadcast questioned allegations by Herbert of an official cover-up of atrocities committed by U.S. troops in Vietnam. Herbert sued CBS, claiming that *60 Minutes* falsely suggested he made up the war-crimes charges to explain why he was relieved of his command. Herbert conceded he was a public figure and therefore had to prove *New York Times* actual malice.

The Supreme Court said that it had not intended, when constitutionalizing libel law, to prevent plaintiffs from obtaining evidence needed to prove actual malice. Indeed, Justice Byron White, who wrote the Court's opinion, said the *New York Times* actual malice rule "made it essential" that public officials and public figures understand both the conduct and state of mind of media defendants. If public officials and public figures were prevented from asking about the thoughts, opinions and conclusions of journalists, White said, the balance between the protection of reputation and the protection for the First Amendment guarantees of freedom of speech and press would be unacceptably skewed in favor of the press.

White rejected the argument that investigations into the journalist's state of mind would have "an intolerable chilling effect" on editorial decision-making. He contended that the media have a self-interest in taking any necessary precautions, including a "frank interchange of fact and opinion," to avoid publishing a knowing falsehood or reckless error. White said he did not believe that discussions between reporters and editors were "so subject to distortion and . . . misunderstanding" that they should be immune from courtroom examination. However, he said, investigations into the editorial process should be permitted only when someone suing for libel has to prove *New York Times* actual malice. Inquiry into the state of mind should not be permitted "merely to satisfy curiosity."[193]

The Supreme Court returned the *Herbert v. Lando* case to the federal district court judge for trial. The trial judge eventually ruled for CBS on most of Herbert's complaint on grounds he could not prove *New York Times* actual malice. In 1986, a federal appeals court dismissed the case.[194]

Modern Challenges to the Actual Malice Standard More than half a century has passed since the landmark *New York Times v. Sullivan* decision, and its influence has been felt around the world. Several countries, including Argentina, Hungary, India, the Philippines and Taiwan, have embraced or even expanded the actual malice standard in their libel jurisprudence.[195] However, the decision that has been the bedrock of American libel law for decades is facing increasing challenges at home. In 2021, two Supreme Court justices called for reconsideration of *Sullivan*, dissenting in the denial of certiorari in a libel case appeal. A man had sued for defamation in Florida, saying he was falsely accused

---

[193] 441 U.S. 153 (1979).

[194] 781 F.2d 298 (2d Cir.), *cert. denied*, 476 U.S. 1182 (1986).

[195] Kyu Ho Youm, "The 'Actual Malice' of New York Times Co. v. Sullivan: A Free Speech Touchstone in a Global Century," 19 *Comm. L. & Pol'y* 185 (2014).

of being a member of the Albanian mafia, but the case was dismissed when the court found he was a "public figure" and would be unable to establish actual malice. Justice Thomas, who had long expressed skepticism of the *Sullivan* standard, again said that the decision lacked historical support, and noted that the actual malice requirement continues "to insulate those who perpetrate lies from traditional remedies like libel suits."[196] Justice Gorsuch, noting "momentous changes in the Nation's media landscape since 1964," said the actual malice standard has "evolved into a subsidy for published falsehoods on a scale that no one could have foreseen."[197]

Other courts have also shown a willingness to soften the actual malice standard. Congressman Devin Nunes, who has filed numerous actions against news media for critical coverage, was allowed to proceed in a case stemming from a news story claiming his family used undocumented labor on their farm. While a federal district court dismissed the case, finding that there was no plausible actual malice in the news report published by *Esquire* magazine, the Eighth Circuit Court of Appeals revived the case on appeal in 2021, not based on the underlying story, but on a tweet about the story posted by reporter Ryan Lizza a few weeks after its initial publication. The court found that Nunes' public denial of the allegations contained in the story after it was initially published was enough to trigger potential actual malice when Lizza tweeted about it later, in essence serving as a republication and thus a plausible new avenue for liability.[198] Appellate victories by Nunes and other politicians, which extended litigation and thus legal defense costs for publishers by months or years, stand as warnings for news media counting on a more robust actual malice standard typical in decades past.

� SUMMARY ▧

Public officials and public figures are required to prove *New York Times* actual malice, knowing falsehood or reckless disregard of the truth to win libel suits. The Supreme Court has said plaintiffs must demonstrate that journalists had serious doubts about the truth of a defamatory story before publication. To determine whether writers and editors are reckless, courts examine whether journalists employ standard news-gathering techniques in the time available to prepare a story. Courts also consider the believability of the story, the depth and breadth of the investigation, the credibility of sources and the motives for publication. Plaintiffs can also establish actual malice if they can prove a journalist fabricated a story or otherwise knowingly printed false defamation. The Supreme Court has ruled that public communicators can be required to testify about what they knew and were thinking when they wrote and edited defamatory stories.

FAULT FOR PRIVATE PERSONS The 1974 Supreme Court case *Gertz v. Welch* not only defined public figures but also eliminated the doctrine of strict liability in libel law for **private figures**. When the law holds the media to strict liability, publishers are automatically liable if they defame a private person, even if the media observe normal journalistic practices. Just as *New York Times v. Sullivan* established that the media could not be held liable by public officials who simply proved they had been defamed, *Gertz* established that the media could not be held liable by private persons who proved only that they had been defamed. Justice

---

[196] Berisha v. Lawson, 141 S. Ct. 2424 (2021) (J. Thomas, dissenting).
[197] Berisha v. Lawson, 141 S. Ct. 2424 (2021) (J. Gorsuch, dissenting).
[198] Nunes v. Lizza, 12 F.4th 890 (8th Cir. 2021).

Powell, writing for the majority, said that private libel plaintiffs, who are more vulnerable and have less access to the media than public figures, should perhaps not have to prove *New York Times* actual malice as public officials and public figures must to collect general damages. On the other hand, Powell said, publishers and editors should not be automatically liable—subject to strict liability—if they defame a private person while observing the normal standards of journalism. Powell said holding the media strictly liable for libel of private persons would threaten the vigorous public debate the Court wanted to protect in *New York Times v. Sullivan*.[199] Since *Gertz v. Welch*, every person suing the media for libel must prove some level of fault.

All plaintiffs, public or private, must prove actual malice to collect punitive damages, but the Court in *Gertz* said the states may decide what level of fault private libel plaintiffs must meet to collect general damages. Four states require private persons involved in matters of public interest to prove actual malice, the same high standard that public officials and public figures must meet.[200] New York sets a slightly lower standard, requiring private persons to prove "gross irresponsibility,"[201] a standard more rigorous than negligence but less demanding than actual malice. Most states, the District of Columbia and Puerto Rico impose the lesser standard of negligence, requiring private persons to prove that defamation was published with a lack of due care.

Negligence Negligence, the fault requirement most states have adopted for private persons suing for libel, is a standard of liability that is used widely in tort law. Negligence means a failure to act as a reasonable person would in similar circumstances. In libel law, the issue is whether a writer exercised reasonable care in determining whether a story was true or false.[202]

States apply the term *negligence* in one of two ways. Many states define negligence by an *average person standard*: the failure to do what "a reasonably prudent person" would do.[203] Other states define negligence by a professional *standard*: a failure to be as careful as an ordinarily prudent person in the same occupation.[204] For journalists and professional communicators, then, the difference between the two standards is whether communicators' efforts to be accurate are to be judged by the standards of an average person who is perhaps unfamiliar with communications or by what professional writers and editors would ordinarily do in similar circumstances. The average person standard does not take into consideration the daily difficulties of journalism, such as deadline pressures or uncooperative sources. When the professional standard is used, witnesses can testify to the kinds of behavior considered acceptable within the profession.

No court has provided a definitive list of professional communication practices considered to be negligent. The Supreme Court suggested in *New York Times v. Sullivan* that a failure to check facts may be negligent. In *Sullivan*, the *Times'* advertising staff may have acted negligently, the Court said, when it failed to check

---

[199] 418 U.S. 345-48.
[200] Alaska, Colorado, Indiana, and New Jersey. *See* John McCrory and Robert Bernius, "Constitutional Privilege in Libel Law," 1 *Communications Law* 53, 427–9 (1997).
[201] *See* Chapadeau v. Utica Observer-Dispatch, Inc., 341 N.E.2d 569 (N.Y. 1975).
[202] *See Restatement (Second) of Torts* § 580B comment g.
[203] Memphis Publishing Co. v. Nichols, 569 S.W.2d 412 (Tenn. 1978). For lists of states adopting each standard, *see, e.g.*, John McCrory and Robert Bernius, "Constitutional Privilege in Libel Law," 1 *Communications Law* 53, 433–9 (1997).
[204] Martin v. Griffin Television, Inc., 549 P.2d 85 (Okla. 1976).

the paper's news columns to verify the accuracy of an advertisement calling for support for civil rights activities in the South.[205]

A single lapse in generally accepted reporting practices may constitute negligence, while it probably would not constitute actual malice. Negligence can arise through errors in note taking and mistakes in typing. Negligence often occurs because journalists rely on the wrong sources or fail to check facts. One academic study reported that juries are likely to decide a journalist is negligent if they determine the journalist failed to verify information through the best available sources.[206]

A South Carolina reporter made several mistakes that constituted negligence when he erroneously reported that James Jones pleaded guilty to pirating tapes in violation of copyright laws. Jones had been arrested and arraigned with his father, an uncle named Jack Jones and two others. Two months later, the father and uncle pleaded guilty, but the charges against James Jones were dismissed. The reporter who wrote the defamatory story said a U.S. attorney had told him that James Jones pleaded guilty. But the official said he had read the reporter the names of the guilty directly from the record, a record that did not include the name of James Jones.

The South Carolina Supreme Court said a jury understandably decided that the reporter violated acceptable reporting standards because he did not check court records himself or contact the Joneses, whom he knew. The court said the six days between the guilty pleas and publication of the story gave the reporter ample time to check his information. The state supreme court reinstated a jury verdict of $35,000, which had been set aside by the trial judge.[207]

Most courts expect that public communicators will make a good-faith effort to determine the accuracy of a news story. Courts do not usually demand that the media investigate exhaustively before a story is published or broadcast. A journalist who contacts the persons directly affected by a story and checks information carefully with sources known to be reliable will not ordinarily be found negligent, even if a story is false.

While private plaintiffs must prove negligence when suing the news media for defamation, the Supreme Court has never ruled whether private plaintiffs must prove negligence when suing an individual—such as a blogger—not belonging to the institutional press. However, the Supreme Court noted in *Citizens United* that "[w]ith the advent of the internet and the decline of print and broadcast media . . . the line between the media and others who wish to comment on political and social issues becomes blurred." Citing the Supreme Court, the Ninth Circuit Court of Appeals in 2014 joined its sister appeals court's ruling that private libel plaintiffs must prove negligence when suing a blogger just as they would if suing a broadcaster or newspaper involving an issue of public concern. The Ninth Circuit ruled Kevin Padrick, senior principal in the Obsidian Finance Group, must prove negligence in his suit against "investigative blogger" Crystal Cox, over accusations on her blog, Bankruptcycorruption.com, that Padrick enriched himself illegally as an appointed trustee of a bankrupt company, an issue of public concern.[208]

---

[205] New York Times Co. v. Sullivan, 376 U.S. 287–8.
[206] W. Wat Hopkins, "Negligence Ten Years After Gertz v. Welch," *Journalism Monographs*, Aug. 1985, at 93.
[207] Jones v. Sun Publishing Co., 191 S.E.2d 12, *cert. denied*, 459 U.S. 944 (1982).
[208] Obsidian Finance Group, LLC v. Cox, 740 F.3d 1284 (9th Cir. 2014); Citizens United v. Federal Election Commission, 558 U.S. 310 (2010).

Wire Services and Live Transmissions

More than a century ago, serial libel plaintiffs would travel from town to town, filing lawsuits against local newspapers that had picked up a story off of a wire service that turned out to be defamatory. Perhaps most famous among these was the entertainer Annie Oakley, a Western sharpshooter who performed for Buffalo Bill's Wild West Show. An AP news report out of Chicago in 1903 said Oakley had been arrested for stealing a man's trousers to help her buy cocaine. The report turned out to be false; the woman in question was actually an Oakley impersonator who went by the name "Any O'Klay." Oakley brought 55 lawsuits against newspapers that published the story, winning most of them for sums totaling tens of thousands of dollars. But courts and legislatures started to realize the flaws of allowing this kind of serial litigious behavior for one mistake that was repeated unknowingly by subscribers to a news wire. This resulted in the development of the "wire service" defense.[209]

Courts in several states have held the media are ordinarily not negligent if they publish defamatory wire service stories without checking facts in the stories.[210] In one case, Massachusetts courts affirmed a summary judgment for newspapers sued for publishing wire service stories about a criminal investigation of Kenneth Appleby. Appleby, of West Springfield, said the media published false defamatory stories about an investigation culminating in his conviction for rape, kidnapping, and assault and battery. Appleby said he was damaged by false statements about his homosexuality, the torture and murder of young homosexual men and his interest in the Nazi Party. In all, Appleby sued 94 newspapers and broadcast stations in the region as well as the AP and United Press International (UPI).

The Massachusetts Supreme Judicial Court, affirming the judgment of the trial court, said that the media's "reasonable reliance" on stories obtained from a "reputable wire service" was not negligence, even in the case of the *Holyoke Transcript-Telegram*, located about ten miles from West Springfield, near the sources for the story. The court noted that both the AP and UPI had excellent reputations for accuracy. The court said requiring individual newspapers and broadcast stations to corroborate wire service stories would be impractical, imposing a heavy burden on the media's ability to report national and world news.[211]

The Massachusetts court did not, however, indicate that newspapers and broadcast stations could always rely on wire service copy without checking it. If a newspaper or broadcast station has reason to doubt a wire service story, the Massachusetts court said, publication without verification could become the basis of a negligence suit. However, the court noted that none of the Appleby stories was "so inherently improbable or inconsistent" that the newspapers should have doubted their accuracy. Nor, said the court, was there evidence that the newspapers knew, or should have known, information about Appleby that raised doubts about the truth of the wire service stories.

The Michigan Supreme Court ruled the wire service defense protected the *Detroit Free Press* against a libel suit. The paper published an article quoting a former professional baseball player saying his cocaine addiction was due to the player's father having a drinking problem. The *Free Press* received the article from

---

[209] *See* Patrick File, *Bad News Travels Fast: The Telegraph, Libel, and Press Freedom in the Progressive Era* (2019).

[210] At least 13 states have recognized the wire services defense. *See* Kyu Ho Youm, "The 'Wire Service' Libel Defense," 70 *Journalism Q.* 682 (1993).

[211] Appleby v. Daily Hampshire Gazette, 478 N.E.2d 721 (Mass. 1985).

the Knight Ridder Tribune News Wire and republished it.[212] The state supreme court said the news service was reputable, the *Free Press* did not know the article contained any false information, and nothing in the story could have alerted the *Free Press* to any potential inaccuracies.[213]

The requirement that libel plaintiffs prove fault also provides broadcast stations with protection for defamatory statements on call-in shows and other live broadcasts. Some states have adopted statutes that protect broadcast stations exercising "reasonable care." A few states have passed laws that either provide broadcasters with immunity for defamation by callers or require private persons who sue to prove *New York Times* actual malice when libelous statements are made during controversial programs. Some states also limit damages for defamatory broadcasts.[214]

In the states that do not protect defamatory statements made during call-in shows, the courts have provided inconsistent guidelines for precautions broadcasters should take. In cases in which recklessness was at issue, courts have disagreed whether the failure to use a delay system during live broadcasts was reckless. The Montana Supreme Court said that a broadcaster is not reckless in failing to install a delay device that allows a talk show host a few seconds to censor calls before they are broadcast. In *Adams v. Frontier Broadcasting Co.*, Bob Adams sued radio station KFBC after an anonymous caller said on a talk show that Adams had been discharged as state insurance commissioner because he was dishonest. The Montana Supreme Court said that use of a delay system could restrict a robust public debate because the device might be used to screen out only those ideas unacceptable to the broadcaster.[215] However, in Louisiana, a state appeals court said the direct broadcast of anonymous defamatory remarks without any attempt to monitor or delay them constituted reckless disregard for the truth.[216] Conduct that is not reckless may be negligent.

■ SUMMARY ■

In *Gertz v. Welch*, the U.S. Supreme Court said that even persons who are not public officials or public figures must show fault to win their libel suits. Most states have said that private persons must prove negligence or a lack of reasonable care on the part of journalists. Negligence often involves the failure to check information adequately or to use the most appropriate sources.

Falsity

Public officials, public figures and private persons involved in matters of public concern must prove not only recklessness or negligence to win libel suits but also falsity.

PROOF OF FALSITY The Supreme Court made clear in *New York Times v. Sullivan* and its progeny that public officials and public figures must prove falsity

---

[212] Jack Weiss and Amy Neuhardt, "Recent Developments in the Law of Defamation," 2 *Communications Law* 21 (1998).

[213] Howe v. Detroit Free Press, 586 N.W.2d 85 (Mich. 1998).

[214] *See* Robert Hughes, "Radio Libel Laws: Relics That May Have Answer for Reform Needed Today," 63 *Journalism Q.* 288 (1986); Bruce Sanford, *Libel and Privacy* § 9.4.3, at 447–8 (2nd ed. 1999).

[215] 555 P.2d 556 (Mont. 1976).

[216] Snowden v. Pearl River Broadcasting Corp., 251 So. 2d 405 (La. Ct. App. 1971).

in order to document *New York Times* actual malice.[217] But the Court did not establish in *Gertz v. Welch* that private persons must also demonstrate falsity to win libel suits. In *Gertz*, the Court said only that a private plaintiff must show fault, often negligence, when suing the media. In 1986, the Supreme Court declared that private persons must prove falsity as well as fault if they are involved in matters of public interest.

In *Philadelphia Newspapers, Inc. v. Hepps*, the Supreme Court ruled that the private persons suing—rather than the media defending—bear the responsibility for proving their version of a case.[218] In *Hepps*, a corporation that franchised a chain of Thrifty stores sued the *Philadelphia Inquirer* for linking the chain to organized crime. The *Inquirer* said the Thrifty chain, which sold beer, soft drinks and snacks, used its criminal connections to obtain favorable rulings from the state liquor control board. Pennsylvania law, consistent with *Gertz*, required the corporate plaintiff, General Programming, to prove negligence to win its suit. However, Pennsylvania common law did not require General Programming or other plaintiffs to prove the defamatory language to be false. Rather, Philadelphia Newspapers, Inc., and other defendants had the burden of proving truth to avoid losing the suit.

The Supreme Court ruled, in a 5–4 decision, that the Constitution required General Programming to prove the falsity of defamatory remarks as well as negligence. Justice Sandra Day O'Connor, who wrote the majority opinion, noted that public officials and public figures already had to prove falsity as part of *New York Times* actual malice. To ensure that truthful speech was not deterred, O'Connor said the Constitution requires that private libel plaintiffs involved in matters of public interest must also establish falsehood. O'Connor said the question of who has the burden of proof in private-person cases becomes important only when the evidence is ambiguous—when truth or falsity cannot be proven in court. She said when it is impossible to "resolve conclusively" whether speech about matters of public concern is true or false, the Constitution requires the scales to be tipped in favor of protecting speech that might be true.

O'Connor said that as a practical matter, requiring private persons to prove falsity will not significantly add to their burden of proof. She said that if plaintiffs can prove that defamation was false, they will ordinarily have an easier time proving the media acted negligently. Justice O'Connor said the Court was not deciding whether a plaintiff, even one involved in matters of public interest, would have to prove falsity when suing a nonmedia defendant. Although private persons claiming to be defamed in a speech or an unpublished memo must prove negligence, they may not have to prove falsity.

MATTERS OF PUBLIC CONCERN The ruling in *Hepps* does not apply to all defamation involving private persons, only to defamation about matters of public interest. Private persons who are not involved in matters of public concern still must prove negligence but not necessarily falsity. The Supreme Court in *Hepps* said that it provided extra protection to speech about issues of public interest to encourage debate.

The U.S. Supreme Court has never defined "matters of public concern." In *Hepps*, the state licensing of a chain of stores that sold beer was a matter of public concern. In *Rosenbloom v. Metromedia*,[219] the Court said that a police campaign

---

[217] N.Y. Times Co. v. Sullivan, 376 U.S. 279; Garrison v. Louisiana, 379 U.S. 64 (1964); Herbert v. Lando, 441 U.S. 153 (1979).
[218] 475 U.S. 767 (1986).
[219] 403 U.S. 29, 31 (1971).

against obscenity was an event of "public or general interest." Other matters of public concern include investment reports sent to a readership of 200,000,[220] comments about product reliability on *60 Minutes*,[221] and criticism of the refereeing of a boxing match reported in the *National Sports Daily*.[222]

Private plaintiffs not involved in matters of public concern do not have to prove actual malice to collect punitive damages. In *Dun & Bradstreet v. Greenmoss Builders*, the Court ruled that Greenmoss Builders did not have to prove actual malice to collect punitive damages after the firm was libeled in a confidential credit report that was not a matter of public concern.[223] Dun & Bradstreet, a credit reporting agency, had mistakenly told five subscribers confidentially that Greenmoss Builders had filed for bankruptcy. Dun & Bradstreet inadvertently attributed the bankruptcy petition of a former Greenmoss employee to Greenmoss itself.

The Court said the private credit report was not a matter of public concern and did not affect the debate on public issues, including "the free flow" of information about business. The Court did not indicate what other kinds of speech might be considered private. The term *matter of public concern* could refer to any issue discussed in the mass media but not to private conversations or materials released only to those with a direct personal interest in the information.

■ SUMMARY ■

In 1986, the Supreme Court ruled that private persons involved in matters of public concern must also prove that defamation is false.

Damage, Injury or Harm

Under American libel law, persons who have been defamed are prohibited by the First Amendment from halting a publication or forcing publication of a retraction, but they can sue for monetary rewards for the harm they have suffered. Proof of harm is the sixth element of a plaintiff's libel case. A plaintiff cannot sue successfully over a harmless libel, although some harm to reputation may be "presumed." Libel plaintiffs may sue for *presumed damages*, the loss of reputation that a defamation is assumed to cause. They may also sue for two kinds of *compensatory damages*: **actual damages**, which are awards for proven loss of good name, shame, humiliation and stress, and **special damages**, which compensate for lost revenues and other out-of-pocket losses resulting from defamation. A libel plaintiff may also sue for **punitive damages**, awards imposed not to compensate for lost reputation but to punish the libeler.

PRESUMED DAMAGES Since *New York Times v. Sullivan*, the Supreme Court has made it more difficult for libel plaintiffs involved in public affairs to receive awards for presumed damages. Before *Sullivan*, successful libel plaintiffs won damages on the presumption that their reputations were damaged because a publication had defamed them. When libel damages were presumed and fault did not have to be proven, juries had wide latitude to make large damage awards to plaintiffs who were not necessarily harmed. If juries wished, they could punish unpopular ideas, thus inhibiting the press.

---

[220] Straw v. Chase Revel, Inc., 813 F.2d 356 (11th Cir. 1987).
[221] Unelko Corp. v. Andy Rooney, 912 F.2d 1049 (9th Cir. 1990).
[222] Don King Productions, Inc. v. James Buster Douglas, 742 F. Supp. 778 (S.D.N.Y. 1990).
[223] 472 U.S. 749 (1985).

In *New York Times v. Sullivan*, the Supreme Court held that public officials could be awarded damages, including presumed damages, only if they proved *New York Times* actual malice. In *Gertz*, the Court said that public figures and private plaintiffs too must prove actual malice if they are to collect presumed damages from the media. Writing for the Court, Justice Powell said that the First Amendment required curbing the "uncontrolled discretion of juries to award damages" when the plaintiff has not been harmed.[224] However, private plaintiffs who are not involved in a matter of public concern may collect presumed damages without proving fault. In *Dun & Bradstreet*, a divided Supreme Court upheld a jury award of $50,000 for presumed damages to a building company libeled in a private credit report.

COMPENSATORY DAMAGES Compensatory damages compensate a plaintiff for the harm a libel causes a reputation. When determining compensatory damage awards, juries consider the degree of fault, the number of people who may have read or heard the defamation, the seriousness of the defamatory charge, the degree of injury suffered, and the character and reputation of the litigants. Two forms of compensatory damages are actual damages and special damages.

Actual Damages In *Gertz*, the Supreme Court said plaintiffs who cannot prove *New York Times* actual malice can collect only for "actual injury." Actual injury may include financial loss, such as a restaurant might suffer after a defamatory review. But the Court in *Gertz* used the term *actual injury* more broadly. "Actual injury," the Court said, includes "impairment of reputation and standing in the community, personal humiliation, and mental anguish and suffering." The Court said that such actual injuries must be supported by "competent evidence," although the Court said plaintiffs do not have to assign a dollar value to their actual injuries.

Elmer Gertz, the Chicago lawyer called a Communist by a John Birch Society publication, won $100,000 in actual damages. A federal appeals court said that Gertz had demonstrated actual injury in part by testifying to his own mental distress, anxiety and embarrassment. Several attorneys testified that lawyers' professional reputations would be damaged by false claims that they were Communists.[225]

The Supreme Court's requirement that injury to reputation be proven rather than presumed has had little practical effect on the size of damage awards. The Court has provided no guidelines for acceptable proof of injury. Proof of damage to reputation is necessarily speculative when monetary loss is not demonstrated. Personal humiliation and mental anguish, in particular, do not carry price tags. If a jury is convinced that a plaintiff has not been seriously damaged by a defamatory remark, the jury may award only *nominal damages*—an award as little as $1. Nominal damages also may be awarded when libel trials are held before judges, without juries. Comedian Rodney Dangerfield won his libel suit against *Star Magazine*, which had falsely written, "Rodney Dangerfield Swills Vodka by the Tumblerful, Smokes Pot All Day and Uses Cocaine." The judge said Dangerfield had not proven serious damage to his reputation and was awarded $1 in nominal damages. However, the judge also gave Dangerfield $45,000 in presumed damages because *Star Magazine* had acted with actual malice.[226]

Special Damages Special damages, unlike actual damages, require proof of out-of-pocket loss, such as financial harm to a business. Monetary loss is the only kind of injury sufficient to justify special damages. Evidence of special damages is required before plaintiffs can win trade libel or product disparagement suits. Some

---

[224] 418 U.S. 349–50.
[225] Gertz v. Robert Welch Inc., 680 F.2d 527 (7th Cir. 1982).
[226] Dangerfield v. Star Editorial, Inc., 25 Media L. Rep. 1379 (9th Cir. 1996).

states also require plaintiffs to prove special damages when suing for slander or *libel per quod*, libel based on circumstances not apparent to the reasonably prudent publisher.[227] Plaintiffs often have difficulty proving that their loss of business was due to a defamatory article.

Punitive Damages The large money awards in libel cases are usually assessed for punitive damages. Punitive damages are intended to punish a publication for defamation and to deter other publications from bad behavior rather than to compensate the plaintiff for injury to reputation. Justice Powell said in *Gertz* that punitive damages are "private fines" levied by juries "to punish reprehensible conduct and to deter its future occurrence." Justice Powell and many commentators have said that punitive damages fail to serve the social interest of libel law: that of vindicating reputation.

Richard DiSalle, a former judge, was awarded $2.2 million, of which $2 million was for punitive damages, for an article in the *Pittsburgh Post-Gazette* saying DiSalle helped to draft a fraudulent will.[228] Vic Feazell, a former district attorney, won $58 million when he sued Dallas television station WFAA for accusing him of taking bribes to fix drunk driving cases. Forty-one million dollars of the verdict, the largest ever in a libel trial, was for punitive damages. The suit was eventually settled for $20 million.[229] If large jury verdicts are not cut back through out-of-court settlements, they are often reduced by judges.

Many commentators and the Supreme Court itself have been concerned that large punitive damage awards lead journalists to censor themselves.[230] To reduce the chances of self-censorship, the Supreme Court requires that all libel plaintiffs, except for private plaintiffs involved in private issues, prove *New York Times* actual malice to collect punitive damages. Some states, including Washington, Oregon and Massachusetts, do not permit punitive damages.[231] Other states require plaintiffs seeking punitive damages to prove not only actual malice but also that the media intended to harm their reputations.[232]

The Supreme Court has upheld the right of plaintiffs to sue for "reasonable" punitive damages. Reasonable punitive damages can be very high. In a case that did not involve the media, a divided Supreme Court affirmed a $10 million award of punitive damages, an award more than 500 times greater than the compensatory awards in the case.[233] In 1989, the Supreme Court denied review of a newspaper's argument that punitive damage awards violate not only the First and Fourteenth Amendments but also the Eighth Amendment's prohibition against excessive fines. The Court rejected a petition for certiorari by the *Pittsburgh Post-Gazette*, appealing a $2.2 million libel judgment, all but $200,000 for punitive damages.[234]

In 1996, the Supreme Court for the first time overturned an award of punitive damages as "grossly excessive" in violation of the Fourteenth Amendment. In a 5–4 decision, the Court overturned a $2 million punitive damage award to an Alabama

---

[227] *E.g.*, Rodney Smolla, *Law of Defamation* § 9.07, at 9–16.1 (1998).
[228] "Aftermath of Libel Case Bodes Ill for Media," *Broadcasting*, July 10, 1989, at 37.
[229] "$58 Million Libel Award Against TV Station," *Editor & Publisher*, Apr. 27, 1991, at 16; Kim Cobb, "Attorney Considered by Turner Gains Prestige in Libel Lawsuits," *Houston Chronicle*, Feb. 10, 1992, at A11.
[230] *See* Gertz v. Robert Welch, Inc., 418 U.S. 349.
[231] *E.g.*, Stone v. Essex County Newspaper, 330 N.E.2d 161 (Mass. 1975); Taskett v. King Broadcasting Co., 546 P.2d 81 (Wash. 1976).
[232] *E.g.*, Rodney Smolla, *Law of Defamation* § 9.08(3)(b)(ii), at 9–20.2 (1998).
[233] TXO Prod. Corp. v. Alliance Resources Corp., 509 U.S. 443 (1993).
[234] *See* DiSalle v. P.G. Publishing Co., 544 A.2d 1345 (Pa. Super. 1988), *appeal denied*, 557 A.2d 724 (Pa. 1989), *cert. denied*, 492 U.S. 906 (1989).

doctor, an amount that had been awarded because the manufacturer of his new BMW failed to tell him that his car had been repainted before it was sold. The Court did not define what is "grossly excessive" but said courts should consider the reprehensibility of the defendant's conduct, the disparity between the award and the harm suffered, and the difference between the award and the civil penalties authorized in comparable cases.[235]

The Court said the $2 million BMW award was not reasonable because the car manufacturer's failure to inform the doctor of the paint job was not particularly "reprehensible." Furthermore, there was a great disparity between the $2 million award and the minor economic harm—about $400—the doctor suffered, and there was a great difference between the $2 million award and the maximum civil penalty of $2,000 the doctor might have collected under Alabama's Deceptive Trade Practices Act.

Many states have enacted statutory caps on the amount of punitive damages that may be awarded, often through tort reform efforts to limit the unpredictability of jury awards. Nebraska does not allow punitive damage awards at all. In 2008, the Supreme Court examined the state laws with punitive damage caps, finding that the most common cap was a 3:1 ratio, meaning punitive damages could at most be three times the amount of actual or compensatory damages. In that case, the court struck down a $2.5 billion award against Exxon regarding the *Valdez* supertanker accident and resulting oil spill that caused massive environmental damage off the coast of Alaska, finding that in that case, a 1:1 punitive damage ratio was proper as a matter of federal common law, rather than the nearly 5:1 ratio the jury had awarded.[236]

OTHER REMEDIES Libel cases are often not just about money. Rather, libel plaintiffs are seeking to be made whole again through damage to their reputations, a feat not easily accomplished. In the digital age, once an item has been published, it can be difficult for that to go away, even if it is established that the item is untrue and defamatory. First Amendment protections against prior restraint make it difficult for courts to order takedowns or injunctions against harmful speech.[237] In recent years, courts have considered what law professor Eugene Volokh calls "anti-libel injunctions" as a potential remedy.[238]

Because libel involving private citizens is not clearly within the scope of the First Amendment, courts do have some ability to force websites to remove libelous content after it has proven to be defamatory at trial. The Texas Supreme Court, for example, found that such an order was permissible under the First Amendment because the online material had been found by a court to be defamatory. However, the court also noted that plaintiffs could not get a similar injunction against potential future libels, which would be an unconstitutional prior restraint.[239] In 2019, the U.S. Court of Appeals for the Ninth Circuit used similar logic to permit an injunction to require a speaker to take down statements found to be libelous and to avoid repeating statements "the same or effectively identical" to the ones in the case at hand.[240]

[235] BMW of North America, Inc. v. Gore, 517 U.S. 559 (1996).
[236] Exxon Shipping Co. v. Baker, 554 U.S. 471 (2008).
[237] Sindi v. El-Moslimany, 896 F.3d 1 (1st Cir. 2018).
[238] *See* Eugene Volokh, "Anti-Libel Injunctions," 167 *U. Pa. L. Rev.* 73, 80 (2019).
[239] Kinney v. Barnes, 443 S.W.3d 87 (Tex. 2013).
[240] Eugene Volokh, "Ninth Circuit Affirms Anti-Libel Injunction, Rejects Overbroad Portion," *The Volokh Conspiracy*, Jan. 21, 2020 (case comment about an unpublished opinion in *Ferguson v. Waid*, No. 2:17-cv-01685-RSM, Jan. 8, 2020).

▓ **SUMMARY** ▓

The U.S. Supreme Court has said that public officials, public figures and private persons involved in matters of public concern can collect presumed and punitive damages only if they prove *New York Times* actual malice. Presumed damages do not require proof of harm. Punitive damages are intended to punish a publication for false defamatory remarks. Public officials, public figures and private persons involved in matters of public concern who do not prove *New York Times* actual malice must show actual injury in order to be eligible for damage awards. Actual injury is proof of damage to reputation or mental anguish as well as actual monetary loss. Special damages are awarded only after proof of monetary loss, though these damages are often capped in relation to the amount of compensatory damages.

THE DEFENDANT'S CASE

Although the media are protected by the high evidentiary burdens placed on libel plaintiffs, media are not required to passively observe whether libel plaintiffs can meet their constitutionally imposed burdens of proving defamation, falsity and fault. Libel defendants also have a number of defenses they can actively assert.

A complete defense in a libel suit is the truth, although truth may be difficult to prove. Besides, the truth is often unknown or unprovable, particularly in statements made during official proceedings. Thus, a common-law privilege allows the media to accurately report to the public about the courts, legislature and executive branch, even when reporters are repeating defamatory statements from trial testimony, courthouse filings, senate speeches and executive press conferences. Communicators also have common-law and constitutional protection to express opinions about the quality of public presentations, including films, books, lectures, restaurant meals, video games and recitals.

This section discusses libel defenses that predate and often overlap the constitutional protections established in *New York Times v. Sullivan* and related cases. This section covers the defenses of truth, the media privilege to report official records and proceedings, and the protection for opinion. Other defenses that are discussed in this section are statutes of limitations, the absolute privilege enjoyed by government officials, a privilege for broadcasters fulfilling political programming requirements, consent, neutral reportage, self-defense and a qualified privilege for internal communications. Any one of the defenses may defeat the plaintiff seeking damages.

Before the media defend themselves in court, however, they try to prevent a trial from starting. Often they seek to use state anti-SLAPP laws or file motions for summary judgment, asking a judge to terminate a case before it starts because the plaintiff has no chance of winning.

Anti-SLAPP

News media are not the only libel defendants. Nonmedia businesses and nonprofit corporations are also sued for comments they make about employee performance or for comments to reporters when trying to protect their own business interests. Citizen activists have been the subject of libel suits by the businesses and government officials they criticize.

Libel suits intended to silence citizen activists or news media reporting on matters of public concern by abusing the legal process are called **SLAPP suits** (strategic lawsuits against public participation). Even though SLAPP suits are seldom successful, they often discourage citizen activism because defending libel suits is so time-consuming and expensive. As of early 2022, more than 30 states and the District of Columbia had enacted statutes to provide procedural remedies for victims of SLAPP suits, often called **anti-SLAPP** laws, while some state legislatures were considering adding them or enhancing the ones already in place.[241] Congress has not passed a federal version of the law, and federal courts are split on whether state anti-SLAPP laws can be raised to fend off meritless libel suits filed in federal court.[242] Anti-SLAPP statutes are becoming increasingly important for journalists and citizens who are threatened with meritless defamation actions.[243]

The strongest anti-SLAPP laws provide a deterrent against meritless defamation actions through fee-shifting provisions and expedited hearings that allow for early dismissal. For example, the Texas version of the law, called the Texas Citizens Participation Act, gives defendants a chance for a hearing within 120 days of the filing of a lawsuit regarding speaking out about a matter of public concern. If the defendant can establish that the case is without merit or otherwise has no chance of success, the judge can dismiss the case. Additionally, the mandatory–fee shifting provision requires the judge to order the plaintiff filing the frivolous lawsuit to pay attorney fees and costs to the defendant to make them whole after wasting their time with a baseless action.[244] Additionally, judges have discretion to sanction the losing plaintiffs to deter them from bringing similar actions in the future.[245]

In 2018, Donald Trump received nearly $300,000 in attorney fees under the Texas Citizens Participation Act after the adult film actress Stephanie Clifford's libel lawsuit against him was dismissed. Clifford, perhaps more famously known by the name "Stormy Daniels," had revealed that Trump had an affair with her years before and had been paid hush money by Trump as he sought the presidency in 2016. She claimed that Trump had hired someone to threaten her to keep her silent in 2011, and Trump responded by tweeting that her accusations were "a total con job" about a "nonexistent man." While the lawsuit was heard by a federal district court in California, the court applied the Texas law because Clifford was a Texas resident when she filed the case, and this court decided to allow state anti-SLAPP motions in federal diversity cases. The district court ruled that Trump's tweet "was not meant to be understood as a literal statement" about Clifford, but was rather a "one-off rhetorical comment" against a political adversary, and thus was not a valid basis for a defamation suit.[246]

In Texas, plaintiffs have the burden to establish a "prima facie" case supported by evidence to avoid dismissal under the anti-SLAPP law.[247] California places a heavier burden on plaintiffs, who must prove a probability of prevailing on their

---

[241] *See* Public Participation Project, "State Anti-SLAPP Scorecard," https://anti-slapp.org/your-states-free-speech-protection/ (accessed Jan. 29, 2022).

[242] See Godin v. Schencks, 629 F.3d 79 (1st Cir. 2010) (requiring a district court to allow a motion under Maine's anti-SLAPP to proceed in a state law defamation case); Klocke v. Watson, 936 F.3d 240 (5th Cir. 2019) (not applying the Texas Citizens Participation Act in a defamation case brought under Texas state law on diversity jurisdiction).

[243] Kristen Rasmussen, "SLAPP Stick: Fighting Frivolous Lawsuits Against Journalists," *Reporters Committee for Freedom of the Press*, Spring 2011, https://www.rcfp.org/wp-content/uploads/imported/ANTISLAPP.pdf?msclkid=93114fb3a77611ecb1b0c7649d290651.

[244] Laura Prather, "The Texas Citizens Participation Act—Five Years After Passage," *Haynes and Boone* (2016).

[245] Tex Civ. Prac. & Rem. Code § 27.009(a)(2) (2019).

[246] Clifford v. Trump, 339 F. Supp. 3d 915, 927 (C.D. Cal. 2018). *See also* Clifford v. Trump, 2018 U.S. Dist. LEXIS 211297 (C.D. Cal. 2018).

[247] Tex. Civ. Prac. & Rem. Code § 27.005 (2016).

claims in a pretrial hearing in order to avoid dismissal of lawsuits that may chill speech on matters of public concern.[248]

California and Texas are recognized as having some of the stronger anti-SLAPP laws. In many states, however, these laws are more limited in scope. New York's law, for example, only applied to lawsuits about application for permits from government agencies until 2020, when the state legislature expanded the law to cover any action "in connection with a matter of public interest."[249] Pennsylvania's law is only available to people "petitioning the government about environmental issues."[250]

Defendants in SLAPP suits can also claim their statements are protected opinion. The online review website Yelp, for instance, has lobbied to enhance anti-SLAPP protections for its reviewers, typically citizens who face lawsuits as a way to make them take down critical comments of restaurants, landlords or other services.[251] Whether filing a SLAPP suit or not, corporate libel plaintiffs often seek the identity of critics who the companies say defame them anonymously on the Internet. Courts have ruled companies can subpoena names of anonymous critics if the plaintiffs demonstrate the strong likelihood that they have been harmed by anonymous defamation. An Illinois court ruled a business couple could seek the identity of persons who anonymously accused them of bribery on a newspaper website.[252]

States without anti-SLAPP protections now find themselves as destinations for domestic "libel tourism." There is a reason that plaintiffs bring defamation actions with no hope of success—either because the statements are opinion, or rhetorical hyperbole, or are protected under Section 230 of the Communications Decency Act—in certain jurisdictions. Several of the aforementioned lawsuits by Congressman Devin Nunes were brought in Virginia, which has become a "magnet for questionable legal claims," according to the Electronic Frontier Foundation. Nunes is a California resident, and his lawsuits against California-based Twitter and his hometown newspaper the *Fresno Bee* were filed in Virginia because it, unlike California, had no robust anti-SLAPP protections allowing quick dismissal and attorney fee awards for meritless litigation.[253]

Summary Judgment

For plaintiffs to win libel suits, they must prove defamation, identification, publication, fault, harm to reputation and usually falsity. If judges are satisfied before trial that plaintiffs cannot prove their cases, the judges may terminate the case before trial by awarding defendants **summary judgment**. Media defendants understandably favor summary judgments because libel cases that end before trial do not go to juries; when cases do go to juries, publishers are apt to lose more often than they win. Summary judgments, which avoid lengthy trials, not only save time, avoid stress and preclude big damage awards but also save lawyers' fees.

---

[248] Cal. Civ. Proc. Code § 425.16(b)(1) (2016).

[249] N.Y. Civ. Rights Law § 76-a(1).

[250] Kristen Rasmussen, "SLAPP Stick: Fighting Frivolous Lawsuits Against Journalists," *Reporters Committee for Freedom of the Press*, Spring 2011. *See* 27 Pennsylvania Consolidated Statutes Sec. 7707 (2021).

[251] Josh Harkinson, "Yelp Is Pushing a Law to Shield Its Reviewers from Defamation Suits," *Mother Jones*, July 20, 2015.

[252] Maxon v. Ottawa Publishing Co., 402 Ill. App. 3d 704 (2010); *see* Dendrite International, Inc. v. Doe No. 3, 342 N.J. Super. 134 (App. 2001).

[253] Joe Mullin, "Virginia Needs a Strong Anti-SLAPP Law to Stop Bogus Lawsuits," *Electronic Frontier Foundation*, Jan. 13, 2020.

A judge should issue a summary judgment if the plaintiff's case is too weak to prevail and there is no "genuine" dispute over a "material" fact that the jury must decide. Judges cannot resolve factual disputes, such as whether the defendant published defamatory language or the plaintiff is a public figure. But if both parties agree on the facts, then judges can determine as a matter of law whether the plaintiff lacks any realistic chance of winning. If so, the judge may issue summary judgment for the media.

Summary judgments have been particularly useful in cases involving public officials and public figures, who must prove *New York Times* actual malice. The Supreme Court has ruled that trial courts must issue summary judgment for the media unless public officials and public figures can make their case with "clear and convincing evidence." Thus, the Court requires that libel plaintiffs meet the same demanding standards of proof before trial as during trial. In *Anderson v. Liberty Lobby, Inc.*, the Supreme Court approved a district court's decision to require the founder of a self-described citizens lobby to prove with clear and convincing evidence before trial that investigative journalist Jack Anderson libeled him with actual malice.[254] Anderson called the lobbyist an "American Hitler." The district court had issued summary judgment for Anderson, ruling that Anderson's thorough investigation precluded a jury from finding *New York Times* actual malice.

Statutes of Limitations

A state's **statute of limitations** is a sure and often easy way to defeat a libel suit. For almost all criminal and civil actions, prosecutors and plaintiffs must file a suit within a specified period, which in a libel suit is usually from one to two years from the date of publication. A plaintiff may not initiate an action after the deadline for filing a suit has passed. Statutes of limitations serve freedom of expression by narrowing the period during which publishers must be concerned that a libel suit will result from the mass of information disseminated through many different media.[255]

In most jurisdictions, the statute of limitations is governed by the *single-publication rule*. This means the clock starts running when the libel is first published. Would-be plaintiffs may not claim a new publication—and bring a new libel suit—each time a defamatory publication is sold or displayed.[256] However, a new edition of a publication or a new newscast may allow a person a second opportunity to sue over the same libel.[257]

Most courts adopt the single-publication rule for online defamation, ruling that the statute of limitations clock begins ticking when defamation is published online, rejecting the position that online publication is "continuous." However, the statute of limitations clock is reset when a website is republished, including when its content is "substantially modified."[258]

---

[254] 477 U.S. 242 (1986).

[255] For a list of state statutes of limitations, *see* Bruce Sanford, *Libel and Privacy*, App. C, at 819–822.1 (2nd ed. 1999).

[256] *E.g.*, W. Page Keeton et al., *Prosser and Keeton on the Law of Torts* § 113, at 800 (5th ed. 1984); *Restatement (Second) of Torts* § 577A (3) and comment on subsection (3).

[257] *Restatement (Second) of Torts* § 577 comment d; *e.g.*, Cox Enterprises, Inc. v. Gilreath, 235 S.E.2d 633 (Ga. Ct. App. 1977).

[258] *E.g.*, Atkinson v. McLaughlin, 462 F. Supp. 2d 1038 (D.N.D. 2006); Firth v. New York, 775 N.E.2d 463 (N.Y. 2002).

A few states cling to the common-law rule that a libel is published every time the article is displayed, sold or circulated to a third party.[259] In these jurisdictions, the media are in constant jeopardy because a plaintiff can sue any time after the first publication date, even long after the statute of limitations has run out on the original publication. How is the date of original publication decided? Most states use the date that the libelous publication is released for sale. For magazines and books, the release date—the date the magazine is generally available for readers—is usually before the date on the cover. Paperback books, too, are often distributed to the public before the dates their publishers declare as publication dates. Attorney Michael J. Morrissey unwittingly waited too long to sue the publishers of the book *Spooks: The Haunting of America—The Private Use of Secret Agents*. Morrissey sued on December 1, 1980, within a year of December 19, 1979, the official publication date of the paperback edition of the book in which he claimed to be libeled. However, a federal appeals court said the one-year clock for the statute of limitations began running on November 20, 1979, the date the paperback version "was generally available for sale in bookstores throughout the United States."[260]

■ SUMMARY ■

Libel defendants may turn to procedural remedies to dismiss actions before trial. In strategic lawsuits against public participation (SLAPPs), defendants in many states have the option to use an anti-SLAPP law to dismiss a case and be awarded attorney fees when the lawsuits have no merit or chance of success at trial. Judges issue summary judgments, in effect dismissing libel cases, when there are no factual issues in dispute and plaintiffs lack sufficient evidence to succeed at trial. Under most statutes of limitations, persons who wish to sue for libel must file suits within a year or two of the publication of the alleged defamation.

Truth

In most states, libel defendants will win if they can prove the defamation they published is true. Although proving the truth will still defeat a libel suit, the defense of truth is less important than it was before 1964, when defamation was presumed and defendants bore the burden of proving the truth. Truth became less important to media defendants when *New York Times v. Sullivan* and the constitutional cases that followed required libel plaintiffs to prove falsity and fault. Now, if a plaintiff fails to establish that a remark is false, the defendant wins without having to prove the publication is true.

The truth of a publication or broadcast may be hard to prove because evidence is unavailable. A reporter's confidential sources may refuse to testify or may lack credibility if they do testify. Furthermore, reporters who testify about events they witnessed have no certainty that a jury will believe them. Convincing witnesses for the opposing party and skilled attorneys on the other side can cloud the truth.

The determination of truth rests on the overall impression, or "gist," of a statement. A story must be substantially true but need not be true in every detail. Minor errors will not destroy the defense of truth. In 2011, the Georgia Court of Appeals

---

[259] *See* W. Page Keeton et al., *Prosser and Keeton on the Law of Torts* § 113, at 800 (5th ed. 1984); Bruce Sanford, *Libel and Privacy* § 13.2.4, at 630–1 (2nd ed. 1999).

[260] Morrissey v. William Morrow & Co., 739 F.2d 962 (4th Cir. 1984), *cert. denied*, 469 U.S. 1216 (1985).

concluded that the *Atlanta Journal-Constitution* published essentially true stories in 1996 reporting that security guard Richard Jewell was a suspect in the bomb explosion at Centennial Olympic Park. Jewell, who was first a hero, then a suspect, was eventually cleared of suspicion. The record establishes, the court said,

> that at the time of the publications, investigators did, in fact, suspect that Jewell may have planted the bomb and were actively investigating that theory. . . .. Because the articles in their entirety were substantially true at the time they were published—even though the investigators' suspicions were ultimately deemed unfounded—they cannot form the basis of a defamation action against the Media Defendants.[261]

Similarly, the Texas Supreme Court found that the "gist" of a broadcast news investigation potentially harmed a surgeon who had been disciplined by the state medical board. KEYE asked the question, "Would you want to know if your surgeon had been disciplined for prescribing himself and taking dangerous drugs?" regarding Dr. Byron Neely, a physician who had been under investigation. The Texas Medical Board, however, had only found that he had self-prescribed medications, not that he had been taking them in a way that harmed his practice. Even though some of the people interviewed by KEYE said on air that Neely had likely used the drugs improperly, there was no finding in the record that it had happened, and Neely provided evidence that he had not used the drugs improperly. The court allowed Neely's case against KEYE to proceed, finding that the "gist" of the broadcast could have caused him harm, overcoming the news station's argument that the broadcast was substantially true.[262]

The media will not be able to prove the truth of a story if important omissions create a false, defamatory impression even though the story contains true statements. In *Memphis Publishing Co. v. Nichols*, a case discussed earlier, the Tennessee Supreme Court said a jury could find the *Memphis Press-Scimitar* liable because it omitted critical facts from an article about a shooting.[263] The *Press-Scimitar* truthfully reported that a Mrs. Newton shot Ruth Nichols when she found Nichols and Mr. Newton in the Nichols home. However, the paper mistakenly implied that Nichols and Mr. Newton were having an affair because the paper failed to report that Nichols, Mr. Newton and two neighbors were sitting and talking in the living room when Mrs. Newton arrived at the Nichols' house. The court said the paper's failure to report the innocent conversation between Mr. Newton and Nichols created the false impression that Mr. Newton and Nichols were committing adultery. The Tennessee Supreme Court said that literal truth of statements in a story does not protect an article that conveys a defamatory meaning.

▦ SUMMARY ▦

Libel suits can be successfully defended with proof that defamatory statements are substantially true. Minor errors will not defeat the truth defense. Although defendants were once required to prove truth to win libel suits, the Supreme Court has shifted the burden so that libel plaintiffs must now prove falsity.

---

[261] Bryant v. Cox Enters, Inc., 311 Ga. App. 230 (2011).
[262] Neely v. Wilson, 418 S.W.3d 52 (Tex. 2013).
[263] 569 S.W.2d 412 (Tenn. 1978).

Protection for Opinion

Libel plaintiffs, as we have seen, must prove that a defamatory statement is false and published with fault. If plaintiffs can't prove falsity, they can't win their libel suit. Often plaintiffs can't prove falsity because the story they claim libeled them consists of **opinion** that can't be proven to be false. Thus, a Southern chef had no libel suit, even though he felt "defamed," when a newspaper reviewer wrote that his dinner was covered with "hideous sauces" and that he had been served "trout à la green plague."[264]

The chef had no libel suit because the reviewer had stated an opinion that could not be considered a false, defamatory fact. The reviewer did not say the chef was transmitting communicable diseases, a statement that could be proven true or false in a laboratory. The reviewer simply said his taste buds rebelled at the sauces and entrees. Diners at the next table might have loved the food. How the food tasted is a matter of nondefamatory opinion.

The Supreme Court has established constitutional protection for statements of opinion. Indeed, the Supreme Court once said, "there is no such thing as a false idea. However pernicious an opinion may seem, we depend for its correction not on the conscience of judges and juries but on the competition of other ideas."[265] While constitutional protection for opinion is generous—extending to biting, caustic criticism inevitable in a democratic society—the First Amendment, the Supreme Court has said, has not created a "wholesale defamation exemption for anything that might be labeled 'opinion.'" Statements of purported opinion, such as "in my opinion, John Jones is a child molester," are not protected opinion, the Supreme Court says, if they connote provably false statements of fact.[266] When a speaker says, "In my opinion, John Jones is a child molester," the speaker implies he or she knows unstated facts about Jones's activities.

Distinguishing opinion from false facts is no easy undertaking. Traditionally, courts have distinguished fact from opinion by considering such factors as the ordinary meaning of words, their verifiability, the social context in which they were uttered and the media in which they were disseminated. Although the Supreme Court is mindful of these factors—and indeed employs some of them in its analysis of opinion—the Court has refused to adopt these criteria as a formal test for determining constitutionally protected opinion. Instead, the Court has proclaimed that an assertion is protected as opinion unless it contains "a provably false factual connotation."

The Supreme Court ruled the term *liar* might be a defamatory false fact when employed by an Ohio journalist in a column. The Court said a jury should determine whether journalist Theodore Diadiun made a false factual statement when he wrote that a high school wrestling coach lied to a panel investigating a brawl following a wrestling match. In *Milkovich v. Lorain Journal Co.*, the Court said a jury might conclude that the term *liar* in a column by journalist Theodore Diadiun was a false fact because it could be read to mean that the coach committed perjury.

The Court ruled 7–2 that wrestling coach Michael Milkovich may have been libeled when Diadiun wrote in the Willoughby, Ohio, *News-Herald* that anyone attending the wrestling match "knows in his heart" that Milkovich "lied at the hearing after . . . having given his solemn oath to tell the truth." Diadiun said in

---

[264] Mashburn v. Collin, 355 So. 2d 879 (La. 1977).
[265] Gertz v. Welch, 418 U.S. 339–40.
[266] Milkovich v. Lorain Journal Co., 497 U.S. 1 (1990).

his column that Milkovich inspired fans to attack opponents from Mentor High School, although Milkovich testified that he was not responsible for the brawl in which seven were injured following a wrestling match between Maple Heights and Mentor. After the hearing, Diadiun wrote that Milkovich taught Maple Heights students a lesson: "If you get in a jam, lie your way out."

Writing for the Supreme Court, Chief Justice Rehnquist saw in Diadiun's column a factual statement—Milkovich committed perjury—that could be proven true or false. Diadiun's use of the term *liar*, the Court said, "is not the sort of loose, figurative or hyperbolic language which would negate the impression" that Diadiun "was seriously maintaining" that Milkovich "committed the crime of perjury." The Court remanded the case so that a lower court could examine testimony in an earlier hearing and trial to determine the truth of Diadiun's charge that Milkovich lied. Milkovich later settled out of court with the *News-Herald* for an estimated $100,000.[267]

There are no connotations of false facts, the Supreme Court has said, when a writer employs exaggerated or figurative terms that are incapable of a factual meaning. Thus, the Court ruled the terms *blackmail* and *traitor* were constitutionally protected opinion when the speaker used the terms figuratively or to exaggerate.

When people involved in a newsworthy situation have different views on what happened at an event, reporting on those different perspectives may be a matter of opinion. This issue arose in a confrontation in Washington, D.C., during a March for Life event in 2019. Students from a Catholic high school in Kentucky attended the event, wearing "Make America Great Again" hats near the Lincoln Memorial when they were approached by a group that had been at an Indigenous Peoples March at the National Mall the same day. Photos and videos from this interaction, generally focusing on student protester Nicholas Sandmann and Native American activist Nathan Phillips, quickly became the subject of intense media and political scrutiny. Several portrayed Sandmann in a negative light, as he appeared to be smirking when approached by Phillips, who was singing and beating a drum; one Twitter account posted a video recorded by one of the Native American marchers and described Sandmann as a "MAGA loser gleefully bothering a Native American protester." News reports differed on whether Sandmann and other students were standing calmly, were yelling or were actively blocking the Native American marchers. Sandmann filed defamation lawsuits against several news outlets, including the *Washington Post*.[268] A federal judge dismissed the case against the *Post* on grounds that the 33 statements Sandmann claimed were false and defamatory either were not about him specifically or were matters of opinion rather than "objectively verifiable fact." For instance, one Native American protester said the students were engaged in a "aggressive display of physicality" and were "rambunctious and trying to instigate a conflict," which the court said were matters of his opinion rather than fact. "[T]erms such as 'ugly,' 'swarmed,' 'taunting,' 'disrespect,' 'ignored,' 'aggressive,' 'physicality,' and 'rambunctious'" are protected by the First Amendment, the court said, because they are not "susceptible of being proven true or false."[269] The ruling was later revised to allow the case to proceed on three specific statements in the *Post* that said that Sandmann had "blocked" Phillips and "would not allow him to

---

[267] "Wrestling Coach Settles Suit Over Column," *News Media & L.* (Spring 1991), at 23.
[268] Cameron Knight, "CNN Confirms a Settlement Has Been Reached with Nick Sandmann," *Cincinnati Enquirer*, Jan. 7, 2020.
[269] Sandmann v. WP Co., LLC, 401 F. Supp. 3d 781, 792 (E.D. Ky. 2019).

retreat," which the judge said were possibly statements of fact that could be proven or disproven through further discovery.[270]

Suits on opinion pieces published by news organizations are seemingly on the rise. In 2020, the re-election campaign of then–President Donald Trump filed three separate lawsuits against CNN, the *New York Times* and the *Washington Post*, based on columns by opinion writers. The CNN lawsuit was based on one sentence in a 37-paragraph column that said, "The Trump campaign assessed the potential risks and benefits of again seeking Russia's help in the 2020 election and decided to leave that option on the table." While dismissing the case on other grounds, a federal district court said this was a statement of fact rather than opinion, saying it has a "precise meaning" and a "reasonable reader could readily understand the first part as alleging the weighing of the risks and benefits," and that while "left on the table" is figurative, it also is capable of precise meaning. And even though the column was printed in the Opinions section of CNN and had rhetorical flourishes that would signal that it was opinion to a reasonable reader, the fact that this one sentence did not contain the same "softening language" such as "appeared to be" or "might well be" that paragraphs around it suggested that it was factual rather than opinion.[271] Like the CNN lawsuit, the *New York Times* suit was dismissed, though the lawsuit against the *Washington Post* was still pending almost two years after it was filed. The litigiousness of anti-media politicians like Trump and Sarah Palin, whose lawsuit against the *New York Times* based on an editorial took five years to go to a trial before a jury ruled against her in 2022, continues to have chilling effects on journalists. As Tony Norman, then-president of the National Society of Newspaper Columnists, said, "I don't know anyone who'd write about Palin now, even if they're totally in the right. I don't even mention her name in my columns if I can help it."[272]

EXAGGERATION AND FIGURATIVE TERMS Some words are so exaggerated or are used in such a figurative sense that the Supreme Court has said they are incapable of a factual interpretation. One case of exaggeration is that of Charles Bresler, a land developer in Maryland, who lost a libel suit against the *Greenbelt News Review* because the newspaper published "rhetorical hyperbole," not fact, when it said Bresler might have engaged in "blackmail." The paper repeated the epithet hurled by citizens who charged that Bresler blackmailed the city when he offered to sell land to the city only after the city rezoned a different parcel he owned.

In *Greenbelt Cooperative Publishing Association v. Bresler*,[273] the Supreme Court said the term *blackmail* clearly did not imply the false, defamatory fact that Bresler was guilty of a crime. "Even the most careless reader," the Court said, "must have perceived that the word was no more than rhetorical hyperbole, a vigorous epithet used by those who considered Bresler's negotiating position extremely unreasonable." As a matter of constitutional law, the Court said, the word *blackmail* was not libelous, at least in the context of a heated city council debate over a political and economic issue of intense public interest. However, the term *blackmail*

---

[270] Paul Farhi, "Federal Judge Reinstates Libel Lawsuit Filed by Covington Catholic Teen Against Washington Post," *Washington Post*, Oct. 28, 2019.
[271] Donald J. Trump for President v. CNN Broadcasting, 500 F. Supp. 3d 1349 (N.D. Ga. 2020).
[272] Bill Grueskin, "Three Trump Campaign Lawsuits Put Opinion in the Crosshairs," *Columbia Journalism Review*, March 8, 2021.
[273] 398 U.S. 6 (1970).

could be defamatory if it was intended to mean that a person employed criminal means to gain advantage.

In another case of exaggerated language, the Supreme Court ruled that a newspaper did not defame a laborer in the charged context of a labor dispute when the paper referred to him as a "scab" and a "traitor to his God, his country, his family and his class." Noting that exaggerated rhetoric is "commonplace in labor disputes," as it is at city council meetings, the Supreme Court said the word *traitor* in a union newsletter did not convey a defamatory meaning when applied to an employee who crosses a picket line. Rather, the Court said in *National Ass'n of Letter Carriers v. Austin*, the word was used in a "loose, figurative sense."[274] It is impossible to believe, the Court said, that any reader "would have understood the newsletter to be charging" the workers "with committing the criminal offense of treason." The case might have come out differently if the word *scab* had been taken out of context to create a false impression.

The Virginia Supreme Court held the phrase "Director of Butt Licking" inadvertently published by a student newspaper did not have a literal meaning and therefore was not defamatory. The state supreme court rejected the plaintiff's argument the words implied "that she curries favor with others by disingenuous behavior" or "performs the duties of her job in an artificial, shallow, or other manner that generally lacks integrity." The court said the "phrase is disgusting, offensive, and in extremely bad taste" but "cannot reasonably be understood as stating an actual fact."[275]

In 2019, Tesla and SpaceX founder Elon Musk won a defamation case brought by a British man who had helped rescue children trapped in an underwater cave in Thailand. On Twitter, Musk called the man "pedo guy" and in emails called him a "child rapist," but a jury in Los Angeles ruled in favor of Musk, apparently agreeing with Musk's attorney's argument that the statements were not intended to be statements of fact, but rather mere insults.[276]

OPINION BASED ON FACT If writers understandably prefer to avoid exaggerated, hyperbolic and vague language, they can ensure that their expression is understood as opinion by stating the facts on which the opinion is based. Readers of opinions based on stated facts, like readers of hyperbole, have no reason to think that statements are factual. Opinion based on stated facts is sometimes called "pure opinion."[277]

The U.S. Court of Appeals for the First Circuit ruled that two columns by *Boston Globe* writer Kevin Kelly were protected opinion in part because Kelly fully disclosed the facts supporting his conclusion that producers of a touring version of the musical *The Phantom of the Opera* were deliberately confusing the public.[278] Kelly said producers of the touring version were trying to make the public think they were seeing a more popular, non-touring version produced by Andrew Lloyd Webber. Kelly wrote that Phantom Touring, Inc., was trying to boost the popularity of its modestly successful road version of *Phantom* by causing patrons to mistakenly think the show was related to Webber's smash London hit of the same name.

---

[274] 418 U.S. 264 (1974).

[275] Yeagle v. Collegiate Times, 497 S.E.2d 136 (Va. 1998).

[276] Lora Kolodny, "Elon Musk Found Not Liable in 'Pedo Guy' Defamation Trial," *CNBC*, Dec. 6, 2019.

[277] *See id.; see also* KCNC-TV, Inc. v. Living Will Ctr., 879 P.2d 6 (Colo. 1994).

[278] Phantom Touring, Inc. v. Affiliated Publications, 953 F.2d 724 (1st Cir.), *cert. denied*, 504 U.S. 974 (1992).

Kelly spelled out in his columns why he thought the touring company was "trying to score off the success" of Webber's play by deliberately employing "confusing marketing." In his columns, Kelly recounted how the touring company proclaimed in large type that its production was "The Original London Stage Musical," a headline that was technically true but, Kelly said, deceptively overlooked the fact that Webber's *Phantom* was the only version popular in London. Kelly also made clear he doubted the touring company sincerely wished to distinguish its *Phantom* from Webber's *Phantom* because the touring company's advertisements employed small type to state that the plays were different. Kelly also admitted in his column that he was being subjective when he concluded the success of Phantom Touring's show must be tied to the reputation of Andrew Lloyd Webber because the road show "lacked artistic merit" and any recognizable stars.

Because Kelly presented the facts on which he based his opinion, the court said Kelly's allegations against the touring company "could only be understood" as personal opinions, not facts that might be proven true or false. Just as exaggeration and rhetorical hyperbole are incapable of being considered factual, the court said, statements are recognizable as "pure opinion because their factual premises are revealed."

Although opinions based on facts are protected, the facts must be stated accurately and interpreted plausibly. "Even if the speaker states the facts upon which he bases his opinion," the Supreme Court has said, "if those facts are either incorrect or incomplete, or if his assessment of them is erroneous, the statement may still imply a false assertion of fact."[279]

TOTALITY OF THE CIRCUMSTANCES By the time the Supreme Court established constitutional protection for rhetorical hyperbole and opinion that does not connote verifiable fact, many courts had developed a more comprehensive protection for opinion that they were reluctant to abandon. Indeed, the Supreme Court does not escape contextual analysis when it distinguishes fact from opinion. Following a tradition reaching back into common law, courts examining the totality of circumstances distinguish fact from opinion by evaluating various factors, usually including an examination of the ordinary meaning of the statement, whether the statement is verifiable, and the linguistic and social context in which a statement occurs. These factors in various mutations are often called the "totality of the circumstances" test.

There is much overlapping of analysis whether courts distinguish opinion from fact by searching for factual connotations or by examining the totality of circumstances. When courts do distinguish fact from opinion by reviewing the circumstances, one factor they often analyze is the common usage or meaning of words, that is, whether a statement has a "precise core of meaning for which a consensus of understanding exists, or, conversely, whether the statement is indefinite and ambiguous."[280] Average readers are more likely to consider vague, subjective terms such as *undistinguished* and *embarrassing* to be opinion than they are more precise, definable terms such as *robber* or *child molester*. Journalists need to be wary of terms that have a legal (and therefore factual) meaning—terms such as *obscene* publication, *substandard* housing and *thief.*

A second criterion often examined in the multifactor distinction between fact and opinion is whether a statement is verifiable, that is, whether it is objectively

---

[279] Milkovich v. Lorain Journal Co., 497 U.S. 1 (1990).
[280] Ollman v. Evans, 750 F.2d 970 (D.C. Cir. 1984).

capable of proof or disproof. Value-laden, subjective words such as *scumbag*, *dandy* or *shrill* are unverifiable opinion, whereas more objective, verifiable statements are factual. The Supreme Court in *Milkovich v. Lorain Journal Co.* said the term *liar* connoted facts the truth of which could be determined by a jury. The professional reviewer and critic should avoid statements that imply the existence of derogatory facts the writer cannot verify.

A third factor is the social context in which a statement occurs. Abusive words that in some contexts might be understood literally as fact in other contexts are understood to be exaggeration, rhetorical hyperbole or opinion. The Supreme Court recognized the importance of social context when it ruled the word *traitor*, as applied to an employee who crossed a picket line, was protected hyperbole because "such exaggerated rhetoric was commonplace in labor disputes."[281] Readers expect opinion in heated political debates and public controversies.

Another criterion for distinguishing fact from opinion is the linguistic context. Adding verbal cues such as "in my opinion" or "it seems to me" may indicate opinion but not, of course, if the statement implies false facts. Courts are more likely to find opinion where statements are phrased as hypotheses rather than assertions. The First Circuit said that Kevin Kelly's *Boston Globe* columns about the Phantom Touring company established a tone of opinion by raising rhetorical questions— instead of making bald statements—about the integrity of the touring company's marketing. The Supreme Court considered linguistic context in *Milkovich* when it noted that Diadiun's article did not contain the "hyperbolic language" that might "negate the impression" that Diadiun was asserting as fact that Milkovich committed perjury.

Courts also consider the format of a statement when distinguishing fact from opinion. Readers are more apt to expect opinion in bylined columns and reviews than in objective news stories. The First Circuit noted that Kevin Kelly's *Boston Globe* columns appeared in a regularly published theater column, "a type of article generally known to contain more opinionated writing than the typical news report." The Supreme Court considered the whole of Diadiun's column in *Milkovich* when Chief Justice Rehnquist noted that the "general tenor" of the article did not negate the impression that Diadiun was asserting a fact about Coach Milkovich.

The Sixth Circuit Court of Appeals ruled that user-generated content resulting in TripAdvisor's yearly listings of the "dirtiest" hotels was opinion rather than factual. Thus, the Grand Resort Hotel in Pigeon Forge, Tennessee, a hotel that appeared on the list, could not sue successfully for libel. Citing *Milkovich*, the court said "dirtiest" is a loose, hyperbolic term because it is the superlative of an adjective that conveys an inherently subjective concept. Furthermore, the "general tenor" of the site also implies opinion, the court said. The TripAdvisor site states clearly the "Dirtiest Hotels" are reported by travelers, thus creating rankings based on the subjective views of the site's users. Readers would discern, the court said, that TripAdvisor did not conduct a scientific study to determine which ten hotels were objectively the dirtiest in America.[282]

Although largely obsolete, the common-law protection of opinion, known as the privilege of fair comment and criticism, also relies on an evaluation of several contextual factors to distinguish fact from opinion.[283] Long before the First Amendment protected statements of opinion, the defense of fair comment and

---

[281] National Ass'n of Letter Carriers v. Austin, 418 U.S. 264 (1974).
[282] Seaton v. TripAdvisor LLC, 728 F.3d 592 (6th Cir. 2013).
[283] Robert Sack and Sandra Baron, *Libel, Slander, and Related Problems* 234–42 (2nd ed. 1994).

criticism protected critics, reviewers, reporters and essayists who criticized public officials, persons involved in public issues, cultural presentations, consumer goods and other matters of public interest. The common-law defense of fair comment and criticism, like state constitutions and statutes, may supplement the constitutional protection for opinion. But the media rely on fair comment and criticism infrequently because the common law often imposes the difficult and perhaps unconstitutional burden on the media to prove that facts are reasonable, that an opinion reflects the writer's actual beliefs and that opinion is offered without ill will.[284]

▓ SUMMARY ▓

Opinion is protected by the First Amendment, by state constitutions and statutes, and by common law. Statements may be protected as opinion, the Supreme Court said in *Milkovich v. Lorain Journal Co.*, provided they do not connote false facts. Protected expression includes exaggerated and vague expression that cannot be understood as factual. Also protected are statements reasonably based on known or stated facts. To distinguish fact from opinion, courts sometimes examine the circumstances surrounding a statement, including the common meaning of a statement, its verifiability, its social and linguistic context, and the format in which it appears. Opinion is apt to be found when terms are used hyperbolically or figuratively in columns and reviews.

Absolute Privileges

Some false and defamatory statements are completely protected by law. **Absolute privileges** protect the speaker of a defamatory message regardless of the speaker's accuracy or motives. Three absolute privileges are important to professional communicators. First, the spoken and written words of public officials acting in their official capacity are privileged. Second, the media have an absolute privilege to defame a person who consents to be defamed. Third, broadcasters have been granted an absolute privilege to air the false defamatory speech of political candidates.

    PRIVILEGE FOR GOVERNMENT OFFICIALS Government officials acting in their official capacity have absolute privilege from libel litigation. The courts have decided that open and uninhibited communication in government must be protected at the risk of damaging individual reputations. Public officials, it has been said, must be able to do their jobs without "the constant dread of retaliation."[285] Therefore, the official statements of executive branch officers and the remarks of legislators during official proceedings are privileged. Also privileged are all of the comments made during judicial proceedings—including those by judges, lawyers and witnesses.[286]

    U.S. senators and representatives are protected from libel suits by the Constitution, which declares that they "shall not be questioned in any other place" for "speech or debate in either house" of Congress.[287] This privilege, however, is not confined to statements made within the legislative chambers. Federal legislators enjoy the privilege when they communicate in committee hearings, legislative

---

[284] Bruce Sanford, *Libel and Privacy* § 5.2, at 142–3 (2nd ed. 1999).

[285] Gregoire v. Biddle, 177 F.2d 579 (2d Cir. 1949).

[286] *See* Bruce Sanford, *Libel and Privacy* § 10.4, at 491–8 (1999).

[287] U.S. Const. art. I, § 6.

reports and other activities integral to the consideration and adoption of legislation. However, the Supreme Court has said the federal legislative privilege does not extend to written and spoken statements beyond the legislative process. In *Hutchinson v. Proxmire*, the Court said that Senator William Proxmire's libelous criticism of Dr. Ronald Hutchinson's research on monkeys was privileged on the floor of the Senate but not outside the Senate.[288] Proxmire could be sued for defamatory remarks repeated in press releases, in his constituent newsletter and during a nationally televised talk show. The Constitution shields senators and members of Congress from libel suits only for matters that are an "integral part of the deliberative and communicative processes," the Court said. Communication with constituents and promotional activities are not privileged.

States have enacted privileges for state legislators similar to those granted to members of Congress by the U.S. Constitution. Many states also provide either an absolute or a **qualified privilege** for lower-level legislators, such as city council members. A qualified privilege protects speech only on certain conditions that vary from state to state. A qualified privilege can be defeated by such "abuses" as inaccuracies or common-law malice, to be discussed later.[289]

Federal executive branch officials with policymaking authority have a broader absolute privilege than members of Congress. In *Barr v. Matteo*, the Supreme Court said public officials are absolutely privileged for libelous comments made in the line of duty. Defamation by an official is protected, the Court said, even if the speech or document is not mandated by the job and is disseminated beyond the office. In *Matteo*, the Court ruled that William Barr, acting director of the U.S. Office of Rent Stabilization, was protected from a libel suit arising from a press release in which Barr condemned two agency officials.[290] The press release said that the two officials, John Madigan and Linda Matteo, would be suspended for violating the spirit, if not the letter, of a federal law when they permitted employees to receive cash for accumulated leave time. Members of Congress called the cash payments "a conspiracy to defraud the Government of funds."

When Madigan and Matteo sued, the Supreme Court ruled that Barr's press release was absolutely privileged. It has long been thought important, the Court said, that "officials of government should be free to exercise their duties unembarrassed by the fear of damage suits" for libel they disseminate in the course of their duties. In issuing the press release, Barr was operating within the sphere of his responsibilities.

It would be an unduly restrictive view of the scope of the duties of a policymaking executive official to hold that a public statement of agency policy in respect to matters of wide public interest and concern is not action in the line of duty, the Court said.

The *Barr* ruling has also been extended to protect officials when they send libelous letters or make libelous statements to grievance boards. States have also adopted an absolute privilege for governors and cabinet-level officers. In addition, most states provide a qualified privilege to lower-echelon officers of state and local government.[291]

---

[288] 443 U.S. 123–30.

[289] *E.g.*, Rodney Smolla, *Law of Defamation* § 8.09[3], at 8–33, and 8.10[3], at 8–43 to 8–45 (1998).

[290] 360 U.S. 564 (1959).

[291] *E.g.*, *Restatement (Second) of Torts* § 598A; Rodney Smolla, *Law of Defamation* § 8.05[2] [a], at 8–19 to 8–20, 8.07[2], at 8–20.2 to 8–20.3 (1998).

CONSENT A settled area of law prohibits people from collecting compensation if they are harmed by activities they agree to. In libel, this means that people cannot successfully sue for libel if they initiate or authorize publications that damage their own reputations.[292] Explicit consent to defamatory publication is rare. Few people authorize the publication of remarks that may damage their reputations. However, in addition to explicit consent, the courts have, on rare occasions, recognized an implied consent. Consent can be inferred when the person suing for libel encouraged or participated in the defamatory publication, knowing what was about to be printed.

The Tennessee Supreme Court said that the Reverend Robert Langford consented to a defamatory publication when he agreed to talk to the Vanderbilt student newspaper, *Hustler*, about his suit for libel and privacy against the campus humor magazine. Langford, a Methodist minister, was suing *Chase*, the humor magazine, for falsely implying that his wife was sexually promiscuous and his one-year-old daughter wanted to be. Langford told the newspaper reporters that he wanted publicity about his suit against *Chase*. Langford encouraged the students to see his lawyers for details of the suit. Subsequently, *Hustler* published that Langford was suing *Chase*, reproduced the page in *Chase* that triggered the suit, describing the charges in Langford's words. Langford sued the paper and the magazine, but the Tennessee court said that *Hustler*'s presentation of the dispute was privileged because Langford had invited and consented to it.[293]

PRIVILEGE FOR BROADCASTS BY POLITICAL CANDIDATES Broadcast stations have been granted an absolute privilege to air libel during political broadcasts. In 1959, the Supreme Court said that broadcasters would not be held accountable for defamatory remarks made by political candidates during time provided under the equal opportunities provision, Section 315, of the 1934 Communications Act. Section 315 requires stations to provide time to all candidates for an office once it has provided time to one. Yet the Communications Act also prohibits stations from censoring the remarks of political candidates.

In the 1959 case of *Farmers Educational and Cooperative Union of America v. WDAY*, the Supreme Court ruled that broadcasters are immune from liability if political candidates defame someone while the broadcaster is providing airtime under Section 315. The Court ruled that WDAY-TV of Fargo, North Dakota, was not liable when W.C. Townley, a colorful independent candidate for the U.S. Senate, accused the North Dakota Farmers Union of being controlled by Communists. Townley was granted time on WDAY under Section 315.[294]

In a 5–4 vote, the Supreme Court ruled that stations could not be held responsible for libelous comments they were required to air and could not censor. The Court said it would be "unconscionable" to hold broadcasters liable for defamation by candidates after compelling the stations to grant the candidates airtime.

■ SUMMARY ■

Defamatory statements made by public officials in their official capacity are absolutely privileged and cannot be the basis of a successful libel suit. In addition, persons who have consented to the publication of defamation about themselves

---

[292] *See* W. Page Keeton et al., *Prosser and Keeton on the Law of Torts* § 114, at 822 (5th ed. 1984); Bruce Sanford, *Libel and Privacy* § 10.4.6, at 513–16 (2nd ed. 1999).
[293] Langford v. Vanderbilt University, 318 S.W.2d 568 (Tenn. 1958).
[294] 360 U.S. 525.

cannot successfully sue for libel. Broadcasters are also protected from liability when providing time to political candidates under the equal opportunities rule of the 1934 Communications Act.

Qualified Privileges

Whereas participants in official government activities may be absolutely protected from libel suits, reporters have a qualified privilege to report on official activities. Journalists do not enjoy an absolute privilege, but they too are typically protected from libel suits if their reports on legislative, judicial and executive proceedings are fair and accurate. Professional communicators are also protected if they employ defamation in self-defense while discussing matters of "mutual interest," and sometimes in news reports of public, but unofficial, events of public concern.

FAIR REPORT PRIVILEGE A qualified privilege protects journalists who report defamatory comments made in official proceedings as long as the stories are fair and accurate. In many states, the stories also have to be attributed and printed without ill will. The reporter's privilege to repeat libel is justified by the public's need to be informed about government actions. Because most citizens cannot observe government directly, they depend on journalists who might not report on city council meetings, court sessions and legislative hearings if the journalists were liable for repeating defamatory statements at these official government proceedings.

The reporter's qualified privilege, the most important common-law defense in the post–*Times v. Sullivan* era, is one of the few protections for the publication of false defamatory statements by news sources. The defense not only defeats libel claims but also frustrates the filing of many suits.

The privilege usually protects only the reports of official proceedings, including legislative, executive and judicial activities at all levels of government. The privilege covers reports of government actions and records as well as reports of meetings and hearings. For the privilege to apply, proceedings must have a legal basis and must deal with a matter of public concern. Usually, meetings must be open to the public, and documents must be available to the public.[295] Some states limit the privilege to the press.[296]

Official Proceedings: Legislative Branch The reporter's qualified privilege protects news reports of official proceedings of governmental bodies authorized to enact or repeal statutes. The privilege applies to reports of the activities of the U.S. Congress, state legislatures, county commissions, city councils, community school boards and university boards of trustees.[297] There is usually no privilege from libel suits for reports of organizations, such as a local parent-teacher association, that do not enact enforceable legislation.

The privilege applies to fair and accurate stories about official meetings, hearings and reports of legislative bodies and their committees. The privilege protects reports of the comments of anyone recognized to speak during official meetings. Reporters need not worry about the truth of the remarks in official proceedings or reports. Hence, the Barton County, Missouri, *Democrat* was privileged when it reported that a man speaking at a city council meeting accused Gregg Shafer, a local police officer, of "knocking up" the man's 16-year-old daughter. The comments

---

[295] *Restatement (Second) of Torts* § 611 and § 611 comment d.
[296] *See* Medico v. Time, Inc., 643 F.2d 134 (3d Cir. 1981), *cert. denied*, 454 U.S. 836 (1981).
[297] *Restatement (Second) of Torts* § 611 comment d.

came during a discussion of who should run the police department. A Missouri appeals court said the *Democrat* was not responsible for investigating the truth or falsity of the accusation. If a newspaper were responsible, the court said, it would be fearful of fully reporting derogatory statements made at public meetings of official bodies.[298]

Journalists will probably be protected by the privilege as long as a quorum is present, minutes are being taken and the legislative body appears to be conducting official business. The *Passaic (New Jersey) Daily News* was privileged when it reported a defamatory comment made during an official meeting even though the meeting was not held in its usual place and the defamatory comment was beyond the subject for which the meeting was called.

The New Jersey Supreme Court recognized a privilege for the *Daily News* to report defamatory statements made by the Clifton city manager during a special meeting of the city council convened in a conference room rather than the usual chamber to consider fiscal issues. In response to a question during the meeting, City Manager John Fitzgerald said he did not promote Chester Swede and Raymond DeLucca to the rank of police sergeant because Swede and DeLucca had been "insubordinate" and "should have been fired." Fitzgerald admitted to having a few drinks before the meeting. After Fitzgerald retired a few months later, the council exonerated Swede and DeLucca of all charges. When the officers sued the *Daily News* for printing Fitzgerald's charges, the New Jersey court said the report of the council meeting was privileged. The court said that although the meeting took place in a conference room rather than the regular meeting room, the council conducted official business and minutes were taken. The meeting was not only official but also public, because the press was allowed to attend.[299]

The reporter's privilege applies to reports of defamatory statements in petitions or complaints officially received by a legislative body. Defamatory petitions to recall a public official may not be protected until the documents are accepted by the appropriate government office. In addition, reports of meetings and discussions by citizens' groups planning to submit petitions may not be protected before the petitions are submitted. Also unprotected are reports of defamatory comments in the halls outside a council meeting or legislative session. The remarks may not be considered part of a legislative proceeding, even if they are made by a council member or legislator and relate to the official proceedings.

Official Proceedings: Executive Branch The reach of the privilege to report executive branch activities is not always clear, but stories based on official reports are usually privileged. For example, the *New York Times* was protected when it reported the damaging conclusions of an investigation by New York City's Department of Consumer Affairs into the sales practices of air conditioner repair shops.[300] Likewise, the *Tampa Tribune* was privileged when it reported that the Stable Lounge was identified as a "trouble spot" in information provided by the county sheriff.[301] Also privileged, by a Massachusetts court, was an accurate report of defamatory statements contained in a commissioned government report prepared by private contractors.[302]

---

[298] Shafer v. Lamar Publishing Co., 621 S.W.2d 709 (Mo. Ct. App. 1981).
[299] Swede v. Passaic Daily News, 153 A.2d 36 (N.J. 1959).
[300] Freeze Right Refrigeration & Air Conditioning Servs., Inc. v. City of New York, 475 N.Y.S.2d 383 (N.Y. App. Div. 1984).
[301] Hatjioannou v. Tribune Co., 8 Media L. Rep. 2637 (Fla. Cir. Ct. 1982). *See also Restatement (Second) of Torts* § 611 comment d.
[302] *E.g.*, Bruenell v. Harte-Hanks Communications, Inc., 23 Media L. Rep. 1378 (Mass. Super. Ct. 1994).

Generally speaking, accurate stories about officials acting and speaking in their official capacity will be protected. Most legal authorities argue that the reporter's qualified privilege is triggered when official conduct is clothed by an official's absolute privilege.[303] The higher the position of the officials, the more likely the reporter will enjoy a qualified privilege to report them. Articles based on official press conferences often will be privileged.[304] The California Supreme Court recognized a privilege for media to report libelous statements contained in a document released at a press conference convened by the state attorney general. The court said the press was privileged to report the names of 92 people named in a report by the state's Organized Crime Control Commission as being suspected of connections to organized crime. The court ruled against Gerald Hay Kilgore, who sued several media for reporting that he was identified in the report as a bookie. The court said that the media reports were privileged because they were accurate stories about a public meeting legally convened by a public official for a lawful purpose.[305]

In many jurisdictions, journalists are not privileged to report defamation contained in informal remarks by public officials made independently of an official proceeding or report. Journalists had no privilege to repeat libelous accusations contained in an argument between Anthony Mitchell, a prosecuting attorney in Camden County, New Jersey, and a local police chief. The argument took place in a judge's chambers after court had been adjourned. The New Jersey Supreme Court said the media had no privilege to report Mitchell's assertions that Les Rogers, a prominent Camden politician, had ordered the police to "fix" criminal cases. The court said Mitchell's comments were not made during official court proceedings and did not constitute an official statement of the county prosecutor's office.[306]

Stories about quasi-judicial proceedings in the executive branch are usually protected. The *Louisville Times* was protected for most of a story reporting that Dr. Charles Pearce was being investigated for prescribing excessive or unneeded drugs. The article was primarily based on proceedings before the Kentucky Board of Medical Licensure.[307] Stories about public hearings may be privileged if the hearings are supervised by an official with the power to investigate complaints.[308] However, stories based on pending government investigations and on nonpublic investigatory documents have generally not been privileged.[309]

Arrest reports are privileged but usually only after a suspect has been officially booked.[310] The suspect usually must be officially charged with a crime, and the name of the suspect must be entered on a police blotter. The blotter itself—the suspect's name, address, age and charge—is privileged in those states where it is a public record.

Journalists need to be particularly careful not to report arrests prematurely. It may be libelous to say that police "arrested" someone if police only question a suspect or "invite" someone to the police station. Furthermore, journalists may not

---

[303] *See* W. Page Keeton et al., *Prosser and Keeton on the Law of Torts* § 114, at 793 (5th ed. 1984); *Restatement (Second) of Torts* § 612 comment c.

[304] *See, e.g.,* Rodney Smolla, *Law of Defamation* § 8.10[2] [d], at 8–41 to 8–42 (1998).

[305] Kilgore v. Younger, 640 P.2d 793 (Cal. 1982).

[306] Rogers v. Courier Post Co., 66 A.2d 869 (N.J. 1949).

[307] Pearce v. Courier-Journal & Louisville Times Co., 683 S.W.2d 622 (Ky. Ct. App. 1985).

[308] *Restatement (Second) of Torts* § 611 comment d.

[309] *But see* Medico v. Time, Inc., 643 F.2d 134 (3d Cir. 1981).

[310] *See* W. Page Keeton et al., *Prosser and Keeton on the Law of Torts* § 115, at 836–7 (5th ed. 1984); *Restatement (Second) of Torts* § 611 comment h.

have a privilege against a libel suit if no charges are filed against a suspect after the media report that police plan to file charges.

Reports of informal disclosures by law enforcement officers may not be privileged. Reporters may not be privileged when they rely on an officer's word at a crime scene, obtain information from an officer over the phone, or take information from a police hotline. For example, a court ruled that there was no privilege attached to information provided by a hotline in the District of Columbia that provided recorded crime reports. The *Washington Evening Star* relied on the hotline to write that John Phillips was charged with homicide after shooting his wife during an argument. The police later classified the shooting as an accident. The Court of Appeals for the District of Columbia said the hotline consisted of unofficial police statements rather than a privileged official police report. The appeals court allowed a jury award of $1 in nominal damages to Phillips to stand.[311]

Informal police reports may not only lack privilege but may also be unverifiable. The media often have no protection for defamatory statements if the police officer on the scene or the desk officer on the telephone denies a reporter's version of a conversation.

Journalists must also be careful not to lose a privilege to report from official proceedings by adding defamation from unofficial sources. Although the *Louisville Times* was privileged when it reported from official proceedings that the drug prescriptions written by Dr. Charles Pearce were being investigated, other information in the same story was not privileged. The *Times* was not protected for a paragraph reporting that 79-year-old Hattie Rose Ludwig contended she became a drug addict while a patient of Dr. Pearce. Although Ludwig's allegation had been used only to illustrate the charges under investigation in an official proceeding, it arose during an interview that was not privileged. When Dr. Pearce sued the paper for libel, a Kentucky appeals court affirmed a summary judgment for the newspaper in the case of the information taken from official proceedings. However, the court allowed Pearce to sue for the information obtained from Ludwig.[312]

Journalists should have little faith that the word *alleged* will protect them from a libel suit if the journalists are not quoting official sources. Journalists cannot claim a privilege to report that a crime is "alleged" if they lack an official source that the press is privileged to report, even if the source is wrong. The use of *alleged* may tell readers that the reporter is not the source of a charge, but reporters can still be sued for libel if they have no privilege to repeat false, defamatory charges originated by others. If journalists choose to employ the verb *allege* in a crime story, the subject of the sentence should be "police," "the grand jury," "an indictment" or some other official source, which is then accurately reported. Many good police reporters avoid the legalistic term *alleged*, preferring instead to report that "police charge" or "the indictment says."

Official Proceedings: Judicial Branch The privilege to cover judicial proceedings is particularly important because almost every issue taken to court is potentially defamatory. The reporter's privilege pertains to any statements during the official judicial process by all legitimate participants, including judges, witnesses, jurors, litigants and attorneys. The *Flint Journal* successfully relied on the

[311] Phillips v. Evening Star Newspaper Co., 424 A.2d 78 (D.C. 1980), *cert. denied*, 451 U.S. 989 (1981), *aff'g* 2 Media L. Rep. 2201 (D.C. Super. Ct. 1977).

[312] Pearce v. Courier-Journal & Louisville Times Co., 683 S.W.2d 633 (Ky. Ct. App. 1985). *See Restatement (Second) of Torts* § 611 comment f.

privilege after it reported from defamatory court testimony that a former local law enforcement officer had offered to protect drug activities.[313]

Also protected are opinions and conclusions that fairly represent court testimony. Federal courts in Massachusetts ruled that television station WCVB-TV fairly and accurately linked Willis Brown Jr. to the disappearance and death of his wife in a report based on a divorce trial. The court said the station accurately reflected testimony at the trial when the station reported that Brown was a prime suspect even though Brown was never charged with a crime. Linking Brown to his wife's disappearance accurately reflected the "gist" of trial testimony that Brown was an abusive husband whose wife feared for her life, the courts said.[314]

The privilege applies to fair and accurate reports of all judicial proceedings, no matter how minor the court. The privilege covers the report of indictments, trials, judicial orders, verdicts and judgments entered at the court clerk's office. The privilege also covers reports of documents filed to support requests for search warrants. California courts ruled that the *Los Angeles Herald-Examiner* was protected from a libel suit by nightclub owners named as arson suspects in a police request for a search warrant. Arson investigator Gary Cooper's request suggested that the club owners had set fire to their own club.[315]

Courts have held that the privilege pertains to any aspect of a legal proceeding, from the beginning to end. In California, for example, a news story about the filing of a complaint in a civil proceeding is privileged,[316] but the same would not be true in every jurisdiction. The reporters' privilege may also protect reports of depositions, which are sworn statements by witnesses under oath.

The press might not have a privilege to report about documents that are irrelevant to the case they are filed with. The New Jersey Supreme Court said that a newspaper was not privileged to report an unsigned document charging a male policeman with fondling a female suspect in violation of federal law. The document containing the allegations was attached to one filed in an unrelated state court proceeding involving disorderly conduct. The New Jersey court recognized no privilege for a misleading and unfair newspaper report and headline falsely implying that federal charges were pending against the officer for improper treatment of the female suspect.[317]

In some states, the press has a privilege to report only after a judge takes action in a case by setting a court date or meeting with the parties in chambers. In these states, if a judge has not taken action, news stories about the instigation of a civil lawsuit may not be privileged even though a complaint is filed with the court clerk.[318] Courts historically were reluctant to provide a privilege for news stories about the filing of civil complaints because the courts wanted to discourage frivolous suits filed only to obtain news coverage protected by libel law. For example, the courts did not want to allow vindictive divorced spouses to file complaints falsely charging their ex-spouses with various wrongs and then withdraw the suits after the press reported the charges. More recently, judges and legal scholars have

---

[313] Dicks v. Fiedler, 16 Media L. Rep. 2391 (Mich. Ct. App. 1989).

[314] Brown v. Hearst Corp., 862 F. Supp. 622 (D. Mass. 1994), *aff'd*, 54 F.3d 21 (1st Cir. 1995).

[315] Cox v. Los Angeles Herald-Examiner, 286 Cal. Rptr. 419 (Cal. Ct. App. 1991).

[316] *See, e.g.*, Dorsey v. National Enquirer, Inc., 17 Media L. Rep. 1527 (C.D. Cal. 1990).

[317] Costello v. Ocean County Observer, 643 A.2d 1012 (N.J. 1994).

[318] *See* W. Page Keeton et al., *Prosser and Keeton on the Law of Torts* § 115, at 837 (5th ed. 1984); *Restatement (Second) of Torts* § 611 comment e.

expressed doubts that withholding the privilege to report judicial filings can frustrate a frivolous suit.[319]

Reports based on copies of court documents may not be privileged even though the copies are identical to filed documents for which coverage is privileged. A California appeals court ruled that a faxed copy of a civil complaint filed against a computer company was not privileged because the copy faxed to the press was not part of the judicial process.[320]

Ordinarily, the privilege to cover the judicial process extends only to proceedings that are public. Closed court sessions for juvenile cases and for the testimony of victims in sexual assault cases are often not privileged. Similarly, in most states, stories relying on documents or records officially withheld from the public are not privileged.[321] Nonpublic documents often include papers filed in juvenile and divorce cases.

Although journalists should know the breadth of privilege in their state, they are not expected to make technical determinations of what constitutes an official legal proceeding. If a proceeding appears to be legal and if the officials participating act as if it is legal, an accurate report of the proceeding should be protected even if false, defamatory statements are made at a proceeding during which the tribunal exceeds its authority.[322]

Unofficial Proceedings In some states, reporters are privileged to report unofficial but open meetings held to discuss matters of public concern.[323] The privilege may apply to public meetings of union members, churches, political parties, civic groups, and medical and bar associations. The privilege could be used to report a chamber of commerce "forum" or a meeting to discuss the removal of public officials. The U.S. Court of Appeals for the Ninth Circuit ruled that the *Moscow Idahonian* was privileged when it reported defamatory comments made at an unofficial public meeting of citizens at Moscow High School. Some at the meeting had argued that a grand jury ought to investigate the legal maneuvers that followed a fight between a University of Idaho student and a lawyer named Murray Estes. One speaker had implied that Judge John Borg acted unethically when he dismissed a charge brought against Estes for assault with a deadly weapon. Borg sued the paper for libel, using Estes as his attorney. After a trial court ruled that the story in the *Idahonian* was accurate, the Ninth Circuit said the press was privileged. The court said the newspaper performed "its most valuable function" when it truthfully reported proceedings related to the administration of law. The court said the public in a representative government must be informed.[324]

Reports of private gatherings, such as the annual meetings of corporations, are not generally privileged. Such meetings usually are not concerned with public problems but with private interests, such as those of stockholders. However, in some states, a report of a meeting of a private organization may be privileged if the meeting pertains to matters of public interest and is open to the public.[325]

---

[319] *E.g.*, Hoelficker v. Higginsville Advance Inc., 818 S.W.2d 650 (Mo. Ct. App. 1991); Bruce Sanford, *Libel and Privacy* § 10.2.3.1, at 469 (2nd ed. 1999).

[320] Shahvar v. Superior Court, 30 Cal. Rptr. 2d 597 (Cal. App. 1994).

[321] *See* W. Page Keeton et al., *Prosser and Keeton on the Law of Torts* § 115, at 837 (5th ed. 1984).

[322] *See* Lee v. Brooklyn Union Publishing Co., 103 N.E. 155 (N.Y. 1913); *Restatement (Second) of Torts* § 611 comment g.

[323] *See Restatement (Second) of Torts* § 611 comment i.

[324] Borg v. Boas, 231 F.2d 781 (1956).

[325] *See* W. Page Keeton et al., *Prosser and Keeton on the Law of Torts* § 115, at 836 (5th ed. 1984); *Restatement (Second) of Torts* § 611 comment i.

Conditions of Privilege: Accuracy and Fairness Any story and headline based on an official proceeding must accurately reflect what was said. Relatively minor errors will not defeat the privilege, but a substantial error or distortion can. *Time* magazine could not claim a privilege when it erroneously reported the reason Russell Firestone was granted a divorce from his wife Mary Alice, a case discussed in the section on public figures.[326] *Time* mistakenly reported that the divorce was granted because of Mrs. Firestone's adultery. Unfortunately, the *Time* reporter apparently did not know that, under Florida law, Mrs. Firestone could not have been granted the alimony the court awarded her had adultery been the justification for the divorce.

To be privileged, a story must not only be accurate but also provide a balanced presentation of the proceeding. A federal appeals court refused NBC a privilege when the network presented only one side of the famous trial of the "Scottsboro Boys." The court said that NBC's portrayal of the trial was not balanced enough to justify a privilege against a libel suit by Victoria Price Street, the white woman who had accused the nine black "Scottsboro Boys" of raping her in 1931. The court said NBC's docudrama inaccurately emphasized the boys' defense. NBC failed to include witnesses who corroborated the story of the former Victoria Price, the court said, while emphasizing portions of the trial that portrayed Price as promiscuous and a perjurer. The flashbacks the network used to dramatize events before the trial reflected only the story of the defense, the court said.[327] Of course, journalists can report the events in court for a day even if only the prosecution is presenting its case. However, reporters will be expected to report the case when the defense is presenting its side.[328]

Conditions of Privilege: Attribution and Common-Law Malice In most cases, the media can claim a privilege only if they inform readers, viewers and listeners that a story reports an official proceeding. This means that both the story and the headline must include an attribution. The former *Washington Daily News* lost a libel suit because it failed to attribute a counterfeiting charge to the Secretary of the Treasury. The *Daily News* printed a story without attribution, asserting that William and Josephine Hughes were charged with making bogus money and passing the bills during an air tour of the country. The newspaper told the court it had obtained the information from an announcement by the U.S. Secretary of the Treasury. The Court of Appeals for the D.C. Circuit said, however, that the newspaper had no privilege to publish an unattributed defamation even though the newspaper report was similar to the official announcement.[329]

A few courts have ruled that journalists can rely on the reporter's privilege only if they base their stories on official documents rather than media reports about the documents. In Louisiana, a court ruled that the Baton Rouge *State Times* had no privilege to report false defamatory information from another newspaper, the *Morning Advocate*. The *Morning Advocate* was privileged when it made a "reasonable interpretation" of an ambiguous press release reporting that Ronald Melon had been arrested on three drug charges. However, the court said it could not grant a privilege to the reporter for the *State Times* who did not see the press release and relied on the report of the other paper.[330]

---

[326] Time, Inc. v. Firestone, 424 U.S. 457–8.
[327] Street v. NBC, 645 F.2d 1223.
[328] *Restatement (Second) of Torts* § 611 comment f.
[329] Hughes v. Washington Daily News Co., 193 F.2d 922 (1952).
[330] Melon v. Capital City Press, 407 So. 2d 85 (La. Ct. App. 1981).

NEUTRAL REPORTAGE Historically, the media have not been privileged to report newsworthy but defamatory charges made outside an official proceeding. However, a few courts have adopted a legal defense that protects reporters who accurately repeat defamatory charges made about public figures. A doctrine called **neutral reportage** allows the media to report newsworthy statements by reliable sources even if the reporter doubts the accuracy of the remarks. Indeed, in the give-and-take of public controversy, reporters often know that one side or the other is lying, although they often don't know who.

The few courts that have adopted neutral reportage say the protection is important to permit the public debate of controversial issues encouraged by the First Amendment. Critics of neutral reportage oppose a legal defense for publishing statements a reporter knows might be false. Knowingly publishing falsity, after all, is actual malice, the critics of neutral reportage observe.

Legal recognition of neutral reportage arose from the controversy over the pesticide DDT. Three scientists sued the *New York Times* for reporting that the National Audubon Society called them "paid liars" when the society said "scientist-spokesmen" of the pesticide industry were being paid to say that DDT did not kill birds. The *Times* obtained the names of the scientists from officials of the Audubon Society, which earlier had accused unnamed industry scientists of misusing bird-count data to conclude that bird life in North America was thriving in spite of pesticides. The scientists' claims, the society said, were "false and misleading, a distortion of the facts for the most self-serving reasons."

A federal jury awarded $20,000 to each of the scientists, but the U.S. Court of Appeals for the Second Circuit reversed the judgment. The appeals court said the First Amendment protected the "accurate and disinterested reporting" of charges made by a "responsible, prominent organization" such as the National Audubon Society, even if a reporter believes the accusations are untrue, which was not the case in the Audubon story. The court said the public interest in being informed about "sensitive issues" requires that the press be able to accurately report, without fear of liability, newsworthy accusations made by responsible, well-noted organizations.[331]

Other courts have adopted the privilege of neutral reportage in narrowly defined circumstances. Usually, the charges must be

1. newsworthy and related to a public controversy.
2. made by a responsible person or organization.
3. about a public official or public figure.
4. accurately reported alongside opposing views.
5. reported impartially.

In addition to the Second Circuit, neutral reportage has been adopted in only a few jurisdictions, including the Eighth Circuit, several federal district courts and state appellate jurisdictions in Florida, Ohio, Vermont and Wyoming. The privilege has been rejected by the state supreme courts in Kentucky and South Dakota and an appeals court in Michigan.[332] Courts rejecting neutral reportage object to protecting the media when they print statements known to be, or suspected to be, false. Indeed, some courts say they cannot shield knowingly false statements from liability

---

[331] Edwards v. National Audubon Soc'y, Inc., 556 F.2d 113 (2d Cir.), *cert. denied*, 434 U.S. 1002 (1977).
[332] *See* John McCrory and Robert Bernius, "Constitutional Privilege in Libel Law," 1 *Comm. Law* 53, 500–12 (1997).

because the Supreme Court has ruled that constitutional protection for defamation crumbles when statements are published with knowing falsehood.

Without a statute or recognition in the common law, journalists should be careful not to expect the neutral reportage defense to be of any help. The Pennsylvania Supreme Court delivered a cautionary tale in 2004, rejecting the neutral reportage defense by a reporter for the Chester County *Daily Local* reporting on libelous comments made by a member of the Parkersburg Borough Council during and after a public meeting. The council member accused two other council members of being "queers and child molesters" and of making homosexual advances toward him, and the reporter accurately quoted those comments in his story, under the headline, "Slurs, Insults Drag Town Into Controversy." The court rejected the reporter's argument that the Pennsylvania legislature had not approved a neutral reportage defense, and that neither the First Amendment nor the Pennsylvania Constitution required recognition of the defense as a matter of state law, allowing the case by the council members to proceed against the publisher in a trial court.[333]

SELF-INTEREST OR SELF-DEFENSE People can use reasonable means to defend themselves against an assault, an unfair business practice or libel. Thus, individuals and businesses are protected from defamation suits when they publish libelous statements to combat attacks on their own reputations.[334] For example, a manufacturer has a qualified privilege to defame a critic in response to charges the company puts the safety of its employees at risk.

Courts have held that the news media can use the self-defense privilege not only to reply on their own behalf but also on behalf of others whose character or professional competency have been maligned in their newspapers and broadcast programming. For example, the Virginia Supreme Court of Appeals ordered a trial court to consider whether libelous attacks by the *Virginia Beach Sun-News* on a competing paper's editor were privileged publications in self-defense and in defense of public officials criticized by the editor. The Virginia Supreme Court said a trial court had not adequately considered self-defense when it awarded $30,000 in damages to the competing editor, J. Willcox Dunn, after the *Sun-News* called him a "deliberate liar" and a "fugitive from truth." The *Sun-News* defamed Dunn, editor of the *Princess Anne Free Press*, after Dunn charged that the *Sun-News* and a majority of local officeholders were part of a political machine associated with criminals.[335]

■ SUMMARY ■

The reporter's qualified privilege to report official proceedings is the most important of the common-law defenses. Reporters will be protected from libel suits as long as they report official proceedings and records fairly and accurately, with proper attribution and, in some jurisdictions, without ill will. The privilege does not protect the reporting of an official's informal comments outside of an official meeting. A few courts have declared that the defense of neutral reportage protects journalists who accurately report false defamatory statements by responsible parties about public officials and public figures. The charges usually must be newsworthy, related to a public controversy and reported impartially, including a reaction from

---

[333] Norton v. Glenn, 580 Pa. 212 (2004); *cert. denied*, 544 U.S. 956 (2005).
[334] *Restatement (Second) of Torts* § 594 comment k; W. Page Keeton et al., *Prosser and Keeton on the Law of Torts* § 115, at 825 (5th ed. 1984).
[335] Haycox v. Dunn, 104 S.E.2d 800 (Va. 1958).

the person defamed. The courts also protect libelous remarks that are communicated only among members of a group with a strong common interest. The courts also protect defamatory information provided to individuals or organizations for their well-being. Businesses can publish defamation to protect their interests. An individual or mass medium cannot be successfully sued for libel if the defamatory remarks were made in reply to libelous remarks first uttered by the plaintiff. Communicators critical of government and business have been harassed by libel suits designed to intimidate, but some communicators have successfully sued back.

PREVENTING LIBEL SUITS

Legal defenses may protect a publication once a libel suit is filed, but litigation is expensive and exhausting. Often communicators can avoid libel suits if they respond promptly and respectfully to disgruntled readers and viewers. People who think the media have defamed them might decide not to sue if they believe the media take their complaints seriously, respond to their questions and, if warranted, publish a retraction. In some states, communicators lessen damage awards for libel if they publish a retraction.

Handling Complaints

A study published by three scholars at the University of Iowa suggests that old-fashioned courtesy may be one of the best deterrents to a libel suit. Professors Randall Bezanson, Gilbert Cranberg and John Soloski found that libel plaintiffs usually sue only after they decide that they have been treated rudely by the press. Plaintiffs typically do not sue immediately after seeing what they believe to be an inaccurate story about themselves in the media. The Iowa researchers found that about half of the 160 libel plaintiffs studied said they asked the media for an explanation before contacting a lawyer or filing a complaint. The readers became plaintiffs, the researchers said, after media personnel assured them the media make no mistakes, gave them the bureaucratic runaround, or cursed them for complaining.[336]

The Iowa project stressed communicators' need to become less defensive about complaints. People agitated by news coverage want to believe they have been listened to. The researchers said that editors should teach reporters how the press can damage reputations, and journalists should respond promptly and courteously to complaints. The professors also suggested the media develop systematic procedures for handling complaints, a recommendation that many media organizations have followed.

Retractions

Publishers may also avoid a libel suit by printing a retraction. Some people who believe they have been defamed refrain from suing if a newspaper or broadcast station corrects the error.

A retraction can be a part of a written settlement, signed by both parties, in which the person complaining agrees not to sue. In addition, more than 30 states have retraction statutes providing protection to media willing to retract false defamatory publications. The retraction statutes vary widely. Some prohibit the recovery

---

[336] Gilbert Cranberg, "Fanning the Fire: The Media's Role in Libel Litigation," 71 *Iowa L. Rev.* 221, 222 (1985).

of punitive damages if a newspaper or broadcast station retracts a defamatory false-hood. Other statutes restrict the plaintiff to recovering special damages through proof of out-of-pocket loss if a retraction is published.[337]

In many states, a reader or viewer must request a retraction within a certain time after the publication. Often, a statute requires that the media be given an opportunity to retract before a suit is filed. Even if a retraction does not reduce damages by law, a jury may award lower damages if the media publish a retraction.

Wisconsin prohibits plaintiffs from suing a "newspaper, magazine or periodi-cal" before first allowing the publication a chance to correct the error. Plaintiffs are denied punitive damages if a proper, timely correction is published. However, a Wisconsin appeals court recently ruled that a libel plaintiff could sue the SportsNet electronic bulletin board without first asking for a retraction that would preclude punitive damages. The court said a plaintiff need not ask a bulletin board for a retraction before filing suit because a bulletin board is not a newspaper, magazine or periodical. An electronic bulletin board is a "random communication," the court said, not a publication that appears at regular intervals.[338]

To reduce damages, retractions must ordinarily be complete, fair and free of damaging innuendoes. Retractions need to be an honest effort to repair dam-age. They often need to be published within a limited amount of time and given the same emphasis and prominence as the defamatory statement. A California court said the *San Francisco Examiner* did not meet the statutory requirement that a retraction be given the same prominence as the defamation when the paper retracted on a Wednesday a libel that was published on a Sunday. A Sunday edition of the paper with a circulation of 450,000 erroneously identified the suspect in a shooting as Willie Lee Beasley instead of Willie Ray Beasley. The court was not sat-isfied when the paper published a retraction in a Wednesday edition with a circula-tion of 150,000. The court said the retraction was not published "in as conspicuous a manner" as the libel.[339]

It is usually best for communicators to consult an attorney before printing a retraction. A lawyer can ensure that a retraction does not exacerbate a complaint. A retraction that repeats a libel may provoke a suit instead of keeping a publica-tion or broadcast station out of court. In addition, a retraction written without legal assistance might not meet state statutory requirements.

■ SUMMARY ■

The media may avoid libel suits if they respond to informal complaints promptly and courteously. Sometimes the media can avoid damages by printing retractions, particularly if the retractions meet the requirements of state retraction statutes.

---

[337] *E.g.*, Bruce Sanford, *Libel and Privacy* § 12.3, at 589–94; App. B, at 773–812 (2nd ed. 1999).
[338] Its in the Cards, Inc. v. Fuschetto, 535 N.W.2d 11 (Wis. App. 1995).
[339] Beasley v. Hearst Corp., 11 Media L. Rep. 2067 (Cal. Super. Ct. 1985).

5

Privacy

The right of privacy is a relatively new area of the law. Unlike libel law, the roots of which go back centuries, privacy law is largely a development of the twentieth century. The origin of privacy law is often traced to an 1890 article in the *Harvard Law Review* written by two Boston attorneys, Samuel Warren and Louis Brandeis. Warren and Brandeis argued that advances in technology and the voyeurism of urban newspapers necessitated new legal protections for privacy. "Instantaneous photographs and newspaper enterprise have invaded the sacred precincts of private and domestic life," Warren and Brandeis declared. "Numerous mechanical devices threaten to make good the prediction that 'what is whispered in the closet shall be proclaimed from the house-tops.'"

Gossip had become a business, in the opinion of Brandeis and Warren, and details of sexual relations were "broadcast in the columns of the daily papers."[1] Warren, who belonged to a socially prominent family, and Brandeis, who would

---

[1] Warren and Brandeis, "The Right to Privacy," 4 *Harv. L. Rev.* 193 (1890).

DOI: 10.4324/9781003264736-5

later sit on the U.S. Supreme Court, argued that the individual had a "right to be let alone," a right to be free from publication of intimate information by a callous and increasingly powerful press.

It has been suggested that the two law partners were motivated to write their article by lurid press coverage of the Warren family, particularly by the *Saturday Evening Gazette*.[2] However, the *Gazette* seldom mentioned the Warrens' social life and then not in intimate detail. The *Gazette* did call Warren's father-in-law, Senator Thomas Francis Bayard, a "pompous turkey-cock," but such political hyperbole hardly invaded anyone's privacy.[3]

Whatever their motivation, Brandeis and Warren argued that a right of privacy is rooted in the dignity of the individual, a dignity then recognized in the law of trespass and copyright. The lawyers said a person's right to prevent trespassers on private property protects the integrity of the personality in a way that should also be protected from journalists who would disclose intimate information. The two authors saw the same personal dignity inherent in the copyright law, which protects writing and other creative expression from unauthorized copying. If the creative expression of one's personality can be protected by law, the Boston lawyers argued, so, too, should the privacy essential to the integrity of the personality.

The seeds that Warren and Brandeis planted were slow to take root in the law, but today nearly all 50 states and the District of Columbia recognize a legal right of privacy. The core of privacy still is, as Warren and Brandeis described it, the right to be let alone. The right to be let alone by the government is recognized in the Fourth Amendment to the Constitution which—though never mentioning "privacy" by name—prohibits unreasonable government searches of citizens' homes and papers. Broadly speaking, the Constitution protects from government intrusion places and personal effects in which a citizen has a "reasonable expectation of privacy."[4] Common law and statutes, too, protect a citizen's spatial or physical privacy from snooping, peeping, and secret electronic and photographic surveillance.

In many states, privacy law also includes the right to be portrayed accurately in the media and the right to prohibit the unauthorized commercial exploitation of one's name or picture in advertising and public relations. The Supreme Court has also extended the constitutional right of privacy to protect one's ability to make important decisions about marriage and the family, including decisions about employing birth control,[5] having an abortion[6] and choosing one's sexual practices.[7]

Beyond spatial and decisional privacy, the law protects informational privacy, the ability to control information about oneself, an increasingly important arena as electronic databases store vast amounts of personal data gathered by banks, schools, credit card companies, brokerage houses, retailers and the government. Privacy concerns become more urgent as computers—whose security is sometimes breached—amass private information in central databases that can be disseminated instantaneously over the Internet. Notably, in Europe, the General Data Protection Regulation (GDPR) went into effect in 2018. It is a set of privacy regulations that applies to any organization worldwide that serves European Union residents and

---

[2] Alpheus Mason, Brandeis, a Free Man's Life 70 (1946); William Prosser, "Privacy," 48 *Calif. L. Rev.* 383 (1960).
[3] Lewis Paper, *Brandeis* 33–5 (1980).
[4] *See* Will Thomas DeVries, "Annual Review of Law and Technology: III. Cyber Law: A. Privacy: Protecting Privacy in the Digital Age," 18 *Berkeley Tech. L.J.* 283 (2003).
[5] Griswold v. Connecticut, 381 U.S. 479 (1965).
[6] Roe v. Wade, 410 U.S. 113 (1973).
[7] Lawrence v. Texas, 539 U.S. 558 (2003).

collects data about them. One of its provisions says, for example, that such organizations must obtain advance consent from their users before collecting data about them through ads or analytics scripts. As a research report put it, "[The GDPR] is a major piece of EU legislation" that "will have the greatest impact on technology companies and advertising networks that directly monetize user data," along with "the media companies that often depend on them for both reach and revenue."[8]

The Fourth Amendment recognizes citizens' reasonable expectation of privacy in their "papers," an interest in controlling information about oneself. Federal and state statutes, too, recognize a privacy interest in information by permitting citizens to inspect, correct and control the release of medical, tax and other personal information held by businesses and government. Statutes protecting information privacy include the Fair Credit Reporting Act, the Right to Financial Privacy Act, the Children's Online Privacy Protection Act and the Health Insurance Portability and Accountability Act. These laws and others will be discussed in later chapters on commercial speech and access to information. This chapter is concerned with four areas of common law and statutory privacy that affect the media. One is the publication of intimate private facts, a concern of Warren and Brandeis. A second is intrusion, a physical or technological invasion of a person's privacy. A third is "false light," which is the public portrayal of someone in a distorted or fictionalized way. The fourth is appropriation, the unauthorized commercial exploitation of someone's identity.[9] Related issues, which will also be discussed in this chapter, include the media's rare infliction of emotional distress and violation of civil rights.

PRIVATE FACTS

Brandeis and Warren were concerned over dissemination of what they considered to be intimate information. One outgrowth of their concern is the private-facts or embarrassing-facts tort. The private-facts tort is defined in the *Restatement (Second) of Torts*, a summary of the common law, as a publication of private information that "(a) would be highly offensive to a reasonable person and (b) is not of legitimate concern to the public."[10] In other words, the private-facts tort involves the disclosure of very personal information, a disclosure that is not justified by the newsworthiness of the information. The U.S. Court of Appeals for the Second Circuit said the private-facts tort is publication of information that is "so intimate" and the publication of which is "so unwarranted" as to shock or "outrage the community's notions of decency."[11] In California, the line between legitimate public interest and invasion of privacy is drawn where publicity "becomes a morbid and sensational prying into private lives for its own sake, with which a reasonable member of the public, with decent standards, would say that he had no concern."[12]

Relatively few courts have found publication of private information sufficiently offensive and sufficiently lacking in newsworthiness to justify punishing the media. The Supreme Court has further diminished successful suits against the media by establishing a nearly impermeable right for the media to publish truthful information if the information is lawfully acquired—usually from public records

---

[8] Susan McGregor and Zylberberg Hugo, "Understanding the General Data Protection Regulation: A Primer for Global Publishers," *Colum. J. Rev.*, Mar. 7, 2018.
[9] William Prosser, "Privacy," 48 *Calif. L. Rev.* 383 (1960).
[10] *Restatement (Second) of Torts* § 652D (1977).
[11] Sidis v. F.R. Publishing Corp., 113 F.2d 806, 809 (2d Cir. 1940).
[12] Virgil v. Time, Inc., 527 F.2d 1122, 1129 (9th Cir. 1975).

and public officials—and the information involves an issue of public importance.[13] Yet, there are instances when the media may be liable for the highly offensive publication of private information.

Unlike a libel plaintiff, the private-facts plaintiff does not sue for lost reputation resulting from false statements. Successful private-facts plaintiffs sue over publication of truthful information that is so intimate that revelation robs them of a part of their personality. Truth, therefore, is not a defense in private-facts cases. The successful private-facts plaintiff sues for shame, humiliation and mental anguish. Also unlike libel, the publication of private facts is usually a tort only if dissemination is widespread. A defamation plaintiff can sue if a defamatory statement is communicated to one other person, but a private-facts plaintiff must usually show that a wide audience was exposed to the publication. The publication of private facts is a tort of publicity.

Highly Offensive Disclosure of Private Information

For a private-facts plaintiff to be successful, he or she must establish that the information publicized is in fact private and that dissemination of that information is highly offensive to the average person. It is generally true, as the *Restatement (Second) of Torts* concludes, that "There is no liability when the defendant merely gives further publicity to information about the plaintiff that is already public"[14] or if publication is not offensive.

The media are most likely to be held liable for the private-facts tort if they reveal intimate information about illnesses, mental disorders, intimate medical procedures and hospitalizations without the consent of the subject. Because offensiveness is a jury question, what constitutes a highly offensive revelation of private facts varies from community to community.

In one well-known case, the Missouri Supreme Court ruled that *Time* magazine invaded the privacy of Dorothy Barber when the magazine published Barber's picture and a story about her unusual eating disorder. *Time* published a photo of Barber taken against her wishes as she lay in a Missouri hospital room. Barber's disease caused her to lose weight even though she consumed large amounts of food. *Time* referred to her as the "starving glutton."[15]

The Missouri Supreme Court considered *Time*'s acquisition and publication of the picture and story to be an invasion of Barber's privacy, a privacy supported by the legally recognized confidential relationship between a doctor and a patient. The Missouri court said the public could be told of Barber's newsworthy disease without the embarrassing revelation of her identity. Because Barber's unusual malady was not contagious, there was no need to reveal Barber's identity to the public in order to alert people who had been in contact with her.

In a blockbuster case, a Florida jury in 2016 awarded Terry Bollea, known as Hulk Hogan, $140 million after Gawker.com, a gossipy, no-holds-barred online site posted a story and excerpts from a video of the former pro wrestler having sex with the wife of a friend. The jury concluded that the posting of a most intimate act was highly offensive, causing Hogan emotional distress and lost endorsements. The jury rejected Gawker's claim that the video contained constitutionally protected news and that Hogan waived some of his privacy by bragging about his sexual

---

[13] Florida Star v. B.J.F., 491 U.S. 524 (1989).
[14] *Restatement (Second) of Torts* § 652D comment b (1977).
[15] Barber v. Time, Inc., 159 S.W.2d 291 (Mo. 1942).

prowess. Gawker also claimed Hogan knew of the recording.[16] Bollea later settled for $31 million.

The jury's privacy decision and high damage award followed earlier rulings by two courts that ruled the First Amendment barred them from removing the Bollea story and video from the Gawker website. A federal district court in Florida and a state court refused to enjoin further publication of content the courts said contained newsworthy information of great public interest. Both courts noted that Bollea had frequently bragged about his sex life and that the story and video attracted much public comment. The federal court noted that a prior restraint—which is almost always prohibited by the First Amendment—would be ineffective trying to halt Gawker's salacious, much-discussed posts because the "cat is out of the bag."[17]

The Public Domain

Private-facts plaintiffs can successfully sue only if the highly embarrassing information revealed about them is, in fact, private. In common law, courts refused the claims of private-fact plaintiffs whose "private" information appeared on public records, thus placing the information in the public domain. Robin Howard provides an example of the plaintiff denied relief because her deeply personal information—a sterilization—appeared on a public record and therefore was not private. The Iowa Supreme Court ruled that Howard could not sue for invasion of privacy when a newspaper published that she had been sterilized involuntarily while a patient at a government home. The fact of her sterilization, the court said, was a public fact because it was part of a record forwarded to the governor's office in a file of complaints against the home. "Because the documents were public," the court said, "the information which they contained was in the public domain," and Howard could not sue for invasion of privacy.[18]

OPEN COURT RECORDS In 1975, the U.S. Supreme Court created a constitutional right for the media to report information contained in records available in an open courtroom. In *Cox Broadcasting Corp. v. Cohn*,[19] the Court established nearly complete First Amendment protection for the media to report information from official records available in open court. The Court ruled 8–1 that a Georgia father could not bring a privacy suit against a television station for reporting the name of his daughter in violation of a Georgia statute. The statute made publication or broadcast of the name of a rape victim a misdemeanor.

The case arose from the 1971 rape and murder of a 17-year-old girl. Six youths were indicted for murder and rape, but the murder charges were later dropped. The victim's name was never publicized during the initial media coverage of the crime. Eight months after the murder, the six youths appeared in court to enter pleas to indictments for rape. During a recess in the proceedings, a reporter for Atlanta station WSB-TV learned the name of the rape victim by reading the indictments provided by the court clerk. Later that day, the station named the victim in a report about the court proceedings. The victim's father brought a civil suit claiming that his privacy was invaded by WSB's broadcast of his daughter's name.

---

[16] Erik Eckholm, "Legal Experts See Little Effect on News Media from Hulk Hogan Verdict," *N.Y. Times*, Mar. 19, 2016.

[17] Bollea v. Gawker Media, LLC, 2012 U.S. Dist. LEXIS 162711 (M.D. Fla. Nov. 14, 2012); Gawker Media, LLC v. Bollea, 129 So. 3d 1196 (Fla. App. 2014).

[18] Howard v. Des Moines Register, 283 N.W.2d 289 (Iowa 1979), *cert. denied*, 445 U.S. 904 (1980).

[19] 420 U.S. 469 (1975).

The Georgia Supreme Court ruled that the father's privacy suit should go to trial, but the U.S. Supreme Court reversed. The Supreme Court said the First Amendment does not permit a privacy suit against the media for disseminating private information contained in public records that are part of an open court proceeding. "The commission of crime, prosecutions resulting from it, and judicial proceedings arising from the prosecutions," Justice Byron White wrote for the majority, "are without question events of legitimate concern to the public and consequently fall within the responsibility of the press to report the operations of Government." By their very nature, the Court said, public records "are of interest to those concerned with the operation of government, and a public benefit is performed by the reporting of the true contents of the records by the media." Punishing the press for disseminating "offensive" public records "would invite timidity and self-censorship," denying the public important information, White said. If there are matters at a trial that should remain private, the government should not put them in the public domain, White said.

VOLUNTARY DISCLOSURE People have no privacy claim if they willingly disclose private information about themselves on blogs, Facebook, Twitter or other media. People who post their own photos of drinking or disrobing consent to public disclosure. Personal information made available beyond "friends only" may be further disseminated by Google and other websites. A federal judge dismissed the First Amendment suit of a Pennsylvania university student who was denied teaching certification after she posted a picture of herself online sipping alcohol over the caption "Drunken Pirate." She was a student teacher at the time at a Pennsylvania high school. The university granted the student an English degree but denied a degree in education because of the photo and what the university said was other unprofessional conduct.[20]

Matters of Public Importance

Justice White noted in *Cox v. Cohn* that court records, which belong in the public domain, contain information about crime, prosecutions and judicial proceedings that are "events of legitimate concern to the public." The *Restatement of Torts* defines private facts as information *not* of legitimate concern to the public. In 1989, the Supreme Court extended First Amendment protection to publication of nearly all information dealing with matters of public importance if the information is truthful and lawfully acquired. In *Florida Star v. B.J.F.*, the Court said the First Amendment protects publication of lawfully acquired truthful information about a matter of public importance unless prohibiting publication will further a state interest "of the highest order." The First Amendment requires that each privacy case be weighed individually, the Court said.

In *B.J.F.*, the Court reversed a judgment against a weekly Jacksonville newspaper for publishing the full name of B.J.F., a rape victim, in violation of a 1911 state statute.[21] The statute barred an "instrument of mass communication" from printing, publishing or broadcasting the name of the victim of a sexual offense. A reporter-trainee for the weekly *Florida Star* acquired the name of B.J.F. from a government news release prepared by the Duval County sheriff's department. Although the

---

[20] Snyder v. Millersville University, 2008 U.S. Dist. LEXIS 97943 (E.D. Pa. Dec. 3, 2008); Jeanette Borzo, "Companies Face Legal Pot Holes of Social-Media Use, Discipline," *Wall St. J.*, Jan. 21, 2011; Jack Stripling, "Panelists Debate How Far Colleges Should Go to Monitor Online Behavior," *Chronicle of Higher Education*, Feb. 7, 2011.
[21] 491 U.S. 524 (1989).

sheriff's department distributed B.J.F.'s name, a sign at the department warned that names of rape victims were not matters of public record. The *Star* published B.J.F.'s name in violation of the paper's own policy not to publish names of rape victims.

In her privacy suit, B.J.F. claimed that publication of her name caused her emotional distress. She testified that her mother received phone calls in which a man threatened to rape B.J.F. again. She testified she had been compelled to move to a new residence, change her phone number and begin mental health counseling. A jury awarded B.J.F. $75,000 in compensatory damages and $25,000 in punitive damages for the paper's violation of the statute. A Florida appeals court affirmed the jury award, and the Florida Supreme Court refused review. The U.S. Supreme Court reversed.

Relying on an earlier decision in *Smith v. Daily Mail Publishing Co.*, a case discussed in Chapter 10, the Supreme Court said the government may constitutionally punish a newspaper for publishing lawfully obtained, truthful information about a matter of public significance only if the government can show that punishment is "narrowly tailored to a state interest of the highest order." The Court agreed that the newspaper published lawfully obtained, truthful information about a matter of public importance. The *Florida Star* acquired B.J.F.'s name lawfully from the sheriff's department. Indeed, the department disseminated the information about B.J.F.'s rape, information about a violent crime that the Supreme Court said was of "paramount public import." The press would censor itself, the Court said, if it feared liability for publishing news stories based on government press releases. If the government wishes to keep information confidential, the Court said, it should establish stronger safeguards on disclosure, not punish the press.

The Court also seemed to agree that the Florida statute served a state interest of a very high—if not the highest—order. The goals of the Florida statute—to protect rape victims' privacy and safety and encourage victims to report rapes without fear of exposure or reprisal—were "highly significant," the Court said. Nevertheless, the Court ruled for the newspaper because the Florida statute was not narrowly tailored.

First, the Court objected to the categorical nature of the statute's prohibition. The Florida law made the press liable whether or not the rape victim's name was already public, regardless of whether publication was offensive or inoffensive to anyone, and without consideration of the publisher's motives. Such automatic liability, without case-by-case weighing of competing values, motives and damages, is unconstitutional when important First Amendment interests are at stake, the Court said.

Second, the statute would be ineffective, the Court said, because it punished only one means of publication: "instruments of mass communication." The statute permitted dissemination of rape victims' names by other methods, including word of mouth, thus failing to serve the purpose of protecting a rape victim's privacy. The Court went on:

> When a State attempts the extraordinary measure of punishing truthful publication in the name of privacy, it must demonstrate its commitment to advancing this interest by applying its prohibition evenhandedly, to the smalltime disseminator as well as the media giant.

Justice White, in a dissenting opinion joined by Chief Justice William Rehnquist and Justice Sandra Day O'Connor, argued that the majority opinion would "obliterate" liability for publication of private facts. "If the First Amendment prohibits wholly private persons . . . from recovering for the publication of the fact that she was raped, I doubt that there remain any 'private facts' which persons may assume will not be" disseminated by the media, Justice White wrote.

Although the *B.J.F.* court ruled that media cannot be held liable automatically for publishing the names of sexual assault victims, the Court said the media might be punished under a narrowly drawn statute or under common law. In either case, the courts must balance privacy interests against the public interest, the Court said.

Newsworthiness

Long before the Supreme Court ruled that the First Amendment protects publication of court records and matters of public importance, the common law had protected publication of an ever-widening range of newsworthy information. Many newsworthy events involved crime, official actions and events of significant public importance. Some newsworthy events are more ephemeral, in which case the disclosure of private information is usually less embarrassing.

A man who saved President Gerald Ford's life lost a private-facts case because the fact of his homosexuality was ruled to be in the public domain and was related to significant newsworthy issues. Oliver Sipple, a decorated Vietnam veteran and a well-known leader in the San Francisco gay community, deflected the hand of Sarah Jane Moore as she aimed a gun at President Ford during his visit to San Francisco in 1975. Sipple unsuccessfully sued several newspapers for revealing his homosexuality to friends and family far from San Francisco.[22] Sipple agreed that saving the president's life was newsworthy but contended that his sexual life was not.

A California appellate court ruled that Sipple's sexual orientation was not a private matter. Sipple's homosexuality was part of the public domain in San Francisco because of his activism in the gay community. His homosexuality was also of legitimate public interest, the court said, because his courageous act cast often-stereotyped homosexuals in a positive light. There was also a newsworthy question whether President Ford delayed public expression of gratitude because of Sipple's homosexuality.

Publishing Sipple's sexual identity was ethically complicated. Although Sipple said he was embarrassed, other members of the gay community, seeking positive publicity about gays, had urged the media to tell the public of Sipple's homosexuality. In ruling against Sipple in his privacy suit, the court said the publication was not intended to embarrass him. The court said publication was an attempt to "dispel the false public opinion that gays were timid, weak and unheroic figures."

Private-facts plaintiffs often lose their cases because they have the misfortune of being involved in significant newsworthy events that reveal personal or embarrassing information. Hilda Bridges lost a privacy suit against a Florida newspaper over publication of a photograph of her fleeing the apartment where her husband had just committed suicide. The photo in *Cocoa Today* showed Bridges running nude across a parking lot on the arm of a police officer. Bridges was rushed from her former apartment after her estranged husband fatally shot himself. He had earlier forced Bridges to disrobe and threatened to kill her. Police surrounded the apartment when they learned that Bridges was a hostage. The media arrived shortly thereafter. Police stormed the apartment at the sound of gunfire from within.

---

[22] Sipple v. Chronicle Publishing Co., 201 Cal. Rptr. 665 (Cal. Ct. App. 1984).

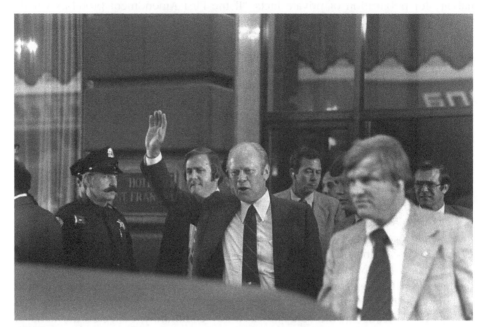

PHOTO 5.1   President Gerald Ford waves moments before shots were fired and Sipple intervened.

Source: Getty Images. Used by permission.

Although Bridges was holding a towel over her front as she fled the apartment, her hips were exposed in the published picture. The jury awarded Bridges $10,000 in her privacy suit against *Cocoa Today*, but an appellate judge ruled for the newspaper because the picture recorded a newsworthy event in a public place. Bridges's public exposure in an event involving a suicide, threatened murder and police was of legitimate public interest, the court said, just as other crimes, arrests, police raids, accidents and fires are of public interest.[23]

Courts have also cited newsworthiness to justify rulings against private-facts plaintiffs in cases in which the public was merely curious. Newsworthiness has proven to be an elastic term, encompassing the sad, the macabre, the hair-raising and the tasteless. "News" has been said to include "all events and items of information that are out of the ordinary humdrum routine, and which have 'that indefinable quality of interest which attracts public attention.'"[24] Courts have found newsworthiness in the family of a man kicked to death by a youth gang,[25] in pictures of auto accident victims,[26] and in the picture of the juvenile victim of a street accident.[27] News can include not only information in official records and events of significant public interest, but also revelation of people's skills, talents, oddities and foibles.

NEWSWORTHINESS OVER TIME   Once people are newsworthy, they may remain newsworthy. Unusual intellectual talents made William James Sidis

[23] Cape Publishing, Inc. v. Bridges, 423 So. 2d 426 (Fla. Dist. Ct. App. 1982), *cert. denied*, 464 U.S. 893 (1983). *See also* Taylor v. KTVB, 525 P.2d 984 (Idaho 1976).
[24] William Prosser, "Privacy," 48 *Calif. L. Rev.* 383, 412 (1960) (*quoting* Sweenek v. Pathe News, 16 F. Supp. 746, 747 (E.D.N.Y. 1936)).
[25] Jenkins v. Dell Publishing Co., 251 F.2d 447 (3d Cir. 1958).
[26] Kelley v. Post Publishing Co., 98 N.E.2d 286 (Mass. 1951).
[27] Leverton v. Curtis Publishing Co., 192 F.2d 974 (3d Cir. 1951).

a newsworthy public figure as a boy, newsworthiness that he retained into adulthood. A child prodigy, Sidis lectured to the faculty of the Harvard math department when he was only 11. Several years later, the *New Yorker* published a "Where Are They Now?" article on Sidis. The article described the life of a man who had become a reclusive clerk who collected streetcar transfers and lived in a simple room in a shabby Boston neighborhood.[28] As a child prodigy, the court said, Sidis inspired both admiration and curiosity. Nearly three decades after he lectured at Harvard, the question of whether Sidis had fulfilled his early promise remained a matter of public concern, the court said.

The court continued:

> Regrettably or not, the misfortunes and frailties of neighbors and "public figures" are subjects of considerable interest and discussion to the rest of the population. And when such are the mores of the community, it would be unwise for a court to bar their expression in the newspapers, books, and magazines of the day.

Sidis died shortly after the article was published.

Information from old public records may retain its newsworthiness even if the information is published in stories of little newsworthiness. The Louisiana Supreme Court ruled a weekly newspaper, the *Iberville South*, did not invade Carlysle Roshto's privacy when it republished a 25-year-old story about Roshto's conviction for cattle theft. Publication of Roshto's criminal record had no relation to any current public issue; the item appeared in the paper's "Page from Our Past" feature, which was made up of randomly chosen stories from earlier issues. Roshto sued for invasion of privacy because he had worked hard after his release from prison, had been pardoned and had hidden his conviction from the people in the community. The court suggested that the paper was insensitive to publish Roshto's story but ruled that the paper would not be punished for publishing truthful, accurate and nonmalicious information.[29]

RIGHT TO BE FORGOTTEN Once private information or misinformation finds its way to the Internet, it may be stored there forever, available indefinitely to remind the world of a person's past indiscretions, private disclosures or crimes. But citizens in the European Union have a "right to be forgotten" that allows an individual to ask Internet companies such as Google to remove links to stories or data that name the individual and are "inadequate, irrelevant, or no longer relevant." In *Google v. Spain*, the European Court of Justice ruled—in a decision with worldwide implications—a Spaniard had the right to ask Google to delete links to an old newspaper story connected to a bankruptcy, a story that the court agreed was no longer relevant or in the public interest.[30]

In 2016, Google challenged a French order that Google remove links from all of its websites—including American—not just from websites in the country from which the request to be forgotten originates. If the French order were upheld, a Google lawyer argued, "Other countries could demand global removals based on

---

[28] Sidis v. F-R Publishing Corp., 113 F.2d 806 (2d Cir. 1940). *See also* Cohen v. Marx, 211 P.2d 320 (Cal. Ct. App. 1949).

[29] Roshto v. Hebert, 439 So. 2d 428 (La. 1983). *See also* Shifflet v. Thomson Newspapers, 431 N.E.2d 1014 (Ohio 1982).

[30] Google, Inc. v. Agencia Española de Protección de Datos (AEPD), Case C-131/12, ECLI:EU:C:2014:317, May 13, 2014, *discussed in* Electronic Privacy Information Center, "The Right to Be Forgotten (Google v. Spain), https://epic.org.

their idea of what the law should be around the world."[31] Since then, in 2019, the European Court of Justice limited the reach of the right to be forgotten to the European Union, meaning that European authorities cannot enforce the right to be forgotten in non-EU countries that do not recognize the right.[32]

Consent

Besides asserting a First Amendment or newsworthiness defense, defendants in private-facts cases may also argue that the plaintiff consented to publication. Consent may be explicit or implied. One who is involved in a newsworthy public event, whether voluntarily or involuntarily, will usually be held to have given an implied consent to be photographed and written about. Similarly, people who talk to a reporter give implied consent for use of their names because they should anticipate publication. However, consent might not be implied if people interviewed fail to understand who they are talking to or that their interview might be published or broadcast.[33]

The more private the facts, the stronger the need for a journalist or public relations practitioner to obtain explicit written consent to publish a name or picture. Journalists and public relations practitioners should be particularly careful to obtain consent when intending to publish information about medical and psychological conditions and private facts about children. Legally, minors cannot give consent.

It can be difficult to know who has authority to give consent to disseminate private information at institutions housing the sick, the intellectually disabled and the young. Releases obtained by television journalist Bill Moyers permitting CBS to film mental patients at Creedmoor State Hospital in New York were invalid because they were not signed by the proper authority. The hospital's Consent for Patient Interview form required that a patient's consent be witnessed by a physician who had determined that a patient was capable of giving consent. The court said that permission forms secured by Moyers were invalid because they were signed by a psychologist, not by a medical doctor.[34]

The media may invade an individual's privacy if they exceed the bounds of the consent granted. For example, a book publisher that has permission to publish the picture of a woman bathing should not pass the picture to a newspaper for publication to a much broader audience.[35] Consent to have one's picture published in news columns does not include consent to have the picture used in a commercial context. And when proper consent is lacking, a court may enjoin dissemination of intimate private information.

■ SUMMARY ■

The private-facts tort is the highly offensive revelation of true, private information that is not newsworthy. Information in the public domain, including information submitted in open court or voluntarily disclosed, is not private. The Supreme Court has ruled the First Amendment protects publication of truthful, lawfully acquired information of significant public interest. Newsworthiness is also a broad defense,

---

[31] Sam Schechner, "Google Appeals French 'Right to Be Forgotten' Order," *Wall St. J.*, May 20, 2016.
[32] Adam Satariano, "'Right to Be Forgotten' Privacy Rule Is Limited by Europe's Top Court," *N.Y. Times*, Sept. 24, 2019.
[33] Prahl v. Brosamle, 295 N.W.2d 768 (Wis. Ct. App. 1980).
[34] Delan v. CBS, 445 N.Y.S.2d 898 (N.Y. Sup. Ct. 1981), *modified*, 458 N.Y.S.2d 608 (N.Y. App. Div. 1983).
[35] McCabe v. Village Voice, 550 F. Supp. 525 (E.D. Pa. 1982).

including information gathered in public places and information about public figures and interesting events. However, information about the ill or the intellectually disabled and private information about children might not be newsworthy and publication may be highly offensive. Consent may be explicit or implied. The media should be most careful to get written consent when acquiring information about mental and physical illness and minors.

INTRUSION AND TRESPASS

Even the most well-known public figures have a right to private retreats where they are free to talk, joke and lower their guard without being accountable to the outside world. A person has a justifiable expectation in a private place to be free from the telephoto lens,[36] the hidden microphone and the trespasser crouching below the window. The law has long held that it is illegal to peep, snoop or eavesdrop on people in private places. Peering in someone's window or pressing one's ear to the door may be trespass, intrusion or both.[37] It is also an invasion of privacy to open someone's mail or to tap someone's telephone or illegally access their computer files.

The tort of intrusion is the highly offensive physical, electronic or mechanical invasion of another's solitude or seclusion.[38] Intrusion includes the secretly recorded conversation, the overly aggressive surveillance and the intimate photograph shot with a telephoto lens. The common law protects citizens from intrusion into private domains, places where people have a legitimate expectation that they are not being watched or recorded. Intrusion is part of privacy law because an intrusion violates citizens' rights to be left alone and to control information about themselves.

Intrusion is an information gathering tort, not a tort of disseminating information by publishing, broadcasting or tweeting. Journalists gathering information with a secret camera or recorder may be liable for intrusion regardless of what they learn or whether they publish or broadcast the information acquired. "Where there is intrusion," a federal circuit judge said, the intruder should

> generally be liable whatever the content of what he learns. An eavesdropper to the marital bedroom may hear marital intimacies, or he may hear statements of fact or opinion of legitimate interest to the public; for purposes of liability that should make no difference.[39]

Privacy interests are also protected by the law of trespass. Trespass law excludes everyone from entering property without consent of the owner or "possessor" of the property.[40] Merely entering private property or posted public property without permission may be a trespass, whether or not the trespasser employs secret recorders, cameras or other intrusive technological devices. As with intrusion, the trespass lies in the act of trespass, not in what is learned or published as a result of the trespass.

---

[36] Souder v. Pendleton Detectives, Inc., 88 So. 2d 716 (La. Ct. App. 1956).
[37] Alan Westin, *Privacy and Freedom* 333–4 (1967); Souder v. Pendleton Detectives, Inc., 88 So. 2d 716 (La. Ct. App. 1956).
[38] *Restatement (Second) of Torts* § 652B (1977).
[39] Pearson v. Dodd, 410 F.2d 701 (D.C. Cir. 1969).
[40] *Restatement (Second) of Torts* § 158 at 277 (1965).

A person has no claim of privacy once personal information is made public, whether willingly or not. People, including the police, usually have no legitimate expectation of privacy in public settings. However, even public figures can be protected from aggressive reporters and paparazzi who harass, interfere and bully them.

Public Places

Generally, the more public the surroundings, the less the expectation of privacy. A California statute reflects the law generally when it says tape-recording at public meetings is not an intrusion when "the parties to the communication may reasonably expect that the communication may be overheard or recorded."[41]

A person dining in a public restaurant may have little expectation of privacy. A federal court in Maine ruled that a *National Enquirer* reporter did not intrude when she persistently sought to interview and photograph Henry Dempsey at a restaurant as well as outside his home.[42] The court said it is not intrusive to attempt to take a photograph in a restaurant open to the public or to attempt interviews without passing the threshold of the home. The reporter's attempts to interview may have been "annoying," the court said, but they were not "highly offensive" and therefore did not constitute intrusion. Similarly, a crime victim has no legitimate expectation of privacy if photographed by a photographer standing in a public park,[43] nor does an accident victim have an expectation of privacy as she is being removed from a rescue helicopter easily visible from a public highway.[44]

However, streaming mobile video may challenge and complicate some of these principles.[45] In the intrusion context, courts look closely at whether an invasion would be highly offensive to a reasonable person. And successful claims typically involve "unusually brazen insensitivity into a scene of grief, violence, or injury in which society is outraged by the distress caused to the victim or the victim's family."[46] You can imagine a livestream video meeting that standard. But it may prove difficult to establish offensiveness in an era of expanded surveillance and ubiquitous digital-information collection.

RECORDING POLICE If accident victims have no expectation of privacy in a public place, one might assume police conducting public duties in public places would also have no expectation of privacy if journalists or citizens record their actions and voices. Indeed, courts are increasingly ruling that citizens do have a right—a First Amendment right—to record police carrying out their duties in public places.

In an important decision, the U.S. Court of Appeals for the First Circuit ruled that Simon Glik had a First Amendment right to film Boston police officers with the video and audio recorder in his cell phone. Standing ten feet from the officers, Glik recorded them arresting a young man on the Boston Common, a public park.[47] Glik said he was concerned the police were using excessive force. Glik was charged with violating the Massachusetts wiretap statute—like statutes is

---

[41] Cal. Penal Code § 632(c).
[42] Dempsey v. National Enquirer, Inc., 702 F. Supp. 927 (D. Me. 1988).
[43] Deteresa v. American Broadcasting Co., 121 F.3d 460 (1997).
[44] Shulman v. Group W. Productions Inc., 995 P.2d 469 (1998).
[45] Jonathan Peters, "Could Facebook Live Change the Way Courts Think About Privacy Law?" *Columbia Journalism Review*, July 14, 2016.
[46] Rodney A. Smolla, "Accounting for the Slow Growth of American Privacy Law," 27 *Nova L. Rev.* 289 (2002).
[47] Glik v. Cunniffe, 655 F.3d 78 (1st Cir. 2011).

several states—that prohibits the secret recording of conversations. Police confiscated Glik's cell phone and computer flash drive. Charges were later dropped, but Glik sued for violation of his civil rights.

The First Circuit said the public has a First Amendment right to film government officials in public spaces. "It is firmly established," the court said, "that the First Amendment's aegis extends further than the text's proscription on laws 'abridging the freedom of speech, or of the press,' and encompasses a range of conduct related to the gathering and dissemination of information." The First Circuit said the filming of government officials engaged in their duties in a public place "fits comfortably" within principles recognized by the Supreme Court that citizens have a right to gather news. Law enforcement officers, the appellate court said, must permit "videotaping that memorializes, without impairing, their work in public spaces." The court ruled that officials lacked grounds to arrest Glik for secret recording because he recorded the officers "openly and in plain view" from ten feet without interrupting them. It was not necessary that Glik be a journalist or that he contest police actions.

Three years later the First Circuit ruled citizens' First Amendment right to record police extends to roadside stops, with the qualification that recording might not be allowed if the driver who has been pulled over is armed or if the act of recording interferes with police.[48] A federal appeals court in Illinois also ruled that citizens have a First Amendment right to record official police actions in public places.[49] A model policy of the International Association of Chiefs of Police states that people have a First Amendment right to record things in plain sight or hearing, including police activity.[50]

While there is strong precedent for a First Amendment right for citizens to record public events, including law enforcement officers, not all federal courts recognize a First Amendment newsgathering right, and the Supreme Court has never explicitly recognized such a right. Whatever the right to record police, it does not include the right for journalists or citizens to obstruct police, to interfere at a crime scene, to jeopardize public safety or to impede emergency equipment or personnel. A federal court in Connecticut ruled that police did not violate the First Amendment rights of a photographer when they protected public safety by halting drone coverage at a restricted accident scene. The court said Hartford police acted reasonably when they stopped the low-flying drone photography because the drone might endanger public safety as it hovered over the scene. The court said the drone was, in effect, trespassing over the cordoned-off area from which the public was excluded.[51]

HARASSMENT AND STALKING Whatever the right of citizens and journalists to record in public places, it does not include a right to engage in overzealous surveillance, harassment, intrusion or trespass. The public is repulsed by egregiously aggressive newsgathering, such as the paparazzi car chase that contributed to the death in Paris of Diana, Princess of Wales.

---

[48] Gericke v. Begin, 753 F.3d 1, 7 (1st Cir. 2014). *See* Clay Calvert, "The Right to Record Images of Police in Public Places: Should Intent, Viewpoint, or Journalistic Status Determine First Amendment Protection?" 64 *UCLA L. Rev. Disc.* 230 (2016).

[49] American Civil Liberties Union of Illinois v. Alvarez, 679 F.3d 583 (7th Cir. 2012), *cert. denied*, 133 S. Ct. 651 (2012); Illinois v. Melongo, 2014 IL 114852 (2014).

[50] International Association of Chiefs of Police, "Model Policy: Recording Police Activity," Dec. 2015, https://www.theiacp.org/sites/default/files/2018-08/RecordingPolicePolicy.pdf?msclkid=9f18b3f6a77911 ec9e50a23b1a340845.

[51] Rivera v. Foley, 2015 U.S. Dist. LEXIS 35639 (D. Conn. Mar. 23, 2015).

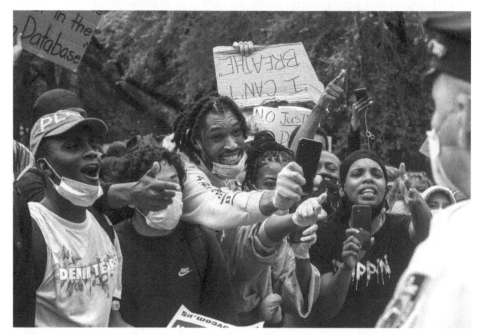

PHOTO 5.2 Protesters clash with police during a rally following the death of George Floyd, a black man who was murdered by a police officer in Minneapolis in 2020. Floyd's death was captured in videos that went viral.

Source: Getty Images. Used by permission.

A famous case involving Jacqueline Onassis, the widow of President John F. Kennedy, illustrates how aggressive journalism can cross over to illegal harassment.[52] Photographer Ron Galella, in his pursuit of photos and information about Onassis, bumped the parents of the Kennedy children's schoolmates, blocked passages, impersonated family employees, spied with telephoto lenses and trailed Onassis hour after hour. When Onassis sued over this list of intrusive activities, Galella complained that Onassis was camera-shy and uncooperative. However, the court ruled that Galella was liable for assault, battery, harassment and infliction of emotional distress. "The essence of the privacy interest," the federal district court said, includes a general "right to be left alone" and to define one's circle of intimacy, to shield intimate and personal characteristics and activities from public gaze, to have moments of freedom from the unremitted assault of the world and unfettered will of others in order to achieve some measure of tranquility. A federal appeals court ordered Galella to remain at least 25 feet from Onassis.[53]

Paparazzi California, home to many celebrities, has passed increasingly stringent laws in an attempt to curb harassment and intrusion by the large band of paparazzi who have been known to drive recklessly, tailgate, surround and corral their quarries and sometimes collide with celebrities' vehicles to acquire newsworthy pictures and stories. In 1998, shortly after Princess Diana's death, the California legislature enacted an anti-paparazzi statute outlawing offensive trespassing with the intent to capture an image or sound recording of a person engaged in "personal or familial activity."

---

[52] Galella v. Onassis, 353 F. Supp. 196 (S.D.N.Y. 1972), *aff'd*, 487 F.2d 986 (2d Cir. 1973).
[53] Galella v. Onassis, 533 F. Supp. 1076 (S.D.N.Y. 1982).

The law also prohibits the offensive intrusion—not necessarily including physical tres-pass—with an enhanced visual or audio device to capture familial activity in a venue where the target has a reasonable expectation of privacy. A 2005 amendment to the California paparazzi law requires photographers who assault a celebrity to forfeit prof-its from the sale for publication of the resulting photo. A 2009 amendment imposes steep financial penalties on publishers who publish photos they know have been acquired in violation of the anti-paparazzi statute. A 2010 amendment prohibits "false imprisonment," that is, boxing in celebrities by blocking their cars, surrounding them or ramming their vehicles so that they cannot escape.[54] Another 2010 amendment—to the California Vehicle Code—increases penalties for reckless driving if undertaken with the intent to capture an image or recording for a "commercial purpose."[55]

In 2015, California once again amended the anti-paparazzi law to prohibit intrusion by low-flying drones. The California law now prohibits not only physically entering land without permission but also knowingly entering into "the airspace above the land of another" without permission to capture images or recordings of private, personal or familial activity.[56] The law was designed to prohibit the use of drones "to cross over fences, bypass gates and travel into private sanctuaries in order to peer into windows, capture goings on and otherwise spy on the private lives of public persons."[57]

The California Press Association and other journalism organizations have opposed many of the anti-paparazzi laws, arguing they inhibit press activities because they are unconstitutionally broad and vague. But in 2015 a California appeals court upheld the 2010 amendment providing higher penalties—up to 6 months in jail and a $2,500 fine—for reckless driving with the intent to take photos for a commercial purpose.

The case involved photographer Paul Raef, who allegedly drove more than 80 miles per hour and cut across Los Angeles freeway lanes chasing a vehicle driven by singer Justin Bieber.[58] A California trial court ruled the statute was unconsti-tutionally overbroad, punishing newsgathering activities protected by the First Amendment. But a California appeals court reversed, ruling the enhanced penal-ties for reckless driving were not targeted only at those driving recklessly to gather news for public dissemination. The court said the law was aimed at all reckless drivers who intended to acquire images of public—or private—interest for a com-mercial purpose, including reckless driving by the private detective who takes a photo to sell to a client, or reckless driving by a blackmailer who takes a photo to extort money. "Driving is not an expressive activity, and driving in violation of traf-fic laws is not an accepted news or information gathering technique entitled to any special protection," the court said.

CYBERBULLYING Stalkers and harassers may follow, annoy and physically threaten their victims, but increasingly stalkers and harassers, bullies and flam-ers employ electronic communications—the Internet, email, blogs and tweets—to threaten, harass and bother their victims. Stalkers and harassers of any stripe usu-ally wish to exercise control over their targets. With the growth of the Internet, it is increasingly easy for hardened stalkers and lovelorn teens to acquire personal

---

[54] Cal. Civ. Code § 1708.
[55] Cal. Veh. Code § 40008.
[56] Cal. Civ. Code § 1708.
[57] Clay Calvert, Charles D. Tobin and Matthew D. Bunker, "Newsgathering Takes Flight in Choppy Skies: Legal Obstacles Affecting Journalistic Drone Use," 26 *Fordham Intell. Prop. Media & Ent. L.J.* 535 (2016).
[58] Raef v. Appellate Division, Superior Court, 240 Cal. App. 4th 1112 (2015).

information about their subjects—often from Facebook and other social networking sites—and to harass, threaten or embarrass their victims anonymously with repeated cyber messages.

The broad range of antisocial Internet communications is sometimes labeled "cyberbullying," which is not a legal term. One expert defines cyberbullying as the sending or posting of cruel or harmful material or engaging in other forms of social aggression using the Internet or other digital technologies.[59] In one study, more than half of mental health professionals surveyed on Internet mental health issues said they had treated a patient with "problematic Internet experience."[60] In another study, 47 percent of high school students reported being the target of bullying.[61]

A federal cyberstalking law makes it a crime to use an interactive computer service to kill, injure, harass, intimidate or cause substantial emotional distress.[62] But a federal judge in 2011 ruled the federal government could not use the cyberstalking law to punish tweeters who tweet messages on issues of public importance, even if the tweets are offensive or obnoxious. Judge Roger W. Titus dismissed an indictment against William Lawrence Cassidy, who had been charged with harassing and causing substantial emotional distress to Alyce Zeoli, a Buddhist religious leader. Cassidy had posted thousands of messages predicting—even encouraging—Zeoli's violent death. "Do the world a favor," said one tweet, "go kill yourself."

Judge Titus said the tasteless, hateful tweets were protected comment about the performance of a religious leader. Titus said blogs and Twitter posts are modern bulletin boards where all manner of pointed, sometimes outrageous, commentary is posted. "Cassidy's speech may have inflicted substantial emotional distress," Judge Titus wrote, "but the government's indictment here is directed squarely at protected speech: anonymous, uncomfortable Internet speech addressing religious matters." Citizens are free to read protected content on the modern bulletin boards, ignore it or, in the case of tweets, refuse to "follow" the tweeter, the judge said.[63]

Missouri, like other states, strengthened its online harassment statute after prosecutors unsuccessfully attempted to prosecute a notorious cyberbullying case under a computer fraud statute. Lori Drew's case was dismissed because her cyberbullying, which preceded a teenage suicide, did not include computer fraud. Under a false identity, Drew had upset an unstable teenage girl, who committed suicide after receiving messages that included the suggestion the "world would be a better place without you." A federal judge threw out Drew's computer fraud conviction, which did not punish frightening and intimidating conduct. After the suicide, Missouri followed several other states that have updated their harassment laws, making it a crime to knowingly frighten, intimidate or cause emotional distress anonymously by any electronic communication.[64]

Internet service providers are shielded from liability for cyberbullying under Section 230 of the Communications Decency Act. In 2009, the U.S. Court of Appeals for the Ninth Circuit relied on Section 230 to affirm dismissal of Cecilia Barnes's

---

[59] Nancy Willard, "Educator's Guide to Cyberbullying and Cyberthreats," *Center for Safe and Responsible Use of the Internet*, Apr. 2007, https://education.ohio.gov/getattachment/Topics/Other-Resources/School-Safety/Safe-and-Supportive-Learning/Anti-Harassment-Intimidation-and-Bullying-Resource/Educator-s-Guide-Cyber-Safety.pdf.aspx?msclkid=d3e13896a77911ecbf084dac47e8e0dd.

[60] Courtney Holliday, "MySpace-hoax Trial Shines Light on Federal Cyberbullying Bill," *FirstAmendmentCenter.org*, Nov. 20, 2008.

[61] Ann Lukits, "Anti-Bullying Legislation Has Mixed Results," *Wall St. J.*, Sept. 5, 2016.

[62] 18 U.S.C. § 2261A(2).

[63] United States v. Cassidy, 814 F. Supp. 2d 574 (D. Md. 2011).

[64] Mo. Rev. Stat. § 565.225.

cyberbullying case against Yahoo! Yahoo! was not liable for failing to remove nude pictures of Barnes taken without her knowledge and posted by her former boyfriend.[65] Section 230 immunizes Internet service providers from any editorial decisions, the court said, because ISPs are not publishers or speakers under the federal statute.

States are grappling with the appropriate punishment for jilted lovers and mean-spirited ex-boyfriends who post nude photos of former girlfriends on "revenge porn" websites.[66] (See discussion of revenge porn in Chapter 9.) Other counterattacks on cyberbullying include YouTube's online "Abuse and Safety Center," which tells users how to report bullying. MySpace improved its capacity to delete hate speech and other harmful postings. Facebook promises users to respond promptly to complaints about nudity, pornography or harassment of minors.[67] Social websites also reserve the right to remove offensive content, terminate the service of customers who violate terms of service, and report illegal content to law enforcement authorities.[68]

■ SUMMARY ■

Intrusion is the highly offensive physical or technological violation of another's privacy. Intrusion occurs when enhanced electronic or photo devices are employed to capture information in a venue where a person has a legitimate expectation of privacy. Generally, the media can record or take pictures of what is easily seen or heard in public and quasi-public places, including recording the actions of police carrying out their duties. Lawful newsgathering and free speech do not include stalking, assault, relentless paparazzi harassment or cyberbullying.

Private Domains

A person's most justifiable expectation of privacy exists in those places of retreat and intimate association, such as the home and the doctor's office. A secretly recorded conversation may be an intrusion, particularly if subterfuge is employed to bring electronic eavesdropping equipment into a private place. In *Dietemann v. Time, Inc.*, the Ninth Circuit Court of Appeals ruled secret transmitting and photographing by two journalists in a private California home were an intrusion. The Ninth Circuit Court ruled that A.A. Dietemann, a quack doctor, could collect damages from Time, Inc., for invasion of his privacy by two *Life* magazine employees who secretly used a voice transmitter and camera in the doctor's den. The journalists gained entrance to Dietemann's house by giving false names. One *Life* staffer secretly photographed the doctor as he waved a wand over bottles of body tissue and rubbed what he said was the cancerous breast of the other journalist. Meanwhile, a transmitter in the journalist's purse transmitted the conversation to a recorder in a nearby police car.[69] Dietemann did not advertise or charge for his "services."

The federal appeals court affirmed a lower court ruling awarding $1,000 to Dietemann for the journalists' electronic intrusion into a private place. Dietemann's den, the Ninth Circuit said, "was a sphere from which he could reasonably expect

[65] Barnes v. Yahoo! Inc., 37 Media Law Reporter 1705 (9th Cir. 2009).
[66] Erica Goode, "Victims Push Laws to End Online Revenge Posts," *N.Y. Times*, Sept. 23, 2013.
[67] Sue Shellenbarger, "Cyberbully Alert: Web Sites Make It Easier to Flag Trouble," *Wall St. J.*, Dec. 16, 2008.
[68] *E.g.*, MySpace.com, Terms of Use Agreement, ¶8.
[69] Dietemann v. Time, Inc., 449 F.2d 245 (9th Cir. 1971).

to exclude eavesdropping newsmen." When a person invites another into a private place, the court observed,

> he does not and should not be required to take the risk that what is heard and seen will be transmitted by photograph or recording, or in our modern world, in full living color and hi-fi to the public. . ... A different rule could have a most pernicious effect upon the dignity of man and it would surely lead to guarded conversations and conduct where candor is most valued, *e.g.*, in the case of doctors and lawyers.

The court rejected *Life*'s claim that concealed electronic instruments are essential to investigative reporting and that their use is protected by the First Amendment. "We agree," the court said, "that newsgathering is an integral part of news dissemination. We strongly disagree, however, that the hidden mechanical contrivances are 'indispensable tools' of newsgathering."

In a passage that has been cited frequently, the court wrote:

> The First Amendment has never been construed to accord newsmen immunity from torts or crimes committed during the course of newsgathering. The First Amendment is not a license to trespass, to steal, or to intrude by electronic means into the precincts of another's home or office.

In another case, one involving a business, where the expectation of privacy is usually less than in a home or hospital room, ABC paid more than $900,000 to settle an intrusion claim brought by an employee of a telephone psychic service whose office conversations were secretly recorded and broadcast. ABC settled the case with Mark Sanders, an employee of Psychic Marketing Group, after the California Supreme Court ruled that Sanders had an expectation of privacy against recording by the media during the secretly recorded workplace conversations, even though Sanders's coworkers could overhear his conversations. An appellate court also ruled that ABC could be asked to pay damages not only for its intrusive secret recording but also for broadcasting the recordings. Damages from the intrusion were increased by the broadcast, the court said. Sanders was secretly recorded during conversations at his work cubicle by ABC's Stacy Lescht, who took a job temporarily as a tele-psychic.[70]

Of course, hotel rooms are places where guests have a legitimate expectation of privacy. In 2016, a jury awarded TV sportscaster Erin Andrews $55 million for a nude video shot through a peep hole in her Nashville Marriott hotel room and viewed by 17 million people in social media. Michael Barrett, who served 27 months in jail for stalking, was told to pay 51 percent of the award. The hotel paid 49 percent because it assigned Barrett a room next to Andrews.[71]

WIRETAPPING AND PHONE RECORDS In some of the cases discussed, secret recorders and transmitters were the instruments of intrusion. Federal and state laws spell out when officials, journalists and citizens can and cannot lawfully

---

[70] Sanders v. American Broadcast Cos., 978 P.2d 67 (Cal. 1999); Sanders v. American Broadcast Cos., 28 Media L. Rep. 1183 (BNA) (Cal. App. 1999) (unpublished); Reporters Committee for Freedom of the Press, "Network Pays Out $900,000 in Hidden Camera Claim," www.rcfp.org/browse-media-law-resources/news/network-pays-out-900000-hidden-camera-claim.

[71] Meghan Keneally, "Jury Awards Erin Andrews $55 Million In Lawsuit," *ABC News*, Mar. 7, 2016.

record, when citizens do and do not have a legitimate expectation of privacy in their conversations and emails and in the records of those conversations and emails.

Under the Fourth Amendment, law enforcement officials seeking evidence of crime must get a warrant if they are to search for and seize evidence in a home, office or other private place where a citizen has an expectation of privacy. The search warrant, a fundamental element of a criminal suspect's rights of due process, is issued after law enforcement officers have convinced a judge there is probable cause to believe that the search of a specific place or monitoring of specific conversation will reveal evidence related to a specific crime. Warrants are required to authorize government bugging, wiretapping and eavesdropping because these intrusions are a form of **third-party monitoring** often conducted without the knowledge of parties to a conversation. Third-party monitoring of conversations is a particularly intrusive monitoring because, as Justice Douglas observed, it may intrude "upon the privacy of those not even suspected of crime and intercepts the most intimate of conversations."[72] While law enforcement officers with a warrant may place a bug in a bedroom or tap a telephone, all other citizens, including journalists, are prohibited from placing a bug, tapping a phone or secretly recording a conversation as a third party.

Under the Federal Wiretap Act, it is illegal for anyone to intentionally intercept or disclose any wire, oral, or electronic communication, including wireless, microwave, cellular phones, electronic mail and data.[73] And the government is supposed to get a search warrant, authorized by a judge, to intercept emails in transit, stored on a home computer or unopened and stored in a data bank.[74] The government must meet lesser standards to access older emails and stored data about who is placing and receiving phone calls, sending and receiving emails, and to access data documenting the duration of phone calls and the time that calls are placed and emails sent. Citizens, journalists and business people have an interest in keeping private who they call and when. But the law provides less privacy protection for phone and email records than the law provides for the content of a phone call and email message.

Following the attacks on the Twin Towers in 2001, Congress passed the Patriot Act, greatly increasing the government's subpoena power to acquire data about phone calls and emails. Section 215 of the Patriot Act permits the government to subpoena "any tangible things"—including records—that are "relevant" to an authorized investigation "to protect against international terrorism or clandestine intelligence activities."[75] (Chapter 11 discusses in more detail the recent revisions of the Patriot Act.) Secret FISA courts, created before 9/11 by the Foreign Intelligence Surveillance Act, quickly approved National Security Agency requests for data about phone calls and emails between Americans and potential terrorists. Even without a court order, American phone companies and Internet service providers could turn over phone and email data if they "reasonably believed" an emergency existed.

In 2013, Edward Snowden, an employee of a subcontractor of the National Security Agency, passed thousands of records to journalists revealing the NSA was collecting vast quantities of metadata—telephone numbers called, the time and duration of calls—not just records of communications linked to terrorism. The

---

[72] Berger v. New York, 388 U.S. 41, 64–5 (1967) (concurring opinion).
[73] 18 U.S.C. §§ 2511(1)(c), 2510 et seq.
[74] Stored Communications Act, 18 U.S.C. §§ 2701 et seq., 2516.
[75] 50 U.S.C. § 1861(a)(1).

Snowden data revealed the government was collecting "bulk" data about virtually every call and email by every American to, from, or within the United States. (Chapter 3 discusses the constructive trust imposed on Snowden.) In 2015, President Obama signed into law the USA Freedom Act, halting NSA's bulk collection of citizens' call records, requiring instead that telephone companies maintain the data to be accessed by government officials only after they acquire a warrant from the Foreign Intelligence Surveillance Court.[76] The act also requires the secret court to declassify some of its decisions and permit outside voices to argue for privacy rights before the court.[77]

Hacking Besides prohibiting tapping phones and intercepting wireless calls, federal and state laws prohibit hacking into telephone systems to acquire previously recorded conversations. Michael Gallagher, a former reporter for the *Cincinnati Enquirer*, pleaded guilty to violations of Ohio wiretap and computer access laws for stealing voice mail messages from Chiquita Brands International, Inc. Gallagher used the recordings to write unflatteringly about Chiquita's operation of banana plantations in Latin America. *The Enquirer* apologized to Chiquita for the reporter's intrusion and theft and reportedly paid Chiquita $10 million.[78] Similarly, it is illegal to implant "keylogging" software on computers so that users unknowingly transmit private and confidential information—such as passwords and account numbers—to outside monitors.[79]

It is also illegal to acquire a person's phone records from a phone company by "pretexting," falsely posing as someone authorized to see the records. Congress passed legislation in 2006 outlawing pretexting after a scandal in which private investigators used pretexting to acquire phone records of Hewlett-Packard board members and journalists covering boardroom fights.[80] Telephone pretexting is illegal in about a dozen states. Hewlett-Packard agreed to a $14.5 million settlement approved by a California Court after private investigators hired by HP executives engaged in pretexting to find the source of company leaks.[81]

PARTICIPANT MONITORING Participant monitoring occurs when at least one party to a conversation is aware of a secret recorder or transmitter. Some people contend that secret participant tape-recording is unethical and unnecessary. Much of the public disapproves. But lawyers, businesspeople, public relations practitioners and journalists may sometimes secretly record conversations to establish an accurate record without inhibiting candor. Unannounced recording protects journalists against false charges that a source was misquoted. Investigative reporters, like police informants, will occasionally carry a secret recorder or transmitter to document drug deals and other wrongdoing. Federal law and most states permit participant monitoring if not conducted for criminal purposes.

Federal Law Federal law permits one party to a conversation to record or transmit a conversation without telling the other party. Participant recording is considered no more intrusive than orally retelling a conversation to a third party.

---

[76] Pub. L. No. 114–23.
[77] Jennifer Steinhauer and Jonathan Weisman, "U.S. Surveillance in Place Since 9/11 Is Sharply Limited," *N.Y. Times*, June 2, 2015.
[78] *See Communications Law 1998* at 466–8 (Practising Law Institute).
[79] Tom Zeller Jr., "Cyberthieves Silently Copy Your Passwords as You Type," *N.Y. Times*, Feb. 27, 2006, at 1.
[80] David Rogers and Robert Guy Matthews, "Congress Approves Bill to Criminalize Pretexting," *Wall St. J.*, Dec. 11, 2006.
[81] Reporters Committee for Freedom of the Press, "HP to Pay $14.5 Million Settlement in 'Pretexting' Scandal," Dec. 8, 2006, www.rcfp.org.

Citizens are generally free to recount conversations, even private conversations, to friends, neighbors, colleagues or journalists. Doctors, lawyers and ministers are prohibited by law from divulging confidential conversations with their clients, but other citizens are not.

Although federal law permits participant recording, Section 2511 of the federal wiretap statute forbids a participant to secretly record a conversation for the purpose of committing a crime or a tort.[82] Civil penalties for violation of the act can result in a fine of $10,000.[83] It is a crime or a tort for a participant in a conversation to make a recording with the intent to blackmail or threaten someone with the recording.[84] However, Congress intended that the federal statute not be invoked against journalists simply because their surreptitious recordings may result in news stories that "embarrass" someone.[85]

An exception to the participant monitoring law, broadcasters must notify callers immediately if a telephone conversation is being broadcast live or is being recorded for broadcast.[86] The FCC assessed a $5,000 penalty against radio station WXLO in Fitchburg, Massachusetts, for recording a telephone conversation for broadcast without telling the party called.[87] But broadcasters, like anyone else, need provide no notice of a secret participant telephone recording not intended for broadcast, provided that participant recording is legal under state law. Furthermore, the FCC rule requiring notice of telephone conversations recorded for broadcast does not require notice of recorded face-to-face conversations intended for broadcast.

State Prohibitions The law in 38 states, like the federal law, permits participant monitoring. However, statutes in 12 states require all parties to consent to a recording.[88] Several state courts have upheld the constitutionality of prohibitions on participant monitoring, most recently the Supreme Court of California in 2021. Earlier, in a case involving a reporter's unannounced telephone recordings, the Florida Supreme Court rejected journalists' arguments that secret recording was needed to corroborate a journalist's story. The court said that secret recording is not an "indispensable" tool of newsgathering and that the First Amendment does not include a right to corroborate news stories with secret recordings.[89]

Disclosing Illegally Recorded Conversations While intercepting and disclosing wire and wireless communications are illegal, the U.S. Supreme Court ruled in 2001 that the First Amendment allows journalists to disseminate illegally recorded conversations if the conversations are of great public interest and if the journalist breaks no law to acquire them. In *Bartnicki v. Vopper*, the Court ruled that radio talk show host Frederick Vopper could not be punished under federal and Pennsylvania statutes for broadcasting an illegally recorded cell phone conversation between two participants in negotiations over teacher pay raises.[90] In the surreptitiously recorded tape, the head of a local teachers' union suggested blowing

---

[82] 18 U.S.C.S. § 2511(2)(d) (1999); Katz v. United States, 389 U.S. 347 (1967).

[83] 18 U.S.C.S. § 2520(c)(2)(B). *See* United States v. Turk, 526 F.2d 654 (5th Cir. 1976).

[84] United States v. Phillips, 540 F.2d 319, 325 (8th Cir.), *cert. denied*, 429 U.S. 1000 (1976).

[85] *See* Boddie v. American Broadcasting Cos., 694 F. Supp. 1304 (N.D. Ohio 1989).

[86] 47 C.F.R. § 73.1206.

[87] *In re* Montachusett Broadcasting, Inc., 7 F.C.C.R. 3594 (1992).

[88] California, Connecticut, Florida, Illinois, Maryland, Massachusetts, Michigan, Montana, Nevada, New Hampshire, Pennsylvania, and Washington. Reporters Committee for Freedom of the Press, "Reporter's Recording Guide," Summer 2012.

[89] Shevin v. Sunbeam Television Corp., 351 So. 2d 723 (Fla. 1977), *appeal dismissed*, 435 U.S. 920, *reh'g denied*, 435 U.S. 1018 (1978).

[90] 532 U.S. 514 (2001).

up the porches of school board members if they failed to offer higher raises. The tape was left anonymously in a mailbox and then passed to the radio station.

Relying on *Smith v. Daily Mail* and *Florida Star v. B.J.F.*,[91] the Supreme Court ruled 6–3 that the media's dissemination of lawfully acquired information about an issue of public importance outweighs the legislature's interest in discouraging unlawful interceptions and protecting the privacy of wire and electronic conversations. To deter unlawful recordings, it is better to punish the interceptors than the journalists who innocently acquire and disseminate the recordings, Justice Stevens wrote for the majority. Stevens suggested the First Amendment might not protect dissemination of some private conversations and trade secrets, but the majority ruled the public interest outweighed privacy when a station broadcast a secret recording of a conversation by participants in an issue of public importance. Negotiations over teacher pay, the subject of the conversation recorded in *Bartnicki*, was an issue of public importance. "One of the costs associated with participation in public affairs is an attendant loss of privacy," the Court said. In *Bartnicki*, no one was charged with violating the federal statute prohibiting knowingly receiving a stolen recording, as journalists sometimes do. The radio station acquired the tape from a source who received it from an anonymous provider.

■ SUMMARY ■

Bugging, wiretapping and other "third-party monitoring" are prohibited. But secret recording by one party to a conversation is permitted by federal law and statutes in 38 states. Phone and email records enjoy less privacy protection than the contents of phone conversations and email messages, but the government exceeded its authority when it collected electronic metadata in bulk, a practice terminated with the Freedom Act. The First Amendment protects dissemination of illegally recorded conversations involving subjects of important public interest.

Trespass

A journalist who intrudes into private places may also physically trespass on property. The ancient law of trespass prohibits entering onto another's land without consent. It is not a trespass to enter private property with the consent of the owner or the possessor of the property. Usually, the possessor of private property is the owner, but a person who rents also "possesses" property. A tenant may grant or deny access to an apartment or rental house, regardless of the wishes of the property owner.[92] For brief periods during emergencies, fire and police officials may also control access to private property, but even during an emergency, the owner of property can deny access to the media.[93] Once journalists enter private property to ask questions, they gain an implied consent to remain if the property owner agrees to talk.[94] However, journalists may become trespassers if they refuse to leave when asked. They may also be trespassers if they misrepresent the purpose of the interview with a private person,[95] fail to identify themselves as reporters,[96]

---

[91] Bartnicki v. Vopper, 532 U.S. 514 (2001).

[92] Lal v. CBS, 551 F. Supp. 356 (E.D. Pa. 1982), *aff'd*, 726 F.2d 97 (3d Cir. 1984).

[93] Prahl v. Brosamle, 295 N.W.2d 768 (Wis. Ct. App. 1980); Anderson v. WROC-TV, 441 N.Y.S.2d 220 (Sup. Ct. 1981).

[94] Machleder v. Diaz, 538 F. Supp. 1364 (S.D.N.Y. 1982).

[95] Belluomo v. KAKE TV & Radio, Inc., 596 P.2d 832 (Kan. Ct. App. 1979).

[96] Prahl v. Brosamle, 295 N.W.2d 768 (Wis. Ct. App. 1980).

unnecessarily disrupt a business[97] or enter property at the request of officials.[98] Flying an unmanned aerial system (a drone) at low altitudes over private property may also be a trespass.

But the law does not require that journalists or anyone else always represent themselves as who they are. The Seventh Circuit Court of Appeals ruled there was no trespass in a case where journalists misrepresented themselves to acquire information from public, commercial businesses. The Seventh Circuit upheld dismissal of trespass and fraud claims against ABC for allowing reporters to pose as patients to investigate Midwest eye clinics after allegedly promising not to work surreptitiously. The appeals court dismissed trespass and other claims by the Desnick Eye Center against ABC and *Prime Time Live* reporter Sam Donaldson for using reporters with hidden cameras at Desnick facilities in Wisconsin and Indiana to gather information about allegedly unnecessary cataract operations. This deception occurred after ABC gained the cooperation of the Desnick Center in Chicago by promising no "ambush" interviews or "undercover" surveillance.[99]

The appellate court said ABC reporters did not trespass when they posed as patients any more than food critics trespass when they conceal their identity from restaurant owners. Owners of restaurants and eye clinics consent to entry by customers, knowing that some might not be who they say they are, the court said. Desnick should have remained skeptical, the court said, when ABC promised not to employ investigative journalists as patients. The court noted that the journalists did not disrupt the business or invade any private places. The court distinguished the commercial eye clinics from the private home in the Dietemann case discussed earlier, a case in which a federal appeals court found invasion of privacy in a much more private setting than the public space of a business.

However, in another case involving a business, a federal appeals court ruled that two reporters hired in a supermarket meat department breached a duty to the supermarket and trespassed when they secretly videotaped in nonpublic areas. The two ABC reporters trespassed when they violated a duty to their employer—Food Lion—by secretly gathering information for a report about low-quality meat. The reporters were disloyal to Food Lion, the court said, because they acted contrary to Food Lion's interests while serving the very different interests of ABC, interests of journalistic exposure.[100] The case was unusual because the journalists went to considerable effort to become employees of Food Lion by misrepresenting their true intentions.

AERIAL SURVEILLANCE Householders have an expectation that their homes are protected from the peeping tom, the hidden recorder, the telephoto lens. But what about people and belongings visible on their property from airplanes, helicopters, nearby apartments and low-flying drones? Drones have provided dramatic news images of exploded buildings in New York City, clashes of police and demonstrators in Ukraine, Louisiana flood sites and Michigan water contamination zones. Businesses are projected to attract millions of new drone operators in the coming years to be used to inspect buildings and bridges, spray crops and search for downed powerlines.[101] Eventually, journalists may deploy "flocks" of drones,

---

[97] Le Mistral, Inc. v. Columbia Broadcasting Sys., 402 N.Y.S.2d 815 (App. Div. 1978).
[98] Wilson v. Layne, 526 U.S. 603 (1999).
[99] Desnick v. ABC, 44 F.3d 1345 (7th Cir. 1995).
[100] Food Lion, Inc. v. Capital Cities/ABC, Inc., 194 F.3d 195 (4th Cir. 1999).
[101] Andy Pasztor, "Business-Drone Rules to Take Effect," *Wall. St. J.*, Aug. 28, 2016.

controlled from vans or helicopter motherships.[102] But, at present, the deployment of drones is tightly restricted by privacy and trespass law and the Federal Aviation Administration (FAA).

Householders have a claim to privacy in the "curtilage" of their property—the property immediately adjacent to a home—as well as the airspace immediately above the house, a privacy claim recognized by Constitutional law, trespass law, statutes and aircraft regulations. The Supreme Court ruled in *United States v. Causby* that property owners control the airspace immediately above their property, or as the Supreme Court phrased it, the "immediate reaches of the enveloping atmosphere."[103] An aircraft trespasses when it enters that immediate airspace above the property, the Court said, if that entry also "interferes substantially" with the owner's use and enjoyment of the land.[104] In *Causby*, the Court said the flight of low-flying airplanes—at that time large, loud, rumbling, fixed-wing airplanes—"which skim the surface but do not touch it, is as much an appropriation of the use of the land as a more conventional entry upon it." Invasions of low-altitude airspace, the Court said, "are in the same category as invasions of the surface." The large planes in the *Causby* case flew at 83 feet, 67 feet above the house, shaking the property and distressing the residents. The Court did not define the height of the airspace a property owner controls.

High above the immediate airspace of a person's property is the "public highway" where interstate air traffic flows. Courts have ruled that householders and businesses have little expectation of privacy in property that can be observed from aircraft flying in public airspace at 500 feet or above. In *California v. Ciraolo*,[105] a Fourth Amendment case, the Supreme Court ruled 5–4 that a homeowner with a 10-foot fence around his backyard had no legitimate expectation of privacy when police flying a fixed-wing aircraft at 1,000 feet took photos of marijuana plants without a search warrant. Similarly, a divided Court ruled police in a helicopter needed no warrant to observe marijuana plants from 400 feet above a greenhouse behind a home in a rural area. Four hundred feet was a height at that time at which any member of the public could have been flying, the Court said.[106] The Supreme Court also said a company had no expectation that buildings on the firm's 2,000 acres could not be observed and photographed from public airspace.[107]

The Supreme Court said in *Causby* that even flights relatively close to a home may not be a trespass if the flights do not substantially interfere with the property owner's use of the property. In a media case, a Texas appeals court concluded a broadcast station did not substantially interfere with a woman's residence when the station's drone hovered above the home one time for ten minutes at an altitude between 300 and 400 feet to gather footage for a story on rental properties.[108] There was no attempt by the broadcaster to intrude into the privacy of the home with cameras or listening devices.

States and municipalities have enacted drone regulations, too. As noted earlier, a California anti-paparazzi statute prohibits knowingly entering into "the airspace above the land of another" without permission to capture images or recordings of

---

[102] Henry H. Perritt, Jr., "Flocks of Drones," *Radio, Television, Digital News Association*, http://rtdna.org/.
[103] 328 U.S. 256 (1946).
[104] *Restatement (Second) of Torts* § 159(2) (1965).
[105] 476 U.S. 207 (1986).
[106] Florida v. Riley, 488 U.S. 445 (1989).
[107] Dow Chem. Co. v. United States, 476 U.S. 227 (1986).
[108] Bevers v. Gaylord Broadcasting Co., 2002 Tex. App. LEXIS 5083 (July 18, 2002).

private, personal or familial activity.[109] A Florida statute requires written consent before pilots can capture images of private property "with the intent to conduct surveillance" and in violation of a person's reasonable expectation of privacy.[110] Under a Texas statute, one of the most stringent laws, it is a misdemeanor not only to employ an unmanned aircraft to capture an image of an individual or privately owned property with the intent to conduct surveillance but also to disclose or distribute the image.[111] An Oregon trespass statute enacted in 2013 allows property owners to bring claims against anyone who flies a drone over their parcels a second time at a height of less than 400 feet after being asked not to.[112] Property owners who prevail under Oregon's drone trespass statute can recover treble damages for any injuries to persons or property caused by unwanted drones.

In 2016, the FAA issued rules for the commercial use of drones, small unmanned aerial systems (UAS) under 55 pounds. A primary goal of the FAA is to protect public safety.[113] Unless a news organization had a waiver, FAA regulations limited flights to daylight hours at altitudes under 400 feet and speeds under 100 miles per hour. Particularly limiting for news organizations were regulations prohibiting flights over people and requiring that the aircraft always be within sight of the pilot or an observer.[114] However, in late 2020, the FAA released two final rules intended to accelerate the integration of drones into the national airspace system. One of them allows for drones to be flown over people, at night and over moving vehicles—without the need to seek operation-specific waivers from the FAA. This will offer significantly enhanced opportunities for aerial news gathering.

ACCOMPANYING OFFICIALS Much of the news that journalists report results from the day-to-day activities of police, firefighters, rescue crews and others who protect and serve—and are often paid by the community. What better way to get close to the news than for journalists to ride along with police on a drug raid or with the medic on an emergency mission? Journalists have a long history of watching public servants at close range as they search for evidence, arrest suspects, rescue the injured and revive the stricken. Public servants often perform their duties on public streets and in public buildings, but they are often called into private homes and businesses, where journalists accompanying them are trespassers.

A New York court ruled that WROC-TV employees trespassed when they accompanied Ronald Storm of the Humane Society of Rochester and Monroe County on an investigation of a private home. Storm, who had a search warrant, was investigating a complaint that animals were being mistreated at the home of Joy E. Brenon.[115] Brenon objected when the TV crew accompanied Storm into the house and shot footage.

The New York court said the authority of officials to enter private property to perform their duty "does not extend by invitation, absent an emergency, to every and any other member of the public, including members of the news media." The court rejected a Florida Supreme Court ruling that had recognized a custom for journalists to accompany fire officials into fire scenes. The authority of state officials

---

[109] Cal. Civ. Code § 1708.
[110] Fla. Stat. § 934.50(3)(b).
[111] Tex. Gov't Code Ann. § 423.003(a).
[112] Or. Rev. Stat. § 837.380.
[113] Operational Rules, www.faa.gov/uas/media/Part_107_Summary.pdf.
[114] 14 CFR § 107.25.
[115] Anderson v. WROC-TV, 441 N.Y.S.2d 220 (N.Y. Sup. Ct. 1981).

to enter private property with a search warrant, the New York court said, does not extend to people the officials might invite to accompany them.[116]

Not only might journalists trespass and intrude if they accompany officials into private places, but they might also be considered to be officials themselves, the Supreme Court has said, violating a citizen's Fourth Amendment protections against unreasonable searches and seizures.

OFFICIALS' LIABILITY In 1999, the U.S. Supreme Court ruled unanimously that officials violate citizens' Fourth Amendment rights when they invite journalists to accompany them into private places while executing a warrant. In *Wilson v. Layne*, the Court ruled that U.S. marshals violated the rights of Charles and Geraldine Wilson in 1992 when the officers allowed two *Washington Post* reporters to observe and photograph an early-morning attempt to arrest the Wilsons' son at their home in Rockville, Maryland. The marshals were participating in "Operation Gunsmoke," a national program to apprehend dangerous criminals. A *Post* photographer took pictures of Charles Wilson, dressed only in undershorts, held face down on the floor, and of his wife in a sheer nightgown. The Wilsons' son was not at his parents' home. No photographs were published.[117]

The Supreme Court agreed with officials that the presence of journalists might beneficially publicize law enforcement efforts to combat crime. But the Court said, "the possibility of good public relations for the police is simply not enough . . . to justify the ride-along intrusion into a private home." Furthermore, the need for accurate reporting on police issues "bears no direct relation" to the constitutionally permissible police intrusion into a home to execute an arrest warrant, the Court said.

The Court also rejected arguments that the presence of reporters during a search might minimize police abuses and protect suspects and officers. Although the presence of third parties might be constitutionally permissible in some cases, the Court said that the *Washington Post* reporters were not in the Wilsons' home to protect the Wilsons or the officers; the reporters were working on a story for their own purposes. Although the Court held that officials violate the Fourth Amendment when they invite the media into private places, a nearly unanimous Court also ruled that the federal marshals in the Wilson case would not be held liable because they did not know in 1992 that they would violate the Fourth Amendment if they invited journalists to accompany them.

Meanwhile, the Ninth Circuit once ruled that journalists accompanying officials act under color of law and therefore may also be liable for violating a citizen's Fourth Amendment right of privacy.[118] The court ruled that CNN personnel were not acting as independent journalists but were acting under color of law when they signed an agreement with officials and closely coordinated the search of the Bergers' property for evidence the couple were illegally killing eagles. Conversations inside the home were transmitted to CNN recorders from a microphone worn by agent Joel Scrafford. The agreement signed earlier with officials left editorial control of CNN broadcasts with the cable network, while CNN agreed to withhold broadcasts until a potential defendant's rights to a fair trial had been secured. In no other

---

[116] *See also* Miller v. National Broadcasting Co., 232 Cal. Rptr. 668 (Cal. Ct. App. 1987); Green Valley Sch., Inc. v. Cowles Florida Broadcasting, Inc., 327 So. 2d 810 (Fla. Dist. Ct. App. 1976); and Prahl v. Brosamle, 295 N.W.2d 768 (Wis. Ct. App. 1980).
[117] 526 U.S. 603 (1999).
[118] Berger v. Hanlon, 129 F.3d 505, on remand from the Supreme Court, *aff'd in part, rev'd in part, and remanded*, 188 F.3d 1155 (9th Cir. 1999).

cases, the Ninth Circuit said, "did law enforcement officials engage in conduct approaching the planning, cooperation and assistance to the media that occurred in this case." The court remanded the case to see whether CNN could be liable for trespass and infliction of emotional distress. Paul Berger was acquitted of all charges except for failing to follow the label when using a toxic chemical.

Journalists, like other private citizens, do not become arms of the police simply because they voluntarily help officials[119] or, at their own initiative, accompany officials onto private property to gather news but play no official role.[120] To act under **color of law**, a journalist must act in "collusion" with[121] or willingly participate in joint activities with state officials.[122] The Ninth Circuit found sufficient coordination between CNN and wildlife officials for journalists to act "under color of law."

Even in those cases in which journalists might act as agents of the government, they are not liable for a civil rights violation unless they violate the Constitution or a federal law. A journalist's defamation or invasion of privacy will generally not give rise to a civil rights claim because neither reputation nor most privacy interests are protected by the Constitution or by federal law.[123]

In 2008, a federal judge ruled that a jury might find that Dateline NBC collaborated so closely with police in a Texas raid that they violated the civil rights of William Louis Conradt Jr., who was suspected of soliciting minors. Conradt committed suicide during a raid before he could be arrested. Judge Denny Chin said a reasonable jury could conclude that Dateline NBC and police conducted an unreasonably intrusive search in violation of the Fourth Amendment and may have recklessly contributed to the suicide in violation of Conradt's civil rights.[124]

A ten-member Dateline NBC crew waited on November 5, 2006, outside Conradt's house in Rockwell County, Texas, to film Conradt's arrest for a segment of "To Catch a Predator"—a show that works with local police departments and an online "watchdog" group called Perverted Justice to identify and arrest "sexual predators." Dateline NBC recorded police officials as they decided how to execute a warrant that NBC had requested. Although officials did not suspect that Conradt had a gun, a seven-member SWAT team was called in to augment the five members of the police force already present. Conradt could see this activity from inside the house. Shortly after the SWAT team entered the home, Conradt shot himself. The segment was broadcast three months later. Conradt's sister filed a $100 million suit against NBC.

Until that time, Conradt, 56, was known as an upstanding citizen. An assistant district attorney, he had practiced law for 30 years. The court said a jury might find the search unreasonable because Dateline was so deeply involved and because the search served so few legitimate law enforcement purposes. The court noted that publicizing arrests can be beneficial, but the court said the "Texas police officers' actions were motivated not by a genuine law enforcement need, but by Dateline's desire for more sensational footage." The Dateline crew did not have a "passive role, as observers," Chin said, but "were involved in the planning, and . . . purportedly pushed the police officers into dramatizing their actions for the benefit

---

[119] *E.g.*, Marshall v. United States, 352 F.2d 1013 (9th Cir. 1965).
[120] Prahl v. Brosamle, 295 N.W.2d 768 (Wis. Ct. App. 1980).
[121] United States v. Gibbons, 607 F.2d 1320 (10th Cir. 1979).
[122] Adickes v. S.H. Kress & Co., 398 U.S. 144 (1970).
[123] *See* Paul v. Davis, 424 U.S. 693 (1976).
[124] Conradt v. NBC Universal, Inc., 536 F. Supp. 2d 380 (S.D.N.Y. 2008).

of the television cameras." The search warrants may have been void, the court said, because the judges who issued them were not fully apprised—if at all—of Dateline's involvement.

▓ SUMMARY ▓

Trespass, the physical entry onto private property, is closely related to the tort of intrusion. States and the federal government are passing laws and regulations to prevent increasingly prevalent drones from trespassing in private airspace. Journalists may be trespassers, and possibly acquire the color of law, if they accompany officials onto private property, a partnership the Supreme Court has ruled violates the Fourth Amendment.

FALSE LIGHT

A third privacy tort, after embarrassing facts and intrusion, is called *false light*. It is illustrated by the case of John W. Gill, whose picture was snapped as he sat with his arm around his wife, Sheila, at the counter of their ice cream concession at the Farmers' Market in Los Angeles. As Gill leaned forward, touching his cheek to his wife's, the famous photographer Henri Cartier-Bresson took a photograph without the Gills' knowledge or consent.

The photograph was published a short time later in the *Ladies Home Journal* to illustrate a story about love. But the story didn't portray love as affectionate gestures, like the one Cartier-Bresson caught between the Gills. Under the Gills' picture in the *Journal* appeared the caption, "Publicized as glamorous, desirable, 'love at first sight' is a bad risk." The accompanying story said that love at first sight, the kind the Gills were portrayed as representing, is the "wrong" kind because it is founded on "100% sex attraction."[125]

The Gills sued the publisher of the *Journal* for invasion of privacy. Their complaint was not that their affectionate moment was captured and publicized, but that their picture, with the caption and article, portrayed them falsely. The California Supreme Court ruled the Gills had a cause of action for invasion of privacy. "It is not unreasonable," said the court, to believe that the portrayal of the couple's relationship as based solely on sex "would be seriously humiliating and disturbing."

The *Restatement (Second) of Torts* defines the false-light tort as the dissemination of highly offensive false publicity about someone with knowledge of, or reckless disregard for, the falsity.[126] The interest protected by the law, the *Restatement* says, "is the interest of the individual in not being made to appear before the public in an objectionable false light or false position, or in other words, otherwise than he is."

The false-light tort provokes disagreement over its relationship to libel and other privacy torts, over what constitutes a "highly offensive" publication and over how much the First Amendment should protect the media from plaintiffs, like the Gills, who assert difficult-to-prove injuries of mental anguish and emotional distress. "False light invasion of privacy has caused enough theoretical and practical problems," one commentator concludes, "to make a compelling case for a stricter standard of birth control in the evolution of the common law."[127]

---

[125] Gill v. Curtis Publishing Co., 239 P.2d 630 (Cal. 1952).
[126] *See Restatement (Second) of Torts* § 632E (1977).
[127] Diane Zimmerman, "False Light Invasion of Privacy: The Light That Failed," 64 *N.Y.U. L. Rev.* 364, 366 (1989).

As the Gill case illustrates, the false-light tort has much in common with libel. Dean William Prosser contended the interest protected by the false-light tort, like the interest protected by libel law, "is clearly that of reputation with the same overtones of mental distress as in defamation."[128] Not surprisingly, false-light claims are often filed at the same time as defamation suits. In their suit against the *Ladies' Home Journal*, the Gills claimed that the picture, caption and story not only cast them in a false light but also hurt their reputation for industry, decency and morality.

In libel and false-light litigation, a plaintiff claims to be the victim of falsehood. Defenses are also similar. False-light defendants, like libel defendants, may claim that the plaintiff is not identified by the publication and that the publication is true. Furthermore, because false-light privacy, like libel, has been "constitutionalized," false-light defendants, like libel defendants, may claim that the plaintiff must prove fault, usually actual malice as required in *New York Times v. Sullivan*.

Although false light shares similarities with libel, the false-light plaintiff does not sue for lost reputation but, like someone suing over publication of embarrassing facts, is seeking recompense, as the Gills were, for the psychic harms of mental distress and humiliation. The late law professor Melville Nimmer thought the false-light tort was a natural derivative of the private-facts tort. Comparing false light and embarrassing facts, Nimmer said an individual has the same privacy interest in "maintaining a haven from society's searching eye" whether true or false information is being revealed.[129] "The injury to the plaintiff's peace of mind which results from the public disclosure of private facts may be just as real where that which is disclosed is not true."

The false-light tort also shares similarities with the embarrassing-facts tort. One similarity is the requirement that a plaintiff in both cases prove the offending material is widely disseminated. Libel plaintiffs must prove that a defamatory remark is "published" to at least one other person besides the plaintiff. But a false-light plaintiff, like an embarrassing-facts plaintiff, must prove that the false information is widely disseminated. False-light privacy is a tort of publicity.

Numerous states refuse to recognize the "amorphous" false-light tort.

Highly Offensive Publications

Although there is substantial inconsistency in judicial rulings in false-light cases, the highly offensive publications that result in false-light suits may be seen to belong to two broad categories: distortion and fictionalization. Cases of only minor falsification do not support a false-light claim.

DISTORTION The most common false-light claim against the media is for the distortion resulting when a broadcaster or publisher omits information or uses it out of context. In a Pennsylvania case, a federal district court refused to set aside a nominal jury award to Clare Randall Uhl, who sued CBS over editing of a documentary that Uhl claimed falsely suggested he was an unsportsmanlike hunter.

In the documentary titled *The Guns of Autumn*, CBS opened a sequence with wild geese walking in a clearing next to a field. Next, the viewer saw Uhl and other hunters, their guns aimed nearly parallel to the ground, firing from behind nearby cornstalks. Finally, Uhl was shown picking up a goose from the ground. Uhl said the editing erroneously portrayed him shooting birds on the ground instead of in

---

[128] William L. Prosser, "Privacy," 48 *Calif. L. Rev.* 383, 400 (1960).
[129] Melville B. Nimmer, "The Right to Speak from *Times* to *Time*: First Amendment Theory Applied to Libel and Misapplied to Privacy," 56 *Calif. L. Rev.* 935, 958 (1968).

flight. A federal district court agreed with the jury finding that falsely suggesting that a hunter shoots birds on the ground is highly offensive to the average person, at least in areas of the country, such as western Pennsylvania, where wild geese "darken the noonday sky."[130]

The context in which information is used can also distort, particularly when one is portrayed in an offensive sexual milieu. The U.S. Court of Appeals for the Fifth Circuit ruled that Mrs. Ed Braun was portrayed falsely when her picture was published in Larry Flynt's *Chic* magazine, a publication devoted to sex. The picture Flynt published showed Braun in a conservative bathing suit feeding a diving pig named Ralph at a family amusement park in Texas where Braun worked. *Chic* acquired the picture of Braun from the park management by misrepresenting the nature of the magazine. Although *Chic* did not alter Braun's picture, Braun objected to its publication next to stories and pictures about enlarging men's breasts, preparing a Chinese concoction from animals' sexual organs and demonstrating navel jewelry on nude models.[131] Braun said she was terrified, embarrassed and humiliated when she learned of the publication.

The court ruled that a jury could have reasonably found that *Chic* cast Braun in a false light by the unauthorized publication of her picture in a magazine "devoted exclusively to sexual exploitation and to disparagement of women." The court said that it could consider the "overall impression" of the magazine in determining that the publication cast Braun in a false light. The court agreed that publication of the photo might erroneously imply that Braun consented to publication of her picture or that she approved of the opinions expressed in *Chic*. A jury might reasonably conclude, the court said, that either misrepresentation was highly offensive.

File photos and television footage of street scenes used to illustrate stories may cast a person in a false light if offensive characteristics are wrongly ascribed to individuals shown. A federal court allowed Linda K. Duncan to pursue a suit against a Washington, D.C., television station for broadcasting scenes falsely suggesting she had herpes. The suit arose from footage WJLA shot of pedestrians, including Duncan, in the capital. Duncan had no false-light claim for the 6 o'clock news broadcast that showed her walking down K Street with other pedestrians. It was not an invasion of privacy for the station to show a close-up of Duncan while the reporter made general statements about herpes. These statements did not suggest Duncan had the disease.

The false-light claim arose from an edited version of the report shown on the 11 o'clock news. As the camera focused on Duncan in the late-night newscast, the reporter said, "For the 20 million Americans who have herpes, it's not a cure." In refusing summary judgment for WJLA, the court said the juxtaposition of the close-up of Duncan and the commentary about 20 million Americans with herpes supported an inference that Duncan had the disease. A jury could decide whether the false inference was sufficiently offensive for Duncan to prevail in a false-light suit.[132]

In contrast, the New York Court of Appeals ruled that Clarence Arrington had no false-light suit against the *New York Times* because characteristics of blacks that Arrington found offensive in an article were not attributed to him. Arrington's picture ran on the cover of the *New York Times Magazine* to illustrate a story about

---

[130] Uhl v. CBS, 476 F. Supp. 1134 (W.D. Pa. 1979).
[131] Braun v. Flynt, 726 F.2d 245 (5th Cir. 1984). *But see* Faucheux v. Magazine Management, 5 Media L. Rep. 1697 (E.D. La. 1979).
[132] Duncan v. WJLA-TV, Inc., 106 F.R.D. 4 (D.D.C. 1984).

middle-class blacks. Arrington's picture was snapped without his knowledge as he walked down a Manhattan street in a dark business suit. The article portrayed middle-class blacks as "materialistic, status-conscious and frivolous individuals without any sense of moral obligation to those of their race who are economically less fortunate."

Arrington said the cover photo falsely cast him as one of the insensitive, callous blacks discussed in the article.[133] However, the New York Court of Appeals, while not ruling whether New York recognizes the false-light tort, said the article did not portray Arrington himself as holding the ideas or opinions of insensitive blacks. Furthermore, unlike the *Braun* case, in which the sexual context was offensive, Arrington's photo was not published in a news context. The picture and article about the upward mobility of minorities, a newsworthy social issue, were not sufficiently offensive to allow Arrington to sue, the court said.

FICTIONALIZATION A second category of false light is fictionalization, the addition of fictional dialogue or characters to what are otherwise essentially factual works. Fictionalization ranges from the relatively limited embellishment of news stories to the much more elaborate addition of dialogue, characters, scenes, mannerisms, beliefs and thoughts in fictionalized books, short stories and "docudramas." An example of embellishment of the news is a story in the *Cleveland Plain Dealer* about Margaret Cantrell and her family five months after the Silver Bridge crashed into the Ohio River, killing Cantrell's husband, Melvin. *Plain Dealer* reporter Joseph Eszterhas wrote the story after a visit to the Cantrell home in Point Pleasant, West Virginia. The article implied that Eszterhas had interviewed Cantrell when he hadn't. Without seeing or interviewing Cantrell, who was not at home when Eszterhas visited, the reporter wrote, "Margaret Cantrell will talk neither about what happened nor about how they are doing. She wears the same mask of non-expression she wore at the funeral."[134]

Margaret Cantrell sued for invasion of privacy, arguing that she was cast in a false light through Eszterhas's deliberate falsifications that implied she was interviewed. She also charged that the article exaggerated the family's poverty. Cantrell said the article made the family objects of pity and ridicule and caused her and her son mental distress, shame and humiliation. Agreeing with Cantrell, a majority of the Supreme Court ruled that Eszterhas placed Margaret Cantrell in a false light with *New York Times* actual malice through his "significant misrepresentations," primarily the false implication that the reporter interviewed Cantrell during his visit and that he observed her wearing "the same mask of non-expression" that he had seen at Melvin Cantrell's funeral.

Fictionalization that portrays a plaintiff falsely need not be negative or disparaging to be highly offensive. The Hill family was portrayed positively but falsely in a 1955 *Life* magazine article that led to a false-light suit. In the article "True Crime Inspires Tense Play," *Life* reported on a Broadway play that depicted the "ordeal" of the Hill family when three convicts held the Hills hostage in their home for 19 hours during a weekend in 1952. *Life* said that the play was a "heart-stopping account of how a family rose to heroism in a crisis." *Life* photographed scenes from the play that were said to be reenacted at the house where the Hills were "besieged." One picture, over the caption "brutish convict," showed the son being

---

[133] Arrington v. New York Times, 5 Media L. Rep. 2581 (N.Y. Sup. Ct. 1980), *aff'd*, 433 N.Y.S.2d 164 (App. Div. 1980), *aff'd in part*, 449 N.Y.S.2d 941 (N.Y. 1982), *cert. denied*, 459 U.S. 1146 (1983).

[134] Cantrell v. Forest City Publishing Co., 419 U.S. 245 (1974).

"roughed up." Another picture, captioned "daring daughter," showed the daughter biting the hand of a convict.[135]

Although the weekend in 1952 was most unpleasant for the Hill family, the convicts, contrary to the *Life* article, did not mistreat the family. In fact, the three convicts treated the Hills courteously and released them unharmed. The Hills neither displayed the heroics nor endured the intimidation portrayed in the article. After their captivity, the family moved from Pennsylvania to Connecticut, but the fictionalized article in *Life* renewed memories that the Hill family was trying to forget. The lower courts upheld the false-light claim, but the Supreme Court reversed on other grounds.

The Supreme Court in *Time, Inc. v. Hill* recognized the false-light tort but ruled that plaintiffs, even private plaintiffs like the Hills, must, like public-figure libel plaintiffs, prove *New York Times* actual malice if they are involved in a newsworthy issue. The fault requirement in false-light cases will be discussed shortly.

MINOR FALSIFICATION Minor falsehoods that offend only hypersensitive individuals are not sufficiently offensive to support a false-light suit. A federal court ruled that a false statement that parents "instituted a suit" against a psychiatrist for the death of their daughter "but later abandoned" it was too insignificant an error to support a false-light suit. The story should have said that the parents consulted an attorney about bringing a suit but had not begun legal action.[136]

A federal district court ruled that a photo and story that falsely suggested a couple resold American consumer goods in Latin America was also insufficiently offensive to permit a false-light suit. The photo appeared in *Forbes* magazine, illustrating a story about Latin American tourists who boost the Miami economy by buying consumer goods in Florida and reselling them at high profits in Latin America. In the photo, Maxwell Fogel, a Philadelphia dentist, and his wife, Anna, were shown standing at an airport counter in Miami next to several boxes. The photo accompanied an article about the benefit to the Miami economy of sales to Latin Americans who ship their purchases home, sometimes reselling them at four times the purchase price. The caption under the Fogels' picture said, "The Load: Some Latins buy so much in Miami they've been known to rent an extra hotel room just to store their purchases."[137]

The Fogels, who said they were photographed while waiting to acquire ticket information, charged in their false-light and libel suit that the photograph created the false impression that they were buying merchandise for resale in Latin America and were masquerading as citizens of another country. A federal judge granted summary judgment for the magazine on both libel and false-light claims. The judge said the Fogels' appearance in the photo at the ticket counter did not imply that the couple participated in the Latin American trade. Furthermore, the judge said neither the Fogels' reputation nor privacy would be violated if the photo and story did imply they bought goods in the United States for legal resale elsewhere.

Clearly unbelievable falsification will usually not support a false-light suit. The U.S. Court of Appeals for the Tenth Circuit ruled that a beauty queen had no libel or false-light suit against *Penthouse* magazine because the story that offended her was so obviously unbelievable. The story told of a fictional Miss Wyoming's memories of making men levitate during sex.[138] The court said the story was nei-

---

[135] Time, Inc. v. Hill, 385 U.S. 374 (1967).
[136] Rinsley v. Brandt, 700 F.2d 1304 (10th Cir. 1983).
[137] Fogel v. Forbes, Inc., 500 F. Supp. 1081 (E.D. Pa. 1981).
[138] Pring v. Penthouse Int'l, Ltd., 695 F.2d 438 (10th Cir. 1982), *cert. denied*, 462 U.S. 1132 (1983).

ther libelous nor an invasion of the privacy of a real Miss Wyoming who sued. The court said the story "described something physically impossible in an impossible setting." The reader would realize, the court said, that the offensive sections of the story were "pure fantasy and nothing else."

■ SUMMARY ■

The false-light tort is the knowing dissemination of highly offensive false publicity. A person may be placed in a false light through highly offensive distortion resulting from omissions and from the use of pictures and broadcast footage out of context. Plaintiffs may also be cast in a false light through embellishment of news and fictionalization in books, short stories, docudramas and other media. One is not necessarily cast in a false light by minor or fanciful fictionalization or by creative embellishment.

Fault

The media are protected in false-light suits by the First Amendment fault requirement imported by the Supreme Court from the law of libel. In *Time, Inc. v. Hill*, decided three years after *New York Times v. Sullivan*, the Court ruled that false-light plaintiffs involved in issues of public interest may not successfully sue for false light without proving that publication was made with *New York Times* actual malice.

As in *Sullivan*, the *Hill* Court said that the press would be saddled with too great a burden if it had to verify "to a certainty" the accuracy of the facts in news articles. The Court said that sanctions against either innocent or negligent misstatement in stories of public interest could discourage the press from exercising its First Amendment freedoms. Thus, the Hills had to prove malice even though they were private persons involuntarily drawn into an issue of public interest.

Malice in false-light cases, like malice in libel, comprises a combination of reckless or knowing practices, such as fabrication of quotes, reliance on unreliable sources and failure to heed warnings. Eszterhas published with actual malice in the *Cantrell* case because he misrepresented that he had interviewed Cantrell. Similarly, the author of an unauthorized biography of baseball player Warren Spahn published with malice when he invented dialogue, created imaginary incidents and attributed imagined thoughts and feelings to Spahn. The author of the Spahn book, like Eszterhas, failed to interview the subject of the work. The author of the Spahn biography also failed to interview any members of Spahn's family or any baseball player who knew him.[139]

A federal court also found actual malice in the case of Larry Flynt's *Chic* magazine and its publication of Braun's photo. The magazine "acted with entire disregard for the falsity of their portrayal of Mrs. Braun," the court said. Not only was her picture published in an offensive sexual context, but the editor misrepresented the nature of the magazine to acquire permission to publish the picture.[140]

Since *Cantrell*, some courts, citing *Gertz v. Welch*, have argued that private false-light plaintiffs, like private libel plaintiffs, should have a lesser burden of proof than actual malice. These courts, which see the false-light tort as paralleling libel,

---

[139] Spahn v. Julian Messner, Inc., 221 N.E.2d 543 (N.Y. 1966), *appeal dismissed*, 393 U.S. 1046 (1969).
[140] Braun v. Flynt, 726 F.2d 245 (5th Cir. 1984). *But see* Faucheux v. Magazine Management, 5 Media L. Rep. 1697 (E.D. La. 1979).

focus on the status of the plaintiffs—whether they are private persons or public figures—rather than on public interest in the subject. These courts see a natural symmetry in requiring private plaintiffs in libel and false-light cases to shoulder a similar burden of proof.

Other courts require private and public false-light plaintiffs to prove reckless disregard as public figures must in libel suits. Courts requiring all false-light plaintiffs to prove malice focus on protecting publication of newsworthy issues. These courts argue that the First Amendment imposes a heavier burden on private false-light plaintiffs than on private libel plaintiffs because the false-light plaintiffs' claims of mental suffering and shame are less demonstrable than the reputational harm asserted by private libel plaintiffs. The press would be exposed to excessive liability to private false-light plaintiffs, it is argued, if the plaintiff were not required to prove malice.

The fault requirement poses a particularly troublesome problem when real people recognize themselves as "fictional" characters in novels and docudramas. Fiction writers usually write from their own experience, but they disguise the real people on whom their work is based by transforming them, making composite characters and using other literary devices. However, real people may be identified in works that purport to be pure fiction or fictionalizations of real events. Plaintiffs identified in either type of work might sue for libel or false-light privacy.

The identification problem is illustrated in a libel case in which author Gwen Davis Mitchell, in her popular novel *Touching*, did not adequately disguise a psychologist who conducted nude encounter groups. *Touching* was a fictionalized account of the author's experiences in a California nude therapy group called the "Nude Marathon." The encounter group was conducted by Dr. Paul Bindrim.

Mitchell thought she had transformed her experiences in the Nude Marathon sufficiently that she created a work of fiction in which Bindrim could not be identified. The leader of the therapy group in the novel was a Dr. Simon Herford, a crude, vulgar psychiatrist who used four-letter words frequently with his patients. Herford was "a fat Santa Claus type" with "long white hair, white sideburns, a cherubic rosy face and rosy forearms." Bindrim was a clean-shaven, trim psychologist—not a psychiatrist—who did not use profanity with his patients.[141]

Despite the differences between Herford and Bindrim in speech, physical appearance and professional credentials, a few witnesses said that they recognized Bindrim in the character of Herford by the pattern of Herford's conduct in situations similar to actual occurrences in the Nude Marathon. Thus, fabricated dialogue that Mitchell thought would increase the distance between her fictional doctor and the real one was ruled to have libeled Bindrim by making him out to be crude and unprofessional. Bindrim won $75,000 in damages from Doubleday and Mitchell.

The *Bindrim* case is a warning that once real people convince a jury they are identified in a fictional work, the author's attempts at disguise become evidence of falsification and, in the *Bindrim* case, defamation. Attempts to disguise real people may also be evidence of malice because malice is knowing falsehood. As the court said in *Bindrim*, "Mitchell's reckless disregard for the truth was apparent from her knowledge of the truth of what transpired at the encounter, and the literary portrayals of that encounter."

---

[141] Bindrim v. Mitchell, 155 Cal. Rptr. 29 (Cal. Ct. App. 1979), *cert. denied*, 444 U.S. 984 (1979).

▨ SUMMARY ▨

All false-light plaintiffs must meet a fault requirement. Public figures must prove actual malice, but courts divide over whether private plaintiffs must prove actual malice or some lesser degree of fault.

COMMERCIALIZATION

The fourth branch of privacy law is appropriation. The *Restatement (Second) of Torts* says that a person is liable for invasion of privacy if he or she "appropriates to his own use or benefit the name or likeness of another."[142] An appropriation is usually the unauthorized commercial use of another's name or picture in an advertisement, poster, public relations promotion, or other commercial context.

The injury suffered by an appropriation plaintiff may take two forms. A plaintiff whose identity is used for commercial purposes may suffer shame and humiliation similar to that suffered by a private-facts plaintiff, or the plaintiff may suffer loss of a commercial property. Celebrities, in particular, lose the "publicity" value in endorsements and other commercial opportunities when their identities are appropriated without their consent.

Appropriation and Unauthorized Publicity

Appropriation was the first branch of privacy law to develop following publication of Brandeis and Warren's 1890 article in the *Harvard Law Review*. Although Brandeis and Warren did not discuss commercial appropriation, the appropriation tort, as it developed at the turn of the century, is consistent with Brandeis and Warren's concern that people be able to control what is said about them. To publish peoples' names or pictures in commercial contexts without their permission is, in a sense, to deny them the right to be left alone. Pirating someone's identity for commercial gain may cause the same mental distress as the revelation of personal information, the disclosure that concerned Brandeis and Warren.

The law of appropriation originated in New York, where a disproportionate number of appropriation cases are still filed because of the concentration there of publishing, broadcasting, public relations and advertising companies. Under the New York civil rights statute, adopted in 1903, it is a tort and a misdemeanor to use a person's name, portrait or picture without consent for "advertising purposes or for the purposes of trade."[143]

The appropriation sections of the New York civil rights statute were adopted in response to a case in 1902 in which the New York Court of Appeals, the state's highest court, refused to recognize a right of privacy. In *Roberson v. Rochester Folding Box Co.*, the Court of Appeals ruled that Abigail Roberson of Albany had no legal claim to assert when the Franklin Mills Company used the young girl's picture, without her permission, in advertisements for the company's flour.[144] The Franklin Mills advertisements, which referred to Roberson as "The Flour of the Family," were circulated in stores, warehouses, saloons and other public places. Roberson said she had been "greatly humiliated by the scoffs and jeers of persons who recognized her face and picture."

---

[142] *Restatement (Second) of Torts* § 652C (1977).
[143] N.Y. Civ. Rights Law § 50–1.
[144] 63 N.E. 442 (N.Y. 1902).

When the Roberson family sued for invasion of privacy, the New York court ruled in a 4–3 decision that there was no law of privacy. While sympathetic to the Roberson claim, the court was unwilling to recognize a legal remedy for such a purely mental injury as invasion of privacy. The court feared it could not contain the privacy tort if the new category of legal wrong were recognized. If the commercial publication of unauthorized photos may be barred, the court said, what is to prevent the courts from halting the publication of unauthorized photos in news columns? If the unauthorized publication of a person's likeness can be barred, then why not a description or commentary about a person's looks?

Furthermore, the court wondered how it could adequately distinguish between public figures, who abandon much of their right of privacy, and private persons like Abigail Roberson, who do not. Not the least of the court's fears was a deluge of litigation by plaintiffs with ill-defined claims of mental suffering. This imagined barrage of lawsuits would place too great a burden on the press to defend itself, the court said.

After a storm of public disapproval over the court's refusal to recognize a right of privacy, the New York legislature passed a privacy statute prohibiting the unauthorized commercial use of a person's name, portrait or picture. About the same time, the Georgia Supreme Court became the first state supreme court to recognize commercial appropriation as a violation of a right of privacy.[145] On learning of the Georgia decision, Louis Brandeis wrote he was glad that the right to privacy was finding judicial recognition.[146]

Since the early 1900s, many courts have compensated private citizens like Abigail Roberson for the shame, humiliation and mental distress suffered when their privacy is invaded through the unauthorized commercial exploitation of their identities. Celebrities and public figures, too, have sued successfully for invasion of privacy when their names, pictures, acts and talents have been commercially appropriated without their permission. However, some courts have balked at compensating baseball stars, movie actors, singers and other celebrities for loss of privacy when their identities are commercially appropriated. These courts argue that celebrities, who make their living from public performances, do not suffer a loss of privacy as a private person does when their identities are appropriated for commercial purposes. Celebrities, these courts say, suffer a commercial loss, not the shame and humiliation of an invasion of privacy. In a word, celebrities lose their right of publicity.

The right of publicity, recognized in more than 20 states, is the right of celebrities and public figures to exploit the significant commercial value in their names, pictures, styles, voices and other distinctive features and talents. Unlike a right of privacy, the right of publicity is a property right that can be marketed and, in some jurisdictions, willed to one's heirs. "[I]nfringement of the right of publicity looks to an injury to the pocketbook," one commentator notes, while "an invasion of appropriation privacy looks to an injury to the psyche."[147] Unauthorized appropriation of celebrities' identities does not necessarily cause mental distress but may diminish their publicity value, particularly if the appropriation is extensive or tasteless.

A privacy right, tied as it is to a person's personality, dies when the person dies. However, the right of publicity, which is a property right, does not necessarily

---

[145] Pavesich v. New England Life Ins. Co., 50 S.E. 68 (Ga. 1905).

[146] *Letters of Louis D. Brandeis* 1, 306 (Melvin Urofsky and David Levy eds., 1971).

[147] J. Thomas McCarthy, "Public Personas and Private Property: The Commercialization of Human Identity," 79 *Trademark Rep.* 681, 687 (1989).

die with the owner.[148] The right of publicity may be willed to one's heirs. In legal jargon, the right of publicity may be "descendible." Several states have adopted statutes allowing people to will the publicity value in their name or identity to their estate or heirs.[149]

States recognizing the inheritability of publicity rights tend to emphasize one's right to enjoy and pass to one's heirs the fruits of one's industry. In California, a publicity statute prohibits for 50 years after death the commercial use of the name, voice, signature, photograph or likeness of any "deceased personality" without prior consent of the person or his agent. A deceased personality is anyone who has commercial value in his or her identity at the time of death. However, it is not a violation of the California law or other state statutes recognizing the descendibility of publicity rights to use the identity of a dead person in news, public affairs, sports stories or political campaigns or in a book, magazine, musical work, film or television program.[150]

Some states do not recognize a right for people to will publicity rights to their heirs, whether or not the celebrities exploit the rights commercially during their lifetime.[151] In these states, rights of publicity die with the person. Instead of emphasizing the right of individuals to pass the product of their work to their descendants, these states tend to emphasize the personal nature of the right of publicity and the difficulties in treating such rights as independent of the people who made them valuable.

Whether an unauthorized commercial appropriation violates privacy or publicity, the appropriation most often involves the unauthorized use of a person's name or identity in an advertisement, including look-alike and sound-alike advertisements. Appropriation may also occur in other commercial trade contexts.

ADVERTISEMENTS In a typical case, businessperson Donald Manville was allowed to collect damages for invasion of privacy when his picture ran without his permission in newspaper advertisements for Norge self-service laundries. Manville had posed for a picture in front of a laundry with the understanding that the photo would be used in a news story, not as it was published, as an advertisement in which he endorsed Norge laundries as good investments.[152]

Identification resulting in commercial appropriation can also be made through nicknames and slogans. The S.C. Johnson & Son Company violated football player Elroy Hirsch's right of publicity by using his nickname, Crazylegs, as the name of a women's shaving gel.[153] The comedian Johnny Carson's right of publicity was violated by the manufacturer of portable toilets. The manufacturing company never used Carson's full name or picture but appropriated his identity by using the phrase "Here's Johnny," the same phrase used to introduce Carson on his nightly television program. The company also appropriated Carson's personality by calling its portable toilet "The World's Foremost Commodian."[154]

LOOK-ALIKES AND SOUND-ALIKES A celebrity might successfully sue if he or she is identified through a "look-alike." Jacqueline Onassis obtained an

---

[148] W. Page Keeton et al., *Prosser and Keeton on the Law of Torts* 778 (5th ed. 1984).
[149] *See* American Law Institute, *Restatement (Third) of Unfair Competition* § 46–7 (1995).
[150] Cal. Civ. Code § 990.
[151] *E.g.*, N.Y. Civ. Rights Law § 50; R.I. Gen. Laws § 9–1–28; *see generally* Peter Felcher and Edward Rubin, "The Descendibility of the Right of Publicity: Is There Commercial Life After Death?" 89 *Yale L.J.* 1125 (1980).
[152] Manville v. Borg-Warner Corp., 418 F.2d 434 (10th Cir. 1969).
[153] Hirsch v. S.C. Johnson & Son, Inc., 280 N.W.2d 129 (Wis. 1979).
[154] Carson v. Here's Johnny Portable Toilets, Inc., 698 F.2d 831 (6th Cir. 1983).

injunction to stop magazine fashion advertisements in which Barbara Reynolds, an Onassis look-alike, was shown at a "legendary" private wedding—"no tears, no rice, no in-laws, no smarmy toasts, for once no Mendelssohn." Reynolds appeared in the Christian Dior ad with actress Ruth Gordon and television personality Gene Shalit. A *Newsweek* magazine story characterized the actors in the much-discussed ads as "idle, rich, suggestively decadent, and aggressively chic."[155]

In ruling for Onassis in her appropriation suit, the court said that imitators can simulate the voice or hairstyle of the famous in noncommercial settings but that "no one is free to trade on another's name or appearance and claim immunity because what he is using is similar to but not identical with the original." Reynolds "may capitalize on the striking resemblance of facial features at parties, TV appearances, and dramatic works," the court said, but she may not use her face in commercial advertisements that are deceptive or would promote confusion.

In a "sound-alike" case, a California jury awarded Bette Midler $400,000 for an automobile advertisement in which a singer imitated Midler's voice.[156] The U.S. Court of Appeals for the Ninth Circuit had earlier held that a jury should determine whether the Ford Motor Company and the advertising agency Young & Rubicam, Inc., appropriated Midler's identity by broadcasting an ad with a singer who was hired because she sounded like Midler when she sang "Do You Want to Dance."[157] Several people testified that they thought Midler was singing in the commercials.

The Ninth Circuit said it is a tort in California for advertisers to deliberately imitate the distinctive voice of a widely known professional singer to sell a product. Young & Rubicam had acquired permission to use the song but not to imitate Midler's voice. The Ford Motor Company was dropped from the suit. In a similar case, the Ninth Circuit upheld an award of more than $2 million to singer Tom Waits for imitation of his distinctive singing voice in radio ads for SalsaRio Doritos.[158] In 2006, Waits was awarded damages in a case against the Audi division of Volkswagen for a Spanish commercial in which a voice like Waits's sang music similar to Waits's "Innocent When You Dream."[159]

Video Games In cases asserting commercial rights for student athletes, two federal appeals courts have ruled that Electronic Arts, manufacturer of interactive video games, violated the publicity rights of collegiate athletes by portraying them in video games. The Third and the Ninth Circuit ruled that video game companies violate the publicity rights of celebrity athletes if the companies build interactive video games around the identities of the athletes without permission or payment.[160] The Ninth Circuit affirmed a district court that ruled Electronic Arts violated the publicity rights of former Arizona State University and, later, University of Nebraska quarterback Sam Keller by emphasizing the similarities between Keller and the virtual football player in the game *NCAA Football*.

While noting that video games are constitutionally protected expression, the court concluded—as the Third Circuit did in a case involving former Rutgers quarterback Ryan Hart—that the EA game merited no First Amendment protection because it "literally recreates Keller in the very setting in which he has achieved renown." Keller's avatar shared many similarities with the real Keller, including his

---

[155] Onassis v. Christian Dior-New York, Inc., 472 N.Y.S.2d 254 (Sup. Ct. Spec. Term 1984).
[156] Midler v. Young & Rubicam, 944 F.2d 909 (9th Cir. 1991), *cert. denied*, 503 U.S. 951 (1992).
[157] Midler v. Ford Motor Co., 849 F.2d 460 (9th Cir. 1988).
[158] Waits v. Frito-Lay, Inc., 978 F.2d 1093 (9th Cir. 1992), *cert. denied*, 506 U.S. 1080 (1993).
[159] Ben Sisario, "Still Fighting for the Right to His Voice," *N.Y. Times*, Jan. 20, 2006.
[160] Hart v. Electronic Arts, Inc., 717 F.3d 141 (3d Cir. 2013); Keller v. Electronic Arts, Inc. 724 F.3d 1268 (9th Cir. 2013).

college teams, his jersey number, height, weight, skin tone and playing style. The interactive game lacked sufficient creative elements to "transform" Keller's identity into a new work that is more than mere celebrity likeness or imitation, the court said. In 2013, Electronic Arts discontinued *NCAA Football* and agreed with Collegiate Licensing to pay $40 million to athletes for violating their rights of publicity.

In a related antitrust case, the Ninth Circuit in 2015 overturned a district court ruling requiring big college football and basketball programs to pay athletes up to $5,000 a year from revenues earned from broadcasting and marketing athletes' names, images and likenesses. The court said NCAA schools could be required to pay all the costs of athletes attending universities—not just tuition, books and fees. But the court said the NCAA does not act anti-competitively when it prohibits universities from paying athletes for their publicity rights, payments the NCAA says would undermine amateurism in college sports.[161]

Most recently, in 2021, the Supreme Court decided a landmark case, *NCAA v. Alston*, that signaled serious changes for the ability of student athletes to monetize themselves. The justices, in a 9–0 opinion, addressed antitrust claims filed by current and former student-athletes challenging the NCAA's compensation limits for student-athletes. They struck down the limits, against a century-long "no pay for play" college sports tradition, and effectively cemented the NCAA's new reality—one in which the NCAA "must prepare for a changing landscape that will undoubtedly require universities to develop 'all of the above' strategies for student-athlete monetization."[162] Indeed, "*Alston* alone . . . did not revolutionize the college sports landscape, but it may well serve as a fulcrum for the massive change that the system is set to undergo and that . . . is already underway."[163] Roughly a week after *Alston* came down, the NCAA announced a uniform interim policy suspending its name, image and likeness rules for all incoming and current student-athletes.[164] That change also came amid an increasing focus on state and federal legislation challenging the NCAA's name, image and likeness rules, making it clear that the organization's restrictions on athlete compensation were under attack on multiple fronts.

TRADE PURPOSES Appropriations do not always occur in advertisements for commercial products. It is also possible to appropriate peoples' identities or violate their right of publicity through the unauthorized use of their names or likenesses in public relations promotions, posters and other commercial purposes that do not advertise a product. The New York privacy statute bars the unauthorized commercial use of someone's name not only in advertising but also for other "purposes of trade."

The model Christie Brinkley sued successfully under the trade section of the New York law to stop unauthorized use of her picture on posters sold in stores. The posters did not advertise any products but traded on Brinkley's good looks and popularity without her consent.[165] In another trade case, a man was allowed to bring an appropriation suit when his picture was used without permission in a Minox camera manual. The manual served an educational purpose but also was ruled to be an appropriation of the man's identity for commercial purposes.[166]

---

[161] O'Bannon v. NCAA, 802 F.3d 1049 (9th Cir. 2015), *cert. denied*, 137 S. Ct. 277 (2016).

[162] Gregory A. Marino, "NCAA v. Alston: The Beginning of the End or the End of the Beginning?" *Foley & Lardner*, Aug. 4, 2021, www.foley.com/en/insights/publications/2021/08/ncaa-v-alston.

[163] *Id.*

[164] Michelle Brutlag Hosick, "NCAA Adopts Interim Name, Image and Likeness Policy," *NCAA*, June 30, 2021, www.ncaa.org/news/2021/6/30/ncaa-adopts-interim-name-image-and-likeness-policy.aspx.

[165] Brinkley v. Casablancas, 438 N.Y.S.2d 1004 (App. Div. 1981).

[166] Selsman v. Universal Photo Books, Inc., 238 N.Y.S.2d 686 (App. Div. 1963).

It is not an appropriation to make an *incidental* reference to a real person in a book, film, play, musical or other work, whether fact or fiction. Even identifying persons in a corporate documentary that builds goodwill but does not advertise a product has been ruled not to be a misappropriation. The U.S. Court of Appeals for the Fifth Circuit ruled that Anheuser-Busch Companies did not appropriate Roy Benavidez's identity by depicting him as a hero in a documentary about valiant Hispanic soldiers. Benavidez appeared in an 80-second segment of the 13-minute film titled *Heroes*. The documentary recounted the exploits of Hispanic Congressional Medal of Honor recipients.

The Corporate Relations Department of Anheuser-Busch Companies supervised and paid for the film, which was developed at the request of the National Association of Latino Elected and Appointed Officials from information supplied by the Department of Defense. The film was made available to schools, government agencies, veterans' organizations and Hispanic organizations. It may also have been shown at Anheuser-Busch hospitality centers where the company distributes free beer.[167]

The appeals court said there was insufficient commercial benefit to Anheuser-Busch to support a misappropriation claim. No beer was sold at the hospitality centers, no orders were taken or solicited, and no one was forced to watch the film. Undoubtedly, Anheuser-Busch "may enjoy increased good will in the Hispanic community" as a result of the film, the court said, but the "incidental" commercial benefit did not support a claim for misappropriation.

■ SUMMARY ■

Appropriation is the unauthorized commercialization of another. Appropriation may or may not be accompanied by the mental stresses associated with invasions of privacy. A violation of one's right of publicity, however, is the taking of the marketable, sometimes inheritable, property interest celebrities own in their looks, voices and talents. Appropriation and violation of publicity rights may occur in unauthorized advertisements, promotions and video games.

Defenses

Traditional defenses in appropriation and publicity suits have been newsworthiness and consent. However, the First Amendment is appearing more frequently as a defense for disseminating someone's name, picture or identity without their consent.

THE FIRST AMENDMENT An important defense in publicity cases is the First Amendment right to disseminate and discuss information of public importance. The Utah Supreme Court ruled that the First Amendment protected a U.S. senator from a publicity suit when he published constituents' pictures in campaign literature. Postal workers who posed with Senator Orrin Hatch said the picture reproduced in reelection literature constituted an implicit endorsement of the senator, which they did not intend and which they said violated their publicity rights. But the Utah court ruled that the campaign literature was newsworthy information protected by the First Amendment. The court said persons who pose with, or inadvertently appear with, public officials or candidates may not claim their identity has been appropriated if the picture is taken in a public or semipublic place.[168]

---

[167] Benavidez v. Anheuser-Busch, Inc., 873 F.2d 102 (5th Cir. 1989).
[168] Cox v. Hatch, 761 P.2d 556 (Utah 1988).

In the only publicity case on which the Supreme Court has ruled, the high court held in a narrow and unusual case that the First Amendment does not protect the media from appropriation suits if the media appropriate an entertainer's entire act. In *Zacchini v. Scripps-Howard*, the Supreme Court ruled that the First Amendment did not bar a human cannonball from pursuing a publicity suit under Ohio law against a television station that broadcast his entire act during a news program.[169]

WEWS-TV in Cleveland broadcast Zacchini's act on the news even though Zacchini asked the news team not to. The WEWS coverage consisted of a 15-second news clip of Zacchini from the time he blasted from the cannon until he landed safely in a net. The Supreme Court held the First Amendment did not provide a privilege to broadcast someone's whole act, what the Court called Zacchini's entire "professional property." Broadcasting his entire act, the Court said, posed "a substantial threat to the economic value of that performance" because viewers of the broadcast might not pay to see Zacchini in person.

In 2016, the Ninth Circuit affirmed dismissal of a suit by Jeffrey Sarver, who claimed the Oscar-winning film *The Hurt Locker* violated his right of publicity because it was based on his experiences in Iraq disposing of improvised explosive devices (IEDs). The court ruled the film is an expressive work protected by the First Amendment, not commercial speech. Furthermore, the court said Sarver, unlike an athlete or performer, had no publicity value in his Army experience exploding IEDs.[170]

NEWSWORTHINESS The traditional defense at common law in commercialization cases is newsworthiness. Newsworthiness is a broad defense in appropriation cases as it is in private-facts cases. Publication or broadcast of names and pictures in news reports of political, social and entertainment events are not commercial appropriations. The fact that the media are commercial enterprises motivated by profit and supported by advertising does not diminish the newsworthiness of the items they publish and broadcast. "It is the content of an article or picture, not the media's motive to increase circulation, which determines whether an item is newsworthy," the New York Court of Appeals has said.[171]

Events may be newsworthy even if they are commercially sponsored. The newsworthiness of an Elvis Presley press conference allowed producers of a "talking magazine" to reproduce and distribute large segments of the conference even though the event was staged as a commercial promotion by Presley's record company.[172] The recorded segments of the conference appeared in *Current Audio*, a magazine that included written and photographic material supplemented with a stereo record that included interviews and commentary. RCA Corporation, which sponsored the press conference, said the extensive coverage of the conference, including the voice recording, violated the company's exclusive contract with Presley. But the court said a press conference of a popular singing star is newsworthy:

> To hold, as [RCA] urges, that one who has freely and willingly participated in a press conference has some property right which supersedes the right of its free dissemination . . . would constitute an impermissible

---

[169] Zacchini v. Scripps-Howard Broadcasting, Co., 433 U.S. 562 (1977).
[170] Sarver v. Chartier, 813 F.3d 891 (9th Cir. 2016).
[171] Stephano v. News Group Publications, Inc., 474 N.E.2d 580 (1984).
[172] Current Audio, Inc. v. RCA Corp., 337 N.Y.S.2d 949 (Sup. Ct. 1972).

> restraint upon the free dissemination of thoughts, ideas, newsworthy events, and matters of public interest.

The picture on the cover of a book or magazine is newsworthy if the subject is a newsworthy event or is reasonably related to a newsworthy subject inside the publication. *New York* magazine won an appropriation suit brought by Duncan Murray after the magazine published a cover photo of Murray at the city's St. Patrick's Day parade. In a picture taken by a freelance photographer, Murray was dressed in the "striking attire" of an Irish hat, a green bow tie and a green pin. The New York Court of Appeals said the picture was newsworthy because Murray participated in "an event of public interest to many New Yorkers." Furthermore, the picture was related to a newsworthy article on Irish immigrants in the magazine.[173]

The movie *Borat* is also newsworthy, thus denying New York City pedestrian Jeffrey Lemerond compensation when he sued under New York's appropriation statute. Lemerond appeared in the film running away screaming "Get away!" when Borat greeted him unannounced on Fifth Avenue. Lemerond also appeared, but with his identity blurred, in a film trailer. A federal appellate court easily concluded the newsworthiness of Borat, the tale of a bizarre and boorish fictional Kazakh television personality sent to "report" on the U.S. Though childish and vulgar, the film "fits squarely" within the newsworthiness exception to the New York law prohibiting the unauthorized commercial appropriation of one's identity, the U.S. Court of Appeals for the Second Circuit ruled. The film "attempts an ironic commentary of 'modern' American culture," the court said, contrasting the "backwardness" of Borat with the social ills of a supposedly sophisticated society.[174]

Twenty-year-old nude pictures of a female wrestler were not newsworthy when *Hustler* published them accompanying a story about the woman's murder, a federal appellate court ruled. Thus, *Hustler* was not protected by the newsworthiness exception to Georgia's right-of-publicity law when the magazine published the photos of wrestler Nancy Benoit at the time she was murdered. She was killed by her husband, Christopher Benoit, in a widely publicized murder-suicide. The federal court denied *Hustler* protection of the newsworthiness exemption because the old photos were irrelevant to the very newsworthy murder-suicide. One's entire life is not legitimately opened to public scrutiny, the court said, just because one is the victim of an infamous murder. A $20 million punitive damage award was later dismissed because *Hustler* mistakenly believed the photos were newsworthy.[175]

Media Promotion Courts have consistently ruled that it is not an appropriation for publishers and broadcasters to promote the media's own publications and programs with advertisements containing previously published or broadcast news and photos. In one well-known case, *Holiday* magazine successfully defended itself against an appropriation suit brought when the magazine advertised itself with previously published pictures of actress Shirley Booth.

Holiday had photographed Booth wearing a fashionable hat and immersed in water up to her neck at a resort in the West Indies.[176] After the picture was published in a newsworthy travel story, *Holiday* published the photo again in an

---

[173] Murray v. New York Magazine, 267 N.E.2d 256 (N.Y. 1971).

[174] Lemerond v. Twentieth Century Fox Film Corp., 2008 U.S. Dist. LEXIS 26947 (2d Cir. 2008).

[175] Toffoloni v. LFP Publishing Group, 572 F.3d 1201 (11th Cir. 2009); Toffoloni v. LFP Publishing Group, 483 Fed. App'x 561 (11th Cir. 2012), *cert. denied*, 2012 U.S. LEXIS 9546, Dec. 10, 2012.

[176] Booth v. Curtis Publishing Co., 223 N.Y.S.2d 737 (App. Div.), *aff'd*, 182 N.E.2d 812 (N.Y. 1962). *See also* Namath v. Sports Illustrated, 363 N.Y.S.2d 276 (Sup. Ct. 1975), *aff'd*, 371 N.Y.S.2d 10 (App. Div. 1975), *aff'd*, 352 N.E.2d 584 (N.Y. 1976).

advertisement for the magazine. Booth sued for appropriation under the New York Civil Rights Statute. In ruling for *Holiday*, New York Appellate Judge Charles Breitel said:

> so long as the reproduction was used to illustrate the quality and content of the periodical in which it originally appeared, the statute was not violated, albeit the reproduction appeared . . . for purposes of advertising the periodical.[177]

Such commercial uses are not an appropriation because they do not imply that the person pictured endorses the publication. The use of the person is said to be only "incidental" to the media advertisement for its news and entertainment.

The media may also advertise books, broadcasts and other presentations with photos and footage not previously disseminated. The U.S. Court of Appeals for the Second Circuit said that the First Amendment may require that a book publisher be allowed to publish in an advertisement the picture of the author of a competing book. The Second Circuit said Random House could publish the picture of Robert Groden, the author of a book arguing that several conspirators killed President Kennedy, in an advertisement for Random House's *Case Closed* by Gerald Posner. Posner's book rejected conspiracy theories.

The Second Circuit concluded that the ad fell within the incidental use exception to the appropriation law. What drives the incidental use exception, the court said, "is the First Amendment interest in protecting the ability of news disseminators to publicize, to make public, their own communications."[178]

▧ SUMMARY ▧

Newsworthiness is a broad defense allowing the use of information of public interest in commercial contexts. Newsworthiness has been recognized in reports of commercially staged press conferences and in the photos on book covers. Newsworthy names and photos may also be used in incidental advertising for a publication or broadcast.

CONSENT Besides the First Amendment and newsworthiness, consent is a defense in commercialization cases. A broadcaster or publisher generally need not acquire consent to present people in newsworthy reports because newsworthy uses of a person's identity are not considered commercial appropriations. However, advertisers and public relations practitioners normally should acquire written consent from participants in commercial advertisements and public relations promotions. As with any contract, consent agreements should be written, should state the parties to the agreement, state the scope and duration of the terms, and should provide for consideration. Consideration is the payment for the use of the name or picture.

A name or picture should not be used commercially after consent has expired. Actor Charles Welch was awarded $1,000 compensatory damages and $15,000 punitive damages because the Mr. Christmas company broadcast Welch's commercials after his contract expired. Under terms of the contract, Mr. Christmas could run the ads for two years, but the company ran them for three.[179]

---

[177] 223 N.Y.S.2d 744.

[178] Groden v. Random House, 61 F.3d 1045 (2d Cir. 1995).

[179] Welch v. Mr. Christmas, Inc., 447 N.Y.S.2d 252 (App. Div. 1982), *aff'd*, 57 N.Y.2d 971 (1982).

Altering or falsifying materials may also violate a consent agreement. Maryland Manger, the author of a prize-winning letter on "Why I Am Glad I Chose Electrolysis as a Career," won an appropriation suit against the Kree Institute of Electrolysis because the institute changed her letter into an endorsement for the institute's electrolysis machine.[180] Manger won a contest conducted by Kree, an institute that taught electrolysis and sold the Radiomatic electrolysis machine that permanently removed superfluous hair. Manger signed a consent form permitting Kree to publish her winning letter and picture. But a jury ruled Kree appropriated Manger's identity when the institute's publication referred to her as a "Kree operator" and changed her letter into an endorsement of the Radiomatic, an electrolysis machine she did not use.

Releases must be signed by mentally competent adults. Parents must sign for minors. Actress Brooke Shields learned that agreements signed by parents on behalf of minors are usually binding. When Shields turned 17, she tried to enjoin publication of nude photos taken of her in a bathtub when she was ten. Shields's mother had signed a contract granting photographer Gary Gross unlimited rights to take and use the innocent photos of Brooke in return for $450.

Shields, who as a teen made provocative advertisements for Calvin Klein clothes, said the nonpornographic bathtub photos embarrassed her simply because "they are not me now." But the court ruled that a parent's consent is binding for a minor. "A parent who wishes to limit the publicity and exposure of her child," the court said, "need only limit the use authorized in the consent."[181]

Whether an oral or implied agreement is satisfactory will depend on the jurisdiction, and in general consent often takes the form of a broad model release. The broadest releases give the advertiser unrestricted rights to take, copyright, alter, sell and publish a model's or actor's photograph. Unrestricted-use contracts allow great flexibility to advertisers and the media, but a model who signs such an open-ended contract may later regret the broad terms.

A New York court ruled that a model who signed an unrestricted consent form was blocked from suing for appropriation when her photo was sold for uses she disliked. The highly paid model, Mary Jane Russell, was barred from an appropriation suit when Springs Mills retouched one of her photos the company bought from Marboro Books. Russell signed a release granting unrestricted use of her picture to photographer Richard Avedon, who took several pictures of Russell for advertisements of Marboro Books. Russell had no objection to Marboro's use of her picture showing her in bed, next to her "husband's" bed, reading an educational book. The caption said, "For People Who Take Their Reading Seriously."

Russell objected, however, when the picture was sold to Springs Mills, Inc., a manufacturer of bed sheets, and retouched so that Russell appeared to be reading a pornographic book. Springs Mills also added captions suggesting a "lost weekend" and other risqué activities. Russell said the bed sheet ad contradicted her modeling image as an intelligent, well-bred young wife in socially approved situations.

A New York court said the unrestricted consent form Russell signed barred an appropriation suit for Marboro's sale or Springs Mills' purchase of the original photograph. However, the court said unrestricted consent did not block a suit for libel. The court said Springs Mills might have so altered the emphasis, background

---

[180] Manger v. Kree Institute of Electrolysis, Inc., 233 F.2d 5 (2d Cir. 1956).
[181] Shields v. Gross, 451 N.Y.S.2d 419 (App. Div. 1982), *aff'd as modified*, 58 N.Y.2d 338 (1983). A federal court also refused an injunction in Shields v. Gross, 563 F. Supp. 1253 (S.D.N.Y. 1983).

and context of Russell's picture as to make it an essentially different—and perhaps libelous—picture.[182]

▣ SUMMARY ▣

Communicators should have written consent to use a person's name or picture for commercial purposes. Oral consent may be unsatisfactory. Consent agreements, signed by competent adults, should state the parties to the agreement and the scope and duration of the terms and should provide for consideration. A name or picture should not be used commercially after consent has expired.

EMOTIONAL DISTRESS AND PERSONAL INJURY

As the libel and privacy chapters illustrate, plaintiffs suing the media for libel and invasion of privacy often claim anxiety, humiliation and other emotional distress. Sometimes, however, plaintiffs claim emotional distress as a separate tort, independent of defamation, invasion of privacy or other wrong. Courts have been reluctant to recognize liability for the intangible harms of emotional distress just as they have been reluctant to recognize liability for the mental suffering of the privacy plaintiff. Damages are not easily awarded when, as in emotional distress and privacy cases, it may be difficult to prove what, if anything, a plaintiff suffers. Besides, minor insults and threats are an unfortunate fact of life. "It would be absurd," a legal text notes, "for the law to seek to secure universal peace of mind."[183] Law may be an especially inappropriate remedy when the source of mental discomfort is a publisher or broadcaster with a First Amendment mandate to promote robust debate that may be disquieting.

Nevertheless, courts do occasionally recognize the tort of intentional infliction of emotional distress where "outrageous" conduct by the media is thought to cause severe anxiety in private persons. Of related concern are cases in which plaintiffs argue, usually unsuccessfully, that the media cause physical harm either by "inciting" readers and viewers to illegal action, or through negligence, where the media fail to foresee that members of an audience will emulate violent acts they see or read about. A few courts have held the media liable for failing to foresee physical harm that would result from publication.

Intentional Infliction of Emotional Distress

A plaintiff can sue for intentional infliction of emotional distress when another's conduct is "so outrageous in character, and so extreme in degree, as to go beyond all possible bounds of decency, and to be regarded as atrocious, and utterly intolerable in a civilized community."[184] The intentional infliction tort is also called "outrage." Conduct is sufficiently shocking to support an emotional distress suit when, for example, a person delivers a rat to a customer who ordered bread[185] or harasses a debtor with repeated abusive threats of lawsuits and ruined credit.[186]

---

[182] Russell v. Marboro Books, Inc., 183 N.Y.S.2d 8 (Sup. Ct. 1955).
[183] W. Page Keeton et al., *Prosser and Keeton on the Law of Torts* 56 (5th ed. 1984).
[184] *Restatement (Second) of Torts* § 46 comment d (1965). *See* Robert Drechsel, "Negligent Infliction of Emotional Distress: New Tort Problem for the Mass Media," 12 *Pepp. L. Rev.* 889 (1985).
[185] Great Atl. & Pac. Tea Co. v. Roch, 153 A. 22 (Md. 1931).
[186] W. Page Keeton et al., *Prosser and Keeton on the Law of Torts* 61 (5th ed. 1984).

The victim suffers rather ill-defined, subjective mental anguish and emotional upset. The victim may also suffer tangible damages such as ulcers and lost wages.

The media have been sued several times for intentional infliction of emotional distress, but usually unsuccessfully. Whether a publication or broadcast constitutes outrageousness is a subjective judgment based on the facts of a case. Statements insufficiently outrageous to sustain a lawsuit include disclosing the identity of undercover narcotics agents,[187] publishing the details of a loved one's death in an emergency room,[188] calling a leading opponent of pornography the "Asshole of the Month,"[189] and saying that a murdered daughter had "no family support."[190] In 2018, a federal judge dismissed claims against Fox News over its retracted coverage of the murder of Democratic aide Seth Rich. His parents brought claims for intentional infliction for reports that Rich was murdered for leaking sensitive emails from DNC servers to WikiLeaks. The judge held that Fox's reporting was deficient but did "not rise to the level of extreme and outrageous conduct."[191]

However, several courts have refused to dismiss intentional infliction claims in cases involving irresponsible and offensive commentary or aggressive news coverage. Most recently, in 2019, a Texas judge ordered InfoWars founder and conspiracy theorist Alex Jones to pay legal fees to a parent of a school shooting victim suing Jones for intentional infliction of emotional distress.[192] Jones said repeatedly the 2012 Sandy Hook shooting was a hoax. The claim was brought by the father of a six-year-old boy who was among the first-graders and school staff members killed. The fees were imposed partly because Jones failed to produce witnesses and provide information to opposing counsel as ordered by the judge, who also denied a motion filed by Jones to dismiss the case. In another case, in 2008, a federal court refused to dismiss a claim that Dateline NBC intentionally inflicted emotional distress when a broadcast crew collaborated with police to arrange and cover a raid that ended in the suicide of a Texas assistant district attorney.[193]

In 1993, CBS settled a suit with Yolanda Baugh, who claimed the network intentionally inflicted emotional distress by broadcasting a videotape of her made shortly after she was allegedly attacked by her husband.[194] A federal district judge in California had earlier ruled that Baugh might have an emotional distress claim against a CBS news crew that broadcast the recorded conversation between Baugh and a crisis intervention worker at Baugh's home after the alleged attack.[195] The judge denied CBS' motion for summary judgment in a suit in which Baugh charged that a CBS crew acted "outrageously" when it recorded her for segments of *Street Stories*. The court said CBS might have acted outrageously when the news crew recorded Baugh, knowing that she was psychologically vulnerable shortly after an alleged incident of domestic violence. In addition, the court said the CBS team may have contributed to the emotional distress by acting fraudulently if the CBS

[187] Ross v. Burns, 612 F.2d 271 (6th Cir. 1980).

[188] Reichenbach v. Call-Chronicle, 9 Media L. Rep. 143 (Penn. Ct. C.P. Lehigh County 1982).

[189] Ault v. Hustler, 13 Media L. Rep. 2232 (D. Or. 1987), *aff'd*, 860 F.2d 877 (9th Cir. 1988), *cert. denied*, 489 U.S. 1080 (1989).

[190] Holtzscheiter v. Thomson Newspapers, Inc., 411 S.E.2d 664 (S.C. 1991).

[191] Alan Feuer, "Judge Dismisses Two Lawsuits Against Fox News Over Retracted Seth Rich Story," *N.Y. Times*, Aug. 2, 2018.

[192] Jonathan Tilove, "Court Orders Alex Jones to pay $100,000 in Sandy Hook Legal Costs," *Austin American-Statesman*, Dec. 31, 2019.

[193] Conradt v. NBC Universal, Inc., 536 F. Supp. 2d 380 (S.D.N.Y. 2008).

[194] Baugh v. CBS, No. C93–0601 FMS (ARB), 1993 WL 280319 (N.D. Cal. July 20, 1993).

[195] Baugh v. CBS, 828 F. Supp. 745 (N.D. Cal. 1993).

employees misrepresented themselves—as Baugh claimed they did—as a camera crew from the district attorney's office.

Although private persons may occasionally be allowed to pursue outrage suits against the media, the Supreme Court has all but eliminated such suits by public figures and officials. For a time, public figures viewed intentional infliction of emotional distress suits as an alternative to libel and false-light privacy claims because the person claiming emotional distress, unlike the plaintiff suing for libel or false-light privacy, did not have to prove the media published with malice.

However, in a case pitting *Hustler* magazine against the Reverend Jerry Falwell, the U.S. Supreme Court ruled that public figures may not successfully sue the media for intentional infliction without proving—as in a libel suit—that they are the subject of a false statement of fact published with *New York Times* actual malice. The Court's decision, in the case of a crude parody portraying Falwell as an incestuous drunkard, means that public officials and public figures will be unable to sue successfully for even the most biting satire or criticism unless it contains a provably false fact and is published with actual malice.[196]

Falwell charged that *Hustler* magazine engaged in outrageous conduct by publishing an advertisement satirizing an advertisement for Campari Liqueur. In the real Campari advertisement, celebrities talk about their "first time," that is, their first encounter with Campari Liqueur, often in glamorous settings. But in the *Hustler* parody (see Figure 5.1), Falwell's "first time" is a sexual encounter with his mother in a Lynchburg, Virginia, outhouse. Falwell's mother is portrayed as a drunken and immoral woman, and Falwell appears as a hypocrite and habitual drunkard. At the bottom of the page is a disclaimer stating, "ad parody—not to be taken seriously."

Falwell sued for libel, invasion of privacy and intentional infliction of emotional distress. The U.S. Court of Appeals for the Fourth Circuit ruled that the parody did not invade privacy under Virginia law because it was not used for commercial purposes. There was no libel, the court said, because no reasonable person would believe that the statements about Falwell in the parody were factual. However, the Fourth Circuit did rule the outrageous language of the parody caused Falwell emotional distress. In *Hustler Magazine, Inc. v. Falwell*, the Supreme Court reversed in a unanimous decision written by Chief Justice William Rehnquist.

Chief Justice Rehnquist agreed with Falwell that the *Hustler* advertisement was "doubtless gross and repugnant in the eyes of most." But the Court said the caricature of Falwell contained constitutionally protected ideas and opinions about a public figure. The ad did not contain "actual facts" about Falwell "or actual events in which [he] participated." Rather, the ad contained statements about Falwell that were so outrageous that they could not be true, the Court said. The very outrageousness of the parody placed it in the realm of ideas and opinion, not false and possibly defamatory facts. The Court said that the *Hustler* cartoon was a tasteless version of political cartoons that have flayed public figures through American history. Justice Rehnquist compared the advertising parody to political cartoons of Thomas Nast castigating the Tweed Ring in New York and cartoons of George Washington portrayed as an ass. Cartoons may be offensive, but they contain constitutionally protected ideas and opinion.

The Court said an "outrageousness" standard of liability is unconstitutional because it is too subjective and would punish the publisher's motives. Rehnquist said public debate might suffer no harm if courts could punish outrageous cartoons,

---

[196] Hustler Magazine, Inc. v. Falwell, 485 U.S. 46 (1988).

Jerry Falwell talks about his first time.*

FALWELL: My first time was in an outhouse outside Lynchburg, Virginia.

INTERVIEWER: Wasn't it a little cramped?

FALWELL: Not after I kicked the goat out.

INTERVIEWER: I see. You must tell me all about it.

FALWELL: I never *really* expected to make it with Mom, but then after she showed all the other guys in town such a good time, I figured, "What the hell!"

INTERVIEWER: But your mom? Isn't that a bit odd?

FALWELL: I don't think so. Looks don't mean that much to me in a woman.

INTERVIEWER: Go on.

FALWELL: Well, we were drunk off our God-fearing asses on Campari, ginger ale and soda—that's called a Fire and Brimstone—at the time. And Mom looked better than a Baptist whore with a $100 donation.

INTERVIEWER: Campari in the crapper with Mom . . . how interesting. Well, how was it?

FALWELL: The Campari was great, but Mom passed out before I could come.

INTERVIEW-ER: Did you ever try it again?

FALWELL: Sure . . .

lots of times. But not in the outhouse. Between Mom and the shit, the flies were too much to bear.

INTERVIEWER: We meant the Campari.

FALWELL: Oh, yeah. I always get sloshed before I go out to the pulpit. You don't think I could lay down all that bullshit *sober*, do you?

© 1983—Imported by Campari U.S.A. New York, NY 48°proof Spirit Aperitif (Liqueur)

Campari, like all liquor, was made to mix you up. It's a light, 48-proof, refreshing spirit, just mild enough to make you drink too much before you know you're schnockered. For your first time, mix it with orange juice. Or maybe some white wine. Then you won't remember anything the next morning. **Campari. The mixable that smarts.**

CAMPARI® **You'll never forget your first time.**

*AD PARODY—NOT TO BE TAKEN SERIOUSLY

FIGURE 5.1 Parody advertisement from Hustler Magazine provided by LFP Publishing Group, LLC.

but the chief justice said he doubted there is any principled way to make a distinction between outrageous and reasonable cartoons. "'Outrageousness' in the area of political and social discourse," he said,

> has an inherent subjectiveness about it which would allow a jury to impose liability on the basis of the jurors' tastes or views, or perhaps on

the basis of their dislike of a particular expression. An "outrageousness" standard thus runs afoul of our longstanding refusal to allow damages to be awarded because the speech in question may have an adverse emotional impact on the audience.

The Court also said that holding *Hustler*'s publisher, Larry Flynt, liable for outrageous political opinions would unconstitutionally punish him for bad motives. In debate about public affairs, the First Amendment protects many things "done with motives that are less than admirable," the Court said. Indeed, the Court noted, a political cartoon is often "intentionally injurious"; the purpose of a political cartoon is to be "a weapon of attack, of scorn and ridicule and satire." In a word, the cartoonist's motive is to be outrageous.

Relying on *Falwell*, the Southern District of New York in 2021 granted summary judgment to defendants Sacha Baron Cohen, Showtime and ViacomCBS, dismissing with prejudice intentional infliction of emotional distress claims, among others, brought by Roy Moore, the far-right Alabama politician, lawyer and jurist who served as chief justice of the Supreme Court of Alabama, before being removed from office for judicial misconduct. Moore was subjected to a fictitious pedophile-detection wand in an episode of Cohen's satirical show "Who Is America?"[197]

Also relying on *Falwell*, the Supreme Court ruled in 2011 that picketers denigrating homosexuality could not be punished for inflicting emotional distress on mourners at a military funeral. The Court ruled 8–1 in *Snyder v. Phelps* that members of the Westboro Baptist Church were engaging in constitutionally protected speech when they picketed the Maryland funeral of Marine LCpl. Matthew Snyder, who was killed in Iraq.[198] The church members, who believe that God hates and punishes the United States for its tolerance of homosexuality, particularly in the American military, carried signs stating "Fags Doom Nations," "Thank God for Dead Soldiers" and "Priests Rape Boys."

Chief Justice Roberts, writing for the Court, said the hurtful signs were protected for their content, form and context because the picketers expressed opinions on issues of public concern in a public forum, as they had many times before. The Chief Justice wrote:

> The placards highlighted issues of public import—the political and moral conduct of the United States and its citizens, the fate of the Nation, homosexuality in the military, and scandals involving the Catholic clergy—and Westboro conveyed its views on those issues in a manner designed to reach as broad a public audience as possible.

As in *Falwell*, the Court refused to allow punishment for "outrageous" expression because jurors might then punish viewpoints on public issues with which they disagreed. Speech on public issues has always been protected, Roberts said, no matter how "vehement, caustic, and sometimes unpleasant."

The Court noted that the Westboro picketers did not intrude into the funeral. They were on public property, 1,000 feet from the church where the funeral was held, and they could not be heard during the service. Snyder's father could see only

---

[197] Carl Mazurek, "Court Dismisses Roy Moore's Claims Against Sacha Baron Cohen Satire," Media Law Resource Center (July 2021), https://medialaw.org/court-dismisses-roy-moores-claims-against-sacha-baron-cohen-satire/.
[198] 131 S. Ct. 1207 (2011).

the tops of signs as he drove to the funeral. "The record confirms," Roberts wrote, "that any distress occasioned by Westboro's picketing turned on the content and viewpoint of the message conveyed, rather than any interference with the funeral itself." In dissent, Justice Alito argued the Court was permitting a vicious verbal assault on a private individual. Mr. Snyder, Alito said, was denied the right of any parent to bury his son in peace.

▓ SUMMARY ▓

The media seldom are sued successfully for intentional infliction of emotional distress, conduct so outrageous as to be beyond human decency. However, several courts have recently permitted private persons to pursue intentional infliction suits over aggressive reportorial practices. Attempts by public figures to employ intentional infliction suits as substitutes for libel and privacy suits were stalled when the Supreme Court ruled that the First Amendment bars outrage suits by public figures who cannot prove the statements are false and published with actual malice.

Physical Harm

Besides being charged with inflicting emotional distress, the media are also accused of causing physical harm, the most frequent instances being when someone emulates or copies what they have seen or read. Some plaintiffs argue the media "incite" harm when mimics of the media harm themselves or others. Courts have tended to reject the incitement arguments as they have also rejected claims that the media should be held liable for negligence, that is, failing to foresee that audience members might hurt themselves or others by copying what they read and hear.

INCITEMENT When stories or programs appear to cause physical harm, some courts have ruled that the First Amendment prohibits holding the media responsible unless it can be shown that the media "incited" the harmful action. The U.S. Court of Appeals for the Fifth Circuit ruled that *Hustler* magazine was not liable for the death of a 14-year-old because the magazine story that led to the death by hanging did not incite the dangerous act. In *Herceg v. Hustler*, the appeals court reversed a $169,000 jury award to Diane Herceg for the death of her son, Troy D., from experimenting with "autoerotic asphyxia," the dangerous practice of masturbating while choking the blood supply to the brain.[199]

The appeals court first determined that the article on autoerotic asphyxia was constitutionally protected speech because it was not obscene or otherwise outside of First Amendment consideration. The court then ruled that *Hustler* should not be held liable because it did not incite the death. Indeed, the Court questioned whether a magazine purchased for solitary reading could ever incite a reader to action.

With similar reasoning, a California appeals court ruled that CBS Records and singer Ozzy Osbourne did not incite the suicide of a young listener. The court ruled that the First Amendment barred the parents of 19-year-old John McCollum from suing Osbourne and the record company for the suicide of their son after he listened to an Osbourne song with the lyrics:

> Ah know people
> You really know where it's at

---

[199] Herceg v. Hustler Magazine, Inc., 814 F.2d 1017 (5th Cir. 1987).

You got it
Why try, why try
Get the gun and try it
Shoot, shoot, shoot.[200]

There is no incitement, the court said, in art that evokes "a mood of depression as it figuratively depicts the darker side of human nature."

The incitement requirement has protected the media not only when members of the audience hurt themselves but also when they hurt others by imitating or copying media violence. An NBC program in which a girl is raped with a "plumber's helper" was ruled not to have incited four youths, who had seen the program, to rape a girl with a bottle shortly after the program aired.[201] Similarly, CBS was not liable for the death of a woman killed by a youth who argued the network had inspired the deed by saturating him with violent episodes.[202] The California court also ruled that CBS was not negligent. In 2019, the Sixth Circuit held that relatives of victims of the mass shooting at the Pulse night club in Orlando, Florida, could not recover damages under the Anti-Terrorism Act in claims against Twitter, Facebook and Google. The plaintiffs had argued that the Islamic State of Iraq and Syria (ISIS) used the platforms to recruit Americans to commit terrorist attacks and, therefore, the platforms were responsible.[203]

Although media offerings are seldom held to incite physical harm, a federal appeals court ruled that a publisher might be liable for disseminating a book that, in effect, incites crime by aiding and abetting murder. The Fourth Circuit reversed summary judgment for Paladin Enterprises, publisher of *Hit Man: A Technical Manual for Independent Contractors*, a book James Perry relied on as a guide when he murdered three members of a family.[204] Relatives of the family sued Paladin for aiding and abetting murders by contract. *Hit Man* taught would-be killers how a professional "gets assignments, creates a false identity, makes a disposable silencer, leaves the scene without a trace, watches his mark unobserved and more." Perry followed *Hit Man* closely.

The court rejected Paladin's claim that *Hit Man* was protected speech because it did not incite anyone to murder. The Fourth Circuit overturned a district court ruling that *Brandenburg v. Ohio* barred liability for Paladin because the book only "advocated" or "taught" lawlessness but was not "directed to inciting or producing imminent lawless action." The Fourth Circuit determined that although *Brandenburg* protects "abstract" teaching, it does not protect the intentional, detailed direction of murderers the court found in *Hit Man*. Paladin's book was not protected because the publisher "intended that *Hit Man* would immediately be used by criminals and would-be criminals in the solicitation, planning, and commission of murder and murder for hire." The court said few other publications describing potentially illegal activities would be unprotected by the First Amendment because few other publishers would demonstrate the specific intent to aid criminality that Paladin demonstrated. As part of a settlement, Paladin agreed to take *Hit Man* off the market.[205]

---

[200] McCollum v. CBS, 249 Cal. Rptr. 187 (Cal. Ct. App. 1988).
[201] Olivia N. v. NBC, 178 Cal. Rptr. 888 (Cal. Ct. App. 1981).
[202] Zamora v. CBS, 480 F. Supp. 199 (S.D. Fla. 1979).
[203] Crosby v. Twitter, Inc., No. 18–1426 (6th Cir. 2019).
[204] Rice v. Paladin Enters, Inc., 128 F.3d 233 (4th Cir. 1997), *cert. denied*, 523 U.S. 1074 (1998).
[205] "'Hit Man' Case Settles," *News Notes: 27 Media L. Rep.*, June 15, 1999.

NEGLIGENCE People act negligently if they breach a duty of care owed to the plaintiff and that breach causes injury.[206] Surgeons, for example, are negligent if they leave scissors in a patient. Surgeons have a duty to their patients to foresee that forgetting scissors will cause serious injury.[207] Plaintiffs have argued that the media are negligent when they fail to foresee that publications and programs containing violence and antisocial behavior may inspire readers and viewers to cause harm to themselves or others. Courts, however, generally hold the media owe no duty of care under the common law of negligence to a general audience, either for physical harms or for financial losses.

In *McCollum*, the California court said that CBS owed no duty to the McCollums or to anyone else to foresee all the harms that listeners and viewers might inflict on themselves and others. CBS and Osbourne owed no duty of care to the McCollums because the company and the artist could not reasonably have foreseen that suicide would result from listening to the song, the court said. The music and lyrics had been recorded and distributed years before McCollum killed himself.

Furthermore, the court said, Osbourne and CBS had no relationship with the public creating a duty to prevent harm. Unlike the relationship between doctors and their patients, there was no "dynamic interaction" between the singer and his audience justifying media liability, the court said. In addition, the court said, the social costs of imposing a duty on the media to withhold a song that might inspire suicide would be too burdensome. "[I]t is simply not acceptable to a free and democratic society," the court said, to impose a duty upon performing artists to avoid the dissemination of artistic speech, "which may adversely affect emotionally troubled individuals."

Courts have also ruled the media are not liable when false information causes financial harm. In *Gutter v. Dow Jones, Inc.*, the Supreme Court of Ohio ruled that the owner of the *Wall Street Journal* was not liable to a reader for an error in listings of corporate bond interest. Phil Gutter, an investor, lost nearly $1,700 when the interest rate turned out to be different than the paper reported. However, the Ohio Supreme Court dismissed a suit for negligent misrepresentation.[208]

The court said that the newspaper owed no duty to Gutter, a member of the broad newspaper readership. Like other courts, the Ohio court said holding a newspaper liable to the public imposes too great a burden on freedom of expression. Furthermore, the court said it was not justifiable for Gutter to rely on the mistaken news account to buy his bonds without first checking the status of the bonds with a broker. Similar legal rulings have been reached when unintentional errors have appeared on a ticker tape,[209] in commercial loose-leaf summaries of corporate finances,[210] and in advertisements for investment opportunities.[211]

FORESEEABLE HARMS A few courts have ruled that the media may be liable for causing serious physical harm to an individual. In two commercial cases, courts have held the media liable when particularly serious risks—in one case murder—were thought to be too obvious for the media to ignore. In another case, a newspaper placed a crime victim at risk of further violence by publishing her name.

---

[206] W. Page Keeton et al., *Prosser and Keeton on the Law of Torts* 164–5 (5th ed. 1984).
[207] *Id.*
[208] Gutter v. Dow Jones, Inc., 490 N.E.2d 898 (1986).
[209] Jaillet v. Cashman, 194 N.Y.S. 947 (App. Div. 1922), *aff'd*, 139 N.E. 714 (N.Y. 1923).
[210] First Equity Corp. v. Standard & Poor's Corp., 869 F.2d 175 (2d Cir. 1989).
[211] Pittman v. Dow Jones, Inc., 662 F. Supp. 921 (E.D. La. 1987), *aff'd*, 834 F.2d 1171 (5th Cir. 1987).

In the most significant media negligence case, the U.S. Court of Appeals for the Eleventh Circuit upheld a jury verdict finding *Soldier of Fortune* magazine liable for negligently publishing an advertisement that resulted in a contract killing. Saying that a magazine has a legal duty to refrain from publishing advertisements that subject the public to a "clearly identifiable unreasonable risk of harm," the court upheld an award of more than $4 million to Michael and Ian Braun, the sons of a man murdered by an assassin hired through a classified ad.[212]

A jury determined that *Soldier of Fortune* negligently published an advertisement that resulted in the killing of Richard Braun and the wounding of his 16-year-old son in front of the family's Atlanta home. The killer, Michael Savage, was hired after he placed a "Gun for Hire" ad in the personal services section of *Soldier of Fortune*. In the ad, Savage said a "37-year-old professional mercenary desires jobs. Vietnam Veteran. Discrete [sic] and very private. Body guard, courier, and other special skills. All jobs considered."

The court ruled that *Soldier of Fortune* violated a public duty not to publish a clearly identifiable unreasonable risk of harm that in fact led to Richard Braun's death. One determines whether a risk is unreasonable, the court said, by balancing the risk of a serious harm against the costs of guarding against it. *Soldier of Fortune* was held liable because the advertisement presented a grave risk—murder—that outweighed the burden of requiring the publisher to foresee the likely consequences of the ad.

The court said its holding did not violate the First Amendment because publishers were not being subjected to burdensome responsibilities to check the danger and legality of each advertisement. The court said a publisher could be held liable only if an advertisement on its face, without further investigation, would alert a reasonably prudent publisher to the unreasonable risk.

The Savage ad presented a clearly identifiable unreasonable risk, the court said, because it

> (1) emphasized the term "Gun for Hire," (2) described Savage as a "professional mercenary," (3) stressed Savage's willingness to keep his assignments confidential and "very private," (4) listed legitimate jobs involving the use of a gun—bodyguard and courier—followed by a reference to Savage's "other special skills," and (5) concluded by stating that Savage would consider "[a]ll jobs."[213]

In another commercial case, the California Supreme Court ruled that the First Amendment did not bar a negligence action against a radio station whose on-air promotion stimulated reckless conduct among teenage drivers, conduct that resulted in the death of a motorist. The case resulted from a station's public relations promotion in which a popular disc jockey drove from place to place in southern California. Meanwhile, the station encouraged its teenage audience to hurry to the disc jockey's next stop to claim a prize. One youthful listener, following the disc jockey at high speeds on the California freeways, forced another car to overturn, killing the driver.

In *Weirum v. RKO General, Inc.*, the California Supreme Court ruled the station was liable because it was "foreseeable that defendant's youthful listeners,

---

[212] Braun v. Soldier of Fortune Magazine, Inc., 968 F.2d 1110 (11th Cir. 1992), *cert. denied*, 506 U.S. 1071 (1993).
[213] 968 F.2d 1121.

finding the prize had eluded them at one location, would race to arrive first at the next site and in their haste would disregard the demands of highway safety." Although the court did not say that the station "incited" the reckless driving, the station's broadcast promotion stimulated the teenage audience to irresponsible, dangerous conduct that resulted in a death.[214] Giving short attention to the station's First Amendment claims, the court said, "The First Amendment does not sanction the infliction of physical injury merely because achieved by word, rather than act."

The *Soldier of Fortune* and *Weirum* cases involve advertising and commercial promotion that have less constitutional protection than political speech. But a Missouri court ruled that a newspaper might be liable for subjecting a person to violent threats by publishing a crime story. The Missouri Supreme Court ruled that Sandra Hyde could bring an emotional distress suit against the City of Columbia and a Columbia newspaper over a story about her successful escape from an abductor who was still at large. After the story appeared, Hyde was followed and threatened by telephone. In one call, a man said, "I'm glad you're not dead yet; I have plans for you before you die."[215]

The Missouri court imposed an obligation on the press to investigate the risk of publishing information from a law enforcement document the paper argued was a public record. The court said the newspaper could reasonably foresee from the assailant's past conduct, reported character and tendency toward violence that the publication of Hyde's name and address would create a temptation for the abductor to harm her.[216]

■ SUMMARY ■

The media are seldom liable for the physical harms that media users inflict on themselves or others. Some courts have ruled that violent acts on television do not incite members of the audience to harm themselves or others, but one federal appellate court ruled that a book publisher might be liable for distributing a manual for murder.

Some courts find the media have no duty under the common law of negligence to foresee harms to a general audience and that the burden of preventing violence or financial hardship would be too inhibiting. However, the Fifth Circuit has found the media liable for publishing an advertisement containing a "clearly identifiable unreasonable risk" of murder. The media have also been exposed to liability for encouraging reckless behavior in a commercial promotion and for subjecting a woman to threats from an abductor known to be at large.

---

[214] 539 P.2d 36 (Cal. 1975).
[215] Hyde v. City of Columbia, 637 S.W.2d 251 (Mo. App. 1982), *cert. denied*, 459 U.S. 1226 (1983).
[216] Hyde v. City of Columbia, 637 S.W.2d 251 (Mo. App. 1982), *cert. denied*, 459 U.S. 1226 (1983).

Intellectual Property

Whereas privacy law allows people to limit public dissemination of private information about themselves, copyright allows authors to control how their creative expression is copied, distributed and performed. Copyright protects books, musical compositions, videos, newspaper articles, recordings, software, TV programs, advertisements, podcasts, email and other original expression from unauthorized copying and performance. Copyright law punishes those who infringe the rights of authors to control the reproduction, adaptation, distribution, display and performance of their original works.

Copyright is an increasingly important mass communication issue in postindustrial countries whose information economies depend in large measure on the creation and sale—including exports—of intellectual property. In 2015, core copyright industries—including broadcasting, publishing, software, recording and film—added value of more than $1.2 trillion to the U.S. economy, close to 6.9 percent of the nation's gross domestic product. Exports of American copyright products exceed exports of aircraft, pharmaceuticals and agricultural products.[1] In 2022, with the non-fungible token (NFT) art market taking off (and the potential to revolutionize arts patronage), anonymous thieves are stealing digital art and passing it off as

---

[1] Stephen E. Siwek, "Copyright Industries in the U.S. Economy: The 2016 Report," International Intellectual Property Alliance (IIPA) (2016), https://www.iipa.org/files/uploads/2017/12/2016CpyrtRpt Full.pdf.

DOI: 10.4324/9781003264736-6

their own to sell, raising copyright issues in a market where NFT trading volume hit $10.7 billion in the third quarter of 2021.[2]

Intellectual property was protected in the Constitution before adoption of the First Amendment. Article I, Section 8 of the U.S. Constitution gives Congress the power "to promote the Progress of Science and useful Arts, by securing for limited Times to Authors and Inventors the exclusive Right to their respective Writings and Discoveries." Section 8 encourages intellectual creativity of benefit to society by granting creative people exclusive control over their intellectual expression for a fixed period, after which the work passes into the public domain.

Thus, copyright not only benefits society by spurring creative expression; it also benefits "authors" by allowing them to control and profit from their creative expression for a limited time. There is great tension between copyright owners—film studios, record companies and publishers—who tend to emphasize their property rights to control the distribution, copying and performance of their works, and creative entities that want to innovate and create new works by borrowing from works still under copyright protection. The entertainment, music and media companies are also waging a "quiet war" against Google and other giant tech companies to keep copyrighted photos, videos and songs off the Internet. Millions of times each week, web companies try to track and remove Disney films uploaded on YouTube, digital music that pops up online or snippets of Wall Street research notes posted on Twitter. In 2011, Google's web search engine was asked to remove links to a few hundred thousand web addresses. In 2015, the number of requests mushroomed to more than 20 million a week.[3]

Copyright law is implicated when students download iTunes in the dorm or upload videos to YouTube, when Google scans library books and when a magazine scoops a competitive publication with a purloined manuscript. Copyright piracy is a huge illegal business worldwide. Digital pirates can quickly produce unlimited, perfect copies of copyrighted music, video and text. Chinese piracy of American intellectual property has been an issue in American-Chinese relations for many years.[4]

Article I, Section 8 recognizes two kinds of intellectual property: inventions and writings. Inventions are protected under patent law, which provides inventors up to 20 years in which to enjoy exclusive commercial exploitation of the machines, processes, manufactured products and designs they create.[5] "Writings," which include books, poems, screen plays, songs and DVDs, are protected by the federal copyright statute, the primary subject of this chapter.[6] This chapter will also discuss trademark law, which prohibits companies from confusing the public about the origin of a product.

COPYRIGHT

The British originated copyright as a method of censorship after Gutenberg invented the printing press in the 1440s. In 1556, the British Crown granted the Stationers' Company a monopoly on printing, primarily to check the spread of the

---

[2] Kevin Collier, NFT art sales are booming, just without some artists' permission, NBC News (January 10, 2022), https://www.nbcnews.com/tech/security/nft-art-sales-are-booming-just-artists-permission-rcna10798.
[3] Rani Molla and Shira Ovide, "The War on Internet Piracy," *Bloomberg Gadfly*, Mar. 23, 2016.
[4] Edward Cody, "U.S. Warns China on Piracy, Market Access," *Wash. Post*, Nov. 15, 2006, at D8.
[5] 35 U.S.C. §§ 154 and 173.
[6] Federal copyright law is found in Title 17 of the United States Code, chapters 1–13, §§ 101–1332.

Protestant Reformation. By requiring that all published works be registered with the Stationers' Company, the government made it easier to block dissemination of heretical writings that threatened the Crown.

In time, the government's interest in controlling heresy was outweighed by authors' and publishers' desire to curb unauthorized copying of their publications. Under pressure from authors and publishers, the British government relinquished its copyright control. The first statute to recognize the rights of authors was the Statute of Anne of 1710, which granted authors the exclusive right to publish their new works for a renewable 14-year term. Works had to be registered at Stationers' Hall, not so that the government could easily identify the dangerous but so that copyright holders could prove their claims of originality when they believed others had copied their work.

In the United States, the first federal copyright law was adopted in 1790.[7] The first copyright act protected an author of any "book, map or chart" from unauthorized copying for a renewable 14-year term. Protection for prints was added in 1802,[8] musical compositions in 1831,[9] photographs in 1865,[10] and paintings in 1870.[11]

The federal copyright statute was revised twice in the twentieth century, once in 1909[12] and again in 1976,[13] with numerous amendments before and after 1976. The 1909 Act was continually strained by the development of new technologies used to create copyrighted works or exploit them—the motion picture, phonograph, radio, television, computer, tape recorder, photocopy machine, and satellite, cable and other communication technologies.

Congress adopted the 1976 Copyright Act after 20 years of study. The Copyright Act of 1976 included several changes that made it easier for authors to control when and how their works are used by others. The 1976 revision also made copyright law more uniform by preempting state copyright law. Since 1976, technological advances have obliged Congress and the courts to make changes in copyright law in response to the development of cable television, satellite transmissions, home recording of television programs, rental movies, software, cell phones, video games and the Internet.

Copyrightable Works

Copyright, which the Constitution says protects "writings," protects much more expression than words on a page. Copyright subsists in "original works of authorship fixed in any tangible medium of expression . . . from which they can be perceived, reproduced, or otherwise communicated."[14] Copyrightable works of authorship include literary, musical, dramatic, audiovisual, pictorial, graphic and sculptural works. Literary works include books, newspapers, magazines, corporate house organs, newsletters, annual reports and computer programs.

To be original, a work need not be unique, novel or good. Rather, the work must be created independently—not copied from another work—with a modicum

---

[7] 1 Stat. 124 (1790).
[8] 2 Stat. 171 (1802).
[9] 4 Stat. 436 (1831).
[10] 13 Stat. 540 (1865).
[11] 16 Stat. 212 (1870).
[12] 35 Stat. 1075 (1909).
[13] 90 Stat. 2541 (1976).
[14] 17 U.S.C. § 102.

of intellectual effort.[15] Students own copyright in their exam essays, the videos they shoot, and their email postings. One can also copyright dance, musical compositions and recordings. The U.S. Copyright Office in Washington will register a work whether or not it is of high quality. The office will not deny copyright because a work may be obscene[16] or fraudulent.[17]

A work is fixed in a tangible medium of expression as soon as it is created or recorded so that it can be perceived. A short story is fixed when it is saved on a computer disk or printed on paper. A photo is fixed when the shutter snaps. The recording of a televised football game becomes a fixed work of authorship as a camera crew and director select shots and simultaneously broadcast and record the game. An unedited video of a plane crash is also an original work of authorship.[18] Loading expression into the random access memory (RAM) of a computer also "fixes" a copy if the expression resides in RAM long enough to be "perceived."[19]

Copyright protects expression, not the ideas or the facts contained in the expression. An author owns the copyright in a review of a Pink concert but not in the idea of writing the review or in the facts within it. Others are free to write a review of the concert employing the same facts, provided these authors employ their own language, style and sequencing. To be ethical, writers should acknowledge the sources of facts and ideas they borrow from others; borrowing facts and ideas without attribution may be plagiarism. But borrowing of facts and ideas does not violate the first author's copyright. Copyright infringement occurs when an author copies the expression of another without permission or a privilege to copy. Copying an author's copyrighted words, music or other expression without permission infringes copyright in the original work even if the copier acknowledges the source of the expression.

The Supreme Court ruled in 1884 that photographs are "writings" protected by copyright. In *Burrow-Giles Lithographic Co. v. Sarony*, the Court ruled that a photograph of the playwright Oscar Wilde sitting in a Victorian interior with a book in his hand (see Photo 6.1) was an original work authorship.[20] Napoleon Sarony, therefore, could bar unauthorized copying of his photograph by a lithographer. The Court rejected the argument that a photograph is a mere mechanical reproduction requiring no originality and therefore no authorship. On the contrary, the Court said, Sarony gave visible form to his original mental conception by posing Wilde, selecting and arranging the costume and draperies, arranging the light and shade, and thereby evoking the desired expression. Photographers may not protect the idea of taking a picture or the individual elements of the picture under copyright law. Rather, the copyright owner owns the copyright in the composition, the placement of the elements within the whole.[21] An advertiser is given copyright protection, not for the choice of a particular actor or a special editing technique, but for the expression resulting from a combination of artistic choices, including the selection of actors, the composition of each frame, the pace of editing, camera angles, hairstyle, jewelry, decor and makeup.[22]

---

[15] Bleistein v. Donaldson Lithographing Co., 188 U.S. 239 (1903).
[16] *See, e.g.*, Clancy v. Jartech, 666 F.2d 403 (9th Cir. 1982), *cert. denied*, 459 U.S. 826 (1982).
[17] *E.g.*, Belcher v. Tarbox, 486 F.2d 1087 (9th Cir. 1973).
[18] Los Angeles News Serv. v. Tullo, 973 F.2d 791 (9th Cir. 1992).
[19] MAI Systems Corp. v. Peak Computer, Inc., 991 F.2d 511 (9th Cir. 1993).
[20] 111 U.S. 53 (1884).
[21] Bleistein v. Donaldson Lithographing Co., 188 U.S. 239 (1903).
[22] C. Blore & Don Richman, Inc. v. 20/20 Advertising Inc., 674 F. Supp. 671 (D. Minn. 1987).

PHOTO 6.1   Napoleon Sarony's photo of Oscar Wilde.

Copyright is recognized not only for individual stories, photos and programs but also for compilations and derivative works. A **compilation** is a work formed by collecting and assembling preexisting materials or data that are "selected, coordinated, or arranged in such a way" as to create a new original work. A compilation may be the assembly of discrete facts that, individually, would not be copyrightable. Trivia dictionaries, some databases and Dow Jones stock lists are copyrightable compilations even though the individual items in them may not be copyrightable.[23]

An alphabetized list of names in a telephone directory is not sufficiently original to constitute a copyrightable compilation. In *Feist Publications, Inc. v. Telephone Services Company*, the Supreme Court ruled that the publisher of a regional telephone directory did not violate the copyright of a smaller local directory when the publisher of the regional directory borrowed names and addresses from the local book.[24] The publisher of the larger directory merely took facts whose compilation and arrangement were "devoid of even the slightest trace of creativity," the Court said. However, in a different case, the U.S. Court of Appeals for the Eleventh Circuit ruled that the compilation of the Yellow Pages embodied enough originality to merit a copyright.[25] The court found sufficient originality for a copyright based

---

[23] Eckes v. Card Prices Update, 736 F.2d 859 (2d Cir. 1984); Dow Jones & Co. v. Board of Trade of Chicago, 546 F. Supp. 113 (S.D.N.Y. 1982).
[24] 499 U.S. 340 (1991).
[25] Bellsouth Advertising and Publishing Corp. v. Donnelley Information Publishing, Inc., 933 F.2d 952 (11th Cir. 1991).

on the compilers' judgments about which commercial categories to establish and which businesses to place in those categories.

In *Feist*, not only did the Supreme Court fail to find originality in an alphabetized list, but the Court also refused to recognize a copyright based on the time, money and effort—the "sweat of the brow"—the telephone company expended to create the book. The Constitution requires originality, not effort alone, as a condition for successful copyright claims, the Court said.

One kind of compilation that can be copyrighted is a collective work. A **collective work** is a gathering of preexisting works that may already be copyrighted. Collective works include magazines, anthologies and corporate reports, each of which may contain several copyrighted works. The publisher of a magazine or anthology must have permission from the individual copyright holders to compile the collective work. The collective work can be separately copyrighted as original expression while contributions to the collective retain their separate copyrights.

A **derivative work** may also be copyrighted. A derivative work is a transformation or adaptation of an existing work. The copyright owner has the exclusive right to create derivative works. Derivative works include translations from foreign languages, movie versions of plays and novels, and dolls based on cartoon characters. Derivative works are created when a work is recast, transformed or adapted.[26] A federal appeals court ruled that encircling or "framing" another's web page in advertising may constitute a derivative work for which the framer should get permission.[27]

Facts, procedures and processes are too unoriginal to be copyrighted. Also uncopyrightable are systems, methods of operation, concepts, principles and discoveries.[28] A federal appellate court ruled that the user interface—the system of menus and commands—in popular spreadsheet software was an uncopyrightable method of operation, much like the familiar QWERTY arrangement of keys on a computer keyboard.[29] Copyright also does not protect useful items such as tables, chairs and typefaces.

Formats and layouts are also not copyrightable. A format is the general plan or organization of a work, the shape and size of a publication, the length of a broadcast or the number of minutes of music to be included at a certain time each week in a television show. The layout is the plan or arrangement of elements on the page. Formats and layouts cannot be copyrighted because the number of ways in which stories, pictures and type can be placed on a page is too limited to allow one person or company to claim exclusive ownership.

NOTICE, REGISTRATION AND DEPOSIT The term of copyright protection continually lengthens, extending the time at which copyrighted works pass into the public domain and are then available for use by other creative authors without permission or royalty payments. A federal court ruled in 2015 the lyrics to "Happy Birthday to You" are in the public domain because of a faulty registration in 1935, thus ending $2 million yearly royalties to the purported copyright owner, Warner/Chappell Music.[30]

---

[26] 17 U.S.C. § 101.
[27] Futuredontics, Inc. v. Applied Anagramics, Inc., 45 U.S.P.Q.2d 2005 (C.D. Cal. 1998).
[28] 17 U.S.C.A. § 102(b).
[29] Lotus Dev. Corp. v. Borland Int'l Inc., 49 F.3d 807 (1st Cir. 1995), *aff'd by evenly divided vote*, 516 U.S. 233 (1996).
[30] Marya v. Warner/Chappell Music, Inc., 131 F. Supp. 3d 975 (C.D. Cal. 2015).

Copyright protection for works created after 1977 lasts for the life of the author plus 70 years. The benefit of copyright, therefore, can be willed to one's survivors for 70 years after the death of the copyright holder. If a company is the copyright holder, copyright runs for 120 years from the date of creation or 95 years from the date of publication, whichever is shorter.[31]

In 2003, the Supreme Court ruled 7–2 that Congress did not exceed its authority when it lengthened the term of copyright by 20 years to 70 years after the life of the author. Writing for the majority in *Eldred v. Ashcroft*, Justice Ruth Bader Ginsburg said the Constitution did not set a specific duration for copyright terms when it provided for "limited" terms.[32] Ginsburg rejected the argument that Congress unconstitutionally establishes a perpetual copyright when the legislature continually lengthens the term from its original renewable 14-year duration.

Ginsburg also rejected arguments that an extended copyright term violates the First Amendment by excessively delaying the time at which copyrighted works pass into the public domain and can be incorporated into new expressive creations. Ginsburg noted that copyright does not prohibit creators from disseminating ideas and facts contained in copyrighted works. She also noted that the fair use defense (to be discussed later) permits commentators and scholars to publish limited portions of copyrighted works without permission for purposes of discussing and criticizing the original work. Backers of the copyright term extension, which include the Walt Disney Corporation, argue longer protections encourage original and often-expensive creative expression by allowing long-term financial incentives.

Notice Although authors are not required to protect copyright, they should place copyright notices on their works and register them. If a work is published, two copies must be deposited with the Copyright Office in Washington, D.C. Copyright notice is the voluntary sign attached to a work warning would-be copiers that they need permission to reproduce that work. Copyright notice signifies that authors have not abandoned their work to the public domain. Notice has three elements: (1) the letter C in a circle ©, the word copyright, or the abbreviation copr.; (2) the year of first publication; and (3) the name of the copyright owner. A copyright notice looks like this: © 2015 Marvin Dude.

A copyright notice should be placed where it will be easily seen. A copyright notice will normally be placed on, or just after, the title page of a book, on the title page or the masthead of a magazine, near the title of a film or at the bottom of a web page. If notice on the front of a photograph or painting would damage the work, notice can be placed on the back. Notice should be placed on a computer program so that it appears on a user's terminal at sign-on. Although copyright notice is not required on American works distributed after March 1, 1989, placing notice on copyrighted works is advisable. Besides warning would-be infringers that copyright is claimed, a copyright notice also bars infringers from claiming they infringed "innocently." A court may reduce the money paid to a copyright owner by an infringer who "was not aware and had no reason to believe that his or her acts constituted an infringement of copyright."[33] Copyright notice is also necessary for freelancers' bulk registration of works.

Copyright notice on a periodical, anthology, slide show or other collective work covers all contributions to the work except for advertisements inserted on

---

[31] 17 U.S.C. § 302.
[32] 537 U.S. 186 (2003).
[33] 17 U.S.C. § 504(c)(2).

behalf of outside businesses or organizations.[34] For example, one copyright notice on the *New York Times* covers all staff and freelance stories and pictures, even though freelance writers and photographers may retain separate copyright owner-ship in their works. But the overall *Times* copyright notice does not cover advertise-ments, except ads for the *Times* itself.

Individual contributors to collective works may attach separate copyright notice to their contributions if they and the publisher agree. A separate copyright notice on a story or picture can serve as the credit line. Freelance writers and other contributors to collective works will want a separate notice on their contributions if they wish to take advantage of the efficiency and low cost of bulk registration of their work.

Registration and Deposit In the days of the English Star Chamber, the British Crown required registration of all works in London so that the government could more easily check for heresy and sedition. Now, however, registration is not a tool of suppression but a way of establishing who first created a disputed work. The person who first registers a work has strong legal evidence of copyright ownership.

An author may register a work—published or unpublished—with the Register of Copyrights in Washington by submitting the proper form and a registration fee. To obtain all the benefits of registration, it should be done within three months of publication. However, in 2010 the Copyright Office had a backlog of several months. An author must "deposit" two physical copies of a published work and may deposit one copy of an unpublished work. Works published electronically and unpublished works can be deposited electronically. The deposit requirement is separate from the voluntary registration system but is usually fulfilled at the time of registration.

To save time and money, freelance writers and photographers can register 12 months of work in a group for one fee.[35] Publishers of magazines, newspapers and newsletters can register from one to three months of publications with a single application and fee.

Although unregistered works are protected under the copyright law, the law includes incentives for authors to register their work. Authors of works originat-ing in the United States may not sue for infringement until a work is registered, although foreign authors can.[36] Copyright owners of registered works may sue an infringer for "actual damages"—lost sales and for profits the infringer illegally gained. Copyright owners of registered works may also ask courts to enjoin further infringement.

If a copyright owner registered the work before the infringement took place, he or she can seek "statutory" damages instead of actual damages. Statutory dam-ages are awarded to owners of registered copyrights simply because the copyright is infringed, without proof of financial damage. The court may award the copyright owner statutory damages of between $750 and $30,000 for each work infringed and up to $150,000 if the work was infringed "willfully."[37]

COPYRIGHT OWNERSHIP Copyright belongs to the "author" of a work. The author may be an individual or joint author. Joint authors are two or more authors who collaborate with the intent that their contributions be combined into

---

[34] 17 U.S.C. § 404(a).
[35] 17 U.S.C. § 408(c)(2).
[36] 17 U.S.C. § 411(a).
[37] 17 U.S.C. § 504(c).

a unified, copyrightable whole.[38] A composer and a lyricist, for example, may be joint authors of a collaborative song. Each joint author may authorize use of a work without permission of the other, provided both authors receive royalties. An editor usually is not considered to be a joint author of a work. However, publishers sometimes claim joint copyright ownership with freelancers if editors employed by the publishers make creative contributions to works. As computers have become the standard workstation, determining the "author" of digital works becomes more difficult. Working at computers, often in different locations, several writers, editors, photographers and illustrators can make simultaneous contributions to a digital work, contributions that might never be separately identified.

Works Made for Hire The legal author of a work is not necessarily the same as the creator. When a work is "made for hire," the "author"—who owns the copyright—is the party who hires an employee or commissions a freelancer to create a work. A work made for hire is either (1) "a work prepared by an employee within the scope of his or her employment" or (2) "a work specially ordered or commissioned" that falls within one of nine specified categories. Works for hire include freelance contributions to a collective work—such as a magazine—if a work-for-hire agreement is signed.[39] Works created by employees within the scope of their employment include stories, photos and videos created by staff reporters, artists, publicists, photographers and copywriters while on the job. Copyright in those works belongs to the publisher, broadcaster, public relations firm or advertising agency that employs the creators.[40] All rights in works for hire belong to the employer on the theory that the company should own the copyright if the company assigns the task, risks the resources to carry it out and directs the work of the creator. Employers, as copyright owners, may grant permission to employees to publish or display their works elsewhere.

Even an article written in off-hours may be a **work for hire** if the article is the direct result of one's employment. Independent writers and artists are not considered "employees" who create works for hire unless several elements of the employer-employee relationship are present. In *Community for Creative Non-Violence v. Reid*, the Supreme Court said that independent contractors are not considered employees unless they meet several criteria of employment such as being supervised, being provided a place to work, receiving fringe benefits and having a long-term, salaried relationship with an employer.[41] The Court ruled that James Earl Reid, a sculptor working on commission, was not an employee because he was a skilled professional who supplied his own tools, worked in his own studio, received no regular salary or benefits and had only a short-term business relationship with the homeless shelter that commissioned the sculpture. After *Reid*, freelance photographers and writers are seldom considered to be employees.

Even if freelance writers and artists working on commission seldom meet the criteria of "employees," they may create a "work for hire" in which they own no rights if a work is "specially ordered or commissioned" for a collective work—such as a magazine or newspaper—and both parties sign a work-for-hire agreement. Freelancers who are not employees create a work for hire only if both parties "expressly agree" in a written contract that "the work shall be considered a work

---

[38] *See, e.g.*, Childress v. Taylor, 945 F.2d 500 (2d Cir. 1991).
[39] 17 U.S.C. § 101.
[40] *See, e.g.*, United States Ozone Co. v. United States Ozone Co. of Am., 62 F.2d 881 (7th Cir. 1933) (company owns copyright in pamphlet written by employee during working hours).
[41] 476 U.S. 693 (1989).

made for hire."[42] Absent a written contract containing the term *work for hire*, free-lance photographers and writers who sell a work to a publisher, advertising agency or other producer grant permission only for one-time publication. All other rights remain with the freelancer unless a contract states otherwise.

While publishers often demand that freelance writers and artists sign work-for-hire contracts, publishers sometimes demand freelancers transfer copyright to the publisher without signing a work-for-hire contract. In such cases, the law allows freelancers to negotiate the return of the copyright after 35 years.[43] Freelancers prefer if publishers are even less demanding, negotiating only "first North American serial rights," "first English-language serial rights," or "one-time rights," leaving other rights to the author. More established writers, photographers and artists, who them-selves have strong bargaining positions, are better able to negotiate transferring fewer rights to a publisher.

Government and Copyright The copyright statute prohibits the federal gov-ernment or its employees from owning a copyright in works created by government employees as part of their official duties.[44] However, government employees own the copyright in speeches and writings composed on their own time. Meanwhile, private firms that contract with the government may own the copyright in works commissioned by the government if the government agrees. Public television sta-tion WQED in Pittsburgh was permitted to own the copyright of a bicentennial series called *Equal Justice Under Law*, a series that had been commissioned by the Judicial Conference to increase public understanding of the courts.[45]

State executive, legislative and judicial branches may not copyright their stat-utes, judicial opinions or regulations—laws binding on all citizens[46]—but some states do assert copyright in government tax maps and other documents lacking the force of law, thus allowing state and local agencies to control copying of the records after public inspection.[47] However, copyright claims by state and local governments may conflict with citizens' rights to copy records under state open records laws.[48] In addition, in 2020, the Supreme Court ruled that a state may not copyright its entire official code, which includes both the laws and annotations interpreting them. "If everything short of statutes and opinions were copyrightable," Chief Justice John G. Roberts Jr. wrote for the majority,

> then states would be free to offer a whole range of premium legal works for those who can afford the extra benefit. A state could mon-etize its entire suite of legislative history. With today's digital tools, states might even launch a subscription or pay-per-law service.[49]

▨ SUMMARY ▨

Copyright encourages creativity by granting authors exclusive rights in original works of authorship for a limited period. Copyrightable works include literary,

---

[42] 17 U.S.C. § 101.
[43] 17 U.S.C. § 203.
[44] 17 U.S.C. §§ 101, 105.
[45] Schnapper v. Foley, 667 F.2d 102 (D.C. Cir. 1981).
[46] Banks v. Manchester, 128 U.S. 244 (1888).
[47] *E.g.*, County of Suffolk v. First American, 261 F.3d 179 (2d Cir. 2001).
[48] *See* Becky Dale, "Can the Government Copyright Public Records?" *Virginia Lawyers Weekly*, July 26, 2004.
[49] Georgia v. Public.Resource.Org, Inc., 140 S. Ct. 1498 (2020).

pictorial and graphic creations as well as compilations and derivative works. Copyright does not depend on notice or registration, although both are recommended for protection from claims of "innocent" infringement and for eligibility to file suit and receive statutory damages in infringement cases. Works created by employees are works made for hire, and the employer is deemed to be the author and copyright owner. Freelance writers, photographers and video operators create a work for hire—and do not own the copyright—only if a contract specifies that the work is a work for hire. Neither the federal government nor its employees may own the copyright in works created by federal employees on the job, but some states claim copyright in works other than laws and judicial opinions. Private companies sometimes may copyright works created under government contract.

Rights

The Copyright Act grants a "bundle" of rights to copyright owners. These rights include the exclusive right to copy or reproduce a work, to create adaptations or derivative works, to distribute copies of a work and to perform and display the work publicly.[50] These exclusive rights give authors the legal ability to control the use of their work.

COPYING One of the most important rights of the copyright owner is the exclusive right to control the copying, or reproduction, of a work. Photocopying a book is a form of reproduction or copying, as is downloading a copyrighted film, recording from the Internet, or sampling musical phrases from a recording for inclusion in another musical work. The copyright owner of the expression in a book, magazine article, podcast, recorded song, motion picture or computer program has the right to control when and if that expression is reproduced. By prohibiting unauthorized copying, copyright law protects the commercial incentive for authors to produce creative expression that benefits society.

It is particularly hard to prohibit illicit copying of digital information on the Internet because thousands of copies can be produced quickly and flawlessly. American music and film producers say millions of songs and hundreds of thousands of movies are downloaded illegally each day. Pirating is augmented by some copiers' cavalier notion that digital information "ought to be free." YouTube, owed by Google, is cited as the biggest platform for pirating music. With that said, courts and governments do curb some illegal copying. A federal statute prohibits moviegoers from recording motion pictures from a theater screen with portable cameras.[51] American courts have ruled that companies cannot lawfully provide software or servers that allow pirates to download and trade copyrighted works without paying royalties.

The "exclusive" right of copyright owners to control the reproduction of their work is not absolute. The legal doctrine of "fair use," to be discussed shortly, allows critics, commentators, reviewers, scholars and others to copy limited portions of copyrighted expression for comment and criticism. The copyright statute also allows limited copying by public libraries. Public libraries have a statutory privilege to photocopy an article to fill individual requests by noncommercial users.

DERIVATIVE WORKS The owner of a copyright controls the creation of derivative works. Derivative works are transformations or adaptations of existing

---

[50] 17 U.S.C. § 106.
[51] Artists' Rights and Theft Prevention Act of 2005 in the Family Entertainment and Copyright Act of 2005, 119 Stat. 218, § 102.

works.[52] The author of a novel, for example, may create—or authorize others to create—any number of derivative works, including sequels, films, plays and cartoons, all based on the original novel. A separate copyright can be owned in each derivative work, which is important in cases of infringement of the derivative work. Film producers need their own copyrights in motion pictures based on novels so that they can sue if the film is illegally copied. Similarly, book publishers want their own copyrights so that they can protect their commercial interest in their publications.

Because copyright is divisible, authors can authorize separate copyrights on any number of derivative works while retaining copyright in the underlying work. Divisibility of copyright is much like the power of a landowner to grant water rights to one person, oil rights to another and a road right of way to a third, while retaining ownership in the land.[53] Likewise, the author of a novel can authorize creation of a film script and production of a movie. The producer of the film can own a separate copyright. Meanwhile, the author of the novel can retain the right to license the creation of comic strip characters, T-shirts and other works derived from the novel.

Giles Martin and his father, a former producer of the Beatles, derived a new album, *LOVE*, from 80 minutes of "reimagined" Beatles' music. The Martins' album began as a soundtrack for an evening of acrobatics and dance for Cirque du Soleil. Giles Martin took apart some of the Beatles' recordings and put them back together again in different ways with the support and approval of Paul McCartney, Ringo Starr, Yoko Ono Lennon and Olivia Harrison.[54] A reviewer in the *Wall Street Journal* called the reconfigured works "fresh, seamless, and musically cohesive."

A federal court in Colorado ruled that an editing firm did not create derivative works when the company removed "sex, nudity, profanity, and gory violence" from motion pictures for home viewing on DVDs the company sold.[55] The court said the editing changes by Clean Flicks, which consisted of simple deletions, were too unoriginal to result in a derivative work. The court ruled the sanitized DVDs were unauthorized copies of the original films, copies that interfered with the market of such producers as SONY Pictures and Time Warner Entertainment—companies that sold their own edited versions of their films. The court ordered Clean Flicks to stop copying and distributing the Hollywood motion pictures.

DISTRIBUTION The copyright owner's exclusive right to distribute includes the author's authority to publish, sell, loan or rent copies of a copyrighted work. A book publisher, who usually owns the copyright in a book, distributes the work in physical form to bookstores or digitally over the Internet. Musical recordings, or "sound recordings," may be distributed in the physical form of compact discs (phonorecords) or in digital form through electronic dissemination. A webcast, whether by an independent Internet "station" or, more frequently, by websites operated by existing radio and TV stations, distributes and publicly performs copyrighted material. *Playboy*'s distribution right in the magazine's copyrighted photographs was infringed when 170 *Playboy* photographs were made available without authorization on an electronic bulletin board.[56]

---

[52] 17 U.S.C. § 101.
[53] *See* William Strong, *The Copyright Book* 36 (2nd ed. 1984).
[54] Jim Fusilli, Beatles Music, "Reimagined With 'Love'," *Wall. St. J.*, Nov. 29, 2006, at 10.
[55] Clean Flicks of Colorado, LLC v. Soderbergh, 433 F. Supp. 2d 1236 (D. Colo. 2006).
[56] Playboy Enters., Inc. v. Frena, 839 F. Supp. 1552 (M.D. Fla. 1993).

Although distribution rights include the right to sell a copy of a work, distribution rights do not include control over resale of a copy. The author's control and receipt of royalties stop with the "first sale" of each lawfully produced copy of a book, film or other work. The author receives a royalty on the first sale but not on subsequent sales. Thus, a library may sell or loan copies of books it purchased without consulting or paying the copyright owner. Similarly a video store, which pays when it purchases cassettes, may resell or rent videos to private individuals without additional payments. Individuals can give a CD they purchase to a friend but may not distribute copies of the CD. An exception to the "first sale doctrine" prohibits the commercial rental of copies of computer programs and sound recordings without the copyright owner's permission. This is because computer programs and sound recordings are so easily copied, and are likely to be.[57]

The distribution right includes the right to pick the time when, or if, a work will be distributed. The right of copyright owners to pick the time of publication or distribution was reiterated by the Supreme Court in a case in which the *Nation* magazine pirated excerpts from President Ford's memoirs. In *Harper & Row, Publishers, Inc. v. Nation Enterprises*, the Supreme Court ruled that the *Nation* violated the copyright held by Harper & Row by publishing several stolen excerpts of Ford's memoirs that were to be published in *Time* magazine. *Time* had an exclusive contract with Harper & Row to publish excerpts from the memoirs before the hardbound book was distributed. "Publication of an author's expression before he has authorized its dissemination," the Supreme Court said, "seriously infringes the author's right to decide when and whether it will be made public."[58]

In a case involving distribution from electronic databases, the Supreme Court ruled that freelancers should control whether their newspaper and magazine work is republished in electronic databases. In *New York Times Company v. Tasini*,[59] the Court ruled that the *Times, Newsday, Time, Atlantic Monthly* and other publishers infringe freelancers' copyright if they make available freelancers' printed stories and photos in electronic databases without getting the freelancers' permission or paying them for the electronic distribution. As a result of the *Tasini* decision, the *Times* and other publications began removing freelancers' work from databases unless freelancers granted permission for uncompensated online publication. Even before *Tasini*, publishers were requiring freelancers to sign contracts—often work-for-hire contracts—granting electronic distribution rights to publishers.

DISPLAY Copyright owners have a right not only to copy, to authorize derivative works and to distribute copies of their works but also to perform and display their work publicly. To "display" a work publicly means to show a copy "either directly or by means of a film, slide, television image" or other device to a substantial number of people beyond the normal circle of friends and acquaintances.[60] Thus, the copyright owner has a right to control when and if photographs are placed on exhibit, projected on a screen in a public place, or made available to the public browsing the Internet. When 170 *Playboy* photographs were posted without authorization on a bulletin board, not only was *Playboy*'s right to distribute infringed but also the company's right to display the original expression.[61]

---

[57] 17 U.S.C. § 109.
[58] 471 U.S. 539 (1985).
[59] 533 U.S. 483, 29 (2001).
[60] 17 U.S.C. § 101.
[61] Playboy Enters. Inc. v. Frena, 839 F. Supp. 1552 (M.D. Fla. 1993). *See* Working Group on Intellectual Property Rights, Bruce Lehman, chair, *Intellectual Property and the National Information Infrastructure* 70–2 (1995).

Courts have ruled it does not infringe a copyright owner's display rights if one computer links to a website in order for the viewer to see text and images stored there. Even "deep links" that bypass a website's important home page and advertising in favor of pages within a website are not considered to be an infringement. A federal appeals court ruled that Google did not violate the display rights of *Perfect 10*, a magazine and website, when Google linked to *Perfect 10*'s website and "framed" full-size nude pictures stored at *Perfect 10*'s server. The court ruled that pictures are "displayed" by the websites that store and serve them, not by a search engine such as Google that links to a server and frames pictures stored at a distant website.[62] Google, the court said, neither displayed nor distributed *Perfect 10*'s full-size pictures. Nor, the court said, did Google infringe *Perfect 10*'s display rights in reduced or thumbnail photos. Even though Google created and stored the thumbnail photos of *Perfect 10*'s images on Google computers, Google's search engine transformed the use—thus creating a fair use—of the thumbnails from entertainment to an Internet pointer, "directing a user to a source of information."

PERFORMANCE The performance right allows owners of literary, musical and dramatic works, dance and audiovisual works "to perform the copyrighted work publicly."[63] Composers, playwrights, record companies and film producers can authorize—or not authorize—public performances and demand royalties. A public performance can be live, projected from film or tape, broadcast to an audience, webcast or otherwise performed. One may perform a work "publicly" by performing it at clubs, factories, theaters, summer camps and large business establishments. To be a copyright infringement, the work must be performed at public places or transmitted to the public without authorization.[64] An ABC affiliate, for example, performs an episode of a weekly series when the station broadcasts the program over the air.

Performance rights in music have always been complicated because the user must get separate permissions to use copyrighted musical compositions and musical recordings. Music publishers usually own the copyright in the musical composition and lyrics (often referred to as the "song") while a record label is apt to own the copyright in the "sound recording" (the track fixed on a CD or downloaded from the iTunes Store).

Performance Licenses for Musical Compositions Say, for example, an oldies radio station wishes to broadcast a recording of the John Lennon and Paul McCartney song "Yesterday" from the Beatles' album *Help*. The station needs permission to perform the music and lyrics, that is, the song, written by Lennon and McCartney. Rather than negotiate separately with the publisher or owner of copyrighted Lennon-McCartney music, radio stations, film producers and others acquire musical performance rights from one of the performing rights organizations.

The three main performing rights organizations are the American Society of Composers, Authors and Publishers (ASCAP), Broadcast Music, Inc. (BMI) and SESAC, companies that license the majority of the copyrighted music played on the air. BMI represents more than 300,000 songwriters, composers and music publishers, encompassing music styles from classical to hip-hop and songwriters from John Lennon to Faith Hill and Snoop Dogg. The clearinghouses collect the performance fees and distribute them to member composers and copyright holders according to a formula.

---

[62] Perfect 10, Inc. v. Google, Inc., 487 F.3d 701 (9th Cir. 2007).
[63] 17 U.S.C. § 106(4).
[64] 17 U.S.C. § 101.

Theater producers, including producers of campus productions, must get copyright clearance to perform copyrighted music in musical reviews and other nondramatic public performances. A filmmaker, television producer, commercial advertising agency or other creators of audiovisual works must acquire a "synchronization" license controlled by the music publisher. A "synch" license allows use of music in a motion picture, television program, commercial advertisement or music video. Often, the music is timed with (synchronized with) the moving or still visual images in the film or other audiovisual work.[65] General Motors would need a synchronization license to use the underlying music in Bob Seger's "Like a Rock" in Chevrolet truck advertisements. Artists sampling recorded music or remixing recordings in digital "mashups" need authorization to perform copyrighted music. Similarly, a podcaster needs a musical performance right if the podcast contains a copyrighted song disseminated for later playback on an MP3 player. If the podcast contains an audiovisual work, the podcaster should acquire a synchronization license to time the music to the video.[66]

Performance Licensing for Sound Recordings Radio broadcasters with a license to play the McCartney-Lennon song "Yesterday" do not need a separate performance right to broadcast a particular recording of "Yesterday," whether the recording is the Beatles' track on the *Help* album or the "Yesterday" recording by the Cincinnati Pops Orchestra directed by Erich Kunzel. For better or worse, broadcasters have never had to pay performance royalties despite long efforts by the record companies (which usually own the performance rights in a recording) and musicians (who sing and play instruments in a recording) to be paid for performance of their sound recordings.[67]

While radio stations pay royalties for broadcasting a musical composition—but not for broadcasting a specific recording—producers of audiovisual works also must acquire—as mentioned earlier—a license to synchronize a musical composition with the pictures and video in the work.[68] In addition, producers of motion pictures and audiovisual works—including animated films, videos, television shows and video games—must acquire a license to perform a specific recording. This license, called a master use license, is usually acquired from the record label. A television station, for example, would need a master use license to broadcast the Cincinnati Pops' recording of "Yesterday" in a program.

Stand-alone Internet "stations"—whether operated by broadcasters or independently—need licenses to stream digital sound recordings on the Internet if the Internet webcaster is operating like a radio station, with playlists and featured recordings, or is webcasting to subscribers or an interactive audience that chooses the tracks it hears.[69] Napster.com, an Internet webcaster, must acquire performance rights to stream sound recordings for the company's digital jukebox, a service for subscribers who pay a fee to listen to selected recordings.

Webcasters can obtain performance rights for a musical composition from BMI or one of the other performance rights organizations, but the independent webcasters negotiate their own deals to perform copyrighted sound recordings

---

[65] David Powell, "'All Clear?' A Music Clearance Primer," www.themusicbridge.com.
[66] Colette Vogel and Mia Garlick, *Podcasting Legal Guide: Rules for the Revolution*, https://mirrors.creativecommons.org/Podcasting_Legal_Guide.pdf.
[67] 17 U.S.C. § 114(a).
[68] *See* David Powell, "All Clear?—A Music Clearance Primer," *The Music Bridge LLC*, www.themusicbridge.com/id38.htm.
[69] David Oxenford, "Internet Radio—The Basics of Music Royalty Obligations," *First Amendment Law Letter* (Davis Wright Tremaine LLP) (Fall 2006), at 2.

over the Internet. Podcasters downloading audio files should also obtain performance licenses.

Compulsory Licenses If webcasters are not serving subscribers and are not streaming with the regular schedule of a radio station, webcasters can stream music under a compulsory license. A compulsory license is an exception to copyright allowing the media to perform a copyrighted work without explicit permission as long as the user pays royalties. Compulsory licenses save the media the cumbersome and expensive process of negotiating licenses. The time-consuming, costly licensing process reduces public performances of copyrighted works, thereby diminishing the number of public performances of a work the public might otherwise enjoy and cutting royalties for copyright owners. Therefore, Congress concluded that the public and copyright owners would benefit if the media were guaranteed the ability under a compulsory license to perform some copyrighted works without having to ask permission. In return, the media pay royalties.

Cable operators enjoy compulsory licenses that allow cable systems to carry local over-the-air television broadcasts, increasing the reach of over-the-air broadcasts to consumers with poor reception to over-the-air signals.[70] Under the compulsory license, cable operators cannot be refused permission by the copyright owners to retransmit the programs through the cable "facility," but the cable company must pay royalties to "retransmit" the television programs. Courts have ruled that satellite and wireless companies are also communications "facilities" that retransmit television signals to their paying subscribers. Courts have quite consistently ruled that the Internet is not a communication facility entitled to compulsory license, but, rather, the Internet is an amorphous, worldwide network of linked computers.[71] Internet operators, therefore, must get permission from television broadcasters before streaming broadcast programming.

Operators of direct broadcast satellites have a compulsory license to transmit network signals to homes that are not served by over-the-air television.[72] Satellite operators are guaranteed content for which they pay, and broadcasters earn revenues for delivery of their programs to households the broadcasters would not otherwise reach. In 2006, the U.S. Copyright Office ruled that cell phone companies have a statutory license to use copyrighted music in the ring tones announcing cellular phone calls, once the copyright owners have made the music available to the public.

Webcasters have a compulsory license to play copyrighted digital sound recordings if the web system is not interactive and listeners do not subscribe.[73] Musicians and performers benefit from the compulsory license because they receive royalties on the digital web transmissions, royalties they are denied when their performances are broadcast over the air or simulcast by a radio station over the Internet. To qualify for the compulsory license, the webcaster must not operate like a radio station from which it might be easy for listeners to record scheduled music. The webcaster cannot publish a schedule of broadcast plays and must limit the number of songs played by a particular artist or from a single album. The webcaster must also employ technology to discourage illicit copying.

---

[70] 17 U.S.C. § 111.
[71] WPIX, Inc. v. ivi, Inc., 691 F.3d 275 (2d Cir. 2012).
[72] 17 U.S.C.A. § 119(a); Satellite Broadcasting & Communications Ass'n of Am. v. Oman, 17 F.3d 344 (11th Cir. 1994).
[73] Sound Exchange, "Licensing 101," www.soundexchange.com.

Under the Digital Millennium Copyright Act of 1998, half the statutory fee goes to the performers and half to the copyright owner in the performance—usually the record company. Rates for compulsory licenses are set, distributions determined and disputes settled by the three-member Copyright Royalty Board convened by the Librarian of Congress. Cable and wireless systems pay royalties into a general copyright fund that is then distributed to copyright owners. The royalty board determines the shares of the fund to be distributed to each type of work—motion pictures, sports, religious programming—and, if necessary, the appropriate share for individual copyright owners.[74] A clearing agency, SoundExchange, collects royalties under the statutory license for digital Internet music performances.[75]

MORAL RIGHTS Countries that belong, as the United States does, to the Berne Convention for the Protection of Literary and Artistic Works are required to protect artists' and writers' "moral rights" in their work. Moral rights include the right to be known as the author of one's work and to withdraw a work from distribution. Moral rights also allow an author to protect the integrity of a work by preventing others from deforming it or using it in a way that reflects poorly on the author.[76] A related right permits artists to profit from resales of their work. The United States generally considers its moral rights obligations under the Berne Convention to be met when creators seek remedies under the law of libel, privacy, misappropriation and rights of publicity.

The Copyright Act grants additional moral rights for works of visual art under the Visual Artists Rights Act of 1990.[77] The act protects artists' rights of attribution and integrity in some paintings, drawings, prints, sculpture and photographs produced for exhibition. An artist whose work is violated can sue to stop the violation and to claim monetary damages.

The right of attribution gives artists the right to have their names associated with works they create and to prevent use of their names with works they do not create. The law also allows artists to disassociate themselves from their works if the works have been distorted or mutilated. To protect the integrity of a work, the law prohibits intentional distortion, mutilation or other modification of an artist's work if the changes "would be prejudicial to his or her honor or reputation." Several states, including New York[78] and California,[79] have also adopted moral rights statutes for artists.

The Visual Artists Rights Act does not protect the moral rights of journalists or news photographers. Moral rights for journalists must be found in other laws, such as the law of publicity, privacy, libel or misappropriation. It is not a violation of a moral right protected under federal law to reproduce a picture of a painting, sculpture or other artistic work in a book, newspaper, magazine or audiovisual work, although the reproduction may infringe the copyright in the work.[80]

Congress has not prohibited the "colorization" of black-and-white films, a practice that some directors say violates the integrity of their work. Although colorization is permitted if no copyright infringement occurs, some films must be labeled if color has been added. Congress created a National Film Registry of distinguished

---

[74] 70 Fed. Reg. 30901–30916 (May 31, 2005).
[75] David Oxenford, "Internet Radio—The Basics of Music Royalty Obligations," *First Amendment Law Letter* (Davis Wright Tremaine LLP) (Fall 2006), at 3.
[76] Harry Henn, *Copyright Law: A Practitioner's Guide* 176 (1988).
[77] 17 U.S.C. § 106A.
[78] N.Y. Arts & Cult. Aff. Law § 14.03 (McKinney 1996).
[79] Cal. Civ. Code § 986–7.
[80] H.R. Rep. No. 514, 101st Cong., 2d Sess., *reprinted in* 1990 U.S.C.C.A.N. 6915, 6927.

motion pictures that must be labeled if copies are altered. Congress created a National Film Preservation Board that each year selects up to 25 "culturally, historically, or aesthetically significant" films for inclusion on the registry.[81]

▩ SUMMARY ▩

Copyright owners are granted a bundle of rights. These include the rights to reproduce and distribute their works, create derivative works and publicly perform and display their works. The right to copy, perform or exercise the other rights of the copyright owner include the power to deny copying, creation of a derivative work, or a performance. Copyright law recognizes separate copyrights in musical compositions and sound recordings, resulting in a complicated mix of requirements for broadcasters, digital webcasters and producers of audiovisual works. The federal government and a few states have enacted moral rights legislation granting certain artists protection for the integrity of their works of fine art after the works are sold and granting the right for artists to be accurately identified with their work.

Infringement

Plaintiffs in copyright cases must prove they own copyright in an original work and that the defendants violated one or more of the copyright owners' exclusive rights. Infringers may be criminally liable for unauthorized copying whether or not they profit from the copying.[82] Once likely infringement is established, a court may enjoin dissemination of the infringing copies. It does not violate the First Amendment to halt distribution of copies that infringe a copyright.[83] Halting a copyright infringement is viewed by the courts as a protection of a property interest rather than an interference with free speech.

Unless works are so strikingly similar that unauthorized copying is a certainty, it cannot be assumed that a work that resembles another was copied. Copyright protects any original literary or artistic expression even if, by coincidence, it resembles someone else's work. Thus, even if plaintiffs can prove that their work is original, that they own the copyright and that someone else's work is similar, they may have difficulty proving that the defendant's work was copied. Typically, a plaintiff has no witnesses to testify to the copying. Lacking direct evidence, copyright owners can nevertheless prove copying by showing that the defendant had reasonable access to the copyrighted work and that the alleged copy is substantially similar to the original.

ACCESS It is easy to prove access to a widely disseminated work that anyone might see and copy. Thus, Miller Brewing Company had no difficulty establishing that Carling O'Keefe Breweries had access to Miller Lite advertisements that were broadcast on television and on cable.[84] Similarly, Universal City Studios, producer of the movie *Jaws*, easily established that Film Ventures International, producer of the movie *Great White*, had easy access to *Jaws*. Both the movie *Jaws* and the book on which it was based had been seen or read by millions.[85] Copiers have easy access to works distributed online.

---

[81] 2 U.S.C. § 179.
[82] 17 U.S.C. § 506(a).
[83] *In re* Capital Cities/ABC, Inc., 918 F.2d 140 (1990).
[84] Miller Brewing Co. v. Carling O'Keefe Breweries, 452 F. Supp. 429 (W.D.N.Y. 1978).
[85] Universal City Studios, Inc. v. Film Ventures Int'l, Inc., 543 F. Supp. 1134 (C.D. Cal. 1982).

SUBSTANTIAL SIMILARITY Besides proving access, a copyright plaintiff must prove that the works are substantially similar. It is easy to prove substantial similarity in cases in which the pirate copies the original work verbatim. There was no question of substantial similarity in *Quinto v. Legal Times of Washington, Inc.* because it was easily demonstrated that a Washington legal publication reprinted, without change, 92 percent of a copyrighted work.[86] More often, however, copying will not be as obvious. Indeed, determining substantial similarity between two works is one of the more difficult questions in copyright law.[87] "[T]he test for infringement of copyright is of necessity vague," Judge Learned Hand observed.[88]

In determining substantial similarity, courts often examine whether the underlying ideas and the manner of expression are similar in the two works.[89] The film *Great White* was so similar to the movie *Jaws* that a court issued a preliminary injunction against infringement of *Jaws*. Both films starred sharks that threatened coastal towns on the Atlantic seaboard. The films shared similar major characters, including teenage victims of the shark, a crusty sea captain and a shark expert. "In light of the great similarity of expression," the court said, "it would seem fair to conclude that the creators of *Great White* wished to be as closely connected with the plaintiff's motion picture *Jaws* as possible."[90]

In contrast, a federal appeals court ruled that ABC's *The Greatest American Hero* was not substantially similar to Warner Brothers' *Superman* movies. The idea of each was similar—a character with superhuman powers battles evil—but the characters were very different. Unlike Superman, ABC's hero, Ralph Hinckley, was slight, informally dressed and weak-chinned, "the antithesis of the Superman character image." Unlike Superman, the flying Hinckley crashed into buildings and penetrated walls only with great difficulty. Although he was impervious to bullets, Hinckley, unlike Superman, feared being shot.[91]

TYPES OF INFRINGEMENT Infringement takes three forms: direct, contributory and vicarious.

Direct Infringement A person directly infringes a copyright by copying, performing or otherwise violating a copyright owner's exclusive rights without permission. It is a direct infringement to photocopy a book or duplicate a DVD without permission. Those who share files of copyrighted music and film without permission are direct infringers. In an online case, Dennis Erlich directly infringed the copyright in the published and unpublished works of L. Ron Hubbard, the late founder of the Church of Scientology, by uploading copies of Hubbard's writings onto an electronic bulletin board without authorization. Expressions posted on the bulletin board, which had 500 paying subscribers, were distributed worldwide on the Internet.[92] Even though Erlich made no money from the Hubbard expressions he placed on the bulletin board, a federal court in California said that he was a direct infringer because he copied copyrighted material into a forum where it would be read by others and more widely distributed and copied.

In 2014 a federal district court upheld a jury award of $1.2 million against Agence France Presse (AFP) and Getty Images for willfully infringing the copyright

---

[86] 506 F. Supp. 554 (D.D.C. 1981).

[87] Melville Nimmer and David Nimmer, *Nimmer on Copyright* § 12.10[3].

[88] Peter Pan Fabrics, Inc. v. Martin Weiner Corp., 274 F.2d 487 (2d Cir. 1960).

[89] Sid & Marty Krofft Television Prods. v. McDonald's Corp., 562 F.2d 1157 (9th Cir. 1977).

[90] Universal City Studios, Inc. v. Film Ventures Int'l, Inc., 543 F. Supp. 1134 (C.D. Cal. 1982).

[91] Warner Bros. Inc. v. American Broadcasting Co., 523 F. Supp. 611 (S.D.N.Y. 1981).

[92] Religious Technology Ctr. v. Netcom On-Line Communication Servs., Inc., 907 F. Supp. 1361 (N.D. Calif. 1995).

of photojournalist Daniel Morel. AFP published and sold eight photos of the 2010 Haitian earthquake Morel uploaded to Twitter via a TwitPic account. Lisandro Suero, a Twitter user, copied the photographs into his own Twitter feed without Morel's consent. AFP and Getty Images ended up distributing eight photos, initially credited to Suero, to thousands of news outlets and other customers around the world.

Morel was awarded the maximum statutory damages under the copyright law for distribution of the eight copyrighted photos by the two organizations because the jury concluded AFP and Getty willfully violated Morel's copyright. The court noted that both organizations were experienced working in an industry where copyright requirements are prevalent. Yet, AFP published the photos while apparently harboring some doubts about whether Suero was authorized to distribute them. AFP continued to distribute the photos after it learned that Morel was the photographer and copyright holder. Getty distributed the photos without clear authorization and continued to distribute Suero-credited photos two weeks after AFP sent Getty a notice to "kill" all of the Morel photos.[93] See Photo 6.2. The Twitter terms of service permit users to tweet and retweet photos but do not authorize third parties such as Suero, AFP or Getty to remove photos from tweets and distribute and sell them without permission.

Contributory Infringement Contributory infringers contribute to the infringement of others or knowingly cause others to infringe, but they do not necessarily infringe directly themselves. A federal appeals court ruled that Napster, the online file-sharing company in a former incarnation, contributed to infringement by computer users who traded music recordings through the Napster online system.[94] Napster, which now sells music legitimately, provided the server from which music files were shared. Without Napster's support services, the court said, "Napster users could not find and download music they want with the ease of which defendant boasts." Driven from hosting a server that contributed to illegal file sharing, Napster reappeared as a service allowing patrons to lawfully download music files for a fee.[95]

A unanimous Supreme Court ruled that providers of free "peer-to-peer" file-sharing software may also be contributory infringers. The Supreme Court ruled that Grokster, Ltd., and StreamCast Networks, Inc., may have been contributory infringers by inducing users through advertising to illegally download copyrighted music and film on what the Court called "a gigantic scale." The Court said Grokster and StreamCast profited from the illegal file trading by directing advertising to an estimated 10 million users of company software, many of them former users of Napster fileservers.[96]

The Supreme Court overturned a lower court, which had held Grokster was not a contributory infringer because the Grokster software was capable of many lawful, non-infringing uses, including trading articles among libraries or trading uncopyrighted music. The lower court relied on a 1982 Supreme Court ruling that the SONY Corporation was not a contributory infringer when it produced and sold videocassette recorders on which home viewers could record programs from their television sets. In *Sony Corporation of America v. Universal City Studios*, the Supreme Court noted that the SONY recorder, the Betamax, had many lawful uses

---

[93] Agence France Presse v. Morel, 2014 U.S. Dist. LEXIS 112436 (S.D.N.Y., Aug. 13, 2014).
[94] A&M Records v. Napster, 239 F.3d 1004 (9th Cir. 2001).
[95] *See* Napster.com.
[96] Metro-Goldwyn-Mayer Studios, Inc. v. Grokster, Ltd., 545 U.S. 913 (2005).

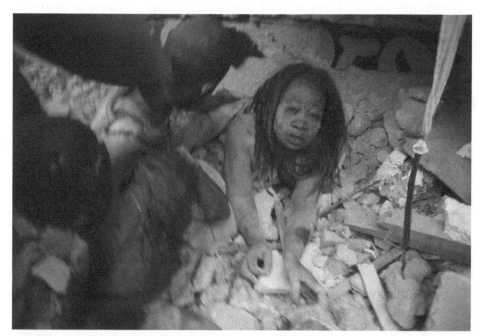

PHOTO 6.2 Photographer Daniel Morel was awarded $1.2 million after Agence France-Presse and Getty Images distributed without permission Morel's photos of the 2010 Haitian earthquake that a photojournalist posted to Twitter.

Source: © Daniel Morel 2010. Reprinted with permission.

and that the SONY Corporation had no intent to encourage illegal copying.[97] The Court concluded the videocassette recorder's principal use was for "time-shifting," allowing viewers to record programs for viewing at times of their choosing.

In contrast, the Supreme Court ruled that Grokster and StreamCast may have been contributory infringers because the companies' intent was to induce users—as a substitute for Napster—to illegally download copyrighted works, a practice from which Grokster would profit by directing advertising to users' screens. The Supreme Court remanded the *Grokster* case for determination whether the two companies should be held liable for "purposeful culpable expression and conduct" constituting contributory infringement.

Four months later, Grokster settled with record producers, agreeing to halt distribution of its file-swapping software and agreeing to pay $50 million in damages.[98] In 2006, a federal court in California ruled against StreamCast Networks. In 2010, a federal judge in New York halted the operations of Lime Wire, a peer-to-peer file-sharing service that the court said encouraged copyright infringement on a "massive scale."[99]

Vicarious Infringement Vicarious liability is found when someone has the right and ability to supervise the infringer's activity—and therefore can stop it—and benefits from the infringement.[100] Vicarious infringement is found when some-

---

[97] 464 U.S. 417 (1984).

[98] Jeff Leeds, "Grokster Calls It Quits on Sharing Music Files," *N.Y. Times*, Nov. 8, 2005, at C1.

[99] Arista Records LLC v. Lime Wire LLC, 2010 U.S. Dist. LEXIS 115675 (S.D.N.Y. Oct. 26, 2010).

[100] Fonovisa, Inc. v. Cherry Auction, Inc., 76 F.3d 259 (9th Cir. 1996); Shapiro, Bernstein & Co. v. H.L. Green Co., 316 F.2d 305 (1963).

one with supervisory powers profits from an infringement. Unlike the contributory infringer, the vicarious infringer does not necessarily encourage or provide the means for infringing.

The federal appeals court determined Napster to be a vicarious infringer as well as a contributory infringer because the company had a direct financial interest in building the user base on which future profits depended. Furthermore, Napster had the ability to police the system by blocking illegal downloads of copyrighted music. Podcasters might also be vicarious or contributory infringers if they profit from or encourage distribution of unlicensed copies of copyrighted recordings or films.

Safe Harbors In 1998, Congress adopted legislation that protects online service providers from liability for money damages for infringement when the service providers merely transmit or temporarily store digital information for their subscribers.[101] Under the statute, online service providers are not liable for monetary damages for copyright infringements on their systems or networks if they act as mere conduits of information sent or received by others. If, like a common carrier, a service provider merely transmits information but does not select or alter the content or choose the recipients, the provider will not have to pay the copyright owner monetary damages for the infringements of others.[102] The provider is also exempt from monetary liability for the temporary storage or "caching" of information—a form of temporary copying—that is, an automatic process designed to reduce congestion on the Internet. ISPs include web-hosting companies, search engines such as Google, e-tailers such as Amazon.com and Vimeo, the website where members post videos of their own creation.

To maintain their safe harbors, Internet service providers must implement reasonable policies to prevent postings by repeat infringers, designate an agent to receive notices of infringement and create standard technical measures to detect infringements. ISPs must also "take down" Internet postings if notified they are hosting or linking to infringing material.[103] To have an allegedly infringing website removed from an ISP, the copyright owner must provide notice containing the name and address of the complaining party and identify the infringing materials.[104] The ISP must return the questionable material to the website if a subscriber who posted it "counter-notifies" the ISP the material is not infringing and the complaining party does not seek a court order to stop the reposting. The party claiming copyright violation can then sue the party posting the materials, but not the Internet service provider. Bloggers, too, can enjoy a safe harbor as a "provider of online services" if the bloggers designate an agent for notification of infringing materials with the Copyright Office and have a policy against repeat copyright infringement by their subscribers and account holders.[105]

Providers could lose their safe harbor if they have actual knowledge, or "red flag" knowledge, of infringement.[106] But it is difficult for an ISP to become liable for illegally posted copyrighted materials. Even if an Internet site knows generally that many user-generated posts contain infringing copyrighted works, the service provider is not obligated under the Digital Millennium Copyright Act to find and

---

[101] Digital Millennium Copyright Act, Pub. L. No. 105–304, codified at 17 U.S.C. § 512.
[102] 17 U.S.C. § 512(a).
[103] 17 U.S.C. § 512.
[104] 17 U.S.C. § 512(c)(3)(A)(i)–(vi).
[105] *See* Electronic Frontier Foundation, "Bloggers FAQ," www.eff.org/bloggers/lg/faqip.php.
[106] Capitol Records, LLC v. Vimeo, LLC, 826 F.3d 78 (2d Cir. 2016).

remove the offending material. In 2014, Google and Viacom settled a seven-year suit in which Viacom had argued that Google should monitor YouTube—which Google purchased in 2006 for $1.6 billion—and take down thousands of hours of Viacom content that had been illegally posted.[107] In its $1 billion lawsuit, Viacom claimed YouTube illegally streamed 79,000 copyrighted videos between 2005 and 2008. Viacom owns cable networks such as Comedy Central and MTV and the Paramount movie studio.

A federal court had ruled in 2013 that YouTube had no obligation to look for materials that might infringe copyright.[108] YouTube had a responsibility to take down materials only if YouTube "had been told of specific infringing materials," the court said. Viacom had not identified the copyright violations with sufficient specificity. No money reportedly changed hands in the settlement.

Copyright Claims Board In 2020, Congress passed the Copyright Alternative in Small-Claims Enforcement Act of 2020 (CASE Act), which directed the Copyright Office to establish the Copyright Claims Board (CCB). It will begin operating in 2022 as a three-member tribunal within the Office, and it will provide an efficient option to resolve certain copyright disputes that involve claims of less than $30,000. CCB proceedings will be streamlined, generally without formal motions, and they will require fewer resources, in money and time, than federal lawsuits. Subject-matter experts in the Office will render the decisions. They will not be precedential, meaning the CCB will not be required to follow them in later cases, and they will have no impact on unrelated federal court proceedings.

■ SUMMARY ■

Authors who think their copyrights have been infringed must prove that their works are original, that they own valid copyrights, that the alleged infringer had access to the copyrighted work and that the alleged copy is substantially similar to the original. In determining substantial similarity, courts examine whether the works have the same idea and manner of expression. Infringers of copyright may violate the law by directly copying, by knowingly contributing to infringement by others, or by vicariously profiting from unlawful copying in circumstances they supervise. Federal law protects online service providers from monetary liability if they merely carry and temporarily store infringing material of cyberspace users and if they take down copyrighted materials when notified that posted materials violate copyright.

Fair Use

The fair use doctrine creates an exception to the law prohibiting unauthorized copying of copyrighted expression. The fair use doctrine is the law's attempt to reconcile the "exclusive rights" granted to authors to encourage creativity with a sometimes conflicting interest in ensuring that knowledge of creative achievement is widely disseminated and discussed. For a journalist or critic to discuss and evaluate a copyrighted work, it is usually necessary to copy at least small portions of the original work. Therefore, the copyright law permits limited copying for comment and criticism under the doctrine of fair use.

---

[107] Leslie Kaufman, "Viacom and YouTube Settle Suit Over Copyright Violations," *N.Y. Times*, Mar. 18, 2014.
[108] Viacom International Inc. v. YouTube Inc., 940 F. Supp. 2d 110 (S.D.N.Y. 2013).

Fair use, one expert declared, is "a privilege in others than the owner of a copyright to use the copyrighted material in a reasonable manner without his consent, notwithstanding the monopoly granted to the owner" by the copyright.[109] To make fair use of a copyrighted work, it is not necessary to ask permission or pay a royalty. The fair use doctrine, which developed in the common law, was embodied in Section 107 of the Copyright Revision Act.[110] Section 107 permits limited copying of copyrighted work, usually only for "productive" purposes such as news reports, criticism and comment. For copying to be a fair use, the copier should usually be "engaged in creating a work of authorship whereby he adds his own original contribution to that which is copied."[111] Copying is a fair use, the Supreme Court has said, when the new work is "transformative," that is, the author "adds something new" by altering the original with "new expression, meaning, or message."[112] It is also important that copying not be so extensive as to damage the copyright owner's commercial market. The factors to be considered when a court is determining if copying constitutes a fair use are

1. the purpose and character of the use, including whether such use is of a commercial nature or is for nonprofit educational purposes.
2. the nature of the copyrighted work.
3. the amount and substantiality of the portion used in relation to the copyrighted work as a whole.
4. the effect of the use on the potential market for, or value of, the copyrighted work.

PURPOSE AND CHARACTER OF THE USE Section 107 of the Copyright Revision Act does not define the uses of copyrighted material that are "fair," but the preamble to Section 107 says that fair use is likely to be found when the purpose is "criticism, comment, news reporting, teaching, . . . scholarship or research." A purpose least favored by courts is "mere reproduction," creating a work in which the new author has contributed little effort or original expression.[113] At the time the copyright law was adopted, the Senate suggested fair use would include

> quotation of excerpts in a review or criticism for purposes of illustration or comment; quotation of short passages in a scholarly or technical work, for illustration or clarification of the author's observations; use in a parody of some of the content of the work parodied; summary of an address or article, with brief quotations, in a news report . . . reproduction by a teacher or student of a small part of a work to illustrate a lesson; reproduction of a work in legislative or judicial proceedings or reports; incidental and fortuitous reproduction, in a newsreel or broadcast, of a work located in the scene of an event being reported.[114]

---

[109] Rosemont Enters., Inc. v. Random House, Inc., 366 F.2d 303, 306 (2d Cir. 1966), *cert. denied*, 385 U.S. 1009 (1967) (quoting Ball, *The Law of Copyright and Literary Property* 260 (1944)).
[110] H.R. Rep. No. 1476, 94th Cong., 2d Sess. 66 (1976), *reprinted in* 1976 U.S.C.C.A.N. 5659, 5680.
[111] Melville Nimmer and David Nimmer, 3 *Nimmer on Copyright* § 13.05[A], at 13–163.
[112] Campbell v. Acuff-Rose Music, Inc., 510 U.S. 569 (1994).
[113] Working Group on Intellectual Property Rights, Bruce Lehman, chair, *Intellectual Property and the National Information Infrastructure* 77 (1995).
[114] S. Jud. Comm. Rep. No. 983, A Report to Accompany S. 1361, Copyright Law Revision, 93d Cong., 2d Sess. 115 (1974).

NEWS AND COMMENT One purpose of the copyright law is to encourage the dissemination of knowledge. The law therefore permits reporters and scholars to quote brief excerpts from copyrighted works without paying royalties. Scholars may quote short passages of a written work or reproduce small sections of a painting for the purpose of discussion and criticism. Journalists may quote briefly from copyrighted works for the purpose of disseminating news. When the Senate said that incidental and fortuitous reproduction of a copyrighted work is fair use, it meant that copyrighted material may appear by chance as background to events being reported. A federal district court in New York City found such incidental copying when WABC, Channel 7, broadcast footage of a high school band playing a copyrighted song, "Dove sta Zaza," in a parade. The court said the station's brief segment of the copyrighted song was fair because the use was incidental to a news event.[115] Similarly, broadcast or publication of a copyrighted painting as background in news footage or a news photograph would be fortuitous and therefore a fair use.

The U.S. Court of Appeals for the Second Circuit ruled in 2015 Google's purpose was "transformative" when it scanned millions of books in their entirety in major public and university libraries. Over the objections of book publishers, the court said the digital copying was a permissible fair use because Google transformed the original works by creating a new digital search function allowing readers and scholars to find references in books, many of which were out of print or hidden on dusty shelves. The search function also allows researchers to read short snippets and determine whether to buy the book or read it at the library, the court said. The court also ruled the digital scanning did not damage the publishers' book market because the digital copies—viewable only in "snippets"—did not substitute for the original publications.[116] In an earlier decision, the Second Circuit had ruled it a fair use for Google to create a searchable database of books.[117]

In 2011, artist Shepard Fairey and the Associated Press settled a copyright suit surrounding Fairey's famous "Hope" poster of presidential candidate Barack Obama, a poster that was based on an AP news photo.[118] Fairey circulated 300,000 of the posters of Obama gazing upward with a determined look. The AP also settled with Obey Clothing, an apparel company that produced 234,000 items bearing Fairey's image of Obama. The Obama presidential campaign welcomed the Fairey posters but never formally adopted or paid for them.

In the settlement, Fairey and Obey agreed not to use AP photographs without permission, but Fairey continued to maintain that his edgy, iconic, red-cream-and-light-blue image of Obama is a transformative fair use of the color news photo. The news agency continued to maintain that Fairey and Obey Clothing violated its copyright by copying the news agency's photograph. Fairey admitted that he used the press agency news photo as a "visual reference." "I respect the work of photographers," Fairey said, "as well as recognize the need to preserve opportunities for other artists to make fair use of photographic images." In the settlement, reached days before a trial was to begin, Fairey and the AP agreed to become business partners, sharing rights to make posters and merchandise bearing the "Hope" image and agreeing to collaborate on a series of images Fairey would create based on AP

---

[115] Italian Book Corp. v. ABC, 458 F. Supp. 65 (S.D.N.Y. 1978).
[116] The Authors Guild v. Google, Inc., 804 F.3d 202 (2d Cir. 2015), *cert. denied*, 2016 U.S. LEXIS 2545 (U.S., Apr. 18, 2016).
[117] Authors Guild, Inc. v. HathiTrust, 755 F.3d 87 (2d Cir. 2014).
[118] Randy Kennedy, "Shepard Fairey and the A.P. Settle Legal Dispute," *N.Y. Times*, Jan. 12, 2011.

photographs.[119] In 2012, Fairey was fined $25,000 and sentenced to 300 hours of community service for lying in court about which AP photo provided the basis for the "Hope" poster.[120]

PARODY Another purpose permitted by the fair use doctrine is parody. A parody distorts or closely imitates another work to make fun of the original work. The Supreme Court acknowledged that parody "needs to mimic an original to make its point."[121] It is unlikely to be a fair use when a communicator uses a copyrighted work merely to "get attention" or "avoid the drudgery in working up something fresh," rather than commenting on the "substance or style" of the original.

The U.S. Supreme Court ruled that a parody may be a fair use even though it has a commercial purpose and copies the "heart" of the original work. Reversing a lower court, the Supreme Court ruled in *Campbell v. Acuff-Rose Music, Inc.*, that 2 Live Crew's parody of Roy Orbison's "Oh, Pretty Woman" could be sufficiently transformative not to violate the copyright held by Acuff-Rose. The lyrics to the original song state: "Pretty woman, walking down the street, Pretty woman, the kind I like to meet." 2 Live Crew's parody, though, restates the original as: "Bald headed woman, girl your hair won't grow, Bald headed woman, you got a teeny weeny afro."

In a unanimous opinion written by Justice David Souter, the Court said the 2 Live Crew parody of "Oh, Pretty Woman" may be a transformative use of the original because it "depart[s] markedly" from the Orbison lyrics, creating its own comment and criticism of the Orbison song. Although the Court did not find the parody to be of "high rank," the Court said the 2 Live Crew version

> juxtaposes the romantic musings of a man whose fantasy comes true, with degrading taunts, a bawdy demand for sex, and a sigh of relief from paternal responsibility. The later words can be taken as a comment on the naiveté of the original of an earlier day, as a rejection of its sentiment that ignores the ugliness of street life and the debasement that it signifies.

The Supreme Court said the lower court placed too much emphasis on the commercial purpose of a parody. Although a commercial use weighs against a finding of fair use, Justice Souter wrote, commercialism is not the only factor. Indeed, the Court said, if a commercial use were presumptively unfair, most copying of copyrighted works for news reporting, comment, criticism, research and parodies would be unfair because these activities are usually conducted for profit. Justice Souter noted Samuel Johnson's adage that "no man but a blockhead ever wrote, except for money."

Although the Court ruled that a parody might be a fair use, it remanded the case for a determination whether 2 Live Crew's repetition of the opening musical phrase from Orbison's song amounted to excessive copying. The Court noted that some quotation of this musical phrase, the "heart" of the Orbison song, would be a fair use. Indeed, a parody, the Court said, must quote "the original's most distinctive or memorable features" if the audience is to recognize the original. "It is the heart at which parody takes aim," the Court said.

---

[119] Janon Fisher, "Obey Clothing Will Now Partner with the Wire Service," *Adweek*, Mar. 16, 2011.
[120] L. Gordon Crovitz, "How a Poster Got a Legal Shredding," *Wall St. J.*, Sept. 17, 2012.
[121] Campbell v. Acuff-Rose Music, Inc., 510 U.S. 569 (1994).

The Supreme Court also remanded the case for a determination whether 2 Live Crew's rap version of "Oh, Pretty Woman" would interfere with the potential market for other rap versions of "Oh, Pretty Woman" should Acuff-Rose ever wish to produce and distribute its own rap versions. However, the Court concluded that the 2 Live Crew parody would not interfere with a potential market for parodies of "Oh, Pretty Woman" that Acuff-Rose might wish to produce. The Court doubted that Acuff-Rose would ever want to market a parody of its own copyrighted song. It is unlikely, the Court said, for creators of imaginative works to license parodies, critical reviews or lampoons of their productions.

The Court also noted that Acuff-Rose cannot complain if the success of the 2 Live Crew parody diminishes the value of the Orbison song. Copyright violation is found when the copy becomes a substitute for the original, not when the copy successfully lampoons the original. "Parody may quite legitimately aim at garroting the original, destroying it commercially as well as artistically," the Court said. On remand, the parties settled.[122]

Following the decision in *Acuff-Rose*, courts have emphasized that parodies must make fun of the original work, not some other target or people's foibles. Thus, drawing on copyrighted work to create satire is less likely to be a fair use than drawing on copyrighted work to create a parody. "Parody copies from the object it mocks, while satire uses recognizable elements from the original work to mock something else or society in general."[123]

TEACHING AND NONCOMMERCIAL RESEARCH Teaching and noncommercial research are also purposes for which limited copying is permitted under the fair use doctrine. The Classroom Guidelines developed in 1976 and often cited by courts allow a teacher or researcher to make a single copy of a chapter in a book or to copy a single article from a periodical or newspaper. The guidelines also permit a teacher to make multiple copies for a class, provided that the copies are short and maximum teaching effectiveness does not allow time to obtain permission from the copyright owner.[124]

Copying excerpts of academic writings for free use by college students is an educational purpose, but a federal appeals court ruled that educational copying may not be a fair use if a court "mechanically" applies equal weight to all four fair use factors. A federal appeals court was particularly concerned that a lower court reviewing copying at Georgia State University improperly presumed that copying no more than 10 percent, or one chapter, of a work favored fair use. Fair use analysis does not produce bright-line rules, the court said, but "must be performed on a case-by-case/work-by-work basis."[125]

PERSONAL ENTERTAINMENT Copying a work, particularly a whole work, for one's own pleasure or entertainment is normally not a fair use. Such copying is not a fair use because it has no transformative purpose. Photocopying a book or sharing a digital music file simply to avoid the cost of purchasing it violates copyright, even if the copier intends only to read the book or listen to the music, not lend it, sell it or make more copies.

Thus, one may ask, is it lawful to record a song or television program for one's personal use? Yes, if one is making a single recording of a song or program that is broadcast free of charge to the listener or viewer. The Audio Home Recording

---

[122] "Acuff-Rose Settles Suit with Rap Group," *The Commercial Appeal* (Memphis), June 5, 1996.
[123] Electronic Frontier Foundation, "Bloggers FAQ," at 4, www.eff.org/bloggers/lg/faqip.php.
[124] H.R. Rep. No. 1476, 94th Cong., 2d Sess., 68–70 (1976), reprinted in 1976 U.S.C.C.A.N. 5659, 5681–3.
[125] Cambridge University Press v. Patton, 769 F.3d 1232 (11th Cir. 2014).

Act of 1992 authorized listeners to make single recordings of music on recording machines programmed to block serial recording, machines on which royalties are paid for the benefit of copyright owners.

In 1984, the Supreme Court ruled in *Sony Corp. of America v. Universal City Studios, Inc.*, that homeowners can record complete copyrighted television shows off the air for their personal, noncommercial use. The case is known as the Betamax decision after Sony's home recorder, the Betamax. The Court ruled that home recording for the purpose of "time-shifting"—watching the program at a more convenient time—is a fair use.[126] Instead of requiring that living room copiers justify their recording of entire broadcast programs with a transformative purpose, the Supreme Court was satisfied that home copiers do not have a commercial purpose and that copying does not damage the market for Hollywood films. "If the Betamax were used to make multiple copies for a commercial or profit-making purpose, such use would presumptively be unfair," the Court said. But most people record television shows so that they can watch them at a later time. This time-shifting is "a noncommercial, nonprofit activity," which constitutes fair use, the Court said.

The limited legal protection for single copies made for individual use does not extend to multiple copies. The Betamax case was decided at a time when analog videocassette recorders were relatively new. The Supreme Court thought it "speculative" whether millions of householders creating home libraries of recorded programs would damage Hollywood's commercial market. There was little fear in 1982 of serial copying of copyrighted television programs because successive copies produced on analog copiers rapidly diminished in quality. The Audio Home Recording Act permitted digital recordings for individual use, but the 1992 Act prohibited serial recording and did not contemplate widespread distribution of perfect digital copies via computer networks and DVDs.

Record companies attempt to require consumers to purchase even single musical tracks from an authorized subscription service, such as iTunes, often at 99 cents per track. Company contracts may authorize subscribers to make digital copies for use on other platforms or at other locations but prohibit file sharing, a practice that demonstrates no transformative use.

SCOOPING A NEWS COMPETITOR The Supreme Court has ruled that a news organization that steals and publishes a competitor's news may infringe copyright. In *Harper & Row, Publishers, Inc. v. Nation Enterprises, Inc.*, the Supreme Court held that the political magazine *Nation* violated Harper & Row's copyright when the *Nation* printed 300 to 400 words from President Ford's then-unpublished memoirs, *A Time to Heal*.[127] After the *Nation* published its article, *Time* canceled an agreement with Harper & Row to publish excerpts from the book just before the hardbound edition went on sale. The *Nation*'s purpose, to "scoop" *Time*, weighed heavily in the Court's decision that the use was not fair. The Court did not question that the passages the *Nation* published were newsworthy; the quoted passages explained Ford's pardon of President Nixon. Nevertheless, the Court said that the passages infringed copyright because the *Nation*'s purpose and effect of the use were not to report news but to beat Harper & Row and *Time* to the marketplace. "The *Nation*'s use," wrote Justice Sandra Day O'Connor for the majority, "had not merely the incidental effect but the intended purpose of supplanting the copyright holder's commercially valuable right of first publication." The *Nation*, in the Court's

---

[126] 464 U.S. 417 (1984).
[127] 471 U.S. 539 (1985).

opinion, was less interested in reporting news than in creating a news event of its own. Furthermore, the character of the use was hardly fair, the Court said, when the *Nation* acted in bad faith by knowingly exploiting a stolen manuscript.

CORPORATE COPYING Corporate copying for commercial purposes is generally not a fair use. Thus, corporations that copy journal articles for different internal departments violate a publisher's copyright. A federal appeals court ruled that Texaco violated the copyright in scientific journals when company scientists photocopied articles from several scientific and technical journals for their research files.[128] Copying entire articles for one's files is not a transformative use, the court said. On the contrary, the court said that copying by a profit-making corporation was for a commercial purpose and that it damaged the publishers' market. The court suggested that if the company did not wish to purchase a subscription for each of its scientists, it could negotiate licenses with individual publishers, buy copies of articles from a document delivery service that would pay royalties to the publishers, or acquire a license to copy through the Copyright Clearance Center.

Commercial copying of broadcast programs, even segments of news programs—like commercial copying of printed articles—is generally not a fair use. The U.S. Court of Appeals for the Eleventh Circuit ruled that a commercial broadcast "clipping service" infringed the copyright in newscasts that the service copied off the air. WXIA-TV in Atlanta obtained an injunction against Carol Duncan's TV News Clips, a company that recorded the evening news and sold segments to individuals and institutions that wanted a record of televised coverage of their activities. The Eleventh Circuit said Duncan's "unabashedly commercial" purpose heavily influenced the court's decision to rule that the recording and sale of broadcast news segments was not a fair use.[129] The court distinguished TV News Clips from a newspaper clipping service that buys the newspapers it clips and sends the clippings to customers. TV News Clips was buying nothing. In fact, the court said that TV News Clips could impair WXIA's market for news clips if the station chose to sell them.

In 2013, a federal district court in New York ruled that an online news monitoring service that provided news excerpts to paying customers violated the copyright of the Associated Press.[130] Meltwater News copied the titles and verbatim quotes, including the lead, from AP stories. In one of 33 examples cited by the district court, Meltwater copied 61 words from a 544-word AP story under the title "Wikileaks Suspect's Trial Near Super-Secure NSA." Quoting verbatim from AP, Meltwater told its subscribers:

> FORT MEADE, Md. (AP)—The military intelligence complex an hour outside Washington where the WikiLeaks case goes to court this week is known as a cloak-and-dagger sanctum off-limits to the public—a reputation that's only partly true . . . low-level clearance and a Lady Gaga CD. The prosecution can only hope that their arguments, or the evidence, will reveal the secrets of how. . . .

The court ruled that Meltwater News was not a search engine, as the company claimed, but a clipping service that violated AP's copyright by providing excerpts

---

[128] American Geophysical Union, Inc. v. Texaco, Inc., 60 F.3d 913 (2d Cir. 1994).
[129] Pac. & S. Co. v. Duncan, 744 F.2d 1490 (11th Cir. 1984).
[130] Associated Press v. Meltwater U.S. Holdings, Inc., 2013 U.S. Dist. LEXIS 39573 (S.D.N.Y. Mar. 21, 2013).

of AP news reports to customers without paying a license fee. Neither the purpose nor use of Meltwater News Reports is a transformative fair use, the court said.

> Meltwater uses its computer programs to automatically capture and republish designated segments of text from news articles, without adding any commentary or insight in its News Reports. Meltwater copies AP content in order to make money directly from the undiluted use of the copyrighted material.

Meltwater's clipping service is a substitute for the AP news service, thus diminishing AP's market, the court said.

NATURE OF THE COPYRIGHTED WORK Besides considering the purpose and character of copying, courts ruling on fair use also consider the nature of the copyrighted work: its length, its factual or fictional nature, the effort involved in creating it and its availability. Some works, because of their nature, are subject to more fair use than others. Works such as databases, lists and stock tables, which require much effort but not much originality, in effect receive less copyright protection than works such as novels and plays that embody more originality.[131] News reports are less protected than movies and novels because the news contains facts, which cannot be copyrighted and which are used in comment and criticism of public events.

Some works are of such a nature that copying even a small amount might not be a fair use. A few words from a brief poem or song, for example, might be an infringement. Copying a small excerpt from a commercial newsletter might also be an infringement, particularly if the copying is for a commercial purpose. Commercial newsletters typically have only a few pages, a modest circulation and a hefty subscription price. Publishers of newsletters of this nature cannot afford much free copying by others. Copying even a few lines might significantly damage the market value of the newsletter.[132] Courts are quite protective of unpublished manuscripts and letters. In the case in which the *Nation* published excerpts from Gerald Ford's memoirs, the Supreme Court said that the unpublished nature of the memoirs was a "key, though not necessarily determinative, factor" tending to negate a defense of fair use. In the *Nation* case, the Court was concerned that the copyright owner had lost the right of first publication.[133]

The U.S. Court of Appeals for the Second Circuit twice ruled that publishers of biographies violated the copyright in unpublished letters by copying or paraphrasing significant portions.[134] Copyright in letters belongs to the person who writes them. However, after complaints from historians and journalists, Congress passed legislation clarifying that courts were placing too much emphasis on the unpublished nature of works. The Court reminded that copying portions of an unpublished work might be a fair use. All four of the fair use factors must be weighed to determine whether copyright in an unpublished work has been infringed, Congress said.[135]

---

[131] N.Y. Times Co. v. Roxbury Data Interface, Inc., 434 F. Supp. 217 (1977).

[132] Wainwright Sec., Inc. v. Wall Street Transcript Corp., 558 F.2d 91 (2d Cir. 1977), *cert. denied*, 434 U.S. 1014 (1978).

[133] Harper & Row, Publishers, Inc. v. Nation Enters., 471 U.S. 539 (1985).

[134] Salinger v. Random House, Inc., 811 F.2d 90 (2d Cir. 1987), *cert. denied*, 484 U.S. 890 (1987); New Era Publications Int'l, ApS v. Henry Holt & Co., 695 F. Supp. 1493 (S.D.N.Y. 1988), *aff'd*, 873 F.2d 576 (2d Cir. 1989), *cert. denied*, 493 U.S. 1094 (1990). *But see* Wright v. Warner Books, Inc., 953 F.2d 731 (2d Cir. 1991).

[135] 17 U.S.C. § 107.

AMOUNT AND SUBSTANTIALITY OF THE PORTION USED The greater the amount of work copied, the weaker is the fair use defense. But determining substantiality is more than a question of the quantity copied; it is also a question of the quality of the portion used.

Quantity It is generally not a fair use to copy all or most of a copyrighted work, regardless of the purpose. For example, the *Legal Times* of Washington violated the copyright of Dave Quinto when it published 92 percent of an article Quinto wrote for the *Harvard Law Record*.[136]

The Betamax case is unusual because the Supreme Court ruled it was a fair use for householders to record entire copyrighted television programs off the air for shifting the time of viewing. In this atypical case, the court reasoned that home copying by individuals for noncommercial purposes is a fair use that would not damage the commercial market for the copyright holder. As a general rule, one is prohibited from copying whole works. A critic or reporter should not quote more than a few paragraphs of a book or a few lines from an article at one time in a criticism or review. A reviewer might copy a few lines from a poem or a single chart or graph from a technical treatise, even if the copying is for the purpose of criticism or comment.

A continually perplexing question is whether it is a fair use for composers and artists to "sample" from copyrighted songs. Digital music sampling is the exact reproduction in a new work of an existing musical phrase. Sometimes whole musical compositions are created with bits and snippets sampled from other works. On the one hand, sampling would appear to be a fair use because the sampler usually "borrows" only a few bars of music and transforms them into a new work. However, sampling suggests infringement because the sampler copies a musical phrase exactly, often a distinctive musical phrase, possibly the "heart" of the work. Several courts have ruled that sampling music is not a fair use.

A federal district judge ruled that musician Biz Markie violated the copyright in the song "Alone Again (Naturally)" when he digitally copied and repeated a ten-second phrase without authorization.[137] Courts in the federal Sixth Circuit have been particularly protective of copyright owners, ruling that even the briefest sampling may constitute a copyright infringement. In 2006, a federal judge in Nashville halted distribution of the million-selling classic hip-hop album "Ready to Die" after a jury determined that the producer, Sean "Diddy" Combs, had failed to get permission to include a three-note horn riff lasting only a few seconds from the 1992 recording, "Singing in the Morning," by the Ohio Players.[138] The jury awarded the copyright owners $4.2 million. Because of the risk that musical sampling might not be deemed a fair use, many record companies go through the time-consuming, expensive process of negotiating an agreement for each musical phrase borrowed from another composition.[139]

Visual artists, like musicians, can also infringe copyrights by physical and digital sampling for collages, magazine covers and montages. *Newsday* reportedly paid FPG International, a stock photo agency, $20,000 to settle a copyright infringement

---

[136] Quinto v. Legal Times, Inc., 506 F. Supp. 554 (D.D.C. 1981).
[137] Grand Upright Music Ltd. v. Warner Bros. Records, Inc., 780 F. Supp. 182 (S.D.N.Y. 1991).
[138] K. Matthew Dames, "Uncleared Sample Halts Sales of Seminal Hip Hop Album," *Copycense*, Mar. 20, 2006, www.copycense.com/2006/03/uncleared_sampl.html.
[139] Carl Falstrom, "Note: Thou Shalt Not Steal: Grand Upright Music Ltd. v. Warner Bros. Records, Inc. and the Future of Digital Sound Sampling in Popular Music," 45 *Hastings L.J.* 359, 361 (1994).

claim and agreed to give proper credit for two digital photos *Newsday* edited for a front-page montage.[140]

Quality Even if the amount of material copied is small, copying may be an infringement if the "quality" of material taken is high. In *Harper & Row v. Nation*, the Supreme Court said that the 300 to 400 words quoted by the *Nation* from President Ford's memoirs constituted a small portion of Ford's book but were substantial because they were "the heart of the book." The *Nation* took "the most interesting and moving parts" of the manuscript, the Court said. The quoted passages qualitatively embodied Ford's distinctive expression.

The Supreme Court said the *Nation*'s copying was similar to CBS' infringement of Charlie Chaplin films when the network copied brief but important segments. CBS used no clips longer than four minutes from Chaplin films in a broadcast running more than an hour. But a federal court found an infringement because the network took the highest-quality scenes.[141]

The U.S. Court of Appeals for the Second Circuit ruled that biographer Ian Hamilton violated the copyright in novelist J.D. Salinger's unpublished letters, in part, because the passages Hamilton quoted and paraphrased "make the book worth reading." The biography copies "virtually all of the most interesting passages of the letters, including several highly expressive insights about writing and literary criticism."[142]

EFFECT ON THE PLAINTIFF'S POTENTIAL MARKET The effect of copying on the plaintiff's commercial market is the most important factor for determining fair use.[143] This last criterion is a question of the effect of copying not only on the present market but also on the potential market for the copyrighted work. Critical to a determination of the commercial effect of copying is whether the copy has the same function as the original and therefore competes with, or supplants, the original work in the marketplace.

In *Wainwright Securities, Inc. v. Wall Street Transcript Corp.*, the U.S. Court of Appeals for the Second Circuit ruled that summaries of commercial reports infringed a copyright because they made it unnecessary to purchase the original.[144] *The Wall Street Transcript*, a financial newspaper, printed 250- to 300-word abstracts of research reports published by Wainwright Securities. Each year, Wainwright wrote 275 in-depth analyses of corporations, evaluating their financial characteristics, ability to take advantage of changes in their industry, growth prospects and profit expectations. *The Wall Street Transcript* summarized Wainwright Securities' reports very effectively—so effectively that the *Transcript* advertised that it was not necessary to buy the reports.

In ruling that the *Wall Street Transcript*'s summaries violated Wainwright's copyright, the Second Circuit said that the *Transcript* was not making its own analysis and was not commenting on or criticizing Wainwright's work. Nor was the *Transcript* taking only brief quotes or seeking the opinions of others on the work. Instead, the *Transcript* "appropriated almost verbatim the most creative and original aspects of the reports, the financial analyses and predictions, which represent a substantial investment of time, money and labor." By summarizing the reports, the

---

[140] "Photo Suit Settled," *National Law Journal*, Jan. 16, 1995, at A10.

[141] Roy Export Co. v. Columbia Broadcasting Sys., Inc., 672 F.2d 1095, 8 Media L. Rep. 1637 (2d Cir. 1982), *cert. denied*, 459 U.S. 826 (1982).

[142] Salinger v. Random House, Inc., 811 F.2d at 99, 13 Media L. Rep. at 1960.

[143] Harper & Row, Publishers, Inc. v. Nation Enters., 471 U.S. 539 (1985); Triangle Publications, Inc. v. Knight-Ridder Newspapers, Inc., 626 F.2d 1171 (5th Cir. 1980).

[144] 558 F.2d 91 (2d Cir. 1977), *cert. denied*, 434 U.S. 1014 (1978).

Transcript lowered the commercial value of Wainwright's reports. The *Transcript*'s summaries were, in effect, serving the same function as Wainwright's reports, the court said.

A detrimental commercial affect also figured in the infringement found in *Harper & Row v. Nation*. The Supreme Court ruled that the 300 to 400 words quoted in the *Nation* from President Ford's memoirs had a potential and actual effect on the market for the Ford book.[145] Almost immediately, Harper & Row lost $12,500 as a result of the *Nation*'s publication because *Time* magazine canceled a contract to serialize parts of the memoirs. The *Nation*, by quoting from sections of the book licensed to *Time*, took the part of the market *Time* would have had. More important, the Court said, the *Nation*'s publication of portions of the unreleased manuscript "poses substantial potential for damage to the marketability of first serialization rights."

More recently, courts have ruled viewers do not infringe copyright when they record in the cloud for personal use. A federal appeals ruled that Cablevision Systems Corporation did not infringe TV networks' and film companies' copyrights by allowing viewers to digitally record individual shows on servers operated by Cablevision. The court found no infringement, not only when a viewer recorded a specific program on Cablevision's remote recorder but also when the viewer ordered the program for personal viewing.[146]

Meanwhile, Google won two cases in which federal appeals courts ruled Google's digital copies of entire works constituted fair use, not having a significant effect on the potential market or the value of the original copyrighted works. In these cases, Google employed the copies for a new function, thus transforming the copies into a new work. The Ninth Circuit Court of Appeals ruled that Google did not damage the potential market in nude photos published by *Perfect 10*, an adult magazine and website, when the search engine company employed low-resolution thumbnail photos as pointers—Internet pathways—to *Perfect 10*'s original photos. The court ruled that Google's thumbnails did not provide a substitute for *Perfect 10*'s full-size nude photos or for cell phone downloads, but rather provided an Internet route to those photos.[147]

Similarly, the Second Circuit Court of Appeals ruled that Google did not damage the potential market of book publishers when Google copied millions of library books in their entirety, not so that readers could download or access them for free, but so that Google could transform the copies by providing search tools and access to limited "snippets" of books. The court conceded that readers could find facts and some "authorial expression" through Google searches, but the court found it highly unlikely that the "cumbersome, disjointed, and incomplete nature" of aggregated snippets could provide a significant substitute for the purchase of an author's book.[148]

▦ SUMMARY ▦

The fair use doctrine attempts to balance the competing social interests of encouraging creativity by granting authors exclusive rights in copyright while allowing

---

[145] 471 U.S. 539 (1985).

[146] The Cartoon Network, LP v. CSC Holdings Inc., 536 F.3d 121 (2d Cir. 2008), *cert. denied*, 129 S. Ct. 2890 (2009).

[147] Perfect 10, Inc. v. Google, Inc., 487 F.3d 701 (9th Cir. 2007).

[148] The Authors Guild v. Google, Inc., 804 F.3d 202 (2d Cir. 2015), *cert. denied*, 136 S. Ct. 1658 (2016).

limited copying for comment and criticism. In determining fair use, courts consider the purpose of the copying, the nature of the copyrighted work, the substantiality of the copying and the effect of the copying on the market for the copyrighted work. Courts are least likely to find a fair use when works are copied for a commercial purpose and the copyright owner's commercial market is damaged. Courts are most likely to find a fair use when the original work is transformed into a new work that does not damage the potential market of the original.

UNFAIR COMPETITION

Copyright protects the property value in the expression of information and ideas. However, copyright does not protect the property value in signs, titles, names and slogans that businesses use to differentiate themselves. These commercial symbols are considered too "trivial" for protection under copyright law. Nevertheless, the considerable originality and commercial value of these symbols can be protected from theft and misleading uses by the law of unfair competition.[149]

In early common law, unfair competition was often equated with "passing off." A company passes off or "palms off" when it offers a product as someone else's by using similar labeling, packaging or advertising. Unfair competition now has a broader consumer orientation, encompassing several commercial practices that confuse or mislead the consumer. Prohibited forms of unfair competition include misappropriating the work of others, using similar titles in a misleading way, stealing trade secrets and advertising falsely. False advertising is discussed in the chapter on advertising. Theft of trade secrets is treated in the chapter about access to government records. Misappropriation and trademark infringement are discussed here.

Misappropriation

Misappropriation is the unauthorized taking of the benefit of someone else's investment of time, effort and money. In media cases, misappropriation usually involves the taking of "hot news," "free riding" on the valuable, time-sensitive information that someone else has gathered, assembled, edited and disseminated, or plans to disseminate. In misappropriation cases, the free rider competes with the originator of the information, and the aggregate of free riders might substantially threaten the viability of the information producer's business.[150]

The tort of hot news misappropriation originated in a 1918 case in which the Supreme Court ruled that the International News Service (INS) misappropriated hot news from the Associated Press. INS employees misappropriated AP breaking news by taking fresh World War I dispatches from the AP office bulletin boards and newspapers and putting the stories on the INS wire—sometimes after rewriting them, sometimes not.[151]

The Court said INS misappropriated AP's expenditure of time and effort in gathering and assembling facts. The Supreme Court noted that facts in a news report cannot be copyrighted. Nor can the effort and money expended to gather news be copyrighted. However, INS was liable for misappropriation of hot news,

---

[149] J. Thomas McCarthy, 1 *McCarthy on Trademarks and Unfair Competition* § 1.2.
[150] National Basketball Ass'n v. Motorola, Inc., 105 F.3d 814 (2d Cir. 1997).
[151] International News Serv. v. Associated Press, 248 U.S. 215 (1918).

which, the Court said, "is taking material that has been acquired . . . as the result of organization and the expenditure of labor, skill, and money, and which is salable."

A news organization, the Court said, may use a story by another news agency as a tip from which a new story can be developed through independent effort and expense. But the "bodily appropriation of a statement of fact or a news article, with or without rewriting, but without independent investigation or other expense" is misappropriation.

Reflecting new technologies, a federal court in New York found evidence of misappropriation when All Headline News (AHN) searched out AP news stories on the Internet, removed evidence of AP's ownership, and redistributed the stories under the AHN banner. The court saw evidence that AHN did no original news gathering or reporting.[152]

The AP case, later settled, followed AP's warnings to search engine companies, aggregators and competitive websites that the news cooperative would digitally track its stories and bring suit against those who used association members' products without paying.[153] AP's aggressive stance reflects the concern of many newspaper publishers and wire services in the United States and abroad, which struggle to profit through advertising from their own websites while newspaper circulation and advertising decline.

In 2011, a federal appeals court ruled that Flyonthewall (Fly), an Internet business-news company, did not misappropriate the valuable, time-sensitive stock recommendations of Merrill Lynch and other investment firms. Fly distributed the recommendations and paraphrased summaries of reports to its own customers, often before markets opened and before the investment firms could distribute the recommendations to all of their customers.[154] Fly received the recommendations from its own employees' emails and from Internet postings by clients of the investment firms who had received the reports. Reversing a lower court, the Second Circuit ruled that Fly was not free-riding off the investment firms' costly, time-sensitive recommendations. Rather, the court said Fly was exerting its own energy and expense to find, summarize and distribute the investment firms' research. "A firm's ability to make news—by issuing a recommendation that is likely to affect the market price of a security—does not give rise to a right for it to control who breaks that news and how," the court said. All parties agreed that Fly did violate the firms' copyrights when Fly copied one- and two-sentence summaries verbatim from the firms' reports.

In a 1997 case, the Second Circuit ruled that a pager company did not misappropriate NBA basketball game scores when the pager company retransmitted scores to individual subscribers. The court said the pager company was not competing with the NBA when it gathered and retransmitted facts (scores) that the NBA had broadcast in copyrighted programs.[155] The court was satisfied that the pager company expended its own effort and expense to gather and retransmit the scores which the court said were in the public domain.[156]

Sports teams and organizations control what can be broadcast, blogged and messaged from sports venues through contractual agreements and by controlling

---

[152] Associated Press v. All Headline News Corp., 608 F. Supp. 2d 454 (S.D.N.Y. 2009).

[153] Saul Hansell, "Start-Up Plans to Make Journalism Pirates Pay Up," *N.Y. Times,* July 27, 2009.

[154] Barclays Capital Inc. v. Theflyonthewall.com, Inc., 650 F.3d 876 (2d Cir. 2011).

[155] Paul Farhi, "Under NFL Rule, Media Web Sites Are Given Just 45 Seconds to Score," *washingtonpost. com*, June 30, 2007.

[156] National Basketball Ass'n v. Motorola, Inc., 105 F.3d 841 (2d Cir. 1997).

the conditions for access to events. The National Football League told news organizations they could post no more than 45 seconds per day of video shot at the facilities of the league's 32 teams. Major League Baseball limited the number of photos journalists can post online from each game and restricted audio and video coverage.

Trademarks

Another form of unfair competition is misuse of another's trademark so as to confuse the public. A trademark is the word, name or symbol a company uses to identify itself as the source of goods. The amended Lanham Trademark Act of 1946 defines a trademark as "any word, name, symbol, or device" used by a manufacturer in commerce "to identify and distinguish his or her goods . . . from those manufactured or sold by others and to indicate the source of the goods."[157] Familiar trademarks include Apple, M&M's, McDonald's, Scrabble and Kleenex. Slogans such as "Where There's Life There's Bud" can also be trademarks, as can titles of newspapers and columns. Trademarks associate a product with a specific source, whether or not the consumer can name the company that distributes M&M chocolate candies or Budweiser beer. iTunes is a trademark belonging to Apple Computer Incorporated.

Closely related to trademarks are service marks. A service mark is a symbol that is used in sales or advertising to identify services instead of products. "Elvis" and "Elvis in Concert" are service marks identifying entertainment services that Elvis Presley provided while alive and that Presley's estate owns rights to.[158] A broadcaster's call sign, such as "WXBQ," may also be registered as a service mark identifying the source of news, entertainment and advertising services. Titles, character names and other distinctive features of radio and television programs may also be service marks.

Trademarks and service marks have value as intellectual property because they represent a portion of the goodwill of a company. Trademarks and service marks are signals to consumers of the quality of goods and services. Trademarks and service marks reduce the time and effort customers expend to buy products. Because of the commercial value of trademarks and service marks, a company can acquire exclusive use of a distinctive mark.

REGISTRATION Trademark and service mark rights are created through adoption and use on goods in trade. Unlike copyright and patent, trademark does not depend on originality, invention or discovery, although a company's trademark may indeed embody imagination. Owners of trademarks and service marks are given exclusive use of their marks because of their marks' distinctiveness. The distinctiveness depends on the ability of the mark to cause the public to associate a product or service with the company that provides it.

Trademarks and service marks are protected under common law, but registration with the federal government under the Lanham Trademark Act provides recorded notice worldwide of a company's claim to ownership in a trademark or service mark. Trademark registration applications include a drawing of the mark and payment of a fee. A registered mark is denoted with a circled "R" (®) and the phrase *Registered in the U.S. Patent and Trademark Office* or the abbreviated version *Reg. U.S. Pat. & Tm. Off.* If a trademark registration is pending, companies

---

[157] 15 U.S.C. § 1127.
[158] Estate of Presley v. Russen, 513 F. Supp. 1339 (D.N.J. 1981).

sometimes print "Trademark Pending" or "TM." Once the mark is used, the Patent and Trademark Office can issue a registration certificate.[159] Registration must be renewed every ten years and can be renewed for as long as the mark is used.[160] Trademarks can also be registered in each state, usually with the secretary of state's office.

Inherently Distinctive Marks   To be registered, either a mark must be inherently distinctive or it must be a descriptive mark that has acquired a "secondary meaning." Words such as *reader, best* or *nationwide* cannot normally be registered as trademarks because they merely describe the function, use, size or quality of goods. Names such as "Tasty" candy, "Oyster House" restaurant and "Ivy League" clothes cannot be registered as trademarks because, as merely descriptive terms, they are in the public domain.

A mark is inherently distinctive—a strong mark—if it is fanciful, arbitrary or suggestive.[161] A mark is fanciful if it is coined specifically to be a trademark. "Kodak" photographic equipment and "Clorox" bleach are coined terms that have no meaning other than to identify the source of certain products.

A mark is also inherently distinctive if it is arbitrary. An arbitrary mark consists of common words or symbols whose usual meaning has no relation to the product or service to which the words are attached. The "Stork Club" restaurant is an arbitrary trademark because storks have nothing to do with a restaurant. "Old Crow" whiskey, the "Flash" music group and "Apple" computers are all arbitrary marks. These are strong marks, immediately identifying the source of specific products or services.

Suggestive marks, a third type of inherently distinctive or strong marks, are distinctive because they suggest what a product does without describing it. "Brilliant" furniture polish suggests the quality of the product. The polish in the bottle is not brilliant, but the mark suggests one's furniture will be. The same word, *brilliant,* could not ordinarily be a trademark for a diamond because brilliant would merely describe a gem. "Vanish" toilet bowl cleaner and "Coppertone" suntan lotion are other suggestive trademarks that do not merely describe a product.

Secondary Meaning   Although marks cannot be registered if they merely describe goods or services, descriptive marks can be registered if they acquire a secondary meaning. A secondary meaning is the drawing power or the commercial magnetism that develops over time in a title or in a corporate, business or professional name. A secondary meaning is the mental association in a buyer's mind between a mark or symbol and the source of a product, even though the mark is not inherently distinctive.[162] A mark acquires a secondary meaning when the name and the business become one in the public mind.

Vogue is a word of common usage, but it has acquired a secondary meaning, at least when the term appeared on a magazine. Over time, *Vogue* acquired an association between the magazine and the clothing and accessories "worn by the American woman of discriminating and fashionable tastes."[163] Other marks that began as descriptive names but developed secondary meanings include American

---

[159] 15 U.S.C. § 1051.
[160] *Id.* at § 1058.
[161] J. Thomas McCarthy, 1 *McCarthy on Trademarks and Unfair Competition* §§ 11:1–11:4, at 11–5 to 11–18.
[162] J. Thomas McCarthy, 2 *McCarthy on Trademarks and Unfair Competition* § 15.01, at 15–4 to 15–7.
[163] Conde Nast Publications, Inc. v. Vogue Sch. of Fashion Modeling, Inc., 105 F. Supp. 325, 331 (S.D.N.Y. 1952).

Airlines, Kentucky Fried Chicken and Payless drugstores. The Supreme Court has ruled that a distinctive color may be a trademark.[164]

INFRINGEMENT The purpose of a trademark is to protect consumers from being misled about the source of goods or services. When one company infringes the trademark of another, it confuses the consumer. In deciding whether a trademark has been infringed, courts consider such things as the strength of the marks, the similarity in appearance of the products, the meaning of the marks, the kinds of goods in question and the intention of the defendant in using the mark. A plaintiff in a trademark case may sue to have the infringing use stopped and to collect illegal profits, damages, attorneys' fees and court costs.

A federal court in New Jersey found sufficient likelihood of confusion to constitute infringement when Bob Russen used trademarks belonging to Elvis Presley's estate in promotions for Russen's "The Big El Show," an entertainment program imitating the dead singer's performances. Promotion for "The Big El Show" included use of "Elvis Presley," "TCB" and the "Elvis Pose," all words and symbols that are registered to Presley's estate. TCB with a lightning bolt is a trademark Presley placed on letterheads, jackets and the tails of airplanes to identify his entertainment services. The Elvis Pose is an image of Elvis in a jumpsuit hunched over a microphone and singing.[165]

The federal court said that "Elvis Presley," the "Elvis Pose" and "TCB" are strong marks distinguishing entertainment services provided first by Presley and then by his estate. Russen was using marks essentially identical to Presley's. Furthermore, the services Russen offered were very similar to Presley's. "The Big El Show" was a careful imitation of Presley's performances, and Russen's intent was to capitalize on Elvis's popularity. In finding a likelihood of confusion, the court did not suggest that people who bought tickets for "The Big El Show" would think that Elvis was alive (even though some of them might). But, the court said, the ordinary ticket buyer would likely believe incorrectly that "The Big El Show" was "related to, associated with, or sponsored by" Elvis Presley's estate.

The *Washington Post*, CNN and other media stopped a company from "framing" their web pages in a manner that the media companies said infringed their trademarks. In a negotiated settlement, Total News, Inc., which operates an Internet news site, agreed to discontinue making it appear that the *Washington Post* and other prominent news sources were associated with *Total News* on the World Wide Web.[166] *Total News* agreed to stop framing web pages belonging to the *Post, CNN* and other news sources with the *Total News* name and advertising. In a trademark and copyright infringement suit,[167] the *Post, Cable News Network, Wall Street Journal* and other news organizations claimed that *Total News* pirated their products and reduced the value of their business by presenting their web pages diminished and partially obscured by the *Total News* frame. The news organizations that argued the public would be confused when they saw the companies' news and advertising under the *Total News* name next to *Total News* advertising. In the settlement, *Total News* agreed to avoid any practices that are "likely to imply" that *Total News* is affiliated with the *Post, CNN* or the other news organizations. Visitors to the *Total News* site are able to jump to the web pages of the news organizations by

---

[164] Qualitex Co. v. Jacobson Products Co., 1514 U.S. 159 (1995).

[165] Estate of Presley v. Russen, 513 F. Supp. 1339 (D.N.J. 1981).

[166] "Settlement Halts Internet Framing and Permits Text-Only Hyperlinking," 54 *Pat., Trademark & Copyright J.* (BNA) 165 (June 19, 1997).

[167] Wash. Post Co. v. Total News, Inc., 97 Civ. 1190 (S.D.N.Y., filed Feb. 20, 1997).

clicking on plain text hyperlinks. But the news organizations' pages appear with no names or advertising associated with *Total News*.

FIRST AMENDMENT If a trademark is used in an unauthorized comedy, parody or criticism, the use may be protected by the First Amendment. The U.S. Court of Appeals for the Second Circuit has ruled that the rights of the trademark owner must be balanced against the interests of free speech when the unauthorized use is for expressive purposes.

The Second Circuit ruled that the public interest in free expression and parody outweighed the slight risk of consumer confusion when *Spy* magazine published a parody of *Cliff's Notes*, the trademarked college study guides to the great books.[168] The parody, *Spy Notes*, purported tongue-in-cheek to summarize *Slaves of New York* and other hip urban novels.

Noting that "the expressive element of parodies requires more protection than the labeling of ordinary commercial products," the Second Circuit determined that consumers would not be confused because *Spy Notes* used red, blue and white on the cover, colors very different from the distinctive yellow cover of *Cliff's Notes*. In addition, *Spy Notes*, which condensed trendy novels instead of great books, contained the word satire five times on the front cover and sold for twice the price of *Cliff's Notes*. Whatever minimal likelihood of confusion *Spy Notes* presented, it was insufficient to justify an injunction against a constitutionally protected parody, the court said.

Disparaging Trademarks A trademark not only identifies the origin of a product, but often communicates political and social messages in its own right, sometimes positively (e.g., "Asian Efficiency") and sometimes negatively (e.g., "Christian Prostitute"). Because of the expressive content in trademarks, a federal appeals court in Washington ruled in 2015 the Patent and Trademark Office (PTO) cannot refuse to register a trademark for an Asian band named "The Slants." The appeals court held, and the Supreme Court affirmed in 2017, that the PTO violated the First Amendment when it denied trademark registration for The Slants because it was said to be "disparaging."

The Lanham Act permits the PTO to deny registration to marks that disparage, slight or are scandalous or deceptive. A company or group whose trademark is denied registration can continue to use the mark, but registration creates legal benefits. A registered trademark is presumed to be valid; it becomes incontestable, and it confers exclusive use nationwide, even for regional entities. The owner of a registered trademark can sue willful infringers in federal court for treble damages.

The PTO said "Slants" had a "long history of being used to deride and mock a physical feature" of people of Asian descent. But Simon Tam, the band's front man, said members of the band "want to take on these stereotypes that people have about us, like the slanted eyes, and own them. We're very proud of being Asian—we're not going to hide that fact."

The appeals court ruled the PTO's failure to issue the registration was an unconstitutional viewpoint discrimination because the government registers trademarks whose content it approves (e.g., CelebrAsians) but refuses to register those whose content it disapproves (e.g., Slants). "It is a bedrock principle underlying the First Amendment," the court said, "that the government may not penalize private speech merely because it disapproves of the message it conveys."

---

[168] Cliff's Notes, Inc. v. Bantam Doubleday Dell Publishing Group, Inc., 886 F.2d 490, 16 Media L. Rep. 2289 (1989).

When the PTO denies registration to a "disparaging" trademark, the agency regulates expression well beyond a commercial symbol, the court said. The PTO denies Tam the ability to create a dialogue on controversial political and social issues, the court said. The band name is expressive speech through which Tam

> makes a statement about racial and ethnic identity. He seeks to shift the meaning of, and thereby reclaim, an emotionally charged word. He advocates for social change and challenges perceptions of people of Asian descent. His band name pushes people. It offends.

The Washington Redskins found support in the Slants decision for the football team's challenge to the PTO's cancellation of Redskin trademarks the PTO said offended Native Americans.[169]

Most recently, in 2019, the Supreme Court ruled in *Iancu v. Brunetti* that the Lanham Act's prohibition against registration of "immoral or scandalous" trademarks violated the First Amendment.[170] The respondent, Erik Brunetti, was an artist who founded a clothing line using the trademark FUCT. Brunetti said the mark is pronounced as four letters, but the PTO read it differently and decided that the mark was "highly offensive" and "vulgar" and that it had "decidedly negative sexual connotations." The Supreme Court, citing *Matal v. Tam*, held that the "immoral or scandalous" clause, like the disparagement clause, discriminated improperly on the basis of viewpoint.

DILUTION Even if use of a trademark would not deceive or confuse the public, a use might be prohibited if it would tarnish or dilute the value of a mark. The dilution theory has frequently been successful in preserving the value of a trademark that has been used in an unwholesome or degrading context. At the request of the Coca-Cola Company, a federal district court in New York enjoined a company from selling posters reading "enjoy cocaine." The posters were printed in a script and color identical to those used by Coca-Cola. The poster company said that the posters were only a satirical spoof, but the court said that the unwholesome association of Coca-Cola with an illegal drug could dilute the value of the Coca-Cola trademark. The court did not suggest that consumers would confuse Coca-Cola with cocaine. Rather, the court said consumers might be offended in their mistaken belief that the Coca-Cola Company treated a dangerous drug humorously.[171]

About half the states have antidilution statutes. Federal trademark laws also protect the aura and uniqueness of famous trademarks from dilution. The Federal Trademark Dilution Act protects famous trademarks such as Kodak from uses that would lessen the distinctiveness of the mark.[172] While state antidilution statutes require that a trademark owner only prove a "likelihood" of harm, the federal statute requires proof of actual dilution.

The U.S. Supreme Court held that the owners of the Victoria's Secret trademark had not proven that Victor's Little Secret, an adult video and "novelty" store, diluted the value of the Victoria's Secret trademark.[173] A federal district court had enjoined Victor's Little Secret from using that name, assuming that its continued

---

[169] In re Tam, 808 F.3d 1321 (Fed. Cir. 2015), *aff'd*, Matal v. Tam, No. 15–1293 (U.S. June 19, 2017). Richard Sandomir, "Ruling Could Help Washington Redskins in Trademark Case," *N.Y. Times*, Dec. 22, 2015.

[170] 139 S. Ct. 2294 (2019).

[171] Coca-Cola Co. v. Gemini Rising, Inc., 346 F. Supp. 1183 (E.D.N.Y. 1972).

[172] 15 U.S.C. § 1125(c).

[173] Moseley v. Victoria's Secret Catalogue, Inc., 537 U.S. 418 (2003).

use would likely tarnish the Victoria's Secret mark, the mark of a national chain of stores selling high-end, sexy clothing and beauty products. The Supreme Court, however, held that the dilution act requires proof of harm, such as a loss of a mark's distinctive identity, rather than speculation about future harm.

A growing number of dilution and infringement claims are resulting from the unauthorized use of trademarks as Internet domain names. Domain names tell Internet users where an individual or company is located in cyberspace. Sometimes the names are used in an unsavory context. A federal judge in Washington enjoined a company from using the domain name "candyland.com" to identify a sexually explicit website. The Hasbro company, manufacturer of children's toys and games and owner of the "Candy Land" trademark, argued successfully that the value of its mark was diminished by the unsavory "candyland.com."[174] Similarly, Toys "R" Us, the toy store chain, convinced a federal judge to enjoin use of the name "Adults R Us" to identify a website for adult entertainment.[175]

Cybersquatting, another practice relating to Internet domain names, became common in the 1990s. Cybersquatters profit by registering domain names of well-known trademarks and then selling the domain names back to the trademark owners. Cybersquatting became profitable because registration was inexpensive and domain name registrars did not require that requesters of famous domain names own the trademarks. Once a cybersquatter registered a domain name, the trademark owner was prohibited from using its brand name for electronic commerce and was often forced to pay "ransom" to get its name back.

To halt cybersquatting, Congress passed the Anticybersquatting Consumer Protection Act of 1999.[176] The act makes a person liable for profiting from the domain name registration of another's trademark. Under the act, a court may order the cybersquatter to forfeit the domain name and transfer it to the owner of the mark. The U.S. Court of Appeals for the Fourth Circuit ruled that Virtual Works violated the act when it registered vw.net as a domain name. The firm was ordered to relinquish vw.net to Volkswagen, owner of the VW trademark.[177]

ABANDONMENT Unlike copyrights and patents, which are protected for limited times, a trademark lasts as long as it is used in commerce. Trademarks are lost when they are abandoned. A company can deliberately abandon its trademark by ceasing to use it or by willingly giving it up. More likely, a mark will be lost because companies do not guard against use of the mark as a generic term. Words such as aspirin, cellophane and linoleum were once trademarks but gradually passed into the public domain because people used the terms to signify generic pain relievers, food wrappings and synthetic floor coverings. Escalator, shredded wheat and thermos were also once trademarks but lost their association with a particular manufacturer and passed into the public domain.

Companies place great value in their trademarks and go to great lengths to keep them from passing into the public domain. A company lawyer might call a journalist, reminding him to avoid using a trademark as a generic term. Trademark owners frequently buy advertisements reminding the media to use trademarks as proper adjectives, not as nouns or verbs. (See the Kimberly-Clark advertisement, Figure 6.1.) A writer may refer to a photocopying machine or a Xerox photocopying machine, but one should not refer to the xerox or write that a person xeroxed

---

[174] Hasbro, Inc. v. Internet Entertainment Group, Ltd., 40 U.S.P.Q.2d (BNA) 1479 (W.D. Wash. 1996).
[175] Toys "R" Us, Inc. v. Akkaoui, 40 U.S.P.Q.2d (BNA) 1836 (N.D. Calif. 1996).
[176] 15 U.S.C. § 1125(d).
[177] Virtual Works, Inc. v. Volkswagen of America, Inc., 238 F.3d 264 (4th Cir. 2001).

You may not realize it, but by using the name **Kleenex®** as a generic term for tissue, you risk erasing our coveted brand name that we've worked so hard for all these years. **Kleenex®** is a registered trademark and should *always* be followed by a ® and the words 'Brand Tissue'. Just pretend it's in permanent marker.

®Registered Trademark of Kimberly-Clark Worldwide Inc. ©2013 KCWW.

FIGURE 6.1   Kimberly-Clark, "Do Not Erase." Reprinted with permission.

a copy. Xerox and other trademarks are proper adjectives that should appear capitalized or in distinctive type with a lowercase generic noun such as photocopying machine. One wears a Stetson hat or perhaps a Stetson but not a stetson. One plays Scrabble crossword game or Scrabble but not scrabble. Journalists can avoid infringing trademarks and providing free advertising by describing students wearing western hats who photocopy their class assignments before playing a crossword game.

■ SUMMARY ■

The law of unfair competition protects intellectual property not protected by copyright. Under the common law of misappropriation, a person can sue for damages if someone steals uncopyrightable facts or appropriates the time and expense invested in gathering and disseminating information. Trademark law protects trademarks and service marks—including slogans and titles that identify the source of a product—from misleading use by others. Both strong marks and descriptive marks that have acquired a secondary meaning can be protected from infringement. When trademarks are used in parodies, newsgathering and other expressive purposes, the public's First Amendment interest in free expression may outweigh the trademark owner's property interests. Trademarks may be diluted through unsavory, though not necessarily confusing, associations. Owners of trademarks insist that their marks be capitalized and used as proper adjectives so that the marks do not lose their property value by acquiring a generic meaning.

Political Speech

Corporations have long been held to be "persons" entitled to equal protection and due process of the laws.[1] Like individuals, corporations are protected by the Fifth Amendment against being charged twice for the same crime.[2] Yet corporations, unlike individuals, have no personality and no way to achieve personal fulfillment. A corporation is, as Chief Justice John Marshall observed in 1819, a "mere creature of law" and therefore possesses "only those properties which the charter of creation confers upon it."[3] Because corporations are artificial creations of the state, they have never enjoyed all the rights of personhood. For example, corporations,

---

[1] Santa Clara County v. Southern Pac. R.R., 118 U.S. 394, 396 (1886) (equal protection); Smyth v. Ames, 169 U.S. 466, 522 (1898) (due process).
[2] United States v. Martin Linen Supply Co., 430 U.S. 564 (1977).
[3] Dartmouth College v. Woodward, 17 U.S. (4 Wheat.) 518, 636 (1819).

DOI: 10.4324/9781003264736-7

unlike individuals, can be required to testify against themselves[4] and have no right of privacy.[5]

For many years, profit-making nonmedia corporations also had no First Amendment rights. Thus, government regulations of corporate expression in elections, ballot propositions and lobbying raised few First Amendment issues. The law reflected Justice Byron White's view that speech by impersonal, state-chartered corporations deserves little or no First Amendment status because it does not further the First Amendment values of "self-expression, self-realization and self-fulfillment."[6] Accordingly, in decisions issued in 1990 and 2003, the Court limited the ability of nonmedia corporations to speak about candidates.

Yet, although nonmedia corporations are impersonal entities, they contribute social and political commentary as well as commercial information to public debate. The ExxonMobil Corporation, for example, has a YouTube channel featuring commentary on social issues. Other corporations contribute to public communication through advertisements, corporate reports, video productions and websites.

The Supreme Court first recognized in 1978 that profit-making nonmedia corporations have First Amendment interests in speaking and that consumers have First Amendment interests in hearing corporate messages. A short time later, the Court held that a New York utility could not be stopped from telling customers about the advantages of nuclear power. In a landmark 2010 decision known as *Citizens United*, the Court overturned its earlier precedents restricting corporate-funded speech about candidates.[7] The use of corporate funds to pay for speech about candidates is now fully protected by the First Amendment. Corporate involvement in elections remains a highly controversial topic. Indeed, overturning *Citizens United* via a constitutional amendment was a key aspect of the Democratic Party's 2020 platform.

The first section of this chapter examines corporate speech rights in the context of ballot measures and social issues. In addition to expressing their views on public issues, corporations are protected from having to disseminate messages they oppose. The second section examines the new legal environment for corporate speech in candidate elections. The third section explains the regulation of political broadcasting and the unique obligations imposed on corporations operating broadcast stations. Finally, the chapter discusses lobbying.

BALLOT PROPOSITIONS AND OTHER PUBLIC ISSUES

The First Amendment rights of nonmedia corporations were first developed in cases involving ballot propositions and public issues. In ballot propositions, citizens vote on issues ranging from the mundane, such as banning plastic bags, to issues representing cutting edge social change, such as abolishing the death penalty. Newsworthy ballot propositions in 2020 included legalization of medical or recreational marijuana, election policy, and the employment status of app-based rideshare drivers. Twenty-four states allow citizens to collect signatures and place propositions on the ballot concerning proposed laws or repeal of existing laws. All states, except Delaware, require state constitutional amendments to be approved by

---

[4] Andresen v. Maryland, 427 U.S. 463 (1976); Wilson v. United States, 221 U.S. 361 (1911).
[5] California Bankers Ass'n v. Shultz, 416 U.S. 21 (1974); United States v. Morton Salt Co., 338 U.S. 632 (1950).
[6] First Nat'l Bank of Boston v. Bellotti, 435 U.S. 765, 804–5 (1978) (White, J., dissenting).
[7] 558 U.S. 310 (2010).

voters. At the national level, there is no provision for ballot propositions. However, many municipal and county governments frequently utilize ballot propositions. Ballot propositions were initiated early in the 1900s to neutralize the power of well-financed lobbyists over legislatures. The reform was supposed to provide citizens a direct voice in governmental policy and discourage legislators from acting only in response to powerful, narrow interests.

States also have expressed concern that commercial corporations may dominate political debate through the ballot proposition process. To prevent this, several states, including Massachusetts, passed statutes prohibiting corporate financial participation in ballot propositions. The Massachusetts law said corporations could not buy ads supporting or opposing a ballot issue unless the ballot measure related directly to the business of the corporation. The First National Bank of Boston challenged the law because the bank wanted to buy newspaper advertisements opposing a personal income tax. The attorney general of Massachusetts, Francis Bellotti, said First National's ads would violate the statute because the personal income tax proposal did not relate directly to the bank's business. First National then sued Bellotti, arguing that the state law infringed the company's First Amendment rights.[8]

In ruling for the bank in *First National Bank of Boston v. Bellotti*,[9] and for other corporations in later cases, the Supreme Court has created an almost unlimited First Amendment freedom for nonmedia corporations to spend money to support ballot propositions and other social issues. *Bellotti* is founded on the right of citizens to receive political speech by corporations.

The Right to Receive Political Content

Central to the Court's ruling in *Bellotti* was the political nature of First National's proposed advertisement. Speech about a tax referendum, the Court said, is constitutionally protected speech "at the heart of the First Amendment's protection." The constitutional question, the Court said, was "whether the corporate identity of the speaker deprives this proposed speech of what otherwise would be its clear entitlement to protection." Because the Court concluded that political speech retains its constitutional status regardless of its corporate source, the Court declared the Massachusetts statute unconstitutional.

Although the Court recognized the constitutional value of the bank's political advertisements, the Court also recognized citizens' rights to receive corporate information. Corporate speech on a referendum is constitutionally protected, the Court said, "not so much because it pertains to the seller's business as because it furthers the societal interest in the 'free flow of commercial information'" to the public. Explaining the First Amendment right to receive information, the Court drew on recent cases emphasizing the right to receive expression, such as *Virginia State Board of Pharmacy v. Virginia Citizens Consumer Council*,[10] an advertising case decided two years before *Bellotti*. In *Virginia Pharmacy*, the Court said a state statute prohibiting price advertising of prescription drugs violated citizens' First Amendment right to receive information and make thoughtful choices. Similarly in *Bellotti*, the Court said citizens have a right to receive political information about a tax referendum, information that is "indispensable to decision-making in a

---

[8] *See* William E. Lee, "Inside the *Bellotti* Court," 39 *Cardozo Arts & Ent. L.J.* 55 (2021).
[9] 435 U.S. 765 (1978).
[10] 425 U.S. 748 (1976).

democracy." According to the *Bellotti* opinion, the government could not discriminate against certain speakers because the "inherent worth of the speech in terms
of its capacity for informing the public does not depend upon the identity of its
source, whether corporation, association, union, or individual."

To the Supreme Court, a ballot proposition is just one of many social and
political issues about which corporations might speak. "The freedom of speech and
of the press guaranteed by the Constitution," the Court said in *Bellotti*, "embraces
at the least the liberty to discuss publicly and truthfully all matters of public concern without previous restraint or fear of subsequent punishment."[11] The Court's
broad vision of constitutionally protected corporate speech was confirmed two
years later when the justices ruled that the Public Service Commission of New
York could not bar a regulated utility from telling its customers about the benefits
of nuclear power. The Court in *Consolidated Edison Co. of New York, Inc. v. Public
Service Commission of New York, Inc.*[12] struck down a state regulation barring the
utility from including political brochures in its monthly bills. As a general matter,
the Court said, "the First Amendment means that the government has no power
to restrict expression because of its message, its ideas, its subject matter or its
content."[13]

The Court did not rule in *Bellotti* that all corporate political speech is constitutionally protected. The government might regulate corporate expression, the Court
said, if the government demonstrates a compelling interest, such as the need to
preserve the integrity of the electoral process from corporate domination. However,
the Court saw no evidence that "the relative voice of corporations has been overwhelming or even significant in influencing referenda in Massachusetts, or that
there has been any threat to the confidence of the citizenry in government." To be
sure, the Court said, corporate advertising may influence the outcome of a ballot
proposition, but "the fact that advocacy may persuade the electorate is hardly a
reason to suppress it." People in a democracy, the Court said, bear the responsibility to judge which speech they choose to believe, whether that of the powerful or
the weak.

Justice White, who dissented in *Bellotti*, argued that nonmedia corporations
enjoy no First Amendment right to speak or publish about matters unrelated to
their businesses. White thought the Massachusetts statute prohibiting corporate
spending in ballot propositions should prevail because speech by an impersonal
corporation, chartered by the government, does not serve the First Amendment
value of self-fulfillment. The ideas expressed by a company "are not a product of
individual choice," White said.

Freedom From Compelled Speech

Corporations not only may express themselves on public issues but also are protected from having to disseminate messages they oppose. In *Pacific Gas & Electric
Co. v. Public Utilities Commission of California*, the Supreme Court ruled a California
utility could not be forced to include a newsletter from a consumer group in the
company's billing envelopes.[14] In *Pacific Gas & Electric*, the Court overturned a

---

[11] 435 U.S. at 776 (quoting Thornhill v. Alabama, 310 U.S. 88, 101–2 (1940)).
[12] 447 U.S. 530 (1980).
[13] *Id.* at 537 (quoting Police Dep't v. Mosley, 408 U.S. 92, 95 (1972)).
[14] 475 U.S. 1 (1986).

Public Utilities Commission regulation requiring the utility to include materials from a consumer group that often challenged PG&E in rate-making proceedings.

In a 5–3 decision, the Supreme Court ruled it was unconstitutional for the Public Utilities Commission to force PG&E to carry political views with which the utility disagreed. In an opinion written by Justice Powell and joined by three other justices, the Court said forcing a utility to carry unwanted consumer messages was unconstitutional, just as the Court had earlier ruled in *Miami Herald Publishing Co. v. Tornillo* that it was unconstitutional to force a newspaper to publish a reply by a political candidate the paper attacked editorially.[15] As will be discussed later in this chapter, broadcasters are required to carry speech by political candidates.

In dissent, Justice Rehnquist argued PG&E was not forced to associate with views it opposed because the utilities commission required Toward Utility Rate Normalization (TURN) to publish a disclaimer saying PG&E did not necessarily agree with the consumer group's messages. Justice Stevens, in his dissent, argued that consumer messages are little different from other messages that corporations have traditionally been required to carry without First Amendment problems. Corporations often have been required to disseminate legal notices, print messages on loan forms and publish proposals by dissident stockholders.

▪ SUMMARY ▪

The Supreme Court has created a First Amendment right for nonmedia corporations to speak on matters of public importance. Included among corporate rights is freedom from compelled dissemination of someone else's political messages.

Corporate First Amendment protections are based primarily on the right of citizens to receive messages on ballot propositions and other political and social issues. A corporation can use its own channels of communication, such as billing envelopes and newsletters, or it can buy advertising in another medium, as the First National Bank of Boston sought to do.

ELECTIONS

If the First Amendment permits corporations to buy advertising to support referenda and other political and social issues, it might seem likely that corporations also could buy advertising to support political candidates. After all, the Supreme Court has said, freedom of expression "has its fullest and most urgent application precisely to the conduct of campaigns for political office."[16]

Until the *Citizens United* ruling in 2010, however, corporations were not allowed to spend from their treasuries to buy advertising on behalf of a federal candidate or contribute money directly to federal candidates. After *Citizens United*, corporations can buy advertising on behalf of candidates, but still cannot contribute directly to candidates. **Contributions** are gifts of money or services given directly to the candidate. Contributions to candidates are thought to present a much greater danger of corrupting the political process than **independent expenditures**, which are monies spent independently of candidates to advocate their election. Contributions, it is feared, will create a *quid pro quo*; office holders will take actions, such as sponsoring legislation, favoring their large contributors. In

---

[15] 418 U.S. 241 (1974).
[16] Monitor Patriot Co. v. Roy, 401 U.S. 265, 272 (1971).

contrast, corporate expenditures for advertising are not believed to create a *quid pro quo* arrangement. In *Citizens United*, the Supreme Court ruled that corporations, like citizens and political groups, have a constitutional right to expend money for advertising supporting or opposing a candidate.

Prior to *Citizens United*, federal law concerning corporate and union political expression was extraordinarily complex, rife with complicated rules and exceptions. For example, press corporations such as the *New York Times* could editorialize in favor of candidates, but nonmedia corporations, such as General Motors, were precluded from purchasing advertising concerning candidates. Certain nonprofit corporations were allowed to spend funds on behalf of a candidate, but only if the organization had the sole purpose of promoting an ideology and did not accept donations from businesses or labor organizations. Unions could spend unlimited amounts of money encouraging members to vote for a candidate, but only if this partisan message was delivered solely to union members and their families. *Citizens United* eliminated these restrictions, opening the way for all corporations and unions to freely spend to speak to the public about candidates.

Citizens United overturned two relatively recent cases in which the Supreme Court had upheld the constitutionality of statutes prohibiting corporate expenditures relating to candidates. Some of those prohibited expenditures, now legal, were called "electioneering communications," broadcast, cable or satellite advertisements that were prohibited during the weeks before a general election or primary. Gone now are technical rules permitting corporations to broadcast issue ads before an election, but only if those ads did not serve as the "functional equivalent of express advocacy" for or against a candidate. Now corporations can buy ads in any media, at any time, proclaiming "Vote for Mary." The *Citizens United* majority displayed much less fear of corporation-funded candidate speech than previous courts and legislatures. Opponents of *Citizens United*, such as President Obama, claimed the ruling "opens the flood-gates for an unlimited amount of special interest money into our democracy. . . . I can't think of anything more devastating to the public interest."[17] As each election since 2010 demonstrates, the fear of corporate expenditures was unfounded.

The *Citizens United* ruling places a new emphasis on disclosure of campaign expenditures, a requirement central to campaign finance law. Under *Citizens United*, campaign law may not limit the amount of money a corporation, union or individual spends on behalf of a candidate, but campaign law does require prompt disclosure of how much was spent by whom. The theory of disclosure is that citizens are entitled to know who is funding campaign messages and can better judge the credibility of a message if they know who paid for it.

The *Citizens United* ruling leaves untouched the ability of corporations to create **political action committees** (PACs) to raise and spend large amounts of money voluntarily contributed by management and shareholders. While corporations, after *Citizens United*, are no longer required to use PACs for campaign speech instead of their own treasuries, some corporations may prefer to do so for public relations purposes. And, because *Citizens United* left intact the ban on contributions to candidates from corporate treasuries,[18] PACs will continue to be the vehicle through which corporate officers and shareholders pool money for contributions to candidates.

---

[17] President's Weekly Radio Address, Jan. 23, 2010.
[18] *See* United States v. Danielczyk, 683 F.3d 611 (4th Cir. 2012) (*Citizens United* does not affect the ban on corporate and union contributions to candidates), *cert. denied*, 2013 U.S. LEXIS 1810 (Feb. 25, 2013).

Expenditures

Campaign finance reformers have sought to limit how much money could be spent by a federal candidate and a candidate's supporters, and banned corporate and union spending on behalf of a candidate, but the Supreme Court has consistently struck down limits on how much money may be spent by candidates and groups such as PACs, ruling it is unconstitutional for the government to limit speech to equalize the relative power of the rich and poor in an election. As the Court said in *Buckley v. Valeo*, "the concept that government may restrict the speech of some elements of our society in order to enhance the relative voice of others is wholly foreign to the First Amendment."[19] Until *Citizens United*, though, the Court supported restrictions on corporate and union spending relating to candidates. The ban on corporate and union candidate-related speech has been justified by reformers as preventing *quid pro quo* corruption and preventing "distortion" of the electoral process. *Citizens United* rejected both rationales.

QUID PRO QUO CORRUPTION Justice Kennedy's majority opinion in *Citizens United* agreed with the Court's earlier conclusion in *Buckley* that independent expenditures do not create the danger of *quid pro quo* corruption. The hallmark of corruption, Justice Kennedy stated, "is the financial *quid pro quo*: dollars for political favors." Although Congress compiled a record of more than 100,000 pages when it enacted the Bipartisan Campaign Reform Act in 2002 (BCRA), it was unable to uncover any examples of votes being traded for independent expenditures. While entities making large independent expenditures might gain influence over or access to elected officials, this did not mean that those officials are corrupt. "Ingratiation and access," Justice Kennedy wrote, "are not corruption."

Independent expenditures are made by non-candidates and must not be controlled by or coordinated with the candidate. An example of an independent expenditure would be Citizens United producing and advertising *Hillary: The Movie*, asserting that Hillary Clinton was unfit to be president. The movie and supporting ads would be an independent expenditure if Citizens United produced the movie and ads without consulting with any candidate's campaign. A coordinated expenditure would be considered an illegal campaign contribution. The *Buckley* Court found that independent expenditures by individuals and PACs "may well provide little assistance to the candidate's campaign and indeed may prove to be counterproductive," and Justice Kennedy applied this conclusion to corporate independent expenditures in *Citizens United*. Quoting *Buckley*, Justice Kennedy wrote that independent expenditures lack "prearrangement and coordination" with the candidate, and this "not only undermines the value of the expenditure to the candidate, but also alleviates the danger that expenditures will be given as a *quid pro quo* for improper commitments from the candidate."

DISTORTION The *Citizens United* Court also downplayed the distorting effects of corporate and union expenditures in elections, overturning bans first adopted by Congress in 1947, continued in a comprehensive overhaul of election law known as the Federal Election Campaign Act of 1971 (FECA),[20] and refined in the BCRA.[21] A central purpose of these restrictions of corporate and union expen-

[19] 424 U.S. 1, 48–9 (1976). *See also* Randall v. Sorrell, 548 U.S. 230 (2006) (finding unconstitutional Vermont's limits on the amounts spent by state candidates).
[20] 2 U.S.C. § 441b(a).
[21] 2 U.S.C. § 441b(b)(2).

ditures is to prevent the "distortion" that might result if massive corporate and union capital enters the electoral process. Congress sought to "eliminate the effect of aggregated wealth on federal elections."[22] Law in 24 states, now unconstitutional because of *Citizens United*, also prohibited corporations and unions from using treasury money to support candidates for state office.[23]

Prohibitions on corporate expenditures to prevent distortion had been upheld by the Court in *Austin v. Michigan Chamber of Commerce*,[24] a 1990 decision upholding a state restriction on corporate spending on behalf of candidates, similar to FECA's restriction, and in *McConnell v. FEC*,[25] a 2003 decision upholding BCRA's "electioneering communication" provision. In *Austin*, the Court by a 6–3 vote said Michigan's desire to avoid the distorting effects of corporate wealth was a compelling interest justifying a prohibition on election expenditures. The *Austin* Court viewed the "corporate form" as the primary danger to the integrity of the elections that Michigan wished to preserve. Operating with special privileges granted by the state, such as favorable tax treatment, corporations have the potential to develop power that should not be permitted to dominate and distort the political marketplace, the Court said.

Justice Kennedy, who wrote the *Citizens United* opinion, dissented in *Austin*, calling the ruling "the most severe restriction on political speech ever sanctioned by this Court." When Kennedy wrote for the majority in *Citizens United*, he announced that *Austin*'s distortion rationale interfered with the "open marketplace" of ideas protected by the First Amendment.[26] By suppressing the speech of corporations, the government "prevents their voices and viewpoints from reaching the public and advising voters on which persons or entities are hostile to their interests." The First Amendment, Kennedy wrote, "confirms the freedom to think for ourselves."

The ban on corporate expenditures at issue in *Citizens United* was flawed because it suppressed the speech of millions of corporations, most of which were "small corporations without large amounts of wealth." Justice Kennedy cited statistics showing that more than 75 percent of the corporations subject to federal income tax have less than $1 million in receipts per year, a fact that belied the government's argument that the statute was needed to prevent the distortion caused by large amounts of money. The law was also an ineffective means of preventing the "distorting effects" of aggregated wealth because wealthy individuals and unincorporated associations could spend unlimited amounts on independent expenditures, while "certain disfavored associations of citizens—those that have taken the corporate form—are penalized for engaging in the same political speech."

Justice Kennedy also feared that the distortion rationale could serve as the basis for a restriction on political speech by the press. The fact that FECA and BCRA allowed press corporations to editorialize about candidates[27] undercut the government's proclaimed fear of the corrosive impact of corporate wealth. It would be unconstitutional to restrict the political speech of wealthy press corporations to reduce the impact of that speech, Kennedy wrote. Yet press corporations were not entitled to greater First Amendment protection than other corporations. The government commits a "constitutional wrong" when "by law it identifies certain

---

[22] Pipefitters Local Union No. 562 v. United States, 407 U.S. 385, 416 (1972).

[23] *See* American Tradition P'ship v. Bullock, 132 S. Ct. 2490 (2012) (Montana law prohibiting corporate expenditures in state elections violates *Citizens United*).

[24] 494 U.S. 652 (1990).

[25] 540 U.S. 93 (2003).

[26] 558 U.S. 310 (2010).

[27] 2 U.S.C. § 431(9)(B)(i).

preferred speakers. By taking the right to speak from some and giving it to others," Justice Kennedy wrote, the government deprives the public of the right "to determine for itself what speech and speakers are worthy of consideration."

The Court majority in *Citizens United* distrusted government regulation of political speech. The First Amendment, Justice Kennedy wrote, is "premised on mistrust of governmental power." The speech-restrictive hand of government could be seen in the complex regulatory apparatus that had evolved to regulate corporate political speech. Prior to the enactment of BCRA, corporations were allowed to refer to federal candidates in issue ads if so-called magic words such as "Elect Jane Doe" were not used. In 2002, Congress found many corporate issue ads lacking the "magic words" were nonetheless intended to influence candidate elections by condemning or supporting a candidate's record. Congress in BCRA banned corporations and unions from even referring to candidates in issue ads broadcast near elections; the Court in *Wisconsin Right to Life v. FEC* narrowed the statute, ruling that corporate issue ads could refer to candidates unless the ad was the "functional equivalent of express advocacy."[28] Given the complexity of determining whether prospective corporate-sponsored speech, such as *Hillary: The Movie*, was "the functional equivalent of express advocacy," Kennedy noted that cautious speakers would seek an advisory opinion from the FEC before political speech took place. The FEC's power in this process, Kennedy said, was analogous to licensing laws implemented in sixteenth- and seventeenth-century England, "laws and governmental practices of the sort the First Amendment was drawn to prohibit."

Speakers should not be required to hire a campaign finance attorney or seek declaratory rulings before "discussing the most salient issues of the day," Kennedy wrote.

Justice Kennedy was also hostile to the government's effort in BCRA to target broadcast, cable and satellite political communication. "Rapid changes in technology—and the creative dynamic inherent in the concept of free expression—counsel against upholding a law that restricts political speech in certain media or by certain speakers," he wrote.

Justice Stevens's dissenting opinion, joined by Justices Ginsburg, Breyer and Sotomayor, said the majority erred in treating corporations like human beings. Stevens wrote that corporations have "no consciences, no beliefs, no thoughts . . . they are not themselves members of 'We the People' by whom and for whom our Constitution was established." Corporate speech does not promote any individual's interest in self-expression, rather, it is "derivative speech, speech by proxy," Stevens argued. Moreover, Stevens believed corporate expenditures threatened "democratic integrity" by undercutting public confidence in the fairness of elections. Finally, Stevens believed the law did not impose a serious burden on expression because corporations could use PACs to convey candidate-related messages.

The fear that *Citizens United* would result in a Super Bowl–style deluge of political ads sponsored by businesses was proven false in every election since 2010. As prominent First Amendment attorney Floyd Abrams observed, "It turns out the apocalyptic forecasts were not just inaccurate but utterly insupportable."[29]

---

[28] 551 U.S. 449 (2007).

[29] Floyd Abrams, "The *Citizens United* Disaster That Wasn't," *Wall St. J.*, Oct. 17, 2017, at A17. *See also* Conference Board Committee on Economic Development, "The Landscape of Campaign Contributions" (Nov. 2016) (concluding that businesses have not responded to *Citizens United* by engaging in independent expenditures); Bradley Smith, "Celebrate the *Citizens United* Decade," *Wall St. J.*, Jan. 21, 2020, at 18 (corporations contribute well under 10 percent of political spending).

Before Citizens United

Permitted	**Prohibited**
• Issue advertising	• Contributions to candidates
• Sponsorship of a PAC to solicit contributions from executives and shareholders or members to fund ads supporting or opposing a candidate, and make contributions to candidates	• Express advocacy ads concerning a candidate or issue ads that were the "functional equivalent of express advocacy" broadcast in the period before an election

After Citizens United

Permitted	**Prohibited**
• Express advocacy ads in any medium at any time, including the weeks before an election	• Contributions to candidates
• Issue advertising	
• Sponsorship of a PAC for political contributions and ads as before	

FIGURE 7.1 Corporate and union federal campaign activities before and after *Citizens United*.

Major business corporations do not spend treasury money on candidate ads, due to an awareness of the dangers of appearing excessively partisan. Large expenditures may alienate employees, shareholders and customers. Instead, businesses seeking to participate in political campaigns funnel money through third parties, such as Super PACs and 501(c) groups, which are discussed later in this chapter.

Unions, however, have seized upon *Citizens United* to change their political operations. Previously prohibited from using treasury funds to communicate with non-union members, unions have begun using those funds for candidate-related broadcast ads, contributions to liberal Super PACs, and outreach to non-union members by telephone and door-to-door campaigns. Among the top organizations giving money to Super PACs in the 2020 election were unions such as the Communications Workers of America.

As shown in Figure 7.1, the *Citizens United* ruling did not affect the ban on corporate and union contributions to candidates. As discussed later in this chapter, corporations and unions are still required to establish PACs to raise money for contributions to candidates.

Contributions

The Court in *Buckley* accepted the legislative purpose of contribution limits, which is to discourage political favoritism for large contributors. The *Buckley* Court distinguished contribution limits from expenditure limits, stating that a limit on the amount of money an individual gives to a candidate "involves little direct restraint on his political communication, for it permits the symbolic expression of support evidenced by a contribution but does not in any way infringe the contributor's freedom to discuss candidates and issues." A limit on contributions still allows contributors to fund speech independent of the candidate. In contrast, because expenditures are more like "pure speech" than are monetary contributions, limits on expenditures, the Court said, "impose direct and substantial restraints on political speech." A limit on campaign expenditures "necessarily reduces the quantity of expression by restricting the number of issues discussed, the depth of their exploration, and the size of the audience reached," the *Buckley* Court said.

The *Buckley* Court found that preventing *quid pro quo* corruption or the appearance of such corruption were sufficiently important interests to justify contribution limits for individuals and PACs. "To the extent that large contributions are given to secure a political *quid pro quo* from current and potential office holders, the integrity of our system of representative democracy is undermined," the Court said.

In 2000, the Supreme Court again said campaign contributions limits are constitutional,[30] upholding a Missouri law restricting campaign contributions to candidates for statewide office to $1,075. As in *Buckley*, the Court found the concern for corruption, or the appearance of corruption justified campaign contribution limits. Justice Souter, writing for the 6–3 majority, said, "Leave the perception of impropriety unanswered, and the cynical assumption that large donors call the tune could jeopardize the willingness of voters to take part in democratic governance."

In 2006, however, the Court found Vermont's low contribution limits to be unconstitutional. Under Vermont law, individuals, parties and committees could contribute only $400 to a candidate for governor during a two-year general election cycle.[31] Justice Breyer's plurality opinion in *Randall v. Sorrell* argued that contribution limits that were "too low" would prevent candidates from amassing the resources necessary for effective campaigns, especially against incumbents.

Contribution limits must be equal for all candidates for an office, the Court ruled in *Davis v. FEC* in 2008.[32] Under the "Millionaire's Amendment" of BCRA, if a wealthy candidate spent more than $350,000 in personal funds, that candidate's opponents qualified to receive larger individual contributions, triple the normal amount ($6,900 rather than the $2,300 limit in effect in 2008). The Court ruled that the law creating different contribution limits on candidates vying for the same seat unconstitutionally penalized the right to spend personal funds for campaign speech.

Similarly, an Arizona law providing public funds to candidates in response to the privately financed campaign speech of opponents or independent groups was found unconstitutional in 2011. Candidates for state office in Arizona who chose to have their campaigns publicly financed received an initial allotment. Once a privately funded candidate's expenditures exceeded the level of the initial allotment, "equalizing" funds were made available to publicly financed candidates. Roughly one dollar was made available to publicly financed candidates for every dollar spent by an opposing privately financed candidate or independent expenditure group. The Court found the law impermissibly burdened the speech of privately financed candidates and groups. A level playing field "sounds like a good thing," the Court wrote in *Arizona Free Enterprise Club's Freedom Club PAC v. Bennett*.[33] However, freedom is the guiding principle of the First Amendment, "not whatever the State may view as fair."

PERMISSIBLE CONTRIBUTIONS AND LIMITS PACs can contribute only $5,000 to each candidate per year, but they can contribute to as many candidates

---

[30] Nixon v. Shrink Missouri Government PAC, 528 U.S. 377 (2000).
[31] 548 U.S. 230 (2006).
[32] 554 U.S. 724 (2008).
[33] 564 U.S. 721 (2011).

as they want. They can also contribute $15,000 per year to national political parties and up to $5,000 per year to other committees.

In the 2021–2022 election cycle, individuals may contribute no more than $2,900 to a candidate's primary campaign and $2,900 for the general election; individuals may also contribute up to $5,000 to a PAC per year. While the Court in *Buckley* ruled base limits on contributions to a particular candidate to be constitutional, in 2014 the Court found unconstitutional a cap on aggregate contributions by an individual to all candidates, PACs and parties. In *McCutcheon v. FEC*, the Court addressed a challenge by a donor who complied with the base limits but sought to give to more candidates than allowed by an aggregate limit of $123,200.[34] Chief Justice Roberts wrote that the government "may no more restrict how many candidates or causes a donor may support than it may tell a newspaper how many candidates it may endorse." As in *Citizens United*, the Court said the only legitimate governmental interest in regulating campaign finance was in preventing *quid pro quo* corruption. While the base limits prevented *quid pro quo* corruption, the aggregate limit did not serve that interest.

The Supreme Court in 2022 heard arguments challenging a statute providing candidates could use no more than $250,000 in post-election contributions to repay loans candidates made to their campaigns before the election. The government claimed the law was necessary to prevent *quid pro quo* corruption, but a three-judge district court panel found there was no evidence of such corruption, and the law was not properly tailored. Due to the base limit of $2,900 per individual contribution, the contributions of 86 individuals, totaling $249,400, could be legally used to repay a candidate's loan. "It is hardly clear," the district court wrote, why the eighty-seventy or eighty-eighth contributor "poses a particular danger" of corruption.[35] At the Supreme Court, Charles Cooper, attorney for Senator Ted Cruz who is challenging the law, said Congress gives a "corruption hall pass" to the first 86 donors, "but abruptly closes the window on donor No. 87."[36] Several justices expressed skepticism toward the law during oral argument; a decision is expected by June 2022.

Although contributions to candidates by individuals and PACs are limited as to amount, and corporate and union contributions are prohibited, wealthy individuals, like PACs, and now corporations and unions, may make unlimited expenditures independent of a candidate.[37] The unlimited expenditures for PACs and individuals are the result of *Buckley; Citizens United* opened the doors for the unlimited corporate and union expenditures, but retained the existing ban on contributions by these organizations. Beginning in 2010, a new type of PAC, known as a Super PAC, can accept unlimited amounts from individuals, other PACs, corporations and unions.

PROHIBITED CONTRIBUTIONS Corporations and unions are barred from making contributions to federal candidates. Prohibited contributions include coordinated expenditures, gifts of money, advertising, securities, discounts, membership lists, use of facilities, broadcast time and services to candidates and their campaigns.[38] Thus, a corporate-owned advertising firm that gives free or reduced-price services to a candidate or takes a loss to benefit a candidate makes an illegal contribution. Advertisers and public relations firms may provide services to

---

[34] 572 U.S. 185 (2014).
[35] Ted Cruz for Senate v. FEC, No. 19-cv-908, 2021 WL 2269415, at 26 (D.D.C., June 3, 2021).
[36] Adam Liptak, "Justices Set to Back Cruz in Campaign Finance Case," *N.Y. Times*, Jan. 20, 2022, at A15.
[37] 2 U.S.C. § 441a(a).
[38] 11 C.F.R. § 100.52(d)(1).

candidates at regular prices. A corporate-owned broadcaster who gives free time or news tapes to one candidate but not to his or her opponent makes an illegal campaign contribution.[39]

It is also an illegal contribution for a corporation or union to allow its stockholders, employees, or members the free use of its facilities for more than an "occasional, isolated, or incidental" amount of time to voluntarily produce election materials.[40] In 2006, the FEC amended its rules, allowing employees to use corporate computers and Internet facilities for voluntary Internet political activities, such as email and blogging. These voluntary Internet activities are permissible provided the activity does not prevent the employee from completing the normal amount of work and does not increase overhead or operating costs.[41]

Disclosure

Although *Citizens United* struck down bans on corporate and union expenditures, the Court by an 8–1 vote upheld a law requiring disclosure of the sponsors of corporate and union political messages. Disclosure, the Court believed, would help citizens understand who is funding campaign messages.

A central aspect of the campaign finance laws is the requirement that the identity of donors and amounts of contributions and expenditures be publicly disclosed. The Federal Election Campaign Act (FECA) requires each political committee and federal candidate to register with the FEC and to keep detailed records of both contributions and expenditures made "for the purpose of . . . influencing" the nomination or election of a person to federal office.[42] The records must include the name and address of everyone making a contribution of more than $200, along with the date and amount of the contribution.

Federal law also requires disclosure of the source of funding for advertising that "expressly advocates the election or defeat of a clearly identified candidate, or that solicits any contribution, through any broadcasting station, newspaper, magazine, outdoor advertising facility, poster, yard sign, direct mailing or any other form of general public political advertising."[43] The identity of the sponsor must be presented clearly and conspicuously, telling who paid for the ad and whether the ad was authorized by the candidate.

Candidates and their committees also must file periodic reports containing the name of each person who has contributed to a campaign and the names of candidates and committees that have received more than $200 in a calendar year. Reports filed with the Federal Election Commission and similar reports filed under state disclosure laws must be made available for public inspection and copying. A person who fails to comply with the requirements on making, receiving or reporting contributions or expenditures aggregating $2,000 or more in one year may be imprisoned for up to a year and fined up to $25,000.[44]

The Supreme Court upheld the constitutionality of the election disclosure requirements in *Buckley v. Valeo*. The Court noted that disclosure requirements, unlike limitations on expenditures, impose no ceiling on campaign-related activities. The disclosure requirements are justified, the Court said, because they tell a

---

[39] A.O. 1978–60, Fed. Election Camp. Fin. Guide (CCH) ¶ 5350 (Sept. 1, 1978).
[40] 11 C.F.R. § 114.9.
[41] Internet Communications, 71 Fed. Reg. 18589 (Apr. 12, 2006) (modifying 11 C.F.R pts. 100, 110, 114).
[42] 2 U.S.C. §§ 431(9)(A)(i), 432(e)(1), (f)(1).
[43] 11 C.F.R. § 110.11(a)(1).
[44] 2 U.S.C. § 437g(d)(1)(A).

voter to whom a candidate may be responsive when in office. Furthermore, the disclosure requirements deter corruption by exposing large contributions and expenditures and providing the records essential for monitoring contributions.

The *Buckley* Court admitted disclosure requirements may limit the right of association by deterring some contributions. But the Court said the minor infringement on the right of association was justified by the importance of disclosure to the political process. Nevertheless, the Supreme Court said that minor political parties would not have to disclose contributions and expenditures if there was "a reasonable probability" that disclosure of contributors would subject the party to threats or harassment from government or private individuals.

In a case involving potential harassment of a political organization, the Supreme Court allowed the Socialist Workers Party to withhold the names of contributors. In *Brown v. Socialist Workers '74 Campaign Committee*, the Court forbade the state of Ohio to require disclosure of contributors to the Socialist Workers Party because there was a history of government and private harassment of the party.[45] Similarly, the U.S. Court of Appeals for the Second Circuit ruled that the Communist party was exempt from record-keeping and disclosure requirements because there was undisputed evidence of a reasonable probability that disclosure would subject contributors to threats, harassment or reprisals.[46]

Even without threats or harassment, some disclosure requirements may violate the First Amendment, particularly as applied to individuals. The U.S. Supreme Court struck down an Ohio law banning the distribution of anonymous campaign literature in *McIntyre v. Ohio Elections Commission*.[47] The 7–2 decision by the Court upheld the right of an Ohio woman to hand out anonymous leaflets opposing a proposed school tax levy. The Supreme Court pointed out the importance of anonymous political tracts throughout American political history, including the *Federalist Papers*, written by James Madison, Alexander Hamilton, and John Jay but attributed to "Publius." Authors might seek anonymity to avoid economic retribution or social ostracism or for other reasons, the majority opinion pointed out. "Anonymity is a shield from the tyranny of the majority," the Court wrote.

The implications of the *McIntyre* opinion, however, are limited. The Court noted that its ruling did not pertain to disclosure requirements that apply to political communications over the broadcast media. In *McConnell v. FEC*, the Supreme Court upheld a statute requiring disclosure of individuals or organizations spending $10,000 or more a year for broadcast advertisements referring to candidates in pre-election periods. All individuals who contribute $1,000 or more for such purposes must also be identified.[48] In *Citizens United*, the Court by an 8–1 vote reaffirmed BCRA's disclosure requirements as constitutional, rejecting claims that disclosure requirements chill donations to a group by exposing donors to retaliation. There was no proof that donors to Citizens United had faced threats or reprisals and that prompt disclosure promoted transparency. "With the advent of the Internet," Justice Kennedy wrote, prompt disclosure "can provide shareholders and citizens with the information needed to hold corporations and elected officials accountable for their positions and supporters."

---

[45] 459 U.S. 87 (1982).
[46] Federal Election Comm'n v. Hall-Tyner Election Campaign Comm., 678 F.2d 416 (2d Cir. 1982), *cert. denied*, 459 U.S. 1145 (1983).
[47] 514 U.S. 334 (1995).
[48] 2 U.S.C. § 434(f).

In 2010, the Supreme Court also rejected claims that disclosure of the names and addresses of those signing **referendum** petitions would chill the exercise of First Amendment rights.[49] Washington law treats submitted referendum petitions as public records available for public inspection.[50] Two anonymous petition signers and an organization called Protect Marriage Washington sought to prevent disclosure of the names and address of those signing a petition seeking voter approval of a new law expanding the rights of domestic partners. The plaintiffs feared that the signatories would be subject to threats, harassment and reprisals. However, by an 8–1 vote, the Supreme Court in *Doe v. Reed* found that disclosure of the typical petition would not generate reprisals against signatories. Writing for the Court, Chief Justice Roberts claimed public disclosure helps prevent petition fraud, such as forgery. Protecting the integrity of the petition process was a sufficiently important governmental interest to justify the disclosure law, Roberts said.

The continuing validity of *Doe* was undercut in 2021 when the Supreme Court, by a 6–3 ruling, found that California may not require charities soliciting contributions in the state to disclose the identity of their major donors. Writing for the Court in *Americans for Prosperity Foundation v. Bonta*, Chief Justice Roberts concluded the disclosure requirement unconstitutionally burdened donors' First Amendment rights and was not narrowly tailored.[51] The Court did not question the validity of the state's interest in preventing fraud, but the enormous amount of information the state collected was not an integral part of the state's fraud detection efforts. Although it was convenient for the state to have the donor information "close at hand," mere administrative convenience did not justify the burden on donors' rights. Measures such as a subpoena offered a more tailored approach to investigating fraud.

The parties challenging the California law said the issues were distinct from campaign disclosure laws, but the sweeping theory of *Bonta*, especially the requirement that disclosure laws be narrowly tailored, could erode political disclosure requirements. To Justice Sotomayor, writing a dissenting opinion joined by Justices Breyer and Kagan, the majority's analysis "marks reporting and disclosure requirements with a bull's-eye." Similarly, Justice Breyer commented during oral argument, "This case is really a stalking horse for campaign finance disclosure laws."

Political Action Committees

Federal election law permits corporations and unions to form and support political action committees (PACs) that can raise and spend substantial amounts of campaign money. A PAC is the political arm organized by a corporation, labor union or trade association to support candidates for elective office. PACs raise funds for their activities by seeking voluntary contributions from members and pooling them into larger, more meaningful amounts that are contributed to favored candidates and political party committees or used to fund independent expenditures. Several media corporations, including Google, Comcast and Time Warner, have their own PACs.

PACs are the most visible and controversial outgrowth of the campaign finance reform of the 1970s. There were 8,855 PACs active in the 2020 election, and except for Super PACs, they contributed $448 million to federal campaigns. Some

---

[49] 130 S. Ct. 2811 (2010).
[50] Wash. Rev. Code § 42.56.001.
[51] 141 S. Ct. 2373 (2021).

PACs favor Republicans. During the 2020 election cycle, the National Auto Dealers Association PAC gave 70 percent of its contributions to Republicans. Other PACs, especially those associated with organized labor, favor Democrats. For example, the American Federation of Teachers PAC gave 99 percent of its 2020 contributions to Democrats. Many PACs, however, support both parties. In the 2020 election cycle, Democrats and Republicans, respectively, received 48 and 52 percent of the campaign contributions from the National Association of Realtors PAC.[52]

PACs generally favor incumbents over challengers. Thus, even Democrats, especially those with powerful leadership positions or assignments on committees overseeing regulated industries, can tap business interests for campaign contributions. For example, 61 percent of $4.5 million raised for the 2020 election by Democrat Steny Hoyer, House majority leader, came from business PACs such as Comcast and Dominion Energy.

Although PACs may make both contributions and independent expenditures, most PACs focus on contributions to candidates. A special type of PAC that makes only independent expenditures, known as a Super PAC, is discussed later in this chapter.

SPONSORSHIP OF PACS Corporations, unions and trade associations can provide sponsorship critical to the success of PACs. A sponsoring company or union can pay for all costs of establishing and operating the *separate segregated funds*, as sponsored PACs are known legally. The sponsoring corporation, union or trade association may pay the salaries, overhead and costs of soliciting contributions. Corporate and union officers also may control company PACs and direct their contributions to candidates.[53] In 2020, there were 1,669 corporate PACs, 275 labor PACs and 726 trade association PACs.

PACs also may be unsponsored or independent of corporations, unions and trade associations. Independent PACs, also known as non-connected PACs, are established by independent organizations, partnerships or unincorporated associations such as Emily's List, which promotes the election of pro-choice Democratic women. Unlike sponsored PACs, which can receive unlimited funds for overhead and administrative expenses, unsponsored PACs must pay for overhead and administrative expenses out of money solicited. For example, the Microsoft-sponsored PAC paid nothing for rent and utilities in the 2020 election cycle; Emily's List paid $3.4 million for rent and utilities during that same period. However, independent PACs can solicit money from a wider range of contributors than sponsored PACs can. In 2020, there were 2,252 non-connected PACs.

SOLICITATION OF FUNDS Corporate PACs can solicit voluntary contributions from management, stockholders and their families; union PACs can solicit funds from members and their families; trade association PACs can solicit funds from individual members of the association and management and stockholders of member corporations and their families. Sponsored PACs are not supposed to solicit funds beyond their donor class. Neither management nor union PACs may solicit funds from the general public. Non-connected PACs are not subject to these solicitation restrictions; they may solicit contributions from the general public.

---

[52] The Center for Responsive Politics operates a website, OpenSecrets.org, detailing campaign finances and expenditures. *See* www.opensecrets.org/pacs/index.php.
[53] 2 U.S.C. § 441b; 11 C.F.R. § 114.5(b), (d); Pipefitters Local Union No. 562 v. United States, 407 U.S. 385 (1972).

Solicitations by non-connected PACs through public advertising must indicate who paid for and authorized the solicitation.[54]

Super PACs

In a significant shift in federal election law because of *Citizens United*, in 2010 it became legal for advocacy groups to receive contributions of unlimited amounts. Shortly after the Supreme Court issued its *Citizens United* ruling in January 2010, the Court of Appeals for the D.C. Circuit in March 2010 held that individual contributions to advocacy groups may not be limited.[55] The appellate court, however, held that SpeechNow.org, an advocacy group, could be required to register as a PAC and comply with reporting requirements relating to contributors and expenditures expressly advocating the election of federal candidates.

SpeechNow sought to make independent expenditures in the 2008 elections backing federal candidates whom it viewed as supporting the First Amendment; these expenditures were to be funded by contributions from individuals, some of whom sought to give as much as $110,000 to the group. Prior to the 2008 elections, the FEC advised SpeechNow that it must register as a PAC and limit individual contributions to $5,000 per year.

Writing for a unanimous en banc panel of the D.C. Court of Appeals, Chief Judge David Sentelle ruled that groups formed solely to make independent expenditures may receive individual contributions of unlimited amounts. Sentelle said the analysis in *SpeechNow.org v. FEC* was "straightforward" due to the *Citizens United* decision. Because *Citizens United* held that independent expenditures do not corrupt officeholders or create the appearance of *quid pro quo* corruption, the appellate court held that "contributions to groups that make only independent expenditures also cannot corrupt or create the appearance of corruption." The FEC argued that large contributions to groups that make independent expenditures could lead to undue influence over officeholders, but Sentelle said those claims "plainly have no merit after *Citizens United*." While limits on contributions to candidates were an acceptable means to prevent *quid pro quo* corruption, the government had no anti-corruption interest in limiting contributions to an independent-expenditure group such as SpeechNow," Sentelle wrote.

The *SpeechNow.org* ruling is narrow, applicable only to those advocacy groups making only independent expenditures. The ruling does not apply to PACs that make contributions to candidates. Nor does the ruling affect limits on individual contributions directly to candidates. And, the ban on union and corporate contributions to candidates remains in effect.

The Circuit Court held that the organizational and disclosure requirements applicable to PACs imposed minimal burdens and could be validly applied to SpeechNow. Because the *Citizens United* Court upheld disclosure requirements as promoting public awareness of who is funding candidate-related speech, the appellate court similarly held the public "has an interest in knowing who is speaking about a candidate and who is funding that speech." Further, requiring disclosure of such information "deters and helps expose violations of other campaign finance restrictions," such as those barring contributions from foreign citizens.

---

[54] 11 C.F.R. § 110.11(a)(3).
[55] SpeechNow.org v. FEC, 599 F.3d 686 (D.C. Cir. 2010).

PHOTO 7.1 Sheldon Adelson, founder and CEO of the Las Vegas Sands, and his wife Miriam at a January 28, 2020, White House event as President Trump welcomed Israeli Prime Minister Benjamin Netanyahu and announced details of a Middle East peace plan. The Adelsons were the top individual contributors to federal elections in 2019–2020, donating $3 million to candidates and party committees and $215 million to Super PACs.

Source: Getty Images. Used by permission.

The explosive growth of independent expenditure groups, now known as Super PACs, is transforming the federal electoral landscape.[56] Eighty-four Super PACs raised nearly $85 million for the 2010 elections. In the 2020 elections, 2,318 Super PACs raised $3.5 billion and spent $2 billion on independent expenditures. A handful of Super PACs outpaced others raising and spending money. The leading conservative Super PAC, the Senate Leadership Fund, raised $475 million and spent $293 million. The leading liberal Super PAC, Senate Majority PAC, raised $372 million and spent $230 million.

Most Super PAC expenditures are for "attack" messages opposing candidates. During the 2020 presidential election, American Bridge 21st Century, the leading pro-Biden Super PAC, spent $51 million on ads attacking Donald Trump and only $40,000 for pro-Biden ads. America First Action, the leading pro-Trump group, spent $133 million attacking Joe Biden and $45,000 in favor of Trump.

Super PAC spending has been derided as setting fire to piles of donor cash; many voters are skeptical of ads by groups unconnected to a candidate. Indeed, the campaign landscape is littered with massive expenditures that were futile. For example, the 2016 Republican presidential primaries show that substantial amounts of Super PAC money do not guarantee a candidate's success. In the primaries, Right to Rise USA raised and spent more money than any other Super PAC in an ill-fated

---

[56] Data concerning Super PACs comes from the FEC and OpenSecrets.org.

effort to support Jeb Bush. Despite Right to Rise's more than $83 million in ad spending, Bush withdrew after finishing poorly in three primaries.

Critics fear a handful of Republican billionaire "super donors" will exercise undue political influence through multimillion dollar donations to Super PACs. For example, Sheldon and Miriam Adelson gave $215 million to conservative Super PACs in 2020. However, liberal billionaires Michael Bloomberg and Thomas Steyer collectively gave $161 million to liberal Super PACs in 2020. Moreover, liberal Super PACs are the beneficiaries of large contributions by labor organizations. For example, the Carpenters and Joiners Union, the Service Employees International Union, the Laborers Union and the National Education Association collectively gave $143 million to liberal Super PACs in 2020. Thus, pro-Biden outside groups outspent pro-Trump groups by $260 million in 2020.

Super PACs are required to disclose their donors and expenditures to the FEC. Corporations, unions and wealthy individuals who wish to keep their political activities anonymous use a variety of techniques, known as "dark money." Significantly, in 2020 liberal-oriented dark money groups outspent conservatives.[57]

Dark Money Groups

Political spending and donations by groups not disclosing their donors is an increasingly important part of elections. These groups, known as dark money groups, spent more than $1 billion in the 2020 elections. Of donations and spending reported to the FEC, liberal groups injected more than $514 million in dark money into the 2020 elections, overshadowing the $200 million supporting Republicans. Dark money groups preferred to contribute to Super PACs rather than sponsor ads themselves. Opponents of dark money believe citizens should know who is funding political expression, but when a Super PAC reports a contribution from a dark money group, the identity of the donor to the dark money group is unknown.

Wealthy individuals create limited liability corporations (LLCs) to receive protection from legal and tax liabilities. An LLC may receive unlimited contributions; in turn, an LLC may make unlimited independent expenditures on political ads, or it may make an unlimited contribution to a Super PAC. LLCs are private corporations whose ownership can be difficult to trace. When an LLC makes an independent expenditure, the source of the money is disguised. Similarly, when an LLC contributes to a Super PAC, the Super PAC merely discloses that it received a contribution from the LLC, but the identity of those who funded the LLC is not disclosed. For example, in 2016 Priorities USA, a pro-Clinton Super PAC, received a contribution of $2 million from the Emerson Collective LLC, an organization created by Laurene Powell Jobs, widow of Apple co-founder Steve Jobs. Whether the money contributed by the Emerson Collective came from Ms. Jobs or another donor is unknown.

The most controversial sponsors of political ads are nonprofit tax-exempt groups organized under section 501(c) of the Tax Code. Examples of these nonprofits are 501(c)(4) social welfare groups, such as Planned Parenthood and the National Rifle Association; 501(c)(5) labor groups, such as the AFL-CIO; and 501(c)(6) trade associations, such as the U.S. Chamber of Commerce and the American Medical Association. Nonprofit 501(c) groups may receive unlimited contributions; donors are no longer reported to the Internal Revenue Service (IRS) because of a policy adopted in 2018. These groups may not have political activities as their

---

[57] Kenneth Vogel and Shane Goldmacher, "Denouncing Dark Money, Then Deploying It in 2020," *N.Y. Times*, Jan. 30, 2022, at A1.

primary purpose; the de facto rule is that no more than 49 percent of a group's expenditures may be for political purposes. In recent years the IRS has done little to enforce this limit, and groups often categorize as "educational activities" those ads discussing political issues but not supporting or opposing a candidate. These groups also avoid reporting their activities to the FEC by airing issue ads prior to 30 days before a primary or 60 days before a general election.[58]

Until 2018, 501(c) groups had to disclose donors of more than $5,000 a year to the IRS. A federal judge in 2019 found the IRS violated the Administrative Procedure Act because the agency had not allowed public comment on the 2018 rule change.[59] Consequently, in late 2019 the IRS reissued the rules but allowed for public comment as mandated by the APA. Despite receiving many comments from opponents of dark money, in 2020 the IRS formally adopted new rules that exempt almost all types of 501(c) groups from having to identify donors. In its explanation of the rules, the IRS stated it was "aware of concerns raised regarding campaign finance laws; however, Congress has not tasked the IRS with the enforcement of campaign finance laws."[60] Because the IRS had previously inadvertently disclosed the identity of donors, in violation of the Tax Code, reducing filing requirements on tax-exempt organizations would reduce the potential for inadvertent disclosure.

Due to a stalemate at the FEC, currently composed of three Democratic and three Republican commissioners, the agency in 2022 is unlikely to adopt regulations requiring donor disclosure of 501(c) organizations. Despite a 2020 ruling by the Court of Appeals vacating an FEC rule that enabled such organizations to withhold the identity of donors unless the donor had earmarked money for a *specific* independent expenditure,[61] the FEC has shown no interest in requiring greater donor disclosure.

To break the FEC stalemate, some members of Congress have proposed changing the agency from six members to five; no more than two would be affiliated with the same political party, and a tie-breaking fifth commissioner would be an independent. In addition, Democrats, who have sought for a decade to unveil the identity of dark money donors, have proposed legislation to achieve greater donor disclosure. Altering the structure of the FEC and enhanced donor disclosure are parts of a wide-ranging bill, titled the For the People Act, which barely passed the House in March 2021 over the opposition of all Republican House members. The bill faces strong opposition from Senate Republican leader Mitch McConnell, who believes increased disclosure would chill free speech rights. Democrats in 2022 do not have the 60 votes necessary to move the bill forward in the Senate; majority leader Charles Schumer sought to alter the Senate's filibuster rules in January 2022, but this attempt failed due to opposition from all Republican Senators and two Democrats, Senators Joe Manchin III and Kyrsten Sinema.

Dark money creates a "stark tension" between efforts by Democrats to win elections "and their commitments to curtail secretive political spending by the superrich."[62] As noted by Amy Kurtz, president of the Sixteen Thirty Fund, a 501(c)

---

[58] Wesleyan Media Project/Center for Responsive Politics, "Outside Group Activity, 2000–2016," Aug. 24, 2016, https://mediaproject.wesleyan.edu/disclosure-report/?msclkid=e38b9721a77f11ecae85ada2abf d2ec9.

[59] Bullock v. IRS, 401 F. Supp. 3d 1144 (D. Mont. 2019).

[60] Dep't of Treasury, *Guidance Under Section 6033 Regarding the Reporting Requirements of Exempt Organizations*, 85 Fed. Reg. 31,959 (May 28, 2020).

[61] Citizens for Responsibility and Ethics in Washington v. FEC, 971 F.3d 340 (D.C. 2020) (vacating 11 C.F.R. § 109.10(e)(1)(vi)).

[62] Kenneth Vogel and Shane Goldmacher, "Denouncing Dark Money, Then Deploying It in 2020," *N.Y. Times*, Jan. 30, 2022, at A1.

(4) group that in 2020 was a top dark money donor to liberal Super PACs, "While we are dedicated to reducing the influence of special interest money in our politics, we are also committed to level the playing field for progressives."[63]

▨ SUMMARY ▨

Campaign finance laws prohibit corporate and union contributions to candidates; gifts of "anything of value" are prohibited, including free advertising, airtime and tapes. The Supreme Court, however, ruled in *Citizens United* that prohibitions on candidate-related independent expenditures by business corporations and unions are unconstitutional. Corporations and unions can also participate in elections by forming and soliciting funds for PACs. Contributions to PACs and the amount that PACs may contribute to candidates are limited by election law, which was upheld by the Supreme Court in *Buckley v. Valeo*. However, PACs, individuals, and now corporations and unions may spend unlimited amounts independent of a candidate. The Court has also upheld the constitutionality of laws requiring disclosure of campaign contributions and expenditures, although requiring individual advocates to identify themselves may be unconstitutional. Given the polarized political environment of 2022, it is unlikely that Congress will enact laws requiring dark money donor disclosures.

Judicial Elections

Unlike federal judges who are nominated by the president and approved by the Senate effectively for life, state court trial and appellate judges are elected for limited terms in 39 states. Until recently, judicial elections were generally low-key. However, judicial elections have become increasingly contentious, with extensive spending by both candidates and outside groups. In 2018, judicial candidates and outside groups spent $39.7 million on ads; the biggest-spending outside groups predominately used dark money.[64]

To protect the independence and integrity of the judiciary, states have codes of conduct regulating what judicial candidates may say and how they raise money. The U.S. Supreme Court has addressed issues surrounding judicial elections in three cases. In each case, the Court split 5–4, highlighting the complexity of balancing judicial integrity and free expression in the context of judicial elections.

There are two competing views of judicial elections within the Court. The first rejects the special context of judicial elections as justifying abridgement of candidate speech or activities. As Justice Scalia wrote, debate on the qualifications of candidates is at the "core of our electoral process," not at the edges. The second view differentiates judicial elections from legislative and executive office elections. "Judges are not politicians," Justice Ginsburg wrote, "and the First Amendment does not require that they be treated as politicians simply because they are chosen by popular vote."

REGULATING WHAT JUDICIAL CANDIDATES SAY Every state with judicial elections has a code of judicial conduct restricting what candidates may say. Nearly every state prohibits candidates from making a pledge or promise with respect to a case or issue likely to come before the court, such as "I will always rule in favor of our hard-working law enforcement officials." These "pledge" clauses

---

[63] *Id.*
[64] Douglas Keith, *The Politics of Judicial Elections, 2017–2018* (2019).

have withstood First Amendment challenges.[65] Separate provisions prevent candidates from announcing their positions on legal or political issues, such as "I think the legislature should legalize marijuana." These so-called announce clauses, however, are unconstitutional because of *Republican Party of Minnesota v. White*, a 2002 U.S. Supreme Court opinion.[66]

The Supreme Court ruled 5–4 that judicial candidates have a right to express their views when campaigning for office. In *White*, the Court struck down a Minnesota code of judicial conduct prohibiting judicial candidates from announcing their views on "disputed legal or political issues." Under the announce clause, candidates were free to discuss their character, work habits, education and general discussions of the role of law and the courts, but they were prohibited from making position statements, even if they did not promise to maintain that position after an election. The announce clause was designed to maintain the impartiality of the state judiciary.

Justice Scalia, writing for the Court, found the announce clause failed strict scrutiny, either because the law did not advance the interest in impartiality or the definition of impartiality was implausible. If impartiality meant lack of bias toward either party to a proceeding, the announce clause was poorly tailored because it did not restrict speech for or against particular *parties* but rather speech for or against particular *issues*, Scalia said. Impartiality was not a compelling interest if it meant a lack of preconception toward any particular legal view because it is virtually impossible to find a judge who does not have preconceptions about the law. "Proof that a Justice's mind at the time he joined the Court was a complete *tabula rasa* in the area of constitutional adjudication would be evidence of lack of qualification, not lack of bias," the Court stated. Justice Scalia rejected the idea a state may choose to have judicial elections and then prevent candidates "from discussing what elections are about."

Justice Scalia noted that the Court was not addressing the "pledges and promises" clause, but Justice Ginsburg in a dissenting opinion claimed the "announce clause" and the "pledges and promises" provisions were interdependent and equally vital to promoting confidence in the impartiality of the state's judges. Ginsburg differentiated judicial elections from those of the political branches; judges represent the interests of the law, not the interests of persons or political parties. Just as states could decide that partisan elections were incompatible with the position of trust of judges, so could states balance the interests in judicial integrity and free expression within the unique setting of an elected judiciary, Ginsburg wrote.

RESTRICTIONS ON SOLICITATION As judicial candidate expenditures have increased, so have fundraising efforts of candidates and their supporters. For example, Alabama's Supreme Court campaigns cost $7.5 million in 2004, increasing to over $13 million in 2006.[67] Judicial candidates rely upon contributions, often from lawyers or business groups with issues likely to be before the judge. Sue Bell Cobb, who served as Chief Justice of the Alabama Supreme Court from 2007 to 2011, wrote, "It's terribly awkward and uncomfortable for a judge to have to ask for campaign money. But how are you going to win without it? My biggest concern

---

[65] *See, e.g.*, Carey v. Wolnitzek, 614 F.3d 189 (6th Cir. 2010) (finding pledge clause regarding "cases" and "controversies" constitutional but remanding for consideration of "issues"), *on remand*, 2012 U.S. Dist. LEXIS 142830 (E.D. Ky. Sept. 29, 2012) (finding pledge clause regarding "issues" constitutional); Pa. Family Institute v. Celluci, 521 F. Supp. 2d 351 (E.D. Pa. 2007) (upholding narrowly construed pledge clause); In re Kinsey, 842 So. 2d 77 (Fla. 2003) (same); In re Watson, 100 N.Y.2d 290 (2003) (same).
[66] 536 U.S. 765 (2002).
[67] Jed H. Shugerman, *The People's Courts: Pursuing Judicial Independence in America* 252 (2012).

is how shameful all of this looks to the public.[68] Or, as an Ohio Supreme Court justice colorfully stated, "I never felt so much like a hooker down by the bus station . . . as I did in a judicial race. Everyone interested in contributing has very specific interests. They mean to be buying a vote."[69]

To preserve public confidence in the judiciary, most states with judicial elections restrict how judicial candidates raise money. In 2015, by a 5–4 vote, the U.S. Supreme Court in *Williams-Yulee v. Florida Bar* upheld a Florida rule preventing judicial candidates from personally soliciting campaign funds.[70]

In upholding the Florida rule, Chief Justice Roberts emphasized that "judges are not politicians, even when they come to the bench by way of the ballot. And a state's decision to elect its judiciary does not compel it to treat judicial candidates like campaigners for political office." The Florida rule, preventing personal solicitation, but allowing the formation of a fundraising committee, was supported by the compelling interest in protecting the integrity of the judiciary. Judges "cannot supplicate campaign donors without diminishing public confidence in judicial integrity," Roberts wrote.

Applying strict scrutiny, the Court found the law was narrowly tailored. The solicitation ban aimed "squarely at the conduct most likely to undermine public confidence in the integrity of the judiciary; personal requests for money by judges and judicial candidates." The ban allows judicial candidates freedom to discuss any issue.

They cannot say, "Please give me money," Roberts noted.

THE INFLUENCE OF MONEY ON JUDICIAL IMPARTIALITY Businesses and interested groups, such as trial lawyers, have poured money into important judicial races, either in the form of contributions or independent expenditures. The U.S. Supreme Court concluded in 2009 that the extraordinary involvement of Don Blankenship, CEO of Massey Coal Company, in the election of a West Virginia Supreme Court justice required that the justice **recuse** himself from hearing a case involving Massey Coal.

A West Virginia jury found Massey liable in 2002 for $50 million in compensatory and punitive damages due to actions harmful to a competitor, Harman Mining. Knowing that the state's Supreme Court would consider an appeal of the verdict, Blankenship recruited Brent Benjamin to challenge Justice Warren McGraw, who was up for reelection in 2004. Blankenship contributed the statutory maximum $1,000 to Benjamin's campaign committee, gave nearly $2.5 million to "And For the Sake of the Children," a group that blanketed the state with television ads attacking McGraw as too soft on crime, and spent just over $500,000 on independent expenditures supporting Benjamin. Blankenship's $3 million in contributions and expenditures was three times the amount spent by Benjamin's own committee.

Benjamin defeated McGraw and cast the deciding vote to overturn the $50 million jury verdict in 2007 and on rehearing in 2008. Justice Benjamin denied recusal motions, asserting that he had no personal pecuniary interest in the case. Other justices, however, claimed that Blankenship had created "a cancer in the affairs of this Court."

The U.S. Supreme Court ruled 5–4 in *Caperton v. Massey Coal Co.* that due process requires a judge's recusal from a case involving a significant campaign

---

[68] Sue Bell Cobb, "I Was Alabama's Top Judge. I'm Ashamed by What I Had to Do to Get There," *Politico Magazine*, Mar.–Apr. 2015.
[69] Jed H. Shugerman, *The People's Courts: Pursuing Judicial Independence in America* 4 (2012).
[70] 135 S. Ct. 1656 (2015).

supporter.[71] Writing for the Court, Justice Kennedy found that Blankenship's "disproportionate influence," combined with the temporal relationship between the election and the pending case, created a risk of bias requiring Benjamin's recusal.

Not every campaign contribution by a litigant or attorney creates a probability of bias that requires a judge's recusal, but Justice Kennedy said this was an "exceptional case." Blankenship's contributions and expenditures "eclipsed" the total amount spent by all other Benjamin supporters and exceeded by 300 percent the amount spent by Benjamin's campaign committee. Blankenship spent $1 million more than the total amount spent by the campaign committees of both candidates combined. The temporal relationship between Blankenship's efforts and the pendency of the case was critical: "Although there is no allegation of a *quid pro quo* agreement, the fact remains that Blankenship's extraordinary contributions were made at a time when he had a vested stake in the outcome." Given these circumstances, there was an unconstitutional risk that Benjamin was biased toward Blankenship.

Chief Justice Roberts, in a dissenting opinion, questioned the "probability of bias" standard for recusal as failing to provide clear, workable guidance for future cases. Roberts posed 40 questions, such as "How much money is too much money?" to point out the uncertainties created by the majority. He believed the majority opinion requires judges "simultaneously to act as political scientists (why did candidate X win the election?), economists (was the financial support disproportionate?), and psychologists (is there likely to be a debt of gratitude?)."

Some states seek to reduce the conflicts created by money in judicial elections by limiting the amount any person may contribute to a candidate. For example, Florida limits contributions to no more than $1,000 per election to trial court candidates, and no more than $3,000 per election to a Supreme Court justice.[72] Other states require recusal when the case involves donations above a certain level. California, for example, requires that judges disclose contributions from parties and attorneys in cases before them and are disqualified from participating in a case if they received a contribution of more than $1,500 from a party or attorney for an election within the last 6 years or for an upcoming election.[73] States may not, however, limit independent expenditures by non-candidates, as such expenditures are constitutionally protected under *Buckley*.

■ SUMMARY ■

The Supreme Court has addressed issues arising from judicial elections on three occasions, each time splitting 5–4. The Court struck down an "announce clause" prohibiting judicial candidates from making position statements. The Court upheld a rule preventing judicial candidates from personally soliciting campaign funds. Where campaign donations and independent expenditures are extreme, due process requires a judge's recusal from a case involving a significant campaign supporter.

---

[71] 556 U.S. 868 (2009).
[72] Fla. Stat. § 106.08(1)(a).
[73] Cal. Civ. Proc. Code § 170.1(a)(9)(A). *See also* California Code of Judicial Ethics, Canon 3E(2)(b).

REGULATION OF POLITICAL CANDIDATE BROADCAST PROGRAMMING

In the 2019–2020 election cycle, political advertisers spent $8.5 billion across television, radio and digital media. Like most federal candidates, Joe Biden and Donald Trump spent most of their advertising dollars on television. Trump, however, spent 39 percent of his ad dollars on digital platforms such as Facebook, a sign of the increasing importance of these platforms which in 2012 accounted for only a 1.7 percent share of all political ad spending.[74] Yet Congress in 2022 remains committed to policies regulating how broadcasters treat political candidates, policies that do not apply to Internet-based media such as Facebook.

Campaign strategy for decades has relied on broadcasting as the critical advertising vehicle, although the candidate purchasing the most broadcast ads has no certainty of winning. Billionaire Michael Bloomberg's unsuccessful campaign for the Democratic presidential nomination spent a total of $505 million on broadcast, cable, radio and digital ads before he withdrew from the race after disappointing results in the March 2020 Super Tuesday primaries. Bloomberg's massive spending was unable to overcome a widely criticized performance in a February debate. Also consider the 2020 general elections, where Democrats outspent Republicans by $2 billion in the presidential, U.S. Senate, and U.S. House races. Pro-Biden television ads outnumbered pro-Trump ads two to one or even three to one in most battleground states. Yet the vote totals did not match this spending differential.[75] Despite the uncertain effectiveness of broadcast ads, the overwhelming sense among current members of Congress is that broadcast advertising is essential to their political survival.

From the inception of broadcast regulation in 1927, broadcasters have been subject to regulations concerning candidate use of their stations. Today, the FCC settles disputes involving two requirements of the 1934 Communications Act that provide access to the airwaves for political candidates. One, the equal opportunities law, requires a broadcast station to provide time for a political candidate if it has provided time for an opponent. The other, the reasonable access law, requires broadcasters to provide reasonable amounts of time for candidates running for federal office.

Both laws also apply to local cable system operators and direct broadcast satellite (DBS) system operators. FCC rules, however, sharply limit the equal opportunity and reasonable access laws to "origination programming," which is under the *exclusive* control of the cable operator or satellite provider.[76] The bulk of the programming services carried by cable and satellite systems, such as CNN or Fox News, are under the control of companies separate from local cable and satellite system operators. Hence, programming services like CNN are not subject to the political broadcasting laws. Because cable and DBS system operators originate little of their own programming, FCC interpretations of the cable and DBS "origination programming" rules have been rare; consequently, this discussion focuses on broadcasting.

Significantly, the equal opportunities and reasonable access laws do not apply to social media and other Internet-based platforms; these platforms are free to

---

[74] Steve Passwaiter, "Political Ad Spending This Year Reaches a Whopping $8.5 Billion," *Ad Age,* Nov. 23, 2020.
[75] Howard Homonoff, "2020 Political Ad Spending Exploded: Did It Work?" *Forbes,* Dec. 8, 2020. *See also* Wesleyan Media Project, "Political Ads in 2020: Fast and Furious," Mar. 23, 2021.
[76] 47 C.F.R. § 76.5(p) (cable); 47 C.F.R. § 25.701(b)(2) (DBS).

determine whether ads will be sold for political purposes. Since 2019 Twitter has banned political advertising. In 2020 Google announced it would no longer allow political ads to be directed to specific audiences based on people's public voter records or political affiliations. Facebook in 2020 prohibited political ads in the week before the November presidential election to prevent last-minute misinformation campaigns and limit the potential for civil unrest. Advocacy groups have called for government oversight of digital political ads after revelations that Russian groups purchased digital ads designed to influence the 2016 election; such regulation is unlikely to be approved unless Democrats change Senate filibuster rules, a task they failed to accomplish in January 2022.

Equal Opportunities for Political Candidates

The **equal opportunities** requirement (see Figure 7.2), initially a part of the 1927 Radio Act, states that broadcasters who provide airtime for "legally qualified" political candidates must "afford equal opportunities to all other such candidates for that office."[77]

The equal opportunities law, sometimes inaccurately called the equal time law, requires that candidates for the same office have the same opportunity to purchase broadcast time during a period of the day when they are likely to attract the same size and type of audience. However, broadcast stations do not have to limit the time provided for one candidate because an opponent cannot afford to buy the same amount of time. The FCC has recognized that Section 315 does not "equalize disparities in the financial resources of candidates."[78] If a station provides free time to one candidate, it must offer free time to any qualified opponents for the same office.

Critics of the equal opportunities law, Section 315 of the 1934 Communications Act, complain the law does not stop a rich candidate from buying far more time than an opponent can afford. Nor does Section 315 require equal treatment for independent and minority party candidates, often excluded from televised debates between candidates of the major parties, for reasons explained later in this chapter.

In enforcing the political broadcasting requirements, the FCC only responds to complaints about programs or advertisements that have been broadcast. The agency will not intervene prior to a broadcast. During the 2004 presidential election, 18 senators, all Democrats, questioned the legality of an anti-Kerry documentary *Stolen Honor* that Sinclair Broadcasting intended to air on 62 of its television stations. FCC Chair Michael Powell responded, "Don't look to us to block the airing of a program. I think it would be an absolute disservice to the First Amendment and I think it would be unconstitutional if we attempted to do so," Powell said.[79] Faced with intense public and advertiser pressure, Sinclair backed down from airing *Stolen Honor* in its entirety. Instead, Sinclair aired portions of the documentary, along with pro-Kerry material.

The FCC and federal courts have exclusive jurisdiction of Section 315 cases. In 2008, the Nevada Supreme Court overturned a lower state court's injunction ordering MSNBC to either include Representative Dennis Kucinich in a scheduled debate among Democratic Party presidential candidates or not televise the debate.[80]

---

[77] 47 U.S.C. § 315(a). 65 *See* Hon. Thomas Eagleton, 81 F.C.C.2d 423, 426 (1980).
[78] *See* Hon. Thomas Eagleton, 81 F.C.C.2d 423, 426 (1980).
[79] "FCC Won't Block Anti-Kerry Film," *Associated Press*, Oct. 15, 2004.
[80] NBC Universal v. Dist. Ct., 124 Nev. 1495 (2008).

> If any licensee shall permit any person who is a legally qualified candidate for any public office to use a broadcasting station, he shall afford equal opportunities to all other such candidates for that office in the use of such broadcasting station: Provided, That such licensee shall have no power of censorship over the material broadcast under the provisions of this section. No obligation is imposed upon any licensee to allow the use of its station by any such candidate. Appearance by a legally qualified candidate on any—
>
> 1 bona fide newscast,
> 2 bona fide news interview,
> 3 bona fide news documentary (if the appearance of the candidate is incidental to the presentation of the subjects covered by the news documentary), or
> 4 on-the-spot coverage of bona fide news events (including but not limited to political conventions and activities incidental thereto),
>
> shall not be deemed to be use of a broadcasting station within the meaning of this subsection. Nothing in the foregoing sentence shall be construed as relieving broadcasters, in connection with the presentation of newscasts, news interviews, news documentaries and on-the-spot coverage of news events, from the obligation imposed upon them under this chapter to operate in the public interest and to afford reasonable opportunity for the discussion of conflicting views on issues of public importance.

FIGURE 7.2 The Equal Opportunities Statute.

MSNBC's lawyers successfully argued Kucinich was trying to make an "end run" around the FCC and federal courts by seeking an injunction from a state court; the Nevada Supreme Court held the lower court had no jurisdiction over the matter. Kucinich's proper remedy was to complain to the FCC after the televised debate, the court said. The state supreme court also said the lower court's order was also an unconstitutional prior restraint because it prohibited MSNBC from televising the debate unless Kucinich participated. (The Nevada court did not address MSNBC's argument that Section 315 was inapplicable to a cable network.)

QUALIFIED CANDIDATES Section 315 requires broadcasters to provide equal opportunities only to "legally qualified" political candidates once other "legally qualified" candidates have been given or sold airtime. The FCC has said a person must meet three requirements to qualify as an official political candidate.

First, a candidate must have publicly announced an intention to run for office. The commission considers filing for office or fulfilling state requirements to appear on the ballot the equivalent of a public announcement. Extensive news coverage of incumbents does not mean that they have announced their intention to run again for office. The FCC said then–President Lyndon Johnson was not a candidate for the 1968 Democratic presidential nomination when the television networks broadcast an interview with him in December 1967 because he had not publicly announced his bid for reelection.[81] Senator Eugene McCarthy, who had announced his candidacy, complained he should have received airtime because he and Johnson were the opposing candidates for their party's nomination. The commission said it would be "unworkable" for the FCC to decide which potential but undeclared candidates

---

[81] Sen. Eugene J. McCarthy, 11 F.C.C.2d 511, *aff'd sub nom.* McCarthy v. FCC, 390 F.2d 471 (D.C. Cir. 1968).

in fact were candidates. In March 1968 Johnson announced he would not seek reelection.

The second requirement to be met before triggering Section 315 requirements is that a candidate meets the qualifications prescribed by law for the office. For example, any candidate for president of the United States must be a "natural born citizen" and be at least 35 years old. For example, Arnold Schwarzenegger, who was born in Austria and became an American citizen after immigrating to the United States, is not eligible to be president and therefore could not be a "legally qualified" presidential candidate.

The third requirement for a legally qualified political candidate under Section 315 is the most complicated. A candidate seeking an elective office must qualify for a place on the ballot or publicly commit to seeking election as a write-in candidate. For example, a state may require candidates for any statewide office to represent parties receiving 5 percent of the vote in the preceding election or submit a nominating petition signed by a required number of registered voters.

Under Section 315, a person seeking election as a write-in candidate must meet any legal requirements for write-in candidates. A write-in candidate also must make a "substantial showing" as a candidate—that is, engage in such campaign activities as making speeches, distributing literature, maintaining a campaign committee and establishing a headquarters. A candidate seeking nomination to public office by a convention or caucus must also make a "substantial showing" to be considered an official candidate.[82] A broadcast station cannot deny equal opportunities to any candidate simply because the person appears to have little chance of winning.

Broadcasters must provide equal opportunities only to legally qualified candidates who are competing for the same votes in a specific election. In a November general election, anyone running for the same office, regardless of party affiliation, is an "opposing candidate." In primary elections, candidates can claim equal opportunities for appearances by opponents within their party, but not for appearances by candidates running for the same office in another party.

TIME REQUIREMENTS The FCC has said emphatically that Section 315 requires stations to provide candidates with equal broadcast opportunities rather than only equal time. When a station sells time to one candidate, it must be willing to sell opponents the same amount of time at a time of day when a comparable audience can be reached. An hour of television time at 9 A.M. on Sunday is not equivalent to one hour during prime time on Sunday evening because substantially fewer people are likely to watch the morning program.

Under Section 315, political candidates cannot demand that broadcast stations allow them to go on the air at any time the candidates choose. A candidate for mayor in Chicago could not demand hour-long blocks of time instead of the five-minute segments and spot announcements the station offered.[83] Nor are stations required to provide any individual candidate free time unless free time first was given to an opponent.

In fact, under Section 315, a broadcaster need not offer any time at all to political candidates. However, broadcasters cannot avoid election coverage completely. The FCC has said broadcast licensees must provide "substantial" amounts of time for political candidates as part of the stations' requirement to serve the public

---

[82] 47 C.F.R. § 73.1940(3)(f).

[83] Martin-Trigona, 64 F.C.C.2d 1087 (1977). However, federal candidates may have some control over the kind of time they can demand, as discussed in the next section of this chapter.

interest. In addition, the federal candidate access law, discussed later in the chapter, requires broadcasters to provide "reasonable" amounts of time to each candidate running for federal office.

A broadcast station is not required to notify a legally qualified political candidate when an opponent has been granted airtime. It is up to the candidate to request the time within a week of the broadcast triggering the statute.[84]

"USE" OF BROADCAST TIME Section 315 provides that any "use" of a broadcast station by a political candidate entitles opponents to an equal opportunity. Any positive presence of candidates in a 60-second ad or a 30-minute program, including their pictures or voices, triggers Section 315. Candidates "use" broadcast time under Section 315 even if they only announce the sponsorship of an ad in a voice that can be recognized.

Campaign advertising that does not "use" a candidate's image or voice, however, does not trigger the equal opportunities doctrine. For example, it is not a "use" when an ad describes a candidate's voting record but the candidate does not appear.

Only a "positive" appearance of a candidate's voice or picture constitutes a "use" under Section 315.[85] An unfavorable depiction of a candidate by an opponent or other critic is not a "use" of a broadcast station that triggers the equal opportunities requirements, the FCC has said. The commission wanted to ensure that candidates could not claim equal opportunities after airing ads critical of their opponents but containing their opponents' pictures and voices.

A candidate's appearance need not be political to be a "use" for the purpose of Section 315. The FCC has said that distinguishing between political and nonpolitical broadcasts would require highly subjective judgments about content and could lead to increased governmental oversight of programming content. Therefore, public officials "use" the airwaves when they appear on-air on behalf of charities such as the United Fund campaigns. Television evangelists also "use" the airwaves when they participate in televised worship services if the evangelists are candidates for office.

Candidates who appear in televised entertainment programming, including movies, "use" the airwaves whether they approve of the timing of a broadcast. The airing of Ronald Reagan's movies when Reagan was an official candidate for president allowed opponents to claim equal opportunity for airtime even though Reagan was probably not consulted before the broadcasts.[86] Indeed, the FCC has ruled that an opponent may be granted time equal to the duration of a broadcast movie or radio or television program if the candidate's appearance is "substantial" and "integral" to the plot. If the candidate's appearance is not "substantial," opponents receive under Section 315 time roughly equal to the candidate's airtime.

A candidate's control over a broadcast is a key criterion in determining whether an appearance requires a broadcaster to offer opponents equal opportunity for the time of an entire program or only for the amount of time a candidate appears. A candidate's presence in a political spot, however brief, obligates a broadcaster to provide the opponent time equivalent to the entire ad. If a candidate is present in only 10 seconds of a 60-second ad, the opponent has the right to 60 seconds. Political campaign ads are presumed to be controlled by the candidate or

---

[84] 47 C.F.R. § 73.1920(b).
[85] Codification of the Commission's Political Programming Policies, 9 F.C.C.R. 651 (1994).
[86] Adrian Weiss, 58 F.C.C.2d 342, *review denied*, 58 F.C.C.2d 1389 (1976); Walt Disney Productions, Inc., 33 F.C.C.2d 297, *aff'd sub nom.* Review of the Pat Paulsen Ruling, 33 F.C.C.2d 835 (1972), *aff'd*, Paulsen v. FCC, 491 F.2d 887 (9th Cir. 1974).

the candidate's political campaign staff. However, if a candidate appears as part of a talk show controlled by a host, an opponent is entitled only to the amount of time the candidate is "on camera or on mike."[87]

EXEMPT PROGRAMMING Some programming is exempt from the equal opportunities requirement. In a 1959 amendment to the 1934 Communications Act, Congress said broadcasters do not have to provide equal opportunities for candidate appearances during newscasts, news interviews, news documentaries and "on-the-spot coverage" of news events, including political conventions and many political debates.[88]

NEWSCASTS In 1959, Congress adopted the equal opportunities exemption for political candidates on newscasts to override a decision by the FCC. The commission had decided that a third-party mayoral candidate in Chicago should be granted airtime comparable to the news coverage accorded incumbent Mayor Richard Daley and his Republican opponent. Third-party candidate Lar Daly, no relation to the incumbent, said he was entitled to time when the mayor appeared in news film accepting his nomination and meeting the president of Argentina at the Chicago airport. The FCC agreed.[89]

The Daly decision created such a furor that Congress amended the Communications Act the same year. Congress feared the FCC's interpretation of Section 315 would "dry up" broadcast coverage of political campaigns. A Senate report said broadcasters would be reluctant to show a political candidate on a news program if broadcasters would have to offer free time to opponents.[90]

For a news program to qualify as a newscast under the 1959 amendment, it must be regularly scheduled and emphasize news. The content must be determined by network or station personnel rather than by a candidate. The FCC has ruled that the *Today* show on NBC qualifies as a news show because it is regularly scheduled and emphasizes news coverage. The FCC also has ruled that *Entertainment Tonight* and *Entertainment This Week*, syndicated programs that provide spot news coverage and news interviews about entertainment, are bona fide news programs that do not trigger the equal opportunities requirement. The commission said the news exemption from Section 315 is not based "on the subject matter reported" in a show but on "whether the program reports news of some area of current events." The commission said determining the value of subjects covered by a program would be "suspect under the First Amendment."[91]

When a journalist seeking elective office appears on a news show in the role of reporter or anchor, the newscast exemption does not apply. A federal appeals court affirmed an FCC decision that on-the-air appearances by reporter William Branch would have required a Sacramento television station to provide equal opportunities to Branch's opponents.[92] Branch wanted to keep his job while he ran for a town council position in Loomis, California, but KOVR said he would have to take an unpaid leave of absence during his political campaign. The station said it would not provide the airtime necessary to meet the equal opportunities requirements of Branch's opponents during the election campaign.

---

[87] *See, e.g.*, Robert R. Benjamin, 51 P & F Rad. Reg. 2d 91 (1982).

[88] 47 U.S.C. § 315(a).

[89] CBS, 26 F.C.C. 715, 18 P & F Rad. Reg. 238, *reconsideration denied*, 18 P & F Rad. Reg. 701 (1959).

[90] S. Rep. No. 562, 86th Cong., 1st Sess. 9, 10 (1959).

[91] Paramount Pictures Corp., 3 F.C.C.R. 245 (1988).

[92] Branch v. FCC, 824 F.2d 37 (1987), *cert. denied*, 485 U.S. 959 (1988).

News Interviews and Documentaries News interviews are exempt from the equal opportunities requirement if they take place on a bona fide news interview program. Shows such as *Meet the Press, Face the Nation* and similar local programs are considered bona fide news interview programs. The FCC also considers news interview segments appearing on programs such as *The Tonight Show* to be exempt from equal opportunities requirements.

The FCC, when deciding whether a news interview program should be exempt, considers how long the program has been on the air and whether

1. the program is regularly scheduled.
2. broadcasters or broadcast journalists control the program content and format.
3. the decisions about content and format are based on reasonable journalistic judgments rather than an intention to advance a candidate's political career.
4. the selection of persons to appear is based on their newsworthiness.

The FCC regards "innovative" approaches to interview programs as acceptable. Thus, programs with extensive audience participation, such as *Jerry Springer*, have qualified for the news interview exemption. Other programs with distinctive formats, such as *Politically Incorrect* and *The Howard Stern Show*, have also qualified for the news interview exemption.[93]

In 2006, the FCC ruled the news interview segments of *The Tonight Show* qualified for the news interview exemption.[94] An interview with California governor Arnold Schwarzenegger airing during the 2006 campaign period was exempt because *The Tonight Show* was regularly scheduled; the producers controlled all aspects of the program; and decisions about format, content and participants were based on the producers' independent news judgment and not motivated by partisan purposes. The FCC's decision did not apply to all aspects of *The Tonight Show;* skits, comedy monologues, musical entertainment and similar segments did not serve the congressional intention in adopting the news interview exemption.

In 1994, the U.S. Court of Appeals for the D.C. Circuit upheld an FCC decision that allows news interviews produced by independent producers, as well as those provided by stations and networks, to qualify for the news interview exemption under Section 315.[95] The court affirmed the FCC's judgment that Congress, when it adopted the news interview exemption in 1959, intended that professional journalists rather than candidates produce and control news interview programs. An independently produced show would lose its exempt status if the producers permitted political candidates to control the program for their own political advantage.

Although an interview on a bona fide news interview program is exempt from equal opportunities requirements, an appearance by a candidate in a news documentary is exempt only if the appearance is incidental to the discussion of an issue of genuine news value. The FCC rejected a request for equal time by Richard Kay, who was competing against Robert A. Taft Jr. and Howard M. Metzenbaum in 1970 for a seat in the U.S. Senate. Taft and Metzenbaum appeared for 93 seconds in a CBS news documentary, *Television and Politics*. The commission ruled that the

---

[93] *See, e.g.*, Infinity Broadcasting Operations, Inc., Declaratory Ruling (DA-03–2865) (Sept. 9, 2003).
[94] Equal Opportunities Complaint Filed by Angelides for Governor Campaign Against 11 California Television Stations, Order (DA 06–2098) (Oct. 26, 2006).
[95] Telecommunications Research & Action Center v. FCC, 26 F.3d 185 (D.C. Cir. 1994).

program focused on the use of television by candidates rather than on either of Kay's opponents.[96]

On-the-Spot Coverage of News Events The 1959 exemption for on-the-spot coverage of news events includes live broadcasts of presidential speeches such as the State of the Union and reports to the nation during international crises. Spot news events include candidates' announcements that they are running for office and candidate appearances at parades, court proceedings and baseball games. The spot news exemption also applies to political conventions, press conferences held by political candidates and many debates among political candidates.

For example, broadcasts of press conferences are exempt news events if (1) a broadcaster made a good-faith judgment that the press conference is a bona fide news event and (2) the licensee does not intend to provide one candidate with an advantage over another.[97]

Applying those guidelines, in 1980 the FCC said that the broadcast of a press conference held by President Jimmy Carter was a bona fide news event. Senator Edward Kennedy, who was challenging Carter's renomination, complained that the president had used more than five minutes of a press conference to attack him. The networks refused to give Kennedy time under the equal opportunities rule, and the FCC affirmed the broadcasters' decision. The commission said it would not overrule the news judgments of broadcasters absent evidence they intended to promote one candidate over another.[98]

In addition to exempting live press conferences under Section 315, the FCC has decided in a series of rulings to exempt the broadcast of many debates between political candidates. Before 1975, presidential debates had not been televised since the 1960 broadcasts featuring Richard M. Nixon and John F. Kennedy. Congress had temporarily suspended the equal opportunities rule to allow broadcasters to carry the Nixon-Kennedy debates.

However, beginning in 1975, the commission gradually has exempted debates sponsored by civic organizations, broadcasters, political parties and the candidates themselves. The commission has said the factor determining whether a debate is exempt under Section 315 is its bona fide news value and not its sponsor. In 1988, the commission ruled that debates between presidential candidates George H.W. Bush and Michael Dukakis were exempt from the equal opportunities requirement even though the two major political parties sponsored them. The FCC said debates can be exempt if broadcasters make good-faith journalistic decisions that the debates are newsworthy. Televised debates, the commission said, do not give the candidates "unbridled power" to advance their candidacies. "Indeed, the adversarial nature of the debate format reduces greatly the chance of any broadcast favoritism."[99] Sponsors may define which candidates appear in debates; consequently, minor party candidates have no right to appear in debates.[100]

The U.S. Supreme Court has ruled that government-owned public broadcast stations may exclude candidates from debates as long as the exclusions are not made on the basis of a candidate's views.[101] A public station may limit debate

---

[96] Richard B. Kay, 26 F.C.C.2d 235 (1970).

[97] Petitions of Aspen Institute and CBS, 55 F.C.C.2d 697 (1975), *aff'd sub nom.* Chisholm v. FCC, 538 F.2d 349 (D.C. Cir.), *cert. denied*, 429 U.S. 890 (1976).

[98] Kennedy for President Comm., 77 F.C.C.2d 64 (Broadcast Bureau), *review denied*, 77 F.C.C.2d 971, *aff'd*, Kennedy for President Comm. v. FCC, 636 F.2d 432 (D.C. Cir. 1980).

[99] *In re* Fulani, 65 P & F Rad. Reg. 2d 644, 645 (1988).

[100] Johnson v. FCC, 829 F.2d 157 (D.C. Cir. 1987).

[101] Arkansas Educational Television Commission v. Forbes, 523 U.S. 666 (1998).

participants to candidates who are viable and "serious" without infringing the First Amendment rights of candidates not invited to participate, the Court said.

The Court upheld the decision of the Arkansas Educational Television Commission (AETC) to invite only major party candidates and others "who had strong popular support" to participate in a 1992 debate. Independent candidate Ralph Forbes, who was not included, sued AETC, claiming his First Amendment rights were abridged. The U.S. Court of Appeals for the Eighth Circuit ruled for Forbes, saying he could be excluded only if AETC had a compelling reason.[102]

Holding that political debates on public television are not a public forum, the Supreme Court said journalists need not demonstrate a compelling interest to justify excluding candidates the journalists consider unnewsworthy. As long as the publicly funded stations do not try to stifle a particular point of view, they may exercise editorial discretion when broadcasting debates among political candidates, the Court said. The station's decision to exclude Forbes was based on viewpoint-neutral journalistic discretion, not on an unconstitutional judgment to exclude Forbes because of his political views. Any other result could lead the approximately 230 government-supported public television stations not to carry any candidate debates, the Court said.

LIMITS ON BROADCASTER CENSORSHIP OF POLITICAL CONTENT
A broadcast station has no control over the content of programming aired by political candidates. Section 315 prohibits broadcasters from censoring the candidates even if their statements are racist, vulgar or defamatory. Hence, the FCC refused to tell stations they could reject the spot announcements of Georgia Senate candidate J.B. Stoner, who proclaimed himself to be a "white racist" candidate. Stoner's ad campaigned against a law he said "takes jobs from us whites and gives those jobs to the niggers." Stoner, chairman of the neo-Nazi National States Rights Party, said he was for "law and order with the knowledge you cannot have law and order and niggers too." The commission said it could not, under the First Amendment, override the provision of Section 315 prohibiting stations from censoring candidates without evidence of a "clear and present danger of imminent violence."[103] The prohibition against censoring candidate programming applies only when the candidate's voice or picture is a part of the broadcast.

Nor may broadcasters restrict offensive candidate messages to times of day when audiences are small. The Court of Appeals for the D.C. Circuit rejected an effort by a broadcaster to place candidate advertising showing pictures of aborted fetuses only in the 10 P.M. to 6 A.M. time period.[104] The appellate court feared candidates might not reach potential voters if their ads could be seen only late at night.

The station claimed the images were "harmful to children," but the appellate court found it would be difficult in some instances to separate a broadcaster's objection to a commercial's graphic images from objections to a candidate's message. A candidate might engage in self-censorship by changing the content of a commercial to ensure it would escape being channeled into the late-night hours. The court held stations are to broadcast political commercials containing graphic material just as they would advertisements without such images.

Because candidate ads cannot be edited under Section 315, the U.S. Supreme Court ruled licensees are not responsible for libelous remarks occurring during

---

[102] Forbes v. Arkansas Educational Television Communication Network Foundation, 93 F.3d 497 (8th Cir. 1996).
[103] Letter to Lonnie King, 36 F.C.C.2d 635 (1972).
[104] Becker v. FCC, 95 F.3d 75 (D.C. Cir. 1996).

equal opportunities "uses." If the licensees were liable for the defamatory remarks of a candidate they could not edit, the Court said, they would be penalized for doing what the law intended them to do—provide broadcast time for political candidates.[105] Of course, the candidates themselves are legally responsible for defamatory or other illegal remarks they make over the air.

Broadcasters are responsible for libel conveyed by non-candidates, such as Super PACs. Consequently, stations may request changes to submitted ads by non-candidates and refuse to carry ads by these groups.

RATES AND SPONSOR IDENTIFICATION The equal opportunities provision requires broadcasters to charge political candidates the station's lowest advertising rates 45 days before a primary election and 60 days before a general election. Before the 45- and 60-day time periods, broadcasters can charge candidates what they normally charge advertisers buying the same amounts of time.[106] Stations are under no obligation to provide discounted rates to Super PACs. During recent elections, Super PACs have paid up to nine times what candidates paid.

When fulfilling equal opportunities obligations, broadcasters can charge candidates only what they charge their largest-volume advertisers for the same amount of time at the same time of the broadcast day. If a radio station charges $200 for a single one-minute commercial but $125 for each of 15 one-minute commercials sold as a package, the station must sell a single one-minute commercial to a candidate for $125. Federal candidate advertisements referring to an opponent qualify for the reduced rates only if the candidate's voice or image appears, accompanied by a statement that the candidate approved[107] of the ad. Federal law also requires that an announcement specify who paid for the ad. In *Citizens United*, the Supreme Court by an 8–1 vote upheld a requirement that televised "electioneering communications" paid for by non-candidates must include a disclaimer stating the ad was not authorized by a candidate and must identify the sponsor.[108] There was no showing that these requirements would chill speech, the Court stated.

FCC rules concerning sponsorship identification impose enhanced disclosure obligations for ads on "controversial issues of public importance." The ad must state it was "paid for" or "sponsored by" the organization that paid for the ad. In 2016 Cumulus Radio agreed to pay a $540,000 penalty for airing ads promoting a hydroelectric project without the language "paid for" or "sponsored by" Northern Pass Transmission, the company behind the project.

Broadcasters must make available for public inspection extensive records documenting purchase requests for ads relating to elections, national legislative issues or other controversial issues.[109] These requirements were ruled constitutional in *McConnell v. FEC*. In late 2019, the FCC clarified the "public file" requirements for broadcasters who accept ads on issues of national importance paid for by non-candidates. First, the file must list all the issues described in the ad, even if there are multiple issues. Second, in disclosing the governing board of an organization sponsoring an ad, the broadcaster cannot accept a single name as making up that board without making an inquiry asking if there are more officers.[110]

---

[105] Farmers Educ. & Co-op. Union of America v. WDAY, Inc., 360 U.S. 525 (1959).

[106] 47 U.S.C. § 315(b).

[107] 47 U.S.C. § 317. *See also* Codification of the Commission's Political Broadcast Rules, 9 F.C.C.R. 5288 (1994) (visual but not audio identification required for television).

[108] 2 U.S.C. § 441(d).

[109] 47 U.S.C. § 315(e); 47 C.F.R. § 73.1212.

[110] Complaints Involving the Political Files of WCNC-TV, Inc., Licensee of Station WCNC-TV, Charlotte, NC, et al., Memorandum Opinion and Order, FCC 19–100 (Oct. 16, 2019).

Access for Federal Candidates

Although Section 315 of the Communications Act requires broadcasters to provide equal opportunities to political candidates, it does not require broadcast licensees to provide time to political candidates in the first place. If only Section 315 regulated political campaign advertising, stations could avoid equal opportunity requirements by refusing to run any political ads. To ensure that broadcasters accept ads from each legally qualified candidate running for *federal* office, Congress adopted Section 312(a)(7). Under the law, a broadcast station could lose its license for willfully or repeatedly refusing to provide "reasonable access" or to permit the "purchase of reasonable amounts of time" by federal candidates. Section 312(a)(7) does not require broadcast stations to provide airtime to candidates for state or local offices.

Section 312(a)(7) was adopted in part to offset the fact that Congress was amending Section 315 to require broadcasters to charge political candidates the station's lowest advertising rates. Congress feared that imposing the low advertising rates would discourage broadcasters from selling time to political candidates. In 2000, Congress exempted non-commercial educational broadcast stations from Section 312(a)(7). Federal statutes prohibiting noncommercial educational broadcast stations from supporting or opposing any candidate for public office, or accepting payment for advertising concerning candidates, remain in effect.[111]

The FCC has said the best way to balance the desires of the candidates for airtime and the interests of the broadcasters under Section 312(a)(7) is "to rely on the reasonable, good faith discretion" of broadcast licensees. Therefore, the commission has not established a set of rules interpreting "reasonable access" in Section 312(a)(7). However, the commission has said reasonable access means that broadcasters should try to accommodate the requests for airtime of individual candidates and avoid "blanket bans" of candidate advertising except during newscasts. The commission has said "reasonable access" to broadcast facilities for candidates to federal office means that broadcasters ordinarily must provide some time for advertising during prime listening and viewing hours.[112]

The FCC also has said broadcasters are not obligated to disrupt contracts with commercial sponsors to give candidates their choice of time.[113] Additionally, in 1994, the FCC said broadcasters need not sell political candidates odd blocks of time—such as 5 minutes or 20 minutes—that might disrupt station program schedules and station contracts with networks and program syndicators. However, in 1999, the FCC said stations' decisions not to sell odd blocks of time should not be based "solely" on whether a program schedule will be disrupted. Rather, stations and candidates should engage in "good-faith negotiations" about commercial lengths.[114]

The FCC says stations deny "reasonable access" if they refuse to run any federal candidate advertising once a political campaign begins. The commission requires that broadcasters decide "reasonably," when campaigning has begun. In a decision upheld by the U.S. Supreme Court, the commission ruled that three national television networks violated Section 312(a)(7) when they turned down

---

[111] 47 U.S.C §§ 399, 399b. *See* Minority TV Project v. FCC, 736 F.3d 1192 (9th Cir. 2013) (upholding § 399b). *See generally* FCC v. League of Women Voters, 468 U.S. 364 (1984) (finding unconstitutional a ban on all editorializing by public broadcast stations receiving government funding).
[112] 1984 Political Primer, 100 F.C.C.2d at 1524–5.
[113] *Id.*
[114] Section 312(a)(7), 17 P & F Rad. Reg. 186 (1999).

requests by the Carter-Mondale Presidential Committee to buy time 11 months before the 1980 election.

The case, *CBS v. FCC*, reached the Court after the networks refused to broadcast a 30-minute Carter-Mondale campaign film in December 1979.[115] Campaign officials wanted the broadcast to coincide with President Carter's announcement that he would seek reelection. CBS offered the committee only five minutes of prime time. NBC and ABC said that they were not yet prepared to sell any time for the 1980 campaign. The networks said that demands for equal opportunity to the Carter-Mondale presentation by other presidential candidates so long before the election would disrupt their programming schedules.

The Court, following its reasoning in *Red Lion*, said the First Amendment rights of the candidates and the public outweigh those of the broadcasters. Chief Justice Burger, for the Court majority, said the access requirement "makes a significant contribution to freedom of expression by enhancing the ability of candidates to present, and the public to receive, information necessary for the effective operation of the democratic process."

Burger said the FCC reasonably decided that once a campaign has begun, broadcasters must weigh the merits of each request for time from a federal candidate. However, to justify a refusal of a candidate's request, a broadcaster must make a counteroffer or be able to explain to the commission why access would pose "a realistic danger of substantial program disruption."

Burger also concluded that the FCC may reject broadcaster determinations of whether a campaign has begun. In the Carter-Mondale case, Burger said, the FCC's decision that the 1980 presidential campaign had begun by late 1979 was reasonable because 12 candidates had formally announced their intentions to run and were actively campaigning. They were collecting endorsements and otherwise campaigning.

After the Carter-Mondale decision, one federal appeals court said the ruling that broadcasters cannot refuse all candidate advertising does not mean that broadcasters must provide free time to federal candidates. The U.S. Court of Appeals for the D.C. Circuit rejected a plea by Senator Edward Kennedy that he receive free time to offset network coverage of President Carter, whom Kennedy was opposing in the 1980 Democratic primaries. The networks said they would be willing to sell Kennedy time but would not grant him free time. The FCC and the D.C. Circuit agreed, stating that broadcasters can either provide reasonable access free or sell reasonable amounts of time.[116] Since free ad time for one candidate under Section 312(a)(7) will trigger equal opportunities obligations for all opponents under Section 315, commercial broadcasters generally refuse to provide free ad time.

■ SUMMARY ■

Section 315 of the 1934 Communications Act requires broadcast licensees to provide equal opportunities to legally qualified political candidates. The equal opportunities requirement does not apply to newscasts, news interview programs, news documentaries or live coverage of news events, including political debates.

---

[115] 453 U.S. 367 (1981).
[116] Kennedy for President Comm. v. FCC, 636 F.2d 432, 436 (D.C. Cir. 1980).

Broadcast licensees must charge political candidates the lowest advertising rates within 45 days of primary elections and 60 days of general elections. Broadcasters cannot censor the remarks of legally qualified candidates during political broadcasts and are not liable for defamatory candidate comments.

Section 312(a)(7) of the Communications Act requires commercial broadcast licensees provide "reasonable access" or permit the "purchase of reasonable amounts of time" by legally qualified candidates for federal office. Stations are not required to provide free time to federal candidates. However, in the Carter-Mondale case, the Supreme Court affirmed an FCC determination that broadcasters cannot categorically refuse all candidate ads once a political campaign begins.

LOBBYING: THE RIGHT TO PETITION

Lobbying is part of everyone's First Amendment right to petition the government for redress of grievances. The right to petition also applies to corporations or unions whose motives might be no loftier than to seek legislation to damage a competitor.[117] In 2020, $3.5 billion was spent on lobbying the federal government; among the top spenders were the pharmaceutical and health care industries, both subject to intensive interest by Congress due to the COVID-19 pandemic. Traditionally, heavily regulated industries such as telecommunications have been among the top spenders on lobbying. Recently, social media companies, facing intense Congressional criticism regarding the harmful impact of their platforms on young children and adolescents, have markedly increased their lobbying expenditures. Facebook, for example, spent $14.6 million on lobbying in 2021, up from $1.3 million a decade earlier.

Lobbying the government may be carried out through direct contacts with legislators or through indirect public relations campaigns, sometimes called *grassroots lobbying*. Either form is protected by the First Amendment. However, lobbyists are required to comply with extensive disclosure requirements. For many years, lobbying was regulated by the Federal Regulation of Lobbying Act of 1946. However, in 1995, Congress passed a new law—the Lobbying Disclosure Act of 1995 (LDA)—designed to oversee lobbying more effectively and increase public confidence in government.[118] The old law, Congress found, had been "ineffective because of unclear statutory language, weak administrative and enforcement provisions, and an absence of clear guidance as to who is required to register and what they are required to disclose."[119] Congress amended the LDA in 2007.

Lobbying Disclosure Act of 1995

The LDA requires registration by any person whose total income for lobbying "contacts" with government is expected to exceed $2,500 over a quarterly reporting period. The act also requires organizations with in-house lobbyists to register if the organization's lobbying expenses will be more than $10,000 over a quarter. Lobbying "contacts" are defined as any oral or written communication, including electronic communication, with legislative or executive branch officials, designed to influence federal policy. As a result of this definition, grassroots lobbying is not

---

[117] Eastern R.R. Presidents Conference v. Noerr Motor Freight, Inc., 365 U.S. 127 (1961).
[118] 2 U.S.C. §§ 1601–12.
[119] *Id.* at § 1601(2).

covered by the act. About 10,000 Washington lobbyists were registered prior to the 1995 passage of the LDA, increasing to nearly 15,000 lobbyists in 2007. The number of registered lobbyists sharply declined beginning with the 2007 recession and dropped to 11,538 in 2020. Moreover, due to changes in the lobbying law enacted in 2007 and restrictions on lobbying imposed in 2009 by the Obama administration, discussed later in this chapter, some firms that previously registered many staff members, even if they did little lobbying, began limiting the number of employees registered. Nearly 3,000 registered lobbyists deregistered in 2009. The attitude has changed from "when in doubt, report" to "don't report unless clearly required."[120]

Nonprofit organizations, such as labor unions and trade associations, often must register because their principal purpose may be to influence legislation. Registered lobbyists are required to file quarterly statements identifying their clients and detailing the general areas and specific issues on which they have lobbied, including specific references to legislative bill numbers and executive branch actions. Registered lobbyists need not, however, report the names of legislators or executive branch officials they lobbied. Under the act, lobbyists must give estimates of income and expenses, although for amounts larger than $5,000, these estimates need only be rounded to the nearest $10,000. The reports are filed with the Secretary of the Senate and the Clerk of the House of Representatives. Violation of the act can result in fines; in 2015 the Carmen Group paid $125,000 to settle allegations it failed to properly disclose its activities.

Excluded from registration requirements are public officials acting in an official capacity and persons who testify on legislation before a congressional committee. Congress excluded those who testify from registering as lobbyists because Congress did not want to discourage testimony and thereby impair its ability to gather information necessary to legislate. Also excluded from registration are persons for whom lobbying makes up less than 20 percent of their work for a particular client per quarter. For example, a lawyer whose main responsibilities involved legal work for a client but who also did some lobbying for the client would not have to register if the lobbying involved less than 20 percent of the lawyer's total time spent working for that client.

Foreign Agents

Lobbyists who work for foreign "principals" are also supposed to disclose their activities. Just before World War II, Congress was disturbed to learn of well-organized, pro-German groups distributing "antidemocratic material" in the United States. To mitigate the efforts of these "subverters of democracy, and foreign-policy propagandists," Congress passed the Foreign Agents Registration Act of 1938 (FARA).[121]

The FARA, like the domestic lobbying act, relies on disclosure of agents' activities, not on suppression of their speech. Under the act, agents must report their affiliations, the way they carry out their activities, how they receive and spend money, and how they disseminate information. However, foreign agents are prohibited from spending money to influence an American political election. In *Communist Party v. Subversive Activities Control Board*, the Supreme Court said

---

[120] Peter Baker, "Groups to Push for Exceptions to Lobby Rule," *N.Y. Times*, Apr. 21, 2009, at A1. See *also* Brody Mullins and T.W. Farnam, "Recession Thinned Ranks of Washington Lobbyists Last Year," *Wall St. J.*, Mar. 12, 2009, at A4.
[121] 22 U.S.C. §§ 611–22.

Congress could require registration or disclosure when "secrecy or the concealment of associations has been regarded as a threat to public safety and to the effective, free functioning of our national institutions."[122]

Foreign "agents" who are supposed to register include any person or organization that acts "at the order, request, or under the direction or control" of a foreign principal. Foreign principals include governments, political parties, businesses and organizations. The foreign principal may be a friend or enemy of the United States.[123] A foreign agent also includes anyone in the United States who acts "as a public relations counsel, publicity agent, information-service employee or political consultant" for a foreign principal. For example, if a foreign government hires an American public relations firm, the firm becomes an agent subject to registration because the firm is "indirectly supervised, directed, controlled, financed, or subsidized" by a foreign principal. In 1995 Congress amended FARA, enabling those who lobby on behalf of a foreign commercial or other private-sector foreign entity to register under the LDA, whose disclosure requirements are less extensive than FARA's.

In addition to registration requirements, foreign agents are also required to label the "informational materials" they distribute and file copies of the material with the U.S. Justice Department.[124] "Informational material" is any communication designed to influence the American public about the interests or policies of a foreign government or to influence the foreign policy of the United States. These materials must be labeled with information about the agent's identity and the identity of the principal for whom he or she acts. The Supreme Court upheld the labeling requirement in *Meese v. Keene*,[125] stating that the labeling requirement did not involve censorship or a restraint on distribution. "To the contrary," the Court stated, "Congress simply required the disseminators of such material to make additional disclosures that would better enable the public to evaluate" the materials.

Until recently, FARA has rarely been enforced; between 1966 and 2015, only seven criminal cases were brought. Special Counsel Robert Mueller, investigating Russian meddling in the 2016 election, used FARA as a prosecutorial tool, most prominently getting Trump's former campaign manager Paul Manafort to plead guilty to violating FARA for failing to disclose his lobbying on behalf of the government of Ukraine. After Manafort's conviction, FARA registrations increased by 50 percent from the previous year. DOJ officials emphasized in late 2019 that increased enforcement of FARA remains a top priority.

Lobbying Reform

Jack Abramoff, once regarded as among the most powerful lobbyists in Washington, pleaded guilty on January 3, 2006, to charges of fraud, tax evasion and conspiracy to bribe public officials.[126] Abramoff used his close ties to Republican leaders to collect $82 million in lobbying fees from casino-rich Indian tribes. As part of his lobbying practice, Abramoff offered "things of value" to public officials in exchange for official acts. "Things of value" included lavish trips, meals and entertainment, and employment for relatives of officials. Abramoff stated, "I can't imagine there's

---

[122] 367 U.S. 1, 97 (1961).
[123] 22 U.S.C. § 611(c)(1).
[124] 22 U.S.C. § 614.
[125] 481 U.S. 465 (1987).
[126] Susan Schmidt and James Grimaldi, "Abramoff Pleads Guilty to Three Counts," *Wash. Post*, Jan. 4, 2006, at A1.

anything I did that other lobbyists didn't do and aren't doing today." In October 2006, Representative Bob Ney pleaded guilty to charges that he sponsored legislation to benefit Abramoff's clients in exchange for lavish golf and gambling trips.

Congress responded to the Abramoff scandal by enacting the Honest Leadership and Open Government Act of 2007.[127] Under the law, lobbyist-sponsored travel and gifts are severely restricted. House candidates are prohibited from flying on private aircraft; Senate and presidential candidates must pay the fair market value for flights on private aircraft. Lobbyists are prohibited from giving gifts or meals that violate House or Senate rules. Meals must be of nominal value, such as light appetizers; within the lobbyist community, this is known as the "toothpick test." Members of Congress who are convicted of accepting bribes lose their retirement benefits.

The 2007 act seeks to restrict the "revolving door" between former legislators and the lobbying industry. For example, in 2003 former Representative Billy Tauzin began negotiating for a job as head of the lobby for drug companies shortly after President George W. Bush signed a Medicare drug law authored by Tauzin. The 2007 act requires departing members of Congress to disclose negotiations with potential employers and to recuse themselves during their final months in the case of a conflict of interest. Former Senators must wait two years before they lobby Congress; former House members are banned for one year. Due to this ban, Christopher Dodd, who left the Senate in 2011 to head the Motion Picture Association of America, was unable to lobby his former colleagues during 2012 congressional debates about copyright legislation.

The 2007 act also requires disclosure of "bundling," the practice whereby lobbyists combine campaign contributions from multiple donors. Candidate committees, political parties and PACs controlled by candidates (known as leadership PACs) must disclose to the FEC the identities of registered lobbyists who provide two or more bundled contributions exceeding $15,000 per six-month period. The FEC is required to make this information available on its website. The 2007 Act also requires the disclosure of any organization that "actively participates" in the planning, supervision or control of lobbying activities. The National Association of Manufacturers (NAM) challenged this provision, claiming NAM members would be chilled from participating in public policy initiatives for fear of the consequences of disclosure. The D.C. Circuit Court of Appeals found that law to be constitutional because it did not prohibit lobbyists from saying anything; it only required disclosure.[128]

The new law requires the Secretary of the Senate and the Clerk of the House to maintain searchable electronic databases of the reports filed by registered lobbyists. Senate and House members must also file travel reports, and this information is also publicly available on the Internet. A 2009 study of these reports by the *New York Times* revealed that the new rules have reduced the number of privately financed trips taken by lawmakers, but some lawmakers and lobbyists have learned how to exploit the loopholes in the rules.[129] For example, while lobbyists themselves are not allowed to pay for lawmakers' trips, their corporate clients can. And, while lobbyists are not allowed to travel on the same plane as a lawmaker, they can meet the lawmaker at a destination.

---

[127] Pub. L. No. 110–81, 121 Stat. 735 (2007).
[128] Nat'l Ass'n of Mfrs. v. Taylor, 582 F.3d 1 (D.C. Cir. 2009).
[129] Eric Lipton and Eric Lichtblau, "Ethics Rules for Congress Curb but Don't End Paid Trips," *N.Y. Times*, Dec. 7, 2009, at A1.

Barack Obama campaigned on promises to reduce the influence of lobbyists and his administration issued a series of lobbying restrictions in 2009. On January 21, 2009, President Obama issued an executive order prohibiting executive branch appointees from receiving gifts from lobbyists, imposing a two-year ban on working on issues affecting a former employer, and imposing a two-year ban on lobbying the executive branch after leaving government service.[130] The Obama White House also announced that lobbyists would be banned from serving on federal advisory committees. These committees advise agencies on trade rules, environmental regulations, consumer protection and thousands of other government policies. In 2014, an appellate court held the advisory committee ban possibly interfered with lobbyists' First Amendment rights and remanded to a lower court;[131] in response, the Obama administration changed the policy to allow lobbyists to serve on advisory committees.

The American League of Lobbyists, the American Civil Liberties Union (ACLU) and Citizens for Responsibility and Ethics in Washington (CREW) asked that the other bans be rescinded. The restrictions discouraged registrations among lobbyists who once filed disclosure forms out of an abundance of caution. Moreover, registered lobbyists turned work over to nonregistered lawyers and business executives who can call or meet with officials without the restrictions applicable to lobbyists.[132]

Critics of the Obama reforms described the effort as "pasting a new façade onto an old game." Suddenly, working as a "strategic advisor" sounded better than lobbyist. "It's clear at this point it was a branding exercise," said Jack Quinn, a lobbyist.[133]

Donald Trump promised to "drain the swamp" in Washington, and shortly after his inauguration he issued an executive order regarding lobbying activities by executive branch appointees.[134] Appointees were barred for five years after they left office from lobbying the agency where they worked. They were allowed, however, to lobby other parts of the government. Lobbyists could join the Trump administration, but for two years they were prohibited from working on any issues they had been involved in while in the private sector. Critics noted the five-year ban would be easily evaded by masking ex-officials' activities as "consulting" once they left government. Trump repealed his executive order on the last day of his presidency, enabling members of his administration to immediately accept lucrative lobbying positions.

President Biden, on his first day in office, signed an executive order prohibiting officials who leave their government posts from lobbying the executive branch or registering as foreign agents for two years.[135] Biden's order also prevents ex-officials from advising registered lobbyists, an attempt to crack down on "shadow lobbying." This is a common practice where former officials influence policy by advising others who lobby, rather than making lobbying contacts themselves. Key Biden administration officials, such as Secretary of State Antony Blinken and Secretary of Defense Lloyd Austin, however, worked with former Obama administration officials at WestExec Advisors representing clients such as Boeing. Neither

---

[130] Executive Order 13490, "Ethics Commitments by Executive Branch Personnel," 74 *Fed. Reg.* 4673 (Jan. 26, 2009).

[131] Autor v. Pritzker, 740 F.3d 176 (D.C. Cir. 2014).

[132] Elizabeth Williamson, "Some Lobbyists Try to Skirt Stimulus Ban," *Wall St. J.*, Apr. 28, 2009, at A6.

[133] Elaina Plott, "How the Obamas Changed Washington," *Washingtonian*, Dec. 2016.

[134] Executive Order: Ethics Commitments by Executive Branch Appointees (Jan. 28, 2017).

[135] Executive Order: Ethics Commitments by Executive Branch Personnel (Jan. 20, 2021).

registered as lobbyists. The Biden order prevents for two years those appointees who were formerly registered lobbyists from participating in any matter in which they formerly lobbied. This provision does not apply to former shadow lobbyists.

The Clinton, Obama, Trump and Biden administrations have each required appointees to sign an "Ethics Pledge" acknowledging the authority of the attorney general to bring a civil action against them for violating ethics rules. Remedies for violations include forfeiting money obtained by breaching the ethics code. Neither the Clinton, Obama, nor Trump administrations brought any civil actions to enforce their codes. Despite the use of lofty language regarding maintaining public trust in government, ethics policies have been subject to lax enforcement.

▓ SUMMARY ▓

Although petitioning the government is a right guaranteed by the First Amendment, Congress requires disclosure of lobbying to prevent corruption of democratic processes. Lobbyists are supposed to register and disclose income and expenditures as well as the laws or regulations they have attempted to influence. Foreign agents, too, are supposed to register and disclose their income and expenditures. Congress enacted lobbying reforms in 2007; the Obama, Trump and Biden administrations implemented a series of restrictions on lobbying activities that are poorly enforced.

CHAPTER

8

Commercial Speech

Until the late nineteenth century, advertisements were usually simple announcements much like classified ads. In the 1700s and 1800s, artisans and merchants used small notices to tell their patrons that fabrics and other manufactured goods had arrived from abroad. The truth of advertisements was seldom an issue because consumers could usually examine the products and shun merchants who sold inferior merchandise.[1]

With the growth of mass production, advertising became more sophisticated. By the beginning of the twentieth century, manufacturers were using national advertising to convince consumers in distant markets to buy mass-produced, undifferentiated products. As markets grew and became impersonal, opportunities for profitable misrepresentations increased. Patent medicine manufacturers, in

---

[1] Daniel Pope, *The Making of Modern Advertising* 4–5 (1983).

DOI: 10.4324/9781003264736-8

particular, were notorious for their exaggerated advertising promises. Some patent medicine makers bragged that with the right advertising, they could sell dishwater.

As mass marketing developed, truth in advertising took on new importance to reputable companies. Procter & Gamble, Burpee Seeds, Quaker Oats and other producers of brand-name products wanted consumers to have faith in the truth of national advertisements. Believing the "rotten apple theory," reputable national advertisers feared that false advertising by one company damaged the credibility of the others.

Manufacturers' concerns for truth in advertising led to the formation of regulatory organizations within the business community. Truth in advertising was a major theme at the 1911 convention of the Associated Advertising Clubs of America. In 1912, the National Vigilance Committee—later the Better Business Bureau—was created. By the 1930s, a movement within the industry to clean up advertising had resulted in several codes discouraging false and misleading advertising.[2]

New legal regulations were an important tool in the effort to keep advertising honest. Most states adopted a law similar to one proposed in 1911 by the trade magazine *Printers' Ink*. The *Printers' Ink* statutes, which still form the basis for much state regulation, made it a misdemeanor to disseminate misleading advertising. On the national level, the Federal Trade Commission Act of 1914 established federal authority to outlaw deceptive acts and practices, including false advertising. Later, the Food and Drug Administration was established to oversee labeling of food, drugs, cosmetics and medical devices and to regulate the advertising of prescription drugs. The Bureau of Alcohol, Tobacco and Firearms (ATF), a division of the Treasury Department, oversees advertising and promotion of alcoholic beverages.

For many years, state and federal regulation of advertising evolved without raising questions of freedom of expression. Until the mid-1970s, commercial advertising was outside First Amendment consideration. Today, however, the Supreme Court has established limited First Amendment protections for commercial advertising, recognizing the important right of advertisers and publicists to communicate truthful information about products and services to consumers, balanced with the people's interests in being protected from untruthful, misleading or incomplete information as they make purchasing decisions.

THE FIRST AMENDMENT AND ADVERTISING

The Supreme Court first ruled that "purely" commercial advertising enjoys constitutional protection in a 1976 case involving advertising for prescription drugs. In *Virginia State Board of Pharmacy v. Virginia Citizens Consumer Council*,[3] the Court struck down a state statute prohibiting pharmacists from advertising the prices of prescription drugs. Since then, the Court has developed a complicated "commercial speech" jurisprudence that has limited government regulation of billboards, "For Sale" signs, lawyers' advertisements and other commercial messages, including advertisements for abortion referral services. A Supreme Court ruling in 2015 made government efforts to regulate commercial speech even more difficult, when the court struck down a town ordinance restricting the size of political, religious

---

[2] *See* S. Watson Dunn, Arnold M. Barban, Dean M. Krugman, and Leonard N. Reid, *Advertising: Its Role in Modern Marketing* 24–8 (1990).
[3] 425 U.S. 748 (1976).

and business signs on First Amendment grounds (see Chapter 3).[4] However, until shortly before the *Virginia Pharmacy* decision, commercial advertising had always been outside constitutional consideration.

Commercial Speech Doctrine

The Supreme Court placed advertising outside First Amendment protection in 1942, in a case called *Valentine v. Chrestensen.*[5] In that case, the Court ruled that F.J. Chrestensen had no First Amendment right to distribute handbills advertising tours of a former Navy submarine. Chrestensen distributed handbills to pedestrians in lower Manhattan, advertising 25-cent tours of his $2 million submarine moored at a state-owned pier in the East River in New York City. The handbills promised visitors a glimpse of the kitchen, torpedo compartment and crew's sleeping quarters on the S-49 submarine, also known as the "fighting monster." Children could take the tour for 15 cents.

City officials, however, told Chrestensen to stop distributing his handbills because he was violating the New York City Sanitary Code, which prohibited the distribution of "commercial and business advertising." Chrestensen then added a message to the back of his flyers protesting the restrictions imposed on him under the sanitation code. With a "political" message on one side of his submarine handbills, Chrestensen sought an injunction barring police from interfering with distribution of what he argued was constitutionally protected expression.

The U.S. Supreme Court, in a four-page decision, ruled that New York officials could stop distribution of Chrestensen's flyers without violating the First Amendment. The Court said the flyers were "purely commercial" advertising that fell outside constitutional protection. The Court dismissed the political message appended to the flyers as a ruse not to be taken seriously. With its curt decision in *Valentine v. Chrestensen*, the Court originated the "commercial speech doctrine," which was to deny constitutional protection to commercial advertising until the mid-1970s.

In 1964, the Supreme Court took a small step toward constitutional protection for advertising when it ruled in *New York Times Co. v. Sullivan* that political criticism of public officials is protected by the First Amendment, even if it is paid for (see Chapter 4 for more detail about this case). The Supreme Court rejected Police Commissioner Sullivan's argument that the criticism of Alabama law enforcement officers should have no constitutional status because the criticism was part of a paid advertisement. Another commercial element of the advertisement, according to Sullivan, was its solicitation of funds to support the civil rights movement. The Supreme Court, however, said that it was "immaterial" whether the editorial advertisement was purchased; the ad was protected political speech because it "communicated information, expressed opinion, recited grievances, protested claimed abuses, and sought financial support on behalf of a movement whose existence and objectives are matters of the highest public interest and concern."[6]

Although *Times v. Sullivan* established that paid political speech enjoys constitutional protection, the case did not create constitutional protection for "purely commercial advertising" such as a dog food ad or Chrestensen's original handbills.

---

[4] Reed v. Town of Gilbert, 135 S. Ct. 2218 (2015); *see also* Adam Liptak, "Consequences Ripple After Court Expands Free Speech," *N.Y. Times*, Aug. 18, 2015, A15.
[5] 316 U.S. 52 (1942).
[6] 376 U.S. 254 (1964).

The Supreme Court came a bit closer to protecting commercial speech in 1973 when it suggested in *Pittsburgh Press Co. v. Pittsburgh Commission on Human Relations* that it might be willing to grant constitutional status to "an ordinary commercial proposal."[7] But the Court in *Pittsburgh Press* upheld an advertising regulation that prohibited unnecessary discrimination by gender in newspaper classified advertisements.

A short time later, in *Bigelow v. Virginia*,[8] the Court struck down a state statute that prohibited advertising of abortion referral services. But ads for abortion referral services too were not "purely commercial" speech. Unlike product ads, the abortion referral ads contained factual material similar to the political content of editorials and news columns. For example, the ad at issue in *Bigelow* declared, "Abortions are now legal in New York." The *Bigelow* ad was also different from purely commercial advertisements because the service advertised was itself constitutionally protected after the court's *Roe v. Wade* decision in 1973.[9] It is more difficult to square advertising restrictions with the First Amendment if the service advertised is itself constitutionally protected.

The Supreme Court established First Amendment protection for "purely commercial" advertisements in *Virginia State Board of Pharmacy v. Virginia Citizens Consumer Council*,[10] a case in which the Supreme Court struck down a Virginia statute prohibiting licensed pharmacists from advertising the prices of prescription drugs. The pharmacists' ads were purely commercial because they did "no more than propose a commercial transaction," the Court said.

The Virginia State Board of Pharmacy argued that the prohibition on price advertisements for prescription drugs did not violate the First Amendment because purely commercial speech had not been protected by the First Amendment since *Valentine v. Chrestensen*. The board also argued that aggressive price competition among pharmacists would harm consumers because pharmacists would have less time to compound and dispense drugs. The pressures of advertising, the board said, would force conscientious pharmacists either to diminish their painstaking professional services or to go out of business. Furthermore, the Board of Pharmacy argued that competitive advertising would not necessarily result in the lower drug prices anticipated by the Virginia Citizens Consumer Council.

The Consumer Council, representing a number of prescription drug users, particularly the elderly and infirm, argued that the Virginia statute was a violation of consumers' First Amendment right to receive information necessary to their good health. The Consumer Council also argued that prohibitions on advertising forced consumers to spend more time and money finding the best drugs at the cheapest prices.

In *Virginia Pharmacy*, the Supreme Court recognized a constitutional protection for purely commercial speech motivated by a desire for profit. Justice Blackmun, writing for the Court, said that the price advertising of prescription drugs is protected by the First Amendment even though a pharmacist does not wish to editorialize on any subject, cultural, philosophical or political. He does not wish to report any particularly newsworthy fact, or to make generalized observations even about commercial matters. The "idea" he wishes to communicate is simply this: "I will sell you the X prescription drug at the Y price."

---

[7] 413 U.S. 376 (1973).
[8] 421 U.S. 809 (1975).
[9] 410 U.S. 113 (1973).
[10] 425 U.S. 748 (1976).

Although price advertising for drugs is "purely commercial," the Court said commercial advertising, like editorial comment, contributes to democratic decision-making served by the First Amendment. In a statement merging the commercial marketplace and the marketplace of ideas, the Court said:

> Advertising, however tasteless and excessive it sometimes may seem, is nonetheless dissemination of information as to who is producing and selling what product, for what reason, and at what price. So long as we preserve a predominantly free enterprise economy, the allocation of our resources in large measure will be made through numerous private economic decisions. It is a matter of public interest that those decisions in the aggregate be intelligent and well informed. To this end, the free flow of commercial information is indispensable.

The Court's First Amendment protection for commercial advertising depended very little on the right of pharmacists to speak or publish. After all, the professional association representing pharmacists opposed lifting the ban on advertising. Of more importance to the Court than a right to speak was the consumer's constitutional interest in receiving information about drug prices. The right to receive would be honored, Justice Blackmun said, because the individual consumer's interest "in the free flow of commercial information may be as keen, if not keener by far, than his interest in the day's most urgent political debate." The Court rejected as "paternalistic" the State Board of Pharmacy's claim that allowing pharmacists to advertise prices of prescription drugs would undermine their professionalism and thereby hurt consumers.

In a very sharp dissent, Justice Rehnquist feared that the "logical consequences" of the *Virginia Pharmacy* decision would be to elevate "commercial intercourse between a seller hawking his wares and a buyer seeking to strike a bargain to the same plane as has been previously reserved for the free marketplace of ideas." Rehnquist did not agree with the majority's assertion that commercial advertising should be protected by the First Amendment because purchasing decisions based on advertising contribute to public decision-making in a democracy. To Justice Rehnquist, the First Amendment protects public decision-making on political, social and other public issues. It does not protect "the decision of a particular individual as to whether to purchase one or another kind of shampoo." Justice Rehnquist thought the Court's decision in *Virginia Pharmacy* devalued the First Amendment.

Advertising's Lower Status

According constitutional status to advertising has not necessarily devalued the First Amendment, but advertising itself still does not enjoy the full First Amendment protection of political speech. Although the majority of justices in *Virginia Pharmacy* appeared to equate commercial advertising with political speech, in fact commercial speech came under the constitutional umbrella in *Virginia Pharmacy* as a second-class form of expression. Starting in *Virginia Pharmacy* and continuing through other commercial speech decisions, the Court has permitted many regulations on commercial speech that would not be tolerated on political speech. For example, although the government must demonstrate a compelling interest to justify restraints on political speech, the government needs to demonstrate a lesser "substantial" or "important" need to justify restraints on commercial advertising.

A major difference in the protection of political and commercial speech can be seen in the Court's tolerance for falsehood in each. Although considerable falsehood is permitted in the political arena because government censorship is considered worse than false political speech, the Court said in *Virginia Pharmacy* that the government may constitutionally ban commercial promotions that are "false or misleading in any way" or that promote products or services that are illegal. The Court also said that prior restraints, which are presumed to be unconstitutional in the political arena, may be invoked to halt misleading commercial speech. Furthermore, although political expression may not be compelled, the Court said that commercial advertisers might be required to disseminate warnings, disclaimers and other messages to ensure that commercial speech is not misleading. Since *Virginia Pharmacy* was decided, the Supreme Court has ruled that even truthful advertising may be prohibited to serve a substantial government interest.[11]

The constitutional protections for commercial speech are weaker than those for political speech, the Supreme Court said, because of "common sense" differences between commercial and political speech. First, the Court said that commercial speech is hardier than other kinds of expression because of the need of businesses to advertise in a market economy. Advertisers will not be as intimidated by government regulations as political speakers might be, the Court said, because of the unrelenting economic pressure on businesses to advertise. In other words, commercial advertising may be regulated more than political speech because advertising can more easily withstand regulation.

The other "commonsense" difference between commercial and political speech is that commercial speech is more easily verified. Advertisers, the Court said, know their products well and often make factual statements that can be proven objectively, perhaps by scientific test. Political statements, in contrast, are often assertions of fact or opinion that cannot be proved and should not have to be. But because advertisers easily may verify their statements, the Court said there is less reason to tolerate false and misleading statements in commercial ads than in political debate.

Although commercial speech has occupied a second-class status constitutionally since *Virginia Pharmacy* was decided in 1976, the Supreme Court has issued a number of decisions broadening the range of commercial content protected—at least partially—by the First Amendment. In 1977, the Court ruled that attorneys have a constitutional right to advertise the prices of routine services, such as a simple will or uncontested divorce.[12] The Court has also extended constitutional protection to illustrations and pictures in attorneys' ads,[13] "For Sale" and "Sold" signs on private houses,[14] advertisements for contraceptives,[15] and promotions for electrical power by a utility.[16] However, the Supreme Court has also ruled that the First Amendment does not protect ads for casinos[17] or sales promotions in college dormitories.[18]

---

[11] Posadas de Puerto Rico Assocs. v. Tourism Co., 478 U.S. 328 (1986).
[12] Bates v. State Bar of Arizona, 433 U.S. 350 (1977).
[13] Zauderer v. Office of Disciplinary Counsel, 471 U.S. 626 (1985).
[14] Linmark Assocs., Inc. v. Township of Willingboro, 431 U.S. 85 (1977).
[15] Bolger v. Youngs Drug Prod. Corp., 463 U.S. 60 (1983); Carey v. Population Servs. Int'l, 431 U.S. 678 (1977).
[16] Central Hudson Gas & Elec. Corp. v. Public Serv. Comm'n, 447 U.S. 557 (1980).
[17] Posadas de Puerto Rico Assocs. v. Tourism Co., 478 U.S. 328 (1986).
[18] Board of Trustees v. Fox, 492 U.S. 469 (1989).

The Court's commercial speech decisions have been criticized for being inconsistent and therefore providing little guidance for advertisers who want to know whether government restrictions are constitutional. The Court employs a four-part analysis when determining the constitutionality of advertising regulations.

The Four-Part Test

The four-part test for determining the constitutionality of regulations on commercial speech was set forth by the Supreme Court in *Central Hudson Gas & Electric Corp. v. Public Service Commission*,[19] a case in which the Court upheld a utility's right to promote the use of electricity. In *Central Hudson*, the Court struck down a state regulation that prohibited electric utilities from running all advertisements promoting the use of electricity. The prohibition, which was instituted to conserve energy, barred ads promoting efficient uses of electricity as well as those advocating inefficient or wasteful uses. The Supreme Court ruled that a blanket ban on all electricity ads violated the First Amendment.

Under the four-part test promulgated in *Central Hudson* and later cases, a court must determine first whether speech is commercial expression eligible for First Amendment protection. Second, a court examines whether the government asserts a substantial interest in regulating the expression. If the speech is eligible and the government asserts a substantial interest, a court next considers whether the regulation directly advances the governmental interest asserted. If so, the court in the fourth step decides whether the regulation is sufficiently narrow.

COMMERCIAL SPEECH ELIGIBLE FOR CONSTITUTIONAL CONSIDERATION Speech passes the first part of the *Central Hudson* test and is eligible for constitutional protection if it is accurate and advertises a lawful product or service. False and misleading advertising and advertising for illegal products and services are not eligible for constitutional consideration. The first task of a court, therefore, is to determine whether the expression at issue is commercial speech for a lawful product or service.

Defining Commercial Speech An advertisement is commercial speech, the Court said in *Virginia Pharmacy*, if it does "no more than propose a commercial transaction."[20] The Court also has said that commercial speech is expression "related solely to the economic interests of the speaker and its audience." Similarly, Justice Brennan once referred to "pure advertising" as "an offer to buy or sell goods and services or encouraging such buying and selling."[21] Although these definitions do not encompass all commercial speech, they adequately describe ads that expressly offer a product or service for sale, particularly at a specific price.

Price advertising for prescription drugs, the Supreme Court said in *Virginia Pharmacy*, was a purely commercial proposal. Similarly, a lawyer's offer to write a will at a predetermined price, a homeowner's offer to sell a house and a salesperson's attempt to sell Tupperware in a university dormitory are purely commercial speech because they do no more than "propose a commercial transaction."

Associating an advertisement with a political issue does not necessarily transform commercial speech into political speech, the Supreme Court has said. F.J. Chrestensen's commercial flyers for submarine tours remained commercial advertisements, the Supreme Court said, even though he appended a political protest

---

[19] 447 U.S. 557 (1980).
[20] 425 U.S. 762.
[21] Dun & Bradstreet v. Greenmoss Builders, 472 U.S. 749 (1985) (Brennan, J., dissenting).

to the back. In *Central Hudson*, the Court said that an electric utility's bill inserts promoting the efficient use of electricity were commercial speech even though the inserts served a political plan, the state-approved energy conservation program.

Likewise, in *Bolger v. Youngs Drug Products Corp.*,[22] the Court ruled that leaflets distributed by a condom manufacturer were commercial speech even though they contained political and social information about preventing venereal disease (VD). Leaflets distributed by a condom manufacturer were not transformed into fully protected political speech simply because they "link a product to a current public debate," the Court said. The Court said in *Bolger* that a condom manufacturer's "direct comments" on public issues such as venereal disease would merit full constitutional protection, but not statements "made in the context of commercial transactions." The Court said it feared advertisers would try to immunize false or misleading product information from government regulation if commercial messages were considered to be political when the two were blended.

The informational pamphlets at issue in *Bolger* did not propose that readers buy Youngs' condoms. One pamphlet discussed the use of condoms generally as a method of preventing the spread of venereal disease. At the end, the pamphlet identified Youngs as the distributor of the flyer. Another pamphlet about VD described various Trojan-brand condoms manufactured by Youngs without offering them for sale. Nevertheless, the Court ruled the pamphlets were commercial speech because they (1) were conceded to be paid advertisements, (2) made reference to a specific product and (3) were economically motivated. Not all of these three criteria must be met for an advertisement proposing no commercial transaction to be considered commercial speech. Corporate image ads, for example, might be considered commercial speech even though they mention no products, the Court said.

The definition of commercial speech was clouded in 2004 when the Supreme Court let stand a California ruling that corporate reports, press releases and letters to the editor are less protected commercial speech—subject to penalties if found to be false—rather than the more protected political speech.[23] The California Supreme Court had ruled that Marc Kasky, a consumer activist, should be allowed to prove in court that Nike Inc. violated a state consumer protection law by issuing false statements about workers' conditions in the footwear company's Southeast Asian manufacturing plants. When the U.S. Supreme Court dismissed review, Nike settled with Kasky for $1.5 million to be used to educate workers, increase training and monitor manufacturing in Southeast Asia.[24]

Nike issued several press releases and comments in response to charges that its manufacturing operations in Southeast Asia were "sweatshops" that paid low wages and exploited women and children. The California court said Nike's public comments were not fully protected political speech, but were commercial speech—like product advertising—because they were directed "to an audience of persons who may be influenced by that speech to engage in a commercial transaction with the speaker." Nike claimed its press releases and letters were political speech because they did not attempt to sell athletic footwear, but responded to politically motivated criticism about its manufacturing processes. (See excerpts from a Nike release in Figure 8.1.) More than 40 entities, including Microsoft, the *New York Times* and public relations organizations, supported Nike's claim.

---

[22] 463 U.S. 60 (1983).

[23] Kasky v. Nike, 27 Cal. 4th 939 (2002), *cert. dismissed*, 539 U.S. 654 (2003).

[24] Stephanie Kang, "Nike Settles Case with an Activist for $1.5 Million," *Wall Street Journal*, Sept. 15, 2003, at A10.

BEAVERTON, Ore.—June 6, 1996—NIKE, Inc. today responded to claims made by Joel Joseph, chairman of the Made in the USA Foundation, of underage Indonesian workers making NIKE's line of Air Jordan shoes for 14 cents an hour by stating that his allegations are completely false and irresponsible.

"Perhaps Mr. Joseph should have looked at an Air Jordan shoe on store shelves to learn that the product is made in Taiwan," said Donna Gibbs, NIKE's director of corporate communications. "One has to question the credibility of an individual whose organization is largely financed by labor unions opposed to free trade with developing nations," she said. "It's also too bad that Kathie Lee Gifford has found it necessary to avoid the media spotlight by pushing Michael Jordan onto it."

Wherever NIKE operates around the globe, it is guided by principles set forth in a code of conduct that binds its production subcontractors to a signed Memorandum of Understanding. This Memorandum strictly prohibits child labor and certifies compliance with applicable government regulations regarding minimum wage, overtime, as well as occupational health and safety, environmental regulations, worker insurance and equal opportunity provisions.

NIKE enforces its standards through daily observation by NIKE staff members. Every factory in the world that manufactures NIKE components and finished goods has NIKE staff assigned to it who are responsible for monitoring adherence to the Memorandum of Understanding. The next level of enforcement is a system of third-party audit, conducted by Ernst & Young. These thorough reviews conducted over several days include interviews with workers, examination of safety equipment and procedures, review of free health-care facilities at the work site, investigation of worker grievances and audits of payroll records.

The average line-worker's wage in Asian subcontracted facilities is double the government-mandated minimum. In addition, compensation extends beyond wages to include subsidies for transportation, housing, free meals and health care, bonuses for attendance and improved skills; and legally mandated paid holidays, pregnancy and menstrual leave. These benefits significantly increase the value of the daily wage.

The income level of an Indonesian entry-level worker at a NIKE subcontracted facility is five times that of a farmer, and in China, an assistant line-supervisor earns more than a surgeon with 20 years of experience.

FIGURE 8.1   Excerpts from a Nike press release responding to sweatshop allegations.

When the U.S. Supreme Court dismissed the Nike appeal, Justice Breyer dissented, arguing the high court should rule Nike's communications are protected speech about controversial public issues. Breyer, joined by Justice O'Connor, noted that Nike's letter to college presidents and athletic directors was not in an advertising format, proposed no product purchases and contained facts, and responded to criticism about Nike's labor practices. Breyer warned that fear of lawsuits would chill corporations' willingness to engage in public debate.[25] Afterward, Nike said it would withhold a report on corporate responsibility.

Lawful Products and Services   Once a court has determined that commercial speech is at issue, it asks whether the expression promotes a lawful product or service. Under the first part of the *Central Hudson* analysis, commercial expression

---

[25] 539 U.S. 654.

entitled to constitutional protection must promote products and services that are themselves legal. Ads for prescription drugs, houses and lawyers' services are eligible for constitutional consideration because they promote lawful products and activities. Similarly, ads promoting electricity and condoms also meet the first part of the test. However, ads for obscene materials, criminal activities and discriminatory job opportunities are outside constitutional consideration because they promote illegal products or services.

Federal appellate courts have disagreed whether housing ads omitting pictures and references to minorities discriminate in violation of federal law. The federal Fair Housing Act prohibits advertising "indicat[ing] any preference . . . based on race." In one case, the U.S. Court of Appeals for the Second Circuit refused to dismiss a discrimination suit against the *New York Times* by minorities who claimed housing ads in the newspaper violated the federal law. Plaintiffs in the case, several black individuals joined by the Open Housing Center of New York, charged that *Times* real estate ads published over a 20-year period violated the Fair Housing Act because they rarely depicted blacks as potential home buyers or renters. In refusing to dismiss the case, the Second Circuit said a jury "plausibly may conclude" that ads with models of a particular race and not others violate the Fair Housing Act by indicating a racial preference. Ads demonstrating a racial preference would not be protected by the First Amendment, the court noted, because they would "further an illegal commercial activity." The Supreme Court refused to review the Second Circuit's ruling to let the *Times* be sued.[26]

In contrast, the Sixth Circuit dismissed a similar discrimination suit against the *Cincinnati Enquirer*, ruling that the Fair Housing Act is not violated merely because minority models are absent from housing advertisements.[27] Unlike the Second Circuit in the *New York Times* case, the Sixth Circuit ruled that housing ads would violate the Fair Housing Act only if they constituted a discriminatory "campaign" by a specific realtor or if the ads illegally promoted discrimination at specific housing projects. But ads that are independent of a campaign are not discriminatory merely because they contain white models only, the court said. Indeed, the Sixth Circuit concluded that independent housing ads depicting whites only are lawful statements protected by the First Amendment.

In another twist to the question of what constitutes commercial speech for lawful products, the Supreme Court has ruled that ads and logos promoting unlawful uses of lawful products may be unprotected by the First Amendment. In *Village of Hoffman Estates v. Flipside, Hoffman Estates*, the Court ruled that logos and slogans on cigarette papers, water pipes, "roach clips" and other drug paraphernalia were outside First Amendment protection because the paraphernalia were marketed for illegal purposes.[28] In *Hoffman Estates*, drug paraphernalia were displayed next to books and magazines entitled *High Times, Marijuana Grower's Guide, A Child's Garden of Grass* and *The Pleasures of Cocaine*. A sign in the store referred to the "head" supplies used by frequent drug users. A design on cigarette papers showed a person smoking drugs.

The *Hoffman Estates* decision did not say that commercial speech may be prohibited for all products that might be used for an illegal purpose. Such reasoning could lead to prohibitions on almost all commercial expression. "Peanut butter advertising cannot be banned," a federal judge once observed, "just because

---

[26] Ragin v. New York Times Co., 923 F.2d 995 (2d Cir.), *cert. denied*, 502 U.S. 821 (1991).
[27] Housing Opportunities Made Equal v. Cincinnati Enquirer, Inc., 943 F.2d 644 (6th Cir. 1990).
[28] 455 U.S. 489 (1982). *See also* Camille Corp. v. Phares, 705 F.2d 223 (7th Cir. 1983).

someone might throw a jar at the presidential motorcade."[29] However, the commercial expression in *Hoffman Estates* was not protected commercial speech because it promoted the illegal use of drugs.

False, Misleading and Deceptive Advertising To merit constitutional consideration, commercial speech not only must promote a lawful product or service but also must be true and not misleading. The state has a legitimate interest, the Court said in *Virginia Pharmacy*, in ensuring that the "stream of commercial information flows cleanly as well as freely." The Supreme Court ruled that ads offering prescription drugs, simple legal services and houses for sale were eligible for constitutional protection because the ads were not false, misleading or deceptive. The promotion of electricity by Central Hudson Gas & Electric was also eligible for constitutional protection because it did not mislead consumers. A later section will discuss deception in detail.

Generally, ads mislead if they make important false statements or leave the wrong impression. A federal appeals court ruled that the term *invoice* in a car dealer's advertisement is inherently misleading because many customers mistakenly believe that a car dealer's profit is the difference between the sale price to the customer and the invoice price to the dealer. In fact, a dealer's invoice may have little relationship to the cost of a car to a dealer.[30]

The Supreme Court has said advertising the price of a drug or simple legal procedure is not misleading but that price advertising of complex services is. In *Bates v. State*,[31] the Court said that price advertisements for complex legal services, such as complicated divorces and estate settlements, could be prohibited because they would be misleading. Ads for complex services are misleading, the Court said, because attorneys cannot accurately fix a price before work begins on open-ended, time-consuming tasks. Only routine legal services that take a fixed amount of time can be accurately priced in advertising that does not mislead, the Court said. Routine services for which the price might be advertised include uncontested divorces and simple adoptions.

The Court also has ruled that attorneys' use of in-person sales talks can be prohibited because of the potential for deception. In-person solicitations can be prohibited because they, unlike lawyers' advertisements in the media, present dangers of coercing, intimidating, misleading and invading the privacy of potential clients. The Court said an attorney's in-person appeal for business—often to a vulnerable potential client who is distraught by a divorce, an accident or a death—is deceptive because it "may exert pressure and often demands an immediate response, without providing an opportunity for comparison or reflection."[32]

In 2003, Congress enacted the CAN-SPAM Act to reduce unsolicited commercial email messages.[33] The law makes it illegal to send commercial email messages, known as spam, with intent to deceive recipients about who is sending the message or the subject of the message. The CAN-SPAM Act also requires commercial emailers to provide a functioning address and an opportunity for recipients to stop the commercial messages. The law does permit companies to send warranty and safety information to customers who have purchased products.

---

[29] Dunagin v. City of Oxford, 718 F.2d 738 (5th Cir. 1983), *cert. denied*, 467 U.S. 1259 (1984).

[30] Joe Conte Toyota, Inc. v. Louisiana Motor Vehicle Comm'n, 24 F.3d 754 (5th Cir. 1994).

[31] 433 U.S. 350 (1977).

[32] Ohralik v. Ohio State Bar Ass'n, 436 U.S. 447, 457 (1978).

[33] Pub. L. No. 108–197, 117 Stat. 2699 (2003) (codified at 15 U.S.C. §§ 7701–7713).

LEGITIMATE GOVERNMENT REGULATORY INTEREST Once it has been determined that an advertisement is eligible for constitutional consideration because it accurately promotes a legal product or service, a court's analysis focuses on the constitutionality of the proposed government regulation. The second criterion of the *Central Hudson* test is whether a regulation serves a legitimate or substantial government interest. If the speech in question were political rather than commercial, government suppression would require proof of a compelling state interest under the standards of strict scrutiny. The lesser value of commercial speech is reflected in the more relaxed standard that the government demonstrate only a legitimate or substantial interest to justify regulation.

The government frequently has met the second part of the *Central Hudson* test quite easily by demonstrating an interest in preserving the health, safety, morals or aesthetic quality of the community. In *Central Hudson*, the Supreme Court recognized the legitimacy of the New York Public Service Commission's desire to conserve energy. The Public Service Commission tried to curb Central Hudson's promotional advertising for electricity as part of a national policy of energy conservation. The Supreme Court declared the commission's complete ban on the utility's electricity promotions to be unconstitutionally broad, but not before recognizing the legitimacy of the Public Service Commission's goal of saving energy. The Supreme Court also has said that traffic safety and the physical appearance of a city are sufficient state interests to justify banning commercial billboards if the other criteria of the *Central Hudson* test are met.[34]

In *Posadas de Puerto Rico Associates v. Tourism Co.*, a case in which the Supreme Court upheld a ban on truthful casino advertising, the Court recognized as a legitimate state interest a desire by the government of Puerto Rico to preserve the morality and welfare of the Puerto Rican people by discouraging gambling.[35] The gambling promoted by the casino ads on the island, Justice Rehnquist said for the Court majority, could result in "disruption of moral and cultural patterns, the increase in local crime, the fostering of prostitution, the development of corruption, and the infiltration of organized crime." Although the Supreme Court has struck down laws prohibiting the advertising of alcoholic beverages, the Court has recognized that governments have a legitimate interest in curbing the consumption of alcohol.[36]

DIRECT ADVANCEMENT OF THE GOVERNMENT'S REGULATORY INTEREST The third part of the *Central Hudson* test is whether a regulation on commercial speech "directly and materially" advances the government's legitimate interest. It is one thing to conclude that the government has a legitimate interest in establishing a regulation; it is a more demanding requirement for the government to then establish that the proposed advertising regulation would directly advance the state's interest. In *Central Hudson*, the Court said there is an "immediate connection between advertising and demand for electricity." Therefore, a ban on the electricity promotions would advance the state's interest in conserving electricity. Thus, when the Supreme Court struck down the blanket prohibition on energy advertising in *Central Hudson*, it was not because the Court was convinced the ban would ill serve the goal of conserving energy. The ban was struck down because

---

[34] Metromedia, Inc. v. City of San Diego, 453 U.S. 490 (1981).
[35] 478 U.S. 328 (1986).
[36] 44 Liquormart, Inc. v. Rhode Island, 517 U.S. 484 (1996); Rubin v. Coors Brewing Co., 514 U.S. 476 (1995).

it was overbroad, barring all advertising for electricity, even ads that promoted efficient uses of electricity.

Sometimes the Supreme Court has assumed, without hard evidence, that a regulation on advertising would advance a governmental interest. In the *Posadas* case, the Court assumed, without concrete data or anecdotes, that barring casino advertising in Puerto Rico would serve the government goal of keeping Puerto Ricans out of the casinos. Writing for the majority, Justice Rehnquist said it was "reasonable" for the Puerto Rican legislature to believe that advertising gambling on the island would increase the number of gamblers. Therefore, Rehnquist concluded that banning casino advertising would directly advance the state interest in curbing prostitution, crime and other demoralizing activities the legislature said gambling spawned.

Since *Posadas*, the Supreme Court has been less willing to assume, without evidence, that a government regulation will serve a government interest. Instead of deferring to state regulators, the Court now says states must present evidence that a regulation will advance a legitimate interest. The government's burden, the Supreme Court has said,

> is not satisfied by mere speculation and conjecture; rather, a governmental body seeking to sustain a restriction on commercial speech must demonstrate that the harms it recites are real and that its restriction will in fact alleviate them to a material degree.[37]

Federal courts have grappled with the requirements of proof in several cases regarding compelled disclosure requirements in marketing and labeling products. In 2015, for example, the Court of Appeals for the D.C. Circuit reviewed a Securities and Exchange Commission (SEC) requirement that companies trading in gold, tungsten, tin and tantalum from the Democratic Republic of the Congo disclose that fact on their websites and reports. Advocacy groups have opposed allowing imports of these materials from the Congo and other war-torn areas in a way that benefits militias that commit genocide and other human rights atrocities. A trade group, the National Association of Manufacturers, sued to strike down the requirement, arguing that the government had failed to prove any benefits that the conflict minerals disclosure requirement would advance.[38]

The court of appeals considered this to be a commercial speech matter under *Central Hudson* rather than merely being a matter avoiding deceptive advertising, as was the case when the court previously upheld a U.S. Department of Agriculture regulation requiring meat producers to put country-of-origin labels on meat products.[39] While the court recognized that ameliorating the humanitarian crisis in the Democratic Republic of the Congo was sufficient as a government interest, it also found a lack of proof by the government that the regulation would serve that interest. A potential effect of the regulation, the court suggested, would likely be billions of dollars in compliance costs by companies and a boycott of companies using minerals from those regions, perhaps preventing millions of dollars from flowing into the region. However, the court said this outcome was "entirely unproven and rests on pure speculation." Indeed, it was unclear whether the rule either alleviated

[37] Edenfield v. Fane, 507 U.S. 761 (1993).

[38] National Association of Manufacturers v. Securities and Exchange Commission, 800 F.3d 518 (D.C. Cir. 2015).

[39] American Meat Institute v. United States Department of Agriculture, 760 F.3d 18 (D.C. Cir. 2014).

or aggravated the human rights problems in the region. Because "the SEC was unable to quantify any benefits of the forced disclosure regime," the court struck down the requirement.[40]

The Supreme Court has not been convinced that prohibitions on alcohol advertising would further the government's legitimate interest in curbing drinking. In *Rubin v. Coors Brewing Co.*, the Court struck down a federal regulation prohibiting statements of alcohol content on beer labels because the ban would not sufficiently advance a government interest in preventing "strength wars,"[41] contests in which brewers attempt to increase market share by advertising the high alcohol content of their beverages. In an opinion written by Justice Clarence Thomas and joined by seven other justices, the Court said that the government ban on labels containing the alcohol content of beer would not prevent strength wars because the regulations were so contradictory as to be "irrational."

The Court recognized that the labels were accurate and that the government had a substantial interest in protecting the health, safety and welfare of its citizens by preventing brewers from competing on the basis of alcohol strength, a competition that might increase alcoholism. However, the Court said it could not uphold the constitutionality of irrational regulations that prohibited statements of alcohol content on beverage labels but permitted them in beverage advertising. Justice Thomas also found it irrational that federal law would prohibit alcohol statements in beer labels but permit them on labels of wines and spirits. There is little chance, Thomas said, that a statute combating strength wars will advance its aim "while other provisions of the same act directly undermine and counteract its effects."

Similarly, the Court struck down a Rhode Island ban on advertising alcohol prices in part because the government did not demonstrate that the ban would discourage drinking. In *44 Liquormart, Inc. v. Rhode Island*, the government of Rhode Island argued, but did not document, that competing advertisements would lower the prices of alcohol, thus encouraging consumption.[42] In the principal opinion for the Court, joined by three other justices, Justice John Paul Stevens said that "without any findings of fact, or indeed any evidentiary support whatsoever, we cannot agree with the assertion that the price advertising ban will significantly advance the State's interest in promoting temperance." Furthermore, there was no evidence that eliminating the ban on advertising would raise alcohol consumption. With no evidence that the ban would curb alcohol consumption, the Court was unwilling to uphold what Stevens considered a paternalistic ban on truthful speech about a lawful product.

In 2011, the Supreme Court ruled pharmaceutical companies have a First Amendment right to use data identifying doctors' drug prescriptions to market drugs to doctors. Ruling that the prescription data is protected commercial speech, the Court struck down a Vermont statute prohibiting use of the data for marketing. The court said the ban would not advance legitimate state interests in protecting public health and reducing health costs.[43]

NARROWLY DRAWN BAN Besides directly advancing a legitimate state interest, a constitutional regulation on truthful commercial speech for a lawful product must be narrowly drawn. Courts have sometimes interpreted the fourth *Central Hudson* requirement to mean that a regulation on commercial speech has

---

[40] 800 F.3d at 525.
[41] 514 U.S. at 479.
[42] 517 U.S. 484 (1996).
[43] Sorrell v. IMS Health Inc., 564 U.S. 552 (2011).

to be the "least restrictive" possible. However, the Supreme Court ruled in *Board of Trustees v. Fox* that restrictions on commercial speech may be constitutional even if they are not the least restrictive.[44] The *Fox* Court said there should be a reasonable "fit" between legislative interests and the regulations employed to achieve them.

The Court remanded the *Fox* case for a determination whether university regulations barring all private commercial activities in dorm rooms represented the proper fit of legislative goal and regulatory means. The regulations were challenged by companies prohibited from selling housewares in university dorms. The State University of New York at Buffalo defended the regulations, designed to prevent commercial exploitation of students and to create an educational atmosphere at the university. The Supreme Court recognized the legitimacy of the state's goals but returned the case to the lower courts for determination of the reasonableness of the ban.

In *Central Hudson*, the Court found the ban on electricity promotions to be unconstitutionally broad because it was more extensive than necessary to further the government interest in energy conservation. The Court recognized that the New York Public Service Commission had a legitimate interest in regulating advertising to conserve energy. But the ban was unconstitutional, the Court said, because it barred promotional information about efficient as well as inefficient uses of electricity.

The Court said the Public Service Commission had failed to demonstrate that its interest in energy conservation could not be advanced adequately by more limited regulation. Rather than ban all promotions, the Court said the Public Service Commission might further its conservation policy by ensuring that the utility's advertisements include information about the relative efficiency and expense of different uses of electricity.

The city of Cincinnati also failed to constitutionally match a regulation to a legitimate government goal. In *Cincinnati v. Discovery Network, Inc.*, the Supreme Court ruled unconstitutional a city ordinance that prohibited 62 newsracks distributing commercial handbills but allowed more than 1,500 other newsracks containing newspapers.[45] The ordinance was challenged by companies that distribute real estate and adult education booklets.

The Court agreed that the city had a legitimate goal of preserving the safety and aesthetics of the community by limiting the number of newsracks. However, the Court saw no relationship between the total ban on 62 commercial newsracks and the city's interests in preserving safety and aesthetics. Removal of the 62 racks would be a minuscule improvement, the Court said, if more than 1,500 equally ugly newspaper racks were allowed to remain. After struggling unsuccessfully to find a clear distinction between noncommercial newspapers and "commercial" real estate and education promotions, the Court was "unwilling to recognize Cincinnati's bare assertion that the 'low value' of commercial speech is a sufficient justification for its selective and categorical ban on news-racks dispensing 'commercial handbills.'"

In a case of alcohol advertisements, eight justices of the Supreme Court agreed that Rhode Island's total ban on truthful price advertising for alcohol did not fit properly with the state's goal of reducing drinking. Rhode Island had several alternatives to a ban on price advertising, alternatives that would reduce drinking without curbing speech, the Court said. The state could discourage drinking by raising prices of alcoholic beverages, raising taxes on alcohol, putting limits on

---

[44] 492 U.S. 469 (1989).
[45] 507 U.S. 410 (1993).

purchases of alcohol as the government limits the purchase of prescription drugs, and conducting education campaigns to discourage drinking.

While striking down the Rhode Island law, the Supreme Court rejected a contention from the *Posadas* case that the government's power to regulate the sale of a product includes the right to ban commercial expression about the product. "The First Amendment directs that government may not suppress speech as easily as it may suppress conduct, and that speech restrictions cannot be treated as simply another means that the government may use to achieve its ends," Justice Stevens wrote in *Liquormart*. Under the Twenty-First Amendment, states may regulate—even prohibit—the sale of alcohol. But the Twenty-First Amendment does not permit states to restrict truthful speech about a lawful product, the Court said.

The Supreme Court also emphasized the importance of truthful speech about lawful products when it struck down tobacco advertising regulations. In *Lorillard Tobacco Company v. Reilly*, the Court found that Massachusetts had a compelling interest in protecting the health of children, but a prohibition of outdoor advertising of cigars and smokeless tobacco products within 1,000 feet of schools or playgrounds failed the fourth prong of the *Central Hudson* test.[46]

Writing for the Court, Justice O'Connor held that the breadth and scope of the outdoor restrictions did not represent a "careful calculation" of the burden on speech. Massachusetts had not appropriately considered the varying impact of the 1,000-foot boundary in rural, suburban and urban locations. In a large city such as Boston, tobacco manufacturers and retailers would be unable to advertise in 87 percent to 91 percent of the city. To Justice O'Connor, the geographic reach of the restrictions would "constitute nearly a complete ban on the communication of truthful information about smokeless tobacco and cigars to adult consumers."

The Court also struck down a Massachusetts prohibition on indoor smokeless tobacco and cigar advertisements lower than five feet from the ground. This regulation failed both the third and fourth prongs of the *Central Hudson* test. "Not all children are less than 5 feet tall, and those who are certainly have the ability to look up and take in their surroundings," O'Connor said.

Although states have the authority to enact narrowly tailored advertising restrictions on smokeless tobacco and cigars, a federal statute governing the advertising of cigarettes preempts states from restricting cigarette advertisements to promote health. The Federal Cigarette Labeling and Advertising Act, however, does not preempt state power to control the sale of cigarettes. Thus, a Massachusetts ban on self-service displays of tobacco products was found to be constitutional.

▨ SUMMARY ▨

The First Amendment protects commercial speech but to a lesser degree than it protects political expression. The Supreme Court has said that the hardiness and verifiability of commercial speech justify lesser constitutional protections on advertising than on political and social commentary. Commercial speech has been defined as expression promoting a commercial transaction.

Under a four-part test developed by the Supreme Court, restrictions on commercial speech are permitted even if the expression is accurate and promotes a lawful product or service. Under the four-part test, truthful commercial speech may be restricted if the government asserts a substantial interest that will be advanced

---

[46] 533 U.S. 525 (2001).

by a regulation. The regulation must also be narrowly tailored to serve government objectives.

UNFAIR AND DECEPTIVE ADVERTISING

Because false and deceptive commercial advertisements are outside constitutional protection, they may be banned. Advertisers also may be ordered to alter ads so that they cease to be deceptive. The required alterations may include warnings, disclosures and corrections of earlier deceptive ads. Advertisers are also required to substantiate advertising claims.

Advertisements are regulated under a number of federal and state laws. The leading regulatory body is the FTC, which operates under the Federal Trade Commission Act of 1914 and is a five-person commission whose members are appointed by the president to staggered seven-year terms. The commission has a large staff of attorneys, economists and accountants who originate inquiries, issue reports and conduct investigations.

The FTC's rulings and reports not only define the scope of federal regulation but also determine standards for state and industry regulatory bodies. In some states, an advertiser who complies with the Federal Trade Commission Act may not be penalized under state antideception laws.

The FTC's primary mission is to protect consumers from unfair or deceptive market practices and to promote vigorous competition. The primary statutory authority for the FTC's activities is the Federal Trade Commission Act, which prohibits unfair methods of competition and unfair or deceptive acts or practices in or affecting commerce. The Federal Trade Commission Act gives the FTC authority not only over advertising but also over monopolistic and other anticompetitive activities. In recent years, the FTC has been especially concerned with preventing deception in advertisements claiming environmental, nutritional and other health benefits.

The FTC shares jurisdiction or coordinates with the Department of Justice, the Food and Drug Administration, the Environmental Protection Agency, the Consumer Product Safety Commission and numerous other federal agencies. The FTC also works with state agencies, notably the National Association of Attorneys General.

The Federal Trade Commission originally had jurisdiction only over unfair and deceptive acts or practices that hurt competing companies. In 1938, however, the scope of the Federal Trade Commission Act was broadened to provide protection for consumers as well as competitors.[47] At the heart of FTC advertising regulation is its power to require that advertisers substantiate the accuracy of advertising claims.[48] Since the 1980s, the FTC has narrowed the definition of deception and demanded more empirical evidence than before to establish that an advertisement is deceptive or misleading.

Unfairness

The FTC may stop both unfair and deceptive advertising. Section 5 of the Federal Trade Commission Act declares unfair competition and unfair or deceptive acts or practices in commerce to be unlawful.[49] The Federal Trade Commission has

---

[47] 15 U.S.C. § 53.
[48] Kenneth Plevan and Miriam L. Siroky, *Advertising Compliance Handbook* 109 (2nd ed. 1991).
[49] 15 U.S.C. § 45(a)(1).

referred to its authority to stop unfairness as its "general law of consumer protection for which deception is the one specific but particularly important application."[50]

In the early 1970s, unfairness was described very broadly as whether a practice offended public policy, was immoral or unethical, or caused substantial injury to consumers or businesses.[51] In 1980, the FTC narrowed the focus of its unfairness inquiries to whether an advertisement or commercial practice causes substantial consumer injury.[52] In 1994, Congress defined an unfair act or practice as one that "causes or is likely to cause substantial injury to consumers which is not reasonably avoidable by consumers themselves and not outweighed by countervailing benefits to consumers or to competition."[53] The Federal Trade Commission Act permits the FTC to issue broad rules curbing unfairness in a whole industry if the harmful acts or practices are "prevalent." These "Trade Regulation Rules" and the advertising industry's resentment of them will be discussed in a later section.

Unfairness is more likely to arise in a company's treatment of customers than in advertising. Because the commission looks for substantial harm, the FTC is not concerned with trivial or merely speculative harms. In most cases of unfairness, substantial injury involves monetary harm, as when sellers coerce consumers into purchasing unwanted goods or services. In one case, a company acted unfairly by requiring consumers to buy expensive parts before company service personnel would reassemble furnaces they had dismantled.[54]

Unwarranted health and safety risks also may support a finding of unfairness. A razor blade manufacturer was found to have acted unfairly when it distributed free samples of blades in newspapers, thus creating the possibility that small children might hurt themselves.[55] A tractor manufacturer also was found to have acted unfairly when it failed to tell customers that opening the gas cap after the engine was hot might result in dangerous "geysering" of gasoline.[56]

In 2012, Facebook settled FTC charges that the social network company was unfair and deceptive in its online privacy practices. The FTC had charged Facebook with changing user information—such as users' Friends lists—from private to public without warning or user approval; representing that apps would not have access to most user information when they did; sharing "Friends Only" data more widely than Facebook policy stated; sharing information with advertisers after promising not to; and making photos and videos accessible after an account had been deactivated.[57]

In the agreement, Facebook agreed to establish a comprehensive privacy program, to obtain consumer consent before changing consumers' privacy preferences, and to prohibit access to user information more than 30 days after the user deletes an account.[58] Facebook was also deemed to be liable for penalties of $16,000 a day for each count if it violated the terms of the settlement.[59] Indeed, Facebook continued to violate the order for years, making consumers' personal data accessible

[50] International Harvester, Inc., 104 F.T.C. 949 (1984).
[51] FTC v. Sperry & Hutchinson, 405 U.S. 223 (1972).
[52] "Statement of Policy on the Scope of Consumer Unfairness Jurisdiction," 4 *Trade Reg. Rep.* (CCH) 13,203 (Dec. 17, 1980).
[53] 15 U.S.C. § 45(n).
[54] Holland Furnace Co. v. FTC, 295 F.2d 302 (1961).
[55] Philip Morris Inc., 82 F.T.C. 16 (1973).
[56] International Harvester Co., 104 F.T.C. 949 (1984).
[57] FTC, "Facebook Settles FTC Charges That It Deceived Consumers by Failing to Keep Privacy Promises," *Press Release*, Nov. 29, 2011.
[58] Somini Sengupta, "F.T.C. Settles Privacy Issue at Facebook," *N.Y. Times*, Nov. 29, 2011.
[59] *Id.*

to advertisers and third-party app developers, including information about "the news and books they were reading, their relationship details, their religious and political views, their work history, their photos, and the videos they watched." The company also misrepresented the extent to which it allowed use of personal data for building facial recognition technology tools. In 2019, the continued violations resulted in a $5 billion civil penalty, the largest ever issued by the FTC, as part of a settlement with Facebook recognizing its flouting of the 2012 order. The settlement also required Facebook to create an independent "Privacy Committee" to oversee personal data handling within the company, as well as an external monitor approved by the FTC to provide additional oversight of privacy practices.[60] It is questionable whether the record-breaking fine and privacy protection practices would deter future bad conduct by the company. Critics, including two dissenting FTC commissioners, noted that the fine was so small compared to the revenue the company generated for its privacy violations that the settlement announcement actually resulted in Facebook stock value jumping drastically the same day.[61]

The FTC has also investigated Google, which agreed to refund at least $19 million the company unfairly billed to consumers for unauthorized charges by the consumers' children. Google agreed to reimburse parents for charges by children made through apps downloaded from the Google Play app store. It was unfair, the FTC said, to bill consumers for unauthorized charges incurred by their children. Google also agreed to obtain express, informed consent from account holders for all in-app charges. In a similar case, Apple agreed earlier to pay at least $32.5 million for unauthorized in-app charges by children.[62]

Deception

The FTC is more concerned with deception than with unfairness. Although deception is not defined in the Federal Trade Commission Act, the FTC has defined a deceptive ad as one that is likely to mislead a reasonable consumer with a material statement or omission.[63]

LIKELY TO MISLEAD Deceptive advertisements are those that either contain express falsehoods or create false impressions that tend to mislead. Courts and the FTC have long held that ads do not have to deceive someone to be deceptive; rather, ads must possess a "tendency," or "capacity," or be "likely" to mislead a reasonable consumer.[64] It does not matter whether the advertiser intends to mislead; an advertisement may have a tendency to deceive regardless of the advertiser's intent. Deceptiveness is determined by the overall impression of an advertisement, not by isolated statements within it. Statements that might be susceptible to both a misleading and a non-misleading interpretation will be considered deceptive. A box of Cheez-It crackers including the words "Whole Grain" prominently featured on the front was found to be deceptive by the U.S. Court of Appeals for the Second Circuit, when the Cheez-It in question actually had "enriched white flour" as the primary ingredient. Even though elsewhere on the box, in smaller print, the actual amount of whole grain was given in more detail, the court said that consumers

---

[60] Lesley Fair, "FTC's $5 Billion Facebook Settlement: Record-Breaking and History-Making," *Federal Trade Commission*, July 24, 2019.
[61] Devin Coldewey, "9 Reasons the Facebook FTC Settlement Is a Joke," *TechCrunch*, July 24, 2019.
[62] FTC, "Google to Refund Consumers at Least $19 Million to Settle FTC Complaint It Unlawfully Billed Parents for Children's Unauthorized In-App Charges," Sept. 4, 2014.
[63] FTC, "Policy Statement on Deception," appended to Cliffdale Assocs., Inc., 103 F.T.C. 110, 165 (1984).
[64] *Id*. at 184.

would find the actual ingredient list "[c]ontrary to the reasonable expectations communicated by the large, bold-faced claims of 'WHOLE GRAIN'" on the front.[65]

REASONABLE CONSUMER Whether an advertisement is deceptive depends on the likelihood the ad will deceive a consumer "acting reasonably in the circumstances."[66] An advertisement is not deceptive if it would mislead only a few particularly gullible consumers. After all, the FTC has said, a company "cannot be liable for every possible reading of its claims no matter how far-fetched."[67] Thus, for example, the law does not help the consumer who thinks Danish pastry is always made in Denmark.[68] Likewise, a federal appeals court in 2021 found no deception by the grocery store chain Trader Joe's for marketing its store brand honey as "100% New Zealand Manuka Honey" and labeled the product with Manuka honey as the sole ingredient, even though tests revealed the Manuka flower nectar content ranged between 57.3 and 62.6 percent. The court said reasonable consumers would be aware that "busy bees cannot be prevented from foraging on different kinds of flowers, despite their keepers' best efforts." Also, the court explained, the relatively low cost of the honey ($1.59 per ounce, compared to the usual $21.55 per ounce cost of pure Manuka honey) would be a signal to a "reasonable consumer in the market for Manuka honey."[69]

Sometimes the FTC determines an advertisement is deceptive simply by reading or viewing it. However, often the FTC relies on the testimony of experts and the results of consumer surveys to determine the likelihood of deception. An ad is deceptive if it is likely to deceive a "substantial number" of consumers in the group to which it is directed.[70] An ad that tends to deceive 20 percent to 25 percent of the consumers in a survey is said to deceive a "substantial number."

Although many ads are aimed at the reasonable consumer in the general public, others are targeted at subgroups, such as children, the aged or the ill. An ad that exaggerates the medicinal powers of a product might not deceive average, healthy adults but could be deceptive if directed to terminally ill consumers desperately seeking a cure.[71] Misleading promises of easy weight loss might not deceive the consumer of average weight but could deceive the obese consumer to whom it is directed.[72]

The FTC also has taken action against alcohol and tobacco advertising that appears to threaten youth, including e-cigarettes.[73] In one case, the FTC halted the use of logos and messages for Redman smokeless tobacco in televised tractor- and truck-pulling contests watched by young people. The commission said televising Redman logos, flags and other commercial symbols at the contests violated the federal law prohibiting televised advertising of smokeless tobacco products.[74] Similarly, the Philip Morris Company agreed to stop placing signs behind scoring tables and other locations at baseball, basketball, hockey and football games

[65] Mantikas v. Kellogg Co., 910 F.3d 633, 637 (2d Cir. 2018).
[66] *Id.*
[67] International Harvester Co., 104 F.T.C. 949, 1057 (1984).
[68] *See* Heinz W. Kirchner, 63 F.T.C. 1282, 1290 (1963).
[69] Moore v. Trader Joe's, 4 F.4th 874, 877 (9th Cir. 2021).
[70] Patricia Bailey and Michael Pertschuk, "Deception Policy Statement Prepared by Commissioners Bailey and Pertschuk and Transmitted on Feb. 29 to the House Energy and Commerce Committee," 46 *Antitrust & Trade Reg. Rep.* 372, 393 (1984).
[71] Travel King, Inc., 86 F.T.C. 715, 719 (1975).
[72] Porter & Dietsch, Inc., 90 F.T.C. 770, 864–5 (1977), *aff'd*, Porter & Dietsch, Inc. v. FTC, 605 F.2d 294 (7th Cir. 1979), *cert. denied*, 445 U.S. 950 (1980).
[73] *E.g.*, Canandaigua Wine Co., 56 Fed. Reg. 32,575 (consent order, July 17, 1991).
[74] Pinkerton Tobacco Co., 57 Fed. Reg. 4634 (consent order, Feb. 6, 1992).

where television cameras would fix on them.[75] In 2019, the FTC ordered vaping companies such as Juul to turn over information about how they have been marketing e-cigarettes, in response to spikes in use among high school–age children. Materials sought include e-cigarette giveaway programs, use of online influencers and promotions on college campuses. Juul, fearing potential regulation including a possible federal ban on flavored e-cigarette pods, voluntarily halted all advertising efforts in response.[76]

Advertisers are not liable if accurate ads aimed at doctors, lawyers and other specialists are misunderstood by the average consumer. Laypersons read at their own risk the technical language in ads directed to experts.[77]

MATERIALITY To be deceptive, advertising that has a tendency to deceive the average consumer must be material. A material statement in advertising, like a material statement in corporate securities transactions, is one that is likely to affect a purchasing decision. A material advertising claim need not actually influence a consumer's decision to buy a product; nor must the consumer lose money for the ad to be considered deceptive. An ad is deceptive if it is likely to, or has the capacity to, affect consumer choices.

Material statements include express claims and deliberately implied claims about a product or service. An omission in an advertisement may also be material if the seller knows or should know that consumers need the omitted information to form an accurate impression. The FTC has found advertising claims or omissions about health, safety, durability, performance, warranties, quality and cost to be material. Indeed, the FTC considers most factual advertising claims about a product to be material. After all, the commission has observed, advertisers would not make factual claims if the advertisers did not intend to influence consumers' choices.[78]

Consumer decisions would be affected, for example, by a material claim that only one brand of air conditioner ensures cooling on extra hot, humid days.[79] Likewise, a claim that aspirin relieves pain better than other pain relievers is material,[80] as is a claim that a skin cream contains aspirin. However, it would not be material to say in a tire advertisement that the tire manufacturer's main office is red when it is white. The color of the building would not be germane to a consumer's decision to buy tires.

Material statements that are likely to deceive may consist of express falsehoods. More often, deceptive ads contain statements that are literally true but create a false implication.

EXPRESS FALSEHOODS Expressly false statements about product attributes are almost always deceptive. The FTC has defined express claims as ones that make a direct representation. The meaning of express falsehoods, like the meaning of *libel per se*, can be determined from the plain meaning of the words.[81] The message is stated unequivocally. Express falsehoods include claims that merchandise is "antique" when it is not old enough to qualify as antique,[82] that coffee is

---

[75] "Phillip Morris Agrees to Settle DOJ Charge of Violating Ban on Cigarette Advertising," *BNA Management Briefing*, June 7, 1995.

[76] Matthew Perrone, "Consumer Watchdog Agency Probes Juul and 5 More Vaping Firms," *Associated Press*, Oct. 3, 2019.

[77] Koch v. FTC, 206 F.2d 311 (6th Cir. 1953).

[78] *See* "Policy Statement on Deception," appended to Cliffdale Assocs., Inc., 103 F.T.C. at 182 (1984).

[79] Fedders Corp. v. FTC, 529 F.2d 1398 (2d Cir.), *cert. denied*, 429 U.S. 818 (1976).

[80] American Home Prods., 98 F.T.C. 136 (1981), *aff'd*, American Home Prods. Corp. v. FTC, 695 F.2d 681 (3d Cir. 1982).

[81] Thompson Medical Co., 104 F.T.C. 648, 788 (1984).

[82] State v. Cohn, 188 A.2d 878 (Conn. Cir. Ct. 1962).

"caffeine free" when the brew contains caffeine, or that goods are "fireproof" when they are only fire resistant.[83] Explicit falsity has also been found when merchandise was called "genuine" when it was a simulation or imitation.[84]

An ad also is deceptive if it contains an expressly false demonstration of a product. In the famous sandpaper shave case, Rapid Shave was made to appear in a television commercial to have the moistening power to soak sandpaper for an effortless shave. The voice in the television commercial told viewers they were seeing proof that Rapid Shave could shave "tough dry sandpaper." However, viewers were not shown sandpaper being shaved. Instead, they saw a piece of Plexiglas on which sand had been spread. After Rapid Shave was applied, a razor whisked the sand away.[85]

The ability of Rapid Shave to soften sandpaper was not disputed, at least if considerable time was allowed. But the viewer was not seeing sandpaper shaved. The FTC and the Supreme Court ruled the Plexiglas mock-up was materially deceptive because it was used as "actual proof of an advertising claim." Even though Rapid Shave could shave sandpaper if enough soaking time were allowed, the Supreme Court said the demonstration was deceptive because it falsely told viewers they were seeing objective proof of a product's performance.

Colgate-Palmolive, the makers of Rapid Shave, said it substituted Plexiglas for sandpaper only to compensate for the technical distortions of television. Colgate-Palmolive said sandpaper on television looked like unattractive, plain, brown paper. But the Court said simulations should not be employed if they cannot represent a product truthfully. The Rapid Shave case indicates, the Court said, "that television is not a medium that lends itself to this type of commercial, not that the commercial must survive at all costs."

IMPLIED FALSEHOODS More common and more difficult to identify than express falsehoods are statements or omissions in advertisements that create a false impression by implication. The FTC defines implied claims circularly as claims that are not express.[86] An implication can be thought of as a false meaning added to a truthful advertisement by the reader or viewer because of an impression the advertisement creates. Advertising claims that are technically true but deceptive because they create a false implication can be divided into at least 15 categories.[87] Several categories are discussed in the following sections.

Reasonable Basis Implication The Federal Trade Commission requires that advertisers have a reasonable basis for the objective claims in their advertisements. Advertisers should be able to support all material claims with results from scientific tests or other appropriate evidence. Thus, an advertiser who says its tires stop faster than others should have scientific evidence to substantiate the claim.

An advertiser's ability to support substantive claims is a material element, the absence of which is deceptive. Consumers, the FTC says, are less likely to rely on claims for products and services if they know that the advertisers have no reasonable basis for making them.[88] Thus, the FTC may find an advertisement deceptive,

[83] Perfect Mfg. Co., 43 F.T.C. 238 (1946).
[84] Masland Duraleather Co. v. FTC, 34 F.2d 733 (3d Cir. 1929).
[85] FTC v. Colgate-Palmolive Co., 380 U.S. 374 (1965).
[86] Thompson Medical Co., 104 F.T.C. 648, 788 (1984).
[87] *See* Ivan Preston, "The Federal Trade Commission's Identification of Implications as Constituting Deceptive Advertising," 57 *U. Cin. L. Rev.* 1243 (1989).
[88] "FTC Policy Statement Regarding Advertising Substantiation," *in* Thompson Medical Co., 104 F.T.C. at 839–40 (1984).

even if the claim is true, if the advertiser has no reasonable basis for making the claim.

The FTC originated the substantiation requirement in 1972 when it ruled that an advertising claim by Pfizer Pharmaceutical lacked a reasonable basis.[89] Although *Pfizer* was technically an unfairness case, the FTC has frequently cited *Pfizer* for the proposition that advertising claims must be substantiated if an advertiser is to avoid deception.[90] In *Pfizer*, the FTC was not satisfied that the pharmaceutical company had adequate substantiation for its claims that Unburn suntan lotion "actually anesthetizes nerves" to relieve pain. In fact, the company could offer no scientific data to support the claim.

The FTC said that "failure to possess substantiation amounts to a lack of reasonable basis, which in turn is an unfair act or practice under Section 5" of the Federal Trade Commission Act. The FTC said in *Pfizer* that substantiation might be provided through scientific studies, existing medical literature, tests conducted by makers of similar competing products, or in some cases, the successful wide use of a product. Pfizer, however, had virtually no evidence for its claims for Unburn tanning lotion.

Advertisers should possess substantiation before they make claims about safety, performance, efficiency, quality and price. If an advertisement asserts a certain level of scientific support by saying "tests prove" or "studies show," the advertiser must be able to provide supportive results for the claim from two scientifically valid tests. If an ad does not claim a certain level of supporting data, the FTC determines a reasonable basis for claims by considering the type of claim, the product and the consequences for consumers of a false claim. The FTC also considers the benefits to consumers of a truthful claim, the cost to the company of developing substantiation, and the amount of substantiation experts in the field believe is reasonable.[91]

The Firestone Tire & Rubber Company was found to have issued deceptive and unfair advertisements by failing to substantiate a claim that the company's Super Sport Wide Oval tires "stop 25 percent quicker." The tires did stop a car more quickly than other tires on wet concrete, but the company lacked "substantial scientific test data" to prove that the tires performed significantly better in the many different road conditions American motorists encounter.[92] Similarly, a company marketing Acne-Satin, a skin medication promoted by singer Pat Boone, lacked substantiation for its claims that the product "cures acne, eliminates or reduces the bacteria and fatty acids responsible for acne blemishes."[93]

Proof Implication Another deceptive advertisement is one that falsely creates the impression that evidence presented proves a claim. A false implication of proof is created if an advertiser misrepresents the evidence presented to substantiate an advertising claim. Ads are deceptive if they misuse test data, create a phony aura of scientific support or otherwise imply proof that does not exist. In the Firestone advertisement just mentioned, the company created a false implication of proof by saying that the company's "racing research" established that Firestone tires "stop 25 percent quicker." The implication was deceptive because, although

---

[89] Pfizer, Inc., 81 F.T.C. 23 (1972).
[90] Gary Ford and John Calfee, "Recent Developments in FTC Policy on Deception," 50 *J. of Marketing* 98 (1986).
[91] "FTC Policy Statement Regarding Advertising Substantiation Program," *in* Thompson Medical Co., 104 F.T.C. at 839–40 (1984).
[92] Firestone Tire & Rubber Co. v. FTC, 481 F.2d 246 (6th Cir. 1973), *cert. denied*, 414 U.S. 1112 (1973).
[93] *In re* National Media Group, Inc., 94 F.T.C. 1096 (1979).

the company had conducted tests, it had no tests comparing the ability of Firestone and other tires to stop a car under normal driving conditions.[94]

Bayer Corporation agreed to undertake a $1 million campaign telling viewers the company had made unsubstantiated claims for Bayer aspirin. The Federal Trade Commission said Bayer had no substantiation for its advertised claims that taking an aspirin daily can prevent heart attacks and strokes. The FTC said a regular aspirin regime will not benefit some adults and others will be adversely affected by taking an aspirin each day. Bayer's aspirin-a-day advertisements ran for three years. Bayer consented to distributing brochures and running advertisements providing substantiated information about aspirin's effectiveness in preventing heart attacks and strokes.[95]

Demonstration Implication Product demonstrations in advertisements may also create deceptive implications. In the Rapid Shave case discussed earlier, a mock-up was misleading because it falsely demonstrated the moistening power of a shaving cream. More often, however, a demonstration is true but nevertheless creates a false impression about how the product will perform in normal circumstances. The FTC found misleading an advertisement in which a sandwich was kept dry under water in a Baggies lunch bag while the sandwich in a competitor's bag was soaked. The demonstration was accurate, but it falsely implied that Baggies were superior to other sandwich bags for keeping food fresh in a refrigerator or lunchbox. "Dunking the sealed bags in a sink of water and swishing them vigorously . . . is not proof of the comparative abilities of the two bags to prevent food spoilage," the FTC said.[96]

The Standard Oil Company of California falsely implied through a demonstration of clean air and a pollution meter that Chevron gasoline with F-310 removed all or most pollutants from engine exhaust. In one ad, a car burning Chevron with F-310 emitted clear exhaust into a large see-through balloon tied to the exhaust pipe of the car. In another ad, the exhaust was contained in a transparent bag encircling the car. In a third, a meter dial labeled "exhaust emissions" pointed to "100" at the "dirty" end of the scale before Chevron with F-310 was used. After "just six tankfuls," the meter pointed to "20," four-fifths of the way toward "0" at the "clean" end of the scale. Meanwhile, another car in the ads, a car whose gasoline did not contain F-310, continued to emit dirty exhaust that clouded the balloon and bag.

The balloon ads were deceptive, the FTC said, because the clear Chevron exhaust appeared to contain no pollutants, when in fact it contained invisible but significant amounts of carbon monoxide and hydrocarbons. Independent scientific tests revealed that the F-310 additive did reduce pollutants but not as much as the balloon and bag demonstrations indicated. The ads were deceptive, the FTC said, "because of the substantial disparity between the visual impact of the demonstrations and the evidence which showed the actual average reductions."[97] The meter, too, was misleading because the drop of 80 units from the dirty end to the clean end did not correspond to the much smaller percentage reduction in pollutants a typical motorist would experience from using Chevron with F-310.

The U.S. Court of Appeals for the Ninth Circuit ruled that BBD&O, the advertising agency in the Chevron case, bore responsibility for the deceptive demonstrations. It is not enough that an advertising agency know that products will perform

---

[94] Firestone Tire & Rubber Co. v. FTC, 481 F.2d 246 (6th Cir.), *cert. denied*, 414 U.S. 1112 (1973).

[95] Caroline Mayer, "Bayer Settles Ad-Claim Dispute," *Washington Post*, Jan. 12, 2000, at E2.

[96] *In re* Colgate-Palmolive Co., 77 F.T.C. 150 (1970).

[97] *In re* Standard Oil Co., 84 F.T.C. 1401, 1470 (1974).

as the manufacturer claims, the court said. The agency also has a responsibility to represent that performance accurately. BBD&O argued that it should not be liable because it based the ads on information that had been validated by independent tests and approved by several departments at Chevron, including engineering, research and law.

However, the Ninth Circuit said it was not sufficient for BBD&O to satisfy itself only that F-310 did in fact reduce pollution. The agency also had a responsibility to ensure the accuracy of the implicit representations the ads conveyed. Said the court:

> No specialized engineer was needed to put BBD&O on notice that a gauge which drops from a reading of 100 ("dirty") to 20 ("clean") implies a sweeping representation with reference to the change in level of pollution discharge. In light of the advertising agency's active participation in developing this advertising, it was BBD&O's responsibility to assure itself not only that the gauge was not rigged, but also that use of the gauge did not convey a distorted impression.[98]

No Qualification Implication Advertisements are also misleading if they omit a necessary qualification. The FTC ruled, for instance, that a Firestone tire advertisement was misleading because it claimed without qualification that Firestone was "The Safe Tire." The company's claim was supported by the statement that Firestone tires pass all of the company's inspections.[99]

However, although it was true that Firestone marketed no tires that failed company inspections, the FTC ruled that the unqualified claim that Firestone tires were "safe" was deceptive because it falsely implied that the tires were free of all defects. Indeed, 15 percent of the respondents in a consumer survey thought the company was claiming that its tires were free of defects. But tests available at the time of the advertisement were insufficiently accurate to detect all defects in a tire.

Effective Qualification Implication Consumers are always warned to read the small type in an advertisement for qualifications, but the FTC says ads may be deceptive even if they contain accurate but ineffective qualifications. "A qualification presented weakly has the same impact as a qualification completely absent," Professor Ivan Preston observes.[100]

The FTC ruled that the advertisements for Chevron gasoline with F-310 were deceptive not only because the clear bags belied scientific tests for pollution, but also because the visual impact of the clear bags overwhelmed the verbal and written qualifications in the broadcast and print versions of the ads. The verbal and written parts of both balloon ads did not claim that the Chevron exhaust was completely "clean," only that it was "cleaner" than the other exhaust. Nor did the ads claim that Chevron eliminated pollution, only that it reduced it. Despite this qualifying language, the Federal Trade Commission ruled that the ads were misleading because the "strong, predominant visual message" of the clear balloons and bags implied a complete reduction in pollutants. "The net impression," the FTC said, "is overwhelmingly influenced by the striking visual portions of the advertisements."[101]

---

[98] *In re* Standard Oil Co. v. FTC, 577 F.2d 653, 660 (1978).

[99] *In re* Firestone Tire & Rubber Co., 81 F.T.C. at 457 (1972).

[100] "The Federal Trade Commission's Identification of Implications as Constituting Deceptive Advertising," 57 *U. Cin. L. Rev.* 1243 (1989).

[101] *In re* Standard Oil Co., 84 F.T.C. at 1471 (1974).

Significance Implication Insignificant facts stated so that they appear to be significant also create a false implication in advertising. In one case, advertisements for Old Gold cigarettes were deceptive even though they truthfully claimed that Old Golds were found "lowest in throat-irritating tars and resins." Though true, the ads created the false implication that smokers would benefit from choosing Old Golds over other brands.[102]

The study on which the cigarette ad claims were based was reported in *Reader's Digest*. In its report of the study, *Reader's Digest* concluded that the difference in tar and nicotine among cigarette brands was too insignificant to be important to smokers. One cigarette is "just about as good as another" to "nail down" a smoker's coffin, the *Digest* said.

The FTC ruled, in a decision upheld by a federal appeals court, that the Old Gold ads were deceptive because they falsely implied a significant difference among cigarettes. The advertisements, the court said, used the truth in a perverted way "to cause the reader to believe the exact opposite of what was intended" in the *Reader's Digest* article.

Puffery Implication Although advertising claims are supposed to be factual and represent the experience of the people making them, the law of advertising, like the law of libel, leaves room for subjective statements of opinion. Advertisers may exaggerate or "puff" their products on such subjective matters as taste, feel, appearance and smell. The commission assumes that ordinary consumers do not take **puffery** seriously.

It is acceptable puffery for an advertiser to say that a foreign sports car is "the sexiest European,"[103] that "Bayer works wonders,"[104] or that a motor oil is the "perfect" lubrication, allowing a car to travel an "amazing distance" without an oil change.[105] "So far as we know," a federal appeals court said, "there is nothing 'perfect' in this world, which undoubtedly means nothing more than that the product is good or of high quality." Such exaggeration is recognized as puffery and creates no false implication.

Puffery becomes deception when exaggerated claims falsely imply material assertions of superiority. However, determining when puffery becomes a materially misleading statement is very difficult. The FTC ruled that Jay Norris Company went beyond acceptable puffery when it advertised that a television antenna was an "electronic miracle." The FTC said the statement was one of several exaggerated claims that could lead consumers to believe falsely that the antenna was generally superior.[106]

One of the most famous puffery cases involved a man who insisted that Pepsi made an offer that he could have a Hawker Harrier jet if he turned in enough "Pepsi Points" as part of a marketing campaign the company launched in 1996. Pepsi's television ad featured teenagers browsing the "Pepsi Stuff" catalog in school, with items such as a Pepsi T-shirt for 75 points or a leather jacket for 1,450 points. At the end of the ad, a Hawker Harrier jet lands in front of the school, with a kid in the cockpit, and the note "Harrier Fighter 7,000,000 Pepsi Points" at the bottom of the screen. While Pepsi Points were typically gathered through

---

[102] P. Lorillard Co. v. FTC, 186 F.2d 52 (4th Cir. 1950).

[103] *In re* Bristol-Myers Co., 102 F.T.C. 21 (1983), *aff'd*, 738 F.2d 554 (2d Cir. 1984).

[104] *In re* Sterling Drug, Inc., 102 F.T.C. 395, *aff'd*, 741 F.2d 1146 (9th Cir. 1984).

[105] Kidder Oil Co. v. FTC, 117 F.2d 892 (7th Cir. 1941).

[106] *In re* Jay Norris, Inc., 91 F.T.C. 751 (1978), *aff'd*, Jay Norris, Inc. v. FTC, 598 F.2d 1244 (2d Cir.), *cert. denied*, 444 U.S. 980 (1979).

purchasing soft drink products, people could also buy a point for 10 cents, which a Washington man exploited by sending Pepsi a check for $700,000 and insisting he was accepting their offer to exchange 7 million Pepsi Points for the jet. When Pepsi declined to provide him the jet, valued at about $23 million, he sued. A federal district court ruled that the advertisement makes exaggerated claims common to television ads, that for example, buying a product will make the viewer "attractive, stylish, desirable, and admired by all," and that "a reasonable viewer would understand such advertisements as mere puffery, not as statements of fact" rather than literal truth. Because the ad was "clearly in jest," the court found that it was not really an offer, thus no contract existed, and Pepsi did not have to give the man a jet.[107]

Endorsements The FTC regulates product endorsements by consumers, experts, organizations and celebrities, requiring disclosure of "material connections" between advertisers and endorsers. The FTC requires advertisers to inform consumers if product endorsements are paid for with money or products. An endorsement is misleading if consumers would think the product evaluation is independent when in fact statements are sponsored advertising messages. FTC endorsement guidelines also include disclosure requirements to bloggers and others in social media who endorse products.[108] It may be particularly difficult for consumers to distinguish independent product evaluations from paid endorsement-advertisements in informal, interactive social media. Companies increasingly send products to bloggers to generate buzz about new commercial offerings.

Bloggers must disclose payments they receive in exchange for reviewing a product. "The post of a blogger who receives cash or in-kind payment to review a product is considered an endorsement," the FTC says. "Thus, bloggers who make an endorsement must disclose the material connections they share with the seller of the product or service."[109] A member of Elevenmoms.com, a bloggers group organized by Walmart, must disclose the merchandise they receive from Walmart retailers and suppliers if they review Walmart merchandise. A blogger who receives a car for a favorable review must disclose the material connection to the sponsor. A blogger who receives a free book probably does not.

Celebrities do not have to disclose their relationship to an advertiser if the relationship would be obvious to a consumer, as when a celebrity endorses a product in a prime-time television commercial. But the celebrity must disclose his or her material relationship to an advertiser if the celebrity is paid to endorse a product during a talk show conversation or other venue in which a consumer might not expect a favorable comment about a product was paid for. Under the new guidelines, celebrity endorsers as well as advertisers may be liable for false or unsubstantiated claims in an endorsement.

An expert is someone who has acquired superior knowledge of a subject as a result of experience, study or training. If experts claim in an advertisement that a product is superior, FTC guidelines require that the experts have expertise relevant to their product endorsements. Experts are also supposed to have compared a product they endorse with others. Astronaut Gordon Cooper's endorsement of a

---

[107] Leonard v. PepsiCo, 88 F. Supp. 2d 116, 128 (S.D.N.Y. 1999).
[108] FTC, "Guides Concerning the Use of Endorsements and Testimonials in Advertising," 16 C.F.R. § 255.0(b).
[109] FTC, "FTC Publishes Final Guides Governing Endorsements, Testimonials," Oct. 5, 2009: "What People Are Asking," May 2015.

fuel-saving automobile engine attachment was ruled to be deceptive because the astronaut's expertise was not in the field of automobile engines.[110]

If an organization endorses a product, the product should meet professional standards set by the organization.[111] Thus, mattresses endorsed by a chiropractic association should perform to standards set by the profession. Neither celebrities nor ordinary citizens need to possess special expertise to endorse a product.

For example, the FTC has also cracked down on video game companies that pay influencers to promote their products on YouTube. In 2016, Warner Bros. settled with the FTC after it was revealed that the company had paid individual YouTubers hundreds to thousands of dollars to promote its *Middle Earth: Shadow of Mordor* video game. The sponsored videos, which were viewed an estimated 5.5 million times, did not include any clear disclosure that they were sponsored. A text box that revealed the video was sponsored only if a viewer clicked on a "show more" button was inadequate, the FTC said. The settlement mandated clearer endorsement disclosures by Warner Bros. in future videos.[112]

In 2019, the FTC issued new guidelines for disclosure requirements to online influencers. These make it clear that "as an influencer, it is your responsibility to make these disclosures," rather than relying on companies to do it for you. Guidelines include disclosing "any financial, employment, personal, or family relationship with a brand," going beyond payments to include receiving free or discounted products or other perks. Endorsement activities include "tags, likes, pins, and similar ways of showing you like a brand." Disclosures should be placed so they are "hard to miss." For example, disclosures should not be buried in a mass of hashtags or hidden on an "About me" page away from the content where the endorsement activity is made. As an example, the FTC said on a photo account like Snapchat and Instagram, one should "superimpose the disclosure over the picture and make sure viewers have enough time to notice and read it." Endorsements made on live streams should be repeatedly regularly so they are not missed by people who do not watch the whole thing.[113]

Native Advertising Web platforms such as Facebook, Buzzfeed and Vice, as well as traditional news operations such as the *New York Times* and the *Atlantic*, have offered companies the chance to pay tens of thousands of dollars for content to be published that has the appearance of being an independent journalism effort.[114] However, studies have shown that, regardless of efforts by publishers to make sponsorship of content transparent, readers and viewers are often still confused about whether content is an advertisement.[115] FTC guidelines regarding native advertising—often also known as "sponsored content," "advertorials" or "brand publishing"—are in place to ensure that the relationship between sponsor and publisher is made clear to the audience. In the policy statement, the FTC noted that native advertisements "are deceptive if they mislead consumers into believing they are independent, impartial, or not from the sponsoring advertiser itself."

---

[110] *In re* Cooper, 94 F.T.C. 674 (1979).

[111] "Guides Concerning the Use of Endorsements and Testimonials in Advertising," 16 C.F.R. § 255.4.

[112] Austen Hufford, "FTC Says YouTube Gamers Didn't Adequately Disclose Payments," *Wall St. Journal*, July 11, 2016.

[113] "Disclosures 101 for Social Media Influencers," *Federal Trade Commission*, Nov. 5, 2019, www.ftc.gov/influencers (accessed Jan. 30, 2020).

[114] John Hermann, "In Media Company Advertising, Sponsored Content Is Becoming King," *N.Y. Times*, July 25, 2016, B1.

[115] Joe Lazauskas, "Study: Article or Ad? When It Comes to Native, No One Knows," *Contently*, Sept. 8, 2015.

These include, for example, publishing advertisements that are in the same format as news content, such as content with a byline and in the same font and column width as a news story or a video that resembles other video content usually produced by journalists on a news site. To avoid confusion, the FTC recommends native advertisements make the sponsorship relationship clear, with the word "advertisement" featured prominently.[116] Also helpful in distinguishing sponsored content are "visual cues such as the borders around or background shadings of ads or ad groupings."[117]

The FTC brought an enforcement action in 2016 against the retailer Lord & Taylor, which paid the online magazine *Nylon* to publish an article and to post photos of its fashion collections on Instagram without requiring *Nylon* to disclose the connections. In addition, Lord & Taylor paid 50 "influencers" between $1,000 and $4,000 to wear dresses from the collection and post photos of themselves on Instagram, also without requiring disclosure of the payments. As part of a settlement, Lord & Taylor was required to make future endorsement relationships on such platforms clear and conspicuous.[118]

State Regulations

All 50 states have enacted legislation that, like the Federal Trade Commission Act, prohibits unfair competition and unfair acts and practices or otherwise allows citizens and companies to sue over deceptive advertising.[119] Under many state laws, consumers as well as competitors can sue not only to stop deceptive advertising but also to recover damages and attorneys' fees.

Although states can regulate advertising only within their borders, regulations in important commercial states, such as Texas or Florida, have a national impact. During the many years of deregulation by the federal government, state attorneys general became more aggressive, suing airlines, car rental companies and other corporations over advertising that violated state laws, laws that sometimes reflected guidelines issued by the National Association of Attorneys General. National advertisers objected that they could not meet 50 different state standards for deception. State attorneys general also enforce regulations on tobacco marketing.

In a blow to state efforts to regulate national advertising, the Supreme Court ruled that states could not regulate airline advertising because federal airline rules preempt state law.[120] Because Congress claimed federal jurisdiction for regulation of airline advertising, the Court said that states could not sue airlines for failing to disclose ticket restrictions and charges in their advertisements. Congress has not claimed exclusive federal jurisdiction over all national advertisements. For example, the federal Food, Drug, and Cosmetic Act (FDCA) does not preempt state laws that allow lawsuits by consumers for deceptive claims on labels. A Massachusetts resident filed a national class action lawsuit in federal court against the New England Coffee Company for selling "Hazelnut Crème" coffee that did not actually have any hazelnut in the product. In 2019, the U.S. Court of Appeals for the First Circuit

---

[116] Enforcement Policy Statement on Deceptively Formatted Advertisements, Federal Trade Commission, Dec. 22, 2015.

[117] "Blurred Lines: An Exploration of Consumers' Advertising Recognition," *Federal Trade Commission Staff Report*, Dec. 2017.

[118] "FTC's Lord & Taylor Case: In Native Advertising, Clear Disclosure Is Always in Style," *Federal Trade Commission*, Mar. 15, 2016.

[119] Kenneth Plevan and Miriam Siroky, *Advertising Compliance Handbook* 289 (2nd ed. 1991).

[120] Morales v. Trans World Airlines, Inc., 504 U.S. 374 (1992).

allowed the case to proceed, finding that a reasonable customer would not necessarily go to the list of ingredients to confirm that it contained real hazelnut, but rather "would find in the product name sufficient assurance so as to see no need to search the fine print on the back of the package," and further finding that the class action under Massachusetts state law was not preempted by the FDCA.[121]

ONLINE CHALLENGES Enforcing state and federal commercial speech laws online can be a challenge because of the safe harbor provisions for providers and users of interactive computer services under Section 230 of the Communications Decency Act (see Chapter 4), by not treating them as a "publisher or speaker" of information provided by others. While this immunity from liability has been broadly applied in the context of libel claims, some courts have found ways around the shield to allow civil and criminal investigations of web hosts to proceed.

A website may lose its immunity under Section 230 if it creates or helps third parties to develop illegal content. A federal appeals court ruled that Roommate.com was not immune from liability under Section 230 because it required subscribers to state possibly discriminatory preferences before they could search listings or post housing opportunities on the site that matched people seeking a roommate to those offering a room for rent.[122]

Roommate.com required subscribers to answer a questionnaire disclosing their sex, sexual orientation and whether they would bring children to a household, as well as their preferences on those three matters and others. These were in drop-down menus built into the website. The court said Roommate.com lost its immunity under Section 230 by becoming a content provider, helping to create content that was possibly discriminatory in violation of federal and California fair housing laws.

The court said Section 230 does not grant immunity for "inducing" third parties to express illegal preferences. "By requiring subscribers to provide the information as a condition of accessing its service. . . . Roommate becomes much more than a passive transmitter of information provided by others. It becomes the developer, at least in part, of that information." The message to website operators is clear, the court said: "If you don't encourage illegal content, or design your website to require users to input illegal content, you will be immune."

While Roommate.com lost its immunity under Section 230 for inducing possibly discriminatory preferences, it did not lose its immunity for encouraging subscribers to provide "Additional Comments" that were sometimes provocative. Roommate.com was not responsible when subscribers wrote that they preferred white male roommates, only "BLACK, GAY, MALE" roommates, no "drugs, kids or animals," or, in one posting, a woman who "hopefully wont mind having a little sexual incounter [*sic*] with my boyfriend and I."

The Roommate.com ruling, however, has been widely criticized and largely seems to be limited to its unusual facts, which involved active participation by the web host in forcing consumers to reveal discriminatory information that violated fair housing laws. Ultimately, after years of litigation and appeal, Roommate.com was found not to have violated housing discrimination laws, rendering the Section 230 question of potential liability for illegality moot.

Typically, under Section 230, web hosts will not be held liable for the acts of their users, even if it allows distasteful content on the web to go unpunished. Sex trafficking victims and advocates have long tried to deter sex trafficking under

---

[121] Dumont v. Reily Foods Co., 934 F.3d 35, 40 (1st Cir. 2019).
[122] Fair Housing Council of San Fernando Valley v. Roommate.com, 666 F.3d 1216 (9th Cir. 2012).

federal and state laws, targeting websites that run advertisements enabling connections between sex dealers and buyers. Craigslist shut down its adult services advertising section in 2010, but Backpage.com continued to run advertisements for "adult entertainment" and "escorts," using Section 230 as a shield from civil liability. In 2016, a federal court of appeals bolstered Section 230 immunity for Backpage.com, in a lawsuit brought by sex trafficking victims who said they were minors at the time they were being featured in the "escorts" section and that Backpage.com facilitated these advertisements to maximize profits.[123] Congress responded in 2018 by passing the Fight Online Sex Trafficking Act (FOSTA), which amended Section 230 to remove protections for websites that opponents believed promoted prostitution and sex trafficking. The revisions permitted states and the federal government to enforce their laws against these actions and also added penalties, including up to ten years in prison for a website hosting content "with the intent to promote or facilitate the prostitution of another person."[124] The law led to the immediate shutdown of Craigslist's "personals" section, and the FBI seized Backpage.com in an enforcement action. Advocates for consensual adult sex workers said FOSTA put them in danger by removing the possibility of any safe platforms for them to offer their services.[125] FOSTA has been challenged on grounds that it violates the First Amendment by being overbroad and vague with mixed results. In 2020, the U.S. Court of Appeals for the D.C. Circuit allowed a First Amendment challenge aiming to stop enforcement of the law to proceed, but the court had not issued a final ruling two years later.[126] Meanwhile, a federal district court in Texas ruled in 2021 that the law was not unconstitutionally vague or overbroad and could be enforced against a man accused of facilitating sex trafficking on the website Cityxguide. com.[127]

▦ SUMMARY ▦

A number of federal and state agencies prohibit harmful trade practices. However, the Federal Trade Commission is the main enforcer of truth in advertising. Deceptive advertisements contain material statements or omissions that are likely to mislead reasonable consumers. Ads are deceptive if they contain expressly false statements or demonstrations. Ads are also deceptive if they contain true statements that convey a misleading implication. Deceptive implications may be found in advertisements that lack substantiation, lack sufficient qualification, contain misleading proofs or demonstrations, imply false significance, puff excessively and rely misleadingly on expertise and endorsements. Plaintiffs may also bring suits for deceptive advertising under state law. Web hosts of advertising, however, are largely shielded from such lawsuits by Section 230 of the Communications Decency Act.

FEDERAL REMEDIES

The FTC has a number of powers to prevent or remedy deceptive advertising. Some are future-looking, providing guidance to advertisers so that they can avoid deceptive advertising. These powers include staff opinion letters, industry guidelines and

---

[123] See Doe v. Backpage.com, 817 F.3d 12 (1st Cir. 2016).

[124] Allow States and Victims to Fight Online Sex Trafficking Act of 2017, Pub. L. No. 115–164.

[125] Rose Conlon, "Sex Workers Say Anti-trafficking Law Fuels Inequality," *Marketplace*, Apr. 30, 2019.

[126] Woodhull Freedom Foundation v. United States, 2020 U.S. App. LEXIS 2217 (D.C. Cir. 2020).

[127] United States v. Martono, 2021 WL 39584 (N.D. Tex. 2021).

rules. Some FTC powers focus on the present, permitting the agency to halt or correct a misleading or deceptive ad. These include consent decrees, cease-and-desist orders, affirmative disclosure and corrective advertising. In addition, the FTC, advertisers and consumers can seek court injunctions to halt deceptive ads. One of the FTC's most important powers is the authority to require advertisers to substantiate advertising claims before they are disseminated.

The FTC has been very active in investigation and enforcement efforts involving online advertisement and marketing. When social media companies violate the privacy promises they make in their terms of service, the FTC has been the federal agency taking enforcement action, including multimillion-dollar settlements with companies such as Facebook, Google and Snapchat. Cryptocurrency scams have been the target of FTC enforcement actions in recent years, with $80 million in losses reported by consumers in a six-month period starting in October 2020, a median of $1,900 per complaint. Scammers use online marketing through websites and social media to lure investors with "tips" or "secrets," or sometimes fake celebrity support. In 2021, the FTC reported consumers were defrauded out of $2 million on scams involving Elon Musk impersonators alone.[128] Social media are a "gold mine" for fraud, causing $770 million in reported losses to consumers in 2021, with more than 60 percent of those losses reported to the FTC stemming from marketing for investment scams and online shopping.[129]

Prospective Remedies

The FTC's opinion letters, advisory opinions, industry guides and trade regulation rules are broad statements that tell advertisers before they disseminate advertisements the kinds of statements and practices that may be deceptive. These are *prospective*, or future-looking, guidelines that help advertisers to avoid deceptive practices.

STAFF OPINION LETTERS Staff opinion letters are not specifically mentioned in the FTC's rules. They are a form of quick, free advice that does not bind the commission. If an advertiser wants an informal opinion on whether an ad might violate the law, the advertiser can ask for an opinion letter from the commission.

ADVISORY OPINIONS If advertisers want to know more than they can learn in a staff opinion letter about whether a contemplated activity would be legal, they can write to the FTC for an advisory opinion. An advisory opinion, which is more formal than a staff opinion letter, is placed in the public record and protects the requesting party who follows the advice from litigation until such time as the commission might shift its position.[130] However, although the advertiser who follows an advisory opinion is protected from a suit, an advertiser might find the commission's advice burdensome because the commission tends to be stricter in its advisory opinions than in its litigation.

INDUSTRY GUIDES Under Section 18 of the Federal Trade Commission Act, the FTC may prescribe "interpretive rules and general statements of policy with respect to unfair or deceptive acts or practices." One form of general statement is an industry guide. Unlike an advisory opinion, an industry guide is written for a whole industry. An industry guide is the FTC's interpretation of federal law but does

---

[128] Federal Trade Commission, "FTC Data Shows Huge Spikes in Cryptocurrency Investment Scams" (May 17, 2021).
[129] Federal Trade Commission, "Social Media a Gold Mine for Scammers in 2021" (Jan. 25, 2022).
[130] Advisory Opinions, 16 C.F.R. § 1.1–1.4 (1995).

not itself have the force of law. An advertiser who violates an industry guide may or may not be charged with deception or some other violation of federal law.[131]

FTC industry guides prescribe, often in minute detail, acceptable advertising and labeling of products as diverse as adhesives,[132] dog food[133] and toupees.[134] FTC regulations on product endorsements and testimonials are issued in the form of industry guidelines, as are regulations on deceptive pricing, fuel economy advertising for new automobiles, the women's handbag industry and cigarette labeling.[135]Sometimes industry guides are required by Congress. For example, a section of the Fur Products Labeling Act required the FTC to establish a fur products name guide so that animals used for furs would be uniformly identified. One FTC industry guide specifies that the word *free* may be used in an advertisement even if a consumer is charged a small fee for postage and handling.[136]

The FTC has issued guidelines to limit deception when advertisers claim environmental benefits from their products.[137] The guidelines prohibit general environmental claims such as "Eco-Safe" if the environmental benefits are not specifically listed. Use of the term *biodegradable*, the FTC said, should be reserved for advertising claims that can be substantiated with competent scientific evidence that the product will decompose in nature within a reasonably short period.

The FTC also has issued guidelines explaining when the agency will consider health and nutrition claims such as "low fat" or "high fiber" to be deceptive or misleading.[138] The FTC's policy derives from regulations issued by the Food and Drug Administration (FDA) for the labeling of foods.[139] Under FDA regulations, food labels must tell consumers what nutrients, fat, calories, cholesterol, salt and fiber are contained in labeled food, and the FDA sets criteria allowing food manufacturers to describe a food as "low fat" or "high fiber." The FTC looks to the FDA for guidance when determining whether health and nutrition claims in food advertising are deceptive.

The FTC has also issued a "Dot Com Disclosures" guide, telling advertisers how to avoid deceptive advertising on smartphones and social media. Disclosures necessary to avoid deception must be "clear and conspicuous" on any device, large or small, the FTC said. If a disclosure cannot be made clearly on a small screen, then that platform should not be used. It would be deceptive, the FTC said, if smartphone users had to zoom and scroll to read small type disclosing the monthly fee for a house-monitoring camera, or had to click a hyperlink to learn that a portable cooler would not keep food safe in a hot car.

Further, the Dot Com Disclosures guide gave examples for advertisements on social networking sites such as Twitter and Instagram. It is inadequate to merely link to the advertiser's website for full disclosures because readers may not be expected to click through. Additionally, making the ad pitch in one tweet and the disclosure in the next may not be adequate because the delay could make the two disconnected on the reader's timeline or stream. Instead, the FTC recommends

---

[131] *See generally* George Rosden and Peter Rosden, 3 *Law of Advertising* § 32.04[2] (1995).

[132] Guides Against Deceptive Labeling and Advertising of Adhesive Compositions, 16 C.F.R. § 235.

[133] Guides for the Dog and Cat Food Industry, 16 C.F.R. § 241.

[134] Guides for Labeling, Advertising, and Sale of Wigs and Other Hairpieces, 16 C.F.R. § 252.

[135] *See* George Rosden and Peter Rosden, 3 *Law of Advertising* § 32.04[2] (1993).

[136] Guide Concerning Use of the Word "Free" and Similar Representations, 16 C.F.R. § 251.

[137] Guides for the Use of Environmental Marketing Claims, 16 C.F.R. § 260.

[138] Enforcement Policy Statement on Food Advertising, 59 Fed. Reg. 28,388 (1994).

[139] "Food Labeling Regulations Implementing the Nutrition Labeling and Education Act of 1990: Opportunity for Comments," 58 *Fed. Reg.* 2066 (1993) (codified in part at 21 C.F.R. pts. 5, 20, 104, 105, 130).

beginning the tweet with "Ad:" or using #ad or #sponsored in the social media post.[140]

RULES A more sweeping and legally potent FTC power is the agency's rule-making authority. Rules may be required by statute or may be issued under the FTC's broad authority to prevent unfair and deceptive practices. The commission favors rules, like industry guides, because they allow for a more uniform and efficient policy than individual commission decisions. Rules, like industry guides, affect whole industries, not just an individual company or advertiser.

Rules are more potent than industry guides because they have the force of law. Advertisers who violate a rule may be sued for engaging in deceptive acts or practices in violation of Section 5 of the Federal Trade Commission Act. Violators may be required to refund money, return property, pay damages and pay civil penalties of up to $10,000 a day.[141]

When the FTC wishes to issue a rule, it must publish the text of the rule and reasons for proposing the rule. Advertisers, manufacturers and the public can then present written comments and testify at hearings. A final rule can be challenged in a federal appeals court within 60 days of its promulgation.

Several rules are mandated by statute. For example, the Comprehensive Smokeless Tobacco Health Education Act of 1986 requires health warnings on smokeless tobacco products and advertising.[142] The Hobby Protection Act of 1973 requires that imitation political posters, literature and buttons be marked with the year of publication.[143]

The FTC has issued a rule required by statute to curb misleading telemarketing. Under the Telemarketing Sales Rule, telemarketers must disclose "promptly and clearly" in their telephone calls their identities and that they are attempting to make a sale.[144] The caller must also disclose the nature of the goods or services offered. Costs of purchasing, receiving or using any good or service must also be conspicuously disclosed. The rule also prohibits calls before 8 A.M. and after 9 P.M. and prohibits threats and intimidation, profane or obscene language and repeated calling that abuses or harasses. However, the rule does permit telemarketers, including publishers and cable operators, to call more than once within any three-month period.

In 2008, the FTC amended its Telemarketing Sales Rule to allow consumers to easily opt out of receiving automated, recorded voice messages from commercial and charitable organizations. The amendment to the National Do-Not-Call Registry allows consumers to refuse future recorded messages by pressing a key or saying a particular word as the message is delivered. Consumers who find recorded solicitations on their answering machines can call a toll-free number to block future messages. Telemarketers must acquire written consent to send recorded telephone solicitations. The rules do not allow consumers to opt out of recorded political calls and market surveys because those calls are beyond the FTC's jurisdiction.[145] The law forbids automated calls or text messages to cell phones.

---

[140] FTC, ".com Dislosures: How to Make Effective Disclosures in Digital Advertising," Mar. 2013, https://www.ftc.gov/business-guidance/resources/com-disclosures-how-make-effective-disclosures-digital-advertising?msclkid=64b69b99a7a111eca14e08b1653d7956.
[141] 15 U.S.C. § 45(m)(1).
[142] Regulations Under the Comprehensive Smokeless Tobacco Health Education Act of 1986, 16 C.F.R. § 307.
[143] Rules and Regulations Under the Hobby Protection Act of 1973, 16 C.F.R. § 304.
[144] 16 C.F.R. pt. 310.
[145] *Id.*

Besides issuing rules mandated by statute, the FTC also issues trade regulation rules, often called *TRRs*, under its own authority. The commission first asserted
the power to issue trade rules in the early 1960s, when it issued the rule requiring
a health warning on cigarette packages.[146] In the years following, the commission
issued a number of rules, often specifying detailed requirements such as what information must be included in advertising about the power output of a home ampli-
fier[147] and how the size of television screens is to be measured (diagonally).[148]

Backed by a Supreme Court decision[149] and legislation,[150] the FTC in the
1970s issued several broad rules to prevent unfairness in advertising for eyeglasses,
vocational schools, funeral homes, used cars, and other products and services.
Businesses objected, arguing that rules based on "unfairness" were too vague to
follow without undue uncertainty and expense. Opposition to the FTC prevailed
when the agency proposed to ban all televised children's advertising as unfair. The
ban was justified, the FTC argued, because the relationship between powerful,
sophisticated corporate advertisers and susceptible children was inherently unfair.
The networks, advertisers and toy manufacturers, with $661 million in advertis-
ing revenues at stake, disagreed. If corporate advertising to children is inherently
unfair, they asked, why isn't all advertising unfair? Is even the average adult a match
for the refined marketing and psychological skills of Madison Avenue professionals
with millions to spend on an ad campaign?

Responding to the criticism of the FTC's aggressive campaign against unfairness, Congress passed legislation requiring the FTC to halt issuing broad unfairness rules, including its proposed ban on televised children's advertising.[151] By
1994, after years of acrimony, Congress again authorized the FTC to issue TRRs but
not vague rules attempting to prohibit a generalized "unfairness." The FTC is now
authorized to issue TRRs to halt unfair acts and practices that cause or are likely to
cause "substantial injury" to consumers, when consumers cannot reasonably avoid
the injury, and when the injury is not outweighed by countervailing benefits to
consumers or to competition.[152]

To reduce the likelihood of vague rules, Congress limited FTC discretion in
two ways. First, the Federal Trade Commission Act bars the FTC from relying on
"policy" considerations alone in determining what is unfair. The FTC must base a
TRR on a likelihood of substantial injury that the consumer cannot avoid.

Second, the Federal Trade Commission Act permits the FTC to issue a TRR
only to halt harmful acts and practices that are "prevalent," such as those that present a "widespread pattern of unfair or deceptive acts or practices."[153]

Halting Advertisements

If the FTC's warnings in advisory opinions, industry guides and rules fail to prevent deceptive advertising, the FTC can halt illegal ads through the use of consent
decrees and cease-and-desist orders. In addition, competing advertisers who might
be hurt by a deceptive advertisement can seek a court injunction.

---

[146] FTC, "Trade Regulation Rule for the Prevention of Unfair or Deceptive Acts or Practices in the Sale of
Cigarettes," 29 *Fed. Reg.* 8325 (1964).
[147] Trade Regulation Rule: Relating to Power Output Claims for Amplifiers Utilized in Home Entertainment
Products, 16 C.F.R. § 432.
[148] Deceptive Advertising as to Sizes of Viewable Pictures Shown by Television Receiving Sets, 16 C.F.R.
§ 410.
[149] FTC v. Sperry & Hutchinson Co., 405 U.S. 233 (1972).
[150] Magnuson-Moss Warranty Federal Trade Commission Improvement Act of 1975, 15 U.S.C. § 45.
[151] Federal Trade Commission Improvements Act of 1980, Pub. L. No. 96–252 (1980).
[152] 15 U.S.C. § 45(n).
[153] 15 U.S.C. § 57a(b)(3).

CONSENT DECREES More than 90 percent of FTC cases are settled by consent decrees in which a party agrees to discontinue an advertising practice.[154] Advertisers have a strong incentive to sign consent decrees. If they do not, the FTC may file a formal complaint against them. The formal complaint is often accompanied by considerable bad publicity, much more than accompanies a consent decree. In addition, an advertiser who signs a consent decree is not required to admit to false or deceptive advertising. Furthermore, a consent decree saves the costs and time of litigation. A signed consent order is published for public comment and becomes final after 60 days. Failure to abide by a consent order subjects a company to fines of up to $10,000 a day for as long as the advertising campaign continues.

The FTC seeks consent agreements to halt misleading infomercials and require advertisers to reimburse consumers who are misled. In response to the first complaint filed by the FTC against an Internet advertiser, Brian Corzine, who operated as Chase Consulting on America Online, agreed to refund the $99 customers paid him for advice to repair bad credit ratings. Corzine allegedly advised customers to use new federal taxpayer identification numbers on credit applications in place of their social security numbers. The FTC said customers who followed Corzine's advice would be providing false information.[155]

The FTC also finds violations of native advertising and sponsorship guidelines to be deceptive. The commission ordered Creaxion, a marketing and public relations company, and Inside Publications, a magazine publisher, to stop engaging in misrepresentations of their content and business relationship. Creaxion had worked with a company selling mosquito repellent during the 2016 Zika outbreak to market the product by paying former Olympic gold medal-winning gymnasts Carly Patterson and Jake Dalton to endorse the product on Instagram accounts. Creaxion also paid *Inside Gymnastics* magazine to publish "ads disguised as features or other articles of interest to its readers" about the product, but neither the company nor the magazine made it clear that this was sponsored content.[156]

Most consent decrees originate when a citizen or—more frequently—a competitor sends a letter to the FTC complaining about an advertising practice. Commission staff members, either in Washington, D.C., or at one of the several regional FTC bureaus, may also originate an inquiry. If it appears that ads are deceptive, the staff conducts an investigation. If the investigation reveals that corrective action may be necessary, a proposed complaint may be submitted to the commission. The commission notifies the party of the proposed complaint and asks whether the party would sign a consent order agreeing to discontinue the deceptive practice.[157] If so, the complaint can be abandoned.

CEASE-AND-DESIST ORDERS If consent cannot be reached, the FTC may issue a formal complaint leading to a cease-and-desist order. Once the formal complaint is issued, the advertiser loses the opportunity to sign a consent order. The commission begins the cease-and-desist proceedings if it determines that the action would be "to the interest of the public" as required by Section 5 of the Federal Trade Commission Act. As Justice Brandeis said, that interest must be "specific and

---

[154] George Rosden and Peter Rosden, 3 *Law of Advertising* § 33.01 (1999).
[155] Stuart Elliott, "Court Halts Ad for Credit Repair," *N.Y. Times*, Sept. 15, 1994, at D17.
[156] "PR Firm and Publisher Settle FTC Allegations They Misrepresented Product Endorsements as Independent Opinions, Commercial Advertising as Editorial Content," *Federal Trade Commission*, Nov. 13, 2018.
[157] George Rosden and Peter Rosden, 3 *Law of Advertising* § 33.02[2] (1999).

substantial."[158] If deception is trivial, the commission may decide that seeking a cease-and-desist order is not in the public interest.

The FTC has wide discretion to decide whether the public interest would be served by legal action against an advertisement. In deciding whether to take action, the FTC will answer such questions as how many consumers were deceived, how much money they lost, whether market forces would fix the problem without government intervention, and whether government intervention would be an effective deterrent.[159]

When the FTC issues a complaint against an advertiser, an investigation proceeds to adjudication. The FTC announces the complaint in a widely distributed press release sometimes accompanied by a press conference, either of which may damage a company's sales.[160] When the complaint is issued, the case is assigned to an FTC administrative law judge, who conducts a hearing much like a trial. The agency has the burden to establish substantial evidence that an advertiser has violated the law. The administrative law judge either dismisses the case or issues a cease-and-desist order that can be appealed to the full commission and then to a federal appeals court.

A cease-and-desist order becomes final after all appeals or after time runs out to make an appeal. Failure to abide by a cease-and-desist order, as with failure to abide by a consent decree, can lead to fines of up to $10,000 a day, but the fines are usually much less. In fact, a company might decide it makes better business sense to continue the ads and sustain the fines than to stop a successful ad campaign.

In one of the most famous and long-running cases, the FTC won a judgment against the makers of Geritol 14 years after a complaint was filed to halt misleading advertisements. The FTC filed a complaint in 1962 charging that the J.B. Williams Company's television advertisements for Geritol were misleading. The FTC said the ads for the vitamin-and-iron tonic misleadingly said the product was an effective remedy for tiredness, loss of strength and that "run-down" feeling. The FTC found the ad deceptive because Geritol is effective only in a minority of cases, in which tiredness is caused by a lack of the iron and vitamins in Geritol. In most cases, fatigue is caused by factors not affected by Geritol.

In 1964, the FTC issued a cease-and-desist order telling J.B. Williams to include statements in its ads that the vast majority of people who are run down do not suffer from iron or vitamin deficiencies that Geritol might correct. Two years later, the case was given to the Justice Department when J.B. Williams did not comply with the cease-and-desist order. The company was fined $800,000 in 1973 for violating the FTC's order, but a court of appeals ordered a new trial.[161] In 1976, 14 years after the complaint was filed, the FTC won a $280,000 judgment against the makers of Geritol.

INJUNCTIONS In some cases of deceptive advertising, particularly when public health might be at risk, the most important FTC goal is to stop the offending advertisement quickly. This can be accomplished with an injunction. Under Section 13 of the Federal Trade Commission Act, the commission can ask a federal district judge for an injunction to stop deceptive advertising for items such as food, drugs, cosmetics and financial products. For example, in *FTC v. National Commission on Egg Nutrition*, the FTC obtained a temporary injunction stopping

---

[158] FTC v. Klesner, 280 U.S. 19, 28 (1929).
[159] Deceptive and Unsubstantiated Claims Policy Protocol, 4 Trade Reg. Rep. (CCH) 39,059 (1975).
[160] George Rosden and Peter Rosden, 3 *Law of Advertising* § 34.03 (1999).
[161] United States v. J.B. Williams Co., 498 F.2d 414 (2d Cir. 1974).

statements asserting there is no scientific evidence linking egg consumption and heart disease.[162]

In recent years, the FTC has been taking actions against marketing of investment scams online involving cryptocurrency. In 2018, the FTC got an order against four people it accused of promoting "deceptive money-making schemes" through posts on social media sites and YouTube, where they asserted that their "Bitcoin Funding Team" could turn a $100 investment into $80,000 in monthly income. A federal district court issued a restraining order against the men from proceeding with their fraudulent marketing efforts and freezing their assets. The men ultimately settled with the FTC and agreed to pay more than $470,000 to refund to consumers.[163]

Although the commission obtained a temporary injunction in the *Egg Nutrition* case, the agency usually does not seek a permanent injunction, preferring to act through the slower and more thorough administrative process of seeking consent decrees or cease-and-desist orders. However, these processes are much too slow for consumers whose health is being harmed by a product or for companies being hurt commercially by a competitor's deceptive advertisements. Advertisers damaged by competitors' ads often seek injunctions in federal court under the Lanham Act, a subject addressed shortly.

Required Statements

Not only can the FTC halt deceptive advertising and punish the advertiser, but the agency can also order alterations in advertisements to make them accurate. Besides requiring substantiation, the FTC can tell advertisers that they must include certain words or phrases in their ads and correct false impressions created by deceptive ad campaigns.

The FTC's power to alter the content of advertisements is a power not usually enjoyed by the government. Critics charge that such a power violates the First Amendment as well as the purpose of the Federal Trade Commission Act. The FTC, critics say, is supposed to prevent deception, not to require the dissemination of information. But defenders of affirmative disclosure requirements say that the FTC cannot meaningfully prohibit deception unless it can sometimes require that statements be added to advertisements.

AFFIRMATIVE DISCLOSURE The Federal Trade Commission Act does not explicitly grant the FTC power to order disclosure. But Congress did recognize that advertisers must reveal facts necessary to keep ads from being deceptive.[164] Silence by an advertiser is not always deceptive, but silence is deceptive if it means a consumer might be hurt.[165]

Often a consent decree contains an affirmative disclosure requirement. In one case, the Morton Salt Company agreed to stop advertising Lite Salt in such a way that consumers would think it was more healthful than ordinary salt. In signing the consent order, the company agreed that future advertising of Lite Salt would contain the statement: "Not to be used by persons on sodium- or potassium-restricted diets unless approved by a physician."[166] In another case of affirmative disclosure,

---

[162] 517 F.2d 485 (7th Cir. 1975).
[163] Federal Trade Commission, "Promoters of Deceptive Chain Referral Schemes Involving Cryptocurrencies Agree to Settlement With FTC" (August 22, 2019).
[164] Committee on Interstate and Foreign Commerce, H.R. Rep. No. 1613, 75th Cong., 1st Sess. 5 (1937).
[165] Alberty v. FTC, 182 F.2d 36 (D.C. Cir. 1949), *cert. denied*, 340 U.S. 818 (1950).
[166] Morton-Norwich Products, Inc. [1973–1976 Transfer Binder] Trade Reg. Rep. (CCH) ¶ 20,891 (1975).

the FTC ordered the J.B. Williams Company to tell customers in Geritol ads that a vitamin-and-iron supplement will probably not correct a run-down feeling. Health warnings on cigarette packages are also a form of affirmative disclosure.

CORRECTIVE ADVERTISING In rare cases, the FTC requires that advertisements contain statements to correct misrepresentations created by a long-term, misleading advertising campaign. In a case involving Doan's pills, the FTC may impose corrective advertising if consumers develop false beliefs due to an advertising campaign and if consumers are likely to hold those false beliefs into the future.[167] To determine whether corrective ads are necessary, the FTC considers consumer surveys, the duration of the ads, the persuasiveness of the ad claims and how sophisticated the audience for the ads is.

In the Doan's case, the FTC imposed a corrective advertising requirement on the maker for eight years of advertisements that said that Doan's was an effective remedy for back pain and that the pills contained special ingredients not found in other nonprescription pain relievers. The FTC said that the ads made an unsubstantiated claim that Doan's pills were better for relieving back pain because of special ingredients. The FTC said the pills do contain ingredients not found in other nonprescription pain relievers, but there was no evidence Doan's pills were more effective because of the ingredients. The FTC told Novartis Corporation, Doan's pills' manufacturer, to stop making the "special ingredients" claims. The FTC also ordered Novartis to include a disclaimer in their ads: "Although Doan's is an effective pain reliever, there is no evidence that Doan's is more effective than other pain relievers for back pain."

The Court of Appeals for the D.C. Circuit upheld the FTC's Novartis decision.[168] The court said the FTC may impose a corrective advertising requirement if (1) deceptive advertising substantially has helped to create false beliefs in the public's mind, (2) the false beliefs likely will remain after the advertising campaign stops and (3) consumers continue making purchase decisions based on the false beliefs. The court said the FTC supported its finding that the Doan's pills advertisements met this test. The court said the FTC's use of survey research results and expert testimony was sufficient.

In the well-known Listerine case, the FTC required the Warner-Lambert Company to make statements in its advertising to correct a long-running campaign claiming that use of Listerine mouthwash would help to prevent colds.[169] The FTC ordered Warner-Lambert to include in $10 million of its advertising the statement that Listerine "will not help prevent colds or sore throats." The FTC also ordered the company to use the phrase, "Contrary to prior advertising." However, the Court of Appeals for the D.C. Circuit said requiring that phrase violated Warner-Lambert's First Amendment rights. The court said the FTC had required more speech than needed to correct the false impression. The court did uphold the FTC's requirement that Warner-Lambert say Listerine would "not help prevent colds or sore throats."

In a long-running fraud and racketeering case, federal District Judge Gladys Kessler in 2012 issued the final text of corrective messages to be published by major tobacco companies that had been found to have communicated for decades false and deceptive statements amounting to fraud under the racketeering laws. Judge Kessler ordered Philip Morris, R.J. Reynolds and other cigarette manufacturers to publish corrective statements about the adverse health effects of smoking,

---

[167] Novartis Corp., 1999 FTC LEXIS 90 (May 13, 1999).
[168] Novartis Corp. v. FTC, 223 F.3d 783 (D.C. Cir. 2000).
[169] Warner-Lambert Co. v. FTC, 562 F.2d 749 (D.C. Cir. 1977), *cert. denied*, 435 U.S. 950 (1978).

the addictiveness of smoking and nicotine, and the lack of any significant health benefit from smoking "low tar," "light," "ultra-light," "mild" and "natural" cigarettes. The companies were also ordered to disclose their manipulation of cigarette design and composition to ensure optimum nicotine delivery and the adverse effects of exposure to secondhand smoke.[170]

On appeal, the Court of Appeals for the D.C. Circuit ruled most of Judge Kessler's corrective disclosures could be required of the cigarette companies under the racketeering law because they are forward-looking disclosures that prevent future violations of the statute. Thus the appeals court approved Judge Kessler's requirement that cigarette companies publish statements proclaiming that

- Smoking kills, on average, 1,200 Americans every day.
- Smoking causes heart disease, emphysema and many cancers.
- Cigarette companies intentionally designed cigarettes with enough nicotine to create and sustain addiction.
- Smokers of "low tar" and filtered cigarettes inhale essentially the same amount of tar and nicotine as they would from regular cigarettes.
- Cigarette companies design filters and select cigarette paper to maximize the ingestion of nicotine.
- Secondhand smoke kills over 38,000 Americans each year.

While upholding many of Judge Kessler's required disclosures, the appeals court did overturn the requirement that cigarette companies announce they "deliberately deceived the American public" about the dangers of cigarettes. Requiring a disclosure of past misconduct might have been permissible in a Federal Trade Commission proceeding, the court said, but the court ruled the racketeering statute only allows corrective statements that will prevent future violations.

Competitor Remedies

Consumers, of course, are not the only people hurt by deceptive advertisements. Advertisers, too, may be hurt by the false and deceptive claims of competing companies. However, the FTC offers little immediate relief for a competitor whose major concern is to quickly stop a deceptive ad that may hurt business. Even if the FTC agrees to seek an injunction, the process may be too slow to be of much help to the damaged competitor. Therefore, companies often seek court injunctions themselves to stop the deceptive ads of competing companies.

Companies seek injunctions under Section 43(a) of the Lanham Trademark Act of 1946, the same act discussed earlier in the intellectual property chapter. Besides protecting trademarks, the Lanham Act, as amended in 1988, prohibits any person's "false or misleading representation of fact" in "commercial advertising or promotion" that "misrepresents the nature, characteristics, qualities, or geographic origin of his or her or another person's goods, services, or commercial activities."[171] Anyone, whether a competitor or not, who believes that he or she "is or is likely to be damaged" by deceptive advertising may seek an injunction. Courts, however, have often restricted recovery under the Lanham Act to those who have suffered "competitive injury." The U.S. Court of Appeals for the Third Circuit has ruled

---

[170] United States v. Philip Morris USA, Inc., 907 F. Supp. 2d 1 (D.D.C. 2012); United States v. Philip Morris USA Inc., 2015 U.S. App. LEXIS 8469 (D.C. Cir. May 22, 2015).
[171] 15 U.S.C. § 1125(a).

that consumers may not sue sellers for false advertising under the Lanham Act.[172] Plaintiffs usually seek to halt an offending ad, but they may also be entitled to significant monetary damages.

Before the 1988 amendments to the Lanham Act, competitors could sue under Section 43(a) only if the defendant's advertisement contained false statements about his or her own products. After the 1988 amendments, anyone may sue to stop advertisements in which defendants make false claims either about their own products or about the plaintiff's.

Employing the law before 1988, the makers of Minute Maid orange juice halted Tropicana orange juice ads that contained falsehoods about Tropicana. In the ads, Olympic champion Bruce (now Caitlyn) Jenner squeezed fresh oranges and poured the juice into a Tropicana carton as a voice proclaimed, "It's pure, pasteurized juice as it comes from the orange."[173]

The Coca-Cola Company, which sells Minute Maid, claimed the Tropicana ads were misleading because Tropicana orange juice, like most ready-to-serve orange juices, is not packaged as it "comes from the orange." It is pasteurized and sometimes frozen before packaging. Even though the Tropicana ad said the juice was pasteurized, the U.S. Court of Appeals for the Second Circuit granted a preliminary injunction to stop the ads because they were likely to harm Minute Maid. A "not insubstantial" number of consumers surveyed mistakenly believed Tropicana juice came unprocessed from the orange.

Often competitors attempt to stop deceptive comparative advertisements under Section 43(a). All ads invite comparison, but so-called comparative ads point out the similarities and differences between an advertiser's product and its competitors'. The FTC has defined comparative advertising as ads that compare named or identified competing brands for objectively measurable attributes or price.[174] Although advertisers, the networks and the FTC once frowned on comparative advertisements, the FTC now encourages companies to name and compare competitors' products in advertisements.[175] Comparative ads, which are popular today, are thought to help consumers make better choices.

Johnson & Johnson, the manufacturer of Tylenol, obtained an injunction against Anacin ads that falsely claimed Anacin was a superior pain reliever.[176] The televised ads claimed Anacin could reduce inflammation from muscle strain, backache and tendonitis faster than other pain relievers. "Your body knows the difference between these pain relievers . . . and Adult Strength Anacin," the ad said. Unlike the Tropicana ad, which did not mention Minute Maid by name, the Anacin ad showed the competing products—Datril, Tylenol and Extra Strength Tylenol—on the screen. A federal court enjoined the Anacin ads because they left the impression with consumers surveyed that Anacin was a better pain reliever overall. The real superiority of Anacin, if any, was its ability to reduce inflammation.

Although companies usually seek an injunction under Section 43(a) to stop a competitor's deceptive advertisement, plaintiffs may also seek monetary damages—large monetary damages. In 1986, the U.S. Court of Appeals for the Ninth Circuit upheld a $40 million damage award against Jartran rental truck company for

---

[172] Serbin v. Ziebart Int'l Corp., 11 F.3d 1163 (3d Cir. 1993).
[173] Coca-Cola Co. v. Tropicana Prods., Inc., 690 F.2d 312 (2d Cir. 1982).
[174] 16 C.F.R. § 14.15(b) n.1.
[175] 16 C.F.R. § 14.15(b).
[176] American Home Prods. Corp. v. Johnson & Johnson, 577 F.2d 160 (2d Cir. 1978).

its deceptive ads during a marketing battle with U-Haul.[177] Jartran's ads deceptively portrayed the company's rates as lower and its trucks as newer than U-Haul's. The court awarded U-Haul $6 million in benefits that Jartran received from its deceptive advertising campaign and $13.6 million that U-Haul had to spend to counter Jartran's deceptive ads. Then the court doubled the award to U-Haul, as the Lanham Act allows when ads hurt a competitor.

The authors of a treatise on advertising have offered several suggestions for avoiding litigation over comparative advertisements, including the following:[178]

- Make comparative ads truthful.
- Avoid subjective claims. Use objective claims that can be substantiated.
- Use reliable independent testing services or public surveying firms to substantiate claims.
- Keep the results of the substantiation.
- Present the comparison fairly.
- Avoid knocking the competitor's business practices.

Tobacco Advertising

In 2009, Congress passed major legislation to reduce the health hazards of smoking, especially to youth. Many of the provisions of the Family Smoking Prevention and Tobacco Control Act regulate the advertising and promotion of cigarettes and other tobacco products which, as Judge Kessler said, have often been aimed at young people. Most new smokers, Congress noted in the statute, are under 18.[179] Congress in its "findings" concluded that tobacco use is "the foremost preventable cause of premature death in America," causing more than 400,000 deaths in the United States each year. Congress said reducing the use of tobacco by minors by 50 percent would prevent "well over 10,000,000 of today's children from becoming regular, daily smokers, saving over 3,000,000 of them from premature death due to tobacco-induced disease," and saving $75 billion in health care costs. "In 2005, cigarette manufacturers spent more than $13 billion to attract new users, retain current users, increase current consumption, and generate favorable long-term attitudes toward smoking and tobacco use," Congress found.[180]

The Family Smoking Prevention and Tobacco Control Act authorizes the Food and Drug Administration to control the manufacturing, marketing, advertising and labeling of tobacco products. Congress concluded the FDA is the only agency with the scientific expertise to regulate lawful products known to contain an addictive drug—nicotine—and other ingredients known to cause cancer. Advertisements that violate the Smoking Prevention Act are also deceptive or unfair in violation of the Federal Trade Commission Act, the law that regulates most advertising. The new law requires the Federal Trade Commission to coordinate with the Food and Drug Administration on enforcement of FTC regulations on advertising of cigarettes and smokeless tobacco. The FDA consults with the FTC to revise labeling requirements, normally under FDA jurisdiction. The FDA was also to reissue 1996 regulations on the sale, distribution and use of cigarettes and smokeless tobacco, rules the agency was not able to enforce when first issued because the Supreme

---

[177] U-Haul Int'l, Inc. v. Jartran, Inc., 793 F.2d 1034 (9th Cir. 1986).
[178] George Rosden and Peter Rosden, 3 *Law of Advertising* § 31.05 (1999).
[179] Family Smoking Prevention and Tobacco Control Act, Pub. L. No. 111–31.
[180] *Id.* Congressional findings are contained in Section 302 of the statute.

Court ruled Congress had not then authorized the agency to regulate tobacco marketing.[181]

The Smoking Prevention Act gives the FDA power to restrict tobacco advertising and promotions, to collect user fees from tobacco companies to support tobacco control, and to stop illegal sales of cigarettes and other products to children. Under the law, the FDA can reduce—but not eliminate—nicotine in tobacco products and require elimination of harmful additives and prohibit the use of most flavorings.

The law prohibits outdoor advertising within 1,000 feet of a school or playground, bans brand sponsorships of sports and entertainment events, and bans free samples. The law also requires that outdoor cigarette advertising be black text on a white background. Tobacco ads in print publications must also be black and white unless the adult readership is high—above 85 percent—or readership under age 18 is low—fewer than two million for a national publication.

The Smoking Prevention Act requires the FDA's prior approval before a tobacco company can sell or advertise new products, including products that claim to offer less risk of disease or to be less harmful than other products. The FDA will demand scientific proof to verify such claims. No advertising or labels will be allowed that suggest the FDA approves a tobacco product. Health warnings now must cover half of a cigarette package and include graphic images of the harm caused by smoking. Advertisements and labels are supposed to identify a tobacco product as a "nicotine delivery device."

Shortly after the Smoking Prevention Act was adopted, the National Association of Attorneys General promised to collaborate with the Food and Drug Administration enforcing regulations on the tobacco industry.[182] The state attorneys general had 11 years of experience enforcing the Master Settlement Agreement of 1998 in which the tobacco industry gained some protections from lawsuits, agreed to stop marketing tobacco to youth and agreed to pay states $206 billion compensation for medical costs of smoking. Under the master settlement, the tobacco companies also agreed to finance a $1.5 billion antismoking campaign and to open previously secret industry documents. The master agreement contains many marketing and advertising provisions that are similar to, or identical to, those the Food and Drug Administration is expected to enforce.

In the Smoking Prevention Act, Congress declared that advertising and labeling regulations must be consistent with First Amendment speech protections. But six tobacco companies quickly filed suit challenging the constitutionality of the statute.[183] See editorial advertisement, "Protecting Our Speech," published by the Lorillard Tobacco Company, Figure 8.2. Philip Morris was the lone cigarette company to back passage of the law, perhaps hoping FDA controls on advertising and limits on new tobacco products will solidify the market dominance of Philip Morris' Marlboro cigarette.[184]

The U.S. Court of Appeals for the D.C. Circuit ruled in 2012 that color graphics required by the government to illustrate the dangers of smoking were not

---

[181] FDA v. Brown & Williamson Tobacco Corp., 529 U.S. 120 (2000).

[182] National Association of Attorneys General, Letter regarding Docket No. FDA-2009-N-0294, Dec. 9, 2009.

[183] Commonwealth Brands, Inc. v. United States, No. 1:2009cv00117 (W.D. Ky. filed Aug. 31, 2009).

[184] Duff Wilson, "Philip Morris's Support Casts Shadow Over a Bill to Limit Tobacco," *N.Y. Times*, Mar. 31, 2009.

FIGURE 8.2 Editorial advertisement published by the Lorillard Tobacco Company challenging the constitutionality of tobacco advertising restrictions in the Family Smoking Prevention and Tobacco Control Act. Reprinted with permission.

constitutional. The D.C. Circuit said the graphic pictures, which were to be emblazoned on cigarette packages, contained emotional appeals to discourage smoking rather than uncontested factual statements required to counter the misleading and deceptive advertising disseminated by the tobacco companies.[185] Furthermore, the court said the FDA provided not a "shred" of evidence the graphic images would advance the government's interest in reducing smoking.

---

[185] R.J. Reynolds Tobacco Company v. Food & Drug Administration, 696 F.3d 1205 (D.C. Cir. 2012).

The graphic images showed people dying from smoking-related disease and mouth and gum damage linked to smoking. One image of a mother holding a baby encircled in smoke warned: "Tobacco smoke can harm your children." Another image showed smoke escaping from a hole in the neck of a man holding a cigarette. "Cigarettes are addictive," the caption said.

In early 2013, the government determined not to appeal the D.C. Circuit opinion but, rather, to abandon the graphic images and reconsider the government's efforts to warn citizens of the dangers of smoking.[186] Meanwhile, the Centers for Disease Control and Prevention renewed a series of television ads in which ex-smokers harmed by smoking warn smokers to quit.[187]

In 2015, major tobacco companies sued the FDA, claiming the agency violated the First Amendment by requiring companies to get prior approval for nearly all changes in cigarette labels. The FDA guidance issued in March required preapproval if the labels would make a product already on the market "distinct," including changing the background color of an existing product from green to red, changing its logo or adding words such as "premium tobacco."[188]

■ SUMMARY ■

The Federal Trade Commission has several powers and remedies to keep the flow of commercial information clean. The forward-looking powers include staff opinion letters, advisory opinions, industry guides and trade regulation rules. In addition, the FTC can halt deceptive advertising through consent decrees, cease-and-desist orders and injunctions. The FTC can also require that advertisements contain statements necessary to leave an accurate impression or to correct misrepresentation. In addition, companies may seek injunctions under the Lanham Act to halt false or misleading advertisements and promotions by competitors. Consumers may not sue advertisers under the Federal Trade Commission Act or the Lanham Act, but they may sue under state law and may eventually prevail in a suit under the Racketeer Influenced and Corrupt Organizations Act (RICO). The Family Smoking Prevention and Tobacco Control Act puts regulation of tobacco advertising and marketing under control of the Food and Drug Administration and adds significant new restrictions on advertising of tobacco products.

OTHER FEDERAL REGULATIONS

While deception and unfairness are major concerns in the regulation of advertising, consumers claim protection from fraud and misuse of electronic data in the modern media. This section examines regulations on the amount and content of broadcast advertising, the control and security of personal data and the regulation of contests and the depiction of money in advertising.

Children's Television

Parents and citizen groups often contend that children's television programs contain too much advertising. In response, the 1990 Children's Television Act limits the quantity of advertising aired during children's programs. The 1990 legislation limits

---

[186] Jennifer Corbett Dooren, "FDA Scraps Graphic Cigarette Warnings," *Wall St. J.*, Mar. 19, 2013.
[187] CDC.gov/Quitting/Tips.
[188] Tripp Mickle, "U.S. Tobacco Companies File Suit Against FDA Over Label Regulations," *Wall St. J.*, Apr. 14, 2015.

commercial time during children's programming to ten-and-a-half minutes an hour on weekends and 12 minutes on weekdays. The FCC said half as much advertising would be allowed during half-hour programs. The commission said the commercial limits pertain only to programming for children ages 12 and younger, "children who can neither distinguish commercial from program material nor understand the persuasive intent of commercials."

Television broadcast stations and cable operators must abide by the commercial limits, and they must keep records to verify compliance with the statute. Cable operators are responsible for limiting children's advertising in locally originated programming and cable network programming, but they are prohibited by other laws from editing programming, including advertising, transmitted by over-the-air broadcast licensees. The commercial limits apply to advertising just before and after programming but not to public service announcements and noncommercial mini-programs fewer than five minutes in length.[189]

In 2006 the FCC adopted rules prohibiting the display of website addresses during children's programming if the website is selling a product. A website address may be displayed during programs directed to children ages 12 and under only if it meets four criteria establishing that the site supplements the program and is not a sales promotion:

1. The website offers a substantial amount of program-related content or other noncommercial material.
2. The website is not primarily intended for commercial purposes, including either e-commerce or advertising.
3. The website's home page and other menu pages are clearly labeled to distinguish noncommercial from commercial sections.
4. The website page to which viewers are directed by the website address is not used for e-commerce, advertising or other commercial purposes.[190]

The FCC regards the display of the address of a website that sells a product as the "equivalent of a commercial encouraging children to go to the store and buy the product." Thus, including the web address during a program converts the program into a commercial, "just as a host telling children to race to their local toy store would," the agency wrote.[191]

Broadcasters are allowed to display the addresses of commercial websites during allowable commercial time. However, during both programs and commercials, broadcasters are not allowed to display the address of a website that uses characters from the program to sell products or services.

The FCC imposes serious fines on broadcasters for violating the commercial time limitations. The FCC fined KTTU (TV) of Tucson $125,000 because the commission found KTTU exceeded commercial limits 581 times in a 16-month period.[192] The commission also granted the station only a short-term license renewal of two years.

PRODUCT-BASED PROGRAMMING AND PROGRAM-LENGTH COMMERCIALS Parents not only protest the quantity of advertising in children's programming but also complain about what they call "program-length commercials," programs based on toys and other commercial products during which ads

---

[189] Children's Television Programming, 6 F.C.C.R. 2111, 68 P & F Rad. Reg. 2d 1615 (1991).

[190] 47 C.F.R. § 73.670 (broadcasting); 47 C.F.R. § 76.225 (cable).

[191] Clear Channel Television, Inc., 10 F.C.C.R. 3773 (1995).

[192] Mass Media Bureau Advises Commercial Television Licensees Regarding Children's Television Commercial Limits, 13 F.C.C.R. 10265 (1998).

for the same products are broadcast. Citizen groups complain that children's shows featuring commercial products, including *The Adventures of the Gummi Bears* and *Captain N: The Game Master*, are nothing more than program-length commercials for candy, video games and other products. The groups want the FCC to require that the shows be labeled as commercials, which would mean that the half-hour shows would violate the limits of ten-and-a-half or 12 commercial minutes an hour for children's programming.

The FCC has ruled, however, that a program based on a commercial product is not, by definition, a "program-length commercial." The FCC said that a product-based program is a program-length commercial only if both the show and the ads feature the same product. In 1993, the commission fined WFTS-TV of Tampa $10,000 for running a program-length commercial. The station ran two advertisements for G.I. Joe toys during a 30-minute *G.I. Joe* program featuring cartoons based on the toy. The commission said the entire program counted as commercial time because both the program and the ads in the program featured the same product line.[193]

The FCC also prohibits "host-selling," in which a character in a program promotes a product or service that is financially connected to the program. A program character would engage in host-selling if it promoted the virtues of saving at First Bank when First Bank has a relationship to the show or the character. Host-selling is thought to take unfair advantage of the trust children place in program characters. To further prevent confusion in young minds, the FCC requires that commercials be separated from children's program content with a buffer, such as "It's now time for a commercial break."[194]

SPONSOR IDENTIFICATION The FCC also has said companies that give programs to broadcast stations in return for advertising time do not have to be identified as sponsors of the programs under Section 317 of the Communications Act. Section 317, the sponsorship identification requirement, mandates that broadcasters identify anyone who pays to have a commercial or a program broadcast. A station must identify on the air anyone who pays for a program to air or provides a program free if the program promotes a product, service or trademark. Sponsorship identification is intended to prevent deception by telling viewers who is paying for a program or commercial.

In a case involving one of the most popular children's programs of the late 1980s, the FCC held that broadcast stations did not have to identify the companies providing *He-Man and the Masters of the Universe* to stations if the companies received advertising time in return. The commission rejected the contention of a citizen group, the National Association for Better Broadcasting (NABB), that KCOP-TV of Los Angeles should have told viewers the program *He-Man* had been given to the station by makers of the toy of the same name. *He-Man*, based on an invincible animated hero, had been given to the station by Mattel and Group W in exchange for two minutes of advertising time during children's programming. The NABB said the *He-Man* cartoon amounted to a gift to the station because the advertising time provided by KCOP-TV was worth only a small proportion of the program's value. Mattel and Group W spent $14 million on the first 65 episodes of *He-Man* and received commercials from KCOP-TV worth about $300,000.

---

[193] Children's Television Obligations of Digital Television Broadcasters, Second Order on Reconsideration and Second Report and Order (FCC 06–143) (Sept. 29, 2006).
[194] Children's Television Programming, 6 F.C.C.R. 2111, 68 P & F Rad. Reg. 2d 1615, *modified on reconsideration on other grounds*, 6 F.C.C.R. 5093, 69 P & F Rad. Reg. 2d 1020 (1991).

In 1989, the FCC said that stations need not identify the source of a program as long as the stations gave something of value, including advertising time, in return. In a decision upheld by a federal appeals court, the commission said a station would have to identify the source of a toy-based program only if it had been given to a station free or for only "trifling" consideration.[195] The more than $300,000 worth of advertising exchanged by KCOP-TV for *He-Man*, the commission said, was of substantial value and not an insignificant, or "trifling," amount. The commission said no single station would be expected to pay the entire cost of a nationally ranked children's program.

Broadcast Advertising

Although advertising can be limited during children's programs, the amount of commercial time in other programming is not restricted. The FCC has said that marketplace forces can better determine the number and length of commercials than FCC rules can. The commission said that if stations air more commercials than the public will tolerate, "the market will regulate itself"—viewers will not watch and advertisers will not buy time.[196]

However, a few federal statutes still regulate commercials. Section 317 of the 1934 Communications Act, for example, requires that broadcasters identify anyone who has purchased broadcast time, a provision that was just mentioned in this chapter.[197] In commercials, use of an advertiser's name or product constitutes sufficient identification of the sponsor.[198] In 2008, the FTC sought comments on whether the agency should require more disclosure of payments when companies place their products in television programs or embed their products in program plot lines. Companies increasingly embed their products in television programs as viewers increasingly employ technology to avoid commercials.

Two federal statutes ban broadcast advertising of cigarettes, little cigars and chewing tobacco.[199] Wine and beer have been advertised on broadcast stations for years, but liquor usually has not been. Liquor advertisements are not prohibited by statute or the FCC; liquor ads have been kept off the air voluntarily by trade associations representing broadcasters and the alcoholic beverage industry. States often place limits on advertising in all media for happy hours, two-for-one specials and other ad content that might encourage irresponsible drinking.

Broadcast beer advertisements are generally aimed at audiences where at least 70 percent of the listeners or viewers are above the legal drinking age. The FTC has ruled that advertisements may be unfair or deceptive if aimed at audiences too young to use the products lawfully. Ads show safe, moderate drinking, in compliance with FTC decisions and trade association rules.[200]

The FDA oversees advertising for prescription drugs, including the billions of dollars pharmaceutical companies spend annually in their advertising campaigns aimed directly to consumers (DTC). Some televised ads raise serious health

---

[195] *In re* Complaint of Nat'l Ass'n for Better Broadcasting Against Television Station KCOP(TV), 4 F.C.C.R. 4988, 66 P & F Rad. Reg. 2d 889 (1989), *aff'd*, 902 F.2d 1009 (D.C. Cir. 1990).
[196] Television Deregulation, 98 F.C.C.2d at 1105, 56 P & F Rad. Reg. 2d at 1028.
[197] 47 U.S.C. § 317(a)(1).
[198] 47 C.F.R. § 73.1212(f), (g), (h).
[199] 15 U.S.C. §§ 1335, 4402(f). The ban on cigarette advertising was upheld in Capital Broadcasting Co. v. Mitchell, 333 F. Supp. 582 (D.C. Cir. 1971), *aff'd without opinion*, 405 U.S. 1000 (1972).
[200] Davis Wright Tremaine, "Broadcast Law Blog," www.broadcastinglawblog.com, Nov. 30, 2007.

concerns. Merck and Company's heavily advertised Vioxx enjoyed annual sales of $2.5 billion despite evidence that it caused heart problems.

Under FDA regulations, direct-to-consumer ads

1. cannot be false or misleading.
2. must present a fair balance between the risks and benefits of the drug.
3. must reveal facts that are material to the representations made in the ad or the consequences of using the product.
4. must—if printed—disclose the risks listed in the product's labeling or—if broadcast—make "adequate provision" through toll-free telephone numbers, websites, brochures and other means to disclose risks.[201]

The FDA has also drafted guidance to the medical industry about making statements on social media. For example, because platforms such as Twitter have a limited character count, the FDA suggests balance in communicating benefit and risk information both within the same tweet while also including a link to more complete information about the drug or product.[202]

Personal Data

Control of personal data online is an increasingly nettlesome issue. In one of the earliest publicized cases of stolen personal data, it was revealed that sham businesses purchased the personal records—names, addresses, social security numbers—of 150,000 consumers from ChoicePoint, an information services company that sold personal data to credit card companies, mortgage companies and banks that offer loans and mortgages to consumers.[203] By one estimate, data companies, media companies, universities and other data handlers collectively mishandled nearly 94 million private records in one two-year period.[204] In addition, search engines like Google and social media companies like Facebook collect and store billions of bits of information from their users, building "big data" profiles that are extremely valuable to third parties such as advertisers and political campaigns. With such vast information, advertisers can profile the preferences of consumers and target ads instantaneously as consumers click on related websites.

In 2008, the FTC issued revised principles for advertisers' self-regulation of online behavioral advertising,[205] principles that are continuously revised in a dynamic advertising environment.[206] Of most concern to the agency is behavioral advertising itself, which the agency defines as "the tracking of a consumer's online activities over time—including the searches the consumer has conducted, the web pages visited, and the content viewed—in order to deliver advertising targeted to the individual consumer's interests." Behavioral ads account for about $1 billion of the $23 billion online ad revenue.[207] Of lesser concern to the FTC are "first party"

---

[201] "Congress Passes FDA Bill Without DTC Ad Limits," *Manatt, Advertising Law*, Oct. 19, 2007, https://manatt.com/insights/newsletters; "Prescription Drugs: FDA Oversight of Direct-to-Consumer Advertising Has Limitations," *U.S. General Accounting Office*, GAO-03-177, Oct. 2002.

[202] Thomas Abrams, "FDA Issues Draft Guidance for Industry on Social Media and Internet Communications About Medical Products: Designed with Patients in Mind," *FDA Voice*, June 14, 2014.

[203] Steve Lohr, "Surging Losses, but Few Victims in Data Breaches," *N.Y. Times*, Sept. 27, 2006.

[204] Tom Zeller, Jr., "Link by Link: 93,754,333 Examples of Data Nonchalance," *N.Y. Times*, Sept. 25, 2006.

[205] FTC, "Self-Regulatory Principles for Online Behavioral Advertising," 2008.

[206] *See* FTC, "FTC Staff Revises Online Behavioral Advertising Principles," Feb. 12, 2009, https://www.ftc.gov/news-events/news/press-releases/2009/02/ftc-staff-revises-online-behavioral-advertising-principles?msclkid=47dfbb4ba80111ecb4cdde86630065b3.

[207] FTC, "FTC Grapples with Privacy at Roundtable with Industry Professionals, Privacy Advocates, Academics," *Online Media Daily*, Dec. 7, 2009.

advertising, where no data are shared with third parties, and contextual advertising, where delivery of an advertisement is based on a single visit to a web page or a single search query.

One of the principles for behavioral advertisers seeks "transparency and consumer control," requiring websites to provide a clear, concise statement about data being collected and allowing consumers to opt out of providing data. A second principle provides for "reasonable security" and limited retention of consumer data. The third requires consent from consumers if a company plans to make material changes to existing privacy agreements. The fourth principle allows consumers to refuse to allow tracking of health, financial, family and other sensitive information.

In an illustrative case, the FTC settled a complaint with Sears Holdings Management Corporation—owned by Sears, Roebuck and Company and Kmart Management Corporation—in which Sears agreed to make fuller disclosure of its behavioral tracking program and to destroy research data collected through a company software program.[208] The FTC had charged that Sears software monitored consumers' online secure sessions even though consumers thought the software was only monitoring their "online browsing." In fact, the software collected data on the contents of a consumer's online shopping carts, online bank statements, drug prescription records, video rental records, library borrowing histories, and the sender, recipient and subject of web-based emails.

According to the FTC's complaint, Sears invited consumers to "participate in exciting, engaging, and on-going interactions—always on your terms and always by your choice." Sears paid consumers $10 to participate. Sears then asked consumers to download "research" software that the company said would confidentially track their "online browsing." But consumers would not know, unless they read deep into a lengthy license agreement near the end of the registration process, that Sears was tracking much more than their browsing. The complaint charged that Sears' failure to adequately disclose the scope of the tracking software's data collection was deceptive and violated the FTC Act.

Under the settlement, Sears admitted no wrongdoing but agreed to destroy information collected and to clearly disclose the types of data the company will collect in the future. The disclosure must be made separately from any user license agreement; no burying disclosures in the fine print. Sears must also disclose whether any of the data will be used by a third party.

Today, user privacy enforcement is largely left up to the Federal Trade Commission on grounds that Internet companies are violating the privacy promises they make in their terms of service agreements. This has, for example, resulted in the large fines and penalties for Facebook after repeated violations over the past decade, as discussed earlier in this chapter.

Lotteries and Contests

For many years, Americans feared that laws prohibiting gambling were needed to "protect the citizen from the demoralizing or corrupting influence" of solicitations to gamble.[209] Therefore, federal law long prohibited all advertising of lotteries.[210] However, as more states conduct lotteries to raise revenue, the federal law has

---

[208] FTC, "Sears Settles FTC Charges Regarding Tracking Software," *Federal Trade Commission*, June 6, 2009, https://www.ftc.gov/news-events/news/press-releases/2009/06/sears-settles-ftc-charges-regarding-tracking-software?msclkid=ebcd8e8fa80111ecbb91e7f23a04e17d.
[209] United States v. Horner, 44 F. 677 (S.D.N.Y. 1891), *aff'd*, 143 U.S. 207 (1892).
[210] 18 U.S.C. §§ 1301–6.

been modified to permit the media to advertise lotteries in states that conduct them. Congress also has adopted other exemptions to the lottery advertising ban.

LOTTERIES A lottery has three elements: (1) prize, (2) chance and (3) consideration. The prize is the reward, money, trip, merchandise or other remuneration given to the winner. Chance means that luck, not skill, will determine the winner. Consideration, which is often more difficult to recognize than chance or prize, is the effort or expense required of the participant. Consideration is the time one spends to play a game or the money paid to enter a contest. All three elements must be present for a promotion to be considered a lottery.

The ban on lottery advertising was relaxed by two 1988 laws. First, Congress permitted broadcasters to carry ads for legal gambling, including casino gambling, conducted by Native American tribes.[211] Second, Congress permitted publishers and broadcasters operating in states where lotteries are legal to advertise and disseminate information about lotteries in those states and in adjoining states if lotteries are also lawful there.[212]

The media may also print or broadcast advertising and prize lists of lotteries conducted by nonprofit organizations and by commercial companies, if these lotteries are legal under state law. The commercial lotteries, however, must be conducted only occasionally and not be related to the company's usual business.

In 1993, the Supreme Court upheld the constitutionality of the federal prohibition against advertising of lotteries by broadcast stations licensed in states where lotteries are illegal. In *United States v. Edge Broadcasting Co.*, the Court ruled 7–2 that the federal prohibition was constitutional in a case involving WMYK-FM, a station licensed in Moyock, North Carolina, where lotteries are illegal.[213] The station was located only three miles from the state of Virginia, where lotteries are legal. Edge Broadcasting argued that the federal prohibition on lottery advertisements in North Carolina unconstitutionally barred WMYK from broadcasting lawful commercial information, particularly to Virginians, who constitute 98 percent of the North Carolina station's audience. Applying the *Central Hudson* test for commercial speech, the Supreme Court concluded that the federal prohibition on lottery broadcasts advances the significant state interest of discouraging gambling in North Carolina.

The Supreme Court in 1999 said a ban on radio and television stations carrying ads for legal casino gambling violated broadcasters' First Amendment rights.[214] Louisiana broadcasters argued they should be permitted to carry ads for Louisiana and Mississippi casinos. Writing for the Court, Justice Stevens agreed, saying the ban could not pass the third and fourth parts of the *Central Hudson* test.

The Court said the government's interests were substantial, thus passing the second part of the *Central Hudson* test. The government said its interests were to reduce social costs associated with gambling and protect states in which gambling is illegal. However, the Court said the exemptions Congress adopted—permitting advertising for state-conducted lotteries, casinos operated by Native American tribes and certain occasional casino gambling—meant the law could not directly advance the government's interests. The Court said it is not clear that permitting advertising for some casino gambling but not others would reduce the number of people who gamble or the amount of gambling. Rather, the Court said, the congressional

---

[211] Indian Gaming Regulatory Act, 25 U.S.C. § 2720.
[212] 18 U.S.C. § 1307.
[213] 509 U.S. 418 (1993).
[214] Greater New Orleans Broadcasting Association v. United States, 527 U.S. 173 (1999).

exemptions only would persuade gamblers to go to one casino rather than another. The law, then, failed to satisfy the third part of the *Central Hudson* test.

The Court also said the law was broader than necessary to serve the government's interest, failing *Central Hudson*'s fourth part. Gambling's social ills will not be reduced by forbidding ads for some casinos while permitting ads for others, the Court said. Thus, banning broadcast casino gambling ads restricted more truthful speech about lawful activities than the law's results could justify, the Court said.

CONTESTS Although publishers and broadcasters may conduct only occasional lotteries unrelated to their businesses, they can conduct promotional contests and advertise the contests of others as long as the promotions are not false or deceptive. To be legal, contests may not consist of all three elements of a lottery: prize, chance and consideration. Contests may include two elements of a lottery, such as a prize and chance, as long as they do not require the third element, consideration. Many contests avoid the prohibitions on lotteries by basing winning on knowledge or skill rather than chance. Common contests conducted by publishers, broadcasters and retailers include treasure hunts, drawings, word games, picture coloring, name-that-tune competitions and cash call-in jackpots.

The FTC generally does not regulate lotteries, but it does issue rules regulating contests, particularly in food retailing and the gasoline industry. The Federal Communications Act of 1934 also regulates contests. The communications act prohibits broadcasters from deceiving the public by providing any "special and secret assistance" to a contestant in a contest or from fixing or rigging a contest through "any artifice or scheme."[215] In addition, FCC rules require broadcasters who conduct or advertise contests to

> fully and accurately disclose the material terms of the contest, and . . . conduct the contest substantially as announced or advertised. No contest description shall be false, misleading or deceptive with respect to any material term.[216]

FCC rules require that stations reveal who is eligible to win, the nature and value of prizes, how to enter, how winners will be determined and dates of the contest. A disc jockey, television host or broadcast promotion director could be subject to a fine of $10,000 and a year in jail for participating in a false or misleading contest. Furthermore, a station could lose its license for willful or repeated violation. Contests may also be prohibited under state law.

The FCC revoked the license of WMJX-FM in Miami, Florida, because of deception in two contests. In one, the station announced that contestants could win a $1,000 prize in an Easter egg hunt. The station's program director allowed the promotional announcements to be broadcast even though the station had no prize money to award. In the other contest, the station announced a $500 reward for the listener who found disc jockey Greg Austin, reported to be wandering around the Miami area in a daze, "his mind boggled," after a trip to the Bermuda Triangle. However, station announcers knew that Austin was in the studio, safely returned from a brief charter boat excursion.[217]

---

[215] 47 U.S.C. § 509.
[216] 47 C.F.R. § 73.1216.
[217] WMJX, Inc., 85 F.C.C.2d 251 (1981).

Money

The U.S. Supreme Court has ruled that the government can constitutionally regulate the manner in which money is pictured in advertisements and news stories. In *Regan v. Time, Inc.*, the Court upheld a federal statute requiring that money be pictured only in black and white and only either larger or smaller than actual size.[218] Color images are now permitted, but the Treasury Department fears that color photos of money in actual size would aid counterfeiters. Therefore, the law prohibits picturing money unless the reproduction is one sided and either less than three-fourths or more than one-and-a-half times the actual size of money.[219]

▦ SUMMARY ▦

The Children's Television Act of 1990 limits the amount of time devoted to commercials during children's programming. The FCC also regulates program-length commercials and requires sponsor identification.

The collection, control and dissemination of personal data is regulated by a number of laws that attempt to prohibit fraud and misuse of data.

The media may advertise all official state lotteries in any state that operates one. The media may also print or broadcast advertising and prize lists of lotteries conducted by nonprofit organizations and occasionally by commercial companies if the lotteries are legal under state law and if the commercial lotteries are not related to the company's usual business. A lottery has three elements: chance, prize and consideration. A contest usually requires the participant to demonstrate a measure of skill or effort. The media may reproduce U.S. money in an advertisement or illustration if the money is pictured either larger or smaller than real money.

MEDIA'S RIGHT TO REFUSE ADVERTISING

It is well established that the media choose what to broadcast or publish. As Chief Justice Burger said in *CBS, Inc. v. Democratic National Committee*, "For better or worse, editing is what editors are for; and editing is selection and choice of material."[220] In *Democratic National Committee*, the Court ruled that a Washington, D.C., television station had a First Amendment right to refuse to sell airtime for a business group's editorial advertisements.

Before the Supreme Court established the media's First Amendment right to refuse advertising, lower courts had ruled in common law that the media are private businesses free to accept or reject advertising, provided publishers do not violate contracts with their advertisers, monopolize or restrain trade in violation of the antitrust statutes, or discriminate on the basis of race or sex. In *Chicago Joint Board, Amalgamated Clothing Workers of America, AFL-CIO v. Chicago Tribune Co.*, the U.S. Court of Appeals for the Seventh Circuit ruled that newspapers are private enterprises that can refuse even editorial advertisements.[221]

The First Amendment and the common law do not free the media entirely from required publishing and broadcasting. The Federal Communications Act imposes obligations on broadcasters to provide airtime for candidates during elections. The

---

[218] 468 U.S. 641 (1984).
[219] Treasury Directive No. 15–56, FR 48539 (Sept. 15, 1993).
[220] 412 U.S. 94, 124 (1973).
[221] 435 F.2d 470 (7th Cir. 1970), *cert. denied*, 402 U.S. 973 (1971).

media are also required to provide access to advertisers with whom contracts have been signed. In addition, media that collude to refuse advertisements may violate antitrust laws.

▓ SUMMARY ▓

The media may refuse to publish or broadcast advertisements because of First Amendment and common-law precedents. The media's refusal to disseminate an advertisement is not deemed a government refusal in violation of the First Amendment just because the media receive government benefits. However, the media, like other businesses, must honor their advertising contracts, the antitrust laws and other legal obligations.

SECURITIES TRANSACTIONS

Corporations not only have a right to speak but may also be required to speak or publish. A number of laws require banks, insurance companies and other businesses to disclose to the public the details of their financial offerings and the financial strength of their institutions.

Probably the most far-reaching corporate disclosure laws are the securities acts passed during the Roosevelt administration to eliminate abuses that contributed to the stock market crash of 1929. Under the laws, corporations whose stock is publicly traded must disclose financial information to the government, shareholders and the public when the corporations register and trade securities.

For public relations practitioners, federal and state disclosure requirements mean jobs writing periodic reports and press releases, preparing for annual stockholders' meetings and advising corporate executives about their disclosure responsibilities. For business journalists, corporate filings with the Securities and Exchange Commission have been said to compose "the single most intensive research tool" for learning about the operations of American companies.[222]

The fundamental purpose of the federal statutes, the Supreme Court said, "was to substitute a philosophy of full disclosure for the philosophy of *caveat emptor* and thus to achieve a high standard of business ethics in the securities industry."[223] One of the most important securities reforms passed during the New Deal was the Securities Act of 1933, which regulates the initial offering and sale of securities.[224] A year later, Congress enacted the Securities Exchange Act of 1934, which regulates the trading of securities on stock exchanges after they have been offered.[225] Another relevant measure that was enacted during the Roosevelt administration is the Investment Advisers Act of 1940, which regulates some financial publications.[226]

The securities acts are administered by the SEC, created in 1934. The SEC is an independent, bipartisan, quasi-judicial agency. The SEC has five members, not more than three of whom can belong to the same political party. They are appointed by the president for five-year staggered terms. The SEC oversees the

---

[222] Donald Kirsch, *Financial and Economic Journalism* 241 (1978).
[223] SEC v. Capital Gains Research Bureau, Inc., 375 U.S. 180, 186 (1963).
[224] Ch. 2A, 48 Stat. 74 (codified as amended at 15 U.S.C. § 77a).
[225] Ch. 2A, 48 Stat. 881 (codified as amended at 15 U.S.C. § 78a).
[226] Ch. 2A, 54 Stat. 847 (codified as amended at 15 U.S.C. § 80b–1).

financial disclosure that is required of companies traded on the stock exchanges, cities and public agencies that issue municipal bonds,[227] and investment advisors.[228]

Mandated Disclosure

The securities statutes mandate disclosure of financial information about securities that are bought and sold on the stock exchanges. The Securities Act of 1933 requires disclosure in connection with registering securities for sale. The Securities Exchange Act of 1934 mandates corporate disclosure in connection with the trading of those securities. *Security* has been defined broadly under federal law to include stocks, bonds and a variety of other investment vehicles where the purchaser does not take an active role in managing the investment.[229]

REGISTERING SECURITIES The 1933 Securities Act was passed to provide investors with the information they need to make intelligent decisions when purchasing new stock offerings. To achieve this goal, Section 5(c) of the Securities Act prohibits a company from "going public" by offering its stock for sale before it has filed a registration statement with the SEC containing extensive financial information about the company.[230] A company whose shares are already traded on an exchange must file registration statements if a new stock offering is made. After a company files a registration statement with the SEC, there is a brief waiting period during which a company cannot advertise or offer to sell the securities the company hopes investors eventually will buy. The waiting period allows investors "to become acquainted with the information contained in the registration statement and to arrive at an unhurried decision concerning the merits of the securities." After the waiting period, a company may advertise the shares for sale.

While a company is waiting to offer shares of stock to the public, it may issue press releases, advertise its products and continue its other usual communications. However, the company may not seek purchasers of its new shares of stock until the SEC declares its registration "effective."

In a famous case, the Arvida Corporation violated Section 5(c) of the Securities Act by inviting investors to purchase Arvida stock before a registration statement had been completed.[231] Arvida was formed by the industrialist Arthur Vining Davis when he transferred much of his extensive Florida real estate holdings to the corporation. Davis planned to raise additional capital through an offering of stock to the public. When the financing proposal reached final form but before registration was filed with the SEC, a press release was issued on the letterhead of Loeb, Rhoades & Co., a New York brokerage.

The Loeb, Rhoades press release said Arvida would have assets of more than $100 million. The release also said that Davis would transfer to Arvida more than 100,000 acres near the Florida "Gold Coast" for development. To help ensure wide dissemination of the press release in the most prestigious papers, the public relations counsel for Loeb, Rhoades invited reporters from the *New York Times*, the *New York Herald-Tribune* and the *Wall Street Journal* to its offices in time to meet the papers' deadlines. A company official told the reporters that the stock would sell for about $10 a share but declined to answer questions about debt on the

---

[227] Municipal Securities Disclosure, 59 Fed. Reg. 59,590 (1994).
[228] SEC, "SEC Adopts Rules to Enhance Information Reported by Investment Advisors," Aug. 25, 2016.
[229] *See* Donald Langevoort, "What Is a Security? Some Things You Won't Believe," in *Nuts and Bolts of Securities Law* at 33 (1995).
[230] SEC v. Arvida Corp., 169 F. Supp. 211 (S.D.N.Y. 1958).
[231] *Id.* at 213–14.

property, capitalization of Arvida, the company's balance sheet, or control of the corporation. The substance of the press release appeared in the three New York newspapers and numerous other news media throughout the country.

The SEC charged that the release violated Section 5 because it, along with earlier publicity, was calculated "to set in motion the processes of distribution" of stock before registration "by arousing and stimulating investor and dealer interest in Arvida securities."[232] To the SEC, the "arresting references" in the press release to assets in excess of $100 million and to over 100,000 acres on the Florida Gold Coast were part of an illegal selling effort. Indeed, an SEC survey found that within two business days, the publicity had resulted in investor interest worth at least $500,000.

The SEC rejected Loeb, Rhoades's contention that the release and publicity about Arvida were legal because they were legitimate news. Section 5(c), the SEC said, "is equally applicable" whether or not "astute public relations activities" make an illegal stock offering appear to have news value. Indeed, the SEC reasoned,

> the danger to investors from publicity amounting to a selling effort may be greater in cases where an issue has "news value" since it may be easier to whip up a "speculative frenzy" . . . by incomplete or misleading publicity.

Thus, the publicity would aid distribution of an unsound security at inflated prices. This, the SEC concluded, "is precisely the evil which the Securities Act seeks to prevent." The SEC did not want to dam up the normal flow of information, but, the SEC said, the company and its underwriters cannot be part of a publicity campaign that constitutes an offer to sell or solicitation of an offer to buy before registration of a security.

When Arvida's final prospectus was made public, the SEC found support for its decision to enforce Section 5(c). Whereas the press release had stressed the great acreage owned by Arvida, the final prospectus describing the stock revealed that the bulk of the land was not usable in its present condition and was located in areas remote from existing development. The final prospectus also revealed significant debt, indicating that the bulk of the money raised through the stock offering might be used to retire the debt rather than to develop the land. The fuller truth disclosed in the final prospectus proved to the SEC's satisfaction the superiority of the mandated disclosure system over investment decisions "brought about by press releases."

The *Arvida* case raised no First Amendment issues, but the SEC noted that Section 5(c) of the 1933 act "in no way restricts the freedom of news media to seek out and publish financial news." The Section 5(c) prohibition does not violate the First Amendment rights of underwriters because they are in the business of distributing securities, not news, the SEC said. The restrictions of Section 5(c) do not apply to reporters, who presumably "have no securities to sell."

TRADING SECURITIES Whereas the Securities Act of 1933 is concerned primarily with financial disclosure before a security is traded on an exchange, the Securities Exchange Act of 1934 is principally concerned with the trading of securities from one purchaser to another after distribution on the nation's stock exchanges. Under the 1934 act, large publicly traded corporations are required to file annual,

---

[232] *In re* Carl M. Loeb, Rhoades & Co., 38 S.E.C. 843, 851 (1959).

quarterly and other reports with the SEC about the company's operations.[233] Other sections of the act regulate the solicitation of proxies and tender offers.[234] *Proxy statements* announce annual and special shareholder meetings. *Tender offers* are offers by one company to buy controlling shares of another company.

Annual and Quarterly Reports Annual reports, which must be sent to shareholders and filed for public inspection with the SEC, are one of the most effective media through which information is disseminated to the investment community. Corporate reports contain information about management, net sales, earnings, dividends and other information about the financial condition of the company. The annual report also contains the "management discussion and analysis" that describes in detail the capital resources, results of company operations and projected performance. If a projection turns out to be wrong, a businessperson may be protected from a fraud suit if the projection (1) was prepared with a reasonable basis and (2) was disclosed in good faith.[235]

Much of the information in an annual report is updated in required quarterly reports. Between quarterly reports, publicly traded corporations are also mandated to report a few significant developments within 15 days of their occurrence. Between quarterly reports, companies are required to report to the SEC on Form 8-K changes in control of the company, the buying or selling of significant assets, filing for bankruptcy or receivership, changes in the company's certified public accountants and the resignation of directors.[236] The SEC says that a corporation may, "at its option," report other important occurrences, but the law does not require the company to do so unless disclosure is necessary to avoid fraud.

The SEC also allows disclosures to be made online on their websites or, as of 2013, on social media platforms such as Facebook and Twitter, as long as investors have been made aware of the platforms the company uses to make such announcements. The SEC, for example, opened an investigation against the streaming movie service Netflix after the company's CEO revealed on his Facebook page that Netflix had surpassed 1 billion hours of streaming content in a month for the first time in the company's history. The same disclosure was not announced through traditional channels such as a press release or an 8-K form, leading to concern that only certain investors knew this positive information while the company's stock price increased about $10 per share in a day. Investors should have been made aware, the SEC said, that company information of this kind was going to be shared on Facebook.[237]

Proxies and Annual Meetings Besides reporting regularly in quarterly and annual reports, publicly traded companies must tell shareholders in proxy statements when and where the shareholder meetings will be held and what business will be conducted.[238] Proxy statements must also include extensive information about the compensation of chief executive officers and other highly paid executives. Shareholders who will not attend the annual meeting can vote by proxy on various proposals, including management changes and proposals submitted by shareholders. When shareholders vote by proxy, they give their proxy holder, often a committee designated by management, the authority to vote their shares as they

---

[233] 15 U.S.C. § 78m; 17 C.F.R. § 240.13a-1 et seq.
[234] 15 U.S.C. § 78n; 17 C.F.R. § 240.14a-1.
[235] 17 C.F.R. § 230.175.
[236] 17 C.F.R. § 240.13a-11.
[237] SEC, "SEC Says Social Media OK for Company Announcements If Investors Are Alerted," Apr. 2, 2013.
[238] 15 U.S.C. § 78n; 17 C.F.R. § 240.14a-1.

instruct on their proxy statement. Through "proxy fights," dissident directors or minority stockholders may "solicit" shareholders to vote their proxies against management. Through proxy fights, dissident shareholders can sometimes vote management out of office, thus gaining control of a company without buying a majority of shares. Under securities law, neither corporations nor dissident stockholders may issue false or misleading statements to shareholders in an effort to sway their votes.

False or misleading proxy solicitations may be halted whether they are targeted directly at shareholders or are communicated more indirectly through speeches, press releases and television scripts for the public. The U.S. Court of Appeals for the Second Circuit ruled that even a newspaper advertisement placed by a citizens group might be halted if it contained false statements published in an attempt to influence shareholders in a proxy fight.[239] The case involved a newspaper advertisement purchased by a citizens group opposed to the Long Island Lighting Company, known as LILCO. The citizens group was associated with dissident stockholders who hoped to oust LILCO management in a proxy fight. The ad accused LILCO of mismanagement and of attempting to saddle ratepayers with the needless costs of constructing the controversial Shoreham Nuclear Power Plant. The ad urged that LILCO, a company owned by shareholders, be managed by a public authority.

LILCO tried to halt the advertisement, claiming that it contained false statements attempting to sway LILCO shareholders to vote against management. But a federal district court ruled that the newspaper ad purchased by a citizens group was constitutionally protected political expression.[240] However, the U.S. Court of Appeals for the Second Circuit reversed the lower court. Avoiding the First Amendment issue, the appellate court treated the case as a narrow issue of securities regulation, noting, "The SEC's authority to regulate proxy solicitations has traditionally extended into matters of public interest." The appeals court remanded the case, asking the lower court to determine whether the ad in a general-circulation newspaper actually solicited shareholders' votes.

▓ SUMMARY ▓

The securities laws require stock companies to disclose financial information before shares are offered and while they are being traded. Mandated disclosure includes prospectuses before a stock is offered for sale and periodic reports after trading begins. Although companies must disclose a few significant events if they occur between annual reports, corporations may withhold much information if there is no intent to conceal fraud. Rules regulating communications to shareholders have been held to extend to political advertisements that might affect shareholders' votes.

Fraud

Corporations that knowingly make false or misleading statements in their annual reports, proxy statements and other communications mandated by the securities acts commit fraud. It is also fraudulent for corporate executives to knowingly make false statements in speeches and press releases if the statements would affect the price of the company's stock. Both federal law and individual states' laws—so-called *blue-sky laws*—outlaw fraud in connection with securities transactions.

---

[239] Long Island Lighting Co. v. Barbash, 779 F.2d 793 (2d Cir. 1985).
[240] Long Island Lighting Co. v. Barbash, 625 F. Supp. 221 (E.D.N.Y. 1985).

Most fraud litigation is brought under Section 10(b) of the 1934 Securities Exchange Act and Rule 10b-5 of the Code of Federal Regulations. Section 10(b) makes it unlawful for a corporation or its agent to be manipulative or deceptive in connection with the purchase or sale of securities. Under Rule 10b-5, it is manipulative or deceptive for a company to make a deliberately misleading material statement. It is also fraudulent for a company to fail to clarify a statement to avoid misleading investors. Investors may sue to enjoin deception and to recover money lost because of reliance on deceptive statements.

MATERIALLY DECEPTIVE FACTS For a statement to be fraudulent, it must involve a material fact. Material facts are facts important to the decision of a reasonable investor to buy, sell or hold a security. A fact is material in a proxy statement, the Supreme Court said, "if there is a substantial likelihood that a reasonable shareholder would consider it important in deciding how to vote." To be material, a fact must not necessarily change an investor's decision to buy or sell. A fact is material if it would be significant to reasonable shareholders in the "total mix" of their information.[241]

Material facts include a sharp change in company earnings, the imminence of a very profitable transaction and information about a possible merger or bankruptcy.[242]

Material facts also may include the illness or disability of a key executive.[243] A non-material fact would be the color of the chief executive's office. Thus, a company might falsely state the color of the boss's office without committing fraud because the color is not important to investors' decisions to buy or sell.

The merger of two companies is usually important to investors, thus raising the question at what point merger negotiations become material and therefore can no longer be lawfully denied. Are casual lunches at which executives gently probe the possibility of a merger material? Or does a merger become material only when the documents joining two companies are signed?

The Supreme Court has ruled that merger negotiations become material either when they are so advanced as to make a merger very probable or at an earlier point in the discussions if the magnitude of the merger would dramatically alter the company.[244] Thus, discussions of big mergers become material before discussions of insignificant mergers, and discussions that seem likely to result in mergers are material before discussions in which mergers seem improbable. Until mergers and other developments become material, companies can lawfully deny them.

Following major corporate financial scandals, Congress in 2002 passed important legislation to increase corporate accountability and restore confidence in the markets.[245] Just before the fall elections, Congress passed the Sarbanes-Oxley Act to increase trust in corporate accounting, which was undermined repeatedly by unreported sweetheart loans, off-the-books entities and insider dealing at infamous companies such as Enron, Arthur Andersen, ImClone, Global Crossing, WorldCom and Adelphia.

The major focus of Sarbanes-Oxley is to strengthen independent accounting at publicly traded companies. Sarbanes-Oxley also requires faster and more

---

[241] TSC Indus., Inc. v. Northway, Inc., 426 U.S. 438, 449 (1976).

[242] Dirks v. SEC, 463 U.S. 646 (1983); Northern Trust Co. v. Essaness Theatres Corp., 103 F. Supp. 954 (N.D. Ill. 1952); *In re* Ward La France Truck Corp., 13 S.E.C. 373 (1943).

[243] Wesley Walton and Charles Brissman, *Corporate Communications Handbook* 4–37 (1990).

[244] Basic, Inc. v. Levinson, 485 U.S. 224 (1988).

[245] Sarbanes-Oxley Act of 2002 (Pub. L. No. 107–204, 116 Stat. 745), also known as the Public Company Accounting Reform and Investor Protection Act of 2002 and commonly called SOX or SarbOx.

complete disclosure of important changes at publicly traded companies. From now on, companies must disclose in their annual reports material transactions and special-purpose entities that are not reported on the corporate balance sheet.[246] Other material changes to a company's financial condition must be reported on a "rapid and current basis."

Sarbanes-Oxley also increased criminal penalties greatly. Penalties for corporate mail and wire fraud were quadrupled from five years in prison to 20 years.

Misstatements Materially deceptive facts can be positive misstatements or omissions. It was a material misstatement for the director of the Livingston Oil Company to overstate the corporation's income during a speech to securities analysts. The speech was later distributed to shareholders to encourage more sales of stock.[247]

The Supreme Court has ruled it is materially misleading for management to give advice to shareholders that is not based on generally accepted fact. In *Virginia Bankshares, Inc. v. Sandberg,*[248] the Court agreed, 8–1, that a Virginia bank misled minority shareholders when it urged them to approve a buyout of their stock at $42 per share as part of a merger. Management told the shareholders in proxy statements that $42 per share was a "high" value and that terms of the merger were "fair."

Management's "conclusory terms in a commercial context" were misleading, the Court said, because they were not based in fact. The Court agreed with lower-court conclusions that management's statements were misleading because the $42 share price was neither high nor fair "when assessed in accordance with recognized methods of valuation." Management's evaluation, the Court said, "was open to attack by garden-variety evidence."

However, the Court ruled against the shareholders seeking payment above $42 per share from the bank. A five-member majority of the Court ruled that the minority shareholders were not entitled to additional compensation because they could not prove that they lost money as a result of the misleading statements soliciting their proxies. The Court said that the misleading proxy statements did not cost the shareholders money because the shareholders' proxies were not legally necessary for the bank merger to occur.

Public relations firms cannot avoid liability for fraud if they blindly pass along misleading investment information for their corporate clients. A federal judge in Illinois told a corporate financial relations firm it could rely on corporate clients' representations only if the public relations firm also made a "reasonable investigation" to satisfy itself that the statements were true.[249] The SEC has reiterated the financial public relations firm's responsibility to withhold corporate information it knows or has reason to know is false.[250]

A 1995 amendment to the federal securities laws provides a "safe harbor" for predictions by corporations as long as they are accompanied by adequate cautionary statements.[251] The safe harbor provision—called a "pirate's cove" by detractors—allows companies to make predictions about earnings or new products without liability for fraud if the predictions are subsequently proven wrong.

---

[246] 17 C.F.R. §§ 228, 229, 232, 240, 249, 270, 274.

[247] Sprayregen v. Livingston Oil Co., 295 F. Supp. 1376 (S.D.N.Y. 1968).

[248] 501 U.S. 1083 (1991).

[249] SEC v. Pig 'N' Whistle Corp. [1971–1972 Transfer Binder] Fed. Sec. L. Rep. (CCH) ¶ 93,384 (N.D. Ill. 1972).

[250] *In re* Howard Bronson & Co., SEC Release No. 21138 (July 12, 1984).

[251] 104 Pub. L. No. 67, 109 Stat. 737 (1995).

However, to benefit from the safe harbor, the prediction must caution investors about important factors that could create results different from those envisioned by management.

Omissions More common than misstatements of material facts are deceptive half-truths or omissions. The Electric Autolite Company misled shareholders when it disclosed a proposed merger but failed to tell them in proxy statements that the Autolite board of directors, which recommended a merger with the Mergenthaler Linotype Company, was already under the control of Mergenthaler.[252]

In one of the most famous public relations fraud cases, the Texas Gulf Sulphur Company (TGS) issued a materially deceptive press release to dampen rumors of a major copper discovery. In its press release, TGS said that press reports of the company's substantial copper discovery in Timmins, Ontario, were exaggerated. The release said public estimates about the size and grade of ore were "without factual basis and have evidently originated by speculation of people not connected with TGS."[253] Relying on this negative release, several investors sold shares in the company, only to learn from a Texas Gulf Sulphur press release 12 days later that the company had made a 10-million-ton ore strike, one of the largest in history.

In court, Texas Gulf Sulphur said it would have been premature and possibly misleading for the company in its first release to speculate on the size and grade of ore at the mining site. The company had not yet had the ore samples analyzed chemically. But a federal appeals court ruled that the known richness of the ore samples even before chemical analysis was material and did not justify a press release as negative as the company first issued. As evidence that the ore samples were material to investors' decisions even before the samples were chemically analyzed, the court noted that several Texas Gulf Sulphur executives bought additional shares of the company before the ore strike was announced.

The U.S. Court of Appeals for the Second Circuit said the TGS press release misleadingly suggested there was no basis for investor optimism. The court did not require a company to issue a press release to quell rumors but said that material facts should be complete and accurate once a company issues a public statement. Instead of saying speculation about a major ore find was without factual basis, Texas Gulf Sulphur should have said nothing, told how promising the ore samples were by visual inspection, or said the situation was in flux.

How much to reveal, if anything, during searches for raw materials, merger negotiations, land acquisitions and other delicate periods may be a difficult corporate decision. Nevertheless, silence may sometimes be the best policy to keep negotiations on track and to avoid charges of fraud for partial revelations. Silence may be difficult to maintain when a company would like to be forthcoming and when securities analysts and the media are clamoring for information.

Failure to Disclose Payment for Publicity Another fraud securities law prohibits is the failure of publishers and public relations practitioners to disclose payments they receive for corporate publicity affecting a security. Such failure can violate Rule 10b-5 or Section 17(b) of the Securities Act. Section 17(b) makes it illegal to "publish, give publicity to, or circulate any notice, circular, advertisement, newspaper, article, letter, investment service, or communication about a security without revealing payments received."[254] The purpose of the section is to halt

---

[252] Mills v. Electric Autolite Co., 403 F.2d 429, 434 (7th Cir. 1968), *vacated and remanded*, 396 U.S. 375 (1970).
[253] SEC v. Texas Gulf Sulphur Co., 401 F.2d 833, 845 (1968), *cert. denied*, 394 U.S. 976 (1969).
[254] 15 U.S.C. § 77q(b).

articles in newspapers or periodicals that appear to be unbiased opinion about a company but that in fact are purchased.[255]

Stock Market Magazine was charged with fraud for failing to reveal that it published corporate features for companies that bought advertising and story reprints.[256] The Court of Appeals for the D.C. Circuit sent the case to a federal district court for a determination as to whether the magazine, which offered financial news to some 12,000 subscribers, was publishing the articles in exchange for corporate purchases of advertising and reprints. If so, the magazine could be required to disclose these payments. The magazine contended there was no *quid pro quo* that needed to be revealed under the securities laws.

The Court of Appeals told the district court that although the lower court was investigating whether articles were published in return for advertising and reprint sales, the court could not demand to know who wrote the articles in question. The SEC had argued that the magazine should be required to reveal not only that it sold advertising and reprints but also that featured companies sometimes wrote the articles, paid public relations firms to write them, or paid editors of *Stock Market Magazine* to write them. The appeals court said the First Amendment prohibits inquiry into who pays a writer or how much of a published article is written by someone outside a magazine. Such inquiry, the court said, would impermissibly interfere with editorial judgments about constitutionally protected content.

The First Amendment protects the publisher's right to determine who writes and edits published material, the court said. Content is protected whether the writer is paid by a publisher, a public relations firm or a featured company. A magazine might be required to disclose that it received payments or sold advertising and reprints as a condition for publishing an article, the court said, but the First Amendment bars requiring a magazine to disclose who wrote which parts of a business article.

Public relations practitioners are also supposed to disclose payment from companies they promote. The SEC has warned public relations firms that they violate the Securities Act if they do not reveal payment for preparation and dissemination of material designed to make a new stock offering look like an attractive investment.[257]

IN CONNECTION WITH A PURCHASE OR SALE Under Rule 10b-5, not only must fraudulent statements be material, they must also be "in connection with the purchase or sale of any security." The *in-connection-with* test is met if a corporation issues a materially false or misleading statement on which other investors rely for their purchases or sales. But reliance by investors may be presumed when a company makes materially false or misleading statements. In the *Texas Gulf Sulphur* case, the Second Circuit Court of Appeals said the in-connection-with test was met when Texas Gulf Sulphur issued a misleading statement "reasonably calculated to influence the investing public."[258]

Courts have ruled the in-connection-with requirement is also met when materially false statements are made in corporate annual reports,[259] product

---

[255] H.R. Rep. No. 85, 73d Cong., 1st Sess. 24 (1933), *cited in* United States v. Amick, 439 F.2d 351, 365 n.18 (7th Cir. 1971), *cert. denied*, 404 U.S. 823 (1971).

[256] SEC v. Wall St. Publishing Inst., 851 F.2d 365 (D.C. Cir. 1988), *cert. denied*, 489 U.S. 1066 (1989).

[257] Howard Bronson & Co., SEC Release No. 21138 (July 12, 1984). *See also* SEC v. Pig 'N' Whistle Corp. [1971–1972 Transfer Binder] Fed. Sec. L. Rep. (CCH) ¶ 93,384 (N.D. Ill. 1972).

[258] SEC v. Texas Gulf Sulphur Co., 401 F.2d 833, 862 (2d Cir. 1968).

[259] Heit v. Weitzen, 402 F.2d 909 (2d Cir. 1968), *cert. denied*, 395 U.S. 903 (1969).

promotions,[260] speeches by corporate directors to securities analysts,[261] and advertisements.[262] In each case, investors might rely on the statements when buying or selling securities. The SEC has also warned companies that statements made during rate-filing hearings, during labor negotiations and in other public circumstances must be factual because they too can be heard and relied on by investors.[263]

DUTY TO CORRECT STATEMENTS ATTRIBUTED TO THE COMPANY

A publicly traded corporation has an affirmative duty to correct a published material misstatement if the error originates with the corporation or its agent. In *Green v. Jonhop*,[264] a federal court said that a corporation had an obligation to correct falsely optimistic earnings projections made by an underwriter who marketed the company's securities. Corporate silence in the face of falsely optimistic earnings projections, the court said, could fraudulently encourage investors to rely on the underwriter's statements.

A corporation also has a responsibility to correct misstatements if the company approves or helps to draft reports by stock analysts or public relations firms containing material misinformation. The U.S. Court of Appeals for the Second Circuit noted that corporate officials who review outside analysts' reports engage in "a risky activity, fraught with danger" because officials, by their participation, make "an implied representation that the information they have reviewed is true or at least in accordance with the company's views."[265] In addition, corporate officials must treat with caution any activity that suggests that the company has "ratified" a particular analysts' projections. One corporate communication manual suggests that "the company should avoid disseminating analysts' reports."[266]

A corporation may also have a duty to correct its own statements if changing conditions transform accurate statements into misleading statements. A U.S. district court said the A.H. Robins Company had a duty to update statements in its stockholder annual reports indicating that the company's Dalkon Shield contraceptive was safer and more effective than other similar devices on the market. A study that was published after Robins' first reports indicated that the contraceptive was not as safe or effective as Robins first indicated.[267] Another court ruled that the Shattuck Denn Mining Corporation had an obligation to tell investors that a previously announced merger deal had fallen through. Without the update, investors could buy Shattuck's stock with the mistaken belief that the merger would increase profits.[268] Courts have generally been vague about how long an initial corporate communication remains "alive" and thus subject to correction, although it is clear that eventually a statement will become stale and thus not require correcting.[269]

---

[260] SEC v. Electrogen Indus., Inc. [1967–1969 Decisions] Fed. Sec. L. Rep. (CCH) ¶ 92,156 (E.D.N.Y. 1968).

[261] Sprayregen v. Livingston Oil Co., 295 F. Supp. 1376 (S.D.N.Y. 1968).

[262] *See* Donald Feuerstein, "The Corporation's Obligations of Disclosure Under the Federal Securities Laws When It Is Not Trading Its Stock," 15 *N.Y. L. Forum* 385, 393 (1969).

[263] SEC Release No. 34–20560 (Jan. 20, 1984).

[264] 358 F. Supp. 413 (D. Or. 1973).

[265] Elkind v. Liggett & Myers, Inc., 635 F.2d 156, 163 (2d Cir. 1980).

[266] Wesley Walton and Charles Brissman, *Corporate Communications Handbook* 4–9 (1990).

[267] Ross v. A.H. Robins Co., 465 F. Supp. 904 (S.D.N.Y. 1979), *rev'd*, 607 F.2d 545 (2d Cir. 1979), *cert. denied*, 446 U.S. 946, *reh'g denied*, 448 U.S. 911, *on remand*, 100 F.R.D. 5 (1982).

[268] SEC v. Shattuck Denn Mining Corp., 297 F. Supp. 470 (S.D.N.Y. 1968). *See also* Financial Indus. Fund, Inc. v. McDonnell Douglas Corp., 474 F.2d 514 (10th Cir.) (per curiam) (en banc), *cert. denied*, 414 U.S. 874 (1973).

[269] Wesley Walton and Charles Brissman, *Corporate Communications Handbook* 2–11 (1990).

One way to limit the "life" of a press release might be to use phrases such as "at present" or "right now."[270]

A corporation generally has no duty to respond to market gossip and rumors not attributable to the company.[271] Similarly, a corporation has no duty to respond to an inaccurate interpretive article that is not attributable to the company. The U.S. Court of Appeals for the Second Circuit ruled that the International Controls Corporation (ICC) had no duty to respond to Dan Dorfman's report in the *Wall Street Journal* about ICC's plan to buy the Electronic Specialty Company. The speculation about the plan turned out to be true, but the price per share that Dorfman quoted was considerably higher than ICC was offering. ICC had no duty to respond because the company was not the source of the speculation.[272]

Even if an inaccurate news article is attributed to a company, a corporation probably has no duty to correct the article if information the company provided was accurate. In *Zucker v. Sable*, a federal district court said it would be unreasonable to require a company "to examine every financial publication to ascertain whether the reports of its admittedly accurate press release have been misinterpreted so as to mislead members of the public."[273] In *Zucker*, the newspapers had published misleading stories about the Sable company by omitting the word *investigational*, which had been included in Sable's press release. Sable had filed an investigational application with the Food and Drug Administration for development of plastic lenses. The word *investigational* was a critical omission in the news reports because investigational applications, which indicate time-consuming product research is not complete, can take many years for FDA approval.

DUTY TO DISCLOSE INSIDER TRADING Besides a duty to correct its own false or misleading statements, a corporation and its "insiders" also have a duty to disclose material information when they plan to base purchases or sales of company stock on nonpublic information. This duty to disclose to avoid fraud arises from executives' financial responsibility to shareholders and the markets. Publishers of personal investment advisories and some financial journalists may also have a duty to disclose nonpublic information they intend to profit from.

Insiders An assumption underlying the securities laws—although not all legal scholars agree—is that it is unfair for insiders to buy and sell a company's stock for their own benefit if they base their decision on nonpublic material facts. The theory is that every investor should have equal access to material information about a stock. Insiders have a duty to disclose material information before trading because of the fiduciary nature of their positions. Fiduciaries are people who have a position of trust that prohibits them from acting only in their own self-interest. In the corporate context, an executive is entrusted by shareholders with responsibility to manage the shareholders' assets and is therefore supposed to act in the shareholders' interest. To avoid a conflict of interest, Rule 10b-5 imposes a duty on insiders who possess valuable nonpublic information either to disclose the information or to refrain from trading.[274]

---

[270] Donald Langevoort, "Corporate Disclosure and Insider Trading: Keeping Your Client Out of Trouble," in *Nuts and Bolts of Securities Law* at 304 (1995).

[271] *See* John Sheffey, "Securities Law Responsibilities of Issuers to Respond to Rumors and Other Publicity: Reexamination of a Continuing Problem," 57 *Notre Dame Law* 755 (1982).

[272] Electronic Specialty Co. v. International Controls Corp., 409 F.2d 937, 949 (2d Cir. 1969). *See also* Greenfield v. Heublein, Inc., 742 F.2d 751 (3d Cir. 1984).

[273] 426 F. Supp. 658, 663 (1976). *See also* Mills v. Sarjem Corp., 133 F. Supp. 753 (D.N.J. 1955).

[274] *See* SEC v. Texas Gulf Sulphur Co., 401 F.2d 833 (2d Cir. 1968), *cert. denied*, 394 U.S. 976 (1969). *But see* Henry G. Manne, *Insider Trading and the Stock Market* (1966).

Securities statutes do not define *insider*, and congressional attempts to define it have failed. But the Supreme Court, agreeing with the SEC, has defined an insider as one who, by virtue of his or her position with the issuer of stock, has access to nonpublic corporate information that is supposed to be used only for corporate purposes, not for personal benefit.[275] This definition covers corporate officers, directors, controlling stockholders and corporate public relations executives.

Certain outsiders may acquire the duties of insiders if they "have entered into a special confidential relationship in the conduct of the business of the enterprise and are given access to information solely for corporate purposes."[276] These temporary insiders or quasi-insiders include accountants, lawyers and public relations counsel who have access to nonpublic material information that is intended only for corporate use. These quasi-insiders, like permanent insiders, are supposed to make true and accurate statements about material aspects of a company and are supposed to abstain from trading if they have not disclosed the material information on which trades might be based.

A variation of illegal insider trading is *tipping*. Tipping is the practice of passing nonpublic material information to friends or brokers so that they can trade. The "tipper" may be liable for fraud along with the "tippee." The *Texas Gulf Sulphur* case is a well-known example of both insider trading and tipping. In *Texas Gulf Sulphur*, the federal appeals court found that executives of the mining company violated insider trading prohibitions by buying stock in the company and also by tipping friends when the insiders learned ahead of the public of the very promising copper ore samples taken at a site in Timmins, Ontario. In ruling that the insiders' stock purchases were illegal, the court said the investing public should have the same access to material corporate information as a corporate insider. Under legislation passed since *Texas Gulf Sulphur* was decided, inside traders may have to repay three times their illegal profits.

In an effort to curb insider trading, Congress passed legislation that increased penalties, extended liability and encouraged revelation of insider trading. Under the Insider Trading and Securities Fraud Enforcement Act of 1988, not only are illegal traders and tippers liable, but so also are those brokers, investment advisers and other supervisors who fail to take appropriate steps to prevent illegal trading.[277] The act also increases criminal penalties and allows the Securities and Exchange Commission to pay persons who provide information about insider trading.

One example of insider trading that has drawn SEC scrutiny is the "**pump-and-dump**" scheme, in which a company promotes the stock publicly, sometimes using misleading information, to increase share values, with a plan of selling the stock when it has sufficiently increased its value. Pump-and-dump schemes often use the Internet, including social networks, to reach a broad audience rapidly. In 2011, the rapper 50 Cent promoted a penny stock on Twitter in which he had a large ownership interest, saying, for example, "HNH1 is the stock symbol for TVG there launching 15 different products. they are no joke get in now" to his nearly 4 million Twitter followers. The stock price soared, increasing 290 percent in value, and earning 50 Cent more than $5 million in increased stock value. Because he did

---

[275] Dirks v. SEC, 463 U.S. 646, 653 (1983), *citing* Chiarella v. United States, 445 U.S. 222, 227 (1980), and *in re* Cady, Roberts & Co., 40 S.E.C. 907 (1961).

[276] Dirks v. SEC, 463 U.S. at 655, n.14. *See also* Elkind v. Liggett & Myers, Inc., 635 F.2d 156 (2d Cir. 1980); SEC v. Texas Gulf Sulphur Co., 401 F.2d 833 (2d Cir. 1968).

[277] 15 U.S.C. § 78u-1. *See also* H.R. Rep. No. 910, 100th Cong., 2d Sess., reprinted in 1988 U.S.C.C.A.N. 6043.

not immediately sell the stock, and because it was not based on clearly inaccurate information, this was not an illegal pump-and-dump scheme.[278] Additionally, he followed his tweets with several disclaimers that may have helped him avoid an SEC investigation, including one saying, "I own HNH1 stock thoughts on it are my opinion. Talk to financial advisor about it."[279]

Quasi-insiders People using confidential information to buy or sell securities violate the insider trading laws, even if the traders have no direct association with the company whose shares they trade. The U.S. Supreme Court said that a company owns its nonpublic information just as it does the rest of its property, and the information is for the company's exclusive use.[280] A person violates the securities laws by misappropriating insider information, such as the unpublished fact that a company is targeted for a takeover. The Court's decision came in a case that arose when James O'Hagan bought shares of the Pillsbury Company before the flour miller was purchased by a British company. The Court ruled O'Hagan had misappropriated information belonging to his Minneapolis law firm when he bought the shares. O'Hagan's firm represented Grand Metropolitan PLC (Grand Met), a British company, which hired a Minneapolis law firm to represent it while it was considering its takeover bid for Pillsbury. Pillsbury's share value increased dramatically when Grand Met announced that it would bid for the company. O'Hagan sold his shares for a profit of more than $4.3 million.

Although O'Hagan was not involved directly in representing Grand Met, he was convicted of violating securities, federal mail fraud and money-laundering laws. The Supreme Court upheld the convictions. The Court said that in addition to the "traditional" theory of insider trading, which is applicable when, for example, a company director or officer uses nonpublic information to trade in the company's stock, there is a second approach—the "misappropriation" theory. A person violates securities laws when she or he "misappropriates confidential information for securities trading purposes in breach of a duty owed to the source of the information."

In the *Grand Met* case, O'Hagan did not represent Grand Met, but his law firm did. The firm's connection allowed O'Hagan to learn nonpublic information— that Grand Met intended to make a bid for Pillsbury. It also created a fiduciary responsibility for him to let Grand Met know he would use that information to purchase Pillsbury stock or to refrain from buying the stock. Because he did neither, he misappropriated Grand Met's information to trade in Pillsbury's stock, and in doing so, he violated insider trading laws. The Court noted, however, if O'Hagan had found in a park trash can information about Grand Met's takeover plans, he would have no fiduciary duty. He could trade freely in Pillsbury stock.

Investment Advisers Stockbrokers and financial advisers have a fiduciary relationship with their clients, much like that of a corporate insider with shareholders. Stockbrokers and financial advisers have a personal responsibility to their clients, imposing on the advisers a duty to register with the Securities and Exchange Commission and to avoid misleading customers for personal gain.

Although many publications offer advice about stocks and finances, most financial publications lack the personal relationship to investors and the direct involvement in investors' portfolios that create fiduciary responsibilities. In *Lowe*

---

[278] Jesse Eisinger, "What Do 50 Cent, Carmen Electra & Shaquille O'Neal Have in Common? Touting Penny Stocks," *ProPublica.org*, Jan. 12, 2011.
[279] Joe Weisenthal, "50 Cent's Most Hysterical Penny Stock Tweets Yet," *Business Insider*, Jan. 11, 2011.
[280] United States v. O'Hagan, 521 U.S. 642 (1997).

v. SEC,[281] the Supreme Court ruled that Christopher L. Lowe's *Lowe Stock Advisory* was not an investment advisory that must be registered with the Securities and Exchange Commission. Lowe's newsletter contained general commentary about the securities markets, reviews of investment strategies and specific recommendations for buying, selling or holding stocks. Lowe, however, did not manage individual investment portfolios through the newsletter.

A financial publication must register with the SEC as a personal investment advisory, the Court said, only if it offers "individualized advice attuned to any specific portfolio or any client's particular needs." Lowe's newsletter was not a personal investment advisory, the Court said, because it offered completely disinterested advice to the general public on a regular publication schedule. A financial newsletter, the Court said, is not so much like an investment adviser as it is like a newspaper; newspapers, newsmagazines and general-circulation business publications are exempt from registration requirements of the SEC. The Court in *Lowe* suggested, but did not hold, that a telephone hotline Lowe offered to readers might be subject to the Investment Advisers Act even though his newsletter was not, because the hotline might be considered "personalized advice" about buying and selling securities.

Financial Journalists and Market Insiders There is another level of information processors who have access to corporate information but who do not have the fiduciary duties of a corporate insider, a quasi-insider or an investment adviser. People in this group include financial journalists, publishers of impersonal financial newsletters, printers, bank employees, public relations practitioners and employees of financial brokerage houses. These information handlers are sometimes called *market insiders* because they have access to information about mergers, tender offers and other sensitive financial intelligence, but they do not have the fiduciary relationship of insiders and quasi-insiders to companies issuing stock or of investment advisers to their clients.[282]

Although market insiders have no fiduciary duty to market traders, courts have ruled that employees of investment banking firms, financial printers, newspaper publishers and other processors of market information violate Section 10(b) and Rule 10b-5 if they misappropriate information about mergers, acquisitions and other confidential information for their own gain. Under a theory of misappropriation, market insiders have been ruled to engage in fraud in violation of Section 10(b) by taking market information belonging to their employers and using it to tip and trade for their own enrichment.[283]

By a 4–4 vote, the Supreme Court upheld the securities fraud conviction of R. Foster Winans, a *Wall Street Journal* reporter, who engaged in a form of "scalping."[284] (The 4–4 split means that the appeals court decision is precedent only in the Second Circuit.) A scalper manipulates the market, usually by buying stock, touting it in a publication and then selling it when the price of the stock rises.[285] Winans passed financial information to a stockbroker, Peter Brant, who acted on the information before it appeared in the *Journal's* "Heard on the Street"

---

[281] 472 U.S. 181 (1985).

[282] *See* Maria Galeno, "Drawing the Line on Insiders and Outsiders for Rule 10b-5: Chiarella v. United States," 4 *Harv. J. L. & Pub. Pol.* 203, 207 (1981).

[283] SEC v. Materia, 745 F.2d 197 (2d Cir. 1984), *cert. denied*, 471 U.S. 1053 (1985). *See also* United States v. Newman, 664 F.2d 12 (2d Cir. 1981), *aff'd after remand*, 722 F.2d 729 (2d Cir.), *cert. denied*, 464 U.S. 863 (1983).

[284] Carpenter v. United States, 484 U.S. 19 (1987).

[285] SEC v. Capital Gains Research Bureau, Inc., 375 U.S. 180 (1963).

column, a column containing public information about companies' financial prospects. The influence of the *Wall Street Journal* is such that the price of a company's stock might fluctuate because of a favorable or unfavorable mention in the "Heard on the Street" column. Winans's tips resulted in a net profit of $690,000 for Brant and his clients. Winans and his roommate, who was also involved in the scheme, made about $31,000.

The Supreme Court upheld a ruling by the Second Circuit Court of Appeals that Winans violated Section 10(b) by misappropriating information belonging to his employer in violation of the *Journal's* conflict-of-interest policy. The conflict-of-interest policy forbade staff members to trade on information before it is published. Like most newspapers, the *Wall Street Journal* claims ownership in all information gathered by its staff.[286]

Although Winans was not a corporate insider and was not trading on insider information, he was not exempt from the fraud provisions of the securities law. The Second Circuit said the securities laws are not aimed "solely at the eradication of fraudulent trading by corporate insiders." The fraud provisions also reach trading activity, such as trading on the basis of improperly obtained information, a practice that the court said is "fundamentally unfair."

The court said Winans's duty to abide by the *Journal's* conflict-of-interest policy created another duty under Section 10(b) to avoid trading or tipping on the basis of misappropriated information. Winans's misuse of the *Journal's* information before publication defrauded the newspaper, the court said, by sullying its reputation for ethical journalism.

The Second Circuit said that holding a journalist liable under a securities fraud statute did not violate the First Amendment because no government restrictions were placed on publication of the "Heard on the Street" column. The securities law required only that journalists, like other citizens, not engage in fraudulent transactions.

Winans was also convicted of violating federal statutes prohibiting use of interstate mail or wire communication for fraud, a conviction that the Supreme Court unanimously affirmed. The wire and mail fraud statutes prohibit use of either form of interstate communication to obtain money or property by false pretenses. The Court said Winans defrauded the *Wall Street Journal* by taking the publisher's confidential information in violation of an employee pledge and using the mails and telephones to profit from the information. The Court said the *Journal* had an exclusive right to use its property, including confidential business information.

▧ SUMMARY ▧

Publicly traded corporations are subject to fraud suits under Section 10(b) of the Securities Exchange Act of 1934 if they deliberately make a misleading statement of a material fact or fail to disclose material information when they have a duty to do so. Materially deceptive statements include misstatements and omissions that would affect an investor's decision to buy, sell or hold a security. In addition, a corporation may have a duty to disclose material information if misleading information circulating in the media originated with the corporation. Corporate insiders and publishers of personal investment advisories also have a duty to disclose material information before using it as a basis for buying or selling securities. Financial journalists and

---

[286] United States v. Carpenter, 791 F.2d 1024 (2d Cir. 1986).

market insiders have also been ruled to have a duty not to trade on market information acquired from their employers.

ADEQUATE DISCLOSURE The duty to disclose corporate information includes a requirement that disclosure be timely and broad. When a corporation makes a disclosure, whether it is mandated by statute or is made to avoid fraud, the disclosure must be prompt and adequately distributed so that shareholders and other investors will have time to digest the information before insiders buy and sell.

Breadth of Disclosure Information must be disseminated, the SEC has said, "in a manner calculated to reach the securities marketplace in general through recognized channels of distribution, and public investors must be afforded a reasonable waiting period to react to the information."[287] The procedures to be followed for sufficient dissemination of material information will depend on the market for the corporation's securities. If the corporation has a national market, information should be directed to the national financial press, the major financial communities and to other areas where the corporation knows there will be interest in its securities. Many documents must be filed electronically with the Securities and Exchange Commission and can be posted on corporate websites.[288] In addition, publicly traded companies can make "fair disclosure" to the public through widely circulated press releases, announcements made through press conferences or conference calls and by electronic transmission, including the Internet.[289]

The New York Stock Exchange (NYSE) requires a listed company to disclose material information to the public quickly. Ordinarily the fastest means will include a release to the public press by telephone, facsimile or hand delivery, including dissemination through Dow Jones & Company, Inc., Reuters Economic Services and Bloomberg Business News.[290] In addition, the NYSE suggests dissemination to newspapers in New York City and in cities where the corporation has headquarters or plants.

The SEC has said that release of material information over a private wire service to a limited number of institutional subscribers is not adequate dissemination.[291] In *SEC v. Texas Gulf Sulphur Co.*, the U.S. Court of Appeals for the Second Circuit said it was not sufficient for an NYSE corporation to publish news of a large mineral discovery only in a Canadian newspaper of limited circulation.[292] Issuing a news release "is merely the first step in the process of dissemination required for compliance with the regulatory objective of providing all investors with an equal opportunity to make informed investment judgments."

Timeliness While disclosure is supposed to be broad, it is also supposed to be prompt. But the SEC, the courts and the exchanges permit a company to withhold material information temporarily if the decision to withhold is a good-faith business judgment. Disclosure may be delayed where it would prejudice the ability of a company to pursue corporate objectives or where facts are in a state of flux. The objectives of a corporation might be jeopardized, for example, if negotiations for land were disclosed before acquisition was complete. In the *Texas Gulf Sulphur* case, officers of the company fraudulently misled investors while insiders bought stock, but the appeals court said it was not wrong for the company to withhold

---

[287] *In re* Faberge, Inc., 45 S.E.C. 249, 255 (1973).
[288] SEC Release No. 33–8230 (May 7, 2003).
[289] SEC, Selective Disclosure and Insider Trading, 17 CFR pts. 240, 243, 249.
[290] NYSE Manual ¶ 202.6(C).
[291] *In re* Faberge, Inc., 45 S.E.C. at 255.
[292] 401 F.2d 833, 856 (2d Cir. 1968) (en banc), *cert. denied*, 394 U.S. 976 (1969).

disclosure of the promising drilling results until adjoining land could be acquired.[293] Disclosure of information might also be delayed to allow acquisition of another company[294] or liquidation of a portion of a company's business.[295]

When circumstances are in a state of flux, corporations may exercise their business judgment to withhold information until the situation has stabilized. In a rapidly changing situation, a series of press releases could cause undesirable fluctuations in the price of a corporation's stock. In such circumstances, it is better to wait until the situation has calmed.

The U.S. Court of Appeals for the Tenth Circuit ruled that a corporation can wait to release information until it is "available and ripe for publication."[296] The court said that the McDonnell Douglas Corporation did not mislead shareholders when it waited several days for results of an internal evaluation of reduced earnings in the company's aircraft division before issuing a special report. "To be ripe," the court said, information "must be verified sufficiently to permit the officers and directors to have full confidence" in its accuracy. The hazards from an erroneous statement are "obvious," the court said, but it is "equally obvious that an undue delay not in good faith, in revealing facts, can be deceptive, misleading, or a device to defraud." McDonnell Douglas, the court concluded, investigated the expected shortfall as soon as it became known and wasted no time evaluating the information and preparing a release.

▓ SUMMARY ▓

When publicly traded corporations disclose information, it should be disseminated broadly in a timely fashion. But disclosure may be delayed until information is complete and accurate.

---

[293] 401 F.2d at 850, n.12.
[294] Matarese v. Aero Chatillon Corp. [1971–1972 Transfer Binder] Fed. Sec. L. Rep. (CCH) ¶ 93,322 (S.D.N.Y. 1971).
[295] Segal v. Coburn Corp. [1973 Transfer Binder] Fed. Sec. L. Rep. (CCH) ¶ 94,002 (E.D.N.Y. 1973).
[296] Financial Indus. Fund, Inc. v. McDonnell Douglas Corp., 474 F.2d 514, 519 (10th Cir. 1973), *cert. denied*, 414 U.S. 874 (1973).

Obscenity and Indecency

"Sex," Justice Brennan once observed, "has indisputably been a subject of absorbing interest to mankind through the ages." This "great and mysterious motive force in human life," he said, is "one of the vital problems of human interest and public concern."[1] Sex has been a subject of art since humankind originated artistic expression. Even before the Roman Empire, every sexual practice that is today considered acceptable and unacceptable had been sketched, painted, carved, or sculpted.[2]

The commercialization of sex is big business and a significant part of contemporary American mass media. In 2020, the U.S. adult entertainment industry generated an estimated $15 billion in revenue from DVDs, magazines, fantasy phone sex services, Internet sites, satellite and cable services, hotel pay-per-view services and

---

[1] Roth v. United States, 354 U.S. 476, 487 (1957).
[2] D. Byrne and K. Kelley, "Introduction: Pornography and Sex Research," in *Pornography and Sexual Aggression* 2 (Neil Malamuth and Edward Donnerstein eds., 1984).

DOI: 10.4324/9781003264736-9

erotic dance clubs. To put this figure in perspective, adult entertainment industry revenue is larger than the revenue of the domestic box office receipts of the major Hollywood film studios, $11.4 billion in 2019.[3] While the major Hollywood film studios and independents released 987 feature length films in 2019, the adult industry released more than 13,000 films. Consumers are shifting from DVDs to the Internet, especially to online content-sharing platforms such as OnlyFans, where content creators earn money from subscribers. While OnlyFans also features topics such as fitness and fashion, 70 percent of the content on the site is sexually explicit.[4] There are approximately 4.2 million sexually oriented websites on the Internet; Pornhub, the world's most visited pornography site, receives 100 billion views per year, more than Amazon, Netflix and Twitter. *Playboy* magazine, which had been on the cutting edge of depicting female nudity in the 1950s, briefly abandoned nudity in 2015 due to the ready availability of hard-core sexual content on the Internet, in favor of more demure photos of barely clad women. *Playboy* returned to topless photographs of women in 2017, but the magazine's circulation is sharply declining in the face of more explicit competitors.[5] Despite the widespread availability of material depicting sexuality in America in 2022, there remain sharp cultural and political disputes about the harmfulness of this material and whether government should restrict its availability.

The terms **pornography, obscenity** and **indecency** are often mistakenly used interchangeably; each term has a distinct meaning. Pornography is a generic reference to sexually explicit material intended to cause sexual excitement. Pornography has no legal definition. Obscenity is legally defined as a narrow class of "hard-core" pornography that is so "offensive" and so lacking in "social value" that it is denied First Amendment protection. Obscene expression is unprotected in all media. Indecent materials are less graphic or erotic than obscenity. Indecency is fully protected in the print media and on the Internet but may be restricted in the more intrusive broadcast media and may be limited in some ways on cable television and in telephone communications. This chapter is largely concerned with two matters: first, discussing the difficult task of defining obscenity, and second, considering the restrictions that may be placed on indecency.

Some justices have argued that obscenity should be protected by the First Amendment because obscenity is a matter of taste.[6] Today, though, obscenity is outside of legal protection by the First Amendment.[7] However, enforcement of obscenity law is sharply waning as Americans increasingly accept adult consumption of sexual materials depicting adults. The exploitation of children in sexual materials is the focus of current enforcement efforts, along with efforts to limit children's access to sexual materials.

OBSCENITY

Obscenity is the most graphic form of sexual expression and is banned in all media distributed in the United States. The Supreme Court regards obscenity as unworthy of constitutional protection because obscene depictions do not contribute to the exposition of ideas.

---

[3] Motion Picture Association of America, *2020 THEME Report: A Comprehensive Analysis of the Theatrical and Home Entertainment Environment* at 41.
[4] Jason Wise, "OnlyFans Statistics," *Earthweb*, https://earthweb.com/onlyfans-statistics.
[5] Jessica Bennett, "Can Millenials Save Playboy?" *N.Y. Times*, Aug. 4, 2019, at BU 1.
[6] Paris Adult Theatre I v. Slaton, 413 U.S. 49, 70 (1973) (Douglas, J., dissenting).
[7] Roth v. United States, 354 U.S. 476 (1957).

Defining Obscenity

Arriving at a definition of obscenity has been a difficult task for the Supreme Court. From 1957 until 1973, the justices could not agree on a test for determining whether sexual materials are obscene. The difficulty of defining obscenity was captured by Supreme Court Justice Stewart, who said simply, "I know it when I see it."[8] Under Chief Justice Burger, the Supreme Court settled on a definition, announced in 1973 in *Miller v. California*. The *Miller* test remains, and the case provides the foundation for discussing obscenity.[9]

California convicted Miller under state law for conducting a mass-mailing campaign to advertise four books and a film depicting sexual activity. The advertising brochures contained depictions of men and women, their genitals prominently displayed, engaged in a variety of sexual activities. The Supreme Court, applying the three-part test, now known as the *Miller* test, found the materials to be obscene.

To determine whether a work is obscene, the Court said, it is first necessary to establish that "the average person, applying contemporary community standards" would find that the work, taken as a whole, appeals to the prurient interest. Second, the materials must depict or describe sexual conduct in a "patently offensive" way that is specifically defined by state law. Third, the work, taken as a whole, must lack serious literary, artistic, political, or scientific value. The test is "conjunctive"; all three parts must be met if a work is to be ruled obscene and therefore outside of constitutional protection.

PRURIENT INTEREST To be obscene, materials taken as a whole must appeal to the prurient interest as determined by "the average person, applying contemporary community standards." To be obscene, materials must appeal to a lascivious, shameful, or morbid interest in sex. Materials are not obscene simply because people may find them to be disgusting; they also must have a sexual appeal.

The Average Person In *Miller*, the Supreme Court held that patent offensiveness and prurient interest should be determined by what would be obscene to the average person, not to the youngest and most vulnerable. The average person is the normal adult, not a highly sensitive prudish person. Nor is the average person someone with strange or perverted tastes.

Community Standard The Supreme Court under Chief Justice Burger and Chief Justice Rehnquist has reflected the decentralization of power favored by Republican administrations, tending to leave substantial decision-making powers to the states. Each state, for example, can determine the degree of fault a private person must prove in a libel suit against the media. In the law of obscenity, too, the Burger Court augmented the power of localities by ruling in *Miller* that the average person determining whether sexual materials are obscene is supposed to apply a "contemporary community standard." Jurors can draw on their own understanding of the views of the average person in the community to decide what is patently offensive and prurient.[10] The "community" reflecting the average person's values may be the juror's city, county, or state. The community standard may be interpreted by a public opinion poll. Not surprisingly, urban populations are more tolerant of pornography than are people in smaller communities.[11] The availability of sexual material via the Internet is not evidence that it is acceptable under

---

[8] Jacobellis v. Ohio, 378 U.S. 184, 197 (1964) (Stewart, J., concurring).
[9] 413 U.S. 15 (1973).
[10] Hamling v. United States, 418 U.S. 87 (1974).
[11] Marc Glassman, "Community Standards of Patent Offensiveness: Public Opinion Data and Obscenity Law," 42 *Pub. Opinion Q.* 161 (1978).

community standards. As the Court of Appeals for the Fourth Circuit wrote in 2009 in affirming the conviction of a man who trafficked in bestiality films, "the availability of certain materials in the fringe of a community is no indication of community acceptance of it."[12]

Miller rests on the idea that community standards vary throughout the nation. Chief Justice Burger said it is neither "realistic nor constitutionally sound to read the First Amendment as requiring that the people of Maine or Mississippi accept public depiction of conduct found tolerable in Las Vegas, or New York City." Burger admitted that using different state and local standards might cause some distributors to censor their sexual materials to conform to the tastes of the most conservative markets.

Although laws proscribing the sale, distribution or exhibition of obscene materials are substantially alike in almost all states, the enforcement of those laws varies markedly, reflecting different community values and political realities. In many communities, voters currently perceive the prosecution of obscenity crimes as being of lesser importance than the prosecution of other types of crimes. As one lawyer noted, "If you talk to prosecutors on the front lines, they've got fraud, gang activity, organized crime and drug cartels to contend with. Nobody wants resources redirected to dirty movies."[13] In addition, sentences in obscenity cases are often minimal, leading prosecutors to conclude that obscenity prosecutions as "high risk and low reward ventures."[14] At the federal level, enforcement of obscenity laws, such as the ban on the mailing or interstate shipment of obscene materials, varies from administration to administration. The George W. Bush administration sought to punish the distributors of adult materials; under the Obama, Trump and Biden administrations, the Department of Justice has focused on the exploitation of children. For example, in 2021, the DOJ obtained convictions in 33 cases involving child pornography. It obtained only one conviction involving the depiction of adult sexuality.

Because some communities are more conservative than others, federal officials prosecuting pornographers sometimes practice *venue shopping*, picking a jurisdiction—or venue—in which prosecutors think they have the best chance of finding a jury that will convict for obscenity. People connected to the film *Deep Throat*, for example, were prosecuted and convicted under federal obscenity laws in Memphis.[15] Memphis was also the venue of the first conviction for interstate transmission of obscenity over the Internet. A California couple was sentenced to more than two years in prison for distributing digital images of bestiality, incest, rape and sex scenes involving sadomasochistic abuse from their electronic bulletin board on the West Coast to people in Memphis. A federal court in Memphis sentenced Robert Thomas to 37 months in prison and his wife Carleen to 30 months for transmitting obscenity via a computer network and for selling obscene videotapes through the mail.[16] As the Thomas case illustrates, the materials may have been acceptable in California but were illegal in Memphis due to varying community standards.

Minors and Variable Obscenity Although the average adult applying contemporary community standards determines what appeals to prurient interests and

[12] United States v. Adams, 337 F. App'x 336 (4th Cir. 2009).
[13] Jason Krause, "The End of the Net Porn Wars," *ABA Journal*, Feb. 1, 2008.
[14] Attorney General's Commission on Pornography: Final Report 55 (1986).
[15] United States v. Battista, 646 F.2d 237 (6th Cir.), *cert. denied*, 454 U.S. 1046 (1981).
[16] United States v. Thomas, 74 F.3d 701 (6th Cir.), *cert. denied*, 519 U.S. 820 (1996).

otherwise meets the obscenity definition, there is a different or variable standard for material available to minors. The states, the Supreme Court has said, have a compelling interest in "safeguarding the physical and psychological well-being of a minor."[17] Some states prohibit the display of lewd materials where children might see them.[18] In 1998, Congress prohibited a broad range of sexual materials on the Internet in legislation known as the Child Online Protection Act (COPA); the fight over COPA is discussed later in this chapter.

Under what is known as **variable obscenity**, the Supreme Court allows prohibition of materials that are obscene to children but not to adults. The principle of variable obscenity was established in 1968 in *Ginsberg v. New York*.[19] In *Ginsberg*, the Supreme Court upheld the conviction of Sam Ginsberg for selling minors "girlie" magazines that had been found not to be obscene for adults. The magazines showed female buttocks and breasts without full opaque covering as required by a New York statute prohibiting distribution of materials harmful to minors under age 17.

Instead of applying the average-person standard in *Ginsberg*, the Court, in an opinion written by Justice Brennan, held that a state might bar materials as obscene if they appeal to the prurient interests of minors, provided the materials also meet the other criteria of obscenity—patent offensiveness to minors and lack of serious social value to minors. Serious literature and objects of art that contain only nudity or sexual information are not obscene to children any more than they are to adults.

The Court in *Ginsberg* did not demand scientific proof that pornography leads to antisocial conduct among children. Instead, the Court deferred to the determination of the New York legislature that materials could be obscene to minors even if they were not to adults.

Exploitation of Children To protect young minds and bodies, the Supreme Court also has ruled a state may prohibit the distribution and possession of pictures and films in which children perform sexual acts. It is not necessary to determine whether such sexual materials are obscene, only that the children are exploited sexually, the Court said in *New York v. Ferber*.[20] Ferber was convicted for selling to an undercover police officer two films of young boys masturbating. The Court said that "the exploitative use of children in the production of pornography has become a serious national problem."

In *Ferber*, as in *Ginsberg*, the Court required no scientific proof of harm to children. The *Ferber* Court noted, "the legislative judgment, as well as the judgment found in the relevant literature, is that the use of children as subjects of pornographic materials is harmful to the physiological, emotional, and mental health of the child."

Because the distribution of child pornography "is intrinsically related to the sexual abuse of children," the Court said the distributors of children's pornography could be punished even though they did not produce the materials portraying children. Closing the distribution network would cut off the financial incentives essential to pornographic filmmakers, the Court said.

The social interest in protecting children is so compelling the Supreme Court has ruled it is illegal to even possess child pornography.[21] Similarly, a federal

---

[17] New York v. Ferber, 458 U.S. 747 (1982).
[18] *See, e.g.,* Ga. Code Ann. § 16–12–103.
[19] 390 U.S. 629 (1968).
[20] 458 U.S. 747 (1982).
[21] Osborne v. Ohio, 495 U.S. 103 (1990).

court ruled it illegal for a person to receive films depicting teenage girls in provocative poses, even though the girls were wearing bikini bathing suits and underwear.[22] Reporters also are unprotected by the First Amendment if they send and receive child pornography over the Internet while preparing news stories about the child pornography industry.[23]

In 2002 the Supreme Court ruled that the harm-to-children rationale does not support prohibitions of computer-created virtual child pornography or performances involving young adults who look like minors. The law can punish the creation, sale and distribution of child pornography, the Court said in *Ashcroft v. Free Speech Coalition*,[24] only if the materials involve real children, not simulations. In *Free Speech Coalition*, the Court struck down a section of the Child Pornography Prevention Act (CPPA), a law making it illegal to produce, distribute or receive any visual depiction that "appears to be" of a minor engaging in sexual conduct.[25] The statute, which the Supreme Court ruled was overbroad, was an attempt by Congress to prohibit virtual child pornography that was already proliferating on the Internet.

As the Court noted in *Ferber*, children are harmed when they are used in the illegal production of pornography. But virtual child pornography, the Court said in *Free Speech Coalition*, "records no crime and creates no victims by its production." The Court did not address a separate federal statute punishing "morphing," the practice of altering innocent pictures of real children to make it appear the children are engaged in sexual activity. Federal appellate courts have found that child pornography created by taking the heads of children from innocent photographs and superimposing them on photographs of the bodies of adults engaged in sexual conduct harms children and is not protected expression.[26]

A federal statute requiring those who create and distribute materials depicting "actual sexually explicit conduct" to maintain records of their models' ages and identities[27] was found to be constitutional by the Court of Appeals for the D.C. Circuit in 1995[28] and the Sixth Circuit Court of Appeals in 2009. These records, containing each model's photo identification, must be available for inspection by the government upon request. Sexually explicit publications must include a statement noting where the relevant records are kept and who maintains them. The law also applies to "secondary" producers who publish, reproduce, or upload sexual images to a website.

The Sixth Circuit noted in *Connection Distributing Co. v. Holder* that Congress had not banned images of sexually explicit conduct that appeared to involve minors, on the theory that some would involve minors.[29] Instead, Congress chose to regulate the records of those creating and distributing sexually explicit images. The appellate court found the law promoted the interest in protecting children in a reasonably tailored manner.

Due to the prevalence of online pornography depicting young-looking performers, the statute can be applied to most creators of sexual imagery, but according to a 2020 ruling by the Third Circuit, the statute violates the First Amendment rights of "niche players" who do not depict performers who are at least 30 years

---

[22] United States v. Knox, 32 F.3d 733 (3d Cir. 1994), *cert. denied*, 513 U.S. 1109 (1995).

[23] United States v. Matthews, 209 F.3d 338 (4th Cir.), *cert. denied*, 531 U.S. 910 (2000).

[24] 535 U.S. 234 (2002).

[25] 18 U.S.C. § 1256(8)(B).

[26] United States v. Hotaling, 634 F.3d 725 (2d Cir. 2011) (upholding 18 U.S.C. § 2256(8)(C)).

[27] 18 U.S.C. § 2257.

[28] Am. Library Ass'n v. Reno, 33 F.3d 78 (D.C. Cir. 1995).

[29] 557 F.3d 321 (6th Cir. 2009).

old. In *Free Speech Coalition v. Attorney General*, the Third Circuit ruled the government's interest in protecting children was not advanced when explicit depictions show performers whom no reasonable person could mistake for a child. Thus, the appellate court found the law could not be validly applied to ten plaintiffs—producers of sex education materials, artists and a journalist—who the court said were not "ordinary pornographers" because they produced "unique and often creative approaches to sexually explicit conduct" featuring performers who did not resemble children.[30]

The appellate court's ruling, its fourth in a decade-long challenge to the law, vacated a nationwide injunction that prevented the government from enforcing the law against anyone. The injunction afforded more relief than necessary to protect the ten plaintiffs. Given that the law could be validly applied to an extensive number of creators using young-looking performers, the Third Circuit found the statute was not overbroad.

Legislators and prosecutors are grappling with sexting—the sending or posting of nude or seminude photos via cell phones or the Internet. Earlier academic studies downplayed the prevalence of sexting among teenagers,[31] but a 2021 study revealed that sexting is becoming viewed as normal among 9- to 17-year-olds.[32] Many prosecutors recognize that child pornography laws—aimed at pedophiles—are too blunt an instrument for today's adolescent cyberculture. Unless there are aggravating circumstances, such as the involvement of adults, coercion or revenge, prosecutors are unlikely to bring life-altering felony charges.[33]

By 2020, 26 states had enacted laws separating teen sexting from child pornography.[34] For example, Vermont treats as delinquents, subject to juvenile court proceedings, those minors who transmit nude photos of themselves. Minors found guilty under the Vermont sexting law are not required to register as sex offenders, and their records are expunged when they turn 18.

In response to the problem of youth sexting, Apple in 2021 announced an iPhone update that warns users under 18 before they open or send text messages with nude photos.[35] Apple initially included a feature that notified parents when children shared or received nude photos. After strong backlash from privacy advocates, Apple dropped the parental notification feature.

Pandering In determining whether sexual materials are obscene, the Supreme Court will consider the methods by which they are marketed. If the materials are aggressively marketed for their prurient appeal, known as pandering, they are more likely to be termed obscene.[36] So offensive is pandering to the Supreme Court that the justices have upheld obscenity convictions for the commercial promotion of sexual materials when neither the promotion nor the materials advertised were clearly obscene.

In *Ginzburg v. United States*, one of the most controversial cases in obscenity law, the Supreme Court held that in "close cases" evidence of "commercial

---

[30] 974 F.3d 408 (3rd Cir. 2020).
[31] Kimberly Mitchell, David Finkelhor, Lisa Jones, and Janis Wolak, "Prevalence and Characteristics of Youth Sexting: A National Study," *Pediatrics* 129(1), 13–20 (Dec. 2011).
[32] Thorn, *Self-Generated Child Sexual Abuse Material: Youth Attitudes and Experiences in 2020* at 3 (2021).
[33] Erik Eckholm, "Prosecutors Weigh Teenage Sexting: Folly or Felony?" *N.Y. Times*, Nov. 14, 2015, at A13.
[34] *See, e.g.*, Neb. Rev. Stat. Ann. § 28–1463.03; 13 Vt. Stat. Ann. § 2802b.
[35] Julie Jargon, "Apple Plans to Warn Kids on Nudes, Won't Notify Parents," *Wall St. J.*, Dec. 6, 2021, at A12.
[36] Pinkus v. United States, 436 U.S. 293 (1978); Frederick Schauer, *Law of Obscenity* 83–4 (1976).

exploitation of erotica solely for the sake of their prurient appeal" may be decisive in the determination of obscenity.[37] One of publisher Ralph Ginzburg's publications, *EROS*, a hardbound magazine dealing with sex, featured some explicit material but also photographs described by Professor H.W. Janson, a New York University art historian, as "outstandingly beautiful and artistic."[38] Nonetheless, the Court found an emphasis on prurient appeal in Ginzburg's promotional efforts, such as an advertisement describing *EROS* as "*the* magazine of sexual candor."

The ads announcing Ginzburg's publications contained no erotic or explicit pictures or foul language, but Justice Brennan, writing for the Court, found pandering because Ginzburg's enterprise was permeated with the "leer of the sensualist." Even the postmark from Middlesex, New Jersey, was suggestive. Justice Douglas, who dissented, later remarked that Ralph Ginzburg went to jail "not for what he printed, but for the sexy manner in which he advertised his creations."[39]

After the *Ginzburg* ruling, some states amended their obscenity statutes to outlaw the commercial exploitation of erotica solely for the sake of its prurient appeal.[40] The Supreme Court in the 1970s affirmed two obscenity convictions that relied on the pandering concept.[41] In 2002 and 2008, the Court addressed the pandering of child pornography.

In 2002, the Court in *Free Speech Coalition* struck down a provision of the Child Pornography Prevention Act of 1996 that prohibited the possession of a sexually explicit image that is "advertised, promoted, presented, described, or distributed in such a manner that conveys the impression" it depicts a child engaging in sex. The Court said this provision was overbroad because the law not only punished possession of illegal images of child sex that had been advertised as child sex, but the law also punished possession of lawful sexual images *if* the images had been advertised and promoted to "convey the impression" that the materials contained child sex. Thus, possession of a film containing no child sex might be prosecuted criminally if the film trailers conveyed the impression that a viewer would see child sex in the film.

Congress responded to *Free Speech Coalition* by enacting the Protect Act of 2003, outlawing the promotion or advertising of child pornography.[42] In 2008, the Supreme Court upheld the constitutionality of the Protect Act's prohibitions on illegal advertising. Unlike the CPPA, the Protect Act does not criminalize the possession of sexual images because of the way they are advertised. Instead, the Protect Act punishes the advertising of child pornography, regardless of whether a defendant possesses child pornography. The Protect Act does not prohibit the advertising of lawful sexual materials, including virtual pornography that does not involve real children and is not obscene.

In *United States v. Williams*, the Court ruled that offers to provide or receive child pornography are "categorically excluded from the First Amendment."[43] Advertisers or solicitors of sexual materials can be punished if they believe they are offering illegal sexual materials or if they fraudulently offer legal materials they advertise as child pornography. Writing for a seven-person majority, Justice Scalia noted that the constitutional defect the Court found in the pandering provision in *Free Speech Coalition*

---

[37] 383 U.S. 463 (1966).

[38] Peter Magrath, "The Obscenity Cases: Grapes of Roth," *S. Ct. Rev.* 7, 27 (1966).

[39] Paris Adult Theatre I v. Slaton, 413 U.S. at 70 (1973) (Douglas, J., dissenting).

[40] *See, e.g.*, Ga. Code § 16–12–80.

[41] Splawn v. California, 431 U.S. 595 (1977); Hamling v. United States, 418 U.S. 87 (1974).

[42] 18 U.S.C. § 2252A(a)(3)(B).

[43] 553 U.S. 285 (2008).

"was that it went *beyond* pandering" to prohibit possession of protected virtual pornography. In contrast, the Protect Act narrowly focuses on speech that proposes an illegal transaction, where that speech seeks to introduce "material into the child-pornography distribution network." Fraudulent offers to provide illegal products are "doubly excluded" from the First Amendment, Justice Scalia noted.

As will be discussed later in this chapter, the FCC considers whether broadcast sexual content is presented in a titillating manner—which the FCC considers pandering—when defining broadcast indecency.

Atypical Tastes Material may be obscene if it appeals to people with atypical sexual tastes, even when it does not appeal to average adults and minors. In *Mishkin v. New York*, the Supreme Court ruled that material with little appeal to an "average" person may nonetheless be obscene if the dominant theme of the work as a whole appeals to the prurient interests of the "clearly defined deviant sexual group" to which it is disseminated. In *Mishkin*, the Court upheld the conviction of a man who produced and sold books dealing with sadomasochism and fetishism, such as *Cult of the Spankers*.[44]

As noted in Chapter 2, Congress in 2010 amended the "depiction of animal cruelty" statute to punish animal crush videos that were obscene. Congress found that depictions of extreme acts of animal cruelty, such as intentional crushing, impaling, or burning, appeal to a specific sexual fetish. Although the term *obscenity* generally applies to materials depicting sexual acts, Congress said the term also covers "unusual deviant acts" appealing to prurient interests.[45]

A federal appeals court in 2014 found the statute to be a facially constitutional means of targeting speech that promotes and requires the wanton torture and killing of animals.[46]

PATENT OFFENSIVENESS To be obscene, sexual materials must be more than sexually stimulating or titillating. They must also be patently offensive depictions of sexual conduct specified by the legislature. In *Miller*, the Supreme Court provided examples of what a statute could define as sexual conduct: (1) patently offensive representations or descriptions of ultimate sex acts, normal or perverted, actual or simulated, and (2) patently offensive representations or descriptions of masturbation, excretory functions and lewd exhibition of the genitals.

Patently offensive materials feature an excess of repetitive sexual detail, often in a commercial context. Although textual material may be obscene, recent enforcement efforts focus on visual depictions. In *Hamling v. United States*, the Supreme Court held that advertising brochures including explicit photographs of heterosexual and homosexual intercourse, fellatio, cunnilingus, masturbation and group sex were patently offensive.[47]

Mere nudity is not patently offensive. When the Georgia Supreme Court ruled that the nudity in the film *Carnal Knowledge* was obscene, the U.S. Supreme Court reversed. In an opinion written by then-Justice William Rehnquist, the Court said the film did not show details of sexually intimate encounters that might be obscene. There was no exhibition "of the actors' genitals, lewd or otherwise."[48] Therefore, the film was not patently offensive.

---

[44] 383 U.S. 502 (1966).
[45] Animal Crush Video Prohibition Act of 2010, 18 U.S.C. § 48.
[46] United States v. Richards, 755 F.3d 269 (5th Cir. 2014), *cert. denied*, 2015 U.S. LEXIS 2046 (Mar. 23, 2015).
[47] 418 U.S. 87 (1974).
[48] Jenkins v. Georgia, 418 U.S. 153 (1974).

Similarly, "four-letter words" are not obscene. Four-letter words may be offensive or indecent, but generally they are not sexually arousing and therefore are not obscene. The Supreme Court ruled that opposition to the military draft, expressed by the phrase "Fuck the Draft," lacked erotic content.[49] Four-letter words may be part of graphic and lewd sexual portrayals that are patently offensive, but four-letter words by themselves are not obscene.

Because obscenity law focuses on hard-core depictions of sexual activities, it poses few restraints on most journalists, advertisers and public relations practitioners. One danger for people in the media, however, is using the term *obscenity* too loosely. It is libelous to say a person distributes obscene materials if the materials in question do not meet the narrow definition of obscenity.

SOCIAL VALUE Finally, for a work to be obscene, it must not only be patently offensive and appeal to prurient interests but also lack social value when viewed as a whole.

The Whole Work By requiring that the work be looked at as a whole, the Court in *Miller* reaffirmed its 1957 decision in *Roth v. United States*[50] that a determination of obscenity should not be made based on only a few isolated passages or pictures. The *Roth* decision rejected the holding in the nineteenth-century English case, *Regina v. Hicklin*,[51] in which an English court ruled that works could be declared obscene if only a few passages endangered children and other sensitive people. Under the *Hicklin* rule, many literary classics were ruled to be obscene because they contained a few offensive passages. Among the books banned in this country on that basis were James Joyce's *Ulysses*, D.H. Lawrence's *Lady Chatterley's Lover* and Theodore Dreiser's *An American Tragedy*.

The *Hicklin* rule was challenged in an American court in a case involving the importation of Joyce's *Ulysses*. In a decision upheld on appeal, Judge John Woolsey, a federal judge in New York, ruled that *Ulysses* could be imported because, taken as a whole, the book was not obscene. Judge Woolsey found the book to be a serious literary effort of which explicit descriptions of sexual acts were a necessary part.[52] The Supreme Court reiterated Judge Woolsey's view when it ruled in *Roth* and *Miller* that a work should be judged as a whole.

Defining Social Value In First Amendment analysis, courts generally avoid judging the value of expression. In the political arena, for example, the courts make no effort to determine whether a politician's promises are false, impractical, far-fetched or naive. Listeners decide the value of what they hear. But in obscenity cases, the Supreme Court requires a social value test to determine whether materials are constitutionally protected. In the *Miller* decision, the Supreme Court said that to be obscene, sexual content taken as a whole must lack "serious literary, artistic, political, or scientific value."

The value of sexual expression—unlike its offensiveness and its appeal to prurient interests—is not determined by the average person applying contemporary community standards. In *Pope v. Illinois*, the Supreme Court ruled that the value question of the three-part *Miller* test should be decided by a "reasonable person" rather than by the "average person."[53] The Court's decision in *Pope* increases

---

[49] Cohen v. California, 403 U.S. 15 (1971).

[50] 354 U.S. 476 (1957).

[51] 3 Q.B. 360 (1868).

[52] United States v. One Book Called "Ulysses," 5 F. Supp. 182 (S.D.N.Y 1933), *aff'd*, 72 F.2d 705 (2d Cir. 1934).

[53] 481 U.S. 497 (1987).

First Amendment protection for sexual materials; the reasonable person might find literary, artistic, political, or scientific value in a work where the average person, representing the majority, might not. In practice, critics, scholars and other experts frequently help to determine the value of a disputed work. For example, a federal appeals court reversed a ruling that a rap album "As Nasty As They Wanna Be" was obscene because the lower court judge had not relied on expert opinion to determine the social value of the work.[54] The Eleventh Circuit said a judge could not assess social value simply by listening to the recording.

Under the *Miller* standard, works dealing with political and historical subjects have social value even if the works are crude and offensive. The movie *Caligula*, for example, was ruled to have artistic value even though it contained endless scenes of tasteless sex and violence. Although a federal court found the film to be patently offensive, the film was not obscene because the violence and sex did not appeal to the prurient interest and because, taken as a whole, the film contained artistic effort and creativity to portray themes such as the abuse of power.[55]

▨ SUMMARY ▨

For a work to be obscene, it must, taken as a whole, appeal to the prurient interest of the average person applying contemporary community standards. It must also depict specified sexual conduct in a patently offensive manner according to contemporary community standards. Works are patently offensive if they are "hardcore" depictions of lewd displays of the genitals or sexual acts. To be obscene, materials also must lack serious literary, artistic, political, or scientific value, as determined by a reasonable person. Materials that appeal to the prurient interest of minors or deviants may also be obscene even though the materials might not be obscene to the average adult. Materials that are not obscene but "pander" in an intense commercial promotion of their sexual appeal also may be prohibited as obscene.

Revenge Porn

In an era when it is commonplace for couples to share nude photos digitally, it is "just as easy for a jilted lover to find a pornographic website to post them online."[56] Although some advocates for victims prefer "nonconsensual pornography," the more widely used phrase "revenge porn" refers to the distribution of sexually explicit images of individuals without their consent. Ninety percent of the victims of revenge porn are female; when they discover that explicit photos have been posted, the damage includes diminished employment prospects, devastating emotional distress and a loss of a sense of personal safety. As one victim recounted, the posting of an explicit photo by her ex-boyfriend "made me feel bad, to the point that I even told my mother that all I wanted to do was go get in the car and go kill myself."[57] Victims sometimes find that they must pay to have the images removed.[58]

---

[54] Luke Records, Inc. v. Navarro, 960 F.2d 134 (11th Cir. 1992).
[55] Penthouse Int'l, Ltd. v. McAuliffe, 7 Media L. Rep. 1798, 1804 (N.D. Ga. 1981), *aff'd by an evenly divided court*, 717 F.2d 517 (11th Cir. 1983), *cert. denied*, 465 U.S. 1108 (1984).
[56] Matthew Goldstein, "Law Firm Founds Project to Fight 'Revenge Porn,'" *N.Y. Times*, Jan. 30, 2015, at B1.
[57] People v. Iniguez, 202 Cal Rptr. 3d 237 (Cal. App. Dep't Super. Ct. 2016). *See also* State v. Austin, 2019 IL 123910 ¶ 67 (2019) (describing the harm experienced by victims of revenge porn).
[58] People v. Bollaert, 203 Cal. Rptr. 3d 814 (Cal. Ct. App. 2016).

Prior to 2013, only Alaska, New Jersey and Texas had laws punishing revenge porn. In other states, existing laws such as unauthorized computer use or harassment were found not to apply to revenge porn.[59] Remedies such as a federal copyright infringement lawsuit are problematic; often the victims either do not own the copyright to the images because they are not the person who took them, or they do not want to publicly register the images they wish no one ever sees. Similarly, filing takedown notices under the provisions of the Digital Millennium Copyright Act of 1998 is tedious and expensive since "images proliferate swiftly online and takedown notices have to be filed with each site separately."[60] Despite a few recent multimillion-dollar damage awards, civil actions are often not viable because most potential defendants are unable to pay a damage award.

In response to the severity of the problem and the lack of adequate legal remedies, most states have recently enacted revenge porn statutes. Currently, 46 states and the District of Columbia have criminal statutes punishing those who post sexual images without the consent of the individual depicted. Some states also provide for civil damages.

State revenge porn laws generally focus on the following elements: (1) non-consensual disclosure of images, whether still photos or video; (2) depicting nudity or sexually explicit conduct; and (3) causing harm, such as financial loss or mental anguish. A minority of states limit their statutes to images depicting adults;[61] the majority of states punish disclosure of images of a person of any age.[62] Some states specify that the image must be obtained or created under circumstances where the person depicted had a reasonable expectation the image was to remain private.[63] Where the image is related to a newsworthy event, it is generally not punishable,[64] nor are images depicting activity occurring in a public setting punishable.[65] Images do not have to be obscene, as defined by the *Miller* test, to be punishable under state revenge porn statutes. Considerations such as artistic merit are irrelevant; it is sufficient if the imagery depicts nudity or sexually explicit conduct.

The Illinois statute punishing the "non-consensual dissemination of private sexual images,"[66] considered to be the strongest anti-revenge porn law yet enacted, was found by the Illinois Supreme Court to be constitutional in 2019.[67] The Illinois court viewed the statute as a privacy regulation like laws regulating the unauthorized disclosure of other types of private information, such as medical records. The core of the statute was the lack of consent to dissemination; to obtain a conviction, the state must show "the disseminator obtained the image under circumstances in which a reasonable person would know that the image was to remain private and knows or should have known that the person in the image has not consented to the dissemination." There was no criminal liability for dissemination of the very same image obtained and distributed with consent. Thus, "the *manner* of the image's acquisition and publication" was crucial to the illegality of its dissemination. The Illinois court found the interest in privacy would be less effectively served

---

[59] *See, e.g.*, Crapps v. Florida, 180 So. 3d 1125 (Fla. Dist. Ct. App. 2015); People v. Barber, 992 N.Y.S.2d 159 (N.Y. Crim. Ct. 2014).

[60] Margaret Talbot, "Taking Trolls to Court," *New Yorker*, Dec. 5, 2016, at 59.

[61] *See, e.g.*, Ga. Code. Ann. § 16-11-90.

[62] *See, e.g.*, Fla. Stat. § 784.049.

[63] *See, e.g.*, Texas Penal Code § 21.16(b)(2).

[64] *See, e.g.*, Colo. Rev. Stat. § 18-7-107(2).

[65] *See, e.g.*, Ga. Code. Ann. § 16-11-90.

[66] 720 ILCS 5/11-23.5(b).

[67] State v. Austin, 2019 IL 123910 (2019). *See also* State v. VanBuren, 214 A.3d 791 (Vt. 2019) (finding Vermont revenge porn statute to be constitutional).

by alternatives such as civil suits, which do not deter judgment-proof perpetrators who are unable to pay court-ordered damages, or copyright, which requires the victim to be exposed again in the Library of Congress' public catalog. Moreover, because the law did not affect speech on matters of public concern, it did not pose a potential for censorship.

Websites hosting nonconsensual images posted by users have Section 230 immunity, but as *People v. Bollaert* illustrates, the immunity can be lost if the website develops content by requiring that users input information as a condition of posting material.[68] Kevin Bollaert created a website UGotPosted.com hosting nude images submitted by users; Bollaert reviewed all content before it was posted and required that a user who wanted to post pictures of another person had to input that other person's full name, age, location and Facebook link.

Bollaert was convicted of identity theft and invading privacy. A California appellate court rejected Bollaert's Section 230 defense, finding that like the website in *Roommates*, discussed in Chapter 8, UGotPosted.com was designed to solicit unlawful content. By forcing users to answer questions before posting, Bollaert's actions materially contributed to identity theft and privacy invasions, thus eliminating his Section 230 defense. Bollaert also created a website, ChangeMyReputation. com, to which individuals who had pictures posted on UGotPosted.com would be directed and told they could pay money to have the photos removed. This was extortion because Bollaert obtained money by threatening the continued display of private nude images, and further humiliation, unless victims paid for removal.

Google in 2015 took steps to attack revenge porn by posting a form in which victims can ask the search engine to remove from its search results a link to a website with these images. If Google deems an image revenge porn, it will still be accessible to those who know the web address of the image; once delisted from Google, however, the image would not be found through the search engine. The company announced that although its philosophy has always been that Google Search should reflect the whole web, revenge porn serves "only to degrade the victims—predominantly women." Google stated, "This is a narrow and limited policy, similar to how we treat removal requests for other highly sensitive personal information, such as bank account numbers and signatures, that may surface in our search results."[69] The posting of revenge porn on websites such as Facebook and Instagram also violates the terms of service of those companies and victims may ask those companies to remove such images.

Privacy and Possession of Obscenity

Prohibitions on obscenity include bans on the sale, importation and interstate transport of obscene materials,[70] including child pornography.[71] The U.S. Court of Appeals for the Eighth Circuit has ruled that ordering obscenity through the mail also is illegal.[72] There is, however, a limited right to possess obscene materials in the privacy of the home.

---

[68] 203 Cal. Rptr. 3d 814 (Cal. Ct. App. 2016).

[69] "Revenge Porn and Search," *Google Public Policy Blog*, June 19, 2015, https://publicpolicy.googleblog. com/2015/06/revenge-porn-and-search.html.

[70] *See* United States v. Reidel, 402 U.S. 351 (1971); United States v. Thirty-Seven Photographs, 402 U.S. 363 (1971); 18 U.S.C. §§ 1461–65.

[71] Osborne v. Ohio, 495 U.S. 103 (1990).

[72] United States v. Kuennen, 901 F.2d 103 (8th Cir.), *cert. denied*, 498 U.S. 958 (1990). It is illegal for the government to entice citizens to order obscene material through the mails. *See* Jacobson v. United States, 503 U.S. 540 (1992).

Although the law is quite clear that obscene material cannot be bought or transported lawfully, in 1969 the Supreme Court unanimously ruled in *Stanley v. Georgia* that a First Amendment–based right of privacy protected a citizen who merely possessed sexual materials in the home.[73] Stanley was convicted for possession of obscene films found while police were searching his residence for evidence of illegal bookmaking. In ringing language, Justice Thurgood Marshall wrote, "If the First Amendment means anything, it means that a State has no business telling a man, sitting alone in his own house, what books he may read and what films he may watch."

In several obscenity cases decided after *Stanley*, such as *United States v. Reidel*, the Court emphasized that the right to possess obscenity in the home did not also mean that someone had a right to distribute or receive obscenity.[74] The limitations placed on the reach of *Stanley* in cases such as *Reidel* prompted Justice Black's comment that *Stanley* would be "good law only when a man writes salacious books in his attic, prints them in his basement, and reads them in his living room."[75]

The right recognized in *Stanley* to possess obscenity is further limited by the Court's ruling in *Osborne v. Ohio* upholding the constitutionality of prohibitions on the possession of child pornography. In *Osborne*, the Court upheld an Ohio statute that prohibited the possession or viewing of materials showing nude minors.[76] The U.S. Supreme Court said the statute was constitutional because the Ohio Supreme Court said it did not prohibit possession of all nude depictions of children. The state law prohibited only those pictures in which the nudity constituted "a lewd exhibition" or a "graphic focus on the genitals." The goal of the Ohio legislature in adopting the statute was to diminish the economic incentives to exploit children in sexually explicit films and pictures by punishing those who possess them.

Whatever tenuous right Stanley had to possess obscenity in his home, the Supreme Court has ruled the right does not extend to areas outside the home, such as public theaters. In *Paris Adult Theatre I v. Slaton*, the Court ruled that a downtown Atlanta theater could be barred from showing two obscene films, *Magic Mirror* and *It All Comes Out in the End*, to willing adults.[77] Signs outside the theater announced that the movies were "mature feature films" for adults 21 and older. "If viewing the nude body offends you," one sign said, "Please Do Not Enter." There was no evidence that minors had entered the theater.

The Supreme Court rejected the theater management's argument that adults should have as much right to attend an explicit movie in a theater as Stanley had to possess obscene materials in his home. A public theater, unlike a home, is not a private place, the Court said. The state can regulate a theater as it can regulate any other business. It was immaterial, the Court said, that the management of the public theater limited the audience to consenting adults. There are many activities, including prostitution and bare-fist prizefighting, that the state prohibits even though adults are willing to participate. The state has an interest, the Court said,

---

[73] 394 U.S. 557 (1969).

[74] United States v. Reidel, 402 U.S. 351 (1971); United States v. Thirty-Seven Photographs, 402 U.S. 363 (1971).

[75] Thirty-Seven Photographs, 402 U.S. at 382 (Black, J. dissenting).

[76] 495 U.S. 103 (1990).

[77] 413 U.S. 49 (1973).

in protecting "the quality of life and the total community environment, the tone of commerce in the great city centers, and, possibly, the public safety itself."

In 2003, in *Lawrence v. Texas*, the Supreme Court struck down a Texas homosexual sodomy law, holding that a person's decisions about the intimate relationships he will have in the home are not to be criminalized because society finds such relationships to be immoral.[78] The Court believed decisions about intimate relationships lie within a zone of personal liberty, which the government may not enter.

Lawyers were quick to use *Lawrence* as a defense against prosecutions for distributing obscene materials, but these efforts have not been successful. In 2005, in *United States v. Extreme Associates*, the Court of Appeals for the Third Circuit held that federal laws proscribing the distribution of obscene materials do not violate the privacy rights of willing adults.[79] Closely examining the Supreme Court's post-*Stanley* rulings about the distribution of obscenity, the court of appeals found the Court had consistently recognized that the right to possess obscene material in the privacy of the home did not mean there was a correlative right to distribute that material.

The defendants in *Extreme Associates* used various techniques to screen out unwilling adults and children from their Internet site, but the court of appeals found the Internet, like the theater in *Paris Adult Theatre*, was subject to obscenity law. The state has a legitimate interest in stemming the tide of commercialized obscenity, even to consenting adults, the court of appeals said.

Due Process and Prior Restraints

Because obscenity is outside First Amendment protection, it can be enjoined before distribution as well as punished afterward.[80] To identify potentially obscene films, local governments have the legal authority to review films before exhibition. However, as was discussed in Chapter 3, local governments no longer do so, largely because the Supreme Court established strict procedural safeguards to protect expression. Injunctions on obscene materials are also rare because of these procedural safeguards.

The Supreme Court has said a prior restraint may be imposed before judicial review only if the restraint is imposed for a specified brief period, a court can review the restraint "expeditiously," and the censor bears the burden of going to court to suppress the speech and prove that the expression is not constitutionally protected.[81] In *Freedman v. Maryland*, the Supreme Court said theater owners and film distributors may not be compelled to prove their productions are not obscene. Rather, the government agency that would stop the expression must prove the materials are obscene.

Although the *Freedman* standards were developed in the context of film licensing, the Supreme Court has required these standards in cases where customs agents seized imported materials,[82] postal officials restricted use of the mails,[83]

---

[78] 539 U.S. 558 (2003).

[79] 431 F.3d 150 (3d Cir. 2005), *cert. denied*, 547 U.S. 1143 (2006).

[80] Steven Catlett, "Enjoining Obscenity as a Public Nuisance and the Prior Restraint Doctrine," 84 *Colum. L. Rev.* 1616 (1984).

[81] Freedman v. Maryland, 380 U.S. 51 (1965). *See also* Vance v. Universal Amusement Co., 445 U.S. 308 (1980); Southeastern Promotions, Ltd. v. Conrad, 420 U.S. 546 (1975).

[82] United States v. Thirty-Seven Photographs, 402 U.S. 363 (1971).

[83] Blount v. Rizzi, 400 U.S. 410 (1971).

and managers of a municipal auditorium refused use of the auditorium for a production of the musical *Hair*.[84] In each of these cases, the Court said the due process of prior restraint law requires that administrative decisions be made rapidly
and that the administrator not have the final word on what is obscene. Only the
courts, the Supreme Court said in *Freedman*, have the necessary sensitivity to freedom of expression to determine when prior restraints might be imposed.[85] As the
Court noted in the *Hair* case, "an administrative board assigned to screening state
productions—and keeping off stage anything not culturally uplifting or healthful—
may well be less responsive than a court, an independent branch of government, to
constitutionally protected interests in free expression."

Government agents violate a citizen's due process rights if the agents move
too slowly to review a prior restraint, which includes the period while a businessperson waits for the government to issue a business license. Context determines
how quickly the government must make a ruling. A theater owner who already has
rented films of brief popularity is entitled to a quicker administrative decision than
a businessperson who is asking whether the site of a proposed adult bookstore
conforms to zoning laws. The Supreme Court said it is constitutional to require that
a film distributor wait 14 days for an appeal of a ruling that his films are obscene
but that a delay of 40 days may be unconstitutionally long.[86] A federal appellate
court ruled that 150 days is too long for the owner of an adult bookstore to wait
for administrators to decide whether his store conforms to zoning laws and protects
children from obscenity.[87]

If the government is to seize sexual materials, a judge first must rule them to
be obscene. In *Fort Wayne Books, Inc. v. Indiana*, the Supreme Court overturned
a decision of the Supreme Court of Indiana holding that all sexual materials might
be removed from an adult bookstore before a trial for racketeering if officials had
reason to believe that the owners were circulating obscenity.[88] The Supreme Court
said the risk of prior restraint on constitutionally protected expression is too high
if sexual materials may be seized before they are found to be obscene. The Court
said officials may seize a single copy of a book or film as evidence, but they may
not take all materials from an adult bookstore before an obscenity determination
is made.

However, the Supreme Court has ruled that the First Amendment allows the
government to seize a defendant's entire entertainment business, including constitutionally protected books and films, after a racketeering conviction. In *Alexander
v. United States*, the Court said the government did not violate the First Amendment
when it seized 13 bookstores and video stores and nearly $9 million from Ferris
Jacob Alexander after he was convicted of racketeering by transporting and selling obscenity.[89] A five-justice majority rejected Alexander's argument that seizing
his entertainment business constituted an unconstitutional prior restraint. First, the
racketeering law did not prevent Alexander from selling any particular book, movie
or magazine, nor was he required to obtain government approval before doing so.
After forfeiting the assets that were related to his prior racketeering convictions,
Alexander was free to open new stores, restock his inventory and sell sexually

---

[84] Southeastern Promotions, Ltd. v. Conrad, 420 U.S. 546 (1975).
[85] *See also* Henry Monaghan, "First Amendment 'Due Process'," 83 *Harv. L. Rev.* 518, 522–3 (1970).
[86] United States v. Thirty-Seven Photographs, 402 U.S. 363 (1971).
[87] 11126 Baltimore Boulevard, Inc. v. Prince George's County, 58 F.3d 988 (4th Cir.), *cert. denied*, 516
U.S. 1010 (1995).
[88] 489 U.S. 46 (1989).
[89] 509 U.S. 544 (1993).

explicit materials. Second, the racketeering statute did not target expressive materials; books, like nonexpressive assets such as sports cars and cash, could be forfeited because of their role in the operation of a racketeering enterprise. The Court said the seizure of Alexander's assets, unlike the unconstitutional pretrial seizure in *Fort Wayne Books*, was not premature because a trial court already had determined that Alexander's entertainment business was linked to racketeering in obscenity.

▨ SUMMARY ▨

The Supreme Court has ruled that adults may receive obscene materials in the privacy of their homes. However, the right to receive and possess obscenity is severely curtailed by constitutional prohibitions on the distribution and sale of obscenity. The right to possess obscenity is further limited by the Court's ruling that possession of child pornography may be barred. The Supreme Court also has held that obscene films may be prohibited in theaters even if admission is limited to consenting adults.

When the government attempts to show a work is obscene, the First Amendment requires due process be followed. This includes placing the burden of proof on the government and providing for rapid judicial review.

INDECENCY

As was discussed earlier in this chapter, obscene content has no First Amendment protection. If material appeals to the prurient interest, is patently offensive and has no serious social value, the government may ban the material, criminally punish its creators and distributors, or take a variety of other actions.

Indecent material is sexually oriented but does not meet the *Miller* definition of obscenity. Indecency, much like obscenity, depicts or describes sexual or excretory activities or organs in a patently offensive manner. Indecency, in contrast to obscenity, need not arouse a prurient interest in sex. In addition, an indecent broadcast program, unlike one that is obscene, can have serious value and still violate the law. The FCC has said that the "serious merit" of a program will be considered as a factor, but not necessarily the deciding factor, in determining whether a broadcast is indecent.

Unlike obscenity, indecency receives some First Amendment protection, which varies from medium to medium. Courts analyze indecency regulations according to the technological attributes of a medium and the level of effort required of the reader or viewer to receive messages. For example, the Supreme Court regards the Internet as similar to the highly protected print media because both require affirmative effort by the recipient to receive a message. In contrast, broadcast indecency is restricted because broadcasting is "uniquely accessible to children," even those who are too young to read.

Broadcasting

As was noted in Chapter 3, in 1969, the Supreme Court held in *Red Lion Broadcasting Co. v. FCC* that spectrum scarcity justified regulations designed to promote the presentation of a range of views.[90] The regulation of broadcast indecency, however, is not justified on spectrum scarcity grounds. Instead, the Supreme Court's decision in

---

[90] 395 U.S. 367 (1969).

FCC v. Pacifica Foundation, upholding the FCC's power to punish a broadcaster for airing indecent content, justifies broadcasting's reduced First Amendment protection in this context because broadcasting is intrusive and accessible to children.[91] Writing for the Court, Justice Stevens said that broadcasting "is a uniquely pervasive presence in the lives of all Americans." Broadcasting "confronts" citizens in public but also "in the privacy of the home, where the individual's right to be left alone plainly outweighs the First Amendment rights of an intruder." Even though listeners could change channels or turn off the receiver after encountering offensive depictions of sexuality, this was "like saying that the remedy for an assault is to run away after the first blow." Justice Stevens also said that society's interest in protecting children, coupled with the ease with which even young children could gain access to broadcasting, justified broadcasting's special treatment. In a dissenting opinion, Justice Brennan questioned whether listening to broadcasts, even in the home, implicated "fundamental" privacy interests.

Although a federal statute outlaws the broadcasting of obscene, indecent, or profane material,[92] the FCC's enforcement has focused on indecency. Broadcasters almost never air hard-core sexual depictions that meet the *Miller* test for obscenity. Also, the statutory reference to profane material has rarely been enforced. In the 1930s, blasphemous statements such as *By God* were regarded as profane.[93] Since the 1960s, however, statements such as *God damn it* have been treated as protected expression.[94] In a 2004 decision treating the word *fuck* as both indecent and profane, the FCC announced a new approach that classifies "vulgar and coarse" language as profane.[95] The FCC left the status of words other than *fuck* unsettled; broadcasters were warned that the agency would analyze other potentially profane words or phrases on a case-by-case basis. Subsequently, in two 2005 decisions discussed later in the chapter, the FCC ruled that words such as *dick* are not sufficiently graphic to be profane and that blasphemous statements, such as *God damn it*, are not actionable as profanity. In 2006, though, the FCC ruled that *shit* was sufficiently vulgar to be both indecent and profane. By treating *fuck* and *shit* as both indecent and profane, the FCC was not authorizing additional fines or sanctions; rather, the agency was emphasizing the harmfulness of even a single utterance of these words.

Enforcement of indecency is a highly politicized process. The FCC chair's political party affiliation is a major factor affecting indecency enforcement. From 1969–2004, when the FCC chairman was a Republican, there were 53 proposed fines; when the chairman was a Democrat, there were 39 proposed fines. The average proposed fine during the tenure of Republican chairmen was $98,667. The average proposed fine when a Democrat chaired the agency was $39,096.[96] The pressure put on the FCC by Congress and outside groups also affects the ebb and flow of FCC enforcement. In 2001, for example, the FCC received just 346 indecency complaints and the agency levied $91,000 in fines. As shown in Table 9.1, from 2003 to 2006, indecency and profanity in broadcast programming were issues of intense political interest to Republicans. The FCC's enforcement bureau ruled in

---

[91] 438 U.S. 726, 748–9 (1978).
[92] 18 U.S.C. § 1464.
[93] *See, e.g.,* Duncan v. United States, 48 F.2d 128 (9th Cir. 1931).
[94] Gagliardo v. United States, 366 F.2d 720 (9th Cir. 1966); Raycom, Inc., 18 F.C.C.R. 4186 (2003).
[95] Complaints Against Various Broadcast Licensees Regarding Their Airing of the "Golden Globe Awards," Memorandum Opinion and Order, 18 F.C.C.R. 4975 (2004).
[96] The FCC vs. Indecency, www.washingtonpost.com/wp-dyn/content/custom/2005/10/28/CU2005102800826.html.

Table 9.1 Indecency Complaints and Fines 2000–June 2006		
	Number of Complaints	**FCC Proposed Fines**[*]
2006 (Jan.–June)	327,198	$3,962,500
2005	233,531	0
2004	1,405,419	2,428,080
2003	166,683	440,000
2002	13,922	99,400
2001	346	91,000
2000	111	48,000

Source: FCC Enforcement Bureau.

[*] In some instances, the fine may be reduced or rescinded. Also, the fine may relate to a complaint from a prior year.

October 2003 that an isolated utterance of *fuck* in a live entertainment broadcast was not indecent; this ruling prompted 237,215 letters of protest. Amid intense political pressure, the FCC in March 2004 overturned its enforcement bureau and held that even a single utterance of *fuck* in live entertainment programming is indecent and profane. The FCC also received more than 542,000 complaints about Janet Jackson's "wardrobe malfunction" exposing her breast at the 2004 Super Bowl halftime show; in September 2004, the FCC fined CBS-owned television stations $550,000 for the Super Bowl broadcast.[97] The agency also negotiated consent decrees with the Viacom, Emmis and Clear Channel broadcast groups in 2004.[98] In exchange for dismissal of pending indecency cases, these broadcasters agreed to collectively pay $5.5 million in "voluntary contributions" to the U.S. Treasury. Each broadcaster also agreed to implement indecency compliance plans including training of on-air talent and producers, use of time-delay equipment on live programming, and suspension or termination of employees involved in future indecency violations. Howard Stern decried the FCC's actions as a "witch hunt" and moved his program in 2006 to Sirius, an unregulated subscription satellite service.

Until the early 2000s, FCC fines for indecent broadcasts have been rare and only a small amount.[99] As discussed later, a law enacted in 2006 increased the amount of fines tenfold. Faced with a difficult regulatory environment and the loss of audience to cable and satellite services that can legally carry graphic programs, like *Game of Thrones*, the major television networks in 2006 filed suit against the FCC, claiming it is time to revisit the indecency rules. In 2012 the Supreme Court unanimously held the FCC's enforcement was vague as applied to three broadcasts of isolated expletives or fleeting nudity. The Court did not decide whether the indecency rules in their entirety violate the First Amendment.

Even prior to the 2012 ruling, the FCC had scaled back indecency enforcement in the face of strong broadcaster opposition and a changing political landscape; Democrats, who generally regard broadcast indecency as a less important

---

[97] Complaints Against Various Television Licensees Concerning Their February 1, 2004 Broadcast of the Super Bowl XXXVIII Halftime Show, Notice of Apparent Liability for Forfeiture, 19 F.C.C.R. 19230 (2004). This order was vacated by the Court of Appeals for the Third Circuit. CBS Corp. v. FCC, 663 F.3d 122 (3d Cir. 2011), *cert. denied*, 132 S. Ct. 2677 (2012).

[98] Viacom, Inc., Order (FCC 04–268) (Nov. 23, 2004); Emmis Communications Corp., Order (FCC 04–199) (Aug. 12, 2004); Clear Channel Communications, Inc., Order (FCC 04–128) (June 9, 2004).

[99] *See, e.g.*, Frank Aherns, "Delays, Low Fines Weaken FCC Attack on Indecency," *Wash. Post*, Nov. 10, 2005, at A1.

issue than do Republicans, controlled the House from 2007 through 2010 and the Senate from 2007 to 2014. On April 1, 2013, the FCC announced it had dismissed more than 1 million indecency complaints. In 2014 the FCC issued only two indecency findings, and in recent years the agency has often issued no indecency findings. With the House narrowly under control of Democrats and the Senate split evenly between Democrats and Republicans as a result of the 2020 elections, the current political environment does not support robust FCC enforcement. Only extreme cases, such as the case discussed later involving the display of an erect penis during a newscast, are likely to be pursued.

LIMITING INDECENT BROADCASTS The First Amendment protects indecency because the Supreme Court has said only those sexually oriented materials meeting the *Miller v. California* test for obscenity fall outside constitutional protection. However, in 1978, in *FCC v. Pacifica Foundation*, the Supreme Court ruled that the FCC could regulate the times of indecent broadcasts without violating the First Amendment.[100]

The dispute in *Pacifica* began with an afternoon broadcast of a George Carlin recording, "Filthy Words," on New York City radio station WBAI (FM). A New York father complained to the FCC after hearing the Carlin satire on the use of language while driving with his son.[101] Carlin began his 12-minute monologue by saying he would talk about "the words you couldn't say on the public, ah, airwaves, um, the ones you definitely wouldn't say, ever." Then he frequently repeated in a variety of contexts seven "dirty" words: *shit*, *piss*, *fuck*, *cunt*, *cocksucker*, *motherfucker* and *tits*.

The FCC said Carlin's "dirty" words were indecent because they repeatedly depicted sexual and excretory activities and organs in a patently offensive manner during the early afternoon when children were "undoubtedly" in the audience. Although the FCC did not penalize the Pacifica Foundation, the WBAI licensee, for the Carlin broadcast, the commission said additional complaints about indecent programming from listeners could lead to sanctions. Broadcasters airing indecency not only risk fines and the loss of their licenses under the 1934 Communications Act,[102] but they also can be fined and jailed for up to two years under the federal criminal code.[103]

The FCC's decision to warn Pacifica for the broadcast of the Carlin monologue was reversed by the Court of Appeals for the D.C. Circuit but reinstated by a divided U.S. Supreme Court. Justice John Paul Stevens, in an opinion supported in part by four other justices, said the FCC's warning to WBAI did not violate the 1934 Communications Act or the First Amendment.

Stevens said the FCC did not "censor" WBAI's broadcast of the Carlin monologue, as Pacifica contended. As was discussed in Chapter 3, the prohibition on censorship in the 1934 Communications Act has never forbidden the FCC to evaluate broadcasts after they were aired. The commission had not edited the "Filthy Words" monologue in advance. Rather, the FCC had reviewed the program after the broadcast as part of the commission's responsibility to regulate licensees in the public interest. Stevens said review of program content after a broadcast is not censorship.

[100] 438 U.S. 726 (1978).
[101] Pacifica Foundation Station WBAI (FM), 56 F.C.C.2d 94 (1975).
[102] 47 U.S.C. § 312(a)(6).
[103] 18 U.S.C. § 1464.

Stevens also rejected Pacifica's argument that Carlin's monologue could not be regulated because it was not obscene. Pacifica had argued that *obscenity* and *indecency* mean the same thing under federal law; both require an appeal to the prurient interest before punishment. Stevens, though, said the words *obscene* and *indecent* have different meanings when applied to broadcasting. The term *indecent* refers "to nonconformance with accepted standards of morality," the justice said.

Stevens said important considerations in indecency cases include the time of day of the broadcast, the nature of the program containing the offensive language, the composition of the audience, and perhaps the differences among radio, television and closed-circuit transmissions. The Court said the Carlin monologue could be regulated because of the repetitive use of the offensive words at a time when children could reasonably be expected to be a part of the audience.

Justice Brennan in a dissenting opinion, said the FCC's regulation of the Carlin speech was unconstitutional. In an opinion joined by Justice Marshall, Brennan said the Court's majority was for the first time prohibiting minors from hearing speech that was not obscene and therefore is protected by the First Amendment. Brennan said that "surely" preserving speech entitled to First Amendment protection is important enough that listeners could be required to suffer the "minimal discomfort" of briefly hearing offensive speech before they turned off the radio. Brennan accused the Court of attempting "to impose its notions of propriety on the whole of the American people."

DEFINING BROADCAST INDECENCY As noted above, the FCC's interest in enforcing indecency ebbs and flows according to the political environment. For nine years after *Pacifica*, the FCC emphasized it would only punish repetitive use of the words in Carlin's monologue and found no broadcasts deserving sanctions.

In 1987, the FCC developed a broader contextual analysis that emphasizes three factors; the explicitness or graphic nature of the material, the extent to which there was repetition and whether the material was presented to "pander" or "shock."[104] The commission uses a national standard for determining whether a program is patently offensive, not a local community or statewide test. The FCC also considers the "full context" of the program. For example, a newscast employing explicit language might not be indecent, but a disc jockey repeatedly using language implying sexual activity might be indecent programming. From the late 1980s until the early 2000s, indecency fines were rare and generally a small amount. The biggest fines targeted a handful of radio "shock jocks," such as Howard Stern, who made explicit discussions of sex the dominant theme of their programs.[105]

Under Republican leadership, the FCC's interest in punishing indecency markedly increased in the early 2000s. Figure 9.1 contrasts FCC indecency rulings from 2001 to 2006. These rulings reveal that the FCC has no bright-line test to define indecency. Instead, the agency makes case-by-case determinations, balancing several factors to decide whether a program is indecent. Critics, who believe the FCC's indecency decisions are arbitrary and inconsistent, claimed that indecency determinations reflect "little more than the personal tastes" of the commissioners.[106] These

---

[104] Industry Guidance on Broadcast Indecency, 16 F.C.C.R. 7999 (2001).

[105] Sagittarius Broadcasting Group, 10 F.C.C.R. 12 (1995).

[106] Stephen Weiswasser and Robert Sherman, "*Oprah* and Spielberg vs. *Without a Trace* and Scorsese: Indecent Inconsistency at the FCC," 24 *Comm. Lawyer* (2006).

Consistent or Inconsistent?		
Indecent		*Not Indecent*
Fuck	vs.	**Fuck**
Uttered by U2's Bono on an awards show. The FCC regarded the remark as "gratuitous."		Uttered repeatedly by actors during *Saving Private Ryan*. The FCC concluded the language was "integral" to the film.
Shit	vs.	**Bullshitter**
Uttered by Nicole Richie on an awards show. The FCC regarded the remark as "gratuitous."		Uttered by a *Survivor* contestant during a news interview. The FCC said the news context weighs against indecency findings.
Janet Jackson's Breast	vs.	**Nicollette Sheridan's Naked Back**
Briefly exposed during the *Super Bowl Halftime Show*. The FCC regarded the segment as overtly sexual.		Shown during an introduction to *Monday Night Football*. Despite the sexually suggestive nature of the segment, there was no graphic depiction of sexual organs.
Howard Stern's discussions of sex	vs.	**Oprah Winfrey's discussions of sex**
Stern discusses various sexual activities such as oral sex. The FCC concluded Stern was pandering to the audience interest in sexuality.		Winfrey discusses various sexual activities such as oral sex and terms used by teenagers. The FCC claimed the segment was designed to help parents.
A teenage girl wearing a bra and panties	vs.	**A couple in bed passionately kissing, caressing and rubbing**
Briefly shown straddling a teenage boy during an episode of *Without a Trace*. The FCC found the scene to be "highly sexually charged."		Briefly shown during an episode of *Alias*. The FCC said there was no display of sexual organs.

FIGURE 9.1 FCC rulings on indecency (2003–2006).

criticisms led to challenges of new policies announced in 2004 concerning isolated expletives and fleeting images of nudity.

   ISOLATED EXPLETIVES AND IMAGES Although the FCC is unlikely to challenge expletives in news programs, the commission announced in 2004 that it considers even a single utterance of what is called "the F-word" both indecent and profane in live entertainment programs.[107] In its 2004 ruling, the FCC overturned its own enforcement bureau, which had ruled that U2's Bono had not expressed indecency when he exclaimed, "This is really, really, fucking brilliant," upon winning the 2003 Golden Globe Award for best original song. The enforcement bureau found that in this context the word *fucking* did not describe sexual activities. Moreover,

---

[107] Complaints Against Various Broadcast Licensees Regarding Their Airing of the "Golden Globe Awards," Memorandum Opinion and Order, 19 F.C.C.R. 4975 (2004).

drawing upon the FCC's guidelines, the bureau concluded that fleeting and isolated remarks did not warrant FCC sanctions.[108]

In overturning the enforcement bureau's decision, the FCC announced that its precedents allowing isolated or fleeting use of the F-word in similar contexts were no longer good law. Any use of the F-word inherently has a sexual connotation, the commission said. Furthermore, use of the F-word was patently offensive because it "is one of the most vulgar, graphic and explicit depictions of sexual activity in the English language." The FCC described Bono's use of the F-word as gratuitous, and indicated that political, scientific, or other uses of the F-word might mitigate its offensiveness. The FCC noted that a factor in its decision to target isolated use of the F-word was the ease with which broadcasters can delay live broadcasts and bleep offending material. In response to this ruling, many broadcasters began using delays on live broadcasts.

In another 2004 decision concerning the brief exposure of Janet Jackson's breast during the 2004 Super Bowl halftime show, the FCC announced that an isolated visual image of nudity could also be indecent.[109] This departed from an earlier policy requiring more than an isolated presentation of nudity for a broadcast to be indecent.

The FCC's isolated expletives and images decisions created uncertainty among broadcasters. Sixty-six ABC television network affiliates preempted the November 2004 Veteran's Day broadcast of the film *Saving Private Ryan*, which has numerous uses of the F-word. In early 2005, the FCC dismissed complaints filed against some of the ABC affiliates airing the film, holding the film's coarse battlefield language, unlike that of Bono, was neither gratuitous nor intended to shock. "Indeed, it is integral to the film's objective of conveying the horrors of war through the eyes of these soldiers, ordinary Americans placed in extraordinary situations," the agency stated. ABC provided parents with ample warnings about the film's content; thus, the FCC concluded the presentation was not intended as family entertainment. Also, the FCC ruled that uses of the words *God damn* and similar blasphemous phrases were not profane.[110]

In another decision issued in 2005, the FCC held that the words *dick, penis, testicles, bastard, bitch, hell, damn, orgasm, breast, nipples, pissed* and *crap* were not profane when used in a fleeting manner in entertainment programs such as *Friends, Will and Grace* and *Scrubs*. The FCC claimed these words, in context, were not sufficiently graphic to be patently offensive.[111]

In 2006, the FCC ruled that *shit*, "one of the most offensive words in the English language," was both indecent and profane.[112] Nicole Richie, a presenter at the *2003 Billboard Music Awards* program, asked, "Have you ever tried to get cow shit out of a Prada purse?" Even when used in an isolated manner in entertainment programming, the FCC found "the S-word" was likely to "disturb the peace and quiet of the

---

[108] Complaints Against Various Broadcast Licensees Regarding Their Airing of the "Golden Globe" Awards, Memorandum Opinion and Order, 18 F.C.C.R. 19859 (Enf. Bur. 2003). *See generally* Anne Marie Squeo, "A Job for Solomon: Was Bono's Blurt a Verb or Modifier?" *Wall St. J.*, Mar. 11, 2004, at A1.

[109] Complaints Against Various Television Licensees Regarding Their February 1, 2004, Broadcast of Super Bowl XXXVIII Halftime Show, 19 F.C.C.R. 19230 (2004).

[110] Complaints Against Various Television Licensees Regarding Their Broadcast on November 11, 2004, of the ABC Television Network's Presentation of the Film "Saving Private Ryan," Memorandum Opinion and Order, 20 F.C.C.R. 4507 (2005).

[111] Complaints by Parents Television Council Against Various Broadcast Licensees Regarding Their Airing of Allegedly Indecent Material, Memorandum Opinion and Order, 20 F.C.C.R. 1931 (2005).

[112] Complaints Regarding Various Television Broadcasts Between February 2, 2002 and March 8, 2005, Notices of Apparent Liability and Memorandum Opinion and Order (FCC 06–17) (Mar. 15, 2006).

PHOTO 9.1   Janet Jackson and Justin Timberlake performing at the Super Bowl XXXVIII Halftime show on February 1, 2004. Immediately before this photo was taken, Timberlake sang "Gonna have you naked by the end of this song" from "Rock Your Body" and pulled off part of her costume, exposing her right breast for 19/32 of a second. The brief exposure of Jackson's breast resulted in an unprecedented 540,000 complaints to the FCC and a fine of $550,000, which was rescinded in 2011.

Source: Getty Images. Used by permission.

home." The FCC cautioned broadcasters that only in rare circumstances would the S-word, like the F-word, be regarded as essential to an artistic, educational, or political message. To emphasize its view that the S-word was almost always indecent, the FCC found a documentary about blues musicians airing on a public television station to be indecent. The licensee failed to demonstrate to the FCC's satisfaction that phrases such as "that shit is crazy" were essential to informing the public about a matter of public importance. In setting aside the artistic judgment of acclaimed film-maker Martin Scorsese, the FCC said the documentary's educational purpose could have been fulfilled "without the repeated broadcast of expletives."

In an important clarification of its policy on isolated expletives, the commission announced in November 2006 that live news programs provide a context that weighs against an indecency finding. At issue was a live interview on *The Early Show*, a two-hour morning program airing on the CBS television network. During the interview, a contestant in the CBS program *Survivor: Vanuatu*, described another contestant as a "bullshitter." The FCC explained that news programs were at the core of the First Amendment's protection. The FCC cautioned broadcasters that "there is no outright news exemption from our indecency rules." Nevertheless, considering the important First Amendment interests at stake, the FCC announced it would "proceed with the utmost restraint when it comes to news programming."[113]

The FCC's new policy on "isolated expletives" was sustained in 2009 by the Supreme Court in a 5–4 ruling based on administrative rather than constitutional law.[114] The majority in *FCC v. Fox Television Stations (Fox I)* concluded the FCC did not act arbitrarily in violation of the Administrative Procedure Act when it began punishing single utterances of *fuck* and *shit*. "The Commission could reasonably conclude," Justice Scalia wrote for the majority, that the "coarsening of public entertainment in other media such as cable" justifies more stringent regulation of broadcast programs to provide a "relatively safe haven" for children.

The Supreme Court in 2009 also vacated another appellate court ruling that the FCC had acted arbitrarily in fining CBS $550,000 for the brief display of Janet Jackson's breast during the 2004 Super Bowl halftime show.[115] On remand in 2011, the appellate court again found the FCC's action invalid, and the Supreme Court denied certiorari in 2012.[116]

The Supreme Court did not consider broadcasters' First Amendment arguments in the isolated expletives and isolated images cases and remanded the cases to appellate courts to address those issues. The first appellate court to answer constitutional questions, the Second Circuit, in 2010 found the FCC's policy invalid due to vagueness.

On remand, the Second Circuit noted the vagueness doctrine requires that broadcasters be given fair notice of what material is indecent.[117] Fair notice is particularly important with respect to content-based restrictions because of their chilling effect. The court found ample evidence in the record that broadcasters have cancelled programs due to uncertainty about whether the FCC would find the program to be indecent.

The appellate court also criticized the FCC for engaging in subjective decision-making. Noting that the FCC had concluded that explicit language was "integral" to some programs such as *Saving Private Ryan*, while not "integral" to other programs, such as Martin Scorsese's blues documentary, the court wrote, "There is little rhyme or reason to these decisions and broadcasters are left to guess whether an expletive will be deemed 'integral' to a program." With millions of dollars and core First Amendment values at stake, the FCC's policy was "simply not good enough," the court wrote.

---

[113] Complaints Regarding Various Television Broadcasts Between February 2, 2002 and March 8, 2005, Order, (FCC 06–16) (Nov. 6, 2006).
[114] FCC v. Fox Television Stations, Inc., 556 U.S. 502 (2009).
[115] FCC v. CBS Corp., 556 U.S. 1218 (2009).
[116] CBS Corp. v. FCC, 663 F.3d 122 (3d Cir. 2011), *cert. denied*, 132 S. Ct. 2677 (2012).
[117] Fox Television Stations v. FCC, 613 F.3d 317 (2d Cir. 2010).

The Supreme Court in 2012 unanimously ruled in *FCC v. Fox Television Stations (Fox II)* that the FCC failed to give Fox and ABC fair notice that fleeting expletives and momentary nudity could be found indecent.[118] Therefore, the FCC's standards as applied to these broadcasts were unconstitutionally vague in violation of the Fifth Amendment.

In an opinion written by Justice Kennedy, the Court noted the FCC's policy at the time of Fox's broadcasts of the *Billboard Music Awards* in 2002 and 2003 required repetition of expletives before material could be found indecent. Similarly, when ABC in 2003 aired an episode of *NYPD Blue* featuring seven seconds of nudity, FCC policy treated fleeting images as not indecent. As noted above, the Commission changed its policy toward isolated expletives and brief nudity in 2004. Sanctioning the earlier broadcasts under new rules was equivalent to changing the rules in the middle of the game. Under the Due Process Clause of the Fifth Amendment, "regulated parties should know what is required of them so they may act accordingly," Justice Kennedy wrote.

The Court's decision was exceedingly narrow, holding only that the broadcasters were denied fair notice of the FCC's standards. The Court declined the broadcasters' request to find that the FCC's entire indecency policy violated the First Amendment and that *Pacifica* should be overturned. However, Justice Kennedy said the FCC and courts were free to review the indecency policy. In effect, the First Amendment questions were postponed for another day.

There was little appetite in the Obama administration to deal with broadcast indecency. In the first official action in response to *Fox II*, the Department of Justice on September 21, 2012, dropped efforts to collect a fine from Fox for a 2003 program that featured whipped cream, spanking and pixilated images of topless strippers.[119] Then-FCC chair Julius Genachowski announced he had directed the agency's enforcement bureau to "focus its resources on the strongest cases that involve egregious indecency violations." Accordingly, on April 1, 2013, the FCC announced it had reduced its backlog of pending indecency complaints by dismissing more than one million complaints, principally by closing cases that were beyond the statute of limitations, contained insufficient information or were foreclosed by precedent. The agency also announced it was seeking public comment on whether it should make changes to its indecency policies or maintain them as they are. Although the FCC did not find a single broadcast to be indecent between 2009 and 2013, a 2015 ruling, discussed later, shows that extreme cases will be severely punished. As of early 2022, the FCC has yet to revise its indecency policies. This is an issue that has largely faded from the agency's current priorities.

FINING INDECENCY On June 15, 2006, President Bush signed the Broadcast Decency Enforcement Act, which increased the maximum penalty the FCC can impose per indecency violation from $32,500 to $325,000.[120] This tenfold increase was necessary, President Bush stated, because the prior amount was not a deterrent to many broadcasters, and in recent years "broadcast programming has too often pushed the bounds of decency."

Although Congress sets the maximum amount that can be assessed for an indecency violation, the FCC can impose a lesser amount if it concludes the violation is not egregious. The agency also has substantial discretion in determining

---

[118] 132 S. Ct. 2307 (2012).

[119] Amy Schatz, "U.S. Drops Efforts to Collect 2003 Indecency Fine from Fox," *Wall St. J.*, June 21, 2012, www.wsj.com/articles/SB10000872396390444165804578010831575210340.

[120] Pub. L. No. 109–235, 120 Stat. 491 (2006).

whether any fine is assessed. For example, in 2006 the FCC resolved complaints about programs, such as the *2003 Billboard Music Awards* show, involving isolated use of expletives such as *fuck* and *shit*. These programs aired prior to the FCC's decision in the Bono case; the agency found the broadcasts to be indecent but imposed no fines because FCC policy at the time of the broadcasts tolerated isolated use of expletives.[121]

The FCC first proposed a maximum fine in a 2015 decision involving a Virginia television station's 6 P.M. newscast featuring a three-second clip of a hand stroking an erect penis during a story about a former porn actress who had joined a local volunteer rescue squad.[122] Screen shots obtained from an adult website showed the clip in a box to the side of images of the actress's face. The journalist who obtained the images did not notice the box and station management reviewed the story on equipment that did not show the entire screen. Despite the news context, the FCC imposed a maximum fine because the station failed to take adequate precautions to ensure explicit material was not aired. The case may be an outlier due to the extreme nature of the content and its presentation at 6 P.M. However, if Republicans in 2022 regain control of the House and the Senate, the shifting political winds may bring indecency again to the forefront of the FCC's agenda.

CHANNELING INDECENCY Although the FCC has said broadcasters can air indecency only during the hours when children are not expected to be listening and watching, currently between 10 P.M. and 6 A.M., it has had difficulty finding a **safe harbor** for indecency that is acceptable to both Congress and the courts. All three branches of government have struggled to find a time for broadcast indecency that shields children from offensive programming but allows adults access to constitutionally protected speech.

In 1992 Congress sought to limit the safe harbor from midnight to 6 A.M., but this law was flawed because it allowed certain public radio and television stations to begin broadcasting indecency at 10 P.M. The D.C. Circuit, sitting en banc, voted 7–4 that Congress had not properly justified treating commercial and public broadcasting stations differently. The court said Congress had not explained how the disparate treatment of broadcasters met the compelling governmental interest of protecting children from indecent broadcast programming.[123]

The D.C. Circuit's majority said it had to set aside the midnight standard in favor of the 10 P.M. standard—the hour that some public broadcasters could begin airing indecent programming—so all broadcasters would be treated the same. Congress, the court said, did not provide evidence that minors are less likely to be corrupted by sexually explicit material broadcast by a public station than by a commercial station. The court said allowing public broadcasters to air indecency before midnight undermined the argument for prohibiting indecent speech before midnight on other stations.

Telephone

For years, there was little concern about content communicated over the telephone. However, when dial-a-porn services proliferated in the 1980s, parents complained the services were readily available to children, who may try to imitate the sexual

---

[121] Complaints Regarding Various Television Broadcasts Between February 2, 2002, and March 8, 2005, Notices of Apparent Liability and Memorandum Opinion and Order at 101–45 (FCC 06–17) (Mar. 15, 2006).

[122] WDBJ Television, Inc., Notice of Apparent Liability (FCC 15–32) (Mar. 23, 2015).

[123] Action for Children's Television v. FCC (Act III), 58 F.3d 654 (D.C. Cir. 1995), *cert. denied*, 516 U.S. 1043 (1996).

activities described and who sometimes incurred charges of thousands of dollars listening to dial-a-porn. In 1988, Congress banned obscene and indecent messages delivered via commercial telephone services.

The U.S. Supreme Court held that Congress could constitutionally ban obscene sexual messages provided by commercial telephone services. At the same time, however, the Court said a ban on indecent dial-a-porn services violated the First Amendment.

In *Sable Communications v. FCC*, the Supreme Court ruled that sexually explicit phone messages that are indecent but not obscene cannot be banned but can be regulated. The Court said that because indecency, unlike obscenity, is constitutionally protected, Congress invalidly banned indecent dial-a-porn instead of only restricting access by children. Justice White said the 1988 statute was "another case of burning the house to roast the pig."[124]

The Court acknowledged Congress has a legitimate interest in preventing children from being exposed to dial-a-porn. However, the Court said that because indecent speech is constitutionally protected, as the Court first held in *FCC v. Pacifica Foundation*, the regulation of indecent dial-a-porn must be limited so that access by children is restricted without barring access by adults. In *Sable*, the Court distinguished telephone services from broadcasting:

> The context of dial-in services, where a caller seeks and is willing to pay for communication, is manifestly different from a situation in which a listener does not want the received message. Placing a telephone call is not the same as turning on a radio and being taken by surprise by an indecent message. Unlike an unexpected outburst on a radio broadcast, the message received by one who places a call to a dial-a-porn service is not so invasive or surprising that it prevents an unwilling listener from avoiding exposure to it.

Also, telephone service providers were able to use methods such as access codes to make their messages available to adults but not to children.

Shortly after the Supreme Court ruled in *Sable* that a blanket ban on indecent dial-a-porn is unconstitutional, Congress enacted more limited legislation. Congress adopted a statute prohibiting dial-a-porn services from providing indecent messages to persons younger than 18 years old and to nonconsenting adults.[125] The law also requires telephone companies that bill for adult messages to block indecent dial-a-porn from the phones of customers who have not subscribed to the service in writing. The statute also allows dial-a-porn services to insulate themselves from prosecution by adhering to FCC procedures limiting children's access to explicit sexual messages.

The FCC, under the authority of the law, adopted rules requiring dial-a-porn providers to restrict access to their services by requiring callers to use credit cards or access codes or by scrambling their calls so that they can be heard only through a descrambling device.[126] Two circuits of the U.S. Courts of Appeals, the Second and the Ninth, have upheld the law and the FCC's interpretation of it. Both courts said the rules were narrowly tailored to meet the compelling government interest in protecting the "physical and psychological well-being of minors."[127]

---

[124] 492 U.S. 115 (1989).

[125] 47 U.S.C. § 223.

[126] Regulations Concerning Indecent Communications by Telephone, 5 F.C.C.R. 4926 (1990).

[127] Dial Information Servs. Corp. v. Thornburgh, 938 F.2d 1535 (2d Cir. 1991), *cert. denied*, 502 U.S. 1072 (1992); Information Providers' Coalition for Defense of the First Amendment v. FCC, 928 F.2d 866 (9th

Cable Television

When determining the constitutionality of cable regulations, the Supreme Court grapples to protect the First Amendment rights of system operators to control their content, to protect the rights of adults to access constitutionally protected content, and to protect children from indecency. At the same time, Congress and the courts want to encourage the development of new technologies.

In some ways, cable is like print, suggesting that cable operators can be accorded maximum First Amendment freedoms without exposing children to great amounts of indecency. Cable systems, like print, offer diverse voices through scores of channels, enough channels to distinguish cable from broadcasting, which is licensed and regulated because of the limited broadcast frequencies. Cable is also like print because householders control entry of the medium into the home. Cable subscribers, like newspaper and magazine readers, order cable and pay for it regularly. Therefore, cable is an invited guest into the home, unlike free broadcasting, which the Supreme Court in *Pacifica* described as an intruder. Cable is also unique because system operators can block channels at the command of individual subscribers, permitting subscribers to protect children from unwanted content.

Although cable can be analogized to print, the medium also embodies qualities of the more ubiquitous and intrusive broadcasting medium, suggesting that cable might be more regulated than print to protect children. Since cable and broadcast channels are both available at the click of a remote, cable channels such as MTV can appear every bit as pervasive and intrusive as over-the-air broadcast channels, such as local television stations, even though the cable service is invited into the home.

Generally, the courts have ruled that cable operators enjoy nearly the same First Amendment rights as publishers or Internet operators. The Court has noted that cable companies originate programming and exercise editorial discretion.[128] In another case, the Court referred to cable as "part of the press" because cable operators deliver news, information and entertainment to their subscribers.[129] In yet another case, the court said cable operators are entitled to largely the same First Amendment protection as publishers.[130]

Of course, cable operators, like operators of other media, have no right to disseminate obscenity. But cable operators may transmit indecency. In a case emphasizing the similarity between cable operators and publishers, the Supreme Court upheld lower court rulings that indecency cannot be banned on cable. In *Wilkinson v. Jones*, the Court upheld lower court rulings striking down a Utah statute barring indecency on cable.[131] The federal district court said that cable could not be regulated like broadcasting because cable offered so many more channels. The court also said that cable, unlike broadcasting, is invited into the home. Indeed, cable subscribers pay extra for HBO, Showtime and other premium channels that sometimes carry sexually oriented programming, the court noted. Furthermore, cable subscribers can control children's access to indecency by installing "lockboxes" provided by cable companies, the court said.

In *United States v. Playboy Entertainment Group, Inc.*, the Court reaffirmed the rights of cable operators by striking down part of a statute designed to protect

---

Cir. 1991).

[128] Los Angeles v. Preferred Communications, Inc., 476 U.S. 488 (1986).

[129] Leathers v. Medlock, 499 U.S. 439 (1991).

[130] Turner Broadcasting Sys., Inc. v. FCC, 512 U.S. 622 (1994).

[131] 800 F.2d 989 (10th Cir. 1986), *aff'd without opinion*, 480 U.S. 926 (1987).

children from inadvertently being exposed to sexual video and audio.[132] The Court struck down a section of the Telecommunications Act of 1996 that attempted to halt the "bleed" of sexual pictures and dialogue from adult cable channels to channels children might be watching in the basic cable service tier. The statute required cable operators carrying Playboy channels, AdulTVision, Spice and other channels "primarily dedicated to sexually oriented programming" either to completely scramble the signals, to block them entirely, or to cablecast them between the hours of 10 P.M. and 6 A.M., to lessen the possibility that children might glimpse a bare breast or hear suggestive dialogue bleeding from an imperfectly scrambled transmission. Another alternative allowed cable operators to block delivery of the sexually oriented channels only to cable subscribers who requested the block. However, only a tiny fraction of cable subscribers requested the house-by-house block. Most cable systems therefore chose the time-shifting alternative—cablecasting indecency after 10 P.M.—because establishing a bleed-proof scrambling technique was too expensive, a complete block ended the transmission of constitutionally protected sexual expression, and few households requested individual blocks.

Playboy and other adult programmers challenged the statute, arguing that even the required time-shifting was unconstitutional because it restricted cable operators, programmers and adult viewers who desired nonobscene sexual programming before 10 P.M., when 30–50 percent of adult programming is normally viewed. In a 5–4 ruling, in which the Supreme Court applied strict scrutiny to the regulations, the Court held that the required scrambling, total blocks and time-shifting were unconstitutional content restraints because a less restrictive method was available to protect children from a signal bleed, a problem the Court was not convinced was very serious in the first place. The Court ruled that cable operators' and programmers' First Amendment rights could be served and children protected if cable operators followed the less restrictive alternative of notifying subscribers that the cable companies would block indecent programming to individual homes if subscribers asked. Requiring notification allows subscribers to take advantage of cable's unique technology, the Court said, the ability of cable operators to block individual channels to individual homes. Through notification and blocking, programmers could provide sexual content via cable 24 hours a day to adult viewers with a right to view it. At the same time, children would be protected, the Court concluded.

Although cable operators have broad First Amendment rights to control the types of programs they will carry, cable systems are monopolies in most localities and are required to provide channels for voices that the cable operator does not choose. To diversify voices in often-monopolistic cable systems, the federal government requires larger cable systems to lease up to 15 percent of their channels to anyone who will pay to rent a channel.[133] Through local franchises, cities and counties require cable systems to set aside "PEG" channels for public, educational and government programming.[134] The Supreme Court has ruled that cable operators can ban indecency on leased access channels but not on public, educational and government channels.

LEASED ACCESS Under a 1984 cable act, Congress requires larger cable systems to designate 10–15 percent of their channels for use by others on a commercial or "leased" basis. Smaller cable systems are not required to lease channels.

---

[132] 529 U.S. 803 (2000).
[133] 47 U.S.C. § 532.
[134] 47 U.S.C. § 531.

A section of a 1992 law permits cable operators to ban indecency on leased channels if the cable system provides written policies that explain the law and the cable company's procedures.[135] The law also allowed cable operators to permit sexually oriented programming over leased channels, but only if the cable operators "segregated" indecent programming on a single channel that would be available within 30 days if subscribers requested it in writing. In a decision affirming the First Amendment rights of cable operators, the Supreme Court ruled that cable operators can permit or forbid indecency on leased access channels but cannot be required to segregate the sexually oriented programming onto a single channel that would be blocked to all subscribers or opened only to those who requested it. In *Denver Area Educational Telecommunications Consortium, Inc. v. FCC*, the Court struck down the segregation requirement because it unconstitutionally restricted sexual content of the cable system operators, programmers and adult viewers.[136]

In a plurality opinion that most justices concurred in, the Court ruled that the law allowing cable operators to ban or allow indecency on cable channels was constitutional. But the portion of the statute requiring the segregation and written request was unconstitutional, the Court said, because it restricted protected programming entirely during the 30-day period while subscribers were waiting for activation of leased channels. The Court also said the written-request requirement was unconstitutional because it inhibited subscribers whose reputations might be damaged if a cable operator revealed they requested a restricted channel.

PEG CHANNELS Local governments may require cable systems to provide public, educational and government channels as a repayment to the community for being allowed to lay cables under city streets and to use city rights-of-way. PEG channels are used for the cablecast of city council and school board meetings, educational programming and public announcements. In *Denver Consortium*, the Supreme Court ruled the First Amendment permits the government to bar cable operators from restricting indecency in PEG channels. The Court concluded that a cable operator's "veto" over indecency was much less necessary to protect children on public access channels than on leased access channels. Unlike leased access channels, which are controlled by a third party who rents a channel, public access channels typically are operated cooperatively by local community and governmental organizations, often including an access channel manager appointed by the municipality. Elaborate screening and certification processes protect children from indecency on public access channels, the Court concluded, precluding the need for content controls by cable operators.

Internet

In 1996, Congress attempted to prohibit indecency on the Internet, but the U.S. Supreme Court found the law unconstitutional. The Court said the Internet should have the same level of First Amendment protection as the print media have. Because indecency is not prohibited in the print media, it may not be proscribed on the Internet.

The Communications Decency Act (CDA), which was part of the Telecommunications Act of 1996, prohibited deliberately using the Internet to send indecent, patently offensive, or obscene material to people under 18 years old. The CDA also made it illegal for any person or company to allow dissemination

---

[135] 47 U.S.C. § 532(b).
[136] 518 U.S. 727 (1996).

of obscene or indecent material to minors over Internet facilities it controlled. Violators could be fined or imprisoned for up to two years. Internet providers could defend themselves if they acted "in good faith" to take "reasonable, effective, and appropriate actions" to prevent minors from receiving indecent material through the Internet.[137]

In *Reno v. ACLU*, the Supreme Court found the CDA unconstitutional, saying that the Internet should receive expansive First Amendment protection.[138] The government argued that the Internet should be subject to extensive regulatory control, as is broadcasting. The Court disagreed, stating that the Internet is not as "invasive" as broadcasting. Based on the dial-up technology of that era, the Court said gaining access to content on the Internet requires a user to take deliberate actions, from turning on a computer to connecting to an Internet service provider such as AOL to accessing a specific website. The Court said because certain steps must be taken, it is unlikely that an Internet user would accidentally encounter indecent material.

The Court also distinguished the Internet from broadcasting because there was no spectrum scarcity justifying government regulation. The Internet did not have physical limitations like those of broadcasting. At any given time, tens of thousands of people are discussing a range of subjects on the Internet, where content is "as diverse as human thought." And the Internet provides a low-cost means for "publishers" to reach a global audience.

Applying strict scrutiny in the *Reno* decision, the Court agreed the government had a compelling interest in protecting children from obscene and indecent material. But the Court said the CDA was unconstitutional because it was not narrowly drawn to restrict speech as little as possible.

Justice Stevens, writing for the 7–2 Court majority, said important words in the CDA were unconstitutionally vague. The Court said that criminal laws limiting speech must define terms carefully, yet the CDA was imprecise, the Court said, not allowing Internet users to know what speech was illegal. For example, the term *patently offensive* was defined as material involving "sexual or excretory activities or organs" as taken "in context" and "measured by contemporary community standards." The Court said these phrases, meant to give context to "patently offensive," are themselves not defined.

Without clear definitions, the Court said, the words "will provoke uncertainty among speakers about . . . just what they mean." The Court said the statute's undefined terms would cause self-censorship. Some speakers would silence themselves, fearing they would violate the law, even though their "messages would be entitled to constitutional protection," the Court said. Also, the CDA was flawed because, the community using the narrowest, most confining definitions would set the standard for the entire country. Justice Stevens said an email message about birth control a parent sent to a child at college might violate the law if people in the college town considered birth control to be indecent or patently offensive.

The Court also found the CDA was overbroad, prohibiting communications that are constitutionally protected, as well as content that lawfully can be prohibited. The Court noted the CDA constitutionally prohibited obscenity on the Internet but unconstitutionally banned indecent and patently offensive material. The First Amendment does not protect obscene material in any mass medium, including the Internet. But the CDA also banned offensive or indecent material that has literary,

[137] Pub. L. No. 104–104, § 502, 110 Stat. 56 (1996).
[138] 521 U.S. 844 (1997).

artistic, political, or scientific value, the Court said, although that material would be protected for adults if published in other media.

The Court did follow its reasoning in *Sable Communications v. FCC*, discussed earlier in this chapter, in which it upheld a congressional ban on obscene messages transmitted by telephone.[139] But in *Sable* and in the CDA decision, the Court said the First Amendment protects indecent messages transmitted from adults to adults when users must take affirmative steps to receive indecent material, as both "dial-a-porn" customers and Internet users do.

The Court suggested parental control or blocking software would be constitutionally acceptable ways to prevent children's access to indecent material. The Court majority said a more precisely and narrowly drawn statute preventing children's access to indecent material on the Internet might be constitutional.

COPA After the Court ruled the CDA unconstitutional, Congress attempted to protect children on the Internet with a narrower law. In 1998, Congress enacted the Child Online Protection Act (COPA) prohibiting commercial material "harmful to minors" on the World Wide Web. The overbroad CDA had prohibited noncommercial as well as commercial materials on the whole Internet.

To overcome vagueness and overbreadth, Congress drew on the Supreme Court's ruling in *Miller v. California* to define "harmful to minors" in COPA. A commercial work was harmful to minors under COPA if jurors applying "contemporary community standards" would find the work "as a whole" appeals to the prurient interest of minors, is patently offensive and lacks serious value. COPA provided a defense to website operators who used age verification techniques to prevent minors from gaining access to prohibited materials. COPA was the subject of a 10-year battle that culminated in a ruling of unconstitutionality.

In *Ashcroft v. American Civil Liberties Union II*, the Court held that the government failed to prove that age verification techniques were more effective than software filters installed by parents. Justice Kennedy, writing for the majority in *Ashcroft II*, noted that COPA was suspect because a blue-ribbon commission created by Congress concluded that filters were more effective than age verification techniques.[140] Kennedy concluded that if Congress promoted the use of filters, parents could control what their children see "without subjecting protected speech to severe penalties."

The Court remanded the case so the trial court could consider the effectiveness of various technical methods of controlling children's access to harmful material. After a trial, a federal district court in March 2007 held COPA violated the First Amendment because software filters were a more effective but less restrictive means of blocking access to sexual materials than the age verification schemes authorized by COPA.[141] Additionally, the court ruled that COPA was unconstitutionally vague because it did not define how terms like "as a whole" would apply to the World Wide Web. "There is no question that a printed book or magazine is finite, and, as a result, it is very easy to discern what needs to be examined in order to make an 'as a whole' evaluation," the district court wrote. The same is not true for a web page or websites because pages and sites are hyperlinked to other pages and sites. A publisher of a website could only guess at what undefined portion of the "vast expanse" of the web would be considered to be the whole work by a

---

[139] 492 U.S. 115 (1989).
[140] 542 U.S. 566 (2004).
[141] ACLU v. Gonzales, 478 F. Supp. 2d 775 (E.D. Pa. 2007), *aff'd*, 534 F.3d 181 (3d Cir 2008), *cert. denied*, 555 U.S. 1137 (2009).

court, and this imprecision was unconstitutional, the district court wrote. The Third Circuit affirmed this ruling in 2008; when the Supreme Court denied certiorari in 2009, the ten-year battle over COPA ended.

CIPA Public libraries that accept federal funds may be required to limit access to sexually explicit Internet material, the Supreme Court ruled in 2003. By a 6–3 vote, the Court upheld a federal statute requiring that public libraries use filtering software or risk losing federal subsidies for Internet access.

By 2000, 95 percent of public libraries in the United States provided public Internet access. Patrons of all ages regularly searched for online pornography, often exposing other patrons unwillingly to pornographic images. In 2001, Congress required libraries receiving federal funds to install software filters to block adults from accessing obscenity or child pornography and children from accessing material harmful to minors. But software filters are imprecise, often "overblocking" materials adults and children have a First Amendment right to see. Thus, Congress, in the Children's Internet Protection Act (CIPA), also permitted libraries to disable filters for patrons engaged in "bona fide research or other lawful purposes."[142]

In *United States v. American Library Association*, the Supreme Court upheld CIPA, ruling that libraries may restrict patrons' access to Internet material of "requisite and appropriate quality," just as librarians have traditionally decided which books to purchase.[143] Writing for the Court, Chief Justice Rehnquist noted that most libraries already exclude pornography from their print collections because they deem it inappropriate. "It would make little sense to treat libraries' judgments to block online pornography differently, when these judgments are made for just the same reason," Rehnquist said.

The majority of the Court concluded that CIPA does not seriously burden library patrons' access to constitutionally protected Internet content. The Court was unsympathetic to the claim that some patrons would be too embarrassed to ask librarians to unblock sites or disable filters. "The Constitution does not guarantee the right to acquire information at a public library without any risk of embarrassment," the Court said.

■ SUMMARY ■

Obscenity is prohibited in any medium of expression. The regulation of nonobscene sexual depictions varies from medium to medium. In *FCC v. Pacifica Foundation*, the Supreme Court ruled that broadcasters can be constitutionally restricted to airing indecency only at those times of day when children are not likely to be in the audience. The current "safe harbor" for broadcasting indecent material is between the hours of 10 P.M. and 6 A.M.

Dial-a-porn services can transmit indecent material at any time of day. However, these services must employ techniques, such as access codes, to limit their audiences to adults. Cable systems may transmit indecent material at any time of day on channels controlled by the cable operator. Cable companies may prohibit indecent material on leased access channels; municipal officials overseeing PEG channels may also prevent these channels from being used for indecent programs. Finally, the Supreme Court has ruled that communicators using the Internet, like print publishers, have a First Amendment right to disseminate indecency.

---

[142] 20 U.S.C. § 9134(f)(3).
[143] 539 U.S. 194 (2003).

VIOLENT PORNOGRAPHY

Violence in the media is a recurrent concern among the public and politicians. Congress periodically holds hearings to determine if violence in the media contributes to violence in society. As will be shown later in this chapter, industry organizations have adopted various systems of labeling movies, recordings and video games in response to political pressure. In 1996, Congress passed legislation requiring violent television programming to be labeled and parents to be afforded the technology to block it from home TV screens. In 2005, Congress authorized the use of software to render "imperceptible" portions of films displayed in homes.

American courts have never found that violence alone lacks First Amendment protection. Violence is not included in the definition of obscenity. If violence is combined with sexual content and the material is found to be obscene, it is the sexual matter, not the violence, which is the basis for the finding.

Effects of Violent Pornography

Social science research is not conclusive about the effects of violent pornography. Nonetheless, in 1986 the Attorney General's Commission on Pornography (the Meese Commission) asserted that exposure to violent pornography depicting the degradation, domination or coercion of women increases aggressive behavior toward women, including sexual violence. The Meese Commission lacked solid scientific proof for this claim and acknowledged that its conclusions were based in part on its members "own insights and experience" with violent pornography.[144] Two commissioners objected to the commission's efforts to "tease the current data into proof of a causal link."[145]

Social scientists questioned the Meese Commission's conclusions, arguing that a causal relationship between exposure to sexually violent images and aggression toward women is found in laboratory studies measuring short-term effects, but that these studies do not support conclusions about long-term effects. Further, it is unclear whether the adverse effects of violent pornography are caused by the combination of violence and sexual imagery or are due to depictions of violence against women. Social scientific evidence suggests that exposure to violent pornography may increase one's tolerance for sexual crimes, but evidence linking violent crime to pornography is not clear. According to its critics, the Meese Commission used social science studies "selectively to confirm certain moral/political beliefs."[146]

Women and Violence

The Meese Commission advocated stricter enforcement of obscenity law, but feminists claimed that violent and degrading portrayals of women should be illegal even when not obscene. In the 1980s, several feminists argued that violent pornography violated women's civil rights; objectionable portrayals of women contributed to discrimination against women in settings such as employment and education.[147] In response, the city of Indianapolis declared the "graphic sexually explicit subordination of women" to be illegal. The ordinance outlawed the verbal or pictorial

---

[144] Attorney General's Commission on Pornography, Final Report (1986).
[145] *Id.* (separate statement of Commissioners Judith Becker and Ellen Levine).
[146] Daniel Linz, Neil Malamuth, and Katherine Beckett, "Civil Liberties and Research on the Effects of Pornography," in *Psychology and Social Policy* 149 (P. Suedfeld and P.E. Tetlock, eds., 1992).
[147] *See, e.g.,* Catharine MacKinnon, *Only Words* (1993).

representation of women in "subordinate" ways, including as sexual objects enjoying pain or rape or in "scenarios of degradation."

The U.S. Court of Appeals for the Seventh Circuit declared the ordinance unconstitutional because it did not assess a work as a whole, nor did it include the elements of patent offensiveness, prurient appeal and lack of social value as required by *Miller*.[148] Speech treating women in an approved way—premised on equality—was lawful under the ordinance no matter how sexually explicit. Speech treating women in the disapproved way—as submissive in matters sexual or as enjoying humiliation—was illegal under the ordinance "no matter how significant the literary, artistic, or political qualities of the work taken as a whole," the appellate court wrote. The First Amendment "forbids the state to declare one perspective right and silence opponents."

The Seventh Circuit observed that violent pornography, like racist or anti-Semitic speech, is protected expression even though political majorities find it to be insidious. Otherwise, the government would become "the great censor and director of the thoughts which are good for us."

Video Games

For more than two decades, the depiction of violence and sexuality in top-selling video games such as *Grand Theft Auto* has been a matter of great concern to social scientists and legislatures.[149] In response to the belief that these games harm children, several cities and states enacted laws limiting or prohibiting children's access to violent and sexually explicit games; each law has been found to be unconstitutional.

Most prominent among these cases is the Supreme Court's 2011 ruling striking down California's ban on the sale or rental of violent video games to minors. The Court in *Brown v. Entertainment Merchants Association* held that video games, like books, plays and movies, are a protected form of communicating ideas.[150] As in *United States v. Stevens*, discussed in Chapter 2, in which the Court rejected Congress' effort to add depictions of animal cruelty to the list of unprotected speech, the *Brown* Court emphasized that violence may not be added to the list of unprotected speech "by a legislature that concludes certain speech is too harmful to be tolerated." Legislatures may not create new categories of unprotected speech by balancing the value of speech against its social costs, the Court ruled in both *Stevens* and *Brown*.

Justice Scalia, writing for the majority in *Brown*, found that California's law raised the danger that the legislature was motivated by disgust with the ideas expressed by violent video games. Disgust is not a valid basis for regulating expression, he noted, adding that the ideas expressed in violent video games, not the objective effects of those games, may have been the "real reason" for the law. States have the power to protect children from harm caused by exposure to sexual materials, but they lack "a free-floating power to restrict the ideas to which children are exposed." Moreover, the law ran against a long-standing tradition of violent portrayals, such as *Grimm's Fairy Tales*, that have been freely available to children.

---

[148] American Booksellers Ass'n, Inc. v. Hudnut, 771 F.2d 323 (7th Cir. 1985), *aff'd without opinion*, 475 U.S. 1001 (1986).

[149] *See, e.g.*, Craig Anderson et al., "Violent Video Games: Specific Effects of Violent Content on Aggressive Thoughts and Behavior," 36 *Advances Experimental Soc. Psychol.* 199 (2004).

[150] 131 S. Ct. 2729 (2011).

Applying strict scrutiny, the Court found California's evidence in support of the law to be insubstantial. The social science studies relied upon by California did not prove that violent video games cause minors to act aggressively. Moreover, the effects of violent video games, which the Court described as "small," were indistinguishable from effects produced by other media, such as cartoons. The law was also flawed because it did not restrict children's access to violence in other media such as movies and television. The fact that California had no persuasive reason to regulate only video games raised doubts about the legitimacy of the state's purported interest. Moreover, the Court questioned the need for the law because the video-game industry has a ratings system, discussed later, and its dealer association discourages retailers from selling games labeled "M" to minors. The Court viewed this system with approval, stating it "does much to ensure that minors cannot purchase seriously violent games on their own, and that parents who care about the matter" can readily evaluate games.

Brown is in line with a stream of lower court cases emphasizing the First Amendment rights of children[151] and the lack of proof of a solid causal link between violent video game exposure and violence.[152] California sought to defend its law by relying on *Ginsberg v. New York*, discussed earlier in this chapter. In *Ginsberg*, the Court sustained a statute restricting children's access to sexual materials, even when those materials were lawfully available to adults. *Ginsberg* was embedded in a deep tradition of restricting sexual materials and the Court deferred to the legislature's judgment that sexual materials are harmful to children. In *Brown*, however, Justice Scalia emphasized that there was no long-standing tradition of restricting children's access to depictions of violence. Even *books*, a word Scalia italicized for emphasis, "contain no shortage of gore," such as *Grimm's Fairy Tales*, in which "Hansel and Gretel (children!) kill their captor by baking her in an oven." Other media, such as motion pictures and comic books, have faced a "long series of failed attempts" to restrict the portrayal of violence, Scalia noted. By demanding proof of the harmful effects of violent portrayals, *Brown* signals to legislatives that measures restricting violent portrayals in media other than video games are likely unconstitutional.

The V-chip

The FCC has been reluctant to restrict violence in broadcast programming.[153] However, in 1996, Congress adopted legislation requiring ratings of "violent" and "sexual" programming and the installation of computer chips in television sets that would allow parents to block the rated programming.

The so-called V-chip law was enacted as part of the Telecommunications Act of 1996. The law mandates that television receivers with 13-inch or larger screens sold in the United States contain a computer chip allowing television set owners to block programs containing violence, sexual content, "or other indecent material about which parents should be informed before it is displayed to children."[154] The law does not define *violence, sexual content,* or *indecency,* although indecency has been defined by the FCC. The V-chip can be coded by parents to automatically block programming that they find objectionable. In 1998, the FCC said V-chips

---

[151] American Amusement Machine Ass'n v. Kendrick, 244 F.3d 572 (7th Cir. 2001).
[152] Entertainment Software Ass'n v. Blagojevich, 404 F. Supp. 2d 1051 (N.D. Ill. 2005).
[153] Report on the Broadcast of Violent, Indecent, and Obscene Material, 51 F.C.C.2d 418 (1975).
[154] Pub. L. No. 104–104, § 551, 110 Stat. 56 (1996). *See also* 47 U.S.C. § 303(x).

must be installed in half the television receivers made for sale in the United States by July 1, 1999, and in all sets by January 1, 2000.[155]

For the V-chip to block programs, violent or sexually oriented programming must be accompanied by program ratings sent through the television signal. Congress told video program distributors that they had one year to "voluntarily" implement a program rating system that was acceptable to the FCC. Otherwise, the FCC was empowered to create its own advisory committee to develop a ratings system. In 1998, the FCC gave final approval to the television program rating system developed by the National Association of Broadcasters, the National Cable Television Association and the Motion Picture Association of America.[156] The ratings, assigned to all television programs except news, sports and unedited MPAA-rated movies on premium cable channels, alert parents to program material they might not want their children to watch. Commercials are not rated.

The ratings are as follows:

Programs Designed for Children

TV-Y	Appropriate for all children
TV-Y7	Programs directed to children seven years old and above
TV-Y7-FV	Fantasy violence may not be appropriate for children under seven years old

Programs Designed for General Audiences

TV-G	For general audiences
TV-PG	Parental guidance suggested; the program may contain material unsuitable for younger children. The program also may contain (V) moderate violence; (S) some sexual scenes; (L) occasional coarse language; or (D) some suggestive dialogue.
TV-14	Parents strongly cautioned; the program may contain material unsuitable for children under 14 years of age. The program also may contain (V) intense violence; (S) intense sexual scenes; (L) strong coarse language; or (D) intensely suggestive dialogue.
TV-MA	Mature audiences only; the program may contain material unsuitable for children under 17 years of age. The program also may contain (V) graphic violence; (S) explicit sexual scenes; (L) strong coarse language.

Ratings are applied to programs by broadcast and cable networks. Syndicated programs, such as talk shows, are rated by the program distributor. To ensure that program ratings are applied accurately and consistently, the television industry established the Oversight Monitoring Board. The board includes members from broadcast television, cable television, program production and the public. The board has no enforcement power except public pressure.

Despite being available since the late 1990s, use of the V-chip is low. In a 2007 report on television violence,[157] The FCC found that of the 280 million television sets in U.S. households, only 119 million sets are equipped with the V-chip.

---

[155] Blocking of Video Programming Based on Program Ratings, 13 F.C.C.R. 11248 (1998).
[156] Video Program Ratings, 13 F.C.C.R. 8232 (1998).
[157] Violent Television Programming and Its Impact on Children, Report (FCC-07–50) (Apr. 25, 2007).

Additionally, the FCC found few parents used the V-chip and many parents lack understanding of the ratings system. Further, the FCC reported programs are often inaccurately rated.

The Family Movie Act

Congress gave video consumers greater control over the content of movies displayed in private households by enacting the Family Movie Act of 2005 (FMA).[158] The Act allows parents or others to employ software to render objectionable portions of a film "imperceptible" so long as the filtering is controlled by a member of the household and no fixed copy of the altered version of the movie is created.

The Family Movie Act resulted from litigation brought by film directors, such as Steven Spielberg, and Hollywood film studios, against companies that sold unauthorized copies of movies that had been altered to delete "sex, nudity, profanity, and gory violence." The editing techniques included fogging or the use of a black bar to obscure visual content; audio content was redacted or replaced with ambient noise. The directors and studios claimed the edited versions infringed their copyrights. As discussed in Chapter 6, in 2006 a federal district court ruled in favor of the directors and studios and enjoined companies such as Clean Flicks from selling unauthorized edited versions of copyrighted films.[159]

The directors and studios also sued companies that sold filtering software enabling consumers to skip or mute objectionable film content. While the suit was pending, Congress passed the FMA and the defendants selling filtering technology were dismissed from the suit. Companies such as ClearPlay can continue selling specially equipped DVD players and filtering software.

ClearPlay produces software that is used in conjunction with an authorized copy of a movie and a specially equipped DVD player. Parents download software for a particular film and can customize their preferences by adjusting 14 different filter settings relating to violence, sex and nudity, and language. For example, a parent could mute "Vain references to Deity," "Ethnic and Social Slurs" and "Strong Profanity" in the audio track of a DVD.

▇ SUMMARY ▇

Violent pornography in American media may not be prohibited unless it is obscene. The Meese Commission on pornography said it found a causal link between violent pornography and violence in society, but social scientists generally do not go so far. It also has been ruled unconstitutional to bar violent pornography that degrades women. In 2011, the Supreme Court found a California law restricting children's access to violent video games to be unconstitutional. The ruling in *Brown* signals the Court's hostility to efforts to restrict violent portrayals in other media.

Congress enacted the V-chip requirement in 1996; today, all television sets with a screen 13 inches or larger sold in the United States are equipped with a computer chip that allows set owners to block programming based on its rating. In 1998, the FCC approved a rating system developed by the broadcast, cable and motion picture industries. In 2005, Congress authorized the use of software to render "imperceptible" portions of films displayed in homes.

---

[158] Pub. L. No. 109–9, 119 Stat. 223 (2005) (amending 17 U.S.C. § 110).
[159] Clean Flicks v. Soderbergh, 433 F. Supp. 2d 1236 (D. Colo. 2006).

CONTROLLING NONOBSCENE SEXUAL EXPRESSION

Nonobscene sexual expression may be restricted to certain places or times to protect those who wish to avoid pornography and to preserve the tone of the community. The constitutionality of time, place and manner restrictions on nonobscene sexual expression depends on the circumstances in each case. Government restrictions on nonobscene sexual expression should be as narrow as possible and should allow alternative avenues by which the nonobscene materials may find their audience.

Generally, the government's power to regulate or prohibit sexual expression increases as the expression merges with conduct. Some conduct, such as nude sunbathing, topless waitressing and massaging, contains no expression and therefore can be regulated without First Amendment consideration.[160] Other nonobscene conduct, such as nude dancing and nude musicals, contains significant expressive content and therefore may be channeled to certain times and places, if not banned.[161] Three acceptable governmental regulations on the distribution of nonobscene sexual materials are zoning, postal and display laws. The media themselves also self-regulate the sexual content of their offerings.

Zoning Laws

Communities attempt through zoning laws to control the impact of adult theaters and bookstores. Sometimes cities attempt to diffuse the impact of sex establishments by spreading them through different parts of the community or controlling the signs through which they present themselves to the public. Sometimes city zoning concentrates adult bookstores and theaters in one place for easier monitoring and law enforcement.

In 1986, the Supreme Court upheld a Renton, Washington, zoning regulation that prohibited adult movie theaters within 1,000 feet of any residential zone, family dwelling, church, park or school. In *City of Renton v. Playtime Theatres, Inc.*, the Court ruled the law was a constitutional time, place and manner regulation even though it singled out adult movie theaters and bookstores for regulation.[162] The regulation was content-neutral, the Court said, because it was aimed at protecting the community from crime and declining trade and property values, not at the content of the films.

Courts used the *Renton* standard in rejecting challenges to changes in New York City zoning laws. The zoning changes largely were limits on where adult businesses may locate and prohibitions on adult businesses clustering together. The new zoning standards effectively shut down all adult business in Times Square, including adult theaters and bookstores. Several courts found the city's intent was to eliminate neighborhood deterioration, crime and decreased property values that accompany adult businesses. The city's purpose was not to infringe on the adult businesses' speech rights. The courts also said the zoning laws were not broader than necessary to rectify these effects. Finally, courts said the adult businesses had sufficient alternative areas within New York City to conduct their activities.[163]

Although the Supreme Court has approved zoning laws to restrict the location of pornographic theaters and bookstores, the Court generally does not permit

---

[160] *See, e.g.*, South Florida Free Beaches v. City of Miami, 734 F.2d 608 (11th Cir. 1984).
[161] Schad v. Borough of Mount Ephraim, 452 U.S. 61 (1981).
[162] 475 U.S. 41 (1986).
[163] *See, e.g.*, Hickerson v. City of New York, 146 F.3d 99 (2d Cir.), *cert. denied*, 525 U.S. 1067 (1998).

zoning laws to ban nonobscene sexual expression. The Court struck down a New Jersey zoning law that barred all commercial live entertainment, including nude dancing, in the Borough of Mount Ephraim. The zoning ordinance was declared unconstitutional because it provided no place where constitutionally protected nonobscene dancing might be performed. The Court said the borough had not demonstrated that permitting nude dancing would create the difficulties with parking, trash collection and police protection that prompted the ban on commercial live entertainment.[164]

The Court has twice upheld generally applicable laws banning all public nudity, including sunbathing as well as erotic dancing. In a 5–4 ruling in *Barnes v. Glen Theatre*, the Court said Indiana could constitutionally adopt a statute prohibiting public nudity even if this meant that erotic dancers who wanted to dance nude were required to wear pasties and G-strings.[165] The Court upheld a similar Pennsylvania law in *City of Erie v. Pap's A.M.*[166] In both cases, the Court applied the *O'Brien test*, discussed in Chapter 3, concluding that the bans on public nudity were designed to protect public morality and safety, not to suppress freedom of expression, and at most had minimal impact on expressive activity. The Court acknowledged that requiring pasties and G-strings might minimally diminish the erotic impact of otherwise nude dancing, but the First Amendment does not require a city to permit dancers to convey the erotic message "when the last stitch is dropped."

Zoning laws restricting the showing of nonobscene materials must not be too broad. In a Florida case, the U.S. Supreme Court struck down an ordinance prohibiting drive-in movie theaters from exhibiting films showing bare breasts, buttocks, or pubic areas if the screens were visible from streets and sidewalks. By preventing the showing of all nudity, the ordinance would have protected children not only from lewd pornography but also from pictures of a baby's buttocks, the nude body of a war victim, scenes from a culture where nudity was common, art exhibitions and pictures of nude bathers.[167]

Postal Regulations

Whereas zoning may channel nonobscene communications to certain places, postal regulations protect one's privacy from the assault of unwanted sexual materials. Reflecting the special concern of legislators and courts for protecting children and privacy, the Supreme Court permits homeowners to stop sexually oriented advertisements from being delivered to their mailboxes. Under postal law, people who receive a pandering advertisement can contact the post office and have their names removed from the mailer's list. The law also says that the sender can be required to mark on the outside that the advertisements are sexually oriented. Ads do not have to be obscene to be halted. The Supreme Court upheld the constitutionality of the statute in *Rowan v. United States Post Office Department*.[168] The Supreme Court unanimously agreed no one has a right to force even good ideas on an unwilling recipient. Thus, the mailer's right to communicate stops at the mailbox of the unreceptive addressee.

---

[164] Schad v. Borough of Mount Ephraim, 452 U.S. 61 (1981).
[165] 501 U.S. 560 (1991).
[166] 529 U.S. 277 (2000).
[167] Erznoznik v. City of Jacksonville, 422 U.S. 205, 213 (1975).
[168] 397 U.S. 728 (1970).

Display Laws

Statutes and ordinances also may restrict the display to minors of sexually explicit materials that are not obscene for adults. The U.S. Court of Appeals for the Tenth Circuit upheld a Wichita, Kansas, ordinance barring display of sexual materials to minors but permitting the use of so-called blinder racks that hide the lower two-thirds of the cover of sexual publications. Blinder racks effectively shield minors from sexual materials without unconstitutionally depriving adults of access to legal sexual publications.[169] Similarly, another federal appellate court ruled constitutional a Minneapolis ordinance requiring bookstores to keep materials that are harmful to minors in a sealed wrapper or behind an opaque cover.[170] Adults still have access to the materials by asking a clerk to remove the wrapper, by viewing an inspection copy kept behind the store counter, or by viewing the material in an adults-only bookstore that excludes minors.

Informal Restraints

Injunctions are not the only potentially unconstitutional restraints on sexual materials. Informal government pressures also may unconstitutionally suppress sexual materials. In 1963, the U.S. Supreme Court ruled it was unconstitutional for a state commission to threaten magazine and book distributors with prosecution for materials that had not been determined to be obscene. In *Bantam Books, Inc. v. Sullivan*, the Court ruled that the Rhode Island Commission to Encourage Morality in Youth imposed an unconstitutional prior restraint on magazine and book distributors when the commission sent them notices that some of their publications, including *Playboy* and *Peyton Place*, were "objectionable" for sale or display to youths under age 18.[171] The notices thanked distributors on the list in advance for their cooperation and reminded them that the Rhode Island commission had the duty to recommend prosecution for purveyors of obscenity. Officials were then sent to see what action distributors planned to take.

The Rhode Island commission said it wrote letters and visited distributors simply to advise them of their legal rights. But the Supreme Court said the commission engaged in an informal censorship in violation of the First Amendment. The Court said the Rhode Island commission's threats and coercion unconstitutionally suppressed publications. The Court also said the term *objectionable* in the commission's warning notice was vague, leaving distributors to speculate whether the commission considered a particular publication to be obscene.

In a more recent case, a federal appeals court held that Attorney General Edwin Meese and members of his Commission on Pornography did not violate the First Amendment when they sent letters to retail outlets, such as convenience stores, asking them to respond to a witness' allegation they were involved in the sale of pornography.[172]

The D.C. Circuit said the Commission on Pornography's letters were not like the unconstitutional letters sent by the Rhode Island Commission to Encourage Morality in Youth. Unlike the Rhode Island letters, the pornography commission's letters never threatened legal action, the court said. Whereas the Rhode Island letters warned of possible prosecution and were followed by a police visit, the

---

[169] M.S. News Co. v. Casado, 721 F.2d 1281 (10th Cir. 1983).

[170] Upper Midwest Booksellers Ass'n v. City of Minneapolis, 780 F.2d 1389 (8th Cir. 1985).

[171] 372 U.S. 58 (1963).

[172] Penthouse Int'l, Ltd. v. Meese, 939 F.2d 1011 (D.C. Cir. 1991), *cert. denied*, 503 U.S. 950 (1992).

pornography commission's letters only announced the accusations of pornography and asked the companies to respond. Even though the pornography commission was headed by the U.S. attorney general, the court found no threat of prosecution in the letters. The First Amendment is not abridged, the court said, "in the absence of some actual or threatened imposition of governmental power or sanction."

Cutting Funds

Another way for the government to curb nonobscene sexual expression is to bar funding. The government, of course, does not have to support painters, writers, musicians and other artistic creators. Budget cutters may constitutionally limit or eliminate funding for the National Endowment for the Arts, the National Endowment for the Humanities and other agencies that support artistic expression. If the government does fund expression, it is not obligated to support art, dance and writing that is sexually explicit.

In 1998, the U.S. Supreme Court said the government may reject grant proposals for artistic projects that are indecent or do not comply with "values of the American public."[173] The Court said a law requiring the National Endowment for the Arts (NEA) to consider whether artistic projects seeking federal funds show a "respect for diverse beliefs" and are "decent" does not unconstitutionally mandate suppression of certain viewpoints.

In 1990, Congress told the NEA to include among criteria for judging grant applications "general standards of decency and respect for the diverse beliefs and values of the American public."[174] Several artists challenged the law, arguing the statute required the NEA to engage in viewpoint discrimination by rejecting artistic projects defying mainstream values or offending generally accepted standards of decency. The 8–1 Court disagreed, saying the law did not prevent the NEA from funding indecent artistic expression if it chooses. The Court said the law does no more than require the NEA "to take 'decency and respect' into consideration."

Justice O'Connor, writing for the majority, said there was no substantial risk the law would limit expression because many factors, including decency, go into judging the quality of artistic projects. The law only provides additional criteria—decency and respect for American beliefs and values—the NEA may use to make these decisions. The Court said the law "imposes no categorical requirement" that would force the NEA to reject grant proposals because of their viewpoints.

Industry and Citizen Regulation

Politicians frequently blame the media for social ills, especially after tragic events such as school shootings. These accusations are often accompanied by calls for government regulation of media content, especially portrayals of sex and violence. This type of political reaction is long-standing. In the early 1950s, Congress held hearings on the adverse effects of comic books. In the 1960s, the increasingly graphic portrayal of sex and violence in movies and on television was of concern to politicians. In the 1980s, Congress was concerned with sex and violence in recorded music. Most recently, politicians have turned their attention to violent video games. In response to political pressure, media organizations have

---

[173] National Endowment for the Arts v. Finley, 524 U.S. 569 (1998).
[174] 20 U.S.C. § 954(d)(1).

developed schemes of self-regulation. Media organizations, whose PACs are heavy donors to political campaigns, have largely been able to blunt calls for regulation by claiming that self-regulation is preferable to government regulation. Thus far, the only government regulation of violence is the television program rating scheme discussed earlier in this chapter. Currently, the most prominent forms of self-regulation are those adopted by the motion picture, recorded music and video game industries.

MOTION PICTURES The movie rating system was created in 1968 by the Motion Picture Association of America and the National Association of Theatre Owners. This is a voluntary system; filmmakers are under no legal obligation to have their films rated, nor must theater owners restrict their audiences. However, filmmakers have a powerful economic incentive to have a film rated because most theaters will not exhibit unrated films. Because the ratings symbols G, PG, PG-13, R and NC-17 are registered trademarks, filmmakers may not self-apply these symbols to films. (The X rating, which has been replaced by NC-17, is not a trademark and is self-applied in various forms, such as XXX to hard-core sexual films.) Theater owners have political incentives to enforce age restrictions. For example, after the Columbine tragedy, theater owners pledged to increase their efforts to restrict audiences for R-rated films, acknowledging that they were doing this to reduce the prospect of onerous legislation.[175] As most American teenagers know, enforcement of age restrictions for R-rated films varies from theater to theater. Enforcement has been less strict in large cities and on the East and West Coasts and stricter in small towns and suburbs in the South and Midwest.

Ratings decisions are made by a ratings board whose members are parents unaffiliated with the film industry. The board reviews each submitted film, estimating what most parents would consider to be an appropriate rating. By majority vote, the board decides on a film's rating. A producer who is seeking a less severe rating may edit the film and resubmit it. Also, producers may appeal a rating decision to a ratings appeal board, consisting of representatives of the motion picture industry. Only by a two-thirds vote may the appeal board overturn a ratings board decision; few appeals are successful as less than 1 percent of films have their ratings overturned on appeal. From 1968 to 2018, 29,791 films have been rated: 57 percent received R ratings, 18 percent received PG ratings, 16 percent received PG-13 ratings, 5 percent received G ratings and only 1 percent received NC-17 ratings.[176]

In making ratings decisions, the ratings board considers theme, language, violence, nudity, sex and drug use. Films that are classified as G, or general audience, are for all ages and contain minimal violence and no nudity, sex scenes or drug use. A PG, or parental guidance rating, means that some material in the film might be inappropriate for young children. Drug use and explicit sex scenes are absent; any nudity is brief, and violence does not exceed moderate levels. A rating of PG-13, or parents strongly cautioned, means that some material in the film is inappropriate for preteens. Some scenes of nudity and drug use may be present, along with isolated use of sexually derived words. Rough violence is absent in a PG-13 rated film. An R-rated film is restricted to those who are at least 17 years old or accompanied by a parent or guardian. Films rated R may include nudity and sexual scenes, rough and persistent violence, drug use and coarse language. If a

---

[175] David Rosenbaum, "Theaters in U.S. Will Require IDs at R-Rated Films," *N.Y. Times*, June 9, 1999, at A1.
[176] Motion Picture Association of America, *"G" Is for Golden: The MPAA Film Ratings at 50* at 40 (2018).

film receives an NC-17 rating, no one age 17 or under may be admitted to view it. Films that receive this rating have explicit sex scenes, excessive violence, or an accumulation of sexually oriented language. It is important to note that the NC-17 rating is not synonymous with the legal category of obscenity; a film may receive an NC-17 rating because of its violence.

All advertising for films submitted for a rating must be approved by the MPAA (Figure 9.2). If a studio were to broadcast or publish an advertisement that had been rejected by the MPAA, the rating of the film would be revoked. Trailers shown in theaters or on home videos must show the rating for the trailer and the

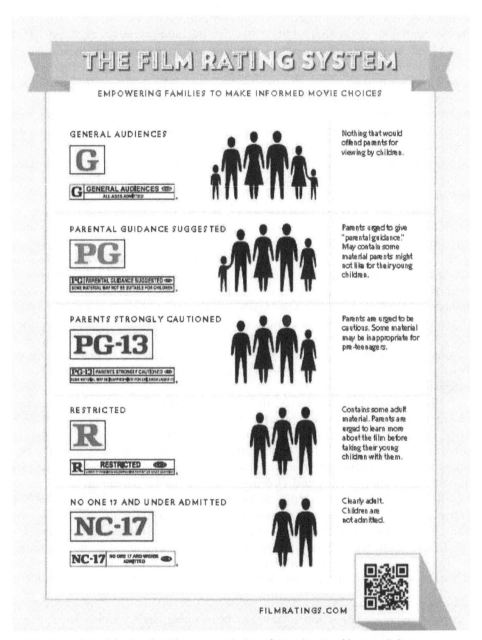

FIGURE 9.2 Copyright, Motion Picture Association of America. Used by permission.

rating of the picture being advertised. A trailer that is rated for "all audiences" contains no scenes that caused a film to be rated PG, PG-13, R or NC-17. Trailers that are rated for "restricted audiences" should precede only films that are rated R or NC-17.

RECORDED MUSIC The recording industry also has a voluntary system of labeling recorded music. In 1985, in response to pressure from the National Parent Teacher Association and the Parents Music Resource Center, the recording industry agreed to place parental advisory labels on recordings that include explicit depictions of violence, sex or drug use. The Recording Industry Association of America (RIAA) owns the mark "Parental Advisory—Explicit Content" and allows record companies to place this label, known as the PAL logo, on the packaging for recordings. Digital distribution platforms are also allowed to display the PAL logo prior to the purchase or distribution of a PAL recording. No record company is required to label its explicit recordings. If a record company chooses to participate in the labeling program, the decision as to which recordings are labeled is made by the record company in conjunction with the artist. The RIAA states:

> In some instances, record companies ask an artist to re-record certain songs or to revise lyrics because a creative and responsible view of the music demands such a revision. Sometimes songs are simply taken off an album. In other instances, the artist and the record company agree that there is musical and artistic credibility in the whole of the work even when the lyrics may be too explicit for mainstream distribution. In those instances, the RIAA's PAL logo is applied prominently to the outside of the permanent packaging. The Logo or a similar PAL Notice may also appear in advertising for the sound recording, and throughout online and mobile products or services that allow consumers to receive and play a sound recording on their personal computer or mobile device.[177]

The RIAA provides record companies with guidelines to determine when a label should be attached to a recording. The guidelines note that labeling "is not a science" and requires consideration of the "context, frequency, and emphasis" of the lyrics. The guidelines ask record companies to consider whether, "in light of contemporary cultural morals and standards and the choices and views of individual parents, the recording might be one that parents may not want their children to listen to." Where the label or artist creates an edited version of a recording, it may have the label "Edited Version." The RIAA does not allow participants in the program to label revised recordings as "Clean" or "Non-Explicit."

The RIAA also recommends that the Parental Advisory label appear in advertisements for labeled recordings. Retailers of physical products, such as CDs, are also encouraged to post notices explaining that recordings displaying the Parental Advisory logo "contain strong language or depictions of violence, sex or substance abuse. Parental discretion is advised." The RIAA also recommends that digital distribution platforms adopt mechanisms allowing parents to control access to PAL content.

---

[177] Recording Industry Association of America, "Parental Advisory Label," www.riaa.com/resources-learning/parental-advisory-label.

VIDEO GAMES Since 1994, the Entertainment Software Rating Board (ESRB), created by the interactive software industry, has rated video and computer games.[178] The ESRB rates more than 1,000 games per year. Each packaged or boxed game is judged by a panel of three raters, such as retired school principals, who have no ties to the interactive software industry. Once a game is rated, a rating icon is displayed on the front of packaging; more detailed content descriptors appear on the back of packaging. Because the ESRB owns the trademarks to its rating icons, game producers may not self-apply the icons to any game that has not been rated by the ESRB.

The ESRB classifies games as follows:

Early Childhood (EC)	Content is suitable for children ages three and older. There is no content that parents would find inappropriate.
Everyone (E)	Content is suitable for ages six and older. These games may contain minimal violence. In 1998, this replaced the previously used Kids to Adults (K–A) category.
Everyone 10+ (E10+)	Content suitable for ages 10 and older. Games may contain mild violence and/or minimally suggestive themes.
Teen (T)	Content is suitable for ages 13 and older. Games in this category may contain violent content and strong language.
Mature (M)	Content is suitable for ages 17 and older. These games include more intense violence or language than games in the Teen category.
Adults Only (AO)	These games include graphic sex and/or violence and are not suitable for those under the age of 18.
Rating Pending (RP)	Games have been submitted to the ESRB and are awaiting final rating. This symbol appears only in advertising prior to the release of a game.

The content descriptors include "Blood and Gore," "Use of Drugs," "Strong Language," Nudity" and "Suggestive Themes."

The ESRB announced in 2011 a new ratings method for digitally delivered games and apps. Publishers of these downloadable games complete a questionnaire designed to assess categories such as violence, sexual content and language. All games rated by this process are later tested by ESRB staff to verify that the publisher's disclosure was accurate. For digitally delivered games and apps, the ESRB also supplies assessments of interactive elements. These include "shares info," which means personal information provided by a user, such as an email address, is shared with third parties; "shares location," which displays a user's location to other users; and "users interact," which includes user-to-user communication.

Publishers who submit games to the ESRB are contractually bound to follow the ESRB's advertising guidelines. These guidelines provide that advertising must accurately reflect the nature and content of the game and the rating issued.

In 2005, the ESRB changed the rating of *Grand Theft Auto: San Andreas* from M to AO after it was disclosed that players were able to unlock explicit sexual content hidden in the game. The ESRB's rating change prompted Walmart

---

[178] Entertainment Software Rating Board, "About ESRB," www.esrb.org/about/.

and Target, the nation's leading sellers of video games, to pull the game from their shelves; most major chain stores do not carry AO-rated games. A new version without the explicit sex was rated M, and the game returned to major retail outlets.

MARKETING PRACTICES After the Columbine tragedy, President Bill Clinton asked the Federal Trade Commission to assess whether the motion picture, recorded music and electronic games industries were marketing to children products that had parental warnings or age restrictions. In its first report, issued in 2000, the FTC concluded that these three industries routinely targeted children under age 17 in advertising campaigns for restricted material.[179] In 2002, the FTC found that the movie and electronic games industries had reduced the advertising of R-rated movies and M-rated games in media popular with teenagers. The record industry continued to advertise music with explicit lyrics in television shows and magazines popular with teenagers, although advertisements in these outlets increasingly displayed the Parental Advisory warning.[180] Subsequent reports reveal that industry practices ebb and flow. For example, in its 2004 report, the FTC found the motion picture industry returned to advertising R-rated films and DVDs on television programs with large teen viewership, a practice that had previously declined.[181] In its most recent report, issued in 2009, the FTC found the movie industry engaged in pervasive targeting of young children by advertising PG-13–rated movies on children's cable networks and through promotional tie-ins with food, toys and other licensed products. Display of the Parental Advisory label for music was inadequate on artist and record company websites, as well as in television advertising. Only music retailers and online download sites prominently displayed the Parental Advisory label. The FTC gave high marks to the electronic game industry, concluding that the industry did not target M-rated games to teens or T-rated games to younger children.[182] The FTC refuses to bring any legal action based on these marketing practices, fearing that this would cause these industries to cease self-regulation. The FTC also recognizes that the First Amendment limits its authority to regulate the marketing and sale of violent material. The agency recommends that Congress continue its support for industry self-regulation programs.

CITIZEN ACTION Several citizens' groups pressure the media, with varying success, to reduce sex and violence. For example, pressure from the Parents Music Resource Center and the National Parent Teacher Association led to the establishment of the record industry's Parental Advisory program. Contemporary groups active in fighting against pornography include Enough is Enough, which seeks to

---

[179] FTC, "Marketing Violent Entertainment to Children: A Review of Self-Regulation and Industry Practices in the Motion Picture, Music Recording & Electronic Game Industries," Sept. 2000, https://www.ftc.gov/reports/marketing-violent-entertainment-children-review-self-regulation-industry-practices-motion-picture-0?msclkid=dec0ac35a80011ec93ef20ac7d3cad54.

[180] FTC, "Marketing Violent Entertainment to Children: A Twenty-One Month Follow-up Review of Industry Practices in the Motion Picture, Music Recording & Electronic Game Industries," June 2002, https://www.ftc.gov/reports/marketing-violent-entertainment-children-twenty-one-month-follow-review-industry-practices-motion?msclkid=1e9d375fa80211ecbbe9fb42b49ae10d.

[181] FTC, "Marketing Violent Entertainment to Children: A Fourth Follow-Up Review of Industry Practices in the Motion Picture, Music Recording, and Electronic Game Industries," July 2004, https://www.ftc.gov/reports/marketing-violent-entertainment-children-fourth-follow-review-industry-practices-motion-picture?msclkid=30599b00a80211ec85c330390e7ad64b.

[182] FTC, "Marketing Violent Entertainment to Children: A Sixth Follow-up Review of Industry Practices in the Motion Picture, Music Recording, and Electronic Game Industries," Dec. 2009, https://www.ftc.gov/legal-library/browse/cases-proceedings/public-statements/statement-chairman-leibowitz-marketing-violent-entertainment-children-sixth-follow-review-industry?msclkid=4771c8b5a80211ec9afb88286aaff81e.

educate the public and policymakers on the dangers of pornography. The Parents Television Council claims to have more than 1 million members; the PTC works to "ensure that children are not constantly assaulted by sex, violence and profanity" on television and other media. The PTC rates programs as family-friendly or unsuitable for children and facilitates complaints to the FCC with an online complaint form. Courts have ruled that citizens have a First Amendment right to picket pornographic establishments and to try to intimidate patrons and employees of the stores by threatening to publish their pictures. Such conduct is constitutional if the pickets do not trespass or block entrances.[183]

■ SUMMARY ■

Sexual communications that are not obscene may be regulated by time, place and manner restrictions such as zoning ordinances, postal regulations and restrictions on the display of materials that would be harmful to minors. In addition, citizens may pressure media to curb sex and violence. Letters threatening government legal action against sexual materials may constitute an unconstitutional prior restraint, but nonthreatening letters are constitutional. The government may choose the art it funds, including denying grants based in part on whether the government considers the artistic project to be indecent. Media industry segments, such as the motion picture, recorded music and video game industries, have developed extensive systems of labeling their products.

---

[183] Eagle Books, Inc. v. Jones, 474 N.E.2d 444 (Ill. App.), *cert. denied*, 474 U.S. 920 (1985).

10

The Media and the Judiciary

Thus far, this book has concentrated on law that punishes injurious publication: broadcasts that hurt individual reputations, ads that mislead consumers and websites that infringe on copyright. This chapter on the media and the courts is the first of three chapters to focus on newsgathering.

News coverage of the courts creates tensions between the advocates of two constitutional rights. The Bill of Rights, in addition to guaranteeing free expression, also guarantees the right to a fair trial for criminal defendants. The Sixth

Amendment provides that anyone who is accused of a crime shall have the right to a trial "by an impartial jury," a jury composed of persons who can decide guilt or innocence on the basis only of the evidence presented in a courtroom. Judges, attempting to ensure fair trials, sometimes curb the speech of lawyers and witnesses and the ability of journalists to obtain information.

In court, judges may control what jurors see and hear. However, outside the courtroom, jurors often see and hear news stories and tidbits of gossip, increasingly on social media, that are protected by the First Amendment but are not allowed into evidence in court. Extensive news coverage may jeopardize the rights of criminal defendants to receive a fair trial, some legal experts contend. In 2021, several high-profile trials illustrated the challenge of selecting an impartial jury in a saturated media environment. For example, the fraud trial of Theranos founder Elizabeth Holmes took place after several years of adverse publicity regarding the collapse of Theranos, including an HBO documentary, podcasts, a best-selling book, and local and national news media coverage. Similarly, the trial of Minneapolis police officer Derek Chauvin was held after cell phone videos showing Chauvin kneeling on the neck of George Floyd went viral. In each case, jurors were selected via a process known as **voir dire**, which elicits information regarding potential jurors' demographic characteristics, attitudes about social and political issues, lifestyle, media usage, and exposure to information about the defendant. In Chauvin's trial, voir dire took two weeks; potential jurors first completed a 14-page questionnaire and then were subjected to one-on-one questioning.

In 2022 the U.S. Supreme Court refused to overturn the death sentence of Boston Marathon bomber Dzhokhar Tsarnaev on the ground that the trial judge did not properly screen jurors for bias due to pretrial publicity. The 2013 bombings and subsequent four-day manhunt received global press coverage. Defense attorneys argued that prejudice must be presumed due to the pretrial publicity and sought to move the trial to a different city, known as a change of venue. The trial judge, following Supreme Court precedent, denied this motion. Boston's large population weighed against a finding of presumed prejudice. Further, community passions diminished in the nearly two years between the bombings and the 2015 trial. Jurors were selected after a three-week voir dire. Once selected, jurors were instructed to avoid media coverage, including social media. During the trial the judge repeatedly renewed his instruction that jurors avoid extraneous influences. As will be shown later in this chapter, the Supreme Court's ruling preserves the discretion of trial judges in conducting voir dire in high publicity cases.

Since the 1960s, the Supreme Court has grappled with the free press–fair trial conflict. Most notably, in 1966, the Court ruled that massive sensational media coverage prevented Dr. Sam Sheppard from receiving a fair trial. As described earlier in Chapter 1, Sheppard's ordeal began on July 4, 1954, when neighbors he had called discovered Marilyn Sheppard's body in the upstairs bedroom of the family home. Sheppard said he woke up in the middle of the night and struggled with an intruder but was knocked unconscious. Sheppard immediately became the object of sensational pretrial publicity. The media also helped turn his trial into what has been called a "Roman holiday."[1]

Local newspapers immediately began publishing a barrage of information and opinions that were never admitted into evidence during Sheppard's trial. Newspapers accused Sheppard of impeding the police investigation, emphasized

---

[1] Sheppard v. Maxwell, 384 U.S. 333 (1966).

his refusal to take a lie detector test and quoted a police detective who said Sheppard's explanation of the death was suspect. One ran a front-page editorial asking, "Why Isn't Sam Sheppard in Jail?" Within 24 hours of the editorial, the authorities arrested Sheppard.

During Sheppard's trial in 1954, the judge seated newspaper reporters so close to Sheppard and his attorney that the pair had to leave the courtroom to talk without being overheard. Often the movement of reporters into and out of the courtroom made it difficult for the lawyers and witnesses to be heard. Photographers jammed the corridors, taking pictures of jurors, witnesses, lawyers and Sheppard.

The jury convicted Sheppard of murder. His unsuccessful appeals to three appellate courts were discussed in Chapter 1. Sheppard spent 12 years in jail before the U.S. Supreme Court, in *Sheppard v. Maxwell*, reversed the original verdict on the ground that he did not receive a fair trial. Sheppard was acquitted in a new trial but died a few years later.[2]

The Supreme Court said that Sheppard did not receive a fair trial because of prejudicial publicity and a carnival-like atmosphere in the courtroom. However, the Court also stressed the media's role in protecting public oversight of the judicial system. In *Sheppard*, the Court emphasized that judges must ensure that defendants receive trials by impartial juries while they restrict the press as little as possible. The Court's *Sheppard* opinion establishes the framework for much of the rest of the chapter.

DEFINING JURY BIAS

The U.S. Supreme Court has said that jurors are biased as a matter of law if they are so affected by prejudicial publicity that they cannot set aside preconceived ideas and decide a case solely on evidence presented during a trial. Judges and lawyers often argue that an impartial jury may be impossible to find if a community has been saturated by news reports of a sensational crime and the arrest of a suspect. However, social scientists have been unable to prove that prejudicial publicity causes biased jurors.

The Supreme Court and Jury Prejudice

Justice Holmes said in 1907 that "the theory of our system is that the conclusions to be reached in a case will be induced only by evidence and argument in open court, and not by any outside influence, whether of private talk or public print."[3] The courts do not require jurors to be completely unaware of the facts and issues of a case. In the treason trial of Aaron Burr, Chief Justice John Marshall first said that impartial jurors might form impressions about a case before trial if those impressions could be changed in light of evidence presented in court.[4]

The Supreme Court has said a defendant can receive a fair trial even if every member of the jury knows the defendant's prior criminal record before the trial begins. The criminal defendant in *Murphy v. Florida*, Jack Roland Murphy, had become notorious after he helped steal the Star of India sapphire in 1964. Murphy

---

[2] In 2000, Sheppard's son lost a lawsuit asking a jury to find that Ohio had wrongfully imprisoned his father. James Erwin, "Sheppard Verdict Is Challenged," *Cleveland Plain Dealer*, May 2, 2000, at 2B.
[3] Patterson v. Colorado, 205 U.S. 454, 462 (1907).
[4] United States v. Burr, 24 F. Cas. 49 (1807).

appealed his conviction for robbery and assault on the ground that the jury had been prejudiced by knowledge of his previous criminal record.

Justice Marshall, writing for the Court, said jurors need not be "totally ignorant of the facts and issues" of a case.[5] He distinguished between "mere familiarity" with a defendant and a "predisposition against him." Marshall said that none of the jurors, when questioned before the trial, indicated that Murphy's past was relevant to the case. Only 20 of 78 potential jurors were excused because they had prejudged Murphy's guilt, suggesting little overt prejudice against Murphy. Neither the atmosphere in the courtroom nor that in the community was inflamed, the Court said.

The Supreme Court has said a conviction will be overturned because of prejudicial publicity only if the Court finds identifiable bias in individual jurors[6] or such an extraordinary amount of prejudicial publicity in the media that the "presumption of prejudice" is raised.[7] For example, in *Irvin v. Dowd*, the Court overturned a murder conviction because publicity created a "wave of passion" and "pattern of prejudice."[8] The Court found a "build-up of prejudice" in the case of Leslie Irvin, who was convicted for a December 1954 murder near Evansville, Indiana. Shortly after his arrest in April 1955, the press announced that "Mad Dog Irvin" had confessed to six murders in four months. Headlines announced he had been placed at the scene of at least one of the murders and identified in a police lineup. In many stories, Irvin was referred to as the "confessed slayer of six." Radio, television and newspaper stories revealed Irvin's criminal history. The local radio station broadcast curbside opinions of Irvin's guilt by members of the public.

U.S. Supreme Court Justice Tom Clark, who wrote for a unanimous Court, said the continued adverse publicity fostered a strong prejudice among the people of the county. Of 430 prospective jurors who were questioned, 90 percent at least suspected Irvin was guilty. A number admitted that if they were in Irvin's place, they would not want themselves on the jury. Of the jurors finally seated, 8 of 12 were familiar with the case, including the fact that Irvin was accused of other murders. All eight said they thought he was guilty. Some jurors said they were going to have to be convinced that Irvin was not guilty, contrary to the principle that a defendant is presumed innocent until proven guilty. One juror said he "could not . . . give the defendant the benefit of the doubt that he is innocent." Another said he had a "'somewhat' certain fixed opinion" of guilt. Yet all 12 jurors told the judge they could be impartial.

Justice Clark said the statements of impartiality could be given little weight when "so many" jurors "so many times, admitted of prejudice." The jurors' statements reflected a "'pattern of deep and bitter prejudice' shown to be present throughout the community." The Court overturned Irvin's conviction and death sentence.

In *Sheppard v. Maxwell*, the Court did not require evidence that jurors were unable to base their verdict on what they saw and heard in the courtroom. The Court said only there could be no doubt that the deluge of extremely inflammatory publicity reached at least some of the jurors. Relying on its own impression of the potential impact of publicity, the Court criticized the prejudicial publicity, community pressure and lack of judicial control over activity in the courtroom that led to Sheppard's conviction.

---

[5] 421 U.S. 794 (1975).
[6] *See, e.g.*, Irvin v. Dowd, 366 U.S. 717 (1961).
[7] *See, e.g.*, Estes v. Texas, 381 U.S. 532 (1965).
[8] 366 U.S. 717 (1961).

The Supreme Court in 2010 emphasized that pretrial publicity only rarely deprives a defendant of a fair trial.[9] By a 6–3 vote, the Court held that former Enron CEO Jeffrey Skilling was not denied a fair trial by extensive publicity preceding his 2006 conviction for conspiracy, securities fraud, making false representations to auditors and insider trading. Enron, based in Houston, collapsed into sudden bankruptcy in 2001 amid charges that corporate executives lied about the firm's financial health to ensure that Enron's stock price remained artificially high.

Before his 2006 trial, Skilling asked the court to relocate the trial to a different city, claiming that extensive pretrial publicity in Houston had poisoned potential jurors against him. Skilling supported his motion with a compilation of news reports and commentary expressing anger toward Enron executives, including a column headlined "Your Tar and Feathers Ready? Mine Are." A local rap artist recorded a song imagining Skilling's death. The trial judge refused to move the trial, concluding the pretrial publicity, punctuated by "isolated incidents of intemperate commentary," had mostly been unemotional and objective. The Supreme Court sustained the trial judge, concluding that Skilling's trial was not tainted by inflammatory publicity as Leslie Irvin's trial had been.

Writing for the Court in *Skilling v. United States*, Justice Ginsburg outlined the distinctions between Skilling's trial and those in cases such as *Irvin*. First, Houston, the nation's fourth most populous city, provided Skilling a "large, diverse pool of potential jurors," unlike the small rural community Irvin was tried in. Second, Justice Ginsburg said the news and commentary about Skilling, though "not kind," contained "no confession or other blatantly prejudicial information" readers or viewers could not "shut from sight." Third, unlike cases where a trial rapidly followed a reported crime, Justice Ginsburg concluded the "decibel level of media attention diminished" in the years between Enron's collapse and Skilling's trial. Finally, the jury acquitted Skilling of nine insider-trading counts, proof to Justice Ginsburg that the jury was not affected by prejudicial publicity.

The Supreme Court also rejected Skilling's claim the trial court failed to detect juror bias by properly questioning potential jurors, a process known as voir dire. A 14-page questionnaire, largely developed by Skilling's lawyers, was used by the trial court to prescreen potential jurors, resulting in dismissal of 119. The remaining potential jurors were asked individually in court about various questionnaire answers, such as whether they remembered articles or broadcasts about the case. "This face-to-face opportunity to gauge demeanor and credibility, coupled with information from the questionnaires regarding jurors backgrounds, opinions, and sources of news, gave the court a sturdy foundation to assess fitness for jury service," Justice Ginsburg wrote.

Measuring Prejudice

Although courts and others routinely assume some information will be prejudicial, no one knows for certain whether extensive exposure to media coverage of the criminal justice process has an impact on jury decisions. In contrast to the result of the Sheppard trial, for example, many defendants are found not guilty despite massive nationwide pretrial publicity. Despite the deluge of pretrial publicity surrounding the O.J. Simpson case, a jury acquitted Simpson in 1995 after only a few hours of deliberation. Similarly, Michael Jackson was found not guilty of child molestation charges in 2005 following several years of adverse publicity about his relations with

---

[9] Skilling v. United States, 561 U.S. 358 (2010).

children. And, in 2011 Casey Anthony was found not guilty of murdering her daughter, a case that drew intense media coverage. In 2021, Kyle Rittenhouse was acquitted of all charges stemming from his shooting of three men during a 2020 racial justice protest. The case, touching on contentious issues such as gun rights and self-defense, captured the nation's attention, especially due to broadcast of the court proceedings.

Many observers argue that the values of a fair trial and a free press often are compatible. The Supreme Court acknowledges that the press helps ensure fair trials by allowing public scrutiny of the judicial system.[10] Extensive pretrial publicity is relatively rare; most crimes receive little or no press coverage. Also, there is little evidence linking pretrial publicity to jury bias. The impact of the press on potential jurors is exaggerated, and procedural safeguards are effective in limiting the effect of pretrial publicity.

There is little real-life evidence bearing on this issue. The only time researchers listened to actual jury deliberations, they said they found that jurors did not make capricious decisions because of bias.[11] The secretly taped jury discussions were but one aspect of a massive study of jury performance completed in 1954. The director of the study, Harry Kalven, said the jury was "a pretty stubborn, healthy institution not likely to be overwhelmed by a remark . . . in the press."

Soon after the 1954 study, the courts prohibited studies of real juries, fearing the research would influence deliberations. Hence, most research on the impact of crime reporting on jurors comes from studies of public reaction to news stories and research involving mock juries. Human attitudes are difficult to study even when they can be tested directly by procedures well designed for the research questions being asked. Research on juror behavior is particularly imprecise because it is conducted on nonjurors in circumstances that do not effectively duplicate the experiences of jurors.

The most one can conclude from such research is that publication of a defendant's confession or criminal record could convince some jurors that a defendant is guilty. However, some studies suggest that careful questioning of the jury pool during the jury selection process can help weed out potential jurors strongly influenced by pretrial publicity.[12] In addition, a factor often forgotten by commentators concerned about the impact of prejudicial publicity is people's inability to absorb everything that is published or broadcast. Some people pay little attention to news. Even regular news consumers watch and read selectively and forget much of what they have heard or read as time passes.

Regardless of the lack of research evidence establishing that media coverage of criminal cases influences jurors, courts try to protect defendants against prejudicial publicity.

Prejudicial Publicity, Community Pressure and Decorum in Court

Supreme Court Justice Felix Frankfurter once asked how "fallible men and women" can reach a verdict based only on what they hear in court when their minds are "saturated" by media coverage for months "by matter designed to establish the

---

[10] *See, e.g.*, Sheppard v. Maxwell, 384 U.S. 349–50; Cox Broadcasting Corp. v. Cohn, 420 U.S. 469, 491–2 (1975).

[11] Harry Kalven Jr. and Hans Zeisel, *The American Jury* 492–9 (1966). *See also* Rita Simon, "Does the Court's Decision in *Nebraska Press Association* Fit the Research Evidence on the Impact on Jurors of News Coverage?" 29 *Stan. L. Rev.* 515, 518–20 (1977).

[12] *See, e.g.*, Geoffrey Kramer et al., "Pretrial Publicity, Judicial Remedies, and Jury Bias," 14 *Law & Hum. Behav.* 409 (1990).

guilt of the accused."[13] In the *Sheppard* case, all but one of the jury members who decided that Sam Sheppard was guilty said during the jury selection process that they had read about the case in the newspapers or heard about it on radio or television.

Although legal experts and scholars do not agree on the impact of pretrial publicity, most assume that certain kinds of information may be prejudicial.[14] The U.S. Justice Department, the American Bar Association (ABA) and several state bench-bar-press committees have issued similar guidelines designed to limit reporting of crime and court news. Most mention the reporting of the following:

- *Confessions.* The Fifth Amendment protects against persons being required to testify against themselves. A confession may be ruled inadmissible evidence at trial if it was made under duress or if a defendant was not properly advised of his or her right to an attorney. However, jurors may have a hard time ignoring a confession that is publicized. In *Rideau v. Louisiana*, the Supreme Court overturned the murder conviction of Wilbert Rideau after he confessed to a sheriff in the absence of a lawyer to advise him of his rights. Rideau's filmed confession was seen by an estimated 100,000 television viewers living near Lake Charles, Louisiana. The Supreme Court said the televised confession in a very real sense *was* Rideau's trial—at which he pleaded guilty to murder. The Court added that any subsequent court proceedings would be pointless.[15]

- *Prior criminal records.* A prior criminal record is ordinarily inadmissible because a defendant cannot be convicted based on past criminal history. Prosecutors must prove that defendants committed the crimes for which they are being tried and not past misdeeds. Yet jurors might have a difficult time deciding that a person on trial for burglary or murder is innocent if he or she has been convicted of a similar crime before. In *Irvin v. Dowd*, the media revealed Leslie Irvin's earlier convictions for arson and burglary after he was arrested for murder near Evansville, Indiana. News stories also disclosed Irvin's juvenile record and a court-martial on AWOL charges. The Supreme Court said the stories were part of "a build-up of prejudice" in the community that led the Court to overturn Irvin's 1955 conviction.

- *The results of lie detector tests, blood tests, ballistics tests and other investigatory procedures.* The results of some tests administered by police investigators might not be admitted into evidence in court because the tests were improperly administered. Some tests used to evaluate evidence produce unreliable results. In addition, the fact that a defendant chooses not to take a test might have no bearing on his or her guilt or innocence. Yet in *Sheppard v. Maxwell*, the Cleveland newspapers headlined Sam Sheppard's refusal to take a lie detector test as if it were evidence he must be hiding his role in his wife's murder. The newspapers also reported the results of blood tests that were never admitted into evidence at the trial.

- *Character flaws or lifestyle.* Comments from neighbors or other acquaintances about a suspect's lifestyle will seldom be admitted into evidence in court. Frequently, the comments reflect rumors or hearsay rather than behavior witnessed firsthand. In the *Sheppard* case, the Cleveland newspapers emphasized that Sheppard had extramarital affairs that were not documented in

---

[13] Irvin v. Dowd, 366 U.S. 729–30 (Frankfurter, J., concurring).
[14] *See, e.g.,* John Walton, "From O.J. to Tim McVeigh and Beyond," 75 *Denver U.L. Rev.* 549 (1998).
[15] 373 U.S. 723 (1963).

court. During the trial, the jurors had access to a newspaper story claiming that Marilyn Sheppard had said her husband had a "Dr. Jekyll and Mr. Hyde" personality. No evidence of the accusation was presented during the trial.

- *Potential witnesses, testimony or evidence.* Pretrial statements of potential witnesses may or may not be heard by jurors in court. In the *Sheppard* case, the newspapers quoted a detective who said blood had been washed from the floor of the Sheppard home before investigators arrived but who never testified about the blood in court.

- *Speculation by officials.* Sometimes law enforcement officers and judges are purveyors of prejudicial publicity. They might make statements about the character, innocence or guilt of defendants that probably will not be admitted into evidence. In the *Sheppard* case, a newspaper headline reported that a police captain had called Sheppard a "bare-faced liar." The police officer was never called to the witness stand to explain the comment. In the *Irvin* case, the media reported that at least two officials were determined to make certain that Leslie Irvin was executed.

- *Other sensational and inflammatory statements.* Judges fear press coverage so inflammatory and pervasive that it contributes to a "deep and bitter pattern" of community prejudice. Although an accumulation of publicity can contribute to a public perception that the suspect is guilty, particular kinds of media coverage can foster community fears and prejudices. Media use of nicknames such as "Mad Dog Irvin" can suggest guilt. Headlines that demand the arrest of a suspect, as occurred in the *Sheppard* case, can inflame a community. Strong community bias not only makes selecting impartial jurors difficult but also can pressure jurors into convicting the defendant. When the Cleveland papers published the names of potential jurors, all received calls and letters from "cranks and friends" with opinions about the upcoming trial.

Finally, legal experts contend a defendant not only needs to be tried by jurors who are unaffected by prejudicial publicity but also needs to be tried in solemn and ordered proceedings free of a carnival-like atmosphere. The Supreme Court once said the preservation of an atmosphere in court necessary for a fair trial "must be maintained at all costs."[16] In the *Sheppard* case, the judge did not adequately preserve the decorum of the courtroom when he seated reporters inside the rail that separates the public from the trial participants. Reporters could overhear conversations between Sheppard and his lawyers and between the lawyers and the judge. The Court said the arrangements made for the press inside the courtroom caused Sheppard "to be deprived of that 'judicial serenity and calm to which [he] was entitled.'"[17]

▓ SUMMARY ▓

The Sixth Amendment guarantees criminal defendants the right to a trial by an impartial jury. The Supreme Court has said that an impartial juror is one free from strong impressions that close the mind to evidence presented in court. Jurors can know something about a defendant if they can decide a case on evidence they hear in court. However, the Court has overturned criminal convictions on evidence of massive publicity that has created a "presumption of prejudice" among jurors.

---

[16] Estes v. Texas, 381 U.S. at 540.
[17] 384 U.S. at 355 (quoting Estes v. Texas, 381 U.S. at 536).

Many judges and lawyers contend that information published before a trial but not introduced into evidence can lead to a biased jury. In addition, maintaining order in the courtroom itself is considered essential to guarantee the rights of a defendant.

REMEDIES FOR PREJUDICIAL PUBLICITY

The Supreme Court's decision in *Sheppard v. Maxwell* in 1966 marked the fifth time in seven years that the Court had reversed a criminal conviction because of prejudicial publicity or press behavior in the courtroom.[18] In *Sheppard*, the Court responded to the issues raised by prejudicial publicity not by lecturing the press but by delivering a stinging rebuke to the trial judge for failing to protect Sheppard's right to a fair trial.

Justice Clark said the Supreme Court did not want to impose direct limitations on the reporting of public trials because of the role of the press in guarding against abuses in the criminal justice system. Clark said justice cannot survive secret trials. He also said that the press guards against the miscarriage of justice by subjecting the police, prosecutors and the entire judicial process to public scrutiny. But, he continued, no one ought to be punished for a crime without being "fairly tried in a public tribunal free of prejudice, passion, excitement, and tyrannical powers."

The Supreme Court said the trial court judge in *Sheppard* had failed to protect the defendant in three ways, including two involving the judge's lack of control over the trial itself. The Court said the trial judge (1) did not control the atmosphere of the courtroom and (2) did not control information released to the press during the trial. Both concerns will be discussed later in the chapter.

The third judicial error, said the *Sheppard* Court, was the judge's failure to protect jurors from the impact of prejudicial pretrial publicity. The Court recommended remedies for prejudicial publicity, such as changing the location of the trial, that do not directly interfere with reporting court news but may limit the impact of pretrial news on jurors.

Change of Venue

One of Justice Clark's suggestions for protecting a trial against the impact of news stories is a change of venue, which means a shift in the location of the trial. State judges have the authority, within limits specified by state law, to move a trial from the jurisdiction of the crime to another jurisdiction in the state.[19] Moving a trial can be expensive for the county responsible. Changing the location of a trial is supposed to move the trial away from the scene of the most damaging publicity, but in notorious cases may not be effective. For example, the judge in the 2021 trial of Derek Chauvin denied a motion for a change of venue, stating, "I don't think there's any place in the state of Minnesota that has not been exposed to extreme amounts of publicity on this case."

In *Rideau v. Louisiana*, the Supreme Court held that the trial court's denial of a change of venue for Wilbert Rideau violated his constitutional right to a "fair and impartial trial." Rideau had asked that the trial be removed from the Calcasieu Parish trial court after his confession was televised three times in the parish. Justice Stewart, writing for the Supreme Court, said the televised confession became

---

[18] *See also* Marshall v. United States, 360 U.S. 310 (1959); Irvin v. Dowd, 366 U.S. 717 (1961); Rideau v. Louisiana, 373 U.S. 723 (1963); Estes v. Texas, 381 U.S. 532 (1965).
[19] *See, e.g.*, Ga. Code. Ann. § 17–7–150.

Rideau's trial to "tens of thousands of people." Stewart said further court proceedings "in a community so pervasively exposed to such a spectacle could be but a hollow formality."

Federal judges can move a trial to a different state.[20] It may be difficult in a case receiving nationwide attention to move the trial far enough away to find unaffected jurors, but national coverage of an event may differ from local coverage where the event takes place. For example, in 1996, a federal judge moved the trial of Timothy McVeigh and Terry Nichols, charged in the 1995 bombing of the federal office building in Oklahoma City, from Oklahoma City to Denver.[21] The judge noted that the bombing had generated enormous national publicity but reasoned that the national news coverage of the tragedy was significantly different from the local coverage. The national coverage, the judge said, was more "factual," pertaining to the "who, what, where, why, and when" of the bombing. The local coverage in Oklahoma, by contrast, was more "personal, providing individual stories of grief and recovery," as well as being more intense than the national coverage. The judge concluded that these differences suggested that a more impartial jury could be found outside the Oklahoma City area, even though no part of the country was unfamiliar with the bombing.

Change of Venire

A change of venire changes the jury pool rather than the location of a trial. Occasionally, a judge will request that potential jurors be brought in from a nearby community. In the sensational murder trial of John Wayne Gacy, accused of the sex-related murders of 33 boys and young men in the 1970s, jurors were bused from Rockford, Illinois, to Chicago. Similarly, in the 2011 Casey Anthony trial, jurors were brought to Orlando from another part of Florida.

In 1995, a state appellate court affirmed a Trenton, New Jersey, judge's order that a jury from a nearby county should be bused in to consider a highly publicized murder trial, although the appellate court also ruled that the racial demographics of the potential jury pool must be carefully examined to ensure fairness. A Trenton newspaper had engaged in a "stream of invectives" against the defendant, a black man accused of raping and murdering a white female artist. The *Trentonian* had referred to the defendant as "monster," "maggot" and "artist slayer" and stated that the defendant would eventually be put to death and that "the world will be a better place for his passing."[22] On appeal, a New Jersey appellate court agreed that the trial judge had properly decided, on the basis of the prejudicial publicity, that the case should be tried before a jury from another county. However, the appellate court held that the judge should have considered the racial composition of the county from which the jury would be drawn.[23]

Theoretically, jurors who have been imported have had less exposure to potentially damaging publicity. However, regional newspapers and national television news ensure that information about major crimes achieves widespread circulation.

---

[20] Fed. R. Crim. P. 21.

[21] United States v. McVeigh, 910 F. Supp. 1467 (W.D. Okla. 1996).

[22] "Judge Lambasts Paper's 'Invective' in N.J. Murder," *Editor & Publisher*, May 13, 1995, at 23; Michael Booth, "Race Demographics Must Be Considered in Venue Challenges," *N.J.L.J.*, June 19, 1995, at 1.

[23] State v. Harris, 660 A.2d 539 (N.J. App. Div. 1995).

Continuance

A judge who believes that publicity might damage the chances for a fair trial can postpone the trial until publicity subsides. Continuance, the legal term for postponement, was mentioned by Justice Clark in *Sheppard v. Maxwell* as an alternative when a trial judge is faced with "a reasonable likelihood that prejudicial news prior to trial will prevent a fair trial." The Court noted in *Irvin v. Dowd* that the trial court had denied eight motions for a continuance.

Postponement can effectively remove the trial from the publicity surrounding the arrest. Of course, there is likely to be renewed publicity when the trial finally takes place. There are other practical problems. Defendants asking for a postponement might have to waive their constitutional right to a speedy trial. In addition, defendants unable to raise bail wait in jail during the continuance. Furthermore, the longer a trial is postponed, the more likely witnesses or evidence will disappear.

Lawyers for Timothy McVeigh, charged with the Oklahoma City federal building bombing, argued news stories—in particular, reports in the *Dallas Morning News* and several other publications that McVeigh had confessed to his lawyers—had made a fair trial impossible. McVeigh's lawyers asked Judge Richard Matsch, who presided over McVeigh's trial, to grant a year's continuance, among other suggested procedural remedies. Matsch denied the requests.[24] The judge conceded the media had covered "every angle of the story," but he said he had "full confidence that a fair minded jury" would "return a just verdict based on the law and evidence presented to them." The jury found McVeigh guilty of 11 counts of murder and conspiracy.

Severance

Severance is a remedy available only when more than one person has been charged with the same crime or related crimes. Two or more defendants are tried separately to prevent the publicity related to one trial from affecting the other.

Voir Dire

Voir dire is the term used for the process of questioning potential jurors before selecting a jury for a trial. Potential jurors are asked questions designed to detect bias. The prospective jurors might be asked whether they know the defendant or any of the witnesses. They also might be asked about their occupation, media habits or religious beliefs. They might be asked whether they have racial prejudices or believe in the death penalty. In theory, the purpose of voir dire is to find persons able to judge a defendant only because of information presented in the courtroom. In practice, each lawyer looks for jurors who might lean toward his or her client or who might be suspicious of the opposing lawyer. In most federal courts, the judge asks the questions, although counsels sometimes participate.[25] In state courts, the opposing attorneys usually ask the questions during voir dire.

The lawyers on each side of a case can challenge any number of jurors "for cause." Prospective jurors will be excused if the judge is convinced they are unfit to serve. For example, a juror might be dismissed for an obvious prejudice or because he or she is a relative of the crime victim. The Supreme Court noted in *Rideau v.*

---

[24] United States v. McVeigh, 955 F. Supp. 1281 (D. Colo. 1997).
[25] Fed. R. Crim. P. 24.

Louisiana that the trial judge had wrongly refused to excuse two deputy sheriffs from the jury although Rideau had confessed to the sheriff.

In addition to the challenges for cause, each side in a case also can dismiss a limited number of jurors through peremptory challenges without giving a reason. The number of peremptory challenges varies with the state and with the nature of the case. Lawyers use peremptory challenges to excuse prospective jurors when the lawyers cannot persuade a judge to excuse them for cause. Attorneys might excuse a juror because they have a "gut feeling" that a potential juror has hidden biases. The gut feeling could be based on answers to questions, facial expressions, clothes, or rumor. Peremptory challenges are also used to excuse jurors who have socioeconomic characteristics that suggest a probable bias, though one that might be hard to detect. The Supreme Court has held, however, that discriminatory use of peremptory challenges based on race or gender violates the Fourteenth Amendment's Equal Protection Clause.[26]

The Supreme Court has ruled that the Sixth Amendment does not require that potential jurors be asked to disclose their exposure to prejudicial publicity. In *Mu'Min v. Virginia*, the Court said it was constitutionally sufficient for a judge to ask prospective jurors generally whether they could decide guilt based on courtroom testimony, without asking them specifically what they knew about the case. The Court said judges do not necessarily have to ask such questions as "What have you seen, read, or heard about this case?" It is sufficient for a judge to ask, "Given what you have seen, read, or heard about this case, can you enter the jury box with an open mind and be impartial in this case?" Judges can ask more precise questions if they choose, the Court said, but the Sixth Amendment does not require them to do so.[27]

As discussed earlier in this chapter, the Supreme Court in 2022 refused to find fault with the voir dire conducted in the Boston Marathon bomber trial. Prior to the 2015 trial, 1,373 prospective jurors completed a 100-question questionnaire about their backgrounds, social-media habits, views on the death penalty, and whether because of media exposure had formed an opinion that the defendant was guilty and should receive the death penalty. The trial judge refused to include a question in the questionnaire asking what facts prospective jurors had learned from the media, claiming the question was "too unguided." From the questionnaire responses, 256 prospective jurors were brought for individual voir dire, which took place over three weeks. During this process, the judge again refused to ask a blanket question about what prospective jurors had learned from media accounts. The judge was guided by *Mu'Min*: the critical inquiry was whether jurors could approach the case with an open mind and base their verdict on courtroom evidence.

The First Circuit set aside Tsarnaev's death penalty, holding that in cases where there is extreme prejudicial publicity, the judge must assess both what a juror has learned and the effect of such exposure on the juror's ability to be impartial.[28] The Supreme Court, however, reinstated the death penalty, holding that because voir dire is "committed to the district court's sound discretion, there is no blanket constitutional requirement that it must ask each prospective juror what he heard, read, or saw about a case in the media." The trial judge instead must evaluate whether each prospective juror "is to be believed when he says he has not formed an opinion about the case."

---

[26] Batson v. Kentucky, 476 U.S. 79 (1986) (race); J.E.B. v. Alabama, 511 U.S. 127 (1994) (gender).
[27] 500 U.S. 415 (1991).
[28] 968 F.3d 24 (1st Cir. 2020).

Drawing upon prior cases, the Court in *United States v. Tsarnaev* emphasized that the right to an impartial jury "does not require *ignorance*."[29] The trial court concluded that a media-content question focused on what a juror knew before coming to court, rather than on potential bias. The Supreme Court agreed with the trial court, holding that the court of appeals departed from Supreme Court precedent by mandating media-content questions in all high-profile cases. Justice Thomas, writing for the Court, said "Tsarnaev committed heinous crimes. The Sixth Amendment nonetheless guaranteed him a fair trial before an impartial jury. He received one."

The prescreening of potential jurors via questionnaires has become increasingly commonplace in high-profile cases and abbreviates jury selection. Questionnaires are sent to potential jurors; the answers are then used to reduce the number of potential jurors questioned in person. In addition to the Tsarnaev case, questionnaires were used in the 2021 trials of Elizabeth Holmes and Derek Chauvin. In the 2006 criminal trial of former Enron executives Kenneth Lay and Jeffrey Skilling, 283 prospective jurors received questionnaires asking detailed questions about their opinions of Enron, Lay and Skilling. Based on the answers, 119 people were eliminated from the jury pool.

In some trials, behavioral scientists have been used as "jury consultants" to help lawyers choose jurors. These jury consultants conduct extensive research to determine what kind of jurors might be sympathetic to the lawyer's case. Then the lawyer tries to seat jurors who fit the profile.

Sequestration

Sequestration is the "locking up" of the jury during a trial. A judge can order that the jurors be isolated under guard. They usually are housed together at a hotel at government expense. They are generally not allowed to see friends or family or to see news stories about the case. Guards screen and monitor phone calls.

Sequestration prevents jurors from hearing others evaluate the evidence or predict the outcome of the trial. Although sequestration cannot be used until a jury is chosen, it effectively keeps jurors from obtaining information from outside the courtroom during the trial. The Supreme Court implied that the judge in the Sheppard trial should have sequestered the jury. Because the judge did not sequester jurors, they were exposed to rumors and opinions during the trial as well as before. Two jurors heard a radio broadcast in which a woman claimed that Sheppard had fathered her illegitimate child.

However, sequestration is very expensive, and it seriously disrupts the lives of jurors, particularly during long trials. The jurors in the O.J. Simpson prosecution, for example, suffered significant hardship during their nine-month sequestration. One Simpson juror, who had to be treated for high blood pressure during the trial, told the *Los Angeles Times* that the sequestration made him "stir-crazy."[30] Defense attorneys often worry that a sequestered jury will resent the defendant for keeping them from family and friends. Moreover, questions have been raised about sequestration's effectiveness. Some experts contend that even sequestered jurors are rarely completely isolated from prejudicial information, which can seep in to affect jurors despite the best safeguards.[31]

---

[29] No. 20–443, slip op. at 8 (U.S. Mar. 4, 2022).
[30] "The Simpson Legacy," *Los Angeles Times*, Oct. 8, 1995, at S4.
[31] "Sequestering Juries," *N.J.L.J.*, Oct. 9, 1995, at 26.

Judicial Admonition

Once a jury has been chosen, a judge can instruct jurors to render their verdict based on evidence presented in the courtroom. A judge may tell jurors to avoid reading, watching, or listening to anything about the trial. In 2020, the Judicial Conference, which sets policy for the federal courts, issued model jury instruction to combat an epidemic of Internet research and social media posts by jurors. The new model instructions advise judges to start warning jurors about social media and Internet research before they are empaneled and to keep reminding jurors at the beginning and end of each day.

In 2011, the Arkansas Supreme Court tossed out a murder conviction and ordered a new trial because a juror tweeted about the case during the trial.[32] Not all social media usage is problematic, however, as the Fourth Circuit in 2021 found in a case where a juror accessed Twitter, liked a tweet, retweeted a tweet and tweeted one of her own, all related to football. Jurors had been instructed not to use social media to learn about or discuss the case, and the juror's activity was not related to the trial.[33]

The Supreme Court criticized as inadequate the admonitions to the jury issued by the Sheppard trial court judge. He "suggested" and "requested" that jurors avoid reading newspapers, listening to the radio, or watching television. He said that "we shall all feel very much better" if the jurors paid no attention to the media. But, the Court said, the judge failed to "instruct" or "admonish" jurors to avoid the media.

Judges who admonish jurors want to keep them from seeing or hearing inadmissible information and commentary that may affect their decisions while at the same time avoiding the cost and inconvenience of sequestration. Many judges believe, and one important study found, jurors take such admonitions very seriously.[34]

New Trial

As a last resort, a criminal conviction can be overturned, as occurred in *Irvin*, *Sheppard* and *Rideau*. A retrial involves all the expense and personal trauma of the first trial. Defendants may have to remain in jail if they cannot post bond. In his *Sheppard* opinion, Justice Clark noted that reversals are but palliatives; the cure lies in those remedial measures that will prevent the prejudice at its inception. The courts must take such steps by rule and regulation that will protect their processes from prejudicial outside interferences.

■ SUMMARY ■

The Supreme Court in *Sheppard v. Maxwell* criticized the trial court judge for failing to protect against prejudicial pretrial publicity, failing to control the courtroom and failing to restrict the release of prejudicial information during the trial. The Court's opinion suggested that the judge in the Sheppard trial should have used tools available to judges to protect against prejudicial publicity. The devices available include change of venue, change of venire, continuance, severance of related trials, voir dire, sequestration, admonitions to the jury and a judicial order for a new trial.

---

[32] Dimas-Martinez v. Arkansas, 2011 Ark. 515 (2011).
[33] United States v. Loughry, 996 F.3d 729 (4th Cir. 2021).
[34] Harry Kalven, Jr. and Hans Zeisel, *The American Jury* (1966).

CONTROLLING CONDUCT IN COURT

The Supreme Court stressed in *Sheppard v. Maxwell* that judges must ensure a dignified atmosphere in the court, including control over the behavior of journalists; the judge in the Sheppard trial should have kept reporters from areas of the courtroom where they could disrupt the defendant, lawyers and jurors and the number of reporters in the courtroom should have been reduced when it became evident they were disrupting the trial.

Judges also can control the use of cameras in court. However, restrictions on cameras in state courts have been significantly relaxed in the last 40 years.

Both television and still cameras have long been perceived by some judges and lawyers as a threat to the dignity of courtrooms. After the Supreme Court in 1981 said that states can develop their own rules if the presence of cameras does not violate a defendant's right to a fair trial, most states adopted rules allowing camera coverage. Cameras still were prohibited in most federal trial courts in 2022.

The Early Ban on Cameras

The hostility to cameras in court is often traced to the sensational trial of Bruno Hauptmann in 1935. Hauptmann was accused of kidnapping and killing the 18-month-old son of Charles Lindbergh, who had become famous as the first person to fly nonstop across the Atlantic. More than 800 journalists from around the world attended the trial; the press hired messengers who disrupted the trial by running into and out of the courtroom with copy. Reporters and photographers who could not get into the courtroom jammed the halls. However, only a few cameras were allowed inside the courtroom, and photographers largely obeyed a judicial order barring pictures while court was in session.[35]

In 1937, two years after Hauptmann's conviction, the American Bar Association (ABA) recommended banning cameras in courtrooms as one of several efforts to curb trial publicity. To the ABA, cameras "detract from the essential dignity of the proceedings, degrade the court and create misconceptions . . . in the mind of the public." Although ABA recommendations are not law, they are significant because states often adopt them as rules governing court proceedings.[36]

The ABA's opposition to cameras continued for more than 40 years. For most of that time, photographers were generally kept out of courtrooms. In the mid-1950s, only one state—Colorado—allowed cameras in court. In the early 1960s, Texas also permitted courtroom television and still photography. In 1962, televising live events was still relatively new and spectacular, and television coverage of the trial of Billie Sol Estes created a major controversy.

Estes, a Texas grain dealer, became the focus of national media attention when he was charged with fraudulently inducing farmers to buy nonexistent fertilizer tanks. A two-day pretrial hearing in Tyler, Texas, was broadcast live by radio and television. The scene was vividly described by the *New York Times*:

> A television motor van, big as an intercontinental bus, was parked outside the courthouse and the second-floor courtroom was a forest of

---

[35] *See generally* State v. Hauptmann, 180 A. 809, 827, *cert. denied*, 296 U.S. 649 (1935); Marjorie Cohn and David Dow, *Cameras in the Courtroom* (1998); Ronald Goldfarb, *TV or Not TV: Television, Justice and the Courts* (1998).

[36] *See* Criminal Justice Standards Committee of the American Bar Association, *ABA Standards for Criminal Justice: Fair Trial and Free Press* 10–12 (3rd ed. 1992).

equipment. Two television cameras had been set up inside the bar and four more marked cameras were aligned just outside the gates.

A microphone stuck its 12-inch snout inside the jury box, now occupied by an overflow of reporters from the press table, and three microphones confronted Judge Dunagan on his bench. Cables and wires snaked over the floor.[37]

By the time the trial itself began, the judge had moved television cameras to a booth constructed in the back of the courtroom. This prompted Estes's counsel to remark, "This doesn't look like a courtroom to me, it looks like a movie theater."[38] Live coverage was permitted only occasionally during the trial, and reports of the trial were confined primarily to news programs. However, despite the more limited camera coverage, Estes appealed his conviction on the ground that broadcast coverage denied him a fair trial. The Supreme Court agreed, 5–4, and ordered a retrial. Estes later was convicted again.

The Supreme Court's majority in *Estes v. Texas* said the press must be allowed as much freedom to report court proceedings as possible, but the preservation of the atmosphere necessary to guarantee a fair trial "must be maintained at all costs."[39] Four of the five justices in the majority believed that the mere presence of television cameras in court violated the defendant's Sixth Amendment guarantee of a fair trial. The fifth justice, John Harlan, said television coverage must be banned at that time in criminal trials of "widespread public interest" and "great notoriety."

Justice Clark, who wrote the Court's majority opinion, listed the concerns still voiced by those opposing cameras in court. Cameras would distract jurors and inevitably lead to the pressure "of knowing their friends and neighbors have their eyes upon them." Cameras were also a form of mental harassment resembling a police line-up, Clark said. A defendant "is entitled to his day in court, not in a stadium or a city or nationwide arena," he added. Clark also said the presence of cameras impaired the quality of testimony because it could frighten some witnesses and encourage others to exaggerate.

Whereas four of the justices in the majority suggested television cameras inherently endangered the constitutional rights of any criminal defendant, Justice Harlan said in a concurring opinion that he was limiting his judgment to only "heavily publicized and highly sensational" trials. Harlan, whose vote was necessary to overturn the first Estes conviction, suggested he might permit cameras in "run-of-the-mill" criminal trials and for educational purposes. Harlan did not want to prohibit the states from experimenting with cameras in the courtroom. He said that television may eventually become "so commonplace an affair in the daily life of the average person" that it would not likely damage the judicial process.

Cameras Move Into Courtrooms

After the *Estes* decision, every state but Colorado barred cameras from court for nearly a decade. Meanwhile, cameras became smaller and quieter and therefore less intrusive. They became less dependent on special lighting. The media kept

---

[37] Homar Bigart, "Estes Goes on Trial in Texas with TV in Courtroom," *N.Y. Times*, Sept. 25, 1962, at 46.
[38] *Newsweek*, Nov. 5, 1962, at 5.
[39] 381 U.S. 532 (1965).

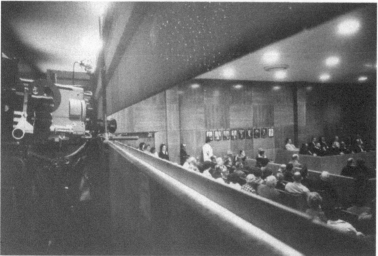

PHOTOS 10.1 AND 10.2   In September 1962, two days of pretrial proceedings were held to consider whether the trial of Billie Sol Estes would be televised. Cameras were set up inside the bar during the first day's proceedings. Judge Otis T. Dunagan subsequently ruled that cameras would not be allowed inside the bar for the second day's proceedings; the top photograph shows the array of television and news photographers covering the second day of the pretrial hearings. (Estes and his attorney are seated in the foreground.) The pretrial hearings were carried live by local television stations. Judge Dunagan ruled that television coverage of the October 1962 trial would be allowed but blocked live coverage of the voir dire of prospective jurors or testimony of witnesses. Television cameras were restricted to a booth built at the back of the courtroom, shown in the bottom photograph. Except for the prosecution's closing argument and the return of verdict by the jury, there was no live television coverage of the trial.

Source: Getty Images. Used by permission.

pushing for the acceptance of cameras in court. By the end of 1980, 22 states had experimented with cameras and another dozen were studying the issue.[40]

A pilot program in Florida led to the Supreme Court test of whether states could allow cameras in court. Beginning in 1977, Florida conducted a year-long test of electronic coverage; at the conclusion of the test, the Florida Supreme Court said that physical disturbance by the cameras "was so minimal as not to be an arguable factor" during trials.[41]

Florida's rules were challenged by two defendants who had objected to the presence of cameras at their trial. On appeal, the U.S. Supreme Court held 8–0 that the Constitution does not prohibit states from experimenting with cameras in state courts. In *Chandler v. Florida*, the Court said it would not invalidate state rules permitting cameras in court unless criminal defendants can prove their Sixth Amendment rights to a fair trial were violated.[42]

Writing for the Court, Chief Justice Burger noted in *Chandler* that only four justices in *Estes* had declared that cameras in the courtroom automatically denied a defendant a fair trial. Burger, in asking again whether cameras in court violated the rights of criminal defendants, noted technological changes since *Estes*. He acknowledged there was still a heated controversy over whether the mere presence of cameras in court "invariably and uniformly affected the conduct of participants so as to impair fundamental fairness." Yet, said the chief justice, whatever potential cameras had for interfering with the judicial process, no one had presented data establishing that the "mere presence" of broadcast media "inherently has an adverse effect on that process."

The Supreme Court said a complete constitutional ban of cameras could not be justified simply because a fair trial might be jeopardized in some cases. To overturn a conviction in a trial with cameras present, a defendant must demonstrate the cameras impaired a jury's ability to decide his or her case fairly, the Court said, or a defendant must establish that the presence of cameras or the possibility of televised coverage adversely affected any participants, including witnesses. In the *Chandler* case, the majority opinion noted, the defendants had not provided any evidence that their trial was tainted by broadcast coverage.

Shortly after the *Chandler* decision, the ABA modified its ban on cameras in the ABA Code of Judicial Conduct; if an appellate court or "appropriate authority" approves, a judge may allow camera coverage if it is "unobtrusive, will not distract trial participants, and will not otherwise interfere with the administration of justice."[43]

By 2022, 46 states allowed television coverage of trials and appellate proceedings. Four states—Delaware, Indiana, Louisiana and New York—limited camera coverage to appellate arguments, which are heard solely by judges. In 2005, the New York statute banning cameras in trial courts was found constitutional by New York's highest court, which stated the law was merely a restriction on the means of gathering news, not a restriction on the openness of court proceedings.[44] (Illinois, which previously limited coverage to appellate proceedings, adopted a policy allowing limited trial coverage in 2016.) Only the District of Columbia bans the press from using cameras and microphones when covering both trial and appellate proceeding. The district's court of last resort, the D.C. Court of Appeals, however, itself streams audio of all oral arguments on its website and streams live video of

---

[40] Chandler v. Florida, 449 U.S. 560, 565 nn. 5–6 (1981).

[41] *In re* Post-Newsweek Stations, Inc., 370 So. 2d 764 (Fla. 1979).

[42] 449 U.S. 560 (1981).

[43] American Bar Association, *Code of Judicial Conduct* Canon 3A(7) (1982).

[44] Courtroom Television Network v. New York, 833 N.E.2d 1197 (N.Y. 2005).

Table 10.1 Cameras in Courts		
TIER I: STATES THAT ALLOW THE MOST COVERAGE		
California	Montana	Utah
Colorado	Nevada	Vermont
Florida	New Hampshire	Washington
Georgia	New Mexico	West Virginia
Idaho	North Dakota	Wisconsin
Kentucky	South Carolina	Wyoming
Michigan	Tennessee	
TIER II: STATES WITH RESTRICTIONS PROHIBITING COVERAGE OF IMPORTANT TYPES OF CASES, SUCH AS SEXUAL OFFENSE, OR PROHIBITING COVERAGE OF ALL OR LARGE CATEGORIES OF WITNESSES WHO OBJECT TO COVERAGE OF THEIR TESTIMONY		
Alaska	Massachusetts	Oregon
Arizona	Mississippi	Rhode Island
Connecticut	Missouri	Texas
Hawaii	New Jersey	Virginia
Iowa	North Carolina	
Kansas	Ohio	
TIER III: STATES THAT ALLOW APPELLATE COVERAGE ONLY OR THAT HAVE SUCH RESTRICTIVE TRIAL RULES THAT COVERAGE IS LARGELY PREVENTED		
Alabama	Louisiana	New York
Arkansas	Maine	Oklahoma
Delaware	Maryland	Pennsylvania
Illinois	Minnesota	South Dakota
Indiana	Nebraska	

Note: The District of Columbia is the only jurisdiction that prohibits trial and appellate coverage entirely.

Source: Copyright by Radio Television Digital News Association. Used here with permission of RTDNA. For detailed information about each state's rules, see www.rtdna.org.

some arguments. During the COVID-19 pandemic, the D.C. Court of Appeals began streaming videoconferences of oral arguments on YouTube. Indeed, the COVID-19 pandemic has resulted in many courts adopting temporary policies as in-person proceedings moved to forums such as teleconferences.

As part of the general trend toward more electronic coverage of judicial proceedings, nearly all state supreme courts have recently begun live webcasting or cablecasting of their oral arguments. The majority allows video coverage, but a small number, such as Maine, Missouri, Rhode Island, South Dakota, Vermont, Virginia and Wyoming, restrict coverage to audio. Most courts allowing electronic coverage also have archives of recordings available on the Internet.[45]

States vary in trial coverage allowed, as is illustrated in Table 10.1. Ostensibly to preserve a fair trial, some states prohibit or limit camera coverage of criminal trials. For example, Pennsylvania prohibits any broadcast coverage of criminal trials,

---

[45] For a summary of state supreme court policies regarding video and audio coverage of their oral arguments, see United States Government Accountability Office, *U.S. Supreme Court: Policies and Perspectives on Video and Audio Coverage of Appellate Court Proceedings* at 51–2 (2016).

and Maine allows broadcast coverage only of nontestimonial aspects of criminal proceedings, such as arraignments and sentencing. Other states generally allow coverage of criminal and civil proceedings but protect privacy by prohibiting coverage of sensitive cases or vulnerable witnesses. Virginia, for example, prohibits broadcast coverage of sex offense cases, and Missouri prohibits coverage of participants who are victims of crime. Kansas and Ohio prohibit coverage of witnesses who object. Many states leave broad discretion with the trial judge to determine what cases or witnesses will be subject to broadcast coverage. In Florida, a judge can exclude electronic media coverage only if it will have a "substantial effect" that would be "qualitatively different" from that of other media coverage.

To ensure the dignity of court proceedings, state court rules typically limit the number of photographers and electronic media personnel and their location in the courtroom and specify the types of equipment that may be utilized. For example, Florida allows one television camera at trials and appellate proceedings; only one still photographer is allowed at trials and appellate proceedings. The cameras must not produce distracting sound or produce artificial light. To protect attorney-client privilege, no audio pickup is allowed of conferences between attorneys and their clients, between co-counsel, or between the judge and the attorneys held at the bench.[46]

Whether journalists may use laptop computers and similar devices in state courtrooms depends upon local rules or the discretion of the judge. Some states have adopted statewide rules governing use of laptops and similar devices. Connecticut and Utah recently adopted statewide rules allowing silent use of portable electronic devices such as laptops in courtrooms. In the 2012 sex abuse trial of former Penn State assistant football coach Jerry Sandusky, the judge allowed journalists to bring portable devices into the courtroom but banned live tweeting or texting. Such activities would be "broadcasting" in violation of Pennsylvania's rules, the judge concluded.

FEDERAL TRIAL COURTS As of 2022, cameras were not allowed in federal criminal trials. The rules banning cameras in federal criminal trials[47] have withstood First Amendment challenges.[48] Federal policy on camera coverage of civil trials is complex, reflecting the federal judiciary's deep ambivalence on the question. In essence, local courts may adopt rules authorizing camera coverage, although the Judicial Conference, the policymaking body for the federal courts, prefers that there be no camera coverage of civil trials. In 2020, though, the Judicial Conference authorized a pilot program allowing livestreaming of audio in certain civil cases. The 2020 pilot program is the third time the Judicial Conference has explored electronic coverage of court proceedings. Also, the COVID-19 pandemic has resulted in a temporary policy change allowing the use of video and teleconferencing for certain criminal and civil proceedings.

In 1990, the Judicial Conference authorized a pilot program allowing camera coverage in six district courts and two courts of appeals. Although the results of this study were positive,[49] the Judicial Conference voted in 1994 to reject a proposal allowing still photography and radio and television coverage of civil trials in

---

[46] "Technological Coverage of Judicial Proceedings," *Fla. R. Jud. Admin.* 2.450 (2021).

[47] Fed. R. Crim. P. 53.

[48] *See, e.g.,* United States v. Hastings, 695 F.2d 1278 (11th Cir.), *cert. denied,* 461 U.S. 931 (1983).

[49] Federal Judicial Center, *Electronic Media Coverage of Federal Civil Proceedings: An Evaluation of the Pilot Program in Six District Courts and Two Courts of Appeals* (1994).

ILLUSTRATION 10.1   Theranos, founded in 2003, was a high-flying Silicon Valley startup, valued at over $9 billion in 2014. Elizabeth Holmes, the firm's founder, received star treatment, often appearing on magazine covers such as *Fortune*. After the *Wall Street Journal's* John Carreyrou reported in 2015 that Theranos' blood testing machine was unreliable, Theranos quickly unraveled. Holmes was indicted on federal fraud charges in 2018 and the firm dissolved that same year. Her 2021 trial was preceded by massive publicity, including top-selling books, television documentaries and podcasts.

In this illustration by courtroom artist Vicki Behringer, Holmes breaks into tears during cross-examination by Assistant U.S. Attorney Robert Leach on November 30, 2021. In one of the most pivotal moments of the four-month long trial, Holmes was asked about private romantic notes sent between her and Ramesh Balwani, whom she claims controlled and abused her. Jurors found unpersuasive her attempt to blame Balwani for her actions as head of Theranos— of the 32 witnesses, jurors rated Holmes as the least credible—and convicted her on four counts of defrauding investors.

Because the criminal trial was held in federal court where cameras are banned, news outlets hired courtroom sketch artist Vicki Behringer to provide visual journalism. She has more than three decades of experience; among the noteworthy trials she has sketched include the 1996–1998 Unabomber proceedings, the 2004 Scott Peterson trial, the 2005 Michael Jackson trial, and the 2011 Barry Bonds trial. She is known for her ability to quickly capture emotions and actions in the courtroom. She states, "All of this is done from my seat in the audience as fast as I possibly can to meet my extremely tight deadlines. My sketches are then seen in news stories, sometimes all over the world. I really love the immediacy and spontaneous flow of my work."

Source: Copyright 2021 Vicki Behringer. Used by permission.

all courts.[50] The Judicial Conference concluded "the intimidating effect of cameras on some witnesses and jurors [is] a cause for concern."[51] And, in 1996 the Judicial Conference urged, but did not require, the governing bodies of each federal circuit,

---

[50] "Judicial Conference Votes Down Cameras," *News Media & L.* (Fall 1994), at 3.
[51] *Report on the Proceedings of the Judicial Conference of the United States* at 47 (Sept. 20, 1994).

known as Judicial Councils, to repeal any local rules permitting judges to authorize cameras in civil proceedings. Consequently, only two federal district courts have local rules authorizing camera coverage of civil proceedings. Civil proceedings in the District Courts for the Eastern and Southern Districts of New York have been televised a few times since 1994.[52]

In early 2010, the Supreme Court by a 5–4 vote prevented the broadcast of a trial in San Francisco of a civil lawsuit challenging Proposition 8, the initiative banning same-sex marriage in California.[53] The Court ruled a district court adopted a local rule permitting broadcasting without following appropriate procedures that provide the public with notice and an opportunity for comment. Although the Court claimed it was not expressing any views on the propriety of broadcasting court proceedings, its view of the harms created by such broadcasts do not indicate favorability toward broadcasting.

The case arose when the federal district court for the Northern District of California announced on January 6, 2010, that an audio and video feed of the upcoming Proposition 8 trial would be transmitted live to certain courthouses in other cities and would be videotaped for delayed release on YouTube. The cameras were to be operated by court personnel; federal district judge Vaughn Walker said he felt strongly that this initial coverage "be absolutely within the court's control."[54] Although a local rule had long banned use of cameras, the district court amended this local rule in December 2009, shortly after the Ninth Circuit Judicial Council, which oversees the federal courts in the western states, announced it had approved a pilot program for the use of cameras in civil non-jury trials.

In a per curiam opinion, the Court's then-conservative bloc (Chief Justice Roberts, Justices Scalia, Kennedy, Thomas and Alito) noted that although district courts have the discretion to adopt local rules, federal law requires a district court to follow certain procedures to adopt or amend a rule. The district court gave the public only five business days to comment on a change in the local rules, a period the majority regarded as inappropriate, especially because the need for a meaningful comment period was "acute" in this case. Due to the concerns the Judicial Conference has expressed about broadcasting court proceedings, it was incumbent upon the district court to adopt a proposed rule only after notice and an adequate period for public comment.

The majority believed that broadcasting the trial "about a contentious issue" would likely cause harm to witnesses. Citing *Estes v. Texas*, discussed earlier in this chapter, the majority noted that broadcasting may chill witness testimony. Some of the witnesses in favor of Proposition 8 had been previously harassed and stated they would not testify if the trial were broadcast. "It is difficult to demonstrate or analyze whether a witness would have testified differently if his or her testimony had not been broadcast," the majority wrote. Justice Breyer, joined by Justices Stevens, Ginsburg and Sotomayor, wrote a dissenting opinion questioning the claim that witnesses would be harmed by a closed-circuit broadcast, especially because the trial was being extensively covered by national and international newspapers. Justice Breyer also believed there was an interest in the public learning about the case and how courts work, an interest completely ignored by the majority.

---

[52] *See, e.g.*, Marisol v. Guiliani, 929 F. Supp. 660 (S.D.N.Y. 1996); Hamilton v. Accu-Tek, 942 F. Supp. 136 (E.D.N.Y. 1996); E*Trade v. Deutsche Bank, 582 F. Supp. 2d 528 (S.D.N.Y. 2008).
[53] Hollingsworth v. Perry, 558 U.S. 183 (2010).
[54] Associated Press, "Court: Gay-marriage Trial to Be Videotaped, Uploaded to YouTube," *Associated Press*, Jan. 7, 2010.

In late 2010, the Judicial Conference approved another pilot program to evaluate the effect of cameras in district courts. Under the pilot, 14 trial courts began recording civil proceedings in June 2011; the program ended in July 2015. In March 2016 the Judicial Conference voted not to change its policy regarding camera coverage. It did, however, agree to let three district courts continue the pilot program.[55] The 2020 pilot program allows audio livestreaming on YouTube of civil proceedings "involving a matter of public interest." Fifteen district courts are participating in the program which will run until early 2023. Proceedings involving live witness testimony are excluded, as are cases involving sealed, confidential, or classified materials.

In response to the COVID-19 pandemic which shut down courthouses, the Judicial Conference in March 2020 approved the temporary use of video and teleconferencing for certain criminal and civil proceedings until the emergency ends. Judges have discretion as to how these are accessed by the public, whether by videoconference apps, call-in lines, or links to audio livestreams.

FEDERAL APPELLATE COURTS The Judicial Conference in 1996 passed a resolution allowing federal courts of appeal to decide for themselves whether to allow still photographs or radio and television coverage of appellate arguments.[56] Two U.S. Courts of Appeals—the Second and Ninth Circuits—have permitted cameras in appellate arguments on a case-by-case basis. In 2013, the Ninth Circuit became the first federal appeals court to begin live video streaming of its en banc cases. Since 2007, the Third Circuit has posted hundreds of audio recordings of its oral arguments; in 2017 it began posting video recordings of some oral arguments. The D.C. Circuit began audio livestreaming of arguments in 2018. Prior to the COVID-19 pandemic, 11 of the 13 courts of appeals posted audio recordings of oral arguments on their websites.[57]

As a result of the COVID-19 pandemic, all the courts of appeals have livestreamed audio of their oral arguments; the Ninth and Eleventh Circuits have livestreamed argument video. It is uncertain if audio livestreaming will continue after the pandemic subsides.

During the 2009 hearings on her nomination to the Supreme Court, Sonia Sotomayor stated that her experience with cameras at the Second Circuit was "positive." Once on the Court, however, Sotomayor changed her views to align with the majority of the Court's members who are vehemently opposed to television coverage of the Court's proceedings. Former Justice David Souter, whom Sotomayor replaced, stated in 1996, "The day you see a camera in our courtroom, it's going to roll over my dead body."[58] In early 2013, Sotomayor said televising oral arguments could be "more misleading than helpful."[59] Justice Alito, who favored camera access when he was a judge on the Court of Appeals for the Third Circuit, indicated in May 2009 that he agreed with Souter's strong opposition to cameras in the Supreme

[55] Report of Proceedings of the Judicial Conference of the United States at 12 (Mar. 15, 2016).

[56] Linda Greenhouse, "Reversing Course, Judicial Panel Allows Televising Appeals Courts," *N.Y. Times*, Mar. 13, 1996, at A1.

[57] For a summary of the video and audio policies of the U.S. Courts of Appeals, see United States Government Accountability Office, *U.S. Supreme Court: Policies and Perspectives on Video and Audio Coverage of Appellate Court Proceedings* at 14 (2016).

[58] Robert Greenberger, "High-Court Shift: Speedy Sound Bits, for Now, but No TV," *Wall St. J.*, Apr. 30, 2004, at B4.

[59] Jordan Teicher, "Sonia Sotomayor No Longer Interested in Bringing Cameras into the Supreme Court," *New York Daily Intelligencer,* Feb. 6, 2013, www.nymag.com/intelligencer/2013/02/sonia-sotomayor-cameras-tv-supreme-court.html.

ILLUSTRATION 10.2   The Supreme Court and most federal courts do not allow camera coverage of their proceedings. These courts do, however, allow artists to sketch their proceedings. One of the most prominent artists specializing in court coverage is Art Lien, who has been sketching the courts since 1976, and for most of that time the U.S. Supreme Court has been his regular beat. Lien writes that "courtroom sketching is a form of visual journalism or reportage drawing that is slowly dying out. Where once upon a time news organizations each had their own artist covering a story, today a "pool" artist often sketches for all. It is a demanding and stressful discipline where the drawing is often done directly and under tight deadline." Lien "travels light. Apart from a small 11" by 15" sketch pad, everything I need I can carry in my pockets. I don't use squeaky markers and I am generally inconspicuous." Here, Lien depicts Margie Phelps arguing *Snyder v. Phelps* before the U.S. Supreme Court. In *Snyder*, discussed in Chapters 2 and 5, the Court ruled that the First Amendment shielded Westboro Baptist Church from tort liability for picketing at military funerals. Writing for the Court, Chief Justice Roberts wrote, "Speech is powerful. It can stir people to action, move them to tears of both joy and sorrow, and—as it did here—inflict great pain. On the facts before us, we cannot react to that pain by punishing the speaker. As a Nation we have chosen a different course—to protect even hurtful speech on public issues to ensure that we do not stifle public debate."

Source: Copyright 2011 Art Lien. Used with permission.

Court.[60] In recent years Congress has considered legislative proposals requiring the Court to allow cameras, prompting public opposition by members of the Court. For example, Justice Kennedy stated the proposed legislation raised sensitive separation of powers issues. He noted that "proposals mandating and directing television in our court are inconsistent with the deference and etiquette that should apply between the branches."[61] The late Justice Scalia was blunter. "We don't want to

---

[60] *See* Comm. on the Judiciary, A Bill to Permit the Televising of Supreme Court Proceedings, S. Rep. No. 110–448 (2008).
[61] Linda Greenhouse, "2 Justices Indicate Supreme Court Is Unlikely to Televise Sessions," *N.Y. Times*, Apr. 5, 2006, at A16.

become entertainment," he said.[62] Chief Justice Roberts acknowledged the argument that the public would benefit greatly from televised proceedings, but added, "We don't have oral arguments to show people how we function. We have them to learn about a particular case, in a particular way that we think is important."[63] In 2019, Justice Kagan joined the justices who fear the impact of televised coverage, stating that if seeing the Court at work came at the expense of the way the institution functioned, "that would be a very bad bargain."[64]

Journalists made some progress in December 2000, when the Supreme Court released audiotapes of the oral argument in the challenge to Florida's handling of presidential ballots.[65] The Court released the tapes immediately after the argument was finished—the first time the Court made audiotapes public before announcing its decision in a case. From 2000–2009, the Court released audiotapes immediately after hearing arguments in 21 important cases challenging affirmative action, federal election laws, the war on terrorism and restrictions on abortion. In 2010, however, the Supreme Court ended the practice of same-day release of audio recordings in high-profile cases. In October 2010, the Court began posting audio recordings of all arguments on its website at the end of each argument week.[66] From 2010 to 2018, the Court deviated from its policy on four occasions, releasing same-day audio recordings in high-profile cases such as the April 2015 arguments in three same-sex marriage cases.

Although the Court remains opposed to camera coverage, in May 2020 the Court's building was closed to the public due to the COVID-19 pandemic, and the Court heard oral arguments via telephone conference in ten cases. The Court provided the media pool a live audio feed of these arguments. This practice continued through May 2021.

The Court resumed holding arguments in person in October 2021, but the sessions were not open to the public. Instead, audio of the arguments was livestreamed, a practice the Court announced would continue at least through April 2022. The Court also posted audio recordings and transcripts on its website each day of oral argument.

Media and transparency groups have asked the Court to make audio livestreaming permanent, noting that as of September 2021 oral arguments from May 2020 have been streamed over 2 million times.

■ SUMMARY ■

Judges have the authority to control the behavior of the press within the courtroom. Whether cameras are allowed in state courtrooms depends on the rules of individual states. Many states allow restricted use of cameras in court, a practice permitted by the U.S. Supreme Court if a defendant's right to a fair trial is not violated. Cameras are still banned in most federal courts, but the Judicial Conference in 2020 began its third pilot program regarding electronic coverage. Due to the COVID-19

---

[62] "Scalia Bars Reporters from Speech to Insurance Execs," *Associated Press*, Oct. 13, 2005.

[63] *See* Comm. on the Judiciary, A Bill to Permit the Televising of Supreme Court Proceedings, S. Rep. No. 110–448 (2008).

[64] Joan Biskupic, "Supreme Court Justices Still Skeptical of TV" (Mar. 7, 2019), www.cnn.com/2019/03/07/politics/supreme-court-kagan-alito.html.

[65] "The Supreme Court Arguments," *N.Y. Times*, Dec. 2, 2000, at A18. Audio recordings of oral arguments in historic Supreme Court cases are available at www.oyez.org.

[66] Office of Public Information, Supreme Court of the United States (Sept. 28, 2010).

pandemic, federal courts including the Supreme Court have livestreamed audio of oral arguments.

CONTROLLING PREJUDICIAL PUBLICITY

In *Sheppard v. Maxwell*, Justice Clark's majority opinion stressed that judges, in addition to protecting the jury from prejudicial publicity and controlling courtroom conduct, must control the disclosure of information by trial participants. At the same time, however, he asserted that the press cannot be prevented from reporting the trial itself. The tolerance for "gagging" trial participants and intolerance for restricting press reports of trials continues to be the Court's policy after more than 50 years of litigation. In addition, the Supreme Court has held since *Sheppard v. Maxwell* that the press cannot ordinarily be punished for reporting lawfully obtained information about the judicial process.

Restraints Imposed on News Sources

In the *Sheppard* opinion, Justice Clark said the trial judge in the case should have tried to control the release of information to the press by lawyers, police and witnesses. Clark applauded the *Sheppard* trial judge's threat to bar from the courtroom one defense witness, Sheppard's brother, who was accused of trying the case in the newspapers. Clark said the judge would have been within his authority to forbid any lawyer, party, or witness to discuss the case with the press.

Even before *Sheppard*, the U.S. Department of Justice had issued a 1965 policy statement governing the release of information by its personnel. Commonly known as the Katzenbach Rules, after then–Attorney General Nicholas Katzenbach, the statement condemned the release of information designed to influence the outcome of a trial. The rules, still federal policy in 2022, instruct Justice Department personnel not to make statements about investigative procedures, evidence, prospective witnesses, confessions, a defendant's character or arguments to be used in the case. Nor were members of the Justice Department to volunteer information about a defendant's prior criminal record or encourage the news media to obtain photographs of defendants in custody. Authorized personnel could release a defendant's identity, age and residence; the criminal charge; the identity of the investigating and arresting agencies; the length of the investigation; and the circumstances surrounding the arrest.[67]

Shortly after the *Sheppard* decision, judges and lawyers released their own recommendations designed to prevent the publication of information like that discouraged by the Katzenbach Rules. In 1968, the ABA recommended contempt citations for lawyers, defendants, witnesses, court personnel and law enforcement officers who made out-of-court statements designed to affect the outcome of a trial.[68] Also in 1968, the Judicial Conference, responsible for developing policy for the federal courts, adopted similar guidelines for the release of information.[69]

Since the 1960s, the ABA and the judicial conference have revised their recommendations to allow for the release of more information than the 1968 documents

---

[67] *See* 28 C.F.R. § 50.2.
[68] American Bar Association Legal Advisory Committee on Fair Trial and Free Press, *The Rights of Fair Trial and Free Press* (1969).
[69] *See* Report of the Committee on the Operation of the Jury System on the "Free Press-Fair Trial" Issue, 45 F.R.D. 391 (1968).

allowed, but both still encourage restrictive orders, particularly for lawyers.[70] The U.S. Supreme Court has refused several opportunities to declare unconstitutional what judges call restrictive orders and what journalists call **gag orders** or **restraining orders**. In fact, in 1991, the U.S. Supreme Court said lawyers' comments about criminal proceedings can be restricted because lawyers, as officers of the court, are bound to protect the integrity of the legal system. In *Gentile v. State Bar of Nevada*, the Court said restrictions of attorneys' comments during trials, in particular, are subject to less First Amendment scrutiny than constraints on the expression of the press or public in general.[71] Chief Justice Rehnquist, writing for a majority, said lawyers' speech may be restricted more than that of the public and press because attorneys have special access to information about judicial proceedings and the discovery process and lawyers' out-of-court statements could threaten the fairness of proceedings because the public is likely to consider lawyers' statements "especially authoritative."

Restrictive orders prohibiting trial participants, and particularly lawyers, from providing information to the press take a variety of forms. They can ban all, or only some, of the persons involved in a trial from discussing a case with journalists. They can prohibit giving the media specific kinds of information or any information at all. In February 2019, federal judge Amy Berman Jackson ordered Roger Stone, charged with lying, obstruction of justice and witness tampering stemming from Robert Mueller's investigation of Russian interference in the 2016 presidential election, to cease any public speech about the investigation, the case or any of the participants. Jackson initially ordered Stone not to talk about the case when entering or exiting the courthouse[72] but modified the gag order after Stone posted a threatening message about Jackson on Instagram and attacked Mueller in a variety of forums. Jackson concluded Stone's statements posed a substantial risk to the administration of justice. Preventing Stone from making "incendiary and threatening" comments was the least restrictive means possible to assure the safety of the people associated with the case.[73] In July 2019, Judge Jackson found Stone had repeatedly violated the order through social media posts designed "to gin up" more controversy about the legitimacy of the Mueller investigation. Jackson issued a blanket ban on Stone's use of social media during the pendency of the case. Stone's appeal of Jackson's order was dismissed by the D.C. Court of Appeals because Stone had failed to file a timely appeal.[74] After a jury convicted Stone on all charges, he was sentenced to three years and four months in jail. At Stone's sentencing hearing in February 2020, Judge Jackson announced that Stone's repeated and willful violation of the gag order and threatening behavior toward the court were factors in determining his sentence. Jackson said Stone "knew exactly what he was doing" as he violated the gag order.

A restrictive order is likely to be overturned if an appellate court decides that the trial judge did not consider alternatives to the order and the order was broader than necessary to protect the rights of a defendant. For example, a federal district court in Connecticut overturned a state court's order prohibiting attorneys from making "any public statement" to the press during a sensational chain-saw murder

---

[70] *See* Criminal Justice Standards Committee of the American Bar Association, *ABA Standards for Criminal Justice: Fair Trial and Free Press* (3rd ed. 1992); Revised Report of the Judicial Conference Committee on the Operation of the Jury System on the "Free Press-Fair Trial" Issue, 87 F.R.D. 519 (1980).
[71] 501 U.S. 1030 (1991).
[72] Order, United States v. Stone, No. 19-CR-018 (D.D.C, Feb. 15, 2019).
[73] Transcript of Hearing, United States v. Stone, No. 19-CR-018 (D.D.C. Feb. 21, 2019).
[74] *In re* Roger Stone, No. 19–3054 (D.C. Cir. Oct. 22, 2019).

ILLUSTRATION 10.3   In this sketch by renowned courtroom sketch artist Art Lien, Assistant U.S. Attorney Jonathan Kravis delivers the government's closing argument at the November 2019 trial of self-proclaimed "dirty trickster" Roger Stone. Judge Jackson issued multiple gag orders prohibiting Stone from making prejudicial comments about the trial. After Stone posted comments threatening the judge, Jackson ordered Stone to cease all use of social media. Stone's violation of the gag orders was a factor in Jackson's decision to sentence Stone to 40 months in prison.

Source: Copyright 2019 Art Lien. Used with permission.

trial. Richard Crafts was accused of cutting up his wife with a chain saw, then putting her body through a wood-chipping machine. The federal court acknowledged that because of the extensive media coverage the case had already received, trial judge Howard Moraghan "could reasonably conclude" that further publicity might endanger the defendant's right to a fair trial. However, the federal court declared the restrictive order unconstitutionally overbroad because it prohibited "any" statements by lawyers about the case rather than only those statements that might "reasonably" be prejudicial. In addition, the federal court said, gag orders must be accompanied by evidence that a judge had considered alternatives to restricting the speech of the attorneys, such as sequestering the jury.[75]

Appellate courts are more likely to overturn restrictions on participants' speech in civil trials and after legal proceedings are concluded. In 1990, the U.S. Supreme Court found unconstitutional a Florida law that punished grand jury witnesses who disclosed their own grand jury testimony. In *Butterworth v. Smith*, Michael Smith, a reporter for the *Charlotte Herald-News*, wanted to include in a news story or book his own testimony before a special grand jury investigating the Charlotte County State Attorney's Office and Sheriff's Department.[76] Smith was called to testify after writing news stories about alleged misconduct relevant to the

---

[75] Connecticut Magazine v. Moraghan, 676 F. Supp. 38 (D.C. Conn. 1987).
[76] 494 U.S. 624 (1990).

grand jury's investigation. The prosecutor conducting the grand jury investigation warned Smith that he could be prosecuted under Florida law if he revealed any of his testimony. When the grand jury concluded its investigation, Smith claimed a First Amendment right to publish his own testimony. The state of Florida argued in part that grand jury testimony should remain secret so that persons exonerated by grand juries would not be held up to ridicule, witnesses would not fear retribution and persons about to be indicted would not flee.

The U.S. Supreme Court held unanimously that the First Amendment protects the right of grand jury witnesses to publish their own testimony once the term of a grand jury ends. The majority opinion, written by Chief Justice Rehnquist, said the Florida statute was unconstitutional because it provided for the punishment of speech central to First Amendment values. Rehnquist noted that under the Florida ban on discussion of grand jury testimony, critics of government could be silenced by calling them before grand juries. The Court did not decide whether grand jury witnesses could publish their own testimony while a grand jury is still sitting or discuss what they had learned about the grand jury proceedings from being a witness, such as the scope and details of the investigation.

▋ SUMMARY ▋

Judicial orders restricting officers of the court and others involved in a case from talking to the press were widely encouraged in the late 1960s. Court orders restricting witnesses, law enforcement officers, lawyers and litigants are usually upheld by appellate courts if the trial judge decides there is a reasonable likelihood that the jury may otherwise be biased, and the judge has considered alternatives.

Restraints Imposed on the Media

Although Justice Clark, in *Sheppard v. Maxwell*, authorized restraints on trial participants' contacts with the news media, Clark said the Supreme Court had not authorized restricting press reports of proceedings in open court.

The Supreme Court's prohibition of prior restraints directed at the news media in criminal proceedings might seem curious considering the Court's tolerance of restrictive orders on news sources such as lawyers, witnesses and law enforcement officers. But the Court frequently draws a line between restricting press access to information and prior restraint, saying that although the First Amendment does not give reporters an absolute right to acquire information, it creates an almost insurmountable bar to prior restraints once material is in the hands of the press.[77]

Protection of the media's right to publish information about criminal proceedings was reinforced in 1976 when five Supreme Court justices said they were not likely to tolerate prior restraints on the news media to stop prejudicial pretrial publicity. In *Nebraska Press Association v. Stuart*, the Court held that a Nebraska court's restrictions on the reporting of a murder investigation and subsequent legal proceedings violated the First Amendment.[78]

The case began with a mass murder in the tiny prairie town of Sutherland, Nebraska, on the night of October 18, 1975. The 850 town residents were told to stay off the streets and to be careful who they admitted to their homes after six members of the Henry Kellie family had been killed. The next day, a neighbor of

---

[77] *See, e.g.,* Pell v. Procunier, 417 U.S. 817 (1974).
[78] 427 U.S. 539 (1976).

the murdered family, 30-year-old Erwin Charles Simants, confessed to law enforcement officers. Simants, charged with six counts of premeditated murder, immediately became the focus of nationwide news coverage.

After four days of publicity, County Judge Ronald Ruff issued an order prohibiting the publication of news obtained during public pretrial proceedings. Members of the press also were ordered to observe supposedly voluntary Nebraska Bar-Press Guidelines. The guidelines, agreed to by representatives of the state bar and news media, discouraged the reporting of prejudicial material such as confessions. Ruff's order, upheld by District Judge Hugh Stuart, was intended to suppress publication of Simants's confession, statements he had made to relatives and the results of medical tests related to a sexual assault. The Nebraska Supreme Court upheld the key elements of the Stuart order. Simants was convicted of first-degree murder in January 1976.

Five months later, a unanimous U.S. Supreme Court said the Nebraska court order barring publication of Simants's confession and other information about the case was unconstitutional. Chief Justice Burger, who wrote for five of the nine justices, did not say that prior restraints could never be imposed to protect the rights of a defendant. However, he said, anyone wishing to restrain the media would have the "heavy burden" of demonstrating that a fair trial would not be possible without prior restraint. He said a prior restraint on publication was "one of the most extraordinary remedies known to our jurisprudence" and should be difficult to obtain.

To determine whether a prior restraint was warranted in the Simants case, Burger applied a form of the clear-and-present-danger test, discussed in Chapter 2. Burger looked at three factors:

1. the nature and extent of pretrial news coverage
2. whether other measures would likely mitigate the effects of unrestrained pretrial publicity
3. the effectiveness of a restrictive order in diminishing the effect of prejudicial publicity

Considering the first factor, Burger affirmed trial judge Ronald Ruff's judgment that there would be "intense and pervasive" pretrial publicity that might impair the defendant's right to a fair trial. However, Burger noted that Ruff found only that the publicity could *possibly* have constituted a clear and present danger to a fair trial. Burger said Ruff's conclusion was necessarily speculative because the judge was dealing with factors "unknown and unknowable." Burger seemed to suggest that it might be impossible to prove that pretrial publicity would lead to a prejudiced jury and thus impossible to meet the burden of proof necessary to justify a prior restraint.

Second, Burger said Ruff had not indicated whether alternatives to prior restraint would have protected Simants. Ruff had not said that remedies such as a change of venue or voir dire would have failed to protect a fair trial. Nor had Ruff closed the courtroom, an alternative that Burger implicitly approved in his opinion.

Finally, Burger said, it was not clear that a prior restraint on publication would have halted pretrial publicity in Sutherland. In a town of 850, word of mouth could be more damaging than news media accounts, Burger said. In addition, by law, Judge Ruff could legally try to limit the publicity only within the county. As a county judge, he did not have jurisdiction over network television news and the national wire services.

Although Burger imposed a form of the clear-and-present-danger test on defendants who want to restrain the press, at least three of the Court's justices would have provided even greater protection for the press. Justice Brennan, who had concurred only in the judgment in the case, said in a separate opinion that prior restraint could never be permitted to ensure a fair trial. Justices Stewart and Marshall joined in Brennan's concurring opinion. In addition, Justices White and Stevens indicated in separate concurring opinions that they might eventually agree to Brennan's absolutist approach.

A year after the Supreme Court's decision in *Nebraska Press Association*, the Court affirmed its reluctance to allow prior restraints on court coverage. In *Oklahoma Publishing Co. v. District Court*, a trial judge had allowed the press to attend the detention hearing of an 11-year-old boy who had been arrested for the murder of a railroad switchman.[79] A few days later, the judge prohibited the media from publishing the boy's name, obtained during the open hearing, and a picture, taken immediately afterward without any objections. The Supreme Court noted that, by statute, juvenile proceedings in Oklahoma were private unless explicitly ordered open. However, the Court said in a per curiam opinion that because the press was permitted to attend the hearing, an order to prohibit the publication of information and pictures obtained there was unconstitutional.

The *Nebraska Press Association* decision has largely meant that prior restraints on court coverage have not been allowed by lower courts. For example, in 2005 the Court of Appeals for the Second Circuit ruled unconstitutional a judge's order barring publication of the names of potential jurors in the trial of Wall Street figure Frank Quattrone.[80] Shortly before Quattrone's trial in April 2004, a state court judge declared a mistrial in the separate prosecution of Dennis Kozlowski, a former high-profile executive of Tyco Corporation. Near the close of Kozlowski's fraud trial, the *Wall Street Journal* and other publications published the name of a juror who in court flashed an apparent O.K. sign to Kozlowski. Soon after, the juror received a frightening letter, and the state court judge declared a mistrial.[81] Jury selection began in the Quattrone case less than two weeks later.

To avoid a mistrial, federal district judge Richard Owen ordered the press not to disclose the names of prospective jurors in the Quattrone case, even though the names were stated in open court. The court of appeals held the order unconstitutional because it failed to meet the standards of *Nebraska Press Association*. First, Owen did not make factual findings that publicity would harm Quattrone's right to a fair trial. Owen based his order solely on the incidents in the Kozlowski trial, and the appellate court held that a prior restraint may not be based on incidents that occurred in a separate and unrelated trial. Second, the record did not demonstrate that Owen had sufficiently considered measures other than a prior restraint. Finally, the appellate court held the ban to be ineffective because it did not prevent members of the public from disseminating the jurors' names.

In 1984, the Supreme Court in *Seattle Times Co. v. Rhinehart* approved an exception to its virtual ban of prior restraints on journalists, an exception triggered when media personnel obtain information because they are participants in a lawsuit.[82] The *Seattle Times* and the *Walla Walla Union-Bulletin* had been sued for defamation by Keith Rhinehart, the leader of a religious group called the Aquarian Foundation. During the pretrial discovery process, the newspapers questioned

---

[79] 430 U.S. 308 (1977).
[80] United States v. Quattrone, 402 F.3d 304 (2d Cir. 2005).
[81] *See* Jess Bravin and Kara Scannell, "Behind the Tyco Mistrial," *Wall St. J.*, Apr. 5, 2004, at B1; Andrew Ross Sorkin, "No O.K. Sign and No Guilty Vote by Juror No. 4," *N.Y. Times*, Apr. 7, 2004, at A1.
[82] 467 U.S. 20 (1984).

whether the foundation had been damaged by its reporting and asked the judge to order the foundation to reveal the names of its members and donors for the previous ten years to determine whether donations declined after the stories. The foundation countered that such an order would violate the First Amendment rights of members and donors to privacy, freedom of association and freedom of religion.

The trial court judge ordered the Aquarian Foundation to provide the names of members and donors but prohibited the newspapers from publishing the information. The newspapers appealed the restriction on publication, but the order was upheld by a unanimous U.S. Supreme Court. Justice Powell, writing the Court's opinion, said the restraint on publication inherent in the trial court's order was not the "classic prior restraint that requires exacting First Amendment scrutiny." Although the order prohibited publication of information obtained through discovery, the same information could be published if acquired in another way, Powell said.

The Court said *Rhinehart* was not a classic prior restraint case, thus the restraint was permissible if supported by a "substantial" interest. The Court concluded the state's interest, preventing information acquired during discovery from being used for other potentially harmful purposes, was "substantial." Legal rules requiring litigants to reveal any information relevant to a suit, the Court said, force trial participants to provide material that may damage an individual's privacy or reputation if published. The Supreme Court accepted the findings of lower courts that the publication of the names of Aquarian Foundation members and donors could lead to adverse consequences for those individuals.

■ SUMMARY ■

The Supreme Court, in *Nebraska Press Association v. Stuart*, said that prior restraints on publication to protect the right to a fair trial are ordinarily unconstitutional. The Court said that before trial judges issue prior restraint orders, they must consider the nature and extent of pretrial news coverage, alternative measures to protect Sixth Amendment rights and whether a prior restraint order would be effective. However, the Court has approved a prior restraint order in a case in which newspapers obtained information only because they were parties in a lawsuit.

PUNISHMENT AFTER PUBLICATION

The Supreme Court, in addition to holding that it is ordinarily unconstitutional to prevent the publication of news about court proceedings, has also ruled it unconstitutional to punish the media after publication of lawfully acquired news about the judicial system. In two cases, the U.S. Supreme Court ruled unanimously that government could not punish the media for truthful news stories about the judiciary or the criminal justice system absent a compelling government need.

In *Landmark Communications v. Virginia*, the Court said the state could not punish a newspaper for printing information about a confidential judicial inquiry.[83] The case arose in 1975 when the *Virginian Pilot*, owned by Landmark Communications, identified a judge who was being investigated by a Virginia commission which reviews complaints about the disability or misconduct of judges. An article in the *Pilot* accurately reported that the commission had not filed a

---

[83] 435 U.S. 829 (1978).

formal complaint against the judge. A month after the article, a grand jury indicted Landmark for divulging the judge's name in violation of state law. A Virginia statute treated dissemination of the confidential information as a misdemeanor. Landmark was found guilty and fined $500.

The Supreme Court of Virginia affirmed the conviction, but the decision was reversed by the U.S. Supreme Court. Chief Justice Burger, writing the Court's opinion, did not discount the need for confidentiality by the judicial review commission. He noted that 47 states, including Virginia, provided for confidential investigations of judicial conduct. Burger said confidentiality protected the credibility of individual judges and the reputation of the judicial system from public disclosure of unsubstantiated complaints.

Burger said accurate reporting of the conduct of public officials "lies near the core of the First Amendment." He said the article published by the *Virginian Pilot* "clearly served those interests in public scrutiny and discussion of governmental affairs which the First Amendment was adopted to protect." Before discussion of the court system can be punished, Burger said, the danger to the administration of justice "must be extremely serious and the degree of imminence extremely high before utterances can be punished."

In contrast, Burger said, Virginia's interest in protecting both the reputation of individual judges and respect for the judicial system did not justify the encroachment on the freedom of the press. Virginia argued that the state's effort to protect confidentiality encourages complainants, witnesses, and judges to take part in the investigations. But Burger noted that only 2 of the 47 states with review boards punished breaches of confidentiality by criminal sanction. In addition, Burger said, the Court had established in libel cases that it would not repress speech that damaged public officials' reputations. States were free to punish participants for breach of confidentiality, but non-parties such as the press were free to disseminate lawfully acquired information.

A year later, the Supreme Court held the state of West Virginia could not punish the *Charleston Daily Mail* and the *Charleston Daily Gazette* for printing the name of a juvenile defendant. The two papers identified a 14-year-old who shot and killed a classmate at a junior high school in St. Albans, a small community outside Charleston. Reporters obtained the name by asking witnesses, the police and an assistant prosecuting attorney at the scene of the incident. A grand jury indicted the two newspapers for violating a West Virginia law prohibiting newspapers from publishing the names of youths charged as juvenile offenders. Under the law, newspapers, but not broadcast stations, could be fined $100 and editors and reporters jailed for up to six months. The West Virginia Supreme Court prohibited county officials from acting on the indictment, and the U.S. Supreme Court, in *Smith v. Daily Mail Publishing Co.*, upheld that judgment.[84]

The U.S. Supreme Court said a state could punish "truthful information about a matter of public significance" only "to further a need of the highest order." The Court's majority opinion acknowledged the validity of West Virginia's interest in facilitating the rehabilitation of youthful offenders by protecting their anonymity. However, the Court said, the state's interest in anonymity was not sufficient to overcome the First Amendment right to publish. The Court noted that every state protected the anonymity of juveniles, but 45 of the 50 accomplished that objective without criminal penalties on nonparties. Moreover, the Court said, the statute

---

[84] 443 U.S. 97 (1979).

was unconstitutional because it restricted only newspapers and not the electronic media, thus failing to protect the identity of juveniles. Three radio stations had also revealed the name of the 14-year-old St. Albans youth who killed his classmate, but none of the stations could be prosecuted under the West Virginia law.

■ SUMMARY ■

The Supreme Court has held the First Amendment ordinarily prohibits punishment of the press for the publication of news stories about judicial proceedings. Absent a compelling governmental interest or an extremely serious and imminent threat to the administration of justice, states cannot punish the media for publishing truthful information that is lawfully acquired.

ACCESS TO COURTROOMS, RECORDS AND JURORS

After the Supreme Court demonstrated in 1976 and 1977 its intolerance for prior restraints on publication, some trial court judges, drawing on Justice Burger's suggestion in *Nebraska Press Association* that courtrooms be closed to ensure a fair trial, did so to prevent reporters from acquiring information that could prejudice the outcome of a trial. Indeed, the Supreme Court seemed to sanction court closures in 1979 when it ruled that the press and the public did not have a constitutional right to attend pretrial hearings. In the 1980s, however, the Supreme Court reversed direction and held that the public and the press have a qualified First Amendment right of access to trials and the jury selection process as well as to pretrial hearings.

Trials

The Supreme Court first ruled in 1980 that the press and the public have a constitutional right of access to courtrooms. In *Richmond Newspapers v. Virginia*, seven justices agreed the public has a limited First Amendment right to attend criminal trials.[85] *Richmond Newspapers* marked the first time the Supreme Court has held that the public has a First Amendment right to observe government proceedings and records.

Richmond Newspapers arose from a series of circumstances that understandably could frustrate a judge. In July 1976, John Stevenson was convicted of the murder of a hotel manager. A few months later, the Virginia Supreme Court overturned the conviction, holding that a bloodstained shirt had been improperly admitted into evidence. A second trial ended in a mistrial in May 1978 when a juror asked to be excused and no alternate juror was available. Stevenson's third trial, in June 1978, also ended in a mistrial when one prospective juror told others about the history of the case.

Before the beginning of the fourth trial, still in 1978, Judge Richard H.C. Taylor closed the trial at the request of the defense. Richmond Newspapers, the corporate parent of the *Richmond Times-Dispatch* and the *Richmond News-Leader*, unsuccessfully protested the closure. Stevenson was found not guilty after a closed trial. Richmond Newspapers' post-trial appeal of the closure was denied by the Virginia Supreme Court, but the U.S. Supreme Court granted certiorari.

Although a majority of the Court agreed that the Virginia closure order violated the public's right to an open trial, the Court was otherwise divided. No more

---

[85] 448 U.S. 555 (1980).

than three justices agreed to join any one opinion. Chief Justice Burger, writing the opinion for the Court, said that although the First Amendment does not explicitly mention a public right to attend criminal trials, such a right is implied. The rights specifically guaranteed in the First Amendment, Burger said, such as freedom of speech and press, the right to assemble peaceably and the right to petition the government for a redress of grievances, ensure free communication about government. "Plainly it would be difficult to single out any aspect of government of higher concern and importance to the people than the manner in which criminal trials are conducted," he added.

Burger said the Bill of Rights was enacted after a long tradition of openness in the Anglo-American judicial system, a tradition based on the indispensable role public trials play in the criminal justice system. Burger, supported only by Justices White and Stevens, said criminal trials have been open "to all who cared to observe" since before the Norman Conquest of England. Public trials inspire public confidence in the fairness of the criminal justice process. In addition, public trials allow the public to see "justice done," helping to defuse community outrage after major crimes.

For Burger, freedom of the press "could be eviscerated" without some protection for gathering news. Although Burger emphasized the First Amendment right to attend trials belongs to the public as a whole and not specifically to the press, he also said that the press often acts as a surrogate for the public, informing people about court activity.

Burger based the right of access to courts not only on the First Amendment right of the public to have information about the courts but also on an expansive interpretation of the First Amendment right to assemble. Burger said that trial courtrooms—like public streets, sidewalks and parks—are public places where the public and representatives of the media have a right to exercise their First Amendment rights. People assemble in public places, Burger said, "not only to speak or to take action, but also to listen, observe, and learn." He added that people exercising their First Amendment right to be present in a courtroom historically have been thought to enhance "the integrity and quality of what takes place."

Because the press and the public have a constitutional right to attend court, Burger said, the trial in a criminal case can be closed only if the state interest in a fair trial overrides the rights of the press and public to attend. Burger criticized Judge Taylor in the *Stevenson* case for failing to explain the need for closure. Burger said, "No inquiry was made as to whether alternative solutions would have met the need to ensure fairness; there was no recognition of any right under the Constitution for the public or press to attend the trial."

Burger did not explain what circumstances and evidence would demonstrate the "overriding interest" that would justify closing the court. In a separate opinion, though, Justice Stewart suggested that courts might be closed to protect trade secrets or youthful rape victims. Justice Brennan, in a separate opinion joined by Justice Marshall, said that national security might warrant closure.

Just two years after the Court decided *Richmond Newspapers*, a 6–3 majority affirmed the Court's commitment to public trials. In 1982, in *Globe Newspaper Co. v. Superior Court*, five justices said states could not require that courts be closed routinely during the testimony of minors in sex offense cases.[86] The Court's opinion said closure could be based only on a "compelling" need in individual cases and could last no longer than necessary.

---

[86] 457 U.S. 596 (1982).

In *Globe Newspaper Co.*, a Massachusetts statute provided that a judge "shall exclude the general public from the courtroom" during a criminal trial "for rape, incest, carnal abuse," or other sex-related crimes when the complainant was less than 18 years old. Relying on the statute, a trial court judge in Norfolk County ordered a rape trial closed in 1979. When the Supreme Judicial Court of Massachusetts dismissed an appeal by the *Boston Globe*, the U.S. Supreme Court granted certiorari.

The state defended closed courtrooms to protect young complainants of sex crimes from further trauma and embarrassment. Justice Brennan, writing for the Court, said that as compelling as that interest was, it did not justify mandatory closure. Rather, he said, the need for closure must be made on a case-by-case basis; the need for closure would depend on the minor's age and psychological maturity, the nature of the crime and the need for the testimony. Brennan said the court should not be closed if the names of the minors were already in the public record or if the minors indicated they were willing to testify in the presence of the press.

The decision in *Globe Newspaper Co.* has generally not affected state efforts to keep juvenile proceedings closed. In *Globe*, the Court said the state may not automatically close the trial of an adult when juvenile witnesses may be called. But the Court did not say that all juvenile proceedings are presumptively open. In fact, juvenile proceedings are presumptively closed to the public in most of the states.[87] States often avoid prosecuting youths in open court as part of an effort to avoid stigmatizing them for life as criminals. The Supreme Court has not ruled that closing courts during juvenile proceedings violates the First Amendment rights of the public and press.[88]

Opponents of closed juvenile justice proceedings say public access to ensure against abuse is as important in the juvenile justice system as it is in adult courts. Indeed, many observers question whether youths who are arrested for violent crimes and repeat offenders should not be treated as adults.

Several state appellate courts have affirmed trial court decisions to open juvenile proceedings to the public. In Ohio, the supreme court said state law allows trial judges to admit the public. The Ohio Supreme Court said a juvenile court judge did not abuse his discretion when he opened a hearing held to consider whether two juveniles should be tried as adults. The juveniles, arrested on charges of murder, argued that their Sixth Amendment rights to a fair trial would be jeopardized if evidence presented in an open hearing was ruled inadmissible during their trial. However, the juvenile court judge said the public's First Amendment right to attend trials includes juvenile proceedings. He said the juveniles had not demonstrated that closing the hearing was necessary to protect their Sixth Amendment rights.[89]

Some federal courts have also noted the value of openness in juvenile proceedings. In 1994, a federal appellate court ruled that the Juvenile Delinquency Act[90] does not require that federal juvenile hearings be closed to the press and public.[91] The U.S. Court of Appeals for the Third Circuit held that judges may decide on a case-by-case basis whether to grant access to juvenile proceedings. The case arose when the *Pittsburgh Post-Gazette* sought access to the detention

---

[87] *See, e.g.,* Ala. Code § 12-15-129.

[88] For an argument favoring opening juvenile proceedings, see Joshua Dalton, "At the Crossroads of *Richmond* and *Gault:* Addressing Media Access to Juvenile Delinquency Proceedings Through a Functional Analysis," 28 *Seton Hall L. Rev.* 1155 (1998).

[89] Ohio *ex rel.* Fyffe v. Pierce, 531 N.E.2d 673 (1988).

[90] 18 U.S.C. §§ 5031–5042.

[91] United States v. A.D., 28 F.3d 1353 (3d Cir. 1994). *See also* United States v. Doe, 22 Media L. Rep. 1693 (E.D. Wis. 1994).

hearing of two juveniles arrested in connection with gang-related armed robberies. After being denied access, the newspaper appealed to the Third Circuit.

The parties to the case disputed the meaning of key sections of the Juvenile Delinquency Act, one section of which suggested that judges had discretion to hold juvenile hearings in open court or in chambers. The appeals court, noting the many civic advantages of open trials pointed out in the *Richmond Newspapers* case, reasoned that mandatory closure of juvenile hearings was unconstitutional. Instead, the Third Circuit ruled that the judge in each case should balance the public interest in openness against the interests of the juvenile, including the harm to rehabilitation that publicity might cause. The appeals court stated that judges who close juvenile proceedings must provide "factual findings related to the circumstances of this particular case" that warrant closure.

If the Supreme Court has not declared that juvenile proceedings must be open to the public, neither has it said that civil trials must be open to the public. However, Chief Justice Burger noted in *Richmond Newspapers* that both civil and criminal trials have historically been presumed to be open.

Civil court cases can often be more important to the public than the prosecution of individual criminals. Civil trials often involve such issues as discrimination, voting rights, antitrust, government regulation and bankruptcy. They also often involve the dangers of cigarettes, drugs, automobiles and chemical-processing plants. Consequently, appellate courts in the post-*Richmond Newspapers* era have recognized a First Amendment right of access to civil trials. The same policy considerations for keeping criminal trials open, such as allowing the public to check for government abuse and fostering public respect for the judicial process, apply to civil courts. Appeals courts often require judges to demonstrate a compelling need before closing civil hearings or trials. Judges must also show a potential for harm to litigants or persons not party to a case and severely limit the closure.

PROTESTING COURT CLOSURES

If a motion is made to close a court proceeding, you should raise your hand, stand and say:

Your honor, I am (your name), a reporter for (your news organization). I respectfully request the opportunity to register on the record an objection to the motion to close this proceeding to the public, including the media. Our legal counsel has advised us that standards set forth in state and federal court decisions give us the opportunity for a hearing before the courtroom is closed. These rulings require judges to demonstrate a compelling need before closing both civil and criminal hearings or trials. Judges must show a potential for harm to litigants or persons not party to a case before they close a court proceeding, and limit closure to only that which is necessary to mitigate such harm. I respectfully request such a hearing and a brief continuance so our counsel may be present to make the appropriate arguments. Thank you.

FIGURE 10.1 This is a sample statement journalists often read to judges if a motion is made to close a court proceeding. A legal confrontation with judges over courtroom closure can often be avoided if journalists ask judges before court proceedings that their media organizations be allowed to challenge motions for closure. Many media lawyers recommend that reporters call their editors as soon as possible after the issue of closure is raised so that editors have the option of calling an attorney. This sample statement is provided by the First Amendment Foundation, Tallahassee, Florida.

In late 2013, in *Delaware Coalition for Open Government v. Strine*, the Court of Appeals for the Third Circuit held that Delaware's government-sponsored arbitration proceedings were essentially civil trials that must be open to the public.[92] To preserve its preeminence as a business-friendly legal environment, Delaware created an arbitration process as an alternative to trial for certain kinds of business disputes. Like private arbitration, Delaware's proceedings were closed to the public. Unlike private arbitration, however, which takes place before private arbitrators in private venues, Delaware's government-sponsored arbitration proceedings took place before judges in courthouses and resulted in binding judicial orders. The Third Circuit observed:

> Delaware's proceedings derive a great deal of legitimacy and authority from the state. They would be far less attractive without their association with the state. Therefore, the interests of the state and the public in openness must be given weight, not just the interests of rich businesspersons in confidentiality.

The First Amendment right of access mandated that the proceedings be open to the public, the appellate court stated. The Supreme Court denied certiorari in 2014.

Jury Selection

A unanimous Supreme Court declared that the selection of the jury, as well as the trial itself, must ordinarily be open to the public. In fact, in the first of two closed-courtroom cases named *Press-Enterprise Co. v. Riverside County Superior Court*, the Court treated jury selection as part of the trial.[93] The Court said that public confidence in the criminal justice system derives in part from public access to the questioning of potential jurors. Public confidence in the courts generally should be given priority over undocumented concerns about the right to a fair trial for the defendant or violations of the privacy of citizens asked to be jurors, the Court said.

In what is known as *Press-Enterprise I*, the Press-Enterprise Company of Riverside, California, successfully appealed the closing of jury selection before the trial of Albert Greenwood Brown Jr, who had been charged with the rape and murder of a teenage girl in California. The judge refused to allow the voir dire examination of jurors to be open to the public and the press to protect Brown's right to a fair trial and the privacy rights of jurors. After a voir dire lasting six weeks, all but three days of which were closed to the press, the judge also refused to release the transcripts of the questioning. California appellate courts refused to review the case, but the U.S. Supreme Court vacated the judge's order and remanded the case for further consideration.

Chief Justice Burger, writing for eight of the nine justices, said the process of jury selection has been presumptively open to the public since the development of trial by jury. Burger contended the selection of jurors has always been an integral part of the public trial. Although Burger said, "no right ranks higher than the right

---

[92] 733 F.3d 510 (3d Cir. 2013). Every federal court of appeals to consider the issue of public access to civil trials has found there is a First Amendment right of access. *See, e.g.*, FTC v. Standard Fin. Mgmt. Corp., 830 F.2d 4040 (1st Cir. 1987); Brown & Williamson Tobacco Corp. v. FTC, 710 F.2d 1165 (6th Cir. 1983).
[93] 464 U.S. 501, 508 (1984). *See also* ABC, Inc. v. Stewart, 360 F.3d 90 (2d Cir. 2004) (closure of voir dire was invalid).

of the accused to a fair trial," he contended the right of the accused and the right of the public to attend the voir dire were closely connected. Burger said:

> The value of openness lies in the fact that people not actually attending trials can have confidence that standards of fairness are being observed; the sure knowledge that *anyone* is free to attend gives assurance that established procedures are being followed and that deviations will become known.

To overcome the presumption that jury selection must be open, Burger said, a judge first must specify an overriding interest, such as the defendant's right to a fair trial or jurors' rights to privacy. Second, the judge must establish that the overriding interest cannot effectively be protected except through closure. For example, Burger said, a judge may decide that closure is the only way to protect the privacy of a prospective juror who, during the voir dire, is asked whether he or she has ever been sexually assaulted. Third, the judge must document in writing why closure is essential to protect a "higher value." That is, the judge will need to explain why the answer of the prospective juror is entitled to privacy. Fourth, the closure can last only as long as necessary to meet the needs of the single juror. Burger said the California trial judge in *Press-Enterprise I* had not supported his closure order by findings that either Brown's right to a fair trial or the privacy of the jurors was threatened by questioning the jurors in public.

The Supreme Court in 2010 again emphasized the importance of public jury selection by holding that a defendant's Sixth Amendment right to a public trial was violated when a Georgia trial court closed jury selection proceedings without considering alternatives to closure.[94] Because the case was brought by a criminal defendant, rather than the press, the Court considered the challenge under the Sixth Amendment, which "was created for the benefit of the defendant." In the context of jury selection, a criminal defendant's assertion of a Sixth Amendment right of openness was no less important than assertion of a First Amendment right of access by the press. "Trial courts are obligated to take every reasonable measure to accommodate public attendance at criminal trials," the Court concluded.

Pretrial Hearings

Since 1984, the Supreme Court has extended a First Amendment right of access to hearings held before the trial begins. Although pretrial hearings are not technically part of trials, they often take on the significance of trials. Legal authorities contend that 90 percent of criminal cases never reach the trial stage, often because they are resolved because of pretrial hearings. Consequently, a pretrial hearing often presents the only opportunity for a public proceeding in a criminal case.

Pretrial hearings are often held to determine whether there is enough evidence for a judge to find "probable cause" that a defendant committed a crime. Judges may also hold pretrial hearings to consider whether potential evidence, such as a confession or a weapon, may be presented to a jury during a trial. Judges also hold hearings to consider whether bail should be denied, or the courtroom closed.

If a pretrial hearing is reported in the media, potential jurors can read about, and perhaps be influenced by, information such as a confession that might not be

---

[94] Presley v. Georgia, 558 U.S. 209 (2010).

admissible as evidence during a trial. Because jurors are not selected until a case comes to trial, judges cannot sequester them or order them not to read or listen to news reports about pretrial hearings.

In the early 1980s, trial courts were reluctant to open pretrial hearings to the public, in part because of a 1979 U.S. Supreme Court decision. In 1979, before recognizing a First Amendment access to courtrooms, the Court said in *Gannett Co. v. DePasquale* that the press and public do not have a right to attend pretrial hearings.[95] Only one year after *Gannett*, the Supreme Court ruled in *Richmond Newspapers* that trials are presumptively open under the First Amendment. However, the Court did not overrule *Gannett* in *Richmond Newspapers, Globe Newspaper Co.* or *Press-Enterprise I*. In 1986, the Court ruled in *Press-Enterprise II* that the public and the press have a First Amendment right to attend pretrial hearings held to determine whether there is probable cause to believe a suspect has committed a crime. Although the Supreme Court did not directly overrule *Gannett* in *Press-Enterprise II*, the Court's reliance on the First Amendment right of access cast considerable doubt on *Gannett*'s continued validity.[96]

In *Press-Enterprise II*, a magistrate in Riverside, California, excluded the press from a preliminary hearing scheduled to determine whether there was probable cause that nurse Robert Dias had murdered a dozen hospital patients with massive doses of the heart drug lidocaine. The magistrate said closure was necessary because Diaz's case had attracted national publicity and "only one side may get reported in the media." After a 41-day hearing, the magistrate ordered a trial because he determined there was probable cause to believe that Diaz committed the murders. The magistrate refused to release transcripts of the hearing.

The California Supreme Court, upholding the magistrate's order to close the courtroom, said that defendants must demonstrate only a "reasonable likelihood" that a public hearing would prejudice their right to a fair trial. However, the U.S. Supreme Court, by a 7–2 margin, said the First Amendment requires that defendants seeking to close pretrial hearings must demonstrate a greater danger to their rights than a "reasonable likelihood."[97] Instead, the Court said, defendants must provide specific evidence that an open courtroom would present a "substantial probability" of endangering their rights to a fair trial. In addition, echoing *Press-Enterprise I*, the Supreme Court said judges must consider whether alternatives to closure could protect the rights of the defendant. Further, closure must be for only as short a time as necessary to ensure a fair trial.

Chief Justice Burger, again writing for the Court, said the public ought to have access to pretrial hearings for the same reasons that access is important for criminal trials and jury selection. In what has become known as the "experience and logic" test, Burger said a First Amendment right of access would be determined by asking (1) "whether the place and process have historically been open to the press and general public" and (2) "whether public access plays a significant positive role in the functioning of the particular process in question." Burger concluded that there had been a tradition of accessibility to preliminary hearings. He added that access had a positive role; the attendance of the public and the press at open hearings is important because, unlike a trial, there is no jury to guard against the "corrupt or overzealous prosecutor" and "the compliant, biased, or eccentric judge."

---

[95] 443 U.S. 368 (1979).
[96] *See also* El Vocero de Puerto Rico v. Puerto Rico, 508 U.S. 147 (1993) (per curiam).
[97] 478 U.S. 1 (1986).

However, as forcefully as the Supreme Court emphasized the importance of access in *Press-Enterprise II* and the other decisions, the Court will not stop all court closures. Trial judges can constitutionally close courts if they can document an overriding interest that cannot be protected by alternative means and if they can narrowly restrict the closure as required in the *Press-Enterprise* cases.

In addition, the Supreme Court's recent emphasis on the presumption of openness for trials and pretrial hearings does not affect the historic secrecy of grand juries. Because grand juries prepare indictments, rather than determine guilt, they play a different role in the legal system than pretrial hearings and trials. Reports about grand jury proceedings could disseminate unsubstantiated charges and hearsay that might not lead to an indictment. No judge is present in a grand jury hearing to ensure that the evidence sought is relevant to the investigation. Further, those who testify generally do not have the right to counsel or the right to cross-examine others who testify, as they would during pretrial proceedings and trials. In *Press-Enterprise II*, all nine justices supported opinions emphasizing the importance of secrecy for grand jury proceedings.

Consequently, the press has no First Amendment or common-law right of access to judicial hearings or documents connected to grand jury proceedings, said the Court of Appeals for the D.C. Circuit.[98] The court denied media access to grand jury hearings and documents that would reveal grand jury issues or processes in the investigation of President Clinton's relationship to former White House aide Monica Lewinsky.

▧ SUMMARY ▧

In 1980, in *Richmond Newspapers v. Virginia*, the Court said that the public and the press have a First Amendment right to attend trials, which are presumptively open unless the state can document an overriding interest in closure. In *Globe Newspaper Co.*, the Court said that statutes providing for automatic closures are unconstitutional. In *Press-Enterprise I*, the Court said that the First Amendment protects against the closure of the jury selection process. In *Press-Enterprise II*, the Court extended the presumption of openness to pretrial hearings. In the series of courtroom-closure cases, the Court has established that judicial proceedings can ordinarily be closed only for compelling reasons that are carefully substantiated. A judge must consider alternatives to closure and must limit closure to only as long as necessary. Thus far, most courts considering closure have not distinguished between criminal and civil cases. Grand jury proceedings remain closed, however. Juvenile court proceedings, traditionally closed, are sometimes open to the public.

Access to Court Records

Official court records long have been open for inspection and copying by the public and the press under common law. Many appellate courts have said access to records also is guaranteed by the First Amendment. The Supreme Court has not directly established a First Amendment right of access to judicial records, but the *Press-Enterprise* cases establishing a right of access to jury selection and pretrial hearings also included access to sealed transcripts. Chief Justice Burger's majority opinions in both cases assumed the public has the same right of access to the transcripts of the pretrial hearings as it has to the hearings themselves.

---

[98] *In re* Motions of Dow Jones & Co., Inc., 142 F.3d 496 (D.C. Cir.), *cert. denied*, 525 U.S. 820 (1998).

Both state and federal appellate courts usually support a right of access to official court documents, particularly to those used as evidence in court, unless a compelling need for nondisclosure is demonstrated. In a prosecution of automobile maker John DeLorean on charges of conspiring to import cocaine, the U.S. Court of Appeals for the Ninth Circuit said that court records could be sealed only if "strictly and inescapably necessary" to ensure a fair trial for the defendant.[99] The Ninth Circuit said a district court judge had improperly sealed records pertaining to whether DeLorean should be confined before his trial and documents containing allegations of government misconduct during the DeLorean investigation.

The Ninth Circuit said such pretrial documents often are important to a public understanding of the judicial process. The appeals court said the district court failed to satisfy all three of the tests that must be applied before documents could be sealed. First, the judge had not demonstrated there was a substantial probability DeLorean would not receive a fair trial if the documents were released. Second, the judge had not established that alternatives to sealing would inadequately protect DeLorean's rights. Finally, the judge did not demonstrate a substantial probability that sealing would be effective in protecting DeLorean's rights.

Several federal courts have found that the presumption of openness extends to the right of broadcasters to copy tapes used as evidence in court. For example, the U.S. Court of Appeals for the Third Circuit said broadcasters could not be prohibited from copying tapes made during a controversial FBI "sting" operation known as Abscam.[100] Broadcasters sought video and audio tapes played in open court during the bribery trial of two Philadelphia city council members. The Third Circuit said the broader dissemination of information already made public increased the chance that the Abscam trial could provide a catharsis for community hostility and ensure that the defendants were treated fairly by judges and lawyers, goals emphasized in *Richmond Newspapers*.

In contrast, both the Fifth and Sixth Circuits of the U.S. Courts of Appeals turned down requests to copy tapes because of perceived risks to the defendants' Sixth Amendment rights.[101] Both courts relied on *Nixon v. Warner Communications, Inc.*, a 1978 Supreme Court decision that prevented the copying of White House tapes of former president Richard Nixon. In *Nixon*, the Supreme Court held that broadcasters and record companies did not have the right to copy the Nixon tapes for broadcasting and sale to the public. The tapes had been used as evidence at the trials of presidential aides charged with obstructing justice during the Watergate investigation. The Supreme Court acknowledged "a general right to inspect and copy public records and documents" at the discretion of the judge.[102] However, the Court held that the public's common-law right of access had been superseded by congressional action creating a procedure for processing and releasing the tapes to the public.[103] The First Amendment had not been violated because the press had been allowed to listen to the tapes and had been given transcripts during the trial.

---

[99] Associated Press v. U.S. Dist. Court, 705 F.2d 1143 (9th Cir. 1983).
[100] *In re* NBC, 648 F.2d 814 (3d Cir. 1981). *See also In re* Application of NBC [United States v. Myers], 635 F.2d 945 (2d Cir. 1980); United States v. Jenrette, 653 F.2d 609 (D.C. Cir. 1981).
[101] United States v. Beckham, 789 F.2d 401 (6th Cir. 1986); Belo Broadcasting Corp. v. Clark, 654 F.2d 423 (5th Cir. 1981). *See also* Oregon *ex rel.* KOIN-TV, Inc. v. Olsen, 711 P.2d 966 (Or. 1985); United States v. Edwards, 672 F.2d 1289 (7th Cir. 1982).
[102] 435 U.S. 589 (1978).
[103] Presidential Recordings and Materials Preservation Act, Pub. L. No. 93–526, 88 Stat. 1695 (1974).

Federal appeals courts have also been divided on the media's right of access to records that have not been introduced into evidence in court. Many of the conflicts over access to records involve materials used by lawyers during the discovery process in cases that never come to trial. Chapter 1 of this book discussed the discovery process, which allows both parties in a legal dispute to investigate documents and question witnesses that might be material to a case. A court can compel one party to disclose discovery information to the other, sometimes accompanying the order with a confidentiality order guaranteeing that the information will not be made public.

A Supreme Court case involving both compelled discovery and a protective order, *Seattle Times v. Rhinehart*, has strongly influenced lower courts since it was decided in 1984. In *Rhinehart*, discussed earlier in this chapter, the Supreme Court said a trial court did not violate the First Amendment when it prohibited newspapers from publishing information obtained during discovery in a libel suit.

Some courts have found the need to protect values such as privacy overcomes the right of access to discovery documents. In an extraordinary 2015 ruling, however, a Pennsylvania court unsealed discovery documents in a lawsuit brought against entertainer Bill Cosby because Cosby's role as "public moralist" narrowed his zone of privacy. Cosby had been sued in 2005 by Andrea Constand for sexual assault and other torts. In a 2005 deposition, Cosby admitted he had sex with another woman after he gave her Quaaludes and agreed to an exclusive interview with the *National Enquirer* in exchange for the magazine suppressing a story about another woman's sexual assault allegations. The deposition was placed under a temporary seal in 2005, but before the court could rule on a permanent seal, the parties settled.

Ten years later, after more allegations of similar misconduct by Cosby were published, the AP sought to unseal the Constand documents. The court weighed the injuries caused by disclosure against the public's interest in the information. Cosby had voluntarily narrowed his zone of privacy because he thrust himself into public controversies by offering his views on childrearing and family life, the court said. The court concluded, "the stark contrast between Bill Cosby, the public moralist and Bill Cosby, the subject of serious allegations concerning improper (and perhaps criminal) conduct" is a matter of significant public interest.[104]

Many courts have held that discovery documents in both criminal and civil cases cannot automatically be sealed. For example, the U.S. Court of Appeals for the First Circuit has said the federal rules governing civil suits create a presumption that pretrial discovery should take place in public. Therefore, in *Public Citizen v. Liggett Group*, the First Circuit said that documents surrendered in pretrial discovery to the relatives of a lung cancer victim could be made public.[105] The court upheld a lower court decision to release to health associations 18 boxes of research documents prepared by a consultant for Liggett & Meyers Tobacco Company even though a trial was never held.

The First Circuit said federal rules permit the courts to seal pretrial documents in civil suits for "good cause" to protect persons "from annoyance, embarrassment, oppression or undue burden or expense." However, the court said the rules also require that pretrial discovery be public unless compelling reasons justify denying public access. The court noted Liggett & Meyers had not argued that documents

---

[104] Constand v. Cosby, 112 F. Supp. 3d 308 (E.D. Pa. 2015).
[105] 858 F.2d 775 (1988), *cert. denied*, 488 U.S. 1030 (1989).

sought by the health organizations contained trade secrets or other "specifically confidential material" that would have prevented them from being made public.

In 2014, in *Company Doe v. Public Citizen*, the Court of Appeals for the Fourth Circuit issued one of the strongest rulings in favor of a First Amendment right of access to court records.[106] A district court sealed all documents and allowed a company to proceed pseudonymously as "Company Doe" in a lawsuit against the Consumer Product Safety Commission. Advocacy groups, such as Public Citizen, were allowed to challenge the orders because the right of access "is widely shared among the press and the general public alike," the Fourth Circuit stated. Because the sealing order was based on speculative claims of harm, the district court was ordered to unseal the record in its entirety. Nor was there justification for the use of a pseudonym; the appellate court ruled the public has an interest in knowing the names of litigants, especially those suing the government.[107]

Whether juror names must be publicly available has not been addressed by the Supreme Court, and lower courts are split on this issue. In 2008, the Court of Appeals for the Third Circuit overturned a trial court order keeping juror names secret. In *United States v. Wecht*, the Third Circuit found that public knowledge of juror names is a well-established part of the American judicial tradition.[108] Further, the judicial system benefits from a presumption of public access to jurors' names. "The prospect of criminal justice being routinely meted out by unknown persons does not comport with democratic values of accountability and openness," the court said. The appellate court rejected the trial court's reasons for withholding jurors' names. The trial court's fear that the press would publish stories about the jurors, making some unwilling to serve, was "conclusory and generic" and insufficient to overcome the presumption of openness.

A different result was reached by the trial court in the high-profile 2007 trial of media tycoon Conrad Black, at which Black was convicted of obstruction of justice and mail fraud stemming from complicated maneuvers diverting money to him from Hollinger International shareholders. To accommodate the more than 400 journalists covering the trial, the judge reserved half of the courtroom seats for journalists and arranged a live audio and video feed in two overflow courtrooms.

During the trial, the judge refused to publicly release the names and addresses of the jurors, claiming disclosure of this information in such a highly publicized case would create the risk that jurors would be subjected to prejudicial contact.[109] Voir dire had been open to the public, as required by *Press-Enterprise I*. But unlike public access to voir dire, which promoted the fairness of the proceedings, the court said disclosure of juror names raised the prospect of jury tampering and other contact harmful to a fair trial. Similarly, the judges conducting the 2010 trial and 2011 retrial of former Illinois governor Rod Blagojevich, the 2011 trial of baseball star Barry Bonds, the 2011 trial of Casey Anthony and the 2019 trial of drug lord Joaquín Guzmán Loera sealed juror names to prevent jury tampering. Juror names are usually released after the trial; Anthony's jurors were identified three months after the conclusion of the trial. The trial judge wanted a "cooling-off" period due to death threats and public outrage stemming from the not guilty verdict.

---

[106] 749 F.3d 246 (4th Cir. 2014).
[107] *But see* John Doe Co. No. 1 v. Consumer Fin. Prot. Bureau, 2016 U.S. Dist. LEXIS 78988 (D.D.C. June 15, 2016) (allowing companies suing the CFPB to remain anonymous because of debilitating injury to their reputations if their identities are disclosed before the CFPB's investigation is completed).
[108] 537 F.3d 222 (3d Cir. 2008).
[109] United States v. Black, 483 F. Supp. 2d 618 (N.D. Ill. 2007).

▓ **SUMMARY** ▓

Most court records are presumed by appellate courts to be open. However, lower court judges may seal records, particularly if the records have not been introduced into evidence in court. Courts have disagreed when asked to decide whether broadcasters may copy videotapes introduced into evidence in court.

Interviewing Jurors

In extraordinary cases such as those involving organized crime figures, juror anonymity is protected, and journalists are prohibited from initiating interviews with jurors who wish to remain anonymous after the verdict. In other high-profile cases in which juror identity is known, judges may still seek to restrict press interviews with jurors. Appellate courts have upheld reasonable restrictions on post-verdict press interviews with jurors.

In a highly publicized Louisiana case, an anonymous jury was empaneled because two of the defendants had previously pled guilty to witness tampering. At the conclusion of the trial, the judge told the jurors that their anonymity would be protected unless they chose to be publicly identified. The judge also prohibited jurors from publicly discussing their deliberations but said they could discuss their general reactions to the trial. None of the jurors wished to be identified publicly. The Fifth Circuit upheld the trial court's action, concluding that the interest in protecting jurors from post-verdict harassment and invasions of privacy justified the restriction on newsgathering. The appellate court added, "If jurors voluntarily waive their anonymity and consent to interviews on matters other than jury deliberations, so be it. They need not become unwilling pawns in the frenzied media battle over these cases."[110]

In 2003, the New Jersey Supreme Court upheld a trial court's order prohibiting media representatives from interviewing jurors after a highly publicized murder trial ended in a mistrial.[111] The trial court feared that interviews with jurors in the mistrial case would chill the free exchange of ideas among jurors in a retrial. The state supreme court found this fear to be too speculative a basis to justify the restriction. However, the supreme court believed that juror interviews "might reveal some insight into the jury's deliberative process" that would give the prosecution a significant advantage at the retrial and violate the defendant's Sixth Amendment rights. The risk that juror interviews would benefit the prosecution was sufficiently important to justify the interview ban. Moreover, the supreme court noted that the ban expired on the return of a verdict in the retrial.

A ban on juror interviews that is not narrowly tailored to serve a sufficiently important interest will be found unconstitutional. For example, the U.S. Court of Appeals for the Tenth Circuit found impermissibly overbroad a judge's order that prevented jurors from discussing the case with anyone.[112] The judge offered no reason for the restriction, nor was the order tailored to protect the confidentiality of jury deliberations. The Tenth Circuit stated:

> It would have been constitutionally permissible for the court routinely to instruct jurors that they may refuse interviews and seek the aid of the court if interviewers persist after they express a reluctance to speak. It

---

[110] United States v. Brown, 250 F.3d 907 (5th Cir. 2001).

[111] State v. Neulander, 173 N.J. 193, 801 A.2d 255 (N.J. 2002), *cert. denied*, 537 U.S. 1192 (2003).

[112] Journal Publishing Co. v. Mechem, 801 F.2d 1233 (10th Cir. 1986).

could have told the jurors not to discuss the specific votes and opinions of noninterviewed jurors in order to encourage free deliberation in the jury room. But the court could not issue a sweeping restraint forbidding all contact between the press and former jurors without a compelling reason.

While acknowledging the trial court's power to impose limited restrictions on juror interviews, the Tenth Circuit concluded that the order impermissibly interfered with the news media's First Amendment right to gather information.

■ SUMMARY ■

Judges have the authority to reasonably restrict interviews with jurors. However, these restrictions must be narrowly tailored to serve an important interest, such as preserving the confidentiality of jury deliberations. In cases where an anonymous jury is empaneled, judges may prevent the press from contacting jurors who wish to remain anonymous.

CONTEMPT POWER

Judicial Authority

American judges inherited from the English courts the power to cite for **contempt of court** any acts of disobedience or disrespect and any acts that interfere with the judicial process.[113] A single judge—often the same judge who was the object of the contempt—can decide what kind of conduct constitutes contempt of court, accuse a person of being in contempt, determine that person's guilt and assess the punishment. In a matter of minutes, a person can be fined or sentenced to jail.

The judicial power to summarily cite for contempt of court is an unusual concentration of authority in our system of government. A holdover from authoritarian rule in England, the contempt power ensures judicial authority and order in the court. It gives judges the enforcement power necessary to protect the constitutional rights of persons under the jurisdiction of the courts. Anyone who disobeys a judge, including a journalist, may be faced with a contempt citation. Even if an appeals court later decides that a contempt order was unconstitutional, it may well uphold the fine or jail term imposed by the trial judge. The appellate courts do not want to encourage doubts about judicial authority in the courtroom.

There are limits on the contempt power designed to curb its abuse. Most of those limits apply to both civil and criminal contempt.

Civil Contempt Versus Criminal Contempt

The differences in the two kinds of contempt, civil and criminal, do not parallel the distinctions between civil and criminal law. Rather, civil and criminal contempt can be distinguished by the purpose of a contempt order and a difference in the assessment of penalties.[114]

A civil contempt citation is coercive; it is applied to get someone to do something. The penalty stays in force until the court's directives are obeyed or become

---

[113] *See* Ronald Goldfarb, *The Contempt Power* 1 (1971).
[114] *See* Luis Kutner, "Contempt Power: The Black Robe: A Proposal for Due Process," 39 *Tenn. L. Rev.* 1, 8 (1971).

moot. Civil contempt is usually imposed on a person who refuses to obey an order intended to protect one of the parties in a court case. In mass media law, judges most often use civil contempt when a reporter refuses to reveal confidential news sources. Journalists are cited for contempt because they refuse to give possible evidence to one of the parties in a legal dispute. Myron Farber of the *New York Times* was sentenced to jail and fined $1,000 a day for civil contempt after he refused to divulge his notes in a murder trial. Farber spent 40 days in jail after refusing to let the judge review the notes.

In civil contempt, a judge can order the person charged with contempt to be locked up until he or she agrees to obey the court. In a sense, people charged with civil contempt hold the keys to their own cells. They can free themselves by complying with the court order. Many states have limited the amount of time a person can serve in jail.

In contrast, a criminal contempt citation punishes disrespect for the court, such as obstruction of court proceedings or verbal abuse of the judge. The penalty could be a fine, a jail sentence, or both. In Colorado, a court held two reporters and their newspaper, the *Boulder Daily Camera*, in contempt after the reporters questioned jurors in a murder trial. As a result of the reporters' actions, the jurors were dismissed and jury selection had to be repeated. In lieu of a fine, the reporters and the newspaper were ordered to reimburse the parties in the case and the state judicial department for the costs of four additional days of trial. The reporters and the newspaper also had to pay the costs incurred by the state for prosecuting them for contempt.[115]

A journalist who refuses to reveal confidential sources could be cited for both civil and criminal contempt. A judge can cite a reporter for civil contempt to coerce a reporter to reveal sources and for criminal contempt for disobeying an order of the court. This happened in the case of Myron Farber, the *New York Times* reporter mentioned earlier. In addition to his fine and jail sentence for civil contempt, Farber was fined $1,000 and ordered to spend six months in jail—a sentence later suspended—for disobeying the court.

The Supreme Court has ruled that those sentenced to jail for criminal contempt for more than six months have a right to a jury trial.[116] Additionally, in cases involving "serious" fines, such as the $64 million fine imposed on a union for out-of-court violations of an injunction, the Court has ruled criminal procedural protections, such as trial by jury, the right to counsel and proof beyond a reasonable doubt, are necessary to prevent the arbitrary exercise of judicial power.[117] The Court has not yet granted the same procedural right to persons cited for civil contempt.

Limits on Judicial Power

The U.S. Constitution and federal law limit the power of judges to cite for contempt of court, particularly for behavior outside of the judge's presence. The limits are important to journalists because they protect the publication of information and comment about the courts.

FIRST AMENDMENT Supreme Court decisions in the 1940s virtually eliminated the use of contempt citations to punish publications or broadcasts about

---

[115] *In re* Stone, 703 P.2d 1319 (Colo. Ct. App. 1985).

[116] Bloom v. Illinois, 391 U.S. 194 (1968).

[117] United Mine Workers of America v. Bagwell, 512 U.S. 821 (1994).

court proceedings, especially for the criticism of judicial behavior. In *Bridges v. California*, the Supreme Court ruled that contempt citations issued in response to published criticism of judges violated the First Amendment.[118] By a 5–4 margin, the Court said that judges could not hold journalists or speakers in contempt absent a clear and present danger of a miscarriage of justice.

In *Bridges*, an official of the International Longshoremen-Warehousemen's Union was held in contempt after newspapers reported that he said that a judge's decision in a union dispute was "outrageous." At about the same time, the *Los Angeles Times* published three editorials commenting about cases pending before judges; the newspaper was found guilty of contempt of court and fined. The convictions of the union official and the newspaper were upheld by the California Supreme Court but overturned by the U.S. Supreme Court. Justice Black, writing the Court's majority opinion, said "the only conclusion supported by history" is that those who adopted the Constitution "intended to give to liberty of the press . . . the broadest scope that could be countenanced in an orderly society." Drawing on language used by the Supreme Court in sedition cases, Black said the criticism of pending court cases could be punished only if there was an "extremely high" degree of imminence of an "extremely serious" evil. Black said neither the union official's remarks nor the newspaper editorials met this standard.

Five years later, in *Pennekamp v. Florida*, the Supreme Court said *Miami Herald* editorials accusing judges of protecting criminals did not present a clear and present danger to the administration of justice.[119] Justice Stanley Reed, writing for a unanimous Court, said, "Free discussion of the problems of society is a cardinal principle of Americanism—a principle which all are zealous to preserve." One year after *Pennekamp*, the Court again overturned journalists' contempt convictions in *Craig v. Harney*.[120] A trial judge concluded newspaper coverage and editorials about a pending case were intended to falsely present to the public the nature of the proceedings and influence the court. The Supreme Court reversed, stating there "is no special perquisite of the judiciary which enables it, as distinguished from other institutions of democratic government, to suppress, edit, or censor events which transpire in proceedings before it."

Bridges, Pennekamp and *Harney* made it clear that the Supreme Court expects judges to have thick skins and that the criticism of judges should not lead to contempt of court charges. As the Court stated in *Harney*, "the law of contempt is not made for the protection of judges who may be sensitive to the winds of public opinion. Judges are supposed to be men of fortitude, able to thrive in a hardy climate." However, courts might uphold contempt citations for other kinds of publications. For example, courts might be less tolerant of publications that seek to influence jury decisions. Courts might decide that jurors could be more easily intimidated than judges. In addition, *Bridges, Pennekamp* and *Harney* did not involve prejudicial pretrial publicity or the violation of a judicial order.

JUDICIAL REACH AND DUE PROCESS The Supreme Court has not been alone in limiting the use of the judicial contempt power. Congress and many state legislatures have passed laws limiting the ability of judges to hold journalists in contempt for the publication of unfavorable stories or commentary. As early as 1831, Congress enacted a statute restricting federal judges to holding persons in contempt only if they refused to obey a judicial order or if their behavior in or near

---

[118] 314 U.S. 252 (1941).
[119] 328 U.S. 331 (1946).
[120] 331 U.S. 367 (1947).

the courtroom could "obstruct the administration of justice."[121] The word *near* probably refers to the hallway outside the courtroom and maybe the sidewalks or grounds just outside the courthouse.[122]

In addition, persons cited by federal judges for contempt for activity taking place outside a courtroom ordinarily have a right to a notice of the nature of the charge and a hearing. In federal courts, persons who are cited for contempt have the right to an attorney, the right to cross-examine witnesses, the right to offer testimony and frequently the right to a jury trial. If the contempt involves criticism or disrespect of a judge, that judge is disqualified from the proceeding.[123]

Limits on Appeals

The power of judges to cite for contempt of court with only limited opportunities for appeal presents problems for journalists when a judge has issued a prior restraint order—that is, a judge has ordered reporters not to print or publish a news story. After the Supreme Court's decision in *Nebraska Press Association*, most prior restraint orders would be considered unconstitutional by appellate courts. However, if reporters do not print the news until they can appeal a judge's order, a story may lose its news value. If journalists do print the story in violation of a judge's order, they may be cited for contempt of court. The rule, known as the **collateral bar rule**, is that a citation for contempt of court stands even if an appellate court declares the original prior restraint order unconstitutional. In other words, a journalist can be jailed or fined for violating an order that infringes on the First Amendment. The reason is that appellate courts want to protect the authority of the trial courts even when the trial courts are wrong. As the U.S. Supreme Court stated in 1967, "respect for judicial process is a small price to pay for the civilizing hand of the law."[124]

Judges rarely enjoin publication, but several cases reveal the danger of contempt when journalists disobey an injunction. In *Dickinson v. United States*, two reporters in Baton Rouge, Louisiana, tried to cover the hearing of a government-sponsored civil rights volunteer accused of conspiring to murder the mayor. A federal district judge ordered the news media not to report testimony given in the public proceedings, an order the two reporters disobeyed. The judge found the reporters in contempt of court and fined them $300 each. The reporters appealed.

The U.S. Court of Appeals for the Fifth Circuit agreed with the reporters that the judge's order was a prior restraint that violated the First Amendment. The Fifth Circuit said that a blanket ban on publication "cannot withstand the mildest breeze emanating from the Constitution."[125] However, the appeals court refused to overturn the contempt order.

Chief Judge John Brown said the principle that an injunction must be obeyed, regardless of the ultimate validity of the court order, was "well-established." Brown suggested that the reporters should have appealed the order rather than violating it. He acknowledged that an appeal created "thorny problems" given the timely nature of news. Brown concluded, however, that a judicial order must be obeyed absent a showing that it was "transparently invalid" or "patently frivolous."

---

[121] 18 U.S.C. § 401.
[122] Nye v. United States, 313 U.S. 33 (1941).
[123] Fed. R. Crim. P. 42(a) (3). *See* Ronald Goldfarb, *The Contempt Power* 68 (1971).
[124] Walker v. City of Birmingham, 388 U.S. 307 (1967).
[125] 465 F.2d 496 (5th Cir. 1972).

The case against the two reporters was returned to the district court judge to determine whether the punishment for contempt was "appropriate" given that the order disobeyed had been unconstitutional. The trial judge upheld his previous contempt order and the fines. The Fifth Circuit affirmed the lower court for the second time.[126]

In 1986, however, the U.S. Court of Appeals for the First Circuit overturned a contempt conviction of a newspaper that disregarded a judge's prior restraint order. In 1986 and in a related opinion in 1987, the court ruled that it was permissible to violate a "transparently unconstitutional" court order if a quick appeal to the order was not available.[127] The First Circuit reversed a contempt citation issued by the District Court for Rhode Island against the *Providence Journal* for printing, contrary to a judicial order, information about Raymond Patriarca, a reputed crime boss in New England. After Patriarca died in 1985, the paper obtained from the FBI the results of an illegal wiretap on Patriarca's phone in the 1960s. However, Patriarca's son obtained a court order barring publication in the *Journal* on the grounds that his own right of privacy would be violated. The *Journal* was cited for contempt of court in November 1986 when it printed a story based on the FBI file in violation of the court order.

A three-judge panel of the First Circuit reversed the contempt order in December 1986. The panel said the order was a "transparently invalid" infringement of the First Amendment because the federal district judge had failed to meet the heavy burden of proof required by the U.S. Supreme Court before imposing a prior restraint. The court acknowledged the "bedrock principle" that court orders—even those later found to be unconstitutional—must be obeyed. However, the panel of judges said that when a court order "transparently" violates the First Amendment, the court "is acting so far in excess of its authority that it has no right to expect compliance," and the interest in preserving the integrity of the judicial system is not served by requiring it.

In May 1987, the First Circuit, after rehearing the case en banc, affirmed the panel's opinion but attached a modification. The full court said that editors in the future who are ordered not to print a story must make a "good faith effort" to appeal a prior restraint before they publish in violation of the order. When editors are ordered not to print a story, the court said, they may publish and still challenge the constitutionality of an order only "if timely access to the appellate court is not available or if [a] timely decision is not forthcoming."[128]

The U.S. Supreme Court dismissed *United States v. Providence Journal* on procedural grounds, leaving intact the First Circuit's ruling in favor of the newspaper.[129] However, the rule in *Providence Journal* holds only for the First Circuit and does not overturn *Dickinson* in the Fifth Circuit. Nor does the First Circuit's decision change the general judicial bias toward upholding a contempt of court order even if it is unconstitutional. Only a few state appellate courts—including those in Illinois,[130] Kansas[131] and Washington[132]—have joined the First Circuit in allow-

---

[126] Dickinson v. United States, 476 F.2d 373, *cert. denied*, 414 U.S. 979 (1973).

[127] *In re* Providence Journal, 820 F.2d 1342 (1st Cir. 1986), *modified*, 820 F.2d 1354 (1st Cir. 1987), *cert. dismissed*, 485 U.S. 693 (1988).

[128] 820 F.2d 1354 (1st Cir. 1987).

[129] 485 U.S. 693 (1988).

[130] Cooper v. Rockford Newspapers, Inc., 365 N.E.2d 746 (Ill. App. Ct. 1977).

[131] State v. Alston, 887 P.2d 681 (Kan. 1994).

[132] State *ex rel.* Superior Court of Snohomish County v. Sperry, 483 P.2d 608 (Wash.), *cert. denied*, 404 U.S. 939 (1971).

ing publishers who defied injunctions to challenge the validity of their contempt citations.

The limited application of the *Providence Journal* ruling is illustrated by contempt proceedings against CNN. In 1994, CNN was temporarily ordered not to broadcast audiotapes of deposed Panamanian President Manuel Noriega's prison telephone calls. While CNN's appeal of the order was pending before the Eleventh Circuit, the network repeatedly cablecast the tapes. Even though the restraining order was eventually vacated, Judge William Hoeveler found CNN to be in criminal contempt of court.[133] In late 1994, Judge Hoeveler gave CNN the option of paying a "substantial" fine or airing an apology and paying a smaller fine. The network chose to pay an $85,000 fine and air the apology, which was drafted by the judge. The apology stated that CNN "realizes that it was in error in defying the order of the court" and that the network should have awaited the results of its appeal rather than violating the court's order. The apology concluded:

> Our justice system cannot long survive if litigants take it upon themselves to determine which judgments or orders of court they will or will not follow. . . . In the event unfavorable judgments are rendered, the right of appeal is provided. This is the course on which we should have relied. We regret that we did not.[134]

◼ SUMMARY ◼

Judges have substantial authority to cite individuals for contempt of court. Criminal contempt citations are used to punish disruptive behavior. Judges issue civil contempt citations to coerce people into following a court order, such as revealing confidential news sources. Congress, state legislatures and the courts have provided substantial protection against contempt citations for persons writing about the courts. However, persons ordered not to publish information about court activity may be punished for contempt even if the order itself is ultimately declared invalid.

---

[133] United States v. Cable News Network, Inc., 865 F. Supp. 1549 (S.D. Fla. 1994).
[134] "CNN Is Sentenced for Tapes and Makes Public Apology," *N.Y. Times*, Dec. 20, 1994, at B7.

11

Protection of News Sources, Notes and Recordings

I n addition to the conflicts between the courts and the press discussed in the previous chapter, there is an ongoing dispute over court orders demanding journalists produce notes, tapes or documents (*subpoena duces tecum*) or orders requiring journalists testify in court (*subpoena ad testificandum*), usually about confidential news sources. On one side, many judges and lawyers believe that reporters should be required to testify in court like everyone else. On the other side, journalists argue that their ability to report the news often depends on protecting the confidentiality of news sources.

Reporters are frequently willing to go to jail and pay fines rather than obey court orders requiring them to reveal the names of confidential sources. In one of the most famous cases, *New York Times* reporter Myron Farber spent 40 days in jail and the *Times* paid $286,000 in fines when Farber refused to produce notes of his investigation into suspicious deaths in a New Jersey hospital. Farber's stories led

DOI: 10.4324/9781003264736-11

to the murder indictment of Dr. Mario E. Jascalevich, who wanted to see Farber's notes for the preparation of his defense.

Farber refused to give up his notes because they would have revealed confidential sources he used to prepare his stories. Farber and other journalists argue that news sources will not talk to the media if they fear their identities will be revealed. Unless reporters can promise confidentiality, they say, people who know about official corruption and criminal activity will keep quiet because they fear for their jobs or their safety if they "blow the whistle." If reporters cannot promise confidentiality to sources, Farber said, there would be less information for the public "on a variety of important and sensitive issues, all to the detriment of the public interest."[1]

Judges sometimes order journalists to turn over notes and the names of sources to protect significant social interests, such as the Sixth Amendment right of criminal defendants to obtain evidence in their favor and to confront witnesses against them. In the case of Farber, Dr. Jascalevich wanted to know what the reporter was told by potential witnesses, such as Dr. Stanley Harris, who Jascalevich believed to be his "principal accuser."

In addition, law enforcement officials contend that journalists have a civic duty to testify about crimes they witness. Videographer Josh Wolf refused to provide a federal grand jury with video he shot of a 2005 San Francisco protest march in which a policeman was injured. Wolf refused to testify before the grand jury and was found to be in contempt of court. He spent 226 days in jail, a record for an American journalist, before he agreed to provide the video.

Finally, plaintiffs and defendants in civil suits sometimes contend that journalists possess information that could determine who wins and who loses their litigation. The testimony of five reporters was deemed to be critical to Wen Ho Lee's suit against the Departments of Justice and Energy for violating Lee's rights under the federal Privacy Act. Anonymous sources revealed to the press that Lee was the target of an investigation into security breaches at the Los Alamos, New Mexico, nuclear research facility. Lee claimed these leaks, which included information about his employment history, finances and results of polygraph examinations, violated the Privacy Act. When government officials proved to be evasive and uncooperative in helping Lee identify the leakers, a court ruled the testimony of reporters was necessary. The reporters balked and were held in contempt of court, a ruling sustained in 2005 by the Court of Appeals for the D.C. Circuit.[2] The reporters avoided jail and fines when their news organizations paid Lee $750,000 to settle the case.

For many years, judges and legislatures have tried to reconcile the need for evidence in court with the desire of communicators to preserve the anonymity of their sources. The result so far is an uneasy compromise. In most states, reporters may withhold sources or notes unless a criminal defendant, a prosecutor or a party in a civil suit proves a compelling reason for demanding them. Hence, much of the protection for reporters is provided on a case-by-case basis only after a court battle.

This chapter discusses the statutes and judicial opinions that shield journalists from contempt citations if they refuse to testify. The chapter also discusses congressional subpoenas, government access to journalists' telephone records and police searches of newsrooms.

---

[1] *In re* Farber, 394 A.2d 330 (N.J. 1978).
[2] Lee v. DOJ, 413 F.3d 53 (D.C. Cir. 2005), *cert. denied*, 547 U.S. 1187 (2006).

TESTIMONIAL PRIVILEGES

Judges and legal scholars argue that few should be exempted from the responsibility of testifying in court. As more people are excused from telling what they know, fewer remain to contribute evidence in the search for truth in court. However, all states provide testimonial privileges to certain communications. The most common of these privileges apply to attorney-client, physician-patient and priest-penitent communications.[3]

Lawyers and doctors, for example, are usually not required to testify in court about their clients or patients because society recognizes they render essential services that depend on confidentiality. Lawyers and doctors cannot effectively provide legal advice or practice medicine if clients and patients cannot be candid, assured that their confidences will not be revealed. Lawyers need to know all information pertinent to a criminal charge to provide the best defense. Doctors sometimes need to know intimate details about a patient's behavior to provide a correct diagnosis. Clients and patients will not be open and forthright or might not seek help in the first place if they believe that embarrassing or incriminating information might be made public.[4]

Journalists also argue that the identity of their confidential sources should be protected from disclosure so the public may receive information about crime and corruption that might otherwise remain unpublished. In *Branzburg v. Hayes* the Supreme Court rejected a First Amendment–based privilege for journalists. However, the *Branzburg* Court emphasized that states were free to enact statutes protecting journalists. Thus far, 40 states and the District of Columbia have granted a statutory testimonial privilege to journalists. There is no federal journalist's privilege statute.

Many federal courts also provide a limited First Amendment privilege. Strangely enough, the source of these rulings is *Branzburg*, a decision that appeared to say that journalists do not have constitutional protection when they refuse to reveal their news sources. Lower courts have relied on the peculiar configuration of concurring and dissenting opinions in *Branzburg* to create a limited First Amendment privilege for journalists.

The law of journalist's privilege is complex. In some cases where a court does not recognize a First Amendment-based privilege, a journalist may nonetheless be protected under a state statute. In other settings, journalists will be protected by the First Amendment in the absence of a statutory privilege. Context is critical in defining a journalist's privilege.

PROTECTION UNDER THE FIRST AMENDMENT

The Supreme Court

In *Branzburg v. Hayes*, a 5–4 majority of the U.S. Supreme Court rejected a privilege under the First Amendment for three reporters who had refused to testify before three different grand juries.[5] The Supreme Court decided the cases from Kentucky, California and Massachusetts with one opinion.

---

[3] *See, e.g.,* Ala. Code §§ 12-21-161 (attorney-client privilege); 34-24-60 (physician-patient privilege); 12-21-166 (priest-penitent privilege).
[4] *See, e.g.,* John Henry Wigmore, 8 *Evidence in Trials at Common Law* §§ 2291, 2380a (McNaughton rev. ed., 1961).
[5] 408 U.S. 665 (1972).

One of the reporters, Paul Branzburg of the *Louisville Courier-Journal*, was appealing two court orders to testify before different grand juries investigating drug use and sales. In 1969, Branzburg had written about two young men he watched making hashish near Louisville. Branzburg promised not to reveal the men's identities and refused to identify them when called to appear before a **grand jury**. In a second article, in 1971, Branzburg described the two weeks he spent watching and interviewing several dozen unnamed drug users in Frankfort, Kentucky. He again refused to testify after being subpoenaed by a grand jury to discuss criminal activity he had witnessed. Although a Kentucky law protects reporters from being forced to reveal sources, a state appellate court said the statute did not protect journalists who personally observe criminal acts.

In another case, Earl Caldwell of the *New York Times* was subpoenaed to appear before a federal grand jury in Oakland, California. The grand jury ordered Caldwell, who covered the militant Black Panther Party, to bring notes and audiotapes of interviews with Black Panther officers and other representatives. The grand jury was investigating allegations of Black Panther threats against President Nixon, their involvement in assassination plots and their participation in riots. Caldwell refused to appear and was found in contempt of the grand jury. The U.S. Court of Appeals for the Ninth Circuit reversed the contempt order, and the U.S. government petitioned for certiorari.

The third case also involved a journalist who had refused to answer grand jury questions about the Black Panthers. Paul Pappas, a television news reporter, covered civil disorders in New Bedford, Massachusetts, in 1970. He had been allowed into a barricaded store serving as the headquarters for the Black Panthers while they waited for a police raid. Two months later, Pappas told a grand jury what he had witnessed outside the Black Panthers' headquarters, but he refused to answer questions about what took place inside.

The reporters argued that if journalists were forced to reveal their confidential sources, people would be reluctant to speak to reporters, harming society's interest in the "free flow of information." Caldwell refused even to enter the grand jury room, arguing that his appearance, even if he said nothing, would destroy his working relationship with the Black Panthers. Because grand jury proceedings are secret, Caldwell said, the Black Panthers could never be sure what he had said or refused to say behind closed doors. A grand jury appearance would drive "a wedge of distrust" between him and the Black Panthers, resulting in less public knowledge about the group.

Denying a First Amendment privilege for journalists, a divided Court in *Branzburg* contrasted the rights of the press with the obligation of every citizen to answer questions relevant to a criminal investigation. Justice Byron White, writing a majority opinion for the Court, said he could not see why the public interest in law enforcement should be overridden by "the consequential, but uncertain, burden on news gathering" that might result from insisting that reporters testify before grand juries.

White, supported by four other justices, emphasized the importance of the long-standing principle that the public "has a right to every man's evidence," particularly during grand jury proceedings, which play "an important role in fair and efficient law enforcement." He said the Court could not adopt the theory "that it is better to write about crime than to do something about it." Moreover, White said the journalists had not demonstrated that substantial numbers of sources would remain silent if journalists were forced to testify before grand juries.

White rejected the arguments of reporters Branzburg, Caldwell and Pappas even though the three argued only for a qualified, rather than an absolute, privilege for reporters to withhold the names of sources. The reporters said they should not have to testify unless the government could establish that (1) a reporter had information relevant to a crime being investigated, (2) the information was not available from other sources and (3) the need for the information was sufficiently compelling to override First Amendment interests. But White said that although a qualified privilege would presumably reduce the number of times that reporters would have to testify, it would not provide the press with the certainty of confidentiality necessary to satisfy sources. Under a conditional privilege, White said, the press could never guarantee a source that confidentiality would be protected by a court.

White did not want to force judges to decide who would qualify for a constitutional press privilege. Defining who was a journalist, he said, was "a questionable procedure in light of the traditional doctrine that liberty of the press is the right of the lonely pamphleteer who uses carbon paper or a mimeograph." He said that lecturers, political pollsters, scholars, and novelists, as well as newspaper publishers, disseminate information gathered from confidential sources. He added that almost any author may quite accurately assert that he is contributing to the flow of information to the public, that he relies on confidential sources of information, and that these sources will be silenced if he is forced to make disclosures before a grand jury.

White said there is "no justification" for officials to harass the press in efforts to disrupt a journalist's relations with news sources and courts could protect journalists from bad faith investigations. White claimed that balancing the need to protect confidential sources against the need for testimony was a task for legislators rather than courts. He noted that Congress and state legislatures have the power to develop a statutory privilege.

Justice Powell, although the fifth vote in the *Branzburg* 5–4 decision, wrote a separate concurring opinion to emphasize "the limited nature" of the Court's ruling. Although Powell voted against Branzburg, Caldwell and Pappas, he emphasized the courts should protect journalists in cases of harassment, such as where the information sought bears "only a remote and tenuous relationship to the subject of the investigation" or does not serve "a legitimate need of law enforcement."

Justice Stewart, writing a dissenting opinion, would have granted the three reporters in *Branzburg* the qualified privilege they sought. Stewart, in an opinion supported by Justices Brennan and Marshall, rebuked the "Court's crabbed view of the First Amendment. Stewart said reporters have a limited First Amendment right to refuse to reveal sources, a right that stems from society's interest "in a full and free flow of information to the public." Stewart, in contrast to White, said the right to publish information would be severely curtailed without protection to obtain it in the first place.

Stewart acknowledged that grand juries must be able to compel "every man's relevant evidence" if the criminal justice system is to function fairly. But Stewart said a qualified privilege for journalists would serve a public interest that parallels the interest served by the privilege accorded doctors and lawyers to withhold confidential information about their patients and clients.

Stewart advocated a three-part test government officials must satisfy to overcome the privilege. His test would require the government to demonstrate there is

1. a probable cause to believe that a reporter has information "clearly relevant" to a specific violation of law.

2. evidence that the information sought cannot be obtained by alternative means less destructive of First Amendment values.
3. "a compelling and overriding interest in the information."

Stewart said the relevance requirement prevents the government from conducting a fishing expedition for information at the expense of the media. Stewart said that in the case of *New York Times* reporter Earl Caldwell, the government had not shown that the grand jury was investigating any specific crime. The relevance requirement also could prevent harassment of reporters and sources.

Stewart also believed that the government must demonstrate a need for a journalist's confidential information. Stewart agreed with the Ninth Circuit that the government had not established a compelling interest in Caldwell's testimony. Stewart said there was no evidence that Caldwell had information about illegal activities of the Black Panthers. On the other hand, Stewart believed that Caldwell had demonstrated that his ability to report on the Black Panthers would be impaired if he were required to appear before a grand jury.

Finally, Stewart said officials should have to prove they could not obtain the necessary information without forcing a journalist to testify. Stewart said that if journalists were required to provide information that was available elsewhere, the flow of information to the public would be disrupted without a resulting benefit to the courts. In the *Caldwell* case, Stewart said, the government had not shown that it had tried alternative means to acquire the information it was seeking; he believed the government must show the information it was seeking could not be obtained through other witnesses such as police informants.

Justice Douglas, the fourth dissenter in *Branzburg*, argued that the First Amendment prohibited the government from requiring journalists to testify. His views, coupled with those of Stewart, Marshall and Brennan, added up to four justices who believed in at least limited First Amendment protection for journalists who refused to reveal their sources. Justice Powell's concurring opinion, which some have interpreted as supporting a limited reporter's privilege, muddied the waters.[6] Justice Stewart later described the vote in *Branzburg* as perhaps "a vote of four and a half to four and a half."[7]

Due to *Branzburg's* ambiguities, many lower courts in the 1970s began to create a qualified First Amendment privilege for journalists who refuse to disclose confidential information. Other courts, however, have followed the view of the majority in *Branzburg*, which denied a constitutional privilege, particularly when the facts of cases mirror the circumstances of Branzburg, Caldwell and Pappas.

Lower Court Denial of Privilege

Courts are most likely to follow the precedent of Justice White's majority opinion in *Branzburg* when journalists are subpoenaed by grand juries, when they are asked to testify about something they witnessed, and when they are being asked to produce non-confidential information rather than sources or information obtained because they promised confidentiality.

Courts ordinarily follow *Branzburg's* majority when asked to decide whether a reporter should testify in front of a grand jury. When the Supreme Court held that

---

[6] *See generally* William E. Lee, "A Revisionist View of Journalist's Privilege: Justice Powell, *Branzburg*, and the 'Proper Balance'," 34 *Cardozo Arts & Ent. L.J.* 113 (2016).
[7] Potter Stewart, "Or of the Press," 26 *Hastings L.J.* 631, 635 (1975).

reporters do not have a First Amendment right to refuse to testify before grand juries, the Court emphasized the importance of grand juries to effective law enforcement and the need for "every man's evidence." Lower courts have since contended that journalists deserve First Amendment protection against testifying only if they can establish that grand jury requests for testimony are conducted in bad faith or constitute harassment.[8] Reporters who are unable to meet this burden of proof are uniformly required to testify about the selling of drugs, the possession of weapons or assaults.

Courts also frequently require reporters to testify when they are asked about events they witnessed rather than about the names of sources or information given to them by sources. In these cases, the reporters themselves are, in a sense, their own sources. Reporters Branzburg, Pappas and Caldwell had been asked to reveal what they witnessed. In *Miami Herald Publishing Co. v. Morejon*,[9] the Florida Supreme Court held that the First Amendment did not protect a *Herald* reporter who refused to testify about events he had witnessed. Accompanying airport police officers, reporter Joe Achenbach watched the arrest of Aristides Morejon for smuggling four kilograms of cocaine into the country. The Florida court, relying on the majority in *Branzburg*, said that there is no privilege for reporters who are subpoenaed for their eyewitness observations of an event relevant to a court proceeding.

For many years, prosecutors, defendants and judges frequently requested reporters' notes, tapes and other information, but usually not journalists' sources. But subpoenas for sources and contempt citations for uncooperative journalists increased dramatically for several years after September 11, 2001. Prosecutors investigating leaks of classified or restricted information became especially aggressive in seeking the identity of journalists' sources.

In Providence, Rhode Island, Channel 10 reporter James Taricani was sentenced to six months' home confinement for refusing to reveal the source of a leaked video showing a city hall official taking a bribe.[10] Also, two reporters for the *San Francisco Chronicle*, Mark Fainaru-Wada and Lance Williams, were sentenced to jail for a period of up to 18 months in September 2006 for their refusal to comply with grand jury subpoenas. The reporters, who obtained secret grand jury transcripts about a government investigation of the distribution of steroids to prominent athletes, were asked to identify their sources in a subsequent investigation into the leak.[11] The judge stayed their imprisonment until the Court of Appeals for the Ninth Circuit could consider an appeal. While the case was on appeal, Troy Ellerman, a lawyer for an executive with the laboratory under investigation, identified himself as the reporters' source. Ellerman agreed to plead guilty to obstruction of justice and disobeying court orders. As part of the plea deal, prosecutors ceased their attempt to imprison the reporters.

Most importantly, in Washington, a three-judge panel of the U.S. Court of Appeals unanimously ruled that two journalists must testify before a federal grand jury investigating unauthorized disclosure of undercover CIA operative Valerie Plame, whose name was leaked to Washington columnist Robert Novak, possibly in violation of federal law.[12] In each case, courts ruled that *Branzburg* precluded recognition of a journalist's privilege.

---

[8] *See, e.g., In re* Lewis, 377 F. Supp. 297 (C.D. Cal.), *aff'd*, 501 F.2d 418 (9th Cir. 1974), *cert. denied*, 420 U.S. 913 (1975).

[9] 561 So. 2d 577 (Fla. 1990).

[10] *In re* Special Proceedings, 373 F.3d 37 (1st Cir. 2004).

[11] *In re* Grand Jury Subpoenas to Fainaru-Wada and Williams, 438 F. Supp. 2d 1111 (N.D. Cal. 2006).

[12] *In re* Grand Jury Subpoena, Miller, 397 F.3d 964 (D.C. Cir.), *cert. denied*, 545 U.S. 1150 (2005). *See generally* Douglas McCollam, "Attack at the Source," *Columbia Journalism Rev.*, Mar.–Apr. 2005, at 29.

Journalists in Jail 2001–2022			
Journalist	*Year*	*Time in Jail*	*Reason for Release*
Josh Wolf	2006–2007	226 days	Provided video
Judith Miller	2005	85 days	Agreed to testify
Jim Taricani	2004–2005	122 days	Complied with conditions of confinement
Vanessa Leggett	2001–2002	168 days	Grand Jury term expired

FIGURE 11.1   Journalists jailed since 2001.

For nearly 50 years, media lawyers have creatively claimed that *Branzburg* does not preclude a qualified First Amendment privilege for journalist-source relationships, especially in cases not involving grand juries. Media lawyers have claimed that Justice White's opinion for the *Branzburg* Court was a plurality opinion, and the crucial opinion was Justice Powell's concurring opinion, which arguably implied that some form of reporter's privilege should be recognized.[13] The court of appeals in the Plame case, however, characterized Justice White's *majority* opinion as "authoritative precedent," which "in no uncertain terms" rejected a reporter's privilege. Moreover, the court of appeals read Justice Powell as emphasizing that a First Amendment privilege to withhold source identity was available only in rare cases of bad faith investigations—a protection available to the public as well as the press. "The Constitution protects all citizens, and there is no reason to believe that Justice Powell intended to elevate the journalistic class above the rest," the appeals court wrote.

As will be discussed later in this chapter, the appeals court did not decide whether a federal common-law privilege exists for journalists. But the court concluded that the government's need for the journalists' testimony outweighed any common-law privilege that might exist.

The prosecutor complicated the Plame case by acquiring "waivers" of confidentiality from key officials. Under this tactic, officials waive confidentiality, thus allowing journalists to discuss with prosecutors conversations the journalists might have had with officials. Some journalists asserted the waivers were coerced by the Bush administration and thus should be ignored by the courts. However, Matthew Cooper of *Time* testified before the grand jury investigating the Plame leak in July 2005 after his source urged him to do so. Judith Miller of the *New York Times* initially refused to testify and was jailed for contempt. While in jail, Miller sought assurances from "Scooter" Libby, her White House source, that the waiver Libby signed was voluntary. Libby urged her to testify and on release after spending 85 days in jail, Miller testified about her conversations with Libby.[14]

Based in part on the testimony of Miller and Cooper, Libby was indicted in October 2005 on obstruction of justice, false statement, and perjury charges for allegedly lying to FBI agents and the grand jury investigating the Plame leak. During the pretrial discovery process, Judge Reggie Walton ruled that *Time* magazine must

---

[13] *But see* McKevitt v. Pallasch, 339 F.3d 530, 532 (7th Cir. 2003) (questioning lower court decisions recognizing a First Amendment–based journalist's privilege).
[14] *See generally* William Lee, "The Priestly Class: Reflections on a Journalist's Privilege," 23 *Cardozo Arts & Ent. L.J.* 635 (2006).

produce drafts of an article by Cooper, along with internal correspondence, to Libby's attorneys. Drawing upon *Branzburg*, Walton rejected the claim that a journalist has a First Amendment privilege to withhold documents from a criminal defendant. Because the indictment of Libby claimed discrepancies exist between Libby's grand jury testimony and that of reporters such as Cooper, the court ruled the "First Amendment does not protect news reporters or news organizations from producing documents when the news reporters are themselves critical to both the indictment and prosecution of criminal activity."[15] After a trial at which Miller, Cooper and other journalists testified, a jury in March 2007 concluded Libby had falsely testified that he learned of Plame's CIA affiliation from reporters and did not leak information about Plame. He was convicted on four counts of obstruction of justice, perjury and making false statements.

The trend of appellate courts reading *Branzburg* narrowly was continued by the Fourth Circuit's 2013 decision in *United States v. Sterling*.[16] As part of its unprecedented crackdown on leaking, the Obama administration in late 2010 charged former CIA officer Jeffrey Sterling with unauthorized disclosure to *New York Times* reporter James Risen of national defense information about a CIA program to disrupt Iran's development of nuclear weapons. A district court ruled that Risen had a First Amendment right to refuse to testify about his confidential sources.

The Fourth Circuit found that *Branzburg* "unequivocally" rejected a First Amendment-based privilege that treats reporters differently from all other citizens who are compelled to give evidence of criminal activity. The appellate court also refused to read Justice Powell's concurring opinion as a tacit endorsement of Justice Stewart's dissenting opinion. If a subpoena is issued in good faith and is based on a legitimate need of law enforcement, *Branzburg* requires that a reporter testify like every other citizen. The appellate court found the subpoena was not issued in bad faith or for the purposes of harassment. Despite this ruling, Attorney General Holder decided in 2015 not to force Risen to testify at Sterling's trial.

Lower Court Reliance on a Three-Part Test

In situations not involving grand juries, some appellate courts have recognized a limited First Amendment privilege based on the three-part test advocated by Justice Stewart in his *Branzburg* dissent. Persons who seek confidential information from reporters are usually asked to demonstrate that the information is relevant to their case, they cannot obtain the information from alternative sources, and their need for the information is "compelling" and should override the First Amendment interest in protecting news sources. The Supreme Court has passed up several opportunities to overturn the lower courts' grant of a constitutional privilege to journalists.

The practical application of a qualified privilege for reporters varies greatly by jurisdiction. Courts disagree over whether the privilege should apply when a criminal defendant is seeking information, when the information is being sought in a libel suit, or when documents and videotape are obtained without a promise of confidentiality.

Courts recognizing a First Amendment–based privilege have not limited the privilege to the traditional news media; the privilege has been applied to specialized

[15] United States v. Libby, 432 F. Supp. 2d 26 (D.D.C. 2006).
[16] 732 F.3d 482 (4th Cir. 2013), *rehearing en banc denied*, 732 F.3d 482 (4th Cir. 2013).

publications, such as an oil industry newsletter,[17] a medical newsletter,[18] and investment analyst reports,[19] as well as academic researchers,[20] a documentary filmmaker,[21] and an investigative book author,[22] if the reporting is independent. For example, in 2011, the Second Circuit ruled the privilege did not apply to Joseph Berlinger, a documentary film producer, because he did not act as an *independent* reporter. Berlinger had been solicited by plaintiffs in an environmental damage suit to tell their story. Berlinger made changes to the film at the direction of plaintiff's counsel. Berlinger was ordered to divulge 600 hours of outtakes because those who "have been commissioned to publish in order to serve the objectives of others who have a stake in the subject of the reporting are not acting as an independent press," the Second Circuit wrote.[23] In contrast, in 2013 a federal court found that documentary film makers Ken Burns and his partners, who produced a documentary *The Central Park Five* about men who were convicted of a 1989 rape and served full prison terms before their convictions were vacated, operated independently and were entitled to the privilege. Although the film presented the men in a sympathetic manner, Burns and his partners retained full editorial control over the film.[24]

CRIMINAL PROCEEDINGS The Reporters Committee for Freedom of the Press found that more than half of the subpoenas issued to reporters in 2001 were from criminal defendants in state court proceedings.[25] In most criminal trials, courts use a three-part constitutional test to determine whether reporters are required to reveal confidential sources or information in their possession. Usually, the deciding factor is whether the person seeking the information can demonstrate a compelling need.

During criminal trials, prosecutors are frequently able to convince judges that journalists have information needed to convict a criminal defendant. However, criminal defendants trying to subpoena reporters often do not obtain the information they seek, despite the Sixth Amendment right to compel testimony in their favor. Criminal defendants sometimes are unable to meet all three parts of Stewart's test in *Branzburg*. For example, a federal appeals court affirmed the quashing of a subpoena served on *Sports Illustrated* because a defendant in a college basketball point-shaving scandal could not demonstrate that the information he sought was necessary to his defense. The U.S. Court of Appeals for the Second Circuit said that James Burke, who had been convicted, also had not shown that he had tried to obtain the information from sources other than *Sports Illustrated*.[26]

---

[17] McGraw-Hill, Inc. v. Arizona, 690 F.2d 5 (2d Cir. 1982).
[18] Apicella v. McNeil Laboratories, Inc., 66 F.R.D. 78 (E.D.N.Y. 1975).
[19] Summit Tech. Inc. v. Healthcare Capital Group, Inc. 141 F.R.D. 381 (D. Mass 1992).
[20] Cusumano v. Microsoft Corp., 162 F.3d 708 (1st Cir. 1998). *But see In re* Request from the United Kingdom, 685 F.3d 1 (1st Cir. 2012) (denying privilege to academic researchers).
[21] Silkwood v. Kerr-McGee Corp., 563 F.2d 433 (10th Cir. 1977).
[22] Shoen v. Shoen, 5 F.3d 1289 (9th Cir. 1993).
[23] Chevron Corp. v. Berlinger, 629 F.3d 297 (2d Cir. 2011).
[24] *In re* McCray, Richardson, Santana, Wise, and Salaam Litigation, 2013 U.S. Dist. LEXIS 22688 (S.D.N.Y. Feb. 19, 2013).
[25] Reporters Committee for Freedom of the Press, *Agents of Discovery: A Report on the Incidence of Subpoenas Served on the New Media in 2001* at 7 (2003). In a study of subpoenas received by the press in 2006, subpoenas in criminal cases also similarly outnumbered those received in civil cases. RonNell A. Jones, "Avalanche or Undue Alarm? An Empirical Study of Subpoenas Received by the News Media," 93 *Minn. L. Rev.* 585, 657 (2008).
[26] United States v. Burke, 700 F.2d 70 (2d Cir.), *cert. denied*, 464 U.S. 816 (1983). *But see* United States v. Criden, 633 F.2d 346 (3d Cir. 1980), *cert. denied*, 449 U.S. 1113 (1981) (ordering reporter to testify in criminal trial).

The Second Circuit blocked Burke's attempt to obtain nearly all the documents and tapes related to a 1981 *Sports Illustrated* article, "How I Put the Fix In," coauthored by Douglas Looney, a staff writer, and Henry Hill, a career criminal. In the article, Hill told his version of a scheme to fix Boston College basketball games during the 1978–79 season.

The scheme to fix Boston College games collapsed when the team came closer than planned to beat Holy Cross and the conspirators lost substantial sums of money. Soon afterward, Hill testified against his partners in exchange for immunity from prosecution. Burke, a reputed mob boss, was sentenced to 20 years in prison for his role in the scheme. He appealed, contending that the trial judge made several errors, including failing to require that *Sports Illustrated* turn over the documents and tapes related to the Hill-Looney article.

When the Second Circuit applied a version of Stewart's three-part test in *United States v. Burke*, the court said Burke satisfied only one prong: that the information sought was relevant to his defense. The court agreed that the documents and tapes being sought could have been relevant because they might have contradicted the trial testimony of Henry Hill. But Burke could not prove that the materials were "necessary or critical" to his defense, an adaptation of the Stewart requirement that there be a "compelling and overriding interest" in the information. The *Sports Illustrated* documents and tapes were not critical to Burke's case because he wanted to use them only to attack Hill's credibility; there was already ample evidence to destroy Hill's credibility as a witness because Hill had been convicted of loansharking, extortion and drug trafficking.

The Second Circuit said that Burke could not fulfill the third requirement of the Stewart test either. Burke had not sought the information from other available sources. For example, he had not subpoenaed a witness to the interviews of Hill by the *Sports Illustrated* writer Looney.

CIVIL TRIALS The Reporters Committee for Freedom of the Press reported that subpoenas in civil suits accounted for 36 percent of the subpoenas issued in 2001 to news media responding to a survey. Nearly 97 percent of those subpoenas were sought by litigants in lawsuits in which the media entity was not a party to the suits.[27] If the newspaper or broadcast station fighting a subpoena is not the defendant in a civil suit, the courts frequently recognize the constitutional privilege and decide in favor of the news medium. In the recent Wen Ho Lee case, however, the Court of Appeals for the D.C. Circuit upheld a lower court ruling that journalists had to reveal the identity of their confidential sources.

Journalist as Third-Party Writers or editors are least apt to be required to disclose information when it is being sought by parties in civil suits that do not directly involve the journalists being subpoenaed. The courts regularly decide that the civil litigants seeking notes or the names of sources in such cases cannot meet the requirements of the three-part test.

Litigants in civil suits often cannot establish that the information they seek is available only from journalists, one of the prongs of the Stewart test. Because the journalists were able to discover the information, judges often reason, attorneys for civil litigants ought to be able to do the same. Civil litigants also have a more difficult time than criminal defendants in proving a compelling need for the information. The Constitution does not provide civil litigants with the same power to

---

[27] Reporters Committee for Freedom of the Press, *Agents of Discovery: A Report on the Incidence of Subpoenas Served on the New Media in 2001* at 7 (2003).

require testimony on their own behalf as it does for criminal defendants. In addition, because defendants in civil suits do not face the possibility of jail or death, they might have less at stake if journalists withhold information. That is, judges often view the interests of parties in civil suits, which are primarily monetary, as less compelling than those in criminal cases. Furthermore, many civil suits involve private disputes such as compensation in accidental injury cases that do not have a direct and substantial impact on public health and safety.

A federal appeals court decided one of the most significant civil cases involving confidential news sources in 1972, less than six months after the Supreme Court decided *Branzburg*. In *Baker v. F & F Investment*, the U.S. Court of Appeals for the Second Circuit used a variation of the three-part test to uphold the right of a prominent magazine journalist to refuse to reveal his source.[28] The court said litigants seeking the source of an article by journalist Alfred Balk had not established the need for the information or that they could not find the information in other ways. Balk wrote "Confessions of a Block-buster" for the *Saturday Evening Post* in 1962. He based the story, which documented discriminatory real estate practices in Chicago, on information supplied by an anonymous source given the pseudonym "Norris Vitcheck." The source told Balk how he scared whites living near black neighborhoods into selling their houses to him at low prices. "Vitcheck" then sold those houses to black homebuyers for substantial profits. Several years after the article appeared, a group of black individuals sued about 60 landlords, real estate companies and real estate investors, contending that they sold homes to blacks for excessive prices. The plaintiffs wanted Balk to identify "Vitcheck."

The Second Circuit said the plaintiffs had not demonstrated a sufficiently compelling need for the information to override the First Amendment values at stake. In civil cases, the court said, the public interest in protecting a journalist's confidential news sources "will often be weightier than the private interest in compelled disclosure." In the case at hand, the Second Circuit did not mention the Stewart three-part test but relied on similar criteria. The court said the identity of the source "did not go to the heart" of the case, a phrase often used when confidential sources are either not relevant or not necessary to a case. The Second Circuit also noted that according to the trial court judge, no alternatives to identifying Balk's source had been tried.

In contrast, the courts addressing Wen Ho Lee's efforts to force journalists to reveal their confidential sources all found that a qualified First Amendment privilege in civil cases had been overcome. The prevailing precedent in the Court of Appeals for the D.C. Circuit, *Zerilli v. Smith* requires that civil litigants seeking information from a nonparty journalist must meet two requirements; they must show that the information sought goes to the "heart of the matter" and that they have exhausted all reasonable alternative sources of the information.[29] In the *Lee* case, the court of appeals held that the lower court properly applied *Zerilli*. The information Lee sought was critical to proving that federal officials violated his rights under the Privacy Act. If Lee were unable to identify the leakers, he would have also been unable to prove the other elements of a Privacy Act claim, such as willfulness and intent. Before seeking information from journalists, Lee used every tactical device in the Federal Rules of Civil Procedure to extract evidence from the government. For example, Lee deposed 20 government officials, including the Secretary of Energy

---

[28] 470 F.2d 778 (2d Cir. 1972), *cert. denied*, 411 U.S. 966 (1973).
[29] 656 F.2d 705 (D.C. Cir. 1981).

and the Director of the FBI. These depositions revealed "a pattern of denials, vague or evasive answers, and stonewalling." Lee's extensive efforts, combined with the unwillingness of government officials to admit to the leaks, meant the testimony of the journalists was necessary, the court said.[30]

Libel Suits Courts are more reluctant to protect journalists' confidential news sources in civil suits involving media defendants than in suits in which the media are not parties. Courts frequently order journalists to reveal sources and notes when they are subpoenaed by libel plaintiffs. Judges generally insist that libel plaintiffs must have the opportunity to prove that newspapers or broadcast stations acted negligently or with actual malice when preparing defamatory stories.

Judges often conclude that it is unfair for journalists to claim that they acted properly in preparing a story and at the same time refuse to divulge sources that would allow a libel plaintiff to prove otherwise. For example, in *Star Editorial, Inc. v. United States District Court*, a federal appeals court said the only way a libel plaintiff could meet his burden of proof in a libel case was to know who had accused him of lewd and drunken conduct. The U.S. Court of Appeals for the Ninth Circuit ordered the *Star*, a weekly supermarket tabloid, to disclose confidential informants used in preparing a story.[31] The *Star* had published a story claiming that the plaintiff, comedian Rodney Dangerfield, had been drunk in a Las Vegas hotel room with two naked women, had "trashed" the hotel room and had chased a female hotel employee around his room with ice tongs stating that he hoped to rip her clothing off.

The court found the need for the identity of the *Star*'s confidential sources overcame a qualified privilege. The Ninth Circuit said the sources for the Dangerfield allegations, sources the *Star* said were employees of Caesar's Palace hotel, were relevant to Dangerfield's libel suit. The court also said that Dangerfield had an important interest in discovering the *Star*'s confidential sources because the comedian, as a public figure, had to prove the tabloid acted with *New York Times* actual malice. This could be demonstrated, the court noted, by showing that the sources were unreliable or that there were in fact no sources. Without knowing the identity of the sources, however, Dangerfield would have an extremely difficult time proving his case.

Courts considering the constitutional privilege in libel cases frequently point out that the U.S. Supreme Court ruled in 1979 that journalists have no First Amendment right to refuse to testify when a libel plaintiff is seeking evidence of *New York Times* actual malice. In *Herbert v. Lando*, discussed in Chapter 4, the Supreme Court ruled that journalists do not have a First Amendment privilege to refuse to provide information about how a story is investigated and written. In *Herbert*, which did not involve confidential sources, *60 Minutes* producer Barry Lando was required to tell Lt. Col. Anthony Herbert how he decided what to include in a broadcast critical of the army officer. The Supreme Court said such an exploration into the journalistic process was justified because public-figure libel plaintiffs could not show knowing falsehood or recklessness if they did not know what writers and editors were thinking when they put a story together.[32] Lower courts have relied on *Herbert* to require journalists to reveal not only nonconfidential notes and newsroom memos but also confidential sources.[33]

---

[30] Lee v. DOJ, 413 F.3d 53 (D.C. Cir. 2005), *cert. denied*, 547 U.S. 1187 (2006).
[31] 7 F.3d 856 (9th Cir. 1993).
[32] 441 U.S. 153 (1979).
[33] *See, e.g.*, Cape Publications, Inc. v. Bridges, 387 So. 2d 436 (Fla. Dist. Ct. App. 1980).

In addition, courts have relied on *Herbert* to justify punitive measures against the media if they refuse to reveal confidential sources and other materials. Several courts after *Herbert* ruled that news organizations refusing to reveal confidential news sources must defend themselves in libel suits as if the sources did not exist.

In New Hampshire, for example, the state supreme court not only affirmed a lower court ruling to compel disclosure of a newspaper's sources but also said the lower court could punish the paper's refusal to reveal the source by assuming that the source did not exist. In *Downing v. Monitor Publishing Co.*, former police chief Clayton Downing of Boscawen sought the names of sources who had told the *Concord Monitor* that he had failed a lie detector test. The New Hampshire Supreme Court relied heavily on *Herbert* when it said that there is "no absolute privilege" that allows the press to refuse to reveal sources of information "essential" to a libel plaintiff's case.[34]

The New Hampshire Supreme Court noted that reporters held in contempt for refusing to reveal sources often choose to go to jail rather than to obey court orders to provide information. Putting journalists in jail "in no way" helps libel plaintiffs obtain sufficient information to prove their cases, the court said. Therefore, the court decided, if a journalist refuses to reveal a source, the court will assume no source was used. Thus, a newspaper or broadcast station might have to prove the lack of recklessness or negligence without using the information gained from the confidential source and even without saying in court that a source existed.

Therefore, in libel suits, journalists not only have to weigh the possibility of fines or jail sentences when deciding whether to make promises protecting the confidentiality of sources but also must consider the possibility of harm to their libel defenses. Before publishing a potentially defamatory story, journalists should be confident they can prove to a jury that they are accurate and have exercised sufficient care in the preparation of the article without reliance on confidential sources. On occasion, newspapers and broadcast stations may face the dilemma of having to decide whether to break a promise of confidentiality or risk losing a libel case.

The First Amendment is not, of course, the only source of protection for journalists who want to refuse to reveal confidential news sources. There are also state statutes and federal court rules and guidelines. Recent efforts to base a journalist's privilege on federal common law, however, have failed. In very rare circumstances, journalists may claim a Fifth Amendment privilege.

■ SUMMARY ■

The Supreme Court decided 5–4, in *Branzburg v. Hayes*, that reporters do not have First Amendment protection to refuse to testify before grand juries. Justice White, writing the majority opinion, said that journalists had not demonstrated that they should have a privilege to refuse to reveal confidential sources. However, Justice Powell, casting the deciding vote, implied that journalists might be entitled to protection in very limited instances. Justice Stewart, in dissent, said that to compel testimony from journalists the First Amendment should be interpreted to require government officials to prove that there is probable cause to believe the information is relevant to a specific investigation, that the need for the information is compelling, and that no alternative way of acquiring the information is available.

---

[34] 415 A.2d 683 (N.H. 1980).

Since *Branzburg*, a First Amendment privilege is seldom granted when journalists are subpoenaed to testify before grand juries, discuss an event they witnessed, or provide nonconfidential information or sources. However, some appellate courts require persons who want to subpoena a journalist to meet a three-part test based on Stewart's *Branzburg* dissent. Using this test, appellate courts sometimes decide that journalists do not have to testify in criminal trials or where information is being sought by parties to civil suits that do not directly involve the media. The courts are more reluctant to grant the privilege when a media outlet is being sued for libel.

A FEDERAL COMMON-LAW PRIVILEGE?

Three years after the *Branzburg* decision, Congress enacted the Federal Rules of Evidence, including Rule 501, which provides the privilege of a witness "shall be governed by the principles of the common law as they may be interpreted by the courts of the United States in the light of reason and experience."[35] In *Jaffee v. Redmond*, the Supreme Court held that confidential communications made to licensed psychotherapists were protected by a federal common-law privilege. In doing so, the Court adopted a multipart test to guide lower courts in other cases in which a common-law privilege is asserted. The test asks whether the asserted privilege would serve significant private and public interests, whether these interests outweigh any evidentiary benefit resulting from rejection of the privilege, and whether the privilege has been widely recognized by the states.[36]

As shown in cases, such as those involving Wen Ho Lee and Valerie Plame, judicial skepticism toward a First Amendment—based journalist's privilege has markedly increased since 2001. To provide judges with an alternative basis for protecting journalists, media lawyers have argued for a qualified reporter's privilege based on federal common law. These efforts have uniformly failed. Appellate courts for the Second Circuit[37] and the D.C. Circuit[38] ruled that even if a common-law privilege existed, it was overcome by the government's need for the journalists' information. The district courts handling the cases of former White House official "Scooter" Libby[39] and the reporters covering the baseball steroids scandal[40] similarly rejected the common-law privilege arguments. Most recently, the Fourth Circuit ruled that the Supreme Court rejected a common-law privilege in *Branzburg*. Therefore, only the Supreme Court, not lower courts, could recognize such a privilege.[41]

In the 2005 case involving Judith Miller and Matthew Cooper, the Court of Appeals for the D.C. Circuit held that *if* there were a common-law privilege, it was not absolute and was overcome by the special prosecutor investigating the leaking of Valerie Plame's CIA affiliation.[42] Judge Tatel's separate opinion offered the strongest support for a journalist's federal common-law privilege. Tatel argued that "reason and experience," as evidenced by state shield laws, supported judicial acknowledgment of a qualified common-law privilege. Judge Tatel proposed a balancing test for leak cases that examined the government's need for the information,

---

[35] Fed. R. Evid. 501.
[36] 518 U.S. 1 (1996).
[37] N.Y. Times Co. v. Gonzales, 459 F.3d 160 (2d Cir. 2006), *stay denied*, 549 U.S. 1049 (2006).
[38] *In re* Grand Jury Subpoena, Miller, 397 F.3d 964 (D.C. Cir. 2005).
[39] United States v. Libby, 432 F. Supp. 2d 26 (D.D.C. 2006).
[40] *In re* Grand Jury Subpoenas to Fainaru-Wada and Williams, 438 F. Supp. 2d 1111 (N.D. Cal. 2006).
[41] United States v. Sterling, 724 F.3d 482 (4th Cir. 2013). A common law privilege is not recognized in military jurisprudence. United States v. Wuterich, 68 M.J. 511 (N.M. Ct. Crim. App. 2009) (en banc).
[42] *In re* Grand Jury Subpoena, Miller, 397 F.3d 964 (D.C. Cir. 2005).

exhaustion of alternative sources, and weighed the harm caused by the leak against the leaked information's value. In this case, he believed the news value of Plame's CIA affiliation was marginal.

Judge Tatel's balancing test was sharply criticized by Judge Rosemary Collyer in a contempt proceeding against Walter Pincus of the *Washington Post*.[43] Pincus relied on anonymous government sources in articles about Wen Ho Lee, a nuclear weapons researcher who was investigated for espionage. (First Amendment aspects of the *Lee* case were discussed earlier in this chapter.) Pincus claimed that Judge Tatel's common-law balancing test should be followed. Judge Collyer found this test to be inherently unworkable and declined to create a federal common-law privilege. She wrote that a judge's evaluation of newsworthiness would create a subjective standard with unpredictable outcomes. "Courts are ill-suited to decide the degree to which information is beneficial or unimportant to the common weal."

As noted earlier in this chapter, the *Washington Post*, along with other media organizations, paid Lee $750,000 in 2006 as part of a settlement that ended contempt citations against Pincus and four other journalists.

PROTECTION UNDER THE FIFTH AMENDMENT

Even when judges reject First Amendment and common-law privilege claims, journalists may assert the Fifth Amendment privilege against self-incrimination *if* they are able to convince a judge there is a reasonable fear their testimony will possibly lead to a criminal prosecution. Those asserting the Fifth Amendment must show their fear of prosecution is not "imaginary, remote, or speculative."[44] Journalists have rarely relied on the Fifth Amendment. In 2015, the Sixth Circuit became the first appellate court to rule that a journalist could refuse to answer questions about confidential sources under the Fifth Amendment because the information sought would be useful in a criminal prosecution.

In 2013 and 2010, a federal district judge in Michigan reaffirmed an earlier ruling allowing a *Detroit Free Press* reporter, David Ashenfelter, to assert the Fifth Amendment as a basis for refusing to answer questions about confidential sources. Ashenfelter relied upon confidential sources for a story he wrote revealing the Department of Justice (DOJ) was investigating possible misconduct by Richard Convertino when he was the lead prosecutor during the 2003 Detroit "sleeper cell" terrorism trial. Like Wen Ho Lee discussed earlier in this chapter, Convertino sued the DOJ, claiming the leak violated the Privacy Act. After efforts to obtain the identity of Ashenfelter's sources from the DOJ proved unsuccessful, Convertino sought from Ashenfelter the identity of the sources cited in his article. Under the Sixth Circuit's precedent, Ashenfelter had no First Amendment–based evidentiary privilege,[45] so when asked for the identity of his sources at a December 8, 2008 deposition, Ashenfelter claimed he had a legitimate basis to fear prosecution under federal statutes punishing the improper receipt of confidential documents and information.[46]

Judge Robert Cleland ordered Ashenfelter to submit an *ex parte* affidavit for *in camera* review to help the judge examine the legitimacy of his fear of prosecution.

[43] Lee v. DOJ, 401 F. Supp. 2d 123 (D.D.C. 2005).
[44] *In re* Morganroth, 718 F.2d 161, 167 (6th Cir. 1983).
[45] *See In re* Grand Jury Proceedings, 810 F.2d 580 (6th Cir. 1987).
[46] *See, e.g.*, 18 U.S.C. § 641. *See generally* William E. Lee, "Probing Secrets: The Press and Inchoate Liability for Newsgathering Crimes," 36 *Am. J. Crim. L.* 129 (2009).

At a closed-door deposition on April 21, 2009, Judge Cleland upheld Ashenfelter's Fifth Amendment claims. The Sixth Circuit affirmed, stating that even though the attorney general might be reluctant to prosecute Ashenfelter, "it is not the likelihood but rather the possibility of prosecution that matters in the assertion of privilege."[47]

PROTECTION UNDER STATE STATUTES

Although the Supreme Court in *Branzburg* said the First Amendment does not protect reporters from being compelled to testify before grand juries, the Court did not say the Constitution prohibits legislative protection for confidential sources. In fact, Justice White invited legislatures to "fashion standards and rules as narrow or as broad as deemed necessary." At the time of *Branzburg*, 17 states had shield laws. By 2022, 40 states had shield laws.

States that have adopted "shield laws" protecting journalists are Alabama, Alaska, Arizona, Arkansas, California, Colorado, Connecticut, Delaware, Florida, Georgia, Illinois, Indiana, Kansas, Kentucky, Louisiana, Maine, Maryland, Michigan, Minnesota, Montana, Nebraska, Nevada, New Jersey, New Mexico, New York, North Carolina, North Dakota, Ohio, Oklahoma, Oregon, Pennsylvania, Rhode Island, South Carolina, South Dakota, Tennessee, Texas, Vermont, Washington, West Virginia and Wisconsin. California is the only state to also provide for a privilege in its state constitution. A shield law has also been adopted by the Council of the District of Columbia. The New Mexico and Utah Supreme Courts have adopted rules of evidence providing protection similar to shield laws. A survey of news organizations by the Reporters Committee for Freedom of the Press found that shield laws provided the basis for more than half of the successful media challenges to subpoenas in 2001.[48]

State shield laws vary widely; about a dozen state statutes are like Alabama's, which is "absolute" because it does not qualify the protection for reporters' sources. The Alabama law provides that no person "connected with or employed on any newspaper, radio broadcasting station or television station" who engages in news gathering "shall be compelled to disclose in any legal proceeding" the sources of any published information.[49]

The Alabama statute is absolute in the sense that it does not list exceptions to the privilege, but the law does not shield all journalists. For example, it does not protect the authors of articles written for magazines. This limitation was an important aspect of a libel lawsuit brought by former University of Alabama football coach Mike Price against *Sports Illustrated*. The centerpiece of a May 2003 *Sports Illustrated* article about Price was a description of a hotel room incident between Price and two women he had earlier met at a Pensacola, Florida, strip club. The article included the following:

> He eventually met up with two women, both of whom he had earlier propositioned for sex, according to one of the women, who agreed to speak to SI about the hotel-room liaison on the condition that her name not be used. The woman, who declined comment when asked if she was paid for the evening, said that the threesome engaged "in some pretty

---

[47] Convertino v. Dep't of Justice, 795 F.3d 587 (6th Cir. 2015).
[48] Reporters Committee for Freedom of the Press, *Agents of Discovery: A Report on the Incidence of Subpoenas Served on the New Media in 2001* at 10 (2003).
[49] Ala. Code § 12-21-142.

aggressive sex." She said that at one point she and her female companion decided to add a little levity to the activity: "We started screaming 'Roll Tide!' and he was yelling back, 'It's rolling baby, it's rolling.'"[50]

Price admitted visiting the strip club but denied having sex with anyone mentioned in the article. In a subsequent libel suit, he sought the identity of the confidential source to establish that *Sports Illustrated* acted with actual malice. The Court of Appeals for the Eleventh Circuit concluded that *Sports Illustrated*, as a magazine, was not covered by the Alabama shield law.[51] However, because a qualified First Amendment privilege applied to the magazine, Price was required to depose four women who had knowledge of the confidential source's identity before the article's author would be compelled to reveal his source. Shortly after this ruling, Price and the magazine settled the suit.

The Alabama statute also appears to require publication before any protection is provided. Unpublished notes and tapes may be subpoenaed. Further, the statute on its face would appear to protect only a journalist who refuses to reveal the name of a source and not a journalist who refuses to reveal information from notes.[52] The limitations the Alabama legislature has imposed on the statutory privilege are typical of the laws of many states.

Seven of the more important points to consider in evaluating a shield law are who is protected, whether confidentiality is required for protection, what kind of information is protected, whether publication is required, in what legal forums the privilege can be asserted, whether the privilege can be waived and whether exceptions to the privilege are specified.

People Protected

Justice White's majority opinion in *Branzburg* questioned how judges could define a journalist entitled to a constitutional privilege. White implied that determining who should be protected by a privilege would be difficult because a variety of communicators, such as "lecturers, political pollsters, novelists, academic researchers, and dramatists" contribute to public knowledge. Legislators adopting shield laws have the difficult task of specifying who ought to be shielded from disclosing sources or information in court. The list must be limited, or it could prove to be a haven for anyone who does not want to testify in court, frustrating legitimate attempts to compel needed testimony.

Most of the 40 states with shield laws allow protection for those connected to "newspapers, radio and television" or the "news media." About a dozen states appear to protect *anyone* employed by the news media. Another dozen protect only persons involved in the news process, including editors and photographers. One state statute, Alaska's, applies only to "reporters."[53]

Most shield laws *exclude* book authors, freelance bloggers and writers, academic researchers and others not working directly in news organizations. For example, the New Jersey shield law protects only those "connected with or employed

---

[50] Don Yaeger, "Bad Behavior: How He Met His Destiny at a Strip Club," *Sports Illustrated*, May 12, 2003, at 38.

[51] Price v. Time, Inc., 416 F.3d 1327 (11th Cir. 2005). *See generally* Stefan Fatsis, "Playing Defense: A Coach's Lawsuit Poses Challenges for Time, Inc.," *Wall St. J.*, July 13, 2005, at A1.

[52] Comment, "Rusty Shields for Those Who Wield the Pen: The State of Alabama's Reporter Shield Law in the Aftermath of Price v. Time," 37 *Cumb. L. Rev.* 263 (2006) (noting limitations of Alabama's shield law).

[53] Alaska Stat. § 09.25.300.

by" the news media. In 2011, the New Jersey Supreme Court ruled that those who post messages on online message boards lacked a connection with the news media, such as newspapers or broadcast stations, identified in the shield law.[54] Arkansas became one of the first states to specifically include web-based journalists when in 2011 it amended its shield law to protect reporters and writers for any "newspaper, periodical, radio station, television station, or Internet news source."[55]

Nebraska has adopted among the broadest descriptions of persons covered by shield laws. Its shield law protects persons engaged in "procuring, gathering, writing, editing, or disseminating" not only news but also "other information." In addition, the Nebraska statute applies to "any medium of communication," which includes, but is not limited to, "any newspaper, magazine, other periodical, book, pamphlet, news service, wire service, news or feature syndicate, broadcast station or network, or cable television system." The Nebraska statute appears broad enough to apply to work of communicators such as public relations professionals.[56]

The growth of Internet-based journalism poses interesting statutory interpretation problems for courts. Laws that narrowly specify protected media, such as Alabama's reference to newspapers, radio and television stations, do not cover journalists producing material solely for websites. Laws that use expansive terms, such as Nebraska's reference to "any medium of communication," cover web journalists. In between these two extremes are state laws that use ambiguous terms, such as "periodical publication," that may be sufficiently expansive to protect web journalists.

The California Court of Appeals for the Sixth Appellate District ruled in 2006 that the state's shield law covered Jason O'Grady, owner and editor of PowerPage, a website devoted to news about Apple computer products.[57] Over a period of several days in November 2004, O'Grady published articles on his website providing details about an Apple product that was under development. Apple claimed O'Grady published its trade secrets, obtained through an Apple employee's breach of confidentiality, and sought to discover the identity of O'Grady's source.

The appellate court easily concluded that O'Grady was an editor/reporter engaged in the dissemination of news. The more difficult question was whether the shield law's protection for journalists working for a "newspaper, magazine, or other periodical publication" applied to PowerPage. Because the terms *magazine* and *e-zine* are now widely used to describe websites that offer regularly updated news, the appellate court concluded that PowerPage could be classified as a magazine. The court stated that web pages like PowerPage "are highly analogous to printed publications: they consist predominately of text on 'pages' which the reader 'opens,' reads at his own pace, and 'closes.'" Even if PowerPage could not properly be classified as a magazine for the purposes of the shield law, the appellate court concluded the legislature intended the phrase "periodical publication" to include all ongoing, recurring news publications. PowerPage differed from traditional periodicals only in its tendency, which flows directly from the technology it employs, to continuously update its content.

Video blogger Josh Wolf is also arguably covered by the California shield law in state cases. However, in April 2006, a federal judge ruled that California privilege law was irrelevant in federal proceedings. A federal grand jury subpoenaed Wolf,

---

[54] Too Much Media LLC v. Hale, 20 A.3d 364 (N.J. 2011).
[55] Ark. Code Ann. § 16-85-510.
[56] Neb. Rev. Stat. § 20-144.
[57] O'Grady v. Superior Court of Santa Clara County, 130 Cal. App. 4th 1423 (Cal. Ct. App. 2006).

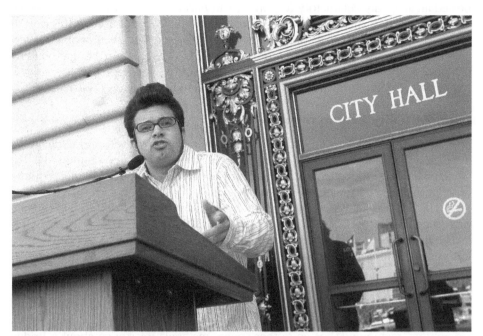

PHOTO 11.1   After his release from federal prison, video blogger Josh Wolf speaks during an April 3, 2007, press conference of the steps of city hall in San Francisco, California. Wolf was imprisoned for 226 days for refusing to comply with a subpoena seeking a video he shot of a 2005 protest. He was released after he provided the video. His lengthy incarceration is a record for an American journalist held in contempt of court.

Source: Getty Images. Used by permission.

seeking video he shot in 2005 of a San Francisco protest march in which a policeman was injured. Wolf filed a motion to quash, arguing that the California shield law provided an absolute barrier to the subpoena. The district court ruled that *Branzburg*, not the state shield law, governed this case and Wolf was ordered to testify.[58] Wolf refused to do so, was imprisoned on August 1, 2006, and was briefly released on September 1 while his case was appealed to the Court of Appeals for the Ninth Circuit. After the appellate court affirmed the contempt order,[59] Wolf returned to jail on September 22. Wolf was released in April 2007 in a deal with prosecutors. Wolf provided the video to the court and in a statement swore he had no information relating to the injury of the police officer. Wolf's incarceration for 226 days is a record for an American journalist held in contempt of court.

State courts increasingly are grappling with the issue of whether those who post information on newspaper websites are "sources" covered by state shield laws. Trial courts in Florida, Montana, North Carolina, Oregon and Texas ruled newspapers did not have to reveal the email addresses and other identifying information of anonymous commentators who posted allegedly defamatory material on the newspapers' websites.[60] However, the only appellate court to rule on this issue held in 2012 that Indiana's shield law did not protect an anonymous commentator who

---

[58] *In re* Grand Jury Investigation, Wolf, No. CR 06–90064 MISC MMC (N.D. Cal. Apr. 5, 2006).
[59] 2006 U.S. App. LEXIS 23315 (9th Cir. Sept. 8, 2006).
[60] Jason Martin, Mark Caramanica, and Anthony Fargo, "Anonymous Speakers and Confidential Sources: Using Shield Laws When They Overlap Online," 16 *Comm. L. & Pol'y* 89 (2011).

posted an allegedly defamatory response to an *Indianapolis Star* news story on the *Star*'s website. The Indiana Court of Appeals found the *Star* did not use this post to further investigate and report on its initial story. The comments section of the newspaper's website was like a bulletin board placed outside the *Star*'s office building for "anyone to tack an announcement." To be a source, the appellate court ruled, one must provide information that is then interpreted by the news organization.[61]

Confidentiality Requirement

A few state shield laws specify that a reporter must have promised confidentiality to a source to be protected by the statute. However, most of the state statutes, like that of Alabama, do not explicitly say whether a promise of confidentiality is required for a journalist to be protected under the law.

The Tennessee Supreme Court, among others, has ruled that the state's statute protecting "any information or the source of any information" from disclosure protects journalists whether they promise confidentiality. The Tennessee court's opinion said the statutory protection for "any" information means that "all" information is protected.[62] The court noted that the legislature had not qualified its protection of "any information" in the statute by requiring that a promise of confidentiality be made. The Tennessee Supreme Court reversed a lower court decision that would have required Memphis newspapers to disclose "any and all correspondence, studies, reports, memoranda, or any other source material" for stories about a bridge collapse.

On the other hand, the Rhode Island Supreme Court strictly construed a state shield law that protects reporters only from testifying about a "confidential association," "confidential information" or the "source of any confidential information."[63] In *Outlet Communications Inc. v. Rhode Island*,[64] the court said the statute did not shield a Providence television station from a grand jury subpoena seeking portions of an on-camera interview that had not been broadcast. The televised interview had taken place on a public sidewalk. The Rhode Island court said the television station could not rely on the statute because the interview "was anything but secret or confidential."

Information Protected

States are divided over whether to shield reporters from revealing notes and other information as well as sources. Some states protect reporters from testifying only when the journalists want to withhold the name of a source. Other states offer protection against disclosure of any information in the possession of a reporter or other media employee. Only a few state statutes specifically say that outtakes, film and photographs are protected from forced disclosure.

The Alabama shield law discussed earlier, if strictly interpreted, would protect only "the sources" of information obtained by news personnel, that is, the identity of confidential sources.[65] The Tennessee statute applies to "any information" as well as "the source of any information" obtained for publication or broadcast.[66]

---

[61] Indiana Newspapers Inc. v. Junior Achievement of Central Indiana, 963 N.E.2d 534 (Ct. App. 2012).

[62] Austin v. Memphis Publishing Co., 655 S.W.2d 146 (Tenn. 1983). *See also* Aerial Burials Inc. v. Minneapolis Star & Tribune Co., 8 Media L. Rep. 1653 (Minn. Dist. Ct. Hennepin Co. 1982).

[63] R.I. Gen. Laws § 9-19.1-2.

[64] 588 A.2d 1050 (R.I. 1991).

[65] Ala. Code § 12-21-142.

[66] Tenn. Code Ann. § 24-1-208(a).

Nebraska protects sources, information and "all notes, outtakes, photographs, film, tapes, or other data."[67]

Most statutes do not protect reporters who have been called to testify about events they have seen rather than to reveal a source or information given to them by a source. More than one court has held that a statute shielding confidential news sources from disclosure does not protect a reporter who witnessed a crime from testifying. Paul Branzburg, the *Louisville Courier-Journal* reporter of *Branzburg v. Hayes*, tried to avoid appearing before two grand juries by arguing he was protected by the Kentucky shield law. Although the Kentucky statute provides without qualification that reporters do not have to reveal their sources, the Kentucky Court of Appeals said the law did not apply to Branzburg's case because Branzburg's own observation was the source of his stories about the making and using of illegal drugs.[68] Branzburg could have been jailed or fined had he remained in Kentucky. However, he had moved to Michigan by the time his case was considered by the U.S. Supreme Court, and Michigan refused to extradite him.

Publication Requirement

Slightly more than half of the 40 state shield laws appear to provide protection whether or not the subpoenaed information is published. About a half-dozen statutes, including Alabama's, require publication for the statutory protection to be triggered. State statutes that require publication will not ordinarily protect information or pictures that reporters and editors leave out of newspapers and news broadcasts.

In contrast, Minnesota's shield law protects against the disclosure of "any unpublished information," and therefore a state court quashed a subpoena for half a page of notes a reporter said she did not use or rely on for a story. Minneapolis freelance journalist Joanna Conners turned over to a plaintiff in a libel case her handwritten notes and a transcription of a tape-recorded interview that contained published information. She deleted from the notes and transcripts information she said she did not use.[69]

Forums Where Privilege Can Be Asserted

Most shield laws protect newspersons asked to testify before any administrative, judicial, or legislative body. A few state statutes cover only civil proceedings or only criminal proceedings. Some do not allow a newsperson to refuse to testify in a libel suit.

A provocative development in privilege law occurred in late 2013 when New York's highest court ruled that New York's absolute shield law protected Jana Winter from a Colorado subpoena seeking her sources regarding James Holmes, the Aurora, Colorado, theater gunman. The New York Court of Appeals ruled that due to the significant disparity between New York and Colorado law, it would offend New York's policy to order Winter to appear in another state where she would likely be compelled to identify her confidential sources.[70] It did not matter, the New York court stated, whether Winter was in Colorado when she spoke with

---

[67] Neb. Rev. Stat. § 20-145(5).

[68] Branzburg v. Pound, 461 S.W.2d 345 (Ky. 1970), *aff'd sub nom;* Branzburg v. Hayes, 408 U.S. 665 (1972).

[69] Aerial Burials Inc. v. Minneapolis Star & Tribune Co., 8 Media L. Rep. 1653 (Minn. Dist. Ct. Hennepin Co. 1982).

[70] In the Matter of Holmes v. Winter, 3 N.E.3d 694 (2013).

her confidential sources; New York-based journalists should not have to consult the law where a source is located before they promise confidentiality.

Waiver

Most state shield laws do not address whether a journalist's privilege is lost, or waived, if the source becomes known or if the journalist discloses part of a confidential conversation. A few statutes indicate that limited disclosure, publication, or testimony by a journalist does not waive the privilege protecting against the forced disclosure of additional information. However, a few shield laws provide that informants can destroy the privilege of a newsperson by revealing their own identity.

Although the New Jersey shield statute does not contain a waiver provision, the state's rules of evidence do. The New Jersey shield law provides for a privilege for information "whether or not it is disseminated." However, the state's evidence rules declare that a person claiming a privilege cannot refuse to testify if any part of the confidential information is disclosed. In the case *In re Schuman*, the New Jersey Supreme Court ruled that the shield law prevailed over the evidence rules. The court said *New Jersey Herald* reporter Evan Schuman did not have to appear in court simply to affirm the truth of a story he wrote about a murder confession. The court said that Schuman was protected from compelled testimony because the state shield law explicitly covered information already disseminated. The court also recognized that the "legislature has continuously acted to establish the strongest possible protection from compulsory testimony for the press."[71]

Exceptions

Some shield laws are absolute in the sense that they do not qualify or limit a journalist's privilege or list exceptions to the statutory protection against the disclosure. In states that list exceptions to their shield laws, the most frequent limitation is a three-part test like the one advocated by Justice Stewart in *Branzburg v. Hayes*. In Tennessee, for example, the state shield law protects a journalist from compelled testimony unless the person seeking the information can demonstrate that (1) the information sought relates to a specific, probable violation of law, (2) the information cannot be obtained through alternative means and (3) there is a compelling and overriding public interest requiring disclosure.[72] Journalists are shielded from testifying if persons seeking the information cannot meet all three criteria.

A few states require disclosure when necessary to prevent "a miscarriage of justice,"[73] a provision that could be used if a judge believed a reporter's testimony was critical to the defense of a criminal defendant. Some states simply indicate that the privilege can be revoked if disclosure is essential to the public interest.[74]

---

[71] 552 A.2d 602 (N.J. 1989).
[72] Tenn. Code Ann. § 24-1-208. *See also* Fla. Stat. § 90.5015(2) (using a similar three-part test).
[73] *See, e.g.*, N.D. Cent. Code Ann. § 31-01-06.2.
[74] *See, e.g.*, La. Rev. Stat. § 45:1453.

Pros and Cons of Shield Laws

In the absence of a clearly defined constitutional protection for journalists, reporters in states with shield laws know that they will not be compelled to testify at least in some circumstances. Although shield laws are generally not absolute, journalists can sometimes determine before they promise confidentiality whether a shield law will protect them. The mere existence of shield laws might help to thwart subpoenas. For example, lawyers might be less likely to seek a subpoena for the purpose of "fishing" for information when a state statute clearly grants a reporter a shield against testifying.

Journalists working in states with shield laws, however, should be cautious before relying on the statutes. Shield laws are limited not only by myriad exclusions and exceptions but also by judges who tend to interpret them strictly. Many journalists and sources who have counted on a shield law found out too late that the statute did not apply to them. Many reporters therefore have faced penalties, including jail, which they had not anticipated and might not have risked had they known no protection existed. Moreover, as Josh Wolf discovered, a strong state shield law is inapplicable in federal proceedings.

Adding to the inherent judicial concern about shield laws limiting the availability of important testimony is a concern for the separation of powers among the branches of government. A few courts have declared that shield laws represent illegal interference by a legislature in the affairs of the judiciary. For example, New Mexico's Supreme Court ruled that the state's shield law violated the state constitution because the legislature could not establish rules for the courts.[75] In addition, courts sometimes rule that shield laws unconstitutionally interfere with the Sixth Amendment rights of criminal defendants. The New Jersey Supreme Court ruled that *New York Times* reporter Myron Farber had to produce subpoenaed materials in the murder trial of Dr. Mario E. Jascalevich despite the state's shield law. The New Jersey court agreed that it was "abundantly clear" that Farber fell under the New Jersey law providing news media employees the privilege of refusing to reveal information collected during their professional activities. However, the court said the state's shield law had to yield to both federal and state constitutional provisions that gave defendants the right "to have compulsory process for obtaining witnesses" in their favor.[76]

The lack of complete protection for confidential sources means that a journalist should carefully consider any promise not to reveal the identity of sources. A reporter may want to promise only conditional confidentiality. That is, a reporter will promise to protect the identity of a source unless ordered to reveal it by a court. Moreover, some lawyers suggest that reporters require sources to sign affidavits as evidence the source exists. Many news organizations require that editors be consulted when reporters wish to promise confidentiality to news sources. Editors might disagree with the promise of confidentiality after the reporter has legally obligated the newspaper, a problem discussed later in the chapter. In addition, news organizations might refuse to help reporters fight subpoenas if the reporters do not adhere to company policy on confidentiality.

---

[75] Ammerman v. Hubbard Broadcasting, Inc., 551 P.2d 1354 (N.M. 1976). The same New Mexico Supreme Court later promulgated a rule providing journalists a limited privilege. N.M. R. Evid. § 11-514.
[76] *In re Farber*, 394 A.2d 330 (N.J. 1978).

▨ SUMMARY ▨

Forty states and the District of Columbia have adopted statutes protecting journalists from revealing news sources. These statutes vary greatly, but none protects every writer in all circumstances. Most apply only to news media employees. A few specify that they apply only when confidentiality has been promised. About half of the statutes apply only to the disclosure of sources and not to notes and other information. Journalists need to be aware of the limitations of their state's shield laws before relying on them for protection against a court order to testify.

PROTECTION UNDER FEDERAL STATUTES AND REGULATIONS

No federal statute explicitly protects reporters from being ordered to testify in court. Shortly after *Branzburg* was decided, both the House and Senate held extensive hearings on proposed shield legislation. The move to enact a federal shield law collapsed because press organizations could not agree on whether the privilege should be qualified or absolute and the DOJ opposed the proposed legislation.[77] By 1975, the sense of urgency had passed as lower courts began recognizing a qualified First Amendment privilege.

As a result of high-profile cases, such as the *Miller* and *Lee* cases discussed earlier in this chapter, proposed shield law legislation was again debated in the House and Senate from 2005 to 2009. A key sticking point was the protection offered to sources of national security leaks. Both the Bush and Obama administrations demanded changes to protect national security. Congress came very close in 2009 to enacting a shield law with provisions acceptable to the Obama administration.[78] In 2010, support for a federal shield law evaporated as WikiLeaks began posting a trove of classified U.S. government documents relating to military actions and diplomatic efforts. President Obama called upon Congress to revive the shield law proposal in May 2013 after press groups criticized the DOJ for obtaining phone records and email of Associated Press and Fox News reporters. The WikiLeaks disclosures, however, have turned Congress against leaks.[79] In 2021, Attorney General Merrick Garland called on Congress to enact a shield law. Although President Biden described government inquiries into reporters sources as "simply, simply wrong," the prospects of a sharply divided Congress enacting a shield law in 2022 are nil.

Despite the absence of a federal shield law, rules governing the federal courts and regulations issued by the DOJ and the Securities and Exchange Commission restrict the use of subpoenas served on reporters.

Several courts have protected reporters from subpoenas under rules of evidence Congress adopted for use in the federal courts. Section 403 of the Federal Rules of Evidence, for example, allows judges to quash subpoenas if information sought from reporters would duplicate information already available. Therefore, a federal judge must consider whether alternative sources of information exist even if the judge does not recognize the qualified privilege developed in the Stewart dissent in *Branzburg*.

---

[77] *See generally Newsmen's Privilege: Hearings before the Subcomm. on Constitutional Rights of the Senate Comm. on the Judiciary*, 93d Cong. (1973); *Newsmen's Privilege: Hearings before Subcomm. No. 3 of the House Comm. on the Judiciary*, 93d Cong. (1973).

[78] Free Flow of Information Act of 2009, H.R. 985, 111th Cong. (2009); Free Flow of Information Act of 2009, S. 448, 111th Cong. (2009).

[79] William E. Lee, "The Demise of the Federal Shield Law," 30 *Cardozo Arts & Ent. L.J.* 27 (2012).

In addition to the rules governing the federal courts, the U.S. attorney general issued guidelines in 1970, revised in 2015, and undergoing revision in 2022, to limit requests for journalists' confidential sources by members of the DOJ. The guidelines were written "to strike the proper balance" between the public interest in an unrestricted flow of information and the public interest in fair and effective law enforcement. The guidelines apply to civil litigation as well as criminal investigations.[80]

The guidelines reflect the protections for journalists recognized in Justice Stewart's three-part test in *Branzburg*. The guidelines state that subpoenas are "extraordinary measures" and that DOJ employees must negotiate with the media and seek alternative sources in most circumstances. The news media are to be given advance notice of subpoenas except in rare situations. Only when there are "reasonable grounds" to believe that the information is essential to an investigation should a subpoena be sought. The scope of the subpoena should be as narrow as possible, limiting the amount of material requested. Subpoena requests generally must be approved by the U.S. attorney general.

Although the guidelines do not apply to terrorists or agents of foreign governments, the terms *reporter* and *news media* are otherwise undefined. Nonetheless, DOJ officials make distinctions about the people subject to the guidelines. For example, aspiring book author Vanessa Leggett was not considered to be a journalist by the DOJ; as an unpublished freelancer working on a book about a high-society murder, Leggett lacked an employer or a contract for publication. Consequently, *all* her notes and tape recordings relating to the murder were subpoenaed by a grand jury without any negotiation between Leggett and the DOJ. A federal appeals court ruled that even if Leggett were a "journalist," she was required to comply with the subpoena absent evidence of harassment or oppression. While the subpoena was not as "narrowly tailored as would be ideal," the appellate court held it was not overly broad. Leggett spent 168 days in federal prison for refusing to turn over her notes and tape recordings.[81]

Recently the DOJ revealed it uses a case-by-case analysis of 12 factors to determine if someone qualifies as a "member of the news media." Factors such as employment by a news organization and possession of press credentials give the DOJ latitude to draw lines between traditional media and new forms such as blogs.[82]

Nor do the guidelines define "newsgathering activities," and DOJ officials seeking to use a subpoena or search warrant must consult with the DOJ's Policy and Statutory Enforcement unit before seeking approval from the attorney general or deputy attorney general.[83] Where behavior is unrelated to newsgathering, approval by top officials for subpoenas or search warrants is unnecessary. For example, in 2021, Owen Shroyer, a talk show host on Infowars, a website known for discredited conspiracy theories, was arrested for entering the Capitol on January 6, 2021, and attempting to prevent certification of the 2020 election results. This disruptive behavior, unrelated to newsgathering, was sufficient to justify his arrest. Similarly, in 2019, in a child pornography and enticement investigation, a search warrant was issued for the email account of a reporter suspected of child enticement. According

---

[80] 28 C.F.R. § 50.10.
[81] *In re* Grand Jury Subpoenas, 29 Media L. Rep. 2301 (5th Cir. 2001), *cert. denied* 535 U.S. 1011 (2002).
[82] Anna Diakun and Trevor Timm, "For the Biden Administration, Who Counts as News Media?" *Columbia Journalism Rev.*, June 9, 2021.
[83] Department of Justice, Justice Manual, Title 9-13-400.

to the DOJ, "Because the target's conduct was not based on, or with the scope of, such individual's newsgathering activities, Attorney General authorization was not required to apply for a warrant."[84]

The DOJ guidelines also limit subpoenas for journalists' telephone and email records and generally require advance notice of a subpoena. These protections exist despite judicial rulings that the news media have no First Amendment right to be notified before telephone companies surrender journalists' records to law enforcement officers. In *Reporters Committee for Freedom of the Press v. AT&T*, several reporters, two newspaper companies and the Reporters Committee for Freedom of the Press tried to block government access to reporters' long-distance billing information if the journalists were not told beforehand.[85] The journalists sued AT&T after the company released toll-call records to government officials five times without informing the media. In one case, the FBI used phone records to try to link Daniel Ellsberg to the publication of the Pentagon Papers, discussed in Chapter 3. In another, the Internal Revenue Service sought evidence to confirm that an IRS employee had illegally divulged information to *New York Times* reporter David Rosenbaum.

The U.S. Court of Appeals for the D.C. Circuit, citing the Supreme Court's decision in *Branzburg*, said that the media have no First Amendment right to prevent the government from seeing telephone records that allow the identification of a news source. In *Reporters Committee*, the court said the First Amendment does not guarantee anyone, including journalists, the right to collect information immune from good-faith investigations by the government.

The DOJ guidelines, amended after *Reporters Committee* and again in 2015, limit any federal subpoena for telephone and email records to information essential to an investigation. The guidelines also say the government should pursue alternative approaches to obtaining the information being sought before officials seek a subpoena. The government must notify the media before subpoenaing telephone records unless notice poses "a substantial threat to the integrity" of an investigation. However, if a news organization is not warned before a subpoena for records, it must generally be notified within 90 days of the time the subpoena is issued. The U.S. attorney general must ordinarily approve a subpoena for records.

Department of Justice attorneys who do not follow the guidelines are subject to internal disciplinary action, but the guidelines specifically state they are "not intended to create any right" in any person. In 2005, the *New York Times* argued the government failed to comply with the guidelines when seeking the telephone records of two *Times* reporters and, as a result, should be barred from receiving the records. A federal district court rejected this argument, holding the guidelines "are just that—touchstones to assist the DOJ in its exercise of prosecutorial discretion—and confer no substantive rights or protections" that may be privately enforced.[86] Similarly, in the case of journalists Matthew Cooper and Judith Miller, discussed earlier in this chapter, the Court of Appeals for the D.C. Circuit held the guidelines, not required by any constitutional or statutory provision, merely "exist to guide the

---

[84] Department of Justice Use of Certain Law Enforcement Tools to Obtain Information from, or Records of Members of the News Media; and Questioning, Arresting, or Charging Members of the News Media, Annual Report for Calendar Year 2019.

[85] 593 F.2d 1030 (D.C. Cir. 1978), *cert. denied*, 440 U.S. 949 (1979).

[86] N.Y. Times Co. v. Gonzales, 382 F. Supp. 2d 457 (S.D.N.Y. 2005), *rev'd on other grounds*, 459 F.3d 160 (2d Cir. 2006), *stay denied*, 549 U.S. 1049 (2006). The *Times* did not appeal this aspect of the lower court's ruling.

Department's exercise of its discretion in determining when to seek the issuance of subpoenas to reporters," not to confer benefits upon reporters.[87]

The DOJ guidelines can be altered by the attorney general and press advocates expressed alarm in 2017 when then–Attorney General Jeff Sessions announced the DOJ was reviewing its policies limiting media subpoenas. As a senator, Sessions had been one of the most ardent opponents of bills proposing a federal shield law, claiming such a law would encourage leaks of classified national security information. The DOJ under President Trump did not issue new guidelines, nor did Sessions markedly increase the number of authorized subpoenas compared to the number authorized by his predecessor Eric Holder.[88] However, William Barr, attorney general in 2019–2020, approved in late 2020 subpoenas seeking the identity of sources who leaked classified information to eight reporters at the *Washington Post, New York Times* and CNN. As in 2013, when the press attacked Holder for seeking the records of Associated Press and Fox News reporters, the Barr-approved subpoenas were widely criticized when they were revealed in May and June of 2021.

When asked by a CNN reporter on May 21, 2021, if he would prevent the DOJ from seeking source information from reporters, President Biden said "It's simply, simply wrong. I will not let that happen."[89] The DOJ, however, did not announce a new policy until the *New York Times* on June 4 revealed the Biden administration had continued the effort to seek email records from *Times* reporters.[90] Faced with intense backlash, on June 5 the DOJ announced it would no longer seek source information from reporters "doing their jobs." This was followed by Attorney General Garland's July 19 announcement that he was asking the deputy attorney general to review and amend the department's regulations to better protect journalists.[91]

Garland's announcement indicated the prohibition on compulsory process would not apply when a reporter was suspected of a crime unrelated to newsgathering activities, or where reporters use criminal methods, such as breaking and entering, to obtain government information. Similarly, subpoenas and search warrants would be allowed when there was an imminent risk of death or serious bodily harm.

Because any regulations developed by the Biden administration can be revised by a new administration, and to ensure that journalist protections continue in succeeding administrations, Garland announced the DOJ would support shield legislation. It is unlikely that a sharply divided Congress will enact a shield law in 2022.

In 2006, the Securities and Exchange Commission issued guidelines concerning subpoenas to members of the news media. The guidelines were prompted by an SEC investigation into stock manipulation by Gradient Analytics in which SEC investigators subpoenaed two Dow Jones reporters who had covered the firm.

---

[87] *In re* Grand Jury Subpoena, Miller, 397 F.3d 964 (D.C. Cir. 2005).
[88] Department of Justice Use of Certain Law Enforcement Tools to Obtain Information from, or Records of, Members of the News Media; and Questioning, Arresting, or Charging Members of the News Media, Annual Reports for Calendar Years 2014–2018.
[89] Charlie Savage, "White House Favors a Ban On Seizing Reporters' Data," *N.Y. Times*, May 25, 2021, at A17.
[90] Charlie Savage and Katie Brenner, "Justice Dept. Waged Secret Fight to Get Emails of Times Reporters," *N.Y. Times*, June 5, 2021, at A1. The story first appeared on nytimes.com on June 4, 2021.
[91] Department of Justice Memorandum, *Use of Compulsory Process to Obtain Information From, or Records of, Members of the News Media*, July 19, 2021.

PHOTO 11.2   President Barack Obama and Vice President Joe Biden stand with Judge Merrick Garland while announcing Garland's nomination to the Supreme Court on March 16, 2016. As discussed in Chapter 1, Garland's Supreme Court appointment was blocked by Senate Republicans, allowing President Donald Trump to fill the vacancy created by the 2016 death of Justice Scalia. When Biden became president in 2021, he nominated Garland as attorney general; Garland was confirmed by the Senate in March 2021. After backlash from the revelation that the Trump administration in late 2020 subpoenaed the email and phone records of eight journalists, Garland announced the DOJ was revising its policy regarding the use of subpoenas and search warrants directed at journalists. He also expressed support for a federal shield law.

Source: Getty Images. Used by permission.

Since the insider trading scandals of the 1980s, discussed in Chapter 8, when reporters were the subject of investigations, the SEC had not subpoenaed any journalists. News of the 2006 subpoenas caused SEC Chair Christopher Cross to publicly scold his staff for failing to give the commissioners prior notice of the subpoenas. Although the SEC had no formal policy in place, Cox stated that "the issuance of a subpoena to a journalist which seeks to compel production of his or her notes and records of conversations with sources is highly unusual." Following Cox's remarks, the SEC decided not to enforce the subpoenas.[92]

In response to the Dow Jones incident, the SEC in April 2006 adopted guidelines for issuing subpoenas to journalists. Like the DOJ guidelines, the SEC guidelines require staff members to seek the information from nonmedia sources and to negotiate with news media to obtain information through informal methods, such as voluntary production, informal interviews or written summaries. A subpoena will be issued only in cases where the requested information is essential to an investigation and all alternative means of obtaining the information have been exhausted. Only the director of the Division of Enforcement, in consultation with the General Counsel, may authorize a subpoena and the chair of the SEC must be promptly

---

[92] Kara Scannell, "Cox Knocks Journalist Subpoenas," *Wall St. J.*, Feb. 28, 2006, at C5.

notified. As with the DOJ guidelines, the SEC guidelines are not intended to create any legally enforceable rights in any person.[93]

■ SUMMARY ■

There is no federal shield law. However, several courts have recognized a privilege for reporters under federal rules of procedure adopted by Congress for the federal courts. In addition, the DOJ and the SEC have adopted guidelines designed to limit the use of subpoenas served on journalists.

CONGRESSIONAL AUTHORITY

The judicial branch is not the only arm of the federal government with the power to subpoena reporters and cite journalists for contempt for refusing to disclose sources or information. Although the First Amendment is frequently asserted by uncooperative witnesses, the Supreme Court has yet to rely on the First Amendment as grounds for reversing a criminal contempt of Congress conviction.[94] A handful of public communicators have been threatened with contempt for refusing to testify before Congress during the last 50 years, but until 2016 those efforts were rebuffed by congressional leaders. In an extraordinary move, the Senate on March 17, 2016, unanimously approved a contempt resolution against Carl Ferrer, CEO of Backpage. com, a classified ad website, for largely refusing to comply with a subpoena from a Senate subcommittee investigating child sex trafficking. Lawmakers claimed the website's screening practices were aimed at helping sex traffickers evade prosecution by avoiding terms like "underage" while using terms like "fresh." Ferrer asserted the subpoena violated his First Amendment rights, but the subcommittee overruled this objection and ordered Ferrer to appear at a hearing and to produce relevant documents. When the CEO did not appear and the company produced documents the subcommittee found to be largely unresponsive, the Senate voted to direct its legal counsel to bring a civil action to enforce the subpoena in federal court.

In August 2016, the District Court for the District of Columbia ordered Ferrer to comply with the subpoena.[95] The district court found the subpoena was related to a legitimate legislative purpose because Congress had previously legislated on website immunity for the postings of third parties and can legislate on sex trafficking. The district court also readily dismissed Ferrer's claim that his First Amendment rights were harmed by the subpoena. Ferrer asserted that even searching for documents would abridge his First Amendment rights, but the court ruled a citizen "does not possess an absolute right to be free from government investigation when there are valid justifications for the inquiry." The court also found Ferrer failed to adequately explain how the subpoena interfered with his First Amendment rights, concluding that the "slight" impact of the subpoena was outweighed by the subcommittee's interest in understanding Internet sex trafficking.

Ferrer immediately filed an appeal. While the appeal was pending in late 2016, Ferrer provided more than 1 million pages of documents to the subcommittee.

---

[93] 17 C.F.R. § 202.10.
[94] Todd Garvey, "Congress' Contempt Power and the Enforcement of Congressional Subpoenas," *Congressional Research Service* (2012). The Court, however, has ruled in favor of a witness who claimed the First Amendment was violated by questioning by a state legislative committee. *See* Gibson v. Florida Legislative Investigative Comm., 372 U.S. 539 (1963).
[95] Senate Permanent Subcommittee on Investigations v. Ferrer, 2016 U.S. Dist. LEXIS 103143 (D.D.C. Aug. 5, 2016), *vacated*, 856 F.3d 1080 (D.C. Cir. 2017).

Based primarily on the documents provided by Backpage, the subcommittee issued a report in January 2017 finding that Backpage knowingly concealed evidence of criminality by systematically editing its adult ads by deleting words and phrases such as "school girl" indicative of an illegal transaction.[96] Congress responded to the Senate report by enacting in 2018 legislation allowing state police and attorneys general to prosecute sites that knowingly host sex trafficking content. Victims of sex trafficking also may sue such sites for damages.[97] The law, known as FOSTA, is discussed in Chapter 8. Apart from congressional action, the DOJ seized Backpage.com in 2018, charging its founders with facilitating prostitution and money laundering.

Ferrer's appeal was ruled to be moot by the appellate court because the Senate subcommittee had completed its investigation and no longer sought to enforce the subpoena. The lower court's judgment was vacated, leaving significant questions about the First Amendment's limitations on congressional subpoenas.

SEARCH WARRANTS

Search warrants are more threatening to confidentiality than a subpoena. Although subpoenas require reporters to testify in court or produce documents for the court, the recipient of a subpoena can challenge it during a hearing before complying. In contrast, a search warrant allows no opportunity for a journalist to prepare a response and no opportunity for a court challenge. A search warrant authorizes law enforcement officers to make unannounced searches for journalists' notes and photographs.

Many law enforcement officers prefer search warrants to subpoenas because the officers believe journalists will seek to quash subpoenas. In addition, the officials fear that journalists will destroy or hide evidence while fighting a subpoena. News personnel fear search warrants because they believe newsroom searches will intimidate potential confidential sources. If law enforcement officers could easily acquire warrants authorizing searches, sources could reasonably conclude that journalists could not honor promises to keep information confidential.

Newsroom searches by law enforcement officers, however, have been relatively rare. In addition, state and federal statutes have largely neutralized a 1978 Supreme Court opinion that permitted police to conduct unannounced searches of newsrooms.

In *Zurcher v. Stanford Daily*, the Supreme Court said the U.S. Constitution permits the police to search without warning the homes and offices of people who are not criminal suspects.[98] The Court said that neither the First nor the Fourth Amendment prohibits law enforcement officers with a search warrant from searching for criminal evidence on property used or owned by law-abiding citizens. The 5–3 decision permitted searches of newsrooms, corporate offices, and private homes and cars.

In *Zurcher*, the Stanford University student newspaper challenged a 1971 search of its office. The search occurred after *Stanford Daily* photographers took pictures of a student takeover of the campus hospital's administrative offices. When police officers tried to remove the demonstrators, violence erupted and several

---

[96] Staff of Senate Permanent Subcommittee on Investigations, Report on Backpage.Com's Knowing Facilitation of Online Sex Trafficking (2017).
[97] Pub. L. No. 115–164, 132 Stat. 1253 (2018).
[98] 436 U.S. 547 (1978).

officers were hurt. The injured officers could not identify most of the people involved.

When the Santa Clara County district attorney saw pictures of the incident in the *Stanford Daily*, he obtained a warrant from the municipal court for a search of the paper's offices for film, negatives and prints showing the events at the hospital. The warrant said officials had probable cause to believe that the *Stanford Daily* offices contained "material and relevant" evidence helpful to identifying the persons involved in the violence. The search of the student newsroom did not produce anything that had not been published. The *Stanford Daily* argued that warrants authorizing searches of places occupied by "third parties," persons not directly suspected of crimes, should not ordinarily be allowed.

The Supreme Court said in *Zurcher* that the Fourth Amendment provides no special exemption for searches involving third parties when authorities have probable cause to believe that they can find criminal evidence. In addition, said Justice White, writing for the Court, the First Amendment does not protect the news media from searches. White said the First Amendment requires only that the courts adhere to Fourth Amendment requirements with "particular exactitude." He said the preconditions for a warrant—probable cause, specificity with respect to the place to be searched and the things to be seized, and overall reasonableness—should provide adequate protection for journalists. Justice White also said that the legislative and executive branches could adopt laws and regulations protecting against the abuse of search warrants.

In response to a major lobbying campaign by the news media, several state legislatures and Congress adopted legislation to protect newsrooms from searches. The federal law, the Privacy Protection Act of 1980, severely restricts the use of search warrants to look for or seize information in the possession of public communicators. Under the Privacy Protection Act, federal, state and local law enforcement officers can search only in exceptional circumstances for criminal evidence in the offices of the news media, book authors and others who intend to disseminate information to the public.

The Privacy Protection Act puts more severe restrictions on searches for "work product materials" obtained and prepared for public dissemination. Work product materials are notes, story drafts, mental impressions and opinions. The statute prohibits searches for work product materials unless federal and state law enforcement officers can establish beforehand that (1) there is probable cause to believe a reporter has committed a crime, (2) there is reason to believe that seizure of the materials is necessary to prevent an injury or death or (3) the materials contain information "relating to the national defense, classified information, or restricted data" as defined under federal espionage laws, or the sexual exploitation of children. The government needs to prove only one of the three to meet its obligation under the statute.[99]

In 1993, a federal district court ruled that Secret Service agents violated the Privacy Protection Act when they searched the offices of Steve Jackson Games, Inc., and seized work product materials such as a draft of a book and drafts of several magazine articles. The District Court for the Western District of Texas awarded Steve Jackson Games $51,000 in expenses and damages to the business after the Secret Service searched the firm's offices looking for a proprietary computer document stolen from Bell South. The Secret Service had no evidence that the company

---

[99] 42 U.S.C. § 2000aa.

had committed a crime, the court said.[100] In contrast, the Privacy Protection Act was not violated when law enforcement officials in 2008 seized cameras, memory cards and an external hard drive containing photographs taken by a photojournalist who was suspected of conspiring with a protest group that vandalized a Washington, D.C., hotel.[101]

As part of a 2021 federal investigation into whether there was a criminal conspiracy to steal and publish the contents of a diary kept by President Biden's daughter Ashley as she underwent treatment for addiction, the FBI in early November 2021 searched the residences of James O'Keefe, founder of Project Veritas, and two former employees. (Project Veritas was discussed earlier in Chapter 3.) A warrant used by federal authorities described Ms. Biden's property as stolen and revealed the government was looking for evidence about how Ms. Biden's property was obtained by Project Veritas. During the search, the FBI seized O'Keefe's cell phones.

Project Veritas claimed it is the target of an overzealous Justice Department, prompting federal Judge Analisa Torres to appoint Barbara Jones, a retired federal judge, as a special master to ensure the government did not gain access to attorney-client–protected materials, or materials covered by the First Amendment. (Special masters are appointed in cases where the government has seized materials it is barred from having due to protections such as attorney-client privilege.) Judge Torres believed a special master would ensure the process was fair.[102]

The U.S. attorney's office for the Southern District of New York, in response to questions posed by a Project Veritas lawyer, said the warrant complied with all DOJ policies regarding searches of members of the news media.

The Privacy Protection Act allows officials to search for "documentary materials" under more circumstances than they may search for "work product materials." Documentary materials are pieces of information recorded in tangible form that are obtained during the preparation of a story. This category includes videotapes, audiotapes, photos and other raw materials of the newsgathering process. Documentary materials do not qualify as work product materials because they do not contain journalists' ideas. Law enforcement officials may search for and seize "documentary materials" not only when there is reason to believe a journalist has committed a crime, when there is reason to believe a life can be saved, when there is national security information to protect, or when children are sexually exploited, but also when a journalist does not produce the materials in response to a subpoena. In addition, law enforcement officers can search for documentary materials if they can demonstrate they have a reason to believe the materials would be altered, destroyed or hidden if a reporter were served with a subpoena.

In a 1995 case involving documentary materials, a Missouri federal district court held that a police seizure of a videotape from a television newsroom violated the Privacy Protection Act.[103] The judge ordered the prosecutor to pay the television station $1,000, the minimum penalty under the act. The controversy began when WDAF-TV of Kansas City, Missouri, obtained a videotape from a

---

[100] Steve Jackson Games, Inc. v. United States Secret Service, 816 F. Supp. 432 (W.D. Texas 1993), *aff'd,* 36 F.3d 457 (5th Cir. 1994).

[101] Sennett v. United States, 667 F.3d 531 (4th Cir. 2012).

[102] Michael Schmidt, "Judge Appoints Special Master to Review Material Seized from Project Veritas," *N.Y. Times* (Dec. 8, 2021), www.nytimes.com/2021/12/08/us/politics/project-veritas-special master.html.

[103] Tom Jackman, "Seizure of Videotape Ruled Improper," *Kansas City Star,* Feb. 2, 1995, at A1.

tourist that showed a man dragging a woman by the hair across a Kansas City street. The woman was later found murdered. After WDAF aired the tape, police sought a search warrant because they said the evidence contained in the tape was crucial to charge the man with the murder before Missouri law required that he be released.

The court ruled that the search warrant violated the Privacy Protection Act because the request for the search warrant failed to state that a search would prevent a death or injury or fulfill other provisions of the act permitting a search for documentary materials. The court rejected officials' attempts to justify the search warrant after the fact.

Although the Privacy Protection Act limits searches by state and local officials as well as by federal officials, several states have enacted provisions that are more stringent than the federal statute.[104] Law enforcement officers ordinarily will have to rely on a subpoena rather than a search warrant to obtain confidential information from the media. However, some exceptions remain. For example, the provision in the federal law allowing searches for national security information would have allowed an unannounced search of the *New York Times* offices for the Pentagon Papers.

The FBI's power to engage in electronic surveillance or to examine records, papers and documents was expanded by the USA Patriot Act, enacted in response to the terrorist attacks of September 11, 2001. Under this act, the FBI may obtain information relating to investigations of "international terrorism or clandestine intelligence activities."[105] The FBI, however, is prohibited from investigating someone "solely upon the basis of activities" protected by the First Amendment, such as speaking against government policy. Under the law, FBI agents could subpoena customer records from telephone companies and Internet service providers (ISPs), as well as customer records held by other businesses.

One type of FBI subpoena is known as a National Security Letter (NSL). Requests for NSLs are approved by Special Agents in charge of the FBI's 56 field offices. The majority of NSLs seek telephone billing records and other records relating to electronic communication. Prior to the Patriot Act, NSL requests were approved by senior FBI officials at FBI headquarters. A March 2008 report issued by the Inspector General of the DOJ found the FBI's use of NSLs grew dramatically in the period shortly after 2001.[106] The FBI issued approximately 8,500 NSL requests in 2000. After the passage of the Patriot Act in 2001, the number of NSL requests averaged approximately 48,000 a year during the 2003–2006 periods. Requests dropped to 9,682 in 2018.[107]

Another type of subpoena, known as a Section 215 order, has rarely been used by the FBI. Section 215 of the Patriot Act allows the FBI to seek orders from the Foreign Intelligence Surveillance Court for "any tangible things" including books, records and other items from any business or organization provided the items are for an authorized investigation to protect against terrorism or clandestine intelligence activities. From 2007–2009, the FBI obtained 51 Section 215 orders for a variety of records such as apartment leasing records and credit card records. The

---

[104] *See, e.g.,* Tex. Code Crim. Proc. art. 18.01(e).
[105] 50 U.S.C. § 1861; 18 U.S.C. § 2709.
[106] U.S. Dep't of Justice, Office of the Inspector General, *A Review of the Federal Bureau of Investigation's Use of National Security Letters*, Mar. 2008.
[107] Office of Director of National Intelligence, *Annual Statistical Transparency Report Regarding the Intelligence Community's Use of National Security Surveillance Authorities* 35 (2019).

FBI, however, abused its Section 215 authority when in 2006 it required telephone companies to produce to the NSA "telephone metadata," records of almost every call made or received in the United States. An appellate court ruled in 2015 that Section 215 could only be used in targeted investigations.[108] Congress prohibited the indiscriminate bulk collection of records in the USA Freedom Act of 2015.[109]

Congress allowed some provisions of the Patriot Act to expire in 2020. Thus, for investigations initiated prior to March 15, 2020, or regarding offenses occurring before that date, the FBI is allowed to obtain records from phone companies, ISPs, and other businesses. For other investigations begun on or after March 15, 2020, the government can only obtain records from transportation companies such as airlines, public accommodations such as hotels, physical storage facilities and vehicle rental companies. The government must prove the records pertain to either a foreign power or an agent of a foreign power. The FBI obtained 28 orders for business records in 2020.

In enacting the Patriot Act, Congress forbade all persons or organizations faced with FBI requests for information from telling others about the investigation. In 2006, Congress renewed key provisions of the Patriot Act and altered the provisions relating to FBI subpoenas. Instead of a blanket prohibition on disclosure, under the new law FBI officials could determine which recipients of subpoenas were gagged, based on FBI assessment of factors such as danger to national security.[110] Nonetheless, in a 2007 case brought by a recipient of an NSL, a federal district court found the amended law was an unconstitutional content-based restriction that excluded the firsthand experiences of NSL recipients from public debate. In 2008 the Second Circuit ruled the nondisclosure provision was constitutional *if* the government initiated prompt judicial review when the FBI sought to prevent a recipient from disclosing an NSL.[111]

Federal judge Susan Illston found in 2013 that the DOJ had not implemented the safeguards mandated by the Second Circuit in 2008; the lack of procedural safeguards violated the First Amendment. Ninety-seven percent of NSLs came with a nondisclosure order and Illston found the pervasiveness of nondisclosure orders unnecessarily restricted speech about government. Rejecting the approach taken by the Second Circuit, Illston said it was for Congress, not a court, to remedy the defects in the law.[112]

Congress did so in the USA Freedom Act of 2015; recipients of nondisclosure orders must receive notice of the availability of judicial review. When review is sought, the burden is on the government to justify nondisclosure. In addition, Congress now allows the disclosure of aggregate data concerning the number of NSLs a communications provider receives.[113] The Ninth Circuit in 2017 found the nondisclosure requirement withstood strict scrutiny as a narrowly tailored means of protecting national security. Further, there were adequate procedural safeguards, such as prompt judicial review, to protect First Amendment rights.[114]

---

[108] American Civil Liberties Union v. Clapper, 785 F.3d 787 (2d Cir. 2015).
[109] 50 U.S.C. § 1861.
[110] 18 U.S.C. § 2709(c); *see also* 18 U.S.C. § 3511.
[111] Doe v. Gonzales, 500 F. Supp. 2d 379 (S.D.N.Y. 2007), *aff'd in part and rev'd in part*, 549 F.3d 861 (2d Cir. 2008).
[112] *In re* National Security Letter, 930 F. Supp. 2d 1064 (N.D. Cal. 2013), *vacated and remanded by unpublished order* (9th Cir. Aug. 24, 2015) (No. 13–15957).
[113] 18 U.S.C. § 2709 (judicial review); 50 U.S.C. § 1874 (disclosure of aggregate data).
[114] *In re* Nat'l Security Letter v. Sessions, 863 F.3d 1110 (9th Cir. 2017).

As a result of the USA Freedom Act of 2015, tech companies now regularly publish reports of the number of NSLs received each year, along with data on other types of government requests. The NSL data is published in numerical ranges, rather than exact numbers, to address concerns by the government that releasing exact numbers might reveal information about investigations. The USA Freedom Act also required the FBI "review at appropriate intervals" the nondisclosure requirement of an NSL to assess whether facts supporting nondisclosure continue to exist.[115] Google, for example, now publishes copies of NSLs where the restrictions on disclosure have been lifted.[116]

National Security Letters are not the only form of government demand for information frequently accompanied by a nondisclosure requirement. The Electronic Communications Privacy Act of 1986 (ECPA) authorizes a government entity seeking electronic communications, such as email and documents stored on remote servers, to seek a court order commanding the provider not to disclose the investigation.[117] In 2016, Microsoft filed suit against the federal government, claiming the routine issuance of secrecy orders violated the constitutional rights of the company and its customers. The DOJ issued new guidelines in 2017 limiting the circumstances under which prosecutors may seek secrecy orders, such as when a suspect poses a flight risk, and limiting orders to a year or less. In response, Microsoft dismissed its suit.[118]

■ SUMMARY ■

The U.S. Supreme Court decided in *Zurcher v. Stanford Daily* that the First Amendment does not protect communicators from authorized searches for criminal evidence, even when they are not suspected of criminal activity. The impact of the decision has been blunted by state and federal statutes encouraging the use of subpoenas rather than search warrants in most circumstances. The FBI's power to engage in electronic surveillance or to examine records, papers and documents was expanded by the USA Patriot Act, enacted in response to the terrorist attacks of September 11, 2001. In recent years, Congress has reduced the FBI's authority to obtain records.

BREACHING CONFIDENTIALITY

This chapter has focused on the efforts of journalists to honor their promises of confidentiality to news sources. On rare occasions, however, reporters or editors reveal the names of sources to whom they have promised anonymity. In 1991, the U.S. Supreme Court said journalists are not protected by the First Amendment when sued by victims of broken promises. In *Cohen v. Cowles Media Co.*, the Supreme Court upheld the constitutionality of a Minnesota state law permitting persons who are injured because of a broken promise to recover damages.[119]

---

[115] FBI, Termination Procedures for National Security Letter Nondisclosure Requirement (Nov. 24, 2015).
[116] Richard Selgado, "Sharing National Security Letters with the Public," Dec. 13, 2016, https:// blog. google/topics/public-policy/sharing-national-security-letters-public/. For copies of NSLs received by Google, and data about the number of NSLs received by Google, see the Google Transparency Report, https:/transparencyreportgoogle.com/user-data/us-nationalsecurity?hl=en.
[117] 18 U.S.C. § 2705(b).
[118] Del Quentin Weber, "New Rules Limit Gag Orders on Tech Firms," *Wall St. J.*, Oct. 25, 2017, at A6.
[119] 501 U.S. 663 (1991).

Dan Cohen, a public relations consultant and spokesperson for the 1982 Independent-Republican gubernatorial candidate in Minnesota, sued the *Minneapolis Star & Tribune* and the *St. Paul Pioneer Press Dispatch*. Even though reporters for the two papers had promised him confidentiality, Cohen was identified as the source of a story disclosing that the candidate for the Democratic-Farmer-Labor Party had been convicted 12 years before of shoplifting $6 worth of merchandise.

Editors of the *Star & Tribune* and the *Pioneer Press Dispatch* named Cohen as the source of the story because, they said, readers needed to know that the shoplifting story came from the opposing candidate's campaign staff. The editors argued that a story revealing that one candidate's campaign released "eleventh hour information" about an opponent was more important than a story about a 12-year-old shoplifting charge that had been vacated.

Cohen lost his job as a public relations executive and sued, claiming the newspapers breached an oral contract and reporters and editors misrepresented the newspapers' commitment to protect confidential sources. A jury awarded Cohen $200,000 in compensatory damages for both claims and $500,000 in punitive damages for misrepresentation. In 1989, the Minnesota Court of Appeals upheld Cohen's contract claim and the $200,000 award for compensatory damages. However, the appeals court overturned the award for punitive damages, saying that the reporters had not misrepresented their intentions at the time the promise of confidentiality had been made.[120]

In 1990, the Minnesota Supreme Court reversed the verdict, saying that the reporters' promises to Cohen constituted neither misrepresentation nor a breach of contract.[121] Both reporters and their sources "understand that a reporter's promise is given as a moral commitment" rather than as a binding offer and acceptance of an offer, thus no genuine contract existed, the state supreme court stated.

The Minnesota Supreme Court also refused to enforce the promises of confidentiality to Cohen through a common-law doctrine protecting people who rely on promises. The doctrine, called *promissory estoppel*, requires that courts enforce a promise if breaking the promise creates an injustice that should be remedied by law. The Minnesota court said that enforcing promissory estoppel against the newspaper would violate the First Amendment because the specter of civil damages arising from promises made during election coverage would chill the public debate.

The U.S. Supreme Court, in a 5–4 decision, overruled the Minnesota court. The U.S. Supreme Court's majority said the First Amendment does not prohibit the use of Minnesota's common law of promissory estoppel when journalists break promises made to sources.[122] Justice White, writing for the Court's majority, cited a long line of cases establishing that the First Amendment does not immunize the press from laws that apply to everyone. White noted that reporters, like all citizens, cannot break and enter an office or residence to gather news. Nor can reporters refuse to reveal a confidential news source before a grand jury. Similarly, White said, reporters, like other citizens, may be held responsible for commitments they break.

The Court's majority discounted as "constitutionally insignificant" any impact of Minnesota's doctrine of promissory estoppel on reporting, including possible self-censorship by the press. Any effect of promissory estoppel to limit news

---

[120] 445 N.W.2d 248 (Minn. Ct. App. 1989).
[121] 457 N.W.2d 199 (Minn. 1990).
[122] 501 U.S. 663 (1991).

coverage, the Court said, was an "incidental" consequence of equally applying laws that ensure promises are kept.

The Supreme Court remanded *Cohen* to the Minnesota Supreme Court to determine whether Cohen could establish that he met Minnesota's promissory estoppel requirements. The Minnesota court, in its second review of the *Cohen* case, upheld the jury's award to Cohen of $200,000 in compensatory damages, ruling that Cohen met all three requirements for promissory estoppel.[123]

First, Cohen had documented that the reporters clearly promised confidentiality. Second, Cohen relied on the reporters' promise to his detriment when he handed them the papers documenting the conviction of the Democratic-Farmer-Labor candidate. The resulting stories, using Cohen's name as the source, cost him his job. Finally, the Minnesota Supreme Court said, the broken promises by the newspapers led to an injustice that should be remedied through the common law of promissory estoppel; denying Cohen recourse for the loss of his job would be unjust, given the long journalistic tradition of protecting confidential sources and the absence of a compelling need "in this case" to break the promise.

In the initial wake of the *Cohen* case, media lawyers feared the prospect of similar suits. This fear has proven to be unfounded as journalists rarely break a promise of confidentiality. In one of the few post-*Cohen* cases, in 1993 a federal appellate court remanded for trial a second Minnesota suit brought by a plaintiff who said her identity could be recognized in a *Glamour* magazine story although she had been promised anonymity. The U.S. Court of Appeals for the Eighth Circuit, reversing a summary judgment issued by a federal district court, said a jury ought to decide whether Jill Ruzicka was unjustly harmed under the common-law doctrine of promissory estoppel.[124] The Eighth Circuit said "there is nothing vague or ambiguous" about a promise to keep Ruzicka from being identified in a story. The appellate court said a jury should determine whether Ruzicka could be reasonably identified in the story, which did not name her but described her career and discussed her allegations of sexual abuse, using her first name and a pseudonym for her last name. The Eighth Circuit also said a jury should determine whether the promise of anonymity must be enforced to prevent an injustice.

On remand, the case was settled for $250,000.[125]

◾ SUMMARY ◾

The U.S. Supreme Court has said the First Amendment does not protect journalists who reveal the names of sources promised confidentiality. The Court said that the state of Minnesota could enforce its doctrine of promissory estoppel, a common-law doctrine protecting people who rely on promises to their detriment.

---

[123] 479 N.W.2d 387 (Minn. 1992).
[124] Ruzicka v. Conde Nast Publications, Inc., 999 F.2d 1319 (8th Cir. 1993).
[125] Ruzicka v. Rothenberg, 83 F.3d 1033 (8th Cir. 1996).

Access to Information

Although the First Amendment protects the right to publish information about public issues, it does not guarantee the right to collect information about the government. The U.S. Supreme Court has refused to provide First Amendment protection for newsgathering beyond the access to criminal trials discussed in Chapter 10. The First Amendment does not ensure that a reporter can gain entry to a city council meeting, obtain a consultant's report about the quality of drinking water, or visit the site of a nuclear power plant accident.

If the U.S. Constitution does not guarantee a communicator's access to information, neither does the common law. Judges traditionally have not required that governmental bodies meet publicly or allow everyone to inspect government records. Nevertheless, many government records and meetings have historically been open to the public. This openness has been codified over the last 50 years in federal and state open records and meetings statutes.

Access law, like the right to publish, is grounded in American political theory. Because government in the United States is based on the will of the public, citizens need to know what government is doing. Thomas Jefferson said that only

DOI: 10.4324/9781003264736-12

an informed electorate could govern effectively.[1] Professor Alexander Meiklejohn wrote that citizens who are denied information will make decisions that are "ill-considered" and "ill-balanced."[2] Professor Thomas Emerson said a democracy without an informed public is a contradiction.[3] An informed public must have access to information not only about government but also about public health, product safety and climate change.

Just as access to information is important to our system of government, so is the security of government records, the effectiveness of law enforcement departments and the privacy of citizens. Therefore, not all government records and meetings are open. National defense sometimes hinges on secret military tactics and capabilities. Law enforcement officers would have difficulty catching criminals if suspects could demand to see police evidence and learn investigatory strategies. Likewise, government would infringe citizens' privacy if it disclosed information about an individual's health or taxes.

Since September 11, 2001, the government has closed records, websites and proceedings in order to deny information to terrorists who might try to harm the United States. Many journalists and civil libertarians think too many records have been stamped "Classified," so many records that American citizens are denied needed information about how the government conducts the war on terror.

However numerous the government's reasons for withholding information, Americans probably have more access to government information than citizens in any other country. In the United States, citizens may see criminal arrest records, property records and census reports. The public also can acquire scientific data on the side effects of prescription drugs and learn how the CIA and the FBI have monitored citizens illegally.

This chapter discusses the law of access to the legislative and administrative branches of government and to news events. The chapter begins with a discussion of the Supreme Court's First Amendment rulings on access to government-controlled installations. Then, the chapter discusses the law of access to public property, quasi-public property and war zones. Next, the chapter treats federal and state laws controlling access to government records and meetings.

ACCESS AND THE CONSTITUTION

For many scholars and journalists, the freedom to publish news means little without the ability to gather information. However, the U.S. Supreme Court has ruled that the First Amendment does not guarantee public access to news to the same degree it guarantees the media the right to publish and broadcast. The Court did rule, however, in *Richmond Newspapers v. Virginia*, that the public and the press have a constitutional right to attend trials. Although a few federal courts have recognized citizens' First Amendment rights to government functions and records, the Supreme Court has not extended a citizen's constitutional right of access beyond proceedings in the courts. Journalists therefore depend on statutes to gain access to government records and meetings. In a series of cases involving access to prisons,

---

[1] *E.g.*, Letter to Edward Carrington, Jan. 16, 1787, in 11 *The Papers of Thomas Jefferson* 48–9 (Julian P. Boyd ed., 1955).
[2] *Free Speech* 26 (1948).
[3] "The Danger of State Secrecy," *The Nation*, Mar. 30, 1974, at 395.

the Supreme Court explained why citizens cannot demand access to governmental buildings and activities in the name of the First Amendment.

The Supreme Court

In the handful of newsgathering cases the Supreme Court has decided, it has set forth three principles: First, the First Amendment does not guarantee the public or the press a right to obtain information. Second, journalists have no greater rights of access to information than anyone else. Third, the public's need for access to information will be balanced against sometimes conflicting social needs, such as effective law enforcement and individual privacy.

The Supreme Court said as early as 1972

> that it has generally been held that the First Amendment does not guarantee the press a constitutional right of special access to information not available to the public generally. . . .. Despite the fact that news gathering may be hampered, the press is regularly excluded from grand jury proceedings, our own conferences, the meetings of other official bodies gathered in executive session, and the meetings of private organizations. Newsmen have no constitutional right of access to the scenes of crime or disaster when the general public is excluded.[4]

The Supreme Court has denied journalists a First Amendment right of access to newsworthy information in three prison cases. In the first two, which were decided on the same day, the Court upheld the constitutionality of prison rules restricting reporters' interviews with inmates. The Court said that the First Amendment does not guarantee the press more access to prisons and inmates than is available to the general public.

In one of the cases, *Pell v. Procunier*, reporters claimed a First Amendment right to interview specific California prisoners.[5] Before 1971 in California, journalists could conduct face-to-face interviews with prisoners on request. However, state prison officials said that the policy of unrestricted interviews was partly responsible for a breakdown in prison discipline. Particularly damaging to prison discipline, officials said, was media attention showered on the Soledad Brothers, three black inmates accused of killing a white prison guard. The Soledad Brothers' influence over fellow prisoners grew with their celebrity, officials claimed, reducing the ability of guards to control the prisons. An escape attempt in 1971 resulted in five deaths.

To tighten control by reducing the celebrity of inmates, California officials revised the corrections manual to prohibit "media interviews with specific individual inmates." In *Pell v. Procunier*, the Supreme Court ruled 5–4 that the new restrictions on reporters' access to prisoners did not abridge the First Amendment rights of the press. The Court came to the same conclusion in *Saxbe v. Washington Post*, a case decided at the same time as *Pell* involving similar regulations at federal prisons.[6]

In *Pell*, the Court said that although the First and the Fourteenth Amendments prevent the government from interfering with a free press, the Constitution does

---

[4] Branzburg v. Hayes, 408 U.S. 665 (1972).
[5] 417 U.S. 817 (1974).
[6] 417 U.S. 843 (1974).

not require the government to provide the press access to information not available to the average citizen. Writing for the Court, Justice Stewart said:

> It is one thing to say that a journalist is free to seek out sources of information not available to members of the general public. . ... It is quite another thing to suggest that the Constitution imposes upon government the affirmative duty to make available to journalists sources of information not available to members of the public generally.[7]

Stewart said the Court would defer to the judgment of corrections officials as long as there was no evidence that prison rules were adopted to control specific kinds of expression. Prison officials have the responsibility to control conduct in the prisons, and they have the expertise to determine which forms of prisoner communications do not interfere with prison security, Stewart said.

A few years later, the Court again upheld restrictions imposed on jail visits, this time regulations adopted by Alameda County, California, Sheriff Thomas Houchins. In *Houchins v. KQED*, the Court denied access to a television station that wanted to see the portion of the Santa Rita jail where an inmate was reported to have committed suicide. A psychiatrist claimed that some of his patient-prisoners were ill because of the conditions there.

Chief Justice Burger, writing the opinion of the 4–3 majority, said the Court had "never intimated" a First Amendment right of access to all sources of information under government control. He said that a constitutional right to enter the jail could not be based on the public's concern for the condition of jails and the media's role in providing information. The issue in the case was not the right of citizens to receive ideas, Burger continued, but a claim by the press of a special privilege of access that the Court had rejected in *Pell* and *Saxbe*. The media have no right of access "different from or greater than" that afforded the public in general, Burger said.

Burger said reporters can learn of prison conditions by interviewing prison visitors, public officials, prison personnel and prisoners' lawyers. He suggested that the public interest in prisons is protected when the Board of Corrections and health and fire officials inspect and report on prisons. Burger said the Constitution left the issue of public access to the "political process." It is a legislative matter, he said, quoting a speech by Justice Stewart. Burger asserted:

> The Constitution itself is neither a Freedom of Information Act nor an Official Secrets Act.
>
> The Constitution . . . establishes the contest [for information], not its resolution. Congress may provide a resolution, at least in some instances. . ... For the rest, we must rely, as so often in our system we must, on the tug and pull of the political forces in American society.[8]

In addition, Burger said, the Constitution provides no standards for determining when access is appropriate. Burger said that he did not want the courts deciding who should have access to what governmental information and under what conditions.

---

[7] 417 U.S. 834 (1974).
[8] 438 U.S. 1 (1978) (quoting a speech found in Potter Stewart, "Or of the Press," 26 *Hastings L.J.* 631, 636 (1975)).

Lower Federal Courts

Although the Supreme Court has not recognized a First Amendment right of access to prisons or other news venues—except the courts—a few lower courts have noted a First Amendment newsgathering right in public places. Several courts have ruled that restrictions on press access cannot be overbroad or capricious. One court said the National Transportation Safety Board violated the First Amendment when it severely restricted access to Logan International Airport after a DC-10 slid off an icy runway, killing two people. The court said the board violated the First Amendment because it offered no "reasonable basis" for limiting press access to one hour per day.[9] However, it would be inaccurate to say that journalists have a First Amendment right of access to news scenes.

Courts have ruled that restrictions on access cannot be too broad. Courts in at least seven states struck down broad restrictions on the access of journalists and pollsters to voting locations. The restrictions were adopted to limit "exit interviews" of voters as they left the polls. The statutes were designed to impede the television networks' projections of winners in presidential elections before the polls close in all states. Officials in Western states argued that voters often failed to vote in local elections when East Coast media projected national winners long before the voting booths closed in California, Oregon and Washington. Officials contended that citizens did not vote if they already knew the winner of the presidential race.

A federal appeals court ruled unconstitutional a Washington State statute prohibiting interviews of voters within 300 feet of a polling place. In *Daily Herald v. Munro*, the U.S. Court of Appeals for the Ninth Circuit said the First Amendment protects the discussion of governmental affairs and the gathering of news that takes place in exit interviews.[10] Therefore, the court said any law regulating exit polling must be narrowly tailored to accomplish a compelling governmental interest. The Ninth Circuit said the state's statute prohibiting exit interviews within 300 feet of a polling place—the length of a football field—was too broad for the state's purpose of maintaining peace and order at polling places. Although an appropriately narrow regulation might prohibit disruptive exit polling, the court said, the unconstitutionally broad statute in Washington prohibited all exit polling. Several laws similar to Washington's have been overturned by federal and state courts.[11]

Governments may not bar journalists' access arbitrarily or capriciously. In Iowa, a federal court said that a police department acted without justification when it refused to show public records to one newspaper after showing them to another.[12] Similarly, a court ruled that a female reporter could not be denied access to a locker room in a city-owned baseball stadium where male reporters were allowed. The exclusion from the New York Yankees' locker room violated the right of *Sports Illustrated* reporter Melissa Ludtke to pursue her profession, the court said. The court said the privacy of male baseball players could be protected while Ludtke was allowed to pursue her profession.[13]

Courts also have ruled that the First Amendment prohibits officials from retaliating or punishing reporters by denying them access to press conferences

---

[9] Westinghouse Broadcasting Co. v. National Transp. Safety Bd., 670 F.2d 4 (D. Mass. 1982).

[10] 838 F.2d 380 (9th Cir. 1988).

[11] *E.g.*, NBC v. Cleland, 697 F. Supp. 1204 (N.D. Ga. 1988); CBS v. Growe, 15 Media L. Rep. 2275 (D. Minn. 1988).

[12] Quad-City Community News Serv., Inc. v. Jebens, 334 F. Supp. 8 (S.D. Iowa 1971).

[13] Ludtke v. Kuhn, 461 F. Supp. 86 (S.D.N.Y. 1978).

or sessions of state legislatures. In *Sherrill v. Knight*, a federal appeals court ruled in 1977 that journalists could not arbitrarily be excluded from White House press conferences, holding that newsgathering interests in the First Amendment required access not to be revoked unless the government could establish a compelling state interest. Additionally, the court required the government to state a factual basis for denying access, with an opportunity for journalists to respond, and a final decision in writing made after the response.[14]

The U.S. Court of Appeals for the Fourth Circuit ruled that Maryland Governor Robert Ehrlich recognized an exception for discretionary disclosure when the governor issued a directive barring members of his administration from talking with two *Baltimore Sun* journalists who the governor concluded were not "objective." The governor told his administration not to return calls or comply with requests of the two *Sun* journalists, but the administration did allow the journalists to be notified of, and to attend, public press conferences.[15] The court said the governor's directive reflected the practice that government administrators have discretion over how and to whom they release information. The directive, the court said, did not unconstitutionally inhibit the journalists' ability to gather information through their enterprise and to write critically about the governor and his administration. Nor did the directive ban officials from returning the phone calls of other journalists, including those from the *Sun*. "Government officials frequently and without liability evaluate reporters and reward them with advantages of access," the court said. After the Ehrlich directive, officials in several communities issued similar notices.[16]

The issue arose again in 2018, when broadcast network CNN sued Donald Trump after the White House revoked the press credentials of reporter Jim Acosta following a heated exchange, claiming that Acosta had not displayed appropriate "respect" to the president. A federal district judge said that the White House had denied him due process suspending his access without clear rules and regulations in place, and ultimately the White House reinstated his credentials[17] (Photo 12.1). Under new rules established after the court ruling to make potential suspensions clearer, the White House press secretary later suspended the credentials of Playboy reporter Brian Karem after he joked that "this is a group eager for demonic possession" at a group of right-wing internet personalities who were shouting at him and ignoring his questions after a White House summit. One of the summit attendees shouted at Karem, "You're a punk! You're not a journalist!" and accused Karem of threatening him. Karem sued over the 30-day suspension, and a federal appeals court agreed in 2020 that he was denied due process, finding that regardless of the new guidelines, he had not been put on adequate notice of "the magnitude of the sanction" of making an attempt at humor, the likes of which had not been subject to punishment in the past. The court responded to the Trump administration's arguments about protecting decorum in the press pool by noting that the White House could "rest assured that principles of due process do not limit its authority to maintain order in White House events by, for example, ordering the immediate removal of rogue, mooning journalists."[18]

---

[14] 569 F.2d 124 (D.C. Cir. 1977).

[15] Baltimore Sun v. Ehrlich, 437 F.3d 410 (4th Cir. 2006).

[16] Kirsten Mitchell, "Ehrlich's Edict," 29 *News Media & the Law* (Spring 2005).

[17] Karem v. Trump, 960 F.3d 656 (D.C. Cir. 2020).

[18] *Id.* at 667.

PHOTO 12.1   Jim Acosta, a reporter for CNN, had his White House press credentials revoked after a heated exchange with President Donald Trump during a press conference in 2018. Acosta ultimately had the credentials restored after CNN sued, claiming his access was revoked based on his viewpoint.

■ SUMMARY ■

Although the Supreme Court has recognized a First Amendment right of access to criminal trials, it has ruled in cases involving access to prisons that the First Amendment does not guarantee a right to gather news. The Court has also said that journalists have no constitutional right of access to government facilities beyond that of the public. Other federal courts have said that the First Amendment prohibits officials from arbitrarily denying access or retaliating against journalists by denying access to news conferences. A federal appeals court, however, has ruled the executive branch can favor some journalists over others with interviews and conversations.

ACCESS TO EVENTS

The limited constitutional protection for newsgathering means that officials are generally not required to grant reporters access to news events on public property, on quasi-public property or in war zones.

Public Property

Everyone, including members of the press, generally has access to public streets, sidewalks, parks and public buildings. Several courts have recognized a common-law right for everyone to observe, photograph and record what can easily be seen or overheard in a public place.[19] However, public officials have the authority to

---

[19] *E.g.,* Harrison v. Washington Post Co., 391 A.2d 781 (D.C. Ct. App. 1978); Jacova v. Southern Radio & Television Co., 83 So. 2d 34 (Fla. 1955).

deny access to public property when it becomes the scene of a public disorder or disaster, such as an automobile accident or fire. Public safety officers often exclude journalists from the scene, sometimes unnecessarily. However, courts often avoid second-guessing police and fire officials who have to make snap judgments while trying to save lives and property.

Anyone who disobeys an official order to move away from the scene of a calamity may be charged with criminal trespass, obstruction or resisting arrest.[20] The First Amendment seldom provides protection in such a situation. Although police and fire officials are not supposed to act arbitrarily or capriciously, the courts tend to provide them with wide discretion during emergencies. California and Ohio are two states that have adopted legislation permitting journalists access to the scenes of disasters.[21]

Journalists have few options if they confront authorities at accident and disaster scenes on public property. If journalists refuse to move when ordered to, they may be arrested for interference, disorderly conduct, assault, failure to move on, or other violations, even if their presence poses no hindrance to officials. Sometimes police and fire officials do not fully appreciate the value of news coverage or do not know the laws protecting news reporting.

A federal court in California ruled an Oakland police officer did not violate the First Amendment rights of a newspaper photographer Raymundo Chavez when the officer arrested Chavez for parking his car on the highway at an accident scene and attempting to take photographs. Citing Supreme Court precedent, the federal district court said journalists have no First Amendment right to access accident or crime scenes if the general public is excluded. It was reasonable, the court said, for an officer to prevent Chavez from taking a photograph when neither he nor the public had a constitutional right to stop their cars on the highway and to take photographs.[22]

President Clinton signed a law making it more difficult for the media to report on airplane crashes. The Aviation Disaster Family Assistance Act requires the National Transportation Safety Board to obtain from the airlines lists of passengers on downed craft and release information only to passengers' families. The act also provides for areas where passengers can grieve in private without questions from the media. A task force was to recommend ways to ensure that journalists and attorneys do not "intrude on the privacy of families of passengers involved in an aircraft accident."[23]

Quasi-public Property

The media's right of access to quasi-public property is even less secure than its right of access to public property. Quasi-public property is land that serves a public purpose but is not available for use by the general public. Army bases are quasi-public property. They belong to the public, but unlike public parks, they are not open for regular public use. The site of a nuclear power plant also might be considered quasi-public. The land and buildings may be owned by either the state or a private company, but the facility is dedicated to a public use and is usually regulated and financed by a public agency. The site of a nuclear power plant is not

---

[20] *See generally* Kent R. Middleton, "Journalists' Interference with Police: The First Amendment, Access to News and Official Discretion," 5 *Comment* 443 (Spring 1983).
[21] Cal. Penal Code § 409.5(d); Ohio Rev. Code Ann. 2917.13.
[22] Chavez v. City of Oakland, 2009 U.S. Dist. LEXIS 46250 (N.D. Calif., June 2, 2009).
[23] "Media Access to Information During Air Disasters Restricted," *News Media & Law* (Fall 1996).

public land in the sense that it is dedicated to public use for recreation, communication or another public purpose.

The administrator of quasi-public property, such as a utility, can restrict use to the purposes for which the property is dedicated. The U.S. Supreme Court refused to review the criminal trespass convictions of nine reporters covering a demonstration at the Black Fox nuclear power plant in Oklahoma. The journalists had accompanied antinuclear demonstrators through a hole in a fence at the plant instead of staying at a company-approved viewing site on the property. The journalists complained that they would have missed much of the story if they were restricted to the observation site provided by the Public Service Company of Oklahoma (PSO), which ran the nuclear power plant. Indeed, the PSO, which had been stung by bad publicity from an earlier antinuclear protest, said it wanted to minimize coverage of the demonstration by restricting press access.

The Oklahoma Court of Criminal Appeals said that the press had no special right of access. The PSO, the court said, had the power to regulate the quasi-public property to conform to designated uses. Nine reporters were fined $25 each for trespassing with the demonstrators.[24]

In 2008, the Department of Defense rescinded a 17-year ban on media coverage of returning war dead. Reversing a policy in place since 1991, Defense Secretary Robert M. Gates said families of the fallen soldiers should determine whether the media would be allowed to cover the arrival of caskets from Iraq and Afghanistan at Dover Air Force Base in Delaware. President George H.W. Bush first prohibited photographs of the flag-draped coffins to protect the privacy of the soldiers' families. Critics charge a ban on press coverage hides the costs of war.[25]

Because journalists have limited rights of access to public and quasi-public property, they need to work with public officials to develop access guidelines before emergencies occur. Reporters will more likely be allowed to do their jobs at the scenes of accidents and protests if journalists and officials meet beforehand to discuss each other's responsibilities and agree to conditions and limits on access. Many news organizations have developed access guidelines with state and local law enforcement officers.

Social Media Accounts

As elected officials have increasingly used social media to speak to the public, courts have determined their accounts to be virtual public forums to which the First Amendment applies, as detailed in Chapter 2. At times, officials have blocked journalists and others from their social media accounts, hampering reporters' ability to cover public officials and matters of public concern, including Texas' then–Governor Rick Perry, who blocked several journalists in 2011, drawing ridicule for his pettiness.[26] Courts have consistently held that officials create a public forum when they use social media accounts such as Twitter and Facebook for government business. In 2019, for example, a federal district court ruled that three Republican members of the Wisconsin state assembly violated the First Amendment when they blocked a liberal advocacy organization called One Wisconsin Now. One legislator said he used his account "to notify the public about topics such as legislation,

---

[24] Stahl v. State, 665 P.2d 839, 9 Media L. Rep. 1945 (Okla. Crim. App. 1983), *cert. denied*, 464 U.S. 1069 (1984).

[25] Julian E. Barnes, "Pentagon Lifts Media Ban on Photos of War Dead," *L.A. Times*, Feb. 27, 2009.

[26] Alexandra Petri, "Gov. Rick Perry Blocks Journalists on Twitter—Really?," *Wash. Post*, March 3, 2011; Andy Barr, "Perry Gets Petty on Twitter," *Politico*, Feb. 28, 2011.

upcoming legislative hearings, and government reports" and considered it a "forum for constituents." Another similarly said he used the account to "communicate with his legislative constituents," and the third, the speaker of the assembly, said he used it to speak "on behalf of the Assembly and Republicans in general." The court ruled the officials were acting "under color of state law" when they created and operated the accounts, and that the interactive nature of the accounts—the ability both to speak and to listen to constituents on Twitter as a platform—made these accounts a "designated public forum," and thus ruled that blocking a citizen group based on their viewpoint violated their First Amendment rights.[27] The Fourth Circuit issued a similar ruling, finding that the chair of a county board of supervisors in Virginia violated the First Amendment rights of a constituent by blocking him from the chair's Facebook page. The court found that the chair used the Facebook page "as a tool of governance" and to "further her duties as a municipal officer," including providing information about public safety issues.[28]

The Knight First Amendment Institute at Columbia University filed the most high-profile lawsuit in this area on behalf of several journalists and other citizens who were blocked by then–President Donald Trump from his personal account (@realDonaldTrump), which he created before taking office but continued to use in an official capacity after becoming president. Trump conceded that he blocked people "after posting replies in which they criticized the President or his policies and that they were blocked as a result of this criticism." The court noted that Trump used the account "almost on a daily basis 'as a channel for communicating and interacting with the public about his administration,'" including hiring and firing staff and announcing changes to national policies. The court reasoned that because he was using the account in his official capacity, it became a public forum, and because he blocked users based on their viewpoint, the court found that blocking them violated the First Amendment.[29] Trump appealed the ruling to the Supreme Court, which ultimately dismissed the case as moot after Trump lost his reelection effort and was no longer in office.[30]

War Zones

Journalists covering news in foreign countries usually need permission of the host government. When journalists cover wars involving U.S. troops, they are also subject to the constitutional authority of the U.S. president as commander-in-chief of the military. The president has the authority to block press access entirely. For example, when Marines landed in Grenada in 1983, they were not accompanied by journalists. Similarly, when American forces invaded Afghanistan in 2001, journalists were not allowed to accompany the troops. Larry Flynt, publisher of *Hustler*, claimed the Pentagon's policy interfered with the right to gather information. A federal district court refused to issue an injunction requiring access and later dismissed the case.[31] The Court of Appeals for the D.C. Circuit affirmed, holding that there was no First Amendment right of media access to combat operations.[32]

---

[27] One Wisconsin Now v. Kremer, 354 F. Supp. 3d 940 (W.D. Wis. 2019).

[28] Davison v. Randall, 912 F.3d 666, 680 (4th Cir. 2019).

[29] Knight First Amendment Institute v. Trump, 928 F.3d 226 (2nd Cir. 2019).

[30] Biden v. Knight First Amendment Institute, 141 S. Ct. 1220 (2021).

[31] Flynt v. Rumsfeld, 180 F. Supp. 2d 174 (D.D.C. 2002) (refusing request for injunction); 245 F. Supp. 2d 94 (D.D.C. 2003) (granting motion to dismiss).

[32] 355 F.3d 697 (D.C. Cir. 2004). *See also* Getty Images News Serv. v. Department of Defense, 193 F. Supp. 2d 112 (D.D.C. 2002) (press has no First Amendment right of access to "unlawful combatants" held at U.S. military facility in Guantanamo, Cuba).

Over the course of American military history, press access to combat operations has varied considerably, depending on the viewpoints of the president, Secretary of Defense and military commanders in the field. During the Vietnam War, journalists had unfettered access to the battlefield. During the Persian Gulf War in 1991, journalists were confined to press pools and largely kept away from most of the fighting. In addition, military escorts accompanied pool reporters, monitoring interviews and sometimes interrupting the interviews. Moreover, pool reports were subject to "security review," which was used in some instances to ensure coverage supported the war effort.[33] News executives said the Gulf War policies made it impossible for journalists to tell the public the full story. Consequently, in 1992 military officials and executives of major news organizations agreed to the principle that "open and independent reporting will be the principal means of coverage of U.S. military operations."

To facilitate coverage of the 2003 U.S. invasion of Iraq, known as Operation Iraqi Freedom, Pentagon officials developed a plan to embed at least 500 journalists with military units. The Pentagon's policy required embedded journalists to agree to a lengthy set of ground rules to protect operational security; violation of the ground rules could result in removal from the war zone. (A summary of the ground rules appears in Figure 12.1.) For example, information about ongoing battles was not to be released until authorized by the on-scene commander.

Military officials were to practice "security at the source," meaning that classified information was not to be disclosed to the press. However, the Pentagon's policy provided that classified information could be disclosed to reporters who agreed to security review of their coverage. The Pentagon's policy stated that security review "will not involve any editorial changes; it will be conducted solely to ensure that no sensitive or classified information" is included in news reports.[34]

After American forces withdrew from Iraq in 2011, the embed program there was discontinued, and it was not renewed when thousands of new troops were sent to Iraq in 2016.[35] When the U.S. withdrew troops from Afghanistan in 2021, the embed program effectively ended there as well, drawing criticism when the military largely ignored or denied requests by organizations such as the *New York Times* to allow journalists to witness the withdrawal or interview troops.[36] While Defense Department officials regarded the embed program as highly successful, journalists raised questions about its administration. Military officials in August 2009 terminated a contract with a public relations company that was rating reporters' war coverage as "positive," "neutral" or "negative." Reporters feared the ratings influenced decisions on requests to embed with military units, a claim Pentagon officials denied.[37] The press has also criticized military decisions to limit certain reporter's access to military units. For example, Army officials in June 2009 refused to allow Heath Druzin, a *Stars and Stripes* reporter, to embed with an Army division in Iraq because he "refused to highlight" good news during a previous reporting tour.[38]

---

[33] Sidney H. Schanberg, "Censoring for Political Security," *Wash. Journalism Rev.*, Mar. 1991, at 23–5.

[34] Office of Assistant Secretary of Defense for Public Affairs, "Public Affairs Guidance on Embedding Media During Possible Future Operations/Deployments in the U.S. Central Commands Area of Responsibility," Feb. 10, 2003, www.defenselink.mil/news/Feb2003/d20030228pag.pdf.

[35] Dan Lamothe, "If the U.S. Military Is Expanding in Iraq, Why Isn't It Embedding Journalists?" *Wash. Post*, Dec. 2, 2014.

[36] Megan K. Stack, "A Near Press Blackout in Afghanistan," *New Yorker*, Aug. 4, 2021.

[37] AP, "US Officials Cancel Contract to Profile Reporters," Aug. 31, 2009.

[38] "Army Bars *Stars and Stripes* Reporter from Covering 1st Cav Unit in Mosul," *Stars and Stripes*, June 24, 2009.

Ground Rules for Embedded Journalists in Operation Iraqi Freedom

What's Allowed

- Approximate friendly force strength figures
- Confirmed numbers of captured enemy personnel
- Types of ordinance expended in general terms
- Generic description of origin of air operations, such as "land-based"

- Date, time, location and results of previous conventional military missions and actions, only if described in general terms
- Number of aerial missions
- Service members' names and home-towns with the individuals' consent

What's Not Allowed

- Specific numbers of troops, aircraft, ships, equipment or supplies
- Information on special operations units, unique tactics
- Information regarding future operations
- Information regarding force protection measures at military installations
- Live broadcasts from airfields or aircraft carriers until safe return of aircraft or until authorized by unit commander

- Photographs or television coverage showing the recognizable face or name tag of a prisoner of war
- Specific information on friendly force troop movements during an operation that would jeopardize operational security
- Rules of engagement
- Information on intelligence collection activities
- Information on missing or downed aircraft while rescue operations are underway

FIGURE 12.1 To be embedded with U.S. military units during Operation Iraqi Freedom, journalists agreed to follow an extensive set of ground rules. The Pentagon required journalists to sign an agreement acknowledging that failure to follow the rules "may result in the immediate termination of the embed and removal" from the war zone. This is a sampling of the ground rules.

Druzin wrote that many Iraqi residents of Mosul want American soldiers to leave. The denial of Druzin's embed request appears to have violated the Pentagon's established ground rules, rules which "recognize the inherent right of the media to cover combat operations and are in no way intended to prevent release of embarrassing, negative, or derogatory information." Other journalists had their access terminated. Photographer Zoriah Miller was removed from a Marine unit in Iraq after he posted photographs of the victims of a suicide bomber, including three Marines. When Miller refused to remove the photographs from his website, he was barred from Marine installations. The Marine Corps claimed Miller published information without approval, including material about "any tactics, techniques and procedures witnessed during operations" or that "provides information on the effectiveness of enemy techniques." Miller's case was not unique, as the *New York Times* reported that the embeds of other photographers were terminated following publication of photographs of dead soldiers.[39]

---

[39] Michael Kamber and Tim Arango, "4,000 Deaths, and a Handful of Images," *N.Y. Times*, July 26, 2008 at A1.

Concern about portrayal of dead soldiers heightened in September 2009 as the Associated Press distributed to news media photographs of a Marine fatally wounded in a grenade attack in Afghanistan. The AP did so despite pleas by Defense Secretary Robert Gates and against the wishes of the Marine's family. The photographs were taken by AP photographer Julie Jacobson, who was embedded with a Marine unit in Afghanistan. "AP journalists document world events every day. Afghanistan is no exception," said Santiago Lyon, director of photography for AP. "We feel it is our journalistic duty to show the reality of war there, however unpleasant and brutal that sometimes is."

Shortly after the AP disseminated the images, military officials in Afghanistan changed the ground rules reporters must agree to before being embedded. The amended rules permit publishing of casualty photographs only if the casualty is not recognizable by "face, name tag or other identifying feature."[40] In 2013, a federal district court dismissed a lawsuit by a reporter whose embed status was terminated because he filed a video showing identifiable faces of wounded soldiers. The court reaffirmed that there was no First Amendment right to be an embedded journalist.[41]

▪ SUMMARY ▪

Courts are often inclined to accept the discretion of officials when they deny journalists access to public and quasi-public property. State statutes specify punishment for those who obstruct authority. The Defense Department, acting under the auspices of the president, controls access to war zones. The Defense Department embedded reporters in military units during the wars in Iraq and Afghanistan.

ACCESS TO RECORDS

Although the law seldom guarantees press access to public places, all states and the federal government have adopted statutes mandating public access to many government records and meetings. Most records laws begin with a statement declaring a government policy to maximize public access to government records. When deciding close cases, courts ruling for public access often cite the legislatures' policy statements urging a presumption of openness. The power and purpose of these laws are clear—to make government work transparent as a way of ensuring informed self-government by the people. Texas provides an example in the opening to its Public Information Act with the following passage:

> Under the fundamental philosophy of the American constitutional form of representative government that adheres to the principle that government is the servant and not the master of the people, it is the policy of this state that each person is entitled, unless otherwise expressly provided by law, at all times to complete information about the affairs of government and the official acts of public officials and employees. The people, in delegating authority, do not give their public servants the right to decide what is good for the people to know and what is

---

[40] Combined Joint Task Force 82, Regional Command-East, Media Ground Rules at ¶ 11, Sept. 15, 2009.
[41] Anderson v. Gates, 20 F. Supp. 3d 114 (D.D.C. 2013).

not good for them to know. The people insist on remaining informed
so that they may retain control over the instruments they have created.[42]

Most laws define public records and describe the government agencies covered
by the law, how records are requested and acquired, copying and search charges,
a list of records exempted from disclosure and penalties, if any, for officials who
improperly withhold public records.

The discussion of records laws begins with an analysis of the federal Freedom
of Information Act, the law controlling documents held by federal agencies. Most
issues raised by the federal law are also issues in state open records laws.

Federal Freedom of Information Act

The Freedom of Information Act (FOIA) requires federal agencies to provide any
person access to records, both paper and electronic, that do not fit one of nine
exempt categories that are discussed in a later section.

HISTORY AND PURPOSE Congress adopted the Freedom of Information
Act in 1966 as a bipartisan effort to increase public access to federal documents.
The Electronic Freedom of Information Act Amendments, adopted in 1996, extend
the open records law to digital information held by federal agencies.[43]

Recognizing the rapid growth of digital information, Congress passed the
Electronic Freedom of Information Act (E-FOIA) in 1996 to "maximize the usefulness of agency records and information collected, maintained, used, retained and
disseminated by the Federal Government."[44] By improving public access to agency
information, the Electronic Freedom of Information Act was supposed to "foster
democracy." But federal records are generally public whether or not their disclosure promotes some obvious democratic purpose. Federal records are open to any
person "for any public or private use," Congress said.

The Freedom of Information Act establishes that the government should disclose whenever possible and withhold only when necessary. Congress included
nine exemptions in the law to balance the government's need to maintain privacy
and confidentiality with the public's right to be informed. The Supreme Court has
said that the exemptions do not obscure that "disclosure, not secrecy" is the "dominant objective" of the act.[45]

Since its passage, FOIA has allowed citizens to uncover a wide range of information important to public welfare. Journalists used FOIA to document how the
Department of Housing and Urban Development during the Reagan administration
used government funds to finance projects for prominent Republican politicians
and their friends. Documents obtained through FOIA also revealed how the FBI
harassed Dr. Martin Luther King Jr., and how the CIA illegally monitored domestic
political groups and experimented on prisoners using mind-control drugs. FOIA
has also been used to disclose unsanitary conditions in food processing plants,
safety hazards at nuclear power plants, the presence of poisonous waste in drinking water, compliance of school districts with antidiscrimination laws, and even
the recipe the president's staff uses to brew its White House Honey Ale. In recent
years, FOIA used to reveal unredacted copies and source materials from the special

---

[42] Texas Gov't Code § 552.001 (2016).
[43] Pub. L. No. 104–231, 110 Stat. 3048, *amending* 5 U.S.C. § 552.
[44] Section 2, Findings and Purposes, 110 Stat. 3048.
[45] Department of Air Force v. Rose, 425 U.S. 352 (1976).

counsel investigating ties between the Trump campaign and Russia,[46] as well as documents revealing the president's efforts to coax Ukraine into smearing his opponent during the 2020 election.[47]

Litigation over FOIA has escalated over the past decade. In 2015, nearly 500 lawsuits were filed against federal agencies regarding access to federal documents, including efforts to reveal former Secretary of State Hillary Clinton's emails stored on a private server.[48] Lawsuits increased even more during the Trump administration, nearly doubling what they were a decade before.[49] BuzzFeed alone touted that they filed 58 FOIA lawsuits against the Trump administration in his four years in office.[50]

FOIA has been heavily criticized. Journalists, citizens and lobbyists invoking the law charge that agencies withhold information by interpreting exemptions too broadly and unnecessarily delaying disclosure. Journalists also complain that agencies "lose" documents and hire insufficient staff to process FOI requests. Law enforcement officers, businesses and others contend the act allows too much disclosure, is unfair to businesses submitting information to the government, and is an undue burden on government.

A survey published in 2009 found that 77 percent of Americans support the Freedom of Information Act, even though few citizens use it. Seven in ten adults also think the federal government is too secretive.[51] Journalists, access advocates and politicians criticized the Bush administration for vastly increasing the number of secret government documents and slowing the process of declassification. In 2004, the government classified 15.6 million documents—about 125 per minute—nearly double the number classified in 2001.[52] Thousands were classified under vague categories such as "sensitive" security information.

Indeed, the administration of President George W. Bush adopted a more constricted view of openness after the attack on the World Trade Center and the Pentagon on September 11, 2001. The Bush administration emphasized the importance of protecting national security, personal privacy and the confidentiality of sensitive business information in government records.[53] The Obama administration promised an administration of more transparency, operating on a presumption that government information is public, though these promises were largely left unfulfilled. By 2016, the House Oversight Committee declared that FOIA was "broken" because of the interminable delays in processing requests and the low levels of compliance with the law throughout the federal bureaucracy.

---

[46] Electronic Privacy Information Center v. Department of Justice, 2021 U.S. App. LEXIS 35271 (D.C. Cir. 2021).

[47] American Oversight, "State Department Releases Ukraine Documents to American Oversight," Nov. 22, 2019.

[48] David Burnham, "FOIA Lawsuits Reach Record High," *The FOIA Project*, Jan. 6, 2016; Robert O'Harrow Jr., "How Clinton's Email Scandal Took Root," *Wash. Post*, Mar. 27, 2016.

[49] Camille Fassett, "The Freedom of Information Act Is Getting Worse Under the Trump Administration," *Freedom of the Press Foundation*, Mar. 14, 2019.

[50] Jason Leopold and Christopher Hickman, "Trump Officials Tried to Keep the Public in the Dark, But Buzzfeed News Never Stopped Fighting for Essential Documents," *BuzzFeed*, Jan. 4, 2021.

[51] "Federal Government Still Viewed as Secretive; Public Supports President's Directive on Transparency," survey conducted by Scripps Howard News Service and Ohio University, Mar. 12, 2009, www.sunshineweek.org.

[52] Scott Shane, "Since 2001, Sharp Increase in the Number of Documents Classified by the Government," *N.Y. Times*, July 3, 2005, at 14.

[53] Dep't of Justice, "New Attorney General FOIA Memorandum Issued," Oct. 15, 2001, www.usdoj.gov/oip/foiapost/2001foiapost19.htm.

Since its adoption half a century ago, FOIA has undergone regular revision and updates to address concerns about the law's inadequacy in handling access to federal records, particularly addressing agency denials and delays that frustrated the purpose of the law. The passage of the E-FOIA in 1996 required federal agencies to host digital "reading rooms" on their websites that included the records most often sought by requesters.[54] In 2009, the federal Office of Government Information Services was established to act as an ombuds overseeing agency compliance with FOIA and to provide mediation services to help facilitate processing of requests.[55] The Obama administration's call for broader transparency included requirements that agencies work toward all federal records being kept and managed in digital formats by 2019.[56] On its fiftieth anniversary in 2016, Congress passed the FOIA Improvement Act, which requires federal agencies to make records available in electronic formats such as PDF or data files, prohibits agencies from charging fees or costs for producing records if they miss deadlines and directs the creation of a central, online portal that will allow citizens to make requests of any federal agency through a single website.[57]

DEFINING "AGENCY" The Freedom of Information Act requires that "agency" records be open. The term *agency* includes any executive department, military department, government corporation, government-controlled corporation, or other establishment in the executive branch of the government, or any independent regulatory agency.[58]

The act applies to cabinet offices such as Defense, Treasury and Justice and agencies such as the FBI and Internal Revenue Service that report to them. Federal records are public, whether housed in Washington, D.C., or in regional offices in Atlanta or San Francisco. Independent regulatory agencies subject to the law include the Federal Communications Commission, Federal Trade Commission, Securities and Exchange Commission and Consumer Product Safety Commission. The act pertains to presidential commissions, the U.S. Postal Service and Amtrak. It applies to the Executive Office of the President, including the Office of Management and Budget, but not to the president himself or to the president's advisers. Therefore, the act does not apply to the Council of Economic Advisers or other agencies established only to advise and assist the president.[59] After a court ruled that the White House's Office of Administration was not an "agency," the Obama administration announced that the office would no longer respond to FOIA requests for items such as staff emails.[60] The act also does not apply to records of Congress or the federal courts.

DEFINING "RECORD" The original FOIA did not define what is included in the term *records*, but the 1996 E-FOIA revisions included in the definition of a record any non-exempt information maintained by an agency "in any format, including an electronic format." Federal records include most information that functions as a record of government activity and can be reproduced. Paper documents, tape recordings, photographs and computerized printouts are records because they

---

[54] Electronic Freedom of Information Amendments of 1996, Pub. L. No. 104–231.

[55] OPEN Government Act of 2007, Pub. L. No. 110–175.

[56] Office of Management and Budget, "Managing Government Records Directive," Aug. 24, 2012, 3.

[57] FOIA Improvement Act of 2016, Pub. L. No. 114–185.

[58] 5 U.S.C. § 552(f).

[59] *See* Rushforth v. Council of Economic Advisers, 762 F.2d 1038 (D.C. Cir. 1985).

[60] Citizens for Responsibility and Ethics in Washington v. Office of Administration, 556 F.3d 219 (D.C. Cir. 2009); Josh Hicks, "A Sunshine Week Surprise: White House Exempts Executive Office from Records Requests," *Wash. Post*, Mar. 18, 2015.

chronicle government activity and can be reproduced. Physical objects, such as weapons, are not records.

Under E-FOIA, requesters are supposed to receive records in the format they choose if that format is readily available. Thus, requesters should be able to receive electronic copies of databases and database queries. An agency is also supposed to make new records available online if the agency has online capabilities.

E-FOIA also requires federal agencies to make reasonable efforts to search for requested records in electronic form unless a search would "significantly interfere" with agency operations. To search electronic databases, agencies may have to engage in at least limited programming. But the law does not require agencies to create "new" records. Administrators may redact electronic records, as they can paper records, to remove private, proprietary or security information before releasing records. However, E-FOIA requires an agency to tell how much of a document, if any, has been deleted.

Backlogs of requests at U.S. agencies have grown, with several agencies reporting that they had requests at least a decade old, including one request that was more than 20 years old.[61] The House Oversight Committee discovered in 2016 that hundreds of thousands of new requests were going unfulfilled each year, and more than 40 percent of FOIA requests resulted in no documents being released.[62]

Regardless of the physical form or format of a record, a federal agency must both possess and control a record for it to be subject to disclosure under FOIA. In a ruling that especially limits public access to studies prepared by private consultants for the government, the Supreme Court said a report about diabetes treatments was not an agency record because a federal agency did not possess it. However, government records maintained by private firms under government contract are open.[63]

The Supreme Court has also ruled that an agency cannot be forced to obtain documents that would fall under FOIA if the agency possessed them. Thus, the State Department was not required to retrieve transcripts of Henry Kissinger's telephone conversations while he was Secretary of State and National Security Adviser. Earlier, Kissinger donated the transcripts to the Library of Congress—which is not subject to FOIA—with an agreement that substantially limited public access.[64] A Court has also ruled an agency may have to make records available to requesters even if the same records can be found elsewhere.[65]

ACCESS FOR WHOM? Under FOIA, "any person" may submit a request for a federal record.[66] "Any person" includes citizens of foreign countries and persons acting on behalf of organizations such as defense contractors, media companies and public interest groups.[67]

A federal agency generally cannot consider the purpose of a FOIA request when deciding whether to disclose records.[68] A requester does not have to justify a request or explain why disclosure might be in the public interest. If release

---

[61] Tom Blanton and Nate Jones, "Eight Federal Agencies Have FOIA Requests a Decade Old, According to Knight Open Government Survey," *National Security Archive*, July 4, 2011.

[62] U.S. House of Representatives Committee on Oversight and Government Reform, "FOIA Is Broken: A Report," Jan. 2016, 39.

[63] Forsham v. Harris, 445 U.S. 169 (1980).

[64] Kissinger v. Reporters Committee for Freedom of the Press, 445 U.S. 136 (1980).

[65] Department of Justice v. Tax Analysts, 492 U.S. 136 (1989).

[66] 5 U.S.C. § 552(a)(3).

[67] James O'Reilly, 1 *Federal Information Disclosure* ¶ 4.06, at 4–24, 4–25 (2nd ed. Nov. 1990).

[68] *See* Department of Justice v. Reporters Comm. for Freedom of the Press, 489 U.S. 749 (1989); *see, e.g.,* Justin Franklin and Robert Bouchard, *Guidebook to the Freedom of Information and Privacy Acts* ¶ 1.03, at 1–26, 1–27 (2nd ed. Aug. 1995).

of records depended on an official's definition of the "public interest," agency personnel could withhold documents because they disapproved how the information might be used. As one judge put it, FOIA grants "the scholar and the scoundrel equal rights of access to agency records."[69]

FOIA REQUESTS The Freedom of Information Act mandates that agencies respond to requests promptly and requires only commercial users of the act to pay full search and copying costs. Denials of FOIA requests can be appealed.

Filing Requests Anyone seeking information from a U.S. government agency may be able to obtain it informally. People can ask an agency's public information officer, even at a local or regional office, without making a formal FOIA request. This informal approach, when it works, is quick and inexpensive.

If informal requests do not succeed, a person can file a formal, written request for the information under FOIA. Each agency must publish a description of its organization and a list of the people a citizen should contact when making an inquiry under FOIA. The agency must explain its FOIA procedures and provide electronic indexes of popular records.[70] A sample request letter is printed as Figure 12.2.

Once a formal FOIA request has been made, an agency must release the documents or demonstrate that they fall into one of the exempt categories. Although the law requires the requester only to "reasonably" describe the documents sought, requests are more likely to be fulfilled quickly, cheaply and completely if the requester describes with some precision the records he or she seeks. When possible, a requester should describe a document by number, date, title and author.

If an agency decides that some of the information requested falls under one of the nine exemptions, only that information can be deleted. The rest of the document should be disclosed.

Response Deadlines Under FOIA, agencies have 20 days to determine whether the agency can fulfill the request. If an agency cannot fulfill a request within the 20 days because of "unusual circumstances," the requester may narrow the request so that an agency can fulfill it within 20 days, or the requester and the agency may negotiate a time at which the request will be fulfilled. "Unusual circumstances" are not supposed to include the lengthy backlogs that delay disclosures at several federal agencies. Nevertheless, delays continue to occur. An audit in 2019 showed that five federal agencies had FOIA requests pending that were made more than ten years before, and one request remained unfulfilled after 25 years.[71]

Agencies are also required to expedite a request when the requester demonstrates a compelling need for the records. Agencies will expedite requests when delay poses an imminent threat to an individual's life or safety or when "a person primarily engaged in disseminating information" can show an "urgency to inform the public concerning actual or alleged federal government activity."[72]

To reduce delays, Congress adopted legislation in 2007 requiring agencies who fail to meet the 20-day deadline for producing records to refund from their operating budgets the search costs incurred fulfilling a request. The law also allows requesters to track requests by phone or Internet if fulfilling a request will require more than ten days.[73]

---

[69] Durns v. Bureau of Prisons, 804 F.2d 701, 706 (D.C. Cir. 1986).
[70] 5 U.S.C. § 552(a)(2)(C), (D), (E).
[71] "25-Year-Old FOIA Request Confirms FOIA Delays Continue Unabated," *National Security Archive*, Mar. 8, 2019.
[72] 5 U.S.C. § 552(a)(6)(E).
[73] Openness Promotes Effectiveness in Our National Government Act, codified at 5 U.S.C. § 552(a)(4), (6).

Your address
Daytime phone number
Date

Freedom of Information Office
Agency
Address

FOIA Request

Dear FOI Officer:

Pursuant to the federal Freedom of Information Act. 5 U.S.C. § 552, I request access to and copies of *(here, clearly describe what you want. Include identifying material, such as names, places and the period of time about which you are inquiring. If you think they will help to explain what you are looking for, attach news clips, reports and other documents describing the subject of your research.)*

(Optional:) I would like to receive the information in electronic *(or microfiche)* format.

I agree to pay reasonable duplication fees for the processing of this request in an amount not to exceed *$(state amount)*. However, please notify me prior to your incurring any expenses in excess of that amount.

(Suggested request for fee benefit as a representative of the news media:) As a representative of the news media I am only required to pay for the direct cost of duplication after the first 100 pages. Through this request, I am gathering information on *(subject)* that is of current interest to the public because *(give reason).* This information is being sought on behalf of *(give the name of your news organization)* for dissemination to the general public. *(If a freelancer, provide information such as experience, publication contract, etc., that demonstrates that you expect publication.)*

(Optional fee waiver request:) Please waive any applicable fees. Release of the information is in the public interest because it will contribute significantly to public understanding of government operations and activities.

If my request is denied in whole or part, I ask that you justify all deletions by reference to specific exemptions of the act. I will also expect you to release all segregable portions of otherwise exempt material. I, of course, reserve the right to appeal your decision to withhold any information or to deny a waiver of fees.

As I am making this request as a journalist *(or author, or scholar) and* this information is of timely value, I would appreciate your communicating with me by telephone, rather than by mail, if you have questions regarding this request.

(If you are a reporter or a person who is "primarily engaged in disseminating information," and your request concerns a matter of "compelling need," a request for expedited review may be honored. If so. include the next three paragraphs:)

Please provide expedited review of this request which concerns a matter of urgency. As a journalist, I am primarily engaged in disseminating information.

The public has an urgent need for information about *(describe the government activity involved)* because *(establish the need for bringing information on this subject to the public's attention now.)*

I certify that my statements concerning the need for expedited review are true and correct to the best of my knowledge and belief.

I look forward to your reply within 20 business days, as the statute requires.

Thank you for your assistance.

Very truly yours,

FIGURE 12.2 Sample FOI Act Request Letter, Reporters Committee for Freedom of the Press. www.ifoia.org

Fees Generally, federal agencies are supposed to charge requesters only the actual costs of finding and copying information, including computerized information.[74] FOIA requires that only persons seeking information for commercial uses pay full search and copying costs as well as the costs for officials to review information for possible deletions. All other requesters pay nothing for the first two hours of search time and the first 100 pages copied. Furthermore, requesters using the information for noncommercial purposes cannot be charged for the review for deletions.

The 1986 FOIA Reform Act also specifies that all fees will be reduced or waived if the disclosure of the information is in the public interest because dissemination is likely to contribute significantly to public understanding of the operations or activities of the government and is not primarily in the commercial interest of the requester.[75] Federal courts have ruled in favor of fee waivers for FOIA requesters determined to be "news media" because they gathered information of potential interest to the public, used editorial skills to create distinct works, and published or otherwise distributed the works. For example, courts found "news media" to include the nonprofit National Security Archive, which exercised editorial judgment to make tools regarding defense and international economic policy available to the public, and the nonprofit Cause of Action, which requested records about the FTC's social media guides on product endorsement and testimonials, as well as its own policies on FOIA fee waivers, to inform the public about its concerns.[76] In 2007, Congress amended the law to permit waivers for "any person or entity that gathers information of potential interest to a segment of the public, uses its editorial skills to turn the raw materials into a distinct work, and distributes the work to an audience."

Persons seeking information through FOIA should request a fee waiver in the initial request if they believe they are eligible. Before agencies begin their searches, requesters should establish a limit on the money they are willing to spend for searching and copying.

APPEALS AND PENALTIES If an agency head denies an appeal for access to a record, or if the agency does not respond within 20 days, a person requesting information can file a complaint in federal district court. FOIA provides that a suit under the act should be given precedence over most other litigation. A court has the authority to examine the documents at issue to decide whether an agency has improperly withheld records.[77] The court's decision can be appealed to one of the circuits of the U.S. Courts of Appeals. The judicial examination of documents, known as *in camera* review, was expanded by Congress in 1974 to include even classified information related to national security. President Ford vetoed the 1974 legislation, contending that the courts should not have the authority to overrule the executive branch on what documents should be classified. Congress overrode the president's veto, asserting that a check on executive branch secrecy was necessary.

If a person seeking information wins in court, a judge can assess the government the requester's attorney's fees and other litigation costs.[78] Under a 2007

---

[74] Paperwork Reduction Act of 1995, codified at 44 U.S.C.S. § 3501 et seq.
[75] 5 U.S.C. § 552(a)(4)(A)(iii).
[76] National Sec. Archive v. Department of Defense, 880 F.2d 1381 (D.C. Cir. 1989), *cert. denied*, 494 U.S. 1029 (1990); Cause of Action v. Federal Trade Commission, 749 F.3d 1108 (D.C. Cir. 2015).
[77] 5 U.S.C. § 552(a)(4)(B).
[78] 5 U.S.C. § 552(a)(4)(E).

amendment, a requester might also win attorney's fees from an agency before litigation if a judge orders disclosure or an agency changes its mind.[79]

■ SUMMARY ■

The Freedom of Information Act makes federal records available to any person. The statute opens paper and digital records of the executive branch, with the exception of the White House, but not records of Congress or the federal courts. A document is a record of a federal agency only if the agency both possesses and controls it. An agency must respond to a written request for a record within 20 working days. When a citizen appeals inaction or denial, an agency head is supposed to answer within 20 working days. Agencies can charge for searches and copying, but fees are waived if a request is in the public interest.

EXEMPTIONS An agency must disclose any record that does not fall within one of the nine categories of information exempted from disclosure under FOIA. But the Supreme Court has ruled that the exemptions permit, but do not require, a federal agency to withhold documents. An agency may disclose a document that fits one of the nine exemptions if another statute does not require the information be withheld.

The most important exemptions for journalists are exemption 1, national security; exemption 6, personnel and medical files; and exemption 7, law enforcement investigation records. The most important exemption for businesses is exemption 4, protecting confidential business information. Businesses are also protected by exemption 8, banking reports; and 9, information about wells. The other FOIA exemptions are 2, internal rules and agency practices; 3, matters required to be withheld by other statutes; and 5, inter-agency or intra-agency memoranda.

The gradual expansion of exemptions under FOIA has often been criticized as a way to increase government secrecy rather than transparency, as courts have sometimes interpreted the exemptions broadly, with the Supreme Court finding exemptions on privacy matters and siding with the government agencies denying access to records in eight out of nine cases, according to a 2014 study.[80] The FOIA Improvement Act revisions in 2016 sought to slow down the expansion of exemptions by requiring that agencies release information unless they "reasonably foresee that disclosure would harm an interest" in core agency matters such as national security or personal privacy.[81]

(1) National Security Exemption 1 protects from disclosure information that an executive order declares could damage the national defense and foreign policy. FOIA grants the executive branch more discretion to withhold national security information than any other category. Exemption 1 is the only exemption that allows the executive branch, rather than Congress, to determine the criteria for the release of documents.

The president and his attorney general determine how national security records will be classified. After the attacks of 9/11, the administration of George W. Bush set a tone of wariness, justifying the closure of many previously open records on the demands of national security in a world of terrorist threats.

---

[79] *Id.*
[80] Martin E. Halstuk, Benjamin W. Cramer, and Michael E. Todd, "Tipping the Scales: How the U.S. Supreme Court Eviscerated Freedom of Information in Favor of Privacy," in *Transparency 2.0* (Charles N. Davis and David Cuillier, eds., 2014).
[81] 5 U.S.C. § 552(8)(a) (2016).

In 2011, a federal appeals court ruled the executive branch could withhold details of the capture, detention and interrogation of "high value" detainees held at Guantanamo Bay—information that, if disclosed, might degrade the ability of the CIA to interrogate detainees, could improve al Qaeda's insight into intelligence activities, and could hinder Americans' ability to obtain assistance from foreign nations.[82]

In December 2009, President Obama issued an executive order declaring that "no information may remain classified indefinitely." In a sweeping review of the system for classifying national security information, Obama ordered agencies to regularly review the kinds of information they classify and to eliminate obsolete secrecy requirements and established a new National Declassification Center.[83]

FOIA authorizes judges to review classification decisions, but the courts rarely order the release of information that the executive branch says should be classified. Judges ordinarily defer to the president, who is given the power by the Constitution to conduct foreign policy and to supervise national security. In addition, most courts seem to share the sentiment of the judge who said that "few judges have the skill or experience to weigh the repercussions of disclosure of intelligence information."[84]

(2) Agency Rules and Practices Exemption 2 allows agencies to withhold documents "related solely to internal personnel rules and practices." Among the records fitting the exemption are those dealing with human resources and employee relations, regulations that might govern hiring, firing, work rules and discipline.[85] The general thrust of the exemption, Justice Brennan wrote in *Department of the Air Force v. Rose*, "is simply to relieve agencies of the burden of assembling and maintaining for public inspection matter in which the public could not reasonably be expected to have an interest."[86]

In *Rose*, the Court ruled exception 2 did not permit the U.S. Air Force Academy to withhold summaries of disciplinary hearings, records of "genuine and significant public interest." These were not merely records dealing with internal practices. Discipline at the Air Force Academy was obviously an issue of public interest, Brennan said, given the importance of discipline to military effectiveness. The Court said the names of participants in the hearings could be redacted.

Over several decades courts had greatly expanded exemption 2 to include a wide range of records, the disclosure of which might jeopardize national security, reveal law enforcement procedures, or generally allow laws or agency regulations to be circumvented.[87] In 2011, the Supreme Court narrowed exemption 2 to its original meaning, permitting agencies only to withhold records dealing with human resources and personnel issues.

In *Milner v. Department of the Navy*, the Court ruled 8–1 that exemption 2 did not allow the Navy to withhold information about damage that might result if bombs stored on a base exploded.[88] Such information, which could be useful to terrorists as well as to neighboring residents, might be withheld under a different FOIA exemption, the Court suggested. However, exemption 2, the Court said,

---

[82] American Civil Liberties Union v. Dep't of Defense, 628 F.3d 612 (D.C. Cir. 2011).

[83] Executive Order 13,526, 75 FR 707, Jan. 5, 2010.

[84] "2 Tell of Radiation Experiments on Them as Boys," *N.Y. Times*, Jan. 14, 1994, at A12.

[85] Milner v. Department of the Navy 2011 U.S. LEXIS 2101, Mar. 7, 2011.

[86] 425 U.S. 352 (1976).

[87] *See* Crooker v. Bureau of Alcohol, Tobacco & Firearms, 670 F.2d 1051 (D.C. Cir. 1981).

[88] 2011 U.S. LEXIS 2101, Mar. 7, 2011.

allows an agency to withhold only records "related solely to internal personnel rules and practices."

(3) Statutory Exemptions The third exemption applies to documents that Congress has declared in other statutes to be confidential. The third exemption is often called the "catchall" exemption because it exempts from disclosure any records Congress has decided to exclude from the general policy of openness under FOIA.

The exemption applies to Census Bureau records, tax returns and patent applications. Exemption 3 allows for the withholding of records by such agencies as the U.S. Postal Service, Central Intelligence Agency, Department of Agriculture and the Federal Trade Commission. The Central Intelligence Agency Act of 1949 provides that the names, titles and salaries of CIA employees and the number of personnel employed by the agency are exempt from disclosure.[89] Statutes permit the government to withhold information if disclosure would compromise homeland security and privacy, including student privacy.

Homeland Security One of the most important restrictions on access to records is found in Section 214 of the Homeland Security Act, the act that creates the cabinet level Department of Homeland Security (DHS). Section 214 prohibits the department from disclosing critical infrastructure information provided by agencies and private businesses. Under the Homeland Security Act, private sector companies in chemicals, nuclear energy, water, finance and communications can avoid public disclosure if they submit vulnerabilities in their critical infrastructure to the DHS. Critical infrastructure includes vital systems and assets whose incapacity would have debilitating impact on security, the economy and public health or safety. Once the DHS possesses information regarding the security of critical infrastructure, the information is private and not to be disclosed or used against a company for wrongdoing.[90]

In 2009, Congress passed an amendment to the Homeland Security law prohibiting the disclosure of photographs, film or video of detainees if the Secretary of Defense certifies disclosure will endanger U.S. citizens, members of the Armed Forces or employees of the U.S. government deployed abroad.[91] The statute allows the government to withhold certified photos and videos shot between September 11, 2001, and January 22, 2009. The statute was adopted to allow the Obama administration to withhold photos of American military personnel abusing detainees in Afghanistan and Iraq, including Abu Ghraib prison. The statute, in effect, overturns an appellate court decision ordering the photos be released under the Freedom of Information Act, a case discussed later in the chapter.[92] The Obama administration originally supported release of the abuse photos but later reversed itself, arguing that release might place American military and civilians in danger from angry Afghans and Iraqis.

In the same legislation exempting disclosure of abuse photos, Congress also made it harder for future legislatures to hide new statutory FOIA exemptions in lengthy proposed legislation. The amended statute requires future legislation to cite section 3 of the Freedom of Information Act—the section providing for statutory

---

[89] 50 U.S.C. § 403g.
[90] *See* Reporters Committee for Freedom of the Press, *Homefront Confidential* 55–7 (3rd ed., Mar. 2003).
[91] Protected National Security Documents Act of 2009, sec. 565 of the Department of Homeland Security Appropriations Act, 2010.
[92] American Civil Liberties Union v. Dep't of Justice, 389 F. Supp. 2d 547 (S.D.N.Y. 2005), *aff'd*, 543 F.3d 59 (2d Cir. 2008), *vacated and remanded*, 130 S. Ct. 777 (2009).

exemptions—if the proposed legislation contains new exemptions.[93] Congress concluded that new FOIA exemptions are too often buried in lengthy appropriation or budget bills, only to be discovered long after the bills are debated and adopted.

Privacy Under the Privacy Act of 1974, individuals have the right to obtain and amend government files containing personal information about them. In addition, the Privacy Act permits government agencies to use a "personally identifiable record" only for the reasons it was collected or for reasons specifically listed in the act itself. Agencies are otherwise prohibited from disclosing personal information without the written consent of the person involved. Agencies must keep track of each disclosure.[94] If there is a conflict between the Privacy Act and FOIA, FOIA is supposed to prevail.

Student Educational Records Another federal statute that protects privacy is the Family Educational Rights and Privacy Act, often called FERPA or the Buckley Amendment.[95] FERPA permits students over age 18—or parents of younger students—to see and correct their "educational records." The Federal Rights and Privacy Act also prohibits educational institutions from releasing educational records to the public under threat of losing federal funding.

Universities, colleges and high schools are permitted by FERPA to release "directory information" unless students object. Directory information includes a student's name, address, telephone number, date and place of birth, attendance record, field of study, degrees and participation in official activities, including sports. Educational institutions can release the weight and height of members of athletic teams but not grades and health information.

Over time, universities have employed FERPA to withhold potentially embarrassing information that seemingly has little to do with privacy. Universities have cited FERPA to withhold flight manifestos and summer jobs held by football players, recruiting violations by coaches and boosters, and campus parking tickets.[96]

Student Law Enforcement Records Federal law requires that most campus crime be disclosed, either as individual incidents or in statistical summary, if the crimes are recorded in law enforcement records. The law says law enforcement records at state college and university police stations—records of arrests, charges and incidents—are public, just as law enforcement records are public at city police stations.[97] Law enforcement records do not become exempt educational records if they are stored in the office of student affairs or other nonlaw enforcement offices.

Under federal law, all public and private colleges and universities that receive federal funding must maintain public logs of criminal incidents reported to their police or security offices.[98] Within two days of an incident, record custodians must add to the log the nature, date, time, location and disposition of each criminal complaint. However, campus officials may withhold information that would jeopardize ongoing investigations or reveal the identity of victims of sex crimes. Federal law also requires institutions receiving federal money to annually report statistics for campus crimes, including murder, manslaughter, sex offenses, robbery, aggravated assault, burglary, motor vehicle theft and arson.

---

[93] Open FOIA Act of 2009, sec. 564 of the Department of Homeland Security Appropriations Act, 2010.
[94] 5 U.S.C. § 552a(b), (c), (d).
[95] 20 U.S.C. § 1232g.
[96] Jill Riepenhoff and Todd Jones, "Secrecy 101: College Athletic Departments Use Vague Law to Keep Public Records from Being Seen," *The Columbus Dispatch*, May 31, 2009.
[97] 20 U.S.C. § 1232g(a)(4)(B)(ii).
[98] 20 U.S.C. § 1092(f).

In recent years, there have been shootings at several campuses, including one that resulted in the deaths of 33 at Virginia Tech in 2007. In 2008, Congress amended the federal disclosure law to require colleges to "immediately notify" the campus community upon confirmation of "a significant emergency or dangerous situation involving an immediate threat to the health or safety of students or staff." Jurors in 2012 found Virginia Tech negligent for delaying notification of the campus, fining the university $32,500.[99]

Student Disciplinary Records Citing FERPA, college and university officials have frequently closed student disciplinary records. College officials, supported by the Department of Education, argue that records of student disciplinary proceedings, often conducted in student judicial courts, should remain closed so that youthful offenders can be educated and rehabilitated, shielded from the glare of publicity. Universities also argue that students who violate laws and regulations should not be required forever to carry the stigma of "guilty" because of youthful indiscretions.

Campus judiciaries often try cases involving university rules and conduct standards, including those that proscribe cheating, hazing or destroying dormitory property. But disciplinary records may also include criminal activity not reported to law enforcement officials. Indeed, colleges sometimes channel criminal complaints into the student disciplinary process to avoid the requirement of disclosing law enforcement records. The media and access advocates argue that student judiciary records and proceedings dealing with campus rules violations and crimes should be open to ensure that justice is served and that the public knows whether a campus is dangerous.

Federal law says student judiciary records are not "educational records" exempt from disclosure if the records document charges of violent crime or unforced sex crimes, such as consensual sex with a minor. Thus, universities will not jeopardize federal funding if they release student judiciary records of violent crimes and unforced sex acts. But colleges and universities are not required to release the records under federal law. Colleges and universities may be required under state open records acts to disclose non-educational records of violent crimes. Of course, records of violent crimes will be open at campus police stations if criminal reports are filed with law enforcement officials.

Student judiciary records involving nonviolent crimes and university rules may be withheld at most campuses as "educational records." The federal Department of Education (DOE) argues that student judiciary records involving nonviolent crimes are educational records that should be exempt from disclosure. In 1998, the DOE sued Miami University and Ohio State University to prevent them from releasing campus judiciary records containing students' names. A federal court ruled for the DOE.[100] In 2012, the Georgia attorney general told state universities they may close student disciplinary hearings because a revised state open meetings law recognizes closure under federal law.[101] Student judiciary meetings in Georgia had been open since a Georgia Supreme Court ruling in 1993.[102]

If a university unlawfully reveals educational records, it might lose federal funding, but FERPA does not allow the injured student to sue the university under

---

[99] Associated Press, "College Judge Negligent in 2007 Massacre," *N.Y. Times*, Mar. 15, 2012.

[100] United States v. Miami University, 91 F. Supp. 2d 1132 (S.D. Ohio 2000).

[101] Associated Press, "Ga. Colleges Can Close Discipline Hearings, State Official Says," Oct. 31, 2012.

[102] Red & Black Publishing Co. v. Bd. of Regents, 427 S.E.2d 257 (Ga. 1993).

FERPA.[103] The Supreme Court overturned a Washington Supreme Court ruling that Gonzaga University should pay a Gonzaga student $1.5 million for unlawfully revealing his educational records and refusing to attest to his good character. The university told representatives of the state teacher-certificate office that the student had been accused of raping another student. However, no charges were filed against the student. The student claimed the university's revelation of false accusations and failure to attest to his good character defamed him, invaded his privacy, and cost him a job. The student could sue for defamation or invasion of privacy, but could not sue under FERPA, the Court said.

Driver's Records In addition to the Buckley Amendment and the Privacy Act, Congress passed a law prohibiting states from releasing personal information from motor vehicle records without a driver's consent. The Driver's Privacy Protection Act of 1994 was passed to protect vehicle owners from being stalked and to curb widespread commerce in personal information gleaned from drivers' records.[104] Under the law, state agencies can be fined if they release to the public such information as a driver's name, address, social security number, telephone number or medical information without the driver's consent. Any individual who violates the act can be sued. The act does not restrict the release of information about accidents, driving violations or a driver's legal driving status. The act provides several exemptions, authorizing states to provide personal information to both businesses and government agencies or for such purposes as market surveys and other research, product recalls, vehicle performance monitoring, protection against business fraud and criminal prosecutions.

(4) Confidential Business Information Regulated businesses such as broadcast stations and drug manufacturing companies must submit voluminous amounts of information to regulatory agencies. In addition, businesses seeking government contracts must provide government officials with proprietary information that could be valuable for competitors and journalists. Exemption 4 protects (1) trade secrets and (2) commercial or financial information that businesses submit to government agencies on a confidential basis.

Businesses seeking information about government regulations and their competitors use FOIA more than any other group of requesters. Businesses have obtained, through FOIA, information about government agency procedures, inspection plans and enforcement policies.

Businesses also use FOIA to engage in "industrial espionage," obtaining information about their competitors that is not otherwise available. For instance, Suzuki Motor Company acquired copies of records submitted to the U.S. government by Toyota, information that Suzuki could not obtain from the Japanese government.[105]

Businesses complain that they are required to provide the government economically sensitive information without being able to control who will see it. Indeed, FOIA allows government agencies the discretion to disclose confidential business information, and agencies sometimes knowingly release confidential business records in response to a FOIA request. In addition, agencies sometimes accidentally release sensitive information. For example, the Environmental Protection Agency (EPA) gave the secret formula for Roundup weed killer, a Monsanto

---

[103] Gonzaga Univ. v. Doe, 536 U.S. 273 (2002).
[104] 18 U.S.C. § 2721–5.
[105] James O'Reilly, "Regaining a Confidence: Protection of Business Confidential Data Through Reform of the Freedom of Information Act," 34 *Admin. L. Rev.* 263 (1982).

herbicide, to a competitor because of an agency processing error. Roundup had provided 40 percent of Monsanto's profits during the previous year.[106]

The less used of the two provisions in exemption 4 allows agencies to withhold documents that contain trade secrets, such as the formula for Coca-Cola. Most of the exemption 4 litigation has focused on protecting confidential "commercial or financial information." Agencies are allowed to withhold commercial information about such things as business sales and operating costs, a company's financial condition, and data about a company's workforce if disclosure is likely to impair the government's ability to obtain necessary information in the future or cause "substantial" harm to the competitive position of the company providing the information.[107] Likewise, a court upheld the Defense Department's refusal to reveal information provided by Norris Industries about ammunition the company manufactures. Norris had submitted financial data, including production costs, for the M549 warhead for artillery. An appeals court ruled that disclosure of Norris' financial data would harm Norris' competitive position by allowing competitors to calculate Norris' future bids and pricing structure.[108]

Companies are increasingly using Exemption 4 to intervene in FOIA requests. After the *Argus Leader* won a FOIA lawsuit against the U.S. Department of Agriculture (USDA) to disclose payments made by grocery stores under the Supplemental Nutrition Assistance Program in 2016, the USDA decided no longer to appeal the federal judge's ruling that speculative or unsubstantial competitive harm was not sufficient to exempt disclosure. However, a trade group for grocery stores, Food Marketing Institute, intervened in the case to appeal the decision. The Supreme Court ruled in the group's favor in 2019, finding that despite 20 years of reliance on lower court decisions that a showing of competitive harm was required to exempt this data from disclosure, the strict language of exemption 4 required no such showing.[109] While the Supreme Court has said there is no explicit legal right for a company to stop an agency from releasing information under FOIA,[110] in *Food Marketing Institute v. Argus Leader*, the USDA said it would follow the wishes of the industry group that intervened and would not to reveal what the Supreme Court determined to be "confidential" business information.

(5) Agency Memoranda The widely used exemption 5 protects the deliberative policymaking process of executive agencies. Exemption 5 incorporates into FOIA what is known as "executive privilege." It exempts from disclosure working documents, circulated within an agency or between agencies, which historically have been considered privileged government communications under common law. Exemption 5 protects opinions and recommendations in order to encourage open and frank discussion on policy matters.

Officials contend that sensitive issues can be discussed more thoroughly in preliminary stages outside the glare of publicity. Decision makers are more likely to suggest unconventional ideas, officials argue, if records of their discussions will not be disclosed. Officials also contend that "premature publicity" confuses the

---

[106] Pete Earley, "EPA Lets Trade Secret Loose in Slip-Up, to Firm's Dismay," *Wash. Post*, Sept. 18, 1982, at A1. *But see* Russell B. Stevenson, Jr., "Protecting Business Secrets Under the Freedom of Information Act: Managing Exemption 4," 34 *Admin. L. Rev.* 207, 220 (1982).

[107] National Parks & Conservation Ass'n v. Morton, 498 F.2d 765 (D.C. Cir. 1974). *But see* Critical Mass v. Nuclear Regulatory Comm'n, 975 F.2d 871 (D.C. Cir. 1992), *cert. denied*, 507 U.S. 984 (1993) (recognizing protection for documents that do not fit the first two prongs).

[108] Gulf & Western Indus., Inc. v. United States, 615 F.2d 527 (1979).

[109] Food Marketing Institute v. Argus Leader Media, 139 S. Ct. 2356 (2019).

[110] Chrysler Corp. v. Brown, 441 U.S. 281 (1979).

public by revealing issues and arguments that have little or nothing to do with final decisions.

However, advocates of government disclosure contend the public needs to be a part of the policymaking process before decisions are made. Important issues may be overlooked or deemphasized, it is argued, if officials make up their minds without public debate.

Exemption 5 shields from disclosure policy drafts, staff proposals, studies and investigative reports. The courts have held the exemption also protects from disclosure reports from consultants and internal investigations used in policy preparation and self-criticism.[111] But, in 2014, the U.S. Court of Appeals for the Second Circuit ordered release of a government memorandum containing the legal reasoning for U.S. drone attacks killing Americans overseas. The court ordered disclosure of the document authorizing the Department of Defense and the Central Intelligence Agency to kill Anwar al-Awlaqi, his son, and another man—all U.S. citizens—in Yemen. The court said the government waived its right to withhold the memo authorizing the targeted killings when government officials publicly relied on the legal reasoning in the memorandum to justify the widely criticized drone killings of American citizens.[112]

(6) Personnel, Medical and Similar Files Exemption 6 protects from disclosure a very wide array of information in personnel, medical and "similar" files that, if released, "would constitute a clearly unwarranted invasion of personal privacy." Agencies have to balance the interest in an individual's privacy against the public interest in monitoring the activities of government. The Supreme Court has interpreted the privacy exemption very broadly.

The threshold issue in an exemption 6 case is whether a record falls within the definition of "personnel," "medical" and "similar" files. "Personnel files" are employment records, including performance evaluations and reports on disciplinary proceedings. "Medical files" encompass any individual's medical records held by federal agencies.

"Similar files" include documents that reveal an individual's social security number, marital status, financial status or welfare payments.[113] In addition, courts have said that "similar files" encompass the addresses of federal employees, persons taking federal exams and persons holding Veterans Administration loans.[114] The Supreme Court has said that the term *similar files* applies to any information about a specific individual held by the federal government. In *Department of State v. Washington Post Co.*, eight of the nine justices said a file does not have to contain intimate information to be withheld. Then-Justice William H. Rehnquist said exemption 6 was intended "to protect individuals from the injury and embarrassment that can result from the unnecessary disclosure of personal information."[115]

In 1994, the U.S. Supreme Court ruled in *Department of Defense v. Federal Labor Relations Authority* that disclosure of the home addresses of government employees to unions requesting the addresses would constitute a clearly unwarranted invasion of the right of federal employees to privacy in their homes.[116] At

---

[111] Justin Franklin and Robert Bouchard, *Guidebook to the Freedom of Information and Privacy Acts*, ¶ 15.11, at 15–27, 15–28; ¶ 15.16, at 15–38.

[112] New York Times Co. v. United States, 752 F.3d 123 (2d Cir. 2014).

[113] *See, e.g.*, Justin Franklin and Robert Bouchard, *Guidebook to the Freedom of Information and Privacy Acts* ¶ 1.09[4], at 1–231.

[114] *See, e.g.*, James O'Reilly, 2 *Federal Information Disclosure* ¶ 16.06, at 2S–4, 2S–5 (2nd ed., June 1995).

[115] 456 U.S. 595 (1982).

[116] 510 U.S. 487 (1994).

the same time, the Court said releasing the addresses of government employees to unions "would not appreciably" advance citizens' rights to be informed about the activities of federal government agencies. Eight of the nine justices on the Court said that "privacy of the home . . . substantially outweighs" a "negligible" public interest in the disclosure of the home addresses, a disclosure that would not help the public understand government operations.

Although the Supreme Court has said that exemption 6 protects a wide range of information about individuals, it has also held the exemption does not create an absolute right to privacy for personnel, medical or similar files. Privacy interests must be balanced against the public interest in knowing about the activities of government, an interest that the Supreme Court has said is the "core purpose" served by the Freedom of Information Act. The Court has said the release of private information is unwarranted unless the information sought "sheds light" on government performance.[117]

In 2006, a federal judge rejected Defense Department claims that transcripts and documents containing the names of detainees at Guantanamo Bay should be withheld to protect the privacy of the detainees and their families. Judge Jed Rakoff ordered transcripts and documents of detainees' appearances before a military tribunal released because, Rakoff said, the detainees participating in the tribunals determining their status as enemy combatants would have no expectation that their names, nationalities, home locales and other identifying information would remain private. Furthermore, the Defense Department presented insufficient evidence, the court said, that detainees and their families would be subject to retaliation or embarrassment if their identities were released.[118]

Later, Judge Rakoff ordered the release to the Associated Press of identifying information and documents of allegations and accounts of detainees' mistreatment at Guantanamo—including assaults, use of pepper spray and verbal abuse—and the disciplinary actions taken. Rakoff said most detainees would want the records released as evidence of their abuse.[119] The court saw a public interest in disclosing records shedding light on American treatment of detainees. Similarly, Judge Rakoff ordered disclosure of the heights and weights of detainees involved in hunger strikes, information that would also shed light on American treatment of detainees.[120]

In contrast, a federal court in California denied the *Los Angeles Times* the names of civilian contractors who worked in Iraq and Afghanistan because evidence showed they and their families might be targeted by people opposed to American forces in those countries. Hundreds of contractors had already been killed in the wars in Iraq and Afghanistan.[121]

A federal appellate court also authorized the release of federal employee's sick-leave records because they would help explain how the government works— or doesn't. The court said the public interest in the disclosure of sick-leave records of a federal administrator would outweigh the individual privacy interest in the documents. The appellate court said that the release of sick-leave and work-attendance records of an employee at the Federal Communications Commission serves the public interest in obtaining information about potential government misconduct.[122]

---

[117] Department of Justice v. Reporters Comm. for Freedom of the Press, 489 U.S. 749 (1989).

[118] Associated Press v. Dep't of Defense, 410 F. Supp. 2d 147 (S.D.N.Y. 2006).

[119] Associated Press v. Dep't of Defense, 2006 U.S. Dist. LEXIS 67913 (S.D.N.Y. Sept. 20, 2006).

[120] Associated Press v. Dep't of Defense, 462 F. Supp. 2d 573 (S.D.N.Y. 2006).

[121] Los Angeles Times Communications, LLC v. Dep't of Labor, 483 F. Supp. 2d 975 (C.D. Cal. 2007).

[122] Dobronski v. FCC, 17 F.3d 275 (1994).

(7) Law Enforcement Exemption 7 of FOIA permits the government to withhold information compiled for law enforcement purposes. Exemption 7 allows information to be withheld if disclosure would interfere with law enforcement investigations, disclose the identity of confidential sources, endanger lives, invade privacy, deprive a defendant of a fair trial or reveal law enforcement techniques.[123]

Agencies cannot withhold records under exemption 7 if the records are not compiled for law enforcement purposes. A federal appeals court ruled the FBI had to disclose documents collected about the Free Speech Movement at the University of California because they were not compiled—contrary to a government claim—for the legitimate law enforcement purpose of investigating Communist subversives. Rather, the records were compiled to gain information on a leader with a "contemptuous attitude" and to harass liberal faculty members.[124]

The Supreme Court has interpreted the privacy exemption very broadly in exemption 7 cases, undermining federal and state precedent establishing that records are presumptively open to anyone for any purpose. In two exemption 7 cases, the Court has ruled that requesters will gain access to records containing private information only if they can demonstrate the records will clarify government operations or reveal misconduct. The Court has also allowed the family of a dead official to assert privacy claims in government records.

Computerized Records In *Department of Justice v. Reporters Committee for Freedom of the Press*, the Court ruled that computerized FBI "rap sheets" on private individuals are exempt from disclosure even though much of the information contained in rap sheets can be found in public records in police stations around the country.[125] The FBI's rap sheets at issue in *Reporters Committee* are national computer compilations of criminal records that have traditionally been kept confidential. The rap sheets combine information about arrests, indictments, acquittals and convictions, information that individually is often a matter of public record in local and state law enforcement agencies and courthouses. The rap sheets are accumulated through a nationwide network of local, state and federal law enforcement agencies that share criminal history information under strict rules governing its use. The rap sheets sometimes contain information that is incorrect or incomplete because it may not be updated. Although most states release information about convictions, most states restrict the disclosure of criminal complaints and arrests that do not result in a conviction. Many states withhold information about individuals in the prison system.

The Court's decision in *Reporters Committee* ended a decade-long search by the Reporters Committee and CBS correspondent Robert Schakne for the criminal records of Charles Medico and his three brothers. Medico Industries, a family company, had been described by the Pennsylvania Crime Commission as "a legitimate business dominated by organized crime figures." Schakne wanted to know the connection between the company's defense contracts and bribery allegations against former Representative Daniel Flood, a Democrat from Pennsylvania. The FBI refused to release records of the only living brother, Charles Medico. Schakne and the Reporters Committee argued the information in the FBI rap sheets was a matter of public record in local government files and therefore ought to be released by the federal government.

---

[123] 5 U.S.C. § 552(b)(7).
[124] Rosenfeld v. United States, 57 F.3d 803 (9th Cir. 1995).
[125] 489 U.S. 749 (1989).

The U.S. Supreme Court, balancing the importance of individual privacy against the public interest in understanding government operations, unanimously ruled that the FBI could withhold Medico's records. The Court's opinion, supported by seven justices, said that the federal government's computerized database of rap sheets was private because, in effect, the facts and incidents from which it was compiled were private. Even though journalists might find much criminal information about citizens in American courthouses and police stations, the Court said the information was effectively private because it was hard to locate.

Writing for the majority, Justice Stevens said bits and pieces of criminal information scattered through counties and states enjoy a "practical obscurity" that would be lost if that information were disseminated from a centralized database. "Plainly there is a vast difference," Stevens said, "between the public records that might be found after a diligent search of courthouse files, county archives and local police stations throughout the country and a computerized summary located in a single clearinghouse of information."

If the information in the rap sheets were "freely available" in other locations, Stevens said, Schakne and the Reporters Committee could have easily acquired it without using FOIA. Stevens also said that Congress had demonstrated it intended to protect the privacy of rap sheets by authorizing only a limited use of rap sheets by law enforcement agencies, banks and the nuclear power industry. In addition, Stevens said, the FBI's regulations specify that it can stop sharing rap sheet information with any agency that discloses the data.

The Supreme Court said in exemption 7 cases the public interest in disclosure might outweigh privacy interests if disclosure revealed how the government operates. Indeed, the Court said the basic policy of full agency disclosure focuses on the citizens' right to be informed about "what their government is up to." However, disclosure of rap sheets on private citizens reveals "little or nothing" about the conduct of a government agency, the Court said. The Court argued that disclosure of Medico's personal criminal records would say "nothing directly" about Representative Flood's behavior or the conduct of the Defense Department when it awarded contracts to Medico Industries.

Family of Deceased In 2004, the Supreme Court narrowed the range of records a requester might acquire if those records contain private information. In *National Archives and Records Administration v. Favish*, a unanimous Court extended privacy rights under exemption 7 to living relatives of a dead official and required a plaintiff seeking photos of a suicide scene to assert not just that the records would reveal what the "government is up to," but would provide evidence of government misconduct.[126]

In an opinion written by Justice Kennedy, the Court denied the request of Allan J. Favish, a California lawyer who sought death scene photographs of Vincent Foster, deputy counsel to President Clinton. Foster was found dead in Fort Marcy Park near Washington. One photo showed a gun in Foster's hand. Five investigations concluded Foster committed suicide, but Favish argued the government's investigations were "grossly incomplete and untrustworthy."

The Court did not view the Foster photographs as presumptively open records of a completed investigation into the death of a public official. Rather, the Court ruled the photographs could be withheld under exemption 7 because disclosure could result in an unwarranted invasion of the privacy of Foster's close relatives.

---

[126] 541 U.S. 157 (2004).

Law and tradition recognize the right of family members to control the body and death images of the deceased, the Court said. The Foster family had a right to secure their own peace of mind, their own "refuge from a sensation-seeking culture."

The invasion of the family's privacy was "unwarranted" because privacy interests were not outweighed by public interests in disclosure. Indeed, the Supreme Court placed considerable new burdens on a requester trying to acquire federal law enforcement records containing private information. When the privacy of a suicide's close relatives is at stake, it is not enough for a requester to demand information for its own sake, or to show "what the Government is up to," the Court said. The requester must show that the "the public interest sought to be advanced is a significant one," and that the "information is likely to advance that interest." Favish claimed a significant public interest—disclosure of government misconduct—but he lacked evidence, the Court said.

Favish presented a "bare suspicion" of government impropriety, not evidence "that would warrant a belief by a reasonable person that the alleged Government impropriety might have occurred." Disclosure of the Foster photos would be unlikely to reveal government impropriety, the Court reasoned, noting that five investigations into Foster's death had found no impropriety.

In 2008, a federal appeals court ruled FOIA required release of photos of prisoners abused by American military personnel in Afghanistan and Iraq, including Abu Ghraib prison. But Congress, as discussed earlier, intervened to block release of the photos. The appeals court said disclosure of the photos posed no unwarranted invasion of privacy because identifying features were redacted.[127] Nor could the court justify withholding the photos under exemption 7(F) of the statute which allows records to be withheld if disclosure "could reasonably be expected to endanger the life or physical safety of any individual." The court imagined "diffuse and speculative risks" to the life and physical safety of many people in many countries, but the court had been presented insufficient evidence of unwarranted risk to any identified "individual." On the contrary, the court said disclosure of the abuse photos served "FOIA's central purpose of furthering governmental accountability, and the special importance the law accords to information revealing official misconduct." While the case was on appeal to the Supreme Court, Congress intervened—with support from the Obama administration—passing a statute exempting detainee photos from disclosure if certified by the secretary of defense that release would endanger American civilians or government troops or employees. The Supreme Court then vacated the appellate decision and remanded the case for further consideration in light of the new congressional exemption.

In 2011, the Supreme Court ruled that corporations have no "personal privacy" under section 7(C) of FOIA that can be violated if a federal agency reveals records collected for law enforcement purposes. Reversing a lower court, the Court ruled 8–0 that corporations have no claim to personal privacy, even though they are defined in FOIA and elsewhere as "persons." In *Federal Communications Commission v. AT&T, Inc.,*[128] the Court said that "personal privacy" refers to the privacy of an individual person—evoking human concerns, not the concerns of a corporate entity created by the state. Thus, AT&T failed in its attempt to require the FCC to withhold AT&T's emails, billing records and employees' names acquired from the company during an investigation.

---

[127] American Civil Liberties Union v. Dep't of Defense, 543 F.3d 59 (2d Cir. 2008), *vacated and remanded*, 130 S. Ct. 777 (2009).
[128] 2011 U.S. LEXIS 1899 (Mar. 1, 2011).

Exemption 7 of FOIA also allows agencies to withhold records that could reasonably be expected to disclose the identity of a confidential source, including victims, prisoners, businesses and state or local law enforcement agencies.[129] The Supreme Court has ruled the FBI can claim confidentiality for its sources only if the sources "spoke with an understanding" that their confidentiality would be protected.[130]

(8) Banking Reports Exemption 8 protects from required disclosure a number of financial reports and audits of banks, trust companies, investment banking firms and other federally regulated financial institutions. The records are held by such agencies as the Federal Reserve System, the Comptroller of the Currency and the Federal Home Loan Bank Board.

(9) Information About Wells Exemption 9 protects geological and geophysical information, including maps concerning oil, gas and water wells. Exemption 9 prevents speculators from easily acquiring valuable information that competitors have collected about the location of gas and oil wells. Exemption 9 is the least invoked exemption.

▦ SUMMARY ▦

In an effort to balance the government's need for secrecy with the presumption of openness that pervades the Freedom of Information Act, FOIA provided nine categories of information that can be exempt from disclosure to the public. An agency must disclose any record that does not fall under one of the exemptions and may disclose information falling into an exempt category. Exemption 1, the national security exemption, protects from forced disclosure items properly classified according to criteria established by the president. Even though Congress has given the courts the authority to review whether the government has properly classified records, the courts have been reluctant to second-guess the executive branch on matters of national security. Exemption 2 protects agency management records of little concern to the general public, such as parking and sick-leave regulations. Exemption 3 allows the government to withhold documents Congress has authorized to be confidential by statute. The Homeland Security Act protects critical infrastructure information and detainees' photos. The Privacy Act of 1974 limits federal agency use of personal information. Colleges and universities are required to provide data on campus crime, but FERPA threatens colleges and universities with loss of federal funds if they improperly release "education records."

Exemption 4 protects trade secrets and confidential commercial and financial information. Exemption 5 allows government agencies to withhold information used in their decision-making processes as long as documents are not publicly revealed to be the bases for decisions. Exemption 6 protects information in personnel, medical and similar files that "would constitute a clearly unwarranted invasion of personal privacy." The courts balance the personal interest in nondisclosure against the public interest in the information about government activities. Exemption 7 applies to records compiled for law enforcement purposes that, if disclosed, could reasonably be expected to interfere with law enforcement efforts, constitute an unwarranted invasion of privacy, disclose the identity of a confidential source, or endanger the safety of law enforcement personnel. Exemption 8 protects

---

[129] Justin Franklin and Robert Bouchard, *Guidebook to the Freedom of Information and Privacy Acts* ¶ 1.10 [4], at 1–299.

[130] United States v. Landano, 508 U.S. 165 (1993).

banking reports submitted to the federal government. Exemption 9 applies to maps of oil and gas wells.

State Records Laws

The federal Freedom of Information Act attracts so much attention that it might be easy to forget that it applies only to federal records, albeit federal records that are located all over the country. Many reporters and business firms, however, rely daily on state laws that give them access to state, county and municipal government records. Reporters depend on state laws to provide them access to county budgets, city data about the number of housing starts and reports on the quality of water leaving the local sewage treatment plant.

All 50 states have adopted statutes requiring disclosure of public records held by state, county and municipal governments. The provisions and effectiveness of these laws vary significantly. State legislatures create hundreds of exemptions to the general proposition that public records are open to the public.

State records laws routinely require records to be open at executive and administrative agencies at the state, county and municipal levels of government. Most states have separate laws or policies regulating access to the records of courts and legislatures. New York's FOI law, for example, covers any state or municipal department, board, bureau, division, commission, committee, public authority, public corporation, council, office or other governmental entity performing a governmental or proprietary function for the state or any one or more municipalities thereof, except the judiciary or the state legislature.[131]

Public funding often determines whether an agency must abide by the public records statute. Under Kentucky law, for example, a "body" must conform to the state's open records law if a state or local government created the agency or provides at least 25 percent of its funds.[132]

Most state laws require the government to disclose records in any physical form, including computer tapes and disks. For example, South Carolina's FOI law defines public records to include "all books, papers, maps, photographs, cards, tapes, recordings or other documentary materials regardless of physical form or characteristics."[133] However, some local officials are reluctant to produce computerized records, want to charge more than the cost of reproduction, or refuse to provide electronic copies of the records instead of paper printouts.

Only a few state open records statutes have authorized direct public access to government data banks. Florida, often at the forefront of access law, encourages government agencies to provide electronic access through private computer terminals to public records "in the most cost-effective and efficient manner available."[134] New York has established the Legislative Retrieval Service, a computerized database providing access to pending legislation and related information.[135]

States define public records not only by their physical form but also in terms of their origin, nature and purpose. Some states define public records expansively to include anything in the possession of a state agency, or a public record can be any record made or received in connection with a state law or the transaction of

---

[131] N.Y. Pub. Off. Law § 86(3).
[132] Ky. Rev. Stat. Ann. § 61.870(1)(g), (h).
[133] S.C. Code Ann. § 30-4-20(c).
[134] 1995 Fla. Laws ch. 296.
[135] *See* Legi-Tech v. Keiper, 766 F.2d 728 (2d Cir. 1985).

public business. In contrast, some states still define records more restrictively, limiting public records to only those identified specifically by law as public records.[136]

All states provide a number of exemptions to records disclosure. Most, if not all, states restrict access to personal records and law enforcement and investigatory information. Several states also exempt trade secrets and other business information, department memoranda and tax return data. States are divided between those that mandate withholding any record exempted from disclosure and those that give an agency discretion to disclose exempted material, as FOIA does.[137] Most state laws allow "any person" access to state records, but a few limit access to state citizens.[138] A "person" includes corporations, citizens groups and associations. Journalists have no greater rights of access than others.[139] In 2013, the Supreme Court upheld a Virginia statute denying access to state records to citizens outside Virginia. The Court ruled Virginia did not violate the Privileges and Immunities Clause of the Fourteenth Amendment when the state open records law denied records to plaintiff Mark McBurney, a former Virginian living in Rhode Island seeking records related to his Virginia divorce. Also denied records was Roger Hurlbert, a resident of California. Hurlbert sought Virginia real estate tax assessment records for clients of his national information services business. The Court ruled the Virginia statute—which is similar to laws in several other states—denied neither plaintiff a constitutionally protected privilege or immunity such as the right to practice their trade or profession, to access Virginia courts, transfer property or obtain medical services in Virginia.

In a unanimous opinion written by Justice Alito, the Court said in *McBurney v. Young* a state has no obligation to treat all nonresidents and residents equally.[140] To do so might be costly to Virginia citizens, as well as inefficient. The state FOI law is not protectionist, the Court said. Rather, "Virginia's FOIA exists to provide a mechanism for Virginia citizens to obtain an accounting from their public officials; noncitizens have no comparable need."

The Court said the Virginia law violates no constitutional right of access to public records because access to public information is not a "fundamental" privilege or immunity of citizenship. "This Court," Justice Alito wrote, "has repeatedly made clear that there is no constitutional right to obtain all the information provided by FOIA laws." The Court also ruled the Virginia statute imposed no burdens on interstate commerce.

In all but a few states, access is not dependent on the reason that a person wants to see a document. For example, a Pennsylvania court said a school district must disclose the names and addresses of incoming pupils to parents opposed to the scheduling of kindergarten classes. The court said the parents had a right to the information even though the parents wanted it to enlist opposition to school policy.[141] However, at least a few states restrict access for "commercial" use.[142]

In 1999, the U.S. Supreme Court upheld a California law denying commercial users access to addresses on police records. In a 7–2 vote, the Supreme Court ruled

---

[136] Burt Braverman and Frances Chetwynd, 2 *Information Law* ¶ 24–4.2.2.2, at 915–16 (1985 & Supp. 1990). *See also* Reporters Committee for Freedom of the Press, *Open Government Guide.*

[137] *See generally* Reporters Committee for Freedom of the Press, *Open Government Guide.*

[138] *See* Burt Braverman and Frances Chetwynd, 2 *Information Law* ¶ 24–3.1, at 903–4 (1985 & Supp. 1990).

[139] *See* James O'Reilly, 2 *Federal Information Disclosure* ¶ 27.03, at 27–8 (2nd ed., June 1991).

[140] 569 U.S. 221 (2013).

[141] Wiles v. Armstrong Sch. Dist., 66 Pa. D. & C.2d 499 (1974).

[142] *See, e.g.,* Ariz. Rev. Stat. Ann. § 39–121.03; R.I. Gen. Laws § 38-2-6.

that the law does not unconstitutionally restrict the speech of lawyers, bail bondsmen and social workers who would use the addresses from police records to seek clients. The law permits access to the addresses for five noncommercial purposes, including journalism.

In *Los Angeles Police Dep't v. United Reporting Publishing Co.*[143] the Court ruled the California statute is not an unconstitutional content regulation because it does not bar speakers from disseminating information they already possess. Rather, the statute limits who may have access to the information, the Court said. The Court said the state, which has the authority to deny records to all users, has the authority to deny access to citizens who would use them for commercial purposes.

State laws typically require agencies to explain their reasons for nondisclosure in writing and provide an appeal process, either through the agency itself, through the attorney general, or through another body overseeing records access. Any person denied access to records may go to court to challenge the denial, and nearly every state allows judges to award successful plaintiffs reasonable attorney fees. Some states, such as Florida and Illinois, mandate attorney fee awards when records requesters win their lawsuits against the government. Most states provide for fines or jail terms for officials who do not comply with the state law, although such stern sanctions are seldom imposed.[144] In what many public records advocates saw as a first, a press secretary to the former mayor of Atlanta was convicted by a jury and ordered to pay a $1,500 fine for criminal violations of the Georgia Open Records Act in 2019. Her text messages revealed that she said she would "be as unhelpful as possible," "drag this out as long as possible" and "provide information in the most confusing format available" in response to a request from a local television station for water billing records.[145]

SUMMARY

Every state has an open records law for executive and administrative agencies of state, county and municipal governments. Most laws begin with statements establishing a state policy of openness. Most state records laws apply to any document in the possession of a state agency, with specifically named exemptions. The most common provisions restricting the disclosure of public documents protect privacy and law enforcement investigations. More recently written laws tend to apply to records in any physical form, including in electronic format. Public officials who do not comply with requests can be punished with civil or criminal penalties, but courts are more likely to award attorney fees for successful lawsuits challenging improper denials of access.

ACCESS TO MEETINGS

Neither the First Amendment nor the common law provides the press and the public access to the meetings of federal, state or local governing bodies. Hence, access can be obtained only through statute.

---

[143] 528 U.S. 32 (1999).
[144] Daxton R. Stewart, "Let the Sunshine In, or Else: An Examination of the 'Teeth' of State and Federal Open Meetings and Open Records Laws," 15 *Comm. L. & Pol'y* 265 (2010).
[145] J. Scott Trubey, "Reed Aide Jenna Garland Seeks New Trial in Atlanta Open Records Case," *Atlanta Journal-Constitution*, Jan. 17, 2020.

A strong statute will declare that the purpose of the law is to open delibera-tions to the public as much as possible and that the law should be interpreted by the courts accordingly. The statute should describe the government agencies that are subject to the law. It will tell how many members must be present for a meeting to be official. It will explain how an agency may close a meeting and under what conditions closure is allowed. It should explain how a citizen can contest a closed meeting and what remedies are available if the law has been violated.

Federal

A federal "sunshine law" requires several executive agencies to meet in public. Congress has adopted separate internal rules opening up most of its sessions and most of its committee meetings to the public.

SUNSHINE ACT In 1976, Congress passed legislation requiring about 50 fed-eral agencies, commissions, boards and councils to meet in public. The Sunshine Act also covers the deliberations of agency subdivisions "authorized to act on behalf of the agency." The Sunshine Act declares that the public "is entitled to the fullest practicable information" about the "decision-making processes" of the fed-eral government.[146] With ten exceptions, any meeting at which a sufficient number of members are required to take action is presumed to be public.

The Sunshine Act pertains only to agencies subject to the Freedom of Information Act. In addition, the agencies must be headed by boards of two members or more, a majority of whom are appointed by the president.[147] Among the agencies subject to the statute are the Federal Trade Commission, Federal Communications Commission, Securities and Exchange Commission and National Labor Relations Board.

The Sunshine Act allows public access to discussions prior to official actions. The U.S. Court of Appeals for the D.C. Circuit has said Congress intended that the decision-making process of government be conducted in the open. The court in 1982 rejected arguments of the Nuclear Regulatory Commission that discussions of budget proposals should be closed. The court said that although FOIA exempted documents prepared as a part of the decision-making process, Congress decided that the discussion of issues prior to decisions must be exposed to public scrutiny.[148]

To close a meeting, a federal agency must determine that remaining open would lead to a disclosure of information protected by one of the Sunshine Act's 10 exempt categories. The agency also must determine that the public interest does not require that the meeting be open. Seven of the ten exemptions to the presump-tion of open meetings parallel exemptions of FOIA: national security, agency rules, matters exempted by other statutes, business information, matters of personal pri-vacy, investigatory records and the reports of financial institutions. The Sunshine Act also exempts accusations of criminal activity or formal reprimands to protect the reputations of persons accused but not yet formally charged. In addition, an exemption permits closure for agencies regulating financial matters if a discussion would (1) lead to financial speculation, (2) "significantly endanger" the stability of a bank or (3) frustrate the implementation of an agency action.

A final exemption to the Sunshine Act allows closed meetings to discuss an agency's issuance of a subpoena or its participation in a court or administrative

---

[146] Government in the Sunshine Act, 90 Stat. 1241 (1976) (declaration of policy).
[147] 5 U.S.C. § 522b(a)(1).
[148] Common Cause v. Nuclear Regulatory Comm'n, 674 F.2d 921 (D.C. Cir. 1982).

proceeding.[149] The exemption is intended to ensure that a premature announcement does not allow people to effectively counter agency plans. The Nuclear Regulatory Commission (NRC) used the last exemption to block public access to a discussion about the reopening of the nuclear power plant at Three Mile Island in Pennsylvania. In 1979, a cooling system at the power plant failed, spreading radiation in the atmosphere up to 10 miles away. Four years later, the *Philadelphia Inquirer* wanted to attend NRC meetings dealing with procedural steps for deciding whether to reopen a portion of the plant. A federal district court ruled that the meetings could be closed because they involved preparation for a formal administrative hearing.[150]

The Sunshine Act requires agencies to place a public notice of meetings in the *Federal Register* at least one week in advance. If an agency chooses to close a meeting, it must do so by a recorded vote of its members, and it must provide reasons in advance. Anyone who objects to a closure can file a suit in a federal district court. A court can enjoin a closed meeting or require that similar meetings be open in the future. The agency must maintain a transcript or recording of any closed meetings. Anyone can sue to obtain a transcript, which can be examined by a judge in chambers to determine if it should be open.

Even if a suit under the act is successful, no financial penalty can be levied against individual members of an agency, and no agency action can be invalidated. However, the government can be forced to pay court costs and lawyers' fees. A person who sues under the act can be assessed court costs and lawyers' fees if the suit is found to be "dilatory or frivolous."[151]

One federal agency commissioner who has argued that the Sunshine Act must be reformed has acknowledged that members of many federal governing bodies often do not debate issues during public meetings. Securities and Exchange Commissioner Steve Wallman said decisions are made out of public view through staff discussions, written memos and one-on-one conversations.[152]

Although some government agencies are subject to the Sunshine Act, government advisory boards—composed of citizens rather than government officials and employees—are subject to a different law requiring open meetings. The Federal Advisory Committee Act (FACA) requires that advisory boards meet in public so that advice to government officials by "outsiders" is open to public scrutiny. A federal appellate court ruled that the meetings of President Clinton's Task Force on National Health Care Reform, headed by Hillary Rodham Clinton, need not be open to the public.[153] The court said the task force's meetings were not subject to FACA because Clinton, as the president's spouse, was considered an "officer or employee of the government" rather than a member of the general public.

The U.S. Supreme Court did not rule on whether public interest organizations could seek records of meetings of an energy task force chaired by Vice President Dick Cheney. Public interest organizations, including press groups, sought information under FACA about meetings of a national task force in which executives from the energy industry participated. The groups wanted to learn if private energy companies significantly influenced federal energy policy. Vice President Cheney argued courts would intrude unconstitutionally into the operations of the executive

---

[149] 5 U.S.C. § 552b(c)(10).
[150] Philadelphia Newspapers, Inc. v. Nuclear Regulatory Comm'n, 727 F.2d 1195 (D.C. Cir. 1983).
[151] 5 U.S.C. § 552b(g), (h), (i).
[152] Lucy Dalglish, "Federal Agencies Look for Shade from Sunshine Laws," *Quill*, Sept. 1995, at 18.
[153] Association of American Physicians & Surgeons v. Clinton, 997 F.2d 898 (D.C. Cir. 1993).

branch even by seeking documents about the membership and structure of the task force. On remand from the Supreme Court, a federal appeals court ordered the complaints be dismissed after ruling that FACA disclosure requirements did not apply to the task force because the energy executives who participated had no vote in, or veto over, task force decisions.[154] Supreme Court Justice Scalia refused to recuse himself from the case after it was revealed he went duck hunting with the vice president.[155]

CONGRESS The U.S. Constitution provides that each house of Congress should publish "a Journal of its Proceedings . . . excepting such Parts as may in their Judgment require Secrecy."[156] Otherwise, the Constitution specifies that each house may determine its own rules. The rules determine which sessions should be open to the public and whether cameras ought to be allowed.

Most sessions of the Senate and House are open to the public. The House of Representatives in 1995 voted to require that all committee meetings also be open to the public unless the committee votes to the contrary. Under the rule, House committee meetings can be closed to prevent disclosure of information that would "endanger national security," "compromise sensitive law enforcement information," "tend to defame, degrade or incriminate" someone, or violate a law or rule of the House.[157] The Senate operates under rules adopted in the mid-1970s, rules that require committee and subcommittee meetings—including bill-drafting sessions—be open to the public unless a majority votes in public to close. The House and Senate have agreed to open conference committee meetings, where representatives of the House and Senate try to reconcile different versions of a bill. A conference committee meeting can be closed only by a vote in public of a majority of the Senate conferees or by a vote of the entire House of Representatives.[158]

Both the House of Representatives and the Senate allow radio and television coverage of their proceedings. The two chambers control the cameras and allow broadcasters to use the footage. The committee hearings of both houses are generally open to broadcast coverage.

■ SUMMARY ■

The Sunshine Act requires about 50 federal agencies to meet in public. The act applies to agencies subject to FOIA and headed by a board appointed by the president. The act allows access to discussions prior to official actions. The act provides for exceptions to openness when the agencies are dealing with any of ten topics, most of them mirroring FOIA exemptions. Each house establishes its own rules for access. Most sessions of the bodies and most congressional committee meetings are now open. Both the House of Representatives and the Senate permit broadcast coverage.

States

All 50 states have adopted open meetings laws. The states' open meetings requirements change often through legislative amendment and court interpretation. Reporters and public relations personnel need to keep track of legal developments in the state where they work.

---

[154] *In re* Cheney 542 U.S. 367, *on remand,* 406 F.3d 723 (D.C. Cir. 2005).
[155] Cheney v. Dist. Court, 541 U.S. 913 (2004).
[156] U.S. Const. art. I § 5.
[157] House Information Resources, 104th Cong., 1st Sess., House Rules XI-2(g)(1) (Sept. 29, 1995).
[158] Congressional Quarterly, *Guide to Congress* 59, 67, 112–13, 458–9, 464 (4th ed. 1991).

Many scholars assert that one of the most important aspects of a strong open meetings statute, as well as a strong records law, is a legislative declaration that the law is intended to open government deliberations and actions to the people.[159] One of the most explicit declarations is from the state of Washington:

> The legislature finds and declares that all . . . public agencies of this state and subdivisions thereof exist to aid in the conduct of the people's business. It is the intent of this chapter that their action be taken openly and that their deliberations be conducted openly.
>
> The people of this state do not yield their sovereignty to the agencies which serve them. The people, in delegating authority, do not give their public servants the right to decide what is good for the people to know and what is not good for them to know. The people insist on remaining informed so that they may retain control over the instruments they have created.[160]

Some states indicate that the meetings of all agencies supported by public funds or performing governing functions are open except for explicitly named exceptions. The other states list or enumerate the kinds of agencies that must hold open meetings. The New York open meetings law, like its records law, applies to

> any state or municipal department, board, bureau, division, commission, committee, public authority, public corporation, council, office or other governmental entity performing a governmental or proprietary function for the state or any one or more municipalities thereof, except the judiciary or the state legislature.[161]

Some open meetings statutes, which list the agencies that must comply but which are less inclusive than New York's, leave the status of any unlisted agencies unclear. For example, a law may enumerate "boards and commissions" but not "councils." Many state laws exempt jury proceedings and parole and pardon boards from their meetings laws. Most state legislatures are required to be open.

A comprehensive definition of the word *meeting* in a state law can help the public and officials know what kind of gathering triggers the statute. For example, the Texas statute defines *meeting* as

> a deliberation between a quorum of a governmental body, or between a quorum of a governmental body and another person, during which public business or public policy over which the governmental body has supervision or control is discussed or considered, or during which the governmental body takes formal action.[162]

A quorum is the number of members who must be present at a meeting before an agency can conduct official business. In Texas, a majority of the members of a public body constitutes a quorum. In 1990, the Texas Supreme Court said that two

---

[159] *E.g., id.* at 1162; Douglas Wickham, "Let the Sunshine In! Open-Meeting Legislation Can Be Our Key to Closed Doors in State and Local Government," 68 *Nw. U. L. Rev.* 480 (1973).
[160] Wash. Rev. Code Ann. § 42.30.010.
[161] N.Y. Pub. Off. Law § 86(3).
[162] Tex. Gov't Code 551.001(4).

of the three members of the Texas Water Commission were in a "meeting" when they discussed a case in the restroom.[163] States usually require either a quorum or a majority to be present for the meeting to qualify under the law. A majority may or may not be a quorum. In some states, any two members talking to each other is sufficient for a meeting under the law, regardless of the size of the government body.

What if members of a public body discuss public business at lunch, during a round of golf, or at a retreat? Social gatherings can be an excuse to do the public's business without the public watching. On the other hand, even many advocates of open meetings believe that a law should not prevent officials from socializing. The Texas open meetings law specifically excludes from its requirements any "social functions unrelated to the public business" and attendance at conventions and workshops as long as there is no public business conducted and if "discussion of public business is incidental to the social function, convention, or workshop." Some states provide no exclusion for social affairs or retreats or conferences. In most states, if a meeting is open to the public, cameras and audio equipment are usually allowed. Typically, "walking quorums" are also improper ways to get around quorum requirements. These involve government officials to avoid public meetings laws by ensuring that they are never entirely in the same room at the same time, cycling members in and out to stay below the minimum number required to make a quorum.

All states allow executive, or closed, sessions. Executive sessions are most commonly allowed for discussions of the hiring, firing and disciplining of personnel; real estate transactions; official investigations; security or safety discussions; labor negotiations; and legal suits. Some states also allow executive sessions for discussions that would tend to damage individual reputations.

Journalists frequently object when public officials appear to stretch the meaning of the "personnel" exemption when they close a meeting. In 1989, the Mississippi Supreme Court said a majority of the Hinds County Board of Supervisors repeatedly violated the state's open meetings law when they went into executive session to discuss "personnel." The court held that under the Mississippi statute, the exemption for "personnel matters" was restricted to "dealing with employees hired and supervised by the board." The board had illegally entered executive session to discuss hiring an architect, an independent professional who was not an employee of the board, the court said. The court added that another item discussed in executive session, an appointment to fill a vacancy on the board itself, was not a "personnel matter" as defined by the court either.[164]

Advocates of open government argue that a decision to close meetings should be a public vote, with the reasons for closure on the record. Although the Mississippi open meetings law requires that votes for closure be public, the Mississippi Supreme Court said the Hinds County Board of Supervisors did not always comply. In addition, the court said, the board violated the law by discussing in executive session business that had not been included in its stated reasons for closure. The court also said the board inadequately explained its reasons for going into executive session because the board "tells nothing" about the reasons for closing a meeting when it "simply" says "personnel matters" or "litigation." In an expansive reading of the Mississippi law, the supreme court said the requirement

---

[163] Acker v. Texas Water Comm'n, 790 S.W.2d 299 (Tex. 1990).
[164] Hinds County Bd. of Supervisors v. Common Cause, 551 So. 2d 107 (Miss. 1989).

that the reason for closure be announced means that a reason must be "of sufficient specificity to inform those present that there is in reality a specific, discrete matter" that needs to be discussed in executive session.

Advocates of open government want not only votes to close meetings to take place in public, but also all final votes on public policy to be in the open. The Mississippi Supreme Court said the Hinds County Board of Supervisors illegally voted to hire an architectural firm in an executive session.

Open meetings laws, to be effective, must include a requirement that the public be notified of meetings. Requirements that meetings be open are meaningless if no one knows when and where the meetings are held. Many statutes require that the times of regularly scheduled meetings be posted and sent to the media. States often mandate that the media, or persons requesting notification, be advised of special or emergency meetings in enough time to attend.[165]

Virtually every state provides a mechanism to enforce the open meetings law, but the enforcement mechanisms are seldom used in many states. Prosecutors are reluctant to take action against fellow officials, and citizens seldom make the effort or spend the money to challenge closed meetings. While prosecutions are rare, Florida has successfully prosecuted dozens of open meetings law violators, though only a few have received jail time as a penalty.[166]

Several state statutes provide for short jail sentences or fines for officials responsible for closing meetings illegally. In 1989, three Longwood, Florida, officials were fined $500 each for discussing outside of an official meeting a proposal for the city to purchase a utility.[167] Florida's law and laws in other states also provide for civil penalties, eliminating the stigma attached to a criminal conviction.

Some states allow a court to enjoin officials from closing a meeting when the officials' intent to do so is known in advance. Other states provide for the nullification of any law or ordinance passed in an illegally closed meeting. A few innovative states remove from office officials involved in illegally closing meetings. One of the Longwood, Florida, officials mentioned earlier, City Commissioner Rick Bullington, was removed from office by the governor under a provision in Florida's general statutes after Bullington participated in policy discussions outside of an open meeting.[168]

■ SUMMARY ■

Every state has an open meetings law. The laws that best protect the public's interest in openness specify that meetings be open during consideration of issues as well as when formal action is taken. Strong state open meetings laws also provide for public notice of meetings. At least a few state laws prohibit public officials from conducting business at social occasions. Many states permit closed sessions for discussing personnel matters, real estate transactions, official investigations, security and labor negotiations. Enforcement of the open meetings statutes is a problem in many states, although most have statutory mechanisms, such as fines or short jail sentences, for illegal closure.

---

[165] *E.g.*, Ark. Stat. Ann. § 25-19-106(b)(2).

[166] *See* "Sunshine Prosecutions and Fee Awards Continue Growth," *Brechner Report*, Feb. 1992, at 1.

[167] A database of prosecutions under the Florida Sunshine Law from 1977–2016, http://brechner.jou.ufl.edu/db_prosecutions.asp.

[168] *Id. See* Fla. Stat. § 112.52.

OBTAINING ACCESS: A FINAL WORD

Laws requiring access help journalists. Because of open meetings and open records laws, reporters do not have to rely totally on their own devices to gain access to government meetings and records. However, laws themselves do not guarantee access to records or meetings. Many officials are not aware of the laws. Others may try to ignore or evade them.

Successful reporters learn that access depends on effectively cultivating sources. Officials are more likely to help reporters they know and trust. Reporters should discuss with public officials the importance of conducting business in the open and make an effort to understand why sources are sometimes reluctant to disclose information. Journalists should develop guidelines with local officials for coverage of news events.

Many reporters also have learned that persuasion, either friendly or stern, is often more likely to open a meeting or a record than the enforcement provision of the state law. Persuasion is more immediate and also less expensive than filing a lawsuit or seeking criminal charges. Sometimes, a reluctant official needs only to be convinced that access is required by law. But journalists can best use persuasion if they know access laws themselves. In many states, press associations distribute wallet-sized copies of open meetings and records laws for reporters to carry to meetings.

Reporters also should consult with lawyers to find out how best to achieve access in their states. The best route in some states may be speaking up when asked to leave a meeting. But in North Carolina, a reporter can be fined and jailed for intentionally disrupting a meeting and then refusing an order to leave. Journalists usually need to record the official reasons given for closure in order for lawyers to challenge it.

GLOSSARY

Absolute privilege A libel defense protecting false and defamatory statements made by certain individuals, such as government officials acting in their official capacities, or in certain documents, such as those filed with courts.

Absolutism A theory of freedom of expression holding that the First Amendment prevents all government interference with speaking or publishing. The absolutist position is associated with Justice Black. *See also* **ad hoc balancing, bad-tendency test, clear-and-present-danger test** and **definitional balancing**.

Actual damages Money awarded in a libel suit to a plaintiff who can demonstrate evidence of harm to reputation. Actual damages can include evidence of emotional distress as well as proof of monetary loss.

Actual malice (*New York Times*) In libel, publication with the knowledge of the falsity of a story or with reckless disregard for the truth. The U.S. Supreme Court has said that both public officials and public figures must prove *New York Times* actual malice in order to win libel suits.

Ad hoc balancing A judicial weighing, case by case, of reasons for and against publishing to determine whether expression may be halted or punished. Ad hoc balancing is flexible but unpredictable because it relies little on previous cases or set standards. *See also* **absolutism, bad-tendency test, clear-and-present-danger test** and **definitional balancing**.

Adjudicate To settle a matter.

Administrative law Rules and decisions of administrative agencies such as the Federal Communications Commission and the Federal Trade Commission.

Admonition A judge's warning to jurors about their duties or conduct, such as instructing jurors to ignore prejudicial publicity when deciding on their verdict.

Anti-SLAPP law A law that provides remedies for defendants facing frivolous or meritless lawsuits intended to silence their public speech. Remedies can include early dismissal of the lawsuit and requiring plaintiffs to pay attorney fees of successful defendants. Such lawsuits are called "strategic lawsuits against public participation" (SLAPPs).

Appeal Asking a higher court to review a lower court's decision.

Appellate court A court that reviews the actions of a lower court after an appeal by one of the parties in a case. Appellate courts consider only errors of law or legal procedure and do not reevaluate the facts of a case.

Bad-tendency test A discredited judicial test halting or punishing speech that presents only a remote danger to a substantial individual or social interest. *See also* **absolutism, ad hoc balancing, clear-and-present-danger test** and **definitional balancing**.

Buckley Amendment Family Educational Rights and Privacy Act that prohibits federally funded institutions from disclosing student educational records to the public.

Burden of proof The responsibility imposed on one side in a legal conflict to prove its version of the facts.

Certiorari The name of a writ asking the U.S. Supreme Court to review a case. If the writ is granted, the Court will order the lower court to provide the record of the case for review.

Change of venire Importing the pool of potential jurors from one community to the location of a trial.

Change of venue Moving a trial from one geographical area to another to, for example, lessen the effects of prejudicial publicity.

Clear-and-present-danger test A judicial test that, if applied literally, halts or punishes expression only where there is objective evidence of an imminent, substantial danger to individual or social interests. Sometimes the test has been used to halt speech that presents no clear, imminent danger. *See also* **absolutism, ad hoc balancing test, bad-tendency test** and **definitional balancing**.

Coaxial cable Used by cable television companies to transmit signals to customers. Progressively being replaced by **fiber-optic cable**.

Collateral bar rule Prevents a person who has disobeyed a court order from challenging the merits of the order, even if the order restricts constitutional rights.

Collective work In copyright law, a gathering of preexisting works, which may already be copyrighted, into a new work, such as a magazine or anthology.

Color of law Journalists and others act under color of law when they willingly act in concert with officials, becoming like officials themselves.

Common carrier In communications, a regulated monopoly, guaranteed profits by the government, that is expected to provide message delivery service to anyone for a fee, without interfering in the content of the message.

Common law The body of law developed from custom and tradition as recognized by judicial decisions. Common law is largely based on previous court decisions.

Common-law malice Hatred, ill will, spite.

Compilation A copyrightable work formed by selecting, coordinating, or arranging pre-existing works into a new, original work, such as a database.

Concurring opinion An opinion written by an appellate court judge stating why the judge agreed with other judges.

Consent decree An agreement between a defendant and the government that the defendant will cease allegedly illegal activities.

Contempt of court Acting impermissibly to interfere with a legal proceeding. Punishable by fine or imprisonment.

Content regulation The regulation of expression based on what is said as opposed to where or when it is said. First Amendment doctrine predisposes courts to consider content regulations unconstitutional. *See also* **time, place and manner test** and **strict scrutiny**.

Continuance Postponing a trial, such as to ameliorate the effects of prejudicial publicity.

Contributions Gifts of money or services to a candidate, political party, or political action committee.

Corporation An artificial entity created under the power of law. Corporations have some, but not all, protections the Bill of Rights gives individuals.

Damages Money awarded to a winning plaintiff in a civil lawsuit. *See also* **actual damages**, **special damages** and **punitive damages**.

Defamation Injury to reputation.

Defendant In civil law, the party against whom a lawsuit is brought. In criminal law, the party accused of a crime by the state.

Definitional balancing Judicial balancing of interests after freedom of expression is broadly defined to give it extra weight. Definitional balancing provides more predictable protection to freedom of expression than ad hoc balancing. *See also* **absolutism, ad hoc balancing, bad-tendency test** and **clear-and-present-danger test**.

Derivative work In copyright law, a transformation or adaptation of an existing work, such as the creation of a filmscript from a novel.

Discovery The process before a trial of gathering information that can be used as evidence in a court case. Discovery includes the exchange of information by the two parties to a case.

Dissenting opinion An appellate judge's opinion explaining the judge's disagreement with the court majority's decision.

En banc A French term used when all of the judges of an appellate court decide a case. More typically, a single judge or a small number of judges, called a panel, decide a case.

Equal opportunities Section 315 of the Communications Act requiring broadcast stations and cable systems to offer a legally qualified candidate access to approximately the same size and type of audience for approximately the same amount of time as the station or system provided the candidate's opponent.

Equity A source of law that allows courts to fashion remedies appropriate to the case at hand. The law of equity enables courts to provide legal remedies other than money damages.

Ex parte A Latin legal term meaning by, for, or from one party. This can refer to a proceeding where one of the parties is not present.

Fault Frequently used to mean the media error that the plaintiff must prove to win a libel suit. Plaintiffs who are judged to be public officials or public figures must prove *New York Times* actual malice. Individual states can determine the level of fault that must be proven by other plaintiffs, but most states have chosen negligence.

Fiber-optic cable Hair-sized strands of clear, flexible tubing, predominantly made of glass, that allow information to be sent through impulses of light.

Fighting words Unprotected words that by their very utterance inflict injury or tend to incite an immediate breach of the peace.

First Amendment due process First Amendment procedural requirements that the government justify prior restraints and other restrictions and that hearings be held at which restrictions may be contested. *See also* **prior restraint**.

Fourteenth Amendment Amendment to the Constitution making states, in addition to the federal government, liable for violation of rights protected by the Bill of Rights. A state government that violates the Bill of Rights usually also violates a citizen's right of due process guaranteed by the Fourteenth Amendment. *See also* **incorporation**.

Franchise Agreement between a city, county, or state and a cable system operator allowing the operator to provide cable television service.

Gag order *See* **restraining order**.

Grand jury A jury determining whether there is sufficient evidence to charge a criminal suspect, or otherwise inquiring into possible criminal activity.

In camera review A judge's review of documents or testimony in private or in the judge's chambers, without the public present.

Incorporation A series of cases in which the Supreme Court made state governments liable for violating the Bill of Rights. The Court incorporated the Bill of Rights into the Fourteenth Amendment by holding that state infringements of free speech and other rights violate a citizen's right to due process, guaranteed by the Fourteenth Amendment. *See also* **Fourteenth Amendment**.

Indecency Nonobscene material depicting or describing sexual or excretory activities or organs. The level of protection for indecency varies: broadcast indecency receives the least protection; Internet indecency receives the strongest protection.

Independent expenditures Monies spent independently of candidates to advocate their election or defeat.

Indictment An accusation issued by a grand jury that charges an individual with a crime and requires the person to stand trial.

Injunction Order from a court telling a person or company to perform or refrain from some act, such as publishing. An injunction is an equitable remedy. *See also* **equity** and **prior restraint**.

Innocent construction rule A rule stating that material must be defined as innocent rather than defamatory if an innocent construction is possible.

Innuendo Implied defamation.

Jurisdiction The authority of a court. A court has jurisdiction over a person when that person must obey the orders of the court. A court has jurisdiction over subject matter when constitutions or statutes give the court the power to decide cases relating to the subject.

Liability Being legally responsible for an act.

Libel Printed or, in some states, broadcast defamation.

Litigant A party in a lawsuit; a participant in litigation.

Lottery A contest involving a prize, chance and consideration.

Native advertising Content paid for by advertisers but often produced by journalism organizations and presented in a way that resembles news stories or videos.

Negligence Not acting as a reasonable person would. In some states, a journalist not acting as a reasonable journalist would.

Net neutrality The requirement that Internet service providers allow equal access to all content and applications without favoring or disfavoring content by blocking, slowing or charging extra.

Neutral reportage A libel defense in a few jurisdictions. Neutral reportage may be found if the defamatory charges are newsworthy and related to a public controversy, made by a responsible person or organization about a public official or public figure, and accurately and neutrally reported, and if the story includes opposing views.

Obscenity Material that appeals to the prurient interest, is patently offensive and is without serious social value.

Opinion A court's written statement explaining its decision, or a judge's written statement explaining agreement or disagreement with a court's decision.

Original jurisdiction A court of original jurisdiction is the first court to decide a case, rather than a court hearing a case on appeal.

Overbreadth A First Amendment doctrine by which courts determine that legislation is unconstitutional because it restricts more expression than necessary. *See also* **strict scrutiny** and **vagueness**.

Participant monitoring Secret recording or transmitting of a conversation in which one party to the conversation is aware of the recording.

Party A participant in a legal action.

Per curiam An opinion issued by and for the entire court rather than by one judge writing for the court.

Peremptory challenge An attorney's right to challenge seating a juror without offering a reason.

Petitioner A person who petitions a court to take action, including the initiation of a civil suit or the initiation of an appeal.

Plaintiff The party bringing the lawsuit; the person complaining.

Plurality With reference to the U.S. Supreme Court, the opinion that is supported by more justices than any other opinion in a single case but not supported by a majority of the justices.

Political action committee (PAC) An organization established by a corporation, union, or others to solicit and spend money on behalf of political candidates and issues.

Pornography Sexually explicit material.

Precedent An established rule of law set by a previous court opinion. A precedent for an individual case is the authority relied on for the disposition of the case. The precedent usually comes from a case involving similar facts and raising similar issues as the case at hand.

Preempt The judicial principle asserting the supremacy of federal over state legislation on the same subject.

Pretrial hearings Conferences among attorneys and the judge before a trial begins attempting, for example, to narrow issues or determine what exhibits will be permitted at trial.

Prior restraint Restriction on expression before publication or broadcast by injunction, agreement, or discriminatory taxation. First Amendment doctrine favors punishment after publication instead of prior restraint. *See also* **injunction**.

Private figure A libel plaintiff who is not a public figure or public official. In most states, a private-figure libel plaintiff need prove only that the defendant acted negligently.

Probable cause A legal standard used by judges, police officers and grand juries to determine whether there are reasonable grounds for believing that a person committed a crime.

Product disparagement *See* **trade libel**.

Public figures The U.S. Supreme Court has said that people become public figures for the purpose of libel suits only if they (1) possess widespread fame or notoriety or (2) have injected themselves into the debate of a controversial public issue for the purpose of affecting the outcome of that controversy.

Public forum Public property dedicated to public discourse, such as a speaker's corner, or public property traditionally open to public debate, such as streets and sidewalks. The law also recognizes a nonpublic forum in public property, such as an army base, dedicated to purposes other than free speech.

Public interest The standard the Federal Communications Commission uses to make decisions, according to the Communications Act of 1934.

Puffery Exaggerated advertising claims that are not misleading, deceptive, or false.

Pump-and-dump A scheme in which a stock owner promotes the value of the stock with inaccurate information and then sells when the price of the stock peaks.

Punitive damages Money damages awarded to punish a defendant rather than to compensate a plaintiff for loss of money or reputation.

Qualified privilege A journalist's libel defense based on another's absolute privilege. A qualified privilege may be lost if the story is not fair and accurate or if the defamatory statements are not accurately attributed.

Recuse To disqualify oneself as a judge in a particular case due to a potential conflict of interest or lack of impartiality.

Referendum A ballot issue allowing voters to accept or reject a state constitutional amendment or a state law.

Remand When an appellate court sends a case back to a lower court, directing the lower court to decide the case consistent with the higher court's opinion.

Reputation What others think of a person or entity.

Respondent An appellee, a party opposing the grant of a petition before a court.

Restatement (Second) of Torts A publication of the American Law Institute that attempts to provide a comprehensive statement of the law of torts.

Restraining order An order issued by a judge commanding reporters and editors not to publish stories about a legal proceeding. A restraining order—often called a gag order by the press—also may restrict trial participants from talking with journalists.

Rulemaking A formal process of making administrative law used by such agencies as the Federal Communications Commission and the Federal Trade Commission. An agency must publish a proposed rule in the *Federal Register* and review comments. The rule as finally adopted must also be published.

Safe harbor In the context of broadcast regulations, the time period from 10 P.M. to 6 A.M. when radio and television stations may air indecent material without incurring Federal Communications Commission sanctions.

Search warrant An order issued by a magistrate directing a law enforcement officer to search a place for unlawful property.

Security review Prepublication review by military officials of wartime press reports to ensure classified information is not disclosed.

Seditious libel Defaming the government.

Sequestration Physically isolating jurors during a trial. Housing jurors under guard so that they will not be exposed to information or opinions about a case outside of the courtroom.

Slander Spoken defamation. However, in most states, defamation spoken on broadcast stations or in motion pictures is considered libel.

SLAPP suits (strategic lawsuits against public participation) Libel suits filed against citizen activists to stop political expression.

Special damages Money damages compensating for the loss of reputation that are awarded only on proof of out-of-pocket monetary loss.

Spectrum Range of frequencies of electromagnetic radiation allowing radio and television signals to be sent from a transmitter to a receiver.

Stare decisis The foundation of common law; the doctrine that judges should rely on precedent when deciding cases in similar factual situations.

State action An action taken by the state or on behalf of the state, as opposed to an action by a private individual or entity. Only state actors can violate—and be sued for violating—a citizen's rights under the Constitution, federal or state laws.

Statute of limitations Time limits established by statute during which lawsuits may be filed or criminal charges brought.

Statutory law The law made by statutes passed by legislative bodies.

Strict scrutiny The judicial requirement that a restriction on protected contents be justified by a compelling government interest and that the regulation not be overbroad or vague. *See also* **overbreadth** and **vagueness**.

Subpoena A court document requiring a person to appear in court and testify at a given time and place.

Summary judgment A ruling by a judge that there is no dispute of material fact between the two parties in a case, and that one party should win the case as a matter of law. A summary judgment precludes the need for a trial.

Third-party monitoring Bugging, wiretapping, or eavesdropping on a conversation without knowledge of the parties to the conversation.

Time, place and manner test Regulation of where and when expression is made as opposed to what is said. First Amendment doctrine is more tolerant of time, place and manner restrictions than of content regulations. *See also* **content regulation**.

Tort A legal wrong, other than a crime or a violation of a contract, that is committed by one person against another. Torts include libel, invasion of privacy and trespass. Relief for a tort is usually sought through monetary damages.

Trade libel Intentionally defaming product quality, causing the product manufacturer to lose money.

True threat Intimidating communication, unprotected by the First Amendment, directed to a person or group with the intent to place the victim in fear of bodily harm or death.

Vagueness The doctrine by which courts determine that laws are unconstitutional because average persons would not know ahead of time whether their expression would violate the law. Vague laws affecting expression violate the First Amendment because the uncertainty they create leads to self-censorship. *See also* **overbreadth** and **strict scrutiny**.

Variable obscenity Prohibition of sexual materials that are obscene to children but not to adults.

Viewpoint discrimination Unconstitutional government regulation of speech expressing a particular view on a subject.

Voir dire The examination of prospective jurors to determine whether they are qualified to sit on a jury.

Work for hire In copyright law, a work prepared by an employee "within the scope of his or her employment," or a commissioned work, perhaps from a freelancer, for which a work-for-hire contract is signed. In either case, the employer owns all rights in the work.

CASE INDEX

SUBJECT INDEX

A

abortion 181, 323
absolute privileges 166–8, 571
access, public 510–11, 529–30,
  563–6
actual malice 45, 53, 108,
  125–33, 138–46, 148–52, 209,
  211–15, 227, 571
Adelson, Sheldon and Mariam
  295, 296
ad hoc balancing 45, 613
administrative law 5–6, 6,
  372, 414
Administrative Procedure Act
  (APA) 7, 310, 414
advertising 4–7, 46–7, 53–6,
  68–9; broadcast advertising
  367–8; commercial speech
  322–4; deception 338–48; the
  First Amendment and 321–35;
  the four-part test 326–35;
  halting advertisements
  354–6; intellectual property
  240, 243–4, 248–9, 254–5,
  268–70, 272–3; lower status
  of 339–41; media's right to
  refuse 324–5; native 347–8,
  573; political speech (see
  elections); privacy 181–2,
  215, 218–23, 234, 270–3;
  puffery 345–6; 574; state
  regulations 348–50; tobacco
  advertising 361–4; unfairness
  336–8
aerial surveillance 203–5; see
  also drones; trespass
agency, government 109, 394,
  404, 430, 541, 551, 560–1,
  564–5
alcohol advertisements 321,
  331, 333
Alien and Sedition Acts (1798)
  123–4
Alito, Samuel 12, 13
animal cruelty 46, 55, 398
anonymous speech 37–9
anti-SLAPP law 154–5, 571
appellate courts 571; the First
  Amendment 41; structure
  and function 10–18 (see also
  fair trial)
appropriation 215–25
Areopagitica (Milton) 31, 85
Assange, Julian 62, 93–4
association, right of 197, 305

B

bad-tendency test 42, 571
balancing test 44–6, 505, 571
Barrett, Amy Coney 13, 14
Barron, Jerome 29
Behringer, Vicki 459
Bill of Rights 4, 31–5; see also
  First Amendment
Bipartisan Campaign Reform
  Act (BCRA) 284–6, 291

Bissonnette, Matt 77
Black, Hugo 32
Blackstone, William 130
Blasi, Vincent 26, 30–1
Bollea, Terry 190
Bollinger, Lee 26
Bolton, John 78–80
Brandeis, Louis 180–2, 215–16,
  371–2
Breyer, Stephen 12–14
broadcasting 107; advertising
  367–8; indecency 406–16;
  408, 411, 413; methods of
  control 84–6; political speech
  302–13
Buckley Amendment 551, 571;
  Family Educational Rights
  and Privacy Act (FERPA)
bullying 66–7, 195–7
burden of proof 20; see also
  libel; plaintiffs

C

cable television 86–8, 418–20
cameras in courtrooms 453–63,
  455, 457
campaigns see elections
cease and desist orders 354–7
censorship 28–9, 35–7,
  64–7; limits on broadcaster
  censorship of political
  content 310–11
Central Hudson test 326–35,
  370–1
Central Intelligence Agency
  (CIA) 62, 76–8, 550, 555
certiorari, writ of 16
Child Online Protection Act
  (COPA) 422–3
child pornography 394–6
children: commercial speech
  364–8; the First Amendment
  47; libel 107; privacy
  182, 190–1 (see also child
  pornography; indecency;
  obscenity)
Children's Internet Protection
  Act (CIPA) 423
Children's Online Privacy
  Protection Act (COPPA) 182
Children's Television Act (1990)
  364–5, 372
civil cases 18–21
classified information 73–81,
  92–5, 517, 521, 538, 547, 575
clear-and-present-danger test
  46–50, 495–6, 571
collateral bar rule 487–9, 571
collective works 240–2, 571–2
colleges 67, 551–2, 560
color of law 206–7, 572
commercialization of identity
  215–25
commercial speech 320–77;
  broadcast advertising 367–8;
  childrens' television 364–7;
  commercial speech doctrine

322–4; federal remedies
  350–9; the First Amendment
  and advertising 324–36;
  the four-part test 326–36;
  fraud 377–88; halting
  advertisements 354–6;
  lotteries and contests
  369–71; lower status of
  advertising 324–6; mandated
  disclosure 374–7; media's
  right to refuse advertising
  372–3; money 372; other
  consumer protections 327,
  337; personal data 368–9;
  prospective remedies 351–4;
  racketeering 358–9; required
  statements 357–9; securities
  transactions 373–4; self-
  regulation 368; tobacco
  advertising 361–4; unfair and
  deceptive advertising 336–48
Communications Decency Act
  (CDA) of 1996 41, 118, 156,
  196, 349–50, 420
corporations 4–6, 614; access
  to information 590–1;
  commercial speech 373–9,
  381–3; elections 282–7;
  the First Amendment 68–9;
  libel 103; see also securities
  transactions
corrective advertising 358
court records 12, 122, 151,
  184–5, 187, 479–83
courts 10–18; see also cameras
  in courtrooms
criminal law 21–3, 128
cross burning 50–1
cyberbullying 195
cybersquatting 275
cyberstalking 196

D

dark money groups 296–8
deceptive advertising 336–50
defamation 99–101, 572;
  defamatory content 105–10;
  the defendant's case 154–78;
  libel and slander 101; the
  plaintiff's burden of proof
  105–46
Delgado, Richard 48
dial-a-porn 416–17
disclosure: access to
  information 540–70; access to
  meetings 563–9; affirmative
  366, 373; agency memoranda
  554; agency rules and
  practices 564–5; appeals and
  penalties 547–8; commercial
  speech 357–8; confidential
  business information 553;
  exemptions 548–60; the
  First Amendment 57; law
  enforcement 557; lobbying
  314–16; national security
  548–9; personnel, medical

584